KU-267-341

Sociology
An Introduction

Second Edition

ALEX THIO

Ohio University

GRIFFITH COLLEGE DUBLIN
South Circular Road, Dublin 8.
Tel.4545640 Fax: 4549265

1817 Harper & Row, Publishers, New York
Cambridge, Philadelphia, San Francisco, London,
Mexico City, São Paulo, Singapore, Sydney

A list of photo and cartoon credits appears on pages 640–641, which are hereby made part of this copyright page.

Sponsoring Editor: Alan McClare
Development Editor: Robert Ginsberg
Project Editor: Carla Samodulski
Text and Cover Design: Leon Bolognese
Text Art: Vantage Art, Inc.
Photo Research: Inge King
Production Manager: Jeanie Berke
Production Assistant: Paula Roppolo
Compositor: York Graphic Services, Inc.
Printer and Binder: R. R. Donnelley & Sons Company
Cover Printer: Lehigh Press

Cover Illustration: *Improvisation 31;* Wassily Kandinsky; National Gallery of Art, Washington; Ailsa Mellon Bruce Fund

Sociology: An Introduction, Second Edition

Copyright © 1989 by Harper & Row, Publishers, Inc.

All rights reserved. Printed in the United States of America. No part of this book may be used or reproduced in any manner whatsoever without written permission, except in the case of brief quotations embodied in critical articles and reviews. For information address Harper & Row, Publishers, Inc., 10 East 53d Street, New York, NY 10022.

Library of Congress Cataloging-in-Publication Data

Thio, Alex.
Sociology: an introduction/Alex Thio.—2nd ed.
p. cm.
Bibliography: p.
Includes indexes.
ISBN 0-06-046688-X (Student Edition)
ISBN 0-06-046692-8 (Teacher Edition)
1. Sociology. I. Title.
HM51.T53 1989
301—dc19 88-21964
CIP

88 89 90 91 9 8 7 6 5 4 3 2 1

Contents in Brief

Contents

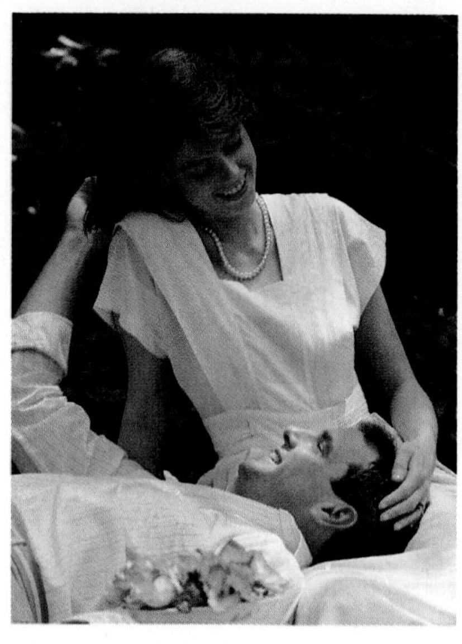

THOMAS
HAYES

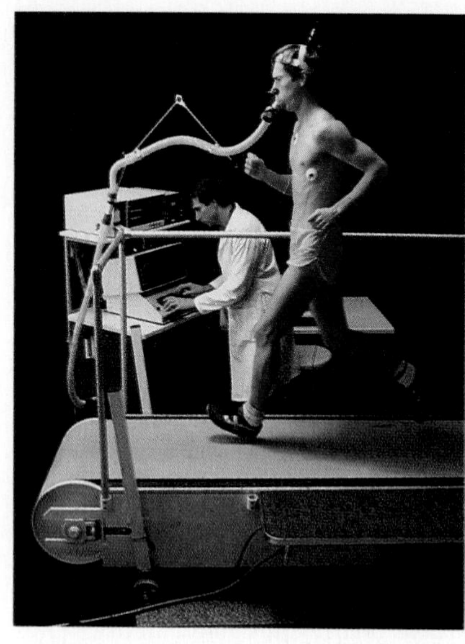

HOPE FOR PEACE
LATIN AMERICA
Therefore Choose Life
LESBIAN GAY CONCERNS
UCC COALITION

Readings

Using Sociological Insight

Looking at Current Research

Understanding Other Societies

Preface

Sociology is an exciting field, and I have tried to convey that excitement in this new edition of *Sociology: An Introduction.* By making sociology come alive for students, I have tried to show them that they can objectively investigate the world in which they live and can gain insight into how it works. By presenting students with current facts and new ideas from sociological research, I want to challenge them to think analytically about the familiar world they think they know. The simple, fast-paced writing style, the frequent use of provocative examples, and the illustrations from current events are intended to do more than make it easier for students to learn sociology. They are also designed to encourage students to question the views about human behavior that they take for granted. Only then can students better understand their own lives and the world they inhabit.

I believe that students will learn more from a book that is clearly written, enjoyable to read, and relevant to their lives. All the elements of the book—the readings, the questions for discussion and review, the photographs and captions, the summaries—are designed to help students involve themselves with the ideas and content of sociology. It has been fun to write this book, and I hope that students will also have fun reading it. When they finish it, they will look at the familiar world around them with a fresh eye and enhanced understanding.

Organization

The book is divided into five parts. Part One introduces students to the nature of sociology, showing them how to think sociologically and how to do sociology. Major sociological perspectives and research methods are presented here. Part Two first examines four social bases of human behavior—culture, social structure, groups and organizations, and socialization. I then discuss two types of behavior—deviance and sexuality—as illustrations of how even seemingly personal actions are socially motivated. Part Three analyzes various forms of human inequality. They include the inequality between rich and poor, between dominant and minority groups, between males and females, and between old and young. Part Four deals with major social institutions—the family, education, religion, politics, economics, medicine, science, and sport. Finally, in Part Five, I discuss those aspects of society that change most visibly. They are population and ecology; urbanization and city life; collective behavior, social movements, and social change.

Features

This book has several features that, I trust, will make the instructor's teaching job and the student's learning experience interesting and rewarding.

Comprehensive Coverage All the standard topics in introductory sociology are covered here. In addition, there are separate chapters on human sexuality, health and medical care, science and technology, and sport. I consider these subjects to be as important as the traditional ones. Health and medical care as well as science and technology are central to understanding modern society, and a sociological analysis can help us better assess how medicine, science, and technology affect our lives. On the other hand, since human sexuality and sport have a special appeal for students, they are ideal for showing how sociology explains human behavior. With the addition of these subjects to the standard ones, the textbook is quite comprehensive. Some instructors may want to cover the whole book. Others may want to cover less, but they still can choose chapters that suit their teaching needs, since each chapter deals with important sociological issues. The Instructor's Resource Manual contains suggestions for four possible sequences for those who wish to teach a shorter course.

Scholarship and Readability This book offers a unique blend of scholarship and readability. I have tried not to gloss over complex sociological issues but to confront them head-on. Although I have taken great care to be fair and accurate in discussing the various theoretical and empirical studies, I have also criticized them, evaluated them, or related them to other studies. Further, I have applied the major sociological perspectives—introduced in the first chapter—throughout the text, wherever they can throw light on a specific subject under discussion. It has been my goal to make complex sociological ideas easy for students to follow. To achieve this, I have written simply and directly, avoiding the use of long and complicated sentences.

Current Research I have taken special care to present the most recent findings from the sociological literature. Sociology is a fast-growing field. In recent years it has produced an abundance of new concepts and data. Perhaps reflecting the significant changes that have taken place in American society since 1980, many of the current sociological studies challenge or supersede those published in the 1960s and 1970s. Thus most of the references cited in this text were published in the 1980s, and many are as recent as 1987 and 1988. I have also discussed important sociological classics, but I have brought them up to date by relating them to the current literature.

Boxed Readings There are three kinds of readings in the text. The "Looking at Current Research" boxes are intended to help students make sense of the fast-changing world in which we live today. The "Using Sociological Insight" boxes are meant to show students how sociology can enrich our lives, helping to solve our social and personal problems. The "Understanding Other Societies" boxes are designed to help students understand our own society better by comparing it with other societies. Readings come from both scholarly and popular magazines. They have been selected for the interest of their topics and for their lively writing. Most important, they strengthen the text by elaborating on specific points that have been discussed in the chapter. For this edition, over 50 percent of the boxes have been replaced with more recent articles.

Pedagogical Aids A number of teaching devices have been incorporated to motivate students and to facilitate learning.

Chapter Introductions. Along with a chapter outline, each chapter opens with a photograph and a brief commentary that highlights a major theme of the chapter. To arouse student interest, some chapters begin with a story, others with a thought-provoking description of the chapter's central theme, and still others with a series of provocative examples or statements. Each chapter introduction is also intended to fix the student's mind on the main themes of the chapter.

Illustrations and Captions. The photographs have been selected to illuminate key ideas throughout the text. The captions have been purposely written to recapitulate those key ideas. Together, the photos and captions reinforce the student's comprehension and retention of the material.

Questions for Discussion and Review. In every chapter there are questions at the end of each main section, and, for this edition, all the questions have been revised. Instructors can use them as a springboard for lively discussions in class. Students can use them to review the main ideas that have just been discussed, before moving on to the next topic. However the questions are used, students will learn more as active thinkers than they would as passive recipients of facts and ideas.

Chapter Summaries. Each chapter ends with a full summary in a question-and-answer format. The standard form of summary in an introductory text tends to turn students into passive consumers of knowledge. In contrast, the question-and-answer format encourages students to become actively involved, by inviting them to join the author in thinking about important issues. Students who have actively thought about what they have read will more easily understand and remember it later.

Key Terms. The most important words are identified in text with boldface type and are defined when they are introduced. They are listed and defined again at the end of each chapter, with a page cross-reference to facilitate study. All key terms are also defined in full in the Glossary at the end of the book.

Suggested Readings. In line with the currentness of the material in the text, the most up-to-date books for further reading are listed at the end of each chapter. These sources enable students to seek additional knowledge about the subject matter of each chapter. Most books are readily available in school libraries.

New to This Edition

I have written a new chapter (Chapter 18) on health and medical care. This is an important subject, and medical sociology is one of the fastest-growing specialties in sociology. The aging of the American population and the growing cost and sophistication of medical treatment are having a major sociological impact on American society. The extensive discussion of AIDS in this chapter is also of extreme importance to today's students and provides a vivid example of sociological forces in action.

Other important new sections are on social interaction and social networks in Chapter 4 (Social Structure) and on war and peace in Chapter 16 (Politics and the State). These topics are sociologically significant, and I have tried to make them interesting and relevant for students. To accommodate this new material, I have combined the last two chapters of the first edition and, in the process, deleted several less important sections.

I have extensively updated the book with new information and research. The new topics include the relevance of sociology to students in recent years, Bellah's research on American individualism, recent critiques of the Sapir-Whorf hypothesis, new critiques of Piaget's theory of cognitive development and Erikson's ideas about the adult life cycle, new evidence on the drift theory of mental illness, the impact of prison overcrowding, the modern mistress ("the new other woman"), the new form of racial prejudice, the conflict view of surrogate motherhood, television evangelism, the birth dearth, and illegal aliens. New materials can be found in every chapter, but they are too numerous to list here.

More than half of the boxed readings have been updated with new topics, and many of the black and white photos have been replaced with more vivid color ones. More important, I have carefully reviewed every photo caption to ensure that it will reinforce students' comprehension and retention of what they have read in the text.

Supplements

Accompanying this text is a highly useful support package for instructors and students.

Instructor's Resource Manual The *Instructor's Resource Manual,* prepared and revised by Peter Morrill of Bronx Community College, provides chapter outlines, learning objectives, a complete summary of chapter topics, and an extensive set of classroom discussion questions keyed to main topics. Each chapter also includes demonstrations, projects, and applications that are designed to develop the thinking skills of students. The *Instructor's Resource Manual* outlines four different sequences of topics for courses of varying lengths, and it ends with an extensive list of audiovisual aids and their sources. The goal of the manual is to enable instructors to show students how to think effectively about sociological topics. In addition, students are helped not only to master the material of the course but also to take an active role in learning it.

Test Bank An entirely new *Test Bank* has been prepared by Jeffrey P. Rosenfeld of Nassau Community College. The *Test Bank* contains 1700 true-false, multiple-choice, fill-in, and essay questions. The *Test Bank* is available as a printed manual and on Harper Test. Harper Test is a computerized test-generation system with full word-processing capabilities. It produces customized tests and allows instructors to scramble questions and/or add new ones. Harper Test is available for the Apple II and IBM PC and PS2 families of computers.

Student Review Manual A *Student Review Manual* has also been prepared by Professor Morrill. It is a substantial book in its own right. Each chapter opens with an outline of the chapter in the text, a list of learning objectives, a detailed review of the material designed to get the student deep into the particulars of the chapter, and numerous questions and answers to check the student's knowledge.

Introductory Sociology Workbook with Software The *Introductory Sociology Workbook,* with accompanying software, by Cornelius Riordan of Providence College and Allan Mazur of Syracuse University, provides a hands-on opportunity for students actually to do sociology. It includes 18 exercises in which students discover correlations between different variables using the highest quality data available. Each exercise links empirical results directly to sociological theory and all exercises use either large national samples or classical experimental data. The program for data analysis is completely menu-driven and easy to learn. It was designed by James Davis, Director of the General Social Survey—from which much of the data is taken. It is available for the IBM-PC and compatibles and the Macintosh and compatibles.

Lecture Supports and Graphics The Lecture Supports and Graphics consist of over 70 transparency masters for use in the classroom. Included are the chapter outlines for each chapter and all tables, graphs, and charts in the text.

Acknowledgments

I am grateful to many colleagues around the country for reviewing the manuscript. Their criticisms and suggestions have enabled me to write a textbook that is both challenging and interesting to students. It should, I hope, meet the requirements of the instructors who teach the course. The reviewers include:

Ravindra G. Amonker, *Southwest Missouri State University*
Philip A. Belcastro, *Borough of Manhattan Community College*
Donald E. Carns, *University of Nevada, Las Vegas*
David L. Decker, *California State University, San Bernardino*
Mary Lee Dennison, *University of South Dakota*
Robin Franck, *Southwestern College*
James R. Henley, Jr., *Texas Christian University*
Robert K. Hirzel, *University of Maryland*
Michael Kupersanin, *Duquesne University*
W. Clayton Lane, *San Jose State University*
David Wendell Moller, *Indiana University*
Donna C. Phillips, *San Bernardino Valley College*
Leo Pinard, *California Polytechnic State University*
M. D. Pugh, *Bowling Green State University*
Roger Salerno, *Pace University*
Frank A. Santopolo, *Colorado State University*
William A. Schwab, *University of Arkansas*
Janet H. Shannon, *St. Joseph's University*
Len Tompos, *Lorain County Community College*
C. Edwin Vaughan, *University of Missouri, Columbia*
Jay R. Williams, *North Carolina State University*
Wayne Zatopek, *Tarrant County Junior College*

I would like to thank a number of people at Ohio University. The librarians have been most helpful in finding the books, articles, and government documents that I needed. My sociology colleagues here have been kind enough to allow me to pursue a project that I greatly enjoyed.

I am particularly thankful to Peter Morrill of Bronx Community College. His tireless pursuit of appropriate essays for the boxes has significantly strengthened the text. His work on the *Student Review Manual* and the *Instructor's Resource Manual* has contributed immensely to the text's support package.

I owe a special debt to several people at Harper & Row. Alan McClare, the sociology editor, gave me the opportunity to have this book published. The editorial supervision of Robert Ginsberg, the development editor, has greatly enhanced the quality of this text and the supplements. Carla Samodulski, the project editor, has efficiently guided the production of the book.

Finally, I am grateful to my wife and children for their understanding and patience. Although I have often robbed them of the time I should have spent with them, they seldom complained about it. They have made it possible for me to take a lot of pleasure, without much guilt, in writing this book.

Alex Thio

PART ONE

The Nature of Sociology

Chapter 1
Thinking Sociologically: A Special Insight

Chapter 2
Doing Sociology: Research Methods

If you were to ask a few typical Americans why they are going to college or planning to marry or having no more than two children, their answers would probably be something like, "because I want to." American traditions encourage us to see our actions as the result of individual choices and individual characteristics. In fact, our actions also reflect the powerful influence of our society. We cannot understand our lives unless we understand how society shapes them. This is what sociology shows us.

The first part of this book provides an overview of the nature of sociology: how sociologists think and what they do. In Chapter 1 we demonstrate that sociology offers a special insight into human life. After tracing the development of sociology, we examine its major theoretical perspectives and discuss its practical uses. Chapter 2 shows how sociologists conduct research to test their theories and build a storehouse of knowledge. It shows the kinds of questions sociologists are interested in, the methods they use to answer these questions, and the special problems they face.

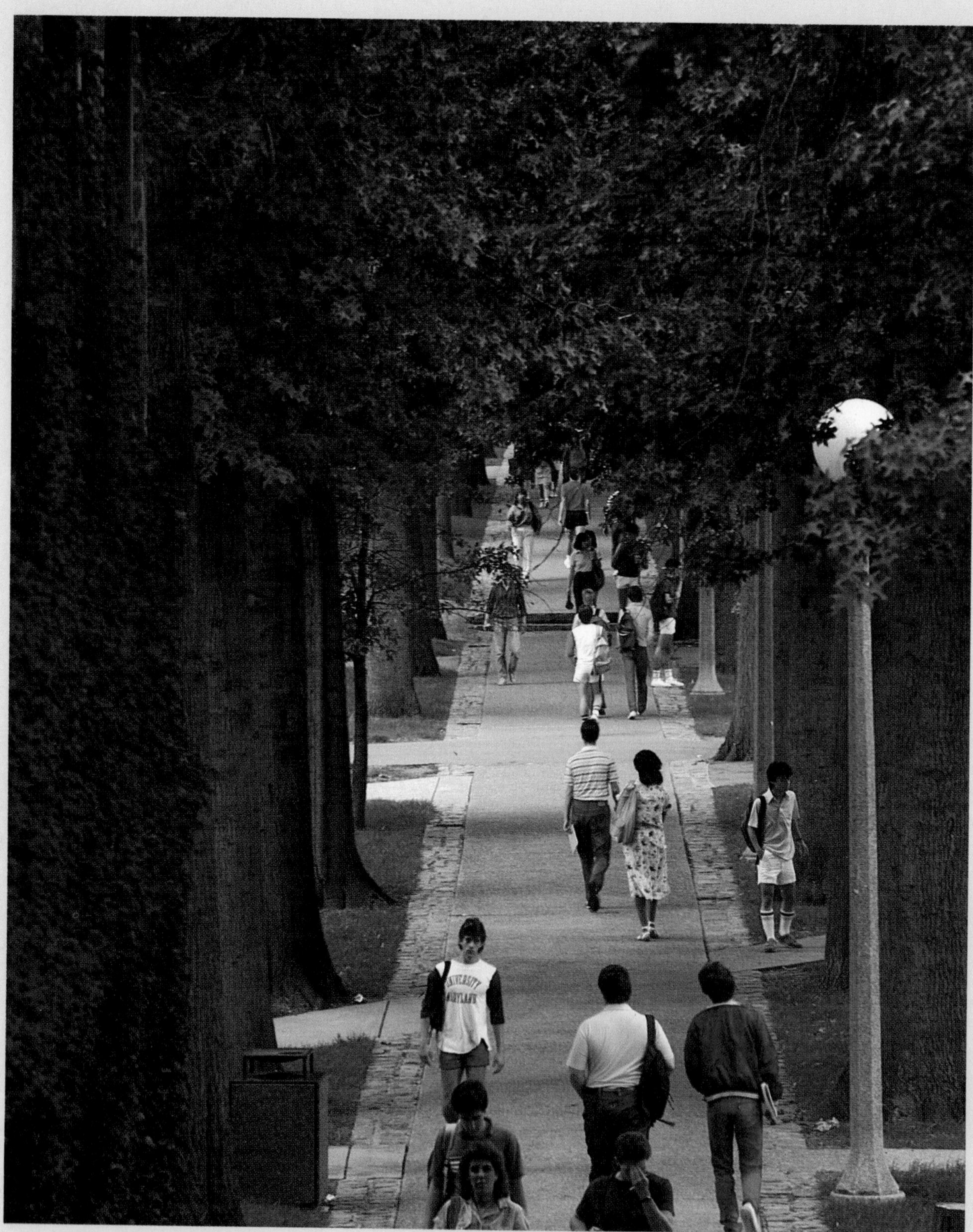
UNIVERSITY

1 Thinking Sociologically: A Special Insight

Sociology is the scientific study of human behavior. It shows us how people interact with each other, how groups or societies differ, and how these social units affect human behavior. Sociology helps us better understand the forces that affect us in all social situations. With this sociological eye, we can see how college students are influenced by the people around them on campus. Obviously, the students are receiving an education that will affect their careers later. But participation in campus life also enables many to find their lifelong friends and even future spouses. This illustrates how a social force such as education has a powerful influence on our lives.

Why are some marriages successful while others end in divorce? Are we born with our personalities already built into us? How will a college education affect your income? Is the American work ethic losing its steam? Why are sports so popular in the United States? Are men naturally tougher than women? Apart from having more money, are rich people different from everyone else? Do cities make people callous and rude? Does the United States encourage high crime rates by coddling criminals? Sociology can help us find answers to questions like these. As the scientific study of human social behavior, **sociology** can show us how people act and react, what the characteristics of groups and societies are, and how these social units affect people.

Thus the subject matter of sociology is familiar. It is, as Peter Berger (1963) said, "the very world in which we have lived all our lives." But sociology casts a new light on this world, offering a unique view on human life. In this chapter we examine that view as well as the history of sociology, its major perspectives, and its uses.

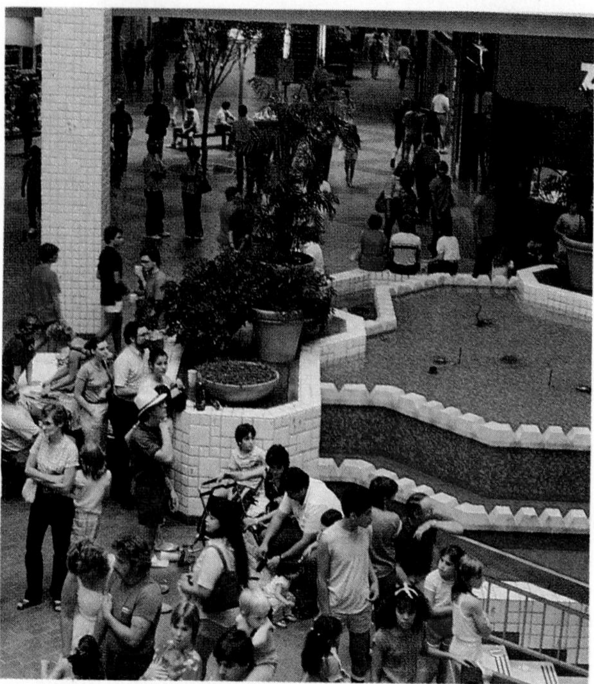

When sociologists look at a peaceful, typically American scene such as this shopping mall in Texas, every element in it suggests interesting and important questions: Why is it typical? Why is it peaceful? What social forces govern how the people in it relate to each other? The questions could be endless, and the answers could tell us much about our lives today. It is the task of sociologists to ask such questions and to look for answers. Sociologists' tools include the various theories about social forces that have been developed over the last 150 years combined with the sociological imagination.

THE STUDY OF SOCIAL LIFE

Virtually everybody has something to say about human social behavior. Because it is the stuff of everyday life, many people think they know all about it. But, as Otto Larsen (1981) notes, "living in a family or working in an organization does not automatically make one a sociologist any more than swimming in the sea makes one an oceanographer or being an animal breeder makes one a geneticist." Sociologists have a special way of looking at human behavior and special tools for studying it.

The Sociological Imagination

When sociologists examine people and their behavior, they focus on how people are influenced by other people and by society. No matter how personal our experiences are, they are influenced by **social forces**—forces that arise from the society we are part of. C. Wright Mills (1959b) referred to the ability to see the impact of social forces on individuals, especially on their private lives, as the **sociological imagination.** This imagination is the essence of the sociological perspective.

Consider the case of suicide, which is certainly a very personal experience. It is reasonable to assume that those who kill themselves are frustrated and unhappy, since happy people rarely want to die. But suicide cannot be explained simply by saying that people who commit suicide are frustrated and unhappy. This explanation does not tell us why, for example, Protestants have higher rates of suicide than Catholics. There is no evidence that Protestants as a group are more unhappy than Catholics. How, then, do we account for the different suicide rates of these two groups?

The sociological perspective leads us to look not at the individual personalities of those who commit suicide but at social forces. When French sociologist Emile

Durkheim (1951) examined suicide in the late nineteenth century, he detailed variations in the rates of suicide among various countries and groups. These rates constitute social, not individual, facts, and to explain them Durkheim turned to social forces. Among the forces he explored was **social integration,** the degree to which people are tied to a social group. When there is either excessive or inadequate social integration, suicide rates are likely to be high.

In the past, when elderly Eskimos committed suicide, the cause was usually extreme social integration. Obedient to the values and customs of their society, they did what they were expected by others to do: killing themselves when they could no longer contribute to the economy of their community. Similarly, Hindu widows used to follow the tradition of their society by ceremoniously throwing themselves onto the funeral pyres of their husbands. These ritual suicides were called *suttee* (literally, "good women"). On the other hand, a lack of social integration can also be found in high suicide rates. Divorced and widowed people, for example, are more likely than married people to be isolated from others and to receive little affection or moral support when they are frustrated. In other words, the divorced and the widowed are more likely to experience inadequate social integration. As a result, they are also more likely than married people to commit suicide. Similarly, Protestants traditionally have been less integrated into their church community than Catholics. Whereas the Catholic church emphasizes salvation through the community and binds its members to the church through its doctrines and rituals, Protestant churches emphasize individual salvation and individual responsibility. This individualism may underlie the higher rate of suicide found among Protestants.

Suicide is an extreme, exceptional act, but all around us we can see ordinary actions that are also molded by social forces. If your family had had only half its actual income, would you be reading this book today? Would you be in college? Would your ambitions be the same? The distribution of income in the United States is a social fact. Your family's position in that distribution is one of your social characteristics. And this characteristic influences your way of living and your chances in life—such as the likelihood that you will attend a college. What career are you planning for yourself? If you had been born in 1900, the chances that you would be a farmer would be much greater than they are now. Suppose you were a Swiss citizen today, your chances of going to war would be much less than they are for you as an American. Our private worlds can never be totally sealed off from the larger world of society. The technology and economy of the United States; it customs, ideals, and beliefs; its government and politics—all these are social characteristics and represent social forces that help shape our lives.

We cannot account for social forces by simply adding up the characteristics of individuals any more than we could describe water by listing the characteristics of its components. When hydrogen and oxygen form water, the water has characteristics different from either hydrogen or oxygen. When people form a sports team, the team develops characteristics (such as teamwork, solidarity, and camaraderie) that are not found in any one of its members. So, too, any social group is more than just the sum of its parts. It has characteristics that are not found in separate individuals but that arise only when these individuals interact. The sociological perspective directs our attention to these social characteristics and the social forces that create them. The sociological imagination grasps the significance of these forces in our lives.

Of course, sociologists do not have a monopoly on this interest in social forces. To understand further what sociology is, we need to consider how it differs from other forms of knowledge.

Sociology and Common Sense

To some people, sociology appears to be the laborious study of the obvious, an expensive way to discover what everybody already knows. As a critic once said to me about a sociologist who had studied prostitution with a large research grant, "He's spent $100,000 just to find out where a whorehouse is." To him and some others, sociology is common sense. But is it? Consider the following statements.

1. Many talented college athletes can expect to become professional players.
2. Since we have the highest divorce rate in the world, marriage must be losing popularity in the United States.
3. Religion and science do not mix. Religion cannot encourage the development of science.
4. Persistent poverty increases the chance that a revolution will erupt.

5. A person is more likely to be murdered by a stranger than by a loved one.
6. Armed robbery is more dangerous to the victim than unarmed robbery.
7. Most of the young people who join cults are different from their conventional peers. They, at the very least, have some problems with their parents.
8. Since Big Business dominates the United States, most Americans work in large companies with more than 1000 employees each.
9. Most elderly Americans live in poverty. If not, they at least consider themselves in poor health.
10. Among college men, the "sexual losers," who have little or no sexual experience, are more likely to rape their dates than the "sexual winners," who have a lot of sexual experience.

Many people would say it's just common sense that all these statements are true. Research has shown, however, that every one of them is false. Here are the facts.

1. No more than 1 percent of college athletes will eventually be lucky enough to turn professional (see Chapter 20: Sport).
2. Marriage remains popular in the United States. We have one of the highest rates of marriage in the world. Even divorced Americans are likely, eventually, to remarry. To most Americans, divorce means rejection only of a specific partner, not of marriage in general (Chapter 13: The Family).
3. Religion may play an important part in the development of science, as it did in seventeenth-century England (Chapter 19: Science and Technology).
4. Revolutions are more likely to occur when living conditions are improving than when they remain consistently bad (Chapter 16: Politics and the State).
5. Murder is committed against family members more often than against strangers (Chapter 7: Deviance and Control).
6. Unarmed robbery is more dangerous than armed robbery. An unarmed robber is more likely to hurt the victim because the victim is more inclined to resist the weaponless robber (Chapter 7: Deviance and Control).
7. The young people who join cults are mostly normal and come from warm, loving families (Chapter 15: Religion).
8. Only a minority of Americans work in large companies. Most work in small firms, especially those with fewer than 100 employees (Chapter 17: The Economy and Work).
9. Most elderly Americans are not poor, nor do they consider themselves in poor health. In fact, when compared to young people, they are more likely to perceive their own health as being good (Chapter 12: The Elderly).
10. The "sexual winners" are more likely to rape their dates (Chapter 8: Human Sexuality).

These and many other sociological findings may surprise you, because they contradict common sense. Of course, not every finding in sociology is surprising, and commonsense ideas are not always false. Some turn out to be true. For example, many people have known all along—and correctly—that the unemployment rate is higher among blacks than among whites, or that the poor are more likely than the rich to end up in prisons. But many commonsense ideas are incorrect, just like the examples given above. Basically, commonsense knowledge has at least two important weaknesses. First, it is not objective. It has not been systematically tested against reality. Instead, it is subjective—based on a person's own feelings, beliefs, or experience. It also represents the accepted wisdom of a community, beliefs so familiar that they are taken for granted. Second, common sense typically gives us timeworn ideas and is often inconsistent. It tells us that "absence makes the heart grow fonder," but also "out of sight, out of mind." Which is right?

A sociologist would approach this question by determining through research the conditions under which separation has a positive or a negative influence on lovers. The sociological approach requires that ideas be systematically checked against evidence, and it offers us the chance to learn something new. Whereas commonsense knowledge is subjective, often inconsistent, and familiar, sociologists seek objective, consistent, new information. To obtain it, they use the methods of science. This is one of the reasons why sociology is exciting. It often shows us that what has long been familiar—or just "common sense"—turns out to be unfamiliar or uncommon. Thus the distinction between sociology and common sense is clear. While common sense merely gives us familiar and untested ideas, sociology offers not only scientific facts and scientifically supported ideas but also the excitement of discovering something new about ourselves.

Sociology as a Science

The goal of science is to find order in apparent chaos. Scientists search for a pattern in what, on the surface, may look like random variations. They look for regularity, something that appears over and over, across time and space. Observation is given the last word in this search. It is true that scientists, like everyone else, have preconceived ideas, beliefs, and values, and they use logic and intuition to understand the world. But scientific methods require scientists to put aside existing views of what the world should be like and to rely, above all, on observation.

When scientists discover a pattern in the world, they describe it in a **hypothesis,** a tentative statement of what the pattern is, of how various events are related to one another. Then they test the hypothesis against systematic observations, producing evidence for or against it. Hypotheses, however, must be related to one another in order to explain a broader range of phenomena. A set of logically related hypotheses that explains the relationship among various phenomena is called a **theory.** A good theory will apply to a wide range of existing observations and suggest testable predictions about what can be observed in the future.

Suppose we are investigating the causes of revolutions. We find that the American Revolution was a struggle against a distant ruler that resulted in the establishment of a democracy. We also find that the Russian Revolution was an uprising against a ruling class that produced a new but still undemocratic government. Despite these differences, we come across some similarities between the two revolutions. In both, the people had experienced a foretaste of liberty. They knew their conditions could be improved. They were enraged by the discrepancy between what was and what they felt ought to be. From these similarities we could devise the hypothesis that revolutions are caused by a discrepancy between expectations and reality. If we test this hypothesis against systematic observations of other revolutions and find that the evidence consistently supports our hypothesis, then we have a theory of revolution.

We would not, however, have proven our theory to be true. A scientific theory is always open to revision in the light of new evidence. Scientific findings are always subject to verification or refutation by other scientists. If the findings cannot be duplicated by other scientists, they are suspect. Scientists routinely check whether their findings confirm or contradict those of their colleagues. This procedure increases the chances that mistakes, oversights, or biases will be detected. It ensures the objectivity of science. Scientists try to see things as they are, not as they want them to be. This is easier said than done because the work of individual scientists is

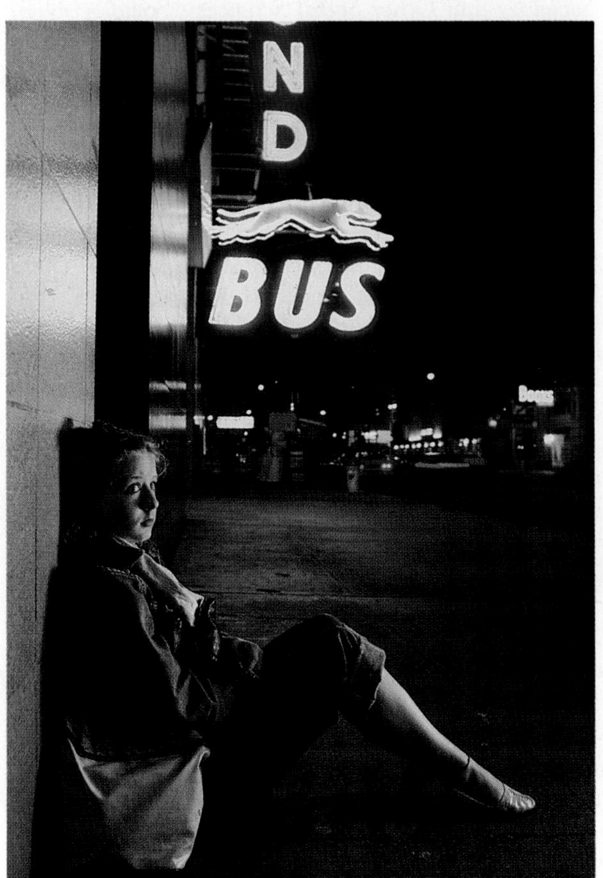

As scientists, sociologists try to see things as they are, not as they want them to be. Consider the problem of teenage runaways. There are over a million of them. Many engage in thievery to survive. Both males and females also sell sex, even though in this age of AIDS, prostitution amounts to slow suicide. Further, they use drugs and court death by sharing needles. Thus every year more than 5000 of them are buried in unmarked graves. A scientific sociological investigation must go beyond our natural sympathy for these youngsters and their parents to examine their lives objectively. This may lead to the discovery that physical, psychological, or sexual abuse causes teenagers to run away from home.

always under the influence of subjective factors such as their values and beliefs. But the objectivity of a body of scientific knowledge can be secured by the constant challenging of findings and theories. Thus scientific methods require not only that evidence be verifiable but also that scientists present their evidence publicly.

Sociology and the Natural Sciences While physical and biological scientists study the physical world, sociologists and other social scientists study various aspects of human behavior. Both types of scientist share the goal of developing scientific knowledge, and both employ scientific methods. But because sociologists deal with human beings, there are important differences between sociology and the natural sciences.

The social world studied by sociologists often seems more complex than the physical world. Unlike rocks or atoms, humans can think, feel, and talk. They can even lie to the scientist observing them. They are conscious and self-conscious. There is, in short, a dimension in human life not found in phenomena studied by physical and biological scientists. This dimension complicates the task of studying human behavior in several ways.

In the first place, human behavior and its causes are often more difficult to observe, define, and quantify than events and objects in the physical world. We can easily identify water and ice and measure the temperature at which water freezes. Identifying which people hold power in a community and measuring that power are more controversial. Furthermore, for any social phenomenon, there are a multitude of possible causes, and elements of the social world are less constant than physical phenomena. They vary from place to place, from time to time, from group to group. Among the possible causes of crime, for example, are poverty, youthfulness, peer pressure, a troubled family life, and so on. The importance of these factors may vary from one society to another. By contrast, in any society and any era, the combination of sodium and chlorine produces the same thing—table salt.

Moreover, unlike natural scientists, sociologists are part of the phenomena they study. They are themselves human beings and members of a society. Sociologists may therefore find objectivity a very elusive goal. As Gunnar Myrdal (1973), a Nobel prize-winning economist, said, "Valuations are, in fact, determining our work even if we manage to be unaware of it. And this is true, however much the researcher is subjectively convinced that he is simply observing and recording facts." Sociologists cannot be totally objective. Furthermore, if sociologists become emotionally involved with the people they study, their subjects may respond to that involvement. Sociologists' subjectivity may influence not only their interpretation of their subjects' behavior but also the behavior itself. In contrast, even if chemists fell in love with the molecules and atoms in their test tubes, their passion could hardly change the behavior of these things.

The interplay between the subjectivity stimulated by the human content of sociology and the objectivity required by scientific methods makes sociology particularly challenging and interesting. Sociologists can seek to minimize the effects of subjective factors by being aware of their biases and acknowledging them. They can also put their subjective involvement to good use, drawing on their feelings to develop a richer understanding of human behavior. As we will see, however, the respective rôles of objectivity and subjectivity in sociology have been a continuing source of controversy.

Sociology and Other Social Sciences Sociologists are not alone in studying social behavior scientifically. They share this endeavor with other social scientists. Although the boundaries between the social sciences have become increasingly blurred, differences remain.

Economics is the study of the production, distribution, and consumption of goods and services. Sociologists are also interested in these activities. They are, however, likely to study the human dimensions of the economy, such as how people work and how their jobs and the distribution of economic goods affect their lives.

History is the study of past events. Historians today not only describe the past but also try to explain historical events by referring to social forces. Sociologists are interested in history too, but they tend to use historical data to explain current social attitudes and behavior.

Political science is concerned with power, the characteristics and operations of governments, and political activities in different societies. Sociologists have learned much from political scientists. But usually sociologists are more interested in how institutions such as the family and the educational system influence political attitudes and voting behavior (a subject that also interests contemporary political scientists).

Psychology is both a biological and a social science. It is the study of the mental processes and behavior of individuals. Areas of interest to psychologists include the physiology of the brain and nervous system, learning, thinking, feeling, motivation, personality, and abnormal behavior. Psychologists tend to deal with these phenomena as individual experiences. When sociologists study these experiences, they are more inclined to examine how they vary among social groups or how they are influenced by society. Psychology and sociology merge in the field of *social psychology,* the study of the relationships between individuals and groups.

Anthropology, like psychology, is both a biological and a social science. Physical anthropologists study the biological evolution of the human species and the physical differences among human groups such as races. Cultural anthropologists examine the culture and ways of life in various societies. Most often, they have studied small, nonindustrial, traditional societies. In contrast, sociologists usually focus on complex, modern societies. But anthropologists have lately become more interested in studying modern ways of life because preliterate societies are fast disappearing.

Social work is often confused in the minds of many people with sociology. Actually they are quite different. While sociology is largely a basic science seeking valid knowledge about human behavior, social work is mostly an applied science studying how sociological knowledge can be used to help people solve such problems as marital discord and alcoholism. Sociology differs from social work in the same way as physics differs from engineering or biology from medicine.

We can see from these comparisons that sociology is a much broader field of study, covering nearly all facets of human social behavior. Thus, it takes in some aspects of each of the other social sciences. Although it overlaps with these other disciplines, it does differ from them in some ways.

QUESTIONS FOR DISCUSSION AND REVIEW

1. How does the sociological imagination clarify the role of the social forces that shape the experiences of individuals?
2. How does sociology differ from common sense?
3. Why does sociology face special problems not encountered by other forms of science?

A street scene in London in the early nineteenth century. The Industrial Revolution quickly transformed England from a rural, agrarian society to an urban, industrial one. The social costs of the transformation—in poverty, crime, inadequate housing, and child labor—stimulated an interest in social reform and challenged thinkers to find explanations and solutions to the problem. One result was the development of sociology as a science and a profession.

THE DEVELOPMENT OF SOCIOLOGY

Sociology has a very short history. Of course, centuries before Christ was born, people like Plato and Socrates had thought and argued about social behavior. But most of them did not make systematic observations to test their speculations against reality. They were social philosophers, not sociologists. The field of sociology emerged in the nineteenth century, when European social philosophers began to use scientific methods.

Two factors combined to convert some philosophers into sociologists: the social upheavals of nineteenth-century Europe and the advancement of the natural sciences. The Western world was radically altered during the nineteenth century, as the Industrial Revolution brought new industries and technologies and new ways of living. Almost overnight, societies that had long been rural and stable became industrialized, urbanized, and chaotic. They confronted problems such as the exploitation of factory workers, migration of people from farms to cities, congestion and poverty in the cities, crowded and squalid housing, broken families, and rising crime. Meanwhile, the political order of Europe had been shaken up. In the aftermath of the French Revolution, many people began to question the legitimacy of their monarchies and the authority of their churches, demanding greater freedom for the individual. Many social philosophers felt challenged to find solutions to their societies' new problems and to understand how and why such radical change could occur. At the same time, the natural sciences were highly respected, because they were providing ways to both explain and control aspects of the physical world. Some social philosophers looked on natural science as a model for how they might go about understanding and controlling the social world.

As sociology developed, these two urges—to improve the world and to apply scientific methods to the study of society—continued to motivate sociologists. As we shall see, however, the value of these goals and their role in sociology have also been a source of controversy.

Herbert Spencer (1820–1913) believed that society corrects its own problems because it is governed by the laws of nature. He argued that government should not intervene to solve social problems.

Pioneers of Sociology

The nineteenth-century French philosopher Auguste Comte (1789–1857) is sometimes called the father of sociology. He coined the word "sociology" in 1838 to refer to the scientific study of society. Comte believed that every society goes through three stages of development: religious, metaphysical, and scientific. According to Comte, reliance on superstition and speculation characterizes the religious and metaphysical stages, and neither is adequate for understanding society or for solving society's problems. What is needed, he argued, is scientific knowledge about society based on social facts, just as scientific knowledge about the physical world is based on physical facts. He envisioned a science of society with two branches: *statics,* the study of the organization that allows societies to endure, and *dynamics,* the study of the processes by which societies change. During the scientific stage, Comte believed, sociologists would develop a scientific knowledge of society and would guide society in a peaceful, orderly evolution.

Auguste Comte (1789–1857) was the first to argue for the need for scientific knowledge about society. He is regarded as the father of sociology.

Herbert Spencer (1820–1913) did not assign such an exalted role to sociologists. This nineteenth-century Englishman had a different view of how society works. He believed that a society can be compared to a living organism. Each part of an animal—its heart, lungs, brains, and so on—has its own function to perform, yet all the parts are interdependent, so that a change in one part affects all the others. Moreover, each part contributes to the survival and health of the animal as a whole. If one organ becomes diseased, others adapt to the crisis, working harder to ensure the animal's survival. Similarly, in Spencer's view, each part of a society performs its own function and contributes to the survival and stability of the whole. The family, religion, the government, industry—all are parts of one "organism," society.

Spencer concluded that society, if left alone, corrects its own problems. It tends naturally toward health and stability. Social problems work themselves out through the natural process of "survival of the fittest." The phrase implies that rich, powerful, or otherwise successful people—the "fittest"—deserve to enjoy their wealth, power, or success because they have been "selected" by nature to be what they are. On the other hand, poor, weak, or otherwise unsuccessful individuals—the "unfit"—should be left to fend for themselves, because nature has doomed them to failure. If government interferes with this natural process by helping the unfit, the society will suffer, because the efforts of its successful people will be wasted. According to Spencer, the best thing government can do about social problems is to leave them alone. The fate of society, in his view, is governed by laws of nature. If nature is left to do its job without government interference, society will not only survive but evolve to become better.

Karl Marx (1818–1883) claimed that conflict and competition are the chief factors in social life. In his view, the primary feature of society is the conflict between capitalists and laborers.

But where Spencer saw harmony and stability, Karl Marx (1818–1883) saw underlying conflict, exploitation, and the seeds of revolution. According to Marx, a German who spent much of his life writing in England and often had money problems, Spencer's stable, interdependent society was a myth. The primary feature of society, Marx claimed, is not stability and interdependence but conflict and competition. Every society, past and present, is marked by social conflict.

In particular, Marx claimed that the primary feature of society is **class conflict.** There is a class of capitalists, the bourgeoisie, who own the means of production, and an exploited class of laborers, the proletariat, who do not own the means of production. These two classes, he said, are inevitably locked in conflict. The laborers, far from being naturally unfit, are destined to overthrow the capitalists and establish a classless society in which everyone will work according to ability and receive according to need.

Marx did not believe, as Spencer did, that the differences between laborers and capitalists are determined by natural selection. On the contrary, Marx believed that they are determined by the economic system. In fact, he argued, the economic system determines a society's religious beliefs, its values, and the nature of its educational system, government, and other institutions. And again unlike Spencer, he urged people not to let society evolve on its own but to change it.

Despite their differences, both Marx and Spencer, like Comte, recognized the value of science in the study of society. But they did not actually use scientific methods. They argued about how society worked and how its troubles might be eased. Nevertheless, they did not conduct scientific observations, much less experiments. It was Emile Durkheim (1858–1917) who pioneered the systematic application of scientific methods to sociology. His ideas about suicide, which we discussed earlier, were not based on speculation. In his study of suicide, he made a research plan. Then he collected a large mass of statistical data on suicide in various European countries. Finally, he analyzed the data in order to discover the causes of suicide. He not only used systematic observation but also argued that sociologists should consider only what they could observe and should look at "social facts as things." They should *not* look, he said, to "the notions" of people in order to explain society. People's subjective experiences should not be a concern of sociologists.

In contrast, the German sociologist Max Weber

Emile Durkheim (1858–1917) pioneered the systematic application of scientific principles to sociology. He was the first to use statistical methods to test hypotheses.

(1864–1920) believed that sociologists must go beyond what people do, beyond what can be observed directly. He argued that individuals always interpret the meaning of their own behavior and act according to these interpretations. Sociologists must therefore find out how people feel or what they think about their own behavior. To do this, according to Weber, sociologists should adopt a method he called **Verstehen**—sympathetic understanding of their subjects. By mentally putting themselves into their subjects' position, sociologists could obtain an "interpretive understanding" of the meanings of particular behavior. Then, he said, they should test this understanding through careful observation.

Max Weber (1864–1920) believed that an objective study of human behavior is insufficient for sociologists. To him, sociologists must also investigate how people feel and think about their own behavior.

American Sociology

By the turn of the twentieth century, sociology had made its way from Europe to the United States. Like their European predecessors, the first American sociologists tried to understand and solve the problems of their time, problems such as crime and delinquency, broken homes, slums, and racial unrest. But they dealt with social problems differently. The Europeans were more interested in developing large-scale social theories. So they examined the fundamental issues of social order and social change, trying to discover the causes of social problems as a whole. In contrast, the Americans were more pragmatic. They were more inclined to focus on specific problems, such as prostitution or juvenile delinquency, and to treat each problem separately. They were mostly religious, many being former ministers. In trying to solve social problems, they hoped to build a heavenly kingdom on earth (Vidich and Lyman, 1985).

For about 40 years, American sociologists studied various problems. Then their religious, reformist fervor began to cool. Some turned their attention to general theories of society. The idea grew that sociology should be a *basic science,* seeking knowledge only, not an *applied science,* putting knowledge to use. Moreover, many people believed that sociology must be objective and free of values. There was then no room in sociology for a commitment to reform society in order to bring it into conformity with certain values. From about 1940 to 1960, sociology was dominated by the attempt to develop scientific methods that could be applied to the study of societies and social behavior. During these two decades, sociologists developed increasingly sophisticated research techniques.

In the 1960s, however, the ideal of objective, value-free knowledge came under fire in just about all fields, including sociology. Renewed awareness of poverty and years of social unrest—marked by race riots, student revolts, and controversy about the Vietnam War—put pressure on sociologists to attack society's ills once again. Meanwhile, attitudes toward the major theoreti-

"It's 'Das Kapital' this and 'Das Kapital' that, but very little of it finds its way into this house."

cal perspectives in sociology were also shifting. The conflict perspective, which emphasizes social conflict as a constant fact of social life, was becoming popular at the expense of the functionalist perspective, which stresses the persistence of social order.

American sociology has thus developed into a diverse discipline. Today, it is both a basic and an applied science, and sociologists use both objective and subjective methods. The soaring number of sociologists—from only about 3,000 in the late 1960s to over 10,000 today—has further splintered sociology into numerous specialties such as mathematical sociology, historical Marxism, phenomenology, ethnomethodology, sociobiology, network analysis, organizational research, clinical sociology, and race and ethnic relations. Each of these specialties has itself differentiated into many subspecialties. The specialty of race relations, for example, has broken down into studies of blacks, Hispanics, Asians, and other specific minorities in the United States (Blalock, 1984; Collins, 1986). Underlying all this diversity are certain theoretical perspectives that sociologists employ to study and understand social behavior. We will examine three major ones in the next section.

QUESTIONS FOR DISCUSSION AND REVIEW

1. How did Karl Marx's understanding of nineteenth-century European society differ from that of Herbert Spencer and Max Weber?
2. What are some of the ways in which the development of American sociology differed from the work of European sociologists?

MAJOR PERSPECTIVES

Sociologists, like just about everyone else, use different levels of analysis. They can look at the "big picture," at one small piece of it, or at something in between. On the lowest level of analysis, we find very specific explanations or descriptions, such as an analysis of the social causes of alcoholism or of the customs of hazing in fraternities. At a middle level of analysis, sociologists develop theories that are broad enough to take in a whole class of activities or events but specific enough to be tested by observation or experiment. Thus we find, for example, theories about the causes of numerous kinds of crime and delinquency. The early European sociologists, however, often developed yet another kind of analysis: they offered a broad vision of what society fundamentally is like or how it works. Their views provided the basis for today's models of society, or **theoretical perspectives.** These perspectives are merely "orienting strategies" (Wagner and Berger, 1985). They show us how to view society and what kinds of questions we should ask about social behavior. Therefore, unlike the more specific theories, they cannot be validated as either true or false. They can only orient or direct us toward what is assumed to be the real nature of society.

Three major theoretical perspectives are used by sociologists today: structural functionalism, conflict perspective, and symbolic interactionism. All three emphasize the influence of social forces on human behavior. But each perspective offers a different view of which social forces are most important.

Structural Functionalism

Both Spencer and Durkheim provided ideas that inspired **structural functionalism.** According to this perspective, which is often called *functionalism,* each part of society—the family, the school, the economy, or the state—contributes something. Each performs certain functions for the society as a whole. Moreover, all the parts are interdependent. The family, for example, depends on the school to educate its children, and the school, in turn, depends on the family or the state to provide financial support. The state, in turn, depends on the family and school to help children grow up to become law-abiding, taxpaying citizens. Out of these interdependent parts of society comes a stable social order, the structure. If something happens to disrupt this social order, its parts will adjust in a way that produces a new stability. Suppose the economy were in bad shape, with high rates of inflation and unemployment. The family would adjust, perhaps by spending less and saving more. The school would probably offer fewer programs and emphasize vocational training. The state might try to cut its budget. As a result, there would be a new social order.

However, what holds the society together, enabling all its part to produce social order? The answer, according to functionalists, is **social consensus,** a condition in which most members of the society agree on what would be good for everybody and cooperate to achieve it. Durkheim assumed that social consensus can come about in the form of mechanical or organic solidarity.

Mechanical solidarity is a type of social cohesion that develops when people do similar work and have similar beliefs and values. It exists in relatively simple, traditional societies. An example of such societies is one in which almost everyone works at farming and believes in the same gods. In contrast, **organic solidarity** is a type of social cohesion that arises when the people in a society perform a wide variety of specialized jobs and therefore have to depend on each other. Organic solidarity is characteristic of complex, industrialized societies. The people in an American city, for example, are likely to hold many very different types of jobs, to have grown up with different family customs, to hold varying beliefs and values. There are bankers, teachers, engineers, plumbers, and many other businesses, professions, and occupations. Among them there will probably be atheists and Christians, Jews and Moslems, reactionaries and radicals, and everything in between. Thus mechanical solidarity among the city's people is not likely to be strong. They cannot be bound together by conformity to the same ideas and ideals. But they can be more easily bound together by their need for each other. The banker needs the secretary who deposits and borrows money, and both need the storekeeper, who needs the trucker who delivers food, who needs the mechanic and gas station attendant and so on. The complex ties of dependence seem virtually endless. These people are bound together by organic solidarity.

During the 1940s and 1950s, structural functionalism became widely accepted by American sociologists. But in its move from Europe to the United States, functionalism had been altered somewhat. Originally, it was used to help explain the social structure as a whole—to clarify how order and stability were maintained. But American sociologists have been more interested in discovering the functions of specific types of human behavior.

The most prominent among these American sociologists is Robert Merton (1957). He classified functions into two types: manifest and latent. **Manifest functions** are those that are intended and seem obvious; **latent functions** are unintended and often unrecognized. The manifest function of going to college, for example, is to get an education, but going to college also has the latent function of enabling many students to find their future spouses.

To study a social phenomenon, we need only common sense to know its manifest functions. Such knowledge is obvious or superficial. But the search for its latent functions requires sociological understanding, which reveals its deeper, underlying reality (Campbell, 1982). Analyses of latent functions, then, can be very provocative. An example is Kingsley Davis's (1976a) functional analysis of prostitution. Guided by common sense, many people would regard prostitution as an evil that threatens the morality of their community. Yet this view does not explain why prostitution has existed for centuries despite many crusades against it. According to Davis, prostitution persists because of its latent function; it guards the sexual morals of society, "protecting the family and keeping the wives and daughters of the respectable citizenry pure." If men can go to prostitutes, they are less likely to persuade "respectable" women to engage in sexual promiscuity. Thus the women can preserve their morals and thereby uphold the sexual morals of their community.

Throughout this book we will see many examples of the usefulness of functionalism, but by itself it cannot lead to a complete picture of society. It has also been criticized for being inherently conservative. In effect, it justifies the status quo. By emphasizing what every current aspect of society does for its citizens, functionalism

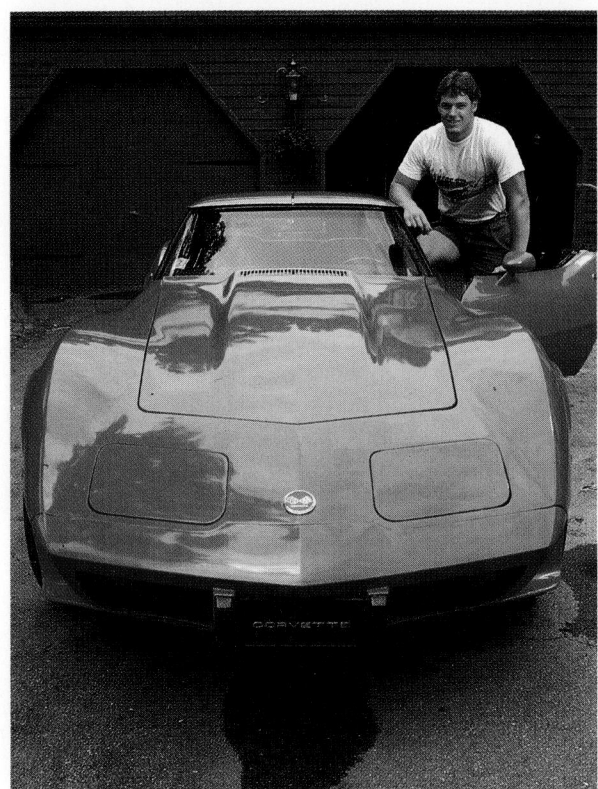

Latent functions are those aspects of things that are apart from their primary purposes. The automobile clearly enables people to go from one place to another. Its manifest function, then, is transportation. But it may also have some latent functions, as does the Corvette here. One latent function of this shiny, expensive sports car is to serve as a status symbol, making its owner feel a great sense of pride. What other latent functions might such a car have?

encourages people to dismiss social change as "dysfunctional" (harmful), even though change may, in fact, produce a better society.

Conflict Perspective

The conflict perspective produces a picture of society strikingly different from that offered by functionalism. Whereas functionalism emphasizes society's stability, the **conflict perspective** portrays society as always changing and always marked by conflict. Functionalists tend to focus on social order, to view social change as harmful, and to assume that the social order is based largely on people's willing cooperation. Implicitly, functionalism defends the status quo. In contrast, proponents of the conflict perspective are inclined to concentrate on social conflict, to see social change as beneficial, and to assume that the social order is forcibly imposed by the powerful on the weak. They criticize the status quo.

The conflict perspective originated largely from Karl

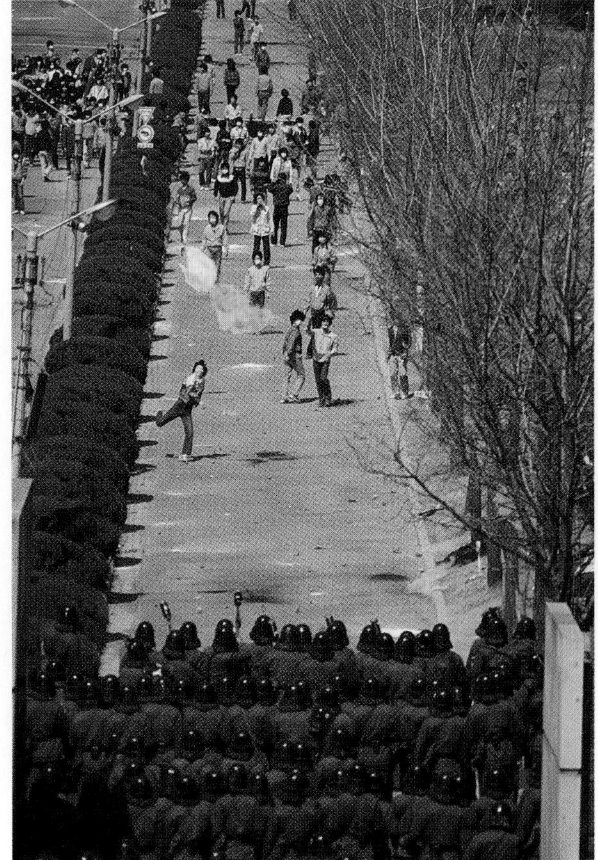

Sometimes conflict is open, as in the battle shown here between South Korean students and the police during a demonstration against the government. But conflict theorists emphasize that all unequal groups—such as management and labor, whites and blacks, or men and women—are in perpetual competition over every aspect of contemporary life. Such competition usually results in the exploitation of the weak by the powerful. Nevertheless, the constant struggle by the weak ensures that society is always changing.

Marx's writings on the class conflict between capitalists and the proletariat. For decades American sociologists tended to ignore Marx and the conflict perspective because the functionalist perspective dominated their view of society. Then came the turbulent 1960s, and the conflict perspective gained popularity among American sociologists. Generally, they have defined conflict more broadly than Marx did. Whereas Marx believed that conflict between *economic* classes was the key force in society, conflict theorists today define social conflict to mean conflict between any unequal groups or segments of society. Thus they examine conflict between whites and blacks, men and women, one religious group and another, and so on. They emphasize that groups within society will have conflicting interests and values and thus will compete with each other. Because of this perpetual competition, society is always changing.

The conflict perspective leads sociologists to ask questions such as: Which groups are more powerful and which are weaker? How do powerful groups benefit from the existing social order, and how are weaker groups hurt? Looking at prostitution, for example, conflict theorists might emphasize that it reflects the unequal social positions of men and women. In prostitution, members of a dominant group, men, benefit from the exploitation of a weaker group, women. This exploitation is made possible by the existence of a social order in which women are subordinate to men. As Edwin Schur (1984) points out, if the sexes were equal, with women having full access to and being equally paid for more "respectable" types of work, women would not become prostitutes. Furthermore, prostitution reinforces the general dominance of men over women because it helps perpetuate the idea that women are inferior beings who can be used as mere objects for pleasure. Whereas the functionalist perspective focuses our attention on how prostitution might reinforce society's moral code, the conflict perspective instead points to how it might reflect and reinforce the power of one group over another. The conflict perspective has been criticized, however, for overemphasizing social conflict and ignoring the order and stability within society.

Symbolic Interactionism

Both functionalist and conflict perspectives tend to focus on abstract concepts and the large social issues of order and conflict. In contrast, **symbolic interactionism** directs our attention to the details of everyday life and the interaction between individuals. We can trace its origins to Max Weber's argument that people act according to their interpretation of the meaning of their social world. But it was George Herbert Mead (1863–1931), an American philosopher, who introduced symbolic interactionism to American sociology in the 1920s.

According to symbolic interactionism, people assign meanings to each other's words and actions. Their actions and attitudes, then, are not determined by some action in and of itself. Instead, they act according to their subjective interpretation of the action. When you speak to a friend, an observer can easily give an objective report of the words you have said. But your friend's response will depend not on the list of words you spoke but on his or her interpretation of the entire interaction, and your friend's response is at the same time influencing what you are saying. If your friend perceives by the way you speak that you are intelligent, this interpretation may make your friend respect and admire you and, perhaps, respond more positively to what you are saying. If you, in turn, catch this interpretation, you may feel proud and speak more confidently. In short, the exchange is a symbolic interaction. It is an interaction between individuals that is governed by their interpretation of the meaning of symbols. In this case, the symbols were primarily spoken words. But a symbol can be anything—an object, a sound, a gesture—that points to something beyond itself. The marks on this paper are symbols because they point to something—they mean something—beyond black squiggles.

The perspective of symbolic interactionism implies two things. First, people do not respond directly to physical "things." Rather, they respond to their own interpretations of them. Second, because people constantly make interpretations—of the world in general, of other people, of themselves and their own interpretations—and then act according to them, human behavior is fluid, always changing. How we act is constantly being altered by how we interpret other people's actions and reactions to our own behavior.

Symbolic interactionists therefore pay very close attention to what, exactly, people do and try to determine what meanings people are giving to their own actions and to those of others. Looking at prostitution, symbolic interactionists do not focus on *why* prostitution exists, as functionalists and conflict theorists do. Instead, they zero in on *how* it exists, examining how prostitutes interact with their clients as well as how they interpret this interaction. In a classic study of how novice call girls learn to deal with their customers, James Bryan (1965) tried to answer such questions as: What do experienced call girls teach novices? (He found that they teach interpersonal skills such as how to engage in telephone conversations and how to discuss and obtain the fee.) Do they teach sexual techniques? (No, even though the novices' previous sexual experiences may have been very limited.) Do the experienced prostitutes teach the novices a certain interpretation of themselves and their clients? (Yes, they are taught to see themselves as honest and their customers as corrupt and hypocritical.) Many more recent studies have found that most prostitutes have learned to regard their sexual activities with customers as simply a job. This enables them to separate sex from emotional involvement, making it easier for them to have sex with many different men whom they see as merely their "tricks" (Heyl, 1979).

In contrast with the relatively abstract concerns of the functionalist and conflict perspectives, symbolic interactionism directs our attention to the concrete details of human life as seen through the eyes of the individuals. It has been criticized, however, for ignoring the larger issues of societal stability and change. It has been faulted, as it were, for examining the trees so closely that it fails to show us what the forest looks like.

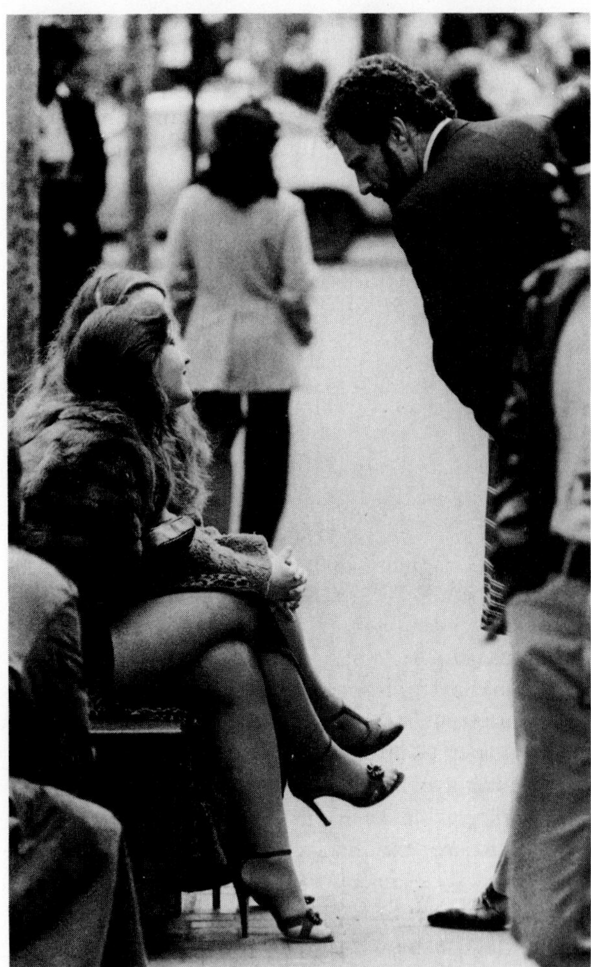

The three sociological perspectives open our eyes to various aspects of the same social phenomenon. From functionalism, we see that prostitution helps keep "respectable women pure" by encouraging men to engage in sexual promiscuity only with prostitutes. From the conflict perspective, we look at prostitution as a reflection of the sexual exploitation of women (a weaker group) by men (a dominant group). From symbolic interactionism, we learn that prostitutes, such as the two women here, regard their sexual activities with customers as simply a business transaction and interact with the men in a businesslike manner.

An Integrated View

By itself, each of the three perspectives can produce a distorted picture of society. In effect, each gives us a view from just one angle. If we overemphasize any one of them, we are likely to miss something about the complex reality of our social world. Each of these perspectives is useful, however, because we cannot take everything about the complex social world into account at once. We need some vantage point. Each perspective tells us what to look for, and each brings some aspect of society and human behavior into sharper focus. Combined, though, these perspectives can enrich our sociological knowledge of the world.

As we shall see in later chapters, the usefulness of each perspective depends on what we are studying, and the three perspectives are not equally helpful in understanding every phenomenon. But often each does have something to contribute to our understanding of the same subject. If we are studying the interaction between black and white Americans, or between upper- and lower-class people, each perspective can be useful. Functionalist and conflict perspectives can lead us to analyses that clarify how the interaction is affected by larger social forces, such as racial prejudice and social inequality.

Symbolic interactionism can give us a richer, more detailed view of specific interactions and an understanding of why people influenced by the same social forces behave in different ways. Sometimes the three perspectives are complementary, sometimes they give contradictory views, and we need to evaluate the merits of each.

QUESTIONS FOR DISCUSSION AND REVIEW

1. What is a "theoretical perspective," and what are the main features of the three perspectives sociologists use today?
2. How do the basic assumptions of the conflict perspective differ from those of structural functionalism?
3. Is any one of the three sociological perspectives better than the others?

THE USES OF SOCIOLOGY

The study of sociology is an intellectual exercise that may be pursued for its own sake, for the pleasure of satisfying curiosity, or for producing scientific knowledge. But sociology also has practical uses for society as a whole and for individuals.

Sociological research can dispel myths and provide a rational basis for choosing public policies. At the end of World War II, sociologists were asked to find a way to reduce the size of American military forces overseas without hurting morale. Their research suggested that if the more experienced soldiers were sent home first, those left behind would not become resentful. In 1954, when the U.S. Supreme Court reached a landmark decision to desegregate public schools, it was influenced by the sociological finding that segregation had harmed black children by causing, among other things, self-hatred. In the 1960s, sociological studies on poverty in the United States helped make a complacent America aware of the problem and encouraged its government to declare the War on Poverty. In the same decade, it was made more difficult than before to commit people to state mental institutions after some sociologists demonstrated that many inmates in those institutions were not dangerous to the public. In the late 1970s, some sociologists discovered that employee ownership could be an effective means for stopping industrial decline. Since then the federal government and many state governments have provided tax advantages to help employees buy and keep the companies where they work. As a result, there are now nearly 7,000 companies having some form of employee ownership and more than 500 companies with most or all of their stocks owned by employees. This is astounding because employee ownership did not exist in the early 1970s. Today many state governments often ask social scientists to do research on how American industry can be revitalized. Many American companies, too, are now trying to regain the competitive edge against foreign rivals by applying the sociological theory of human relations, which essentially calls for participative management and worker participation as a way to boost productivity (Whyte, 1986).

These are only a few well-known examples of how sociology has been used to help our society solve its problems. Based on scientific evidence, such applications of sociology are a far cry from the traditional reliance on untested popular beliefs or haphazard trial-and-error methods to solve social problems. There are at least three ways in which sociologists can serve the public (Rossi and Whyte, 1983). First, they can conduct *applied social research.* Thus they often provide government agencies with more valid estimates of crime, business firms with estimates of worker morale and customers' preferences for certain products, and politicians with data on voter preferences and chances of winning elections. Second, sociologists can serve as *social engineers,* using sociological knowledge to design policies and programs for accomplishing some objectives. For example, sociologists may devise a program for reducing juvenile delinquency, design an effective way for a community to assimilate deinstitutionalized mental patients, and promote worker participation to increase industrial productivity. Third, sociologists can serve as *clinicians,* providing consultation and technical assistance to solve specific problems. They may advise a married couple on how to work together in raising children or show General Motors how to improve worker morale.

Sociology can also benefit individuals directly. The sociological perspective enables us to step outside ourselves mentally, to see how social forces influence our lives so that we may be able to deal with them more effectively. If we have a personal problem, an understanding of the social forces that influence suicide may help us appreciate the value of social integration. We will more likely share our problem with friends and relatives than keep it to ourselves. Thus we will get help and support to solve the problem. Sociology can also help us improve our relations with others—whether they be our parents, lovers, friends, or strangers—by enabling us to analyze our interactions objectively and rationally rather than subjectively and irrationally.

Finally, you can build a career on the study of sociology or use a knowledge of sociology to advance a career in some other field. The opportunities depend on the degree you obtain. About 74 percent of those with a Ph.D. degree in sociology work as teachers at universities and four-year colleges. Those with an M.A. are also likely to teach, usually at junior and community colleges and occasionally at four-year colleges. But increasing numbers have recently been pursuing a wide variety of careers outside the academic community (see box, p. 20). They work as researchers or administrators in public or private organizations such as the Census Bureau, the National Institute of Mental Health, and Population Council, the Urban League, as well as state and federal departments of health, welfare, agriculture, education, and housing. A growing number of sociologists have chosen social engineering or clinical sociology as their specialty. Some sociologists who are teachers, researchers, or administrators double as political analysts, social critics, political lobbyists, or sociological consultants (Huber, 1983b, 1984).

Even if you do not become a sociologist, the study of sociology can help you directly or indirectly in many jobs. A bachelor's degree in sociology can be especially useful if human relations are central to your work. Often such jobs are found in public and private social agencies concerned with child care, juvenile delinquency, drug abuse, and so on. Obtaining related experiences before graduation should increase your chances of being hired by such an agency. Working in a halfway house for juvenile delinquents while in college, for example, will increase your chances of landing a job as a probation officer or drug-treatment worker after graduation. Of course, sociology majors with a B.A. degree also work in business establishments of all kinds—banks, department stores, manufacturing firms, and so on. Most such employers are interested in well-rounded students with good analytical, interpersonal, and communication skills, which you can pick up from sociology courses (Cobb, 1983; Huber, 1983a, 1984). Especially in recent years, numerous companies have been wooing liberal arts graduates with growing enthusiasm. According to a study in 1986, major corporations planned to increase their hiring of new liberal arts graduates by about 20 percent in that year, while they expected to raise the overall hiring of college graduates by less than 1 percent. Even high-tech companies are recruiting liberal arts graduates for jobs in sales, marketing, finance, public relations, and production management. Moreover, after being hired, you are likely to find that your sociological knowledge will help you advance. This has been suggested by a recent study showing that 38 percent of today's top business executives majored in the liberal arts. Another study has also found that 9 out of the top 13 executives at IBM are liberal arts majors. At AT&T, social science graduates move into middle management faster than their engineering counterparts and do at least as well as business and engineering graduates in reaching top management positions (Watkins, 1986; Cheney, 1986).

QUESTIONS FOR DISCUSSION AND REVIEW

1. What is the major difference between applied social research and social engineering?
2. How can sociology help students choose a meaningful career and develop relevant job skills?
3. Why do many government agencies sometimes ignore the policy recommendations provided by applied social researchers?

CHAPTER REVIEW

1. *What is unique about the way sociologists look at human behavior?* They view human behavior, even personal experiences, as being influenced by social forces. This focus on the influence of social forces constitutes the sociological perspective. *How does sociology differ from common sense?* While common sense gives familiar and untested ideas, sociology provides scientific facts and scientifically supported ideas. *How does sociology differ from the natural sciences?* Social phenomena, the subject of sociology, are often more complex and varied than natural events. Sociologists also cannot stand completely detached from the subjects they study. *As a social science, how is sociology unique?* Sociology is a much broader field of study than the other social sciences. It covers some aspect of the human events studied by each of the other social sciences.

USING SOCIOLOGICAL INSIGHT

New Job Opportunities for Sociologists

Most sociologists teach at universities and colleges. But a growing number pursue a wide variety of careers outside the academic community. In the following, Jonathan Turner discusses the social forces behind this trend. What do these new job opportunities tell us about the valuable uses of sociology?

Increasingly, sociologists are working outside the classroom, off the campus, and far away from the ivory tower. One reason for this trend is that the job market in academia is tight. But, more important, the number of jobs for nonacademic sociologists is increasing, especially in state governments. What is occurring is not a mass exodus from academia, but a slow movement. . . . The usefulness of sociology for both government and the private sector is gradually becoming acknowledged.

Why should this be so? The main reason is that the scale of social life—its fluidity, scope, and complexity—has increased. Government is bigger and doing more. Corporations are increasingly large conglomerates. Markets are highly complex and volatile. Social change is incessant. Social protest is frequent. Such transformations of social life create problems of organization. How are people to be coordinated? How are services to be delivered? How are government and industry to get along? How are citizens to be made happy and content? How are potential disruptions to be controlled? How is order to be ensured? How is conflict, when it occurs, to be mediated?

Such questions are the lifeblood of sociology. I am not saying that we have answers to them all, but at least those who must deal with them are beginning to recognize the importance and relevance of sociology. You do not have to have an M.A. or Ph.D. to capitalize on this growing awareness. Just a bachelor's degree can give you what is needed—a general awareness of, and perspective on, the nature of social interaction and social organization.

I see sociology like computer science was two decades ago—a discipline about to take off. There is a growing recognition that the scale of social problems and issues requires new kinds of professionals. Disillusionment with the simple promises of politicians and the failure of economists to manage the economy—to say nothing of the society—has forced the recognition that we now need professionals of a different sort. We require new technologies—not of the whiz-bang, mechanical variety but of the human measure. . . . The understanding of the properties and dynamics of human organization and the knowledge of how to gather and interpret information about human affairs will be increasingly valuable, and, to be blunt, marketable.

To give just a few examples, we

2. *Plato and Socrates discussed social issues. Were they sociologists?* No, they were social philosophers, who thought and argued about the nature of the world but did not test their ideas against systematic observation. *What led to the transformation of social philosophy into sociology?* Seized with the desire to solve social problems and impressed with the contributions from the natural sciences, some nineteenth-century social philosophers tried to apply the scientific method to the study of society in the hope of curing social ills. This attempt to replace philosophical speculation with the scientific method of systematic observation transformed social philosophy into sociology.

3. *What did Spencer mean when he said society is like a living organism?* In Spencer's view, each part of society, like each organ of an animal, performs its own function. If one part of society has problems, the other parts will adapt to the situation, ensuring the survival of the entire society. *What did Marx mean by class conflict?* Marx was referring to the struggle between the class of capitalists, who own the means of production, and the proletariat, who perform the labor. *What is the difference between* Verstehen *and Durkheim's objective approach?* Verstehen requires sociologists to adopt an attitude of understanding or empathy toward their subjects in order to understand how people interpret their own behavior, whereas

will probably be seeing sociologists as data analysts, office heads, sales directors, labor-management facilitators, eligibility workers in the welfare system, heads of adoption agencies, city planning directors, patrol officers on the police force, park and recreation directors, liaison personnel in the various agencies of city government, redevelopment directors, community organizers, census bureau statisticians, social workers, management consultants, advertising executives, insurance agents, and housing developers. Thus, as this very short listing of job options underscores, the provision of many different kinds of human and organizational services will be the avenue of sociological invasion. In all of these jobs, knowledge of organizational dynamics, human behavior, and cultural diversity are essential. . . .

The increasing range of jobs for which sociological training is relevant is the result of the transformation of the economy and government. A postindustrial economy increasingly employs people in service, nonmanual jobs. As machines take on more tasks, the need for personnel to service the productive process grows dramatically. In the private sector, productive activity involves dealing with people, clients, governmental agencies, and other corporate units. Such work has a clear sociological bias. In government, regulatory and service functions are also sociological in character because they involve providing human services and coordination activity.

As sociologically trained individuals assume these service-oriented jobs, they bring with them a perspective that is sensitive to the larger social and cultural forces within which people and organizations operate. This perspective is, I believe, what makes such workers good at what they do, because compared to other professionals, they have fewer blinders. They see more and as a result they can do more. In the long term, I hope, there will be enough sociologically sensitive individuals to supplant the "cost-accountant," "bottom line," "economically rational man" mentality of many organizations. The limitations of this orientation are increasingly evident as this century draws to a close especially as the American economy and government attempt to confront declining per capita productivity and growing competition in world markets. It is these kinds of pressures that have created opportunities for sociologists. And it is for this reason that you should consider sociology seriously as a useful vocation.

Source: Excerpted and adapted from *Sociology: A Student Handbook,* by Jonathan H. Turner. Copyright © 1985 by Jonathan H. Turner. Reprinted by permission of Random House, Inc.

Durkheim, who pioneered the application of scientific methods to sociology, argued that sociologists should deal solely with observable aspects of human behavior.

4. *How did the early American sociologists differ from their European predecessors?* The European sociologists were primarily interested in explaining the nature of society as a whole—the causes of social stability and change. In the United States, interest shifted to the study of specific social problems. Later, American sociologists emphasized the search for sociological knowledge rather than its application to social problems, but their interest in social reform grew again during the 1960s. *What is the nature of modern sociology?* Modern sociology is a diverse discipline, one that is both a basic and an applied science and that uses both objective and subjective methods of investigation.

5. *What are the basic ideas of structural functionalism?* Structural functionalism focuses on social order and assumes that the various parts of a society are interdependent, forming a social structure in which each part serves a function that helps ensure the survival of the whole. *How does the conflict perspective differ from functionalism?* Whereas functionalism focuses on social order and stability, the conflict perspective emphasizes social

change and conflict, showing how one group dominates another. *What is a symbolic interaction?* It is an interaction between individuals that is governed by their interpretations of each other's actions.

6. *Can sociological knowledge be used to solve social problems?* Yes. It has been used to help resolve controversies, to give a sound basis for choosing public policies, and to provide information necessary for intelligent planning. *How can sociology help us in our personal lives?* It enables us to step outside ourselves mentally and see how we and others are influenced by various social forces. *What can you do with a major in sociology?* There are many career opportunities, but some practical experience of supplementary training in college can enhance your chances of finding a good job.

KEY TERMS

Class conflict Marx's term for the struggle between capitalists, who own the means of production, and the proletariat, who do not (p. 11).

Conflict perspective A theoretical perspective that focuses on conflict and change in society, particularly conflict between a dominant and a subordinate group, and emphasizes that conflict is a constant fact of social life (p. 15).

Hypothesis A tentative statement about how various events are related to one another (p. 7).

Latent function A function that is unintended and thus often unrecognized (p. 14).

Manifest function A function that is intended and thus seems obvious (p. 14).

Mechanical solidarity A form of social cohesion that develops when people do similar work and have similar beliefs and values; characteristic of simple, traditional societies (p. 14).

Organic solidarity A form of social cohesion that develops when the differences among occupations make people depend on each other, characteristic of complex, industrialized societies (p. 14).

Social consensus Condition in which most members of society agree on what is good for everybody to have and cooperate to achieve it (p. 14).

Social forces Forces that arise from the society we are part of (p. 4).

Social integration The degree to which people are related to a social group (p. 5).

Sociological imagination C. Wright Mills's term for the ability to see the impact of social forces on individuals, especially on their private lives (p. 4).

Sociology The scientific study of human social behavior (p. 4).

Structural functionalism A theoretical perspective that focuses on social order, which is assumed to be based on the positive functions performed by the interdependent parts of society (p. 13).

Symbolic interactionism A theoretical perspective that focuses on the interaction between individuals and is based on the assumption that their subjective interpretations of each other's actions influence their interaction (p. 16).

Theoretical perspective A set of broad assumptions about the nature of a subject which cannot be proven true or false (p. 13).

Theory A set of logically related hypotheses that explains the relationship among various phenomena (p. 7).

Verstehen Weber's term for the subjective method, which requires sociologists to adopt an attitude of understanding or empathy toward their subjects (p. 12).

SUGGESTED READINGS

Berger, Peter L., and Hansfried Kellner, 1981. *Sociology Reinterpreted: An Essay on Method and Vocation.* Garden City, N.Y.: Anchor Books. Presenting the Weberian, symbolic interactionist approach to social reality.

Bierstedt, Robert. 1981. *American Sociological Theory: A Critical History.* New York: Academic Press. A useful analysis of the major writings of ten functionalist sociologists such as Merton and Parsons.

Collins, Randall. 1985. *Three Sociological Traditions.* New York: Oxford University Press. An insightful analysis of the development of the three sociological perspectives discussed in this chapter.

Horowitz, Irving Louis. 1983. C. *Wright Mills: An American*

Utopian. New York: Free Press. An excellent intellectual biography of the foremost conflict theorist in the 1950s and early 1960s, whose impact on sociology is still felt today.

Vidich, Arthur J., and Stanford M. Lyman, 1985. *American Sociology: Worldly Rejections of Religion and Their Directions.* New Haven and London: Yale University Press. Shows how the religious thought of the last century influences contemporary American sociology and how intellectual and moral problems crop up when sociological concepts are transvalued from religious into secular terms.

45

2 Doing Sociology: Research Methods

As scientists, sociologists look for patterns in our social world. A pattern can be a particular way in which our society has turned us into eager consumers and drivers. If some sociologists hypothesize that heavy advertising is a major factor in the popularity of cars and other consumer goods, they will do research to test the hypothesis. They may conduct a survey by interviewing people. Or they may use some other research method, such as observation, experiment, or analysis of existing data.

From the sociological perspective discussed in the preceding chapter, we can draw many ideas about how social forces shape our lives. Yet these ideas are merely idle guesswork unless they are backed up by scientific facts. This is one important reason why sociologists conduct scientific research to collect data. Social research, however, is not only for checking the presumed validity of existing theories about people and society. It is also for producing information that describes our lives and for developing new theories that explain how our lives are influenced by various social forces. Thus the production of sociological knowledge depends heavily on social research. In this chapter we will find out what social researchers are looking for, what methods they use to gather data, how we may go about doing research, and what kinds of problems sociologists face in trying to be strictly scientific.

BASIC CONCEPTS OF SOCIAL RESEARCH

Sociologists often do research to find out *what* is going on in society, to discover the characteristics of a social phenomenon. Thus they may take a survey, asking people about such things as their attitude toward the Soviet Union, whether they smoke marijuana, and so on. Through the **descriptive research** sociologists gather information that simply describes our lives—though it may stimulate new theories about the social causes of our behavior. They also conduct **explanatory research** to test theories, ideas about *why* or *how* some social event is happening. In either case, social research must be carried out according to a well-established set of scientific rules and procedures.

Different research problems may call for different procedures, but the basic principle remains the same. It requires that all research results be verifiable by other investigators. This goal leads to the first rule of research: we must deal with what is observable.

Operational Definition

If a friend tells us that he has seen a ghost, we can only take his word for it. There is no way we can study the ghost scientifically, because all of us cannot see it. We can, however, study people like our friend who believe in ghosts. We can find out about their family, friends, education, religion, and other social forces in their lives. When we have collected enough data, we can determine whether those factors cause people to believe in ghosts. Other researchers can check to see if our findings are accurate or not, because we are not dealing with ghosts (unobservable) but with ghost believers (observable).

It just so happens that many social phenomena studied by sociologists are like ghosts—hidden from our eyes. What can researchers do? They can resort to operational definitions to beat the problem of trying to study the unobservable. An **operational definition** specifies an action for translating what is unobservable into something that can be observed and measured. The phenomenon called social class, for example, is an unobservable though powerful force in our lives. We may operationally define our social class by asking how many years of schooling we have had, how much money we make a year, or what we do for a living. The operational definition, in effect, tells us to find something concrete that may represent class. That something concrete is an **empirical indicator,** an observable and measurable thing that represents a basically unobservable phenomenon. Thus our education, income, or occupation is an empirical indicator of our class in the same way as a thermometer is an empirical indicator of temperature. Empirical indicators are very important tools for doing social research. Suppose some sociologists use "annual income less than $10,000" as their empirical indicator of lower class; other researchers know exactly what they are talking about and can verify their findings about who the lower-class people are. Developing operational definitions and empirical indicators in social research is not always easy, however (see box, p. 28).

Variable

Although we can use empirical indicators to describe the basic elements of our social world in ways that are precise and verifiable, we want more than a catalogue of facts. We want to know how those elements are related to one another. Usually, we want to know which is the cause and which the effect.

Both causes and effects are known as **variables,** because they refer to characteristics that vary from people to people within the population being studied. A cause is called an **independent variable,** because its presence does not depend on the effect; an effect is referred to as a **dependent variable,** because its presence does depend on the cause. Because people differ with regard to class—some are upper-class, others middle-class, and still others lower-class—social class can be treated as a variable. Gender can also be a variable, because some people are males and others females. Virtually all other social forces and human behaviors may be considered variables. If we are studying a population made up of people of different ages and genders, with different incomes and levels of education, who express different political beliefs, all these characteristics are variables. All these social phenomena can be regarded as variables only because the population being studied is a diverse one, including people of different classes, different genders, or different characteristics of some other kind.

The same phenomena, on the other hand, can also be treated as **constants,** which are characteristics found in *all* members of the population being studied. Suppose we are comparing academic performance between male and female college students. Gender is a variable because our subjects differ in gender, some being males and others females. The characteristic of being in college is a constant because the subjects do *not* differ in education, all being college students. But suppose we want to study social characteristics such as education that influence how women vote. Then gender is a constant because the subjects here do *not* differ in gender, all being women. Education is a variable because the subjects differ in education, some being college-educated and others not.

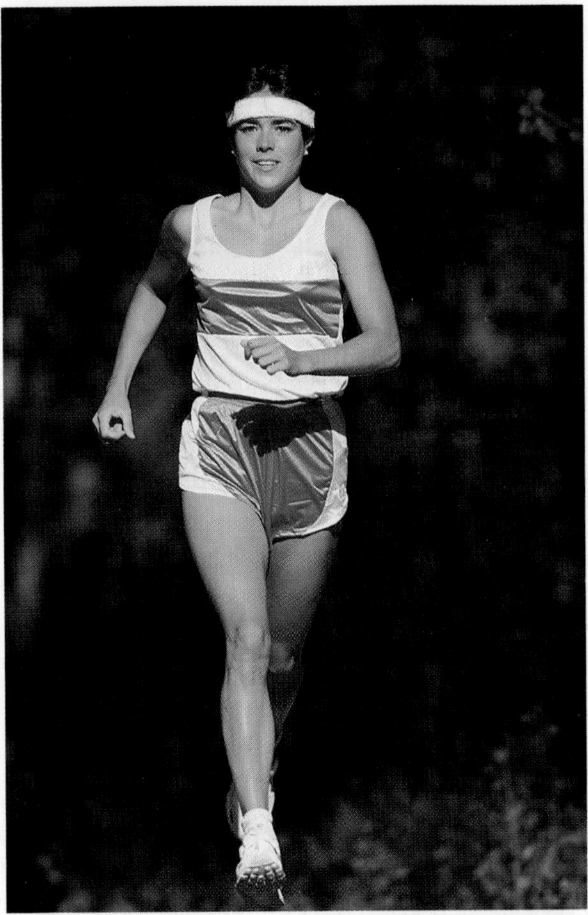

It is not always easy to determine which variable is the cause and which is the effect. If we find that people who exercise regularly are healthier than those who do not, this does not necessarily mean that regular exercise causes good health, because healthy people may be more likely to exercise in the first place. Regular exercise can contribute to good health, but it is only one of many contributing factors and should not be considered the cause of good health.

Correlation

In order to establish one variable as the cause of an effect, we must first be sure that the two variables are *correlated,* both occurring together in some regular way. If two variables are correlated, then when one changes, the other also changes, and there is a pattern to these changes. A *positive correlation* exists when an increase in one variable is associated with an increase in the other variable, as is true in the case of the relationship between education and income: the more education we have, the higher the income we get. A *negative correlation* exists when a decrease in one variable is associated with an increase in the other. Education and racial prejudice, for example, are negatively correlated, in that the more education we have, the less likely we are to be prejudiced. Sometimes a correlation is *curvilinear:* as one variable is changed, another variable first changes in the same direction and then in the opposite. You may recall from Chapter 1 that both very high and very low levels of social integration are associated with high rates of suicide. That is a case of curvilinear correlation, because

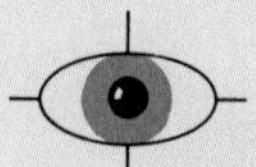

USING SOCIOLOGICAL INSIGHT

Soft Sciences Are Often Harder than Hard Sciences

Human behavior is extremely complex, and the difficulties in measuring it have led some scientists to call fields like sociology and psychology the "soft sciences." This reading compares the methods of the social sciences to the methods of such "hard sciences" as math and physics. Why do social scientists have such difficulty in identifying and operationally defining variables?

To understand the terms soft and hard science, just ask any educated person what science is. The answer you get will probably involve several stereotypes: science is something done in a laboratory, possibly by people wearing white coats and holding test tubes; it involves making measurements with instruments, accurate to several decimal places; and it involves controlled, repeatable experiments in which you keep everything fixed except for one or a few things that you allow to vary. Areas of science that often conform well to these stereotypes include much of chemistry, physics, and molecular biology. These areas are given the flattering name of hard science, because they use the firm evidence that controlled experiments and highly accurate measurements can provide.

We often view hard science as the only type of science. But science (from the Latin *scientia*—knowledge) is something much more general, which isn't defined by decimal places and controlled experiments. It means the enterprise of explaining and predicting—gaining knowledge of—natural phenomena by continually testing one's theories against empirical evidence. The world is full of phenomena that are intellectually challenging and important to understand, but that can't be measured in several decimal places in labs. They constitute much of ecology, evolution, and animal behavior; much of psychology and human behavior; and all the phenomena of human societies, including cultural anthropology, economics, history, and government.

These soft sciences, as they're pejoratively termed, are more difficult to study, for obvious reasons. A lion hunt or revolution in the Third World doesn't fit inside a test tube. You can't start it and stop it whenever you choose. You can't control all the variables; perhaps you can't control *any* variable. You may even find it hard to decide what a variable is. You can still use empirical tests to gain knowledge, but the types of tests used in hard sciences must be modified. Such differences between the hard and soft sciences are regularly misunderstood by hard scientists, who tend to scorn soft sciences and reserve special contempt for the social sciences. Indeed, it was only in the 1970s that the National Academy of Sciences, established by Congress in 1863 to act as official advisor to the U.S. government on questions of science and

with the increase in integration, the suicide rate initially comes down and then goes up. (See box, p. 30, for the ways in which these variables are related.)

Correlation by itself, however, does not prove that changes in one variable are the cause of the changes observed in another. After all, there is a high correlation between hospitalization and death: many more deaths occur in the hospital than at home. But the correlation does not prove that hospitalization *causes* death. Instead, a **third variable** may be at work, such as serious illness, producing the high number of deaths in hospitals. Serious illness often leads to both hospitalization and death and thus may explain the relationship between these variables (Cole, 1976).

In short, when two variables are correlated, it is possible that neither is having an effect on the other. Instead, a third variable, or several other variables, might be the cause of the correlation. When there is no causal connection between two variables that are correlated, the correlation is called **spurious.**

Causal Relationship

A correlation between two variables is necessary but not sufficient to establish that one variable is the cause of another. At least two additional conditions must be technology, began to admit social scientists at all.

An issue that is central to any science, hard or soft, may be termed the problem of how to "operationalize" a concept. To compare evidence with theory requires that you measure the ingredients of your theory. For ingredients like weight or speed it's clear what to measure, but what would you measure if you wanted to understand political instability? Somehow, you would have to design a series of actual operations that yield a suitable measurement—i.e., you must operationalize the ingredients of theory.

All scientists, from mathematicians to social scientists, have to solve the task of operationalizing their intuitive concepts. Physicists have to resort to very indirect (albeit accurate) operationalizing in order to "measure" electrons. But the task of operationalizing is inevitably more difficult and less exact in the soft sciences, because there are so many uncontrolled variables. For example, number of bananas and concentration of sugar can be measured to more decimal places than can habitat complexity and attitudes toward cancer.

Unfortunately, operationalizing lends itself to ridicule in the social sciences, because the concepts being studied tend to be familiar ones that all of us fancy we're experts on. Anybody, scientist or no, feels entitled to spout forth on politics or psychology, and to heap scorn on what scholars in those fields write.

The ingrained labels "soft science" and "hard science" could be replaced by hard (i.e., difficult) science and easy science. The social sciences are much more difficult and, to some of us, intellectually more challenging than mathematics and chemistry. As to the relative importance of soft and hard science for humanity's future, there can be no comparison. It matters little whether we progress with understanding the diophantine approximation. Our survival depends on whether we progress with understanding how people behave, why some societies become frustrated, whether their governments tend to become unstable, and how political leaders make decisions like whether to press a red button. Our National Academy of Sciences will cut itself out of intellectually challenging areas of science, and out of the areas where NAS can provide the most needed scientific advice, if it continues to judge social scientists from a posture of ignorance.

Source: Excerpted from Jared Diamond 8/87 *Discover*, "The Soft Sciences Are Often Harder than Hard Sciences." Jared Diamond/© *Discover* 1987, Family Media, Inc.

met before we can say that a causal relationship probably exists:

1. The independent variable must precede the dependent variable in time.
2. There must not be a third variable that causes both of them.

Often we can determine which variable precedes another through logical assessment. If we look at the high correlation between serious illness and death, we may logically conclude that serious illness precedes death, simply because the alternative notion that death causes serious illness is logically impossible. Similarly, in the case of a high correlation between race and unemployment, we can logically conclude that being black comes first and being jobless comes later, because the alternative possibility—joblessness causes a person's skin to change color—is not logical. Unfortunately, some cases are not so simple. Trying to determine which variable precedes another is sometimes like asking, "Which came first, the chicken or the egg?" If we find that people who exercise regularly are healthier than those who do not, does this mean that regular exercise causes good health? Not necessarily, because healthy people may be more likely to exercise in the first place. Although research has found that exercise can help a person live longer (Clark, 1986), it is only one of many

How to Read a Graph

A graph is a pictorial representation of a set of data. It shows measurements along two axes: a horizontal one, called the *x* axis, and a vertical one, the *y* axis. The label on each axis indicates what is being measured, and the point at which the two axes meet represents either a very low measure or a measurement of zero. As you go up the *y* axis or to the right on the *x* axis, the value of whatever is being measured increases.

Figure 2.1 provides two simple examples. The point at which the *x* and *y* axes meet is at the lower left corner of each of these graphs. Consider the graph on the left. The label on the *x* axis tells us that it represents social integration. The left end of the axis therefore represents very low levels of social integration, which are labeled "inadequate," and the right end represents very high, or "excessive" levels. The *y* axis represents the suicide rate, which increases as you go from the bottom to the top of the axis.

The curve is the part of the graph that contains the information. To see how to read it, let us take one point on the curve, the point labeled "egoistic suicide." In terms of the *x* axis, it is far to the left, so it shows inadequate levels of social integration. At the same time, this point is high on the *y* axis, so it also represents a relatively high suicide rate. Hence, the point indicates that a high suicide rate and inadequate social integration occur together.

Now let us move along the curve and see what it tells us. As we go along the *x* axis, social integration is increasing and the curve is sloping downward, which indicates that the suicide rate is decreasing. In other words, as social integration increases, the suicide rate decreases. But that is only part of the story, because at about the middle of the *x* axis, the curve begins sloping upward again, which indicates that the suicide rate is increasing. According to the labels on the *x* axis, social integration is becoming excessive.

What the curve tells us, then, is that the suicide rate tends to be high when social integration is either inadequate or excessive. The two extreme cases—where the suicide rate is high and social integration is inadequate or excessive—are called *egoistic suicide* and *altruistic suicide,* respectively. By reading the curve in the right-hand graph, you can also see how suicide and social regulation are related.

How accurate are these graphs? Although the total suicide rate might be precisely measured and placed exactly on the *y* axis, social integration and social regulation are not precisely defined or measured, and the terms "inadequate" and "excessive" are value judgments. (We could, however, give operational definitions of integration and regulation and substitute some measurement for the value-laden terms.) Also, the four categories of suicide are not determined with scientific accuracy: they overlap, and these classifications may contain errors.

Despite this lack of precision, the graphs are valuable because they show general patterns of relationships. The curves illustrate that significant personal events are influenced by social forces. They show that extremes of either social integration or regulation are dangerous for society.

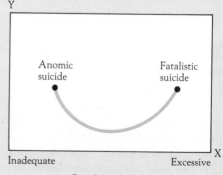

Figure 2.1

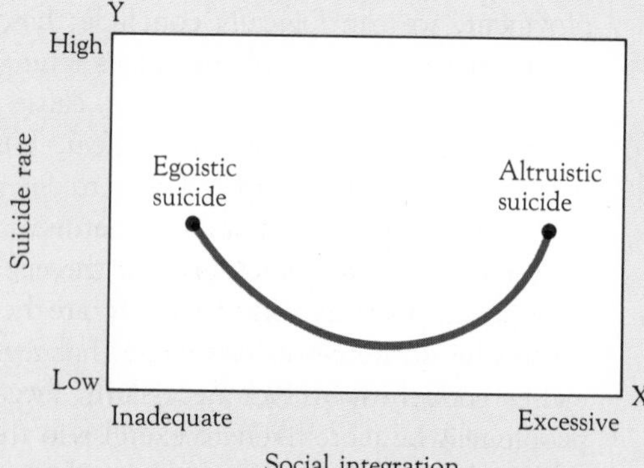

contributing factors. Hence, by itself, exercise cannot be said to cause good health. In another case, students guilty of conduct violations in a dorm were found to have lower grade point averages than their well-behaved peers in the same dorm. The researchers, however, could not answer the question of which came first: clowning around in the dorm or getting lower grades in class (Camer, 1983).

Finally, in order to establish a causal relationship between two variables, we must examine the possibility that a third one is the cause of the correlation between the others. Sometimes the third variable intervenes between the other two, making them apparently rather than genuinely related. Earlier we mentioned the high correlation between race and joblessness. While race precedes unemployment rather than the other way around, this does not necessarily mean that race is the direct cause of joblessness. Instead, it is racial discrimination or some other social problem that may have brought about the high unemployment rate among blacks. Racial discrimination (C), then, is the *intervening variable* that mediates between race (A) and joblessness (B): A→C→B. Sometimes the third variable causes the other to appear correlated in another way. In the previously discussed case of the high correlation between hospitalization (A) and death (B), we noted that the correlation is spurious, brought on by the third variable of serious illness (C):

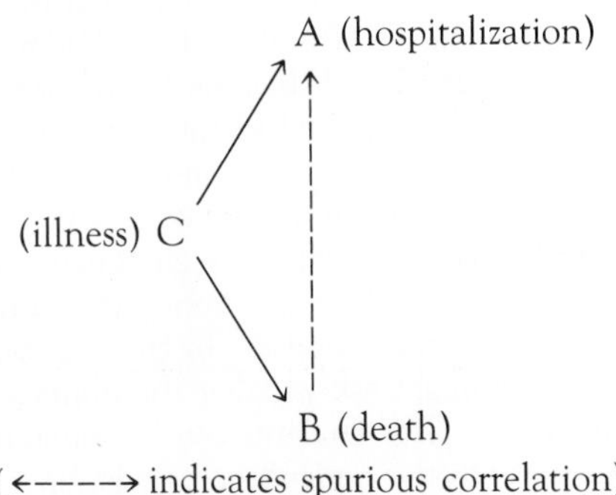

(←----→ indicates spurious correlation)

How can we find out if a correlation is spurious? Often sociologists apply *controls*, procedures for holding certain variables constant. If a correlation disappears when a third variable is held constant, then we have good reason to believe that the correlation is spurious.

Suppose we suspect that the correlation between smoking and lung cancer is spurious and that poverty is a third variable accounting for the correlation. We may try to control the effect of poverty on the correlation by comparing cancer rates among smokers and nonsmokers who are *equally* poor. If the cancer rates of these two groups are the same, we may reason that the correlation between smoking and cancer is spurious. But if the poor smokers have higher cancer rates than poor nonsmokers, then we may conclude that smoking is probably a cause of cancer. Often, complex statistical analysis and other methods are necessary to establish the desired controls, but the specific procedure for establishing controls depends on which of several possible research methods is used. These research methods are the subject of the next section.

QUESTIONS FOR DISCUSSION AND REVIEW

1. Why do sociologists attempt to define and determine relationships between variables?
2. What is the difference between descriptive and explanatory research?
3. What are dependent and independent variables, and how can sociologists establish a relationship between them?
4. How do sociologists determine whether a correlation is spurious or real?

MAJOR RESEARCH METHODS

Variables and correlations are the nuts and bolts of social research. We have examined some rules about which variables and which correlations are meaningful in research—which ones, in essence, count as scientific facts. But how do sociologists collect these facts? There are four basic methods: survey, observation, experiment, and analysis of existing data. Each has its own advantages and disadvantages.

Survey

Of the four research methods, the **survey** is most frequently used by sociologists. Suppose we want to know whether from 1965 to 1980 the percentage of students having premarital intercourse changed. We could take a survey, and we would find, as Table 2.1 shows, that the percentage had increased. (Also see box, p. 32, on how to read the table.) Or suppose a theory suggests that students' social class and geographical background

How to Read a Table

Tables often look boring and complicated, but many sociological data are published in tables, and careful reading can yield fascinating information and ideas for further research. Table 2.1 is a simple one, but we can use it to illustrate six steps to follow in interpreting tables.

Table 2.1 Percentages of 1965, 1970, 1975, and 1980 College Students Having Premarital Intercourse

	Males		Females	
Year	%	n	%	n
1965	65.1	129	28.7	115
1970	65.0	136	37.3	158
1975	73.9	115	57.1	275
1980	77.4	168	63.5	230
Percentage change 1965–1980	+12.3		+34.8	

Source: Ira E. Robinson and Davor Jedlicka, "Change in sexual attitudes and behavior of college students from 1965 to 1980: A research note," *Journal of Marriage and the Family,* 44 (Feb. 1982): 238. Copyright © 1982 by the National Council on Family Relations, 1910 West County Road B, Suite 147, St. Paul, Minnesota 55113. Reprinted by permission.

First, read the title. It should say what kind of information is in this table. It tells us that the table indicates, for four different years, the percentage of college students who had premarital sex.

Second, check the source. The source of the data is cited at the bottom of the table. Sometimes the reputation of the organization that collected the data gives a rough indication of the reliability of the source. But often we will want to know how the data were collected. The report that presents the table usually includes this information.

Third, read the labels. A table has two kinds of labels: column headings along the top of the table and labels down the left side. In this table, the column headings are "Males" and "Females" and the side labels note the year to which each figure applies. Thus each figure in the table describes the response of either males or females in a particular year. To understand what the figures mean, we need to keep both types of labels in mind.

Fourth, understand the figures. Usually, a table gives numbers, percentages, or both. The table here, for example, gives both numbers (the *n* subcolumn) and percentages of people interviewed. Generally, the larger the numbers, the more reliable the information.

Fifth, compare the data. Compare the figures both horizontally and vertically. The table shows that the percentages of college males and females who had premarital intercourse increased from 1965 to 1980, that in each of the four years the percentage of females having premarital sex was less than that of males, and that the increase in the percentage of males who had premarital sex (12.3 percent) was much less than the increase among females (34.8 percent).

Sixth, draw conclusions. If we read the table carefully, we should be able to draw at least some tentative conclusions. We may conclude that the frequency of premarital intercourse among college students increased from 1965 to 1980 and that the sexual behavior of females is becoming more like that of males. The researchers themselves concluded that the larger increase in premarital sex among females reflected increasing equality between the sexes. We should, of course, evaluate such conclusions, looking for questions that warrant further research. In this case we might ask whether the findings on college students can be generalized to the noncollege population.

(say, urban, rural, or suburban) are related to their sexual behavior. Survey data could be collected to determine whether this might be true.

Sampling To take a survey, we first select a **population,** the people whom we want to study. We can choose a population of any size, but all its members must have something in common. Thus a population may consist of all Americans above the age of 100, or all U.S. congresswomen, or all the students at a large university, or all U.S. citizens, or all the people in the world.

If a population is relatively small, all its members can

be approached and interviewed. But if a population is very large, it could cost too much time and money to contact all its members. In such a case, a **sample** of the population, a small number of people taken from the whole population, must be selected. The sample, however, must accurately represent the entire population from which it is drawn. Otherwise the information obtained from the sample cannot be generalized to the population. Failure to heed this may produce misleading conclusions.

A case in point was the famous attempt to predict the outcome of the presidential election in 1936. A popular magazine of that era, *Literary Digest,* selected a large sample of people from telephone directories and automobile registration lists and then asked them whom they would vote for. An overwhelming majority replied that they would choose the Republican candidate Alfred Landon over his Democratic opponent Franklin Roosevelt. So the editors of the magazine concluded that Landon was going to have a landslide victory. But it turned out that Landon was overwhelmingly defeated. Meanwhile, a young man named George Gallup, who had chosen a much smaller but far more representative sample of all the voters, correctly predicted the election's outcome. The *Literary Digest's* incorrect prediction was due to the selection of a sample that did not represent the entire voter population. The sample included only middle- and upper-class people, who could afford telephones and automobiles during those Depression years and who, being largely Republicans, tended to vote for the Republican candidate. The less well-off, who later voted for the winning Democratic candidate, were excluded from the sample.

The *Literary Digest* apparently assumed that since they contacted a huge number of people (10 million), they could accurately predict the election. They did not realize, as Gallup did, that it is not the size but the representativeness of the sample that ensures accuracy. A sample as large as the *Literary Digest's* can be misleading if it is not representative of the population, but a sample as small as Gallup's (only 300,000) can be accurate if it adequately represents the population. In fact, due to today's increased sophistication in sampling, as few as 1500 cases can comprise a representative sample. A representative sample, then, is extremely important for getting correct information on the population as a whole. But how do sociologists go about finding a representative sample?

"And don't waste your time canvassing the whole building, young man. We all think alike."

If a sample is to be representative, all members of the population must have the same chance of getting selected for the sample. The selection in effect must be random, which is why a representative sample is often called a **random sample.** A crude way to select a random sample is to throw the names of an entire population into a hat, mix them up, and then pull out as many names as needed for a sample. This method may be too cumbersome to use if the size of the population is very large. There are more sophisticated and convenient techniques for drawing random samples from large populations. The most commonly used are systematic and stratified sampling.

Systematic sampling involves the use of a system, such as selecting every tenth or hundredth person in the population. We must still make sure that all the members of the population have the same chance of falling into our sample. If every tenth person is taken, then each person in the population has a one-tenth chance of being sampled. The sample would not be representative of, say, a student population if we talk to every tenth student walking into a library, or passing by a street corner, or entering a bar. This is because not all the students are equally likely to go to these places at the time when the survey is taken. Some students may have more than a one-tenth chance of being selected, while others have less than a one-tenth chance. In fact, numerous students would have a zero chance of being included in the sample if they have never gone to those places. To make the sample accurately represent the student population, we should take, say, every tenth name in a list—such as a student directory—where all the students' names can be found.

Stratified sampling is used when the population can be divided into various strata or categories, such as males and females or rural, urban, and suburban residents. To draw a stratified sample, we have to know what percentage of the population falls into each of the categories used and then select a random sample in which each category is represented in exactly the same proportion as in the population. Suppose we know that the population of a city is 52 percent female and 48 percent male; then our stratified sample should also be 52 percent female and 48 percent male.

Types of Surveys Once a random sample is selected, we can ask its members about their opinions, attitudes, or behavior. This is usually done by using self-administered questionnaires, personal interviews, or telephone surveys.

In using *self-administered questionnaires,* the researcher simply gives or sends the people in the sample a list of questions and asks them to fill in the answers themselves. Usually the list consists of true-false and multiple-choice questions. The respondents are asked to answer "yes," "no," or "don't know" or to check one of the answers such as "single," "married," "divorced," or "widowed." There are several advantages to this method. First, it costs the researcher relatively little time and money. Second, since the respondents are assured of their anonymity and fill out the questionnaires in privacy, they may answer the questions more honestly. Third, because they answer the same set of questions, all the respondents can easily be compared with one another as to their attitudes and reported behavior. Such comparison may enable us to know why some people do a certain thing while others do not.

The mailed survey has a big problem, though. Some people will not return the questionnaires. The usual way to tackle this nonresponse problem is to send the subjects a follow-up letter or telephone them and ask them to please fill out the questionnaires. What if this and other remedies do not work and the amount of nonresponse remains substantial? Then the researcher must find out if there is a significant difference in age, education, or some other characteristic between respondents and nonrespondents. If there is no difference, the study may be continued. If there is one, the project may have to be scrapped—or modified by using some other survey method such as personal interviews.

Personal interviews may get greater response from the subjects than does the mailed survey. Fewer people would refuse to cooperate when approached in person than they would when solicited by mail. Personal interviews may be either structured or unstructured. In **struc-**

Before sociologists can draw any conclusion, they must have data. One method of gathering data is the personal interview, which can evoke a more thoughtful and accurate response from respondents than a mailed survey. Personal interviews can be structured or unstructured. In structured interviews, the researcher asks the subject to answer preset multiple-choice questions. But in unstructured interviews, the researcher asks open-ended questions and other questions the situation calls for. The subject is encouraged to answer freely, using his or her own words.

tured interviews, the researcher uses the same kind of questionnaire employed in the mailed survey, with the obvious exception that the interviewer reads the questions to the subject and obtains answers on the spot. Since all the respondents are asked exactly the same questions in exactly the same way and are provided with exactly the same choice of answers, the researcher can compare the subjects with one another on the basis of which answers they choose. Explanations of their attitudes and behavior could then be found. The standardization of questions and answers, however, cannot deal with the great diversity among people and the subtle complexity of human attitudes. Thus respondents with different views are often forced to give the same answer. Some respondents may complain that it is impossible for them to answer the questions with the answers provided in the questionnaire because none of the answers adequately reflects their personal views. Even among those respondents who do not complain, many may simply unthinkingly pick the standardized answers just to get rid of the interviewer.

The researcher could get out of his problem by using an **unstructured interview.** In this kind of interview, open-ended questions are asked—respondents are allowed to answer freely, in their own words. Usually the interviewer starts off by asking a general question, such as "What do you think about political corruption?" Various respondents would interpret this question in varying ways and so would respond differently. Some may focus on the definition of political corruption; others may concentrate on the consequences of political corruption; still others may concern themselves with how to fight political corruption, and so on. The different points raised by different respondents would further lead the interviewer to pursue various issues in different directions. Consequently, the interview with each of the respondents may become a unique case. The interviewer may find that no two answers are alike, since different respondents express themselves differently and mean different things even if they use the same words. All this makes it difficult to compare the answers of many different respondents, which in turn makes it hard to find the causes of whatever is under investigation. Nevertheless, an unstructured interview can produce rich data and deep insights, helping us to gain a profound understanding of the subject.

Whether structured or unstructured, personal interviews can cost much time and money. A complex study may require a bureaucracy with a swarm of administrators, field supervisors, interviewers, and sometimes even public relations personnel. Interviewers must not only be paid for the hours spent in the field but also reimbursed for travel expenses. Interviews are often lengthy and the interviewer may have to travel a long distance (Bailey, 1987). In addition, the interviewer "may drive several miles to a respondent's home, find no one there, return to the research office, and drive back the next day—possibly finding no one there again" (Babbie, 1986).

It is much more convenient to use *telephone surveys,* which have jokingly been called the telephone polls. For many years the telephone has been used merely to encourage respondents to return their mailed questionnaires. In the past, researchers stayed away from telephone surveys because they could produce a biased sample by excluding poor people, who did not own telephones, from the studies. But today the sampling bias has practically disappeared, because at least 97 percent of American households have telephones (Babbie, 1986). As a result, telephone interviewing has recently become very popular in survey research and is routinely used in many public opinion polls. An even more convenient method, computer-assisted telephone interviewing, is sure to become a bigger hit in years to come. The U.S. Census Bureau and commercial survey firms are already using it.

Telephone surveys have certain disadvantages by comparison with face-to-face interviews. Since the interviewer cannot look the respondents in the eye, the latter are less motivated and can more easily end the interview by simply hanging up. Another problem is that people are more distrustful when answering questions from a stranger whom they cannot see. They may suspect that the stranger has a hidden interest, perhaps posing as an interviewer in order to sell magazine subscriptions.

Observation

It is obvious from the preceding section that in surveys we depend on others to tell us what has happened. By contrast, in observation we rely on ourselves to go where the action is—and watch what is happening. There are two ways to observe an ongoing activity. In **detached observation,** we observe as outsiders, from a distance, without getting involved. As detached observ-

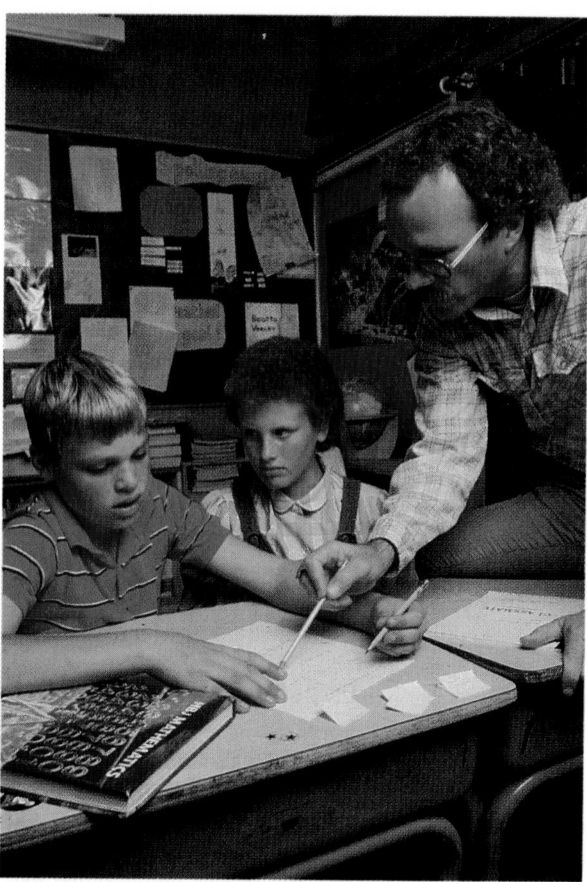

From the theory of self-fulfilling prophecy, we can hypothesize that this teacher's expectations affect his pupils' performance. If he considers them very bright and expects them to do well, they are likely to fulfill his expectation. We can test this hypothesis by conducting an experiment whereby we raise the teacher expectation in the beginning of the school year and check the student performance nine months later. Then we compare the performance of the experimental group with that of a control group. The control group should consist of the other pupils, whom the same teacher has not considered very bright and has not expected to do well.

The intention was to make the teachers expect these supposedly "bright" children to show remarkable success later in the year. Thus the experimental group consisted of these "bright" children, who were exposed to high teacher expectations; the control group included the rest of the pupils. Eight months later the researchers went back to the school and gave all the children another test. They found that the experimental group did perform better than the control group. They concluded that teacher expectations (the independent variable) were indeed the cause of student performance (the dependent variable).

You may notice that the experiments discussed above were carried out in the field—on the street and in the classroom. In these *field experiments,* the subjects could behave naturally. But it is still possible for the experimenter to unconsciously influence the subjects and make them behave unnaturally. This is what happened to one of the most famous field experiments in social science. It was carried out by Elton Mayo in the 1930s at the Hawthorne plant of Western Electric Company in Chicago (Roethlisberger and Dickson, 1939).

Mayo wanted to find out what kinds of incentives and work conditions would encourage workers to work harder. He first systematically changed the lighting, lunch hours, coffee breaks, methods of payment (salary versus piece rate), and the like. He was then surprised to find that no matter what changes were made, the workers increased their productivity. When the light was made brighter, they worked harder than before; but when it was made dimmer, they *also* worked harder. When they were given two or three coffee breaks, they increased their output; when they were not allowed any coffee break, they continued to increase their output. Mayo later discovered that the increased productivity was actually due to all the attention the workers were getting from the researcher. They felt that they were not mere cogs of a machine but instead respected for their work; hence they reciprocated by working harder. The impact of the researcher's presence on subjects' behavior is now known as the **Hawthorne effect.** Social scientists today strive to avoid it by becoming members of the group being studied, by using hidden cameras and tape recorders, or by using various means to prevent subjects from knowing they are being observed.

The Hawthorne effect is particularly threatening to *laboratory experiments.* Unlike the field experiment, which is carried out in a natural setting, the laboratory experiment is conducted under the artificial condition of a lab, where subjects are always aware of being observed. A number of researchers have nevertheless managed to make their laboratory experiments as realistic as real-life situations. Stanley Milgram (1974), for example, told his subjects that he was running a test on the effects of punishment on learning. In fact, he was conducting an experiment on obedience to authority. After asking

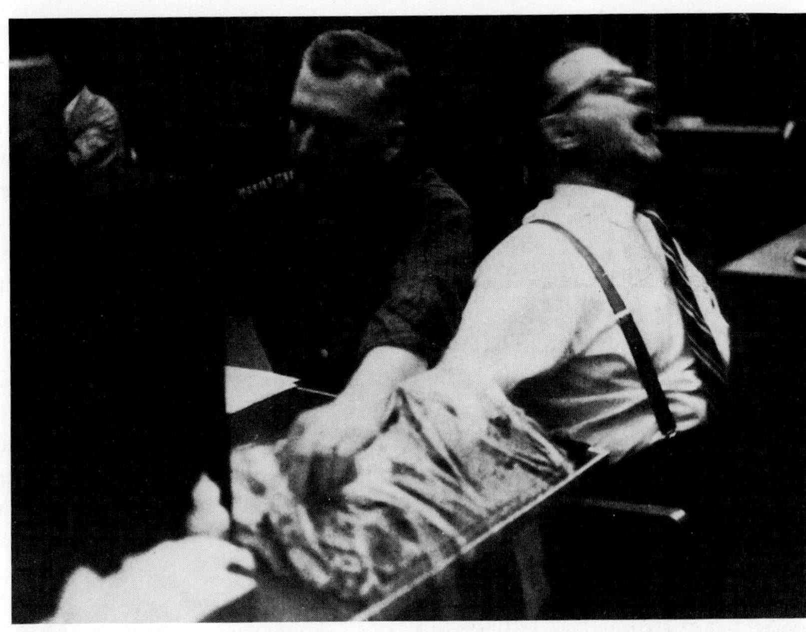

In a field experiment, sociologists can observe subjects acting naturally. But a laboratory experiment presents the problem of observing people in an artificial setting that can color their responses. In Stanley Milgram's famous experiment on obedience to authority, he devised an elaborate simulation to overcome the artificiality of the setting. Thus the subject (in the dark shirt) believes that he is causing the other person to scream with pain when he presses the electric shock machine. Actually, the machine is a fake and the man who is screaming is acting.

each of his subjects to assist in the experiment by taking the role of "teacher," Milgram introduced him or her to another subject playing the role of "student." Actually this "student" was Milgram's research associate. Then Milgram told the teacher to punish the student with an electric shock every time the student gave the wrong answer to a question. Whenever the subject (teacher) obeyed Milgram's command by pressing the shock machine, he or she heard the student screaming with pain. In reality the shock machine was a fake and the student was faking, but all the subjects were led to believe that everything they did or heard was real. They trembled, sweated, and showed other signs of stress when "punishing" the student. Still, a large majority carried out Milgram's order, administering what they believed was great pain. This led Milgram to conclude that ordinary people will follow orders if they come from a legitimate authority, in the same way as the Nazi Germans did when told by their leaders to commit atrocities against the Jews.

Another laboratory experiment, conducted by Philip Zimbardo (1972), was almost as realistic as Milgram's. Zimbardo set up a mock prison in the basement of a university building. Then he recruited student volunteers to participate in an experiment on the effects of prison. Some of them were told to play the role of prisoners, while others became guards. At the end of only six days Zimbardo had to stop the experiment. The "guards" had become extremely cruel and the "prisoners" had become so depressed that they would have become mentally ill if not released soon enough.

The realism of Zimbardo's and Milgram's experiments should not blind us to the disadvantages of experiments as a whole. What happens inside a laboratory will not necessarily happen in the real world outside, where a multitude of other variables are at work. Moreover, most of the larger, important sociological issues cannot be studied through experiments. We cannot create and then study a race riot, a revolution, or a war. Nevertheless, compared with other methods, experiments give researchers more leeway to control and manipulate variables. As a result, by using experiments they are better able to determine the relationship among variables.

Analyzing Existing Data

So far we have discussed methods for collecting data from scratch. Sometimes it is unnecessary to gather new information because there are a lot of "old" data lying around, which have been collected by someone else. Sometimes it is simply impossible to conduct an interview, observation, or experiment because the people we want to study are long dead. Thus sociologists often turn to analysis of existing data.

Secondary Analysis In **secondary analysis** we search for new knowledge in the data collected earlier by another researcher or some public agency. Usually the original investigator has gathered the data for a specific purpose and the secondary analyst uses them for something else. Suppose we want to study religious behavior by means of secondary analysis. We might get our data from an existing study of voting behavior conducted by a political scientist. This kind of research typically provides information on the voters' religion along with education, income, gender, and other social characteristics. The political scientist may try to find out from this research whether, among other things, men are more likely than women to vote in a presidential election and whether the more religious are more politically active than the less religious. As secondary analysts we can find out from the same data whether women attend church more often than men. In the last two decades the opportunities for secondary analysis have multiplied many times over. Various research centers throughout the world have developed a network of data archives whereby they collect and exchange data sets. Since these data sets are stored in computer cards and tapes, they can easily be reproduced and sold for broad circulation and use (Babbie, 1986).

Data suitable for secondary analysis are also available from government agencies. The use of these data has a long tradition. In his classic analysis of suicide in the 1890s, Emile Durkheim relied on official statistics. Finding from the statistics that Protestant countries, regions, and states had higher suicide rates than Catholic ones, Durkheim was able to conclude that many suicides result from a lack of social integration—assuming that Protestantism, a more individualist religious system, makes it harder for unhappy people to get moral support from others. Today many American sociologists employ statistics compiled by the U.S. Bureau of the Census for information on standards of living, migration, differences in incomes of ethnic and racial groups, birth and death rates, and a host of other facts about our society. The Federal Bureau of Investigation, the National Center for Health Statistics, and the Department of Labor are among the other government agencies that provide important statistics. In addition, survey agencies such as the National Opinion Research Center, the Gallup poll, and other public opinion polls publish very useful information. The sources are practically endless. (See box, p. 41.)

Sociologists can save a lot of time and effort by using the information they need from these storehouses of existing data, but secondary analysis has at least two disadvantages. First, the available data may not be completely relevant to the subject being investigated because they have been assembled for different purposes. Data on the median U.S. income, for example, are often given for households, not individuals. If we want to compare the standard of living over the last twenty years, these data can be misleading: they are likely to show an abnormally higher standard of living in recent years because the size of households has been shrinking and the number of two-income families has been expanding. Moreover, secondary data sometimes are not sufficiently accurate and reliable—and some investigators may not be sufficiently sensitized to such problems. Official statistics on crime, for example, overreport lower-class crimes and underreport crimes committed by members of the middle and upper classes.

Content Analysis The data for secondary analysis are usually quantitative, presented in the form of numbers, percentages, and other statistics, such as the *percentage* of women as compared to the *percentage* of men attending church once a week or the Protestants' suicide *rate* (number of suicides for every 100,000 people) as opposed to the Catholics' suicide *rate.* But some of the existing information is qualitative, in the form of words or ideas. This can be found in virtually all kinds of human communication—books, magazines, newspapers, movies, TV programs, speeches, letters, songs, laws, and so on. To study human behavior from these materials, sociologists often resort to **content analysis,** searching for specific words or ideas and then turning them into numbers.

How can we carry out "this marvelous social alchemy" (Bailey, 1987) that transforms verbal documents into quantitative data? Suppose we want to know whether public attitudes toward sex have indeed changed significantly in the last twenty years. We may find the answer from comparing popular novels of today with those of the past to see if one is more erotic than the other. To save time, we will select and study only a representative sample rather than all the novels of the two periods. Before analyzing each of the books, we will also choose a random sample of pages or paragraphs rather than the whole volume. Then we should decide what words will reflect the nature of eroticism. After we settle on a list of words such as *love, kiss,* and *embrace* to serve as indicators of eroticism, we will comb the se-

Understanding Basic Statistics

Statistics are invaluable to sociologists. They use statistics to summarize data; to discover the characteristics of people or events as a group, rather than as separate entities; and to compare groups or events in order to find relationships between variables. To understand better how statistics are used, we will consider one type of statistic: measures of central tendency—that is, measures of what is typical or average for a group. These are among the most frequently used statistics.

Suppose we want to see whether income is related to gender and have the following information:

Income of Males	Income of Females
$ 6,000	$ 4,200
8,100	4,800
12,000	5,000
13,000	7,000
15,200	8,100
15,200	8,100
127,400	15,000

To determine whether gender and income are related, we need a mea-measure that will tell us the typical income of males and of females—in other words, a measure of central tendency. The three most frequently used measurements of central tendency are the mode, the mean, and the median.

The *mode* is that figure which appears most often in a collection of data. Thus in this example the mode of the males' incomes is $15,200 because this figure appears twice while each of the other figures appears only once. The mode of the females' incomes is $8,100. These modes indicate that the males make more than the females.

The mode is the simplest measure of central tendency. But it gives very little information about the group as a whole, because many of the data are not taken into account in computing it. By itself, it does not adequately represent the data. It is therefore misleading to compare these two groups on the basis of their modes of income alone.

Compared with the mode, the mean is more representative of the group, because in computing it we take all the data into account. To calculate the *mean,* divide the total of all the figures by the number of cases. For example, the total of all the males' incomes is $196,900; the number of cases is 7. Dividing $196,900 by 7, we obtain the mean, $28,129. By using the same method, we find that the females' mean income is $7,457. Thus the mean incomes indicate that the male group makes much more than the female.

Like the mode, however, the mean can be misleading. Extreme values distort the picture it gives of the group. In this case, the males' much higher mean income is partly due to one unusually high income, namely, $127,400. Thus the mean, because of this extreme case, still does not adequately represent the group as a whole.

Of the three types of average, the median is the figure most representative of the group. It characterizes the most typical person in the group. If we arrange the numbers from the lowest to highest value, as in our sample data, then the *median* is the number that falls in the middle of the data, with half of the numbers above (smaller than) it and the other half below (larger than) it. In this example the males' median income is $13,000 and females' is $7,000. This clearly shows that males earn more than females, and we may tentatively conclude that there is a relationship between gender and income. For a full analysis, we would want to be sure that third variables are not producing this relationship.

lected pages for them. Finally we will count the number of times those words appear on an average page, and the number will be used as the measure of how erotic the novel is. In repeating the same process with other novels, we will see which ones are more erotic.

This method of examining the *manifest content*—the visible aspects—of a communication is almost like child's play. It merely scratches the surface of the communication, thereby missing its deeper and richer meaning. Thus, in regard to the novels, we should also analyze their *latent content*—underlying meanings—by reading them in their entirety and making an overall judgment of how erotic they are. The problem with this method, however, is that it is more subjective than the analysis of manifest content. Consequently, what is erotic to one researcher may not be so to another. Furthermore, investigators, operating without any clear-cut guidelines, may be inconsistent in interpreting the latent content. They may consider a love scene in some passage erotic but not so a similar love scene on another page, regard explicit language of sex as erotic but not subtle language of love, classify a prolonged rape scene as erotic but not a brief innocent gesture of love, and so forth.

As a whole, content analysis has the big advantage of saving the researcher much time and money. Anybody can do a content analysis, as the materials are available in any school or public library. Even if we botch up a study, it is easier to redo it than is true with other methods. Other methods usually cost too much or are impossible to redo because the event under study no longer exists. A second advantage of content analysis is its unique suitability for historical research. It is like a time machine enabling us to visit people of another time. If we analyze the newspapers published in the last century, we can find out how the people of that period lived, which we cannot do with the other research methods. Finally, content analysis has the distinct advantage of being *unobtrusive*—the analyst cannot have any effect on the subject being studied. There is no way for a content analyst to influence, say, a novel since it has been written. On the other hand, the basic disadvantage of content analysis is its lack of validity. As suggested above, the coding or interpretation of a communication does not necessarily reflect its true meaning, because the analysis of manifest content tends to be superficial and the analysis of latent content is likely to be subjective (Babbie, 1986).

QUESTIONS FOR DISCUSSION AND REVIEW

1. Why do sociologists use surveys more than other kinds of research methods?
2. How does detached observation differ from participation observation?
3. Why does the Hawthorne effect threaten the validity of many laboratory experiments?
4. Where do sociologists find the data they use in secondary and content analysis?

STEPS IN CONDUCTING SOCIAL RESEARCH

When sociologists are doing descriptive research—trying to develop new information—they choose a problem and dig out as much information as possible. But when they are doing explanatory research—testing hypotheses—they usually follow a series of steps. Sociologists disagree about which steps should receive more attention than others, but most try to follow the sequence outlined here.

1. *Choosing a problem.* The first step is to decide what problem to investigate. To make this choice, we may ask ourselves, Does the problem involve something that is observable? How interesting is it? Will an investigation of this issue contribute to sociological knowledge as a whole? Can the knowledge acquired by studying it be put to practical use? Of course, researchers have different beliefs about which of these questions are important, and some even consider all of them equally important. That is why a wide range of subjects is chosen for investigation.

2. *Formulating a hypothesis.* After choosing a subject to investigate, we should formulate a hypothesis that tentatively describes a variable as the cause of some specified effect. Rosenthal and Jacobson, for example, hypothesized that teacher expectations were a cause of student performance. In looking for a hypothesis, researchers usually review the existing theory and research on the problem, rely on their past observation of the subject, or simply speculate about how the phenomenon might have occurred. In formulating a hypothesis, however, we should make sure that it can be tested. This means that the cause of the problem (the independent variable) and the problem itself (the dependent variable) must be operationally defined. The hypothesis that demons cause suicide, for example, is not testable, because it is impossible to find an operational definition of a demon. But we could test Durkheim's hypothesis that a lack of social integration is a cause of suicide, because we can define the variables operationally. We can define the suicide rate (dependent variable) as that reported in official statistics, and we can specify the empirical indicator of a lack of social integration (the independent variable) as being divorced as opposed to being married.

3. *Selecting a method.* To test the hypothesis, we must choose a method for collecting the necessary data. To make this decision, we ask questions such as, How appropriate is each method for this subject? What are the advantages and disadvantages of each? Will any of the possible methods require too much time or money? The survey method, for example, would be inappropriate for studying suicide because dead people cannot be interviewed. Nor can they be observed or experimented with. Thus it is not surprising that Durkheim chose the method of secondary analysis when he studied suicide. Official records are not completely reliable because many suicides go unreported, but these records are easily

available. All things considered, secondary analysis seems an appropriate method for studying suicide.

4. *Collecting the data.* Great care must be taken to ensure that the quality of the data is high. The means for ensuring this quality depends on which research method is being used. If the survey method is being employed, the sample must be as objective as possible. If we conduct an experiment, we must be careful that an artificial situation is not distorting the results. In case we use secondary analysis, we must evaluate the accuracy of the information and avoid either reading too much into the data or missing relevant information. In general, controls are necessary to be sure that some third variables or prior causes are not responsible for a correlation.

5. *Analyzing the results.* A popular saying holds that "the facts speak for themselves." But by themselves facts are meaningless; they must be interpreted. If we find that Protestants have higher suicide rates than Catholics, we must ask, What is the meaning of this finding? In other words, we should explain why religion is related to suicide in our data. In searching for an explanation, we should first make sure that the information is valid and reliable. **Validity** means accuracy: that the study measures what it is supposed to measure or that its data show what they are supposed to show. The finding that Protestants have more suicides than Catholics will be valid if Protestants do in fact have more suicides. It will not be valid if the researcher has misidentified many Catholics as Protestants or mistaken many foul plays and accidental deaths for suicides. **Reliability** (consistency) of a finding will depend on whether the same results are obtained when the researcher or other investigators repeat the study.

After establishing validity and reliability, we should try to determine whether the correlation between religion and suicide is a spurious one. We may be reasonably assured that it is not spurious if we find the suicide rates not only higher in Protestant than Catholic countries but also higher among Protestants than among Catholics within the same country. Finally, we should try to explain why Protestants are more prone to suicide than Catholics. As Durkheim did, we may explain that since Protestantism encourages individualism more than Catholicism does, Protestants are more likely to rely on themselves when faced with a personal crisis and are therefore more likely to kill themselves.

6. *Drawing a conclusion.* Finally, we must determine whether the data have confirmed or refuted the hypothesis and what this confirmation or refutation says about the theory from which the hypothesis was derived. We will also consider how the findings relate to the existing body of knowledge. If they contradict existing theories, we should suggest modifications in these theories and propose future research that might resolve the contradictions. Often, research raises new questions, which we should articulate. In the study of college students' changing sexual attitudes and behavior, for example, Ira Robinson and Davor Jedlicka (1982) found that from the 1960s to the 1970s more students engaged in premarital sex and fewer of them considered it immoral and sinful. But the investigators found that from the 1970s to the 1980s students who had premarital sex were, at the same time, more likely to condemn it as immoral and sinful. This raises the question of why a "sexual contradiction" is emerging in the 1980s. Since their current study does not include the data needed to answer the question, the researchers urge that more research be conducted.

Sociologists do not always follow these six steps closely. Sometimes, for example, they do not formulate a clear hypothesis before collecting data. Nevertheless, this sequence constitutes the model for explanatory research that most researchers try to follow. We should also note that the sequence is usually circular (see Figure 2.2). When sociologists enter the research process through step 1, they ordinarily do not get their problem out of a hat. Instead, their choice of a problem is often

Figure 2.2 How Sociologists Do Research

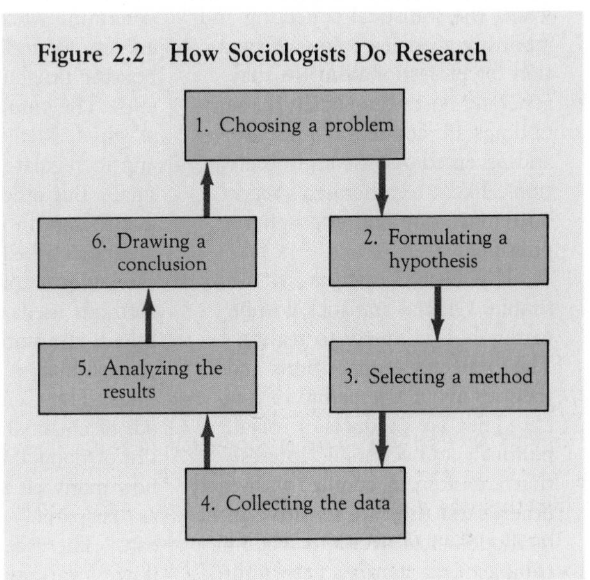

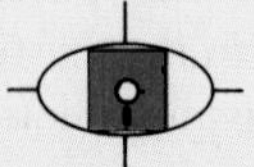

LOOKING AT CURRENT RESEARCH

The Politics of Numbers

The results of social research often take the form of statistics, which are numbers used to describe the world. But the way statistics are created and used is subject to many forces. Some of these forces are political, as is shown in this reading. How might political forces influence the final two stages of the research process?

Every day, from the morning paper to the evening news, Americans are served a steady diet of statistics. We are given the latest figures for consumer prices and the unemployment rate, lagging and leading economic indicators, reading scores, and life expectancies, not to mention data on crime, divorce, and the money supply. Most of these numbers are official in the sense that they are produced by government in what are generally presumed to be impersonal and objective bureaucracies. Of course, in some countries, where the regimes are distrusted, official numbers are also routinely disbelieved. But where the statistical collecting and reporting agencies enjoy a reputation for professionalism (as they generally do in our society), their findings are commonly presented—and accepted—as neutral observations, like a weatherman's report on temperature and atmospheric pressure.

This view, we all know, is too simple. Official statistics do not merely hold a mirror to reality. They reflect presuppositions and theories about the nature of society. They are products of social, political, and economic interests that are often in conflict with each other. And they are sensitive to methodological decisions made by complex organizations with limited resources. Moreover, official numbers, especially those that appear in series, often do not reflect all these factors instantaneously: they echo their past as the surface of a landscape reflects its underlying geology.

Official statistics have always been subject to these influences, but more is now at stake. In the United States, an increased share of federal money is distributed to states and localities according to various statistical formulae and criteria. The making of economic policy as well as private economic decisions hinges on fluctuations in key indicators. Standards for affirmative action in employment and school desegregation depend on official data on ethnic and racial composition.

Official statistics directly affect the everyday lives of millions of Americans. They trigger cost-of-living adjustments of many wages and Social Security payments. They determine who qualifies as poor enough for food stamps, public housing programs, and welfare benefits. They are used to set the rates at which Medicare pays hospitals and to regulate businesses large and small. But official statistics also affect society in subtler ways. By the questions asked (and not asked), categories employed, statistical methods used, and tabulations published, the statistical systems change images, perceptions, aspirations. The Census Bureau's methods of classifying and measuring the size of population groups determine how many citizens will be counted as "Hispanic" or "Native American." These decisions direct the flow of various federally mandated "preferments," and they in turn spur various allegiances and antagonisms throughout the population. Such numbers shape society as they measure it.

Statistics are lenses through which we form images of our society. Our national self-perceptions are regularly confirmed or challenged by statistics on such fundamental matters as the condition of the nuclear family, reading and literacy, and our industrial production and military strength relative to other countries. Whether the meanings that politicians or pundits read into the data are reasonable or fanciful, the numbers provide a basis for popular and specialized discussion. Even when the numbers misrepresent reality, they coordinate our misperceptions of it.

Lest there be any confusion, we should emphasize that to say official statistics are entangled in politics and social life is not to say that they are "politicized" in the sense of being corrupt. In the United States, institutional safeguards for the most part shield the statistical agencies from meddling by politicians and interest groups. Our point is that political judgments are implicit in the choice of what to measure, how to measure it, how often to measure it, and how to present and interpret the results. These choices become embedded in the statistical systems of the modern state and the information they routinely produce.

Source: Excerpted from William Alonso and Paul Starr, "Introduction," *The Politics of Numbers,* edited by William Alonso and Paul Starr, New York: Russell Sage Foundation, 1987, pp. 1–3.

influenced by what other researchers have done (step 6), which they have reviewed shortly before embarking on the project or remembered from their training days in graduate school. Thus, although the individual researcher completes his or her project at step 6, the research process itself continues, starting with step 1 again. Each step is not only influenced by what the researcher has done in the preceding step, as we have just suggested, but is also subject to various forces outside the research process. (See box, p. 44, for how political forces can influence the last two stages of the research process—analyzing results and drawing conclusions.)

QUESTIONS FOR DISCUSSION AND REVIEW

1. What six steps do most sociologists use in conducting explanatory social research?
2. What should sociologists do with the conclusions they draw from a research project?

HUMANIST CHALLENGES TO SOCIAL RESEARCH

The research methods we have described evolved over the years as social scientists tried to adopt the scientific method, which was originally developed to deal with the physical world. In applying this method to the study of people and their social world, social scientists were assuming that people are, in some important ways, like objects and nonhuman organisms. As a result, some social scientists today tend to quantify all kinds of human behavior, including the complex feelings of love and hate and other human phenomena that cannot be meaningfully quantified. Their motto seems to be "If you cannot measure, measure anyhow" (Krenz and Sax, 1986). However, the humanistic content of sociology—the basic qualities of being human as opposed to being subhuman or inanimate—reminds sociologists not to go overboard with quantification. It also challenges sociologists to engage in subjective interpretation, make value judgments, and refuse to do unethical research.

Subjective Interpretation

Rigid adherence to scientific methods may lead us to ignore the humanness of the people we study and to treat them as if they were objects. We would become unwilling to identify ourselves with our subjects and consequently reluctant to subjectively interpret what is going on. But sometimes subjective interpretations are necessary, especially if we want to penetrate into the subjects' inner experiences. This is why Weber, as we noted in Chapter 1 (Thinking Sociologically) advocated the use of the subjective approach, which requires understanding, empathy, intuition, sensitivity, or some other undefinable feeling for the subjects.

Weber himself used the subjective approach to explain how early Protestantism, in particular Calvinism, led to the emergence of capitalism in Western societies. In Weber's view, the Calvinists believed in predestination but did not know whether they were predestined for salvation in heaven or punishment in hell. As a result, they felt quite anxious, which in turn caused them to believe that success through hard work was a sign of being in God's favor. So they worked as hard as they could. After achieving success, they could not spend their money on worldly pleasures because their religion forbade it. They consequently saved as much as they could, reinvested the savings in their businesses, and continued to work hard to acquire new wealth all over again. It was these practices and the accumulation of wealth that eventually gave rise to capitalism.

Now how did Weber know that religious anxiety necessarily motivated the Calvinists to work hard rather than, say, become too discouraged to do anything but get drunk? Weber could only insist that good works "could be considered the most suitable means of counteracting feelings of religious anxiety. . . . They are the technical means, not of purchasing salvation, but of getting rid of the fear of damnation" (Weber, 1930). But how did he know that? Apparently he put himself in the Calvinists' shoes and found that he could have the same fear about damnation if he believed in the same thing—predestination. The validity of this analogy from subjective experience can never be proved, but neither can it be disproved (Andreski, 1968).

Value Judgment

As suggested in Chapter 1 (Thinking Sociologically), scientific methods with their emphasis on the importance of objectivity require that we refrain from making any value judgment. We should deal with "what is" rather than "what ought to be." We should attempt

Sociologists must be aware of their own preconceptions and biases when studying human groups and their behavior. It is easy to approach prison populations from positions of sympathy or disapproval; it is hard to be completely neutral. But awareness of their own biases can help sociologists to keep them under control and to produce objective, accurate data.

to discover what the nature of our society is, rather than what kind of society we ought to create. Sociology, then, should be a value-free science. All this is apparently based on the assumption that it is possible for sociologists to be value-free in the same way natural scientists are. Such a belief in value neutrality was popular with sociologists in the 1950s. Since then it has been challenged by the following argument.

Sociology cannot be value-free because the humanness of its subjects always arouses some feelings in sociologists. Unlike physical scientists, who can easily feel neutral about their nonhuman subjects, sociologists are more apt to feel positive or negative toward their human subjects. Such a feeling tends to show up in sociological research. Suppose we want to study prison life. We would look at it from the standpoint of either the prison administrators or the prison inmates, depending on where our sympathy lies (Becker, 1967). This personal value would also influence how the topic is to be defined, what research method is to be used, how the facts are to be collected, and what conclusions are to be drawn.

Since researchers have varying values, they may approach the same phenomenon from different angles and collect different facts about it. As a result, each fact may reflect a different facet of the phenomenon. In studying American society, for example, conservatives may find it to be the best democracy in the world, but liberals may be more critical. Combined, both views can help us see the complexity—both the positive and negative features, rather than only a small aspect—of American society. If all of us were expected to be value-free, we would have to see the same thing. This is likely to be a narrow aspect of the society, such as the right to vote, that all of us can agree on. Value neutrality, then, may not be appropriate for the study of *human* events, though it is appropriate for nonhuman phenomena. Human events are much more complex, requiring much more than a single fact to deal with it.

There is, of course, the risk that personal values may lead us to distort or ignore disagreeable facts. Nevertheless, this risk can be cut down substantially if we are conscious of our biases. Plato's famous advice, "Know thyself," is particularly appropriate here. Knowledge of our biases can help us control them. If we claim to be value-free, we will cover up our biases and there is no way we can control them. Suppose we are deeply religious and yet claim to be objective. In doing research on dating habits, we may unconsciously ask questions that encourage respondents to condemn premarital sex while they in fact approve it (Hoover, 1984; Borman et al., 1986).

Ethical Problems

Claiming to be value-free can also make sociologists insensitive to at least two kinds of ethical problems in social research, one involving research methods and the other its applications.

First, researchers sometimes lie to their subjects, as Humphreys and Milgram did. Some researchers justify these deceptions as necessary to their pursuit of knowledge. If they did not lie, the subjects might refuse to be studied or their behavior might be altered in a way that would make the experiment useless. Some argue further that the knowledge gained outweighs whatever potential or real harm may befall the subjects. According to Allen Grimshaw (1982), one researcher even asserts that in 99 percent of the cases the worst that could happen to subjects of social research is only "slight embarrassment, bruised egos, umbrage, and ruffled vanity." He adds that this is "the level of trauma that adults, college sophomores, infants, blacks, whites, the educated and the uneducated, the rich and the poor are able to sustain at no great cost." But most sociologists, particularly the humanists, argue that those researchers' scientific ends do not justify deception and invasion of privacy. They believe that respect for personal autonomy and integrity should take priority. In fact, deception by researchers can undermine public trust in them. Suspecting social scientists of being tricksters, subjects may lie to the researcher, pretend to be naive, or do what they think the investigator expects them to do. If deception escalates, we may reach a point where we no longer have naive subjects, but only naive researchers, cranking out bogus data. Moreover, even though only a small minority of subjects have suffered serious harm from experiments like Milgram's, their suffering cannot be nullified by the fact that the majority of subjects have escaped unscathed, just as the harm done victims of drunk drivers cannot be excused by the fact that the majority of pedestrians have been lucky enough to avoid being run over by them (Baumrind, 1985).

A second ethical problem is that some researchers are not concerned that their findings may be used for unethical purposes. They may try to prevent their data from falling into evil hands but would do so only as concerned citizens, not as objective scientists. Claiming to be value-free, they believe that they should be concerned only about producing the best data possible. Most sociologists, however, would try not to get involved in research that they consider unethical.

In 1964 the U.S. Army recruited social scientists for what was called Project Camelot, a $6 million research study of social change in Latin America. It offered social scientists an unusual opportunity to conduct important research on a large scale. About six months later, however, they found out that the Army's real purpose was to obtain data to learn how to prevent revolutions against what many Americans considered repressive governments. After the project was begun in Chile, many social scientists, Chilean officials and journalists, and members of the U.S. Congress and State Department objected to it. Within a year, the project was canceled. By taking part in the research, social scientists would have been helping the United States to interfere in the internal affairs of other countries—a project that many consider unethical. This is why in 1986 a social scientist at Harvard University touched off a storm of criticism when he was discovered to have received a $107,430 grant from the CIA for doing research on Saudi Arabia. Many scholars consider it unethical to work for the CIA because the intelligence agency's dedication to secrecy violates the academic principle of openness. They fear that the CIA will use the findings from its sponsored research to spy on other countries. They are also afraid that the CIA's "dirty tricks" abroad could put them in danger. As one social scientist said, "People's lives could be at stake"; another said, "People in the field now have to worry about their lives." A third canceled his travel plans, declaring, "I don't want to go any place until it's perfectly clear that I'm not associated with the CIA" (Kelman, 1986; Helprin, 1986).

Although most sociologists are sensitive to those ethical problems, they also know that they have a dilemma: Once they have gathered information, they may find themselves powerless to control its applications. No one person can control the ultimate uses to which the knowledge is put. Dependence on institutions for the resources to conduct studies may further reduce researchers' ability to implement their ethical standards. In fact, institutions may determine what is to be studied as well as how information is to be used. As a result, even findings from well-intended research can be used for unethical purposes. A discovery in social science called desensitization technique, for example, can be used to reduce the stress of daily life, but it can also be employed to get individuals to enjoy violence and brutality and increase their efficiency as terrorists and assassins (Reynolds, 1982).

Psychiatrist Thomas Szasz once observed that when you get up in the morning and put on a shirt, "if you button the first buttonhole to the second button, then it doesn't matter how careful you are the rest of the way." So it is with sociology. If the research is sloppy—if the sample is unrepresentative or the control inadequate or the observation biased—then all the brilliant analysis in the world will not make things right. The details of research studies, however, mostly fall beyond the scope of this text, and in the remaining chapters we will emphasize their conclusions.

QUESTIONS FOR DISCUSSION AND REVIEW

1. Who are the humanists, and why do they challenge some methods of social research?
2. In what ways can sociologists use subjective interpretation and value judgments to improve the quality of their research?
3. Under what circumstances can sociologists sometimes justify deceiving subjects or allowing the government to use research results?

CHAPTER REVIEW

1. *What are the purposes of social research?* As part of their efforts to contribute to sociological knowledge, sociologists conduct two kinds of research. One is descriptive research, intended to describe phenomena, which can stimulate new theories. The other is explanatory research, designed for testing existing theories.

2. *What is the primary rule of social research?* All phenomena to be investigated must be observable in some way. Operational definitions are used to make unobservable phenomena observable and measurable.

3. *What are variables and how can their causal relationship be determined?* Various events may be treated as variables if their characteristics vary from one individual or group to another within the population under investigation. The causal relationship between variables can be established if at least three conditions are met: the variables must be correlated; the independent variable must precede the dependent variable in time; and there must not be a third variable causing the correlation.

4. *What research methods do sociologists use?* There are four major methods: *survey,* which gathers information on a population through interviews or questionnaires; *observation,* which provides firsthand experience of the subject being studied; *experiment,* which allows the researcher to manipulate variables; and *secondary and content analyses,* which use existing data.

5. *What steps do social researchers follow?* Generally, they try to follow this sequence: (1) choose a problem, (2) formulate a testable hypothesis, (3) select an appropriate research method, (4) collect data, (5) analyze the result, and (6) draw a conclusion.

6. *How do sociologists meet the humanist challenges to social research?* Primarily because the subjects of sociology are humans rather than things, scientific methods cannot always be as strictly observed in social research as in natural science investigation. Thus sociologists sometimes resort to subjective interpretation, make a value judgment, or simply stay away from unethical research.

KEY TERMS

Constant A phenomenon or characteristic whose value does not change from one individual or group to another within the population being studied (p. 27).

Content analysis The analysis of a communication by searching for its specific words or ideas and then turning them into numbers (p. 40).

Control group The subjects in an experiment who are not exposed to the independent variable (p. 37).

Correlation A consistent association between two or more variables, which may or may not be causal (p. 27).

Dependent variable A variable that is considered the effect of another variable (p. 27).

Descriptive research Research aimed at gathering information in order to describe a phenomenon (p. 26).

Detached observation A method of observation in which the researcher stands apart from the subjects (p. 35).

Empirical indicator An observable and measurable thing that represents a basically unobservable phenomenon (p. 26).

Experiment A research method in which the researcher manipulates variables so that their influence can be determined (p. 37).

Experimental group The subjects in an experiment who are exposed to the independent variable (p. 37).

Explanatory research Research designed to test a hypothesis in order to explain a phenomenon (p. 26).

Hawthorne effect The unintended effect of the researcher's presence on the subjects' behavior (p. 38).

Independent variable A variable that is the cause of another variable (p. 27).

Operational definition A specification of the action needed to translate what is basically unobservable into what can be observed and measured (p. 26).

Participant observation A method of observation in which the researcher takes part in the activities of the group being studied (p. 36).

Population The entire group of people to be studied (p. 32).

Random sample A sample drawn in such a way that all members of the population had an equal chance of being selected (p. 33).

Reliability The extent to which a study produces the same findings when repeated by the original or other researchers; popularly known as "consistency" (p. 43).

Sample A relatively small number of people selected from a larger population (p. 33).

Secondary analysis The analysis of existing data collected by somebody else (p. 40).

Spurious correlation The appearance of a correlation between two variables that are not causally related (p. 28).

Stratified sampling The process of drawing a random sample in which various categories of people are represented in proportions equal to their presence in the population (p. 34).

Structured interview The interview in which the researcher asks standardized questions that require respondents to choose from among several standardized answers (p. 34).

Survey A research method that involves asking questions about opinions, beliefs, or behavior (p. 31).

Systematic sampling The process of drawing a random sample systematically, rather than haphazardly (p. 33).

Third variable A hidden variable that is responsible for the occurrence of a relation between two other variables that are not causally related (p. 28).

Unstructured interview The interview in which open-ended questions are asked and the respondent is allowed to answer freely (p. 35).

Validity The extent to which a study measures what it is supposed to measure; popularly known as "accuracy" (p. 43).

Variable A characteristic that varies from one individual or group to another within the population being studied (p. 26).

SUGGESTED READINGS

Babbie, Earl R. 1986. *The Practice of Social Research,* 4th ed. Belmont, Calif.: Wadsworth. A realistic presentation of social research, showing the compromises that must be made when sociologists attempt to use the ideal research methods.

Blalock, Hubert M. 1984. *Basic Dilemmas in the Social Sciences.* Beverly Hills, Calif.: Sage. An uncommonly readable book by a leading methodologist discussing the common problems, such as the complexity of multiple causation and the fuzziness of social reality, that face social researchers.

Hoover, Kenneth R. 1984. *The Elements of Social Scientific Thinking,* 3rd ed. New York: St. Martin's. A short, readable introduction to the research process, excellent for beginning students.

Labovitz, Sanford, and Robert Hagedorn. 1981. *Introduction to Social Research,* 3rd ed. New York: McGraw-Hill. A short but solid text on the major methods of social research.

Rose, Gerry. 1982. *Deciphering Sociological Research.* London: Macmillan. Useful for learning how to understand published research reports in sociological journals.

PART TWO

Individual and Society

So far we have described what sociology is and how sociologists think and work. Now we begin to examine the substance of sociology. In the next six chapters we analyze four social bases of human behavior and two classes of behavior that illustrate how even seemingly personal actions are socially motivated.

In Chapter 3 we study culture, the design for living that each society transmits to its members. In Chapter 4 we zero in on social structure, the recurrent pattern of relationships among people. Then in Chapter 5 we look at social groups, which consist of people who share some characteristics and interact with each other, and at formal organizations, which are intentionally designed to achieve specific goals. In Chapter 6 we take a close look at how we acquire cultural values.

To see how these social forces influence our behavior, we examine deviant behavior in Chapter 7 and human sexuality in Chapter 8. Contrary to popular belief, tendencies to commit deviant acts and engage in certain sexual practices do not originate from within oneself as an individual only. These tendencies are heavily influenced by various social forces in the society.

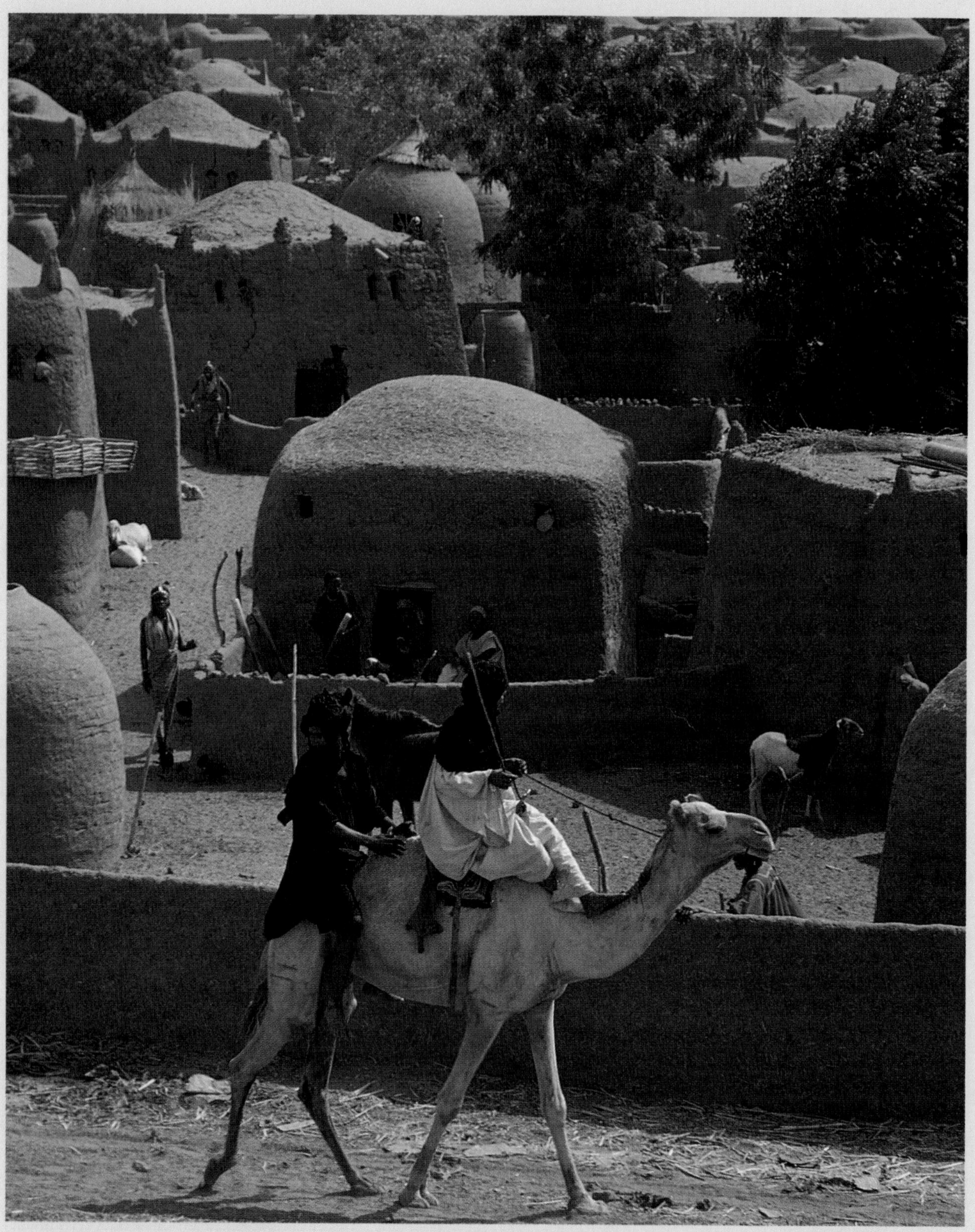

3 Culture

Culture is a design for living. It affects all aspects of our lives and varies from one society to another. Faced with cultural variation, people tend to consider their own culture superior to that of others. To combat this ethnocentrism, *sociologists and other social scientists generally adopt an attitude of* cultural relativism. *It involves judging a culture on its own terms, seeing it through the eyes of its own members. Armed with cultural relativism and further fortified by scientific objectivity, sociologists have developed two perspectives to explain cultural variations. One is the ecological perspective, which attributes cultural variations to differences in physical environment. The other is the functional perspective, which traces cultural variations to differences in the functions of certain cultural practices for the society as a whole.*

Not long ago a social scientist received this rejection letter from an economics journal in China:

> We have read your manuscript with boundless delight. If we were to publish your paper it would be impossible for us to publish any work of a lower standard. And as it is unimaginable that, in the next thousand years, we shall see its equal, we are, to our regret, compelled to return your divine composition, and to beg you a thousand times to overlook our short sight and timidity (Moskin, 1980).

As Westerners, we may find this letter puzzling. If they think the paper is so great, why won't they publish it? Why would they publish inferior ones instead? Unable to find a satisfying answer, we may end up saying, "Ah, the inscrutable Chinese!" To the Chinese, however, the letter is not strange at all. It merely represents a proper way of being polite.

Not only the Americans and the Chinese but also other people around the world tend to see things differently. Obesity may seem unsightly to most Westerners, yet it might appear beautiful to Tonga islanders in the South Pacific. Chopping off a convicted murderer's head may seem barbaric to Westerners but only just and proper to Saudi Arabia's devout Moslems. What lies behind this variation in human perception? To a large extent, it is culture. A **culture** is a design for living or, more precisely, "that complex whole which includes knowledge, belief, art, moral, law, custom, and any other capabilities and habits acquired by [the human being] as a member of society" (Tylor, 1871).

It is obvious from this definition that when sociologists talk about cultures, they are not talking about sophistication nor about knowledge of the opera, literature, or other fine arts. Only a small portion of a population is sophisticated, but all members of a society possess a culture. Neither is culture the same as society, although the two terms are often used interchangeably. *Society* consists of people interacting with one another in a patterned, predictable way. But *culture* consists of (1) abstract ideas that influence people and (2) tangible, human-made objects that reflect those ideas (Velo, 1983). The tangible objects make up what is called the **material culture.** It includes all conceivable kinds of physical objects produced by humans, from spears and plows to cooking pots and houses. The objects reflect the nature of the society in which they were made. If archaeologists find that an ancient society made many elaborate, finely worked weapons, then they have reason to believe that warfare was important to that society. In their study of contemporary societies, however, sociologists are more interested in **nonmaterial culture,** which consists of knowledge and beliefs (its cognitive component), norms and values (normative component), and signs and language (symbolic component).

In this chapter we will begin by examining those three components of culture. Then we will discuss why culture is essential to our survival, what is common to all cultures, and how cultures vary. Finally, we will see how variations in human cultures have been explained.

THE COGNITIVE COMPONENT

Culture helps us develop certain knowledge and beliefs about what goes on around us. **Knowledge** is a collection of ideas and facts about our physical and social worlds that are relatively objective, reliable, or verifiable. Knowledge can be turned into technology, and as such it can be used for controlling the natural environment and dealing with social problems. The high standard of living in modern societies may be attributed to their advanced knowledge and sophisticated technology. Knowledge is best exemplified by science, which we discuss more extensively in Chapter 19 (Science and Technology). On the other hand, **beliefs** are ideas that are more subjective, unreliable, or unverifiable. They may include, for example, the idea that God controls our lives. Beliefs seem to play a greater role in traditional societies. The best example of beliefs is religion, which we discuss in Chapter 15 (Religion).

THE NORMATIVE COMPONENT

Each culture has its own idea not only about what is important in the world but also about how people should act. This is the normative component of a culture, made up of its norms and values. **Values** are socially shared ideas about what is good, desirable, or important. These shared ideas are usually the basis of a society's **norms,** rules that specify how people should behave. While norms are specific rules dictating how people should act in a particular situation, values are the general ideas that support the norms. Thus the specific American norm against imprisoning people without a trial is based on the general American value of democracy. Parents are required by a norm to send their children to school because society places a high value on mass education. We are allowed to criticize our government because we value freedom of speech. Even a norm as mundane as that against pushing to the head of a line is derived from a general value, one that emphasizes fairness and equal treatment for all.

Values and norms also vary together from culture to culture. Since they are subjective in nature, a value and its norms that may be considered good in one society may appear bad in another. As you know, American teachers are relatively inclined to encourage their pupils to think for themselves because we put a high value on individualism. To the Soviets, however, the American norm of self-reliance is dangerous because it encourages antisocial behavior; to them, the American value of individualism means rampant selfishness—the no-holds-barred pursuit of one's own interests, the attitude of "the hell with others." On the other hand, Soviet teachers are more apt to encourage their students to be selfless and serve the state because they believe in socialist collectivism. As Americans see it, though, the Soviet teachers seem to be promoting total obedience to authority, championing a socialist collectivism that amounts to individual enslavement. Consider also one difference between American and Chinese cultures. If someone says to us, "You have done an excellent job!" an American norm requires that we say "Thank you." This may be traced to the value our society places on fair exchange: you scratch my back and I'll scratch yours, so if you praise me I'll thank you for it. In China, however, the same praise will elicit a self-effacing response like "Oh no, not at all" or "No, I've done poorly." The reason is that humility ranks high in the Chinese value system. Thus the Americans might consider the Chinese weird for being unappreciative and the Chinese might regard the Americans as uncivilized for being immodest.

Values and norms also change together over time. In the past most Americans supported the norm of school segregation because they valued racial inequality. Today the norm has given way to school integration because the value has shifted to racial equality. In China before the late 1970s, ideological purity ("We would rather have a poor country under socialism than a rich one under capitalism") was the country's reigning value. One of its resulting norms was to send professors, students, scientists, and other intellectuals to the farm to learn equality from the peasants. After the late 1970s, the new value of pragmatism ("It doesn't matter if the cat is white or black as long as it catches mice") took over, and one of its accompanying norms has been to send many of the intellectuals abroad to learn modernization from the West.

Norms

Day in and day out, we conform to norms. They affect all aspects of our lives. As a result, we are usually not aware of them. If someone asked why we say "Hi"

Sometimes norms persist even after the values from which they are derived have changed. A folkway such as throwing rice at newlyweds can be traced back to ancient beliefs in the importance of having many children. Today we hardly expect newlyweds to have numerous children, but the custom of throwing rice continues to be common. Thus this norm has become separated from the value that inspired it. It is now valued in itself, and we follow the norm simply because it seems the right thing to do. What other norms are associated with weddings?

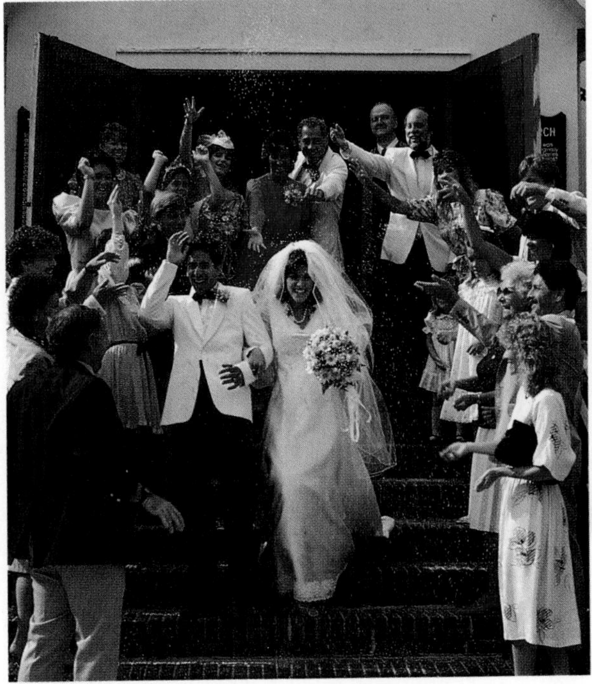

when greeting a friend, we might be inclined to answer, "How else?" or "What a silly question!" We hardly recognize that we are following an American norm. This fact will dawn on us if we discover that people in other societies follow quite different customs. Tibetans and Bhutanese, for example, greet their friends by sticking out their tongues. They are simply following their own norms.

These norms are rather trivial; they reflect one type of norm called a **folkway.** They are relatively "weak," only expecting us to behave properly in our everyday lives. It's no big deal if we violate them; nobody would punish us severely. The worst we would get is that people might consider us uncouth, peculiar, or eccentric—not immoral, wicked, or criminal. Often society turns a blind eye to violations of folkways. Suppose we go to a wedding reception; we are expected to bring a gift, dress formally, remain silent and attentive during the ceremony, and so on. If we violate any of these folkways, people may raise their eyebrows, but they are not going to ship us off to jail.

Much stronger norms than folkways are **mores** (pronounced *mor-ayz*). They absolutely insist that we behave morally, and violations of such norms will be severely punished. Fighting with the bridegroom, beating some guests, burning down the house, and kidnapping the bride are violations of mores, and the offender will be harshly dealt with. Less shocking but still serious misbehaviors, such as car theft, shoplifting, vandalism, and prostitution, also represent violations of mores. In modern societies most mores are formalized into **laws,** which are explicit, written codes of conduct designed and enforced by the state in order to control its citizens' behavior. Hence violations of these mores are also considered illegal or criminal acts, punishable by law. Some folkways—such as driving safely, mowing the lawn, or no liquor sale on Sundays—may also be turned into laws. Laws are usually effective in controlling our behavior if they have strong backing from norms. If there is not enough normative support, the laws are hard to enforce, as in the case of legal prohibitions against prostitution, gambling, teenage drinking, and other victimless crimes.

In fact, all kinds of norms play an important role in controlling behavior, and society has various methods of enforcing them. These enforcement measures are called **sanctions.** They may be positive, rewarding conformity to norms, or negative, punishing violations. Positive sanctions range from a word of approval for helping a child across a street to public adulation for rescuing someone trapped in a burning building. Negative sanctions can be as mild as a dirty look for heckling a speaker or as severe as execution for murder. Some sanctions are applied by formal agents of social control such as the police, but most often sanctions are applied informally by parents, neighbors, strangers, and so on.

Be regularly rewarding us for good actions and punishing us for bad ones, the agents of social control seek to condition us to obey society's norms. If they are successful, obedience becomes habitual and automatic. We obey the norms even when no one is around to reward or punish us, even when we are not thinking of possible rewards and punishments. But human beings are very complicated; we cannot be easily conditioned, as dogs are, by rewards and punishments alone. Thus sanctions by themselves could not produce the widespread, day-to-day conformity to norms that occurs in societies all over the world. To obtain this conformity, something more is needed: the values of the culture.

Values

Since norms are derived from values, we are likely to abide by a society's norms if we believe in its underlying values. If we believe in the value our society places on freedom of religion, we are likely to follow the norm against religious intolerance. If we take to heart the American achievement values, we would accept the norm of studying and working hard. If employers still cling to the traditional belief that a woman's place is in the home, they would violate the norm against job discrimination by not hiring married women. In developing countries parents often carry on the norm of producing many babies because they continue to hang on to the traditional value of big extended families. Why do values have such power over behavior? There are at least three reasons: (1) Our parents, teachers, and other socializing agents (see Chapter 6: Socialization) teach us our society's values so that we will feel it is right and natural to obey its norms. (2) Values contain an element of moral persuasion. The achievement value, for example, in effect says, "It's good to be a winner; it's bad to be a loser." (3) Values carry implied sanctions against people who reject them (Spates, 1983).

People are not always conscious of the values instilled in them, nor do they always know why they obey norms. Sometimes norms persist even after the values from which they are derived have changed. Do you know, for example, why we shower a bride and groom with rice after a wedding? We may feel it is the proper thing to do, or a pleasant thing to do, or in a vague way a sign of wishing the newlyweds well. In fact, the norm is derived from the high value our ancestors placed on fertility, which was symbolized by rice. Thus, over time, a norm can become separated from the value that inspired it. It comes to be valued in itself, and we may follow the norm simply because it seems the right thing to do.

We can easily determine a society's norms by seeing how people behave, but values are not directly observable. We can infer values from the way people carry out norms. When we see that the Japanese treat their old people with respect, we can safely infer that they put great value on old age. When we learn that the Comanche Indians were expected to save their mothers-in-law during a raid by an enemy before trying to save their own lives, then we conclude that the Comanche placed a high value on mothers-in-law. When we see that most American women are dieting, some to the point of becoming anorexic, we know that our culture places an enormous value on slenderness as the model for feminine beauty (Mazur, 1986).

Often, values are not easy to identify. Why is casino gambling illegal in most states, while many of these same states run lotteries? Why do most Americans consider pornography a source of sexual violence but favor the continued sale of pornographic movies and magazines (Press, 1985)? Assessing values in a society is such a complex procedure that sociologists often come up with different, even conflicting, interpretations. But well-reasoned and well-supported analyses can give us insight into a culture. Consider, for example, sociologist Robin Williams's (1970) influential analysis of American values. In his analysis there are fifteen basic values that dominate American culture: success, hard work, efficiency, material comfort, morality, humanitarianism, progress, science, external conformity, individualism, in-group superiority, equality, freedom, patriotism, and democracy (see Table 3.1).

This list does seem to capture something of what is recognizably "American" and to make some of our behavior more understandable. The idea that Americans value freedom and individualism makes more understandable the tendency of politicians to speak out against taxing Americans to support those on welfare.

Table 3.1 Major American Values

Economic Values

1. *Success:* achievement of wealth, power, or fame
2. *Hard work:* readiness to put in long hours if necessary
3. *Efficiency:* the ability to get things done and to do a good job
4. *Material comfort:* a high standard of living, the "good life"

Religious Values

5. *Morality:* the tendency to judge people on the basis of whether they are good or bad, right or wrong
6. *Humanitarianism:* being kind and helpful, providing aid and comfort, contributing time or money to the unfortunate as well as to charitable organizations

Social Values

7. *Progress:* the belief that change is for the good, that the future will be better
8. *Science:* mastery over the external world of things and events as opposed to inner experience of meaning and emotion
9. *External conformity:* emphasizing agreement and avoiding disagreement (hence the dictum, "Never argue about religion")
10. *Individualism:* self-reliance, independence, and the right of each person to develop his or her own personality because each individual has intrinsic worth
11. *In-group superiority:* measuring each person's worth by his or her racial, ethnic, class, or religious background

Political Values

12. *Equality:* treating all people as equals and advocating equal opportunity for everyone
13. *Freedom:* freedom from government controls and freedom to run one's own affairs
14. *Patriotism:* pride in being American and in "the American way of life"
15. *Democracy:* faith in "the people" and their right to govern themselves

Source: From Robin M. Williams, Jr., *American Society: A Sociological Interpretation,* 3rd ed. New York: Knopf, 1970, pp. 452–502.

The notion that Americans value equality is consistent with our relative lack of norms governing interactions between people of different social classes. The idea that Americans value hard work and success explains why athletes work themselves to exhaustion in hope of making it to the Olympics. The American value of efficiency can also explain why we are living in an increasingly impersonal society: we attend very large lecture classes, receive computer letters, seek help from God through pray-TV, work on assembly lines, and eat in fast food restaurants (Ritzer, 1983).

Williams's list further points to some of the areas of conflict in American culture. When external conformity, freedom, and individualism are all highly valued, it is difficult to resolve clashes over whether homosexuality, pornography, or abortion should be prohibited by law. In the business world, the value given to efficiency and success often clashes with considerations of morality: Should companies in pursuing efficiency and success sell adulterated foods and other unsafe products, engage in deceptive advertising, or violate price-fixing laws? Or should they resist these immoralities and risk losing out to competitors? Cultures are basically integrated; they form coherent wholes. But as the inconsistencies among American values demonstrate, that integration is never perfect. This is not surprising because the cultures of large, modern industrial societies are generally less integrated than those of small, traditional ones (Archer, 1985).

Williams's list, however, does not fully reflect the complexity of American culture. It omits the important value of romantic love. It also fails to include three other values in American culture: (1) sociability—the importance of getting along well with others and being able to make friends easily; (2) honesty—the belief that keeping contracts is moral, good for business, or the "best policy"; and (3) optimism—the feeling that the future is hopeful and things will work out for the best (Spindler and Spindler, 1983).

Moreover, some of the values Williams identified have been changing. For one thing, many writers argue that Americans no longer value hard work. According to Daniel Yankelovich (1981), the "ethic of self-denial" (hard work) began to give way to the "ethic of self-fulfillment" ("I've got to love me, enjoy myself, explore myself") in the 1960s and early 1970s, and by the early 1980s as many as 80 percent of all adult Americans had become "self-fulfillers." Marvin Harris (1981) describes the value shift this way:

> Americans have lost their forefathers' work ethic and puritan sense of discipline. In former years Americans worked and saved up for their pleasures. Now young people say they owe it to themselves to have a good life, to get everything that is coming to them—booze, drugs, food, travel, multiple orgasm—right away with no personal entanglements, marriage, or children to worry about.

Actually there is no real abandonment of hard work for easy living. Most Americans still work hard, but they also try to enjoy themselves more—on the job and off. In fact, their work ethic has heavily influenced their pursuit of leisure, so that the harder they work on the job the harder they work at their leisure. In a content analysis of *Fortune* magazine from 1957 through 1979, sociologist Lionel Lewis (1982) found that business leaders, like many other Americans, strive to succeed in their leisure pursuits as well as in their work. As one avid jogger explains, "Running, like business, is full of drudgery. But inherent in our philosophy is the belief that physical fitness gives us a headstart over a less fit competitor" (Lewis, 1982). In short, Americans have not given up the work ethic but have merely added the leisure ethic.

Other values that have also changed in American

Nowadays Americans continue to work hard but also try to enjoy themselves more, whether on the job or off. Work and leisure tend to become inseparable. When people work, they expect to derive pleasure from it, but when they vacation, they do not simply stay idle. In fact, the harder some people work on their jobs, the harder they work at their leisure activities, like this mountain climber.

LOOKING AT CURRENT RESEARCH

Individualism

Americans have always cherished individualism, but in an extensive study of American society, Robert Bellah and associates discovered some major problems with this strong belief. This reading explores individualism and its consequences. How does this strong belief create sharp value conflicts and changes in modern American society?

Individualism lies at the very core of American culture. We believe in the dignity, indeed the sacredness, of the individual. Anything that would violate our right to think for ourselves, judge for ourselves, make our own decisions, live our lives as we see fit, is not only morally wrong, it is sacrilegious. Our highest and noblest aspirations, not only for ourselves, but for those we care about, for our society and for the world, are closely linked to our individualism. Yet, some of our deepest problems both as individuals and as a society are also closely linked to our individualism. We do not argue that Americans should abandon individualism—that would mean for us to abandon our deepest identity. But individualism has come to mean so many things and to contain such contradictions and paradoxes that even to defend it requires that we analyze it critically, that we consider especially those tendencies that would destroy it from within.

The question is whether an individualism in which the self has become the main form of reality can really be sustained. What is at issue is not simply whether self-contained individuals might withdraw from the public sphere to pursue purely private ends, but whether such individuals are capable of sustaining either a public *or* a private life. If this is the danger, perhaps only the civic and biblical forms of individualism—forms that see the individual in relation to a larger whole, a community and a tradition—are capable of sustaining genuine individuality and nurturing both public and private life.

Modern individualism has pursued individual rights and individual autonomy in ever new realms. In so doing, it has come into confrontation with those aspects of biblical and republican thought that accepted, even enshrined, unequal rights and obligations—between husbands and wives, masters and servants, leaders and followers, rich and poor. As the absolute commitment to individual dignity has condemned those inequalities, it has also seemed to invalidate the biblical and republican traditions. And in undermining these traditions individualism also weakens the very meanings that give content and substance to the ideal of individual dignity.

We thus face a profound impasse. Modern individualism seems to be producing a way of life that is neither individually nor socially viable, yet a [illegible] forms would be to return to intolerable discrimination and oppression. The question, then, is whether the older civic and biblical traditions have the capacity to reformulate themselves while simultaneously remaining faithful to their own deepest insights.

Many Americans would prefer not to see the impasse as starkly as we have put it. Philosophical defenders of modern individualism have frequently presumed a social and a cultural context for the individual that their theories cannot justify. Parents advocate "values" for their children even when they do not know what those "values" are. What this suggests is that there is a profound ambivalence about individualism in America among its most articulate defenders. This ambivalence shows up particularly clearly at the level of myth in our literature and our popular culture. There we find the fear that society may overwhelm the individual and destroy any chance of autonomy unless he stands against it, but also the recognition that it is only in relation to society that the individual can fulfill himself and that if the break with society is too radical, life has no meaning at all.

Source: Excerpted from Robert H. Bellah et al., *Habits of the Heart,* New York: Perennial Library, 1986, pp. 142–144. © 1985 The Regents of the University of California.

life include optimism about the future, tolerance of nonconformity, and the importance of material success. In the 1950s there was more optimism, less tolerance of nonconformity, and greater interest in individual success. Between the early 1960s and early 1980s there was less optimism, more tolerance, and greater concern for other people. Today there is a swing back to the values of the early 1950s (Spindler and Spindler, 1983).

However, Americans have also been pursuing their personal ambition so relentlessly that they have little or left for their families, friends, and communities. s leaves them "suspended in glorious, but terrifying, solation." (For more discussion on this and other negative consequences of individualism, see box, p. 59.) Consequently, there is an attempt to move beyond the isolated self by spending more time with the family, seeking meaningful rather than casual relationships, and working to improve community life (Bellah et al., 1986). This tension between concern for oneself and concern for others is an enduring part of American culture. As sociologist Amitai Etzioni tells his interviewer (Kidder, 1987),

> [We have] a continuous, unending conflict where on the one hand the community keeps saying, "There's too much individualism: Listen to me, don't abort, don't smoke, gayness is bad," and on the other hand people saying, "No, I have a need," and feeling inside themselves a tug-of-war. This kind of tug-of-war has been going on in America since "the founding days." We have it today, and we're going to have it in the 21st century.

Studies of American culture have further shown that some of its core values have exhibited remarkable stability and continuity through time. These include equality, honesty, hard work, self-reliance, and sociability (Spindler and Spindler, 1983).

QUESTIONS FOR DISCUSSION AND REVIEW

1. Why is sociology's definition of "culture" different from popular uses of that word?
2. What are cultural values and norms, and how do they combine with sanctions to control people's behavior?
3. How do folkways differ from mores?
4. To what extent do your personal values agree with the list of cultural views identified by Williams?

THE SYMBOLIC COMPONENT

The components of culture that we have discussed so far—norms and values as well as knowledge and beliefs—cannot exist without symbols. A **symbol** is a language, gesture, sound, or anything that stands for some other thing. Symbols enable us to create, communicate and share, and transmit to the next generation the other components of culture. It is through symbols that we get immersed in culture and, in the process, become fully human. We can better appreciate the importance of symbols, and particularly language, from Helen Keller's (1954) account of her first step into the humanizing world of culture. Blind and deaf, she had been cut off from that world until, at the age of seven, she entered it through a word:

> Someone was drawing water and my teacher placed my hand under the spout. As the cool stream gushed over one hand she spelled into the other the word water, first slowly, than rapidly. I stood still, my whole attention fixed upon the motion of her fingers. Suddenly I felt a misty consciousness as of something forgotton—a thrill of returning thought; and somehow the mystery of language was revealed to me. I knew then that "w-a-t-e-r" meant the wonderful cool something that was flowing over my hand. The living word awakened my soul, gave it light, hope, joy, set it free! There were barriers still, it is true, but barriers that could in time be swept away.

Once Helen Keller understood that her teacher's hand sign meant water, once she understood what a word is, she could share her world with others and enter into their world, because she could communicate through symbols. All words are symbols; they have meaning only when people agree on what they mean. Communication succeeds or fails depending on whether people agree or disagree on what their words or signs mean. Helen Keller's experience is a vivid example of the general truth that almost all communication occurs through the use of symbols.

Animal and Human Communication

Animals, too, communicate. If you try to catch a seagull, it will call out "hahaha! hahaha!" to signal its friends to watch out for an intruder. A squirrel may cry out to warn other squirrels to flee from danger. A chimp may greet its fellows by making the "pant hoot" sound, and it threatens them by breaking off and waving branches. When an ant dies, it releases a chemical to induce the surviving ants to carry it to a compost heap. Certain fish signal their presence by sending electric impulses from their muscles. But these signal systems differ in very fundamental ways from human communication.

First of all, our symbols are *arbitrary.* If you do not speak Chinese, you would not know what a *gou* is. *Gou* is the Chinese word for dog. There is no inherent connection between the word and the thing itself. The

Spaniards, after all, call the same animal *perro* and the French call it *chien*. Even "dingdong" is an arbitrary symbol: a bell may sound like "dingdong" to us, but not to the Germans, to whom a bell sounds like "bimbam." The meaning of a word is not determined by any inherent quality of the thing itself. It is instead arbitrary: a word may mean *whatever* a group of humans have agreed it is supposed to mean. It is no wonder that there are a great many different symbols in human communication to represent the same thing (Poog and Bates, 1980). On the other hand, animals are not free to arbitrarily produce different symbols to indicate the same thing because their behavior is to a large extent biologically determined. This is why, for example, all seagulls throughout the world make the same sound to indicate the presence of danger.

Second, animal communication is a *closed system*, whereas human language is an *open system*. Each animal species can communicate only a limited set of messages, and the meaning of these signals is fixed. Animals can use only one signal at a time—they cannot combine two or more to produce a new and more complex message. A bird can signal "worms" to other birds but not "worms" and "cats" together. Animal communication is also closed in the sense of being stimulus-bound; it is tied to what is immediately present in the environment. The bird can signal "worms" only because it sees them. It is impossible for an animal to use a symbol to represent some invisible, abstract, or imaginary thing. As philosopher Bertrand Russell said, "No matter how eloquently a dog can bark, he cannot tell you that his parents are poor but honest." In contrast, we can blend and combine symbols to express whatever ideas come into our heads. We can create new messages, and the potential number of messages that we can send is infinite. Thus we can talk about abstractions such as good and evil, truth and beauty, for which there is no physical thing that is being signaled. It is this creative character of language that leads many people to believe that language is unique to humans. Although several chimpanzees have been taught sign language, it is doubtful that they have created *novel* sentences of their own (Terrace et al., 1979).

Nonverbal Communication

Aside from using words, we also use signs to communicate. But our sign system is quite different from that of animals. Like our language, our nonverbal communication is arbitrary rather than biologically determined, open rather closed. It consists of kinesics and proxemics.

Kinesics is "body language," the use of body movements as a means of communication. Kinesics plays an important role in our social life. To find a pickup in a singles bar, for example, a man typically uses body language. He looks around the room and if he spots a woman he likes, his gaze will rest on her. If the woman is interested, she will hold his gaze, then look away, and again look back at him. The man, getting the message, will move toward her. But the meaning of body language varies from one culture to another. In the United States we nod our heads to mean yes and shake them to mean no. To the Bulgarians, however, the head nodding means no and the head shaking means yes. The Greeks nod their heads to indicate yes but jerk their heads back with their eyes closed and eyebrows lifted to mean no. The Semang of Malaya thrust their heads forward to signal yes and cast their eyes down to signal no. The Ainu of northern Japan do not use their heads at all in saying yes and no, they use their hands.

We are usually less aware of **proxemics**—the use of space as a means of communication—unless someone violates what we consider our personal space. In North America, when talking to a person whom we do not know well, we ordinarily stand about three feet away. If one person moved in closer than that, the other would find it too close for comfort. But South Americans are inclined to stand much closer. We might find them too pushy for being too close to us, and they might find us too unfriendly for being too distant from them. If we converse with Arabs, they might even get closer and literally breathe on us. Their view of public space is also different from Westerners', as Edward Hall (1976) has observed:

> In the Arab world you do not hold a lien on the ground underfoot. When standing on a street corner, an Arab may shove you aside if he wants to be where you are. This puts the average territorial American or German under great stress. Something basic has been violated. Behind this—to us—bizarre or even rude behavior lies an entirely different concept of property. Even the body is not sacred when a person is in public. Years ago, American women in Beirut had to give up using streetcars. Their bodies were the property of all men within reach. What was happening is even reflected in the language. The Arabs have no word for *trespass*, no word for *rape*.

Hall (1966) also noted that the interpersonal distance is small not only among Arabs and Latin Ameri-

Two Arab men in conversation. Nonverbal communication may involve proxemics—the use of space as a means of communication. Proxemics varies from one culture to another. North Americans, when conversing with people whom they do not know well, usually stand about three feet apart from each other. But Arabs, along with South Americans and Southern and Eastern Europeans, tend to maintain a closer conversational distance.

cans but also among Southern and Eastern Europeans, and that it is great among Asians, Northern Europeans, and Northern Americans. Many studies have supported Hall's observation in one way or another. Consider a typical investigation by two social psychologists. They recruited 35 Japanese, 31 Venezuelan, and 39 American students and asked each to have a five-minute conversation on his or her favorite sports or hobbies with a member of the same sex and nationality. The result shows that the Venezuelans sat closer together than did the Americans, who in turn sat closer than the Japanese, the average conversational distance being, respectively, 32.3, 35.4, and 40.2 inches (Sussman and Rosenfeld, 1982). In practically all cultures, however, high-status people tend to invade the personal space of a lower-status person more frequently than the other way around. Professors may pat a student's back but the student rarely reciprocates. Men in general let their hands rest on women's shoulders but women seldom do the same to men. Doctors touch their nurses more often than nurses touch their doctors. Bosses touch their secretaries more often than secretaries touch their bosses (Gillespie and Leffler, 1983). Often, we engage in these and other nonverbal communications without being aware of the messages they covertly transmit to others. Nevertheless, they can have serious consequences for our lives (see box, p. 63).

The Influence of Language

In saying that the Arabs have no words for "trespass" and "rape," did Hall imply that they do not see these acts in the same way as we do? Apparently yes. Many social scientists assume that language influences the way we perceive the world around us. Edward Sapir (1929) was the first to hold this view. Human beings, he said, live "at the mercy of the particular language which has become the medium of expression for their society." Sapir also wrote that language has "a tyrannical hold upon our orientation to the world." When societies speak a different language, "the worlds in which societies live are distinct worlds, not merely the same world with different labels attached to it."

This view was developed by Sapir's student Benjamin Whorf (1956) and became known as the *Sapir-Whorf hypothesis.* It holds that language predisposes us to see the world in a certain way. Sometimes, the hypothesis is put even more strongly: language molds our minds, determining how we think about the world. Whorf found, for example, that the language of the Hopi Indians of the southwest United States has neither verb tenses to distinguish the past and the present nor nouns for times, days, seasons, or years. Consequently, according to Whorf, Hopi- and English-speaking people perceive time differently. While we see the difference between a person working *now* and the same person working *yesterday,* the Hopi do not because their language makes no distinction between past and present.

There are many other intriguing differences among languages. We use the English words "fear" and "shame," which shows our ability to perceive these two feelings as different. But a native tribe in Australia cannot tell them apart because they do not have separate words for them. Instead, they have only one word *(kunta)* to refer not only to fear and shame but also to shyness, embarrassment, and respect. It is therefore difficult for the aborigine to appreciate the differences among those five feelings (Wierzbicka, 1986). The Rus-

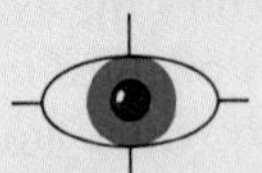

USING SOCIOLOGICAL INSIGHT

The Power of Nonverbal Signals

We do not communicate with words only. We also communicate nonverbally. Whether we are aware of it or not, nonverbal communication can seriously affect our lives, as the following report indicates. How can this knowledge be used to improve job performance?

The nonverbal messages people send, with a look, a gesture, a tone of voice, are very pervasive and important in the workaday world. These covert cues, according to new studies, have a strong impact in key relationships such as those between judge and jury or physician and patient.

One study reveals that the way a judge gives his or her instructions to a jury can double the likelihood that the jury would deliver a verdict of guilty or not guilty—even when on the surface the judge's demeanor seems perfectly impartial. One striking finding of this judicial study concerned trials in which the judge knew that the defendant had a record of previous felonies, a fact that a jury, by law, is not allowed to know unless the defendant takes the stand. When the judges were aware of past felonies, their final instructions to juries were lacking in warmth, tolerance, patience, and competence. The juries in these cases said they were unaware of any bias on the part of the judges, yet their verdicts were twice as likely to be "guilty" than in cases in which the charges were as serious but defendants had no record of felonies. When videotapes were analyzed by independent raters, they found that the judges' tone of voice, rather than anything in their words, communicated the strongest, most negative messages. "Judges can't come out and say, 'This defendant is guilty,'" said Peter Blanck, who did the study. "But they may say it subtly, nonverbally—even if that message is inadvertent."

A judge's charge to a jury is, by law, supposed to be free of such bias. Blanck said that most of the biasing elements he found in his research were unintended. He sees his study as a first step in helping judges to neutralize their hidden messages, as well as, one day, providing lawyers with a new basis for challenging verdicts. "If judges became sensitized to the problem," said Blanck, "they could learn to be more impartial in their demeanor."

According to another study, physicians' rapport with their patients depends to a great extent on their body language. The researchers found that physicians who were rated as having the best rapport sat leaning toward the patient, with arms and legs uncrossed, and nodding as they talked to patients. Another sign of rapport was looking the patient in the eye from time to time, but not staring. The net effect seemed to communicate a desire to be attentive and intimate. The meaning of a given posture or movement, however, is highly specific to a given situation. Thus a physician who leaned back in his chair, which in many social settings would be a sign of feeling relaxed, could be seen by a patient as signaling a lack of interest.

An important implication of this study is for doctors to be more aware of their nonverbal messages so that they can convey the right ones to their patients. Otherwise, the patients would have difficulty recovering. As Robert Rosenthal, the co-author of the study, said, "When a physician gives up on a patient, that patient gets the most negative of nonverbal messages—too bad you're dying—which makes the patient give up hope." On the other hand, as another researcher said, "The most eminent physicians I've observed are exceptionally encouraging to patients. They don't just say, 'We've done all we can,' but rather use the calm assured tones of authority to say, 'I know you'll get better.'"

Source: Excerpted from Daniel Goleman, "Studies Point to Power of Nonverbal Signals," *New York Times,* April 6, 1986, pp. 17, 20. Copyright © 1986 by The New York Times Company. Reprinted by permission.

sian language, on the other hand, has two words for what we call "blue," but we may find it hard to visualize two kinds of blue (Crane et al., 1981). In his novel *1984,* George Orwell (1949) provided a dramatic presentation of the possibilities of the Sapir-Whorf hypothesis. In the dictatorship portrayed in the novel, a language called *Newspeak* had been created. Among other things, Newspeak had no word for freedom, so that people could not even think about freedom, much less want it.

Many scholars, however, have criticized the Sapir-Whorf hypothesis for overemphasizing the power of lan-

Snow and cold have shaped Eskimo culture in countless ways. Eskimos have dozens of words for different kinds of snow, while we have only one. Would a knowledge of the Eskimo words for snow help us to be more aware of different kinds of snow when we see it? Put another way, would knowledge of the words shape the way we perceive reality? The answer is yes, according to the Sapir-Whorf hypothesis. This is why people who speak different languages sometimes think differently and cannot see eye to eye on some issues.

guage. According to the critics, language only influences—rather than determines—how we think. If language determined thought, people who spoke different languages would always think differently. If this were the case, it would be impossible for us to comprehend English translations of foreign languages. But the critics do admit that language does have some influence on cognition. This is why people who speak different languages sometimes think differently, so that they cannot see eye to eye on some issues. Therefore, some scholars today are trying to determine the amount of influence language has on thinking (Ferro-Luzzi, 1986). On the other hand, the Sapir-Whorf hypothesis has stimulated studies of language with the aim of understanding culture. An important finding is that the Eskimo use separate words for different kinds of snow, such as the snow on the ground, falling snow, drifting snow, powdery snow, and slushy snow. They do not have a general term for "snow," as we do. This suggests the greater importance of snow to the Eskimo, who must know the exact condition of the snow to ensure the safety of a sled trip, the success of a hunt, and so on. Similarly, the Garo of northeast India, who live in an environment full of ants, have more than a dozen words for different kinds of ants but no general term for "ant" (Plog and Bates, 1980). The Garo apparently find it useful to distinguish one kind of ant from another. Ants play so small a role in our lives that our language makes no distinction between them. We lump them all together in one word, and to most of us one ant looks just like another.

QUESTIONS FOR DISCUSSION AND REVIEW

1. In what ways do human and animal communication differ?
2. How do kinesics and proxemics function as forms of nonverbal communication?
3. How does the language you use influence the way you see the world?

EVOLUTION AND CULTURE

Having just gone over the various components of culture, we may appreciate the tremendous influence culture has over us. Culture not only surrounds us but gets into us to become an important part of our being human. We are so dependent on culture that we can hardly survive without it. Without culture we would not readily know how to prepare foods, work, raise children, live with other members of society, or do endless other things. Why is culture so important to us but not to animals? An answer can be found in our biological evolution.

Natural Selection

The idea that organisms evolve, that they change gradually over time, is an ancient one, but it was Charles Darwin who proposed a convincing theory of how evolution might occur, the theory of **natural selection.** Organisms vary, Darwin noted, and some of these variations make particular organisms more "fit" than others. Some members of each species are stronger or swifter than others. Thus some are better adapted to their environment than others. In mountain regions, for example, goats that are surefooted are more fit than

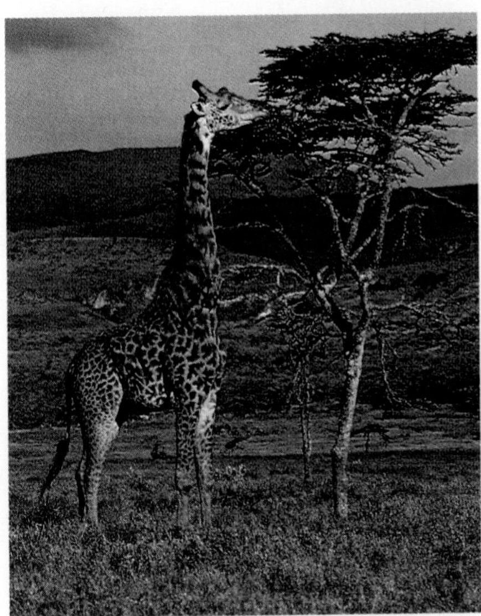

The theory of natural selection tells us that as the environment slowly changes, species either adapt to the changes or die out. When the only food available to giraffes was on high trees, the animals with longer necks could obtain food and survive, whereas those with shorter necks eventually became extinct. This is why today giraffes have very long necks.

their less nimble fellows. On the plains, swiftness rather than nimbleness would likely make some horses more fit than others. The fitter individuals are more likely than others to survive and to produce more offspring than the less fit. Their characteristics are therefore more likely to appear in succeeding generations. Very gradually, the proportion of the population that has these fitter characteristics increases, and the proportion with fewer adaptive traits declines. Ultimately, after many generations, the fit survive and the unfit die out. In other words, nature "selects" the fit for survival and the unfit for extinction.

Consider a simplified version of how the theory of natural selection might explain why giraffes today have very long necks. Originally, neck length might have varied from one giraffe to the next much as body size varies from one human to another. Then suppose there was a shortage of food, and the only food available to the giraffes was foliage on high trees. The longer-necked giraffes would find it easier to obtain food. They would survive and reproduce, and their offspring would have longer necks too. At the same time, short-necked giraffes, having difficulty reaching the high foliage, would eventually die out. The neck length of the surviving population of giraffes would vary, but on the average it would be longer than the neck length of the extinct giraffes (Ember and Ember, 1977; Hitching, 1982).

According to the theory of natural selection, the biological characteristics of every species change over the generations. Sometimes evolutionary change occurs because the physical environment changes, as in our giraffe example. Sometimes it occurs as a response to competition among species. And sometimes change occurs because a species moves to a new environment. This is what probably happened in human evolution (Plog and Bates, 1980; Leakey and Lewin, 1977).

Evolutionary Background of Culture

Humans today are the product of a tremendously long process of evolution, which began with the first living organisms more than 3 billion years ago. By having these same ancestors in the remote past, humans and all other living creatures are related to one another as distant cousins. We therefore share with them certain physical and behavioral characteristics. Even what may seem uniquely human traits can be found in other members of the animal kingdom. We can walk on two feet, so can birds. We can use our hands, so can all apes and monkeys. We can use tools, so can chimps and baboons—even sea otters and some birds. We can live as members of a society, so can some insects. We are not even the only species capable of learning and transmitting behaviors to new generations. Adult chimps can teach their young how to catch ants and termites.

At the same time, however, humans are very different from the rest of the animal kingdom. We are the only species with the capacity for culture—complex language, constant learning, use of sophisticated tools, and a flexible form of social organization. Why are we so different from the other animals who, after all, are descended from the same ancestors? The reason, according to Darwin, is geographical separation. When some members of a species move into a radically different environment, they will evolve into a new species.

Such was the case with the biological evolution of the early humans (Leakey and Lewin, 1977). About 14 million years ago the jungles where the ape's earliest ancestors had been living thinned out, creating a shortage of fruits and nuts. Some of the apes began to venture into the savanna (grasslands), where they could search for new food sources such as seeds, roots, and finally the meat of other animals. The apes that remained in the forest evolved into today's chimps, gorillas, and orangutans. The savanna-dwelling apes evolved into out ancestors, because the environment of the savanna forced them to develop a new set of characteristics.

On the savanna, it is useful to be able to stand upright in order to see over the tall grass to spot oncoming predators and to carry food to a home base. Some of the savanna-dwelling apes failed to develop an erect posture and died out. Those who became bipedal (standing on two legs) began to make tools. It was at this time that these primates began to evolve more quickly into humans. Toolmaking required intelligence and sensitive hands, and living together at a home base further required social interaction involving cooperation, sociability, and vocal communication (Rensberger, 1984). In other words, the erect-walking primates were forced by natural selection to develop those required physical and behavioral characteristics. Eventually, about 100,000 years ago, the primates that did not develop those characteristics became extinct, while the other primates that did survived as humans. At the same time, those very traits that made possible the emergence of humans also made possible the development of a complex culture.

The long evolutionary process has caused us to lose nearly all our **instincts**—biologically fixed traits that enable the carrier to perform complex tasks. Apparently our instincts have been gradually selected for extinction because they did not help our ancestors to adapt to the radically new environment in the savanna—they were useful only for our simian ancestors, left behind in the jungles, to continue dealing in a fixed, automatic way with their relatively unchanging environment. Because we have almost no instincts, we need a culture to survive. This need is most clearly seen in human infants' long dependence on adults. Unlike newly born animals, whose instincts enable them to be on their own in only a few hours or days, human infants must depend on adults for many years—until they have learned enough of the culture to fend for themselves.

We are, then, the only species that depends greatly on complex language, constant learning, sophisticated tools, and a flexible form of social organization—all of which are parts of culture—for survival. The loss of instincts has made us more dependent on each other, and the resulting development of culture has also loosened our bondage to the natural environment. Thus we have adapted to vastly differing environments—from arid deserts and arctic wastelands to rugged mountains and dense jungles—from which various forms of culture have emerged. In short, since evolution gave the human species the capacity for culture, we have moved farther and farther away from our evolutionary home. Today we largely depend on culture rather than instincts to survive (Rindos, 1986).

QUESTIONS FOR DISCUSSION AND REVIEW

1. How does the theory of evolution explain such changes in life forms as the long necks of giraffes or the absence of instincts in humans?
2. To what extent has the process of evolution separated humans from the other primates and created dependency on culture?

CULTURAL UNIVERSALS

Everywhere on the planet, human beings are the product of the same evolutionary process, and all of us have the same set of needs that must be met if we are to survive. Some of these, such as the need for food and shelter, are rooted in biology. Others—such as the need for clothing, complex communication, social order, and esthetic and spiritual experiences—are basic necessities of human social life. Human cultures are the means by which people everywhere meet these needs. Since these needs are universal, there are **cultural universals**—points of similarities in all cultures.

These universals appear in both material and nonmaterial culture. To meet their need for food, all peoples have some kind of food-getting technology, such as food gathering, hunting, or farming. To meet their need for shelter, people in all societies build some kind of housing, such as a grass hut, igloo, wooden house, or brick building. To meet their need for complex communication, all societies develop symbols and language. To meet their need for esthetic and religious experiences, peoples all over the world create art forms—such as music, painting, and literature—and believe in some kind of religion. In fact, George Murdock (1945) found more than 60 cultural universals, including incest taboos, myths, folklore, medicine, cooking, bodily adornment, feasting, dancing, and so on.

a

b

c

d

The activities of human social life that recur in all cultures are called cultural universals. Many of these activities, such as music making, have esthetic as well as practical aspects. Here we see musicians in a variety of cultures: (a) Nigeria, (b) India, (c) South Korea, and (d) the United States. Sociologists are interested in the many different ways that cultural universals express themselves in different cultures. They have found that music can have profound religious significance in some societies, while in others it serves merely to entertain. Although making music is a cultural universal, it is obvious that the music itself will sound very different in each culture.

In the last decade a new Darwinian theory called *sociobiology* has emerged to argue that human behavior is genetically determined. One of the sociobiologist's tasks is to explain how humans have acquired the cultural universals. In regard to incest taboos, for example, the leading sociobiologist Edward Wilson (1980) argues that "human beings are guided by an instinct based on genes" to avoid having sex with their mothers, fathers, or other close relatives. In order to perpetuate and multiply themselves, our genes in effect tell us to stay away from incest. If we do not, our offspring will become less fit than ourselves and less able to produce children. Through the logic of natural selection, then, individuals who avoid incest pass on their genes to more descendants than do those who practice incest. In other words, the prohibition on incest exists practically all over the world because it serves to maximize the fitness and reproductive success of humans.

Most sociologists, however, find the sociobiological argument hard to swallow. In their view, if humans were already compelled by their genes to avoid incest, why would virtually every society in the world bother to prohibit it? It is also unreasonable for sociobiologists to assume that people everywhere are so biologically inclined to avoid incest that it is virtually nonexistent. According to Marvin Harris (1980), there are several hundred thousand cases of father-daughter incest a year in the United States. British anthropologist Edmund Leach (1981) also notes that brother-sister incest is quite common in most Western societies. Of course, most humans do not commit incest, whereas most cats and dogs do, because humans are the only animals prevented by their cultures from doing it. The question, then, is, why do societies find it necessary to prohibit incest—why not just let people engage in it? One sociological explanation is that the incest taboo exists because it brings about marital alliances among many groups that are useful for security against famine and foreign attack. Another sociological explanation is that the incest taboo exists because it ensures family stability—without the taboo, sexual rivalry could tear the family apart. (More in Chapter 8: Human Sexuality.)

Nevertheless, we should remember from our previous discussion that a few cultural universals–notably our use of sophisticated tools and language—can be traced to our evolutionary past. But, as suggested before, we have a paradox here. When natural selection turned humans into a unique species with the capacity for language 100,000 years ago, this cultural capacity left most of our instincts behind. Thus, today much of human activity cannot be explained by the sociobiologist's argument of "instincts based on genes."

QUESTIONS FOR DISCUSSION AND REVIEW

1. What are cultural universals?
2. Which cultural universals are rooted in the necessities of human social life rather than in man's biological nature?
3. Could humans create culture if the theories of sociobiology were true?

CULTURAL VARIATIONS

While cultural universals reflect the *general* means by which all societies meet their common needs, the *specific* content of these means varies from culture to culture. Language, for example, is a cultural universal, but its specific content varies from one society to another, as can be found in the differences among English, Chinese, French, Spanish, and other specific languages.

The variations in human cultures have long fascinated people. In the seventeenth and eighteenth centuries, Europeans read with wonder the tales of American Indians and South Sea islanders provided by missionaries and explorers. But the ability to understand other cultures and how our own culture shapes our lives has been undermined by other equally old reactions. Most important, people tend to use their own culture as a point of reference for judging other cultures. Overcoming this tendency is the first step toward understanding cultural variations.

Ethnocentrism

Almost from the time we are born, we are taught that our way of life is good, moral, civilized, or natural. We feel in our bones that the way we live is right and that other people's ways of life are wrong, uncivilized, or unnatural. This attitude that our own culture is superior to other people's is called **ethnocentrism.** See how you feel about the following practices in other societies.

Among the Alorese people in Indonesia as well as the Hopi Indians in the American Southwest, mothers often masturbate infants to pacify them. Among the Ila-speaking people in Africa and the Trukese people on the Caroline islands in the West Pacific, boys and girls are encouraged to have sex once they reach the age of ten. Copper Eskimo men occasionally have intercourse with live or dead animals. Every male among the Keraki of

Our culture has led us to feel uncomfortable with practices radically different from ours. This ethnocentrism can be so deeply ingrained in us that we may get physically ill if we eat something our culture defines as awful. Thus we may not have the stomach for the millet that these Tuaregs—nomads of North Africa—are eating. On the other hand, influenced by their own culture, they may find some of our favorite foods nauseating. In how many ways does this meal differ from one in your home?

New Guinea customarily engages in homosexual activities during adolescence and in bisexual behavior after marriage. A woman of the Banaro tribe of New Guinea is expected to conceive her first child by one of her husband's friends rather than by her husband. Yanomamo Indian women in Brazil often kill their baby girls by banging their heads against a tree (Ford and Beach, 1951; Harris, 1974).

As Americans, we are inclined to consider all these behaviors strange, uncivilized, or even disgusting. On the other hand, the Siriono Indians of Bolivia find our custom of kissing very disgusting. People of many other societies find it odd that in our preferred position for sexual intercourse the male is on top of the female, a position called the missionary position by South Sea islanders ever since their women copulated with missionaries many years ago (Kluckhohn, 1948).

Ethnocentrism is so deeply instilled in our minds that we tend to condemn cultural practices radically different from ours. Ethnocentrism is also so deeply ingrained in our bodies that we can become physically ill if we eat something our culture defines as sickening. Try to eat toasted grasshoppers, which most Japanese like, or ants, which some tribes in Brazil enjoy; or mice, which the Dahomey of West Africa find delicious. Just the thought of eating any of these things might turn your stomach. Similarly, peoples in other cultures find many of our favorite foods nauseating. The Hindus in India abhor beef, and the Jews and Moslems in many countries spurn pork. The Chinese consider cow's milk fit only for young children. Many Europeans consider corn on the cob fit only for animals. Numerous Asians and Africans recoil from cheese because they find it too smelly (Harris, 1985).

Since ethnocentrism is so powerful, it is bound to make us extremely biased against other cultures and to distort our observation of what they are really like. Witness how distorted the following analysis of *our* behavior in the bathroom and hospital can be if it is done from the perspective of a foreign culture:

> The supplicant entering the temple is first stripped of all his or her clothes. In everyday life the Nacirema [*American* spelled backward] avoids exposure of his body and its natural functions. Bathing and excretory acts are performed only in the secrecy of the household shrine, where they are ritualized as part of the body rites. Psychological shock results from the fact that body secrecy is suddenly lost upon entry into the latipsoh [hospital]. A man, whose own wife has never seen him in an excretory act, suddenly finds himself naked and assisted by a vestal maiden while he performs his natural functions into a sacred vessel. This sort of ceremonial treatment is necessitated by the fact that the excreta are used by a diviner to ascertain the course and nature of the client's sickness. Female clients, on the other hand, find that their naked bodies are subjected to the scrutiny, manipulation, and prodding of the medicine men (Miner, 1956).

Ethnocentrism is so prevalent and runs so deep that even anthropologists find it difficult to shake off. When

Anthropologists who study other cultures are always faced with the problem of how to shed their own biases and to understand things from the point of view of the culture they are studying. Napoleon Chagnon, shown above, wrote a famous account of his first encounter with the fierce Yanomamo Indians of Brazil. Chagnon had to overcome his own deep-seated expectations of how people should behave in order to deal with the Yanomamo on their own terms.

Napoleon Chagnon (1968) first met the Yanomamo Indians in Brazil, he found them horrifying. Being very warlike, the Yanomamo "welcomed" him by aiming their drawn arrows at his face. They had large wads of green tobacco jammed between their lower teeth and lips. Long streams of green mucus incessantly ran down from their noses, the result of having taken a psychedelic drug. They proudly showed off the long scars—which they had painted red—on their heads, the result of constant fighting. "I am not ashamed to admit," Chagnon later said about this encounter, "had there been a diplomatic way out, I would have ended my fieldwork there and then." Another anthropologist, Elenore Bowen, also failed to suppress her feelings of disgust and revulsion toward her subject, the Tiv people of northern Nigeria: "They were all savages. For the first time I applied the term to them in my own thinking. And it fit" (Plog and Bates, 1980).

Both Chagnon and Bowen suggested that they found it hard to be objective in their work because they had not had much experience studying "primitives." But "even with extensive fieldwork experience," observed Paul Turner (1982), "perceptive anthropologists in the 20th century realize the difficulty or impossibility of ridding themselves of all traces of ethnocentrism." This has much to do, according to Francis Hsu (1979), with Western technological superiority, which "still nurtures in many the illusion of Western racial and cultural superiority in general." As a result, some Western anthropologists continue to present inaccurate views of foreign cultures and even to propose policies aimed at changing the cultures of "underdeveloped" countries to make them more like our own (Turner, 1982).

Cultural Relativism

Nevertheless, most social scientists do strive to adopt an attitude of **cultural relativism.** It involves judging a culture on its own terms, which is, in effect, the opposite of ethnocentrism. Since the terms of the culture—the participants' perceptions, feelings, or viewpoints—are either completely or largely unknown to outsiders, social scientists usually try to become insiders so as to understand the natives' point of view. To become insiders, they can use the participant observation technique or simply identify with the subjects (see Chapter 2: Doing Sociology). Only through becoming insiders can social scientists leave behind the blinders of ethnocentrism and take on the stance of cultural relativism. By adopting cultural relativism, we can understand better the cultures of other peoples. From an outsider's ethnocentric perspective, it appears disgusting for Tibetans to cut up their relatives' corpses and then feed them to vultures. But from the Tibetans' own perspective, this practice is necessary to ensure a higher incarnation for their loved ones (see box on p. 71).

A serious problem, however, can arise with cultural relativism. If we evaluate a society's beliefs and practices

UNDERSTANDING OTHER SOCIETIES

Burying the Dead in the Sky

A valuable outcome of studying culture is a better understanding of other people's customs. Sociologists call this ability cultural relativism and use it to analyze practices like those described in the following. How would a sociologist understand the origin of these Tibetan burial practices?

Most Tibetans believe the dead can return to earth in a higher incarnation if their souls are freed from their bodies.

This is said to be achieved when the flesh and bones of the deceased are fed to mountain vultures in "celestial burials."

The corpses, shrouded in white silk, are borne at dawn by farm tractors to the funeral rock. There, relatives and friends are greeted by undertakers and by two Chinese policemen who serve both as witnesses and as guards to ward off unwelcome onlookers.

As the families sip tea, the remains are unwrapped, placed on the rock and carefully carved into pieces. Bones are ground into a powder and mixed with barley.

More barley sprinkled onto fires sends thick, fragrant smoke billowing skyward to attract the vultures from their mountain nests. Soon the huge birds appear. They circle overhead, then swoop in, heading first for the bone meal, next for the human remains.

Corpses must be totally disposed of for the spirits of the deceased to be freed. Anything left behind by the birds must be burned and the ashes scattered.

Most Tibetans favor such a burial, unlike the Chinese, who prefer cremation. Families that cannot afford undertakers sometimes commend their dead to the fish of lakes and mountain streams.

Generally, only criminals are interred in earthen graves.

Source: Excerpted from *U.S. News & World Report* issue of Aug. 29, 1983. Copyright, 1983, U.S. News & World Report, Inc.

by its own standard only, we could never be critical of them. Consider Nazi Germany's belief in its racial purity and practice of exterminating its Jews. There is no way that the cultural relativist, by assuming the Nazi point of view, could condemn them. Similarly, as a cultural relativist, one could not see anything wrong with such horrors as infanticide, cannibalism, torture, dictatorship, and totalitarianism in other countries. To the relativist, "the difference between a vegetarian and a cannibal is just a matter of taste" (Werner, 1986). Relativism may appear on the face of it only a moral issue, irrelevant to the scientific quest for valid and reliable knowledge. But it is not, because it involves trading one kind of ethnocentrism (the researcher's) for another (the subject's). Such is often the case when a Western anthropologist adopts the values of a third-world culture he or she studies, simply because the natives are just as ethnocentric as the Westerner is. The exchange of the anthropologist's ethnocentrism for the natives' can be seen in "accounts that romanticize non-Western cultures while criticizing the industrial societies from which anthropologists come" (Hippler, 1978). It would obviously retard scientific knowledge of culture.

"Do you swear to tell the truth, the whole truth, and nothing but the truth, and not in some sneaky relativistic way?"

This problem can be found in studies on a native tribe in Australia. A number of anthropologists, relying on the aborigines' perspective, have painted a highly favorable picture of them: "Aboriginal infants and young children are extremely well treated and cared for—by any conventional Western standards—and parents are very genuinely concerned for and involved with their children" (Reser, 1981). But this description contrasts sharply with the finding by another anthropologist, who did not use the natives' point of view: "Children are abused by mother and others when they cry. They are shouted at, jerked roughly, slapped, or shaken. The care of children under six years of age can be described as hostile, aggressive, and careless; it is often routinely brutal" (Hippler, 1978).

Most of the time, however, anthropologists do not carry their cultural relativism too far. To get a more accurate analysis, they integrate what they call an *emic* perspective (the natives' viewpoint) with an *etic* analysis (derived from the observer's skills as an objective scientist). Let us see how this approach can help us understand what appears to outsiders as a very strange culture, that of the Yanomamo Indians. Viewed from their own perspective, the Yanomamos' terrible fierceness and female infanticide may not look too strange. According to them, they frequently go to war to capture wives because they have a shortage of women (this is an emic view). Yet, in order to have a constant supply of fierce warriors, they have to kill baby girls to devote more time to raising the future fighters (also an emic viewpoint). But the Yanomamo do not realize that the female infanticide will create a shortage of women when the boys grow up, so they, in turn, will have to go to war to capture wives (this is an etic analysis). At the same time, the infanticide, along with the constant warfare, helps control the Yanomamo population and ensure their survival in the face of chronic scarcity of food sources (also an etic analysis). In the final (etic) analysis, it is the lack of food sources in their environment that causes the Yanomamo to practice warfare and infanticide. Thus the addition of the observer's etic analysis to the participants' emic view enhances our understanding of the Yanomamo culture.

Ecological and Functional Perspectives

The ability to see a culture through the eyes of its members, tempered by scientific objectivity, has allowed social scientists to go beyond the condemnation or fascination that in the past often dominated accounts of distant cultures. It has allowed them to develop scientific explanations for cultural variations. Many of these are based on either the ecological or functional perspective.

The *ecological perspective* attributes cultural variations to differences in the natural environment. Humans must adapt to their environment to survive, and they adapt through their cultures. Thus, as environments vary, so too will cultures.

Let us compare the Eskimo with the Yanomamo. The Eskimo live in an arctic wasteland. It offers limitations and opportunities far different from those in a tropical jungle, where the Yanomamo live. Consequently, the cultural practices of the two peoples differ sharply. While the Eskimo hunt seals as their major source of fresh food, the Yanomamo catch and eat whatever can be found in the forest, such as wild turkeys, wild pigs, monkeys, alligators, anteaters, caterpillars, and spiders. While the Eskimo do not eat vegetables, fruits, or any other plant, which cannot grow in the severe cold, the Yanomamo eat wild fruits, nuts, and seed pods, and they grow some plantains, bananas, and potatoes. While the Eskimo have the advantage of using nature as a giant freezer to save food for future consumption, the Yanomamo do not. The Eskimo live in igloos built with blocks of ice; the Yanomamo live in huts built with branches and leaves. The Eskimo wear multilayered garments and boots to fight off the arctic cold; the Yanomamo wear almost nothing because of the tropical heat.

There is a limit, though, to the utility of the ecological approach. It is obviously true that the Eskimo's and the Yanomamo's natural environments differ greatly. One is extremely cold and the other is hot. But they are also quite similar in one respect: both are equally deficient in game animals, which can be hunted only after many days on a hunting trip. The ecological perspective suggests that just as different environments bring about different cultures, similar environments bring about similar cultures. Hence we would expect that because the Eskimo and Yanomamo face similar shortages of food, they should have developed similar social practices. But they are very different. Old Eskimos are inclined to commit suicide to eliminate their burden on the economic well-being of their village, but the Yanomamo regularly kill their daughters to reduce population pressure on the consumption of scarce foods. The Eskimo men are so hospitable that they would offer their wives to other Eskimo men for the night; the Yanomamo men are so hostile that they would kill other Yanomamo men to kidnap their women. The ecological perspective cannot explain why the Eskimo help one another and the Yanomamo kill one another.

The explanation can be found in the *functional perspective,* which explains cultural practice by referring to its function for the society as a whole. Thus the Eskimo are hospitable because their hospitality serves the function of ensuring similar treatment for themselves at a later time when they, too, travel great distances to hunt in a harsh environment. Without this reciprocal hospitality, it would be impossible for the Eskimo men to be away from home for days and survive in the severe cold. For the Yanomamo, their constant fighting leads to many deaths and thus controls the population. The constant fighting also serves the function of capturing wives from another village to offset their own shortage of women. Without the constant warfare, the male population would become much larger and put more strain on the shortage of food, seriously threatening the survival of the Yanomamo.

The functional approach also helps explain seemingly puzzling cultural practices. In India, which has the largest number of cattle in the world, there are many poor and starving people; yet the slaughter of cows is forbidden. Moreover, their 180 million cows are treated like gods and goddesses. They are given right of way in the street. They are even affectionately retired to "old-age homes" when they begin to become infirm. Why doesn't India feed starving humans by killing these animals for food? The popular explanation is simply that the Hindus consider their cows sacred. But why do they consider their cows sacred? The reason suggested by the functional perspective is that the sacred cows serve several important, practical functions. First, they produce oxen, which Indian farmers desperately need to plow their fields and pull their carts. Second, when the cows die naturally, their beef is eaten by the poor lower castes and their hides are used by non-Hindu Indians to maintain one of the world's largest leather industries. Third, the cows produce an enormous amount of manure, which is used as fertilizer and cooking fuel. Fourth, the cows are tireless scavengers, eating garbage, stubble, and grass between railroad tracks, in ditches, and on roadsides. Thus it costs nothing to raise the cows, while they provide many things of value. In fact, India's peasant economy depends heavily on the cows. If the Indians ate their cows, many more people would starve to death. The Hindu belief in the sacredness of cows therefore saves the lives of people as well as of cows (Harris, 1985).

Many people in India suffer from severe malnutrition, yet will not consider slaughtering and eating the cows that freely roam among them. In fact, they treat the animals like deities. Why? According to a functional analysis, the living cows serve vitally important functions—as draft animals, as producers of fertilizers and fuel—in the peasant economy. Although killing and eating the cows would solve the immediate problem of hunger, it would also eventually destroy the economy, which in turn would cause many to starve to death.

QUESTIONS FOR DISCUSSION AND REVIEW

1. What is ethnocentrism, and why is its influence so powerful?
2. How do the basic assumptions of the ecological and functionalist approaches to human cultures differ?
3. What are some practices in other cultures that you would find odd or disgusting, and how would sociologists explain them?

SUBCULTURAL VARIATIONS

Cultures vary not only from one society to another but also from one group to another within the same society. The unique characteristics shared by members of a group constitute a **subculture.** As shown by Tom Wolfe (1979) in *The Right Stuff,* naval test pilots in the United States share a subculture: they have a sense of belonging to a special fraternity. They talk in a West Virginia drawl even though they come from various parts of the country. They use their own jargon, such as "augured in." They place great value on meeting never-ending tests of courage.

There is, however, no total break between subcultures and the larger culture, because members of the subculture still share characteristics with others in the larger culture. The test pilots, for instance, share with many other Americans values such as a belief in the importance of success and progress, norms such as those against polygamy and murder, and much the same material culture. Thus a person can be a member of both a subculture and the larger, dominant culture.

In a small nonindustrial society in which people have similar backgrounds, experiences, and occupations, there will be few subcultures. People in these societies are primarily differentiated by gender, age, and status, so that they have only the male and female subcultures, adult and adolescent subcultures, and higher- and lower-status subcultures. In modern industrial societies, however, people are likely to be differentiated along many lines. There are not only differences in gender, age, and status but in religious, racial, regional, and occupational background, all of which may provide bases for subcultures. In the United States, for example, there are subcultures of college students, adolescents, Hispanic Americans, Italian Americans, blacks, and many others.

These subcultures are **variant subcultures.** They merely differ from the dominant culture in some way. Their values are still basically acceptable to the society as a whole. Southerners, for example, merely differ from Americans of other regions in leisure-time activities. The southern style of leisure is more centered around the home, family, and church—gossiping, visiting relatives and friends, and attending church services and socials (Marsden et al., 1982). These activities are not objectionable to other Americans at all. On the other hand, there are **deviant subcultures,** which are in sharp conflict with the dominant culture and represent values unacceptable to the dominant culture. They tend to be

Subcultures arise when people with specialized interests form groups. Older women do not usually take part in the motorcycle subculture in California, but since these women enjoyed racing, they have formed their own group—a subculture within a subculture. They have in common their age and their sex, as well as their interest in racing. Members of subcultures often develop their own specialized language and dress code. Subcultures flourish in industrialized democracies, which are usually large and liberal enough to accommodate harmless nonconformity.

illegal or criminal. Examples include the subcultures of professional criminals, prison inmates, delinquent gangs, drug users, and prostitutes. Similar to deviant subcultures are **countercultures.** These also "sharply contradict the dominant norms and values" of the larger society but are not generally considered illegal or criminal (Yinger, 1982). A good example is the youth movement of the late 1960s, which included hippies, flower children, political activists, and rock fans. They believed in peace, love, and cooperation as opposed to militarism, competitiveness, and self-interest.

Sociologists have long recognized ethnocentrism in our subcultures as they have in other cultures. The most obvious case is racial and ethnic prejudice, which the whites in this country hold against blacks and other minorities. Less obvious forms of ethnocentrism have also been observed. In one Chicago slum, sociologist Gerald Suttles (1968) found many examples of one racial group viewing another's behavior through the distorting lens of ethnocentrism. For instance, whites complain that blacks will not look them in the eye, and blacks counter that the whites are impolite and like to stare at people.

Sociologists have also attempted to explain subcultural practices with ecological and functional perspectives. Albert Cohen (1956), for example, has explained the emergence of a delinquent subculture in ecological terms. He showed how the subculture arises from lower-class youth's responses to two environments. First, the poor teenagers are faced with the barriers imposed by middle-class society, where access to status as a high achiever in school is closed to them. They respond by playing hooky or dropping out. Second, they find a lot of opportunities in their poor neighborhood, where access to status as a tough delinquent is open. Having been turned off by the first environment, they find it easy to respond to the second by becoming delinquents. Richard Ball (1968) has also explained the emergence of poor Appalachians' "analgesic subculture" in both ecological and functional terms. According to Ball, the impoverished mountaineers of West Virginia respond to numerous poverty-related problems by developing a way of life that emphasizes mental rigidity, dependency, belligerence, and fatalistic resignation. Although these responses are not adequate adaptations to the barren environment, they are "functional for they provide relief from the pains of frustration."

QUESTIONS FOR DISCUSSION AND REVIEW

1. What separates variant subcultures from deviant subcultures?
2. When do subcultures form and what problems can they cause for the dominant culture?

CHAPTER REVIEW

1. *What is culture?* It is a design for living. It consists of material culture, which includes all the things produced by members of a society, and nonmaterial culture, which comprises knowledge, beliefs, norms, values, and symbols.

2. *What are norms and values?* Norms are social rules dictating how to behave. There are two types: folkways, which simply expect us to behave properly, and mores, which practically force us to behave morally. Both are derived from values, socially shared ideas about what is good, desirable, or important.

3. *How does human communication differ from animal communication?* Animal communication is largely governed by instincts. It is also a closed system, tied to the immediate present. In contrast, human communication is more arbitrarily determined by people. It is also an open system, where people are able to create an infinite number of messages.

4. *How do humans communicate?* Verbally and nonverbally. In nonverbal communication we use kinesics (body movements) and proxemics (space manipulation). In verbal communication we use words, which have significant influence on our thinking and perceptions and can help us understand cultures.

5. *What is the relationship between evolution and culture?* Our evolution from animals to culture-using humans has caused us to lose most of our instincts. Consequently we must depend on culture to survive, and through cultures we have been able to adapt to widely different environments all over the world.

6. *How do cultural universals differ from cultural variations?* As members of the same species, humans everywhere share the same basic needs that they must meet to survive. Cultural universals are the general methods for meeting the common needs, such as the use of language for satisfying the need to communicate. Cultural variations are the specific differences among cultures in using those methods, such as the differences among English, French, Spanish, and many other languages.

7. *What should we do to understand other cultures?* We should get rid of ethnocentrism, the attitude that our own culture is superior to that of others, and adopt cultural relativism, judging other cultures on their own terms. Cultural relativism, however, should be tempered with scientific objectivity.

8. *Why do cultures vary?* The ecological perspective attributes cultural variations to differences in natural environments. The functional perspective explains variations by the functions different cultures perform.

9. *Is culture uniform within a society?* No, within one society, especially within industrial societies, there are variations from one group to another that are called subcultures. Subcultures may merely differ from the dominant culture, or they may be in conflict with it.

KEY TERMS

Belief An idea that is relatively subjective, unreliable, or unverifiable (p. 54).

Counterculture A subculture whose norms and values sharply contradict those of the larger society but which is basically not illegal or criminal (p. 75).

Cultural relativism Evaluating other cultures on their own terms, with the result of not passing judgment on them (p. 70).

Cultural universal A practice that is found in all cultures as a means for meeting the same human need (p. 66).

Culture A complex whole consisting of objects, values, and other characteristics that people have acquired as members of society (p. 54).

Deviant subculture A subculture whose values are in conflict with those of the dominant culture and which tends to be illegal or criminal (p. 74).

Ethnocentrism The attitude that one's own culture is superior to that of others (p. 68).

Folkways "Weak" norms that specify expectations about proper behavior (p. 56).

Instincts Fixed traits that are inherited and enable their carrier to perform complex tasks (p. 66).

Kinesics Use of body movements as a means of communication (p. 61).

Knowledge A collection of relatively objective ideas and facts about the physical and social world (p. 54).

Laws Norms that are specified formally in writing, and backed by the power of the state (p. 56).

Material culture All the physical objects produced by humans as members of society (p. 54).

Mores "Strong" norms that specify normal behavior and constitute demands, not just expectations (p. 56).

Natural selection Process in which organisms that are well-adapted to their environment have more offspring than the less well-adapted, thereby producing evolution (p. 64).

Nonmaterial culture Norms, values, and all the other intangible components of culture (p. 54).

Norm A social rule that directs people to behave in a certain way (p. 54).

Proxemics Perception and use of space as a means of communication (p. 61).

Sanction Formal or informal rewards for conformity to norms, or punishments for violation of norms (p. 56).

Subculture A culture within a larger culture (p. 74).

Symbol A thing that stands for some other thing (p. 60).

Value A socially shared idea that something is good, desirable, or important (p. 54).

Variant subculture A subculture that is different from but acceptable to the dominant culture (p. 74).

SUGGESTED READINGS

Bellah, Robert N., et al. 1986. *Habits of the Heart: Individualism and Commitment in American Life.* New York: Harper & Row. Shows how Americans are torn between a lonely quest for their own success and a desire for close relationships with others.

Brown, Ray B. (ed.). 1981. *Rituals and Ceremonies in Popular Culture.* Bowling Green, Ohio: Bowling Green University Popular Press. A collection of essays analyzing many aspects of American culture, including TV viewing, sports, comic strips, movies, weddings, and funerals.

Harris, Marvin. 1985. *Good to Eat: Riddles of Food and Culture.* New York: Simon & Schuster. A good-to-read book by a leading anthropologist on why people in various cultures relish or reject such foods as cows, pigs, horses, dogs, cats, insects, and human beings.

Kottak, Conrad Phillip. 1982. *Researching American Culture.* Ann Arbor: University of Michigan Press. An interesting collection of articles on various aspects of American culture by professional anthropologists and college students.

Yinger, J. Milton. 1982. *Countercultures: The Promise and the Peril of a World Turned Upside Down.* New York: Free Press. An insightful analysis of the ways countercultures can improve the larger society, by making us appreciate, for example, the rewards of human relationships more than material satisfactions.

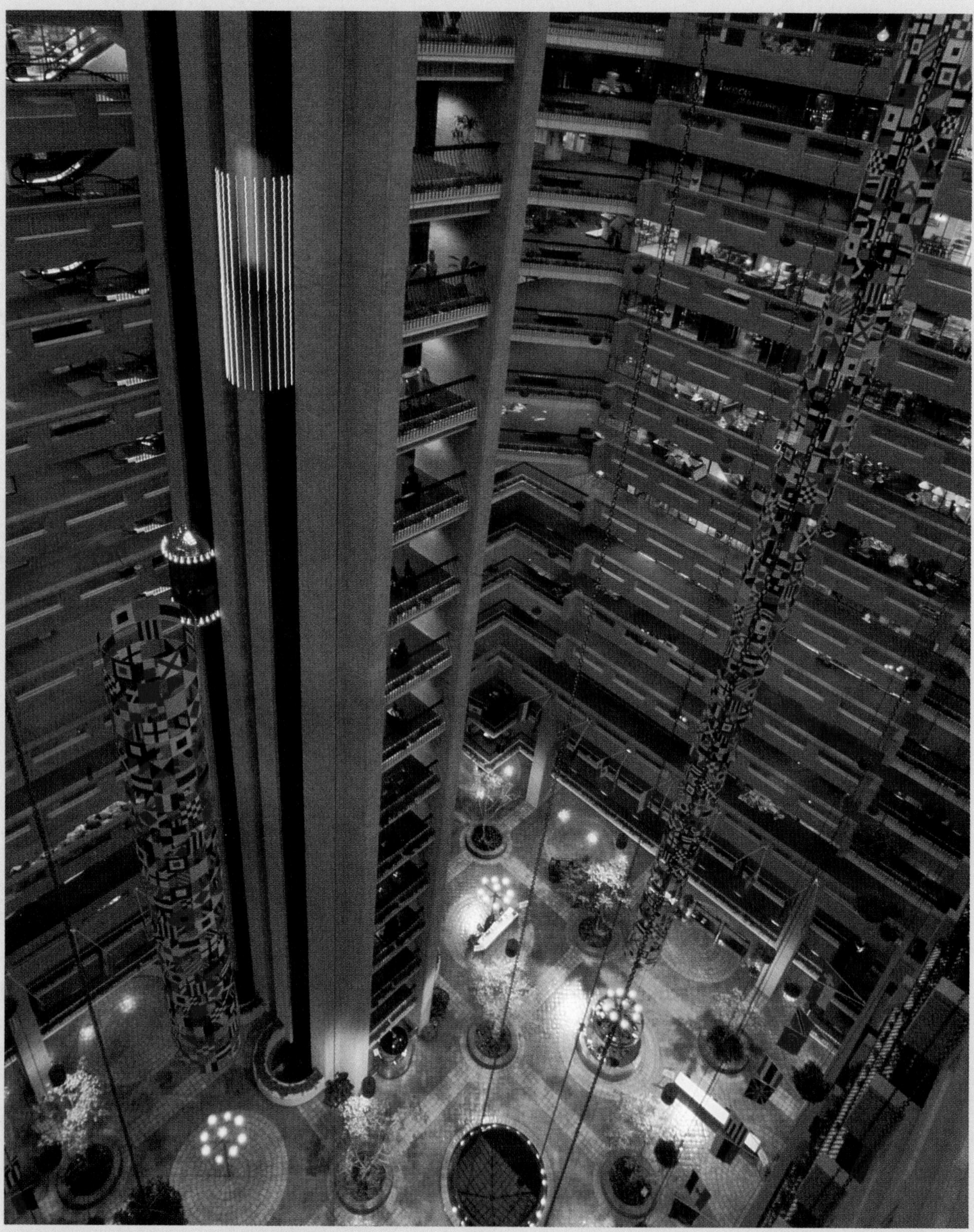

4 Social Structure

Every one of us has a set of statuses and roles. Statuses *are the positions we occupy in society and* roles *are the expectations of what we should do in accordance with our statuses. Thanks to statuses and roles, we know what to expect of others and also what others expect of us. They help us interact with others in certain ways. Out of these social interactions emerges a social network—a web of relationships that ties certain people to one another. All of these recurring patterns of interactions and relationships make up a social structure.*

"No man is an island, entire of itself; every man is a piece of the continent, a part of the main." So wrote John Donne more than three centuries ago. True enough, we are always involved with people in some way. We do something to them, we do certain things with them, and we react to what they do. Even when we are alone, we become involved with them by thinking of them. Without human relationships, we could hardly survive. As infants, we would have died without them. As children, we learned to grow into adults through relationships with others. As adults, we are constantly sustained by social relationships.

Almost like the air we breathe, social relationships are essential to us. And like breathing, these relationships follow recurring patterns, which sociologists call **social structures.** Listen to a parent and teenager and you are likely to hear some echoes of your own adolescence. Walk into your old grade school and you might feel you have taken a trip in a time machine. In friendships and business dealings, in schools, offices, and homes, we find recurring patterns of relationships that constitute social structures. The most common social structure is a *group,* two or more people who interact with one another and share some sense of a common identity. A group may be a clique of friends, a baseball team, a business firm, or a political party. Often groups such as the last three are formed to achieve specific goals, in which case they are called *organizations.* Organizations are supported by **social institutions,** which are stable sets of widely shared beliefs, norms, roles, and procedures that are organized to satisfy certain basic needs of society. Both education and the family, for example, are social institutions. Even beyond these structures, however, we find patterns of stable relationships: groups and institutions form parts of a large social structure called **society.** Societies, in turn, make up an even larger structure—an international community—that is a collection of interacting individuals sharing the same culture and territory.

We will discuss groups, organizations, and institutions in other chapters. Here, we examine societies, along with the dynamic and static aspects of social structure. The dynamic part is **social interaction,** the process by which individuals act toward and react to one another. Social interaction runs through all social structures; it is their lifeblood, making them come alive. In an educational institution, when you ask your instructors questions, they will respond with answers. In a family, when the mother smiles at her son, he will react by smiling back. In a business organization, employees may work hard and their boss may respond by giving them a raise. In the international community, if the Soviet Union decides to build more nuclear weapons, the United States will likely respond by doing the same. Each of these is an example of a social interaction, and each always takes place within a context. This context involves people who have a certain relationship with one another, perhaps characterized by mutual like or dislike or by one liking the other without being liked back. In a loving family, we can see parents and children being connected by affection. In the relationship between the two superpowers, we often observe mutual distrust. However people or groups are tied to one another, their relationships make up the static, fixed aspect of social structure called a **social network.**

SOCIETIES

As large-scale social structures, societies are highly complex. They have so many diverse characteristics—including their cultures, religions, politics, economies, families, schools, and so on—that we may despair of trying to make sense of what they are like. Nevertheless, sociologists have long been aware of certain patterns in the way societies operate. First, all societies can carry on in the face of differences and conflicts among their members because they have developed the foundations of social structure called statuses and roles. And, second, people in different societies have their own ways of making a living and relating to one another. Let us, then, take a closer look at statuses and roles as well as at various types of societies.

Statuses and Roles

When an infant is born in a "yellow baboon" troop in Kenya, the other baboons gather around the mother, but she does not allow them to touch the infant. After about a week, she may allow older juveniles and females to touch the baby baboon briefly, but only after they have sat and groomed her for a few minutes. Younger baboons, however, can seldom get close enough to touch the infant.

Social relations among humans are far more variable than those among animals, but they too follow certain patterns. To a large degree these patterns derive from statuses and roles. As Peter Blau (1977) puts it, "people's positions and corresponding roles influence their social relations." **Statuses** are the positions people occupy in a group or society. **Roles** are expectations of what individuals should do in accordance with their statuses. Thanks to statuses and roles, we usually have some idea of what to expect of other people, and of what other people expect of us. They bring a measure of predictability to our interactions, but statuses and roles also carry the seeds of conflict.

Statuses When you interact with a friend, you are likely to be relaxed, informal, uninhibited. But when you talk with a professor, you are more likely to be a bit stiff, to act in a formal, inhibited way. Being a friend is one status; being a student or professor is another. A status is therefore a definition, an identification, of a person in terms of his or her relationship with another person or group.

In a complex society such as the United States, we have so many statuses it is impossible to name them all. Some of them we are born with. We are born male or female; we are born into some racial group. These statuses of gender and race as well as age are called **ascribed statuses.** They are given to us independently of what we do. All other statuses result from our actions. We earn them in some way. You must do something to be a student or a college graduate or a married person or any one of countless other things. These are called **achieved statuses.** In modern societies such as the United States, achieved statuses have grown in influence at the expense of ascribed statuses. In place of a king or queen who holds the position through inheritance, for example, we have a president who must win the office.

Statuses are sometimes ranked within a social structure; that is, one is considered higher than the other. According to public opinion polls, for example, Americans rank the position of doctors higher than that of plumbers. In a family, the father's status is higher than the son's. In contrast to these *vertical* social structures, some structures are *horizontal.* In these, the various statuses are merely different from each other, not higher or lower. A student's status as a sociology major, for example, is different from but essentially equal to another student's status as a history major. In his analysis of social structure, Blau (1977) refers to horizontal statuses as *nominal parameters* because they have to do with qualitative difference, such as those between genders, races, or religions. Blau uses the term *graduated parameters* for vertical statuses, as they divide people in terms of a rank order that reflects different amounts of an asset such as education, income, wealth, or power.

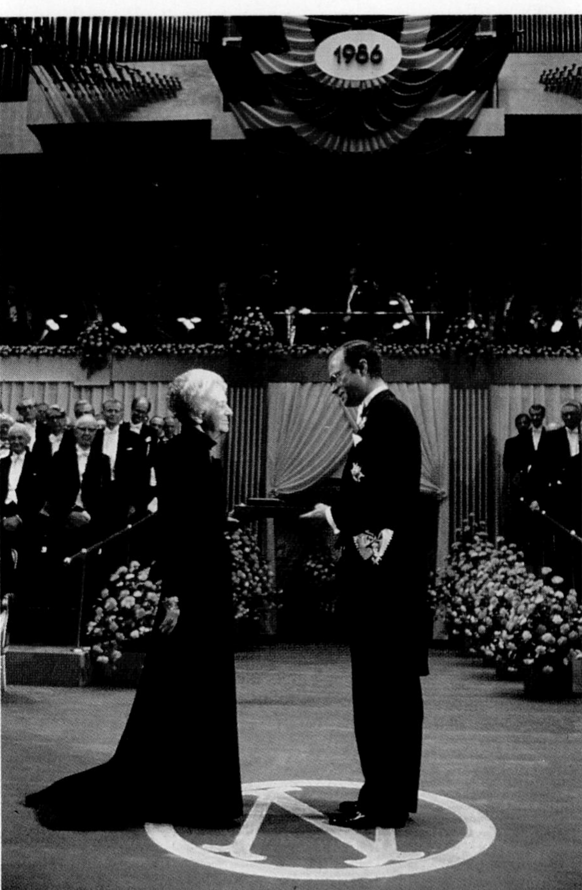

Sociologists have frequently studied the way a status affects our role in society. Ascribed statuses are those with which we are born and which we generally cannot change, such as our gender, race, and age. Achieved status results from our activities. We can see these two types of status here: Professor Rita Levi-Montalcini, former head of the Cell Biology Laboratory at Italy's National Council for Scientific Research, receives the 1986 Nobel Prize for medicine from Sweden's King Carl Gustaf. Professor Levi-Montalcini's status as a Nobel laureate is achieved. Carl Gustaf's status as king is ascribed; it is a consequence of birth.

Despite our many statuses, we are usually influenced by only one status at a time when we relate to another person. When a woman interacts with her husband at home, for example, she will behave primarily as a wife, not as a banker, employer, PTA leader, or athlete. Because the status of wife dominates her relationship with her husband, it is called the **master status** in this interaction. All of her other statuses—as a banker, employer, and so on—are less relevant to the interaction; hence, they are called **subordinate statuses.**

The nature of a society may determine which status becomes the master status. In a racist society such as South Africa, race is the master status and all others are subordinate to it. A white person interacting with a black physician would therefore use race as the master status and profession as the subordinate status. As a result, the white person would not be likely to treat the black physician with the respect usually given doctors.

In our society the master statuses of race and gender also influence the way others treat us. Research has shown that blacks in interracial groups and women in mixed company, when compared with their white and male colleagues, are often given fewer opportunities to interact, are less likely to have their contributions accepted, and usually have less influence over group decisions. This "interaction disability," as imposed by the master statuses of race and gender, is difficult to overcome unless the minorities appear highly cooperative and agreeable to the majority (Ridgeway, 1982). The influence of race and gender also appears in many other areas of social life (see Chapter 10: Racial and Ethnic Minorities and Chapter 11: Gender Roles and Inequalities).

Physical appearance can also function as a master status. Murray Webster and James Driskell (1983) found that, like race and gender, beauty has a profound impact on how individuals are perceived and treated by others. Webster and Driskell discovered, among other things, that attractive persons are expected by college students to be more capable than unattractive ones at most tasks—even piloting a plane—and that good-looking individuals are considered very competent even if they are known to have graduated from an inferior college and to be holding low-paying jobs. Similar findings are duplicated in many earlier studies: Attractive schoolchildren are expected by their teachers to be smarter than unattractive ones; handsome college students are considered by their peers more likely than homely students to get good grades; attractive adults are perceived by many as more likable, friendly, sensitive, and confident. Furthermore, research has shown that others are more likely to agree with the opinions of beautiful people and even to grant them more space on the sidewalk (Clifford and Walster, 1973; Landy and Sigall, 1974; Miller, 1970; Horai, Naccari, and Fatoullan, 1974; Dabbs and Stokes, 1975).

Roles For every status, there are rights and obligations. Children enjoy the right of receiving food, shelter, and love from their parents, but they are expected to show respect, obedience, gratitude, and affection to their parents in return. In other words, every status carries with it a role. Because of your status as a student, you act in certain ways that are part of the student role. Thus status and role seem like two sides of the same coin. But they are distinguishable. A status is basically static, like a label put on a bottle. A role is dynamic, shaped by specific situations and persons.

Consider the role of nurse. In an emergency, nurses must be cool and professional, but they are also expected to convey warmth and concern to their patients. With doctors, nurses are expected to be obedient; with patients' relatives, they may be authoritative. The behaviors demanded by the role change with the situation. (To see how you may change your role behavior to suit a particular situation, see box, p. 84.)

In addition, various people play the same role differently, just as various actors perform the same role on the stage in diverse ways, even though they are working from the same script. The script—the set of expectations or norms about how a person should behave—is the **prescribed role.** How a person actually carries out the role is the **role performance.** The prescribed role of a college student calls for attending classes, reading, thinking, and learning, but people differ in how and to what extent they fulfill these expectations. They may understand the prescribed role differently. They may be more or less successful in fulfilling those expectations. They may simply differ in their manner of carrying out the role. Thus some students may expect to get straight A's while others would settle for C's and B's. The ambitious ones would study harder. Whether ambitious or not, some would end up getting better grades than others. No matter how each individual defines and performs the student role, however, commitment to it is not necessarily total. In fact, as Donald Reitzes (1981) found, only 35 percent of the college students he studied identified strongly with their role. In Reitze's view, most stu-

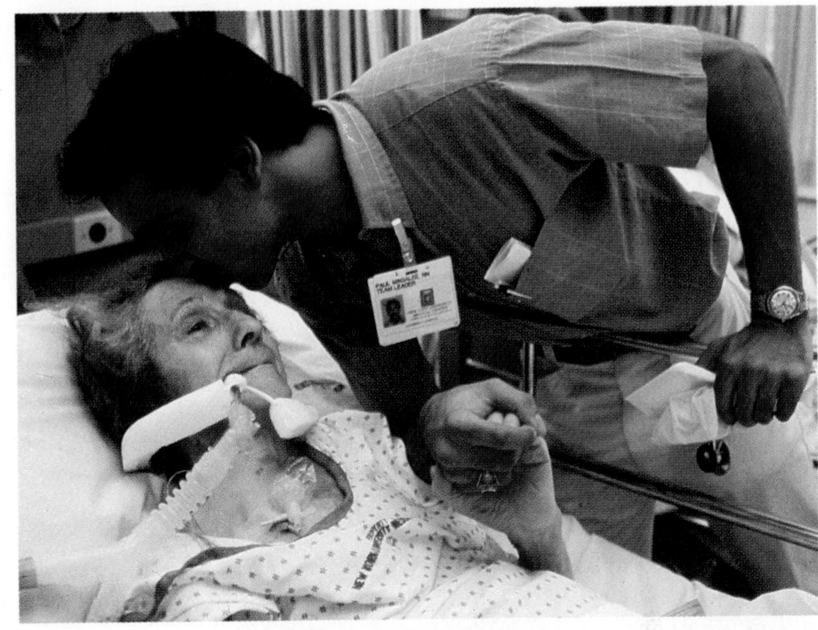

Being a nurse is both an achieved status and a role. His status gives this male nurse a well-defined slot to fill in the hospital hierarchy. His role is to assist the doctor and comfort the patient. Although several nurses might have the same status in a ward, each one has the option of performing the role in a different way. Some nurses may try to appear cool and professional in dealing with patients, but others may exude warmth and concern, as shown here.

dents are not deeply committed to their role because it is "structured for limited or short-term occupancy." A more important reason may be that there are many other roles—such as being a friend, date, leader, and athlete—competing for the student's time.

Indeed, all of us play many roles every day, and some of these roles are bound to impose conflicting demands. The role of judge prescribes an emotionless, objective attitude; the role of father requires emotional involvement. Usually, the conflicting demands of these roles present no particular problem, because a person plays one role at a time. But if a judge found his or her daughter in court as the defendant, there would be a conflict. More commonly, an increasing number of women find themselves caught between the traditional role of homemaker and the modern role of career woman. When we are expected to play two conflicting roles at the same time, we experience **role conflict.** Even a single role may involve conflicting expectations and thus produce what is called a **role strain.** Foremen, for example, are ex-

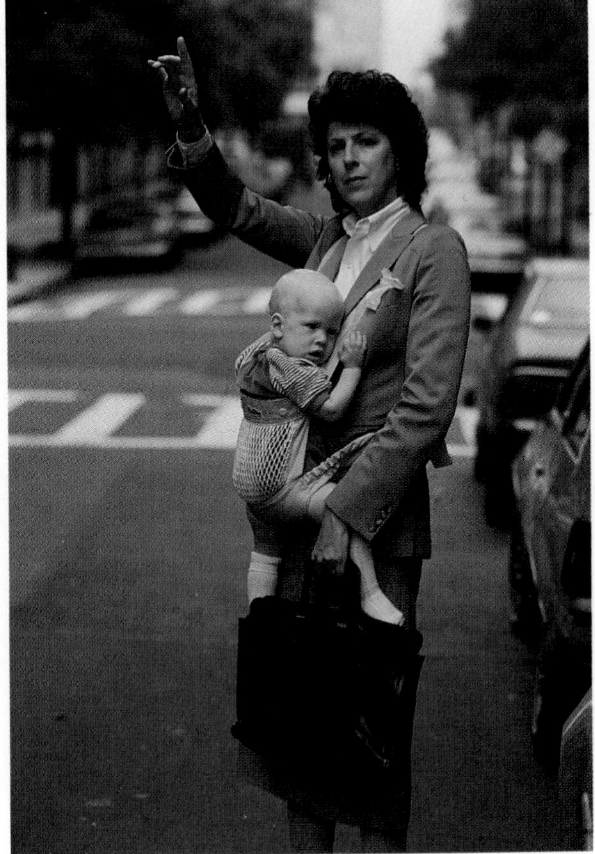

Role conflict results when we must reconcile opposing claims. A growing number of women find themselves caught between the traditional role of a mother and the modern role of a career woman. Such a role conflict is often painful. It tends to produce stress, anxiety, and other psychological aches and pains.

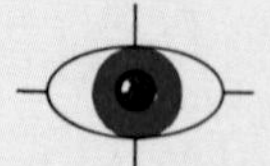

USING SOCIOLOGICAL INSIGHT

Role Behavior at a College Football Game

Role playing involves much more than mechanically conforming to the expectations of a status. Proper emotional expressions are often expected in certain role performances. According to the following analysis, how is emotional role behavior staged at a college football game?

Emotions are not in themselves roles; they are part of the behavioral expectations associated with the roles people enact. We expect parents to display love—not hatred—for their children, social workers compassion—not disgust—for their clients, and clergy empathy for—not envy of—their penitents. An individual enacting a particular role or involved in a particular event does not usually express or feel more than one emotion at a time. However, some social situations call for a series of emotional presentations, often in a programmed order.

I will report the conditions that influenced the emotional responses I both observed and experienced in an elaborate social situation—a college football game. The game was a scheduled conference contest between Alpha University and Beta University. The Alpha-Beta game, always representing a major rivalry, was the last of the season for both teams, each of which had about as many losses as wins. Consequently, the setting provided a major theme for the analysis of emotional role behavior.

College football games are staged events in which the roles of players and spectators are well structured. Their roles, and the expression of emotion associated with the roles, are orchestrated in the game setting. People are expected to take the roles and display the relevant emotions as directed. In order to do so they look to individuals with whom they are interacting for cues about how to act and to feel.

The expectation for an emotional experience, the preparatory mental set for that experience, was being structured for fans throughout the campus and in areas around the campus. The night before, a massive pep rally had promised students that they were certain to share dislike (for the opponents), love (for the team and fellow rooters), and joy (for the victory). Fraternity and sorority parties reinforced the notion that all were to experience an exciting range of emotions at the game. At several settings, such as bars, private homes, and university facilities, graduates of Alpha and Beta universities informed each other about the emotional role expectations they had for the game. It was to be a time for "going wild," and for "letting your hair down."

The pregame interactions

pected to be friendly with their workers, to be one of them. But they are also expected to be part of management and to enforce its rules. Role conflict or strain is usually stressful, causing anxiety and other psychological aches and pains (Biddle, 1986).

In the final analysis, statuses and roles are the foundation of social structure; they determine the pattern of relationships among particular individuals. Thus members of a group (say, a family) can be expected to interact differently from those of another group (say, the opposing teams of a football game). One type of social interaction may be characterized by exchange and cooperation, while the other may be marked by competition and conflict. These patterns of relationships, however, vary from one society to another. Among preindustrial societies, there is more cooperation among hunter-gatherers and more conflict among pastoralists and horticulturalists. But there is still more conflict in industrial than preindustrial societies. Let us explore these various types of societies further.

Preindustrial Societies

Most societies throughout history have been preindustrial. They range from tribes that lived thousands of years before the Roman Empire to the !Kung* people, who live today in the Kalahari Desert of southern Af-

* The ! represents a click, a speech sound not used in English.

among the fans heightened shared expectations for an emotional experience, and defined what the components of the experience were to be. By this time, there was a mutual expectation that loyal Alpha and Beta fans should feel a generalized excitement and should manifest that feeling to each other. Those who had some difficulty getting into the spirit for the game could be helped by readily available alcohol or marijuana. All of these factors worked together to "spiral" the readiness of fans for a proper set of emotional responses to the game.

Cheerleaders can be key orchestrators of fans' emotional role performances. Essentially, the cheerleaders remind the fans of "feeling rules" and help the fans to implement them. The announcer on the stadium public address system can also coordinate emotional responses. Usually there are scattered throughout the crowd several informal cheerleaders who, themselves fans, evoke coordinated emotional performances among other fans in their proximity. Probably they are persons who have had more experience with emotional cueing at games and have received reinforcement for that quasi-leader role.

The formal cheerleaders, the announcers, and the informal cheerleaders function as do "prompters" in a play. The influence of the prompters on the fans can be seen and heard from the field level. In football games, after each down, there are discernible epicenters from which fan response widens. A person jumps up in excitement and others follow suit, not just behind him or her, but in front as well. A person cheers or moans, and there begins around him or her a ripple of similar responses.

The emotions displayed and felt were by no means artificial or shallow. Certainly the depth of feeling and the degree of expression varied among the participants. But the emotional display was real and vivid. That it so rapidly shifted does not detract from its personal significance. Rather, it illustrates the power of the interactive setting for shaping emotional role behavior. Furthermore, it exemplifies the capacity of human beings for accommodating and shaping the settings, and for experiencing and displaying a versatile emotional repertoire within a specific role.

Source: Adapted from Louis A. Zurcher, "Staging Emotional Role Behavior," pp. 53–74 in *Social Roles: Conformity, Conflict, and Creativity.* Copyright © 1983 by Sage Publications, Inc. Reprinted by permission of Sage Publications, Inc.

rica. These preindustrial societies differ from one another in how they obtain their food. They can therefore be classified into four types: **hunting-gathering societies, pastoral societies, horticultural societies,** and **agricultural societies** (Lenski and Lenski, 1987).

Hunting-Gathering Societies Throughout 99 percent of humankind's presence on earth, or until about 10,000 years ago, all societies survived by hunting wild animals, fishing, and gathering wild roots, fruits, birds' eggs, wild bees' honey, and the like. Today, less than 0.1 percent of the world's people live this way. Among the few remaining hunting-gathering societies are the !Kung Bushmen of South Africa, the Batek Negritos of Malaysia, and the Alyawara of central Australia.

Hunter-gatherers move about a great deal in search of food, but they cover only a small area. Because their food sources are thus very limited, hunting-gathering societies are very small, each having only 20 to 50 people. There is a division of labor based on gender: men usually do the hunting; women do the gathering.

Their lives are not necessarily hard. In fact, because their needs are simple, they might work merely two or three hours a day. It has been estimated that a family could easily collect enough of wild cereal grain in three weeks to feed itself for a year. Sometimes the food must be processed, as in the case of some nuts that require roasting and cracking. Hence hunter-gatherers may spend more time feeding themselves than finding the foods (Hawkes and O'Connell, 1981). Nevertheless,

A hunter in the Kalahari Desert, Africa. In hunting-gathering societies there is often a division of labor based on gender: men hunt, women gather. But otherwise most such societies are marked by egalitarianism because possessions are few (limited by the amount that can be carried around) and the people do not accumulate food surpluses. Since no one is rich and everyone shares in the food supply, such societies are marked by peaceful cooperation.

they still have so much leisure time that Marshall Sahlins (1972) has called them the "original affluent societies."

Even so, they do not attempt to accumulate food surpluses. They do not even store food for emergencies, and they tend to share their food with one another. Sharing, in fact, is a central norm and value in these societies. The more successful hunters are denied the opportunity to build prestige and wealth with their skills. They are expected to be self-deprecating about their hunting success, and boasting is met with scorn. Because no one hoards, no one acquires great wealth. And since they have few possessions to fight about, hunter-gatherers are unlikely to engage in warfare. If a strong and skilled hunter tries to dominate others, order them about, or take their wives, he can be secretly killed because there is no effective means of protection (like the police in other societies) and also because everyone has easy access to poisoned arrows, spears, and other hunting weapons. As a result, hunting-gathering societies are generally the most egalitarian in the world. When anthropologist Richard Lee (1979) asked a !Kung hunter-gatherer whether the !Kung have headmen, the man replied, "Of course, we have headmen. . . . In fact, we are all headmen; each one of us is a headman over himself!" This egalitarian trait of a hunting and gathering society is reflected in their religion: they believe in many gods (gods of rain, sunshine, rabbits, sickness, and so on) and consider these gods equal to one another.

Not all of the hunting-gathering societies are egalitarian, though. According to James Woodburn (1982), they fall into two categories: one with "immediate-return systems" and the other with "delayed-return systems." In the first type, people go out hunting or gathering and eat the food on the same day it is obtained; they do not store it for later use. In the delayed-return system, food is elaborately processed and stored. Woodburn found that the !Kung and other hunting-gathering societies with immediate-return systems are profoundly egalitarian for reasons like those discussed above. On the other hand, those with delayed-return systems, such as the aborigines of Australia, are marked by inequality, because stored food can be turned into durable and exchangeable goods—hence leading to accumulation of wealth and power (Yesner, 1983; Testart, 1982). Robert Layton (1986) finds another difference between the two systems. In the egalitarian system, there is an open access to the land or sea from which foods are obtained and a common understanding that anyone has a right to demand the hunter's gain. These ecological and cultural features are absent in the inegalitarian system. In both systems, however, men run the show. They exclude women from hunting activities. They even impose strict and extensive menstrual taboos on women, prohibiting them, when having their period, from touching any man and from handling such "male" things as bows, arrows, and fishing gear. They believe that menstruating women are dangerous to menfolk, that they may cause sickness, injury, or loss of magical power in the man they touch (Kitahara, 1982).

Pastoral Societies In deserts, mountains, and grasslands, plants are difficult to cultivate, but animals can easily be domesticated for use as a food source. About

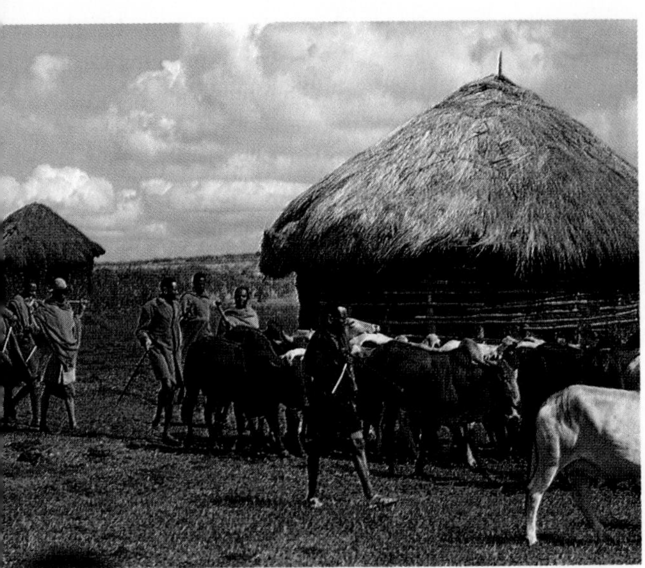

In pastoral societies, animals are domesticated for use as a major source of food. Since pastoralists can accumulate a surplus of food, a great deal of social inequality has developed in their societies. A male individual's social status is based on the size of his herd and the number of his wives. Since they are constantly on the move in search of fresh grazing grounds for their herds, pastoralists have become fiercely independent and tend to disregard land boundaries.

10,000 years ago, some hunter-gatherers began to specialize in the domestication of animals. Today there are a number of pastoral societies, mostly in North and East Africa, the Middle and Near East, and Mongolia. The Africans specialize in keeping cattle; the Arabs, camels and horses; and the Mongols, various combinations of horses, cattle, camels, goats, and sheep. These peoples are different racially and far apart geographically, yet they show a considerable degree of cultural uniformity.

Unlike hunter-gatherers, the pastoralists accumulate a surplus of food. One result is that pastoral societies can be far larger than hunting-gathering bands. Another result is the emergence of marked social inequality, based on the size of an individual's herd and the number of his wives. Some anthropologists argue that animal holdings represent an unstable form of wealth because, as a herder puts it, "Owning animals is like the wind. Sometimes it comes and sometimes it doesn't." When a disaster such as an epidemic or a severe drought strikes, the wealthy herders are assumed to suffer such great losses that social inequality cannot be maintained. But in his study of the Komachi pastoralists in south-central Iran, sociologist Daniel Bradburd (1982) found that disasters cannot wipe out inequalities in animal wealth. "While disasters befall rich and poor alike, they do not befall each with quite the same effect," Bradburd explains. "A poor man who loses half his herd frequently finds it reduced to a size from which recovery is impossible; on the other hand, a wealthy man who loses half his herd will frequently be left with enough animals to rebuild the herd without great difficulty."

Usually, pastoral peoples are constantly on the move, looking for fresh grazing grounds for their herd. Consequently, they become fiercely independent and inclined to scorn land boundaries. They also become rather warlike, and their use of horses greatly enhances their war-making capabilities. They are just as likely to raid settled villages as they are to attack each other. The aim of such aggression is to increase their livestock as well as to warn others against encroachment. Sometimes they take captives and use them as slaves. Their religion and attitude reflect the pastoral way of life. The Hebrews who founded Judaism and Christianity and the Arabs who founded Islam used to be pastoral people, and in each religion we can find the image of a god who looks after his people much as a shepherd looks after his flock. The Mongols have a religious taboo against farming, believing that plowing and planting offend the earth spirit. The African cattle herders, very proud of their pastoralism, regard horticulture as degrading toil.

Horticultural Societies While some hunter-gatherers became pastoralists, others became horticulturalists, growing plants in small gardens. Horticulturalists do their gardening by hand, with hoes and digging sticks. Because their soil cannot support continuous intensive farming, many horticulturalists rely on slash-and-burn cultivation. They clear an area in the jungle by slashing undergrowth and cutting trees, allowing them to dry, and then burning them off, leaving ashes that help fertilize the soil. This procedure also ensures that the plot will be free of weeds. After two or three years of growing crops, the soil becomes exhausted, so new fields are slashed and burned.

Unlike pastoralists, horticulturalists live in permanent settlements. Like that of pastoralists, their society is marked by a sexual division of labor: men clear the jungle and women do the cultivation. Because horticulturalists can produce a food surplus, their societies are usually larger than those of hunter-gatherers. The existence of a surplus also gives rise to inequality in many a horticultural society, where a man can enjoy great prestige by possessing many gardens, houses, and wives.

Warfare, too, becomes very common. Many tribes in a forest often raid each other, torturing, killing, or eating their captives. Victorious warriors receive great honors. They preserve and display their defeated enemies' skulls and shrunken heads, much as athletes today show off their trophies. In advanced horticultural societies, warriors hold power as well as prestige. These societies are usually divided into a small, powerful warrior nobility and a large mass of powerless common people. This social inequality is reflected in religion. Horticultural societies generally believe in capricious gods who must be worshipped. And they perform religious rituals to appease not only the gods but also the spirits of their dead ancestors, perhaps because they live in permanent settlements where the living remain close to their dead. Today, there are still many horticulturalists in the tropical forests of Africa, Asia, Australia, and South America.

Agricultural Societies About 5000 years ago, the invention of the plow touched off the agricultural revolution that radically transformed life in the Middle East and eventually throughout the world. When a field is plowed, weeds are killed and buried efficiently, fertilizing the soil. At the same time, nutrients that have sunk too deep for the plants' roots to reach are brought closer to the surface. Thus the coming of the plow allowed peasants to obtain crop yields many times larger than those horticulturalists obtain with their hoes. If farmers use animals to pull their plows, then their productivity is increased further. As a result, farmers, unlike horticulturalists, can cultivate a piece of land continuously and intensively.

The giant leap forward in food production enables large populations to emerge in agricultural societies. Because each farmer can produce more than enough food for one person, some people are able to give up farming and pursue other occupations. They become tailors, shoemakers, tanners, and weavers. These people help cities emerge for the first time.

The towns, cities, and farms in an agricultural society come under the control of a central government. It is usually headed by a monarch with the power to enslave or even exterminate large numbers of people if he wishes. This centralization of political control coupled with the possession of valuable property provides a strong stimulus for warfare. The common people who fight for their monarch tend to believe that he has divine power. They also believe in a family of gods in which one is the high god and the others are lesser gods. This hierarchy of gods seems to mirror the peasants' experience with various levels of government officials, from the tax collector at the bottom to the monarch at the top.

Agricultural societies are the most complex of all preindustrial societies. They still predominate today in Africa, Asia, and South America. But since the industrial revolution in England 200 years ago, many preindustrial societies have become industrialized and use machinery to till their lands. These industrial societies differ sharply from preindustrial ones.

Industrial Societies

The Industrial Revolution brought many changes in its wake. When a nation industrializes, it supplements human and animal power with machines. With industrialization, cities grow; new occupations are created; social structures and cultures change too. Old ways of life are disrupted.

We may find it easy to understand industrial societies by comparing them to preindustrial societies. This could be the reason why sociologists have long tried to find the basic differences between those two types of societies. As early as 1887, German sociologist Ferdinand Tönnies described the preindustrial society as a **Gemeinschaft,** or "community," meaning that people in such a society have a strong sense of community and relate to each other in a personal way. In contrast, he described industrial society as a **Gesellschaft,** or "society." In such a society, people think of themselves as individuals first and relate to each other in an impersonal way, on the basis of their social roles, and therefore become alienated from one another. Then in 1893 Durkheim used the term *mechanical solidarity* to describe the cohesion underlying preindustrial societies and *organic solidarity* to characterize industrial societies. As we saw in Chapter 1 (Thinking Sociologically), mechanical solidarity is social unity that comes about because people perform the same tasks and have similar values. In contrast, organic solidarity arises when people are forced to depend on one another because their jobs are very specialized. More recently, in 1941, American anthropologist Robert Redfield said that preindustrial societies are small,

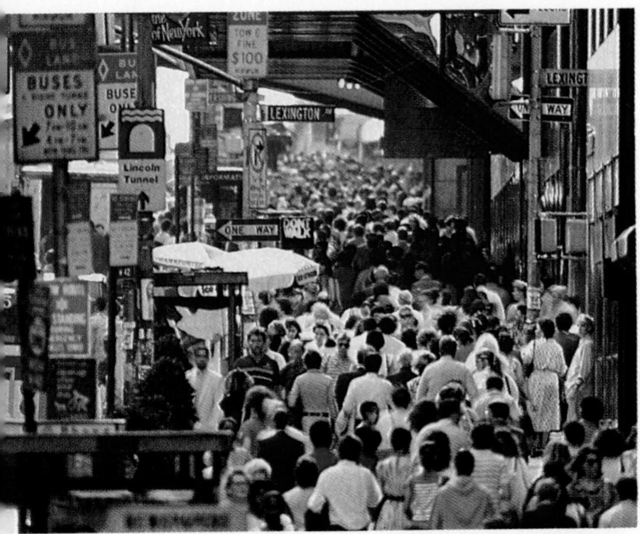

Modern, industrialized societies stand out in comparison with preindustrial societies. In a typical preindustrial society, the social structure is relatively simple, the population is small and homogeneous, the social life revolves around primary groups, and attachment to traditions is strong. But a typical industrialized society is marked by a more complex social structure, a larger and more heterogeneous population, a greater influence by secondary groups, and a greater predilection for social change.

nonliterate, and homogeneous societies in which group solidarity is strong; he called them **folk societies.** On the other hand, he described industrial societies as large, literate, and heterogeneous, with very little group solidarity; he called them **urban societies.**

Today various sociologists have used yet other terms to describe these two types of societies. James Coleman (1982), for example, describes modern industrial societies as *asymmetric,* characterized by the dominance of "corporate actors" (the state, business, labor, and other big organizations) over "natural persons" (the individuals). He contrasts these modern societies with traditional agricultural societies, where person-to-person relations predominate. We can summarize the differences between these two types of societies in reference to four contrasting sets of traits.

1. *Simplicity versus complexity.* The social structure of preindustrial societies is relatively simple. There is very little division of labor, and it is usually based only on age and gender. There tends to be only one clearly defined institution, the family. It is the center of educational, occupational, and religious activities. Technology, too, is simple. The society supports itself by a simple food-getting technique that involves human and animal power.

The social structure of industrial societies is more complex. There is an elaborate division of labor, with thousands of different jobs. There are many social institutions, each more complex than the family. They perform many of the functions of the preindustrial family, as well as new functions. Technology, too, is complex.

2. *Homogeneity versus heterogeneity.* The populations of preindustrial societies are relatively small and homogeneous. Cultural values are so widely shared that social tranquility prevails. In contrast, the populations of industrial societies are larger and more heterogeneous. They include numerous diverse groups that cling to their own subcultures and conflict with each other.

3. *Intimacy versus impersonality.* Social life in preindustrial societies occurs mostly in **primary groups** such as the family. These are small groups in which individuals have strong emotional ties to one another—ties that are intimate and enduring. From these personal relationships comes informal social control, which reinforces social order.

In industrial societies, more social life occurs in **secondary groups,** which consist of people who do not know each other well and who relate to each other in a superficial way. Their relationship is temporary and impersonal. With the growing predominance of impersonal encounters, individuals are more likely to exploit each other, and informal social controls are likely to weaken. Thus formal social control in the form of laws is instituted.

4. *Traditionalism versus modernism.* Preindustrial societies are to a large degree tied to their past and uninterested in social change. They value social stability and emphasize the group's needs rather than the individual's interests. In contrast, industrial societies are more likely to look to the future and to be enthusiastic about social change. They believe in social progress and tend to support the individual's interests above the group's needs.

The four characteristics of each type of society are related. Together they reflect the core nature of each society. Simplicity in social structure, homogeneity in people and values, intimacy in social relationships, and traditionalism in outlook reflect the tendency of preindustrial societies toward *social order.* Complexity in social structure, heterogeneity in people and values, impersonality in social relationships, and modernism in outlook reflect the tendency of industrial societies toward *social conflict.*

We should note that descriptions of various types of societies are merely broad generalizations. They do not necessarily apply to all societies. Also, we should not exaggerate the differences among societies because these are differences only in degree rather than in kind. Many developing nations, for example, are not totally preindustrial—or categorically different from industrial societies—since they have many of the characteristics of industrial societies. They are nonetheless considered preindustrial because their preindustrial features seem more prominent or prevalent than their industrial traits.

Are We Prisoners of Society?

Through its food-getting technology, institutions, formal organizations, social groups, statuses, and roles, society affects the individual. In fact, some sociologists paint a picture of society in which the individual is its prisoner. Other sociologists believe that the individual exercises a great deal of freedom in his or her daily activities. These two views reflect two of the three theoretical perspectives discussed in Chapter 1—structural functionalism and symbolic interactionism.

The Structural Functionalist View The central idea of structural functionalism is that the various parts of society serve the function of contributing to social order. One of these functions is to ensure social order by controlling the individual members of society. Political institutions control us through laws, police, courts, and prisons. Less explicitly, the people we go to school with, work with, or meet in public places control us by being ready to embarrass, ridicule, scold, or hurt us if we do not behave properly. Families and friends control us by threatening to withdraw their love, affection, or friendship if we fail to meet their expectations. All these social pressures push us to conform, to give up our individual freedom. They do not only prevent us from misbehaving, though. They also "systematically constrain our choices to form and maintain relationships" (Feld, 1982). In making friends, for example, we usually associate with people like ourselves. This is because a college, a workplace, or any other social structure typically brings together a homogeneous set of people—with a particular characteristic, such as being relatively young, having a college education, or adhering to the same religion. It appears that we are not as free as we like to think in choosing our friends—or in choosing how to live our lives.

Moreover, we lose our freedom by agreeing and cooperating with the forces that constrain us. We often share in the task of jailor by joining social groups of our own accord because we want to be accepted by others. We even willingly obey the law because we feel like doing so. As functionalists would put it, society ensures order through social consensus—through our willingness to cooperate with the forces that imprison us. As Peter Berger (1963) said, our "imprisonment in society" is carried out largely "from within ourselves":

According to the structural-functionalist view, our society forces us to wait in lines to ensure social order. If we do not wait patiently like everybody else, others will embarrass, ridicule, scold, or hurt us. Through social pressures such as this, we are in effect made prisoners of society. But the symbolic interactionist view suggests that we can exercise our freedom by manipulating interactions, managing others' impression of us, or presenting ourselves in the most favorable light. If we want to be at the front of the line, we can politely ask the people ahead of us for a favor, convincing them with a credible reason that we urgently need to be the first.

> Our bondage to society is not so much established by conquest as by collusion. Sometimes, indeed, we are crushed into submission. Much more frequently we are entrapped by our own social nature. The walls of our imprisonment were there before we appeared on the scene, but they are ever rebuilt by ourselves. We are betrayed into captivity with our own cooperation.

There is certainly truth in the structural functionalist picture. In fact, in much of this text we will be seeing many more of the ways that society confines individuals with their collusion. But the functionalist view may exaggerate the extent to which we are imprisoned. As a macroanalysis, it may focus so much on the forest that it misses the trees. By stressing the social order and the forces that exist before and beyond individuals, it misses the details of everyday life in which we can experience freedom. It is these details that the symbolic interactionist view—a microanalysis—highlights.

The Symbolic Interactionist View The key idea of symbolic interactionism is that human beings interact with each other—not by passively and rigidly following the rules imposed by society but by actively and creatively interpreting each other's actions. In these interactions we exercise considerable freedom.

Erving Goffman (1959) has provided many analyses and descriptions of interactions that demonstrate how people freely manipulate interactions, influencing each other's interpretations. According to Goffman, we are like actors performing on a stage for an audience. Quite often, we try to make a good impression by presenting ourselves in the most favorable light. When out with a new date, we try to appear as charming as possible. When interviewed for a job, we try to appear as bright as possible. Sometimes, in order to ensure a peaceful and orderly interaction, we try to appear friendly or respectful to obnoxious individuals. This is our "on-stage" performance. Backstage—after the date or job interview or workday—we may relax and drop the act. Backstage, we may criticize, ridicule, or curse those obnoxious people we have treated so politely.

On many occasions, we perform with one or two persons as a team. Teachers take care not to contradict each other in front of students. Doctors who consider each other incompetent praise each other when they are with patients. Occasionally, when a president of the United States fires a troublesome cabinet member, both tell the public how much they admire each other, how much they regret the parting, and how much they will miss each other.

Goffman's analysis, however, may mislead us into thinking that the only freedom we have is to deceive each other. Other symbolic interactionists have stressed a different form of freedom to "negotiate" for better social expectations and opportunities associated with certain statuses and roles. This is why bureaucracies often operate in very unbureaucratic ways, with officials of different ranks communicating informally and directly rather than formally and through channels. Even prisoners are able to negotiate the nature of their roles with their captors. Thus many annoying formal rules of the prison are not enforced, and prisoners are allowed to exercise a lot of authority in conducting their own affairs—as long as they do not try to escape or hold the warden and guards hostage (House, 1981; Zurcher, 1983).

In sum, despite the social control imposed on us by society, we can exercise freedom in face-to-face interactions with others. We can turn a social interaction to our benefit by manipulating the other's behavior as well as our own and by negotiating for a better deal in performing our roles. All this implies that we can see personal freedom more clearly if we go beyond society to take a close look at social interaction. Let us examine the nature of social interaction further.

QUESTIONS FOR DISCUSSION AND REVIEW

1. What are statuses and why are they the building blocks of social structure?
2. How do prescribed roles differ from role performance?
3. What types of statuses and groups differentiate preindustrial society from modern industrial society?
4. Do the confinements of the many roles you play make you a "prisoner of society"?

SOCIAL INTERACTION

Interaction is the stuff of social behavior. Society cannot survive without it. That is why we are always engaged in social interaction whenever or wherever we meet someone. We talk, smile, laugh, frown, scowl, scream, or do some other thing to communicate with others, who, in turn, respond in some way. Of course, we do not say and do the same thing with all kinds of people or in all sorts of situations. When a young man is with his parents, he would not tell them a dirty joke that he might use to crack up his buddies. If, at a funeral, you see an attractive person who is weeping for the deceased, you would not approach her or him with a big, cheerful smile and try to make a date. We obviously behave differently with different people or under different circumstances. Given the enormous diversity of social interaction, sociologists have classified it into a few major types. They have also discovered certain patterns of behavior in virtually all kinds of social interaction.

Performing Like Actors

As suggested in the preceding section, Goffman found that people behave in about the same way in all kinds of social interactions. They behave as if they were performing on the stage of a theater. This finding supports the dramaturgical view that Shakespeare made famous with the line "All the world's a stage, and all the men and women merely players." Indeed, when we interact, we behave like actors by following a script that we have learned from our parents, teachers, friends, and others (see Chapter 6: Socialization). The script essentially tells us how to behave in accordance with our statuses and roles, already discussed. But the stage analogy does have limitations. On the stage, the actors have a clearly written and detailed script that allows them to rehearse exactly what they will say and do. In real life, our script is far more general and ambiguous. It cannot tell us precisely how we are going to act or how the other person is going to react. It is therefore much more difficult, if it is possible at all, to be well rehearsed. In fact, as you gain new experiences every day, you constantly have to revise your script. This means that you have to improvise a great deal, saying and doing many things that have not crossed your mind before that very moment. No matter how we interact, however, we always engage in what Goffman calls **impression management—** presenting our "self" in such a way as to make the other person form the desired impression of us.

An example is the management of a vaginal (or "pelvic") examination in the office of a gynecologist. Many women sorely dread this event, when they must subject their most private body areas to "public" scrutiny, very often by a male physician. It is an occasion that obviously carries a certain potential for embarrassment to both doctor and patient. How best to minimize this risk? One way is revealed in a classic study by James Henslin and Mae Briggs (1971). They analyzed the data on several thousand pelvic examinations that Briggs had observed as a trained nurse. A typical examination unfolds like a series of scenes in a play.

In the prologue, the woman enters the doctor's waiting room and thus assumes the role of patient. In the first act, she is called into the consulting room, where she describes her complaints. The doctor assumes his role by responding appropriately. He listens closely, asks the necessary questions, and discusses the patient's problems with her. If a pelvic examination is indicated, he so informs the patient and then departs, leaving the patient in the nurse's hands.

The second act begins as the nurse ushers the patient into an examining room and asks her to disrobe. At the same time, she tries to help the patient make the transition from a dignified, fully clothed person to little more than a scientific specimen. The patient may look nervous, perhaps saying, "What a nuisance! But I guess we women have to put up with this sort of thing." The nurse, of course, is sympathetic and reassuring, telling the patient that there is really nothing to be anxious about and showing her where she may leave her clothes, out of the doctor's sight, and put on her hospital gown. (Many woman are sensitive not only about showing their most intimate selves but also about revealing their intimate apparel to male strangers.) The interaction with the nurse helps defuse any potential embarrassment by creating a strictly clinical situation.

The third act consists of the examination itself. Lying on the table with her body covered, the patient is transformed into a "nonperson"—a mere pelvis, the object of the doctor's scrutiny. She cannot see the doctor, who sits on a low stool. She also avoids eye contact with the nurse. She simply stares at the ceiling and says little or nothing. Similarly, the doctor tries to refrain from talking. All this serves to desexualize the situation, reassuring everybody that it is only a medical examination.

The fourth and final act begins as the examination ends. The doctor now walks out, allowing the patient to dress in solitude. Then, fully clothed, she is ushered back into the consulting room, where both doctor and patient resume the roles they had played in the first scene. The doctor now again treats his patient as a person, and the patient behaves as though nothing unusual had happened. Finally, she departs, going back to her everyday roles.

This analysis suggests that, despite the lack of a script showing how doctor and patient should interact, they nevertheless manage, with the help of the nurse, to play their roles. In a larger sense, their smooth interaction involves exchange and cooperation. The doctor performs a service for the patient, who reciprocates with a payment for the service. If there were no exchange and cooperation, the social interaction could conceivably turn into competition and conflict. Let us discuss these four forms of interaction.

Forms of Interaction

Exchange, cooperation, competition, and conflict can be found in all kinds of social structures—families, corporations, even nations. Exchange and cooperation usually stabilize the social structure. Competition and conflict are more likely to unsettle it and may lead to social change.

Exchange If you help a friend study for an exam and your friend, in turn, types a paper for you, you have engaged in an exchange. An **exchange** is a transaction between two individuals, groups, or societies in which one takes an action in order to obtain a reward in return. The reward may be material, such as a salary or a gift, or it may be nonmaterial, such as a word of praise or gratitude. We find exchanges in all types of situations. Nations trade votes at the United Nations, employees exchange their labor for a salary, friends exchange advice and gratitude, children trade toys, and so on.

Social exchanges are usually governed by the norm of reciprocity, which requires that people help those who have helped them. If a favor has been extended to a person, he or she will be motivated to return the favor. Conversely, if an individual has not been helpful to another, the latter will not be helpful to the former, either (Goldman et al., 1981). Therefore, if social exchanges are fair, the social structure involved is likely to be solid. The exchange reinforces the relationships and provides each party in the exchange with some needed good. But if exchanges are seen as unfair, the social structure is likely to be shaky. A friendship in which one person constantly helps another, expecting but not getting gratitude in return, is likely to be short-lived.

There are, however, a few cases where the norm of reciprocity does not hold. In an *unequal* relationship, unfair exchanges can go on indefinitely, with the more powerful group receiving favors but not returning them. In Iran, for example, the socially advantaged urban Persians often visit the nomadic Qashqai's encampments, where they will get food and a chance to relax from the hosts. But, as anthropologist Lois Beck (1982) found out, "the guests felt no debt, socially or economically, to their hosts; the moral expectation for repayment was absent." Such an unfair exchange simply follows the historical pattern of exploitation of rural populations by the urban dominant classes in Iran. On the other hand, in an *equal* relationship, the participants cannot be too fussy about the fairness of exchange—by demanding an exact tit for tat—unless they want the relationship to be something less than friendship. If you give someone a dollar and twenty cents and expect to get exactly the same amount back from him later, chances are that he is not your friend. Thus, in exchanges between classmates, co-workers, or business associates who are not friends, the participants give benefits with the expectation of receiving precisely comparable benefits in return. In friendships, however, members actively avoid the exactly equitable exchange because it seems too impersonal, businesslike, or unsentimental. Instead, they work out complicated exchanges of noncomparable benefits. Such an exchange would occur if you were to offer consolation to a friend who is ill and later receive $100 from that friend when you are broke (Clark, 1981).

Cooperation In exchange, a task can be adequately performed by only one of the parties. In cooperation, an individual needs another person's help to do a job or to do it more effectively. **Cooperation** is an interaction in which two or more individuals work together to achieve a common goal. Within this very broad category of interactions, there are some interesting differences. Robert Nisbet (1970) has distinguished four types of cooperation.

The oldest type is *spontaneous cooperation.* When neighbors come together to help a family whose house has just burned down, that is spontaneous cooperation. Without this kind of cooperation, human societies would not have emerged.

But spontaneous cooperation is also unpredictable. Over time, some forms of cooperation occur frequently enough for them to become customary in society. It was a custom in parts of the American frontier, for example, for neighbors to work together to build a barn. This type of cooperation, *traditional cooperation,* brings added stability to the social structure.

Because modern societies such as the United States include people with diverse traditions, they are more

Cooperation makes social life possible and therefore is a topic of prime importance to sociologists. Among the Amish it is traditional to join together to raise a barn. Such cooperation brings added stability to the Amish community. In addition to this traditional cooperation, there are three other types: spontaneous cooperation, which is more unpredictable; directed cooperation, which derives from authority; and contractual cooperation, which comes out of a formal agreement between two individuals or groups.

likely to depend on a third type of cooperation, *directed cooperation.* It is based not on custom but on the directions of someone in authority. Thus we are directed by government to abide by the law, pay taxes, and send children to school.

A fourth type of cooperation is equally useful in complex modern societies: *contractual cooperation.* It does not originate from tradition or authority but from voluntary action. Neither does it happen spontaneously; it involves, instead, some planning. In contractual cooperation, then, individuals freely and formally agree to cooperate in certain limited, specified ways. As we can often see, individuals freely decide whether to enter a business project, and they spell out the terms of the cooperation. Or neighbors may agree to work together on a specific community project.

Competition In **competition,** as in cooperation, two or more individuals or groups aim for the same goal. But in a competitive interaction each tries to achieve that goal before the other does. Thus, in a competition, there can be only one winner.

Competition is not the exact opposite of cooperation, though. In fact, a competition involves some degree of cooperation, because the competitors must cooperate with each other by "playing the game" according to the rules. In a boxing match, for example, the fighters must cooperate by not hitting each other on certain parts of the body—by not turning it into a free-for-all. In politics, candidates competing for the same office must cooperate by following certain rules, the major one being that all contenders, especially the losers, must accept the outcome (Boulding, 1981).

It is widely believed that competition brings out the best in us. The economic prosperity of Western capitalist nations, as opposed to the lower standard of living in communist countries, is often attributed to the high value placed on competition. Especially today, faced with serious challenges from Japan and other countries in world markets, American businesses are under great pressure to be more competitive (Reich, 1987). It is apparently true that competition can stimulate economic growth (see Chapter 17: The Economy and Work). Cer-

In a competition between two or more individuals or groups, each tries to achieve the same goal before the other does. In baseball, competition brings out the best in the players. Other athletes, along with politicians and lawyers, also thrive on competition. But for most other tasks, individuals tend to perform less well when trying to beat others than they do when working with them.

In competition, as shown in sports, the contestants play the game in accordance with commonly accepted rules. But deliberate defiance of rules leads to conflict, as demonstrated by an antinuclear demonstration here. Conflict can both harm and help a social structure. It can destroy lives and property, but it can also unify members of each group.

tain types of professionals such as athletes, politicians, and lawyers are well known to thrive on competition. In our everyday life, however, we usually perform less well—or more poorly—when we are trying to beat others than when we are working with them. In one experiment, girls between the ages of 7 and 11 were asked to make collages, some competing and others not. Then seven artists were asked to judge those girls' works. The collages by the competing girls received significantly lower ratings than those by their noncompeting peers. The competing girls' works were, in the eyes of the judges, much less creative—less spontaneous, novel, complex, and varied. In another case, several scholars reviewed over 100 studies conducted from 1924 to 1981 that dealt with competition and cooperation in classrooms. They found that in 65 of the studies, cooperation promoted higher achievement than competition. In only 8 studies did competition induce higher achievement, and 36 studies showed no statistically significant difference. Research on college students, scientists, and workers has produced further data challenging the popular belief in the benefits of competition (Kohn, 1986).

Competition seems to hamper achievement primarily because it is stressful. The anxiety that arises from the possibility of losing interferes with performance. Even if this anxiety can be suppressed, it is difficult to do two things at the same time: trying to do well and trying to beat others. Competition can easily distract attention from the task at hand. Consider a situation where a teacher asks her pupils a question. A little boy waves his arm wildly to attract her attention, crying, "Please! Please! Pick me!" When finally recognized, he has forgotten the answer. So he scratches his head, asking, "What was the question again?" The problem is that he has focused on beating his classmates, not on the subject matter (Kohn, 1986).

Conflict In competition the contestants try to achieve the same goal in accordance with commonly accepted rules. The most important of these rules is usually that competing parties should concentrate on winning the game and not on hurting each other. When competing parties no longer play by these rules, competition has become **conflict.** In conflict, then, defeating the opponent, by hook or by crook, has become the goal. To use an extreme contrast, we can see competition in sports and conflict in wars.

Conflict exists in all forms of social structure. It occurs between management and labor, whites and blacks, criminals and police, but also between friends, lovers, family members, and fellow workers in a common cause (Nisbet, 1970). It can both harm and help a social structure. Wars between nations and violent confrontations between hostile groups clearly are harmful. Yet war may also unify members of a society. This is most likely to occur if various segments of society, such as leaders and the rank and file, agree that the enemy is a real menace to the entire country, that it warrants going to war and defending the nation, or that internal conflict, if any, can be resolved (Markides and Cohn, 1982). Thus the Vietnam War divided the American people because many did not agree with their government that South Vietnam was worth defending, but the Second World War was a unifying force because virtually all Americans looked upon the threat of Nazi Germany and Japan in the same light. Conflict can also stimulate needed change. Consider the black-white conflict in the United States. Spearheaded by the civil rights movement in the 1960s, this conflict has led to greater equality between the races.

Whether social interaction involves exchange, cooperation, competition, or conflict, it always reflects some underlying relationship that has brought the participants together in the first place. As we can see from the foregoing discussion, exchange and cooperation reveal a positive, solid relationship between the interacting parties, while competition and conflict produce a more negative, shaky relationship. Relationships of one type or another usually converge to form a social network, with certain consequences for the lives of its members. Let us, then, find out more about social networks.

QUESTIONS FOR DISCUSSION AND REVIEW

1. In what ways do people use performing skills to manage the impressions others have of them?
2. What are the four forms of social interaction, and how can they stabilize or unsettle the social structure?
3. Why is conflict not always a negative form of social interaction?
4. In what forms of social interaction do Americans most widely participate?

SOCIAL NETWORKS

To the general public, "social networks" refers mostly to small groups of friends, relatives, or co-workers. Sociologists, however, see networks as varying in size and complexity. They run the gamut from a small clique of friends to a huge community of nation-states. Also, the general public always assumes that if you belong to a network, you should expect your fellow members to be nice and helpful to you. We can get this assumption from such popular sayings as "You can get ahead through the old-boy network," "It's not *what* you know but *who* you know," and "Friends in need are friends indeed." To sociologists, however, a network does not necessarily include only members who are friendly to one another. In fact, all kinds of social relationships can be found in networks. There are networks in which individuals express their affection, admiration, deference, loathing, or hostility toward each other (Knoke and Kuklinski, 1982). Finally, the general public often talks about "networks" as if this were merely a fancy word for "groups." Indeed, the two words do appear to mean the same thing. But as sociological terms, they have different meanings. The word "group" refers to only the *people* it comprises. The term "network," however, focuses on the *relationships* among the members. Let us take a closer look at how these relationships form a network and how this affects human behavior.

Characteristics

We are all involved in numerous social networks—webs of social relationships that link specific individuals or groups to one another. Since birth, we have been constantly developing or expanding our social networks by forming social ties with various people who come into our lives. As soon as we were born, our parents drew us into their networks, which became our own. When we began to attend school, we started to develop social ties with children in our neighborhoods, with our schoolmates and teachers, and with children in our churches, synagogues, or other places of worship. As adults, we often get into all kinds of networks, such as those at the college we attend, the place where we work, and the social organizations we belong to. These networks, however, are quite different from the ones that we joined before we turned 17 or 18. Our current adult networks are more diffuse, more loosely organized, and made up of weaker social ties (Shrum and Cheek, 1987). Individuals are not the only ones joining and developing social networks. Groups, organizations, and even whole nation-states also forge ties with each other. That is why there are numerous intergroup networks (such as the relationships among lawyers, judges, doctors, business executives, and other professional groups), intercommunity networks (such as the U.S. Conference of Mayors), and international networks (such as the United Nations).

To make it easier to see what networks look like, sociologists use such devices as points (technically called *nodes*) and lines (or *links*) to represent them. A point can be a person, group, or nation-state. A line can be any kind of social relationship connecting two points. The relationship can be a friendship; an exchange of visits; a business transaction; a romantic entanglement, the flow of information, resources, influence, or power; or an expression of such feelings as affection, sympathy, or hostility (Knoke and Kuklinski, 1982; Cook et al., 1983). Consider what your college network may look like. Let's make A in Figure 4.1 represent you and B, C, D, and E your friends. The lines show that all 5 of you

Figure 4.1 A Social Network

In this network the individuals A, B, C, D, and E are directly linked to one another. This is a dense network because those five individuals know one another or often participate in the same activities. But through E's friendship with F, the other four members (A, B, C, and D) are indirectly connected to F, and all five of them (A, B, C, D, and E) are also indirectly linked to G, H, I, and so on. Thus the whole network consisting of all the people represented here is less dense than the original network of five persons. Since many people are involved in the less dense network, an individual (say A) can even get AIDS from a total stranger (say Q) through a series of sexual contacts between A and E, E and F, F and G, G and K, K and O, and O and Q.

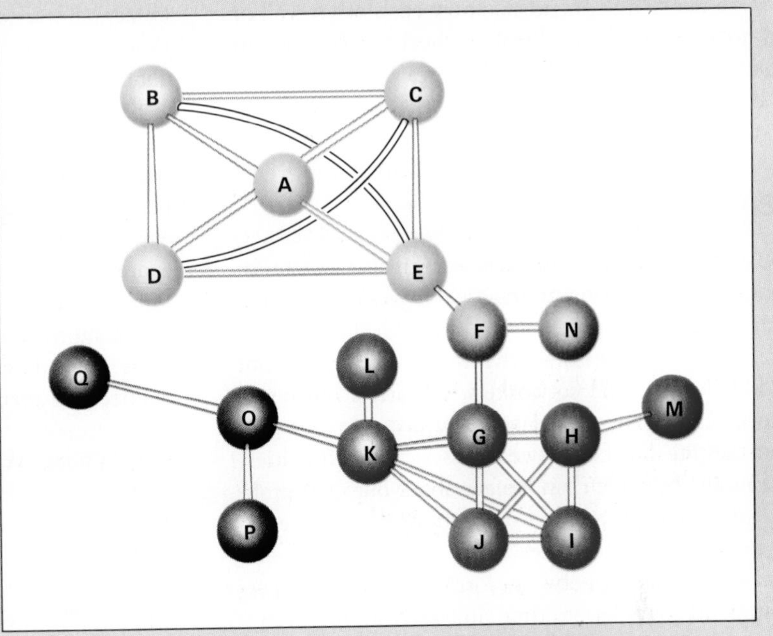

are *directly* connected to one another. Your college network also comprises 12 other people, namely, F through Q. This is because 4 of you—A, B, C, and D—are *indirectly* tied, through E, to those individuals. Due to your (A's) friendship with E and E's friendship with F, you belong to the same network as F and all the other individuals, whom you may not know. Thus a social network can consist of both directly and indirectly connected individuals. Since each of the numerous individuals to whom you are indirectly linked knows, directly and indirectly, numerous other people, you may ultimately belong to a network involving millions of people all over the world. This is especially true today because easily accessible air travel has made it possible for people from many different countries to establish links with one another.

Given the massive network to which we belong, we should not be surprised to meet a total stranger in some faraway city, state, or foreign country and discover that the stranger happens to know somebody that we know. On such an occasion, that stranger and we are likely to exclaim, "Wow, what a small world!" Indeed, a series of classic experiments have demonstrated how small our world is. In one of those studies, the wife of a divinity-school student who lived in Cambridge, Massachusetts, was selected as a "target person." Her name, address, occupation, and other facts about her were printed in a booklet. Copies of this booklet were randomly distributed to a group of people in Wichita, Kansas. They were asked to send it directly to the target person only if they knew her personally. If she was a stranger to them, they were asked to send the booklet to their friends or acquaintances who they thought might know her. Interestingly, many (30 percent) of the booklets sent by strangers did finally reach the target, after passing through the hands of only about five intermediaries (Milgram, 1967; Travers and Milgram, 1969; Lin, 1982). Just as that woman in Massachusetts could receive booklets that had passed through the hands of unknown intermediaries, other Americans today could also get the AIDS virus indirectly from strangers in Africa, Europe, or some other distant land. This is made possible by the huge network that connects us to millions of people all over the world. Of course, such a network is loose, lacking in "density." (A network is said to be dense if its members know each other well or often participate in the same activities.) But it can spread the deadly disease. How else can a loose network—or a dense one—affect our lives?

Effects

A dense network usually acts as a support system for its members. It helps maintain good physical and mental health or prevent physical and mental breakdown. There are several reasons why this is the case. Our friends, relatives, and co-workers, as part of our dense network, can make us feel good by boosting our self-esteem despite our faults, weaknesses, and difficulties. Being more objective than we are about our own problems, they can open our eyes to solutions that we are too emotionally distressed to see. The companionship and camaraderie from our network, fortified by frequent participation in joint leisure-time and recreational activities, can bring us joys and pleasures while chasing away the blue devils of loneliness, worries, and trouble. Finally, our friends and relatives often give us "instrumental support"—money and service—to help us cope with our problems (Vander Zanden, 1987).

However, the network of friends and relatives is not a bed of roses only; it is also full of thorns. For one thing, our intimates place many demands on our time and personal resources. They can further irritate us by criticizing us or invading our privacy. This is why in a study of 120 widows' social networks, the women reported that more than two-thirds of the people who made their lives more difficult were their friends and relatives. In fact, these negative experiences seem to drag down people's sense of well-being more than the positive experiences of receiving social support raise it up. Negative encounters usually have a stronger impact than positive ones because a bad run-in sticks out like a sore thumb against a background of generally pleasant experiences. Thus a pleasant exchange at a wedding already filled with strife between in-laws has some power to restore peacefulness, but a single heated exchange at a tranquil wedding can ruin the whole experience (Fischman, 1986).

On the other hand, the looser networks of mere acquaintances can make our lives more pleasant. If we are unemployed, our loose network is more effective than friends and relatives in helping us find a job. Marked by weak ties among its members, a loose network is usually much larger than a dense one (see Figure 4.1). Hence, an acquaintance in that huge network is far more likely than a close friend in our tiny, dense network to know about the availability of a job (Granovetter, 1983; Lin, 1982; Bridges and Villemez, 1986). A large network, however, can also spread infectious diseases far and wide, as has been suggested. Moreover, its usually impersonal nature can encourage powerful members to exploit weaker ones. In an international network, for example, powerful nations can easily take advantage of smaller, weaker countries (see box, p. 99).

In short, social networks, whether they are dense or loose, can have both positive and negative consequences for people's lives.

QUESTIONS FOR DISCUSSION AND REVIEW

1. What are social networks, and what purposes do they serve?
2. How do loose social networks differ from dense social networks?
3. In what ways do social networks have positive or negative consequences for your life?

CHAPTER REVIEW

1. *What is social structure?* It is a recurrent pattern in the way people relate to each other. *What are the foundations of social structure?* Social structure is based on statuses and roles. Statuses are the social positions occupied by individuals in a group or society. Roles are the expectations of what people should do in accordance with their statuses. *How do we get our statuses?* They are either ascribed or achieved. *Are status and role equivalent?* No, although they are related. Whereas a status is a static label, a role is dynamic, varying with situations and persons. Different people may understand a prescribed role in various ways and perform the same role differently. *How can roles be a source of conflict?* Role conflict occurs when we are expected to play two conflicting roles at the same time. Role strain arises when a single role imposes conflicting demands on us.

2. *What are the two main types of societies?* Preindustrial and industrial. *How can preindustrial societies be classified?* On the basis of how they obtain food, there are four types of preindustrial societies: hunting-gathering, pastoral, horticultural, and agricultural. *How does an industrial society differ from a preindustrial one?* Whereas prein-

UNDERSTANDING OTHER SOCIETIES

The Revolutionary Hamburger

As members of an international network, we form complex social and economic networks with other societies, sometimes with undesirable results. Here, Marvin Harris shows how our recently increased appetite for hamburger has turned America into a "ground-beef imperialist," contributing to the guerrilla uprisings in Central America. How is this "hamburger" network organized, and what are its nodes, links, and effects?

Among everyday events, what could be more humdrum and unremarkable than eating a common American hamburger? Yet in this superindustrial age even the most humble pleasures are likely to depend on a complex global division of labor. The lowly American hamburger is a case in point.

A typical American consumes 50 pounds of ground beef a year, much of it in the form of hamburgers eaten in restaurants, especially fast-food restaurants. Every second, more than 200 hungry customers order one or more hamburgers, resulting in an annual sale of 6.7 billion patties worth $10 billion to the fast-food chains alone. The gastronomic triumph of the fast-food ground-beef patty reflects recent revolutionary changes in American family and work life, namely the demise of families with male breadwinners and stay-at-home mother-cooks. More working mothers, more two-wage-earner childless households, and more footloose, swinging singles add up to a prodigious appetite for quick, cheap burgers served without frills (save the tip, clean your own table). But unbeknown to burger lovers, the success of the fast-food hamburger adds up to another kind of revolution—the shooting kind. Hamburgers are implicated in the guerrilla uprisings that are sweeping across Central America.

By the 1960s, with changes in family eating patterns in full swing, the demand for cheap, lean, hamburger beef began to outstrip the domestic supply. So fast-food interests turned to foreign suppliers. After 1960, regions previously noted for their unexportable scrawny animals suddenly found that Americans were in for lean tough meat in a big way. Central America was one of those regions.

Between 1960 and 1980, ranchers and packers in El Salvador, Guatemala, Nicaragua, and Honduras doubled, tripled, and quadrupled their export of beef to the United States. The boom was good for the ranchers and packers, but it had a destabilizing effect on the peasants and the environment. In less-developed countries, an increase in the production of a food for export often makes that food less available or too expensive to be eaten at home. Despite hefty increases in production, per capita consumption of beef has fallen sharply in Honduras and El Salvador since 1960. In addition, the cattle boom has made land less available for the production of staple food crops such as corn and beans. Millions of acres of forest have been cut down and cleared to give cattle a chance to graze. In regions that already have too much land in too few hands, ranching leads to even greater concentration of land ownership and at the same time provides very little employment for rural workers.

Billie DeWalt, an anthropologist who has studied the spread of cattle ranching in Honduras, reports that peasant farmers now find themselves competing with cattle for access to local resources. Cattle raised for export have already eaten a big chunk of the forest. And if they continue to push the already hard-pressed countryfolk onto smaller and smaller pieces of land, they will end up eating people as well—a revolutionary relationship, to say the least.

Source: Excerpted from Marvin Harris, "The Revolutionary Hamburger," *Psychology Today,* October 1983, pp. 6–8. Copyright © 1983 (APA).

dustrial society is simple, homogeneous, and intimate, industrial society is complex, heterogeneous, and impersonal. Preindustrial society is traditional; it emphasizes the past, social stability, and the interests of the group. Industrial society is modern, stressing the future, social change, and the interests of the individual.

3. *Does society in effect imprison us?* Structural functionalists focus on social order and emphasize the power of its formal and informal sanctions over individuals. Symbolic interactionists concentrate on personal interactions and emphasize the extent to which individuals are free to manipulate and negotiate those interactions.

4. *Is there a pattern to how people interact with each other?* Yes. According to Goffman, people behave in about the same way in all kinds of social interaction. They act as if they were performing on the stage of a theater, engaging in impression management. *In what forms can social interaction appear?* Social interaction can appear in the forms of exchange, cooperation, competition, and conflict. *How does cooperation differ from exchange?* In an exchange relationship, one of the parties can perform a task adequately, but in a cooperative relationship, an individual or group needs another's help in order to achieve a goal, or to achieve it more effectively. *How is competition like and unlike cooperation?* In both there is a common goal; but in competition, each party tries to achieve that goal before the other does. *What is the goal in a conflict relationship?* In a conflict, the objective is to defeat the other party without regard to rules.

5. *How do social networks come about?* As soon as we are born, we are drawn into the network of our parents. As we grow up, we gradually develop social ties with our neighbors, schoolmates, co-workers, and many other people whom we come to know as friends or acquaintances. Since all these people have their own social ties to numerous other people, we become members of their networks as well, though we may not know most of these people. The ties that corral us into a network can be friendship, business transactions, sexual contacts, expressions of admiration or hostility, or some other kind of social relationship. *Can social networks affect our lives?* Yes. The smaller, denser networks of friends and relatives can help us maintain good health by giving us social support. But they can also make our lives miserable by putting many demands on our time and personal resources, criticizing us, and invading our privacy. On the other hand, the larger, looser networks of mere acquaintances are more useful than the smaller, denser networks in helping us find a job. But large networks can also spread infectious diseases to numerous people and encourage powerful nations to exploit weaker ones.

KEY TERMS

Achieved status A status that is attained through an individual's own actions (p. 81).

Agricultural society A society that produces food by relying on plows and draft animals (p. 88).

Ascribed status A status that one has no control over, such as status based on race, gender, or age (p. 81).

Competition A relationship between two individuals or groups in which each strives to achieve the same goal before the other does (p. 94).

Conflict A relationship in which two individuals or groups struggle to achieve a goal by defeating each other without regard to rules (p. 95).

Cooperation A relationship in which two or more persons work together to achieve a common goal (p. 93).

Exchange A reciprocal transaction between individuals, groups, or societies (p. 93).

Folk society Redfield's term for a society that is small, nonliterate, and homogeneous, with a strong solidarity; used to distinguish preindustrial from industrial societies (p. 89).

Gemeinschaft Tönnies's term for a type of society marked by a strong sense of community and by personal interactions among its members (p. 88).

Gesellschaft Tönnies's term for a type of society characterized by individualism and by impersonal interactions (p. 88).

Horticultural society A society that depends on growing plants in small gardens for its survival (p. 87).

Hunting-gathering society A society that hunts animals and gathers plants to survive (p. 85).

Impression management The act of presenting one's "self" in such a way as to make others form the desired impression (p. 92).

Master status A status that dominates a relationship (p. 82).

Pastoral society A society that domesticates and herds animals for food (p. 86).

Prescribed role A set of expectations held by society regarding how an individual with a particular status should behave (p. 82).

Primary group A group whose members interact informally, relate to each other as whole persons, and enjoy their relationship for its own sake (p. 89).

Role A set of behaviors associated with a particular status (p. 81).

Role conflict Conflict between two roles being played simultaneously (p. 83).

Role performance Actual performance of a role (p. 82).

Role strain Stress caused by incompatible demands built into a role (p. 83).

Secondary group A group in which the individuals

interact formally, relate to each other as players of particular roles, and expect to profit from each other (p. 89).

Social institution A set of widely shared beliefs, norms, or procedures necessary for meeting the needs of a society (p. 80).

Social interaction The process by which individuals act toward and react to one another (p. 80).

Social network A web of social relationships that connects specific individuals or groups to one another (p. 80).

Social structure A recurrent pattern in the ways people relate to each other (p. 80).

Society A collection of interacting individuals sharing the same culture and territory (p. 80).

Status A position in a group or society (p. 81).

Subordinate status A status that does not influence a particular relationship (p. 82).

Urban society Redfield's term for societies that are large, literate, and heterogeneous, with little group solidarity (p. 89).

SUGGESTED READINGS

Knoke, David, and James H. Kuklinski. 1982. *Network Analysis.* Beverly Hills, Calif.: Sage. A brief but useful introduction to what social networks are and how sociologists study them.

Kohn, Alfie. 1986. *No Contest: The Case Against Competition.* Boston: Houghton Mifflin. Marshals an impressive array of data to challenge the popular assumption that competition enhances performance.

Lenski, Gerhard, and Jean Lenski, 1987. *Human Societies,* 5th ed. New York: McGraw-Hill. The authors use the perspective of sociocultural evolution to analyze various types of societies, including those that have been briefly discussed in this chapter.

Whyte, William F. 1981. *Street Corner Society: The Social Structure of an Italian Slum,* 3rd ed. Chicago: University of Chicago Press. An enjoyable sociological classic on street gangs, excellent for studying roles and statuses as well as the patterns of social relations.

Zurcher, Louis A. 1983. *Social Roles: Conformity, Conflict, and Creativity.* Beverly Hills, Calif.: Sage. A readable symbolic-interactionist analysis of the diverse ways individuals try to maintain autonomy in role performance.

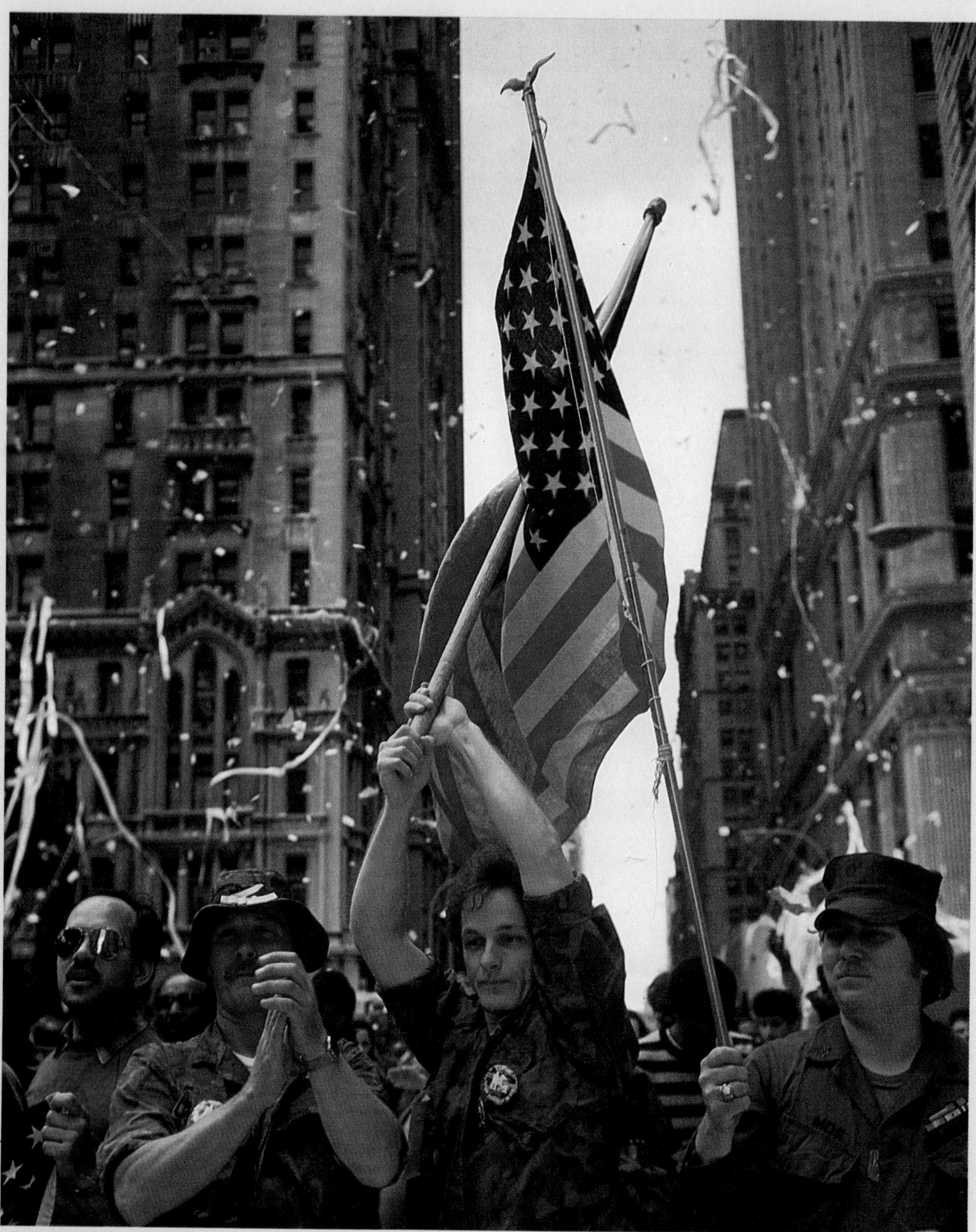

5 Groups and Organizations

We encounter numerous social groups in our lives. They may consist of our relatives, friends, or others to whom we have strong emotional ties. They are what sociologists call our primary groups. On the other hand, we may talk about the weather with a stranger on the street or join a class in listening to a professor's lecture. In doing so, we become part of a secondary group, whose members interact formally. If these people explicitly coordinate their activities to achieve specific goals, they will form a formal organization, as do the veterans of the Vietnam War here. Groups and organizations vary significantly, and they exert different influences on their members.

We live in an organized society. Like the air we breathe, organizations are all around us. They touch virtually every aspect of our lives, from birth to death. A hospital takes care of us when we are born, and a county bureau of records registers our birth. Schools educate us for 13 years; then a college or university takes over for a few more. A state agency gives us a driver's license, and city hall grants us a marriage license. Businesses sell us food, clothing, furniture, and other goods. With the aid of a law firm, a state court will grant us a divorce if we want it. When we die, at least three organizations—a funeral home, a church, and a law firm—will take care of us (Aldrich, 1979; Zucker, 1983).

We apparently need all these and other organizations, but few Americans seem to like them. They are criticized again and again for trampling on our freedom and dignity. Corporations are accused of treating workers like mere cogs in a machine. Government bureaucracies are accused of reducing citizens to numbers and of strangling private enterprise with red tape.

Why? What makes these organizations so central to American society yet so despised? In this chapter we examine the nature, types, and models of organization. But first let us discuss social groups, because organizations are a type of social group.

SOCIAL GROUPS

In a classic experiment Muzafer Sherif (1956) took a group of white, middle-class, twelve-year-old boys to a summer camp at Robbers' Cave State Park in Oklahoma. Sherif pretended to be a caretaker named Mr. Musee. For the first three days the boys lived on one site at the camp and became acquainted. Then they were separated. Half of the boys were given one cabin and one set of activities, and the other half another. Soon each group of boys had chosen a name for themselves, with one group calling themselves "Eagles" and the other "Rattlers." Each had their own insignia on caps and T-shirts, their own jargon and jokes and secrets.

Each band of boys, in short, had formed a **social group**—a collection of people who share some characteristics, interact with one another, and have some feeling of unity. A social group is more than either a social aggregate or a social category. A **social aggregate** is just a collection of people who happen to be in one place but do not interact with one another, such as the boys when they first arrived at the camp. A **social category** is a number of people who have something in common, but they neither interact with one another nor gather in one place. Men as a whole constitute a social category. So do women as a whole, college students as a whole, and so on. A social category becomes a social group when the people in the category interact with one another and identify themselves as members of the group. Thus the boys at Robbers' Cave were members of a social category—twelve-year-old boys—but they became a social group only when they began to interact with one another and consider themselves members of the Eagles or the Rattlers. A closer look at Sherif's experiment can give us a clearer idea of the significance of groups.

Ingroups, Outgroups, and Reference Groups

A few days after Sherif had put the boys in separate cabins, he arranged for the groups to compete against one another in baseball, tug of war, and other games. The winners of the games were awarded points toward a prize—camp knives. At first the Eagles and Rattlers were very friendly with each other, but soon the games turned into fierce competitions. The two groups began to call each other stinkers, sneaks, and cheaters. They raided each other's cabins, and scuffles became common.

The boys' behavior showed that in forming each group the youngsters set up a boundary between themselves as an **ingroup** and the others as an **outgroup.** Every social group defines a boundary between itself and everyone else to some extent, but a cohesive ingroup has three characteristics. First, members of the ingroup normally use symbols such as names, slogans, dress, or badges to identify themselves so that they will be distinguishable from the outgroup. As we have seen, one group of boys in Sherif's experiment called themselves Eagles and the other Rattlers. In the world of adults, more subtle symbols are sometimes used to distinguish one's own group from the outgroup. As Eviatar Zerubavel (1982) has found, the early Christians, intending to dissociate themselves from the Jews, made sure that Easter Sunday (a Christian holiday) would never fall on the same day as Passover Eve (a Jewish holiday). They ruled that Easter be observed on the

Sunday *following* the first full moon in the spring, since Passover Eve always coincided with the full moon. Second, a characteristic of a cohesive ingroup is that its members view themselves in terms of positive stereotypes and the outgroup in negative stereotypes. Sherif's boys, for example, liked to say things like, "We are smart and they are dumb!" A more recent study (Montgomery, 1980) also showed that college students tend to rate their own fraternities, sororities, or organizations higher in prestige than someone else's and to disparage others as "objectionable." Third, the ingroup is inclined to compete with the outgroup or even to get involved in conflict with it.

Sherif's experiment showed how easily loyalty to an ingroup can generate hostility toward an outgroup and even aggression when there is competition for some resource (in this case, prizes). Competition with another group can also strengthen the unity within each group. But there was another phase in Sherif's experiment. He set up situations in which the groups had to work together to solve a common problem. When the camp's sole water tank broke down, he told the groups to work together to repair it. As they cooperated, friendships began to emerge between Eagles and Rattlers. In short, cooperation between groups eroded the hostility and divisions that competition had spurred. According to a more recent study, cooperation can even cause an ingroup's higher-status members to shed their prejudice against and become friends with an outgroup's lower-status members (Johnson and Johnson, 1984).

People often use a group as a frame of reference for evaluating their behavior or forming opinions: the group is then called a ***reference group.*** Members of a street gang, for example, may evaluate themselves by the standards of the gang and feel proud about a successful mugging. This positive self-evaluation reflects the *normative effect* of a reference group whose members share the same view of themselves. If other members of your reference group (say, your parents) have high self-esteem, you too are likely to have high self-esteem. However, reference groups can have "comparison effects" and "associative effects" on self-appraisals. If most of your classmates shine in academic achievement, you are likely to compare yourself with them. As a result, you may have a negative self-evaluation, feeling that your academic performance is not up to par. Being associated with the brilliant group, though, you may feel proud of yourself, "basking in reflected glory" (Felson and Reed, 1986). These reference groups are at the same time ingroups. But we do not have to be members of a group in order to use it as our reference group. As a student, you might have professional athletes as your reference group. If that is the case, you would probably judge your athletic skills to be inadequate—even if they are excellent compared with most amateurs'—and perhaps you would work harder in an effort to meet professional standards.

Whether we are members of reference groups or not, they frequently exert a powerful influence on our behavior and attitudes, as has been suggested. In fact, their impact became well known long ago, after Theodore Newcomb (1958) published his study of the students at Bennington College, a very liberal college in Vermont. Newcomb found that most of the students came from conservative families, and most of the freshmen were conservative. A small minority remained conservative throughout their time at the school. But most became more liberal the longer they stayed at the college. These students, Newcomb concluded, used the liberal faculty or older students as their reference group, whereas the minority continued to look to their conservative families as their reference group.

Primary and Secondary Groups

It is not at all surprising that some students used their families as a reference group. After all, families are the best examples of those groups which Charles Cooley (1909) called *primary* chiefly because they "are fundamental in forming the social nature and ideals of the individual." In a primary group the individuals have strong emotional ties. As discussed in Chapter 4 (Social Structure), it is one of the two main types of social groups. In the *secondary* group, relationships among the members are less personal.

Families, peer groups, fraternities, sororities, neighbors, and small communities are all examples of primary groups. They are marked by what are called *primary relationships.* Communication in these relationships is not limited by formalities. The people in a primary group interact in an informal way, and they relate to each other as unique, whole persons. Moreover, they enjoy the relationship for its own sake.

These characteristics become clearer when we compare them with those of secondary groups. A *secondary group* consists of individuals who do not know each

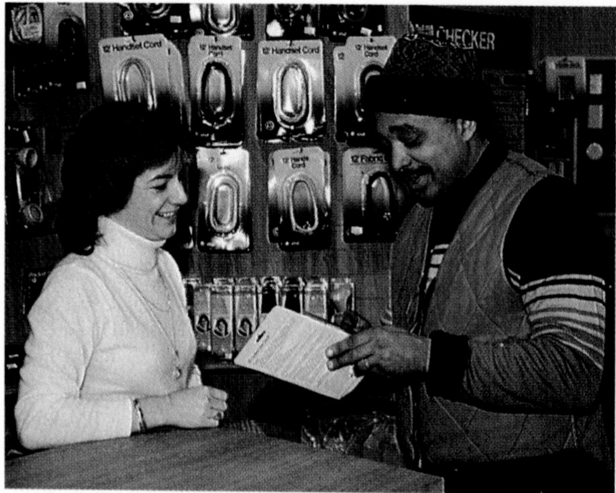

In a secondary group situation, such as a sale, the participants are brought together solely for a specific transaction. They will exchange only minimal, formal, and impersonal pleasantries. Too much personal interest on the part of one person would be inappropriate and might be interpreted by the other as prying. As members of a secondary group, they must relate to each other only in accordance with their roles as salesperson and customer, not as relatives or friends.

other personally; they may have little face-to-face interaction. Members of a secondary group interact formally. They relate to each other only in terms of particular roles and for certain practical purposes.

Consider a salesperson and his clients or a supervisor and her staff. In both of these secondary groups, there are likely to be few if any emotional ties, and the people know little about each other. Their communications are bound by formalities. Sales clerks are not likely to kiss their customers or to cry with them over the death of a relative. The clerk will treat the customer as a customer only—not as a person who is also a mother of three, a jazz lover, a victim of an airplane hijacking, or a person who laughs easily but worries a lot. In contrast, we expect our families to treat us as whole persons, to be interested in our experiences, preferences, and feelings. The clerk is also likely to treat one customer much like another. We expect this attitude in a clerk, but the same attitude in our family or friends would hurt our feelings. Finally, the clerk and the customer have a relationship only because each has a specific task or purpose in mind: to buy or sell something. They use their relationship for this purpose. The relationship among family members, in contrast, is not oriented to a particular task but engaged in for its own sake. In fact, if we believe that a person in a primary group is interested in us only as a means to some end, we are likely to feel "used." Parents are hurt if they feel their children are interested only in the food, shelter, and money the parents provide.

Primary groups are very common in small, traditional societies. But in large industrial societies secondary relationships are pervasive. These do not provide the emotional satisfactions or intimacy of primary groups. Indeed, they can make us feel isolated and lonely. In the prevalence of secondary relationships some observers see the source of the interest in communes, encounter groups, singles clubs, computer dating services, and similar organizations. All these may be attempts to produce primary relationships. But because they often involve strangers who have no emotional commitment to each other, they are not genuine or durable primary groups.

The real primary relationships—with our friends, neighbors, or relatives—are very precious to us. As many studies have shown, they are particularly helpful when we are going through stressful life events. They help ease recovery from heart attacks, prevent childbirth complications, make child rearing easier, lighten the burden of household finances, cushion the impact of job loss by providing financial assistance and employment information (Hanlon, 1982; Albrecht et al., 1982; Brim et al., 1982). (Also see box, p. 107, for the functions of primary groups in Yugoslavia.) However, primary relationships are not always more beneficial than secondary relationships. As suggested in Chapter 4 (Social Structure), our close friends cannot help us get as good a job as our acquaintances can. The reason is that our friends move in the same social circle as we do, but our acquaintances, to whom we have only weak ties, move in different circles. Hence, we may already know the job openings that our friends know, but we may not know the many job opportunities that our acquaintances know.

Although primary and secondary groups differ, they do sometimes overlap. In many families, teenagers may expect their parents to pay them for mowing the lawn or doing some other chore around the house. On the other hand, friendship may blossom among members of a secondary group at a school or workplace.

Small Groups

In discussing the various forms of social groups, whether they are primary, secondary, reference, ingroup

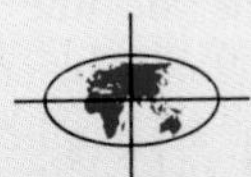

UNDERSTANDING OTHER SOCIETIES

The Social Side of Socialism

Individuals can become overwhelmed by a large and impersonal communist state that attempts to control nearly all aspects of their lives. They can, however, find support and security in their primary groups, as the following report on Yugoslavia shows. Do we get the same benefits from our primary groups in the United States?

The Yugoslav Communists came to power at the end of World War II with definite plans to establish a socialist state and to remodel the economic, political, and social order of the country. Over the next several years, work brigades—young men and women in shorts and work shirts with picks and shovels over their shoulders—marched off to build railroads, highways, and factories. Red banners flew everywhere and "Long Live Comrade Tito" and other political slogans appeared on walls throughout the country.

Because all economic and political institutions were controlled by Communist leadership, it seemed that the government dominated every aspect of Yugoslav life. But centralized planning was one thing; getting nearly 17 million people to carry out the plans was something else. Instead of continuing along a path dictated by a rigid interpretation of Marxist principle or bureaucratic dogma, at crucial points the Yugoslav Communist leaders have accepted and worked with the realities of Yugoslav life.

Among the basic social patterns of prerevolutionary life incorporated into Yugoslav socialism were the *vese*: "connections," or networks of kinship and friendship that cut across time, space, and social status. The use of connections made the Yugoslav transformation possible; the degree of their continued use makes Yugoslavia unique among socialist states. After World War II it would have been logical to station leaders away from their native regions to prevent nepotism and to break down local identifications. But in Yugoslavia, most leaders returned to their native regions to establish the new government.

When Party members returned home to carry out literacy and health programs, and to recruit young people into the work brigades, kinship ties complemented political theory. The appeal by relatives to support government projects softened the conservative stance of their uncles and grandfathers; where a government official would have been suspect, "the son of Jovan Nikolic" was trusted. Communist leaders, knowing the local idioms and attitudes, could translate the ideals and goals of the revolution into terms people could understand and accept. The abstract structures of revolutionary organization were transformed into individual people.

Yugoslavs take pride in their skill at making connections for others and even take offense if they are not asked for their help. There is an element of sport in the otherwise serious business of survival and advancement. Even where routine channels may be equally effective, they lack the challenge and triumph of the connections game.

The process of making contact most often takes place in the guise of gossip and socializing. Each day, relatives drop in uninvited to one another's houses. Midmorning finds several sisters-in-law gathered in one of the kitchens. They have cleaned their houses, been to the market, and now the lady of the house brews a pot of Turkish coffee and pours it into tiny cups. The women chat about their homes, the market, and their plans for the rest of the day. Late afternoon and early evening is the time for those who work to visit other members of the network. Men either join the women in the kitchen or venture off to a *kafana*, a cafe, to meet male friends. Everyone appears to spend an inordinate amount of time socializing, but much of the visiting is far from idle. Business and pleasure are closely tied among kin and friends. It would be rude to visit solely for business, just as it would be rude not to ask a favor of a friend or relative who could help. To reaffirm the sentiment of the relationship, sociable conversation must precede any request. Then the visitor can bring up the purpose of the visit.

Although the business of everyday life is fraught with obstacles, most people face them assertively, confident that they can accomplish what they want. The individual does not feel overwhelmed by vast, impersonal institutions, but faces all challenges with the support of a network of friends and relatives, a series of connections that make his world humane.

Source: Excerpted from Bette Denich, "Yugoslavia: The Social Side of Socialism," *Conformity and Conflict: Readings in Cultural Anthropology*, 4th ed., edited by James P. Spradley and David M. McCordy, Boston: Little Brown, 1980, pp. 135–144.

or outgroup, we have focused on the nature of interaction among the members. The very size of a group, however, may determine how its members interact. This is the most significant finding that has come out of the small-group research.

A *small group* is one whose members are few enough to be able to interact directly with one another. We can see small groups everywhere. In fact, each of us belongs to at least five of them, such as our families, buddies, small classes, discussion groups, weekend parties, fraternities, sororities, and athletic teams (Mills, 1967). Since there are more than 4 billion people on earth, the total number of small groups can be estimated to run as high as 20 billion. Our world indeed is crowded with small groups.

Leadership and Conformity In most small groups, there are two kinds of leaders. *Instrumental leaders* are concerned about achieving goals. They may say something like "Let's get to work!" or "Can't we get on with the job now?" or "I think we're getting off the track." Such tactics show the leaders as overseers, whose exchange with followers involves a "unidirectional downward influence" and a weak sense of common fate. Although this kind of leadership can get the group to move toward a goal, it can also rub people the wrong way (Mabry and Barnes, 1980; Duchon et al., 1986). It is no wonder that most people do not like their instrumental leaders (Slater, 1955). On the other hand, *expressive leaders* are more concerned with members' feelings, making sure that everybody is happy, so that harmony and cohesiveness can reign in the group. The exchange between such leaders and their followers reflects a partnership, characterized by reciprocal influence, a strong sense of common fate, and mutual trust, respect, and liking. A small group needs, however, both types of leaders to function effectively.

Because they are seen as competently performing certain tasks for the group, leaders are usually given an "idiosyncracy credit," which allows them to deviate from the group's norms (Hollander, 1964; Ridgeway, 1981). The rank and file, however, are expected to conform. In a small group the pressure to conform is so powerful that individual members tend to knuckle under. They would go along with the majority even though they privately disagree with it. This point has been driven home by Solomon Asch's (1955) classic experiments. Asch brought together groups of eight or nine students each. He asked them to tell him which of the three lines on a card was as long as the line on another card. In each group only one was a real subject—the others were the experimenter's secret accomplices, who had been instructed to give the same obviously wrong answer. Asch found that nearly a third of the subjects changed their mind and accepted the majority's answer even though they were sure that their own answer was correct and the others' answer was wrong (Figure 5.1).

It may be noted that the small group to which Asch's subjects felt compelled to conform were strangers. The pressure to conform is even greater among people we know. It usually gives rise to what Irving Janis (1982) calls **groupthink,** the tendency for members of a cohesive group to maintain consensus to the extent of ignoring the truth (Hensley and Griffin, 1986). Groupthink may lead to disastrous decisions, with tragic consequences. It caused President Kennedy and his top advisers to approve the CIA's unsound plan to invade Cuba. It caused President Johnson and his advisers to escalate the Vietnam War. It caused President Nixon and his advisers to get involved in the Watergate scandal. (For a more recent example, see box, p. 109.) In each case a few members had serious doubts about the majority decision but did not speak out. It is ironic that although

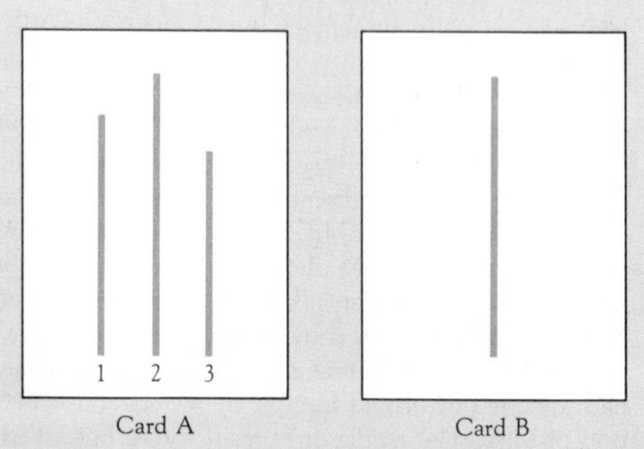

Figure 5.1 Would You Conform?

Asch's experiments suggest that if you are asked privately which line on card A is as long as the line on card B, there is a 99 percent chance that you would correctly pick line 2. But if you find yourself in a group where all the other members choose line 3—an obviously wrong number—there is about a 33 percent chance that you would yield to the group pressure to conform by choosing line 3.

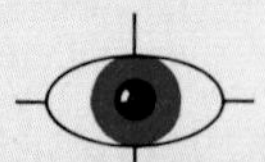

USING SOCIOLOGICAL INSIGHT

How Groupthink Got E. F. Hutton in Trouble

Groupthink is the tendency of persons in a small group to agree with each other even to the extent of ignoring the truth. The following example of an illegal banking practice at a prominent company describes how employees continued to violate the law even when they knew their activities were illegal. What were some of the consequences of groupthink for this company?

When E. F. Hutton speaks, the famous slogan goes, everyone listens. But Hutton's trouble seems to have been a case of no one speaking and no one listening.

What was not spoken about—or at least not in a way that led anyone there to question it—was the practice of check-kiting by Hutton's money managers. And what no one listened to was the still small voice of conscience, whispering misgivings about an unethical and illegal practice.

The whole scheme was simple. A branch of the company would have, say, $70,000 on deposit in a small bank in Ohio. The branch would wire a cash transfer from the account for $1 million. The bank, not wanting to lose Hutton's valuable business, would advance the money, and a day later Hutton would replace it. Hutton got the use of nearly $1 million of the bank's money for 24 hours.

While such oversights happen from time to time in business banking, Hutton made a practice of it: on any given day, the firm overdrew its bank accounts to the tune of millions of dollars; the interest on that money became a major source of company revenue. When the Justice Department finally investigated, Hutton was cited on 2,000 counts of mail and wire fraud, received a $2 million fine, and had to set up a multimillion-dollar fund to reimburse banks for interest payments lost on their funds.

Few at Hutton seem to have questioned the practice before the federal investigation; once established among the Hutton executive echelons, it was taken for granted. In fact, an internal memo from the corporate department in charge of cash management advised, rather blandly, "If an office is overdrafting their ledger balance consistently, it is probably best not to request an account analysis." In other words, the memo said, in effect, We'd rather not know about it—and rather the bank not notice, either.

How could those in Hutton's management let such a practice persist? Quite happily, as it turned out. The group dynamic at play seems to have been one that crops up to one degree or another in groups of all kinds: the group erects barriers against ideas or information that might prove upsetting. At Hutton, presumably, the idea that was out-of-bounds was that the overdraft practice was unethical; the taboo information was that the practice was illegal.

The culture of the workplace, where people are together, day after day, is an arena ripe for implicit agreements not to bring up upsetting facts. Irving Janis has done the most detailed studies of this dynamic, which he dubs groupthink. In groupthink, decison makers tacitly conspire to ignore crucial information because it somehow challenges a collective view with which everyone is comfortable; members of the group cramp their attention and hobble their informaton seeking to preserve a cozy unanimity. Loyalty to the group requires that members not raise embarrassing questions, attack weak arguments, or counter soft-headed thinking with hard facts.

Groupthink, of course, is an especially dangerous pathology for businesses. In making a marketing or product-development decision, for example, a cozy executive group can make costly mistakes. The failure of American auto makers to build high-quality economy cars in response to the oil crisis of the 1970s—and their subsequent loss of market share to the Japanese—is a famous example.

Source: Excerpted from Daniel Goleman, "Following the Leader," *Science 85*, October 1985, pp. 18–20.

leaders are expected to deviate, as we noted earlier, they do not always do so. The reason is that they are as much under the spell of groupthink as their followers, burying their heads in the sand like an ostrich.

The Size Effect Aside from pressuring people to conform, small groups also cause them to behave in other ways. This has a lot to do with the specific size of small groups. The smallest of these groups is a *dyad,* which contains two people. A dyad can easily become the most cohesive of all the groups because its members are inclined to be most personal and to interact most intensely with each other (Wolff, 1950). This is why, as has been shown by the experiment of Ralph Taylor and his associates (1979), we are more willing to share our secrets in a dyad than in a larger group, secrets such as our parents getting divorced or father having been committed to a mental hospital. A dyad, however, is also the most likely to break up. If just one person leaves the group, it will vanish. Such a threat does not exist for a *triad*, a three-person group. If one member drops out, the group can still survive. A triad also makes it possible for two people to gang up on the third one or for one member to patch up the quarrel between the other two. But triads lose the quality of intimacy that is the hallmark of dyads, as described by the saying that "two's company, three's a crowd."

If more people join a triad, the group will become even much less personal, with each individual finding it extremely difficult to talk and relate to each of all the other members. The upshot is the emergence of many different coalitions (made up of two against one, two against three, three against one, and so on) and many mediating roles for various conflicting subgroups. The reason is that even a small growth in the size of a group increases dramatically the number of relationships among its members. If a dyad, for example, grows into a seven-person group, the number of relationships will shoot up from 1 to 966 (Hare, 1962).

Research has also revealed other effects of group size. In a dyad or triad, the host usually has the edge over the visitor, with the host more likely to get his own way. Thus a businesswoman can strike a better deal if she invites the other person to her office. But such territorial dominance—the "home-court" advantage—may go out the window if the group is larger than a triad (Taylor and Lanni, 1981). In public places a large group may also inhibit an individual from helping someone in distress. Over fifty studies have shown consistently that people are less likely to help a victim if others are around than if they are alone with the victim. A major reason is that the knowledge of others being present and available to respond allows the individual to shift some of the responsibility to them (Latané and Nida, 1981). The same factor operates in "social loafing": as the size of a group performing a certain task increases, each member tends to work less hard (Latané et al., 1979; Harkins et al., 1979).

QUESTIONS FOR DISCUSSION AND REVIEW

1. What characteristics of social groups make them different from aggregates and categories?
2. What are some social functions of ingroups and reference groups?
3. Why do sociologists feel that primary groups are fundamental for human existence?
4. How does the concept of groupthink help explain experiences you have had in small groups?

FORMAL ORGANIZATIONS

Some secondary groups are small and transitory, with their goals and rules unstated. A saleswoman and her client or door-to-door salesman and his customer, for example, interact on a temporary basis to achieve a generally known but unstated objective without following any explicitly described rules for carrying out the business transaction. Other secondary groups are large and more permanent, and they have explicit goals and working procedures. Government agencies, for instance, often last well beyond their members' lifetimes, and they are large and complex. Their goals and rules must be stated explicitly so that the work of their many members can be coordinated. These agencies are examples of the kind of social group called a formal organization.

Hospitals and colleges, business firms and political parties, the U.S. Army and the Sierra Club—all these are formal organizations. A **formal organization** is a secondary group whose activities are rationally designed to achieve specific goals. What is the nature of these goals and of the means for achieving them?

Goals and Means

Goals are the raison d'être of organizations. Without goals, organizations would not have come into being. Goals can help an organization determine what it should do. They can further be used as guidelines for measuring its performance—how successful it is in meeting its goals. However, the goals of organizations vary. The primary objective of a labor union is to ensure good wages and working conditions for its members. A political party strives to get its candidates elected. A school

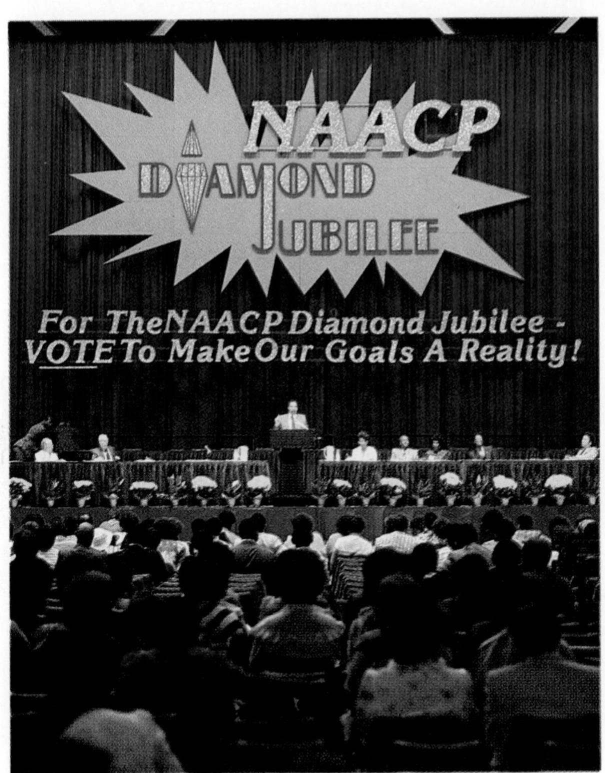

A meeting of the National Association for the Advancement of Colored People (NAACP). Some secondary groups, such as a waiter and a customer, are small and transitory. The individuals interact on a temporary basis to achieve a generally known objective without following any clearly stated rule. But other secondary groups, such as the NAACP, are larger and more permanent. They typically last well beyond their members' lifetimes. Their goals and rules are explicitly stated so that the activities of their numerous members can be coordinated. Such groups become formal organizations.

aims at training young people to become productive citizens.

Whatever their goals, organizations develop certain common means for achieving them. Generally, they engage in *rational planning.* They must decide what specific tasks are necessary for realizing the goals, who are best qualified to carry out the tasks, and how the various tasks are to be coordinated so that costly conflict is avoided and high efficiency achieved.

More specifically, there is first a *division of labor,* whereby workers with different skills are assigned different tasks. This makes it easier for an organization to attain its goals than if all the workers perform the same task. But the division of labor may get out of hand, with each worker producing an item (say, a car door) that cannot be fitted into another item (car body) made by the other worker. This makes it necessary for the organization to establish a *hierarchy of control.* Thus a foreman, a manager, and other administrators are responsible for supervising and directing the workers to ensure that various activities are properly coordinated. The administrators' actions are, however, governed by a set of *formalized rules.* They must deal with the workers in accordance with these rules, without showing any favoritism toward anyone. Their strict adherence to the rules may explain why formal organizations typically appear impersonal. The rules themselves may also explain why the organizations appear to have a life of their own, being able to outlive their members. The departure of certain personnel cannot cause the organizations to collapse because the rules stipulate how replacements are to be found.

Despite their similarities, even organizations that share the same goals may be very different. Both a juvenile training school and a neighborhood public school attempt to control and educate children, but you would not be *equally* willing to be part of these organizations. There are millions of different organizations in a modern society like ours. Sociologists have tried to sort out the essential differences among this multitude of organizations by classifying them into only a few types. One of the best known typologies is Amitai Etzioni's (1975).

Power and Involvement

According to Etzioni, in virtually every organization there are "higher participants" (such as the administrators) and "lower participants" (the rank and file). The function of the higher participants is to exercise power over the lower participants so that the latter will help the organization achieve its goals. Three kinds of power are available to higher participants: (1) *coercive power,* the use of physical force; (2) *remunerative power,* the use of material rewards such as money and similar incentives to ensure cooperation; and (3) *normative power,* the use of moral persuasion, the prestige of a leader, or the promise of social acceptance. There are also three kinds of involvement by lower participants: (1) *alienative,* in which case they do not support the organization's goals; (2) *calculative,* which means they are moderately supportive; and (3) *moral involvement,* in which case they strongly support the organization.

From these three kinds of power exercised by higher participants and three kinds of involvement shown by lower participants, Etzioni constructed a typology of organizations as follows:

	Kinds of Involvement		
Kinds of Power	Alienative	Calculative	Moral
Coercive	(1)	2	3
Remunerative	4	(5)	6
Normative	7	8	(9)

Of the nine types, only three—1, 5, and 9—represent the huge majority of organizations. They are, then, the most common types, while the remaining six are very rare. Etzioni called the three most common types **coercive organizations** (1), **utilitarian organizations** (5), and **normative organizations** (9).

Coercive Organizations Prisons, concentration camps, and custodial mental hospitals are examples of coercive organizations. In each, force or the threat of force is used to achieve the organization's main goal: keeping the inmates in. The inmates obviously do not enjoy being imprisoned; they will run away if they have the chance. They are alienated from the organization and do not support its goals at all. Understandably, the higher participants—prison administrators—have to act tough toward the inmates, seeking compliance by threatening to punish them with solitary confinement if they try to escape. In short, in a coercive organization, coercion is the main form of power used and the involvement by lower participants is alienative.

Utilitarian Organizations Factories, banks, and other businesses are all utilitarian organizations in Etzioni's classification. The higher participants use incentives such as money to ensure that lower participants work to achieve the organization's goals. The rank and file tend to be moderately supportive of those goals. They are likely to calculate whether it is worth their while to work hard, asking "What's in it for me?" In general, the more attractive the remuneration—in money, or fringe benefits, or working conditions—the more committed they are to the organization. Thus the major form of power used in utilitarian organizations is remunerative and the typical form of involvement by lower-level participants is calculative.

Normative Organizations If a Mormon does not pay his tithe, he may be denied access to religious services, but he is not subject to arrest and imprisonment. If the Republican party wants you to vote for its candidates, it may send you letters or knock on your door, and it will certainly advertise; but it does not offer you money. Churches and political parties are examples of a type of organization very different from coercive and utilitarian organizations. Their power over lower participants is based on persuasion, exhortation, social pressure, public recognition, or the appeal of a leader. This normative power is sufficient in these organizations because most of the participants generally want to do what the organization is asking; they are strongly committed to its goals. For this reason normative organizations are sometimes called *voluntary associations.* Typical examples include religious organizations, political organizations, colleges, social clubs, and charitable organizations. In Etzioni's terms, their primary form of power is normative and involvement by the rank and file is moral.

Mixed Organizations In fact, no organization relies entirely on just one type of power. All three types can be found in most organizations. But most use one type of power far more than the other two. Prisons, for example, may use normative power through rehabilitation programs, but they still rely mostly on coercion. A business may use speeches to inspire its workers, but it depends mostly on wages to ensure their involvement.

Nevertheless, some organizations do depend on two types of power to about the same degree. Combat units are a good example. They rely heavily on both normative and coercive powers. First they apply normative powers through basic training, military schools, and patriotic pep talks. It is not practical for the military to offer huge sums of money to induce soldiers to risk limbs and lives, but it can apply effective coercion by withdrawing furlough from AWOLs and by imprisoning or executing deserters.

An Evaluation The Etzioni typology is useful for knowing the characteristics of practically all organiza-

In a voluntary association, such as the men and women who have gathered to march in support of gay rights, the participants join together freely because of a personal, individual commitment to a cause. These people have a strong moral conviction that they are doing the right thing. The power that brings them together is normative, based on their leaders' appeal, persuasion, or exhortation that gays be united to push for their rights. Hence groups such as this are also called normative organizations.

tions. It can also explain why some organizations flounder while others sail smoothly. As Etzioni suggests, organizational effectiveness depends on running an outfit for what it is. If a prison is managed like a coercive organization, a business firm like a utilitarian organization, or a political party like a normative organization, then the organization can be expected to do well. On the other hand, if the prison is run like a political party or if the business firm is operated like a prison, trouble is likely to occur. Research has shown, for example, that when the bosses of business firms or government agencies treat their employees just a little like prison inmates—say, by being unresponsive to their concerns—the lower participants are likely to engage in "whistle blowing," publicly accusing their employing organizations of some wrongdoing (Perrucci et al., 1980). Indeed, most organiza-

In a mixed organization, participants are subjected to several kinds of pressure. In the military, participants may have enlisted voluntarily, but once inside they are subjected to the coercive power of military discipline and to the normative power of basic training and patriotic talks about defending one's country. Though military personnel receive pay, the remunerative power of the military is a secondary factor in organizational control, especially during wartime.

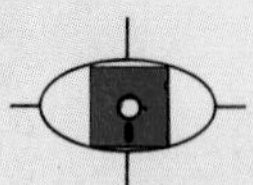

LOOKING AT CURRENT RESEARCH

Nothing Succeeds Like Failure

It is popularly assumed that organizations are bound to break up if they fail to achieve their stated goals. But a number of organizations do continue to operate and even thrive because of their failure to meet their goals. The following research reports how one such organization—skid row rescue missions—succeeds through its program failure. How does consistent failure help the organization to survive rather than break up?

Research Procedures

The data for this paper are derived from attendance at more than 200 rescue mission services while living as a participant observer in many skid row areas in the U.S. intermittently during the course of ten years. The author supported himself as a migratory farm worker and casual industrial laborer and identified himself as such in informal conversations with other skid row residents. Intercity travel was often done by freight train.

Reactions of the skid row residents to the mission program were observed through informal conversations while engaged in employment, drinking in bars, eating in restaurants, standing idly on street corners, listening to the remarks of others while waiting in line to enter the mission chapels, and observations of the congregation during gospel services. Missions were attended in 16 cities across the United States. Missions in all parts of the country were found to be very similar in their hymns, prayers, order of services, and especially in the themes of sermons and in the reactions of the men. The formal policies of the mission programs were learned from personal interviews with directors of missions in Philadelphia, San Francisco, Los Angeles, and Chicago.

Findings

The missions' goal is to convert these "sinful" men [skid row residents] by urging them to accept Christ, which is manifested through taking responsibility, particularly by attending church, abstaining completely from liquor, and above all, by accepting regular and continuous employment.

Through controlling the distribution of food and shelter, the mission management acquires a superior and commanding position. The expression of power and control is apparent upon first entering the building, when individuals are handed a hymn book and directed to designated seats starting from the front row. Although the missions exchange food for an audience of potential converts at gospel services, there is ambiguity in this apparently simple transaction. The missions expect to receive the *attention* of the men during the sermon, while the men anticipate providing only their *presence.* The difference in the definition of the commodity of exchange is apparent soon after the start of the sermon, when many men begin to doze. Lacking the price of a bed, some have walked the streets the entire previous night. Others who had a bed find the mission the first warm place to sit and relax after a day outside in the cold. Since very few have any interest in the sermon, it is not surprising that many men fall asleep as soon as they sit and relax. To insure that the mission obtains its fair value of attention for the food offered, ushers patrol the aisles at frequent intervals and prod dozing men into wakefulness. In

tions will fall by the wayside if their lower participants go so far as to make it impossible for the higher participants to realize their goals. There are some organizations, though, that continue to exist and even thrive on their higher participants' failure to achieve their objectives. A good example is the skid row rescue missions. They continue to function in the face of the higher participants' failure to bring about religious conversion among the lower participants—the skid row residents (see box above).

The major weakness of the Etzioni typology is that it concentrates on what goes on inside the organization; he ignores the environmental, contextual, or external influences. Outside factors do affect the organization significantly (Aldrich, 1979; Marple, 1982; Freeman and Hannan, 1983). Due to societal and cultural differences, for example, Swedish prisons are not as coercive as American prisons, and Japanese firms are run more like normative organizations while American companies more like utilitarian organizations (Ouchi and Wilkins, 1985; Lincoln and Kalleberg, 1985).

Many studies have further revealed the importance of environmental influences on organizations. One study found that the amount of member involvement in missions with long benches, I have seen three-foot sticks used to poke men slumbering in the middle of the benches.

Services invariably end with an emphatic and highly charged appeal for all sinners to come forward to make a profession of faith. Many of the men who attend missions would be expected to be amenable to this religious message due to the basic religious fundamentalism of the lower class, from which most are recruited. Nearly all men on skid row accept the validity and literal interpretation of the Bible. But, paradoxically, the conversion rate is very low. Of the converts, only a fraction remain steadily employed and sober. In addition, there is nearly uniform contempt and condemnation of the mission program.

The invidious implication of moral inferiority connoted by the behavior of mission personnel plus the accusatory content of the sermon directly attack a cherished self-conception for many skid row men: that of being a capable worker. Attributing dependency unequivocally to moral degradation is especially resented in a group which holds self-reliance and economic adequacy as core components of personal worth. The majority react with feelings of guilt and hostility. The desire for adequate nourishment and material comfort is not met in most missions, and most men complain about the poor quality of the food and of their hunger. The men experience a strong feeling of injustice in being subjected to such an unequal exchange. Moreover, they bitterly resent being in the destitute position in which the gospel mission constitutes the best available means of survival.

Conclusion

This analysis has shown that rescue missions fail on a colossal scale in attempting to achieve their primary goal of religious salvation, and that continued failure is necessary for their existence. Failure to convert the vast majority of the members of the congregations leaves a large group of "unsaved" men, which the directors continue to attempt to convert by offering more services, food, and shelter on a continuous basis. This perpetual failure is a necessary condition for the continuation of the mission program on the present scale.

Contrary to the common notion that organizations succeed and are perpetuated by accomplishing their stated objectives, this analysis indicates that certain organizations are in fact perpetuated by *continued failure* to achieve their goals. The implications of this finding extend far beyond the mission program and skid row. Government agencies for enforcing drug laws, for example, continue to exist because they fail to put drug traffickers out of business. Prisons, welfare departments, and mental hospitals also expand inasmuch as their program is ineffective, necessitating retention of those in treatment.

Source: Reprinted from *Social Forces*, 58, (March 1980): 904–924. "Organizational Success Through Program Failure: Skid Row Rescue Missions" by James F. Rooney. Copyright © The University of North Carolina Press.

church affairs depends heavily on the "context variable" of organizational size: the members' commitment is greater in smaller churches than in large ones (Hougland and Wood, 1980). Large size has also been found to depress morale in industrial companies, presumably because it increases the impersonality of relationships and decreases the sense of personal importance in the organization (Zeitz, 1983). A study of highly successful American corporations found that they owe their success to "a rich set of interactions with the environment—namely, customers" (Peters and Waterman, 1982). According to another study, a large and profitable company that made and sold business machines and office furnishings eventually failed because it continued to manufacture mechanical calculators and ignored the electronic revolution in the world at large (Starbuck, 1983). Changes in the larger economic environment can even determine who is likely to rise to the top leadership within large corporations. Early in this century, when large firms had to produce efficiently to succeed against competitors, personnel in charge of manufacturing had the best chance of becoming presidents of their companies. In the middle decades, from 1939 to 1959, when the U.S. economy depended on the expansion of both domestic and international markets, sales personnel were most likely to lead their companies. From 1959 to this day, since further growth of larger companies depends greatly on mergers with and acquisitions of other companies, finance personnel have become increasingly dominant (Fligstein, 1987).

QUESTIONS FOR DISCUSSION AND REVIEW

1. What are the principal features of a formal organization?
2. How do coercive, normative, and utilitarian organizations differ from each other?
3. What features of formal organizations are missing from Etzioni's typology?

ORGANIZATIONAL MODELS

All around us, we find organizations using the types of control Etzioni described. Much as we might try to stay in the warmer world of friends and family, we will bump into these formal organizations and feel their power. Which types of power predominate affects the operation of the organizations as well as our ability to achieve goals we share with these organizations.

There have been many attempts to analyze just how organizations operate and what types of operation are most efficient. Under what circumstances, for example, can an organization do without coercive power? What is the most effective way to offer remunerative rewards? How should the higher-level and lower-level participants interact if the organization is to be effective? Answers to questions like these are contained in organizational models.

Some models describe what organizations are like and others say what they should be like to achieve their goals. No one model yet devised portrays the nature of organizations with complete accuracy. Each tends to focus on certain aspects and obscure others. Taken together, however, organizational models can enhance our understanding.

Scientific Management

Early in this century, American engineer Frederick Taylor (1911) published the first systematic persentation of what was soon called *scientific mangement.* Taylor assumed that the primary goal of an organization is to maximize efficiency. For a manufacturing company, this means getting maximum productivity, the highest possible output per worker per hour. He further assumed that workers are not too bright and can be manipulated. As a result, Taylor argued that the success of an organization depends on three elements: maximum division of labor, close supervision of workers, and an incentive system of piecework wages.

To obtain maximum division of labor, the production of a product must be broken down into numerous simple tasks that are extremely easy to perform. Each of these tasks is then defined down to the tiniest detail, so

Workers on an assembly line in an electronics factory. The scientific management model of industrial organization suggests that a company can achieve maximum productivity if its workers do a simple repetitive task under close supervision. Scientific management works especially well in manufacturing companies, where the work is mostly routine. It has been criticized, however, for treating human beings as machines.

that it can be completed in the shortest time possible. One of Taylor's specific recommendations was that zigzag motions of the hands must be avoided; workers should begin and complete their motions with both hands simultaneously. To ensure that the task is properly carried out, the worker must be closely and continuously supervised. Taylor suggested that there be four types of foremen—setting-up boss, speed boss, quality inspector, and repair boss—and that the foremen in turn be controlled by a planning department. Finally, to be sure they work as hard as possible, workers should be paid by the piece: the more units each produces, the higher his or her pay.

Today many companies still apply Taylor's basic principles (Littler, 1978; Perrow, 1979; Alvesson, 1982). Productivity appears to decline if the basic points of this model are not applied to some degree. Scientific management works particularly well in the world of production, where the work is mostly routine. But the model ignores many aspects of organizations and human behavior. It looks only at the *official* organization, the formal relationships between workers and supervisors. Most sociologists have criticized the model for treating human beings as machines, arguing that this contributes to worker dissatisfaction and ultimately to lower productivity.

Human Relations

In the late 1920s industrial psychologist Elton Mayo challenged practically all the assumptions of the scientific management model. He argued the following: (1) Workers' productivity is not determined by their physical capacity but by their "social capacity," their sensitivity to the work environment. No matter how fast they *can* do their job, they will not produce a lot if their fellow workers frown on the idea of working too fast. (2) Noneconomic rewards, such as friendship with coworkers and respect from management, play a central role in determining the motivation and happiness of workers. Thus wages are less important than Taylor claimed. (3) The greatest specialization is not the most efficient division of labor. Extreme specialization creates problems for those coordinating the work. Supervisors are hard put to know all the details of very specialized tasks. (4) Workers do not react to management and its incentives as isolated individuals but as members of a group. They will reject management's offer of high pay for maximum productivity if their fellow workers are against working too hard (Roethlisberger and Dickson, 1939). These points make up the *human relations model.* In contrast to scientific management, it emphasizes the social forces affecting productivity, especially the infor-

"You know what I think, folks? Improving technology isn't important. Increased profits aren't important. What's important is to be warm, decent human beings."

mal relations among workers. These relations make up what is called the **informal organization,** in contrast to the official organization.

Empirical support for this model came from Mayo's studies at the Hawthorne plant in Chicago in the 1930s. As we discussed in Chapter 2 (Doing Sociology), one of these studies showed that workers increased their productivity regardless of changes in the physical environment. Productivity went up, for example, when the experimenter brightened the workplace, but it also went up when he dimmed the light. Mayo concluded that the employees worked harder because the presence of the researcher made them feel important; management seemed to be treating them as people, not mere machines. Another study at the same plant examined whether output was determined by financial incentives. Surprisingly, it was shaped by an informal norm. The norm forbade working too hard as well as working too slowly. Anyone working too hard was ridiculed as a "rate buster," and anyone working too slowly was scorned as a "chiseler." As a result, each worker tried to produce as much as the other workers, rather than trying to meet management's goals (Roethlisberger and Dickson, 1939).

The human relations model covers parts of the organization ignored by scientific management, but it too has limitations. First, it exaggerates the importance of the informal group life at the workplace. Most workers will not wake up every morning feeling that they cannot wait to go to work in order to be with their co-workers. They are more interested in their families and friends outside the workplace. Second, informal social relations may create more pleasant conditions in the plant, but they cannot significantly reduce the tediousness of the job itself. One may enjoy working with certain individuals, but this cannot turn an inherently boring job into an exciting one. Relations with co-workers, however, may be more significant to white-collar and professional workers than to blue-collar workers, because their jobs often involve a great deal of interaction with their co-workers (Champion, 1975).

Ideal-Type Bureaucracy

Unlike the scientific management and human relations models, Max Weber's organizational model is neither an attempt to say how organizations should work nor a description of how specific, actual organizations do work. Instead, Weber tried to construct what he called an **ideal type.** It does not describe any actual organization, or an average organization, or an "ideal" to be sought. Rather, it describes what are theorized to be the essential characteristics of an organization. It can then be used to determine the extent to which actual organizations have these characteristics. Weber's analysis was so influential, and the type of organization he described is now so widespread, that parts of his model are also part of our definition of formal organizations.

According to Weber, the nature of modern Western society makes a specific form of organization—bureaucracy—necessary. "In the place of the old-type ruler who is moved by sympathy, favor, grace, and gratitude," Weber said, "modern culture requires . . . the emotionally detached, and hence rigorously 'professional' expert" (Bendix, 1962). In every area of modern life there is a tendency toward **rationalization.** Traditional, spontaneous, informal, or diverse ways of doing things are replaced by a planned, unified method based on abstract rules. Applied to organizations, rationalization means the development of bureaucracies. They are, in Weber's view, the most efficient form of organization.

What is a **bureaucracy?** We sometimes use the word to refer to the administration of any organization. Sometimes it is used to mean a government agency. Here we are concerned with bureaucracy as a type of organization. A family farm is not a bureaucracy, but a farm managed by a large corporation is. According to Weber, the essential characteristics of a bureaucracy, which together distinguish it from other types of organization, are as follows:

1. There is a clear-cut division of labor among those in the bureaucracy, assigning to each position certain limited duties and responsibilities.
2. There is a well-defined hierarchy. Those in a higher position have authority to give orders to those below them in the hierarchy, whose work they coordinate (Figure 5.2). The hierarchy resembles a pyramid, with a lot of people at the bottom and progressively fewer as one goes up the pyramid. Authority in the hierarchy is attached to the position, not the person. Orders are issued and obeyed regardless of who occupies the position. This ensures that the organization will not be disrupted by retirement, death, or similar events.

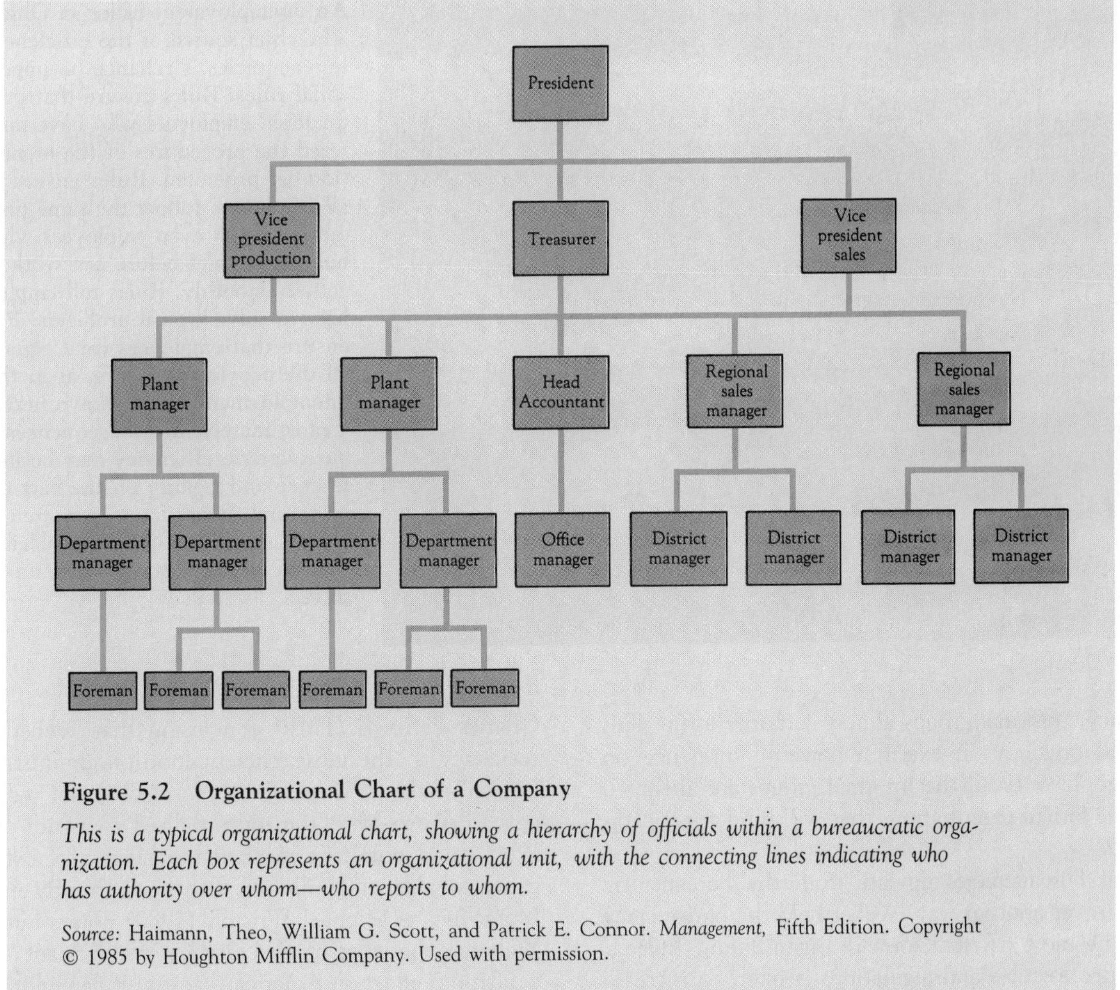

Figure 5.2 Organizational Chart of a Company

This is a typical organizational chart, showing a hierarchy of officials within a bureaucratic organization. Each box represents an organizational unit, with the connecting lines indicating who has authority over whom—who reports to whom.

Source: Haimann, Theo, William G. Scott, and Patrick E. Connor. *Management,* Fifth Edition. Copyright © 1985 by Houghton Mifflin Company. Used with permission.

3. Employees are hired and hold authority on the basis of technical qualifications, which are often determined by examinations. The employees' positions are defined as full-time careers, and to ensure their commitment to the organization, they are rewarded with a salary and the prospect of advancement.
4. The activities of the bureaucrats and their relationships are governed by an elaborate system of explicit, formal, written rules and regulations. This is the most important characteristic of bureaucracies, marking a radical change from informal, more personal ways of organizing work. The reliance on rules in a bureaucracy maximizes efficiency in various ways. First, the rules tell officials what to do. Second, they compel bureaucrats to think and act, not on their own behalf, but as agents of the organization trying to achieve the organization's goal. As a result, bureaucrats become impersonal and objective in dealing with people. They hire, for example, the best-qualified person, not the boss's incompetent son.

This is the bureaucracy in theory. It is marked by specialization, impersonality, and rationalization. In practice, of course, even bureaucrats retain personal interests and feelings that may interfere with their obedience to rules and regulations. And even within a bu-

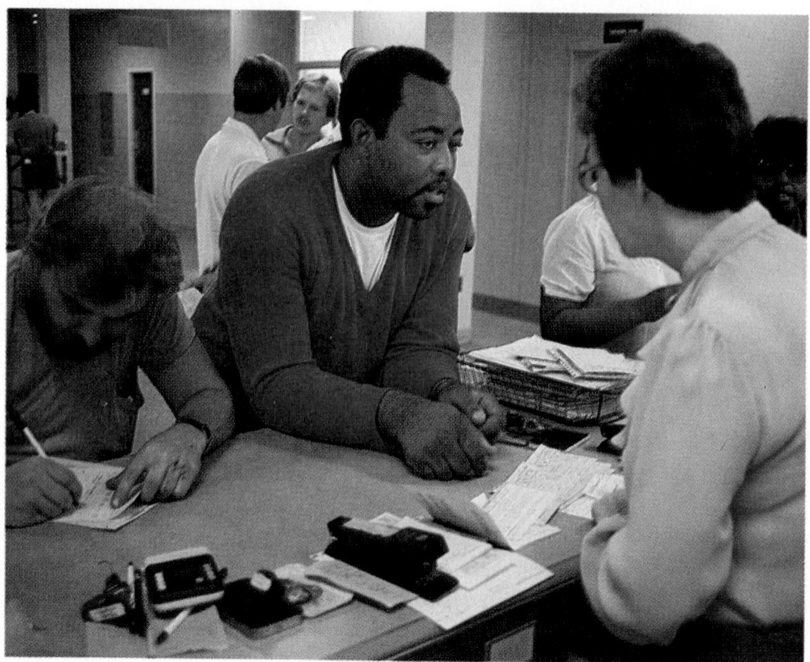

An unemployment office in Ohio. The chief source of the efficiency of bureaucracies is reliance on impersonal rules. Rules ensure that only qualified employees who have mastered the procedures of the organization get promoted. Rules ensure that all employees follow the same procedures so that even employees who have never met before can work together smoothly. Rules tell employees how to solve typical problems. Rules ensure that employees treat equally all the people they serve, as in the unemployment office shown here. Unfortunately, the consequences of bureaucratic efficiency may be indifference and rigidity on the part of personnel. Bureaucrats are often perceived as unsympathetic; problems that are atypical may remain unsolved.

reaucracy, informal groups almost certainly form. This informal organization exerts a powerful influence on how people work. If the informal groups are alienated from the formal organization, they will hinder its operation.

Real bureaucracies deviate from the bureaucratic model in yet another way. Weber held the bureaucracy to be the most efficient form of organization. Indeed, adherence to rules and regulations is likely to increase efficiency when tasks are stable and routine, but it can also produce inefficiency. Rules are based on what is known; they cannot tell people what to do about what cannot be anticipated. When changes occur frequently or when the unusual occurs, rules won't help. A lost I.D. card or birth certificate or other document can bring bureaucratic procedures to a grinding halt. Extreme adherence to rules can be tantamount to inaction. When the Japanese bombed Pearl Harbor in 1941, U.S. military personnel rushed to the armories for weapons. But armory guards refused to issue the weapons unless a formal requisition was properly signed in accordance with regulations (Champion, 1975).

We should, however, put the Weberian model in proper perspective. If we compare the rational-legal form of bureaucracy with traditional, patrimonial, and other similar types of organizations, we may agree with Charles Perrow's (1979) conclusion that Weber's bureaucracy is "the most efficient form of administration known" today. "Without this form of social technology," Perrow says, "the industrialized countries of the West could not have reached the heights of extravagance, wealth, and pollution that they currently enjoy." Moreover, as Michael Wriston (1980) points out, the Weberian model of bureaucracy has a significant "democratizing" effect on American society. It demands unbiased treatment of individuals, helping to ensure equality before the law as well as legal guarantees against arbitrary judicial and administrative decisions.

Collectivist Organization

In Weber's view, bureaucracies emerge because they are an efficient form of organization. In contrast, Karl Marx argued that bureaucracies are the capitalists' tool for exploiting the working class. Eventually, he claimed, bureaucracies will be abolished in a classless, communist society. They will be replaced by collectivist organizations, in which managers and workers work together as equals and for equal pay. In the meantime, an approximation to this organizational model has been tried out in

Table 5.1 Bureaucratic versus Collectivist Models

Bureaucratic Model	Collectivist Model
1. Achieving organizational efficiency through technical competence.	1. Achieving organizational efficiency through worker commitment.
2. Using only technical competence in evaluating member's worth.	2. Using both ideological dedication and technical competence.
3. Maximum division of labor.	3. Minimal division of labor.
4. Maximum specialization of jobs—monopolization of expertise.	4. Generalization of jobs—diffusion of expertise.
5. Emphasis on hierarchy of positions—justifying reward differentials.	5. Striving for egalitarianism—restricting reward differentials.
6. Authority in individual officeholders; hierarchical control; bureaucratic elitism.	6. Authority in collectivity as a whole; democratic control; subordinate participation.
7. Formalization of fixed and universalistic rules.	7. Primacy of ad hoc decisions.
8. Worker motivation through direct supervision.	8. Worker motivation through personal appeals.
9. Impersonality as ideal of social relations in organizations.	9. Comradeship as ideal of social relations in organizations.
10. Informal groups need not be co-opted.	10. Informal groups should be fully co-opted.

Source: Martin King Whyte, "Bureaucracy and modernization in China: The Maoist critique," *American Sociological Review,* 38, 1973, pp. 149–163; Joyce Rothschild-Whitt, "The collectivist organization: An alternative to bureaucratic models," in Frank Lindenfeld and Joyce Rothschild-Whitt (eds.), *Workplace Democracy and Social Change,* Boston: Porter Sargent, 1982.

China. Other types of collectivist organizations can be found in Japan and the United States, but they have not been inspired by Marx. (See Table 5.1 for finer distinctions between bureaucratic and collectivist models.)

During the 1960s and 1970s the Chinese government tried to implement the Marxist model throughout the country. To the Chinese, emphasis on technical competence promotes inequality between managers and workers and among workers as well. It particularly discourages the average workers from meaningful participation in the organization. They will consider themselves incompetent and doubt that they can benefit from the organization. Hence, they will not work hard. Therefore, the government told workers to join administrators and technicians in making decisions, and it required the latter to join the former in working with their hands. All of them also had to attend regular meetings to raise their political consciousness, to heighten their enthusiasm for "serving the people" as opposed to pursuing self-interests (Whyte, 1973; Hearn, 1978).

As a result, all symbols of rank in the military were abolished, all workers received about the same pay, and other trappings of equality appeared everywhere. Meanwhile, China remained economically backward. Since the late 1970s, however, the new government has embarked on a vast modernization program. It seeks out skilled technicians, professionals, and experts to run organizations. It also uses pay incentives to motivate individual workers. In December 1984 it even pronounced that "Marxism is obsolete," and affirmed the role of such capitalist ideas as individual initiative and market competition in China's economic development. Many Westerners suspect that all this might produce a Western-style economy, which in turn would create a Western-style bureaucracy with emphasis on expertise and efficiency but with great inequality between management and labor. We could argue, however, that if the current political situation continues, the Chinese organization would come closer to the Japanese organization than the Western bureaucracy. A basic reason is that China and Japan have about the same collectivist culture, which is more group-oriented than individualistic. But what is the Japanese organization like?

The heart of the Japanese organization is concern with group achievement. Employees begin each workday by singing their company song or reciting slogans of devotion to their company. They work in sections of eight to ten people, headed by the *kacho* (section chief). Each section, now well known as a "quality circle," does not await orders from the top but takes the initiative, and all its members work together as equals. Personnel of different sections often get together to discuss how best to

Japanese companies are collectivist organizations, concerned with group commitment. They are often run like families. They encompass every aspect of the worker's life, even to the point of providing low-cost housing and medical care. Frequently Japanese workers have lifetime job security. In the workplace, employees are given responsibility for product quality, and they are invited to help decide how the work should be done. Sometimes their salaries go up or down in accordance with the profitability of their firm.

achieve company objectives. Executives, then, merely rubber stamp most of the decisions made by employees at the section level. Workers further look upon their company as their family because they enjoy the security of permanent employment. Executives also feel secure and regard their company as their family. The security has "its roots in solid cultural ground and shared meanings" (Peters and Waterman, 1982). Thus both workers and executives are highly committed to their company, working as hard as they can. In such a collectivist environment, the Japanese do not, however, scorn technical competence for fear of generating inequality as the Chinese did in the last two decades. Instead, the Japanese encourage potential innovators to "come forward, grow, and flourish—even to the extent of indulging a little madness" (Peters and Waterman, 1982). But they do so as part of their duty to contribute to the success of their company.

Whether Japanese or Chinese, the collectivist model of organization has a familiar ring to Americans in one sense: the call for participation by all members is a principle of democracy. This contrasts with the bureaucratic model, which is undemocratic because those on top of the organization dictate to those below and those at the bottom may not choose who are above them or influence their decisions. In a collectivist organization, power flows from the bottom up, while in a bureaucracy, it flows from the top down. In the United States this element of the collectivist model can be seen in some 5000 "alternative institutions" established during the 1970s. The free schools, free medical clinics, legal collectives, food cooperatives, communes, and cooperative businesses are a legacy of movements during the 1960s against authority and "the Establishment." These enterprises are collectively owned and managed, without any hierarchy of authority. They tend to be in craft production and other special niches of the economy that exempt them from directly competing with conventional companies. Most are quite small, averaging six employees per organization, but their small size helps preserve full worker participation. The workers are highly satisfied with their jobs and strongly identify with their firms. Since they are also owners, the workers tend to work too hard and often suffer stress and burnout as a result (Rothschild-Whitt, 1982; Rothschild and Russell, 1986).

The collectivist idea of giving workers control over their jobs has also been tried out on a limited basis in some 90 percent of the 500 largest American corporations as a way to combat worker alienation and low productivity. In these companies small groups of employees work together like the Japanese quality circles. They are encouraged with rewards and recognition—merit raises, cash bonuses, and bulletin-board praises—to contribute ideas on how to increase productivity and sales. They operate with the "open door" policy, whereby employees report directly to the top management, which further encourages them to work harder because it makes workers feel important and respected. Practically all of these companies are in the manufacturing sector of the economy. Good examples are IBM and General Motors, which produce computers and automobiles. Recently, the quality-circle style of worker participation has begun to invade the service sector in such areas as the insurance business (Rothschild and Russell, 1986; Scott, 1986).

All this has by and large raised employee morale and advanced the fortunes of many companies. But this has not been the case with a few companies. The problems with the companies that failed, though, came largely from their managements' inability to meet the workers' heightened expectations of wider autonomy and greater self-governance in the workplace. As one worker complained: "This open system has disappointed lots of people. . . . I thought self-management was pretty good until a week ago when I found out my team couldn't decide to make even minor repairs without management approval. . . . Training class created high expectations. There, managers and workers were equal but when you start working you feel managers are different" (Derber and Schwartz, 1983). But in successful companies, workers have a different experience. At IBM, a production-line employee says of his company: "I have a voice here. I've never worked anywhere else where I could speak out, be heard, and they would take action. Here they respect you. They treat you as a person." In a recent year he submitted ten ideas and received bonus checks for four of them. His latest idea was that they could save time by having a robot, rather than workers, remove faulty circuit units from the line. For that suggestion he received more than a week's pay (Kneale, 1986).

In addition to using rewards to stimulate worker participation, a growing number of corporations have enabled their employees to own stock in the companies through employee stock-ownership plans. In 1985, over 6000 corporations had already established employee stock-ownership programs covering more than 10 million workers. But the amount of stock involved is mostly small (Rothschild and Russell, 1986). In fact, the collectivist model is still far from dominating American society as it does the Chinese and Japanese societies. The most influential organizations in the United States—from private foundations to public universities, from multinational corporations to government agencies, and even many religious groups—are still basically organized as bureaucracies.

QUESTIONS FOR DISCUSSION AND REVIEW

1. What are the special features of the scientific management, human relations, bureaucratic, and collectivist models?
2. Why does the ideal-type model of bureaucracy differ from the way bureaucracies operate in real life?
3. Why might American workers resist working in a collectivist-style organization?
4. How can comparison of organizational models help managers improve the operations of business and government?

THE REALITIES OF BUREAUCRACY

Despite widespread dislike of bureaucracy, this form of organization is everywhere. Millions of Americans now work in bureaucracies, and even more must deal with bureaucratic organizations when they wish to enroll in school, to have a phone installed, to get a hospital bill paid, or to handle any number of other countless arrangements that are part of living in a modern society. The prevalence of bureaucratic organization affects both the small details of everyday life and the overall function of the government and economy. The vices and virtues of bureaucracy are thus worth a closer look.

Bureaucratic Vices

In Weber's view, bureaucracy is inescapable but not very likable. "It is horrible," he once said, "to think that the world would one day be filled with nothing but those little cogs, little men clinging to little jobs and striving toward bigger ones" (Bendix, 1962). Finding an American to say a good word about bureaucracy is about as hard as finding a landlord who likes rent control. Why?

We have already noted some of the deficiencies of bureaucracies. The rules and regulations characteristic of bureaucracies are of little help when something unexpected happens. The blind adherence to rules may prevent necessary action. The hierarchies of authority characteristic of bureaucracies are undemocratic. Among bureaucracy's best-known vices, however, is its tendency to produce a seemingly endless number of rules and regulations. Public bureaucracies, in particular, are well known for their mountains of rules. All these rules slow action by government employees and fall like an avalanche on private citizens and businesses that must comply with them. The nation's small businesses alone spend an immense amount of money (about $13 billion) every year in order to complete government forms (Taylor, 1980).

Whenever there are a great many rules, it is virtually inevitable that some of them are irrational and contradictory. Not long ago a millionaire was officially declared eligible for welfare. He was a 31-year-old supermarket employee who had won New York's millionaire lottery. After being laid off from his job, he applied for unemployment benefits. The application was approved because, according to official explanation, lottery winning is no bar to receiving such benefit. Another example is the federal government spending millions of our tax dollars on an antismoking campaign while giving even more money to subsidize the tobacco industry (Peter, 1978). Sometimes the contradictory rules are so tangled up that they can entrap a person. Thus the very compliance with one rule may mean violating another. This is called **Catch-22,** after Joseph Heller's novel by that name. In Heller's book the pilot Yossarian can be excused from flying more bombing missions if a military doctor declares him crazy. That is one military rule. According to another rule, however, Yossarian must first ask the doctor to ground him. But if he asks the doctor to ground him in order to avoid dangerous missions, that is proof that he is *not* crazy. So he must continue flying—Catch-22.

C. Northcote Parkinson (1957) popularized another criticism of bureaucracies. According to what is called **Parkinson's Law,** "Work expands to fill the time available for its completion." Parkinson believed that the natural tendency of bureaucracy is to grow and keep on growing, by at least 6 percent a year. Wanting to appear busy or important or both, officials increase their workload by writing a lot of memos, creating rules, filling out forms, and keeping files. Then, feeling overworked, they hire assistants. If the boss had just one assistant, that person might become a competitor for the boss's job. But if the boss hires two underlings, he or she will be the only person who understands both their jobs. Besides, managers' salaries are sometimes based on how many people they supervise. When two assistants are hired, however, the boss's work increases, because he or she must supervise and coordinate their activities. At the same time, there are powerful incentives for officials to increase their agency work forces, budgets, and missions. As Morris Fiorina (1983) points out, bureaucrats' rewards (such as salary, perquisites, status, and power) depend heavily on the size (employment and budget) of their agencies. The result is an ever-rising pyramid of bureaucracy. Parkinson recently provided an example of how bureaucracies grow inexorably. When Ronald Reagan was governor of California in the 1960s, Parkinson told him about the Bay Bridge, which connects San Francisco to Oakland. When it was first built, 14 painters could paint the bridge from one end to the other and back again. By the time Reagan became governor, the spraying machine, which can do the job much faster, had already been introduced. But the number of people engaged in painting the bridge had jumped to 77. After listening to Parkinson, Reagan valiantly tackled the problem, but he could only cut the staff of painters down to 50. When he became president in the early 1980s, the staff had crept back up to 90 (Train, 1986). To functionalists, bureaucratic growth is necessary for accommodating to changing environments. Without growth, bureaucracies are assumed to be incapable of solving new problems efficiently. To conflict theorists, however, bureaucracies grow in order to serve the interests of those who run the organizations, enabling them to accumulate power, as Parkinson has implied (Meyer, 1985; Hasenfeld, 1987).

There is yet another popular cliché that challenges the functionalist view of bureaucracies as capable of doing a good job. It is known as the **Peter Principle:** "In every hierarchy every employee tends to rise to his level of incompetence" (Peter and Hull, 1969). Competent officials are promoted. If they prove to be competent in their new jobs, they are promoted again. The process continues until they are promoted to a position in which they are incompetent. And there they remain until they retire. The bureaucracy functions only because there are always employees still proving their competence before they are promoted beyond their abilities. Like Parkinson's Law, however, the Peter Principle, though an interesting idea, is based on impressionistic observation rather than rigorous scientific research.

Bureaucratic Virtues

From Peking to Peoria, the vices of bureaucracy are well known. Why then do bureaucracies flourish? In part, it is because they are not all bad. Even red tape has its virtues: what is one person's "red tape," as Herbert Kaufman (1977) said, "may be another person's procedural safeguard." The process of getting a government permit to open a hazardous waste dump may seem an endless, expensive obstacle course of paperwork to the company that wants to operate the dump. But to people living near the proposed site, the rules and regulations that make up the red tape may seem the best guarantee that proper precautions to safeguard their health will be taken.

Similarly, the impersonality of bureaucracies, especially in government, is sometimes welcome. If you need a government-subsidized student loan, you are probably glad that impersonal rules—not political pull or personal friendships—determine whether you can obtain the loan. Bureaucracy encourages equality and discourages discrimination.

Even for employees, bureaucracies may bring some benefits. It is widely assumed that bureaucracies tend to stifle individual creativity and imagination, but this assumption is far from correct. Data collected by sociologist Melvin Kohn (1982) suggest that bureaucracies make their workers intellectually flexible, creative, and open-minded.

Kohn defined bureaucrats as people who work in large organizations with complicated hierarchies of authority, and nonbureaucrats as people who work in small organizations with only one level of supervision. Kohn found that, compared with nonbureaucrats, bureaucrats demonstrated a higher level of intellectual performance on tests administered by an interviewer. Bureaucrats also placed greater intellectual demands on themselves during their leisure time. They were more likely than nonbureaucrats to read books and magazines, attend plays and concerts, and go to museums. They also put greater value on self-direction, rather than conformity, and were more likely to take personal responsibility for whatever they did. Finally, they were more open-minded and more receptive to change than the nonbureaucrats.

Skeptics may argue that the bureaucrats' wonderful traits did not *result* from working in a bureaucracy. Perhaps the bureaucrats were better educated, more intellectually flexible, and more receptive to change in the first place. This argument assumes that bureaucracies hold some special attraction for people with these qualities. But since most people believe that bureaucracies suppress creativity, this assumption is far from convincing.

Kohn contended that bureaucracies themselves encourage the development of the positive traits he found in their employees. The more complex a job is, argued Kohn, the more intellectually flexible the worker becomes, and employees of bureaucracies tend to have more complex jobs than those with comparable education who work for an organization with just one or two levels of supervision. White-collar bureaucrats, such as factory managers, have very diverse responsibilities. They must constantly evaluate information, choose from among a multitude of alternatives, juggle competing interests, reconcile interpersonal conflicts, and move back and forth from meetings to solitary work. Similarly, blue-collar workers in bureaucracies typically perform a variety of tasks and deal with diverse situations. For blue-collar workers, however, Kohn argued that another characteristic of bureaucracies—job protection—is more important than complexity in encouraging the positive traits he found in these workers. In short, compared with a local auto body shop, General Motors is more likely to provide conditions that foster flexibility, creativity, and open-mindedness among employees.

The Future of Bureaucracy

"We are witnessing," wrote Alvin Toffler (1970), "not the triumph, but the breakdown of bureaucracy. We are in fact witnessing the arrival of a new organizational system that will increasingly challenge, and ultimately supplant bureaucracy." Toffler's declaration echoed an analysis presented by Warren Bennis and Philip Slater. In the future, they predicted in 1968, organizations

> will have some unique characteristics. The key word will be "temporary." There will be adaptive, rapidly changing *temporary* systems. These will be task forces organized around problems to be solved by groups of relative strangers with diverse professional skills (Bennis and Slater, 1968).

Toffler called this new type of organization an **adhocracy.** It will be dissolved after completing the task. Moreover, according to Bennis, the temporary organization will be egalitarian, not hierarchical. In Bennis's view, "We should expect the [old] pyramid of bureaucracy to begin crumbling. . . . [New] organizational charts will consist of project groups rather than stratified functional groups."

Toffler and Bennis believe that these temporary, egalitarian organizations will emerge primarily because of two trends. First, the greatly increased rate of social and technological change creates numerous unexpected, nonroutine problems. Bureaucracies are ill equipped to cope with these because they are designed to deal with predictable, routine matters. To survive, organizations must become "adaptive, problem-solving, temporary systems of diverse specialists, linked together by coordinating and task-evaluating executive specialists. . . . " (Bennis and Slater, 1968). In other words, bureaucracies must give way to ad-hocracies.

Toffler and Bennis also predict that bureaucracies will be undermined by the increasing professionalization of employees, especially scientists and engineers. These people have a strong sense of independence, and they resent taking orders from managers who have less technical knowledge. The professionals will be more committed to their own standards of excellence and their professional societies than to their bosses. As a result, the hierarchy of bureaucracy, with power concentrated at the top, will collapse. In its place will emerge more egalitarian organizations, in which employees assume greater responsibility for their own tasks.

The death-of-bureaucracy thesis has come under fire for being based more on wish than hard analysis. Critics argue that only a few experts will tackle the new, nonroutine problems (Shariff, 1979). Most employees will still carry on routine tasks, because everyday production, sales, and accounting tasks cannot be turned over to a robot or a completely automated assembly line. In addition, the experts themselves will return to their original departments and ranks after they have resolved unexpected problems. The critics further contend that only a "microscopic minority" of scientists and engineers are prominent in professional circles and more committed to their profession than to their boss. The overwhelming majority of employees cannot be expected to have this degree of professional loyalty. The critics conclude that there will be more, rather than less, bureaucratization, especially because both public and private bureaucracies are becoming increasingly large and complex.

Both views could be partly correct. There may be more bureaucreatization in the future, particularly in the West, though not in Japan. In becoming larger, already large organizations would be more impersonal, more subject to complex rules and regulations as well as managerial control. Most organizations in the United States already seem to be moving in this direction, as suggested by the recent growth of big government agencies, multinational corporations, multicampus universities, and agribusiness companies (Hage, 1980; Hancock, 1980). Large organizational size usually leads to greater bureaucratic control, requiring numerous workers to follow standard rules and operating procedures so chaos can be avoided (Hsu, Marsh, and Mannari, 1983).

What will be the effect on bureaucratic organizations when it becomes possible for more and more people to work independently at home, on their own computers? This will reinforce the trend toward the replacement of the bureaucratic, hierarchical structure by a more egalitarian organization. The manager will no longer be the "boss" and everybody else "subordinates." Instead, the workers will be the "bosses," and the "manager" will take a supporting role as their planner and coordinator. This is because the workers will possess special knowledge and skills as well as the strong desire for autonomy typical of highly educated people.

At the same time, there may be less bureaucratization among higher-ranked technical experts and specialists within giant organizations. There may also be less administrative control throughout the corporations that are on the frontiers of technology. In many successful corporations in the United States today the highly trained specialists already enjoy a wide range of autonomy. They work in small groups, known as task forces, project teams, quality circles, or skunk works, much like the Japanese, who work together as complete equals to solve a specific problem. In General Motors, for example, there are special project teams, one working on the electric car, another on the overall engine computerization, and a third on labor issues (Peters and Waterman, 1982). While virtually all huge organizations like General Motors are not entirely composed of these small project teams, they may well be in the future. According to Peter Drucker (1986), there has been a significant shift in the composition of the American workforce from manual to knowledge work. Even in today's smokestack, manufacturing industries, only three out of ten employees fit the "labor" category—the rest are mostly in specialized, knowledge work. Given their increasing education, special skills, and desire for autonomy, these knowledge workers will increasingly press for the replacement of the bureaucratic, hierarchical structure of their companies by a much flatter, more egalitarian organization made up of numerous smaller units with six to ten employees each. In this new kind of organization, the manager will no longer be the "boss" and all others the "subordinates." Instead, the knowledge workers will be the "bosses," and the "manager" will play a supporting role as their planner and coordinator.

QUESTIONS FOR DISCUSSION AND REVIEW

1. What vices of bureaucracy do Parkinson's Law and the Peter Principle illustrate?
2. Why does Alvin Toffler feel that bureaucracies will ultimately be replaced by ad-hocracy?
3. What personal experiences illustrate the virtues or vices of bureaucracy?

CHAPTER REVIEW

1. *What is a social group?* It is a collection of people who share some characteristics, interact with one another, and have some feeling of unity. *What are two main types of social groups?* Primary and secondary. A primary group is one whose members interact informally, relate to each other as whole persons, and enjoy their relationship for its own sake. In a secondary group, the individuals interact formally, relate to each other as players of particular roles, and expect to achieve some practical purpose through the relationship. *Does the size of a group matter?* Yes, it does. The pressure to conform is usually very great if a group is small enough for all its members to interact directly with one another. Moreover, the larger a group, the more impersonal it becomes, the more difficult it is for one member to influence another, or the less likely a member is to help someone in distress.

2. *What is a formal organization?* It is a group whose activities are rationally designed to achieve specific goals. *What characteristics do organizations have in common?* In order to achieve their goals, organizations engage in rational planning. This includes a division of labor, a hierarchy of control, and a set of formalized rules. *What are the most common types of organizations?* According to Etzioni, they are coercive, utilitarian, and normative organizations.

3. *According to scientific management, what is the primary goal of an organization, and what must it do to achieve this goal?* Scientific management holds that organizations seek efficiency and that to obtain it they must have maximum division of labor, close supervision of workers, and a piecework system of wages. *How do the scientific management and human relations models differ?* Whereas scientific management focuses on the official organization and the effect of wages on efficiency, the human relations model emphasizes the influence of social forces—in particular the informal relations among workers—on job satisfaction and productivity.

4. *What are the principal characteristics of a bureaucracy?* A bureaucracy is characterized by a division of labor, a hierarchy of authority, the hiring of employees on the basis of impersonal procedures and technical qualifications, and a reliance on formal, written rules. As a result, a bureaucracy is marked by specialization, impersonality, and what Weber called rationalization. In Weber's view it is the most efficient form of organization. *How do collectivist organizations differ from bureaucratic ones?* In a bureaucratic organization, decisions are made by managers. In a collectivist organization, workers participate in the management of the organization.

5. *Why are bureaucracies so little loved?* Bureaucracies are undemocratic organizations that tend to produce an

ever-growing number of rules, rules that may hinder effective action and may be contradictory. Moreover, popular stereotypes of bureaucracies hold that they are inefficient, overstaffed organizations that stifle creativity. *Do bureaucracies have any saving graces?* When tasks are stable and routine, they may be very efficient; their reliance on rules and their impersonality can protect people from the exercise of arbitrary power and favoritism. In addition, there is some evidence that bureaucracies foster among their workers intellectual flexibility, creativity, and openness to change. *Are bureaucracies here to stay?* Some writers have argued that bureaucracies will be replaced by a new type of organization in which *temporary* task forces will be formed to solve specific problems. This prediction of the late 1960s is coming true for a few organizations in the forefront of technological advance. But there is more bureaucratization among most of the ordinary organizations.

KEY TERMS

Ad-hocracy Toffler's term for an organization that assembles temporary groups of experts for solving specific problems (p. 125).

Bureaucracy An organization characterized by a division of labor, hierarchy of authority, the hiring of employees on the basis of impersonal procedures and technical qualifications, and reliance on formal rules (p. 118).

Catch-22 Novelist Joseph Heller's term for the situation in which the very compliance with one rule results in violating another (p. 124).

Coercive organization An organization in which force or threat of force is applied to the lower participants, who in turn are alienated from the organization (p. 112).

Formal organization A group whose activities are rationally designed to achieve specific goals (p. 110).

Groupthink The tendency for members of a group to maintain consensus to the extent of ignoring the truth (p. 108).

Ideal type Weber's term for a description of what are theorized to be the essential characteristics of a phenomenon, which can be compared with actual phenomena (p. 118).

Informal organization A group formed by the informal relations among members of an organization; based on personal interactions, not on any plan by the organization (p. 118).

Ingroup The group to which an individual is strongly tied as a member (p. 104).

Normative organization An organization in which normative power is exercised over the lower participants, who are deeply committed to the organization (p. 112).

Outgroup The group of which an individual is not a member (p. 104).

Parkinson's Law Parkinson's observation—that "work expands to fill the time available for its completion"—for explaining why bureaucracy tends to keep growing (p. 124).

Peter Principle Peter's observation—that "in a hierarchy every employee tends to rise to his level of incompetence"—for explaining the prevalence of incompetence among bureaucrats (p. 124).

Rationalization Weber's term for the tendency to replace traditional, spontaneous, informal, and diverse ways of doing things with a planned, formally unified method based on abstract rules (p. 118).

Reference group A group that is used as the frame of reference for evaluating one's own behavior (p. 105).

Social aggregate A collection of people who happen to be in one place but do not interact with one another (p. 104).

Social category A number of people who happen to share some characteristics but do not interact with one another or gather in one place (p. 104).

Social group A collection of people who share some characteristics, interact with one another, and have some feeling of unity (p. 104).

Utilitarian organization An organization in which remuneration is used to control the lower participants who show calculative involvement in the organization (p. 112).

SUGGESTED READINGS

Abegglen, James C., and George Stalk, Jr. 1985. *Kaisha: The Japanese Corporation.* New York: Basic Books. A well-written and penetrating analysis of how some of the most successful Japanese companies operate.

Homans, George. 1950. *The Human Group.* New York: Harcourt, Brace. In this sociology classic the author analyzes various types of human groups and concludes that they all have three things in common: activities, interaction, and sentiments.

Peters, Thomas J., and Robert H. Waterman, Jr. 1982. *In Search of Excellence: Lessons from America's Best-Run Companies.* New York: Harper & Row. A lively book full of interesting information on the basic characteristics of America's successfully managed companies, remarkably comparable to those of the successful Japanese firms in Abegglen and Stalk's book listed above.

Rothschild, Joyce, and Raymond Russell. 1986. "Alternatives to bureaucracy: Democratic participation in the economy." *Annual Review of Sociology,* 12, pp. 307–328. An uncommonly helpful review of the recent literature on the trend toward greater worker participation in the management of the workplace.

Zucker, Lynn. 1983. "Organizations as institutions," in Samuel B. Bacharach (ed.), *Research in the Sociology of Organizations,* vol. 2. Greenwich, Conn.: JAI Press. An impressive analysis of how Americans over the last two centuries have increasingly relied on organizations to serve their needs.

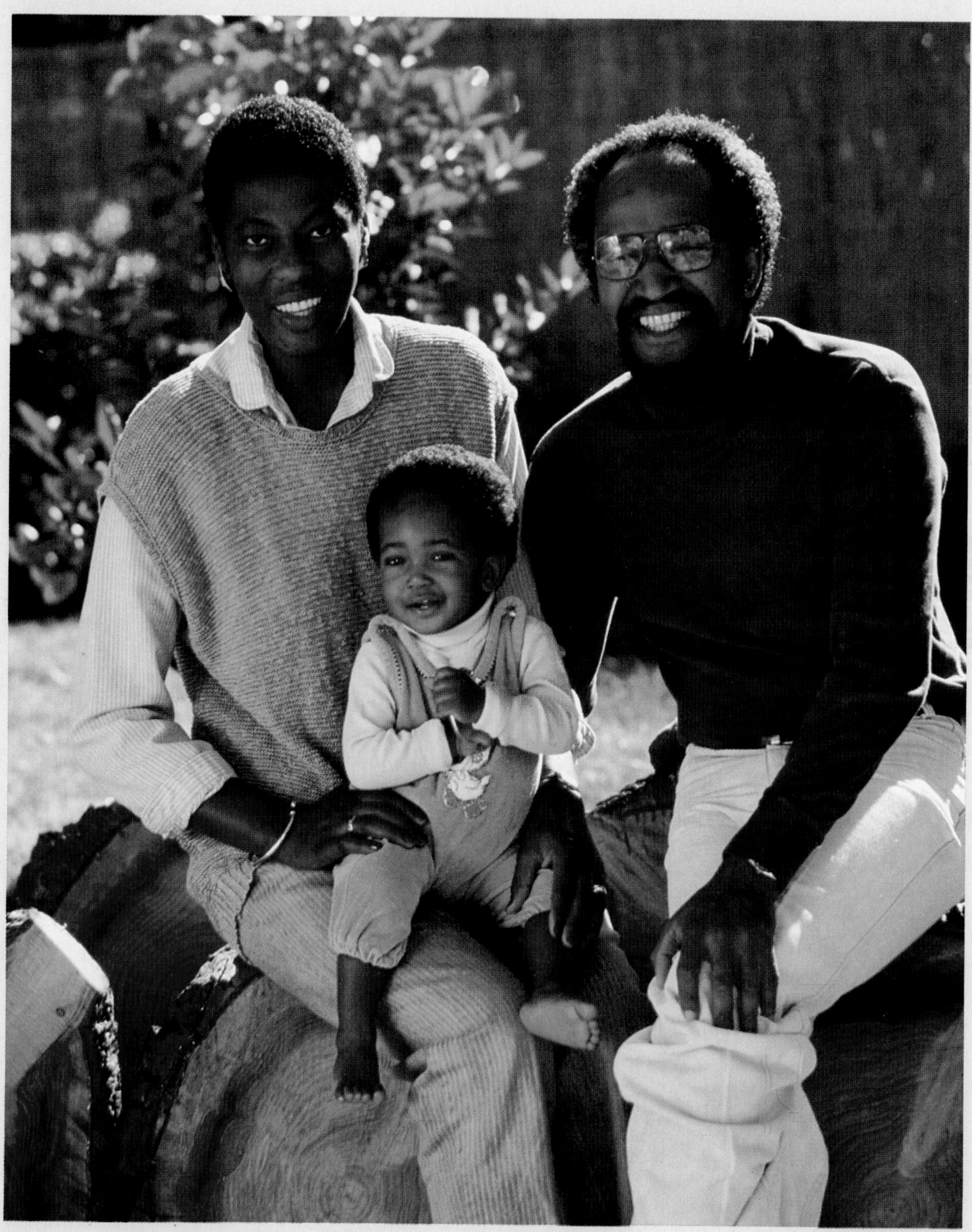

6 Socialization

Socialization is the process by which a society transmits its cultural values to individuals so that they can function properly as its members. Parents play a crucial role in their children's socialization. Intensive socialization can develop children's potential to the maximum, while deprivation of socialization can severely retard their intellectual and physical growth.

Every one of us is born twice. We are first born in the same way as other animals. After this biological birth, the human infant behaves much like a kitten, a puppy, or any other animal infant except that it is more helpless. The human infant eats like an animal, making a mess of itself. It urinates and defecates wherever it pleases. It moves about on all fours. It makes sounds with as little meaning as those made by an animal. Then this little human animal is transformed into a truly human being, a person who can take part in a society and its culture. This momentous transformation is like being born again. It is our sociological birth, made possible by what is called **socialization.**

Socialization is the process by which a society transmits its cultural values to individuals so that they can function properly as its members. It is through socialization that a child learns to be human. It is through socialization, too, that children develop their **personality**—a fairly stable configuration of feelings, attitudes, ideas, and behaviors that characterizes an individual. Even into adulthood, the process of socialization continues, though it usually does not change us as radically as in our early childhood.

If socialization makes us human, are infants like computers waiting to be programed, or even like clay waiting to be shaped? The roles of nature (what we inherit) and of nurture (learning) in making us what we are have long been argued. We begin this chapter by looking at this controversy. Here, we briefly examine the roles of both nature and nurture and several theories of just how they influence our development. Then we turn our attention to who it is that socializes us. Finally, we look at the fundamental question of whether socialization means that freedom is a myth and that we are whatever society makes us.

NATURE AND NURTURE

To the seventeenth-century philosopher John Locke, the mind of a child was like a *tabula rasa* (blank slate). People became what they were taught to be. By the second half of the nineteenth century, a quite different view was popular. Rather than looking to nurture—what people are taught—to explain human behavior, many social scientists looked to nature—what people inherit. The pendulum of opinion has swung back and forth. In retrospect the debate sometimes seems fruitless, but we have learned from it.

From Instincts to Genes

Many social scientists in the late nineteenth century were inspired by Charles Darwin's theory that humans and other animals descended ultimately from the same ancestors. Animals are governed by instincts—fixed traits that are inherited and shared by all members of a species. These inherited mechanisms enable members of the species to perform complex tasks.

The migration of birds provides an example. Twice a year New Zealand cuckoos travel 4000 miles between New Zealand and islands off the coast of New Guinea. The adults leave New Zealand before their eggs are hatched. The young cuckoos later travel the 4000 miles and join their parents—without ever having made the journey and with no one to guide them. Experiments have indicated that other birds also seem to have some inborn sense that guides their migration.

Because animals are governed by instincts and humans are also animals, some people reasoned, human behavior must also be governed by instincts. As a result, many social scientists busily searched for the supposed instincts that would explain all kinds of human behavior. When they saw a mother feeding her baby, they attributed it to the "maternal instinct." When they were asked to explain why nations went to war, they said the cause was the "aggressive instinct." Social scientists eventually discovered more than 14,000 instincts—ranging from a "laughing instinct" to a "religious instinct"—to account for human conduct (Bernard, 1924).

All this classification did little to explain human behavior. In the first place, the concept of instinct was used in a way that was tautological—the explanation was true by definition. The instinct that was "discovered" was merely another name for what was to be explained. The comment that humans had an "aggressive instinct" was just another way of saying that they engage in warfare, in the same way that "high temperature" is another way of saying "hot weather." An aggressive instinct can no more explain warfare than a high temperature can explain hot weather.

The use of instincts to explain behavior had other weaknesses as well. The *same* instinct was used to explain contrary actions. The so-called acquisitive instinct, for example, was used to explain both hard, honest work and bank robbery. Instincts, moreover, are supposed to be in all humans, but human behavior around the world varies greatly. Such supposedly instinctive behavior as aggression, for example, does not appear among the Arapesh of New Guinea. Finally, if humans have an instinct for self-preservation, how do we explain suicide? Many human actions run contrary to our supposed instincts.

As the twentieth century began, the concept of instinct started to lose its popularity. The opposing idea that human behavior is determined by learning or environmental factors began to gain favor. The Russian physiologist Ivan Pavlov had shown that he could teach a dog to salivate at the sound of a bell *only* by repeatedly presenting food along with the sound of the bell. In the 1920s American psychologist John Watson extended Pavlov's experiments with dogs to human infants. In one experiment Watson managed to make a little boy named Albert afraid of a white rabbit that had previously delighted him. He did this by using a nasty trick—frightening poor Albert with a sudden loud noise while the boy was playing with the rabbit.

Watson went on to produce rage in children by hampering their bodily movements. He also produced "love" by patting and stroking their skin. He concluded that all emotions and behaviors are learned through such associations and that environment, not heredity, makes us what we are. He declared:

> Give me a dozen healthy infants, well-formed, and my own specified world to bring them up in, and I'll guarantee to take any one at random and train him to become any type of specialist I might select—a doctor, lawyer, artist, merchant-chief . . . regardless of his tendencies, abilities, vocations, and race of his ancestors (Watson, 1924).

In effect, Watson argued that learning *by itself* determines human personality. Most social scientists today reject this extreme environmental determinism, just as the extreme biological determinism of those who saw instinct as the sole factor has been rejected. While not denying the influence of biological factors, social scientists now consider nurture to be more important than heredity. In recent years, however, the role of heredity has captured increased attention, largely from a group of scientists called sociobiologists.

Edward O. Wilson (1980, 1984), a prominent sociobiologist, defines sociobiology as "the systematic study of the biological basis of all social behavior." According to sociobiologists, human behavior must be explained in the same terms used to explain animal behavior. While they admit that the environment influences our behavior, they emphasize the importance of genetic factors. As sociobiologists Steven Gaulin and Alice Schlegel (1980) state, "The essence of sociobiological theory is that individuals act as if attempting to maximize the representation of their genes in future generations." In other words, virtually all human actions result from our genes trying to protect themselves, to ensure their survival. Thus, when sociobiologists find that natural parents are far less likely than stepparents to commit child abuse, they attribute the difference to "genetic selfishness": natural parents are nice because the children share their genes and stepparents are nasty because the victims do not have their genes. This is similar, in the sociobiological eye, to crows and gulls lovingly brooding and feeding their own chicks but often eating up others' unrelated chicks (Rubenstein, 1980). However, sociobiologists also use the concept of gene selfishness to exlain human compassion for strangers. In rescuing a stranger in trouble, we are said to be genetically motivated because such behavior helps ensure that someday others will do the same favor for us, thereby enhancing the chances of our genes' survival.

As "evidence" for this view, sociobiologists observe that these behaviors can be found not only among all humans but among animals as well. Sociological critics, however, argue that this view overstates the universality of human behavior patterns and ignores the consciousness and culture that set humans apart from animals. They contend that sociobiology is mostly speculation, with little direct evidence to support it. Other scientists agree (Lewontin, Rose, and Kamin, 1984; Kitcher, 1985).

The Significance of Heredity

Obviously, we do inherit something of what makes us who we are. But what? Race and sex are inherited, but their effect on human behavior and personality depends to a great extent on what society makes of them. (We discuss these effects in Chapter 10: Racial and Ethnic Minorities and Chapter 11: Gender Roles and Inequalities.) One important component of our inherited

Obviously we inherit much of our physical makeup. We inherit our physiques; our facial features; our eye, hair, and skin color—all those things that make us resemble our parents and the other members of our immediate families. But there is much dispute over whether we inherit the other personal characteristics that enable us to define ourselves as individuals—such as intelligence, aptitude, and personality. Sociologists maintain that although nature sets limits on what we *can* achieve, socialization plays a very large role in determining what we *do* achieve. Whatever potential is inherited may be developed or stunted through socialization.

makeup is the near absence of instinct within us. As suggested earlier, instincts are biologically inherited capabilities of performing relatively complex tasks. Animals have instincts, which makes it unnecessary for them to learn how to live their lives. Instincts enable birds, for example, to catch worms, find mates, build nests, and raise their young. But humans, largely devoid of instincts, must be socialized to perform similarly complex tasks to survive.

People do appear to inherit temperament—an inclination to react in a certain way. Some people are inclined to be active, nervous, or irritable; others tend to be passive, calm, or placid. Psychologists have found that even infants show consistent temperaments. Some are active most of the time, while others move rather little. Some cry and fuss a lot, and others rarely do. Some react intensely to things like wet diapers, while others have only mild reactions. These differences may influence personality development. Very active infants, for example, are more likely than passive ones to become aggressive and competitive adults.

The role of heredity in determining intelligence and aptitude is more controversial. **Intelligence** is the capacity for mental achievement, such as the ability to think logically and to solve problems. **Aptitude** is the capacity for developing physical or social skills, such as athletic prowess. The extent to which intelligence in particular is inherited has been the subject of some of the most bitter, emotional debates in all of social science. The debate is far from settled. For our purposes here, however, what is significant is that although nature sets limits on what we may achieve, socialization plays a very large role in determining what we do achieve. Whatever potential is inherited may be developed or stunted through socialization.

The Significance of Socialization

It is the lack of instincts that makes socialization both necessary and possible for human beings. As we saw in Chapter 3 (Culture), whatever temperament and potential abilities they are born with, human infants are also born helpless, dependent on others for survival. What may be more surprising, however, is the extent to which traits that seem very basic and essential to "human nature" also appear to depend on socialization. Evidence of the far-reaching significance of socialization comes both from case studies of children deprived of socialization and from instances in which children have been given very special, intensive training.

The Results of Deprivation Since the fourteenth century there have been more than 50 recorded cases of "feral children"—children supposedly raised by animals (Malson, 1972). One of the most famous is "the wild boy of Aveyron." In 1797 he was captured in the woods by hunters in southern France. He was about eleven years old and completely naked. The "wild boy" ran on all fours, had no speech, preferred uncooked food, and could not do most of the simple things done by younger children. A group of experts pronounced him hopelessly retarded. But Jean Itard, a physician, disagreed. He set out to train the boy, whom he later called Victor. After three months Victor seemed a little more human. He wore clothing. He got up at night to urinate in the toilet. He learned to sit at a table and eat with utensils. He started to show human emotions such as joy, gratitude, and remorse. But although he lived to be more than 40 years old, he neither learned to speak nor ever became a normal person (Lane, 1976).

A young girl found in a wolf den suffered a similar fate. Kamala was eight years old when she was discovered in 1921 in India. She snarled and tried to bite her captors, wore no clothes, walked on all fours, ate raw meat, and picked up food with her mouth. Eventually she learned to like other people, eat cooked food, and understand simple language. But she never progressed to the normal level for her age (Singh and Zingg, 1942).

There is some doubt that Victor and Kamala were raised by animals. They were probably old enough to scavenge for food themselves when they were abandoned. Nevertheless, they were certainly deprived of normal socialization, and they bore the marks of this loss throughout their lives. Less extreme cases also illustrate the significance of socialization. In the United States there have been three well-known instances of such deprivation. They involved three children—Anna, Isabella, and Genie—who were kept secluded in their homes with their mothers.

Anna was born in Pennsylvania as an illegitimate child, a fact that outraged her mother's father. After trying unsuccessfully to give Anna away, the mother hid her in the attic. Anna was fed just enough to keep her alive, was neither touched nor talked to, neither washed nor bathed. She simply lay still in her own filth. When she was found in 1938 at the age of six, Anna looked like a skeleton. She could not talk or walk. She did nothing but lie quietly on the floor, her eyes vacant and her face expressionless. Efforts to socialize her were not very successful. Eventually she could do simple things such as walk, feed herself, brush her teeth, and follow simple directions. But she never learned to speak and was far from normal. She died at the age of eleven (Davis, 1947).

Isabella's story is a far happier one. Like Anna, she was an illegitimate child who was six years old when she was found in Ohio in 1938. Her grandfather had kept her and her deaf-mute mother secluded in a dark room. Isabella was more fortunate than Anna because she could interact with her mother. When she was discovered, Isabella showed great fear and hostility toward people and made a strange croaking sound. Specialists who examined her thought she was feebleminded and uneducable. Nevertheless, she was put on a systematic and skillful program of training. After a slow start she began to talk. In only nine months she could read and write, and within two years she was attending school. She had become a very bright, cheerful, and energetic girl. Apparently the intensive training by the specialists, coupled with the earlier interaction with her mother, made it possible for Isabella to develop into a normal person (Davis, 1947).

Intensive training, however, did not work out for Genie, who was found in California in 1970, primarily because she had been deprived of normal socialization for twelve years—twice as long as Isabella. From about one to thirteen years of age, Genie had been isolated in a small quiet room. During the day she was tied to her potty seat, able only to flutter her hands and feet. At night, if she was not forgotten, her father would straitjacket and cage her in a crib with an overhead cover. He would beat her if she made any noise. He never spoke to her except to occasionally bark or growl like a dog at her. Her terrified mother, forbidden to speak to Genie, fed her in silence and haste. When she was discovered, at age 13, she could not stand straight, was unable to speak (except whimper), and had the intelligence and social maturity of a 1-year-old. For the next eight years psycholinguists, speech therapists, and special education teachers worked with her, but at the end, when she was 21, her language abilities could go no further than the 4-year-old level. She was finally placed in an institution (Pines, 1981).

These five cases are, to say the least, unusual. But even less severe forms of deprivation can be harmful. In 1945 psychologist René Spitz reported that children who received little attention in institutions suffered very noticeable effects. In one orphanage Spitz found that infants who were about 18 months old were left lying on their backs in small cubicles most of the day without any human contact. Within a year all had become physically, mentally, emotionally, and socially retarded. Two years later more than a third of the children had died. Those who survived could neither speak, walk, dress themselves, nor use a spoon (Spitz, 1945).

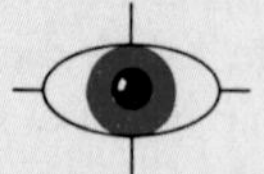

USING SOCIOLOGICAL INSIGHT

The Enigmatic Smile

The smile plays a crucial role in both parent-child bonding and communicating emotion. This reading reviews possible origins of the human smile. How does the author show the links between heredity, environment, and human behavior?

Red deer stags signal their interest in females by prancing about with adolescent exuberance. Greylag geese challenge rivals by extending their necks and then duel until one cries "uncle" by lowering its head to the ground. The three-spined stickleback, a small scaleless fish, woos its consort with a zigzag dance and, having won her interest, swims toward his nest on the chance that she will follow. To ethologists, these are examples of "fixed action patterns"—preset sequences of muscle activity often triggered by specific cues in the environment. They serve the function of "social display," acts of communication that have evolved by virtue of their contribution to survival and reproduction and are apparently under marked genetic control. By contrast, most behavior involved in human social rituals appears to be less a matter of genetic than of cultural inheritance. The handshake is not practiced everywhere. The curtsy came and went. And not even the most strident sociobiologist would argue that applause results from some genetic predisposition to clap the hands together.

What about the smile? The subtlest play of the zygomaticus major—one of the facial muscles that govern the smile—can spell the difference between the passing indifference of strangers and the flowering of lifelong romance, the difference between peaceful coexistence and deadly violence. In an evolutionary sense, the most important things can easily hinge on a smile.

It is difficult to believe that natural selection could have left so important a signal to the vagaries of individual learning. And, as far as we can tell, it did not. If there is one human social display that qualifies as a fixed action pattern, it is the tendency of people in certain well-defined situations to draw back the corners of their mouths and expose their teeth. Smiling, it appears, is something we are born to do.

The evidence for this assertion is diverse. First, there is the sheer universality of the smile. Film studies in remote areas of the world . . . have shown smiling to be a consistent feature of greeting, often in combination with raising of the eyebrows. In France, Bali and Samoa, among the !Kung of the Kalahari and the Waika of South

Since Spitz's pioneering work, many other psychologists have documented the damage done to children who are placed in institutions in which they receive little human contact, attention, or stimulation (Provence and Lipton, 1962). Normal human development seems to require, at the least, that infants have some continuing interaction, some bond of attachment, with another person.

Creating Geniuses The positive effects of specialized socialization are also instructive. According to Thomas Hoult (1974), a young woman named Edith finished grammar school in four years, skipped high school, and went straight to college. She graduated from college at the age of 15 and obtained her doctorate before she was 18. Was she born a genius? Not at all. Ever since she had stopped playing with dolls, her father had seen to it that her days were filled with reading, mathematics, classical music, intellectual discussions and debates, and whatever learning her father could derive from the world's literature. When she felt like playing, her father told her to play chess with someone like himself, who would be a challenge to her.

Like Edith, many geniuses have been deliberately subjected to a very stimulating environment. A well-known example is Norbert Wiener, a prime mover in the development of computers and cybernetics. He entered college at age 11 and received his Ph.D. from Harvard at 18. According to his father, he was "essentially an average boy who had had the advantage of superlative training" (Wiener, 1953). Many musical prodigies of the past, including Mozart and Beethoven, were subjected to rigorous daily training by their parents. Since 1945 a large number of ordinary children have been brought to the famous Japanese music teacher Shinichi Suzuki, and he has successfully "trained every one of

America, this complex sequence of muscular activity runs like clockwork whenever people who enjoy each other come face to face.

Also pointing to a genetic basis of the smile are findings in psychology, zoology and neurology. The smile appears with uncanny regularity in human infants. Even blind and deaf-and-blind children begin social smiling roughly on schedule, by about 3 months of age. Further, we see apparent precursors of the smile in the primates that are our nearest living relatives—a silent, bared-teeth grin in monkeys and a more recognizable "smile" in chimpanzees.

Whatever the brain mechanisms that control the spontaneous smile, they are in place early in life. Unless a 3-month-old has indigestion, or is otherwise indisposed, any halfway intelligent adult prepared to stoop to the child's level can easily elicit a smile. It is as if the infant's brain has matured to the point at which a semireflexive smile has clicked into use—but without any cultural context, social discrimination, hesitancy or ambiguity. The smile is automatic, almost like flinching from pain.

But experience soon begins to play a role. Initially, the visual pattern that will evoke a smile from a 4-month-old is very simple: an oval shape with two dark dots placed where eyes would be if the oval were a face. (An oval with the dots in the wrong place does not work so well.) But during the course of several months, the infant becomes more discerning: The pattern has to be more similar to a real human face to earn a smile. It's as if there were some hard wiring designed to set the infant on a path, after which guidance is left to experience.

Experience will do more than direct the smile; it will also determine its frequency. Experiments have shown that infants who receive no social stimulation after smiling, such as an adult's approving gaze, will begin smiling less often. And infants raised in environments with inadequate social stimulation, such as foundling homes, will smile much less at 8 months or a year than will infants raised in middle-class homes. Nonetheless, the appearance of a reliable social smile by about 3 months of age is affected very little by learning. Maturation initiates, after which experience can differentiate.

Source: Excerpted from Melvin Konner, "The Enigmatic Smile," *Psychology Today*, March 1987, pp. 42–46.

them—*without exception*—to be an excellent string musician" (Hoult, 1979).

Nature may draw the outline of our traits and potential abilities, but that outline is broad and vague. Nurture appears both to determine the actual boundaries and to fill in the details (Nisbet, 1982; Featherman and Lerner, 1985). Consider ace test pilot Chuck Yeager. He may have been born fearless. But if his parents had been overprotective and kept him from jumping off barns, he might never have grown up to be the first flier to break the sound barrier (Wellborn, 1987). Obviously, both heredity and environment are involved in the development of personality. Even something that appears to be an inherited trait, like smiling, also has a social origin (see box above). Which has a greater influence? Sociologists would say environment, and sociobiologists would say heredity. The latest report from the Minnesota Center for Twin and Adoption Research suggests that both factors are about equally influential. The Minnesota researchers gave a battery of personality tests to 248 pairs of twins, including 44 pairs of identical twins who had been brought up in different homes. If twins were found to have the same personality traits, heredity was considered a key factor in personality development. But if twins were found to have different traits, socialization was assumed to have played a larger role. The result showed that the subjects owe about half of their personality to nature and the other half to nurture (Leo, 1987).

QUESTIONS FOR DISCUSSION AND REVIEW

1. What parallels do sociologists recognize in the genetic makeup of animals and humans?
2. How does the contribution of socialization to human personality differ from the contribution of heredity?
3. What do deprived and stimulating environments have in common?

THEORIES OF PERSONALITY DEVELOPMENT

Socialization shapes the development of personality through the influence of biology and environment. How these forces interact to mold personality is a complicated question. There have been many theories. Some emphasize the effect of the environment on personality development, others focus on the significance of inherited factors, and yet others stress the interaction of nature and nurture. Here, we review just a few of the most influential theories.

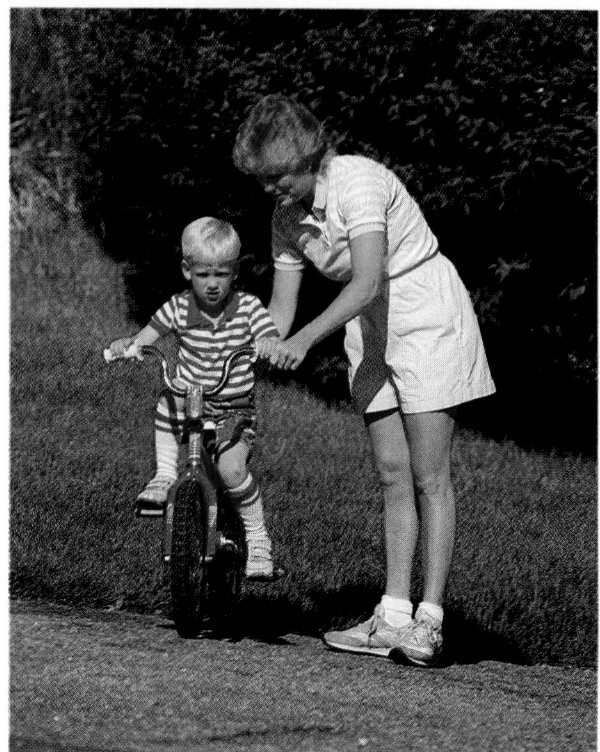

How much of a role does the parent's attitude toward the child play in shaping the child's personality? Some parents encourage children to develop independence; others protect their children so much that they remain dependent. Will this boy grow up with a greater sense of self-confidence because of early exposure to situations in which he must function on his own? The answer is probably yes, according to the behaviorist theory.

Behaviorism

The experiments of Pavlov and Watson convinced many psychologists that behaviors are shaped by the environment. They inspired an approach that dominated American psychology for decades. Because Watson urged psychologists to focus on outer, observable behavior, he called his theory **behaviorism.**

The heart of behaviorism is **conditioning,** the process by which associations are formed between stimuli (from the environment) and responses (from the individual). There are two types of conditioning, classical and operant. In **classical conditioning** a previously neutral stimulus is paired with a stimulus that already evokes a certain response, so that eventually the previously neutral stimulus comes by itself to elicit that response. As Pavlov demonstrated, food naturally elicits a response from a dog—salivation. When he paired a neutral stimulus—a bell—with the presentation of food, the dog eventually salivated in response to the bell alone. Hence the dog was conditioned. In Watson's experiment the sudden loud noise naturally provoked fear from little Albert. When this stimulus was paired with a white rat, which the boy previously did not fear, he eventually became afraid of the animal itself. In the second type of conditioning, **operant conditioning,** a positive reinforcer (reward) or negative reinforcer (punishment) is used to cause the subject to behave in a certain way. Psychologists have employed operant conditioning to train rats, pigeons, and chimps to perform difficult tasks. They reward the animals with food whenever they make a correct response and punish them with an electric shock whenever they make a wrong response.

When applied to socialization, the behaviorist theory suggests that the development of certain personalities depends on classical and operant conditioning. At birth the infant neither loves nor hates its parents; it is emotionally neutral. Only after the parents repeatedly provide it with food, warmth, and alleviation of pain does the infant learn to associate its parents with those pleasurable stimuli. Eventually the child will respond cheerfully to its parents even when the latter do not bring any food, just as Pavlov's dogs salivated at the sound of a bell without the presence of food. Such a child might grow up to have a pleasant and normal personality. On the other hand, some parents are anxious and tense. They handle their infant roughly, stopping the feeding before the infant is full or letting it cry for a long time before feeding it. This kind of parental behavior is a painful stimulus to infants, comparable to the frightening noise that Watson administered to Albert. As a consequence, the parents may arouse unpleasant feelings in the child in the same way as the white rabbit evoked fear in Albert. Such a child might grow up to be unhappy.

Operant conditioning also takes place in the way parents deal with their child. Some parents are permissive and easygoing. They encourage their child to explore and investigate freely. Such a child is likely to develop self-confidence, independence, and a desire to be competent in whatever he or she does. Some other parents, on the other hand, are overprotective, severely restricting their child's freedom of movement and discouraging their child's exploration. Such a child will likely become submissive, shy, and withdrawn.

Behaviorism has given rise to some variations on its ideas. One of these variations was developed by Albert Bandura (1977). To him, it seemed unlikely that human behavior or personality is built up bit by bit by the simple associations suggested by pure behaviorism. It is improbable that "an individual learning to speak would have to be reinforced for every sound that he uttered," or that "a child learning the game of baseball would require separate reinforcement for every movement, swing of the bat, or stop" (Gardner, 1978). Bandura thereby proposed the social learning theory. The environment and reinforcements are still keys to behavior in this theory. But individuals do not learn behaviors response by response. Instead, they may observe a whole sequence or pattern of responses and imitate that pattern. If they find the imitation rewarding, then they will adopt it as their own.

Cultural Determinism

Like behaviorism, **cultural determinism** was explicitly drawn from the environmental perspective. While conceding the influence of biological heritage on personality development, cultural determinists, most of whom are anthropologists, consider cultural factors to be of overriding importance. To support such a view, the late anthropologist Clyde Kluckhohn (1949) told the following story:

> Some years ago I met in New York City a young man who did not speak a word of English and was obviously bewildered by American ways. By "blood" he was as American as you or I, for his parents had gone from Indiana to China as missionaries. Orphaned in infancy, he was reared by a Chinese family in a remote village. All who met him found him more Chinese than American. The facts of his blue eyes and light hair were less impressive than a Chinese style of gait, Chinese arm and hand movements, Chinese facial expression, and Chinese modes of thought.

Cultural determinists hold that culture largely defines what characteristics are rewarded and acquired by

In addition to inheritance and direct parental influence, culture plays a powerful role in shaping our behavior. This is most clear when we compare ourselves to people raised in a radically different environment. An American family would not engage in the formal ritual of bowing that a Japanese family finds conventional. As cultural determinists would suggest, the individuals, whether American or Japanese, are a microcosm of their culture.

members of a society. American culture, for example, puts a high premium on competition, while the Hopi culture values cooperation highly. One consequence is that Americans are more likely to leap with glee and shout "whoopee" when they defeat a competitor. The Hopi might well be reluctant to embarrass others by trying to beat them in the first place. Individual variations exist, and culture does not completely determine the personality of each individual. But in a sense, according to cultural determinists, personality represents an internalized culture. To see how the individual takes on that culture, however, we need to look to other theories.

Freud: Psychosexual Development

Sigmund Freud (1856–1939) believed that biology lays out a certain course of human development and that each child everywhere goes through particular stages. Freud concentrated on emotional development. He saw human beings as compelled by very strong biological drives and constrained by social forces. In his view, the individual personality becomes a battleground for these conflicting demands.

According to Freud, personality is made up of the id, the ego, and the superego. The **id** consists of the desires all humans are born with, which Freud saw as essentially sexual desire. The id is governed by the "pleasure principle." It seeks self-gratification however it can get it, with no regard for reason, logic, or morality. The **ego,** on the other hand, operates in accordance with the "reality principle." It is rational and logical, able to deal with the environment realistically. It therefore sets limits on how far the id can go in gratifying its impulses. The **superego** also seeks to restrain the id, but for moral reasons. It is much the same as what is traditionally called conscience.

In Freud's view an individual's personality depends on how the id gets along in the early stages of a person's life. Are the id's desires blocked out, shunted off into fantasies? Are they denied because of strict moral demands? Or does the ego develop realistic ways of fulfilling many of the id's demands? In a sense, terms for getting along are worked out among the id, the ego, and the superego during childhood through a series of five stages (see Table 6.1).

A crucial step occurs during the third, phallic stage, which begins at about the end of the third year and ends at about the sixth. It is during these years that the notorious **Oedipus complex** develops. Freud used the ancient Greek tale about Oedipus as a metaphor for what goes on in this particular stage of our life. Oedipus was raised as an adopted son who grew up to be a warrior and hero. Not knowing who his real parents were, he killed his father, the king, in a fight and married the queen, his mother. In Freud's view this situation is repeated in every boy's life. The boy is motivated by his id to feel sexual love for his mother and to be jealous of his father and hostile toward him. But he also fears his father's power. As a result, he *represses*—forces aside—both his desire for his mother and hostility toward his father. At the same time, he *identifies* with his father by imitating him and trying to become like him. Little girls go through what Freud called the **Electra complex,** which parallels the Oedipus complex of boys. Girls desire their fathers sexually and are hostile to their mothers. Eventually the girl learns that she must repress her sexual desire for her father, and she begins to identify with her mother. By these identifications, children take on the moral views expressed by their parents. This identification is the basis of the superego. Because the parents' views reflect those of society, the child's superego also reflects the ideals and prohibitions of society.

Freud assumed that the Oedipus complex was a universal phenomenon. But anthropologist Bronislaw Malinowski long ago found that it does not exist among boys on the Trobriand islands in the Pacific. Instead of resenting his father, the Trobriand boy dislikes his maternal uncle, who is required by local custom to discipline the child. This suggests that the key to hostility toward the father in Western society lies not in sexual rivalry, as Freud believed, but in the father's position of authority over the boy. Findings such as Malinowski's led many social scientists to believe that Freud overemphasized the importance of sexuality in personality development. Today followers of Freud tend to give more weight to social and cultural influences on personality.

Piaget: Cognitive Development

Freud dealt with the motivational and emotional aspects of personality—sexual drives and the feelings derived from them. On the other hand, Swiss psychologist Jean Piaget (1896–1980) focused on the cognitive or intellectual part of personality. He argued that there is an inherent structure to the human mind that determines what can be learned and when. Every human

Table 6.1 Freud's Stages of Development

Stage	Characteristics	Effect of Conflict or Frustrations
Oral stage Birth to about one year old	The infant is at the mercy of the id, because the ego and superego have not emerged, and seeks pleasure through oral activities such as sucking.	If the infant's drive for oral pleasure is overindulged or frustrated, as an adult he or she may be excessively interested in oral pleasures, such as eating, drinking, smoking, or oral sex.
Anal stage From about one to three years old	The ego emerges and becomes more influential as the child begins to control its environment through walking, talking, and so on. The growth of the ego is aided by toilet training, through which the child learns self-control and self-dependence. Exercise of the anal muscles is the primary source of pleasure.	If toilet training is overly strict, when the child grows up he or she may be either extremely messy and wasteful or overly concerned with order, cleanliness, and possessions.
Phallic stage From about three to six years old	The child feels sexual love for the opposite-sex parent, learns that this desire must be suppressed, and identifies with the same-sex parent. Through identification the child internalizes the parent's ideals and restrictions, and thus the superego develops.	Failure to develop an adequate superego is one possible outcome; anxiety or confusion about masculinity or femininity may also result.
Latency period From about six to ten years old	The id quiets down, the superego becomes stronger, and the child cultivates relationships with people outside his or her family.	The adult may be withdrawn or extremely individualistic if he or she has had many problems in this stage.
Genital stage Adolescence	The habits of cleanliness, modesty, and sympathy give way to pleasure in disorder, exhibitionism, and aggressiveness, but gradually the adolescent learns to cope with these problems. Gratification becomes centered in the genital area and associated with reproduction.	Frustrations may cause difficulties in getting along with the opposite sex, in marriage, or in parenting.

being, in Piaget's view, goes through certain stages of cognitive development.

1. *Sensorimotor stage (birth to age 2)*: The infant lacks language, cannot think, and cannot make sense of its environment. It also lacks a sense of self and is unable to see itself as the cause of the events in its surroundings. If it shakes a rattle, it does not realize that it causes the rattle to make a sound but acts as if the rattle made the sound by itself. Unlike other people, who interact with the world by using their brains, the infant uses its senses and bodily movements to interact with the environment. The infant, for example, uses its hands to touch, move, or pick up objects, and puts things in the mouth or sucks at some objects. This is why Piaget called this stage *sensorimotor.*

In using its sensorimotor capabilities, the infant does not realize that an object, a human, or a cat has a relatively permanent existence. So in the child's view the mother exists only when she can be seen or touched, but she no longer does when she leaves the child's field of vision.

2. *Preoperational stage (ages 2 to 7)*: The term *preoperational* suggests that the child cannot perform many simple intellectual operations. Suppose we take a boy, two to four years old, for a walk in a park; he may say "dog" every time he comes across one. If we ask him whether he sees the same dog or a succession of different dogs, he might get confused because he cannot distinguish "this particular dog" from dogs as a general category. Suppose we show slightly older children two glasses of the same size containing the same volume of water; they will correctly say that both glasses hold the same amount of water. But if we pour all the water from one of the glasses into a third glass that is taller and thinner, they will incorrectly conclude that the third glass holds more water than the other glass because its water level is higher.

These children are "precausal," unable to understand cause and effect. When Piaget asked 4-year-olds what makes a bicycle move, they replied that the street makes it go. When he asked 6-year-olds why the sun and moon move, the youngsters said that the heavenly bod-

Jean Piaget, the Swiss psychologist, described four stages of cognitive development that each child goes through. At the second, preoperational stage (ages 2–7), children have difficulty grasping the relation between shape and volume. This boy thinks that the tall container has more water than the short one, although he has seen that the water in the tall container has come from a third container of the same size as the short one.

ies follow us in order to see us. These children are also animistic. They attribute humanlike thoughts and wishes to the sun and moon. They even attribute life to such inanimate objects as tables, chairs, and toys, which they believe can feel pain if we hit them. Moreover, they are egocentric, seeing things from their own perspective only. If we ask a young boy how many brothers he has, he may correctly say "One." But if we ask him "How many brothers does your brother have?" he would say "None." He has difficulty seeing himself from his brother's perspective.

3. *Concrete operational stage (ages 7 to 12):* In this stage children can perform all the simple intellectual tasks described above. By 7 or 8 years of age, children are able, for example, to recognize that a given amount of water remains the same regardless of the shape of the glass that holds it. But their mental abilities are restricted to intellectual operations that involve manipulation of concrete objects only. If children of ages between eight and ten are asked to line up a series of dolls from the tallest to the shortest, they can easily do so. But they cannot solve a similar problem put verbally—in abstract terms—such as "John is taller than Bill; Bill is taller than Harry; who is the tallest of the three?" The children can correctly answer this question only if they actually see John, Bill, and Harry in person.

4. *Formal operational stage (ages 12 to 15):* In this stage adolescents can perform "formal operations"; they are capable of thinking and reasoning formally (abstractly). They can follow the form of an argument while ignoring its concrete content. They know, for example, that if A is greater than B and B is greater than C, then A is greater than C—without having to know in advance whether the concrete contents of A, B, and C are vegetables, fruits, animals, or whatever can be seen and manipulated. Not everyone has the capability to progress into this stage of formal operations. In fact, it has been estimated that about half of the American population cannot understand abstract concepts well enough to be regarded as having passed into this stage. We should not, however, equate different stages of cognitive development with different levels of intelligence. In Piaget's view the young child is "neither 'dumber' nor just a few steps behind the older one; rather he thinks about things in a wholly different way" (Gardner, 1972).

Some psychologists have criticized Piaget for underestimating the importance of learning for cognitive development. "If children are *taught* to think" in terms of Piaget's final stage, said one critic, "they can do so" (Watson, 1965). In fact, a new crop of psychological researchers today have tried all kinds of ingenious methods to test children's mental ability and discovered that, contrary to Piaget's belief, most children younger than seven do understand causality (Pines, 1983; Chance and Fischman, 1987). Sociologists have also criticized Piaget for ignoring social factors in cognitive development. The type of family and education that children have does affect their intellectual performance (Simpson, 1980). Studies by Hess and his associates (1968, 1970) suggest that lower-class children are less likely than their middle-class peers to think in causal terms—because their mothers are more "authoritarian" (ordering them around) than "informational" (explaining why they should not do a certain thing). Judith Blake (1981) also finds that in the United States and Europe children from large families are less capable of intellectual performance than those from smaller families—because the intellectual stimulation by parents is spread thinner for each child in the larger families. All these criticisms, however, are valid only because they deal with the rate, amount, or speed of mental development. The rate does vary from one individual or group to another. But the order or sequence of mental development, as laid out by Piaget, does not. Among 10-year-olds, for example, some can think abstractly, like 13-year-olds, while others cannot. But whether or not he or she is able to think like older children, a 10-year-old typically thinks concretely before—not after—learning to think abstractly (Oakes, 1985).

Kohlberg: Moral Development

Picking up Piaget's assumption that the child's mind develops in fixed stages largely on its own, American psychologist Lawrence Kohlberg (1963, 1969, 1981) has argued that children also acquire moral values in the same way. He assumes that children's sense of right and wrong evolves from within themselves rather than from society's attempts to stamp its moral values on their minds.

According to Kohlberg, children go through three levels of moral development. He got this idea from the ways youngsters of different ages deal with moral dilemmas. In his research he presented children with a hypothetical situation, such as the following:

> A woman was dying from cancer. Only one drug might save her. The druggist who had discovered it was charging $2000 for a small dose, ten times what the drug had cost him to make. The dying woman's husband went to everyone he knew to borrow the money, but he could raise only $1000. He begged the druggist to give him credit for the rest or else sell the medicine cheaper. The druggist refused. The husband got desperate and broke into the man's store to steal the drug. Should he have done that?

Some children answered yes; others no. But Kohlberg was more interested in asking further the crucial question *why* they thought so. He found three distinct patterns of response, each reflecting a certain level of moral development.

At the first level, most of the children under age 10 have a *preconventional* morality. They cannot see any moral dilemma in the story—saving the wife versus obeying the law. Some see only the importance of saving the wife, as suggested by this typical response from one of Kohlberg's subjects: "His wife was sick and if she didn't get the drug quickly, she might die." Other children see only the importance of obeying the law: "You shouldn't steal the drug because you'll be caught and sent to jail if you do." None of the children at this level of moral development appreciate the dilemma of both saving the wife and breaking the law or both obeying the law and letting the wife die. The children also define right and wrong according to the *consequence* of the action—on the basis of whether it results in reward or punishment. Stealing the drug is considered right because it can save the wife (reward), or wrong because the individual can be arrested (punishment). Kohlberg calls this kind of thinking *preconventional* or *premoral,* because it is not the way most people define morality.

At the second level, children between 10 and 16 have a *conventional* morality. These youngsters, like the children at the first level, deny the existence of the conflict between the two norms. But they differ in perception of what constitutes right and wrong. While younger children assess an act by its consequences, older ones judge it according to its underlying *motives.* An action is considered right if the motive is good and wrong if the motive is bad. Here is a typical response to the drug-stealing story: "He should steal the drug. He was only doing something that was natural for a good husband to do. You can't blame him for doing something out of love for his wife. You'd blame him if he didn't love his wife enough to save her." Stealing the drug was not judged bad because it was an expression of a nice, altruistic motive.

At the third level, young adults have a *postconventional* morality. They can appreciate the conflict between norms in a moral dilemma and try to make a rational decision that takes into account the importance of *both* norms. In supporting the stealing of the drug, one of Kohlberg's subjects also kept in mind the wrongness of stealing: "The law wasn't set up for these circumstances. *Taking the drug in this situation isn't really right,* but he was justified to do it." Another subject, in opposing the theft, was nevertheless sympathetic to the thief: "*You can't completely blame someone for stealing* but extreme circumstances don't really justify taking the law in your own hands. You can't have everyone stealing whenever they get desperate. The end may be good, but the ends don't justify the means." From these responses we can further detect the postconventional definition of morality: we are doing right if we accept a general principle that is for the good of all even though it may hurt our own interest.

Kohlberg has drawn fire for presenting a biased, male view about moral development, as it has been derived from research on males only. According to Carol Gilligan (1982), Kohlberg focuses on men's interest in the ethics of justice, which is impersonal in nature, and neglects women's lifelong concern with relationships, which are personal. In Gilligan's view, there is a different course for females' moral development. It involves progressing from an interest in one's own survival to a concern for others. Thus women are said to have achieved a great deal of moral maturity if they have developed a compassionate concern for others. But if Kohlberg's view is applied to those women, they will be regarded as morally deficient, because they lack the cold-blooded impartiality that "morally mature" men are supposed to have for judging what is right or wrong. Recent research suggests, though, that the gender difference in moral reasoning is not as great as Gilligan assumes. The fact is that an increasing number of men are just as intrested as women are in such personal matters as love, caring, and relationships, while a growing number of women are just as attuned as men are to the impersonal issues of justice, rights, and fairness (Walker, 1984, 1986; Ford and Lowery, 1986). Other critics have questioned Kohlberg's assumption that his theory is applicable to all cultures. They point out that while the development from preconventionality to conventionality may be universal, the postconventional morality may be more characteristic of future-oriented, liberal, and technologically advanced societies (Loevinger and Knoll, 1983; Snarey, 1987).

Symbolic Interactionism

The developmental theories of Freud, Piaget, and Kohlberg essentially deal with conflict. By contrast, symbolic interactionism emphasizes harmony. Freud pitted the individual against society, concentrating on how the individual seeks sexual gratification against the opposition of society. Piaget set the individual in opposition to the environment, focusing on how the individual strives to manipulate and control the environment. Kohlberg presented the individual with a moral conflict—a conflict between one's own interest and the society's general welfare. On the other hand, symbolic interactionists emphasize the harmonious relationship between the individual and society as the foundation of personality development.

Cooley: The Looking-Glass Process Charles Horton Cooley (1864-1929) was one of the founders of symbolic interactionism. He viewed society as a group of individuals helping each other to develop their personalities. According to Cooley, the core of personality is the concept of oneself, the self-image. And self-image, Cooley said, is developed through the "looking-glass process":

> Each to each a looking glass.
> Reflects the other that doth pass.

We get our self-image from the way others treat us. Their treatment is like a mirror reflecting our personal qualities and Cooley referred to that treatment as our **looking-glass self.** If we have a positive image, seeing ourselves as intelligent or respectable, it is because others have treated us as such. Just as we cannot see our own face unless we have a mirror in front of us, so we cannot have a certain self-image unless others react to our behavior.

The looking-glass process, however, works both ways. While others are judging us, we are judging them in return. The way we judge others affects how we interpret their impressions of us. Suppose certain individuals see us as stupid; we will reject such a view if we consider them stupid in the first place. In fact, as over 50 studies have consistently suggested, we tend to discredit others' negative views of us or to perceive ourselves more favorably than others see us (Shrauger and Schoeneman, 1979).

No matter what kind of self-concept emerges from the looking-glass process, it has a certain impact on our personality and behavior. If we have a favorable self-concept, we tend to be self-confident, outgoing, or happy. If we have a poor self-image, we are inclined to be timid, withdrawn, or unhappy. Research has also shown that low self-esteem has such undesirable outcomes as delinquent behavior and lower academic achievements, and that high self-esteem leads to such favorable consequences as better behavior and greater creativity (Gecas, 1982).

Mead: The Role-taking Process The other founder of symbolic interactionism was George Herbert Mead

(1863–1931). Like Cooley, Mead assumed that the development of a self-concept is made possible by symbolic interaction—by interaction with others through symbols like language and gestures. But while Cooley stressed the importance of using others as our mirrors by observing their reactions to our behavior, Mead emphasized the significance of getting "under the skin" of others by taking their roles.

In their early years, children take the roles of their parents, whom Mead called **significant others,** by pretending to be their mothers and fathers while they play. In this world of make-believe, they learn to see themselves from their parents' perspectives. In the process, they *internalize* their parents' values and attitudes, incorporating them into their own personalities. When they tell their baby dolls not to be naughty, they, in effect, tell themselves not to be naughty. As they grow older, they also come into contact with doctors, nurses, bus drivers, sales clerks, and so on. These people outside the family circle are not as significant as the parents, but they are representative of society as a whole. Mead called them **generalized others.** In playing the roles of the generalized others, children learn to internalize the values of society as a whole. Participation in organized games such as baseball and basketball also promotes this internalization. These games involve a complex interaction among the players that is governed by a set of rules. When they play such games, children are, in effect, playing the game of life. They are learning that life has rules, too.

Internalized social values become only one part of our personality, which Mead called the *me.* Whenever we feel like obeying the law, following the crowd, and the like, we are sensing the presence of the *me.* It represents society within our personality. On the other hand, a portion of our personality cannot be easily "invaded" by society, no matter how often we have played childhood games. Mead referred to this part of our personality as the *I.* It is basically spontaneous, creative, or impulsive. Unlike the *me,* which makes all of us look alike in our behavior, the *I* makes each of us unique. People who live in a relatively free society or have been brought up in a permissive family are likely to have a stronger *I* than *me.* In contrast, those who live in a tightly controlled state or have been raised by overprotective parents tend to develop a more powerful *me* than *I.* But these two aspects of personality are complementary: without the *I* there would be no individual creativity or social progress; without the *me* there would be no social order or individual security. Both are inevitable and necessary.

While Mead explained how the *me* emerges through role taking, he did not say where the *I* comes from. More recently, Norbert Wiley (1979) theorized that we get our *I* from both *me* and *we.* According to Wiley, babies first develop the *me* in the same way as Mead indicated, and through this *me* they identify with their parents so totally that they feel themselves an inseparable part of their parents. Then, through a tactile, giggly love experience between parents and infants, which Wiley calls a *we experience,* the adults are in effect saying to the youngsters, "You exist; you are a different person; and I love the person you are." The infant then learns to see its self as independent from that of its parents, at which point it develops the *I.*

QUESTIONS FOR DISCUSSION AND REVIEW

1. What do the different theories of personality try to explain?
2. How does the theory of behaviorism differ from cultural determinism?
3. How are Piaget's stages of cognitive development similar to Kohlberg's stages of moral development?
4. What is the I and the Me, and why did Mead divide personality into these two parts?
5. What theories of personality seem to guide most parents in their efforts to shape personality?

AGENTS OF SOCIALIZATION

Every society tries to socialize its members. It slips the task into the hands of several groups and institutions, which are therefore called the *socializing agents* of society. Some of them, including the family and school, are in a sense appointed by society to transmit its cultural heritage to the young. Other agents, including the peer group and mass media, are not appointed by society. Their socialization of children is mostly unintentional (Koller and Ritchie, 1978; Elkin and Handel, 1984).

The Family

The family is the most important socializing agent, especially during the first five years of life. Many theorists, such as Freud and Mead, have emphasized the significance of childhood experiences in the family. A review of various studies has concluded that warm,

The cultural heritage is passed on directly from parents to children, which is why the family is the prime socializing agent of society. The family teaches the child to behave as the society expects: Eskimo children behave as Eskimos, Japanese behave as Japanese, and so on. The mother and daughters shown here are Native Americans of the Navajo tribe living in Arizona's Monument Valley. Since their parents follow Navajo traditions, these children will be socialized to behave differently than if they were raised in an urban environment where the main culture predominates and Navajo traditions have been set aside.

supportive, "reasonably constricting" family environments usually produce happy and well-behaving children; while cold, rigid, and "coercively restrictive" families cause youngsters to become rebellious, resentful, and insecure (Gecas, 1981). Research also established the family as the most influential socializing agent for adolescents (Davies and Kandel, 1981; Vandewiele, 1981). Various social forces, however, influence the way parents socialize their children.

A good example is social stratification, as can be seen in the differences between lower- and middle-class families. Research has long shown that lower-class families tend to be more adult-centered, more authoritarian than middle-class families. This might be a vestige of the family pattern that prevailed in our past, when adults treated children as their property, slaves, or pets (DeMause, 1975; Lee, 1982). In these authoritarian families, parents tend to train children to respect and obey parental authority, to follow rules and orders. On the other hand, middle-class parents are more inclined to teach the value of independence. They are more permissive and child-centered (Kohn, 1963, 1977). In one study, for example, middle-class mothers spent twice as much time in mutual play with their three-year-old children as did lower-class mothers (Farran and Haskins, 1980). In the 1980s, however, this class difference seems to be diminishing (Suransky, 1982; *Society*, 1983; Alwin, 1984).

Family size, too, has been found to influence parenting style. In one study, high school students from large families were more likely to describe their parents as authoritarian. They reported that their parents seldom explained the rules imposed on children, were inclined to use physical punishment, and tried to control children longer. But large families are also more likely than

"I'll give you a little tip. Try to be more like me."

small ones to give each child more independence and protection from parental supervision, despotism, and emotional absorption. The reason is that in a large family parental attention is spread over more children, which reduces parental influence on any one child (Gecas, 1981).

Culture further influences how parents socialize their children. In a comparative analysis of over 100 societies, Godfrey Ellis and associates (1978) found that in societies where adults are closely supervised—as in the case of women being directed by mothers-in-law in child care, cooking, and other household chores—parents tend to socialize their children toward conformity. In cultures where adults are not closely supervised, self-reliance becomes the primary objective for socialization. In analyzing similar data, Larry Petersen and colleagues (1982) further discovered that in societies where conformity is emphasized in socialization, parents often resort to physical punishment as a way of teaching children to obey them. In societies where self-reliance is a primary goal for socialization, parents are more inclined to use psychological punishment, such as discontinuing allowances, prohibitions against going out, or otherwise withholding love and making children feel guilty for having misbehaved. (For an illustration of how culture influences the way parents socialize their children, see box, p. 148).

Schools are the chief socializing agency outside the family. In addition to academic instruction, the school teaches a "hidden curriculum." It includes teaching children the behaviors that are acceptable in public life—how to get along with friends, how to work in groups, how to compete. It also includes teaching public virtues such as patriotism, sportsmanship, obedience to laws, and respect for authority.

The School

At home children are treated as unique persons. At school, however, they may be treated impersonally, as mere holders of a role. As a perceptive student put it:

> The main thing is not to take it personal, to understand that it's just a system and it treats you the same way it treats everybody else, like an engine or a machine . . . Our names get fed into it—*we* get fed into it—when we're five years old, and if we catch on and watch our step, it spits us out when we're seventeen or eighteen (Moyer and McAndrew, 1978).

The schools often provide children with their first training in how they are expected to behave in impersonal groups.

Whereas socialization by families often contributes to the diversity of society, the schools are more likely to contribute to uniformity. Society, in effect, officially designates them as its socializing agents. They are expected both to help children develop their potential as individuals and to mold them into social conformity—two goals that may be contradictory. To meet the first goal, the school teaches its formal curriculum of academic knowledge and skills. The pursuit of this goal becomes increasingly important as students rise to progressively higher educational levels (Miller, Kohn, and Schooler, 1986). Thus intellectual performance becomes more important to college students than it is to primary school pupils. By cultivating their intellectual capabilities, students are expected to turn into intelligent citizens capable of making a living while contributing to the prosperity of their society. The pursuit of the second goal—social conformity—is more earnest at the lower grade levels. It involves teaching what has been called a "hidden curriculum," training students to be patriotic, to believe in the society's cultural values, and to obey its laws. This instruction is often made explicit

UNDERSTANDING OTHER SOCIETIES

The "Education-Mama" in Japan

The two great molders of human behavior in modern societies—the family and the school—often work together. When a family member becomes devoted to a child's education, the results can be dramatic. Such is the case in Japan, where the Japanese culture exerts a tremendous influence on the family as a socializing agent. Can American parents also work together with schools to socialize their children?

Ten-year-old Seiji Hashimoto is not doing well in school. Despite his family's high expectations, he is about to flunk out. His mother, who is particularly upset with his scholastic performance, falls ill. Seiji blames himself for his mother's sickness and redoubles his efforts at school. His grades improve, and his mother's illness suddenly disappears.

The Naganos' only son does no chores. "Why?" asks a researcher. "Because," Mrs. Nagano replies, "it would break my heart to take him away from his studies."

Except for the names, these anecdotes sound like those told by many Jewish sons and daughters. The doting Jewish mother may have finally met her match. The Japanese mother is, according to researchers in the vanguard of cross-cultural studies of scholastic effectiveness, a key factor in the Japanese education advantage. Says George De Vos, an anthropologist who has been studying Japanese culture for 25 years, "She is the best 'Jewish mother' in the world."

Harvard University psychologist Jerome Kagan concurs with this analogy. "Until her child goes to school," says Kagan, "the Japanese mother devotes herself to the rearing of the child. In verbal and nonverbal ways, she reminds the child of her deep, warm feelings and that the child is the most important thing in the world to her. Then, she says, 'After all I've done for you, don't disappoint me.' She's like the Jewish mother who says, 'What do you mean you're not hungry—after I've slaved all day over a hot stove for you.'"

The decline of education in the United States has been front-page news for years and may well develop into a prime political issue in the next presidential election. To cite just one statistic, Scholastic Aptitude Test scores have fallen 49 points in verbal aptitude and 31 points in math in the past 20 years. But while politicians search for ways to redress this shortcoming and educators argue the merits of traditional versus progressive education, a few researchers are looking to the Orient for an answer, and at least one is alarmed at the East-West gap. "Americans just don't understand that they are truly behind," says Harold Stevenson. "You talk about Sputnik," referring to the 1957 Soviet orbital launch that jolted Americans into a frenzied effort to catch up in the space race. "Well, there's a similar message in the Japanese advantage in education."

Since 1971, Stevenson has made nine trips to the Far East to determine how the Japanese and

in history and civics classes. But it is also implicit in classroom rituals (such as the pledge of allegiance), in demands that classroom rules be obeyed, in the choice of books to be assigned in English classes, and in a host of other activities (such as glorification of the competition and discipline of sports). The hidden curriculum, then, helps ensure social order and the continuity of a society's values from one generation to the next.

Some schools, of course, are more successful than others in meeting those goals. Generally American schools do better with upper- and middle-class children than with lower-class children. There are at least three explanations (Elkin and Handel, 1984). First, schools with mostly higher-income students tend to have more competent teachers and better resources than schools where poor children predominate. Second, higher-income parents are likely to have developed in their children a higher level of intellectual skills than have lower-income parents. Third, teachers, who usually hold middle-class values, tend to expect middle- and upper-class students to do better than lower-class students. Expectations can be self-fulfilling as we saw in the Rosenthal and Jacobson experiment discussed in Chapter 2 (Doing Sociology).

The Peer Group

As children grow older, they become increasingly involved with their peer group, which consists of chil-

Chinese cultures have won this advantage. The answer is complex, but one factor seems paramount. "The Japanese mother is a very important influence on the education of her children," says De Vos. "She takes it upon herself to be the responsible agent, reinforcing the educational process instituted in the schools."

The most single-minded Japanese mother is known as *kyoiku-mama,* which translates roughly as "education-mama." She approaches the responsibility for her children's education with unrelenting fervor. She pushes her children to excel academically and sends them to ubiquitous after-school classes, known as *juku,* or to private tutors to assure good grades. Mothers are also so highly vocal in the influential Japanese PTA's that some Japanese half-jokingly suggest that the organization be named the MTA.

"To a Japanese," points out Hideo Kojima of Nagoya University in Japan, "the training of children is not simply a technical matter but one that involves the deepest mutual and reciprocal relationships between parent and child." It's not surprising, then, that the Japanese mother, as one researcher wrote, "views her baby much more than do Western mothers as an extension of herself, and psychological boundaries between the two of them are blurred."

When it comes to disciplining her child, the Japanese mother is more inclined than the American mother to appeal to feelings as a coercive tool. Where an American mother might demand that a child stop doing something of which she disapproved, the Japanese mother is more likely simply to express displeasure. Kojima cites the "many Japanese writers (on child rearing) who recommend mildness in the direct verbal teaching of children. They say that children should be admonished in a firm but calm manner, and that adults not use abusive language or show anger and impatience."

If the Japanese mother-child relationship could be summarized in a word, that word would be *amae.* Amae is love combined with a strong sense of reciprocal obligation and dependence.

Amae is at the foundation of Japanese teaching, according to Hiroshi Asuma, Professor of Education at the University of Tokyo. It is the bond between mother and child, and, later, child and teacher, that makes the child "more attentive to what others say, think and feel, more willing to accept the intrusion of significant others into his or her learning, thinking, and feeling; more likely to model after them; better ready to work together; more responsive to recognition from them; and more willing to strive for a common goal."

Source: Reprinted from Perry Garfinkel, "The best 'Jewish mother' in the world," *Psychology Today,* September 1983, pp. 56–60. Copyright © 1983 (APA).

dren who are about the same age and have similar interests. As a socializing agent, the peer group is quite different from the family and school. While parents and teachers have more power than children and students, the peer group is made up of equals.

As a distinctive agent of socialization, the peer group teaches its members several important things. First, it teaches them to be independent from adult authorities, which may speed up their entry into adulthood. Second, it teaches social skills and group loyalties. Third, the peer group teaches its members the values of friendship and companionship among equals—values that are relatively absent in the socialization received from authority figures like parents and teachers. On the other hand, a peer group can socialize its members to thumb their noses at authorities and adults. Some may end up getting into trouble with the law. Many others may only innocently poke fun at adults behind their backs. A group of young children, for instance, may recite among themselves something like: "No more pencils, no more books, no more teachers with dirty looks" (Elkin and Handel, 1984).

Freeing themselves from the grip of parental and school authorities, peer groups often develop distinctive subcultures with their own values, symbols, jargon, music, dress, and heroes. Whereas parents and teachers tend to place great importance on scholastic achievement, adolescent peer groups are likely to put a higher premium on popularity, social leadership, and athletic attainment (Mussen, 1963). The divergence between parental and peer values does not necessarily lead to a hostile confrontation between parents and teenagers. In fact, most youngsters are just as friendly with parents as with peers. They simply engage in different types of activities—work and task activities with parents but play and recreation with peers. Concerning financial, educational, career, and other serious matters, such as what to spend money on and what occupation to choose, they are inclined to seek advice from parents. When it comes to social activities, such as whom to date and what clubs to join, they are more likely to discuss them with peers (Sebald, 1986). This reflects the great importance placed by the peer group on "other-directed behavior"—looking to others for approval and support—as opposed to reliance on personal beliefs and traditional values. The peer groups, in effect, demands conformity at the expense of independence and individuality. Those in early adolescence are most willing to accept conformity; hence they are most deeply involved with peer groups. As they grow into middle and late adolescence, their involvement with peers gradually declines because of their growing predilection for independence (Brown, Eicher, and Petrie, 1986; Shrum and Cheek, 1987).

The Mass Media

The mass media include popular books, magazines, newspapers, movies, television, and radio. They probably exert more influence on children than many other socializing agents. Among the mass media, television appears the most influential. It has been found to affect children in some ways.

First of all, children may come to expect their lives, their parents, and their teachers to be as exciting as those portrayed on television. They are likely to be disappointed and so may find their parents inadequate and their teachers boring. Second, there is some evidence that television tends to impoverish its young viewers' creative imagination. If they watch it frequently, they may find it difficult to create pictures in their own minds or to understand stories without visual illustration. Third, through its frequent portrayal of violence, television tends to stimulate violence-prone children to actual violence, to make normal children less sensitive to violence in real life, and to instill the philosophy that might makes right. Television violence can further heighten children's senses of danger and vulnerability as well as their feelings of alienation and doom (see box, p. 151). On the other hand, television has the redeeming quality of enlarging children's vocabulary and knowledge of the world (Peterson et al., 1986; Friedrich-Cofer and Huston, 1986).

These effects usually wear off as the younger viewer gets older. Although children who have watched television frequently begin school with a better vocabulary and greater knowledge than those who have not, this advantage disappears soon after schooling starts. By the

Television occupies a special place among the agents of socialization simply because children spend so much time watching it. It greatly influences the child's beliefs, values, and behavior. It may make their lives appear boring to children and impoverish their creative imagination. Due to its frequent portrayal of violence, television can also make children less sensitive to violence in real life. But the influence of television becomes weaker as the child grows up.

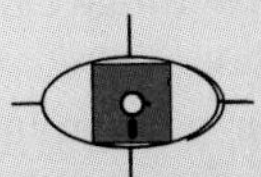

LOOKING AT CURRENT RESEARCH

The Violent Family Hour

Sociological research continues to document the negative impact of television violence on the behavior of children. According to the following report, a recent study indicates that extensive violence is still featured on shows during TV's family hour. What is the nature of television violence and how might it affect its young viewers?

Television's early evening "family hour," 8:00 to 9:00 P.M. Eastern Standard Time, when the greatest number of children are in the viewing audience, is the most violent hour of prime-time programming, according to a report issued by the University of Pennsylvania's Annenberg School of Communications at a Washington, D.C., press conference in September. A research team of the Annenberg School, which has been systematically monitoring television programming since 1967, found that the relatively low level of violence that was achieved during the early evening "family hour" programming of the 1970s has vanished in the 1980s.

Nearly nine out of every ten "family hours" contained violence, and the rate of violent incidents per hour was eight, the highest "violence saturation rate" since 1967, said George Gerbner, dean of Pennsylvania's Annenberg School and one of the authors of the report. The Annenberg School researchers use what they call a "violence index" to compare television shows from season to season. They also survey television viewers' conceptions of reality and have found that the more people watch television, the more they tend to see the world as a mean and gloomy place.

For the past nineteen years, at least, adults and children have been exposed to an average of about sixteen acts of violence (two of them lethal) in each evening's offering of prime-time entertainment programs. The 1984–85 season of network dramatic programming had the highest violence index since the Annenberg researchers began their study in 1967. The index for the 1985–86 season was the fourth highest on record. "This tide of violent representations is historically unprecedented and shows no real sign of receding," said Gerbner.

Weekend daytime children's programs were considerably more violent than the average violence index for all three networks' prime-time programming. Weekend children's programs in the 1984–85 season, which contained an average of twenty-seven violent acts per hour, were the second most violent group of weekend children's programs since 1967. Weekend daytime children's programs have always been at least three times more violent than prime-time programming. Children are exposed to an average of more than twenty acts of violence during each hour that they watch television on Saturday and Sunday mornings. Most of the violence in weekend daytime children's shows is in cartoons. But, the researchers warn, one should not underestimate the effect that humorous and fantasy violence can have on children. "Humor is the sugar coating on the pill," Gerbner said. "If anything, it may make its lessons easier to take."

Television violence has a complex effect on society as a whole, the report stated. "By constantly demonstrating who can get away with what against whom," Gerbner said, "displays of violence confirm an unequal distribution and sense of power in society. Our theory about the dynamics of that demonstration of power and the resulting cultivation of fear is the most important aspect of our research. While research indicates that exposure to violence does occasionally incite and often desensitize viewers to violence, our findings show that for most viewers, the mean and dangerous world depicted on television tends to cultivate a sense of danger, mistrust, dependence, and, despite its supposedly 'entertainment' nature, alienation and gloom."

Source: Reprinted from "The Violent Family Hour," from "Social Science and the Citizen." Published by permission of Transaction Publishers from *Society*, Vol. 24, No. 2, p. 2. Copyright © 1987 by Transaction Publishers.

time children are about twelve years old, they are likely to find commercials unreal and misleading. Older children may become so outraged at being lied to that they are "ready to believe that, like advertising, business and other institutions are riddled with adult hypocrisy." With increased sophistication, older teenagers and adults also take TV violence for what it is—fake and for entertainment only (Waters, 1977; Freedman, 1986).

QUESTIONS FOR DISCUSSION AND REVIEW

1. Why is the family still the most important agent of socialization?
2. What is the hidden curriculum of the school and how does it try to ensure social order?
3. Why are many adolescents more influenced by their peer groups than by their families?
4. In what ways do the positive features of television outweigh the negative?

ADULT SOCIALIZATION

The socialization process does not stop at the end of childhood. It continues with the emergence of adulthood and stops only when the person dies.

Learning New Roles

Being socialized means, in effect, learning new roles. Like children, adults learn many new roles as they go through various stages of life. At the same time, adults' specific socialization experiences do differ from those of children (Mortimer and Simmons, 1978). We can see this in the three types of socialization that all of us undergo.

One is **anticipatory socialization,** which involves learning a role that is to be assumed in the future. Young children learn to be parents in the future by playing house. Young adults prepare themselves for their future professions by attending college. Generally, children tend to idealize their future roles, but adults are more practical about theirs. A child may wish to become the greatest lawyer on earth, but an adult is more likely to want to be one of the best lawyers in a city. Howard Becker and colleagues (1961) found that first-year medical students usually expect to acquire every bit of medical knowledge and then to serve humanity selflessly. Toward the end of their medical schooling, they become more realistic. They are likely to strive to learn just enough to pass exams and to look forward to a lucrative practice as a reward for their years of hard work. In short, as people get closer to the end of their anticipatory socialization, their earlier idealism gradually dies out, to be replaced by realism.

Like children, adults also go through **developmental socialization.** It involves learning roles that are already acquired, much like receiving on-the-job training. Children learn their currently acquired roles as sons or daughters, students, and members of their peer groups. Adults learn their newly assumed roles as full-time workers, husbands, wives, parents, and so on. If we compare these two sets of roles, we can see that adult socialization is more likely voluntary or self-initiated. Children cannot do away with their status of being sons or daughters, are required to go to school, and are largely restricted to hanging around with neighborhood kids. On the other hand, adults can *choose* to marry, become parents, get divorced, change jobs, move, and find friends from a wide area. Moreover, while children are mostly socialized within the confines of primary groups, adults are more likely to go beyond their families and friends and get involved in secondary relationships, such as with their bosses, co-workers, clients, and other members of formal organizations. There is, then, a great deal more self-determination and selectivity in adult socialization (Mortimer and Simmons, 1978).

The experiences that adults receive from their developmental socialization may depend on the nature of the socializing agents as well as the larger society. Business corporations, for example, socialize their workers to achieve high productivity but, at the same time encourage teamwork more than individual creativity, which may reflect the other-directed spirit of American society. The specific nature of a job can also mold adult personality. As demonstrated by Melvin Kohn's (1980) studies, the more complex a job, the more likely it is that the worker will experience self-direction in the workplace and end up valuing autonomy in other aspects of life. On the other hand, the more simple and routine the work, the more likely it is that the individual will be supervised by some higher-up and eventually place a high value on conformity.

A third form of socialization is less common: **resocialization.** It forces the individual to abandon his or her old self and to develop a new self in its place. It happens to adults more often than to children, because the former's personalities tend more to have been developed in the first place. Resocialization can take place in prisons, mental institutions, wars, POW camps, military training centers, or religious cults.

Erikson: Adult Life Cycle

As we saw earlier, Freud and Piaget charted the various stages of personality development that children must pass through until they reach adulthood. More recently, Erik Erikson (1963, 1975) has applied the same concept of developmental stages not only to children but also to adults. Erikson views each stage as a crisis that stems from two opposite human desires. Individuals must resolve the crisis if they expect to lead a normal, happy life.

Erikson found three stages in adult life: early adulthood, middle adulthood, and late adulthood (see also Levinson, 1978). In early adulthood, which lasts from ages 20 to 40, people face the crisis of having to resolve the conflicting demands for love and work. They usually meet the demand for love by falling in love, getting married, and raising a family. If they are too attached to their families, they risk losing the chance of realizing their youthful ambitions. At the same time, they may be eager to work extremely hard to establish themselves in their careers, but in doing so they risk losing intimacy with and incurring isolation from their families. In this stage, then, the young adult is confronted with the conflict between enjoying intimacy and suffering isolation.

In middle adulthood, which lasts from ages 40 to 60, people become acutely aware that their death will come, that their time is running out, and that they must give up their youthful dreams to start being more concerned with others rather than themselves. Usually, they choose to be what Erikson calls *generative*—by nurturing, guiding, teaching, and serving the younger generation. This would give them an elevating sense of productivity and creativity, of having made a significant contribution to others. On the other hand, they are also inclined to continue hanging on to their youthful dreams, to try to be active and feel young again. Since this is difficult to fulfill at this stage, the individuals risk getting weighed down with a depressing sense of disappointment, stagnation, and boredom. In short, the middle-aged adult is faced with the conflict between generativity and stagnation.

In late adulthood, from age 60 till death, people find themselves in the conflict between achieving integrity (holding oneself together) and sinking in despair (emotionally falling apart). Those who are able to maintain the integrity of the self are likely to have accepted whatever they have attained so far. But those who sink in despair do so because they regret that their lives have been full of missed opportunities and that the time is just too short for them to start another life. Therefore, death loses its sting for those who have learned to hold themselves together and to accept death as the ultimate outcome of life. But those who fall apart emotionally cannot accept death and are gripped with fear of it.

Research has established that most people do experience the two conflicting forces in each stage (Varghese, 1981; Ochse and Plug, 1986). We should also note that the word "crisis" does not have the negative connotation in Erikson's theory that it does in our culture. To Erikson, a crisis can be positive. It is basically the same as what the two characters in the Chinese word for crisis *(weiji)* represent: danger and opportunity. When faced with one of Erikson's crises, we need not succumb to the danger of isolation, stagnation, or despair—we could also seize the opportunity for intimacy, generativity, or integrity. According to Erikson (1975), sometimes we have to choose between two opposites, as in the case of integrity versus despair. Sometimes we have to incorporate them and put them in some manageable balance, as in the case of intimacy and isolation, so that we can have, say, both a successful marriage and a high-flying career at the same time. Indeed, many studies have shown that life-cycle changes—new parenthood, the "empty nest" (all children having grown and left home), and retirement—can be positive experiences (Bush and Simmons, 1981). But Erikson's ages-and-stages approach to adult development may not apply to women. Compared with men, women are less likely to pursue a career, hence less likely to risk being isolated from families. If they work, they tend to start doing so at an older age than men—when their children have started going to school. Women also seek and experience greater intimacy than men do. Women, then, are less likely to face the crisis of losing intimacy and suffering isolation as a result of relentlessly pursuing a career (Ochse and Plug, 1985; Rosenfeld and Stark, 1987). Moreover, Erikson has ignored the influence of social forces on those life-cycle experiences (Dannefer, 1984). As the following section suggests, whether the elderly fear death or not depends largely on the nature of society.

Aging and Dying

Unlike the traditional societies, modern societies do not adequately socialize their members for old age and death. In traditional societies, old people are highly valued and respected. It is quite an accomplishment to survive into old age in a traditional society, where most people die relatively young. Further, the experiences

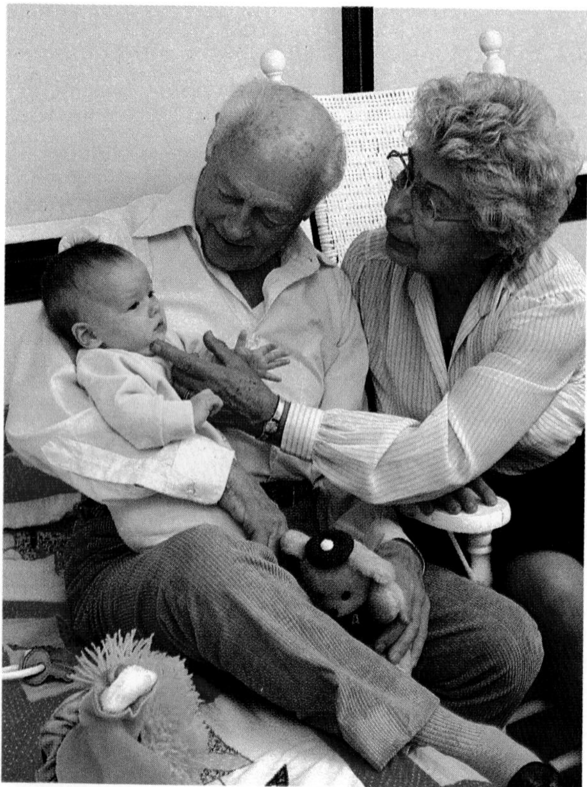

In traditional societies, which change slowly, the old are respected for their wisdom. In modern societies, which change rapidly, it often seems that the old have become obsolete. Most live in their own homes, away from their children and grandchildren. Young people who do not grow up in the company of the elderly have few models for growing old gracefully. Although they often visit their old relatives, they would not relish the prospect of growing old themselves. Nor would they know how to calmly accept death as natural and unavoidable.

that the elderly have accumulated over the years are invaluable to younger generations because their societies change so little and so slowly that old knowledge and values do not seem to lose their relevance. Since the aged live with their children and grandchildren, are given an honored role, and are often observed to dispense wisdom and advice, young people are easily socialized to know how to behave as wise old persons if they themselves become old.

In modern societies, old people typically live alone. Without living with their old parents and grandparents, younger people have little chance of learning how to grow old gracefully. Although they visit their old relatives often, they would not relish the prospect of growing old themselves, because they believe that the aged live an unrewarding, lonely, or even degrading life.

Modern societies also have come up short in socialization for death. In traditional societies, people see their loved ones die at home, handle their corpses, and personally bury them. But in modern societies we seldom witness a dying scene at home because most deaths occur in hospitals. We may even be afraid to touch our relatives' corpses, as we always hire morticians to prepare them for burial. We may never have seen what death looks like, because by the time the mortician has finished making up a dead body, it looks more like a live person sleeping. Although we are often bombarded with television and movie images of death due to war, famine, murder, and other violent acts, we do not weep and grieve over them but instead pull ourselves further away from the reality of death. If we are terminally ill, we would deny our impending death in order to forestall the social stigma associated with dying and to preserve the normal relations with families and friends (Beilin, 1982). Our culture, then, has not taught us to accept death as natural and unavoidable.

This is why, as Elisabeth Kübler-Ross (1969) has discovered, terminally ill patients usually go through five stages from the time when they discover they are dying to the final moment of their death. Kübler-Ross refers to the first stage as "initial denial," because upon being told that they are dying, patients usually express disbelief: "No, not me; it just can't be me." At the second stage—anger—they believe they are dying but get angry with family, doctor, and God, protesting, "Why me?" When they move into the third stage—bargaining—they are no longer angry and ask God to let them live just a little longer in return for good behavior. In the fourth stage—depression—they can no longer postpone their death, so they sink into deep depression. Finally, in the fifth stage—acceptance—they feel calm and ready to die. Most patients, however, do not make it to the final stage.

Since the early 1960s, however, our fear of death has apparently diminished, thanks to a great outpouring of attention to the subject in books, television, and other media. In a 1977 survey of middle-aged and older people in Los Angeles, when asked "How afraid are you of death?" 63 percent responded "not afraid at all" and only 4 percent said "very afraid." The same study also showed that the older ones expressed less fear despite being closer to death (Bengtson, Cuellar, and Ragan, 1977). According to a national survey conducted in the 1960s and then in the 1970s, most Americans of all ages did not find death terrifying. A majority agreed with such statements as "death is sometimes a blessing" and "death is not tragic for the person who dies, only for the survivors," while only one-tenth said that "to die is to suffer." There has also been a turnaround in doctors' attitudes toward death. One study of physicians who often treated terminal cancer patients indicated that in 1961 over 90 percent would *not* tell their patients they were dying. In 1979, however, 98 percent said it was their policy to tell the patients the truth (Riley, 1983).

QUESTIONS FOR DISCUSSION AND REVIEW

1. Why is socialization a lifelong process?
2. How do anticipatory and developmental socialization differ from resocializaton?
3. What three development stages of adult life did Erikson discover, and what personal crisis does each stage contain?
4. Why has the fear of death somewhat diminished in modern American society?

ARE WE PUPPETS OF SOCIETY?

Through socialization we internalize the values of society. Does this imply that we become puppets of society, puppets that even enjoy giving up freedom and following whatever rules society sets down? The answer is yes and no. In some respects, we do behave like society's puppets. Most of us, for example, go along gladly with society's expectation that we be friendly to our friends and love our parents. In all societies, however, there are crimes and other acts that violate society's norms.

Dennis Wrong (1961) has argued that conformity to norms is not total because we are not entirely socialized. There are at least four reasons why socialization can never turn us into total puppets. First, we have certain "imperious biological drives" that always buck against society's attempt to mold us in its image. Second, the socializing influences are not always consistent and harmonious with one another. Our ethnic group, social class, and professional and occupational associations may not socialize us in the same way. They may teach conflicting roles, norms, and values. Third, even if society could consistently and completely socialize us, we would still violate its laws and rules. In the very process of learning to obey the rules, we may also learn how to break them without getting caught, which is a great temptation for most if not all people. Even some of the most "respectable" citizens have committed crimes. Finally, if we were completely socialized, we would become extremely unhappy and probably neurotic or psychotic. No normal person wants his or her drives for self-expression, freedom, creativity, or personal eccentricity to be totally suppressed. This is why Freud held that civilization breeds discontent in individuals.

QUESTION FOR DISCUSSION AND REVIEW

1. What aspects of human life prevent socialization from turning us into total puppets?

CHAPTER REVIEW

1. *What is socialization?* It is the process by which a society transmits its values to individuals so that they can function properly as its members.

2. *Can either nature or nurture alone explain human behavior?* No. Both heredity and environment make us what we are. The importance of heredity can be demonstrated by how our lack of instincts as well as our temperament, intelligence, and aptitude influence the development of our personality. The significance of socialization can be seen in the case studies of children who are feral, isolated, institutionalized, or gifted.

3. *What are the basic themes of the major theories of personality development?* Behaviorism regards human personality as determined by conditioning through the use of rewards and punishments. Cultural determinism emphasizes cultural forces as the determinants of personality. The developmental theories of Freud, Piaget, and Kohlberg show how psychosexual, cognitive, and moral aspects of personality develop through a fixed set of stages. Symbolic interactionism regards interaction between the individual and society as the source of human personality. *How does symbolic interactionism differ from Freud's, Piaget's, and Kohlberg's views of personality development?* Whereas the other three theorists emphasized

conflict between society and the individual, symbolic interactionists view harmonious relations between the individual and society as the foundation of personality development.

4. *What is distinctive about each of the major socializing agents?* The family is the most important socializing agent for the child. It is, however, influenced by other social forces. The school is charged both with helping children develop their potential as individuals and with securing their conformity to social norms. The peer group socializes its members unintentionally. Made up of equals, the peer group often offers a set of values different from that presented by parents and teachers, which helps hasten the child's independence from adult authorities. The mass media, particularly in the form of television, exerts a powerful influence on the child's beliefs, values, and behavior. But this influence usually wears off as the child grows up.

5. *Does socialization stop with the end of childhood?* No. Adults continue to experience socialization as children do. They go through anticipatory socialization, developmental socialization, and resocialization. According to Erikson, adults go through various life stages, each a crisis that the individual must deal with. The most difficult crisis that confronts members of modern society is aging and dying. Generally the aged are not highly respected, and death is not treated as a normal event of life to be accepted.

KEY TERMS

Anticipatory socialization Socialization that prepares a person to assume a role in the future (p. 152).

Aptitude The capacity for developing physical or social skills (p. 134).

Behaviorism The school of psychology that regards behavior as the product of conditioning (p. 138).

Classical conditioning The type of conditioning that involves training the subject to associate two inherently unrelated stimuli (p. 138).

Conditioning The process by which associations are formed between stimuli and responses (p. 138).

Cultural determinism The view that cultural and subcultural factors are the most important determinants of human personality (p. 139).

Developmental socialization The kind of socialization that teaches a person to be more adequate in playing his or her currently assumed role (p. 152).

Ego According to Freud, the rational part of the personality, which mediates between the id and superego (p. 140).

Electra complex According to Freud, the girl's sexual love for her father and hostility toward her mother (p. 140).

Generalized others Mead's term for people whose names are unknown to the child but who influence the child's internalization of the values of society (p. 145).

Id According to Freud, the irrational, pleasure-seeking component of personality (p. 140).

Intelligence The capacity for mental or intellectual achievement (p. 134).

Looking-glass self Cooley's term for the self-image that we develop from the way others treat us (p. 144).

Oedipus complex According to Freud, the young boy's sexual love for his mother and jealousy of his father (p. 140).

Operant conditioning The type of conditioning that involves administering rewards for desired behavior and punishment for undesired behavior (p. 138).

Personality A fairly stable configuration of feelings, attitudes, ideas, and behaviors that characterizes an individual (p. 132).

Resocialization The kind of socialization that is aimed at replacing one's old self with a new self (p. 152).

Significant others Mead's term for specific persons, such as parents, who have a significant influence on the child because the child interacts mainly with them in his or her early years and plays at being these adults (p. 145).

Socialization The process by which a society transmits its cultural values to its members (p. 132).

Superego In Freud's theory, that component of the personality which approximates what is traditionally called conscience. It represents an internalization of the parents' ideals and prohibitions and restrains the id (p. 140).

SUGGESTED READINGS

Corsaro, William A. 1985. *Friendship and Peer Culture in the Early Years.* Norwood, N.J.: Ablex. An observational study of how nursery-school children shape their own developmental experiences through interactions with peers, confirming the views of Piaget, Mead, and others.

Elkin, Frederick, and Gerald Handel. 1984. *The Child and Society,* 4th ed. New York: Random House. A useful basic text for studying childhood socialization.

Lewontin, R. C., Steven Rose, and Leon J. Kamin. 1984. *Not in Our Genes: Biology, Ideology, and Human Nature.* New York: Pantheon. A critical analysis of sociobiology by an evolutionary geneticist, a psychologist, and a neurobiologist, who conclude that "all statements about the genetic basis of human social traits . . . are purely speculative."

Packard, Vance. 1983. *Our Endangered Children: Growing Up in a Changing World.* Boston: Little, Brown. A highly readable book by a well-known social critic arguing that our society is increasingly neglecting our children.

Wilson, Edward O. 1984. *Biophilia: The Human Bond to Other Species.* Cambridge, Mass.: Harvard University Press. An easy-to-read book by a leading sociobiologist, who argues that even such human traits as fear of snakes, sense of beauty, or religious symbolism are genetically determined.

7 Deviance and Control

Broadly defined, deviant behavior is any act that violates a social norm. But how do we know whether an act violates a social norm? For example, is abortion deviant? Is drug use? Some people may think so, but others may not. This suggests that deviance is not absolute, not real in and of itself. It is relative, a matter of definition. Whether a particular behavior is defined as deviant depends on at least three factors: time, place, and public consensus or power. According to this definition, abortion is not a deviant act in our society today because it is not regarded as such by most Americans, but the use of crack by this couple is.

Most of us are probably accustomed to thinking of deviants as creatures foreign to us, as "nuts, sluts, and perverts." But deviance is widespread. Even in a society of saints, as Durkheim long ago suggested, its rules would be broken. In a classic study (Wallerstein and Wyle, 1947) a random sample of Americans were given a list of 49 acts that were actually criminal offenses punishable by at least one year in prison. A whopping 99 percent of them admitted to at least one offense. It is quite possible that the remaining 1 percent had either lied or could not recall, because crime is not something they could be proud of having committed.

Despite the prevalence of deviance, many people's ideas about it are simplistic and erroneous. Virtually everyone thinks that armed robbery is more dangerous in every respect than unarmed robbery. In reality, it is unarmed robbery that is far more likely to result in sending the victim to the hospital. One study, for example, shows that 66 percent of unarmed robbery victims, compared with 17 percent of armed robbery victims, were seriously injured (Feeney and Weir, 1975). Many people also believe that mental illness runs in a family. This may be true for a few patients, but most have acquired the illness through socialization rather than genes. Many people assume, too, that traditional crimes such as murder, assault, and robbery are more harmful to society than corporate crimes such as selling defective cars, industrial pollution, and tax fraud. Actually the reverse is closer to the truth (Thio, 1988).

There are many more popular misconceptions about these deviant acts. We take a closer look at three of them (murder, corporate crime, and mental illness) in this chapter. But let us first discuss what deviance is and what the current indicators of crime are. Then we examine those three examples of deviance, various explanations for its occurrence, and society's attempts to control it.

DEVIANCE IN AMERICA

A man, recently fired, returns to the office where he has worked, rifle in hand, and begins firing. Executives from several companies conspire to keep prices for their products artificially high. In a dark alley, a mugger waits for a victim to pass by. In a nice home, a woman goes through the daily routine of drinking to the point of intoxication. In the pursuit of thinness, a young woman starves herself until she looks like a scarecrow. When two police officers try to arrest a man, he spits on them thinking that he can transmit his AIDS virus to them in this way. These actions may appear to have little in common, but they are all examples of deviant behavior.

What Is Deviance?

Deviant behavior is generally defined as any act that violates a social norm. But the phenomenon is more complex than that. How do we know whether an act violates a social norm? Is homosexuality deviant—a violation of social norm? Some people think so, but others do not. This suggests that deviance is not absolute, not real in and of itself. It is relative, a matter of definition. A deviant act must be defined as such by someone before it can be said to be deviant.

Since many people have different views, they are bound to define deviant behavior differently. It is no wonder that practically all human acts have the potential for being considered deviant. When sociologist J. L. Simmons (1969) asked people what they defined as deviant, he ended up with a list of 252 acts and persons, including homosexuals, prostitutes, alcoholics, murderers, communists, atheists, Democrats, Republicans, movie stars, smart-aleck students, and know-it-all professors. If you are surprised that some of these people are considered deviant, your surprise simply confirms that there are countless *different* definitions of deviance, including your own. Even among sociologists, there is disagreement on what deviance is. Most sociologists define deviance as something negative. To them, deviance is what the public considers negative, objectionable behavior. But a few sociologists argue that deviance can also be positive. To them, then, heroes, saints, geniuses, reformers, and revolutionaries are just as deviant as criminals because they all deviate from being average persons (Thio, 1988).

All definitions of deviance, however, do not carry the same weight. Rock stars may be regarded by some people as deviant, but they are not put in prison. Murderers, on the other hand, are widely considered to be seriously deviant, so that many are put on death row. What determines that murder is more deviant than being a rock star? What determines which definitions of deviance have more serious consequences for the deviants? There are at least three determining factors: time, place, and public consensus or power.

First, what constitutes deviance varies from one historical period to another. Jesus was nailed to the cross as a criminal in his time, but he is widely worshipped as God today. About 30 years after Jesus' birth, the Roman Empress Messalina won a bet with a friend by publicly having a prolonged session of sexual intercourse with 25 different men. At the time, Romans were not particularly scandalized, though they were quite impressed by her stamina. Today, if a person with similar social standing engaged in such behavior, we would consider it extremely scandalous (King, 1985). In the last two centuries, opium was a legal and easily available common drug; today its use is a criminal offense. Nowadays cigarette smoking is legal in all countries, but in the seventeenth century it was illegal in most countries. In fact, in some countries at that time, smokers were punished harshly: their noses were cut off in Russia and their lips sliced off in Hindustan (Goode, 1984a). Second, the definition of deviance varies from one place to another. A polygamist is a criminal in the United States but not in Saudi Arabia and other Moslem countries. Prostitution is illegal in the United States (except in some counties in Nevada), but it is legal in Denmark, West Germany, France, and most other countries. In 1987 the Iran-Contra affair, like the Watergate scandal in the mid-1970s, was considered major news in the United States, especially by the American media and Congress, but people in Europe wondered what the fuss was all about. Third, whether a given act is deviant depends on public consensus. Murder is unquestionably deviant because nearly all people agree that it is. In contrast, long hair on men is not deviant because hardly anybody considers it so. Public consensus, however, usually reflects the vested interests of the rich and powerful. As Marx would have said, the ideas of the ruling class tend to become the ruling ideas of society. Like the powerful, the general public tends to consider, for example, bank robbery to be a crime but not fraudulent advertising, which serves the interests of the powerful.

In view of those three determinants of deviant be-

Lieutenant Colonel Oliver North testifying before a U.S. congressional committee investigating the sale of arms to Iran and diversion of the funds to the Contras, the Nicaraguan rebels. One determining factor in the definition of deviance is the place where the behavior occurs. Whether a certain act is deviant or not varies from one society to another. The Iran-Contra affair was treated as a big scandal in the United States, but many people in Europe could not understand what the fuss was all about. To them, the scandal looked like "another perplexing case of American moralism run wild, a national exercise in self-flagellation."

havior, we may more precisely define **deviant behavior** as any act considered deviant by public consensus or the powerful at a given time and place.

Crime Indicators

Deviance may be either criminal or noncriminal. Noncriminal deviance is less likely to harm someone else. Examples include mental disorders, alcoholism, and suicide. Criminal deviance—such as murder, rape, and price fixing—is generally more serious. More accurately, criminal deviance is behavior that is prohibited by law.

Sinced 1930, when it was first published, the FBI's annual *Uniform Crime Reports* has been a major source of information for studying crime in the United States. Every year it presents a large amount of data on numbers of crimes and arrests, which the police all over the country have sent to the FBI. It has remained the most comprehensive source of official data on crime in the United States, as more than 95 percent of all Americans live in police jurisdictions reporting to the FBI. Even so, it is still far from being an accurate indicator of crime.

First, it reports only what the FBI calls **index offenses,** which it regards as major, serious crimes. There are eight of them: murder, rape, robbery, aggravated assault, burglary, larceny (theft of $50 or more), auto theft and arson. The official statistics do not include victimless crimes such as prostitution and gambling. Neither do they present most of the white-collar crimes, such as income tax evasion, committed by seemingly respectable citizens; fraud against consumers and price fixing

Violent crimes, such as the mugging (above) and the robbery (left), are only the most visible facet of criminality in modern society. White-collar crime also takes a huge toll, though most of it goes undetected. Income tax evasion, bribes taken by public officials, the selling of misleadingly labeled merchandise, working "off the books," and other crimes that do not attract attention to themselves weaken society morally and economically. In addition, even serious crimes can go unreported because victims feel nothing can be done about them.

committed by corporations; and bribe taking and illegal wiretapping perpetrated by government officials.

Second, the FBI statistics even underreport index offenses. To know how much crime has been committed, the police rely heavily on citizens to come forward with the information. In fact, 85 to 90 percent of the offenses appearing in official statistics are based on citizen reports. However, about two-thirds of crime victims fail to report offenses to the police. Most of these victims feel that the offense is not important enough, that it is a private matter, or that nothing can be done about it (U.S. Dept. of Justice, 1983). Moreover, in nearly one-fourth of the cases where a citizen's complaint is received, the police do not consider the incident a crime. In his classic study of police-citizen encounters in three large American cities, Donald Black (1970) discovered a certain bias in the way police handled citizens' complaints. The officers were less likely to define an incident as a crime if it was less serious, if the suspect was not a stranger to the complainant, and if the complainant was not respectful to the police, did not want to have the suspect prosecuted, and was a working-class rather than a white-collar person. Even in serious cases of assault, the police are less likely to make arrests if the victims are black or female (Smith, 1987). Due to victim nonreporting and police discretion, then, the FBI data miss a lot of crimes (see Table 7.1).

Table 7.1 How FBI Statistics Miss the Mark
Most victims of crime do not call the police, who in turn fail to regard some victim-reported incidents as crimes. Thus official data, such as the FBI crime statistics, underreport even major crimes.

	Number of crimes in 1981	
	FBI statistics[a]	Actually occurred[b]
Forcible rape	81,540	178,000
Robbery	574,130	1,381,000
Aggravated assault	643,720	1,796,000
Burglary	3,739,800	7,394,000
Larceny/theft	7,154,500	26,039,000
Motor vehicle theft	1,074,000	1,439,000
TOTAL	13,267,690	38,227,000

[a] As reported by citizens to police.
[b] As told by victims to interviewers, in national surveys.
Source: U.S. Department of Justice, Bureau of Justice Statistics, *Report to the Nation on Crime and Justice: The Data,* 1983, p. 7.

Third, police politics is a major source of bias in the FBI statistics. Law enforcers know that local politicians, businesses, the mass media, and the public at large often find out the crime situation in their areas from official reports. More importantly, they all interpret the reports in a certain way: low crime rates mean police effectiveness; high crime rates mean the problem is out of control. Therefore, when a police department is seeking additional funds or personnel, it is likely to make more arrests and report more crimes. Thus increases in crime rates shown in official statistics may sometimes be misleading (Thomas and Hepburn, 1983).

Given the limitations of official figures, researchers working with the President's Commission on Law Enforcement and Administration of Justice began in 1967 to ask national samples of Americans whether they had been victims of crime. Since 1973 this victimization survey, known as the National Crime Survey, has been providing yearly data on such things as the characteristics of victims and the "dark figure" of crime, which is not reported to the police. The most dramatic finding is the tremendous amount of criminal activity and victimization in the United States. The surveys show, for example, that in 1981 almost 25 million households—a third of all households—fell victim to at least one crime of violence or theft. Since many of these households were victimized more than once, the total number of victimizations—or criminal offenses—was far higher than 25 million; it came up to 41 million, three times the number known to the police. The prevalence of crime also comes across in the finding that the average American runs a higher risk of being victimized by a violent crime than he does of being hurt in a traffic accident.

The crime surveys further reveal who are more likely to be the victims: men more than women; the divorced or never married more than the married or widowed; young people more than elderly; lower-income more than higher-income people; the unemployed and students more than the employed, retirees, and housewives; and city dwellers more than rural residents (U.S. Dept. of Justice, 1983). Most of these differences seem to result from at least three risk factors: exposure (frequent contact with potential offenders), proximity (being in high-crime areas), and lack of guardianship (not having neighbors, police, burglar alarms, barred windows, and so on). Given these factors, people who engage in activities outside of the household, such as going to the movies or attending sports events, are more likely to be victimized than those who stay home to watch television or read a book. Thus young people, for example, suffer a greater chance of being victimized than do older citizens because the former go out more, thereby increasing their exposure and proximity to potential offenders and leaving behind the guardianship against them (Cohen, Kluegel, and Land, 1981; Messner and Blau, 1987).

While they get closer than the FBI statistics to the "true" level of crime, victimization surveys are not perfect, either. When asked whether they have been victimized during the past year, people may give inaccurate reports. An object that has simply been lost may be remembered as stolen. "Memory decay"—poor recall—can creep into victimization survey data. Interviewees may get involved in "backward telescoping," remembering that a crime took place earlier than it did, or they may be given to "forward telescoping," thinking that it occurred more recently than it did. Either way it can reduce the validity of victimization surveys because such studies define crimes as those that have occurred during a specified period of time only (Gottfredson and Hindelang, 1981; Thomas and Hepburn, 1983). Sometimes people simply cannot remember whether they have been victimized within a certain time frame. In one study where the respondents were known from police files to have been victims of crime, about 20 percent failed to report the offenses to survey interviewers (Gottfredson and Hindelang, 1981). These recall problems, however, do not invalidate victimization surveys seriously because they may cancel each other—with some overreporting and others underreporting victimizations.

Another method for measuring crime is the self-report study. While victimization surveys focus on victims, self-report studies concentrate on offenders, asking people whether they have committed a crime. The results have by and large shown that there are no class and race differences in *overall* criminality, which refute the popularly held theory and the FBI finding that lower-class people have higher crime rates than do those of higher classes (see Johnson, 1980; Krohn et al., 1980; Tittle, 1983; but also Thornberry and Farnworth, 1982, for contrasting findings). Other self-report studies, however, have shown status differences in *specific* forms of offenses. Delbert Elliott and Suzanne Ageton (1980), for example, found that lower-class youths are more likely than their middle-class peers to commit serious criminal offenses. In his review of numerous studies, John Braithwaite (1981) concluded that the lower classes are more likely to be involved in "directly interpersonal crimes" such as murder, rape, robbery, and assault, but that the middle and upper classes tend more to commit "less directly interpersonal crimes" such as tax evasion, employee theft, and fraudulent advertising. Let us, then, take a closer look at these two types of crime by analyzing murder and corporate crime.

Murder

Murder is a relatively rare crime. It occurs less often than any of the other major offenses such as rape, robbery, and aggravated assault. We are even less likely to be murdered by others than to get ourselves killed in a car accident. But murder does not appear reassuringly rare if we see it from another angle. According to the FBI (1988), one American is murdered every 26 minutes. The chance of becoming a murder victim for all Americans is 1 out of 157. The odds are especially high for nonwhite males, who have a 1 out of 29 probability of being murdered. Regardless of our race or gender, our chance of murder victimization peaks when we reach the age of 25 (Farley, 1980; Akiyama, 1981).

Homicide occurs most frequently during weekend evenings, particularly on Saturday night. This holds true largely for lower-class murderers but not for middle- and upper-class offenders, who kill on any day of the week. One apparent reason is that higher-class murders are more likely than lower-class homicides to be premeditated—hence less likely to result from alcohol-induced eruptions during weekend sprees (Green and Wakefield, 1979). Research has also frequently shown that most of the murderers in this country are poor. Marvin Wolfgang (1958) estimated that 90 to 95 percent of the offenders came from the lower end of the occupational scale. A more recent study showed that 92 percent of the murderers were semiskilled workers, unskilled laborers, or welfare recipients (Swigert and Farrell, 1976). The latest analysis by Kirk Williams (1984) confirmed these and other similar findings. We should note, however, that the rich and powerful actually cause far more deaths than the poor. Every year, while fewer than 24,000 Americans are murdered mostly by the poor, over 100,000 U.S. workers die from occupational diseases alone, attributable to corporate disregard for safe working conditions (Simon and Eitzen, 1986).

Whatever their class, murderers most often use handguns to kill (FBI, 1988). Perhaps seeing a gun while

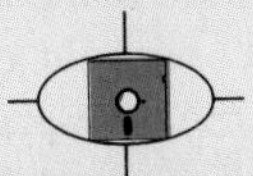

LOOKING AT CURRENT RESEARCH

From Prizefight to Homicide

Does watching two boxers slug it out on TV encourage people to commit murder? The answer is yes, according to sociologist David Phillips. This is based on findings from his current research, as reported below. How does his research help sociologists understand the social forces that create and shape deviant behavior?

The impact of mass media violence on aggression has almost always been studied in the laboratory. In a well-known series of such studies, psychologist Leonard Berkowitz and various associates examined the impact of a filmed prizefight in the laboratory. They found that angered laboratory subjects behaved more aggressively after seeing a filmed prizefight scene. In contrast, angered laboratory subjects exposed to a track meet film displayed a significantly lower level of aggression. However, we cannot generalize with confidence from the impact of mass media violence *in the laboratory* to the impact of mass media violence *in the real world*. Laboratory experiments have been set in highly artificial contexts. Typically, the sorts of aggression studied in a laboratory (like hitting plastic dolls or inflicting electric shocks) have not been representative of serious, real-life violence, such as murder or rape.

The current study, however, examines the effect of mass media violence in the real world. It presents what may be the first systematic evidence suggesting that some homicides are indeed triggered by a type of mass media violence. This study builds on earlier research which showed, among other things, (1) U.S. suicides increase after publicized suicide stories, (2) the more publicity given to the suicide story, the more suicides occur thereafter, and (3) auto fatalities increase just after publicized suicide stories. It was concluded that suicide stories appear to elicit additional suicides, some of which are disguised as auto accidents. It would be interesting to discover whether *homicide* stories elicit additional homicides.

For this study an exhaustive list of championship heavyweight prizefights and their dates was obtained from *The Ring Book Boxing Encyclopedia*. The period 1973–1978 has been chosen for analysis because, for this period, daily counts of all U.S. homicides are publicly available from the National Center for Health Statistics. These data show that, between 1973 and 1978, immediately after heavyweight championship prizefights, U.S. homicides increased by 12.46 percent. The increase was greatest on the third day after the prizefights. It is interesting to note that this "third-day peak" appears not ony in the present study but also, repeatedly, in several earlier investigations: California auto fatalities peak on the third day after publicized suicide stories, as do Detroit auto fatalities. The increase was greatest after heavily publicized prizefights. The most touted of all the prizefights in this period, the so-called "Thrilla in Manila" between Ali and Frazier, displayed the largest third-day peak in homicides. At present, the best available explanation is that the prizefight provokes some imitative, aggressive behavior, which results in an increase in homicides.

Source: Excerpted and adapted from David P. Phillips, "Mass media violence and U.S. homicides," *American Sociological Review*, 48, 1983, pp. 560–568.

embroiled in a heated argument may incite a person into murderous action. As Shakespeare said, "How oft the sight of means to do ill deeds, makes ill deeds done." This may be similar to feeling more inclined to kill after watching a prizefight on TV (see box, above). Of course, firearms by themselves cannot cause homicide, nor can their absence reduce the motivation to kill. It is true that "Guns don't kill, people do." Still, were guns less available, many heated arguments would have resulted in aggravated assaults rather than murders, thereby reducing the number of fatalities. One study suggests that attacks with knives are five times *less* likely to result in death than are attacks with guns (Wright et al., 1983). In fact, the use of less dangerous weapons such as knives in attempted murders has been estimated to cause 80 percent fewer deaths (Newton and Zimring, 1969). Given the enormous number of guns in private hands (about 120 million), it is not surprising that far more deaths result from gun attacks in this country than in Canada, England, and Japan (Rodino, 1986).

Ironically, murder is the most personal crime, largely committed against relatives, friends, or acquaintances. According to the U.S. Department of Justice (1983), at least 55 percent of all murder victims were related to or knew their murderer. An earlier study showed the figure to be 80 percent (Swigert and Farrell, 1976). Many of us may find it incredible that the people we know or even love are more likely to kill us than are total strangers. "This should really not be very surprising," Donald Mulvihill and Melvin Tumin (1969) have explained. "Everyone is within easy striking distance from intimates for a large part of the time. Although friends, lovers, spouses, and the like are a main source of pleasure in one's life, they are equally a main source of frustration and hurt. Few others can anger one so much." The act of murder requires a great deal of emotion. It is a crime of passion carried out under the overwhelming pressure of a volcanic emotion. It may be more difficult for us to kill a stranger for whom we don't have any sympathetic or antagonistic feelings. Only psychotic or professional killers can do away with people in a cold-blooded, unemotional manner (Levi, 1981). But such impersonal killings are rare.

Corporate Crime

Unlike murder, corporate crimes are committed by company executives without the overt use of force, and their effect on the victims is not readily traceable to the culprit. If a miner dies from a lung disease, it is difficult to prove beyond reasonable doubt that he had died *because* his employer violated mine safety regulations (Braithwaite and Geis, 1982). Corporate crimes may be perpetrated not only against employees, but also against customers and the general public. Examples are disregard for safety in the workplace, consumer fraud, price fixing, production of unsafe products, and violations of environmental regulations. Compared to traditional "street crime," corporate crime is more rationally executed, more profitable, and less detectable by law enforcers. In addition, crime in the suite is distinguished from crime in the street by three characteristics.

Three Distinct Characteristics First is the victim's unwitting cooperation with the corporate criminal, which results mostly from carelessness or ignorance. In a home-improvement scheme, the victims do not bother to check the work history of the fraudulent company that solicits them, and they sign a contract without examining its contents for such matters as the true price and the credit terms. Some victims purchase goods through the mail without checking the reputation of the firm. Doctors prescribe untested dangerous drugs after having relied on only the pharmaceutical company's salespeople and advertising. It may be difficult for the victims to know they are victimized, even if they want to find out the true nature of their victimization. Grocery shoppers, for example, are hard put to detect such unlawful substances as residues of hormones, antibiotics, pesticides, and nitrites in the meat they buy.

A second characteristic is the society's indifference to corporate crimes. Generally, little effort is made to catch corporate criminals, and on the rare occasions when they are caught, they seldom go to jail. Even if they do go to prison, they are likely to stay there for less than three days (Clinard, 1979). If their terms are

Deliberately violating safety regulations is one form of corporate crime. Unsafe working conditions, dangerous or faulty products, and price fixing are some of the corporate crimes that cost society money, cause injuries, and claim lives. Here are a few of the numerous people blinded by the toxic fumes that escaped from a Union Carbide pesticide plant in Bhopal, India. The fumes killed more than 2500 people and seriously injured many thousands more. The Indian government has filed a $3 billion suit against the chemical company, which it holds responsible for causing the poison-gas leak.

"Kickbacks, embezzlement, price fixing, bribery . . . this is an extremely high-crime area."

longer, they need not worry too much, either, because their companies will take care of their families and give them their old jobs back when they get out. In recent years there has been less societal indifference toward corporate crime. In price-fixing cases, fines of up to $1 million for the company and $100,000 for individuals can be imposed, and corporate executives can be sent to prison for three years (Clinard and Yeager, 1978). It is doubtful, however, that the government can wage an all-out war against corporate criminals because they are too powerful economically and politically. Moreover, while most people consider corporate crime more serious today than they did in the early 1970s, they still regard it as less serious than traditional crimes such as burglary and robbery (Cullen, Link, and Polanzi, 1982). Therefore, corporate criminals continue to receive lighter punishment than street criminals. In 1985, the giant investment firm of E. F. Hutton was found guilty of 2000 counts of mail and wire fraud, for which it must pay a $2 million fine. This may look like a lot of money, but actually it is peanuts to E. F. Hutton, which has annual revenues of $2.8 billion and profits of $52 million. Besides, not a single Hutton official was indicted. In the same year, the Bank of Boston pleaded guilty to violating a federal law by secretly funneling $1.22 billion in suspected organized crime money to and from European banks. The Bank was fined only $500,000 and not a single one of its officials was indicted (Thio, 1988).

These facts probably account for a third characteristic of corporate crime: the perpetrators often see themselves as respectable people rather than common criminals. Often they maintain their noncriminal self-image through rationalization. Violators of price-fixing laws, for example, may insist that they are helping the nation's economy be "stabilizing prices" and serving their companies by "recovering costs." There is no such crime as price fixing in their book.

Costs of Corporate Crime The economic cost of corporate crime is high—about 27 to 42 times greater each year than the losses from traditional property crimes such as robbery and burglary. Estimates of the total cost of corporate crime range from $50 to $200 billion a year. Price fixing alone costs this nation about $45 billion annually. All this makes the annual estimated loss of $3 or $4 billion from traditional crimes look like small potatoes (Conklin, 1977; Pauly, 1979).

Corporate crime also exacts a high physical cost. Bodily injury and even death may result from violations of health and safety laws, housing codes, and environmental regulations. The violence inflicted on the public by corporate criminals in their pursuit of profit far exceeds the violence by lower-class street criminals. According to the National Commission on Product Safety, 20 million Americans have suffered injuries from using consumer products, and among these victims 110,000 are permanently disabled and 30,000 are dead (Simon and Eitzen, 1986). It has been estimated that each year some 500,000 workers are needlessly exposed to toxic substances such as radioactive materials and poisonous chemicals because of corporate failures to obey safety laws (Anderson, 1981). Of the 4 million workers who have been exposed to asbestos in the United States, about 1.6 million are expected to die from lung cancer, a figure much higher than the total U.S. loss of 372,000 lives during World War II and subsequent wars (Balkan, Berger, and Schmidt, 1980).

There is also a high social cost imposed by corporate crime. Though unmeasurable, the social cost may be more far-reaching than the economic and physical toll. As a former U.S. attorney general wrote: "White-collar crime is the most corrosive of all crimes. The trusted prove untrustworthy; the advantaged, dishonest. . . . As no other crime, it questions our moral fiber" (Clark, 1971). Corporations sometimes weaken the democratic process by making illegal campaign contributions. In foreign countries American corporations operating there often make political payoffs. Such bribes interfere with the political process of those nations by strengthening the existing power structure and reinforce their image of America as an imperialist nation (Jacoby et al., 1977; Simon and Eitzen, 1986).

Mental Illness

While corporate crime and murder are criminal acts, other forms of deviance are not. A clear example is mental illness. Contrary to popular belief, mental illness is extremely common. Surveys have consistently shown that about 20 percent of American adults suffer from mental disorders serious enough to need professional help or hospitalization. It also has been estimated that over 80 percent experience some degree of impaired mental health—in the form of psychosomatic disorder; feelings of nervousness, tension, and restlessness; and difficulties in interpersonal relations (Srole et al., 1962; Weissman et al., 1978; Myers et al., 1984). In fact, all of us have been or shall be mentally ill in one way or another. Of course, most of our mental disorders are not serious at all. We occasionally come down with only a brief anxiety or depression, "the common cold of mental ailments." But the types of mental illness that sociologists—and psychiatrists—study are rather serious. They include **psychosis,** typified by loss of touch with reality, and **neurosis,** characterized by a persistent fear, anxiety, or worry about trivial matters. A psychotic can be likened to a person who thinks incorrectly that 2 plus 2 is equal to 10 but strongly believes it to be correct. On the other hand, a neurotic can be compared to a person who thinks correctly that 2 plus 2 is equal to 4 but constantly worries that it may not be so (Thio, 1988).

Sociologists have long suspected that certain social forces are involved in the development of mental disorder. The one that has been most consistently demonstrated by many different studies to be a key factor in mental illness is social class: the lower the social classes, the higher the rates of mental disorder (Faris and Dunham, 1939; Hollingshead and Redlich, 1958; Srole et al., 1962; Myers et al., 1984).

This finding, however, has prompted two conflicting explanations. One, known as *social causation,* suggests that lower-class people are more prone to mental disorder because they are more likely to have the following experiences: being subjected to social stress such as unemployment, family problems, or threat of criminal victimization; suffering from psychic frailty, infectious diseases, and neurological impairments; and lacking quality medical treatment, coping ability, and social support. The other explanation, called *social selection* or *drift,* suggests that the heavy concentration of mental disorder in the lower-class neighborhood results from the downward drift of mentally ill people into the neighborhood coupled with the upward movement of mentally healthy people out of it. This means that being a member of the lower class is a consequence rather than a cause of mental illness. Both explanations have been found to have some basis in fact, although a majority of the more recent studies favor the social causation interpretation (Eron and Peterson, 1982; Wheaton, 1978, 1980; Mirowsky and Ross, 1983; Kessler, 1979; Rushing and Ortega, 1979; Liem and Liem 1978; Turner and Gartrell, 1978). In general, the evidence for the drift theory comes from studies of extremely serious mental illness such as schizophrenia. The early onset of such illness usually causes individuals to lose their jobs or suffer downward mobility. But the evidence for social causation comes from studies of less severe disorders such as depression and phobia. These problems are more likely to result from the social stresses of lower-class lives (Kessler, Price, and Wortman, 1985).

Is Deviance Always Harmful?

We are accustomed to thinking of deviance as bad. But deviance is not always or completely harmful to society. It can bring benefits if it occurs within limits. Sociologists have noted at least five positive functions of deviance.

First, deviance may enhance conformity in the society as a whole by defining and clarifying norms. Norms are basically abstract and ambiguous, subject to conflicting interrelations. Even criminal laws, which are far more clear-cut than other norms, can be confusing. Through the crime a criminal commits and is punished for, other citizens obtain a concrete example of what constitutes a crime. During the Watergate scandal of the 1970s, for example, both politicians and the public clarified their opinions about which practices, though shady, were just "politics as usual," and which ones were unacceptable. From deviants we can learn the difference

Deviance is not harmful to society in every respect. It can enhance law-abiding behavior by clarifying the law. It can promote social cohesion by focusing collective outrage on the deviant. It can serve as a safety valve for discontented people. It can induce social change by calling attention to unjust laws. It can even provide jobs for many people, such as the judge and lawyers shown here. Judges and lawyers, along with police and prison guards, are only some of the people whose livelihoods depend on society's need to deal with crime and its consequences.

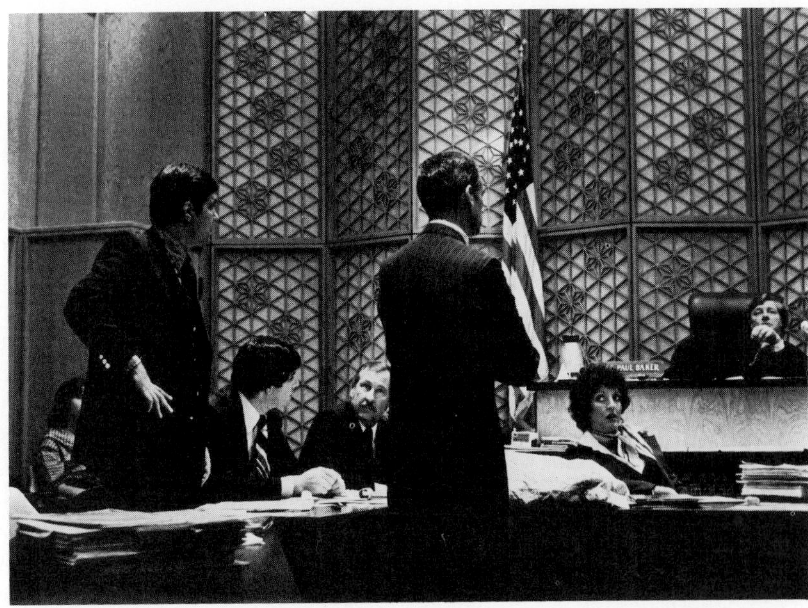

between conformity and deviance—we can see the boundary between right and wrong more clearly. Once aware of this boundary, we are more likely to stay on the side of righteousness (Erikson, 1966).

Second, deviance strengthens solidarity among law-abiding members of society. Differing values and interests may divide them, but collective outrage against deviants as their common enemy can unite them. Because it promotes social cohesion, Durkheim called deviance "a factor in public health, an integral part of all healthy societies" (Durkheim, 1966).

The third function of deviance is the provision of a safety valve for discontented people. Through relatively minor forms of deviance, they can strike out against the social order without doing serious harm to themselves or others. Prostitution, for example, may serve as a safety valve for marriage in a male-dominated society, because the customer is unlikely to form an emotional attachment to the prostitute. In contrast, a sexual relationship with a friend is more likely to develop into a love affair, which would destory a marriage (Cohen, 1966).

Fourth, deviance also provides jobs for many law-abiding people. The police, judges, lawyers, prison wardens, prison guards, criminologists, and others would be out of work if there were no criminals. Criminals also stimulate some useful developments. As Marx (1964) said, "Would locks ever have reached their present degree of excellence had there been no thieves? Would the making of bank notes have reached its present perfection had there been no forgers?"

Finally, deviant behavior sometimes induces social change. Martin Luther King, Jr., and other civil rights leaders were jeered and imprisoned for their opposition to segregation, but they moved the United States toward greater racial equality.

Despite these positive functions, widespread deviance obviously threatens the social order. First, it can destroy interpersonal relations. Alcoholism has torn many families apart. If a friend flies into a rage and tries to kill us, it will be difficult to maintain a harmonious relationship. Deviance can also undermine trust. If there were many killers, robbers, and rapists living in our neighborhood, we would find it impossible to welcome neighbors to our home as guests or babysitters. Finally, if deviance goes unpunished, it can weaken the will to conform throughout society. If we know that most people cheat on their taxes, for example, we may be tempted to do the same.

QUESTIONS FOR DISCUSSION AND REVIEW

1. Why do persons disagree about whether an act is deviant or not?
2. How do we obtain data on criminal forms of deviance, and why is each of these sources somewhat biased?
3. When do murders occur, and who usually commits them?
4. What are the three distinct characteristics of corporate crime?
5. Why is mental illness seen as a form of deviance, and what are some of its causes?
6. What are some of the positive and negative consequences of deviance?

EXPLANATIONS OF DEVIANCE

Obviously society has a large stake in understanding why deviance occurs. At various times and places, deviance has been viewed as a sin or a sickness, as the result of possession by demons or living in a wicked world, as the product of choice or circumstance. We can roughly divide current explanations of deviance into two types: those which look to individual characteristics for the cause, and those which focus on society itself.

Individual Characteristics

Two types of theories attempt to explain deviance by looking at characteristics of the individual. Biological theories say that the source of deviance can be found in the person's body. Psychological theories say the source is in the psyche.

Biological Explanations Early in this century an Italian physician, Cesare Lombroso (1918), studied hundreds of prison inmates in his country. Many appeared to him to have shifty eyes, high cheekbones, strong jaws, receding chins, wispy beards, oversized ears, and overlong arms. These traits, he said, resemble those of apes and savages, and criminals are therefore throwbacks to a more primitive stage of evolution. As such, criminals, he argued, enjoy excessive idleness, love orgies, or have an urge to kill people and then mutilate their bodies, eat their flesh, and drink their blood. He concluded that criminals are born, not made—that deviance is the product of inherited characteristics. But Lombroso had made a very basic error: he had not compared the physical characteristics of criminals and noncriminals. Later when another research made this comparison, he found no difference between the groups: Lombroso's "criminal" physical traits occurred with equal frequency among noncriminals. Lombroso's theory was totally discredited.

Since Lombroso's time there have been many attempts to identify some biological condition as the cause of deviance. In the 1940s an American psychologist, William Sheldon (1949), divided people into three types according to their body shapes: endomorphs (who are plump and soft), mesomorphs (muscular and tough), and ectomorphs (thin and delicate). He argued that each body shape produces certain temperament. The heavy person was considered viscerotonic (stomach-oriented)—given to overeating, passivity, and sluggishness. The muscular person was regarded as somatotonic (body-oriented)—active, assertive, and aggressive. The thin person was believed to be cerebrotonic (brain-oriented)—quite, shy, and withdrawn. From a study of 200 juveniles in Boston, Sheldon concluded that mesomorphs, who have the somatotonic temperament, are most likely to become criminals. Later, criminologists Sheldon Glueck and Eleanor Glueck (1956) compared 500 juvenile delinquents with 500 nondelinquents and found more mesomorphs among the former. Today, however, most sociologists would argue that it is not body type but the social definition of it that influences behavior. In Sheldon's and the Gluecks' studies, the muscular and tough juveniles might have appeared, in the eyes of their peers, more daring than the plump and soft or thin and delicate youngsters. Hence they might have been more encouraged to get involved in rowdy, delinquent activities.

More recently a new version of biological explanation has appeared (Fox, 1971; Shah and Roth, 1974; Mednick and Volavaka, 1980). It holds that a genetic defect called XYY may cause criminal violence. In normal males there are two sex chromosomes, X and Y. The X is inherited from the mother, and the Y comes from the father. It is assumed that the X causes gentle, passive behavor while the Y leads the carrier to be tough and aggressive. In normal males, then, the X and Y balance each other. But XYY males, due to the extra Y, are doubly aggressive and more likely to commit violent crimes. Research has shown that there are more XYYs among prison inmates than among the general population. But the XYY convicts are extremely few, making up no more than 5 percent of the prison population (Shah and Roth, 1974). Even among the few XYY criminals, societal reaction rather than the chromosomal abnormality might have led them to violent crimes. Since in their youth they were large, full of acne, and somewhat retarded, they might have been ridiculed and have learned to respond aggressively (McClearn, 1969).

Psychological Explanations There are also many theories that point to individual psychological characteristics as the cause of deviance. One of the best known is Freud's psychoanalytic theory (see Chapter 6: Socialization). As part of the id, our aggressive drive demands to be expressed. But our superego also demands that the aggressive drive be suppressed. Thus our aggressive drive may want us to cut up another person's body or to defeat him by taking away his life, but our superego in effect says "No!" Our ego has to step in and play the mediating role. It usually employs the "sublimation" approach, which enables us to satisfy our aggressive drive in a socially acceptable way. So *both* our aggressive drive and superego are satisfied when our ego tells us to cut another person's body as a surgeon or to defeat him in sport, politics, or business. Through sublimation, then, we learn to be normal.

However, if we were deprived of love during our childhood, our aggressive drive would become too irrational for our ego to cope with and too powerful for our superego to subdue. We could become emotionally disturbed and commit some extremely violent crime. A case in point is Edmund Emil Kemper III, who, as a child, felt rejected by his divorced parents and abused by his mother, with whom he had to live. At age 21, Kemper murdered eight young women by shooting, stabbing, and strangulation, then cut off their heads and hands, had sexual intercourse with the corpses, and ate flesh from some of them. Finally he went home and killed his mother. He chopped off her head and then cut out her larynx and dumped it down the garbage disposal. "This seems appropriate," he said later, "as much as she'd bitched, screamed, and yelled at me over the years" (Lunde, 1975). Such homicides are usually "the culmination of parental abuse that can no longer be tolerated" (Post, 1982).

On the other hand, if our parents tried too hard to turn us into good boys or girls by severely punishing us for expressing even the mildest form of aggression, such as cursing, we would also become mentally disturbed. Without the normal release of aggressive energy, we would gradually build up a seething caldron of that energy until it caused us to explode. This may explain why a seemingly very nice person can suddenly become a psychotic killer—to the profound shock and disbelief of his family, friends, and neighbors. Anthony Barbaro, age 17, was a nice boy. He was the kind of son parents boast about. He was quiet, considerate, a former Little Leaguer, altar boy, and Boy Scout. He studied hard, worked 20 hours a week as a busboy, and still managed to be in the top 2 percent of his class. He did not take drugs, drink, or smoke. His neighbors all said he came from a good family. On Christmas day of 1975, Barbaro took a rifle and shotgun to the top floor of his school. From there he opened fire at the people on the street. Within two hours, 3 people lay dead and 11 were injured (*Newsweek*, 1975). Earlier, a psychoanalytic study on 13 "sudden murderers" like Barbaro had concluded: "They come from cohesive family backgrounds, where conformity to the rules of the social system was emphasized" (Lamberti, Blackman, and Weiss, 1967; see also Levin and Fox, 1985).

Psychoanalysts ordinarily use logical reasoning and anecdotal illustrations to support their explanations, as presented above. But extremely few deviants are mentally ill. Besides, the psychoanalytic theory cannot be scientifically tested becasue it is impossible to observe and measure the aggressive drive. Thus other psychologists have proposed the testable theory that aggression is a response to frustration (Dollard et al., 1939). They suggest that if we are blocked from achieving a goal, we tend to strike out against others. But frustration rarely leads to deviant acts of aggression (Berkowitz, 1969). If you fail to get the summer job you wanted, you are far more likely to curse or bang a table than to strike a friend. In some instances frustration may lead to violence, but this is more likely to occur through the intervention of social forces. Thus frustrated individuals are more inclined to assault or kill a person if they come from a cultural environment where quick resort to physical aggression is socially approved (Wolfang, 1958) or if they have learned the value of interpersonal violence from their child-abusing parents (Garbarino and Gilliam, 1980).

In short, individual characteristics can certainly play a role in the occurrence of deviance—though under the influence of social factors. Nevertheless, psychology and biology can explain only a tiny fraction of deviance, which occurs largely among the mentally or physically abnormal. To understand the majority of deviants, who are normal, we should turn to sociological explanations. Sociological theories do not assume that there is something wrong with the deviant but instead seek out social environment as the source of deviance.

Anomie

Nearly 50 years ago Robert Merton (1938) developed a theory of deviance that is still very influential today. He built on Durkheim's concept of **anomie,** which literally means "normlessness." More generally, anomie is a condition in which norms are weak or in conflict. Anomie may arise, said Merton, when there is an inconsistency between the culture and the social structure. In the United States such an inconsistency surrounds the issue of success. American culture places great emphasis on success as a valued goal. From kindergarten to college, teachers encourage students to strive for good grades and to be ambitious. Parents and coaches even pressure Little League players not just to play well but to win. The media often glorify winning not only in sports but in business, politics, and other arenas of life. Meanwhile, the social structure does not provide a matching emphasis on the use of legitimate means to achieve this goal of success.

How do people respond when they are taught, in effect, that "Winning isn't everything—it's the only thing"? They may either accept or reject the goal of winning, and they may either accept or reject the use of socially accepted means to that end. Merton analyzed five possible responses to this condition (see Table 7.2).

1. *Conformity* is the most popular mode of adaptation. It involves accepting both the cultural goal of success and the use of legitimate means for achieving that goal.
2. *Innovation* is an adaptation that produces deviance, including crime. When people adopt this response, they accept the goal of success, but they reject the use of socially accepted means to achieve it, turning instead to unconventional methods. The thief and the pimp are, in this sense, "innovators."
3. *Ritualism* occurs when people follow social norms rigidly and compulsively, even though they no longer hope to achieve the goal set by their culture. Working hard by obeying the rules to the letter becomes more important than achieving success. A petty bureaucrat can be considered a ritualist.
4. *Retreatism* is withdrawal from society. Psychotics, alcoholics, drug addicts, and tramps are all retreatists. They care neither about success nor about working.
5. *Rebellion* occurs when people reject and attempt to change both the goals and the means approved by society. The rebel tries to overthrow the existing system and establish a new system with different goals and means. This may involve replacing the current American system of pursuing fame and riches through competition with a new system of enhancing social relations through cooperation.

Table 7.2 How Would You Respond to Goals-Means Gap?

In American society, according to Merton, there is too much emphasis on success but lack of emphasis on the legitimate means for achieving success. Such inconsistency may cause deviant behavior, yet various people respond to it differently.

Modes of Adaption	Cultural Goals	Institutionalized Means
1. Conformity	acceptance	acceptance
2. Innovation	acceptance	rejection
3. Ritualism	rejection	acceptance
4. Retreatism	rejection	rejection
5. Rebellion	rejection of old, introduction of new	rejection of old, introduction of new

Source: Adapted with permission of The Free Press, a Division of Macmillan, Inc., from *Social Theory and Social Structure* by Robert K. Merton. Copyright © 1957 by The Free Press, renewed 1985 by Robert K. Merton.

Anomie is not restricted to any one social group, but is has special implications for the poor. They receive the same message as other Americans: that success is a valued goal, and that how one achieves that goal is less important than reaching it. But society does not provide them with equal opportunities to achieve success. For the poor, in particular, there is likely to be a gap between aspiration and opportunity, and this gap may pressure them toward deviance. According to Merton's theory, it fosters innovation, retreatism, and rebellion because each of these adaptations involves the rejection of socially accepted avenues of success. Each also produces deviant behavior.

Merton's analysis provides an explanation for high rates of property crime in the United States, particularly among its lower classes. But anomie theory cannot explain forms of deviance—such as murder, rape, and vandalism—that are unrelated to success. People who do these things are far from ambitious; they do not commit the crimes as a way of expressing their desire for success. The theory also fails to explain crimes such as embezzlement and tax fraud by those who are already successful. Without taking into account these white-collar crimes, Merton has been criticized for assuming that the poor are more prone to criminality in general than are the rich. Finally, Merton has drawn fire for his assumption of value consensus. As a structural functionalist (Chapter 1: Thinking Sociologically), he assumes that the same value—belief in success—governs various groups in our society. But this runs counter to the pluralistic and conflicting nature of American society, where many ethnic and religious groups do not share the same values. Thus some may engage in deviant acts—such as gambling, cockfighting, violations of fish and game laws, and handling of poisonous snakes to prove one's faith in God—without having been influenced by the cultural goal of success (Thio, 1973, 1988).

Differential Association

In the 1920s Clifford Shaw and Henry McKay (1929) discovered that high rates of crime and delinquency had persisted in the same Chicago neighborhoods for more than 20 years, although different ethnic groups had lived in those neighborhoods. This discovery led Shaw and McKay to develop the theory of **cultural transmission.** The traditions of crime and delinquency, they said, are transmitted from one group to another, much as language is passed from one generation to another. The key assumption is that deviant behavior, like language, is learned.

In the 1930s Edwin Sutherland explained how this cultural transmission might occur (Sutherland and Cressey, 1978). Deviance, said Sutherland, is learned through interactions with other people. Individuals learn not only how to perform deviant acts such as burglary and marijuana smoking but also how to define these actions. Various social groups have different norms, and acts considered deviant by the dominant culture may be viewed positively by some groups. Each person is likely to be exposed to both positive and negative definitions of these actions. How a person ends up defining them depends on **differential association**—the amount of exposure to the differing definitions—and on the person's relationship to those presenting the varying views. The definitions of close friends are likely to have the greatest influence on a person's view of deviant acts.

Note that Sutherland was not saying that "bad company" will turn us into criminals. If this were the case, we would expect lawyers, judges, and police officers to be criminals because they spend so much time with criminals. Rather, differential association theory holds that deviant behavior arises if interactions with those who view these actions positively *outweigh* interactions with those who view them negatively. Which views are most influential depends not just on the frequency and duration of the interactions but also on the relationship between the people in the interaction.

Sutherland developed his theory to explain various forms of deviance, including white-collar crimes such as tax evasion, embezzlement, and price fixing. All these misdeeds were shown to result from some association with groups that considered the wrongdoings acceptable. But it is difficult, according to critics, to determine precisely what differential association is. Most people cannot identify the persons from whom they have learned a procriminal or anticriminal definition, much less know whether they have been exposed to one definition more frequently, longer, or more intensely than the other definition (Sutherland and Cressey, 1978).

Labeling

Both anomie and differential association theories focus on the causes of rule violation. In contrast, labeling theory, which emerged in the 1960s, concentrates on societal reaction to rule violation and the impact of this reaction on the rule violator.

According to labeling theorists, society tends to react to a rule-breaking act by labeling it deviant. Deviance, then, is not something that a person does but merely a label imposed on that behavior. As Howard Becker (1963) said, "Deviance is *not* a quality of the act the person commits, but rather a consequence of the application by others of rules and sanctions to an 'offender.' The deviant is one to whom that label has successfully been applied; deviant behavior is behavior that people so label." The label itself has serious and negative consequences—even beyond any immediate punishment for the deviant—for the individual.

Once a person is labeled a thief or a delinquent or a drunk, he or she may be stuck with that label for life and be rejected and isolated as a result. Finding a job and making friends may be extremely difficult (Link, 1982). More important, the person may come to accept the label and commit more deviant acts. William Chambliss (1973) described what happened to the Roughnecks—a group of lower-class boys—when their community labeled them as delinquents:

> The community responded to the Roughnecks as boys in trouble, and the boys agreed with that perception. Their pattern of deviancy was reinforced, and breaking away from it became increasingly unlikely. Once the

What society considers deviant behavior varies from place to place and time to time. Labeling theorists carry this idea to its ultimate conclusion. They believe that tagging a person as deviant can make the person deviant. A social drinker who gets tagged as an alcoholic can become an alcoholic because people begin to treat him as one and pressure him to live up to that social image. Although the theory has been criticized, it is true that troubled people frequently have difficulty changing their reputations, even when their behavior has changed. Society's reluctance to discard a label may cause the deviant to give up efforts to change. The former alcoholic may resume drinking simply out of frustration because people will not treat him as a sober and responsible person.

> boys acquired an image of themselves as deviants, they selected new friends who affirmed that self-image. As that self-conception became more firmly entrenched, they also became willing to try new and more extreme deviances. With their growing alienation came freer expression of disrespect and hostility for representatives of the legitimate society.

Labeling people as deviants, in short, can push them toward further and greater deviance.

Much earlier, Frank Tannenbaum (1938) had noted this process of becoming deviant. According to him, children may break windows, annoy people, climb over a roof, steal apples, and play hooky—and innocently consider these activities just a way of having fun. Edwin Lemert (1951) gave the name **primary deviance** to such violations of norms that a person commits for the first time and without considering them deviant. Now suppose parents, teachers, and police consider a child's pranks to be a sign of delinquency or evil. They may "dramatize the evil" by admonishing or scolding the child. They may even go further, hauling the child into juvenile court and labeling the child as bad, a delinquent—a deviant. If the child accepts the definition, he or she may be on the same path as the Roughnecks. The child, then, may try to live up to his or her bad self-image by becoming increasingly involved in deviant behavior. Lemert gave the term **secondary deviance** to such repeated norm-violations, which the violators themselves recognize as deviant. Secondary deviants are, in effect, confirmed or career deviants.

Labeling helps us understand how secondary deviance might develop, and it sensitizes us to the power of labels. The theory is actually a version of symbolic interactionism (Chapter 1: Thinking Sociologically). It is based on the assumption that deviance involves a symbolic interaction, with society acting toward certain people by labeling them deviant and these people reacting by becoming secondary deviants. But the theory has been subjected to many criticisms (Harris and Hill, 1982; Thio, 1988). First, it cannot explain why primary deviance occurs in the first place. Second, it assumes that individuals passively accept the label of deviant thrust on them by others. Hence, it cannot explain why some people, such as political leaders and corporate executives, are better able than others like juvenile delinquents to resist accepting the "deviant" label. Third, labeling theory cannot deal with deviance that occurs in secret, which obviously is not labeled deviant by others. Due to the absence rather than presence of a "deviant" label, the secrecy may even encourage a person to continue engaging in deviant activities such as income tax evasion. Conflict theory, however, can deal with these problems.

Conflict

Like labeling theory, conflict theory is concerned with the societal definition of deviance. But it also emphasizes power differentials as determinants of both deviant labeling *and* deviant behavior. Thus it can explain what labeling theory cannot. According to conflict theory, the powerful are more likely than the powerless to commit profitable primary deviant acts (such as tax fraud and price fixing), to resist the label of deviant, and to engage in secret, undetectable deviant activities (Thio, 1973, 1988; Braithwaite and Geis, 1982). There are, however, two versions of conflict theory: traditional and contemporary. One was introduced in the 1930s and the other in the 1970s.

Traditional Conflict Theory Traditional conflict theorists focus mostly on *cultural* conflict as a source of deviant definition and behavior. Cultural conflict arises whenever what is considered right by one subculture is considered wrong by another, more powerful subculture—usually the dominant culture. A classic case of this conflict involved a Sicilian father in New Jersey in the 1930s: After killing his daughter's 16-year-old "seducer," he felt proud of having defended his family honor in a traditional way, but he was very surprised when the police came to arrest him (Sellin, 1938).

The triumph and defeat of Prohibition—which outlawed the sale of alcoholic beverages between 1919 and 1933—has also been offered as another case of cultural conflict (Goode, 1984b). The triumph of Prohibition in 1919 reflected the power and life-style of rural dwellers, southerners, white Anglo-Saxon Protestants, and Americans of native-born parentage, all of whom considered drinking totally disreputable. By 1933 Prohibition was repealed because a new group that became more powerful saw nothing wrong with drinking. This group consisted of urban dwellers, northeasterners, non-Protestants (mostly Irish, Italians, and Jews), and sons and daughters of immigrants. The law, in essence, supports one subculture as worthy of respect and condemns another as deviant (Gusfield, 1967a). In other words, people become deviant because they are on the losing side of a cultural conflict.

Contemporary Conflict Theory Most of the contemporary conflict theorists are Marxists, who focus mostly on class conflict in capitalist society as the mainspring of deviant labeling and behavior.

Many people assume that the law is based on the consent of citizens, that it treats citizens equally, and that it serves the best interest of society. If we simply read the U.S. Constitution and statutes, this assumption may indeed seem justified. But study of the *law in the books,* as William Chambliss (1969, 1973) pointed out, may be misleading. The laws in the books do indeed say that the authorities ought to be fair and just. But are they? To understand crime, Chambliss argued, we need to look at the *law in action,* at how legal authorities actually discharge their duty. After studying the law in action, Chambliss concluded that legal authorities are actually unfair and unjust, favoring the rich and powerful over the poor and weak.

A speakeasy from the era of Prohibition. Between 1919 and 1933, the sale of alcoholic beverages was outlawed by an amendment to the Constitution. A powerful group, rural Americans, considered drinking to be deviant and managed to outlaw it. But the people lumped in the deviant category were largely urban, and later became so numerous and powerful that they had Prohibition repealed. The experience of Prohibition shows clearly that whether a behavior is considered deviant or not can result from a cultural conflict, with the more powerful group imposing its cultural view on others.

Richard Quinney (1974) blamed the unjust law directly on the capitalist system. "Criminal law," said Quinney, "is used by the state and the ruling class to secure the survival of the capitalist system . . . criminal law will be increasingly used in the attempt to maintain domestic order." This involves the dominant class doing four things: First, it defines as criminal those behaviors which threaten its interests. Second, it hires law enforcers to apply those definitions and protect its interests. Third, it exploits the subordinate class so that the resulting oppressive life conditions force the powerless to commit what those in power have defined as crimes. Fourth, it uses these criminal actions to spread and reinforce the popular view that the subordinate class is dangerous, in order to justify its concerns with making and enforcing the law. The upshot is the production and maintenance of a high level of criminality by the powerless (Quinney, 1975).

Other Marxists argue that the capitalists' ceaseless drive to increase profit by cutting labor costs has created a large class of unemployed workers. These people become what Marxists call **marginal surplus population**—superfluous or useless to the economy. They are likely to commit property crimes to survive. The exploitative nature of capitalism also causes violent crimes (such as murder, assault, and rape) and noncriminal deviances (such as alcoholism, suicide, and mental illness). As Sheila Balkan and her colleagues (1980) explained, economic "marginality leads to a lack of self-esteem and a sense of powerlessness and alienation, which create intense pressures on individuals. Many people turn to violence in order to vent their frustrations and strike out against symbols of authority, and others turn this frustration inward and experience severe emotional difficulties."

Marxists further contend that the monopolistic and oligopolistic nature of capitalism encourages corporate crime, because "when only a few firms dominate a sector of the economy they can more easily collude to fix prices, divide up the market, and eliminate competitors" (Greenberg, 1981). Smaller firms, unable to compete with giant corporations and earn enough profits, are also motivated to shore up their sagging profits by illegal means. "One would thus expect," wrote David Greenberg (1981), "consumer fraud, labor law violations (such as hiring illegal immigrants at wages below the legal minimum), fencing operations, and tax evasions to occur more frequently when the economy is dominated by a few giant firms." The highly competitive nature of capitalism is also blamed for pressuring both big and small companies to cross the thin line from sharp to shady business practices (Gordon, 1973; Reiman and Headlee, 1981).

In evaluating conflict theory we can see that it is useful for understanding why certain laws are made and enforced. The law of vagrancy, for example, originated in England as a capitalist attempt to force workers to accept employment at low wages—because a vagrant was, in the eye of the new law, one who does not work. Even laws that appear to protect the powerless may have resulted from the powerful's concern with their own interests. The law against rape, for instance, can be traced to the old days when women were treated as men's property. Rape was in effect considered a property crime against a man—the victim's father if she was unmarried or husband if married.

Conflict theory is also useful for understanding how power differentials pressure the poor to commit less profitable crimes (such as murder, rape, and robbery) and tempt the rich to perpetrate more profitable crimes (such as tax fraud, price fixing, and false advertising). Some sociologists have criticized Marxists for condemning capitalism as the casue of all crimes and ignoring the existence of crime in socialist and communist nations (Goode, 1984b). But Marxists actually assume that some forms of crime always exist in any society. They only argue that such crimes as corporate, employee, and street crimes are far more common under capitalism than under democratic socialism (Young, 1984).

QUESTIONS FOR DISCUSSION AND REVIEW

1. Why can't we explain most forms of deviance by individual characteristics alone?
2. What did Merton mean by anomie, and how can this experience lead to deviant behavior?
3. Why do many sociologists criticize the assumptions of Edwin Sutherland's differential association theory?
4. What factors might push persons from primary to secondary forms of deviance, according to labeling theory?
5. How does conflict theory explain why certain laws are made and enforced?

CONTROLLING DEVIANCE

As we discussed in Chapter 6 (Socialization), society transmits its values to individuals through socialization. If families, schools, and other socializing agents do their jobs well, then individuals internalize the values of their society, accepting society's norms as their own. They become conformists and law-abiding citizens.

Internalization through socialization is the most efficient way of controlling deviant behavior. It produces unconscious, spontaneous self-control. As a result, most people find it natural to conform to most social norms most of the time. Violating the norms makes them feel guilty, ashamed, or at least uncomfortable. Most people act as their own policepersons.

But as we have seen, socialization is never completely successful. A few people commit serious crimes, and everyone deviates occasionally, at least from some trivial norms. Thus control by others—**social control**—is also needed to limit deviance and maintain social order.

Social Control

Social control may be either informal or formal. Teachers, preachers, peer groups, even strangers enforce informal controls through frowning, gossip, criticism, or ridicule. When deviant acts are serious, formal controls are usually imposed. These come from police, judges, prison guards, and similar agents. The formal controllers are specifically appointed by the state, and they can be expected to punish deviants severely.

In small nonindustrialized societies, informal control is the primary or only means of handling deviance. It may involve such mild expressions of disapproval as a frown, scowl, scolding, or reprimand, as in modern industrialized societies. But it may also call for more serious punishment such as beating, maiming, or killing. Such informal control is administered on a private basis, usually by the aggrieved party. This can be seen among the Maya Indians of South Mexico, who believe that you should kill a person who has wronged you. The Eskimos of the American Arctic would also kill people for such offenses as adultery, insult, or being a nuisance. The Ifugao of the Philippines consider it necessary for any "self-respecting man" to kill an adulterer caught red-handed (Black, 1983). Violence in these societies is nonetheless quite rare—so are adultery and other deviances—apparently a testament to the effectiveness of informal control. The deterrent effect of informal control in traditional societies is at least greater than that of formal control in modern societies. As Donald Black (1983) pointed out, in the 1950s the rape incidence among the Gusii of Kenya shot up after the British colonial government prohibited traditional violence against the rapist and started to use the law to deal with the criminal.

In our society, informal control can also be more effective than formal control in deterring deviance. In one study, Richard Hollinger and John Clark (1982) found that informal control in the form of fellow workers' expressions of disapproval constrained employee theft more than did formal control in the form of reprimand or dismissal by management. Earlier studies on shoplifting and marijuana use had also found informal sanctions by peers to be a stronger brake on deviant behavior when compared with the threat of formal—criminal or legal—sanctions (Kraut, 1976; Anderson, Chiricos, and Waldo, 1977).

Nevertheless, our society is marked by an extensive system of formal control. Perhaps formal control has become more important in modern industrialized nations because, as discussed in Chapter 4 (Social Structure), they have become more heterogeneous and more impersonal than traditional societies. This societal change may have increased social conflicts and enhanced the need for formal control. Unfortunately, formal control may backfire, promoting rather than containing deviance (see box, p. 178).

Criminal Justice

The criminal justice system is a network of police, courts, and prisons. These law enforcers are supposed to protect society, but they are also a potential threat to an individual's freedom. If they wanted to ensure that not a single criminal could slip away, the police would have to deprive innocent citizens of their rights and liberties. They would restrict our freedom of movement and invade our privacy—by tapping phones, reading mail, searching homes, stopping pedestrians for questioning, and blockading roads. No matter how law-abiding we might be, we would always be treated like criminal suspects—and some of us would almost certainly fall into the dragnet.

To prevent such abuses, the American criminal justice system is restrained by the Constitution and laws. Americans have the right to be presumed innocent until proven guilty, not to incriminate themselves, and many other legal protections. The freedom of the police to search homes and question suspects is limited. Thus Americans' freedom, especially freedom from being wrongly convicted and imprisoned, is protected. But these laws also make the U.S. criminal justice system less effective than its counterparts in more repressive societies such as the Soviet Union (Sykes, 1978).

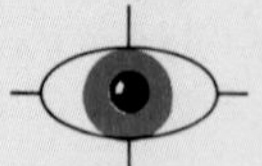

USING SOCIOLOGICAL INSIGHT

Prison and Probation

Our society tries to control deviant behavior mostly through formal social controls. Now enormous numbers of persons are imprisoned, and to reduce the increase in prison populations, growing numbers of criminals are put on probation. But the experience of California described in this reading suggests that both prison and probation do not successfully deter crime. Why do they fail, and what are some alternatives?

Every week, the nation's overcrowded prisons must find room for 1,000 more inmates. The U.S. Government Accounting Office estimates that by 1990 the national prison population will increase to more than half-a-million prisoners. Under federal court orders to ease overcrowding, states released 21,000 prisoners in 1983 before they completed their sentences. To reduce the steady flow into prisons, states choose increasingly to put criminals, even felons, on probation.

In *Prison versus Probation in California: Implications for Crime and Offender Recidivism,* Rand criminologists Joan Petersilia and Susan Turner with Joyce E. Peterson compare 511 criminals sentenced to prison with 511 others who had been put on probation. All came from urban Los Angeles and Alameda counties, and the criminal and personal backgrounds of the two groups were closely matched.

The comparison showed a disheartening rate of failure of *both* prison and probation as a means of reducing the number of crimes committed by the study subjects. In all, the 1,022 probationers and former prisoners had 1,300 new charges filed against them in the two-year study period. About 45 percent of the charges were for crimes against property, 28 percent for violent crimes, 12 percent for violation of drug laws, and 15 percent for other offenses.

Two years following their release from prison, 72 percent of the prisoners had been rearrested, 53 percent had new charges filed against them, and 47 percent had been incarcerated again. The probationers fared only a little better. In the two years following their probation sentences, 63 percent had been rearrested, 38 percent had new charges filed against them, and 31 percent were sent back to jail or prison.

The report estimates that each former prisoner committed twenty crimes compared to twenty-five crimes committed by each probationer during the three years following the subjects' sentencing: "These estimates indicate that society definitely benefited, in terms of crimes prevented, by incapacitating the prisoners for an average of nine months longer than the probationers." But it also costs more to imprison offenders. When all costs of the initial imprisonment or probation were added up, plus the costs of parole supervision, police and court processing for subsequent arrests, and subsequent incarceration, the researchers found that California taxpayers paid about $23,000 per prisoner and about $13,000 per probationer over the three years.

Authorities in a number of locations around the country are experimenting with programs involving intensive supervision of probationers. Some of the elements included in such programs are daily reporting to probation officers, random drug tests, electronic monitoring, house arrest, and performance of community services. Offenders in such programs usually must have jobs and must pay for all or part of the cost of their own supervision, which makes the programs economically attractive. Sometimes they must also reimburse their victims.

Source: Reprinted from "Prisons and Probation," from "Social Science and the Citizen." Published by permission of Transaction Publishers from *Society,* Vol. 24, No. 4, p. 3. Copyright © 1987 by Transaction Publishers.

Herein lies the dilemma of the criminal justice system: if it does not catch enough criminals, the streets will not be safe; if it tries to apprehend too many, our freedom will be in trouble. Striking a balance between effective protection from criminals and respect for individual freedom is far from easy. This may be why the criminal justice system is criticized from right and left. It is attacked both for coddling criminals and for being too harsh.

There is some merit in both criticisms. Most criminals in the United States are never punished. The FBI's annual *Uniform Crime Reports* shows that every year about 80 percent of those who commit such serious "street crimes" as robbery, rape, and auto theft are not arrested. Even a higher percentage of white-collar criminals are left unpunished. Of those few street criminals who are unlucky enough to be caught, many (45 to 55 percent) manage to slip through the court system free, thanks to dropping and dismissal of charges by prosecutors and judges. Of those who are convicted, about 90 percent have taken advantage of **plea bargaining,** whereby the defendant agrees to plead guilty to a lesser charge and thus receive a less severe penalty. As a result, less than 5 percent of all the known perpetrators of serious crimes are eventually sent to prison. Finally, about 80 percent of the prisoners do not serve their full terms, because they are released on parole (U.S. Justice Department, 1983).

Does this mean that the American criminal justice system is soft on criminals? Compared with the Soviet Union, yes. Compared with other democratic societies, no. The United States treats convicted criminals more severely than any other democratic nation. According to Eugene Doleschal (1979), there were 244 people imprisoned for every 100,000 Americans in 1977—the highest imprisonment rate among Western industrialized nations. Most other countries had rates under 100. In Sweden, the rate was 32; in the Netherlands, 28. More recently, due to the introduction of pretrial detention and increased abolition of parole, we have been locking up more people and sentencing them to longer terms. Our prisons are therefore bulging at the seams. In the first half of the 1980s, the prison population had already increased by nearly 60 percent. Today it stands at a record 529,000 and keeps growing by 1,000 a week. Most prisons are now seriously overcrowded (Trott, 1985; Lacayo, 1987). Prison sentences in the United States are indeed the stiffest in the West. Again, Sweden provides a striking contrast. The length of imprisonment in the United States is measured in years; in Sweden it is only in months and weeks. A typical sentence for murder in the United States is life imprisonment; in Sweden, it is two years. The United States is also the only industrialized nation in the West that still executes convicted murderers.

Does the harsh treatment in the United States help to decrease crime rates? Apparently not. We still have more crimes, particularly violent crimes, than other industrialized countries (see box, p. 180). Moreover, our rates of **recidivism**—repeated criminal offenses—are quite high. One study estimated that 74 percent of those released from American prisons are likely to be rearrested three years later (Coleman and Cressey, 1987). According to the U.S. Justice Department (1983), 61 to 64 percent of all adult inmates have been in prison before. To some inmates, American prisons are schools of crime, in which they learn to become more motivated and skillful criminals. These "crime schools" are expensive: it costs more to send a person to prison than to college. The annual cost for keeping a criminal in prison ranges from $7,000 to $30,000 (Lacayo, 1987). The overcrowding in prisons has further made rehabilitation

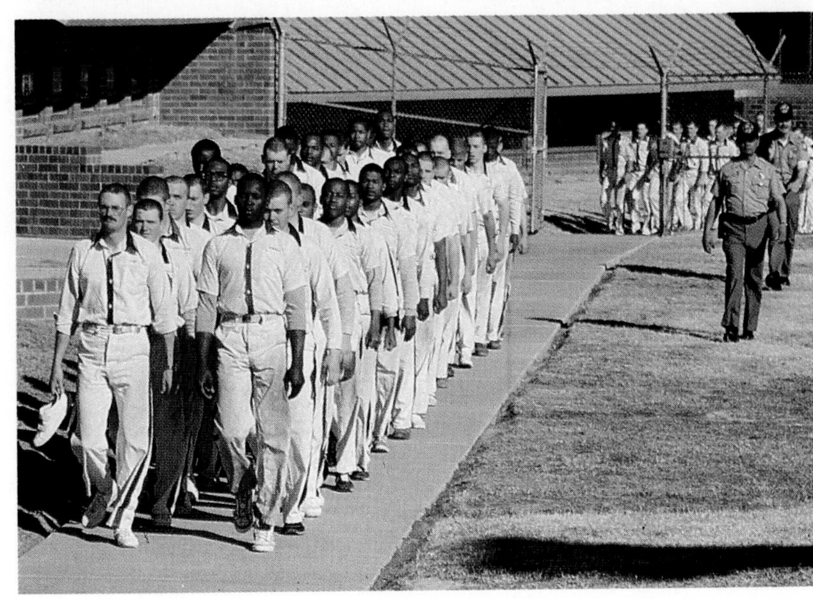

A "correctional facility" in Georgia. In the 1980s our prison population has increased so much that most prisons today are seriously overcrowded. Even before this decade we already had the highest percentage of prisoners per population in the Western world. But we still have more crimes, particularly violent ones, than other industrialized nations. In addition, our rates of recidivism continue to be high.

UNDERSTANDING OTHER SOCIETIES

Why Canada Is Safer than the U.S.

Although our criminal justice system is relatively tough on criminals, we still have higher crime rates than other industrialized countries, such as Canada. The following report suggests some reasons: our nation's violent past, ethnic heterogeneity, and the easy availability of guns. How do these social factors encourage crime?

In a pattern similar to that in the U.S., total crime in Canada rose substantially between 1976 and 1981. Violent crime rose steadily throughout the period, until by 1985 it was up 25.7 percent from the figure for 1976. Yet violent crime remains far below U.S. levels (see table). All of Canada, with a population of 25 million, had 651 murders in 1985. That compares with 18,976 in the U.S. There were 635 homicides in Detroit alone, an economically depressed city of 1.1 million people often described as the nation's "murder capital." Statistics show, however, that property crime rates are not much different than in the U.S. Why, then, is violence so much more prevalent in the U.S.? Can anything be learned from the Canadian experience? There are a variety of explanations. They include:

Safer in Canada
1985 Crime Rates per 100,000 Residents

	Canada	United States
Murder	2.6	7.9
Robbery	90.0	208.6
Rape	10.0	36.6
Break and entry	1,407.0	1,287.3
Motor vehicle theft	324.0	462.0

Source: Canadian Center for Justice Statistics' Federal Bureau of Investigation.

- History and culture: Canada has had a less violent past. It obtained independence from the United Kingdom in an evolutionary rather than revolutionary manner, and had no civil war. The Royal Canadian Mounted Police and their predecessors maintained more law and order in Canada's West than prevailed in much of the American West. "We are more disapproving of violence in Canada," said Frank Porporina, from the attorney general's research division. Nor, he added, is the state violent. Police kill only about 10 people a year.
- Demographics: Canada has more ethnic homogeneity than the U.S. Most Canadians are Caucasian. Some 44 percent are of British stock, and some 29 percent of French origin. The remaining are mostly from other European nations. Toronto's 400,000 people of Italian stock have a generally low crime rate. Asians have arrived in larger numbers among post–World War II immigrants. Like most immigrant groups, they have an extremely low crime rate. Only some 1 percent of Canadians are black, compared with 14 percent of Americans. That disadvantaged minority commits a disproportionately high percentage of violent crime in the U.S.
- Gun laws: Canada's gun laws, always tough, were tightened in 1976. The use of guns in crime has declined even further since then. Local police in Canada issue handgun permits only after an investigation to determine the crime-free status and sanity of the applicant. They also check to see if there is a justifiable need for protection with a gun or for use in a gun collection or registered gun club. A central registry in Ottawa tracks the permits. "It is almost impossible to get a permit to carry a handgun," says Mr. Mosley of the Justice Department. If a gun is used in a crime, the law requires a minimum one-year sentence. For even the possession of an unregistered handgun, a court can sentence an individual to jail for up to five years. Long guns are also controlled. An individual can acquire a rifle only after a check into his criminal status. Further, the police are free to remove firearms from a home if there is a disturbance and get court permission later. This, it is believed, has saved many lives when there is family quarreling.

Source: Excerpted from David R. Francis, "Why Canada Is Safer than U.S.," *Christian Science Monitor*, January 2, 1987, p. 9.

impossible. In fact, it has triggered riots by the inmates. All these problems, however, have led to a few new solutions. A number of states have hired private companies to run some of their prisons at far lower costs than if the states were to do it themselves. Many judges throughout the nation have stopped sending people convicted of nonviolent crimes (such as drunk driving, mail fraud, car theft, and burglary) to prison. These criminals are sentenced to confinement at home or in dormitory halfway houses, with permission to go to work. In Lincoln County, Oregon, some burglars and thieves are given a choice between going to prison and publishing apologies for their crimes, with their photographs, in local newspapers. In Sarasota, Florida, and Midwest City, Oklahoma, motorists convicted of drunk driving are requred to display on their cars bumper stickers announcing the fact (Etzioni, 1987; Lacayo, 1987).

In some states gambling is legal, as shown here. In other states it is illegal. Where it is illegal, gambling is a crime. But since no one is hurt by it, gambling is considered a "victimless crime." This raises important matters of public debate: should we consider an activity criminal if many are willing to take part in it and no one gets hurt? Advocates of decriminalization argue that the law against such an activity can divert law enforcement from more serious crimes, encourage police corruption, and generate many other crimes. But opponents insist that decriminalization will induce more people to engage in the questionable activity.

Decriminalization

Controlling **victimless crimes**—such as prostitution, illegal drug use, and gambling—is especially difficult (Schur, 1979). Laws against these activities are nearly unenforceable, because the evidence necessary to prosecute the offender is extremely difficult to obtain. The "victims" want or need the outlawed goods and services, so they are reluctant to give information on the criminals to the police. The police must therefore rely on investigative methods such as surprise raids, undercover agents, and clandestine surveillance including wiretaps. Even when these methods are used, victimless crimes still flourish.

In fact, many people argue that laws against victimless crimes do more harm than good in several ways. First, they divert very limited resources away from the fight against more serious crimes. Second, laws against victimless crimes encourage police corruption. Because enormous profits are reaped from these crimes, the criminals try to bribe police to "look the other way." Public knowledge of police corruption in turn breeds disrespect for the law. Third, laws against victimless crimes generate many other crimes. As we have discussed, labeling persons as criminals may encourage them to engage in further deviance. Laws against certain drugs and prostitution drive many people out of respectable society and into deviant subcultures.

These two points—that laws cannot control victimless crimes and that these laws often do more harm than good—have led to calls for decriminalization or legalization of victimless crimes (De Leon, 1982). In fact, such victimless crimes as marijuana use, private consensual homosexual acts, and gambling have been decriminalized in a number of states. Especially after eleven states (constituting about 33 percent of the U.S. population) decriminalized marijuana use in the 1970s, an increasing number of Americans have supported decriminalization. As shown by public opinion polls, in 1974 only 36 percent of the general public favored decriminalization but by 1980 it had risen to 52 percent. At the same time, a growing proportion of well-educated and affluent Americans smoke marijuana, which was once popular largely with the lower classes (Goode, 1984).

Nevertheless, in the conservative blacklash of the 1980s, marijuana use—along with prostitution and gambling—is still illegal in many states. Opponents of decriminalization argue that these acts are immoral, that decriminalization cannot get rid of the basic behavioral problem such as drug abuse or sexual deviance, and that decriminalization produces horrible consequences (for example, dope fiends everywhere). While there is no evidence to refute the first two points, there are data to contradict the third: decriminalization did not lead to increased marijuana use in Holland (De Leon, 1982) or in the United States (Johnston, 1980; Single, 1981).

QUESTIONS FOR DISCUSSION AND REVIEW

1. How does internalization of the norms deter deviance in a different way from formal or informal social controls?
2. In what ways can the criminal justice system balance the need to catch criminals with the need to respect individual freedom?
3. How does the United States treat convicted criminals more severely than any other democratic nation?
4. What might happen if victimless crimes such as prostitution or gambling were decriminalized?

CHAPTER REVIEW

1. *What is deviant behavior?* It is an act considered deviant by public consensus or the powerful at a given time and place. *How can we find out about crime in the United States?* From the FBI's *Uniform Crime Reports,* which shows the incidence of various crimes known to the police; the National Crime Survey, which asks people whether they have been victimized by crime; and self-report studies, which ask people whether they have committed criminal or delinquent acts.

2. *In what ways does murder occur?* Murder usually takes place on Saturday night, with the use of a gun. It often involves relatives, friends, or acquaintances.

3. *How does corporate crime differ from street crime?* Corporate crime is more rationally executed, more profitable, and less detectable. The victim often cooperates with corporate criminals unwittingly, society does little to punish them, and they do not see themselves as criminals. Corporate crime further exacts a higher economic, physical, and social cost.

4. *Are the poor more likely to be mentally ill than the rich?* Yes, according to many studies. But there are conflicting explanations on why this is so. One explanation is the stressful life of the poor. The other is that the mentally ill tend to move into the lower-class neighborhood and the healthy ones out of it.

5. *Is deviance always harmful to society?* No. If it occurs within limits, it may help define and clarify norms, strengthen solidarity among law-abiding citizens, provide a safety valve, offer jobs, and stimulate social change.

6. *How do biology and psychology explain deviance?* Such biological and psychological problems as genetic abnormality, uncontrollable aggressive instinct, and frustration have been proposed as causes of deviant behavior.

7. *According to anomie theory, what is the cause of deviance?* American society overemphasizes success as an important goal for all individuals but underemphasizes—and fails to provide to all people—the socially approved means for achieving success. One possible response to this inconsistency is deviance.

8. *According to differential association theory, how does a person become a criminal?* Through learning in interactions with others: when a person's associations with those who view criminal behavior favorably outweigh his or her associations with those who view it unfavorably, criminal behavior results.

9. *How is being labeled deviant likely to affect people?* The label may cause them to look upon themselves as deviant and to live up to this self-image by engaging in more deviant behavior.

10. *How does conflict theory explain deviance?* The traditional version of the theory emphasizes cultural conflict as the source of deviant definition and behavior. The contemporary version traces various crimes to class conflict in capitalism.

11. *How does society control deviant behavior?* Through socialization, but it is never completely successful. It is supplemented by formal and informal social control. Informal control is more common in traditional societies and formal control is more common in modern societies. Informal control, however, seems more effective in deterring deviance. *Is the American criminal justice system soft on criminals?* A low percentage of criminals are ap-

prehended and punished, but compared with other Western countries, the United States imprisons proportionately more people and imposes longer prison terms. *Why are victimless crimes especially difficult to control?* The laws against such crimes are virtually unenforceable and may do more harm than good.

KEY TERMS

Anomie A condition in which social norms are absent, weak, or in conflict (p. 171).

Cultural transmission The process by which the values of crime and delinquency are transmitted from one group to another (p. 173).

Deviant behavior An act that is considered deviant by public consensus or the powerful at a given place and time (p. 162).

Differential association The process by which potential deviants associate more with criminal elements than with noncriminal elements (p. 173).

Index offense The FBI's term for a major, serious crime such as murder, rape, or robbery (p. 162).

Internalization The process by which individuals incorporate the values of society into their personalities, accepting the norms of society as their own (p. 176).

Marginal surplus population Marxist term for unemployed workers who are useless to the capitalist economy (p. 176).

Neurosis Mental problem characterized by a persistent fear, anxiety, or worry about trivial matters (p. 168).

Plea bargaining A pretrial negotiation in which the defendant agrees to plead guilty to a lesser charge in exchange for a less severe penalty (p. 179).

Primary deviance An initial violation of a norm that is not considered deviant by the person committing the act (p. 174).

Psychosis Mental disorder typified by loss of touch with reality (p. 168).

Recidivism Repeated commission of crimes (p. 179).

Secondary deviance Habitual norm violations that the person recognizes as deviant and commits in conformity with his or her self-image as a deviant (p. 174).

Social control Process by which individuals are pressured by others such as teachers, peers, and police to conform to social norms (p. 177).

Victimless crimes Crimes that are without any victim because the offender does not harm another person (p. 181).

SUGGESTED READINGS

Cullen, Francis T. 1984. *Rethinking Crime and Deviance Theory: The Emergence of a Structuring Tradition.* Totowa, N.J.: Rowman & Allanheld. A theoretical statement of how certain social and social-psychological conditions can determine the transformation of a general deviant tendency into a specific form of deviant act.

Pfohl, Stephen J. 1985. *Images of Deviance and Social Control: A Sociolgical History.* New York: McGraw-Hill. Nine perspectives on deviance, ranging from the earliest view of deviance as a demonic act to the latest conception of deviance as an attempt to regain lost power.

Schur, Edwin M. 1984. *Labeling Women Deviant: Gender, Stigma, and Social Control.* New York: Random House. A top-notch text about how women are labeled deviant in a sexist society.

Simon, David R., and D. Stanley Eitzen. 1986. *Elite Deviance,* 2nd ed. Boston: Allyn and Bacon. An excellent book on the nature of numerous deviant activities carried on by the rich and powerful.

Thio, Alex. 1988. *Deviant Behavior,* 3rd ed. New York: Harper & Row. A comprehensive and, according to a UCLA professor writing in the journal *Teaching Sociology,* "remarkably well-written text that takes the student two steps beyond most extant texts."

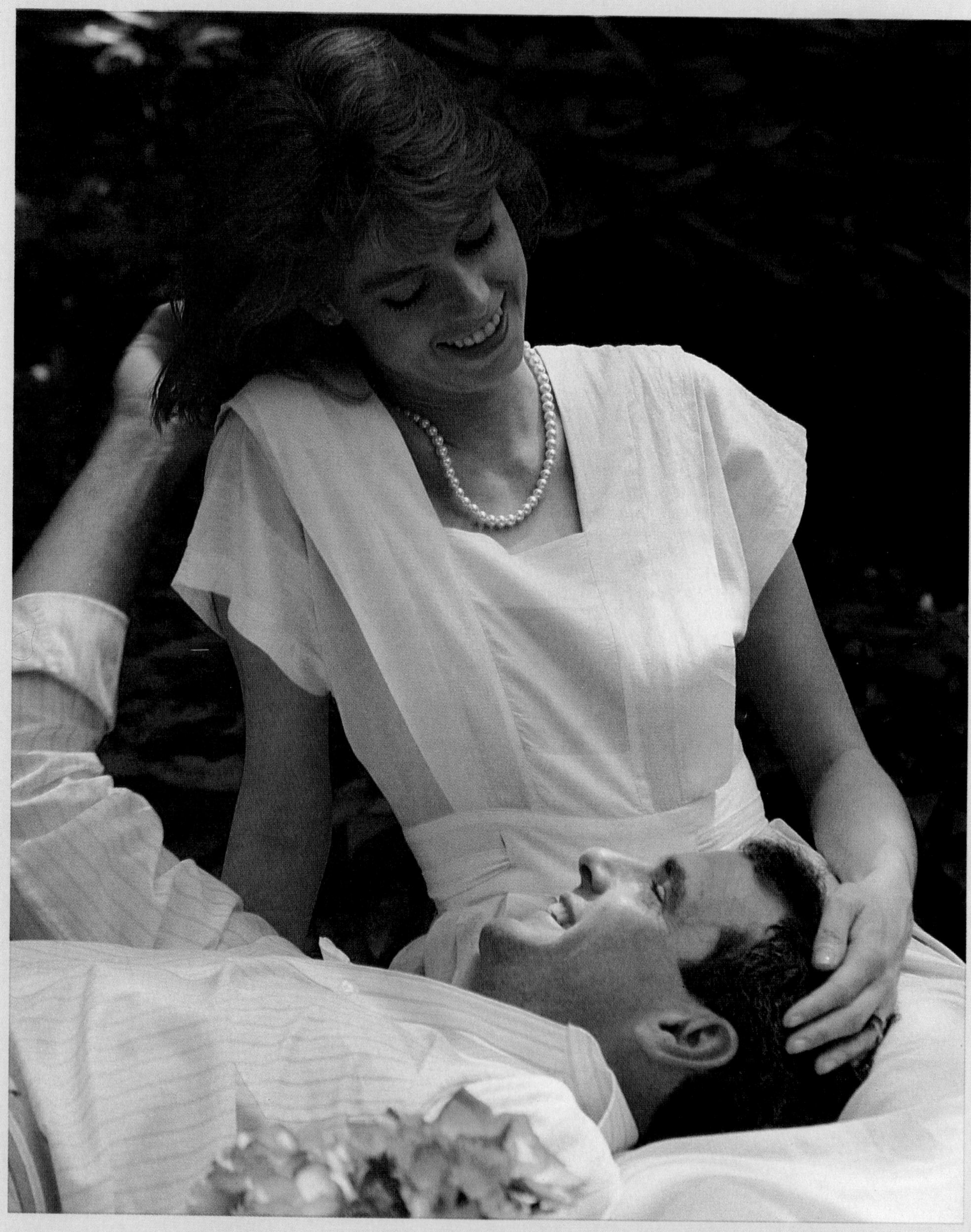

8 Human Sexuality

Many people seem to believe that sex comes naturally, that everybody instinctively knows how to make love. Actually, we must learn how to have sex. This is why sexual behavior varies from one society to another as well as from one group to another within the same society. In Western societies, for example, kissing often accompanies sexual intercourse, but the Balinese of Indonesia and the Thonga of East Africa do not kiss at all. In our society, better-educated and higher-income males are likely to engage in a wider variety of sexual activities (such as extended foreplay) than their less-educated and lower-income peers. Social forces such as culture and social class, then, influence sexual behavior.

Sexuality is one of the most important facets of human life. Without it we would not have been born and the human race would have died out. Aside from fulfilling this biological function of reproduction, human sexuality has recently become a pervasive source of pleasure not only for the married but for the unmarried. We saturate our lives with sexual thoughts, sexual feelings, and sexual activities. Our society, in turn, inundates us with erotic materials via movies, television, advertisements, books, and magazines. While we enjoy sexuality, we also seem to suffer from it. Many people still have sexual hang-ups. Many parents still find it too embarrassing to discuss sex with their children. Many teenagers find their sexual experience "a real downer." Teenage pregnancies, "kiddie porn," and STDs (sexually transmitted diseases such as herpes, chlamydia, and AIDS) are on the rise (Gelman, 1980; Harmatz and Novak, 1983; Smilgis, 1987; Kantrowitz, 1987).

Apparently many people know little about human sexuality. True, there are numerous popular books about sex, but they largely contain sensational stories, flashy claims, misleading information, and wild speculations. In this chapter we will seek out scientific knowledge from scholarly literature on various aspects of human sexuality.

THE SOCIOLOGICAL PERSPECTIVE

According to the sociological perspective, human sexual behavior is learned, the result of a socialization process within a sociocultural context. Without learning anything about sex, humans would not know how to make love. Many people seem to believe just the contrary, that sex comes naturally, that everybody instinctively knows how to have sex. Such a popular belief, however, is false. Only animals are born with a **sex instinct,** which makes them copulate in a certain way and at a certain time only. All dogs and cats, for example, are instinctively programmed to use the same coital position, with the male mounting and entering the female from behind. They also instinctively copulate for reproduction only. They do not have sex unless the female is in heat—the period when she is ovulating and susceptible to pregnancy.

Humans, in contrast, do not have a sex instinct. This is why humans, unlike animals, are able to have sex in many different ways and all year round—in fact, most of the time when the female is not ovulating. What we have is only a **sex drive,** a potential for, rather than a determinant of, sexual desire or action. Whether, when, where, or how we will turn our sex drive into a certain sexual act depends on the nature of our socialization. Since the way we are socialized is subject to the influence of social and cultural forces (see Chapter 6: Socialization), human sexuality tends to vary from society to society and from group to group within the same society.

In the United States, for example, younger, black, or less religious people are more likely to approve of premarital sex than older, white, or more religious Americans (DeLamater, 1981). Among college students, white males masturbate more often than black males, and white females are more likely than black females to perform fellatio, use coitus interruptus, or masturbate their partners (Belcastro, 1985). While men with more education and higher income use a greater variety of sexual techniques—including lengthy foreplay, oral sex, and various coital positions—lower-status men seem more interested in intercourse and orgasm only. Lower-class husbands are also more likely to use sex to relieve tension and frustration and, perhaps as a consequence, less likely to have nocturnal emissions (wet dreams) and sexual fantasies (Pierson and D'Antonio, 1974; Hunt, 1975).

Sexual behavior differs more significantly between societies. In Western societies some form of kissing accompanies sexual intercourse. The Balinese of Indonesia do not kiss at all, and the Thonga of East Africa, to whom kissing is also unknown, said with disgust when they first saw Europeans kiss: "Look at them—they eat each other's saliva and dirt." In the course of sexual intercourse, Western women tend to huff and puff, while Choroti women of Argentina like to spit on their partner's face and Apinaye women of Brazil may bite off bits of their lover's eyebrows and then noisily spit them out. In most societies marital intercourse usually takes place in the privacy of the bedroom, but Yapese couples of a Pacific island sometimes copulate outdoors or in front of others. The Masai of Africa have sex only in the evening because they are afraid that if they do it during the day, the woman's womb will suck up the man's blood. The Chenchu of India, on the other hand, confine sexual intercourse to the day because they believe that children conceived through nighttime copulation will be born blind. In the United States married couples make love two to three times a week, but in most preindustrial societies they do it once daily or nightly. In some, as among the Aranda of Australia, couples engage in coitus as often as three to five times every night (Ford and Beach, 1981). In our society, where premature ejaculation is considered a problem, men strive for prolonged intercourse. But in more male-dominant societies such as East Bay in Melanesia, where delayed ejaculation is considered a hang-up, men try to reach orgasm in 15 to 30 seconds or less. In most societies, homosexuality is condemned as a threat to heterosexuality. However, in some parts of the world, such as the New Guinea Highlands, homosexuality is viewed as a pathway to heterosexuality: preadolescent boys are taught to fellate unmarried men and swallow their sperm because this is believed to be the only way the boys will be able to produce their own sperm in adulthood and impregnate their wives (Reiss, 1986).

There is, however, a limit to the social and cultural variation in human sexuality. This shows up in the abhorrence of incest throughout the world. Since incest avoidance is universal, does it mean that it is innate, biologically based?

QUESTIONS FOR DISCUSSION AND REVIEW

1. How does the sociological perspective differ from popular conceptions of human sexuality?
2. What do the great social and cultural variations in sexual practices imply about the nature of human sexuality?

WHY THE INCEST TABOO?

Practically all societies abhor and prohibit sexual intercourse between close relatives, such as between father and daughter, mother and son, and brother and sister. There are exceptions. In the royal families of ancient Egypt, Hawaii, and Peru, brothers and sisters were required to marry. A famous example is Cleopatra, who was married to two of her brothers at different times while she was herself the product of a brother-sister marriage. According to some anthropologists, the Thonga lion hunters in East Africa were permitted to have sex with their daughters, the Azande chiefs in Central Africa were expected to marry their daughters, and Burundi bridegrooms in East Africa who found themselves impotent on their wedding nights might seek a remedy by having coitus with their mothers (LaBarre, 1954; Albert, 1963). But since these cases have been extremely rare, sociologists generally consider the **incest taboo** universal.

Biological Explanations

The universality of the taboo poses a challenge to the sociological perspective. If social and cultural differences in sexual behavior are taken as proof that human sexuality is sociological rather than biological in origin, how can the sociological perspective account for the universality of the incest taboo? It cannot, argue sociobiologists, who assume that if certain behavior is universal it must be biologically based (see Chapter 3: Culture). This assumption is at the heart of three biological explanations about the taboo.

According to one biological theory, the incest taboo is the result of our instinctive, natural, or inborn revul-

Children who grow up together from infancy in the same family generally do not develop a sexual interest in each other. It has been found, for example, that children who are unrelated by blood but who have been raised together in a communal environment, such as the children in the Israeli kibbutz shown here, do not choose each other as marriage partners. Apparently, childhood familiarity breeds sexual disinterest. This may explain avoidance of sibling incest. But it cannot explain why it is necessary for society to impose the incest taboo if childhood familiarity has made the incest impossible in the first place.

sion against sexual relations with close relatives. But its critics argue that if this were true, not a single society would have found it necessary to enact strict laws to prevent incest. To suggest, as instinct theory does, that all societies would legislate against something that everyone will not do anyway is like arguing that they would make laws to prohibit people from eating dirt. The instinct theory also fails to take into account the fact that some societies define marriage with a first cousin as incestuous, while others do not. As anthropologist Leslie White (1969) said, "Certainly when we consider our own legal definitions of incest, which vary from state to state, to claim that a biological instinct can recognize state boundary lines is somewhat grotesque."

According to a second biological theory, incest is prohibited because inbreeding causes physical degeneration and mental retardation in the offspring. But this explanation does not hold because inbreeding does not necessarily cause biological defects. It only intensifies the inheritance of traits, good or bad. If two incestuous relatives are of superior stock, the quality of their children would be better. As agricultural experts have long known, inbreeding can improve the strains of already superior plants and livestocks. Even if inbreeding could have genetically harmful consequences for the children, it could not have caused some primitive societies to prohibit incest. The reason is that they do not know the causal connection between copulation and birth, as they often consider birth the deed of dead ancestors, spirits and ghosts, or some other supernatural agents. Moreover, the inbreeding theory cannot explain why most societies outlaw incestuous activities that cannot possibly result in birth, as between fathers and preadolescent daughters or fathers and sons.

A third biological theory attributes the incest taboo to **negative imprinting,** which suppresses erotic feelings for individuals with whom one has been familiar since early childhood (Westermarck, 1922; McCabe, 1983). Two ethnographic cases have been used to support this theory. One shows that in the Israeli kibbutz, young men and women who have been raised together in the same children's house never marry each other (Talmon, 1964; Shepher, 1971, 1983). Another case concerns a village in northern Taiwan, where it is customary for rich families to adopt a poor baby girl and raise her as their son's future bride. When these children grow up, they always refuse to marry each other, despite strong parental pressure (Wolf, 1966, 1970). These findings are taken to mean that childhood familiarity breeds sexual disinterest. If this is true, it may explain avoidance of sibling incest only. It cannot explain why most fathers, who cannot possibly have been raised with their own daughter, show no sexual interest in her. Most importantly, like the instinct theory, the negative imprinting theory cannot explain why it is necessary to impose a taboo on sibling (or any other kind of) incest if childhood familiarity has made the incest impossible in the first place.

Sociological Explanations

More satisfactory explanations for the incest taboo are sociological. According to one such explanation, the taboo came into being because it enabled different family groups to work together, thereby enhancing their chances of survival. The early primitive tribes are believed to have been confronted with the serious alternative between marrying out and dying out. The incest taboo, then, was set up as a device for forcing the children of a family to marry into other families. The resulting cooperation among different families became all-important, not only in making daily living easier but also in ensuring survival against famine and security against enemy attack (White, 1969). Although people today, particularly those who live in highly industrialized societies, no longer marry for interfamily cooperation but for love, the norm against incest continues to exist. This is comparable to the persistence of the ancient custom of throwing rice at newlyweds, although we no longer want them to produce numerous babies (see Chapter 3: Culture).

Another sociological explanation is that the incest taboo exists because it serves to keep the family intact. Without the taboo, sexual rivalry and tension would make it impossible for the family to function as an effective unit. If the father has an affair with the daughter, the mother is bound to be jealous and resentful. Consequently the mother can no longer love and care for the daughter as a good mother should. The father will not be able to perform his fatherly duty as his daughter's disciplinarian while, at the same time, being her lover. Moreover, incest can create a great deal of status confusion within the family. As Kingsley Davis (1949) said, "The confusion of statuses would be phenomenal. The incestuous child of a father-daughter union, for example, would be a brother of his own mother; the son of his own sister; a stepson of his own grandmother; possibly a brother of his own uncle; and certainly a grandson of his own father." This family disruption theory, however, is only useful for explaining father-daughter and mother-son incest taboos. It cannot explain the taboo against brother-sister incest because, unlike parent-child incest, it would not cause jealousy among parents or disrupt parental authority; moreover, the status confusion would be minimal.

Sociologists assume that the incest taboo has made most people feel it unnatural to have sex with close relatives. Without the taboo, incest might have been common. As Dorothy Willner (1983) pointed out, brothers and sisters usually avoid physical contact in cultures with stern sibling incest prohibitions but engage in sexual play in cultures with lax or no prohibitions. As a cultural product rather than a fixed biological trait, the incest taboo is itself subject to change. In the last decade there have been a growing number of academic and popular writings that criticize the taboo for causing guilt and uneasy distancing between family members (De Mott, 1980). In the 1970s there were two widely publicized cases of sibling incest that went unpunished. One involved a brother and sister in Sweden who, after being married, were prosecuted but found innocent. The other case involved the marriage between a brother and sister in Massachusetts. They pleaded guilty but were only placed on probation and even allowed to live together—as brother and sister, not as husband and wife. Such a permissive and lenient attitude toward sibling incest may have been a side effect of the sexual revolution that started in the 1960s.

QUESTIONS FOR DISCUSSION AND REVIEW

1. What is the incest taboo, and why is it found in all societies?
2. Why do sociologists assert that the incest taboo appeared for social rather than biological reasons?

CONSEQUENCES OF THE SEXUAL REVOLUTION

Today, sex is no longer the hush-hush matter it used to be. Nudity can be seen in theaters, in movies, and on television. Pornographic magazines and films are easily available. Premarital sex is widespread. Abortion is legal. Homosexuality has come out of the closet; it is no longer "the love that dare not speak its name." These are the obvious consequences of the sexual revolution that swept the United States during the last two decades. But the revolution has brought about some basic changes in our sexual attitude and behavior.

The "sexual revolution" does not mean that Americans have gone wild. Rather, it means that people now show more tolerance for the behavior of others, that the double standard is on the decline, that sex is seen as a recreation as well as a means of procreation, and that the quality of a relationship is as important as its legal status.

First, the sexual revolution has encouraged tolerance for various forms of sexual behavior. An example is the tolerance for homosexuality. Nearly 30 percent of the general public do not find homosexuality morally wrong and as many as 43 percent agree that homosexual acts between consenting adults should be legal, although only 17 to 19 percent have had some homoerotic experience and only 1 to 3 percent are exclusively homosexual (*Public Opinion,* 1978, 1981; Harmatz and Novak, 1983). This suggests that it is all right for others to do what we may not want to do ourselves. The sexual tolerance also comes across clearly in the following illustration:

> Even the girl whose private values dictate that she postpone intercourse until she is married may now feel the mature thing to do is to pick up her mattress and go and sleep in another girl's room if her girlfriend wants to

> have her boyfriend stay the night. Ten years ago she would have been shocked and horrified at the thought. This clearly is a step in the direction of greater sexual permissiveness in the literal sense: she is permitting another person sexual activity which she doesn't approve of herself. She refuses to judge (Broderick, 1972).

Second, the sexual revolution has weakened the **double standard** that allows men to have premarital sex but condemns women for doing so. One indication has been the dramatic increase in women's premarital experience. Between 1965 and 1980, the percentage of college males having had premarital sex climbed from 65 to 77, a difference of only 12 percent, but the percentage of college women with similar experience soared from 29 to 64—a difference of 35 percent (Robinson and Jedlicka, 1982). Moreover, more women than before expect to enjoy sex and reach orgasm. There is, however, a negative side to this increase in female sexual freedom. As one woman said, "I think the 'sexual revolution' basically pushes many women toward having sex more often and with more men than they want to. Now that women are supposed to enjoy sex as equally as men, they are considered 'square' or 'frigid' if they don't rush into bed" (Hite, 1976). Another casualty of the revolution is the upsurge in premarital pregnancies among teenage girls who are "emotionally unready" for intercourse (Shornack and Shornack, 1982).

Third, the sexual revolution has brought a fundamental change in the perceived purpose of sex for married couples. In the past, the primary motive for sex was reproduction. Today most Americans want more than procreation from sex. They also want recreation from it. Thus married couples are now much more inclined to engage in a great variety of sex acts that are aimed more at giving pleasure than at reproduction. The search for pleasure, however, may go too far. Some couples may have forced themselves to use mechanical sex aids, attempt multiple orgasms, or participate in group sex, spouse swapping, or open marriage. Many millions of Americans, according to George Leonard (1983), have plunged into these activities over the last two decades "not because they really *wanted* to, but because they thought they *should.*" The modern use of sex for pleasure, then, may become as obligatory as the traditional use of sex for reproduction.

Fourth, the sexual revolution has largely replaced the old morality with the new. The old was more concerned with the location of sex while the new emphasizes the quality of the partners' relationship. According to the old ethic, a sex act that occurs within marriage is moral and a sex act that takes place outside marriage is immoral. But according to the new ethic, regardless of whether a sex act is marital or nonmarital, it is moral if the couple care for each other and immoral if they sexually exploit each other. Consequently, what is considered right by one ethic is regarded as wrong by the other and vice versa. If a man and woman engage in premarital sex for love, they are immoral to the old moralist but not to the new. On the other hand, if a man forces his wife to have sex with him, he is considered a rapist by the new moralist but not by the old. Thanks to the sexual revolution, the idea that a woman can charge her husband with rape seems less ridiculous today than it did before. There is also an increase in cohabitation—the living together of man and woman without marriage—but the cohabitors are largely similar to married couples in commitment and sexual exclusivity. Premarital sex, too, is on the rise, mostly between couples who are engaged to or love each other rather than between strangers or mere acquaintances (Harmatz and Novak, 1983). There are, of course, a few who are interested only in casual and promiscuous sex, rejecting emotional involvement as the prerequisite for sex. But AIDS has threatened these individuals, leading many of them to stop pursuing one-night stands (Smilgis, 1987).

QUESTIONS FOR DISCUSSION AND REVIEW

1. To what extent has the sexual revolution changed premarital and other forms of sexuality?
2. How does the new sexual morality compare with the old?

NEW SEXUAL MYTHS

In the midst of the sexual revolution, the general public has been bombarded by the mass media with movies, talk shows, books, and articles about sexuality. Quite often the media have made their subject overly provocative and sensational by exaggerating and distorting the findings of sex researchers. As a consequence, while they have destroyed such old myths as the belief that masturbation can cause pimples, blindness, or insanity, the media have, according to the noted sex researcher Wardell Pomeroy (1977), also misled the public into accepting new beliefs that are as foolish as the old. Some of the modern myths that Pomeroy has discussed may still exist today.

Myth 1: Liberated women are causing new sexual problems for men. The old myth that women were uninterested in sex is now replaced by a new one: the liberated woman of today has limitless appetites and expectations for sex. This kind of woman is believed to have created a host of new sexual problems for men, such as impotence and premature ejaculation. There are no data to substantiate this belief. There is, however, some evidence from clinical experiences that men are *not* suffering from sexual inadequacies because women are expecting more.

Myth 2: Women's orgasms should all be out of this world. With the increased awareness of the female's capacity for orgasm, there are more women now than in the past who expect more out of sex, including multiple orgasm. Sex therapists are often forced to tell their female patients to be more realistic. As Pomeroy says, "If I ask a woman who has never had an orgasm what she expects it to be like and she says she expects stars to explode and bells to ring, then I point out that an orgasm simply isn't *that* earthshaking. Lowering her expectations makes it easier for her to achieve the orgasm she is seeking."

Myth 3: Technique is more important than the partners' relationship for achieving sexual pleasure. Nowadays, emphasis on sexual techniques and variety of sexual acts misleads some people into thinking that these alone are the key to sexual pleasure. The notion that sexual techniques are all-important is a myth. "Sexual techniques certainly can be helpful," says Pomeroy, "but it's the quality of that interpersonal relationship that is going to determine the quality of the sex, not the techniques." Besides, sex partners may find some techniques more idiotic than erotic, which is sure to turn them off.

Myth 4: Simultaneous orgasms are always best for a couple. This myth is often propagated by books promoting idealistic concepts such as ideal marriage or perfect sex. Couples are encouraged to strive for **simultaneous orgasms** as a heavenly experience. But grim determination to achieve this objective may actually kill the pleasure of sex because sex is turned into hard work rather than something to be enjoyed. For some people, **sequential orgasms** (one partner climaxing after the other) are more satisfying. They double the pleasure of each partner because each is able to enjoy the other's orgasm vicariously.

Myth 5: Young people today have gone wild sexually. This is the myth that many older adults believe in. They believe that young people engage in freewheeling sex, hopping from bed to bed, with no emotional attachments. It is true that a majority of young men and women today engage in premarital intercourse. Yet this does not mean that they have gone wild. It reflects instead the increasing acceptance of premarital sex among young couples as a means of expressing love or affection for one another.

QUESTIONS FOR DISCUSSION AND REVIEW

1. What are some of the new beliefs about sexuality, and why are they myths?
2. Why did these new sexual myths develop, and what are their consequences?

HETEROSEXUALITY

Having just knocked down the current sexual myths, let us be more positive and examine the data on various forms of sexual behavior. In this section we focus on the more common types of heterosexuality: premarital, marital, extramarital, and postmarital sex.

Premarital Sex

An overwhelming majority of the societies around the world approve of **premarital sex** (sex before marriage): 70 percent permit it for both sexes and nearly all the rest allow it at least for males. Most of the permissive societies are quite different from ours. They do not merely condone premarital sex; they encourage it. As a father in such a society told his adolescent son, "Don't be discouraged by a girl's rebuffs or running away; chase her down. Follow her—it's well worth your while." Our society is obviously not that permissive—and sexist. But it is not as restrictive as the handful (about 5 percent) of societies that *completely* prohibit premarital sex (Murdock, 1967).

Why is one society permissive and another restrictive? The reason, according to George Goethals (1971), is either male dominance or societal complexity. As for the first reason, Goethals observed that sanctions against premarital sex are likely to be severe in patrilineal and patrilocal societies, which are marked by male

"YOU'RE MOVING IN WITH ME? I THOUGHT I WAS MOVING IN WITH YOU."

dominance. In some of these societies premarital sex is allowed, but for males only. Premarital sex for both sexes is more likely to be permitted in matrilineal and matrilocal societies, where male dominance is less prevalent. As for societal complexity, Goethals noted that sexually permissive societies tend to be small, simple, or primitive. Most are tribal communities in developing, third-world countries. More restrictive societies are usually large, complex, or advanced. As suggested by Freud (1961), sexual indulgence can drain a society of the energies necessary for building civilization. Thus simple, primitive societies can afford to permit premarital sex but complex, advanced ones cannot.

The United States is one of the relatively restrictive societies. We have a norm against premarital sex, as suggested by the fact that most older adults—over age 35—consider it morally wrong for young people to have sex before marriage. It is little wonder that many parents are reluctant to discuss sex with their teenage children and are also opposed to the teaching of sex education in schools. As a consequence, teenage pregnancy is common and "initial introductions to direct sexuality are often tense, awkward, unpleasant, anxiety provoking, and, in some cases, traumatizing" (Harmatz and Novak, 1983). Such problems are less likely to occur in sexually permissive societies such as Sweden, where the norm against premarital sex is virtually nonexistent (see box, p. 193).

As has been suggested, however, Americans are more permissive today than they were 30 years ago. There are now proportionately more people, especially the younger ones, who approve as well as practice premarital sex. What kinds of teenagers are likely to have engaged in premarital intercourse? Research has shown that they are typically going steady or engaged, do not attend religious services regularly, or are closer to friends than parents (DeLamater, 1981; Billy and Udry, 1985). Teenage girls who are more influenced by peer groups than parents are also likely to become premaritally pregnant (Shah and Zelnik, 1981). According to another study, those who have engaged in premarital coitus are also more independent, more critical of society, more tolerant of deviance, and more involved in such problem behaviors as alcohol and drug use. On the other hand, those who have remained virgins tend more to see themselves as physically unattractive and incompetent in cross-sex relationships but are more successful academically and, later on, occupationally (Jessor et al., 1983).

Contrary to popular belief, the rising incidence of premarital sex among young people does not mean a corresponding increase in sexual promiscuity. Available comparative data, for women only, indicate that most women today are just like their peers of 30 years ago in having only one premarital sex partner (Harmatz and Novak, 1983). As Herant Katchadourian (1985) concluded, "Although young women now are more likely to engage in premarital coitus than their mothers and grandmothers, their choice of partners is even more likely to be someone they expect to marry." As for men, they are more promiscuous than women and more likely to have sex with two to nine different partners (Keller et al., 1982). But only a minority of men approve of promiscuous, casual sex (Luria et al., 1987). Despite the increase in premarital sex, then, young people of today are not necessarily more promiscuous than before. What a Swedish sociologist says about the prevalence of premarital sex in Sweden is relevant here: it should not be interpreted as evidence of promiscuity (Trost, 1985).

Marital Sex

Compared with their peers of 30 years ago, married people today engage in intercourse more frequently,

UNDERSTANDING OTHER SOCIETIES

Swedish Solutions

American society has made little progress in lowering its rate of teenage pregnancy, and this aspect of adolescent sexuality remains a large problem. In contrast, Sweden, through an aggressive sex education program, has a teenage fertility rate half that of the United States. This reading tells how the Swedes discourage teenagers from getting pregnant. Can we use the same method to solve the problem in the United States?

If pregnancies among teenagers are to be avoided, we should focus on sexual intercourse among teenagers. Abstinence is the best contraceptive, offering 100 percent protection. It is easy to say that teenagers, especially females, should abstain from sexual intercourse, but it is hard to believe that *saying* so would have the intended effect. Most teenagers have a sexual drive that is not easily steered toward abstinence. Even if they tried to follow this advice, they would engage in some emotional sexual behavior, especially when in love. Hugging, kissing, and petting would be the ways for these teenagers to handle their sexual drives. Stopping at petting is difficult, because one petting activity is oral-genital sex, and this can easily lead to sexual intercourse. Thus, the recommendation for emotional-sexual humans to remain abstinent is not effective. Other contraceptive means and techniques are needed for female teenagers and their partners to further reduce the pregnancy rates. Whatever these might be, dissemination of information, availability, and motivation are needed. I offer as an example a look at the Swedish endeavors.

In the mid-1940s the Swedish parliament decided that primary and secondary schools should, in biology classes, inform pupils about the sexual organs of males and females, reproduction, and contraception. Since 1956, such information has been compulsory in all schools, but there have been problems connected with the practice of sex education. A major problem was the heavy emphasis on the physical and technical aspects of sex. About ten years ago, this approach began to be questioned more and more. The social and emotional aspects became more important. Youngsters as well as adults were supposed to show emotions and to develop the emotional aspects of the sexual relationship. Openness, the importance of close relationships, and sexual fidelity were emphasized as being important for a satisfactory sex life.

When sex instruction became compulsory in Sweden in 1956, it was called "sex education"; later it was relabeled "education in sex and life together," and in 1977 it became "education in life together." The word "sex" was abolished, not out of prudishness but to stress the social and emotional aspects and deemphasize the technical and physical aspects that were overemphasized earlier. Over the last one or two decades, improvements have occurred: more teachers have realized the importance of sex education, and more of them are relaxed and interested in their teaching.

The schools and the teachers are not the only transmitters. Television, which in Sweden is an important mass medium for children, has for a number of years shown many informative, sensitive, interesting, and enjoyable programs about sex and life together. Other means indicate society's wish not only to inform but to support the youngsters' sexual, emotional, and social maturity. Connected to many junior high and high schools are school gynecological clinics or youth centers. All youngsters can consult these without cost and with confidentiality—and many do. Often the personnel at these clinics or centers are specially selected and trained midwives. They have the right to prescribe pills to the girls (without cost); they have condoms to give to the girls or boys (also at no cost); and they can be consulted about other matters of importance to the teenager: relationship problems, social pressure toward conformity, fear about a small penis, and other concerns. All counties have family planning clinics or centers to which teenagers as well as adults can go—at no cost and with full confidentiality.

The preferred contraceptive for the teenage girl, the pill, is easily available. The male contraceptive, the condom, is also easily available. The two main distributors of condoms in Sweden, one of them nonprofit, advertise in daily newspapers and weekly magazines, so that those too shy to buy them in the stores can order condoms by mail. Weekend workshops are sporadically organized in many parts of the country as additional support and information for the Swede. Especially during the last decade, there has been a massive and multifaceted endeavor to inform and influence teenagers and adults in so-called family planning matters.

Source: Adapted from Jan Trost, "Swedish Solutions." Published by permission of Transaction Publishers, from *Society,* Vol. 23, No. 1, pp. 44–46. Copyright © 1985 by Transaction Publishers.

Contrary to popular belief, the rising rate of premarital sex does not mean a corresponding increase in promiscuity. Sex within marriage has increased in frequency, and most couples find their marital sex pleasurable. Extramarital sex, often charged with guilt and tension, is not as gratifying as widely imagined. The divorced find their postmarital sex very pleasurable, but most still want to remarry.

spend more time on it, and use more sexual techniques. The average frequency of marital intercourse was about twice a week 30 years ago and is three times a week today. For the married couples of both the past and present, however, there is the same steady decline in coital frequency with increasing age. Usually, after the first four years of marriage, the rate of intercourse begins to decline, largely due to career demands, the arrival of children, and lack of sexual excitement. But wives are increasingly interested in sex while husbands' sexual interest progressively sags. Over the last 30 years the duration of foreplay has changed little, from 15 to 20 minutes, but the duration of coitus has increased impressively. In the past it took married men only two minutes to ejaculate after intromission (vaginal penetration), but now it takes about ten minutes. Couples today are also more willing to experiment with a great variety of sex acts than they were before. In regard to oral sex, for example, more than 90 percent of married people today, as compared with fewer than 50 percent in the past, have tried it (Hunt, 1975; Blumstein and Schwartz, 1983; Jasso, 1985; Luria et al., 1987).

It is therefore clear that married couples today have stronger interest in sex and engage in it more often. But do they enjoy it more? In one survey more than 90 percent of them reported that their marital coitus within the past year had been pleasurable (Hunt, 1975). "Pleasurable" does not, however, necessarily mean attaining orgasm. As far as enabling their wives to achieve orgasm is concerned, today's husbands are not significantly better lovers than their counterparts of 40 years ago. Despite their prolongation of coitus and reliance on greater variety of coital techniques, only about 48 percent of the husbands in 1975 reported that their wives regularly reached orgasm, a figure not significantly higher than the 45 percent reported in the Kinsey survey of 1948. But orgasm is not the sole determinant of sexual pleasure, because love and companionship, in the eyes of most married couples, can also enhance the pleasure of marital sex (Pietropinto and Simenauer, 1977). In fact, couples can get more sexual pleasure from erotic activities without orgasm than with orgasm. Caressing each other, for example, can provide greater pleasure when it does not lead to orgasm. One main reason is that in these sex acts the partners are relaxed, which enhances pleasure, rather than pressured to achieve orgasm, which interferes with enjoyment by turning sex into hard work (Kelvin, 1983).

Until recently lower-class couples did not get as much satisfaction from marital sex as their middle-class counterparts. Among the lower classes, sex was more likely to be regarded as "a man's pleasure and a woman's duty." While lower-class wives seldom enjoyed their marital sex lives, their husbands did not necessarily enjoy theirs either, but were expected to compensate by engaging in extramarital relations. Such relations by the wives, however, were frowned on (Rainwater, 1964). More recent studies, though, suggest that the class differences may be diminishing considerably (DeLamater, 1981).

Religion, however, still has a significant influence on marital sex. When compared with less religious couples, the more religious ones engage in coitus less frequently, are less likely to have oral sex or anal intercourse, and tend to observe the taboo against intercourse during the wife's period. The quality of marital relationship also affects the couple's sex life. If there are problems in a marriage, the couple are less likely to make love frequently (DeLamater, 1981).

Extramarital Sex

Unlike premarital sex, which is prohibited by only a few societies, **extramarital sex**—popularly called adultery or infidelity—is condemned by most societies (Murdock, 1967). Adulteresses, though not adulterers, have often been stoned to death in some of them. In the United States, adultery is still widely disapproved of and still legally considered a sufficient ground for divorce. Despite all this, the actual practice of extramarital sex is relatively common. In the late 1940s Kinsey found that half of the American men and a quarter of the women had had at least one extramarital affair when they reached 40. More recent surveys showed about the same incidence of extramarital relations. The only exception is the threefold increase (from 8 to 24 percent) in the proportion of women under age 25 having sex outside marriage (Hunt, 1975; Tavris and Sadd, 1978).

The affair typically involves another married person, is usually confined to one or two partners, and often lasts only a year or less. A number of social factors seem to lie behind the infidelity. As shown by various studies, extramarital relations are more common among those who have experienced premarital coitus than among those who have not. The religiously inactive are more likely to commit adultery than the active. The better educated are more likely than the less educated to cheat on their spouses. Marital strain and liberal political attitudes are also positively related to extramarital activity (Katchadourian, 1985; Reiss, Anderson, Sponaugle, 1980; DeLamater, 1981). In recent years, an increasing number of single women have become involved with married men, but they differ from the kept mistresses of the past. They are financially independent and pursuing careers. Most are between 25 and 40, an age group that faces a severe shortage of single men as potential mates. At age 25, many single women already find it difficult to find eligible men, and the situation gets worse as they grow older, as single women in their forties outnumber single men by more than two to one (Richardson, 1986).

Extramarital sex is basically a form of deception. It is carried out in secret and often charged with guilt and tension. As a result, the experience is not as gratifying as popularly imagined. According to one study, while 53 percent of women regularly reached orgasm with their husbands, only 39 percent did so in extramarital intercourse. As for married men, while two-thirds rated their marital sex "very pleasurable," fewer than half of the adulterous men gave the same rating to their extramarital coitus (Katchadourian, 1985).

There is another, new form of adultery, variously called "swinging," "mate swapping," or "comarital sex." Unlike the traditional type of adultery, which involves having an affair behind the spouse's back, swinging is an open sexual event in which both husband and wife agree to participate. For this reason, swinging has been referred to as open, consensual, or faithful adultery. Perhaps because it tends to provoke horror or outrage from conventional society, less than 4 or 5 percent of all married couples have ever tried it and only about 2 percent are regular participants (Bartell, 1971; Hunt, 1975; Tavris and Sadd, 1978).

The regular swingers are mostly committed to mate swapping as a way of life. They seek extramarital sex for purely recreational purposes; they avoid falling in love with others' husbands or wives. They seem able to separate sex from love because they usually swing with a particular couple only once or twice and then seek new swinging partners. In a few cases where a couple swings regularly with another, friendship may blossom, much like that between two conventional couples—without sexual jealousy between husband and wife or threat to their marriage. In Brian Gilmartin's (1975) study, swingers reported a higher level of marital happiness than conventional couples. Gilmartin also found more intimacy and affection, more communication, and even more marital sex between swinging spouses than between conventional ones. But most couples who have swung once or twice drop out because they find it too impersonal—like prostitution—or too threatening to their marriage (Denfeld, 1974).

Since mate swapping is extremely deviant, are regular swingers abnormal? Gilmartin (1975) found them no different from conventional couples: "Other than their sexual deviance, the most remarkable thing about swingers is how unremarkable they are." But Gilmartin did find certain social characteristics that distinguish them from conventional couples:

1. Swingers have a much lower rate of church attendance.
2. They tend more to have had an unhappy childhood.
3. Swinging husbands are far more likely than conventional husbands to have divorced or unhappily married parents, though there is not much difference between the wives.
4. Swingers are more alienated from their parents.
5. Swingers began dating earlier, dated more frequently, had their first sexual intercourse at a younger age, were more sexually active before marriage, and married earlier.
6. Swinging couples are more likely to have been divorced before.
7. Swingers are less concerned about social and political issues and less politically active.

In short, swingers are less attached to traditional institutions (such as religion and family) that have a restraining influence on sexuality.

Postmarital Sex

Postmarital sex refers to the coital activity of the divorced, separated, and widowed. Here we will focus on the divorced, because practically all the studies on postmarital sex deal with this group. Postmarital sex is less a social controversy than premarital and extramarital relations. The postmarried's sex lives are less subject to social control—perhaps because, compared to unmarried teenagers, they are considered more socially mature and sexually experienced, less likely to have unwanted pregnancies and venereal diseases. Most importantly, they are no longer under parental control. Also unlike the married, whose extramarital affairs can wreck their marriages, the postmarried may be considered safe because they cannot possibly threaten their nonexistent marriage. Therefore, given the greater sexual freedom enjoyed by the postmarried, it is not surprising that postmarital sex has always occurred more frequently than premarital and extramarital sex. In recent years, however, postmarital sex has even become somewhat more prevalent than marital sex.

In the last 1940s Kinsey found that about 90 percent of the postmarried men had engaged in coitus while 70 percent of the women had done so. By the 1970s Hunt (1975) found that the incidence of postmarital sex had shot up to 100 percent for men and 90 percent for women. Moreover, the postmarried engaged in coitus about twice a week, as compared to three times a week for the married. According to a more recent study (Cargan and Melko, 1982), the divorced have become more sexually active than the married. But the pressure for sex often comes from men, many of whom expect to have sex on the first or second date. Some divorced women are "terrified by what they view as a kind of sexual 'pressure cooker.' They feel pushed and even compelled to perform sexually" (Simenauer and Carroll, 1982). At any rate, divorced women as a whole are quite active sexually, especially more so than widows (Luria, 1987).

The dramatic increase in postmarital sex is largely due to the great upsurge in divorce rates, which are now more than twice as high as in the late 1940s. Another reason could be the rising frequency of premarital and

Postmarital sex is the coital activity of the divorced, separated, and widowed. It occurs more frequently than premarital and extramarital sex. This is probably because postmarital sex is less controversial. Compared with unmarried teenagers, the postmarried are considered more mature, less likely to have unwanted pregnancies and venereal diseases. Also, they are no longer subject to parental control. Compared with the married, whose extramarital sex can destroy their marriages, the postmarried enjoy greater sexual freedom. They obviously do not have a marriage to worry about.

extramarital sex among younger people. As Paul Gebhard (1970) has found, there is a connection between previous experience in premarital or extramarital sex, on the one hand, and a high level of postmarital sexual activity, on the other.

The Hunt survey also suggested that most of the postmarried men and women find their sex lives very pleasurable, and the divorced women even experience more orgasms than the married women of the same age. Nevertheless, the majority of the postmarried eventually remarry. Apparently, they find sex unable to dissolve their loneliness, but expect marriage to do so. Like the never-married who engage in premarital sex, the post-postmarried are more interested in sex with commitment than in one-night stands (Simenauer and Carroll, 1982).

QUESTIONS FOR DISCUSSION AND REVIEW

1. Why aren't young people much more promiscuous than before the sexual revolution?
2. How does premarital sexuality compare with marital sexuality?
3. In what ways is extramarital sex still seen as immoral and the grounds for divorce?
4. Why is postmarital sexuality so prevalent?

HOMOSEXUALITY

Despite the increased tolerance toward homosexuality in recent years, it is still, in 24 states of the union, a criminal offense to make love to a person of the same sex. Even in places where antihomosexual laws have been abolished, gay men are still subject to police harassment. To most people, homosexuality continues to be morally wrong (*Public Opinion,* 1981). Yet homosexuality is relatively common. In the early 1950s, Kinsey found that 37 percent of American men and 13 percent of women had some homosexual experience between adolescence and old age, though only 4 percent of the males and 1 percent of the females became exclusively homosexual throughout their entire lives. About the same incidence of homosexual experience and exclusive homosexuality was found in 1970 (Athanasiou et al., 1970), though somewhat lower figures were obtained in more recent studies (Harmatz and Novak, 1983). In addition, homosexual life-styles have influenced conventional culture. Many heterosexual men, for example, unknowingly behave like gays by wearing long hair, jewelry, men's cologne, or by dancing to disco music. These behaviors were initially popular among homosexuals (Church, 1979). Nevertheless, homophobia—fear of homosexuality—runs deep in society. Out of it have emerged a number of myths about homosexuality.

Myths

According to one myth, male homosexuals are typically effeminate and female homosexuals masculine. Gay men are believed to walk like women, talk like women, or look like women, and lesbians walk, talk, and look like men. Actually it is difficult to distinguish most homosexuals from heterosexuals. Research has shown that gay men are just as masculine as conventional men, and that lesbians are just as feminine as straight women (Storms, 1980).

A second myth is that homosexuals like to molest or seduce young children. The fact, however, is that the great majority of gay men have no more sexual interest in young boys than the great majority of straight men have in little girls. Moreover, most child molesters are *heterosexual* males.

A third myth is that homosexuals consistently play one specific role—either as an active or passive partner—in their sexual activities. The active partner is assumed to perform oral sex on the passive partner. The truth is that most homosexuals engage in a lot of alternation between those two roles. Homosexual couples are also popularly expected to behave like traditional heterosexual couples, one mate playing the role of dominant husband and the other the submissive wife. Again the reality is just the opposite: partners in a homosexual relationship often resemble best friends, who, being equal, "share and share alike," so *both* may cook, make money, or disclose feelings (Peplau, 1981).

A fourth myth is that homosexuals are sick—their homosexuality is a symptom of mental illness. Some homosexuals, particularly those who go to psychiatrists, are perhaps mentally ill, but so are some heterosexuals, particularly those who go to psychiatrists. Therefore, just as it is wrong to conclude that heterosexuals are emotionally disturbed, it is wrong to conclude that homosexuals are.

A fifth myth is that homosexuals, considered abnormal or participants in unnatural sex, cannot be expected

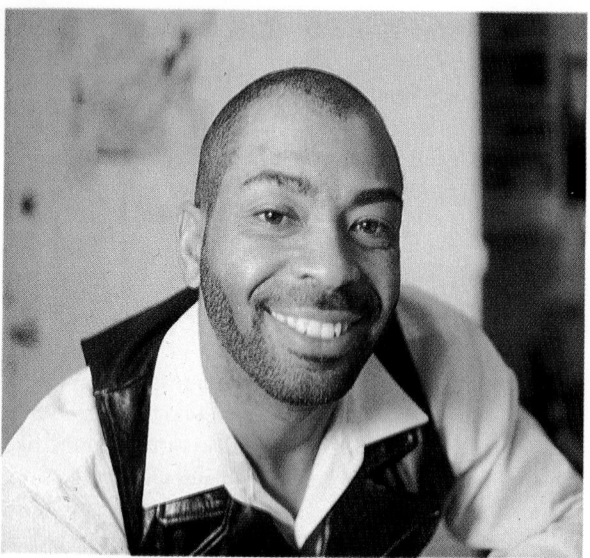

Most homosexuals are indistinguishable from heterosexuals in appearance, manner, and occupation. But homophobia—fear of homosexuality—runs deep in society. It has spawned myths about how gay men and women are different from conventional people. Thus, courts have typically upheld the military's unfair practice of discharging gay soldiers. In a 1988 case, though, Sergeant Perry Watkins (above), who is gay, won his suit against the Army because the court agreed that it is unconstitutional to deny homosexuals the same rights as those enjoyed by other Americans. The Reagan administration, however, was expected to appeal the case to a higher court, possibly the Supreme Court.

to have a satisfactory sex life. Research, however, has shown no real difference between homosexuals and heterosexuals in their physical capacity to enjoy sex. The basic difference has to do with styles of lovemaking. Homosexuals in a love relationship tend to treat sex as play, spending much time on foreplay—focusing on kissing and caressing various parts of the body—before directing attention specifically to genitals for reaching climax. Heterosexual couples are somewhat more likely to work at sex, aiming at a quick orgasm (Testa et al., 1987; Masters and Johnson, 1979).

A sixth myth is that homosexuals are sexually hyperactive. In reality, male homosexuals have about as much sex as heterosexual men—only two or three times a week. In fact, lesbians seem less interested in sex when compared with heterosexual women. While most of the married women engage in sex two or three times a week, the frequency for most lesbians is not more than once a week (Bell and Weinberg, 1978). Gay men, however, are far more promiscuous than heterosexual men. As Alan Bell and Martin Weinberg (1978) found, the majority of male homosexuals have from 100 to more than 500 different partners during their lifetime, as compared with only 1 to 10 for male heterosexuals. We should note, though, that the pronounced promiscuity among male homosexuals has more to do with maleness than homosexuality. Males are typically more promiscuous than women, regardless of their sexual orientation. More importantly, lesbians, despite their homosexuality, have a far lower rate of promiscuity than gay men—most have fewer than nine partners during their lifetime (Meredith, 1984). In the last few years, however, fear of AIDS has caused many gay men to reduce sharply the number of people they have sex with.

Coming Out

In the gay world the process of publicly identifying oneself as a homosexual is called **coming out.** Before they come out, the youngsters do not even privately see themselves as homosexual, although they feel attracted to members of the same sex. In his study of homosexuality, Barry Dank (1971) asked his subjects whether, prior to their graduation from high school, they knew they were homosexual. Some of the typical responses were:

> I would have said, "No, I don't know what you are talking about." If you said "queer," I would have thought something about it; this was the slang term that was used, although I didn't know what the term meant.
>
> I don't think I would have known then. I know now. Then I wasn't even thinking about the word. I wasn't reading up on it.

Young homosexuals, however, acquire their gay identity by going through a number of developmental stages (Troiden, 1979; Coleman, 1982). In the first stage—*sensitization*—homosexuals, when about 13 years old, feel that they are different from their peers. As one gay adult recalled, "I never felt as if I fit in. I don't know why for sure. I felt different. I thought it was because I was more sensitive." Another expressed a similar feeling: "I felt different due to my interest in school, ineptness at sports, and the like."

In the second stage—*dissociation*—homosexuals, about age 17, begin to feel that they might be gay but refuse to define themselves as such. One adult described how he had been in this stage: "Before I was publicly labeled a faggot, I realized that I wasn't very interested in women. I had had enough experiences with girls to realize that while I was aroused by them, I was also aroused by males and wanted to have sex with them. However, I thought this was something I'd outgrow in time, something that would straighten itself out as I matured."

In the third stage—*coming out*—homosexuals, roughly at age 21, regard their sexual feelings as definitely homosexual, get involved in the homosexual subculture, and redefine homosexuality as a positive and viable life-style.

In the final stage—*commitment*—homosexuals, now mature adults, are committed to gayness as a way of life. They insist that they are happy being homosexuals, that they would not change even if given the opportunity, and that they cannot see any benefit in choosing heterosexuality (Troiden, 1979).

Theories

Why have those people become homosexual in the first place? There are many explanations for the development of homosexuality. They may be divided into three major types: biological, psychiatric, and sociological theories.

Biological Theories One of these theories suggests that homosexuality is genetically determined. In the 1950s, studies of twins were made that show that if one of the *identical* twins is homosexual, the chances are 100 percent that the other will also be homosexual, whereas if one of the *fraternal* twins is homosexual, the chances drop to only 50 percent (Kallman, 1952). Such findings have been taken to mean that homosexuality is determined by genes, as identical twins are more genetically alike than fraternal twins. However, sociologists are inclined to argue that social environment is largely responsible for causing homosexuality because, when compared with fraternal twins, identical twins are more likely to be subjected to similar reactions by others. At any rate, there are other studies that show the failure of identical twins to become homosexual together (Kolb, 1963).

Another biological theory suggests that an imbalance between male and female hormones causes homosexuality. This has been derived from several laboratory studies in the 1950s and 1960s. One showed that young homosexual men had lower levels of male hormone than young heterosexual men. Another study indicated that lesbians' daily secretion of androgens (male sex hormones) was considerably higher than their production of estrogens (female sex hormones). Nevertheless, a number of criticisms have been leveled at hormonal theory. First, the findings in support of the theory have not been confirmed in many other laboratories and, in some cases, have actually been refuted (Friedman et al., 1977). Second, even if all the laboratory results showed hormonal differences between gays and straights, we still could not conclude that hormonal imbalances are the *cause* of homosexuality. Hormonal imbalances could well be the *effect* of homosexual practices (Gartrell et al., 1977). Third, when attempts were made to "cure" male homosexuality by administering testosterone (male hormone), the gay man's sex drive increased but he still felt sexually attracted to men rather than women. Fourth, since laboratory studies have been limited to very small self-selected samples of homosexuals, they cannot tell us how common the hormonal imbalance is among the gay population as a whole, as compared with the straight population (Gould, 1974).

More recent analyses, however, have again suggested the possibility of genetic or hormonal influences on homosexuality. Unable to find any strong relationship between childhood experiences and adult homosexuality, a research team has speculated that sexual orientation "may arise from a biological precursor—as do left-handedness and allergies, for example—that parents cannot control" (Bell, Weinberg, and Hammersmith, 1981). Another team has found that after pregnant rats were repeatedly subjected to stress, their male offspring would exhibit female-type behavior when placed with other males. The researchers attribute the homosexual behavior to shortage of male sex hormones, which is assumed to have resulted from the stress suffered by the mothers (Hemming, 1980). Nevertheless, a *direct* connection between the presumed biological factors and human homosexuality has yet to be demonstrated. At best these studies merely suggest that biological factors predispose some individuals toward homosexuality. Whether this biological predisposition leads to homosexuality depends on certain social forces, such as parents and peers, subtly guiding or overtly pressuring individuals into homosexuality.

Psychiatric Theories Psychiatrists have long assumed that homosexuality is a form of mental disorder characterized by "hidden but incapacitating fears of the opposite sex" (Bieber et al., 1962; Socarides, 1978). Male homosexuals are said to suffer from **castration anxiety**—to be afraid of having sexual intercourse with a woman because they regard her vagina "as a castrating instrument capable of biting or tearing off their penis" (Fenichel, 1945).

We may note, however, that the castration anxiety theory runs counter to the fact that the most popular sexual practice among male homosexuals is oral sex (Bell and Weinberg, 1978; Spada, 1979). If they are fearful about getting castrated, gay men would not dare allow others to perform oral sex on them. Moreover, the psychiatric concept of homosexuality as mental illness has been widely and severely criticized. Critics argue that the illness concept is usually based on the study of a biased sample—homosexuals who are psychiatric patients—which has ignored the huge number of normal homosexuals. In fact, comparative studies of gays and straights have failed to find homosexuals "sick or even different, except for sexual preferences" (Gould, 1974). Nevertheless, many psychiatrists continue to regard homosexuality as a mental disturbance (Leo, 1979; Spitzer, 1981) although the American Psychiatric Association removed homosexuality from its list of mental disorders in 1973.

According to another psychiatric theory, a boy will become homosexual if his mother is domineering, overprotective, and seductive and his father weak, detached, and hostile. Alienated from his father, the boy cannot look upon him as a model for learning the masculine role. Instead, driven by his hostile father into the arms of his loving mother, the boy will overidentify with her. As an adult, he will engage in many homosexual acts to seek relief from overidentification with his mother—to prove that he is masculine (Bieber et al., 1962; Socarides, 1978).

We may argue, however, that if gay men were really driven to prove their masculinity, they would have chased women instead, because woman-chasing is widely regarded as a mark of masculinity. In addition, critics have observed that the psychiatric notion of "mama's boy" as a candidate for homosexuality is actually based on the myth that male homosexuals are typically effeminate. Studies of normal homosexuals have further shown that "disturbed parental relations are neither necessary nor sufficient conditions for homosexuality to emerge" (Hooker, 1969; see also Bell, Weinberg, and Hammersmith, 1981).

Sociological Theories It has been suggested that homosexuality, just like heterosexuality, is the result of social conditioning. The assumption is that humans are born with a diffuse, neutral sexual drive that can be directed to any person or object for satisfaction. Thus children are not particularly attracted to the homosexual or heterosexual object choice—a same-sex person is just as sexually exciting as a different-sex person. They are also equally capable of being sexually aroused by their rubber duck, teddy bear, or any other plaything. Only through constant interaction with parents and other socializing agents are they gradually conditioned to restrict their sexual interest to the sexual object choice approved by society—and simultaneously conditioned to kill their interest in the other choices disapproved by society. Since there is a powerful taboo against homosexuality and strong support for heterosexuality in our society, most American adults have been conditioned to heterosexual activity. But some may have been conditioned toward homosexuality in some way. They may have, for example, repeatedly enjoyed the feeling of being attracted to or the actual sexual experiences with same-sex others, which their parents and others, being kept in the dark, could not discourage (Hoffman, 1968; Pomeroy, 1969).

Another sociological theory suggests three related points as important for understanding homosexuality. One, homosexuality is not pathological but merely a variant of sexual expression. Whatever psychological problems some homosexuals may have, they do not cause homosexuality. Two, since homosexuality is a normal form of sexual expression rather than a sickness, there is no need to search for a cure. Attention should instead be directed to the similarities between the processes of becoming homosexual and heterosexual. Three, contrary to psychiatric theories, which overemphasize the importance of early childhood, we should view the adult experience as more important for understanding homosexual behavior. These three points are related to labeling theory. It suggests that homosexuality is not a sickness in itself but only appears as such because it has been stigmatized by society. If it is not a sickness, homosexuality need not be cured. And since it is a social stigma, homosexuality significantly affects the life of the adult who engages in it (Weinberg and Williams, 1975; Gagnon and Simon, 1967).

QUESTIONS FOR DISCUSSION AND REVIEW

1. What is homophobia, and what myths about homosexuals support it?
2. Through what development stages do young homosexuals move as part of the process of coming out?
3. Why do persons become homosexuals, according to biological and psychiatric perspectives?
4. How is becoming homosexual like the process of becoming heterosexual?

RAPE

While homosexuality is not necessarily a crime, rape definitely is. In fact, it is a major, serious crime in the United States. It is also very common. Analysis of the National Crime Surveys has led Allan Johnson (1980) to estimate that 20 to 30 percent of all American girls now 12 years old will suffer a violent sexual attack sometime during their lives. In their surveys of women of all ages in San Francisco, Diana Russell and Nancy Howell (1983) found that 26 percent had been raped and 46 percent had been victims of either rape or attempted rape. The most conservative estimate still puts an average woman's chance of being raped at "an appalling 1 in 10" (Dowd, 1983). Of course, rape may involve a male sexually assaulting another or a female attacking a male. But most of the rapes are committed by men against women, on which we focus here.

Who Are the Rapists?

An answer can be found in Menachem Amir's (1971) classic study of rapes known to the police in Philadelphia. Amir found that, contrary to the myth of black men being more likely to rape white women than black, rape is mostly intraracial—blacks raping blacks and whites raping whites. In about 95 percent of the rapes in Philadelphia, both offender and victim were of the same race; in only 3 percent was the rapist black and his victim white. More recent studies have shown the same intraracial pattern (U.S. Justice Department, 1983).

Most rapists do not randomly, impulsively, or explosively assault their victims. Instead, they do some planning before they strike. Such planning accounted for 71 percent of the rapes analyzed by Amir. Most rapists look for a certain type of female as well as a certain type of location to carry out their plan.

Rapists ordinarily choose females who they believe are vulnerable to attack. Such a female is somehow handicapped or cannot react appropriately or swiftly to the threat of rape, such as a retarded girl, an older woman, a sleeping female, or a girl who is under the influence of alcohol or drugs. Rapists are also likely to select a victim whom they regard as "a loose woman" or "a wild one." If they cannot easily determine the vulnerability of a female, the rapists will likely work out a strategy to test her. They might first try to determine whether or not their selected target is a friendly and helpful person. A rapist might, for example, approach a woman on the street and ask her for a light or for a street direction. If she provides it, he may proceed to ask her an intimate question, make some sexually suggestive remarks, put his arm around her, or touch her in a sexually provocative place in order to see how she reacts. If she reacts submissively or fearfully, he knows that she can be intimidated into submitting to his sexual demands. Another rapist might ask a woman to let him in her house to make an emergency phone call or for any other bogus reason. If the woman falls for such a ploy, the rapist may establish her as his candidate for rape (Selkin, 1975).

As for the location of rape, the assailants look for places that can be easily entered and are relatively safe. Usually these are old houses and apartments in rundown areas of the city, where many women live alone. Rapists may also search empty streets, laundromats, and theater restrooms to find their unsuspecting victims (Selkin, 1975). A more recent study, however, shows that rapes are less likely to happen outdoors than indoors. The reason is that on the street it is easier for women to flee; also, their screams are more likely to draw attention and police (Cohen, 1978).

After they have successfully identified a victim for rape, the attackers *initially* do not resort to intimidation with such violent means as brandishing a weapon or administering a brutal beating. According to Amir, the majority (87 percent) of rapes involved only verbal coercion and nonphysical aggression, such as "Don't scream or I'll cut you to pieces" or "If you don't take your clothes off, I'll kill you!" But when they are ready to carry out the crime, rapists ordinarily become more violent. Amir found that while 15 percent of the rapes did not entail any force, 85 percent involved some degree of violence including roughness, beating, and choking.

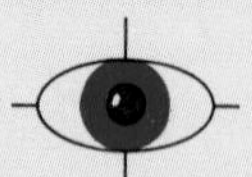

USING SOCIOLOGICAL INSIGHT

When the Date Turns Into Rape

Many studies have shown that most rapists are psychologically normal rather than emotionally disturbed. Not surprisingly, many sociologists today regard rape as an extension of the socially approved male-dominant pattern of sexual behavior. This is particularly true of rapes committed by men against their dates. The following report describes the nature of date rape and efforts made to combat it, especially on college campuses. How does this form of rape differ from other types described in the chapter?

Susan, now 22 and a college senior, was raped almost three years ago on a first date. She met the man in a cafeteria at summer school and went to his dorm that evening to watch television news and get acquainted. After 45 minutes of chitchat about national affairs, he began pawing and kissing her, ignoring her pleas to stop. "You really don't want me to stop," he said, and forced her to have sex.

The attack was an all too familiar incident of date rape. Like many victims, Susan was unwary and alone too soon with a man she barely knew. It took her 18 months to confront the reality that she had, in fact, been raped. Now she is more aware, and her thoughts run to the dangers of dates between women raised to be politely passive and aggressive males who sometimes assume that no means yes. "Women are taught to be nice, to be attractive and appealing," she says, "but we should also teach women to speak up more and teach men to listen more."

Date rape, according to some researchers, is a major social problem, so far studied mostly through surveys of college students. In a three-year study of 6,200 male and female students on 32 campuses, Kent State Psychologist Mary Koss found that 15% of all women reported experiences that met legal definitions of forcible rape. More than half those cases were date rapes. Andrea Parrot, a lecturer at Cornell University, estimates that 20% of college women at two campuses she surveyed had been forced into sex during their college years or before, and most of these incidents were date rapes. The number of forcible rapes reported each year—87,340 in 1985—is believed to be about half the total actually committed. Experts say the victim knows the assailant in at least a third of all rapes. Says Koss: "You're a lot more likely to be raped by a date than by a stranger jumping out of the bushes."

Acquaintance rapes are not always reported because many victims do not define themselves as having been raped. Koss found that 73% of the women forced into sex avoided using the term rape to describe their experiences, and only 5% reported the incident to police. Psychologist Barry Burkhart of Auburn University explains, "Because it is such a paralyzing event, so outside the realm of normal events, they literally don't know what happened to them."

Date rape sometimes occurs after the victim has taken drugs or one drink too many. Whether under the influence or not, victims frequently classify the rape as a hazy, regrettable experience that was somehow their own fault. "And because often they don't even see it as rape, they fail to seek support professionally," says Burkhart. "They are left without a way of understanding it, so they bury it, feeling guilty and ashamed."

The rapists would not merely subject their victims to forced intercourse; they would also force them to submit to such acts as fellatio, cunnilingus, anal penetration, and repeated vaginal intercourse. Sometimes they make jokes at their victims' expense. After he was through, one rapist proclaimed to his victim, "I'll marry you if you get pregnant" (McDonald, 1971).

Rapists can be divided into three types on the basis of motivations for sexual assault. One is the *power* rapist, who seeks to overpower the victim into sexual submission as a way of proving his masculinity. He is primarily uninterested in harming his victim physically. The *angry* rapist, however, wants to hurt his victim and uses the sexual assault as a means of expressing his pent-up anger and rage. Even more violent is the *sadistic* rapist, who can get sexually aroused only by torturing his victim. Nicholas Groth and Jean Birnbaum (1980) found that the majority (55 percent) of their rapists were essentially power-oriented, somewhat fewer (40 percent) were the angry type, and a small minority (5 percent) were sadistic. All this suggests that rape is mostly not sexually motivated. It is instead an expression of male dominance over females.

We have so far discussed only rapists known to the

The use of drugs or alcohol is likely to cloud the issue of consent in a criminal trial. Says Linda Fairstein, a Manhattan district attorney in charge of the sex-crimes unit: "The defense will say she gave consent and just doesn't remember."

In a widely publicized incident last fall, a female student at the University of California, Berkeley, filed a complaint saying she had been gang-raped by a football player she once dated and three of his teammates. The case was dropped, partly because the victim had been drinking. Said Detective Greg Folster of the University of California, Berkeley, police: "I have no doubt that this was a sexual assault, but I don't think the judicial system is quite ready for acquaintance rape."

Researchers compiling profiles of both victims and victimizers find that date rapists are more sexually active than other males and more likely to have a history of antisocial behavior. The rapists and their victims are usually in the 15-to-24 age group. The women are often alone in a new environment, like a college campus. Compared with other women, the victims generally suffer from lower self-esteem and are not very good at asserting themselves. One woman, raped by her date at a fraternity party, said she decided not to scream for help because she did not want to embarrass the rapist.

One theory of date rape is that men and women tend to misread each other's signals, particularly a soft-spoken no that many males assume means yes or at least maybe. Says one student at Pepperdine University in Malibu, Calif.: "There are different kinds of nos. 'Noooo . . . ' is one thing. 'NO, get your filthy hands off me!' is another." Some feminists argue that the U.S. has a "rape culture" in which males are encouraged to treat women aggressively and women are trained to submit. Some surveys back up that dark ideological view of male sexual behavior. In Koss's study, one male in 13 admitted attempting or committing at least one rape. In a 1980 report at UCLA, half the male students admitted that there could be some circumstances under which they would force a woman to commit a sexual act if they were sure of not being punished.

Many campuses and rape crisis centers sponsor speeches and programs aimed at preventing date rape. At Cornell, student actors play the roles of date rapists and victims, then stay in character to restage the scenes along new lines suggested by members of the audience. An increasing number of college campuses now have anti-rape programs. However, as Bernice Sandler of the Association of American Colleges, points out, "many schools are still unsure about whether date rape is rape or not. Schools just don't know what to do about it." But times may be changing. Pi Kappa Phi fraternities around the country now put up posters of *The Rape of the Sabine Women* saying TODAY'S GREEKS CALL IT DATE RAPE. Underneath in smaller type it says, AGAINST HER WILL IS AGAINST THE LAW.

Source: Reprinted from John Leo, "When the Date Turns Into Rape," *Time,* March 23, 1987, p. 77. Copyright 1987 Time Inc. All rights reserved. Reprinted by permission from TIME.

police. They do not, however, represent all the rapists in the United States. According to various surveys, no more than 10 percent of rapes are reported to the police. They tend to overrepresent stranger rapes, because such rapes are far more likely to be reported than acquaintance rapes (Bart, 1975). Among the countless unreported rapes by acquaintances, **date rape**—in which a man commits sexual aggression against a woman he is out with—is the most common. In a study of date rapes, Clifford Kirkpatrick and Eugene Kanin (1957) asked college women whether they had been sexually offended during the academic year. More than half (55.7 percent) replied that they had been, at least once. Their experiences ranged from the relatively trivial to the serious, from forced necking to forced petting to forced vaginal penetration "in the course of which menacing threat or coercive infliction of physical pain was employed." More recently, Kanin and Parcell (1981) did a follow-up study and found the same result. These studies, along with many others, suggest that numerous ordinary men possess "a proclivity to rape" (Malamuth, 1981; Meer, 1987). In fact, most of the rapists, whether strangers or acquaintances to their victims, are normal people. As Susan Brownmiller (1976) put it, "The typical American rapist is no weirdo, psycho schizophrenic beset by timidity, sexual deprivation, and a domineering wife or mother."

The Hidden Culture of Rape

Why do we have so many rapists? Primarily because we live in a "rape prone" culture. In a comparative study of 156 tribal societies, Peggy Sanday (1981) found that a few are "rape free," where women are treated with considerable respect and interpersonal violence is minimized. Most are "rape prone," like our society, characterized by male dominance and interpersonal violence. Indeed, we have a hidden culture of rape that secretly encourages men to rape women. This culture shows itself through the prevailing attitudes toward women.

First, women are treated as if they were men's property. If a woman is married, she is in effect her husband's property. Thus in most of the states in our country a man cannot be prosecuted for raping his wife (Finkelhor and Yllo, 1982; Barden, 1987). Many people seem to reason: how can any man steal what already belongs to him? The property logic may also explain the difficulty of getting a man convicted for raping a "cheap, loose woman" or a known prostitute. Such a female is considered as if she were every man's property, which she is assumed to have proven by having sex with many men. If a "good" woman is raped, we often say that she has been "ravaged," "ravished," "despoiled," or "ruined" as if she were a piece of property that has been damaged. The widespread availability of pornography further reinforces the popular image of women as men's sex objects. Since women are culturally defined as men's property, men may find it difficult to respect women. It is through a lack of this respect that men are encouraged to rape women, since rape expresses the very essence of disrespect for a woman.

Women are also treated as if they were objects of men's masculinity contests. In order for a man to prove his manhood, he is culturally pressured to make out with the largest number of women possible. "The most respected player in the game," wrote Andra Medea and Kathleen Thompson (1974), "is the one who best outwits the most females by coaxing, lying, maneuvering; the one who, with the least actual cost to himself, gets the most females to give him the most sex." The pressure to play this masculinity game often comes from friends who ask something like: "Did you score?" "Had any lately?" If the answer is no, they may say, "What's the matter? Are you queer or something?" Such social pressure tends to make many young men want to show off their "masculine" qualities, such as aggressiveness, forcefulness, and violence. This often involves engaging in sexual violence, of one degree or another, against women. Indeed, as one study shows, the most important factor that distinguishes sexually aggressive males from others is their experience of peer pressure, which comes from aggressive friends (Alder, 1985). Even if the peer pressure does not exist, the popular belief in sexual conquest as a badge of masculinity already encourages men to be aggressive toward women. It is no wonder that the winners of this masculinity contest, such as college men who have a lot of sexual experiences, are more likely to rape their dates than the so-called losers, who have little or no sexual experience (see box, p. 202). All this has caused many sociologists to regard rape as an extension of the socially approved, conventional pattern of male sexual behavior (Kanin, 1983, 1985; Schur, 1984).

There is also a popular myth that, deep down, women want to be raped. One study shows that the majority (71 percent) of the people surveyed believe that women have an unconscious rape wish (Burt, 1980). This is why many people tend to hold the victim responsible for the rape. The victim is assumed to have asked for it by dressing sexily, hitchhiking, accepting a drink in a bar, or accepting a man's invitation to his apartment. A related assumption is that it is impossible to rape a woman if she resists, which is what the defense attorneys of some rapists like to argue. In the courtroom, the victim is often portrayed as a willing partner. In two recent cases, for example, one victim was accused of having a "kinky and aggressive" sex life and another was said to be "sexually voracious" and to have "preyed on men" (Lacayo, 1987). The willing-victim myth is apparently a major motivating force behind many rapes. In one study of convicted rapists, 59 percent deny their guilt and blame their victims instead. They insist that their victims seduced them, meant yes while saying no to the sexual assault, and eventually relaxed and enjoyed the rape (Scully and Marolla, 1984).

QUESTIONS FOR DISCUSSION AND REVIEW

1. What are the three types of rapists, and how do they carry out their crime?
2. Why do many date rapes go unreported?
3. What is meant by the hidden culture of rape, and what sexual myths does that culture support?

CHAPTER REVIEW

1. *What is the sociological perspective of sexuality?* It views sexuality as the result of socialization within a sociocultural context. It explains variations in sexual behavior between and within societies.

2. *Why is the incest taboo universal?* Because, according to biological theories, revulsion against incest is instinctive, inbreeding causes physical and mental weaknesses in offspring, and negative imprinting results from childhood familiarity. But to sociologists the incest taboo exists because it has been necessary for securing interfamily cooperation and keeping the family intact.

3. *What has the sexual revolution brought us?* It has encouraged sexual tolerance, weakened the double standard, changed sexual purposes from procreation to recreation, and emphasized unexploitative sex as more important than whether the partners are married or not.

4. *What are the new myths of sexuality?* Liberated women cause sex problems for men. Female orgasm is earthshaking. Techniques are more important than partners' relationship for achieving sexual pleasure. Simultaneous orgasms are always best for couples. Young people have gone wild sexually.

5. *Why does one society allow premarital sex while another does not?* Male dominance or societal complexity has been linked to sexual restrictiveness; their absence, to permissiveness. *Who is likely to have premarital sex?* Young people who are going steady or engaged, lacking in church attendance, closer to friends than parents, or relatively independent, critical of society, tolerant of deviance, or using alcohol and drugs. *How is marital sex today compared with the past?* The volume and variety of marital sex have increased but the wives' orgasm rate has not improved significantly. *What is extramarital sex like?* The traditional form of extramarital sex is charged with guilt and tension and thus not as gratifying as popularly imagined. Swinging is more satisfying to couples who can separate sex from love but unsatisfactory to those who cannot. *Do divorced people enjoy postmarital sex?* Yes, but the majority eventually remarry because they prefer sex with commitment.

6. *What are the myths about homosexuals?* Gay men are effeminate and lesbians manly. Homosexuals like to molest young children. They characteristically play either an active or passive role in sexual activities. They are psychologically abnormal and cannot have a satisfactory sex life. They are sexually hyperactive. *What are the stages of the "coming out" process?* Sensitization, dissociation, coming out, and commitment. *How do various theories explain homosexuality?* Biological theories attribute homosexuality to genetic abnormality and hormonal imbalance. Psychiatric theories assume homosexuality as pathological and explain it as the result of abnormal parent-son relationships. Sociological theories regard it as the product of social conditioning and suggest a labeling approach for understanding homosexuality.

7. *Who are the rapists?* They may be strangers or acquaintances to the victims. Studies of rape reported to police, which overestimate stranger rapes, show that rapists tend more to victimize women of their race and do some planning before they strike. They may be power-oriented, angry, or sadistic. Studies of acquaintance rapes suggest that there are many rapists in our midst and most are ordinary, normal men. *What is the hidden culture of rape?* It secretly encourages men to rape women by treating women as if they were men's property, as if they were the trophies of men's masculinity contests, and as if they wanted to be raped.

KEY TERMS

Castration anxiety A psychiatric term for the male homosexual's fear of getting castrated while having sex with a woman (p. 200).

Coming out The process of publicly identifying oneself as a homosexual (p. 198).

Date rape Rape committed by a man against a woman he is out with (p. 203).

Double standard The social norm that allows males, but not females, to engage in nonmarital sex (p. 190).

Extramarital sex Having sex with a person who is not one's spouse, popularly called adultery or marital infidelity (p. 195).

Incest taboo The social norm that strongly prohibits sexual relations between close relatives (p. 187).

Negative imprinting A biological mechanism that suppresses erotic feelings for individuals with whom one has become familiar since early childhood (p. 188).

Postmarital sex The sexual experience of the divorced or widowed (p. 196).

Premarital sex Sex before marriage (p. 191).

Sequential orgasms One partner reaching climax after the other does (p. 191).

Sex drive A biological potential for, rather than determinant of, sexual desire or behavior (p. 186).

Sex instinct An innate biological mechanism that causes its carrier to have sexual relations in a certain way and at a definite time (p. 186).

Simultaneous orgasms Both partners reaching sexual climax at the same time (p. 191).

SUGGESTED READINGS

Bell, Alan P., Martin S. Weinberg, and Sue Kiefer Hammersmith. 1981. *Sexual Preference: Its Development in Men and Women.* Bloomington: Indiana University Press. A scholarly but readable study of the childhood and adolescent experiences of both homosexuals and heterosexuals.

Holmstrom, Lynda Lytle, and Ann Wolbert Burgess. 1983. "Rape and everyday life." *Society,* July/August, pp. 30–40. A good summary of the current studies on causes of rape and strategies for stopping it.

Kanin, Eugene J. 1985. "Date rapists: Differential sexual socialization and relative deprivation." *Archives of Sexual Behavior,* 14, pp. 219–231. An interesting analysis of why sexually successful men rape their dates.

Reiss, Ira L. 1986. *Journey into Sexuality: An Exploratory Voyage.* Englewood Cliffs, N.J.: Prentice-Hall. Presents a sociological theory of human sexuality based on the assumption that sexuality is a social product that we acquire in much the same way as we learn to develop friendship and love relationships.

Richardson, Laurel. 1986. *The New Other Woman.* New York: Free Press. A research report on how and why independent single women get involved with married men.

PART THREE

Social Inequality

Chapter 9
Social Stratification

Chapter 10
Racial and Ethnic Minorities

Chapter 11
Gender Roles and Inequalities

Chapter 12
The Elderly

Social inequality exists when we see people having unequal access to valued resources, goods, and services in a society. Such inequality can be found in all societies, including our own, where most people seem to believe that "all men are created equal." Social inequality is a significant force in our lives. It influences our chances of going to college, graduating from it, getting a good job, or living a healthy and long life. It even affects how we think and behave in our everyday activities.

Social inequality may appear between rich and poor, between dominant and minority groups, between the sexes, and between the old and the young. We take a closer look at each of these inequalities in the next four chapters. Chapter 9 focuses on social stratification, a system of inequality in which members of a society are ranked into different strata on the basis of how many social rewards they have. Chapter 10 deals with racial and ethnic minorities, whose physical and social characteristics are used as bases for prejudice and discrimination by the dominant group. Chapter 11 is concerned with gender roles and inequalities, exploring the dominance of men over women. Chapter 12 concentrates on the elderly, showing how they get along in our youth-oriented culture.

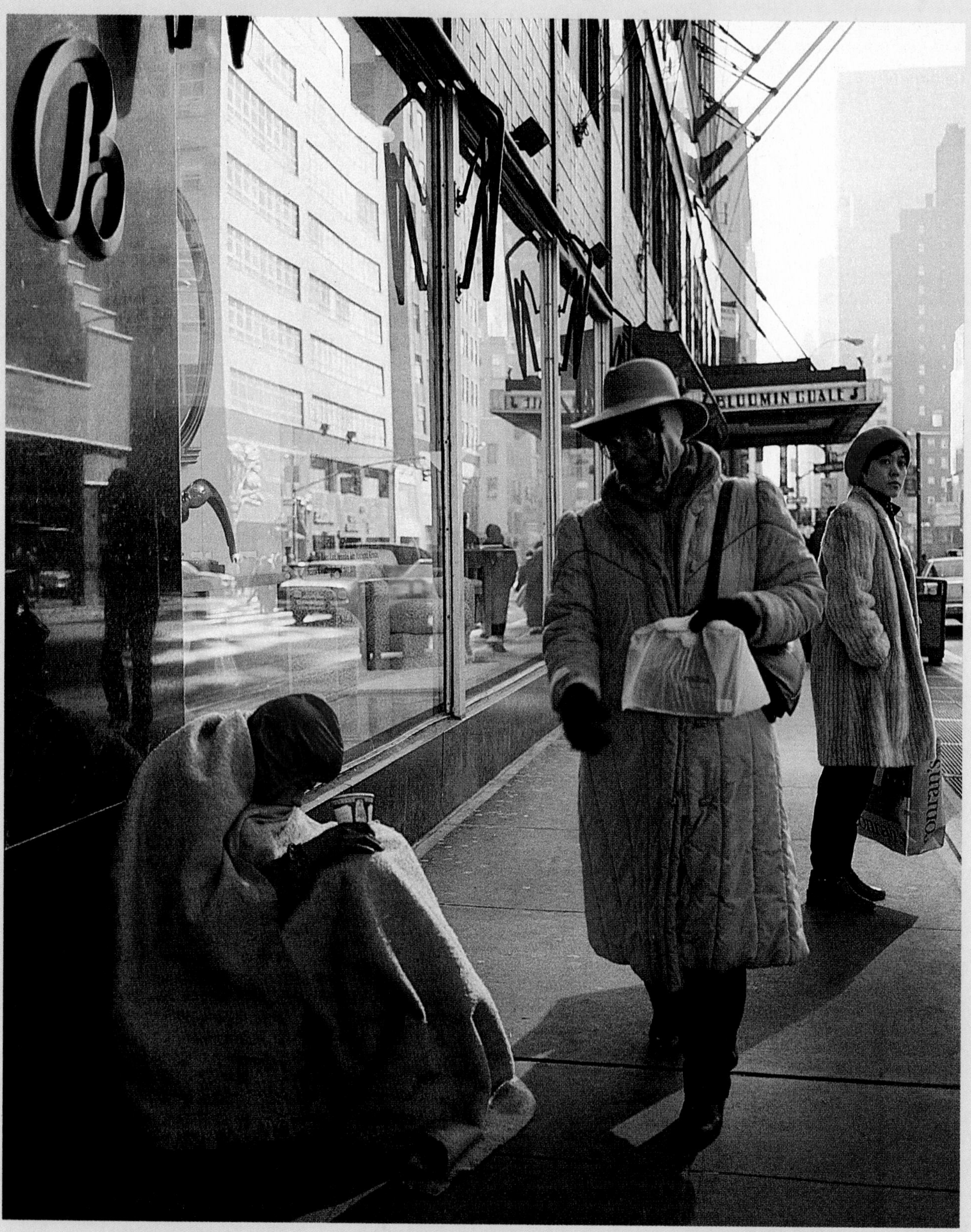

9 Social Stratification

In every society, social rewards such as wealth, power, and prestige are distributed unequally. Having a particular position in this pattern of inequality, called social stratification, *affects how people live. Obviously the rich have far better housing, food, and clothing than the poor. The rich also spend more money on such nonessentials as lavish parties. Thus the rich live better and longer than others. But can poor Americans strike it rich in this land of opportunity? Data suggest that very few Americans rise from rags to riches, but numerous Americans do climb a little way up the socioeconomic ladder—from being a factory worker to being a small-store owner, for example. Most of this upward mobility, then, is very modest, concentrated in the middle portion of the stratification system. Research has further shown that upward mobility has increased during this century. It also happens slightly more often in the United States than in most other industrialized societies.*

Marcia Myshrall is a single mother with three children. She earns only $14,000 per year as an account analyst at a Boston hospital. She has to struggle to make ends meet. She likes to have a vacation once in a while, but the closest she comes is a day at the beach with the kids—if her 7-year-old car is working. "I'm barely surviving," she sighs. By contrast, Ellen and Richard Bellicchi make about $150,000 from their chain of women's health clubs. They reside with their two children in a Connecticut oceanfront house with seven bathrooms, own three boats and four cars, and often vacation abroad. "We live like kings," she says, smiling (Wessel, 1986).

"Those who have, get." This old saying suggests that in every society some people, like Ellen and Richard Bellicchi, get more social rewards than others, like Marcia Myshrall. The specific nature of the rewards may vary from one society to another. The rewards could be in the form of wealth, power, prestige, or whatever is highly valued by the society. All over the world, however, these rewards are distributed unequally. This patterned inequality is called **social stratification.** It is the division of society in such a way that some categories of people get more rewards than others.

In this chapter we first see how these rewards are used as the bases for social stratification in the United States. Then we examine what the social strata, or classes, are in this country, and whether people can move easily from one stratum to another. Finally, we analyze the question of whether it is necessary for society to have this social stratification.

THE BASES OF STRATIFICATION

Social stratification is based on the unequal distribution of many different rewards. Sociologists have long identified three of these rewards as the most important bases of stratification in the United States: wealth, power, and prestige. These three usually go together. If we are rich, we are also likely to have a lot of political power and social prestige. But possession of one reward does not guarantee enjoyment of others. Compared with teachers, some garbage collectors may make more money but have less prestige and power.

Wealth

In the last century Karl Marx divided industrial society into two major and one minor classes: the *bourgeoisie* (capitalists), the *proletariat* (workers), and the *petite bourgeoisie* (small capitalists). Marx differentiated them on the basis of two criteria: whether or not they own the

According to Karl Marx, capitalists seek to maximize profit by exploiting workers. Marx was inspired to develop his analysis of the relationship between capital and labor by the appalling working conditions in factories in the mid-nineteenth century in England. Women and children were employed to work on dangerous machinery for long hours at low pay. Conditions in the United States were not much better, as shown in the famous series of photographs of child laborers taken by Lewis Hine in the first years of the twentieth century. Hine took the photo here, which shows spindle boys working in a Georgia cotton mill.

"means of production"—tools, factories, offices, and stores—and whether or not they hire others to work for them. Capitalists are those who own the means of production and hire others. Workers neither own the means of production nor employ others. Hence they are forced to work for capitalists. As for small capitalists, they own the means of production but do not purchase the labor of others. Examples are shopkeepers, doctors, lawyers, and other self-employed persons. Marx considered these people a minor, transitional class because he believed that they would eventually be forced down into the working class.

In Marx's view, exploitation characterizes the relationship between the two major classes: capitalists and workers. Capitalists, bent on maximizing profit, compel workers to work long hours for little pay. Such exploitation was indeed extreme in Marx's time. Consider his description of child laborers:

> Children of nine or ten years are dragged from their squalid beds at two, three, or four o'clock in the morning and compelled to work for a bare subsistence until ten, eleven, or twelve at night, their limbs wearing away, their frames dwindling, their faces whitening, and their humanity absolutely sinking into a stone-like torpor, utterly horrible to contemplate (Marx, 1866).

Marx believed that eventually workers would rise in revolt and establish a classless society of economic equals. But his prophecy of revolution has not materialized in any highly developed capitalist economy. Writing in the 1860s, Marx failed to foresee that the exploitation of workers would ease and that a large prosperous class of white-collar workers would emerge. Even so, there are still significant economic inequalities in the United States.

Distribution of Income and Wealth In the United States "the income ratio of the top executives to the lowest paid production workers continues to be approximately 100 to 1. A top corporate executive earns far more in one year than a unionized blue-collar worker makes in an entire lifetime of toil" (Blumberg, 1980). For about 30 years, the income distribution in the United States has remained about the same. It is very unequal.

According to the latest data available, the richest 20 percent of the population earn about 44 percent of the total national income. In contrast, the poorest 20 percent earn less than 5 percent of the national income. The distribution of wealth is even more unequal. Whereas *income* is the money people receive over a certain period of time, such as wages and salaries, *wealth* includes the income-producing things they own such as stocks, bonds, savings accounts, and real estate. A large group of Americans own no assets, and most hold little wealth. The richest 20 percent of the population own 76 percent of the total national wealth, but the poorest 20 percent hold far less than 1 percent (see Figure 9.1).

Figure 9.1 Unequal Distribution of Income and Wealth

Income in the form of salaries and wages is unequally distributed among the American people. Wealth accruing from stocks, bonds, property, and the like is even more unequally distributed. The richest fifth of the population owns 76 percent of the national wealth, 380 times more than what the poorest fifth owns—which is a mere 0.2 percent of the nation's wealth.

Sources: Social Indicators, 1973 (Washington, D.C.: Government Printing Office, 1973), p. 182; Census Bureau, *Statistical Abstract of the United States, 1988* (Washington, D.C.: Government Printing Office, 1988), p. 428.

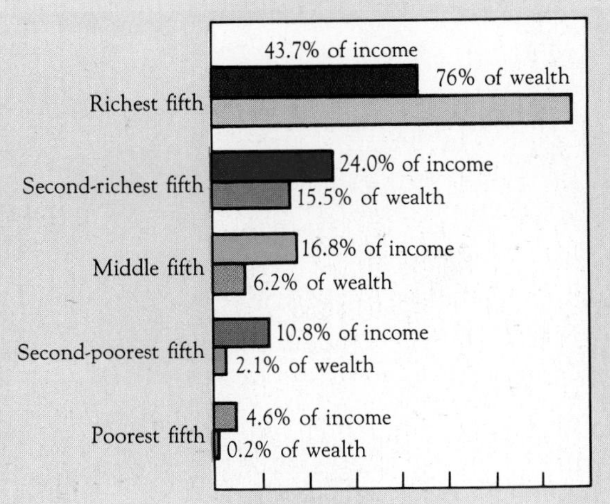

Poverty amid Plenty Although the U.S. income distribution is more equal than that of many nations, especially the developing third-world countries, it is less equal than the distribution in several other industrialized nations such as England, Sweden, and West Germany (Kerbo, 1983). Does this inequality mean that a multitude of Americans live in poverty?

The answer depends on what we consider poor and what we consider a multitude. To determine the number of people who are poor, the government uses an *absolute* definition of poverty. It defines poverty as the lack of minimum food and shelter necessary for maintaining life. It then decides what income is needed to sustain that minimum standard of living and sees how many people fall below it. In 1986, for example, the "poverty

Poverty can be a relative condition, because how poor a person feels depends to a great extent on how other people live. Since the United States is one of the richest countries in the world, poor Americans find their already disheartening poverty even more disheartening when they see the vivid contrast between their own lives and the ways other people live. Moreover, since prosperous Americans tend to blame the poor for their poverty, they are reluctant to support welfare and other programs that supplement income for the very poor. As a consequence, the poor tend to find their conditions worsening, as shown here: (a) a family living in a shelter, (b) a shopping-bag lady living on the street, (c) a couple living in a tent city, and (d) a family living in their car.

a

b

c

d

line" for a nonfarm family of four was $11,203, and 13.6 percent of the population—over 32 million Americans—fell below the poverty line (Census Bureau, 1988). Such figures have stirred up a controversy, however. Conservative critics argue that they overestimate the extent of poverty because they do not count as income many *noncash* benefits, such as food stamps, housing subsidies, and medical assistance, which the poor receive from the government. These noncash benefits account for two-thirds of government programs for the poor. If these benefits are added to cash incomes, many "poor" Americans would rise above the poverty line—hence no longer poor. Liberal critics, on the other hand, contend that government figures underestimate the extent of poverty because the poverty threshold is set too low. It is based on the estimated cost of food for a diet that, if sustained for any period of time, would lead to illness or death. As for the noncash benefits, they help the poor to survive only—rather than lift them out of poverty (Beeghley, 1984). There is yet a third way of looking at poverty. If we define it in terms of its persistence, we can find that only about one-tenth of the so-called poor are persistently poor—having had income below their needs in at least eight of the last ten years. A majority (about 56 percent) are temporarily poor—having been in poverty one or two years. The remaining segment of the poverty population—34 percent—find themselves somewhere between being persistently and temporarily poor (Hill, 1985).

Many social scientists suggest that a *relative,* not an absolute, definition of poverty be used, because how poor or rich we feel depends on how people around us live. Just because we are not starving to death or live far better than, say, the poor in Central America does not mean that we should consider ourselves well-off. According to a widely accepted relative definition of poverty, those who earn less than half of the nation's median income are poor because they lack what is needed by most Americans to live a decent life (Rainwater, 1974; Rodgers, 1982). By that definition, for more than 35 years, the percentage of the nation living in poverty has hovered around 18 to 20 percent (Census Bureau, 1984). Poverty defined in this way exists whenever there are significant economic inequalities.

Still, by the standards of most countries, the percentage of Americans living in extreme poverty is small. Although our country no longer has the highest income per person in the world, it still ranks in the top ten. By some standards, such as taking into account per-capita GNP* or per-capita energy consumption, the United States remains the most prosperous nation. This very prosperity, however, may actually aggravate the plight of the poor. In many developing countries the poor may not find themselves too bad off because most people around them are just as poor (see box, p. 214). But it is tougher to be poor in a sea of affluence, such as the United States. On top of that, most Americans blame the poor for their poverty, stereotyping them as lazy, worthless, and immoral (Kluegel and Smith, 1981). As a result, they condemn welfare programs, even though the money spent on programs for the poor is far less than the tax relief granted the rich. In 1980, for example, the noncash benefits given to the poor cost the federal government $44.1 billion, but tax subsidies, expense accounts, and other such benefits for the rich cost $143.3 billion (Beeghley, 1984). Moreover, all applications for welfare are scrutinized for possible fraud, although only 1.4 percent of the nonpoor's income tax returns are audited despite the much higher cost that the nation pays for tax fraud (Wiener, 1984). In view of these negative attitudes and treatments, the American poor can be assumed to find their economic deprivation greater than it is.

Power

Power—the ability to get people to do things they otherwise would not do—is associated with wealth. Most sociologists agree that people with more wealth tend to have more power. This is evident in the domination of top government positions by the wealthy (Useem, 1980; Kerbo, 1983). Higher-income Americans are also more likely to feel a strong sense of power. Thus they are more likely to be politically active, working to retain or increase their power. Meanwhile, lower-income Americans are more likely to feel powerless to influence major political decisions. They are therefore more indifferent to politics and less likely to participate in political activity—a reaction likely to reinforce their lack of power (Dahl, 1981; Kourvetaris and Dobratz, 1982).

It is clear that power is distributed unequally. But how unequal is that distribution? Does it match the dis-

* Gross national product per person, or the total value of a nation's goods and services divided by its population.

UNDERSTANDING OTHER SOCIETIES

The City of Joy

Poverty in many developing countries is extreme. Yet according to author Dominique Lapierre, who lived in Calcutta for several years, thousands of people exist somehow in that city's slums, and there is widespread sharing among them, especially in an area called the "City of Joy." Why do slums like the one described below exist and how can residents retain and uphold human values?

One of the principal and oldest of Calcutta's slums was wedged between a railway embankment, the Calcutta-Delhi highway, and two factories. Either out of ignorance or defiance, the jute factory owner who, at the beginning of the century, had lodged his workers on this land which he had reclaimed from a fever-infested marsh, had christened the place Anand Nagar, "City of Joy." Since then the jute factory had closed its doors, but the original workers' estate had expanded to become a veritable city within a city. But now more than seventy thousand inhabitants had congregated on an expanse of ground hardly three times the size of a football field. That included some ten thousand families divided up geographically according to their various religious creeds. Sixty-three percent of them were Muslims, 37 percent Hindus, with here and there little islands of Sikhs, Jains, Christians, and Buddhists.

With its compounds of low houses constructed around minute courtyards, its red-tiled roofs, and its rectilinear alleyways, the City of Joy did indeed look more like an industrial suburb than a shantytown. Nevertheless it boasted a sad record—it had the densest concentration of humanity on this planet, two hundred thousand people per square mile. It was a place where there was not even one tree for three thousand inhabitants, without a single flower, a butterfly, or a bird, apart from vulture and crows—it was a place where children did not even know what a bush, a forest, or a pond was, where the air was so laden with carbon dioxide and sulphur that pollution killed at least one member in every family, a place where leprosy, tuberculosis, dysentery and all the malnutrition diseases, until recently, reduced the average life expectancy to one of the lowest in the world. Above all, however, the City of Joy was a place where the most extreme economic poverty ran rife. Nine out of ten of its inhabitants did not have a single rupee per day with which to buy half a pound of rice. Furthermore, like all other slums, the City of Joy was generally ignored by other citizens of Calcutta, except in case of crime or strike. Considered a dangerous neighborhood with a terrible reputation, the haunt of Untouchables, pariahs, social rejects, it was a world apart, living apart from the world.

Everything in this slum combined to drive its inhabitants to abjection and despair: shortage of work and chronic unemployment, appallingly low wages, the inevitable child labor, the impossibility of saving, debts that could never be redeemed, the mortgaging of personal possessions and their ultimate loss sooner or later. There was also the total nonexistence of any reserve food stocks and the necessity to buy in minute quantities—one cent's worth of salt, two or three cents' worth of wood, one match, a spoonful of sugar—and the total absence of privacy, with ten or twelve people sharing a single room. Yet the miracle of this concentration camp was that the accumulation of disastrous elements was counterbalanced by other factors that allowed its inhabitants not merely to remain fully human but even to transcend their condition and become models of humanity.

In this slum people actually put love and mutual support into practice. They knew how to be tolerant of all creeds and castes, how to give respect to a stranger, how to show charity toward beggars, cripples, lepers, and even the insane. Here the weak were helped, not trampled upon. Orphans were instantly adopted by their neighbors and old people were cared for and revered by their children.

Unlike the occupants of shantytowns in other parts of the world, in this slum the former peasants who took refuge there were not marginals. They had reconstructed the life of their villages in their urban exile. An adapted and disfigured life perhaps—but nonetheless so real that their poverty itself had become a form of culture. The poor of Calcutta were not uprooted. They shared in a communal world and respected its social and religious values, maintaining their ancestral traditions and beliefs. Ultimately—and this was of primary importance—they knew that if they were poor it was not their fault, but the fault of the cyclical or permanent maledictions that beset the places where they came from.

Source: Excerpts from *The City of Joy* by Dominique Lapierre. English translation copyright © by Pressinter, S. A. Reprinted by permission of Doubleday, a division of Bantam, Doubleday, Dell Publishing Group, Inc.

tribution of wealth? Power cannot be identified and measured as easily as wealth can, because people with power do not always express it. As a result, sociologists disagree about how it is distributed.

Both Marxist and elite theorists argue that a very small group of Americans holds the most power in the United States. According to *Marxist theorists,* that group consists of capitalists. Even if they do not hold office, say Marxists, capitalists set the limits of political debate and of the government's actions, protecting their own interests. This is why large corporations, through heavy political campaign contributions and congressional lobbying, are able to hold down their taxes. According to *elite theorists,* a lot of power is in the hands of a few hundred individuals who hold top positions in the executive branch of the federal government, in the military, and in corporations. Often, the same people hold power in all of these three centers of power. In any event, they have similar backgrounds, values, and interests, and they form what elite theorists call the **power elite.**

In contrast to both Marxist and elite theorists, *pluralist theorists* argue that power is not tightly concentrated, but widely dispersed. It is more or less equally distributed among various competing groups. The power of big business, for example, is balanced by that of big labor, and government actions are ultimately determined by competition and compromise among such diverse groups. Even ordinary citizens have the power to vote anyone into office or out of it.

In short, while Marxists and elitists see a great deal of inequality in power distribution, pluralists see very little. Both views may be correct. Most of the power in American society is concentrated at the top, but the elite is not all-powerful. It is subject to challenge by voters from below. It is true that the general public is usually powerless—because it does not get organized. But occasionally, when it feels strongly enough about an issue to make its wishes known, as it did about its opposition to the Vietnam War in the 1960s, the government does change its policy to follow public opinion (Burstein, 1981). We examine the theories further in Chapter 16 (Politics and the State).

Prestige

A third basis of social stratification is the unequal distribution of prestige. Following Max Weber, sociologists call this kind of stratification a **status system.**

There is a difference between prestige, on the one hand, and wealth and power, on the other. Wealth and power are objective entities: a person can have them regardless of what other people think of him or her. But prestige is subjective, depending for its existence on how a person is perceived by others. If a person is rich and powerful but is seen by others as unworthy of respect, he or she has low prestige. The boss of an organized crime syndicate may make millions and exercise awesome power, but he might never acquire prestige because most people refuse to hold him in esteem, and they cannot be forced to do so. On the other hand, many college professors may not be rich and powerful, but they do enjoy more prestige.

Although prestige is not as concrete as money and power, most people do seek it. Consciousness of status, Gerhard Lenski (1966) has observed, "influences almost every kind of decision from the choice of a car to the choice of a spouse. Fear of the loss of status, or honor, is one of the few motives that can make men lay down their lives on the field of battle."

How do people obtain such an important social reward? Occupation seems the most important source of prestige. For many years sociologists have found that people have very definite ideas about the prestige of various occupations. In 1947 a team of sociologists asked a large random sample of Americans to evaluate 90 occupations on a scale from "excellent" to "poor." Then in 1963 other sociologists repeated the study with other Americans. They found a nearly perfect correlation between the prestige scores given these 90 occupations in 1947 and in 1963. In those two years, physicians, for example, received one of the highest scores and garbage collectors one of the lowest. Almost all groups of Americans, rich or poor, rated the occupations in the same way (Hodge, Siegel, and Rossi, 1964). About the same finding has appeared in the 1970s and 1980s (see Table 9.1). Even people in many foreign countries—some industrialized and some not—have been found to rank occupations in the same way (Hodge, Siegel, and Rossi, 1964; Treiman, 1977). The exceptions are socialist countries such as the Soviet Union, Poland, and Yugoslavia, where manual jobs are ranked higher than those in the United States, apparently due to the communist ideology that praises the working class (Haller and Bills, 1979; Kerbo, 1983).

How do people evaluate occupations? A quick look at Table 9.1 suggests that the ranking has a lot to do with education and income. In general, the higher the education and income associated with an occupation,

Table 9.1 How Americans Rank Occupations

Occupation is probably the most important source of prestige. All kinds of Americans tend to give the same prestige rating to an occupation. The ranking of various occupations has largely remained the same for the last 40 years. How do people evaluate the occupations? The following table suggests that generally they give higher ratings to those jobs that require more education and offer higher incomes.

Occupation	Score	Occupation	Score	Occupation	Score
Physician	82	Librarian	55	Dancer	38
College professor	78	Statistician	55	Barber	38
Judge	76	Social worker	52	Jeweler	37
Lawyer	76	Funeral director	52	Watchmaker	37
Physicist	74	Computer specialist	51	Bricklayer	36
Dentist	74	Stock broker	51	Airline stewardess	36
Banker	72	Reporter	51	Meter reader	36
Aeronautical engineer	71	Office manager	50	Mechanic	35
Architect	71	Bank teller	50	Baker	34
Psychologist	71	Electrician	49	Shoe repairman	33
Airline pilot	70	Machinist	48	Bulldozer operator	33
Chemist	69	Police officer	48	Bus driver	32
Minister	69	Insurance agent	47	Truck driver	32
Civil engineer	68	Musician	46	Cashier	31
Biologist	68	Secretary	46	Sales clerk	29
Geologist	67	Foreman	45	Meat cutter	28
Sociologist	66	Real estate agent	44	Housekeeper	25
Political scientist	66	Fireman	44	Longshoreman	24
Mathematician	65	Postal clerk	43	Gas station attendant	22
Secondary school teacher	63	Advertising agent	42	Cab driver	22
Registered nurse	62	Mail carrier	42	Elevator operator	21
Pharmacist	61	Railroad conductor	41	Bartender	20
Veterinarian	60	Typist	41	Waiter	20
Elementary school teacher	60	Plumber	41	Farm laborer	18
Accountant	57	Farmer	41	Maid/servant	18
		Telephone operator	40	Garbage collector	17
		Carpenter	40	Janitor	17
		Welder	40	Shoe shiner	9

Source: James A. Davis and Tom W. Smith, *National Data Program for the Social Science: General Social Survey Cumulative File, 1972–1982.* Ann Arbor, Mich.: Inter-University Consortium for Political and Social Research, 1983, Appendix F.

the greater its prestige, as is true of physicians and lawyers. But this is not always the case. Compared with schoolteachers, truck drivers may make more money but rank lower in prestige.

Occupation, of course, is only one of a person's many statuses such as those based on age, race, and gender. These statuses may have different social rankings, creating **status inconsistency.** A black lawyer and a female doctor have high occupational status, but they may have less prestige because of prejudice against their race and gender.

People plagued with status inconsistency usually experience considerable stress. They resent the source of their status inconsistency. They think of themselves in terms of their highest status and expect others to do the same. But others may treat them in reference to their lowest status. Consequently, compared with people who do not experience status inconsistency, those who do are more likely to support liberal and radical movements designed to change the status quo (Lenski, 1966). As research has shown, in the 1960s black bankers and physicians were more militant about changing racial conditions than black janitors and housekeepers (Marx, 1967).

QUESTIONS FOR DISCUSSION AND REVIEW

1. What is social stratification, and what bases are used to stratify American society?

2. How equally is income and wealth distributed in the United States?
3. In what ways is the power basis of stratification different from the system of prestige?
4. Why does status inconsistency create stress?

AMERICAN CLASS STRUCTURE

Despite our cherished belief in social equality, inequality is still entrenched in American society, as we have seen. This inequality can further be observed in the way American society is divided into different social classes, forming a distinctive class structure.

Definitions of Class

What is class? It is an ambiguous concept with several different meanings. Traditional Marxists and European sociologists define class in relation to the means of production, so that they divide society into two major conflicting classes of capitalists and workers only. (Capitalists are those who own the means of production, and workers are those who do not.) But neo-Marxists have modified or extended this concept of class. As a result, people are divided into six classes: employers, petty bourgeois, managers, supervisors, nonmanagerial experts, and workers. They are differentiated according to whether they own the means of production, what organizational positions they hold, and whether they possess the necessary skills or credentials (Wright, 1985; Wright and Martin, 1987). Managing directors, though they do not own but only control the means of production, are considered capitalists because they share many interests with capitalists (Robinson and Kelley, 1979, 1980). Most small-business owners are also considered capitalists even though they were not in Marx's book—because they have too few employees to fit his image of capitalists (Aldrich and Weiss, 1981). Salary earners or nonmanual employees, whom Marx would have regarded as workers, are now considered the "new small capitalists" because they are inclined to ally themselves politically with capitalists (Gagliani, 1981). Self-employed manual workers such as carpenters, electricians, and plumbers, whom Marx regarded as a transitional class doomed to join workers in opposition to capitalists, are considered to have more in common with the capitalist class because they are more affluent, more politically active, and more conservative than the working class (Form, 1982).

But most American sociologists do what Marx would have objected to. They equate class with a status, income, educational, occupational, or socioeconomic grouping. A well-known example is Peter Blau and Otis Duncan's (1967) non-Marxist definition of class as "socioeconomic status" consisting of a certain educational level, occupational status, and income. They also treat class division and social stratification as if they were the same. Thus the major dimensions of stratification (wealth, power, and prestige) can be found in many definitions of class. Consider this typical one by Arthur Marwick (1986): "[Classes are] broad aggregates of individuals distinguished from each other by inequalities in wealth, income, power, authority, prestige, freedom, life-styles, and life chances." Taking both Marxist and non-Marxist definitions into account, we may define **class** as a category of people who own or do not own the means of production, or have about the same amount of income, power, and prestige.

Identifying Classes

How do we know who is in what social class? Since there are no hard-and-fast rules for defining class, sociologists have devised three different methods for identifying what our class is. (1) The reputational method asks: What do others think of us? (2) The subjective method asks: What do we think of ourselves? (3) The objective method asks: What do we do, how much do we have, and how do we live?

Reputational Method Sociologists who use the **reputational method** select a group of people and ask them what classes they think others belong to. These informants are selected as "prestige judges" primarily because they have been living in the community for a long time and can tell the sociologists the standing of many other residents. Presumably, they rank others on the basis of their reputation in the town. If they are asked to rank a man whom they know to be a public drunk, they would put him in a lower-class category. If they are asked to rank a woman whom they know as a respectable banker, they would place her in an upper-class category. To the

Although there is general agreement among sociologists that American society is divided into at least three classes, in practice it is often difficult to specify which class a particular person or family, such as this one, belongs to. There are three different ways to determine a person's class. In using the reputational method, sociologists ask a selected group of people to rank others. In using the subjective method, sociologists ask people how they rank themselves. And in using the objective method, sociologists rank people according to such criteria as income, educational attainment, and occupation.

sociologists, then, whatever class in which the prestige judges place a person is his or her class.

The reputational method is useful for investigating the class structure of a small community, where everybody knows practically everybody else. But it suffers several disadvantages. First, the reputational method cannot be applied to large cities, because it is impossible to find prestige judges who know thousands of other people. Second, it is impossible to generalize the findings from one community to another, because the informants can judge only their own community. Third, it is impossible to find unanimity among the prestige judges in a community. There are always cases in which an individual is considered upper class by one judge but lower class by another.

Subjective Method Rather than asking people what they think of others, sociologists may also ask them what class they themselves belong to. This is called the **subjective method.**

Before 1945 many sociologists who used the subjective method concluded that the overwhelming majority of Americans considered themselves middle class. In 1939, for example, the Gallup survey showed that 88 percent of Americans identified themselves as middle class. Social psychologist Richard Centers (1949), however, argued that these results were misleading, because they were based on surveys that asked people to identify themselves as either upper class, middle class, or lower class. Both "upper class" and "lower class" have connotations offensive to democratic values. To call oneself upper class is to appear snobbish. To call oneself lower class is demeaning, because it implies that one is a loser in this supposed land of opportunity. As a result, many high-status people such as doctors and lawyers would call themselves middle rather than upper class; meanwhile, many low-income and lower-status Americans such as maids and laborers would also say they were middle class. In short, most Americans rejected both the upper- and the lower-class choices, and the only other choice the sociologists gave them was middle class. By including "working class" as a fourth choice in his own surveys, Centers found in 1945 and 1946 that more Americans identified themselves as working class than as middle class. In the 1980s, though, the National Opinion Research Center (1986) found that the number of Americans viewing themselves as working class is about the same as those seeing themselves as middle class. In 1964 Robert Hodge and Donald Treiman (1968) added a fifth choice to Center's list: upper middle class. They found more Americans identifying themselves as middle class than as working class (see Figure 9.2).

These examples suggest some weaknesses of the subjective method. First, the results depend heavily on how the question is asked. Second, the answers are also influenced by the respondents' attitude toward the class system. Despite these very serious problems, the subjective method has at least two advantages. First, it can be used

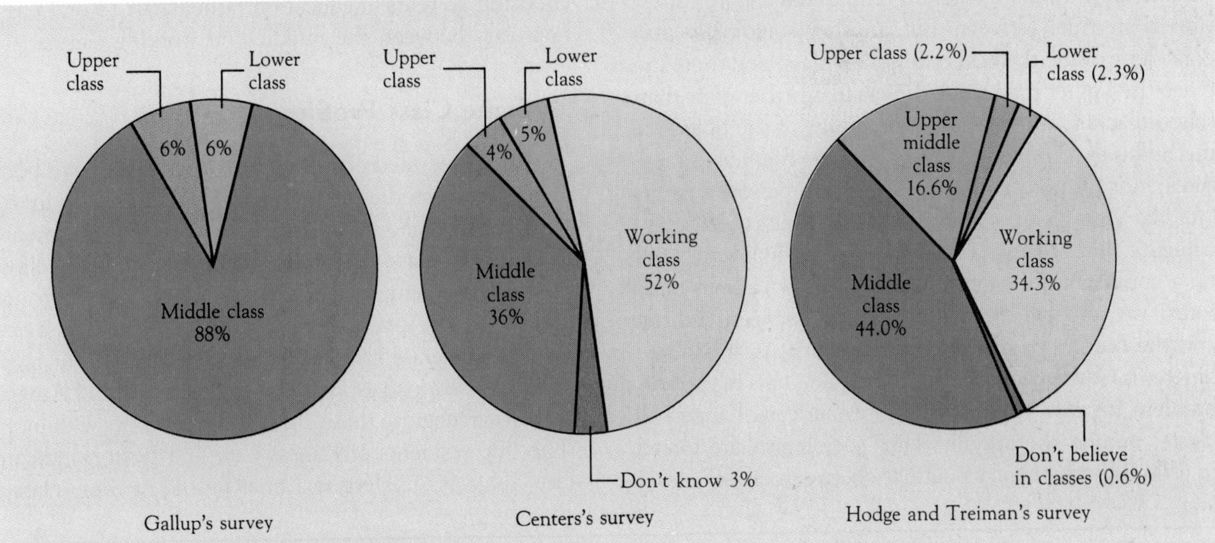

Figure 9.2 Comparison of Three Research Results

By simply adding the "upper-middle class" choice when asking a national sample of Americans to identify their social classes, Hodge and Treiman got a different result than Centers had earlier. Furthermore, when only three alternatives (upper, middle, and lower classes) were listed in the Gallup survey, most respondents who considered themselves "working class" were forced to identify themselves as "middle class," thereby making the middle class appear far larger than it was. It is apparent that the wording of the questions asked in such surveys largely determines the results.

Sources: Richard Centers, *The Psychology of Social Classes* (Princeton, N.J.: Princeton University Press, 1949), pp. 30, 31, 77; Robert W. Hodge and Donald J. Treiman, "Class identification in the United States," *American Journal of Sociology* 73 (1968), p. 536.

fairly easily to investigate large cities or even an entire society. Large numbers of strangers can simply be asked to respond—anonymously if they wish—to a question like, "If you were asked to use one of these names for your social-class standing, which would you say you belong to: middle class, lower class, working class, or upper class?" Second, the subjective method is very useful for understanding and predicting behaviors that are strongly affected by attitudes. If self-employed auto mechanics, electricians, and plumbers identify themselves with the upper class, they can be expected to hold politically conservative views and to vote Republican, just as upper-class people tend to do (Form, 1982).

Objective Method Both the subjective and the reputational methods depend on people's perception of class. The third method depends on objective criteria such as amount of income.

To use the **objective method,** sociologists must decide what criteria are to be used to indicate individuals' class positions. Today most sociologists use occupation, income, and education as the criteria, either singly or jointly. Some sociologists use occupation by itself to divide the population into classes. Others use income or education instead. Still others utilize all three criteria.

Like the subjective method, the objective method is useful for identifying the classes in large cities or an entire society. It has another advantage as well: sociologists can easily obtain the needed data on occupation, income, and education from the Bureau of the Census or by mailing questionnaires to the people themselves.

The objective method has some disadvantages, though. One is that the choice of the criteria for differentiating the classes is arbitrary. One sociologist, believing that education is the best indicator of class, may consequently place schoolteachers in a higher class than truck drivers, because teachers tend to have more education than truck drivers. But another sociologist may consider income the best criterion of class, and therefore place the higher-paid truck drivers in a higher class than schoolteachers. A second disadvantage of the objective method is that the indicators of class are *continuous* measures, not discrete categories. When a person answers "middle class" to a survey question, that is a discrete category, but their incomes and educational levels fall on a continuum of values. With these continuous measures, we can still distinguish clearly between the top and the bottom of the class ladder, but it is difficult to differentiate the people near the middle. This is a serious problem because the majority of Americans happen to cluster around the middle. Thus sociologists are forced to establish an *arbitrary* boundary between classes—say, choosing 12 years of education rather than 11 or 13 as a boundary between the middle and working classes.

Some Class Profiles

The three methods of identifying classes have been used in many studies with roughly the same result: in the United States about 1 to 3 percent of the population are in the upper class, 40 to 55 percent in the middle class, 30 to 45 percent in the working class, and 15 to 20 percent in the poor, lower class. Sociologists disagree about the precise boundaries of these classes, but most accept these broad estimates of their sizes. Other Americans also recognize these classes, as interviews with more than 900 residents of Kansas City and Boston indicate (see Table 9.2). Here is a brief profile of these classes

Table 9.2 A Class Profile

The left column provides a rough stratification of the American population into various classes, made possible by numerous studies using the three class-identifying methods. The names of the classes are not the same in all studies, though. Some refer to upper class as "corporate class" or "capitalist class." Some use the term "working class" for both upper and middle lower classes but others apply it to upper lower class only and call middle lower class the "working poor." "Lower lower class" is variously called "lower class," "underclass," or "the poor." The right column is derived from an analysis of interviews with representative samples of adult residents of Kansas City and Boston.

Social class (with estimated % of total population)		What they are like (as seen by residents of Boston & Kansas City)
Upper class (1%–3%)		"People who have really made it": They include the old rich (e.g., the Rockefellers), the celebrity rich (movie stars), the anonymous rich (millionaire land developers), and the run-of-the-mill rich (well-heeled physicians).
Middle class (40%–55%)	Upper middle class (10%–15%)	"People who are doing very well": They are professional people (dentists, lawyers, corporate executives). They have very large homes, often vacation in Europe, and belong to semiexclusive country clubs.
	Middle middle class (15%–20%)	"People who have achieved the middle-class dream": Although having a lot more than the necessities, they don't have many luxuries. They are suburbanites living in a three-bedroom house with a family-TV room. Each summer, they head for the mountains or the beach.
	Lower middle class (15%–20%)	"People who have a comfortable life": These folks pay their bills on time and even manage to salt something away for a rainy day. They own a six-room, single-family house in a not-too-fashionable suburb.
Lower class (45%–65%)	Upper lower class (20%–30%)	"People who are just getting along": Often the husband is a factory worker, the wife a waitress or store clerk. They rent a small house or large apartment. They own a more-than-ten-year-old car, a TV set, and a clothes washer, but not a dishwasher.
	Middle lower class (10%–15%)	"People who are having a real hard time": These men and women are the working poor, proud that they are working and not on the public dole. They are likely to live in a walkup in an old apartment building. The husband could be a custodian, the wife a cleaning lady.
	Lower lower class (15%–20%)	"People who are poor": Most of these families are on welfare. They live in the poorest section of the inner city. Cockroaches come out at night in the tiny kitchens of their one-bedroom apartments.

Sources: Jack L. Roach, Llewellyn Gross, and Orville R. Gursslin (eds.), *Social Stratification in the United States,* Englewood Cliffs, N.J.: Prentice-Hall, 1969, pp. 154–233; Richard P. Coleman and Lee Rainwater, *Social Standing in America,* New York: Basic Books, 1978.

that has emerged from various studies (Roach, Gross, and Gursslin, 1969; Rossides, 1976; Gilbert and Kahl, 1987; Kerbo, 1983).

The Upper Class Though it is a mere 1 to 3 percent of the population, the upper class possesses at least 25 percent of the nation's wealth. This class has two segments: upper upper and lower upper. Basically, the upper upper class is the "old rich"—families that have been wealthy for several generations—an aristocracy of birth and wealth. Their names are in the *Social Register,* a listing of acceptable members of high society. A few are known across the nation, such as the Rockefellers, Roosevelts, and Vanderbilts. Most are not visible to the general public. They live in grand seclusion, drawing their income from the investment of their inherited wealth. In contrast, the lower upper class is the "new rich." Although they may be wealthier than some of the old rich, the new rich have hustled to make their money like everybody else beneath their class. Thus their prestige is generally lower than that of the old rich. The old rich, who have not found it necessary to lift a finger to make their money, tend to thumb their noses at the new rich.

A party in an upper-class home. Although the upper class constitutes no more than 3 percent of the population, it possesses at least 25 percent of the nation's wealth—and corresponding power and prestige. There are two kinds of people in this class: the "old rich" and the "new rich." The old rich have inherited their wealth from families that have been extremely well-off for several generations. But the new rich have made their fortunes by themselves. Both groups, however, live in luxury and command enormous power and influence in society.

However its wealth is acquired, the upper class is very, very rich. They have enough money and leisure time to cultivate an interest in the arts and to collect rare books, paintings, and sculpture. They generally live in exclusive areas, belong to exclusive social clubs, rub elbows with each other, and marry their own kind—all of which keeps them so aloof from the masses that they have been called the *out-of-sight class* (Fussel, 1983). More than any other class, they tend to be conscious of being members of a class. They also command an enormous amount of power and influence here and abroad, as they hold many top government positions, run the Council on Foreign Relations, and control multinational corporations. Their actions affect the lives of millions.

The Middle Class The middle class is not as tightly knit as the upper class. Middle-class people are distinguished from those above them primarily by their lesser wealth and power, and from those below them by their white-collar, nonmanual jobs.

This class can be differentiated into two strata by occupational prestige, income, and education. The *upper middle class* consists mostly of professional and business people with high income and education, such as doctors, lawyers, and corporate executives. The *lower middle class* is far larger in size and much more diverse in occupation. It is made up of people in relatively low-level but still white-collar occupations, such as small-business owners, store and traveling salespersons, managers, technicians, teachers, and secretaries. Though they have less income and education than the upper middle class, the lower middle class has achieved the middle-class dream of owning a suburban home and living a comfortable life. (These lower-middle class people are referred to as both middle-middle and lower-middle classes in Table 9.2.)

A middle-class family. The designation "middle class" covers extremes of achievement, income, and interests. At the very top, the middle class blends partly into the upper class, and at the bottom it blends partly into the lower class. In general, middle-class people do not have inherited wealth and must earn the money for their homes, education, and life-styles. Middle-class people can be wealthy, if they own a successful business or have risen to the top of their profession. They can command prestige by, for example, holding high elective office. But middle-class people can also be rather poor, such as low-paid church ministers and schoolteachers.

The Lower Class The lower class consists primarily of those who have very little education and whose jobs, if they have them, are manual and carry very little prestige.

There are two strata within the lower class. The working class (referred to as both upper lower and middle lower classes in Table 9.2) consists of skilled and unskilled manual laborers. Some working-class people, such as construction workers, carpenters, and plumbers, are skilled workers and may make more money than those in the lower reaches of the middle class, such as secretaries and teachers. But their jobs are more physically demanding and, especially in the case of factory workers, more dangerous. Other working-class people are unskilled, such as migrant workers, janitors, and dishwashers. There are also many women in this class working as domestics, cleaning ladies, and waitresses, and they are the sole breadwinners in their households. Since they are generally underpaid, they have been called the *working poor* (Gilbert and Kahl, 1987).

The lower lower class, or simply "lower class," is characterized by joblessness and poverty. It includes the chronically unemployed, the welfare recipients, and the impoverished aged. These people live in rundown houses, wear old clothes, eat cheap food, and lack proper medical care. Very few have finished high school. They may have started out in their youth with poorly paying jobs that required little or no skill, but their earning power began to drop when they reached their late twenties. A new underclass has emerged in recent years: skilled workers in mechanized industry who have become unskilled workers in electronically run factories. They have first become helpers, then occasional workers, and finally the hard-core unemployed (Dahrendorf, 1984). Joining their ranks are the growing number of divorced and unwed mothers, who now make up nearly half of all poor families (Goldberg and Kremen, 1987). The poor tend to be isolated from the rest of the community. They are as well hidden as the out-of-sight rich.

A lower-class neighborhood. The lower class is made up of the working poor (skilled and unskilled manual labor) and the nonworking poor. The working poor may rise into the middle class, whereas some members of the middle class may slip into the lower class as they grow older and poorer and can't find work. Many in the lower class have inadequate educations and poor job skills. Female-headed families dependent on welfare and other social programs for food, housing, and medical care are frequently found in the lower class.

There is a different reason for their social invisibility, though. While the rich hide from others, the poor are ignored by others. They are the invisible, "other America" (Harrington, 1962). But in the 1980s a growing number of the poor have become all too visible. They are the homeless. While the government estimates their number to be between 250,000 and 350,000, advocates for the homeless, such as New York's Community Service Society, insist that there are well over 2 million of them. We can easily see them, particularly in large cities, where many sleep on sidewalks, at entrances to public buildings, in train and bus stations, and in parks and plazas as well as other such "public hotels" for the poor (Revlin, 1986).

The Influence of Class

One of the most consistent findings in sociology is that social class is correlated with how people live. Of course, the correlation does not always indicate a causal relationship, but people in different classes do live differently. In fact, the influence of class is so great and pervasive that it is taken into account in nearly every sociological research study. That is why we have discussed, for example, the impact of class on childhood socialization, mental illness, and sexual behavior in previous chapters. We will also examine class differences in religion, politics, sports, and other human behaviors in later chapters. Here we focus on how social class affects life chances and life-styles.

Life Chances Obviously the rich have better houses, food, and clothes than the middle class, who, in turn, live in more comfortable conditions than the poor. The upper classes can also devote more money, and often more time, to nonessentials like giving lavish parties; some rich people even spend more money on their pets than most people earn from their jobs (Parenti, 1977). Their choices are often wider, their opportunities greater, than those of the lower classes. In other words, the upper classes have better **life chances**—a greater likelihood that they will obtain desirable resources and experiences, more opportunities for living a good, long, or successful life.

We can see the impact of class on life chances in the *Titanic* tragedy, which took 1500 lives. In 1912, on the night when the ship sank into the Atlantic Ocean, social class was a major determinant of who survived and who died. Among the females on board, 3 percent of the first-class passengers drowned, compared with 16 percent of the second-class and 45 percent of the third-class passengers. All passengers in first class had been given the opportunity to abandon ship, but those in the third class had been ordered to stay below deck, some of them at the point of a gun (Lord, 1981; Hall, 1986).

Less dramatic but just as grim is the common finding in many studies that people in the lower classes generally live shorter and less healthy lives than those above them in the social hierarchy. An infant born into a poor family is at least three times more likely to die during its first year than an infant born into a nonpoor family. For adults, too, mortality rates—the number of deaths per 1000 people—differ among the classes. Among whites between 25 and 64 years of age, lower-class men have a 48 percent higher mortality rate than middle-class men, and lower-class women have a 61 percent higher mortality rate than middle-class women. The lower classes are more likely to die from heart disease, syphilis, tuberculosis, stomach ulcers, diabetes, influenza, and many other diseases. Lower-class people, for example, are eight times more likely than upper-class people to die from tuberculosis. They are also more likely than higher-class people to obtain their medical care in emergency rooms or public clinics, rather than from a private doctor (Gortmaker, 1979; Kitagawa and Hauser, 1968; Yeracaris and Kim, 1978). Many other studies show the same influence of social class on these and other life chances (see Table 9.3).

Life-Styles Tastes, preferences, and ways of living—called **life-styles**—may appear trivial in comparison to life chances. But sociologists long ago discovered the importance of social class by studying life-style differences among people. In the following we will see how class shapes life-style.

Upper- and middle-class people are likely to be active outside their homes—in parent-teacher associations, charitable organizations, and various community activities. They are also likely to make friends with professional colleagues or business contacts, with their spouses helping to cultivate the friendship. In fact, they tend to combine their social and business lives so much that friendships are no longer a personal matter but are used to promote careers (Kanter, 1977). In contrast, working-class people tend to restrict their social life to families and relatives. Rarely do they entertain or visit

Table 9.3 The Impact of Class on Life Chances

People at the bottom of the American class structure are more likely to die at a given age, to suffer from chronic diseases, and to be victims of violent crime. Those at the top live longer, have more stable marriages, are less likely to be obese, and are more capable of sending their children to college. Not surprisingly, they are more likely to feel very happy.

Life chances	Lower class	Middle class	Upper class
Mortality rate			
White males 45–54 years old	2.12	1.01	.074
Victims of heart disease			
Number per 1000 persons	114	40	35
Obesity in native-born women	52%	43%	9%
Marital instability			
White males, age 25–34, never divorced	23%	10%	6%
Victims of violent crime			
per 1000 population	52	30	27
Children who attend college	26%	37%	58%
Describe selves as "very happy"	29%	38%	56%

Source: Dennis Gilbert and Joseph A. Kahl, *The American Class Structure,* 3rd ed. Homewood, Ill.: Dorsey, 1987, p. 111.

their friends from work. Although male factory workers may "stop off for a beer with the guys" after work, the guys are seldom invited home. Many working-class men and women are also quite reluctant to form close ties with neighbors. Instead, they often visit their parents, siblings, and other relatives, which has prompted Lillian Rubin (1976) to describe the extended family as "the heart of working-class social life." Some observers believe that this kin-oriented sociability arises because working-class people feel less secure in social interactions, fearing or distrusting the outside world (Cohen and Hodges, 1963; Gilbert and Kahl, 1987).

People in different classes also tend to prefer different magazines, newspapers, books, television programs, and movies. Whereas the lower class is more likely to read the *National Enquirer* and watch soap operas or professional wrestling, the upper middle class is more likely to read *Time* and *Newsweek* and watch public television programs. The upper class does not go for TV viewing at all. When the richest 400 Americans were asked what they thought about TV's evening entertainment offerings, their typical responses were condescending: "very mediocre," "99 percent hogwash," "juvenile, boring and insulting" (Hacker, 1983). More generally, when compared with those of higher classes, working-class people read less; attend fewer concerts, lectures, and theaters; participate less in adult education; and spend less on recreation—they are more likely to watch television, work on their cars, take car rides, play cards, and visit taverns (Foner, 1979; Dardis et al., 1981).

There are speech differences between classes, too. The middle class seldom uses the double negative ("I can't get no satisfaction"), while the working class often uses it. The middle class rarely drops the letter "g" in present participles ("doin'" for "doing," "singin'" for "singing") perhaps because they are conscious of being "correct." The working class often drops the "g," probably to show that they are not snobbish. They also tend to pronounce "fact" as "fack," "fewer" as "fure," or "only" as "oney." They like to say "lay" instead of "lie," as in "Let's lay on the beach," without necessarily suggesting a sexual performance. On the other hand, the middle class has a weakness for euphemism. To them, a toilet is a "bathroom," drunks are "people with alcohol problems," madness is "mental illness," an undertaker is a "funeral director," or a prison is a "correctional facility." They also tend to go for "fake" elegance. They would say "vocalist" instead of "singer," "as of this time" rather than "now," "subsequently" rather than "later," "make usage of" rather than "use," or "marketing" instead of "selling." The upper class distinguishes itself by its tendency to use such words as "tiresome" or "tedious" instead of "boring." Upper-class women are inclined to designate something seen in a store as "divine," "darling," or "adorable," while others simply say "nice" (Fussell, 1983). While it is unfair to judge one speech superior to another, research has shown that people tend to find higher-class speakers more credible and likable (Kerbo, 1983).

QUESTIONS FOR DISCUSSION AND REVIEW

1. Why do sociologists have problems defining the concept of social class?
2. What methods do sociologists use to study social class, and what are the strengths and weaknesses of each?
3. What features make each American social class distinctive?
4. How does social class influence life chances and lifestyles?

In every society there is some opportunity to move from class to class, but in a closed society based on a caste system, mobility is severely limited by custom and law. South Africa has a caste system based on skin color. Blacks are prevented by law from achieving their full social, economic, and political potential. It is extremely difficult for the residents of this ramshackle squatter camp in South Africa to live a better life.

SOCIAL MOBILITY

Social class exercises a powerful influence on our lives. But are people stuck in one class, unable to move to another position within the stratification system? In all societies there is some **social mobility**—movement from one occupational status to another. The amount of mobility, however, varies from one society to another.

In a relatively open society such as the United States, whose social stratification is called a **class system,** mobility is easier and more frequent. The positions in this stratification system are supposed to depend more on achieved characteristics such as education or skill than on ascribed status such as race or gender. (For more discussion on achieved and ascribed status, see Chapter 4: Social Structure.)

On the other hand, in a closed society, whose stratification is called a **caste system,** mobility is more difficult. Positions in this hierarchy are determined by ascription more than achievement. People must marry within their caste, children are born into their parents' caste, and movement from one caste system to another almost never occurs. In India's traditional caste system, for example, the outcasts or "untouchables"—people born into the lowest caste—could almost never become members of a higher caste. They were rigidly segregated from the rest of society. Members of other castes feared that they would suffer ritual pollution if they ever touched an outcast, passed through the shadow of an outcast, or were merely seen by an outcast. Although the caste system still dominates the lives of millions in India, it is breaking down. Most importantly, it does not have the sanction of the government. South Africa's caste system, however, is backed by the government. Whereas India's caste system is associated with religion, South Africa's is based on color. Black, white, and "colored" groups are rigidly segregated by law as well as custom. Interracial marriage is prohibited. Schools, housing, hospitals, and other facilities are segregated.

In the following sections, we focus on social mobility in the United States, examining its patterns, its sources, and its consequences for Americans.

Patterns

Social mobility can take several forms. **Vertical mobility** involves moving up or down the status ladder. The upward movement is called *upward mobility* and downward movement, *downward mobility.* The promotion of a teacher to principal is an example of upward mobility, and demotion from principal to teacher is downward mobility. In contrast to vertical mobility, **horizontal mobility** is movement from one job to another within the same status category. If a teacher leaves one school for the same position at another, he or she is experiencing horizontal mobility.

Mobility may also be intragenerational or intergenerational. If an individual moves from a low position to a higher one, it is called **intragenerational mobility**(or *career mobility*). A foreman who becomes the vice-president of a company illustrates intragenerational mobility. If a person from a lower-class family gets a higher-status job, as in the case of a foreman's daughter becoming company vice-president, it is called **intergenerational mobility.**

Of those various forms of mobility, upward intergenerational mobility has attracted the most attention from sociologists. Their research has primarily focused on the question of how much such mobility exists in the United States. This is understandable because when the son of a poor farmer becomes president, politicians and journalists are likely to proclaim, "Only in America." It is an exaggeration, but it reflects the high place that social mobility holds in American values. Rags-to-riches tales make Americans feel good about their country, and they are interesting stories. By publicizing them, the media reinforce the vision of America as a land of opportunity, where through sheer hard work the son of a janitor can become a millionaire. This view of America is further reinforced by the experience of Americans who have achieved moderate, but real, upward mobility.

But is this picture accurate? Is upward mobility common? The answer is yes and no: yes because numerous Americans climb a little way up the social ladder; no because very few Americans rise from rags to riches.

Facts abound to suggest that there is a lot of social mobility in the United States. In a national survey taken in 1982, a large majority (70 percent) of Americans said that they were financially better off than their parents had been. This may not reflect accurately enough the real amount of upward occupational mobility because many blue-collar workers today live better than the white-collar workers of 25 years ago. But another survey clearly shows substantial upward mobility: of all Americans in high-status professions such as science and engineering, 63 percent come from families where the father had a lower-status occupation such as store clerk or factory worker. This study further indicates that 52 percent of all the Americans surveyed have moved up in the occupational hierarchy, compared with 22 percent who have slipped down and 26 percent who have remained in the same occupational status as their fathers (*Public Opinion*, 1982).

Upward mobility also appears slightly more common in the United States than in most of the other industrialized societies. In 1964, for example, 49 percent of Americans moved up and 19 percent down, while 40 percent of French experienced upward mobility and 23 percent downward mobility (Lipset, 1982). A more recent study also found greater mobility in the United States than in France and Austria (Haller et al., 1985). In another study involving 24 countries, most of which are industrialized, the United States ranks third—after Israel and Canada—in upward mobility (Tyree, Semyonov, and Hodge, 1979). In comparing data from the United States, Japan, and five West European nations, Peter Blau and Otis Duncan (1967) also find that "upward mobility is higher in the United States than in other countries." Our country also clearly has a higher rate of mobility than the less developed third-world nations (Lipset, 1982).

Finally, there is some evidence that upward mobility in the United States has increased during this century. In 1900, 45.6 percent of big business executives were sons of wealthy families. But by 1950 it had dropped to 36.1 percent and by 1964 to only 10.5 percent. Meanwhile, the percentage of corporate executives who were sons of *poor* families rose from 12.1 percent in 1950 to 23.3 percent in 1964 (Lipset, 1976). Other studies on workers entering the labor force from 1942 to 1972 further indicate some increase in upward mobility (Blau and Duncan, 1967; Featherman and Hauser, 1978). In the early 1980s, there was substantial upward mobility among young adults from poor families. These successful adults made up the majority (57 percent) of those who used to live in poverty as children (Hill, 1985). In recent years, the middle class seems to have become smaller, though some economists do not think so (Rosenthal, 1985). The proportion of families in the annual income range between $15,000 and $50,000 shrank from 65.1 percent in 1970 to 58.2 percent in 1985. Among the families that have left the middle class, however, more have moved up than down, as shown by the greater increase in the size of the upper class than the lower class (Koepp, 1986).

Most of the mobility in the United States, however, is very moderate, occurring over a small range. It has been concentrated in the middle portion of the stratification system. Americans typically climb only one step up the ladder, as from factory worker to small-store

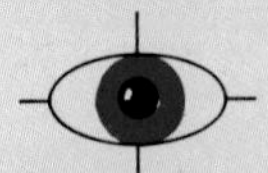

USING SOCIOLOGICAL INSIGHT

Americans in Limbo

Recent shifts in the American economy have changed the pattern of social mobility. For some industrial workers, these changes have meant remaining in the lower statuses. Here, Michael Harrington analyzes what he feels is the most important sociological development of the 1980s. What is the fate of these displaced workers, and what social and economic changes will continue to reshape the work force?

The people of the Monongahela River valley around Pittsburgh are not, as some journalistic reports about them suggested, the "new poor." That term misses the poignance and ambivalence of the present moment for them. They are, they told me over and over, "middle class." "We pay the taxes and take care of the kids and go out for beer and pizza. We're middle class," a steelworker's wife insisted. Or, as Douglas Fraser of the Auto Workers has put it, they are "working people of the middle class," a sociological contradiction and a psychological reality in a country where the working class exists but will not say its own name.

That is ironic in a physical and social setting that all but shouts the name. The landscape of the place is Appalachian, with ridges and hollows, but the industrial geography is the Ruhr or Wales. Mills hulk along the valley floor in the center of grimy towns like Homestead and McKeesport, rows of houses ride the crests of the hills. One can see the ethnicity with the naked eye, the onion spires of a Greek Orthodox church, the Slovak inscription on a school. Everything about the place asserts its working-class character except the workers.

These "working people of the middle class" had to fight, and even die, to win beer and pizza and the possibility that their children could go to college and escape from these valleys. Now that dream is in tatters and the dreamers are suddenly looking into a social abyss.

Homestead is the mill town where the strikers defeated the Pinkertons in a bloody battle in 1892, and where the steelworkers proclaimed their own declaration of independence on July 5, 1936, during the glory days of the legendary Steelworkers Organizing Committee. Now the Jones and Laughlin steel plant, two miles downstream at Hazelwood, lies dead along the river like a beached whale.

In the past, studies of people pushed out of the auto, steel and meat-packing industries show, the workers have indeed found new jobs—jobs that pay about half of what they were making before. Between 1960 and 1978, employment in the steel industry declined by about 100,000 jobs, roughly 20 percent. That process of two decades of attrition was nothing like the ubiquitous, sudden shutdowns that have occurred in the last two or three years. Can hundreds of thousands of people, some in their forties or early fifties, find new jobs when they're all dumped on the market simultaneously?

Upward social mobility has been, in theory and even in practice, the American answer to the problem of inequality. Even when there was no change in social position, a growing national product made it possible for almost everyone to make some gains. The people in McKeesport and throughout "smokestack" America—"working people of the middle class"—are discovering that this postwar pattern no longer holds.

Source: Excerpted from Michael Harrington, "Americans in Limbo," *Harper's*, April 1983, pp. 48–53. Copyright © 1983 by Harper's Magazine Foundation. All rights reserved. Reprinted from the April 1983 issue by special permission.

owner. Only rarely does an American leap from a lowly to a lofty position, as from garbage collector to corporation president. In other words, there is much more short-distance than long-distance mobility, with most of the short-distance mobility occurring in the middle of the occupational hierarchy (Blau and Duncan, 1967; Featherman and Hauser, 1978). This pattern of mobility is not unique to the United States. As a comparative study concludes, "Within all sixteen countries, the picture that emerges is one of severe immobility at the two extremes [top and bottom] of the occupational hierarchy and considerable fluidity in the middle" (Grusky and Hauser, 1984).

A different way of looking at the mobility figures may also make our country look less than a land of opportunity. Earlier we observed that, of all the American workers, 52 percent experience upward mobility and only 22 percent downward. But this reflects, to a large degree, the far greater number of children born into blue-collar families than into white-collar families. The larger number of blue-collar children is likely to result in a higher percentage of upward mobility; the smaller number of white-collar children tends to result in a lower percentage of downward mobility. We should note, however, that most of the white-collar people remain white-collar and many blue-collar workers still stay put among blue collars (Davis, 1982). The difficulty in achieving upward mobility can also be found in other studies (Smith, 1981; Tolbert II, 1982; Jacobs, 1983; Smith, 1983). All this suggests that although the United States is a land of opportunity, it still has a great deal of occupational inheritance (see box, p. 227).

Sources

Why, in the pursuit of the American Dream, are some people upwardly mobile while others stay or fall behind? There are two major factors determining the chances for upward mobility: structural changes in the society and individual characteristics.

Structural Mobility Sometimes large changes in society enable many people to move up the social ladder at the same time. The mobility that results from these social changes is called **structural mobility.**

In the United States there have been at least four sources of structural mobility in this century. First, there was a tremendous expansion of the industrial economy. In 1900 agricultural workers made up nearly 40 percent of the labor force, but massive industrialization reduced the proportion to only 4 percent today. At the same time, many unskilled jobs were gradually taken over by machines. As a result, numerous higher-status jobs—clerical, service, business, and professional jobs—sprang up. This created the opportunity for large numbers of people from farming and blue-collar families to get into those higher-status occupations (Blau and Duncan, 1967; Kerckhoff et al., 1985). The stimulating effect of industrialization on upward mobility can also be seen in many other countries. As has been suggested, there is more mobility in industrialized countries than in less developed ones (Lipset, 1982). However, the enormous industrialization in the United States would have pushed the rate of upward mobility higher than it has if not for our great inequality in income. There is some evidence from cross-national studies to suggest that social inequality is an impediment to the mobility process of industrialization. Those studies indicate that the more inegalitarian a society is, the less mobility it has (Tyree et al., 1979; Grusky and Hauser, 1984).

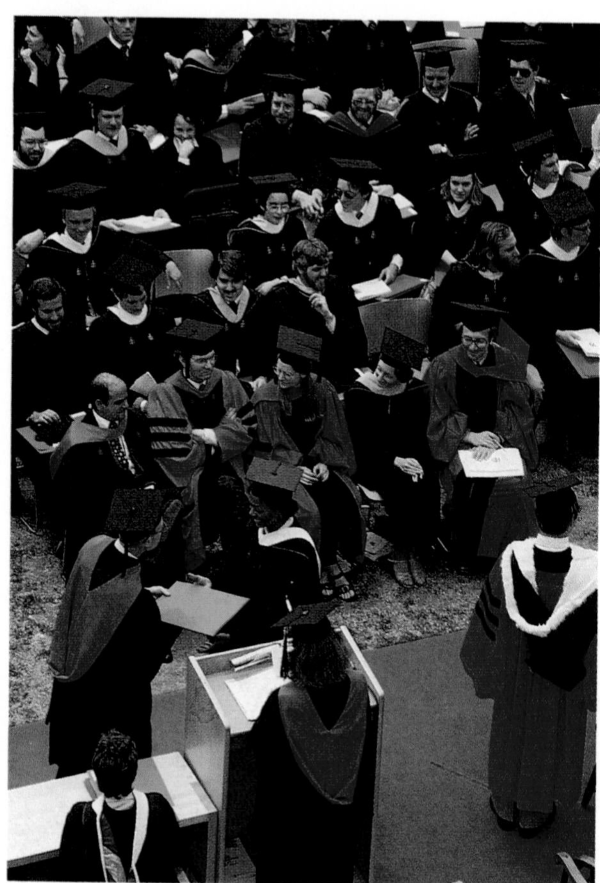

Among the sources of social mobility has been increased educational opportunity. Today over 90 percent of young people are enrolled in high school, and over twelve million are enrolled in college. A college degree enables graduates to obtain high-status and well-paying jobs and professions, so that lower-class or middle-class students who graduate can attain a higher social status than their parents and their peers who did not go to college. Mass education, however, has not brought about total equality in occupational opportunities because members of the higher social classes have gone further in school and consequently obtained higher professional positions.

A second source of structural mobility has been the dramatic increase in the educational attainment of the population. The high school enrollment exploded from a mere 7 percent of the appropriate age group in 1900 to over 90 percent today. College enrollment jumped from only a quarter of a million in 1900 to 12 million today. Thus more people achieved the knowledge and skills needed to fill higher-status jobs (Featherman and Hauser, 1978). We should be careful, though, not to exaggerate the impact of mass education on social mobility. The American system of education has indeed enabled many—at least a third—blue-collar children to go to college and achieve upward mobility. But the same system has simultaneously preserved the rigidity of the higher occupational structure because most of its occupants, the wellborn, have gone much farther in school (Davis, 1982).

A third source of structural mobility has been the lower birthrates in the higher classes than in the lower classes. In the early part of this century professional and other white-collar workers had relatively few children but manual workers, especially farmers, had many. It is estimated that whereas there were 870 sons for every 1000 professional men, there were 1520 sons for every 1000 farmers (Gilbert and Kahl, 1987). Obviously, the sons of professionals were too few to take over their fathers' jobs. In addition, as the economy expanded, there were many more new professional positions. Since there was a shortage of higher-status people to fill all those higher-status jobs, it provided the lower classes with an opportunity to take them. Today, young people who were born in 1965–75, the years when the nation's birth rate fell significantly, can also expect to experience upward mobility in their lifetimes. Since their generation is relatively small—much smaller than the earlier baby-boom generation—they need not compete fiercely with one another for good jobs (see box, p. 230).

A fourth source of structural mobility has been the large influx of immigrants into this country. Immigrants usually took lowly jobs as laborers on the farm, in factories, and in mines, which pushed up many native-born Americans into higher-status occupations. When children of immigrants grew up, they too had the opportunity as native-born Americans to become upwardly mobile. Immigration had also helped open up many higher-status jobs for those people of native birth in at least two ways: by enlarging the population, which stimulated the economy with its greater demands for goods and services, and by directly increasing the productive capacity of the economy with the new arrivals' labor. It is, therefore, no accident that the world's most mobile societies—Israel, Canada, Australia, and the United States—have had unusually large numbers of immigrants (Tyree et al., 1979; Tyree and Semyonov, 1983).

In short, as a result of an industrializing, expanding economy, increasing education, lower birthrates in the higher classes, and considerable immigration, many Americans whose parents were factory and farm workers came to fill higher-status jobs.

Immigration provides the impetus for great social mobility. Poor immigrants such as those working in California's lettuce fields are usually willing to take low-paying jobs, which has the effect of forcing the native poor to rise economically. As populations grow through immigration, the increased demand for goods and services creates new markets and stimulates the economy. The result is more opportunity for everyone to rise economically, including immigrants' children such as this successful architect of Cuban-American extraction.

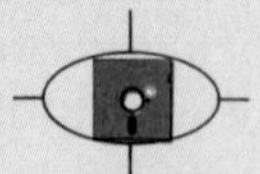

LOOKING AT CURRENT RESEARCH

Who Will Be Rich?

Sociologists have shown that upward mobility is determined not only by individual factors but also by social forces such as a society's economy and demography. This article explores how such forces create better chances for wealth. Why will people of your age group become rich in the 1990s?

When were you born? This question, leading to a generalized prediction of your financial future, is being asked not by astrologers, but by demographers. Over 100 million Americans may hold winning tickets to the affluence expected in the 1990s, simply because they were born at the right time.

If you're 35 today, in ten years, your household may rank among the most affluent; if you're 55, chances are you'll be retired and living well on your nest egg. But if you're 45 today, your employer may push you into early retirement, and if you're 25, making ends meet in 1995 may be downright tough.

Although many details determine your financial health—level of education, occupation, marital status—one of the most important is how old you are, and how many others are in your age group. Some people always have a demographic advantage over others because a person's economic strength depends, in part, on where he or she stands in the population pyramid—the age structure of the overall population.

Generations with few members have an economic edge over large generations because, with people in short supply, there is less competition for entry-level jobs and first houses. A small generation, therefore, has a better chance at prosperity.

This phenomenon was first investigated in the 1950s by Richard Easterlin, a professor of economics at the University of Southern California. His interest piqued by the baby boom, he wrote, in his book *Birth and Fortune*, "As one of the baby-boom parents, I came increasingly to feel that the history of my generation has been importantly affected by its scarcity." Easterlin's hypothesis was that "the effects of generation size, good or bad, persist throughout the life cycle. Every generation follows the pattern of below-average earnings in early working life and above-average earnings later. But the earnings pattern of a small generation is more favorable throughout its career than that of a large generation."

If you were born between 1946 and 1964, you are a member of the largest and most sociologically influential generation in American history, the baby boom. Although its size would theoretically doom this generation to earn less money than a smaller generation, baby-boom women went to work, creating a family affluence that would have been impossible on a single income. The median income of baby-boom couples is $31,000 if the woman works full-time, $26,000 if she works part-time, and only $22,000 if she does not work. Over 70% of baby-boom women are in the labor force today; that number will reach 80% by the mid-'90s.

Beginning in 1965, American fertility dropped sharply and continued to fall for the next ten years. Demographers call the generation born during those years the baby bust. Today baby busters are aged 9 to 19; in 1995 they will be 19 to 29, in their early adult years.

The baby bust, on the basis of its small numbers, can expect a substantial income advantage. Today's teenagers already have their pick of part-time jobs and a lot of spending money. Thirty percent of high school students work at paying jobs and earn between $16 and $56 a week. . . . Because they have few fixed expenses—such as the cost of food, rent, and utilities—most of their money can be spent on whatever they happen to want. Teenagers today have more discretionary dollars than many adults have.

The entry-level employment doors that were closed to the baby boomers of the 1960s and 1970s have been flung open to welcome the baby busters of the 1980s. Companies that hire entry-level workers are scrambling for employees. Burger King, for example, offers its employees a $75 bonus for referring a successful applicant, and both Burger King and McDonalds are hiring retirees to make up for the lack of teenage workers.

The luck of the baby-bust generation will continue throughout its lifetime. "As we move into the late 1980s and 1990s, those born in the recent low birth-rate era will increasingly find, as they reach the labor market, that job openings are plentiful, wage rates relatively good, and advancement rapid," predicts Easterlin.

Source: Excerpted from Cheryl Russell, "Who Will Be Rich?" *Savvy*, May 1985, pp. 64–68.

Individual Mobility Even when structural mobility opens up higher-status positions, some people move up and some do not. Individual characteristics as well as structural changes influence whether a person experiences mobility. The mobility produced by these characteristics is called **individual mobility.**

Among the characteristics that influence individual mobility are racial or ethnic background, gender, education, occupation, fertility, number of siblings, place of residence, physical appearance, and sheer luck. More specifically, being black, Mexican American, Puerto Rican, Indian, or female decreases an American's chances for upward mobility (in the next two chapters we will look at these racial and gender inequalities in detail). College graduates are six times more likely than the uneducated to be upwardly mobile. White-collar workers are four times more likely than blue-collar workers to experience upward career mobility. People with children, perhaps because of family responsibilities that stimulate ambition and diligence, are more upwardly mobile than those with no children. But men from families with fewer than four siblings tend to achieve much higher status than those with more than four siblings. People who live in urban areas have a greater chance of upward mobility than those who live in rural areas. The chances for success are also enhanced for women if they are beautiful and for men if they are tall. Finally, sheer luck often acts as the force pushing a person up the status ladder (Goodman and Marx, 1982; Kasarda and Billy, 1985).

Some of the personal characteristics are *achieved,* such as education, talent, motivation, and hard work. Others are *ascribed,* such as family background, race, gender, and physical appearance. The foregoing discussion suggests that both achieved and ascribed qualities have a hand in determining who gets ahead in American society. But the popular belief in equal opportunity would lead us to expect career success to be attained through achievement more than ascription. Is achievement, then, really the more powerful determining force in upward mobility? According to most sociological studies, achievement may appear on the surface to be the predominant factor, but it is at bottom subject to the influence of ascription (Blau and Duncan, 1967; Jencks et al., 1972, 1979). Blau and Duncan (1967), for example, found that the more education people have, the more successful they are in their career. But they also found that the amount of education people have is related to their family background. Thus, compared with children from blue-collar families, white-collar children can be expected to get more education and then a better chance of career mobility.

Consequences

Although upward mobility may seem to be a dream come true, it can have unpleasant consequences. Adjusting to a new status may be difficult. Upwardly mobile people may feel insecure and anxious in their new positions. They may feel compelled to drop old friends and old tastes, even old beliefs and attitudes, sometimes even their spouses, in order to conform with the habit and style of their new class. They may feel detached from their parents, visiting them less often than before. They may feel compelled to match the possessions of neighbors and friends in their new status, and thus end up financially strapped despite their new, higher position (Reissman, 1959; Tumin, 1967; Hopper, 1981). These adverse effects of upward mobility are especially likely to occur if the individuals are greatly rather than moderately mobile, as in the case of a factory worker becoming a company executive rather than a foreman (Kessin, 1971; Jackson and Curtis, 1972). One study further suggests a somewhat complex relationship between upward mobility and fertility: when on the way up, the individuals tend to restrict their family size, because raising children consumes time and energy—resources needed for realizing aspirations. But after achieving mobility, they tend to have more children, because their higher economic resources makes this more practical (Stevens, 1981).

Downward mobility, too, has negative consequences. Many studies have shown that people who experience downward mobility have higher rates of depression, psychosis, and suicide than other people. Some downwardly mobile individuals need a scapegoat—someone else to blame for their troubles—and become strongly prejudiced against blacks, Jews, or other minorities. Some blame themselves, perhaps because they share the widespread belief that America is a land of opportunity. If opportunity is abundant yet still they are not "a success," then, they feel, the fault must be their own. Others blame society for not giving them a break, and become radical in their politics (Reissman, 1959; Tumin, 1967). In contrast to the upwardly mobile, however, the downwardly mobile interact more frequently with family and friends (Kessin, 1971). Perhaps their occupational failure drives them to seek solace from their primary group. Ironically, the strong ties to this group may have partly contributed to their downward mobility. The weakness of such strong ties, as suggested in Chapter 5 (Groups and Organizations), is that close friends are not very useful in helping us find jobs because they move in the same limited circle as we do and have no more knowledge about job opportunities than we do (Granovetter, 1983).

QUESTIONS FOR DISCUSSION AND REVIEW

1. How does a caste system differ from a class system?
2. How do actual vertical and generational mobility patterns differ from the view that America is a land of opportunity?
3. What structural and individual characteristics influence a society's pattern of mobility?
4. Why does social mobility often have negative consequences?

"Hutchins, what on earth gave you the notion that we want the rich to get poorer and the poor to get richer?"

IS STRATIFICATION NECESSARY?

Social stratification is in essence social inequality, contrary to the American belief in equality. But functionalists have argued that it is necessary. Conflict theorists disagree.

Functionalist Theory

More than 40 years ago, Kingsley Davis and Wilbert Moore (1945) made the most influential statement of the functionalist view that stratification is necessary. Davis and Moore were trying to explain why stratification exists in all societies. The reason, they said, is that stratification serves a useful, positive function—in fact, a function necessary for the survival of a society.

What is this function? According to Davis and Moore, stratification motivates people to work hard by promising them such rewards as money, power, and prestige. The amount of rewards depends on two things: how important a person's job is to society, and how much training and skill are required to perform that job. A physician, for example, must receive more rewards than a garbage collector, not only because the physician's job is more important than the garbage collector's but also because it requires more training and skill. Without this system of unequal rewards, many jobs important to society would never be performed. If future physicians knew they would be paid and respected just as much as garbage collectors, they would not bother to spend years studying long hours at medical school. In short, stratification is necessary for society because it ensures that "the most important positions are conscientiously filled by the most qualified persons."

Conflict Theory

The Davis-Moore theory has been subjected to many criticisms. Some critics argue that it is difficult to see why such large inequalities are necessary to fulfill the functions Davis and Moore described. Why is it functional to pay a corporate executive two or three times more than the president of the United States? The functionalist theory would suggest that the corporate executive's job is more important. But is it really? Many people may disagree. Even the physician's job is not necessarily more important than the garbage collector's, because uncollected refuse can present a serious problem to a society. The functionalist theory also fails to take into account the inherent interest of certain jobs. The intrinsic satisfaction of being a doctor far outweighs that of being a garbage collector. Why, then, should the doctor be given more rewards? More thorough criticisms of the Davis-Moore theory have come from conflict theorists.

According to conflict theorists, stratification occurs not because it is functional but because groups compete for scarce resources. It is not necessary to the society as a whole. Stratification reflects not a just or useful allocation of resources, but an unjust distribution of power. Those who have power exploit those who do not, and the powerful win the competition for resources. The unequal distribution of rewards, then, reflects the interests of powerful groups rather than the basic needs of all people. If other members of society believe that the resulting stratification is right, that belief is simply evidence of the ability of the powerful to shape the ideas and values and laws of a society. They create an ideology justifying their dominance, and other members of society accept that ideology, developing what Marxists call a "false consciousness." But eventually, Marx believed, because of their exploitation they will gain a "class consciousness"—an awareness that capitalism is the source of their common misery—and revolt.

Melvin Tumin (1953), whose views reflected conflict theory, has argued that stratification is dysfunctional for several reasons. First, because it limits the opportunities of those who are not in the privileged class, stratification restricts the possibility of discovering and exploiting the full range of talent in society. When an intelligent teenager is too poor to stay in school and never develops his or her talents fully, society loses. Second, stratification helps to maintain the status quo even when it has become dysfunctional, because the privileged class is able to impose on society the idea that existing inequalities are natural, logical, and morally right. Third, because the stratification system distributes rewards unjustly, it encourages the less privileged to become hostile, suspicious, and distrustful. The result may be social unrest and chaos.

Comparing the Theories

The central views of functionalist and conflict theories of stratification are summarized in Table 9.4. There are facts to support both views. Functional theory, for example, captures the fact that in open societies such as the United States achieved characteristics are an important basis for stratification. In these societies poor people with talents and skills, as functionalist theory correctly suggests, should have a good chance of getting highly rewarding positions. Conflict theory, however, reflects the fact that in some societies ascribed status is the primary basis for stratification. In such societies the privileged, as conflict theory correctly suggests, can continue to maintain their power and keep the poor down. Both theories also fit some facts about the same society. For instance, functionalist theory is useful for explaining the mobility that exists in the United States within the middle stratum. Conflict theory is more useful for explaining the rigidity that characterizes the top and bot-

Table 9.4 A Comparison of Two Theories

Evidence can be found to support both views. They largely reflect two different kinds of social stratification. One is a fluid system with many mobility opportunities and the other is a rigid system with few such opportunities.

Functionalist theory	Conflict theory
1. Stratification is universal and necessary.	1. Stratification may be universal but not necessary.
2. Stratification is an expression of commonly shared social values.	2. Stratification is an expression of the values of powerful people.
3. Tasks and rewards are fairly allocated.	3. Tasks and rewards are unfairly allocated.
4. Stratification facilitates the optimal functioning of society and the individual.	4. Stratification impedes the optimal functioning of society and the individual.
5. Stratification can change gradually, as an evolutionary process.	5. Stratification can change drastically, as a revolutionary process.

Source: Jack L. Roach, Llewellyn Gross, and Orville R. Gursslin (eds.), *Social Stratification in the United States,* Englewood Cliffs, N.J.: Prentice-Hall, 1969, p. 55.

GRIFFITH COLLEGE DUBLIN
South Circular Road, Dublin 8.
Tel.4545640 Fax: 4549265

tom strata, where people tend to inherit their positions of either power or powerlessness.

Finally, both theories assume, though for different reasons, that social inequality is here to stay. Functionalists believe that stratification will persist because it is necessary. Conflict theorists also believe that inequality will continue, but because the powerful will not give up their privileged positions. Thus Alvin Gouldner (1979), a conflict theorist, pessimistically wrote:

> The Communist Manifesto has held that the history of all hitherto existing societies was the history of class struggles: freeman and slave, patrician and plebian, lord and serf, guildmaster and journeyman, and, then, bourgeoisie and proletariat. In this series, however, there was one unspoken regularity: the slaves did not succeed the master, the plebians did not vanquish the patricians, the serfs did not overthrow the lords, and the journeymen did not triumph over the guildmasters. *The lowliest class never came to power.* Nor does it seem likely now.

Indeed, the evidence that we have seen shows the reality and influence of class inequality in American society. What about the inequalities based on race, ethnicity, gender, and age? We examine these in the next three chapters.

QUESTIONS FOR DISCUSSION AND REVIEW

1. How does the functionalist theory of stratification differ from the conflict approach?
2. Why do sociologists agree that stratification is inevitable but disagree about its causes?

CHAPTER REVIEW

1. *What are the key social inequalities?* Inequalities in economic rewards, power, and prestige. The unequal distributions of these social rewards form the basis of social stratification.

2. *How equal is the distribution of wealth and income in the United States?* The distribution has remained about the same for about thirty years, and it is very unequal. The richest 20 percent of the population earn about 44 percent of the total national income, and the poorest 20 percent earn less than 5 percent of the total. The distribution of wealth is even more unequal. *Is poverty widespread in the United States?* By the government's measure of poverty, 11.4 percent of Americans were poor in 1985; if a relative definition of poverty is used, the percentage is higher.

3. *How is power distributed in the United States?* Very unequally, according to Marxist and elite theorists. They argue that power is concentrated in the hands of a very few people. In contrast, pluralist theorists contend that power is widely dispersed among competing groups.

4. *What is the most important source of prestige in the United States?* Occupation, although one's occupational status may be in conflict with one's other statuses, resulting in status inconsistency.

5. *What is a social class?* Marxists define it as a group of people who either own or do not own the means of production. Most American sociologists equate class with a status, income, educational, occupational, or socioeconomic grouping. *How do sociologists determine who is in what social class?* They may use the reputational method, asking a selected group of people to rank others; the subjective method, asking people how they rank themselves; or the objective method, ranking people according to such criteria as income, educational attainment, and occupation.

6. *How is the U.S. population distributed into social classes?* About 1 to 3 percent are in the upper class, 40 to 55 percent in the middle class, 30 to 45 percent in the working class, and 15 to 20 percent in the lower class. *How does social class affect our lives?* People in the higher classes have better life chances than those in the classes below them. They live more comfortably, with a better chance of obtaining desirable resources and experiences, and live longer and healthier lives. Higher-class people also have a different life-style, are more likely to participate in extrafamilial activities, engage in intellectual pastimes, and use "correct" speech.

7. *Is upward mobility common in the United States?* More common than in many other countries, but most of the mobility occurs within the middle segment. Few go from rags to riches. *What factors influence the opportunity for social mobility?* There are structural factors, including an expanding economy, increasing education, low fertility within higher classes, and massive immigration. There are also individual characteristics, such as social and

ethnic background, gender, education, occupation, and luck. *Does upward mobility have drawbacks?* Yes. It may require difficult personal adjustments. This applies to downward mobility as well.

8. *According to Davis and Moore, why is social stratification necessary?* They argue that it serves an essential function. It offers great rewards for those jobs which are relatively important to society and which require considerable training and skill, thus ensuring that these tasks are performed by competent people. *How do conflict theorists view stratification?* It arises from exploitation by the powerful. It is harmful to society—limiting opportunities for those not in the privileged class, deterring useful social change, and producing social unrest.

KEY TERMS

Caste system A relatively rigid stratification system in which one's position is ascribed and there is almost no mobility (p. 225).

Class A category of people who own or do not own the means of production, or have about the same amount of income, power, and prestige (p. 217).

Class system A stratification system in which achieved characteristics play a large role in determining one's position and in which there is considerable social mobility (p. 225).

Horizontal mobility The movement of a person from one job to another within the same status category (p. 226).

Individual mobility Social mobility related to an individual's personal achievement and characteristics (p. 231).

Intergenerational mobility A change in social standing from one generation to the next (p. 226).

Intragenerational mobility A change in an individual's social standing, also called career mobility (p. 226).

Life chances The number of opportunities for living a good, long, or successful life in a society (p. 223).

Life-styles Tastes, preferences, and ways of living (p. 223).

Objective method The method of identifying social classes by using occupation, income, and education to rank people (p. 219).

Power elite A small group of individuals who hold top positions in the federal government, military, and corporations and who have similar backgrounds, values, and interests (p. 215).

Reputational method The method of identifying social classes by selecting a group of people and then asking them to rank others (p. 217).

Social mobility The movement from one social standing to another (p. 225).

Social stratification A system in which people are ranked into categories with some getting more social rewards than others (p. 210).

Status inconsistency The condition in which the individual is given a different ranking in various social categories, such as being high in occupation but low in income (p. 216).

Status system System in which people are stratified according to their social prestige (p. 215).

Structural mobility A change in social standing that affects many people at the same time and results from changes in the structure of society (p. 228).

Subjective method The method of identifying social classes by asking people to rank themselves (p. 218).

Vertical mobility The movement of people up or down the status ladder (p. 225).

SUGGESTED READINGS

Fussell, Paul. 1983. *Class: A Guide Through the American Status System*, New York: Summit. A fun-to-read book about the life-styles of various classes in the United States.

Gilbert, Dennis, and Joseph A. Kahl. 1987. *The American Class Structure: A New Synthesis*, 3rd ed. Homewood, Ill.: Dorsey. A clearly written, insightful analysis of the major studies in social stratification.

Marwick, Arthur, ed. 1986. *Class in the Twentieth Century*. New York: St. Martin's. A historical analysis of social classes in Britain, France, the United States, Czechoslovakia, and West Germany.

Szymanski, Albert. 1983. *Class Structure: A Critical Perspective*. New York: Praeger. A readable text on social stratification, written from the conflict, Marxist perspective.

Wright, Erik Olin. 1985. *Classes*. London: Verso. An uncommon Marxist analysis of social stratification, showing with data the relational, antagonistic, and exploitative nature of classes.

THOMAS
HAYES

10 Racial and Ethnic Minorities

The status of all minorities in the United States is generally better today than before. Coming closest to the American dream of success are Jews, Asians, and white ethnics, followed by blacks and Hispanics. Ironically, Native Americans, who originally owned this land, have experienced the least improvement in their lives. Of course, we still have a lot of prejudice and discrimination. But it is less than before, especially less than in South Africa, where racism is still an official policy. It is also less serious than in India and other third-world countries, where a single incident of ethnic conflict often takes hundreds of lives.

In 1986 and 1987 the media reported a number of events such as the following:

> A black cadet at the Citadel military academy in South Carolina was harassed at bedside in the middle of the night by white students dressed like Ku Klux Klansmen. In Philadelphia, black high school students beat a Cambodian student while onlookers cheered. A Louisiana sheriff issued an order, later rescinded, that all young blacks found in white neighborhoods at night were to be stopped and questioned. And on Dec. 20, Michael Griffith, a 23-year-old black, was beaten with a baseball bat by a mob of white teenagers in the Howard Beach neighborhood of Queens, New York City. As he fled across a busy highway, he was hit and killed by a car (Irwin, 1987).

Mistreatment of minorities does not, however, occur in the United States alone. It can be found all over the world. Some 40 years ago about 6 million Jews were systematically murdered in Nazi Germany. More recently many of the 700,000 Chinese in Vietnam, who made up the majority of the refugees that left the country between 1975 and 1979, were expelled—and forced to pay large sums before expulsion. Many had to leave in small or leaky boats, and as many of them drowned at sea as reached land. At least one-third of the "boat people" were robbed, assaulted, raped, or killed by crews of other vessels from various Southeast Asian countries, which, like Vietnam, have a long history of discriminating against their own Chinese minorities (Sowell, 1983). In Western Europe today, Pakistanis, Turks, Algerians, and other non-European minorities are often subjected to random insults and hostile stares, which tend to escalate into "a gang attack, an anonymous bullet, or a bomb thrown from a passing car" (Nielsen, 1984). In Japan the Koreans, Burakumin (sometimes called *Eta,* meaning much filth), and Konketsuji (American-Japanese mixed bloods) are also targets of considerable prejudice and discrimination (Burkhardt, 1983). In white-dominated South Africa, blacks, coloreds, and Asians continue to be legally segregated and discriminated against. These are only a few of the countless cases of mistreatment suffered by minorities in various countries.

In this chapter we examine the criteria for identifying minorities and the nature of prejudice and discrimination against them. Then we analyze the alternative ways in which a society may accept or reject a minority group and the possible responses by members of the minority. Finally, we find out how various racial and ethnic groups have fared in the United States.

IDENTIFYING MINORITIES

Americans are accustomed to thinking of a minority as a category of people who are physically different and who make up a small percentage of the population. But the popular identification of minorities is often misleading. The Jews in China, for example, do not "look Jewish"—they look like other Chinese. Similarly, the Jews in the United States look like other white Americans. Jews cannot be differentiated from the dominant group on the basis of their physical characteristics, but they are considered a minority (Heilman, 1982). In South Africa, blacks are a minority group, even though they make up a majority of the population (Blalock, 1982). Neither physical traits nor numbers alone determine whether people constitute a minority group. To get a clearer idea of what a minority is, we need first to see what races and ethnic groups are.

Race

As a biological concept, race refers to a large category of people who share certain inherited physical characteristics. These characteristics may include particular skin color, head shape, hair type, nasal shape, lip form, or blood type. One common classification of human races recognizes three groups: Caucasoid, Mongoloid, and Negroid. Caucasoids have light skin, Mongoloids yellowish skin, and Negroids dark skin—and there are other physical differences among the three groups.

There are, however, at least two important problems with such a classification of races. First, some groups fit into none of these categories. Natives of India and Pakistan have Caucasoid facial features but dark skin. The Ainu of Japan have Mongoloid faces but white skin. The Vogul of Siberia have Caucasoid faces but yellowish skin. Some aboriginal groups in Australia have dark skin and other Negroid features but blond hair (Jacquard, 1983). The Polynesians of Pacific islands have a mixture of Caucasoid, Mongoloid, and Negroid characteristics.

Another problem with the biological classification of races it that there are no "pure" races. People in these groups have been interbreeding for centuries. In the United States, for example, about 70 percent of blacks have some white ancestry and approximately 20 percent of whites have at least one black ancestor (Sowell, 1983). Biologists have also determined that all current populations originate from one common genetic pool—

What is a race? Biologically speaking, the term has almost no meaning. Homo sapiens, the only existing human species, evolved about 30,000 years ago, most likely in Africa. All modern human beings descend from the same initial gene pool and share the same genetic endowment. Over the centuries, however, populations became adapted to local environments, which led to the development of real but essentially superficial physical differences such as in eye shape and skin color. Nevertheless, popular perception of these differences has contributed to the sociological definition of race as a social phenomenon. Thus the same person who is considered black in our society may be regarded as white in South American countries.

one single group of humans that evolved about 30,000 years ago, most likely in Africa. As humans migrated all over the planet, different populations developed different physical characteristics in their adaptations to particular physical environments. Thus the Eskimos' relatively thick layer of fat under the skin of their eyes, faces, and other parts of the body provides good insulation against the icy cold of Arctic regions. The Africans' dark skin offers protection from the burning sun of tropical regions. Yet there has not developed a significant genetic difference among the "races." As genetic research has indicated, about 95 percent of the DNA molecules (which make up the gene) are the same for all humans and only the remaining 5 percent are responsible for all the differences in appearance (Vora, 1981). Even these outward differences are meaningless, because the differences among members of the same "race" are greater than the average differences between two racial groups. Some American blacks, for example, have lighter skins than many whites, and some whites are darker than many blacks.

Since there are no clear-cut biological distinctions—in physical characteristics or genetic makeup—between racial groups, sociologists prefer to define race as a social rather than biological phenomenon (Blalock, 1982). Defined sociologically, a **race** is a group of people who are *perceived* by a given society as biologically different from others. People are assigned to one race or another, not necessarily on the basis of logic or fact but by public opinion, which, in turn, is molded by society's dominant group. Consider, for example, an American boy whose father has 100 percent white ancestry and whose mother is the daughter of a white man and black woman. This youngster is considered "black" in our society, although he is actually more white than black because of his 75 percent white and 25 percent black ancestry. In many Latin American countries, however, this same child would be considered "white" (Blalock, 1982). In fact, according to Brazil's popular perception of a black as "a person of African descent who has no white ancestry at all," about three-fourths of all American blacks would *not* be considered blacks. They would be considered white because they have some white ancestry (Sowell, 1983). By sharp contrast, in South Africa some people with fair skin, blond hair, and blue eyes can be classified as colored if one of their ancestors was not white. Several years ago Cynthia Freeman, a South African woman who has those typically Nordic features, had to go to court to prove that she was white in order to continue living in a white neighborhood. But the judge ruled that she was colored because he found her flat nose and high cheekbones not typical of whites (Thurow, 1987). The definition of race, then, varies from one society to another in about the same way as the definition of deviance does (see Chapter 7: Deviance and Control). Sociologists use this societal definition to identify "races" because it is the racial status to which people are assigned by their society—rather than their real biological characteristics—that has profound significance for their social lives.

Ethnicity

Jews have often been called a race. But they have the same racial origins as Arabs—both being Semites—and through the centuries Jews and non-Jews have interbred extensively. As a result, as we noted earlier, Jews are often physically indistinguishable from non-Jews. Besides, a person can become a Jew by choice—by conversion to Judaism. Jews do not constitute a race. Instead, they are a religious group, or more broadly, an ethnic group.

Whereas race is based on popularly perceived physical traits, ethnicity is based on cultural characteristics. An **ethnic group** is a collection of people who share a distinctive cultural heritage and a consciousness of their common bond. Members of an ethnic group may share a language, accent, religion, history, philosophy, national origin, or life-style. They always share a feeling that they are a distinct people. In the United States members of an ethnic group typically have the same national origin. As a result, they are named after the countries from which they or their ancestors came. Thus they are Polish-Americans, Italian-Americans, Irish-Americans, and so on.

For the most part, ethnicity is culturally learned. People learn the life-styles, cooking, language, values, and other characteristics of their ethnic group. Often Americans, in effect, choose ethnicity: they choose whether to continue to consider themselves as members of an ethnic group. Yet members of an ethnic group are usually born into it. The traits of the group are passed from one generation to another, and ethnicity is not always a matter of choice. A person may be classified by others as a member of some ethnic group, for example, on the basis of appearance or accent. In fact, racial and ethnic groups sometimes overlap, as in the case of Afro- or Asian-Americans. Like race, then, ethnicity can be an ascribed status.

Minority

A minority is a racial or ethnic group, but not all racial or ethnic groups are minorities. A **minority** is a group of people who share certain distinctive physical or cultural characteristics *and* are subjected to prejudice and discrimination (Wirth, 1945). They are, in other words, a subordinate group. More specifically, we can identify five characteristics of a minority:

1. A minority possesses racial or ethnic traits that are popularly regarded as different from those of the dominant group.
2. A minority suffers prejudice and discrimination from the dominant group.
3. Membership in a minority is almost always ascribed, not achieved—a person is born into it.
4. Members of a minority feel a strong sense of group solidarity. This bond grows from their common heritage as well as their shared experience of prejudice and discrimination.
5. Members of a minority typically marry other members of their group. They may do so as a result of preference and choice, but rejection by the dominant group often makes marriage outside their own group nearly impossible (Schaefer, 1984).

The key characteristic of a minority group is its experience of prejudice and discrimination. **Prejudice** is a negative attitude toward members of a minority. It includes ideas and beliefs, feelings, and predispositions to act in a certain way. For example, whites prejudiced against blacks might fear meeting a black man on the street at night. They might resent blacks who are successful. They might plan to sell their houses if they expect a black family to move into the neighborhood.

Whereas prejudice is an attitude, **discrimination** is an act. More specifically, it is unequal treatment of people because they are members of a group. When a landlord will not rent an apartment to a family because they are black or Hispanic, that is discrimination.

In general, the more divergent an ethnic group is from the dominant group in society, the more likely it is to confront prejudice and discrimination—and thus to be a minority group. The divergence may be cultural or physical. Asian-Americans, for example, differ from Anglo Americans (the dominant group) culturally as well as physically far more than German-Americans do. The rejection that such divergence may prompt reinforces the consciousness of belonging to a distinct group. As Peter Rose (1981) noted, "Acceptance may loosen the bonds of ethnic identity, as in the case of Scottish and German immigrants to America; rejection and subordination may strengthen them, as among Mexican Americans today."

A minority is not necessarily a small percentage of the population. Blacks are considered a minority in South Africa, even though they make up 68 percent of the population, because they are the subordinate group.

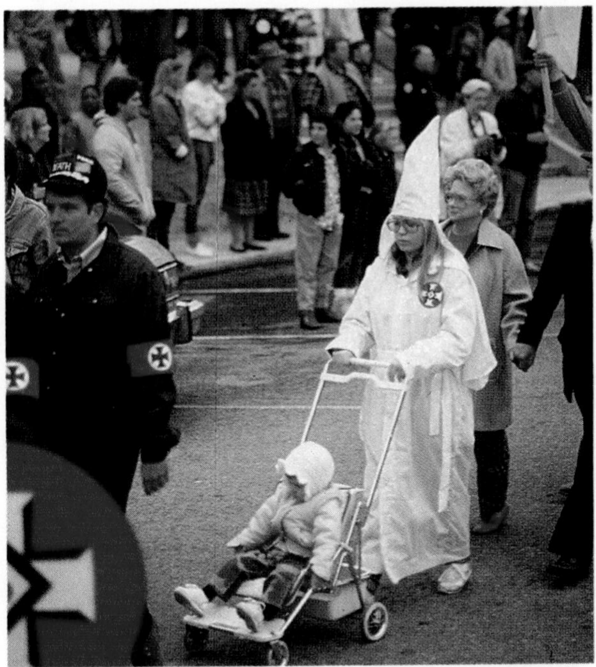

Members of the Ku Klux Klan. Prejudice is a preconceived negative opinion about a group. It can be a powerful force in social relations because the preconceived ideas are often not critically examined. It is therefore easily passed to children from parents, as well as from teachers and peers. In the American South, the Klan has a long history of enormous prejudice—often accompanied by intimidation or violence—against blacks, Jews, Roman Catholics, and foreigners.

Similarly, the dominant group need not make up a large part of the population. The whites in South Africa are the dominant group, although they make up only 18 percent of the population. In the United States, Americans of English descent are today only 22 percent of the population. But because of their continuing social and cultural influence, they are still considered the dominant group—as they were 200 years ago when they constituted more than 90 percent of the population. In the African state of Burundi, the Tutsi make up only 15 percent of the population, but they dominate the Hutu, who comprise the remaining 85 percent. As the dominant group, the Tutsi control the nation's economy and government. In 1972 they asserted their dominance by methodically slaughtering about 150,000 Hutus when the latter tried to take over the government (Sowell, 1981; Hotz, 1984; Brooke, 1987).

QUESTIONS FOR DISCUSSION AND REVIEW

1. Why do sociologists define race as a social rather than a physical phenomenon?
2. What is ethnicity, and why do sociologists prefer to use this concept to explain the diverse behavior of minorities?
3. When does a racial or ethnic group become a minority group?

PREJUDICE AND DISCRIMINATION

We have seen that prejudice and discrimination are not the same. But do they always go together, as many people assume? Do prejudiced people always try to discriminate? Are discriminators necessarily prejudiced? In this section we analyze how prejudice and discrimination are related. We also study their sources and consequences.

Individual Reactions to Minorities

Dr. Martin Luther King illustrated the difference between prejudice and discrimination when he said, "The law may not make a man love me, but it can restrain him from lynching me, and I think that's pretty important" (*New York Times,* 1966). Prejudice is an attitude; discrimination is an act. Robert Merton (1976) has found that the two do not necessarily go hand in hand. In analyzing the possible combinations of prejudice and discrimination, Merton has come up with a description of four possible reactions of dominant group members to minorities (see Table 10.1).

First are the *unprejudiced nondiscriminators.* These people believe in the American creed of equality and put their belief into action—their attitude and behavior are consistent. They are also called *all-weather liberals* because they are likely to abide by their belief regardless of where they are—even if their friends and neighbors are bigots. Theoretically, they could help the cause of racial equality by spreading their belief and practice. But often this potential is not fulfilled because, according to Merton, they tend to commit three related fallacies. First they are likely to commit the "fallacy of group soliloquy": seeking out each other for moral support rather than persuading others to get rid of prejudice and discrimination. This would lead to the "fallacy of unanimity": as like-minded liberals, they would reach the consensus that it is awful to be prejudiced and discriminating but that they themselves are not. As a result, they have the illusion that most people are not

Table 10.1 Individual Responses to Minorities

Dominant group members differ in the way they respond to minorities. Some are prejudiced while others are not. Some discriminate while others do not. But do prejudice and discrimination always go together? The answer is no. It is possible for people to be prejudiced without discriminating against minorities, as shown by type 3 below. It is also possible to discriminate without being prejudiced, as exemplified by type 2. Of course, attitude and behavior can go together, as demonstrated by types 1 and 4.

	Nondiscriminator	Discriminator
Unprejudiced	1. Unprejudiced nondiscriminator (all-weather liberal)—is not prejudiced and does not discriminate, whatever the social pressure might be.	2. Unprejudiced discriminator (fair-weather liberal)—is not prejudiced but, because of social pressure, does discriminate.
Prejudiced	3. Prejudiced nondiscriminator (fair-weather illiberal)—is prejudiced but, because of social pressure, does not discriminate.	4. Prejudiced discriminator (all-weather illiberal)—is prejudiced and does discriminate, whatever the social pressure might be.

Source: From page 103, "Discrimination and the American Creed," by Robert K. Merton in *Discrimination and National Welfare,* edited by Robert M. MacIver. Copyright 1949 by Institute for Religious and Social Studies. Reprinted by permission of Harper & Row, Publishers, Inc.

either. This, in turn, would lead to the "fallacy of privatized solution": they would conclude that if they can free themselves from prejudice and discrimination, the few others who are prejudiced can also do the same. Hence prejudice and discrimination should be treated as a private matter, and people should be left alone to deal with them by themselves. Such a personal approach is a fallacy because racism is not only an individual problem. It is also a social problem and, as such, can be solved only through collective actions such as joining or supporting a civil rights movement. In the final analysis, however, we should not criticize all-weather liberals. After all, they are not prejudiced nor discriminating.

The second type of dominant-group member in Merton's analysis is the *unprejudiced discriminator.* These people's discriminatory behavior is inconsistent with their unprejudicial attitude. Although free from prejudice themselves, they practice discrimination because of social pressure. Hence they are also called *fair-weather liberals.* The unprejudiced homeowner is a fair-weather liberal if he refuses to sell his house to a minority family for fear of offending the neighbors. An unprejudiced executive may also hesitate to promote minority employees to managers lest other employees be resentful. An unprejudiced person might not date another of a different race for fear of being ostracized. Presumably, if they lived in a social climate more favorable to minorities, unprejudiced discriminators would not practice discrimination.

Merton's third category is the *prejudiced nondiscriminator,* the prejudiced person who is afraid to express his or her prejudice through discrimination. Like the fair-weather liberals, these people do not practice what they believe in. They allow social pressure to keep them from doing what they want to do. But since they are prejudiced despite their nondiscriminatory behavior, they are called *fair-weather illiberals* rather than liberals. Under the pressure of antidiscrimination laws, for example, prejudiced people will hire or work with minorities.

Finally, there is the *prejudiced discriminator,* who is deeply prejudiced against minorities and practices discrimination. Like all-weather liberals, these *all-weather illiberals* are consistent: their actions match their beliefs. Members of the Ku Klux Klan provide an example. Strict enforcement of antidiscrimination laws, however, could force them to stop their discriminatory practices. In the late 1950s and 1960s, for example, no-nonsense enforcement of federal laws and court orders, sometimes with the help of federal marshals and troops, forced many state officials in the South to desegregate their schools.

If legislation can compel people to give up discrimination, what about their prejudice? It is true, as many lawmakers believe, that we cannot legislate against prejudice, because such legislation is practically unenforceable. That is probably why we do not have any antiprejudice law. But by legislating against discrimination we can gradually eliminate prejudice. According to cognitive dissonance theory, which has ample support from research data, people tend to change their attitude if it has been inconsistent for some time with their behavior (Festinger, 1957). This usually involves changing their attitude so that it becomes consistent with their behavior. Thus people can be expected to gradually change their prejudicial attitude into an unprejudicial one after they have been legally forced to develop the habit of behaving nondiscriminatorily. Indeed, since 1954 a series of civil rights laws and court rulings have caused many whites to stop their discriminatory practices and to reevaluate their attitude toward blacks. Today significantly fewer whites are prejudiced. Many whites are still prejudiced, though. They do not express their prejudice in the traditional "redneck" way but in a more indirect, subtle manner. This often compels them to see themselves as unprejudiced while trying to project this self-image to others (Hirschman, 1983; Frey and Gaertner, 1986; Ladd, 1987). Nevertheless, blacks can still feel prejudice, as the following indicates:

> As a top student at a black high school in Brooklyn, Ifeachor Okeke inspected several prestigious campuses before choosing a college. "At Amherst, I got the feeling that blacks weren't welcome," she recalls. "At Yale, I also felt a sense of isolation." So she chose Stanford, which "seemed more open and relaxed." Now, after two years on the California campus, she has second thoughts. Her grades are satisfactory—a B average—but it's a struggle to fit in. She was invited to only one party in her sophomore year, and she didn't make a single friend in her dormitory (Taylor, 1987).

Institutionalized Discrimination

Even if every single white were no longer prejudiced and discriminating, discrimination would still exist for some time. Over the years it has been built into various American institutions, so that discrimination can occur even when no one is aware of it. When blacks and whites have long lived in separate neighborhoods, then even though no one tries to discriminate against blacks, neighborhood schools will remain segregated. If employers prefer to hire people who graduated from their own universities that have long denied entrance to blacks, then blacks will not have much chance of being hired. When law and medical schools prefer to recruit children of their wealthy and influential alumni, nearly all of whom are whites, then the students are not likely to be black. When fire and police departments continue to use the height requirements in hiring that were originally intended for evaluating white applicants, then many otherwise qualified Mexican- and Asian-Americans—who are generally shorter than whites—will not get the job (Commission on Civil Rights, 1981; Kimmel, 1986). These are all cases of **institutionalized discrimination.** They are traceable to the long history of discrimination by educational, economic, and other social institutions. They are not the products of individual prejudice.

Recognition of the existence of institutionalized discrimination has led the courts to use busing as a way to desegregate schools. It has also led the federal government to institute affirmative action policies, which require employers and colleges to make special efforts to recruit minorities for jobs, promotions, and educational opportunities. Busing has sparked heated debate and resistance, which we discuss in Chapter 14 (Education). Affirmative action has largely been effective in reducing institutionalized discrimination. But it has also turned into quotas—the requirement that a certain percentage of personnel or students be minority members. This has provoked criticisms that it amounts to "reverse discrimination" against whites. Critics demand that only the best-qualified persons be hired or admitted to college, without regard to race or ethnicity. Most Americans, including the majority of blacks and other minorities, are now opposed to the idea that the government, because of past discrimination, should give special help to minorities (*Public Opinion,* 1981). This reluctance to support government intervention stems largely from the popular American belief that personal success depends on individual efforts (Kleugel and Smith, 1982). Defenders of affirmative action, however, have argued that charges of reverse discrimination mask the continuing institutionalized discrimination against minorities and also reflect white racial hostility (Kluegel and Smith, 1983).

The courts have largely taken a middle position. In 1978 Allen Bakke, a white student, charged that he was denied admission to a medical school in California because of his race. He argued that some minority applicants who were less qualified got admitted under the school's quota system. The Supreme Court expressed its opposition to quotas by ordering the school to admit Bakke. But the Court also supported affirmative action by ruling it constitutional for universities to use race as one—though not the only—criterion in evaluating applicants for admission. In 1986 the Court took a similar action. It ruled it unconstitutional for a Michigan school district to lay off white teachers ahead of blacks with less seniority. But the Court still insisted that it may be necessary to take race into account to remedy the effects of prior discrimination. Thus in 1987 the Court upheld a federal district judge's orders in 1983 and 1984 that required Alabama to promote one black state trooper for each white state trooper. This racial quota, however, could be imposed only if the black trooper was qualified for the promotion. In short, schools and employers are still under government pressure to carry out affirmative action, but they are also expected to evaluate the credentials of minorities more closely than before.

Sources and Consequences

For more than 200 years, the United States has confronted the "American dilemma," proclaiming equality yet practicing discrimination. Since the Supreme Court banned racial discrimination in 1954, however, prejudice and discrimination in our society have been losing steam (Smith, 1981; Hirschman, 1983; Schaefer, 1984). But they are still running strong in many other parts of the world. When racial or ethnic violence erupts in these places, it is usually far more devastating than in our country. In India, for example, the assassination of Prime Minister Indira Gandhi by her Sikh bodyguards in 1984 triggered anti-Sikh riots that took nearly 1,300 lives and left more than 50,000 people without shelter or livelihood. Earlier in the same year, a clash between Hindus and Muslims resulted in 216 dead, 756 injured, and 13,000 homeless. Many of the victims were mutilated with crowbars, swords, and scyths and then doused with kerosene and set afire. A year earlier a similar conflict took more than 3,000 lives (Johnson, 1984). What are the sources of such intergroup hostilities?

One source is social-psychological. Through prejudice and discrimination, members of the dominant group make themselves feel superior to minorities and so build up their self-image. Hostility against minorities is likely to mount when many dominant-group members are beset with unemployment and other problems. They are, in effect, likely to treat minorities as **scapegoats,** blaming them for causing the problems. Thus during the economic crisis of recent years, illegal aliens in the United States and non-European minorities in Western Europe have been blamed for taking away jobs from dominant-group members. During the Middle Ages when thousands of Europeans died in the plague, "rioters stormed Jewish ghettos and burned them down, believing that Jews were somehow responsible for the epidemic. Six centuries later, when Hitler and the Nazis set up extermination camps, Jews were still blamed for the troubles in Europe" (Coleman and Cressey, 1987).

Not all dominant-group members are inclined to use minorities as whipping boys. Are there some personality traits that make one person more likely to be prejudiced than others? In the late 1940s a famous empirical study by Theodore Adorno and his associates (1950) suggested that the answer was yes. Those people most likely to be prejudiced have what Adorno called the *authoritarian personality.* Its characteristics include obedience to authority, admiration of power, great concern for status and toughness, and an inclination to distrust others.

A second source of prejudice and discrimination is socialization. If our parents, teachers, and peers are prejudiced, we are likely to follow their lead. They need not teach prejudice deliberately. In fact, they are more likely to do it unintentionally, by telling ethnic jokes (about, for example, Jewish mothers and Chinese laundrymen) and talking about minorities in terms of racist stereotypes ("lazy Negroes" and "happy-go-lucky Mexicans"). The jokes are especially effective in reinforcing prejudice because, in evoking the listeners' laughter, they make the stereotypes appear completely harmless. Many whites help perpetuate prejudice by bragging "Some of my best friends are blacks," which, in effect, patronizes the minority. Even parents opposed to racism may unknowingly plant seeds of racist thought when they select for their children such popular books as *Mary Poppins* and *The Story of Little Black Sambo,* which contain disparaging images of blacks (Madsen, 1982).

A third source of prejudice and discrimination is the dominant group's drive for economic and political power. According to Marxists, racism can enhance profits for the capitalists. It can ensure a huge supply of cheap labor from among oppressed minorities. It can further force down white employees' wages and break their strikes, as low-paid black workers can be recruited to replace them (Reich, 1981). The dominant group's affluent members also rely on racism to kill business competition from economically successful minorities. In 1913, for example, after the Japanese immigrants in California became successful farmers, legislation was enacted to prohibit them from owning or leasing land so that they could not compete with white farmers. The dominant group's working class also seeks economic benefits from its racism. Thus white labor unions used to withhold memberships from blacks in order to protect their higher-paying jobs (Willhelm, 1980). Today white workers who are in greater competition with blacks for employment also tend to be more intolerant. The government's affirmative action further contributes to this intolerance by sometimes favoring blacks over whites (Cummings, 1980; Giles and Evans, 1986).

For the dominant group as a whole, the greater the economic threat from minorities, the more hostile it is likely to be. This may explain why many of the great mass murders have been of minorities that were economically better off than their murderers, such as the Chinese in Southeast Asia, the Armenians in Turkey, and the Jews in Nazi Germany. There have been many occasions in Southeast Asia when more Chinese were massacred in a few days than blacks lynched in the entire history of the United States. (The number of blacks lynched between 1882 and 1951 was 3,437.) Even more Armenians—about 600,000—were slaughtered by the Turks in one single year (1915). The number of Jews killed in the Nazi holocaust was largest of all (Sowell, 1983).

The dominant group may also be politically motivated, relying on widespread prejudice and discrimination to maintain their power. In South Africa, for example, the white regime denies its black citizens the right to vote. In the American past many state and local governments tried various means to keep minorities out of the political process. They passed laws to forbid blacks from voting. When these laws were overturned by the federal government, they attempted to discourage minorities from political participation by charging a poll tax, by requiring a literacy test, or by printing ballots only in English in areas where many minority people did not know the language. Just as minorities' economic threat can increase the dominant group's hostility, so can their political threat. When southern whites felt threatened by the emerging black power in their counties between 1889 and 1931, the lynching of blacks became more common (Corzine, Creech, and Corzine, 1983). With the rise of political consciousness among the overseas Chinese throughout Southeast Asia since 1910, there had been an increase in discrimination, violence, and bloodshed against the Chinese, culminating in the massive horrors inflicted on the "boat people" in the late 1970s (Sowell, 1983). Growing political interest on the part of Armenians earlier in this century also provoked confiscations by the Russians and deportation and massacres by the Turks.

Obviously, prejudice and discrimination can have extremely negative consequences for the victims, such as wholesale enslavement, mass internment, massacre, and other atrocities suffered by minorities. Such horrors no longer happen in the United States today. But prejudice and discrimination still have some costly consequences for minorities. Blacks, Hispanics, and native Americans, for example, still have higher rates of unemployment and poverty as well as fewer years of schooling and lower life expectancy than whites. For a long time, up to about 1970, racism took a heavy psychological toll on minorities. Most tragically, they developed a sense of self-hatred and dislike for their own groups. But in the 1970s and 1980s their levels of self-esteem have equaled or exceeded that of whites (Porter and Washington, 1979; Hoetler, 1982; Schaefer, 1984), thanks to the civil rights movement and the resulting diminution of prejudice and discrimination.

Prejudice and discrimination do not hold back everyone. The Chinese-American physicist Paul C.W. Chu has risen to the top of his profession in the United States. He is here holding his recent discovery: a disk of ceramic superconductor. Similarly, prejudice and discrimination have not prevented the West Indian blacks in the United States, the Jews in Europe, and the Italians in Argentina from climbing the ladder of economic success higher than the general population.

Severe prejudice and discrimination, however, have not always reduced minorities to poverty. West Indian blacks—immigrants or descendants of immigrants from the Caribbeans—have suffered as much discrimination as other blacks, but they have achieved greater educational, economic, and political success than whites (Beer, 1987). The early Chinese and Japanese immigrants in the United States were subjected to segregation, discrimination, and mob violence, but their descendants today are more economically successful and proportionately better represented in medicine, engineering, and other lucrative professions than whites. In each of the Southeast Asian countries where the Chinese have been denied equal rights, they have also prospered economically while the dominant majority has remained poor. The Jews in Europe have occasionally had their wealth confiscated by governments, but they would just as often produce that wealth again later. Discrimination against the northern Italians in Argentina has not prevented them from climbing the ladder of economic success higher than native Argentines. The ability of these groups to transcend the pauperizing effects of prejudice and discrimination has been attributed to their exceptional cultural emphasis on hard work (Sowell, 1983).

QUESTIONS FOR DISCUSSION AND REVIEW

1. How does prejudice differ from discrimination?
2. What are the four possible combinations of prejudice and discrimination?
3. When does legal discrimination become institutionalized, and why is this form of discrimination hard to change?
4. What social, psychological, and political processes can lead to the growth of prejudice and discrimination?
5. How have some minority groups overcome the pauperizing effects of prejudice and discrimination?

RACIAL AND ETHNIC RELATIONS

We have seen that prejudice and discrimination are an integral part of the relations between the dominant group and minorities. But the amount of prejudice and discrimination obviously varies from one society to another. Hence the racial and ethnic relations may appear in different forms, ranging from peaceful coexistence to violent conflict. In the following sections we analyze the various ways in which a society's dominant group accepts or rejects its minorities, and we also look at minorities' various responses to the dominant group's negative action.

Forms of Acceptance

If a society treats its racial and ethnic groups in a positive way, it will grant them rights of citizenship. Still, its acceptance of these groups is not necessarily total and unconditional. The dominant group, for example, may expect other groups to give up their distinct identities and accept the dominant subculture. Acceptance of a racial or ethnic group may take three forms: assimilation, amalgamation, and cultural pluralism.

Assimilation Frequently, a minority group accepts the culture of the dominant group, fading into the larger society. This process, called **assimilation,** has at least two aspects. The first is **behavioral assimilation,** which means that the minority group adopts the dominant culture—its language, values, norms, and so on—giving up its own distinctive characteristics. Behavioral assimilation, however, does not guarantee **structural assimilation**—in which the minority group ceases to be a minority *and* is accepted on equal terms with the rest of society. German-Americans, for example, have achieved structural assimilation, but black Americans have not. Taken as a whole, assimilation can be expressed as A + B + C = A, where minorities (B and C) lose their subcultural traits and become indistinguishable from the dominant group (A) (Newman, 1973).

When the dominant group is ethnocentric, believing that its subculture is superior to others', then minority groups face considerable pressure to achieve behavioral assimilation. How easily they make this transition depends on both their attitude toward their own subculture and the degree of similarity between themselves and the dominant group. Minority groups that take pride in their own subculture are likely to resist behavioral assimilation. This may explain why Jews and Asians in the United States display "an unusual degree of ethnic solidarity" (Hirschman, 1983). Groups that are very different from the dominant group may find that even behavioral assimilation does not lead to structural assimilation. Skin color is the most striking case of a dissimilarity that hinders structural assimilation. A black, middle-class American, for example, may find structural assimilation more difficult than it would be for a Russian dissident who speaks halting English. Nevertheless, most members of the disadvantaged minorities look upon assimilation as a promise of their right to get ahead—economically and socially—in the United States (Hirschman, 1983).

"Which is it I can't abide—sushi or sashimi?"

Amalgamation A society which believes that groups should go through the process of behavioral assimilation in order to be accepted as equals obviously has little respect for the distinctive traits of these groups. In contrast, a society that seeks amalgamation as an ideal has some appreciation for the equal worth of various subcultures. **Amalgamation** produces a "melting pot," in which many subcultures are blended together to produce a new culture, one that differs from any of its components. Like assimilation, amalgamation requires groups to give up their distinct racial and ethnic identities. But unlike assimilation, amalgamation demands respect for the original subcultures. Various groups are expected to contribute their own subcultures to the development of a new culture, without pushing any one subculture at the expense of another. Usually, this blending of diverse subcultures results from intermarriage. It can be described as A + B + C = D, where A, B, and C represent different groups jointly producing a new culture (D) unlike any of its original components (Newman, 1973).

More than 70 years ago a British-Jewish dramatist portrayed the United States as an amalgamation of subcultures. "There she lies," he wrote, "the great melting pot—listen! . . . Ah, what a stirring and seething—Celt and Latin, Slav and Teuton, Greek and Syrian, Black and Yellow—Jew and Gentile" (Zangwill, 1909). Indeed, to some extent America is a melting pot. In popular music and slang, for example, you can find elements of many subcultures. And there has been considerable intermarriage among some groups—in particular, among Americans of English, German, Irish, Italian, and other European backgrounds. For the most part, however, the amalgamation is made up of these Western European peoples and their subcultures. Brazil, where interracial marriage is common, comes much closer than the United States to being a true melting pot of peoples.

Cultural Pluralism Switzerland provides an example of yet a third way in which ethnic groups may live together. In Switzerland, three major groups—Germans, French, and Italians—retain their own languages while living together in peace. They are neither assimilated nor amalgamated. Instead, these diverse groups retain their distinctive subcultures while coexisting peacefully. This situation is called **cultural pluralism.** It is the opposite of assimilation and requires yet greater mutual respect for other groups' traditions and customs than does amalgamation. And unlike either assimilation or amalgamation, cultural pluralism encourages each group to take pride in its distinctiveness, to be conscious of its heritage, and to retain its identity. Such pluralism can be shown as A + B + C = A + B + C, where various groups continue to keep their subcultures while living together in the same society (Newman, 1973).

To some extent, the United States has long been marked by cultural pluralism. This can be seen in the Chinatowns, Little Italies, and Polish neighborhoods of many American cities. But these ethnic enclaves owe their existence more to discrimination than to the respectful encouragement of diversity that characterizes true pluralism.

For many groups in America, cultural pluralism has become a goal. This became evident during the 1960s and 1970s, when blacks and white ethnics alike denounced assimilation and proclaimed pride in their own identities. But pluralism is not easy to maintain. It requires that society conquer prejudice and respect various groups equally. If it fails to do so, pluralism is likely to give way to either assimilation or outright rejection of minority groups.

Forms of Rejection

When a dominant group rejects racial and ethnic groups, they are restricted to the status of minorities. They are discriminated against to some degree. The three major forms of rejection, in order of severity, are segregation, expulsion, and extermination.

Segregation **Segregation** means more than spatial and social separation of the dominant and minority groups. It means that minority groups, because they are believed inferior, are compelled to live separately, and in inferior conditions. The neighborhoods, schools, and other public facilities for the dominant group are both separate from and superior to those of the minorities.

The compulsion that underlies segregation is not necessarily official, or acknowledged. In the United States, for example, segregation is officially outlawed, yet it persists. In other words, **de jure segregation**—segregation sanctioned by law—is gone, but **de facto segregation**—segregation resulting from tradition and custom—remains. This is particularly the case for blacks in housing (Hirschman, 1983; Logan and Schneider, 1984; Massey and Mullan, 1984). Like the United States, most nations no longer practice *de jure* segregation, but South Africa is a striking exception. Its government enforces an elaborate set of laws to maintain segregation in every aspect of life. They have separate restrooms, separate changing rooms, and separate cafeterias for whites and blacks, who are also separated in residential areas, in schools and universities, in hotels and other public facilities. It is even a crime for a white to visit a black in his home without a permit, which is difficult to get (van den Berghe, 1978).

Expulsion Societies have also used more drastic means of rejecting minorities, such as expulsion. In some cases, the dominant group has expelled a minority from certain areas. In other cases, it has pushed the minority out of the country entirely. During the nineteenth century, for example, Czarist Russia drove out millions of Jews, and the American government forced the Cherokees to travel from their homes in Georgia and the Carolinas to reservations in Oklahoma. About 4000 of the Cherokees died on this "Trail of Tears." During the 1970s Uganda expelled more than 40,000 Asians—many of them Ugandan citizens—and Vietnam forced 700,000 Chinese to leave the country (Schaefer, 1984).

Extermination Finally, the most drastic action against minorities is to kill them. Wholesale killing of a racial or ethnic group, called **genocide,** has been attempted in various countries. During the nineteenth century, Dutch settlers in South Africa exterminated the Hottentots. Native Americans were slaughtered by white settlers. On the island of Tasmania, near Australia, British settlers killed the entire native population, whom they hunted like wild animals. Between 1933 and 1945, the Nazis systematically murdered 6 million Jews. In the early 1970s, thousands of Ibos and Hutus were massacred in the African states of Nigeria and Burundi. Also in the early 1970s, machine guns and gifts of poisoned food and germ-infected clothing were used against Indians in Brazil—twenty tribes were exterminated (Bodard, 1972).

Minority Reactions

A policy of expulsion or extermination leaves a minority group little choice about how to react, but segregation provokes various responses. Sociologist Peter Rose (1981) classifies the possible reactions of minorities by asking two questions. First, do they accept or reject the image of inferior status imposed by the dominant group? Second, do they accept or reject the segregated role imposed by the dominant group? Rose found four possible responses to segregation (see Table 10.2).

Submission If members of a minority group accept both inferior status and a segregated role, they submit to the dominant group. In an extremely racist society, submission may be necessary for survival. For the American slaves, showing submission by bowing to whites and playing dumb was often the only way to stay alive. Minority members might therefore feign submission while inwardly rejecting the image of inferiority. It is more likely, however, that outward submission is matched by

Table 10.2 Minority Responses to Segregation
Victims of expulsion and extermination can hardly do anything except follow orders. But segregation, with its imposition of inferior status on the target group, provokes various responses from minority members. According to sociologist Peter Rose (1981), they may (1) submit to the dominant group, (2) withdraw from their own group, (3) separate themselves from the dominant group, and (4) integrate themselves with the dominant group.

	Segregated Role	
	Accepted	Rejected
Inferior Status		
Accepted	1. Submission	2. Withdrawal
Rejected	3. Separation	4. Integration

inward self-hatred. Before 1970, sociologists used to find evidence of such hatred in black children, who described black dolls as ugly, dirty, or bad, and in black parents, who tried to whiten their skins and straighten their hair (Clark and Clark, 1947; Kardiner and Ovesey, 1962). Today, however, submission by minorities is rare.

Withdrawal People may accept inferior status yet reject segregation by withdrawing from their minority group. Ashamed of their membership in a minority group, they pass as members of the dominant group. Light-skinned blacks may pass as whites, Jews as Gentiles, and Catholic ethnics as WASPs. For white ethnics, one method of passing as a member of the dominant group is to change a foreign-sounding name to an Anglo-sounding one, such as Goldwasser to Goldwater, Schmidt to Smith, or Petropoulos to Peterson.

Like submission, withdrawal may exact a high psychological price. Those who withdraw from their ethnic group may feel guilty for leaving their parents' subculture behind and may fear that the dominant group does not totally accept them. They may become "marginal" people, torn between two cultures. Like submission, however, withdrawal has become less common in the United States in recent years.

Since the 1960s the main thrust in the civil rights movement has been to achieve integration for blacks. As a result, blacks have moved into positions of importance throughout society. Above, for example, a black banker confers with the head of the day-care center that is his client. But integration may threaten ethnic identity. Many are faced with the need to balance their pride in being black and their fear of losing identity in complete assimilation.

Separation Members of a minority may also choose to reject inferior status but to accept segregation. In 1822, for example, freed American slaves chose to leave the United States. They sailed to Africa and colonized Liberia, where, at least until a coup in 1980, their descendants dominated the descendants of the native Africans. More common forms of separation can be seen in ethnic enclaves such as Chinatowns, the Irish and Italian neighborhoods of Boston, the Polish neighborhoods of Chicago, and the Hispanic neighborhoods of San Antonio. Separatism gained popularity among blacks during the late 1960s, when groups such as the Black Muslims urged blacks to seek pride in their own identity and power, not acceptance by whites.

Integration The mainstream of the 1960s civil rights movement urged yet another response: integration. It requires the rejection of both inferior status and segregation and the achievement of equality with the dominant group. Integration, however, threatens ethnic identity. It may lead to assimilation. As ethnic pride increases, full integration becomes less attractive. Many members of minority groups therefore live in two worlds. They enjoy primary relationships with their kin in an ethnic community separated from the dominant social group, and they study or work, carrying on secondary relationships, in the larger society.

QUESTIONS FOR DISCUSSION AND REVIEW

1. In what different ways can the majority group accept members of a minority group?
2. What can happen when a dominant group decides to reject a racial or ethnic minority?
3. How can minority groups accept or reject segregation by a majority group?

MINORITY GROUPS IN AMERICA

The United States is a nation of immigrants. The earliest immigrants were the American Indians, who arrived from Asia more than 20,000 years ago. Long after the

Indians had settled down as native Americans, other immigrants began to pour in from Europe and later from Africa, Asia, and Latin America. They came as explorers, adventurers, slaves or refugees, most of them hoping to fulfill a dream of success and happiness. The British were the earliest of these immigrants and, on the whole, the most successful in fulfilling that dream. They became the dominant group. Eventually they founded a government dedicated to the democratic ideal of equality, but they kept blacks as slaves and discriminated against other racial and ethnic groups. This "American dilemma"—the discrepancy between the ideal of equality and the reality of discrimination—still exists, though to a lesser degree than in the past. Let us look at how the major minority groups have fared under the burden of the American dilemma.

Native Americans have suffered under white oppression and prejudice for over 200 years. Today the majority still experience the effects of this oppression in the form of extreme poverty, poor health, and inadequate social services. They are the most disadvantaged minority in a land that used to belong to them alone. They are, however, reasserting their rights and expressing pride in their unique cultural heritage.

Native Americans

Native Americans have long been called Indians—one result of Columbus's mistaken belief that he had landed in India. The explorer's descendants passed down many other distorted descriptions of the Native Americans. They were described as savages, although it was whites who slaughtered hundreds of thousands of them. They were portrayed as scalp hunters, although it was the white government that offered large sums to whites for the scalps of Indians. They were stereotyped as lazy, although it was whites who forced them to give up their traditional occupations. These false conceptions of Native Americans were reinforced by the contrasting pictures whites painted of themselves. The white settlers were known as pioneers rather than invaders and marauders; their taking of the Native Americans' land was called homesteading, not robbery.

When Columbus "discovered" America, there were more than 300 Native American tribes, with a total population exceeding a million. Of those he encountered around the Caribbean, Columbus wrote: "Of anything they have, if it be asked for, they never say no, but do rather invite the person to accept it, and show as much lovingness as though they would give their hearts" (Hraba, 1979). In North America, too, the earliest white settlers were often aided by friendly Native Americans.

As the white settlers increased in numbers and moved westward, however, Native Americans resisted them. But the native population was decimated by outright killing, by destruction of their food sources, and by diseases brought by whites, such as smallpox and influenza. With their greater numbers and superior military technology, the whites prevailed. Sometimes they took land by treaty rather than by outright force—and then they often violated the treaty.

During the last half of the nineteenth century, the U.S. government tried a new policy. It made the tribes its wards and drove them into reservations. The land they were given was mostly useless for farming, and it made up only 2.9 percent of the United States. Even on the reservation, Native Americans were not free to live their own lives. The federal government was intent on assimilating them, replacing tribal culture with the white settlers' way of life. Indian men were forced to become small farmers, though they had for centuries been hunting and herding while letting women do the farming. Some of the tribal rituals and languages were banned. Children were sent away to boarding schools and encouraged to leave the reservation to seek jobs in cities. In 1887 those Indians who lived away from the tribe and "adopted the habits of civilized life" were granted citizenship. The government also disrupted the tradition of tribal ownership by granting land to the heads of families (Franklin, 1981).

By 1890 the Native American population had been reduced to less than a quarter of a million. Changes in the government's policy toward them came slowly. In 1924 Congress conferred citizenship on all Native Americans. In 1934 the federal government reversed course and supported tribal culture by granting self-government rights to tribes, restoring communal ownership, and giving financial aid. In 1940 the Native American population, which had been reduced to 0.3 million, began to grow.

By 1980 there were 1.4 million Native Americans. Slightly more than half live on 261 reservations, mostly in the Southwest. The rest live in urban areas. After more than two centuries of colonial subjugation, Native Americans today find themselves at the bottom of the ladder—the poorest minority in the United States. Their unemployment rates usually stay at a devastating 40 to 50 percent, compared with less than 10 percent among the general population. In 1982 Native Americans' jobless rate jumped to 80 percent, and in some tribes the average income for a family of four plummeted to a mere $900 a year—way below the nation's official poverty line of $9300 (Beck, 1982). Many are so poor that they live without electricity, heat, or plumbing. As a result, they have serious health problems. Compared with those of the general population, Native Americans' rates of pneumonia, influenza, and diabetes are more than double. Their rate of tuberculosis is 6.2 times higher, and their suicide rate is nearly double. Among Native Americans car accidents are 3.3 times more frequent and alcoholism is 7.7 times more frequent than in the population at large (Huntley, 1983).

Since the early 1960s Native Americans have begun to assert their "red power." In 1963 they started a vigorous campaign to have their fishing rights recognized in northwest Washington; these were eventually granted by the Supreme Court in 1968. In late 1960 they publicized their grievances by occupying Alcatraz, the abandoned island prison in San Francisco Bay, for 19 months. In 1972 they marched into Washington to dramatize the "trail of broken treaties" and presented the government with a series of demands for improving their lives. In 1973 they took over Wounded Knee, South Dakota for 72 days, during which they were engaged in a shooting war with government troops. These dramatic actions were mostly symbolic, designed to foster Indian identity and unity. In the 1980s, however, they have been seeking more substantive goals. Thus, an increasing number of Indian tribes have been filing lawsuits to win back lands taken from their ancestors. They have also been fighting through federal courts to protect their water and mineral resources as well as hunting and fishing rights. Moreover, they are demanding more government assistance with health, educational, and social programs (Zuern, 1983; Jarvenpa, 1985).

All this has sparked a national movement to recapture traditions, to make Native Americans feel proud of their cultural heritage. Virtually every tribe places a heavy emphasis on teaching the younger generation its native language, crafts, tribal history, and religious ceremonies. There used to be a lack of unity among the 300 tribes, but today intertribal visiting and marriage are a common occurrence (Deloria, 1981). Moreover, in the last 15 years, more than 500 Indian men and women have become lawyers—and more have successfully established themselves in the business and professional worlds. Of course, the majority of Native Americans still have a long way to go. Without a viable economic base to draw on, they still find themselves "powerless in the face of rising unemployment, deteriorating health care, and a falling standard of living" (Cornell, 1986). The last 15 years have not been long enough to overcome two centuries of government oppression. In addition, they have to continue struggling with the federal government, which has cut funds for their programs despite its attempt to encourage tribal self-determination and attract private investment to develop reservation economies (Huntley, 1983).

Black Americans

There are more than 28 million black Americans, constituting about 12 percent of the U.S. population. Blacks are the largest minority in the nation. In fact, there are more blacks in the United States than in any single African nation except Nigeria.

Their ancestors were first brought from Africa to North America as slaves in 1619. For the two-month voyage across the ocean they were chained and packed

In the recent past, as prejudice and discrimination have declined in the face of strict laws and changing attitudes, black men and women have achieved greater and greater recognition for their accomplishments. In addition to the large number of talented blacks in sports and entertainment, there are major black figures in politics, literature, and the arts. Above is the famous black novelist Toni Morrison. In 1988, her novel *Beloved,* widely praised for its exuberant language and historical insight, won the Pulitzer Prize for fiction.

like sardines, often lying immobile for weeks in their own sweat and excrement. It was not unusual for half the slaves to die from disease, starvation, and suicide before reaching their destination.

From 1619 to 1820 about half a million of the slaves were taken to U.S. shores. Most lived in the southern states and worked on cotton, tobacco, or sugar-cane plantations. "Slave codes" that restricted their movement and conduct were enshrined in laws. These varied from state to state, but generally slaves could not leave a plantation without a pass noting where they would go and when they would return. Teaching slaves to read and write was forbidden. In seventeenth-century South Carolina, slaves who struck a white person could be punished by being castrated, branded, or burned alive (Unger, 1982). Whipping later became a popular punishment. Even obedient slaves were often abused, and the women were often raped with impunity. The institution of slavery reinforced the prevailing belief that slaves were subhuman and should be treated as such. Even those few blacks who were free faced severe discrimination.

By the time the Civil War broke out in 1861, the number of enslaved blacks had reached 5 million. The end of the Civil War in 1865 brought not only the end of slavery but also other new opportunities for southern blacks. For the first time they could go to public schools and state universities with whites. The greatest black advance came in politics, but little was done to improve the economic position of blacks.

Then, in 1877, federal troops were withdrawn from the South. White supremacy reigned, and whatever gains blacks had made during Reconstruction were wiped out. Many so-called **Jim Crow** laws were enacted, segregating blacks from whites in all kinds of public and private facilities—from rest rooms to schools. These laws were supplemented by terror. If a black man was suspected of killing a white or of raping a white woman, he might be lynched, beaten to death, or burned at the stake. Sometimes blacks were lynched if they married whites.

Lynchings occurred in the North, too. Still, the North offered more opportunities to blacks than did the South. As southern farms were mechanized and as the demand for workers in northern industrial centers rose during World Wars I and II, many southern blacks migrated North. When the wars ended and the demand for workers decreased, however, blacks were often the first to be fired. Even in the North, where there were no Jim Crow laws, they faced discrimination and segregation.

The federal government itself sanctioned segregation. In 1896 the Supreme Court declared segregation legal. In 1913 President Wilson ordered the restaurants and cafeterias in federal buildings to be segregated. Even the armed forces were segregated until President Truman ordered them desegregated in 1948.

A turning point in American race relations came in 1954. In that year the Supreme Court ordered that public schools be desegregated. The decision gave momentum to the long-standing movement against racial discrimination. In the late 1950s and 1960s the civil rights movement launched marches, sit-ins, and boycotts. The price was high: many civil rights workers were beaten and jailed and some were killed. But eventually Congress passed the landmark Civil Rights Act in 1964, prohibiting segregation and discrimination in virtually all areas of social life such as restaurants, hotels, schools, housing, and employment (Schaefer, 1984).

In the last 20 years the Civil Rights Act has ended many forms of segregation and paved the way for some improvements in the position of blacks. Various studies have shown a significant decline in white opposition to such issues as school integration, integrated housing, interracial marriage, and support for a black president. The proportion of black children attending white majority schools in the South rose from less than 2 percent in 1964 to 43 percent in 1980. From 1961 to 1981 the number of blacks going to college soared by 500 percent. Blacks' educational attainment is now virtually the same as that of whites—the median years of schooling completed are already 12.0 for blacks, compared with 12.5 for whites. In the short span of nine years—from 1970 to 1979—the total number of blacks elected to various public offices more than tripled. In 1966, one black was elected to the U.S. Senate, but today there are 21 blacks in the House of Representatives. Blacks are also the mayors of six of the largest American cities. We can see blacks holding positions of prominence in television and films and at major universities and colleges. Most impressive was Jesse Jackson's presidential candidacy, which would have been unthinkable a generation ago. The recent dramatic increase in social recognition for blacks can also be seen in the crowning of a black woman as Miss America, the sending of a black astronaut into space, and the congressional proclamation of a national holiday to honor Dr. Martin Luther King (Reid, 1982; Meer, 1984a; Farley, 1985; Schuman et al., 1985).

Full equality, however, is still far from achieved. Most evident is the continuing large economic gap between blacks and whites. The latest figures on median family income are $13,507 for blacks and $24,654 for whites—blacks earning only about 55 percent of the amount made by whites. The unemployment rate for blacks is more than twice that for whites (17.8 versus 7.1 percent). Black youths also have more than twice the jobless rate as white youths (42.7 versus 18.3 percent). Over 31 percent of blacks live in poverty, compared with fewer than 10 percent for whites. Another glaring racial inequality shows up in housing. Most blacks not only reside in segregated neighborhoods but are more likely than whites with similar incomes to live in overcrowded and substandard housing (Bianchi, Farley, and Spain, 1982; Meer, 1984a; Mare and Winship, 1984; Gelman, 1988).

Less obvious is the fact that, as suggested above, prejudice has become more subtle and complex than before. Many whites today no longer hold the old-fashioned racist idea that "blacks are inferior to whites." But they are more likely to believe that "blacks shouldn't push themselves where they're not wanted" or that "white people have a right to keep blacks out of their neighborhoods if they want to, and blacks should respect that right." While better-educated whites would not ascribe negative attributes (laziness, slovenliness, or stupidity) to blacks, they are more likely to associate positive traits (ambition, intelligence, or cleanliness) with whites than with blacks. Although this mild prejudice rarely turns into overt hostility, it does bother many blacks. According to a recent survey of black college students, 80 percent feel that they experience some form of discrimination during their college years (McConahay, Hardee, Batts, 1981; Gaertner and McLaughlin, 1983; Simpson, 1987).

In sum, prejudice against blacks still exists. They still fall far behind whites in economics and housing, though they have shown impressive gains in education and politics. This is not true for all blacks, however. A black middle class is emerging, now constituting about 40 percent of the black population, as compared with only 5 percent in 1940. While this group is getting richer, the larger number of blacks—the poor underclass—are getting poorer. This is, in William Wilson's (1980, 1987) view, due to the increasing number of well-educated blacks who find it as easy as, or at times easier than, whites of equivalent qualification to get high-paying jobs. As these successful, well-off blacks move to better neighborhoods, they have left behind many ghettos full of poor people (see box, p. 254). These poor blacks have become poorer because they lack education. Since the structure of the national economy has been changing significantly, well-paid industrial jobs available to low-skilled workers are getting scarcer. While there are more and more service jobs, poor blacks cannot get them because they require white-collar skills. All this suggests that it is the changing economy rather than present-day discrimination that worsens the plight of the black underclass. The same economy, however, benefits the well-educated blacks. Thus Wilson argues that the significance of race as an obstacle to upward mobility is declining. While race is no longer as impor-

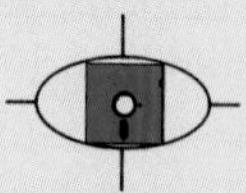

LOOKING AT CURRENT RESEARCH

The Deterioration of Black Ghettos

According to black sociologist William J. Wilson, the emergence of the affluent black middle class has had the ironic affect of transforming many stable inner-city black neighborhoods into disorganized ghettos. Here he explains how this has come about. Can social instability be brought back into the inner-city neighborhoods?

The inner city is less pleasant and more dangerous than it was prior to 1960. Despite a high rate of poverty in inner-city areas during the first half of this century, rates of joblessness, out-of-wedlock births, single families, welfare dependency, and serious crime were significantly lower than they are today and did not begin to rise rapidly until after the mid-1960s, with extraordinary increases during the 1970s. Why have the social conditions of the ghetto underclass deteriorated so rapidly in recent years?

Most unemployed blacks in the United States reside within the central cities. Their situation, already more difficult than that of any other major ethnic group in the country, continues to worsen. Not only are there more blacks without jobs every year; men, especially young males, are dropping out of the labor force in record proportions. Also, more and more black youth, including many who are no longer in school, are obtaining no job experience at all.

However, the growing problem of joblessness in the inner city both exacerbates and is in turn partly created by the changing social composition of inner-city neighborhoods. These areas have undergone a profound social transformation in the last several years, as reflected not only in their increasing rates of social dislocation but also in the changing class structure of ghetto neighborhoods. In the 1940s, 1950s, and even the 1960s, lower-class, working-class, and middle-class black urban families all resided more or less in the same ghetto areas, albeit on different streets. Although black middle-class professionals today tend to be employed in mainstream occupations outside the black community and neither live nor frequently interact with ghetto residents, the black middle-class professionals of the 1940s and 1950s (doctors, lawyers, teachers, social workers, etc.) resided in the higher-income areas of the inner city and serviced the ghetto community. The exodus of black middle-class professionals from the inner city has been increasingly accompanied by a movement of stable working-class blacks to higher-income neighborhoods in other parts of the city and to the suburbs. Confined by restrictive covenants to communities also inhabited by the urban black lower classes, the black working and middle classes in earlier years provided stability to inner-city neighborhoods and perpetuated and reinforced societal norms and values. In short, their very presence enhanced the social organization of ghetto communities. If strong norms and sanctions against aberrant behavior, a sense of community, and positive neighborhood identification are the essential features of social organization in urban areas, inner-city neighborhoods today suffer from a severe lack of social organization.

Unlike in previous years, today's ghetto residents represent almost exclusively the most disadvantaged segments of the urban black community—including those families that have experienced long-term spells of poverty and/or welfare dependency, individuals who lack training and skills and have either experienced periods of persistent unemployment or have dropped out of the labor force altogether, and individuals who are frequently involved in street criminal activity. The term *ghetto underclass* refers to this heterogeneous group of families and individuals who inhabit the cores of the nation's central cities. The term suggests that a fundamental social transformation has taken place in ghetto neighborhoods, and the groups represented by this term are collectively different from and much more socially isolated than those that lived in these communities in earlier years.

Source: Adapted from William Julius Wilson, *The Truly Disadvantaged,* Chicago: University of Chicago Press, 1987, pp. 141–143.

tant in determining who gets ahead, however, it still remains significant today. As the U.S. Commission on Civil Rights reports, black female college graduates still have a higher jobless rate than do their white counterparts (3.1 versus 2.4 percent) and black male college graduates' unemployment rate of 5.5 percent is 3.5 times that of their white peers (Williams, 1983). Moreover, regardless of their economic performance, blacks express less overall satisfaction with their lives than do whites of the same class (Thomas and Hughes, 1986). At any rate, taking into account the long history of black oppression in America, Sowell (1981) concludes: "The race as a whole has moved from a position of utter destitution—in money, knowledge, and rights—to a place alongside other groups emerging in the great struggles of life. None has had to come from so far back to join their fellow Americans."

Hispanic-Americans

In 1848 the United States either won or bought what would become Texas, California, Nevada, Utah, Arizona, New Mexico, and Colorado from Mexico. Thus many Mexicans found themselves living in U.S. territories as American citizens. The vast majority of today's Mexican-Americans, however, are the result of immigration from Mexico since the turn of the century. The early immigrants came largely to work in the farmlands of California and to build the railroads of the Southwest. Then numerous Mexicans began to pour into the United States, driven by Mexico's population pressures and economic problems and attracted by American industry's need for low-paid, unskilled labor.

The United States also added Puerto Rico to its territory in 1898, by defeating the Spaniards in the Spanish-American War. In 1917 Congress conferred citizenship on all Puerto Ricans, but they may not vote in presidential elections and have no representation in Congress. Over the years, especially since the early 1950s, many Puerto Ricans have migrated to the U.S. mainland, lured by job opportunities and cheap plane service between New York City and San Juan.

Thus a new minority group emerged in the United States—Hispanic-Americans. The category actually includes several groups today. Besides the Mexican-Americans and Puerto Ricans, there are immigrants from Cuba, who began to flock to the Miami area since their country became communist in 1959. There are also the "other Hispanics"—immigrants from other Central and South American countries, who have come here as political refugees and job seekers. By 1983 the members of all these groups totaled more than 15 million, constituting over 6 percent of the U.S. population. This made them our second largest minority. Because of their high birthrates and the continuing influx of immigrants, Hispanic-Americans could outnumber blacks in the next decade (Kenna, 1983; Davis, Haub, and Willette, 1983).

The Spanish language is the unifying factor among Hispanic-Americans. Another source of common identity is religion: at least 85 percent of them are Roman Catholics. There is an increasing friction, though, between Mexican-Americans and the newly arrived immigrants from Mexico. Many Mexican-Americans blame illegal aliens for lower salaries, loss of jobs, overcrowding of schools and health clinics, and deterioration of neighborhoods. According to a recent Los Angeles poll, 40 percent of the Mexican-American respondents said there were "too many" Mexican immigrants in California. According to another survey, 66 percent accused illegal immigrants of taking jobs from American citizens and 54 percent believed that cheap immigrant labor had led to lower wages in general. On the other hand, the immigrants consider the Mexican-Americans "lazy" workers and also call them *pochos* (people who ignore their origins) or *Mexicanos falsos.* Whether they are immigrants or not, Hispanics share the distinction of being highly urban. At least 84 percent live in large metropolitan areas, compared with 66 percent of the general population (Kenna, 1983; Montana, 1986).

There are, however, significant differences within the Hispanic community. Mexican-Americans are by far the largest group, accounting for 61 percent of the Hispanics. They are heavily concentrated in the Southwest and West. Puerto Ricans make up 15 percent and live mostly in the Northeast, especially in New York City. As a group, they are the poorest among the Hispanics. Those born in the United States, however, are more successful economically than their parents from Puerto Rico. The Cubans, who constitute 7 percent of the Hispanic population, are the most affluent. They therefore show the greatest tendency toward integration with Anglos. The remaining Hispanics are a diverse group, ranging from uneducated, unskilled laborers to highly trained professionals (Fitzpatrick and Parker, 1981; Nelson and Tienda, 1985).

As a whole, Hispanics are younger than the general population. The median age is 23 for Hispanics, compared with 30 for other Americans. The youthfulness of the Hispanic population is due to relatively high fertility and heavy immigration of young adults. This is particularly the case with Mexican-Americans, who have the most children and are the youngest of all Hispanic groups. At the other extreme are Cubans, who even have fewer children and are older than *non*-Hispanic Americans, with a median age of 41.

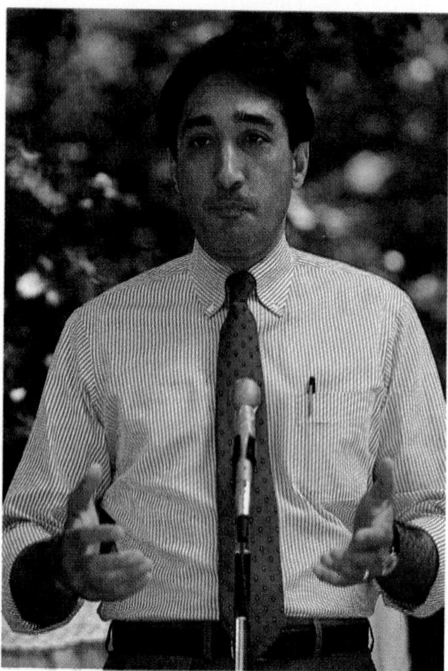

Henry Cisneros, Hispanic Mayor of San Antonio, Texas. Hispanics make up the second largest minority group in the country. They have come to the United States primarily from countries that lie along the Gulf of Mexico and from the islands in the Caribbean. The Spanish language and Catholicism are the major sources of their common identity. Although many Hispanics live in poverty in the United States, they frequently are better off than they were in their country of origin. They find greater opportunities for economic, social, and political improvement here.

Hispanics in general also lag behind both whites and blacks in educational attainment. But some Hispanic groups are more educated than others. Cubans are the best educated, primarily because most of the early refugees fleeing communist Cuba were middle-class and professional people. Mexican-Americans and Puerto Ricans are less educated because they consist of many recent immigrants with much less schooling. The young, American-born Hispanics usually have more education. Lack of proficiency in English has retarded the recent Hispanic immigrants' educational progress. As many as 25 percent of Hispanics in public schools speak little or no English, which has resulted in their having higher dropout rates than non-Hispanic students. Since 1968, however, many schools began to teach academic subjects such as math and science in Spanish while teaching English as a foreign language. But critics argue that bilingual education can slow down students' learning of English. Critics also fear that bilingual education, by fostering the use of Spanish, could hinder Hispanics' assimilation into mainstream American society and create a "Hispanic Quebec" in the United States (Davis, Haub, and Willette, 1983). An increasing number of schools—with backing from Hispanic parents themselves—are now teaching immigrant children in English only (Solorzano, 1984b).

Although Hispanics' economic status has improved in recent decades, they remain primarily clustered in lower-paying jobs. They earn about 70 percent of the amount made by Anglos. They also have a higher rate of unemployment than the general population. The proportion of Hispanic families falling below the poverty line is much larger than that of all white families. Hispanics are much less likely than Anglos of the same socioeconomic status to own homes. Again, Cubans fare better than Mexican-Americans and Puerto Ricans. Cubans are better represented in white-collar jobs and have lower jobless and poverty rates than the other Hispanic groups. This may explain why Cubans tend to vote Republican, while Mexican-Americans and Puerto Ricans are more likely to vote Democratic (Alter, 1983; Krivo, 1986).

In short, Hispanics as a group are still trailing behind the general population in social and economic well-being. However, the higher educational achievement of young Hispanics provides hope that more Hispanics—not just Cubans—will be joining the higher paid white-collar workforce in the future. Even with the present lag behind the general population, Hispanic-Americans have already achieved a great deal. They are "the wealthiest Hispanics in the world," which is the primary reason for the continuing heavy Hispanic immigration to the United States (Davis, Haub, and Willette, 1983). Hispanics are also already a growing force in American politics. They now have nine congressmen, two state governors (in New Mexico and Florida), and mayors in Denver, Miami, and San Antonio. Most importantly, the states with the largest concentration of Hispanics—California, Texas, New York, and Florida—are highly significant for both state and national elections. It is no wonder that Hispanics were eagerly courted by both parties during the 1988 presidential election.

Asian-Americans

During the 1970s there was a large influx of refugees from Southeast Asia, and today there are over 20 different Asian nationalities. The Chinese and Japanese are the largest and best-known groups of Asian-Americans. The Chinese first came during the gold rush on the West Coast in 1849, pulled by better economic conditions in America and pushed by economic problems and local rebellions in China (Kitano, 1981). Soon huge numbers of Chinese were imported to work for low wages, digging mines and building railroads. After these projects were completed, jobs became scarce and white workers feared competition from the Chinese. As a result, violence against the Chinese was sometimes brutal: "Not merely were men scalped and their pigtails cut off. Their ears were amputated. In more than one incident men were branded with hot irons" (Steiner, 1979). Special taxes were imposed on the Chinese, and they were prohibited from attending school, seeking employment, owning property, and bearing witness in court. In 1882 the Chinese Exclusion Act restricted Chinese immigration to the United States, and it stopped all Chinese immigration from 1904 to 1943. Many returned to their homeland.

Immigrants from Japan met similar hostility. They began to come to the West Coast somewhat later than the Chinese, also in search of better economic opportunities. At first they were welcomed as a source of cheap labor. But soon they began to operate small shops, and anti-Japanese activity grew. In 1906 San Francisco forbade Asian children to attend white schools. In response, the Japanese government negotiated an agreement whereby the Japanese agreed to stop emigration to the United States and President Theodore Roosevelt agreed to end harassment of the Japanese who were already here. But when the Japanese began to buy their own farms, they met new opposition. In 1913 California prohibited foreign-born Japanese from owning or leasing lands; other Western states followed suit. In 1922 the U.S. Supreme Court ruled that foreign-born Japanese could not become American citizens.

Worse came during World War II. All the Japanese, aliens and citizens, were evacuated from the West Coast and confined in concentration camps set up in isolated areas. They were forced to sell their homes and properties; the average family lost $10,000. The action was condoned even by the Supreme Court as a legitimate way of ensuring that the Japanese-Americans did not help Japan defeat the United States. Racism, however, was the real source of such treatment. After all, there was no evidence of any espionage or sabotage by a Japanese-American. Besides, German-Americans were not sent to concentration camps, although Germany was at war with the United States and there *were* instances of subversion by German-Americans. In 1976, though, President Ford proclaimed that the wartime detention of Japanese-Americans had been a mistake, calling it "a sad day in American history." In 1983 a congressional commission recommended that each surviving evacuee be paid $20,000. In 1987, when the survivors sued the government for billions of dollars in compensation, the solicitor general acknowledged that the detention was "frankly racist" and "deplorable." And in 1988 the Senate voted overwhelmingly to give $20,000 and an apology to each of the surviving internees (Molotsky, 1988).

Despite this history of discrimination, Chinese- and Japanese-Americans, along with Jewish Americans, are educationally and occupationally the most successful minorities in the United States today. They have higher percentages of high school and college graduates than whites. While Asians are only 1.5 percent of the U.S. population, they make up 8 percent of the student body at Harvard and 21 percent of the student body at the University of California at Berkeley. Among academics, scientists, and engineers, a higher proportion of Asians than whites have Ph.D.'s. Asian professors also publish more than their white colleagues. Moreover, Asian-Americans as a whole have a higher percentage of white-collar jobs and a higher median family income than whites. Thus they have been touted as America's "model minority" or "superminority." The success of Asian-Americans has been attributed to a traditional reverence for learning, parental pressure to succeed, the support of close-knit families, and cultural conditioning for hard work (Kasindorf, 1982; McGrath, 1983; Williams, 1984b; Schwartz, 1987). But white racism, ironically, has also spurred their relentless drive for success. As a Chinese-American says, "Many Asian parents, keenly aware of the obstacles that await their children, instill in them an ambitious drive to be better than everyone else because, in the words of my mother, 'that is the only way that the rest of society won't spit on you'" (Suh, 1986). Such a quietist—as opposed to confrontational—style of responding to racism seems rooted in the Asian culture. It encourages dealing with adversity by way of what the Japanese call *gambare:* simply doing one's best.

Nevertheless, Asian-Americans continue to suffer prejudice and discrimination. In 1986 the Commission on Civil Rights reported that "anti-Asian activity in the form of violence, vandalism, harassment, and intimidation continues to occur across the nation." In that year Asians were attacked in 50 percent of the racial incidents in Los Angeles County and victimized in 29 percent of the racial crimes in Boston, whose Asian-Americans make up less than 1 percent of the population. These attacks come mostly from the bottom of American society—working-class whites and ghetto blacks. But anti-Asian treatment also emanates from the top of society—big corporations and elite universities. Thus Asian college graduates in California find it difficult to get good jobs even though they have done exceptionally well in school. Many Asian-Americans already in private industry find that they lag in salary and promotion behind whites who have less education and fewer skills. At AT&T Bell Laboratories, where Asians make up nearly 10 percent of the 6300-person technical staff, 52 percent of the Asian employees have doctorates, compared with 29 percent of whites. Yet Asians have taken a median of 12 years to reach supervisory positions while whites have taken only 9 years. In 1982 only two Asians have been promoted to the company's 36 executive-director posts (Blackwell, 1982; McBee, 1984). In 1985, in the United States as a whole, Asians made up 4.3 percent of professionals and technicians but only 1.4 percent of officials and managers. White bosses frequently cite language deficiencies as an excuse for denying promotions. Privately, they stereotype the Asians as weak and incapable of handling people, although Japanese-managed companies are well known for outperforming American companies.

Officials at Berkeley, Stanford, Harvard, MIT, and other elite universities have also been charged with discriminating against Asian-Americans. At those universities, admission of Asian-Americans has stabilized or gone down, even though the number of qualified Asian applicants has risen substantially. Today the proportion of admissions among Asian applicants is one-third lower than that among whites, despite comparable or higher academic qualifications. The university officials are apparently fearful of being "swamped" by Asian-American students, often pointing out that there are already numerous Asian-Americans on their campuses. It is true that Asian-Americans are "overrepresented," comprising about 8 percent of the freshman classes, although they constitute less than 3 percent of the U.S. college-age population. But 8 percent is hardly high in comparison to the proportion of Jewish Americans, who make up 25 to 30 percent of the typical Ivy League student body. Yet they, too, constitute less than 3 percent of U.S. youth (Zinsmeister, 1987). The prejudice-driven fear of being swamped by Asian-American students recalls the past fear bout Jews dominating elite universities and about blacks taking over professional sports.

Now that they are being increasingly assimilated into the white culture, however, Asian-Americans have begun to assume a more confrontational stance on the issue of racism. They have complained to the U.S. Justice Department and to the press about discrimination at the universities. They have also sued companies for job discrimination. On the other hand, some corporations have begun to wise up, trying to correct past wrongs. Aware that the Asian nations are becoming ever more powerful in the global economy, they realize that they can get the competitive edge by making use of Asian-Americans' cultural backgrounds and language skills (Schwartz, 1987). Perhaps elite-university officials will follow suit by actively recruiting Asian-American students. These students generally excel in math and science—the very skills that the United States urgently needs today to retain its technological preeminence against the increasing challenge from Japan. But those universities still prejudicially consider such students "too narrowly focused." They continue to use the "academic plus factor" (demonstration of interest in sports, music, and other extracurricular activities) to discriminate against Asian-Americans in admissions.

Jewish-Americans

The first Jews came here from Brazil in 1654—their ancestors had been expelled from Spain and Portugal. Then other Jews arrived directly from Europe. Their numbers were very small, however, until the 1880s, when large numbers of Jewish immigrants began to arrive, first from Germany, then from Russia and other eastern European countries. Here they were safe from the pogroms (massacres) they had faced in Europe, but they did confront prejudice and discrimination.

During the 1870s, many American colleges refused to admit Jews. At the turn of the century, Jews often encountered discrimination when they applied for white-collar jobs. During the 1920s and 1930s, they were accused of being part of an international conspiracy to take over U.S. business and government, and **anti-Semitism**—prejudice or discrimination against Jews—became more widespread and overt. The president of Harvard University called for quotas against Jews. Large real estate companies in New Jersey, New York, Georgia, and Florida refused to sell property to Jews. The Chamber of Commerce of St. Petersburg, Florida, announced its intention to make St. Petersburg "a 100 percent American gentile city" (McWilliams, 1948). Many country clubs and other social and business organizations barred Jews from membership—and some still do.

The Jewish population in the United States rose as European Jews fled the Nazis' attempt to exterminate them. During and after World War II, anti-Jewish activities subsided, but they increased again during the 1960s—including 14 explosions, 9 fire bombings, 4 attempted bombings, and 47 bomb threats against Jewish property (Marden and Meyer, 1978). From 1964 to the present, however, anti-Semitism has declined sharply. Today a sizable minority (about one-third) of Americans still have some negative feelings toward Jews. They believe that Jews stick together too much, that Jewish employers hire other Jews only, and that Jews have too much power in business. But these negative images held by a minority pale in significance when compared with a substantial majority's favorable attitudes toward Jews: 81 percent consider Jews hard-working, 79 percent see them as family-oriented, 71 percent believe Jews to be religious, 64 percent regard them as warm and friendly, and 54 percent feel that Jews have contributed much to our cultural life. The sharp decline in anti-Semitism can further be seen in a number of behavioral changes. There are fewer overt episodes of vandalism and violence against Jews; the membership of anti-Semitic hate groups is extremely small; economic and social discrimination against Jews has practically disappeared; and non-Jews have elected a growing number of identifiable and avowed Jews to high public office (Lipset, 1987).

Despite the past discrimination against them, Jewish Americans as a group have been very successful. Fifty-eight percent of them have college degrees, compared with 29 percent of the total population. Fifty-three percent hold high-paying white-collar jobs, compared with 25 percent of all Americans. The median income of Jewish Americans is 1.7 times higher than the median for the U.S. population as a whole (Gallup Opinion Index, 1978; Sowell, 1981; Waxman, 1981; Rose, 1983). Their success may stem from the emphasis Jewish culture gives to education, from a self-image as God's chosen people, and from parental pressure to succeed. Not all Jews are successful, though. They still have a significant amount of poverty in their midst—over 15 percent of New York City's Jewish population is poor (Schaefer, 1984). This poverty is largely due to the recency of their arrival in America, as can be seen in the experiences of three types of Jews. Most of the poor Jews are Orthodox, the most recent immigrants in the United States. Conservative Jews, who are more successful, have been in this country longer. Reform Jews, the wealthiest of the group, have been here the longest (Waxman, 1981).

Leonard Bernstein, a world-famous and successful composer, pianist, and conductor. Because of their religion, Jews have historically encountered prejudice and murderous discrimination in European countries and subtler but pervasive discrimination in the United States. Nevertheless, in recent years anti-Semitism in America has been on the decline. Jews have become so successfully integrated into American society that they seem to have lost their Jewish identity, as shown by a substantial drop-off in affiliation with synagogues and in ritual observance.

While Jews as a whole are prosperous, they are not conservative or inclined to vote Republican, as other prosperous Americans are. Instead, they tend to be liberal—supporting welfare, civil rights, women's rights, civil liberties, and the like—and to vote Democratic. Perhaps this reflects their ability to identify with the dispossessed and oppressed, people like themselves when they came here to escape hunger and persecution in Europe (Hertzberg, 1984). Jews are so successfully assimilated into American society that they seem in danger of losing their Jewish identity. There has been a substantial decline in affiliation with synagogues and in ritual observance. Today about half of all Jews are not affiliated with a synagogue and only 20 percent attend synagogue regularly. Marriage with non-Jews has increased greatly, with well over half of all Jewish marriages outside New York involving a non-Jew. This has recently intensified the dispute among Jewish leaders over who is qualified to be a Jew. While Reform rabbis would accept as Jews children of intermarriages involving a Jewish father and non-Jewish mother, Orthodox and Conservative leaders would not (Zenner, 1985; Berger, 1986).

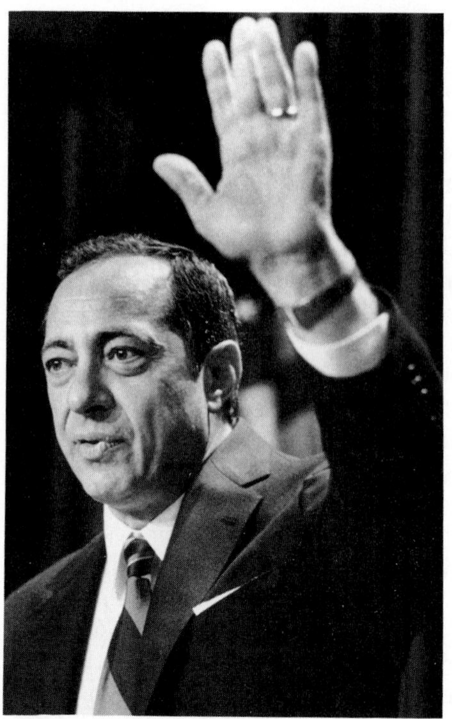

White ethnics generally come from Southern and Eastern Europe. Since they arrived in America very poor and uneducated, they were often regarded as inferior people and treated as such. Even as recently as the early 1970s they were stereotyped as lower-class and ultraconservative. The stereotype, however, has begun to fade as white ethnics move into the mainstream culture. Above is Mario Cuomo, an American of Italian origin who is the governor of New York.

White Ethnics

Jews were not the only European immigrants to face discrimination. From about 1830 to 1860, European immigration surged, and conflict grew between the immigrants—especially Catholic immigrants—and native-born Americans, the majority of whom were Protestants. The Irish immigrants, who tended to be both poor and Catholic, faced especially strong hostility. The notice "No Irish Need Apply" was commonplace in newspaper want ads.

Toward the end of the nineteenth century, there was a new wave of immigrants. These people came not from northern and western Europe, as most of the earlier immigrants had, but from southern and eastern Europe. They were Poles, Greeks, Italians. Many native-born Americans proclaimed these new immigrants to be inferior people and treated them as such. This belief was reflected in the National Origins Act of 1924. It enacted quotas that greatly restricted immigration from southern and eastern Europe, a policy that was not altered until 1965.

Today, Irish, Italians, Poles, Greeks, and others from eastern or southern Europe are called **white ethnics** (Novak, 1973). Even in the 1950s and 1960s, they faced jokes and stereotypes about "dumb Poles" or "criminal Italians"; the Ku Klux Klan included Catholics on its list of hated enemies; and there were countless instances of discrimination against white ethnics who sought high-status jobs. But they are not popularly considered a minority group. If they choose to give up their ethnic identity, most can pass fairly easily as members of the dominant group.

It was politics that brought white ethnics to national attention as a group. During the conflicts in the early 1970s over racial policies and the Vietnam War, liberals sometimes stereotyped white ethnics as racists and unthinking supporters of the war. Richard Nixon and other conservatives applauded them as hard-working patriots and sought their support as the "silent majority." Some spokespersons for white ethnics began to argue that policies designed to aid blacks were discriminating against white ethnics, because they, more than British Protestants, were expected to share their jobs, share their neighborhoods, and pay their taxes (Novak, 1973). Some argued, too, that the media, academics, and many politicians were prejudiced against white ethnics, ridiculing them and their cultures. In response, some white ethnics called on their fellows to assert their power and be proud of their heritage (Mikulski, 1970; Gambino, 1974).

Prejudice against white ethnics has been called "respectable bigotry." Liberal journalists often describe them as ultraconservative and prejudiced against blacks. The stereotype overlaps with the image of uneducated blue-collar workers. In fact, a rising number of white ethnics are middle class, and about half have attended college, the same proportion as many Anglo-Saxon Americans (Alba, 1981, 1985). Several surveys have further shown that white ethnics largely favor "liberal" policies such as welfare programs, antipollution laws, and guaranteed wages. They are also relatively free of racial prejudice, perhaps because they can easily identify with blacks since, like blacks, many have held low-paying manual jobs and been subjected to discrimination (Greeley and McCready, 1974). Most significantly, white ethnics by and large can no longer speak their immigrant parents' language, do not live in ethnic neighborhoods any more, and routinely marry into the dominant group. In short, they have become such an integral part of mainstream American society that it is difficult to tell them apart (Steinberg, 1981). Traces of prejudice toward some white ethnics still exist, though. Most Americans, for example, continue to associate Italian Americans with organized crime, although people of Italian background make up less than 1 percent of the 500,000 individuals involved in such activities (Giordano, 1987).

In conclusion, the status of all the minorities is generally better today than before. Getting closest to the American dream of success are Jews, Asians, and white ethnics, followed by blacks and Hispanics. Ironically, the original owners of this land—Native Americans—have experienced the least improvement in their lives. Of course, we still have a lot of prejudice and discrimination. But it is less than before, especially less than in South Africa, where racism is still an official policy. It is also less serious than in India and other countries, where a single incident of ethnic conflict often takes hundreds or thousands of lives. However, Americans tend to focus on their own current racial problem, without comparing it with how things were in the past or with similar problems in other societies. Interestingly, the lack of historical and cross-cultural concern may limit our understanding of race relations, but it can intensify our impatience with our own racial inequality. This is good for American society, because it compels us—especially the minorities among us—to keep pushing for racial equality. On the other hand, the historical and cross-societal analysis in this chapter, which shows some improvement in our race relations, is also useful. It counsels against despair, encouraging us to be hopeful that racial equality can be achieved. We could even expect blacks and other minorities to achieve economic parity with whites in the near future, if we could learn something from the recent experience of French-speaking Canadians (see box, p. 262).

QUESTIONS FOR DISCUSSION AND REVIEW

1. What different policies has the government adopted toward Native Americans, and why have they often been resisted?
2. Why are large numbers of black Americans still not fully equal?
3. Who are the different groups of Hispanic-Americans, and what factors unify all of them?
4. Why have Asian-Americans gained more educational and occupational success than other minority groups?
5. How have the experiences of Jewish-Americans differed from those of other white ethnic groups?
6. Does the "American Dilemma" still exist, or have American intergroup relations improved?

CHAPTER REVIEW

1. *Do racial classifications mean anything?* Biologically, they have little significance. They do not correspond to genetically distinct groups. Socially, however, racial classifications have had profound meaning, because people often think of themselves and respond to others in terms of race. *How does an ethnic group differ from a race?* People are categorized into races on the basis of their popularly perceived physical characteristics, but ethnic groups are based on shared cultural characteristics.

2. *What is a minority?* It is a group of people who share socially perceived physical or cultural characteristics and who are subjected to prejudice and discrimination.

UNDERSTANDING OTHER SOCIETIES

The Quiet Revolution in Quebec

For many years, French-speaking Canadians (also called francophones) had few job opportunities in Quebec, Canada, even though they made up the majority of the population in the province. But in 1960 this ethnic minority began to fight back against the discrimination they faced because of their language. Today the French Canadians' economic status has improved significantly. How can similar economic gains be obtained by the minorities in the United States?

Before 1960, impoverished French Canadian peasants moved to urban areas, especially Montreal, where they became an industrial proletariat. The majority worked in firms owned by Anglo-Canadians, British, or Americans and operated at management levels in English. "French on the factory floor, English in the boardroom" symbolized the ethnic division of labor in Quebec. French speakers were undereducated, and the small number who had access to higher education in French specialized in theology, law, and the humanities. There were few opportunities to achieve a French language education in engineering or business administration, and francophone businessmen enjoyed very limited access to capital. In 1961 French-owned firms employed only 22 percent of workers in manufacturing and accounted for a mere 15.4 percent of the value added in that sector in Quebec, although the province's population was 80 percent French.

Though French had equal status with English in the parliament and courts of the government of Canada, Canadian institutions, civil and military, operated almost entirely in English, and this included even the offices of federal government agencies in Quebec itself. Francophones held only 13 percent of the positions in the civil service of Canada in 1946, and few of these were in senior posts. French Canadians who wished to work in administrative, professional, or scientific roles in the corporate sector or in the government of Canada, even in Montreal, had to do so in English. The status of the French language was characterized by "inferior duties, small enterprises, low incomes, and low levels of education."

This situation generated considerable discontent among educated intellectuals and professionals who saw their legitimate career aspirations blocked. From their discontent emerged a new version of French Canadian nationalism oriented to modernization rather than mere survival. An important plank in this modern version of French Canadian nationalism was the assertion that Québécois—the new and more positive identity for French Canadians—were not condemned by cultural or genetic disabilities to economic marginality. In their national homeland they were entitled to full participation in the modern economy, if possible in the French language. They would use the powers of their provincial state to catch up and achieve economic equality.

In the provincial general elections of 1960 a group inspired by

Membership in a minority group is generally an ascribed status, and the members usually feel a strong sense of solidarity and marry other members of their group.

3. *Can a person be prejudiced without being discriminatory or be discriminatory without being prejudiced?* Yes, because prejudice and discrimination are not the same—one is an attitude and the other an act. Although the two are related, they do not always go together. *What is institutionalized discrimination?* The practice of discrimination in social institutions that is not necessarily known to everybody as discrimination.

4. *What are the sources and consequences of prejudice and discrimination?* Prejudice and discrimination may bring psychological rewards by allowing individuals to feel superior to minorities or to use them as a scapegoat. They can also be perpetuated by socializing agents. They may bring economic and political advantages to the dominant group as well. The consequences for the victims may range from atrocities to poverty to self-hatred, but prejudice and discrimination have not always been effective in pauperizing their victims.

5. *What are the ways in which a society can accept a mi-*

these views took over the government of Quebec and began to implement what was to become the "Quiet Revolution." Though this movement soon split into competing factions, all agreed that political action and the power of the state must be employed to secure economic justice for French Canadians and to put an end to the ethnic division of labor.

What have been the results of the Quiet Revolution a quarter century after its dramatic inception?

- French Canadians in Quebec have gained confidence that they can indeed participate and compete successfully in managerial roles in a modern economy and that they have a right to demand that the paramount language of work in Quebec should be French. The Quiet Revolution has secularized their predominantly Catholic society and fostered the aspirations and life-styles common to urbanized industrial communities.
- The expansion of Quebec's public services and state enterprises has spawned a large French-speaking technocratic and managerial bureaucracy which is now the core of the Québécois middle class. More than 98 percent of managerial positions in the government and state enterprise sectors are held by francophones.
- Ownership and control of the private sector of Quebec's modern economy remain predominantly in the hands of English speakers, Canadian and foreign, but French speakers have gained an expanding beachhead in higher-level employment and to a lesser extent in the ownership of assets. Enterprises which produce for and serve the Quebec market have been converted almost entirely to the French language, where French-speaking managers enjoy a pronounced advantage.
- As a consequence of the policies of the government of Quebec, ethnic French Canadians have expanded their participation in the modern economy, especially at the higher levels of enterprises. In the private sector French speakers now occupy 58 percent of the senior management positions and 65 percent of middle management posts. (In 1964 a roughly comparable figure for senior posts in the private sector was 14 percent.) In the early 1980s among younger management cadres in the private sector, those in the 20–29 year age cohort, no less than 83 percent are of French Canadian background, indicating that their proportion of managers is likely to increase markedly in the years ahead.

A careful observer has recently concluded that "the socioeconomic status of francophones in Quebec is almost similar to that of their anglophone fellow citizens. It is reasonable to conclude that given the presence of pan-Canadian corporate headquarters in Montreal and the inclusion of Quebec's economy in the economy of North America, the 'catching up' has for all practical purposes been completed."

Source: Adapted from Milton J. Esman, "Ethnic Politics and Economic Power," *Comparative Politics*, vol. 19, July 1987, pp. 396–398.

nority? There are three patterns of acceptance: assimilation, amalgamation, and cultural pluralism. *What are the ways in which a society can reject a minority?* Through segregation, expulsion, and extermination. *How can minorities respond to prejudice and discrimination?* They can accept or reject the idea that they are inferior, and they can accept or reject segregation. These choices produce four major responses: submission, withdrawal, separation, and integration.

6. *Are there indications that Native Americans still experience discrimination?* Their income, employment, housing, and health all fall below the national average. But they have been struggling to protect their land, water, and mineral resources. They have also been recapturing their proud traditions.

7. *Have the civil rights laws of the 1960s made a difference?* Yes, but they did not end inequality. Their positive effects can be seen in the increased educational achievement of blacks and the enlarged number of black elected officials. Remaining inequalities are most obvious in segregated, substandard housing and in high rates of unemployment and poverty among blacks.

8. *What are the origins of Hispanic-Americans?* The category lumps many people together—from the descendants of Mexicans and Puerto Ricans who became Americans because the United States took their lands in wars, to recent immigrants from Cuba and other Central and South American countries. Mexican-Americans are the largest group.

9. *How have Chinese- and Japanese-Americans fared in recent years?* Despite a history of discrimination against them, they, along with Jewish-Americans, are the most successful minorities in education, occupation, and income.

10. *What is the position of Jewish-Americans today?* Their educational, occupational, and economic status is very high. Their affluence, however, has not weakened their traditionally liberal stand on social and political issues.

11. *How did white ethnics come to be looked upon as a minority?* As a result of political conflict, liberals stereotyped white ethnics as racists while conservatives praised them as patriots. This drew national attention to them as a minority.

KEY TERMS

Amalgamation The process by which the subcultures of various groups are blended together, forming a new culture (p. 247).

Anti-Semitism Prejudice or discrimination against Jews (p. 259).

Assimilation The process by which a minority adopts the dominant group's culture, fading into the larger society (p. 246).

Behavioral assimilation The minorities' adoption of the dominant group's language, values, and behavioral patterns (p. 246).

Cultural pluralism The peaceful coexistence of various racial and ethnic groups, with each retaining its own subculture (p. 247).

De facto segregation Segregation sanctioned by tradition and custom (p. 248).

De jure segregation Segregation sanctioned by law (p. 248).

Discrimination An unfavorable action against individuals that is taken because they are members of some category (p. 240).

Ethnic group People who share a distinctive cultural heritage (p. 240).

Genocide Wholesale killing of a racial or ethnic group (p. 248).

Institutionalized discrimination The persistence of discrimination in social institutions, not necessarily known to everybody as discrimination (p. 243).

Jim Crow The system of laws made in the late nineteenth century in the South for segregating blacks from whites in all kinds of public and private facilities (p. 252).

Minority A group of people who share distinctive physical or cultural characteristics and who are subjected to prejudice and discrimination (p. 240).

Prejudice A negative attitude toward some category of people (p. 240).

Race People who share inherited physical characteristics and who are looked upon as forming a distinct biological group (p. 239).

Scapegoat The minority that the dominant group's frustrated members blame for their own failures (p. 244).

Segregation The spatial and social separation of a minority group from the dominant group, forcing the minority to live in inferior conditions (p. 248).

Structural assimilation Social condition in which minority groups cease to be minorities and are accepted on equal terms with the rest of society (p. 246).

White ethnics Americans of eastern and southern European origins (p. 260).

SUGGESTED READINGS

Farley, Reynolds. 1984. *Blacks and Whites: Narrowing the Gap?* Cambridge, Mass.: Harvard University Press. Shows, with data, where blacks have made headway toward equality with whites as well as where they have not.

Rose, Peter I. 1983. *Mainstream and Margins: Jews, Blacks, and Other Americans.* New Brunswick, N.J.: Transaction. A useful collection of sociological articles on racial and ethnic relations by a foremost authority.

Schuman, Howard, Charlotte Steeh, and Lawrence Bobo. 1985. *Racial Attitudes in America: Trends and Interpretations.* Cambridge, Mass.: Harvard University Press. An empirical analysis of how white support for the principle of racial equality has increased substantially but opposition to implementation of the principle has changed little.

Sowell, Thomas. 1983. *The Economics and Politics of Race: An International Perspective.* New York: William Morrow. Uses a cross-cultural analysis to explain why some American minorities have climbed the economic ladder more readily than others.

Wilson, William Julius. 1987. *The Truly Disadvantaged: The Inner City, the Underclass, and Public Policy.* Chicago: University of Chicago Press. A provocative analysis of how poor blacks get poorer, and a proposal for easing their plight.

11 Gender Roles and Inequalities

In the last 10 years American women have made notable advances in education, professions, politics, and other male-dominated careers. They still have a long way to go, however, before winning the battle for equality. Although rising numbers of women have moved into traditionally male professions, they still find most of the top positions held by men, positions such as chairman of the board, senior partner, and police chief. Most important, women still generally earn less than men for the same jobs with the same qualifications.

As soon as a baby is born, parents are likely to ask, "Is it a boy or girl?" They assume that its gender will make a big difference in its future. They may well be right because they expect and teach the baby to play a particular role. If it is a boy, they would have him acquire the male role—to grow up thinking and behaving "like a man." If it is a girl, they would get her to assume the female role—to grow up thinking and behaving "like a woman." **Gender roles,** then, are patterns of attitude and behavior that a society expects of its members because of their gender.

Gender roles, however, mean more than a mere difference between males and females. They also imply inequalities between the sexes. In virtually all societies, women are not only considered different but inferior. They are also taken advantage of. As we saw in Chapter 3 (Culture), the Yanomamo Indians still kill baby girls. Every few days in India there are reports of another "dowry death": 18-year-old Raj Yadav, for instance, was doused with gasoline and burned to death by her husband because neither she nor her parents could pay him an after-the-marriage dowry (Stevens, 1982). Every year in the United States more than 82,000 women are raped and four out of ten female workers are sexually harassed (Sacks and Rubin, 1982). A growing number of single women who live alone or with young children are also sexually harassed by landlords and their agents (Lee, 1987). In the Soviet Union, according to a feminist there, women "have been reduced to child-bearers, sex objects, and general workhorses subject to the degradation of queuing endlessly for foodstuffs while their men go out and get drunk" (Willey, 1980). American women, as we will see, also tend to get the short end of the stick educationally, economically, and politically.

In this chapter we first analyze the nature of gender roles and inequalities. We then examine their roots. Finally we take a look at the current trend toward gender equality.

GENDER ROLES

There are basic differences in what societies expect of men and women. Even when men and women hold the same jobs with the same status, they may face different expectations. In 1982 Svetlana Y. Savitskaya, a Soviet parachutist and pilot, became the second woman in space. But after her space vehicle docked with the orbiting Soviet space station, one male cosmonaut there greeted her by saying, "We've got an apron ready for you. . . . Of course, we have a kitchen for you; that'll be where you work" (Burns, 1982). Such traditional gender-role attitudes have declined in the United States, but many Americans still expect men to be "masculine" and women to be "feminine" (Morgan and Walker, 1983). What is the nature of these gender roles?

Masculine and Feminine in America

For many years American society assigned to men the role of breadwinner and to women the role of homemaker. The American man was expected to work out in the world, competing with other men in order to provide for his family. The "man's world" outside the home was viewed as a harsh and heartless jungle in which men needed strength, ambition, and aggression. "Woman's world" was the home, and her job was to comfort and care for husband and children, maintaining harmony and teaching her children to conform to society's norms.

This basic division of labor has been accompanied by many popular stereotypes of what men and women are supposed to be, and to some extent these stereotypes persist. Men are supposed to be ambitious and aggressive; women, shy, easily intimidated, and passive. Men should be strong and athletic; women, weak and dainty. It is bad form for men, but not for women, to worry about their appearance and aging. Men should hold back their emotions and must not cry, but women are expected to be emotional, even to cry easily. Men are expected to be sexually aggressive and experienced; women, sexually passive and inexperienced. Men are supposed to be independent, fit to be leaders; women are believed to be dependent, in need of male protection. Men are expected to be logical, rational, and objective; women, inconsistent and intuitive (Chafetz, 1978).

These are the traits that most Americans have long associated with each gender. They represent both *stereotypes* about how men and women behave and *expectations* about how they should behave. Today some Americans are more likely than others to hold or reject them. Among women, for example, those who are relatively young, unmarried, well educated, gainfully employed, or who have strong feelings of personal competence tend to reject the traditional gender-role attitudes (Morgan and

Walker, 1983). Among men, lower-class whites are more traditional in gender-role outlook than middle- and upper-class whites. But blacks, especially those who identify themselves as middle class, are more traditional than whites. Blacks tend more to agree with the notion that "most men are better suited emotionally for politics than are most women" or that "women should take care of running their homes and leave running the country to men." This has been attributed to the black nationalism of the 1960s and early 1970s, which often encouraged black men "to take charge of their families, protect their women from white male sexual exploitation, and take on positions of leadership and power in the black community and the larger society" (Ransford and Miller, 1983).

While people may consciously reject the traditional gender roles, they do tend to behave otherwise. Research has shown, for example, that women are more likely to be passive and men aggressive in a number of ways. In interactions between the sexes, the male is more likely to initiate interactions and the female to respond. During a conversation, men tend more to touch women than vice versa. When a man opens the door for women, they tend to say "thank you" or smile their appreciation. But men tend to look confused if a woman opens the door for them, because they are not accustomed to being women's passive beneficiaries (Ventimiglia, 1982). When attacked, women are more inclined than men to withdraw instead of launching a counterattack (Maccoby and Jacklin, 1975). Women are also more "social," more likely to seek security and intimacy in the company of others. As research has shown, there are more women than men calling up a same-sex friend just to talk (Sherman and Haas, 1984). Women are also more likely than men to hug, kiss, or soothe an infant (Rossi, 1984). Other studies have suggested that women are more concerned than men about their physical appearance. Women tend to think of their selves as residing in their bodies; men, in their heads (Stoll, 1978).

Gender Roles in Other Cultures

People have long viewed gender roles as natural, innate, God-given. Indeed, the traditional gender roles in the United States can also be found in many other societies. Studies of other cultures, however, challenge the idea that these roles are universal and dictated by nature.

Many years ago Margaret Mead (1935) found striking differences among three tribes in New Guinea. Among one of them, the Arapesh, both men and women behaved in what many Americans would consider a feminine way. They were passive, gentle, and home-loving. The men were just as enthusiastic as the women about taking care of babies and bringing up children. The Mundugumor were just the opposite: both sexes showed what many Americans consider masculine traits. Both men and women were competitive, aggressive, and violent. In the third tribe, the Tchambuli, there was a sharp difference between male and female roles, and they were the opposite of those traditional in the West. Tchambuli men were emotional, passive, and dependent. They took care of children, did housework, and used cosmetics. The Tchambuli women were the bosses at home. They were the economic providers, doing the hunting, farming, and fishing.

The enormous differences in the gender roles of these three cultures led Mead to conclude:

> Human nature is almost unbelievably malleable, responding to cultural conditions. . . . Standardized personality differences between the sexes are of this order, cultural creations to which each generation, male and female, is trained to conform.

Mead may have overemphasized the power of culture. When George Murdock (1937) analyzed the division of labor in 224 societies, he found a more consistent pattern of gender differences than Mead's analysis suggested. The men in these societies typically did the work that needed muscle power or travel away from home—such as hunting, herding, and boat building. The women generally performed work that required less strength and gave more immediate support to the family—cooking, weaving, gathering fuel, and the like.

Still, Murdock found significant exceptions to this pattern. In 60 percent of the societies women typically carried heavy objects; these tasks were assigned exclusively to men in only 13 percent of the societies studied. Moreover, in many societies, physically undemanding tasks such as trading and fishing were mostly "men's work." In fact, no activity is the preserve of just one sex. Practically any task that is typically done by one sex in some societies is done by the other sex in some other societies (see Table 11.1).

Table 11.1 The Sexual Division of Labor

In most societies men do the heavier physical work and women the lighter work. There are, however, significant exceptions. In some societies the women's work is strenuous, and in other societies the men's job is light. Thus the tasks men or women should perform vary from one society to another.

Activity	Men (usually or always)	Either Sex	Women (usually or always)	Number of Societies
Making weapons	100%	0%	0%	122
Pursuing sea mammals	100	0	0	35
Hunting	100	0	0	179
Building boats	95	4	1	100
Mining and quarrying	94	3	3	38
Working in stone	94	3	3	75
Trapping small animals	94	3	3	148
Lumbering	92	2	6	118
Fishing	84	12	4	158
Herding	84	7	9	55
Building houses	74	15	11	160
Clearing land for farming	73	13	14	130
Trade	69	18	13	114
Making and tending fire	18	19	63	133
Carrying heavy objects	13	27	60	130
Making baskets	22	8	70	126
Making mats	20	7	73	89
Weaving	22	2	76	96
Gathering fruits and nuts	14	14	72	106
Gathering fuel	16	7	77	141
Preserving meat and fish	9	9	82	108
Manufacturing clothing	12	6	82	127
Gathering herbs, roots, and seeds	9	11	80	101
Cooking	3	4	93	201
Carrying water	5	4	91	138
Grinding grain	4	4	92	138

Source: Reprinted from *Social Forces* (15, May 1937). "Comparative data on the division of labor by sex" by George Murdock. Copyright © The University of North Carolina Press.

On the whole, cross-cultural studies suggest that there is a tendency for men and women to do different types of work, but that the precise definition of which sex should do what varies from one society to another. In most societies, however, men are assigned the primary role of breadwinner and women the secondary role of homemaker. The public world is considered a man's domain and the private world a woman's. "Men's work" is more highly valued than "women's work." Even in most of the egalitarian hunting-gathering societies (see Chapter 4: Social Structure), where women often produce more than half of the food supply by gathering nuts, fruits, and plants, men still dominate women (Tavris and Wade, 1984; but see Chafetz, 1984). (Those societies seem to regard the male job of hunting for animal food far away from home as more important—perhaps because meat is a rare resource—and more difficult than the female task of gathering plant foods near the home.) Thus male dominance over females is nearly universal. As Kay Martin and Barbara Voorhies (1975) have observed, "A survey of human societies shows that positions of authority are almost always occupied by males."

QUESTIONS FOR DISCUSSION AND REVIEW

1. What are gender roles, and what traits do most Americans associate with them?
2. How do gender roles in other cultures differ from American conceptions of masculinity and femininity?
3. What pattern of gender roles appears most often in other cultures?

A Ghanaian man weaving cloth. Is weaving a man's or a woman's job? Practically any economic task that is done by one sex ("woman's work") in some societies is done by the other sex ("man's work") in other societies. The task itself is not important in identifying it as a "male" or "female" job; instead, it is whether doing the job makes the individual the primary breadwinner. If the task provides the major source of income, it is likely to be considered an appropriate occupation for a man, and women who want to do it may encounter opposition.

GENDER INEQUALITIES

At one time or another, laws have denied women "the right to hold property, to vote, to go to school, to travel, to borrow money, and to enter certain occupations" (Epstein, 1976). In recent years, there has been significant movement toward gender equality, but large inequalities remain, even in the United States. They are evident in education, in the workplace, and in politics. Underlying these inequalities is **sexism**—prejudice and discrimination against women.

Sexism

A major foundation of sexism is the belief that women are somehow inferior to men. It can be found in all the world's major religions. Buddhism and Confucianism instruct wives to obey their husbands. The Muslim Koran states, "Men are superior to women on account of the qualities in which God has given them preeminence." The Bible says that after Eve had eaten the forbidden fruit and given it to Adam, God told her: "In pain you shall bring forth children, yet your desire shall be for your husband, and he shall rule over you" (Genesis 3:16). And St. Paul noted: "For man . . . is the image and glory of God, but woman is the glory of man. For man was not made from woman, but woman from man. Neither was man created for woman, but woman for man" (1 Corinthians 11:7–9). This may explain why prejudice against women is greater among white Protestants, more religious Baptists, and fundamentalist Protestants than among unchurched whites, less religious Baptists, and nonfundamentalists. The former are more likely to support the idea that "women should take care of running their homes and leave running the country up to men," to agree with the notion that a wife should not expect her husband to help around the house, and to reject the idea of a woman running for president even if she is qualified for the job (Peek and Brown, 1980; Powell and Steelman, 1982; Thornton, Alwin, and Camburn, 1983).

Those who turn to psychology or psychiatry instead of religion for guidance have met sexism, too. A survey of 79 mental health professionals in 1978 found that they applied different definitions of mental health to men and women. A healthy, mature woman was characterized as submissive, dependent, unadventurous, easily influenced, excitable in a minor crisis, susceptible to hurt feelings, and conceited about her appearance. A man with these characteristics would be considered unhealthy and immature (Jaggar and Struhl, 1978). In fact, according to the bible of psychiatric diagnosis, *Diagnostic and Statistical Manual,* such female stereotypes as self-dramatization, overreaction, vanity, and dependence are symptoms of "histrionic personality disorder" (Herbert, 1983). Psychologists and psychotherapists tend to describe men positively—as independent, courageous, and the like—and women negatively—as marked by "sexual timidity" and "social anxiety" (Chafetz, 1978). Their descriptions of male and female traits, like popular stereotypes, often imply that women are inferior (Parker and Parker, 1979).

Sexism is found among women as well as men, as a classic study by Phillip Goldberg (1968) illustrated. Goldberg asked female college students to rate scholarly articles for usefulness, competence, practicality, writing style, and the like. All the students read the same articles. But some were told that the author was "John T. McKay"; others, that the author was "Joan T. McKay." The women who were told the articles were written by "John" gave them high marks; those who believed they were written by "Joan" gave the articles low marks—though the articles were identical. Other researchers found that university administrators gave different responses to the same resumes, depending on whether the author was identified as male or female. Not surprisingly, they judged the fictitious male professors more qualified than the female ones—although the resumes cited the same education and job experience (Fidell, 1970). In a more recent experiment, subjects were asked to view either a man or a woman speaking on chess, interior decorating, or skiing. Although the speakers had read from identical scripts, both male and female subjects who had seen male speakers recalled more information than those who had seen female speakers. The subjects had paid male speakers more careful attention because they expected men to be more competent, intelligent, and knowledgeable than women (Bridgwater, 1980).

Because of sexism, women who are successful in careers outside the home have long been considered deviant. They could expect to pay for this success by both facing the resentment of others and experiencing failure in traditional female pursuits, such as love and marriage. In another classic study, Matina Horner (1969) found that many women indeed have been led to believe that success for them could have high costs. Horner asked 90 college women to write a story about a fictitious woman called Anne who discovers that she has finished at the top of her first-year medical school class. All Horner's subjects had excellent academic records. But nearly two-thirds of them predicted that Anne would become unpopular, unmarriageable, lonely, or otherwise miserable. One wrote that when Anne learns she is at the top of her class, she "starts proclaiming her surprise and joy. Her fellow classmates are so disgusted with her behavior that they jump on her and beat her. She is maimed for life." Another wrote: "Anne feels guilty. . . . She will finally have a nervous breakdown and quit medical school and marry a successful young doctor." In Horner's phrase, the women suffered "fear of success." More recent studies have indicated that fewer women today suffer from this fear—perhaps because gender-role stereotypes were vigorously attacked during the 1970s (Tresemer, 1974). But there are still many sexist men who refuse to support even their own wives' high career aspirations, causing highly educated professional women to have the second-highest rate of separation and divorce among all women in the United States (Houseknecht et al., 1984; Baruch and Barnett, 1986). Apparently, these sexist men feel threatened by their up-and-coming wives. Women, too, can feel threatened if a female co-worker tries to compete with the male majority by being assertive. In one study, 93 male and female managers were asked to listen to a recording of a mild dispute between a male and female manager. Ironically, the female subjects described the woman as more aggressive, "pushy," or unfeminine than the male subjects did (Mathison, 1986).

Despite recently increased respect for women, there remain many subtle expressions of sexism. Studies of nonverbal interaction between the sexes reveal that men often unconsciously exhibit their superiority to women—and women their inferiority. When talking to a man, women typically give such low-status signals as smiling, nodding, holding their arms to their bodies, or keeping their legs together. Men are more likely to use high-status gestures by smiling only occasionally, holding their heads still, and assuming asymmetrical, relaxed body postures (Cory, 1979). Added to this sexist pattern of body language is women's tendency to speak more politely than men, being more careful to say "please" and "thank you" as they are expected to (Kemper, 1984). When men participate in a small-group discussion with women, men tend to have their arguments and decisions accepted more often (Inwald and Bryant, 1981).

Sexism may produce inequality between the sexes by unconsciously biasing evaluations of people's work. When sexism takes the active form of discrimination against women, it obviously creates inequality. Accord-

Woman working in a garment factory. Sexism—prejudice and discrimination against women—springs from the traditional idea that women are somehow inferior to men. This has led to the disparagement of the role women play in society. Thus the majority of working women have been forced to work in low-status jobs for low pay. Even when women hold jobs comparable to those of men, they are frequently paid less than men.

ing to one study, at least 85 percent of the difference between men's and women's earnings is the result of discrimination (Featherman and Hauser, 1976). More recent research has shown that at each level of occupational skill men receive higher pay than women (Miller and Garrison, 1982). Sexism may also foster inequality in a less direct way. If women have been socialized to feel inferior, they may lower their expectations, aiming to achieve less than they otherwise might. Whether through overt discrimination or traditional gender-role socialization, sexism has brought gender inequalities in education, occupation, and politics.

Education

For a long time women were deprived of the opportunities for higher education. They were barred from many colleges and universities, especially graduate and professional schools, far into the 1960s. In general, the more prestigious the institutions, the more strongly they discriminated against women. Harvard, for example, was one of the last to give up sex discrimination. It began to admit women to its graduate business program only as recently as 1963.

The women's movement has made some headway in getting the government to pass laws against sex discrimination in the 1970s. Collectively known as Title IX, the laws require that schools (1) eliminate sex-segregated classes such as all-girl home economics or all-boy shop classes, (2) avoid sex discrimination in admissions and financial aid, (3) end sexist hiring and promotion practices, and (4) provide more opportunities for women's sports. Title IX has given a substantial push to equality in education. This is particularly evident in athletics. In the last ten years, the number of high school girls participating in sports has jumped by 600 percent, and the proportion of college athletic budgets allocated to women's sports has skyrocketed by 1000 percent—from less than 2 percent before Title IX to 20 percent recently. Nevertheless, there is still significant inequality. After all, women's sports get only about 20 percent of the budget, while the remaining 80 percent goes to men's sports (Schaefer, 1984).

Inequality can also be seen in other aspects of education. In high school, girls generally get better grades than boys and are more likely to graduate. In recent years women have also become a little more likely than men to attend college and earn bachelor's or master's degrees. But they are still less likely to receive degrees from graduate or professional schools (see Table 11.2). While starting out with superior academic records, women fall further behind at higher levels of education. In addition, most women undergraduates continue to major in the liberal arts while more men study science, engineering, business administration, and other subjects that will lead to high-paying occupations (Coleman and Cressey, 1987; Census Bureau, 1988).

Inequalities persist, too, on the faculties and in the administration of the nation's colleges and universities. In the early 1980s, the proportion of women on the faculty in most disciplines had not exceeded the level achieved during the 1920s, which was less than 30 per-

Table 11.2 The Gender Gap in Education

In recent years women have caught up with men in getting college degrees, but they are still trailing behind at higher levels of educational achievement.

Educational achievement, 1985	Males	Females
Completing high school	44%	56%
Bachelor's degrees	49	51
Master's degrees	50	50
Ph.D. degrees	64	36
Degrees from law schools	62	38
Degrees from medical schools	70	30

Source: Digest of Educational Statistics, 1987, Washington, D.C.: U.S. Government Printing Office, 1987, pp. 4, 172, 194.

cent. Various studies have consistently shown that, compared with their male colleagues, female academics are less likely to be hired, more concentrated in the lower ranks of institutions, and less likely to be promoted. They are also paid substantially less. At the same time there is evidence that women with Ph.D.'s are just as productive as men in generating research, that female Ph.D. recipients have slightly greater ability than men, and that there is no significant difference in the teaching effectiveness of men and women (Bienen, Ostriker, and Ostriker, 1977; Grant and Snyder, 1984).

Jobs and Money

For years inequality in education has contributed to inequality in the job market. Economic inequality between the sexes was increased too because many people considered housekeeping and child care the only real career for a woman—a job was for women waiting to get married, or for women who could not "find" a husband. Women who did work often had less experience, as well as less education, than men. Consequently, women lagged far behind men in employment and earnings.

These sexual differences have decreased over the years. Forty years ago, only 30 percent of women were employed outside the home. In 1986, more than half (55 percent) of all women were employed, including about 57 percent of those married and with children under 6 years old (Census Bureau, 1988). But the place of women in the workforce is still very far from equal.

Women typically hold lower-status, lower-paying jobs than men. In 1983, for example, 18 percent of employed men were executives, administrators, and managers, but only 7 percent of employed women held these positions (Census Bureau, 1985). Women are also underrepresented in such high-status professions as medicine, law, engineering, and college teaching. On the other hand, women are overrepresented in such low-paying jobs as nursing, public-school teaching, and secretarial work (see Table 11.3). These traditionally female occupations, known in sociology as **women's ghettos,** are subordinate to positions usually held by men. Thus nurses are subordinate to doctors, schoolteachers to principals, and secretaries to executives.

Even when women hold the same jobs as men or have comparable skills and training, they tend to earn less. As a whole, American women earn only about 68 percent of what men make when they do about the same kind of work. Female clerical workers earn only three-fifths as much as males with the same jobs; saleswomen earn only two-fifths of what salesmen make; and female managers' salaries are only half of male managers'. Women often make less than men who have less education. In 1986, for example, the median salary for female college graduates was $21,362, less than the salary of an average male high-school graduate. In fact, the average woman made only slightly more than an average male high-school dropout—$19,241. Even when men and women are matched for age, experience, skill, and time on the job, women earn much less. The gender differ-

Table 11.3 The Women's Ghettos

Despite their increased entrance into the labor force, women are still concentrated in low-status, low-paying positions. Among such jobs are their percentages held by women:

	1972	1986
Secretaries	99%	99%
Registered nurses	98	98
Receptionists	97	97
Child-care workers	96	97
Bank tellers	90	92
Librarians	83	86
Billing clerks	83	85
Waiters, waitresses	92	85
Elementary-school teachers	81	85
Health technicians	72	84
Retail sales clerks	69	69

Source: Census Bureau, *Statistical Abstract of the United States,* 1984, pp. 419–420; Census Bureau, *Statistical Abstract of the United States,* 1988, pp. 376–377.

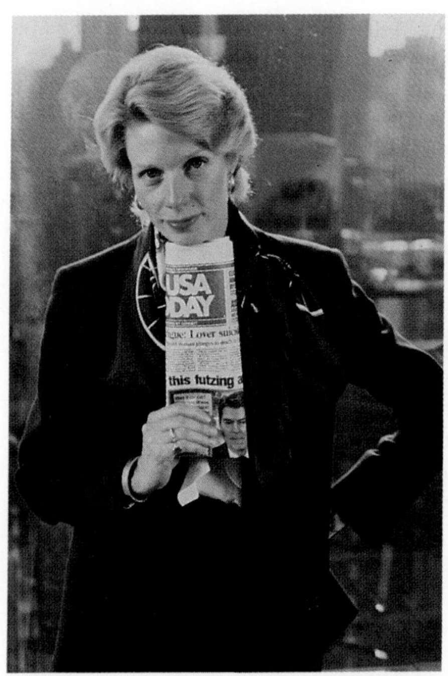

Thanks to the women's liberation movement, a few women such as *USA Today* publisher Cathleen Black (above) have climbed to the top of the ladder of success, a place previously reserved for men. At the same time, though, the positions of many more women have declined sharply, resulting in the "feminization of poverty." Most of these women are single parents. Their number has been growing so fast that they and their children account for three-fourths of the poor today.

ence in earnings has held steady for the last 20 years not only in the United States but in other industrialized societies as well (Treiman and Roos, 1983; Gest, 1984; Welniak and Henson, 1984; Gamarekian, 1987; Census Bureau, 1988).

Economic inequality between men and women is even greater than those figures suggest. The women's movement opened up to some the ladder of succes previously reserved for males, but at the same time the position of many women declined to the point where the phrase "feminization of poverty," coined by sociologist Diana Pearce in 1978, may well become a household expression. A major cause is the rapidly increasing number of families headed by single women. In one year in the late 1970s, when 10 percent of American families fell below the poverty line, 40 percent of families headed by single women were poor (Rich, 1982). The number of these poor families has been growing so fast that today three-fourths of the poor are single women and their children (Peterson, 1987).

Politics

Theoretically, women can easily acquire more political power than men. After all, women voters outnumber men—with 54 percent of the voting population being women. In addition, most of the volunteer workers in political campaigns are women. Yet until recently many women felt that politics is a male activity, that women should not plunge into the dirty world of politics. Sexism also tended to entrap women in a Catch-22 situation to squash their political ambition. If a woman campaigned vigorously, she was likely to be regarded as a neglectful wife and mother. If she claimed to be an attentive wife and mother, she was apt to be judged incapable of devoting energy to public office. But a man in a comparable situation—as a vigorous campaigner or a devoted husband and father—was considered to have a great political asset (Epstein, 1976).

Not surprisingly, women have often helped men get elected, with the result that men have dominated the political process—and women as well. In recent years, however, a growing number of women have assumed political leadership. Since 1980 the percentage of women who vote has surpassed that of men. Differences in the voting patterns of men and women have emerged, with women being more liberal and more likely to favor candidates who are peace-oriented in foreign affairs and caring on social programs and economy (Morrow, 1984b). Women have been developing into an important political force, but they still have a long way to go before reaching equality with men. In 1984 women made up 54 percent of the voting population, but they captured only 5 percent of all public offices. In that same year, just 13 percent of state legislators were women, and there was only one female governor. Only 6 percent of the members of the U.S. House of Representatives and 2 percent of the U.S. Senate were women (Tift, 1984). The number of women in federal and state legislatures has been increasing, though. There are now also more women serving as judges, mayors, city council members, and executives in government agencies. Women seem likely to occupy more and more positions of political leadership in the future.

QUESTIONS FOR DISCUSSION AND REVIEW

1. What beliefs about women give sexism its foundation?
2. What is the current status of women in educational institutions?
3. Why have jobs traditionally reserved for women led to the creation of women's employment ghettos?
4. How might the growing success of women in politics help end sexual discrimination in other areas?

SOURCES OF GENDER ROLES AND INEQUALITIES

Cross-cultural studies of gender roles reinforce a conclusion we reached in an earlier chapter: to explain human behavior, we must look at both biology and culture. The variations in the gender roles established by human societies suggest that these roles are learned, not inherited. But why are women everywhere unequal? Does biology set up some basic inferiority? What gender differences are inherited, and how are gender roles and inequalities related to these differences?

Biological Constraints

There are genetic differences between males and females: males have two different sex **chromosomes,** XY, and females have two similar chromosomes, XX. Males inhert the X chromosome for their mothers and the Y from their fathers, and females get one X chromosome from each of their parents. While a particular composition of sex chromosomes determines a person's sex as a male or female, there is no guarantee that a genetically male person (with XY chromosomes) will look like a man or a genetically female person (with XX) will look like a woman.

Whether a person will develop the appropriate sex characteristics—say, facial hair or breasts—depends on the proportion of male and female sex **hormones.** If a man has more female than male hormones, he would end up with breasts rather than facial hair. If a woman has more male than female hormones, she would have facial hair instead. This is why people who have undergone sex-change operations are injected with a lot of hormones appropriate to their new sex. But in normal men the proportion of male hormones is greater, and in normal females the proportion of female hormones is greater. It is clear that men and women differ chromosomally and hormonally.

The chromosomal and hormonal differences lie behind other biological differences between the sexes. Stimulated by the greater amount of male sex hormones, men are on the average bigger and stronger than women. Yet due to their lack of a second X chromosome, men are less healthy. Men are susceptible to more than 30 types of genetic defects, such as hemophilia and color blindness, which are very rare in women. At birth, males are more likely to die. During the first month after birth, males are much more likely to have one of over 187 physical abnormalities, such as day blindness and progressive deafness. Throughout life males tend to mature more slowly. They also die at a younger age (Stoll, 1978).

There are also sex differences in brain structure. Neuroscience research has established that the left hemisphere, or half, of the brain controls speech, and the right hemisphere directs spatial tasks such as object manipulation. There is more specialization in the male's brain, so that he tends to use just one hemisphere for a given task, while the female tends to use both at the same time. But the male experiences greater cell growth in his spatial perception-dominated hemisphere while the female does so in her language-dominated hemisphere (Restak, 1979; Goy and McEwen, 1980).

The differences in brain structure and hormonal production may have contributed to some behavioral differences between the sexes. Thus female babies are more sensitive than males to certain sounds, particularly their mother's voices, and are more easily startled by loud noises. Female infants are also more quiet, while males are more vigorous and inclined to explore, run, and bang in their play. Female infants talk sooner, have larger vocabularies, and are less likely to develop speech problems—stuttering, for example, is several times more prevalent among males. In the early years of school, girls are superior not only in verbal abilities but also in overall intelligence, while boys excel in spatial performances such as mental manipulation of objects, map reading, and mathematical reasoning. When asked how they have mentally folded an object, boys tend to say simply "I folded it in my mind" but girls are more likely to produce elaborate verbal descriptions. Women are more sensitive to touch, odor, and sound. They show greater skill in picking up peripheral information as well as nuances of facial expression and voice. They are six times more likely than men to sing in tune (Rossi, 1984; Trotter, 1987).

In short, nature makes men and women different, but these differences do not add up to female inferiority. On some measures—such as physical health and early verbal ability—females as a group seem superior to males, and by other measures—especially size and strength—males as a group are superior. Nevertheless, males' dominance over females seems rooted in their larger size and strength. As Penn Handwerker and Paul Crosbie (1982) found in their experimental study of social interaction in small groups, taller people tend to be dominant over shorter ones.

The Role of Culture

These biological differences between males and females seem logically related to the division of labor between the sexes. If men are bigger and stronger, then it makes sense for them to do the work that requires strength. And assigning women the care of the home and children may be a logical extension of their biological ability to bear and nurse children.

However, there are limitations to biological constraints on gender roles and inequalities. Since women have smaller hands and greater finger agility than men, they are logically more fit to be dentists and neurosurgeons. Yet men dominate these high-paying professions because our culture has long defined them as "men's work." Indeed, as we have seen, there are many variations from culture to culture in the details of sex roles. In breadth and depth, social inequalities between men and women exceed by far their biological differences. Especially in industrial societies, biology sets few real constraints, because machines have taken over much of the work demanding physical strength. The cultural definition of gender roles, in fact, exercises awesome power. Because American culture has defined being a physician as men's work, for example, the majority of our doctors are males, and they are among the highest paid professionals. By contrast, in the Soviet Union, where medicine is a "feminine" profession, most of the doctors are women and they are generally paid "women's wages"—less than two-thirds of what skilled blue-collar workers make (Sullerot, 1971). Thus biology may promote the broad outlines of a sexual division of labor, but cultures draw the actual boundaries.

Furthermore, most of the biological differences between males and females (except for those involving reproduction) do not refer to absolute differences between individuals but to where the average male or female is likely to fall on some continuum. There are, after all, many boys who are smaller and weaker than the average girl. Nonetheless, they may conform to a culturally defined gender role, showing a typically "masculine" interest in sports and mechanical toys.

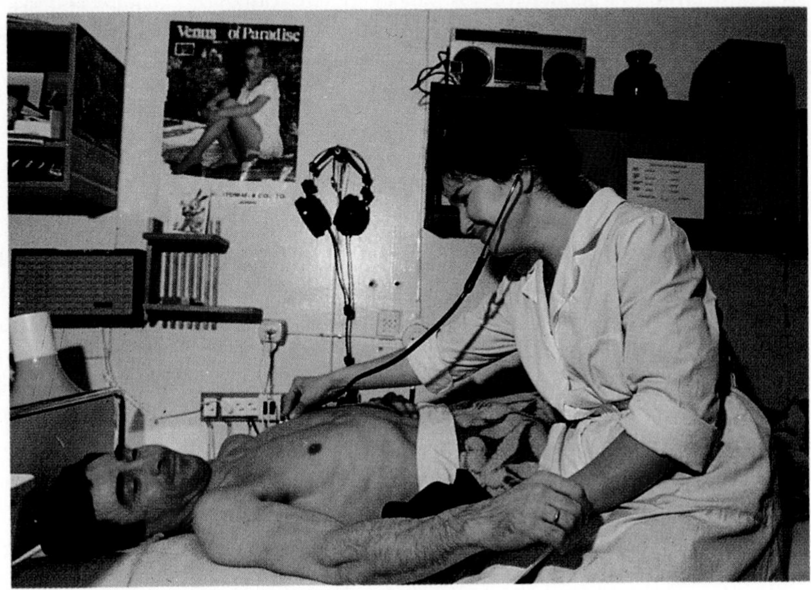

Soviet woman doctor with a male patient. Gender roles vary from one culture to another. What is considered "men's work" in one culture may be regarded as "women's work" in another. But when a field is staffed primarily by women, it is granted lower status than if it were staffed by men. In the United States, medicine is considered a man's profession. Being a doctor is a high-status profession, and doctors are highly paid. By contrast, in the Soviet Union, medicine is a woman's profession and is accorded relatively low status and low pay.

The complicated relationship between the biological characteristics of the sexes and their eventual gender roles is perhaps best illustrated by cases in which a person's sex was ambiguous or mislabeled at birth. In one such case, 38 boys in the Dominican Republic had been raised as girls because they had had an enzyme deficiency that made their external genitals look female when they were born. But at puberty, when they developed the normal male characteristics, they changed their sexual identity, taking on the male role (Kolata, 1979). In other cases, however, adults happily maintained the sex role they had been assigned at birth, even after they had developed characteristics of the opposite sex during puberty (Money and Ehrhardt, 1972). In these cases culture, not biology, seemed to have the last word.

Obviously, biology sets males and females apart. It seems to predispose us to behave in certain ways. But society does much to accentuate gender differences. As Alice Rossi (1984) points out, women may have the natural tendency to handle an infant with tactile gentleness and soothing voice and men may have the natural tendency to play with an older child in a rough-and-tumble way, but these tendencies are often exaggerated through socialization. Thus we are born male or female, but we learn to become men or women.

According to social learning theory, children learn their gender roles by imitating older people of the same sex. After frequently engaging in a gender-stereotyped activity such as baseball, a boy will develop a stable gender identity: "I do boy things. Therefore I must be a boy." But according to cognitive development theory, gender identity is the cause rather than the product of gender-role learning. The boy has first learned from his parents that he is a male. Then he seeks to act and feel like one: "I am a boy. Therefore I want to do boy things."

Socialization

The learning of gender roles is part of socialization. In whatever way a society defines gender roles, its socializing agents pass that definition from generation to generation. In the United States the family, schools, peer groups, and mass media all teach important lessons about these roles.

The Family Newborn babies do not even know their gender, much less how to behave like boys or girls. Thanks to their parents, children very quickly develop their sexual identity and learn their gender roles. Right from birth, babies are usually treated according to their gender. At birth, boys tend to be wrapped in blue blankets and girls in pink. When they are a little older, baby boys are handled more roughly than girls; boys are bounced around and lifted high in the air, but girls are cuddled and cooed over. Boys are often left alone to explore their environment, but girls are protected against any possible accident. Boys are given toy trains, play trucks, and building sets, while girls are given dolls, toy vacuum cleaners, and miniature kitchen appliances. Boys build houses and girls play house. Mothers fuss about how pretty their little girls should look, but they generally care less about their little boys' appearance (Richardson, 1981).

When learning to talk, children become more aware of the gender difference. They are taught to differentiate "he" and "his" from "she" and "hers." When they are older, they sense that males are more important than females, as the word "man" is used to refer to the entire human race as if women did not exist (e.g., "the future of man" rather than "the future of humanity").

Boys are taught to behave "like men," to avoid being "sissies." They are told that boys don't cry, only girls do. If, even in play, they try on makeup and wear dresses, their parents are horrified. Boys tend to grow up with a fear of being feminine, which forces them to maintain a macho image as well as an exploitative attitude toward women. Boys are also encouraged to be self-reliant, to avoid being "mama's boys." They are more likely than girls to receive physical punishment such as spanking, so that they develop a sort of reactive independence. On the other hand, girls are taught to be "ladylike," to be gentle, and to rely on others—especially males—for help. They are allowed to express their emotions freely. Seeing their mothers spend much time and money on fashion and cosmetics, they learn the importance of being pretty—and feel that they must rely more on their beauty than intelligence to attract men (Johnson, 1982; Brownmiller, 1984; Elkin and Handel, 1984).

Parents may deny that they treat their sons and daughters differently, but studies have suggested otherwise. When parents are asked, "In what ways do you think boys and girls are different?" many would say that boys are more active, stronger, more competitive, noisier, and messier and that girls are more gentle, neater, quieter, more helpful, and more courteous. Such gender typing has been found to cause parents to treat their children differently, even when they are not conscious of doing so. If they consider boys stronger, for example, they are likely to handle them more roughly than girls and to protect girls more than boys (Basow, 1980; Richardson, 1981). In recent years, however, there has been a definite trend toward more egalitarian gender-role socialization. Young parents, working mothers, and well-educated parents are particularly inclined to socialize their children into egalitarian gender roles, but parents with regular church attendance and fundamentalist religious identification tend to preserve traditional gender roles (Thornton, Alwin, and Camburn, 1983). At any rate, even if well-educated parents try to socialize their sons and daughters in the same way, their children are still subjected to traditional gender-role socialization outside the home, as the following story suggests:

> A six-year-old child is overheard by her mother explaining to a friend that only boys can be doctors and only girls can be nurses. The mother remarks "But, Sally, you know I'm a doctor." Sally replies "You're no doctor; you're my mother" (Basow, 1980).

"Gosh, Grandma, what a big office you have!"

Let us, then, turn to those socializing agents that have taught Sally and her peers the gender-role stereotypes.

Schools and Peer Groups The socialization of boys and girls into their gender roles gets a boost from schools. Until recently, schools usually segregated courses and sports on the basis of gender. Business and mechanics courses were for boys; secretarial courses and home economics, for girls. Boys played hardball; girls, softball. High school counselors were not very likely to encourage girls to go on to college, because they were expected to get married and stay home to raise children. If a girl was going to college, counselors were likely to encourage her to enter traditionally feminine careers such as teaching, nursing, and social work.

School textbooks, too, have promoted sexual stereotypes. They have long conveyed the impression that males are smarter and more important than females. A study of 134 textbooks in the early 1970s found $2\frac{1}{2}$ times more stories about boys than girls and 6 times more biographies of men than of women. Clever boys were presented 131 times, but clever girls only 33 times. In short, textbooks have presented a world in which females seem to be "merely a ladies' auxiliary to the human species" (U'Ren, 1971; NOW, 1977).

The structure of the school has also helped to reinforce traditional stereotypes of male superiority. In virtually all the elementary and secondary schools, men hold positions of authority (as coordinators, principals, and superintendents) and women are in positions of subservience (as teachers and aides). In 1979, for example, 83 percent of elementary school principals were men while 84 percent of the teachers and 94 percent of the aides were women (Census Bureau, 1984). In such a male-dominant atmosphere, children are subtly led to learn that women are subordinate and need the leadership of men. As Laurel Richardson (1981) observes, "Children learn that although their teacher, usually a female, is in charge of the room, the school is run by a male without whose strength she could not cope; the principal's office is where the incorrigibles are sent."

Title IX, along with continuing pressure from the women's movement, has decreased the sex segregation of classes and sports and produced some changes in counseling and textbooks. But the total elimination of sex-role stereotypes is still a long way off. This is most evident in school athletics. Boys still far outnumber girls in football and baseball, and girls outnumber boys in cheerleading. As mentioned earlier, only 20 percent of the college athletic budget is allocated to women's sports. The difficulty in breaking down the traditional barrier can be seen in this letter to *Time* magazine: "Your profiling women's participation in sports is like encouraging a snail to enter a foot race. Let's face it, women just aren't made right to enter a man's realm of sports" (Basow, 1980).

Such contempt for females in sports also exists among boys' peer group. Before adolescence, boys like to play ball together, excluding girls. Girls learn about male exclusivity and contempt when they are told by boys that "ball games are for boys only because 'girls aren't hardly made' for ball games" (Bernard, 1981). During adolescence, the peer group tends to pressure boys to prove their manhood and sexual prowess with girls and girls to prove their popularity with boys. Dating may become a competitive game for gaining prestige among peers of one's own gender. The result, in Janet Chafetz's (1978) view, is that "in their quest for identity through attachment to a male, all too many young women leave themselves open to crass sexual exploitation and most males are pressured into taking advantage of such a situation."

The Mass Media Of all the sources of sexual stereotypes, the mass media—television, newspapers, magazines, radio—are the most pervasive. In such traditional magazines as *Good Housekeeping* and *Family Circle,* the female role is often defined in terms of homemaking and motherhood, and numerous beauty tips are offered to help attract men or please husbands. The ads in the magazines tell women that "He'll love you for introducing him to the House of Pancakes" and that a particular product can "make your eyes just one thing—sexy, very, very sexy." In less traditional magazines such as *New Woman* and *Working Woman,* we still can see the perpetuation of sexual stereotypes. Although women are portrayed working outside the home, they are nonetheless presented as responsible for housework and children—no protest being raised that women, much more often than men, are expected to perform two jobs simultaneously (Glazer, 1980). If such magazines go all out to demolish the sexual stereotypes, they may lose many of their readers to the more traditional women's magazines. Today the traditional "seven sisters"—*Better Homes and Gardens, Family Circle, Woman's Day, McCall's, Ladies' Home Journal, Good Housekeeping,* and *Redbook*—continue to surpass considerably in readership the new women's magazines, such as *Working Woman, Savvy, Working Mother,* and *Ms.* The traditional magazines have a combined circulation of 40 million, compared with only 3 million for the new magazines (Conant, 1987). While these women's magazines help perpetuate sexual stereotypes, many sports magazines and the sports pages of many newspapers do the same. They often describe male athletes as "great," "tough," "brilliant," "cool," and "courageous" but female athletes as "pretty," "slim," "attractive," "gracious," and "lovely." In popular Sunday comics, too, women are presented as more passive and less important than men. In children's picture books, females, whether as humans, ducks, or frogs, are likely to be portrayed as performing the "feminine" role of pleasing and serving males (Brabant and Mooney, 1986; Williams et al., 1987).

Television commercials also present women as sex objects and dedicated housewives. Young sexy women are shown admiring an old cigar smoker who uses an air cleaner. Housewives are shown in ecstasy over their shiny waxed floors or the sparkling cleanliness of their dishes. Women are shown stricken with guilt for not using the right detergent to get rid of their husbands' "ring around the collar." Prime-time television programs also reinforce traditional gender roles and inequalities. Over the past 15 years, TV researcher George Gerbner has analyzed 1600 prime-time programs including more than 15,000 characters. He concludes that women are generally typecast as either lovers or mothers. They are mostly portrayed as weak, passive sidekicks to powerful, effective men (Waters, 1982). A content analysis of the television portrayals of nurses and doctors in the last 30 years shows that 99 percent of the nurses are females and 95 percent of the doctors are males. Most of these TV nurses are presented not only as subservient to male physicians but also as sex objects. By contrast, the male doctors are mostly portrayed as highly competent professionals (Kalisch and Kalisch, 1984).

The Learning Process We may know much about what a socializing agent teaches, but we still have to know how the child learns the gender role in the first place. As we saw in Chapter 6 (Socialization), there are various explanations of how such learning occurs. According to the psychoanalytic theory, the child turns from unacceptable sexual love of the opposite-sex parent to identification with the same-sex parent—thus taking on an appropriate gender role. While psychoanalysts see the source of gender-role development—libido or sexual love—as biologically determined, social learning theorists point to such environmental factors as conditioning and imitation. Children are rewarded for behaving in ways that parents and others consider appropriate for their gender—and punished for not doing so, so they eventually conform to their society's gender roles. A little boy, for example, learns to hide his fears or pain because he has been praised for being brave and scolded for crying. As discussed in Chapter 6, social learning theorists such as Albert Bandura (1977) offer a modification of this view, arguing that children also learn by imitation. Children tend to imitate their same-sex parent and other adult models, because the latter are powerful, nurturant, and able to reward or punish them. Through reinforcement and imitation, then, children engage in certain gender-typed activities, which lead to the development of a stable gender identity—"I do girl things. Therefore I must be a girl."

According to cognitive development theory, however, gender identity is the cause rather than the product of gender-role learning. As Lawrence Kohlberg (1966) explains, children first learn to identify themselves as a male or female from what they observe and what they are told. Then they seek to act and feel like one: "I am a boy, therefore I want to do boy things." Thus children are not passive objects in the acquisition of gender roles. They are active actors developing their gender identity and performing their gender roles. How clear their gender identity is and how well they perform their gender roles depend significantly on their cognitive skills or the levels of their cognitive development.

Apparently, all the processes discussed above—identification, conditioning, imitation, and cognition—play a part in the learning of gender roles. They are also related to each other. Children cannot rely on their cognition alone to distinguish what is masculine from what is feminine. They have to depend on their parents to serve as models of masculinity and femininity. In serving as such models, the parents are likely to reinforce specific gender-typed behavior ("Boys don't play with dolls" or "See how nicely Janie plays"). Identification with the same-sex parent may also result from, as well as influence, the parents' tendency to reinforce certain gender-typed behavior (Basow, 1980).

Functional Necessity and Exploitation

According to the functionalist perspective, it is functional for society to assign different tasks to men and women. This division of labor was originally based on the physical differences between the sexes. In primitive hunting-gathering societies, for example, men roam far from home to hunt animals because they are larger and stronger, and women stay near home base to gather plant foods, cook, and take care of children because only they can become pregnant, bear and nurse babies. Today muscle power is not as important as brain and machine power. Contraceptives, baby formula, child-care centers, and convenience foods further weaken the constraints that the childbearing role places on women. Yet traditional gender roles persist.

The reason for this persistence, functionalists assume, is that these roles continue to be functional to modern societies. How? Talcott Parsons and Robert Bales (1953) argued that two basic roles must be fulfilled in a group: the **instrumental role** of getting things done and the **expressive role** of holding the group together, taking care of the personal relationships. In the modern family the instrumental role is fulfilled by making money; playing this role well requires competence, assertiveness, dominance. The expressive role requires offering love and affection, and it is best filled by someone warm, emotional, nonassertive. When men are socialized to have the traits appropriate for the instrumental role and women are socialized to have the traits suitable for the expressive role, then the family is likely to function smoothly. Each person fits into a part, and the parts fit together.

The role differentiation may have worked well for many traditional families, and especially for those in traditional third-world societies, as suggested by their lower rates of divorce. But functionalists may have exaggerated the role differentiation because women do perform the instrumental role to a large degree. American housewives spend over 50 hours a week on cooking, dishwashing, housecleaning, laundering, shopping, and other instrumental tasks (Vanek, 1978). Even in many highly sex-segregated primitive societies, women perform a significant instrumental role. As Joel Aronoff and William Crano's (1975) research shows, in nearly half of the preindustrial societies surveyed by Murdock, women contributed at least 40 percent of their societies' food supply. In practically all gathering-hunting societies, women carry out the instrumental task of gathering food, without which the family would risk starvation because male hunters often come home empty-handed (Tanner, 1983). If women's contributions are so important to the family and society, why does gender inequality exist?

Conflict theory suggests that gender inequality arose not because it was functional, but because men were able to exploit women. According to the classic Marxist view, gender inequality is part of the larger economic stratification. By restricting women to childbearing and household chores, men ensured their freedom to go out to acquire property and amass wealth. They also used their power over women to obtain heirs and thus guarantee their continued hold on their economic power. Moreover, men have directly exploited women by getting them to do much work with little or no pay. Thus housewives are not paid for doing housework and child care, which would cost about half of most husbands' income if those services are purchased from others (Vanek, 1978). Gainfully employed wives also do most of the housework, although they work as much as their husbands outside the home (Miller and Garrison, 1982). In addition, as we have seen, they are usually paid less than men for their work outside the home.

Some conflict theorists give greater weight to sexual, rather than economic, exploitation as the source of gender inequality. Randall Collins (1975) argues that "the fundamental motive is the desire for sexual gratification, rather than for labor per se; men have appropriated women primarily for their beds rather than their kitchens and fields, although they could certainly be pressed into service in the daytime too." More recently, according to some feminists, so-called surrogate motherhood has emerged as the ultimate exploitation of women by men because it turns women into mere breeding machines. Although other feminists defend the rights of women to sell their services as surrogate mothers, they do see the men and women who *arrange* surrogacies (for fees of at least $10,000 each) as "the pimps" of the surrogacy movement (Peterson, 1987). Conflict theorists would view surrogate motherhood as a modern way of shoring up gender inequality.

QUESTIONS FOR DISCUSSION AND REVIEW

1. How do females differ biologically from males?
2. Can biological differences alone explain the different and unequal statuses of women?
3. What contributions do the family, the school, peer groups, and the mass media make to sexual stereotypes?
4. How do girls and boys learn gender roles through the processes of identification, imitation, and cognition?
5. Why do followers of the functional and conflict approaches agree that gender inequality is inevitable?

TOWARD GENDER EQUALITY

There has been significant progress toward gender equality in the last two decades. This is largely due to the women's liberation movement. The women's attempt to liberate themselves from the constraints of female-role stereotypes has further induced a growing number of men to free themselves from male-role stereotypes. The end result is that gender roles are becoming less differentiated—or more androgynous—with an increasing number of men assuming traditionally female roles and women taking on traditionally male roles.

The Women's Movement

The women's movement for sexual equality in the United States began in the middle of the last century. It developed out of the larger social movement to abolish slavery. The women who participated in this movement to free the slaves came to realize that they themselves needed freedom too. The women initially attempted to eradicate all forms of sexual discrimination, but gradually focused their attention on winning the right for women to vote. The women's suffrage finally became a reality in 1920. Since then the feminist movement came to a complete halt. Then in the mid-1960s it was put back into motion.

The women's liberation movement has sought to end discrimination based on gender in work, politics, education, and religion. The success of the movement can be measured by the increased opportunities now available to women in almost every sphere of contemporary life. But some feminist leaders themselves have criticized the movement for insisting that the law treat women like men. They argue that working women should be given special benefits such as prenatal care, maternity leave, and child-care services.

Two factors seemed most responsible for the revival of the women's movement. First, since the end of World War II more and more women went to college. After having had so much education, however, the women became unhappy with their jobs as mere housewives or with their low-status, low-paying jobs outside the home. Another factor contributing to the rebirth of feminism was the confluence of the civil rights movement, the student movement, and the antiwar and other political movements in the 1960s. The women who took part in these movements, supposedly fighting for the freedom of the oppressed, found themselves oppressed by the male freedom fighters. The leader of a civil rights group, the Student Nonviolent Coordinating Committee, once suggested in 1964 that the only position for women in SNCC was lying on their backs. At the 1968 Students for a Democratic Society convention, women members were hissed at and thrown off the podium for demanding that women's liberation be added as a goal for the organization. Women in the civil rights and New Left movements, wrote Annie Gootlieb (1971), "found themselves *serving* as secretary, mother and concubine, while men did all the speaking, writing, and negotiating—and these were men who professed to reject the 'oppressive' ritual machinery of their society."

Out of this background emerged a number of all-female organizations. Some might be considered very radical because they hated men, rejected marriage, and vowed to tear down the whole gender-role system. In 1968 they attracted enormous publicity for their picketing of the Miss America Pageant. Their names alone were enough to attract maximum attention, as they called themselves SCUM (Society for Cutting Men) or WITCH (Women's International Terrorist Conspiracy from Hell). Other feminist groups were more moderate, the most famous being NOW (National Organization for Women). NOW seems to have been the most successful feminist organization. It continues to have a strong influence on women's positions today. Its aim is to end sexual discrimination in education, work, politics, religion, and all the other institutions. Consequently, many states have passed laws requiring equal pay for equal work, government departments have issued affirmative action guidelines to force universities and businesses to hire more women, and court decisions in favor of women have been made in many cases of sexual discrimination in hiring, pay, and promotion.

The women's movement has failed, however, to achieve one of its primary objects—passage of the Equal Rights Amendment **(ERA)** to the U.S. Constitution. First proposed as long ago as 1932, ERA was passed by Congress in 1972 and endorsed by 35 states soon thereafter. But its passage requires approval by three-fourths, or 38, of the state legislatures. In 1982 it still failed to get the remaining three state ratifications needed for it to become law. Much of the opposition has come from traditional women. Although ERA is intended simply to prohibit job discrimination against women by the federal, state, and local governments, many traditional women consider it a threat to their cherished status as housewives and mothers. They fear ERA would take away long-enjoyed legal rights such as exemption from military service and economic support from their husbands or ex-husbands. They are afraid that they would have to compete with men in politics, business, and other traditionally male preserves if gender equality becomes a reality. Conservative political and religious groups have further helped to kill ERA. Spending huge sums of money on television commercials, they have told voters that ERA will produce egocentric women, increase abortions, encourage homosexual marriages, and spread AIDS. Nevertheless, the spirit of ERA has recently influenced important judicial actions. In 1986, the Supreme Court upheld the promotion of a woman over a marginally more qualified male employee in California, endorsed a state's right to compel employers to guarantee job reinstatement to women returning from maternity leaves, and ruled that sexual harassment in the workplace is illegal. In 1987 the Court decided that a state may force private all-male clubs to admit female members (Pogrebin, 1982; Smolowe, 1987).

Aside from those Court actions advancing women's rights, there are other signs that the feminist movement has made significant headway toward gender equality. Increased numbers of women are now going to college and graduating with degrees in law, medicine, and other lucrative fields. There are now more women pursuing careers and earning as much as men. Many career women who are married have also achieved economic parity with their husbands (see box, p. 285). The numbers of women in elected office have also increased, and a large majority of Americans are now willing to vote for a qualified woman for president. In 1984 Geraldine Ferraro became the Democrats' vice-presidential candidate. A growing number of women are entering the military, with the United States now having more female soldiers than any other country. The change in gender roles can even be detected in country music. In the 1970s songs like "Stand by Your Man" reflected the traditional expectation among southern white working-class women that they should be nurturing, submissive, and forgiving of their philandering, tough, and insensitive husbands. But in the 1980s there are more songs like "Another Chance," in which the female singers announce their determination not to let their husbands boss them around anymore (Stark, 1986).

Women's lib may have brought about some unintended consequences, though. The crime rates among women have risen. Accordig to the FBI, between 1976 and 1985, the number of women arrested for embezzlement went up 55 percent, compared with a 1 percent decrease for men; and fraud arrests among women shot up 84 percent, nearly twice the rise among men (Burrough, 1987). In marriages where the wives earn more than their husbands, there tends to be tension and chaos, often resulting in divorce (Hays, 1987). Women who want to be called Ms. rather than Miss or Mrs. give the general public the impression of being more ambitious, assertive, and dynamic than those who prefer the traditional forms of address. But they are perceived as less warm and honest (Connor et al., 1986; Dion, 1987). Most significantly, some feminists themselves have begun to criticize the women's movement for overemphasizing equality—for insisting that the law treat men and women alike. Betty Friedan asks rhetorically, "Why should the law treat us like male clones?" Friedan and other critics want feminists to accept the biological differences between the sexes so that they can recognize the unique needs for working women. The critics contend that working women, being the ones who have the babies, must be given special benefits such as prenatal care, maternity leave, and child-care services (Hewlett, 1986; Leo, 1986).

Men's Liberation

A quiet revolution has been going on among some men who want to free themselves from the demands of the traditional male role (Goldberg, 1976). As we have indicated, men are expected to be tough, aggressive, and competitive. They are supposed to suppress their emotions even if they feel like crying when they are sad. The social expectation that they be superior to women makes some men doubt their adequacy as providers or lovers. This is particularly the case when the men's wives do not conform to the traditional notion of femininity—by demanding as much sexual enjoyment as men or making more money than their husbands. The men likely to suffer from these kinds of problems are obviously incapable of fulfilling the male-role demands.

Yet the "tough" men, who feel capable of performing the masculine role to the hilt, are likely to suffer too. They may find it difficult to relate closely to their wives and children, because such a close relationship requires a great deal of sensitivity, warmth, and tenderness—the very qualities discouraged by the masculine role. Their effort to avoid emotion may lead to mechanical sex and,

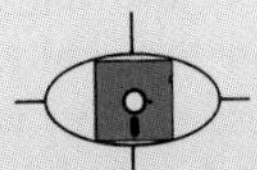

LOOKING AT CURRENT RESEARCH

More Equal than Others

Although women still experience sexual discrimination, a new form of gender equality is emerging. In this reading, sociologist Rosanna Hertz shows that an increasing number of women have found economic equality in two-career marriages. Can this economic equality between husbands and wives promote equality in social, political, and other areas of life?

My objective is to ask a big question in a small way. What will it take for men and women to be truly equal? Philosophers and social critics have answered this question in many complex ways, but most agree that men and women must have equal positions in central social and economic pursuits. More to the point, men and women must be economic equals if they are to be equal in other spheres of social life.

I have studied a small but growing segment of American society in which men and women are economic equals: dual-career married couples in the corporate world. The question is whether success in the work world has fundamentally changed the nature of marriage and family.

Through an analysis of their experiences, I suggest that dual-career couples are "more equal than others" in two senses. First their relative economic equality has made possible important shifts in their roles as husbands and wives. They relate to each other and to their relationship as partners with equivalent goals, aspirations, and pressures. The boundaries between "breadwinner" and "homemaker" are difficult to see when neither spouse can lay claim to higher status or greater influence based on who is working outside the home or who is making more money. Unlike two-paycheck marriages, in which the husband may have a career and the wife a job (or temporary employment), the dual-career couple holds greater potential for equality in marital roles. Second, "more equal than others" also refers to the ways in which equality for some couples may be contingent on the availability of other people, often married couples, for whom equality is not common.

Dual-career couples are by no means the vanguard of the American population in consciously pursuing gender equality. Indeed, they are one of the results of a changing economy: the startling expansion of white-collar employment and the growth of career opportunities for female college graduates have combined to make two careers in one family a more likely option. The composition of the pool of potential mates for well-educated, occupationally mobile men and women has altered over the past two decades. When a career-oriented individual encounters a potential mate today, it is increasingly likely that the candidate will also have a career.

Although only a few of the men and women I interviewed considered themselves "liberated," most are grappling with questions of gender equality and marital equity in response to the pressures of their work. Equally demanding careers, similar incomes, and concerns about finding a balance between work and family have forced these couples to act differently than their more traditional parents and one-career family peers. These two-career couples negotiate household responsibilities and develop innovative solutions to managing finances. They talk about symmetry and equality in the context of her career, his career, and their marriage. They cannot, as often happens in noncareer settings, devalue her career as supplemental without tarring his career with the same brush.

These men and women are participating in an important process of social change. That they do so *behaviorally* more than *attitudinally* argues for an often overlooked perspective on societal change: if behaviors are changed, attitudes congruent with the change will often follow. In this instance men and women who have benefited from the labor market shifts and the achievements of the women's liberation movement are becoming advocates of gender equality even though they were not initially proponents of this cause.

Source: Adapted from *More Equal than Others: Women and Men in Dual-Career Marriages,* by Rosanna Hertz, Berkeley, Calif.: University of California Press, 1986, pp. xi–xiv. © 1986 The Regents of the University of California.

if pushed to extremes, to impotence. They may also find it difficult to develop deep friendships with other men because of the constant pressure to be competitive and to put up a tough, impersonal front (Fasteau, 1975).

As a consequence, many men are ready to support the women's movement. They see the feminists as helpful in reducing the burden of being male. They can also see the benefit of encouraging their wives to pursue careers outside the home if this is what they want. Imprisoning a bored and frustrated wife in the homemaking role, these men believe, is most likely to cause the marriage to fall apart. In addition to having a better marriage, the working wife is expected to increase substantially the family income, especially because she can get equal pay for equal work from her nonsexist employer. Understandably, an increasing number of men have rejected the traditional male-role imperatives: "Be the breadwinner," "Push your way to the top," "Stick in there and fight," "Men don't cry" (Bernard, 1981). Indeed, there is life after Rambo. Men can enjoy a good life when their wives work. For one thing, the wives' earnings have boosted many modest-income families into the $25,000-plus middle and affluent brackets. Nowadays, among 70 percent of couples earning $40,000 to $50,000 a year, both spouses work. Because their wives work, men can now change careers to find one that really interests them rather than getting stuck in a boring job. If such men lose their jobs, their wives' income can mitigate the hardship of unemployment. With working wives' significant contributions to their families' purse strings, men can feel less pressure to knock themselves out. They no longer have to accept overtime, heavy travel, and other unpleasant work obligations. Since they do not have to work so hard to make a living, they now can get to know their children and discover the joys of fatherhood (Fader, 1987).

Androgynous Roles

As we have suggested, the women's movement has largely dealt with the bread-and-butter issue of enlarging educational, economic, and other opportunities for women. A more fundamental effort has emerged to replace the traditional sex-differentiated roles with **androgynous roles.** This effort has been explained by Alice Rossi (1964):

> The traditional conceptions of masculine and feminine are inappropriate to the kind of world we can live in during the second half of the twentieth century. An androgynous conception of sex role means that each sex will cultivate some of the characteristics usually associated with the other in traditional sex role definitions.

Rossi proposes that boys be socialized to be tender and expressive, so they will later feel free to express these qualities in their social relationships. Rossi also recommends that girls be inculcated with need for achievement, good workmanship, and assertiveness, so they will feel free to express these qualities in their adult lives. By thus destroying the traditional gender roles, this socialization strategy is assumed ultimately to enable both men and women to develop the full range of human qualities regardless of their gender.

There are already a sizable number of androgynous men and women in the United States. A series of studies at Stanford University in the 1970s already showed 35 percent of the students to be androgynous. A more recent study also found that students at two other universities are more androgynous in the present decade than in the previous one. These students, whether male or female, can be warm and responsive when they need to be, as well as independent and assertive in appropriate situations. These androgynous students, in other words, can play both masculine and feminine roles equally well. They are also happier than the strongly "masculine" men and strongly "feminine" women, showing behavioral flexibility, better psychological adjustment, and

The counterpart to the women's liberation movement is the increasing willingness of men to assume responsibility for tending the home and raising the children. These androgynous men generally think better of themselves, are happier with their marriages, and consider parenting less stressful when compared with traditional men. But they do find themselves with the same conflicting demands on their time that working mothers have. They have to juggle the roles of parent, spouse, and worker.

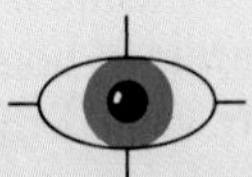

USING SOCIOLOGICAL INSIGHT

Being Male in a Female Profession

A growing number of men have rejected the traditional sex-differentiated roles by assuming some stereotypically female roles. An example is the man who becomes a nurse. Such a man does face some problems, as reported below. How do the expectations of traditional male and female gender roles affect his experiences?

I'm a nurse. I also happen to be a male. Some people believe the two are mutually exclusive.

"Oh, so you're a *male* nurse," they say, not entirely convinced.

Why do we need the qualifier "male" in front of the word "nurse?" After all, there are male and female teachers, doctors, lawyers, chefs, and secretaries. But people don't automatically say "male teacher" or "male doctor," do they?

To the extent that reverse discrimination exists, nowhere does it seem more obvious than in our historically female profession. For example, female co-workers often ask me—a stereotypically "strong" male—to assist them with heavy work. These same nurses, many of them ardent feminists, expect me to care only for male patients, while they care for both sexes. Do they honestly believe that male nurses are not as professional as they are? That's what their actions say.

But professionalism is genderless. It implies the ability to relate to and care for any patient in need. A truly professional nurse—male or female–can effectively care for all patients, male and female, while maintaining their dignity.

Another troubling misconception about male nurses: People believe that because we're men, we have the power to make sweeping changes in the profession. Take salaries, for example. It's said that as more men enter nursing, salaries will increase because "men won't tolerate such low pay." This idea wrongly assigns incredible power to our small group, and it also discredits the efforts of the women who have been working for many years to raise the nursing salary scale.

I'm not prepared for—nor will I accept—the role of financial arbiter for an entire profession just because my shirts button from the right instead of the left. Let the powers-that-be learn the merits on which salary is based from those most capable of teaching them—nurses as a group, not one group of nurses.

Whenever the discussion turns to controversial health-care issues, I find myself in a double bind. If I state an opinion contrary to the prevailing viewpoint, and I often do, I'm called a "typical male." If I sit back and listen to the others without expressing an opinion, I'm scorned for failing to live up to my masculine obligation as group leader. Nobody actually comes right out and *says* this, of course, but nonverbal language makes the meaning pretty clear: If you attempt to lead, we won't follow because you're male; if you choose to follow, we'll think you're not the man you're supposed to be.

How can men who've entered nursing solve the problems we face? We need to break our silence if we want the public to respect us. To change attitudes toward male nurses, we need to teach people who we are and what we do. But we'll also have to go on being ourselves, tending to our patients and our friends. We'll keep on monitoring machines and assessing vital signs. We'll continue to make the ill well and give love to the dying. We will do. We will feel. We will care.

And that, don't you see, is the real equality of the sexes.

Source: Excerpted from Andrew T. McPhee, "Being Male in a Female Profession." Published in the October 1984 *Registered Nursing Journal.* Copyright © The Medical Economics Company Inc., Oradell, N.J. Reprinted by permission.

higher self-esteem (Bem, 1975; Pedersen and Bond, 1985; Bozzi, 1987). Moreover, married men who take a more active "female" role as homemaker and caregiver think better of themselves, are happier with their marriages, and see parenting as less stressful than do traditional men. But parenting is not easy: these androgynous men also reported more strain from having to juggle their roles as parent, husband, and worker (Herbert and Greenberg, 1983). Neither is it easy for such men to enter a traditionally female profession (see box above). This may reflect the larger problem of trying to achieve gender equality in general.

As we have seen, women have made significant advances in education, professions, and politics. But they still have a long way to go before winning the battle for equality. Although increasing numbers of women have moved into traditionally masculine professions, they still find most of the top positions—such as chairman of the board, senior partner, or police chief—held by men. Most significantly, women still earn less than men for the same jobs with the same qualification.

Janet Chafetz (1984) has argued that the degree of gender equality depends on the degree to which women are involved in socially valued economic production. This means that American women will enjoy more equality with men if they move into male-dominated, higher-status occupations. An experimental study further suggests that women can gain more respect from others if they can clearly demonstrate their ability (Wagner et al., 1986). But, to some conflict theorists, all this is not likely to translate into real equality between men and women unless women resort to force—such as legal action—to get equal pay for equal work. As Joan Huber and Glenna Spitz (1983) have observed, the persistent female-male disparity in earnings despite women's increasing labor-force participation suggests that simply moving into male-dominated professions is not enough to ensure gender equality.

QUESTIONS FOR DISCUSSION AND REVIEW

1. How has the women's liberation movement succeeded, and where has it failed?
2. In what ways has the men's liberation movement differed from the women's movement?
3. What are androgynous roles, and why do some men and women feel they will help end gender inequality?

CHAPTER REVIEW

1. *What are the traditional gender roles of American men and women?* Men are expected to be breadwinners, aggressive, and ambitious. Women are expected to be homemakers, passive, and dependent. Consequently, the sexes tend to behave differently.

2. *Are there universal patterns underlying gender roles?* Although gender roles vary from one society to another, there is a tendency for men to do work that requires physical strength and travel, and for women to perform tasks that provide more direct support of the family. In most societies, men are breadwinners and women homemakers. "Men's work" is also more highly valued than "women's work," and men are dominant over women.

3. *What is the nature of sexism?* It involves prejudice and discrimination against women, based on the belief that women are inferior to men. Sexism can be found in religion, from its impact on women, and in the interaction between the sexes.

4. *Do women today match men in educational attainment?* No. Men still outnumber women in more lucrative majors and in graduate and professional schools, though the educational gap has narrowed. *Have women in the workplace achieved equality with men?* No. Although more than half the women are in the workforce, they tend to hold lower-status jobs and to be paid less than men. *How have American women fared in politics?* Better than before. But they are still far from achieving political parity with men.

5. *Do biological differences make females inferior to men?* No, in some ways females seem biologically superior and in other ways inferior. Males do tend to be bigger and stronger, which may give them an edge in establishing dominance over females.

6. *What kind of influence does culture have over gender-role differences and inequalities?* It defines what the gender differences should be, so that the specifics of gender roles vary from society to society.

7. *How do we learn our gender roles?* Through socialization by families, schools, peer groups, and the mass media. *What is the process by which children learn gender roles?* Identification, conditioning, imitation, and cognition have each been proposed as the key process by which this learning occurs.

8. *According to functionalists, why are gender roles still functional in industrial societies?* With men playing the instrumental role and women the expressive role, the family's smooth functioning can be ensured. *How do conflict theorists explain gender inequality?* It stems from economic or sexual exploitation of women.

9. *Has there been significant progress toward gender equality in the last two decades?* Yes, women have made significant

headway in education, professions, and politics, thanks to the women's liberation movement. In addition, a growing number of men have freed themselves from the traditional male role, and many men and women have tried to play androgynous roles.

KEY TERMS

Androgynous role A pattern of attitudes and behaviors combining elements of what are usually considered masculine and feminine patterns (p. 286).

Chromosomes The materials in a cell that transmit hereditary traits to the carrier from his or her parents (p. 276).

ERA Equal Rights Amendment to the U.S. Constitution, intended to prohibit denial of legal rights by the United States or any state on account of gender (p. 283).

Expressive role Role that requires taking care of personal relationships (p. 281).

Gender role The pattern of attitudes and behaviors that a society expects of its members because of their gender (p. 268).

Hormones Chemical substances that stimulate or inhibit vital biological processes (p. 276).

Instrumental role Role that requires performing a task (p. 281).

Men's liberation A quiet movement among some men not to play the traditional dominant male role (p. 284).

Sexism Prejudice and discrimination against women (p. 271).

Women's ghettos Traditionally female low-paying occupations that are subordinate to positions held by men (p. 274).

SUGGESTED READINGS

Brownmiller, Susan. 1984. *Femininity*. New York: Linden Press/Simon & Schuster. A revealing account of what women are forced to do in the pursuit of femininity.

Chafetz, Janet. 1984. *Sex and Advantage: A Comparative, Macro-Structural Theory of Sex Stratification*. Totowa, N.J.: Rowman & Allanheld. A theoretical analysis of how women's involvement in economic production enhances sexual equality.

Fausto-Sterling, Anne. 1985. *Myths of Gender: Biological Theories About Women and Men*. New York: Basic Books. A biologist's critique of the search for biological causes of gender differences, maintaining that people's behavior can alter their physiology.

Rossi, Alice. S. 1984. "Gender and parenthood." *American Sociological Review*, 49, pp. 1–19. A thought-provoking analysis of the biological roots of gender differences, without turning people into passive objects at the mercy of internal genetic forces.

Tavris, Carol, and Carole Wade. 1984. *The Longest War: Sex Differences in Perspective*, 2nd ed. New York: Harcourt Brace Jovanovich. A lively review of various approaches to the study of gender roles and inequalities.

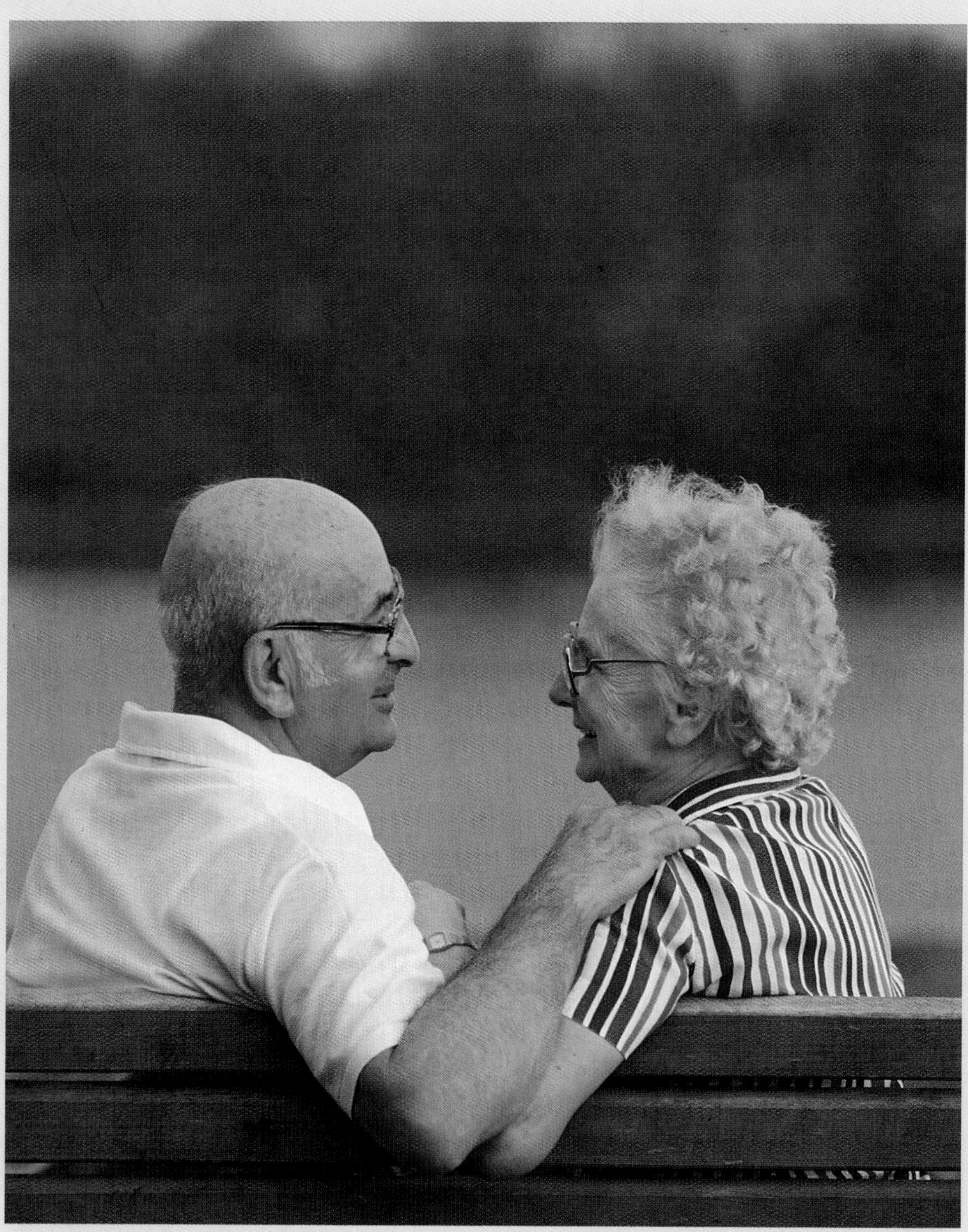

12 The Elderly

In general, the elderly have lower social status in modern societies than in traditional societies. The elderly in the United States, however, are better off than they are popularly believed to be. While they have more health problems than younger people, most of the elderly feel healthy. Although they generally suffer a decline in perception and reaction speed, elderly workers are just as productive as—and often more reliable than—younger workers. Most of the elderly are not poor. Their poverty rate has, in fact, begun to fall below that of the general population in the last few years. Most of the elderly do not live alone, and most of those with children see them frequently. Finally, research has shown no significant differences between elderly and younger people in happiness, morale, or life satisfaction. Nevertheless, poverty is common among the elderly who live alone, those who are women, and those who are black.

There is a Chinese fable that goes as follows:

> In China a family named Lum—grandfather, father, and twelve-year-old son—lived in poverty in a tiny compound. The grandfather was crippled by arthritis and unable to continue his share of work in the rice paddy, so the father decided to [get rid of] him. He trussed him up in a market basket and made for the shore of the Yangtze River. En route he met his son, who cried, "What are you doing to my poor grandfather?" "Quiet," whispered the father, "by lowering him into the stream we will end his suffering and at the same time lighten the load." "I see," nodded the son, "but be sure to bring back the basket. I'll need it one day" (Richman, 1977).

Like race and gender, age can be the basis for prejudice and discrimination. But discrimination against the aged is unlike racism and sexism in one way: the younger generation that now discriminates against the elderly will eventually grow old; like a boomerang, their prejudice may come back to haunt them.

Treatment of the elderly—people aged 65 or older—has received increased attention lately because of the "graying of America": the number of old people has risen sharply, and they now make up a significant part of the population. In 1900 the average number of years an American infant could expect to live was only 47. Today it is 74—a dramatic increase of 27 years. From 3000 B.C. to the beginning of this century, there was a gain of about 29 years of life expectancy. We have achieved in less than 90 years what was gained in the preceding 5000 years (Butler, 1984). Today the elderly make up over 11 percent of the U.S. population, compared with only 4 percent in 1900, and the size of the elderly population is expected to continue growing (see Figure 12.1). In this chapter we will examine how aging affects people and how it changes their role in society. We will also look at how the elderly in America live and at what their position in the future is likely to be.

THE AGING PROCESS

The Heinz ketchup company has tried marketing dietetic food to older people under the name "Senior Foods." It was a flop: "People didn't want to be seen eating the stuff. It was labeling them old—and in our society, it is still an embarrassment to be old" (Mayer, 1977). Johnson & Johnson made a similar mistake when it introduced Affinity shampoo. Its first TV commercial featured a chance meeting between a middle-aged woman and an old boyfriend. He says, "You still look great." By emphasizing age, the commercial failed to sell the product well (Gilman, 1986). The bottom line is that our culture is youth-oriented. Growing old bothers a lot of people. This feeling has much to do with the biological and psychological effects of aging as well as society's definition of the elderly.

Biological Effects

Sooner or later, all of us gradually lose our energies and our ability to fight off diseases. This physical process of aging is called **senescence.** Biologists have been trying to crack the mystery of why it occurs, but without much success. Some believe that we are genetically programmed to age, others point to the breakdown of the body's immunological system, cells, or endocrine and

Old age has many deteriorating effects: wrinkled skin, hair loss, diminution of muscular strength, vulnerability to stroke and heart disease, and so on. But aging does not cause disability in most of the elderly. It also varies from one person to another. Some look younger than their age, whereas others look older. Being physically and socially active generally slows down the aging process, making the elderly look younger.

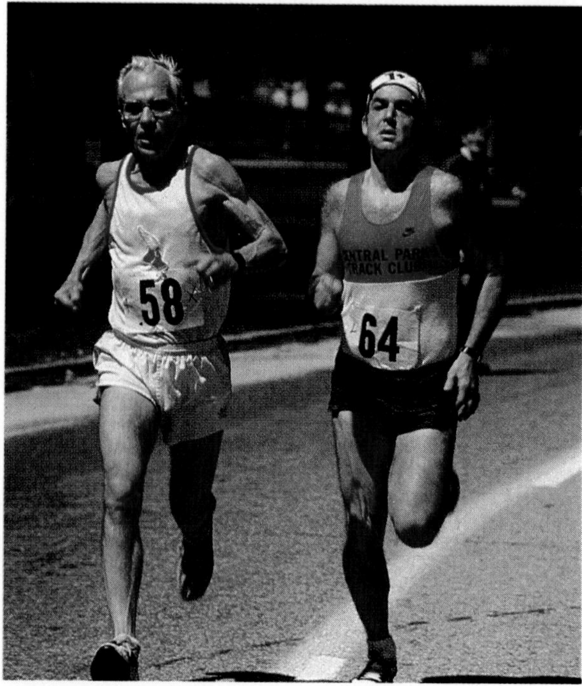

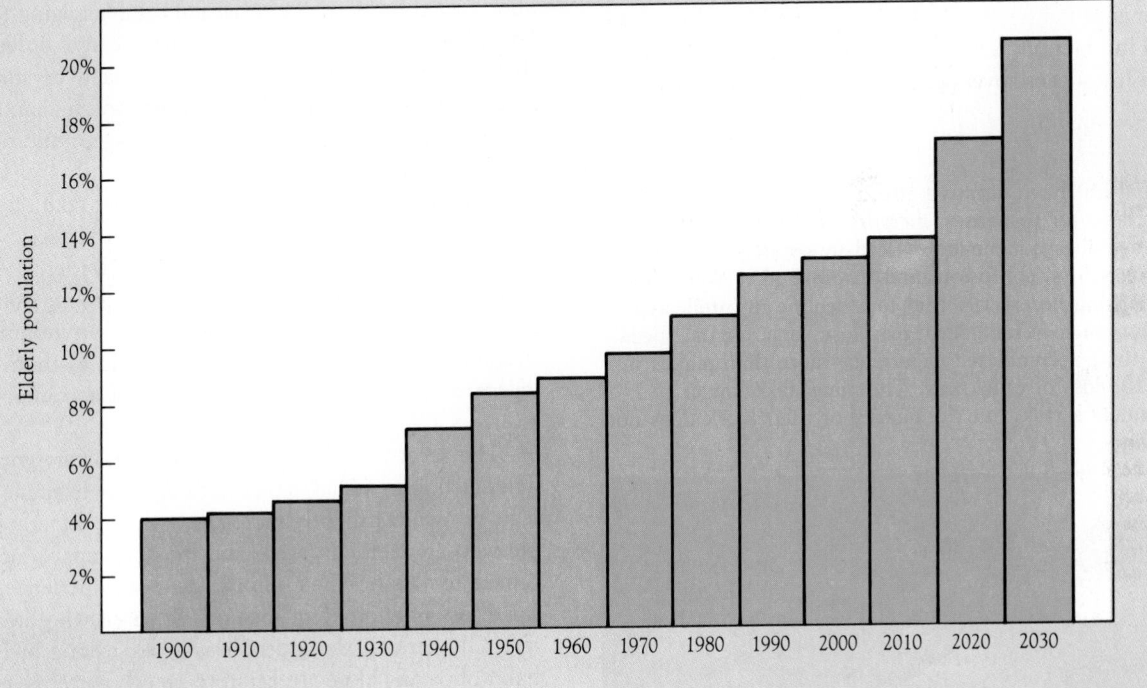

Figure 12.1 The Rise of the Elderly

The elderly, aged 65 or older, are a fast growing minority in the United States. Their proportion in the U.S. population has risen from a mere 4 percent at the turn of this century to over 11 percent today. The elderly population is expected to keep on growing—and estimated to reach 21 percent in only about 40 years from now.

Source: Cynthia M. Taeuber, *America in Transition: An Aging Society,* U.S. Bureau of the Census, Current Population Reports Series no. 128, p. 23 (Washington, D.C.: U.S. Government Printing Office, 1983), p. 3.

nervous systems. In any event, it is clear that senescence involves a decline in the body's functioning, increasing the vulnerability to death. It is a gradual process in which the changes come from within the individual, not from the environment. It is also both natural and universal, occurring in all older people.

Old age has many biological effects. The skin becomes wrinkled, rough, dry, and vulnerable to malignancies, bruises, and loss of hair. Because aging also causes the spinal disks to compress, most elderly people lose one to three inches in height. Another result of aging is a loss of muscular strength. More importantly, blood vessels harden as we age, creating circulatory problems in the brain and heart, which raises the incidence of stroke and heart disease among the elderly. Functioning of the kidneys shows the greatest decline with advancing age (Atchley, 1985; Levin and Levin, 1980).

While aging has all those deteriorative effects, they do not cause disability in most of the elderly. It should further be noted that the speed of aging varies greatly from one individual to another. Thus some people at age 85 look like 65 and others who are 65 look like 85. A number of factors may determine the disparities. The older look, characterized by the sagging and wrinkling of the skin, may stem from too much sun exposure in earlier years. Lack of exercise may speed up the aging process, so that those who sit in a rocking chair waiting for the Grim Reaper usually look and feel older than those who are physically active. Social isolation, powerlessness, and poor health further enhance aging. These largely social, environmental factors suggest that if aging can be accelerated, it can also be retarded (Gelman, 1986).

Psychological Effects

Aging also affects such psychological processes as sensory perceptions, psychomotor responses, memory, and personality. By the time they are 65, more than 50 percent of American men and 30 percent of American women suffer hearing losses severe enough to hinder social interaction. Visual acuity also declines with age: 87 percent of those over age 45 wear glasses, compared with only 30 percent of those under 45. Older people further tend to have slower but more accurate psychomotor responses—such as being able to type at lower speeds but with fewer errors—than young people. Moreover, short-term memory—recall of recent events for a brief time—seems to decline with age, although memory of remote events does not. Old age, however, does not inevitably lead to **senility,** which involves serious memory loss, confusion, and loss of the ability to reason. Senility is an abnormal condition, not a natural result of aging (Butler, 1984). Aging does not necessarily lead to a decline in intellectual performance, either. In fact, **crystalline intelligence**—wisdom and insight into the human condition, as shown by one's skills in language, philosophy, music, or painting—continues to grow with age. Only **fluid intelligence**—ability to grasp abstract relationships as in mathematics, physics, or some other science—tends to stabilize or decline with age (Butler, 1984). With advancing age people also tend to change from an active to a passive orientation to their environment, becoming less inclined to bend the world to their own wishes and more likely to conform and accommodate to it.

Aging can have negative effects on sensory perception, psychomotor responses, memory, and personality. But old age does not inevitably lead to senility—serious memory loss, confusion, and inability to reason. Nor does aging necessarily lead to a decline in intellectual performance. The elderly may lose some mental speed, but their accumulated experience more than makes up for the loss of quickness. They may take longer to complete a task, but the quality of their work does not decline.

The severity and rate of these changes vary greatly. The decline in visual acuity with age, for example, affects nonwhites slightly more than whites. Elderly people who are well educated, and thus presumably accustomed to flexing their minds, do not experience the same loss of short-term memory as those who are not mentally active. Many people who have long had the habit of paying close attention to speech patterns retain much of their hearing ability in old age. For most people, hearing and visual problems are generally inconveniences, not disabilities. Much of the decline in psychomotor and intellectual performance amounts to only a slowing down of work, not a falling off of quality. The elderly may lose some mental speed, but their accumulated experience more than compensates for the loss of quickness. Therefore, contrary to the stereotyped assumption about the aged automatically experiencing mental deterioration, many studies have shown job performance to increase with age (Atchley, 1985; Meer, 1986).

Social Definitions

Physical and psychological aging doubtless have social effects. People confined to wheelchairs may feel isolated. People with impaired hearing may find it difficult to interact with others, so that they withdraw into their private worlds. To a great extent, however, the social effects of aging are society's doing, not nature's. Whereas the effects of age vary greatly from individual to individual, societies tend to lump all people of a particular age together, and to assign them statuses and roles according to their chronological age. The way the elderly are treated, however, varies from one society to another.

Age stratification is found in all societies. In the United States, people younger than 18 cannot vote, and people younger than 30 cannot be members of the U.S. Senate. Children are required to attend school. They are given the status of dependents and are expected to obey their elders, to spend much of their time playing, and to refrain from sexual activities. Similarly, there are **age norms** for the elderly—expectations about what they should and should not do. Basically, they are supposed to be retired, to sit in the rocking chair, and to enjoy the golden years but not to have sexual interests.

In preindustrial societies, the elderly often hold high status. They are esteemed and they assume positions of power. By merely living to be old at a time when few survive past middle age, they earn a certain respect. Because societies change slowly, the knowledge and skills of the aged remain useful. In fact, their experience is greatly valued. They are the community's "experts." Thus throughout Africa, growing old results in rising status and increased respect. Among the Igbo, old people are widely regarded as wise, consulted for their wisdom, and accorded great respect. The Bantu elder is known as "the Father of His People" and revered as such. In Samoa, too, old age is considered "the best time of life," and the elderly are highly respected. Similar respect for older people has also been observed in various other countries, from Thailand to rural Mexico (Cowgill and Holmes, 1972). Of course, there are gaps between the ideal norm of honoring the aged and actual practices. As Peter Yin and Kwok Hung Lai (1983) point out, in traditional China only the relatively well-off could observe the Confucian principle of filial piety—because they were able to ensure respect for elders by having multigenerational households, practicing elaborate ancestor worship ceremonies, or using finances to control children. In India's traditional villages, even the upper-class elderly seldom become leaders because they lose status when their spouses die (Atchley, 1985). Nevertheless, deference to elders remains a social ideal in traditional societies.

In many societies, however, the norm itself changed when industrialization came. The elderly lost their previous role and status. No longer were they the storehouses of a community's knowledge, or the guardians of its traditions, because the knowledge important to the community was changing and traditions were losing their hold. According to modernization theorists, the elderly lose status in modern societies because their skills become obsolete (Cowgill, 1974; Gilleard and Gurkan, 1987). In fact, the elderly's loss of status can be found not only in most of the industrialized countries but also in rural areas that have been touched by modernization. In a remote community in the Nepal Himalayas, for example, the elderly are unhappy with their lot, wishing that they were dead, complaining that their children have abandoned them, and trying to drown their sorrows in home-brewed liquor every day. The reason is that many of their young men have gone to India to work on construction projects and brought back ideas and attitudes that have no room for the traditional value of filial devotion (Goldstein and Beall, 1982).

Modernization does not always have such adverse effects on the elderly, though. Faced with an extremely high level of industrialization, Japan nonetheless continues to embrace its long-standing tradition of respect for old people. This tradition is derived from the Confucian principle of filial duty, which requires children to repay their parents a debt of gratitude for bringing them up. It is further supported by a sharply inegalitarian social structure, which requires inferiors, like servants, students, and children to respect superiors, like masters, teachers, and parents (Palmore and Maeda, 1985). Nevertheless, the case of Japan is only an exception to the rule that modernization reduces the elderly's status. (For another exception, see box, p. 296.)

In contrast to Japan, the United States is founded on the ideology of equality and individualism. With egalitarianism opposing the traditional inequality between old and young, elderly Americans began to lose their privileged status when independence was declared in 1776. Individualism also helped loosen the obligations between young and old (Fischer, 1977). Assisted by this ideological background, extreme industrialization has decisively brought down the status of elderly Americans. Today it sometimes seems as if we expect the elderly to do nothing but wait to die. There is no prestige attached to being old; it is generally seen as a handicap. This is why older people tend to lie about their age. As census takers often find, 55-year-old women suddenly become

UNDERSTANDING OTHER SOCIETIES

The Elderly in China

Historically the Chinese have revered the elderly, but today these 80 million senior citizens face new problems and prospects. This reading surveys the life of the elderly in modern China. How does it compare to the economic and social problems faced by elderly Americans?

China has 80 million people over 60, four-fifths of them living in rural areas. Because of family planning and one-child families, the proportion of elderly in the population will become greater in coming decades.

For centuries China has kept to the Confucian tradition of respect, care and support for old people. As a socialist country China has paid great attention to developing this. The Constitution stipulates that citizens have the right to material assistance from the state and society when they are old, ill or disabled. The government develops social insurance, relief, and medical services required to enable citizens to enjoy this right. The Constitution also states that children who have come of age have the duty to support and assist their parents. Maltreatment of the old is prohibited by law.

The majority of China's old people are physical workers. Only a small number are intellectuals. They include professional revolutionaries before liberation, eminent experts, scholars and experienced workers and farmers who have contributed to the establishment of new China and accumulated much knowledge and experience. They are creators, inheritors and disseminators of China's material and spiritual values.

Men retire at 60 and women at 55 in government offices, while the retirement age is 55 for men and 50 for women in factories and other jobs. Retired workers receive a pension of 75 percent of their wages if they have worked 20 years or more. There are about one million cadres who worked before 1949 and have done special revolutionary work. These retire with 100 percent of their wages.

Most of the retired people in the countryside like to do some light work to support themselves. Others prefer to live with their children. The responsibility system has made big headway and greatly improved the livelihood of the rural people. Yet only 500,000 peasants throughout China have a small pension. Most rural areas do not have retirement systems.

Childless people without incomes in the cities and countryside are guaranteed their livelihood from the collective. There are 23,000 retirement homes in the countryside. In many cities the neighborhood committees have organized to take care of old people with difficulties on a voluntary basis. Some of them even take on their entire support. Newspapers praise these deeds and encourage others to learn from them. Of course, some people have been known to maltreat their parents. But they have been tried and punished.

Society as a whole has tried to provide opportunities for old people to maintain an active role in accordance with their knowledge and ability. Old workers and technicians sometimes keep coming to their factories to help train young workers. Veteran workers and cadres with rich professional knowledge and experience are treasured in society. Forty percent of them work as advisers and consultants in local associations, government offices and enterprises.

Over seventy senior citizen schools have been established. They have turned into activity centers for old folk. Their recreational activities exert a favorable influence on the temperament and character of older people and help them to lead a happy life. They welcome courses on keeping fit, which tell them how to retard the aging process and prolong life.

Many hospitals have special wards for the aged and "home wards" with visiting doctors for those with chronic illnesses. Hospitals spread basic knowledge on health care for the elderly. Over 10 million retired people do physical exercises each day. Many places have clubs and recreation centers for them.

The remarriage of old people has become a new social problem in China. Having lost a partner, and wanting a happy and comfortable life in their old age, it is normal for them to think of remarriage. But under China's deep-seated feudal tradition, widows' remarriage has been regarded as something of an insult to their families. Although the marriage law stipulates that the right of widows to remarry is protected by law, old ideas die hard.

Source: Excerpted and slightly adapted from Zheng She, "New Problems, New Prospects," *China Reconstructs*, July 1986, pp. 8–9.

45, or 75-year-old men are 65 again (Levin and Levin, 1980). The elderly are frequently imprisoned in a **roleless role**—assigned no role in society's division of labor. In fact, mandatory retirement laws have traditionally forced them out of the job market after age 65—now, after 70. It is also very difficult for them to get new jobs again. Little if any value is placed on the elderly's experience. It is often considered irrelevant to the present world.

In short, contemporary American society has not aided the elderly to deal with the biological and psychological effects of aging. Instead it has augmented these effects by defining the aged as people on the fringes of life, as less capable than others of contributing to the work of society.

QUESTIONS FOR DISCUSSION AND REVIEW

1. Why does crystalline intelligence grow with age while fluid intelligence stabilizes or declines?
2. How does the biological process of aging differ from changes caused by age norms and stratification?
3. Why do many sociologists observe that the elderly are trapped in a "roleless role"?

THEORIES OF AGING

To say that the elderly have low status does not tell us a great deal. How do they respond to this status, and just what is their relationship to society? There are many generalizations and theories. Here we look at four of the most influential: disengagement, activity, subculture, and minority theory.

Disengagement

One view of the elderly holds that aging always causes people to disengage from society. Although they do not withdraw totally like hermits, their social interaction declines. According to disengagement theorists, the withdrawal is mutual—aging individuals and younger members of society withdraw from each other. As Elaine Cumming (1963) explains: "The disengagement theory postulates that society withdraws from the aging person to the same extent as the person withdraws from society . . . the process is normatively governed and in a sense agreed upon by all concerned." Thus disengagement occurs when older people retire, when their grown children leave home, when their spouses, friends, and relatives die, when they lose contact with friends and fellow workers, and when they turn their attention to personal rather than societal concerns.

Disengagement theorists further hold that this mutual withdrawal is, on the whole, beneficial both to society in general and to the elderly. It is as if two friends, knowing that separation is imminent, gradually drift apart, easing the pain of separation. Society benefits in at least two ways: disengagement renders the eventual death of the elderly less disruptive to the lives of friends and relatives and it avoids the harmful effects of the older workers' increasing incompetence or sudden death on the economy because younger people have already replaced them in the workplace. The elderly themselves benefit because disengagement relieves them of responsibilities, making their lives easier, and encourages them to begin preparing for their inevitable death. Being "well adjusted" to old age, then, means accepting that one is outside the mainstream of life and coming to terms with one's mortality. Therefore, according to the theory, the disengaged elderly tend to be happier and healthier than those who try to ignore their age and remain as active as before (Cumming and Henry, 1961; Cumming, 1963).

Disengagement theory has stirred up much controversy. The theory does not explain why, for example, powerful members of Congress decline to "disengage," instead remaining in their jobs well past the usual retirement age. More important, critics challenge the assumption that disengagement is universal, inevitable, mutual, and beneficial. James Dowd (1975, 1980) argues that while society may benefit from disengagement, the elderly do not. After all, they are forced into a lower social position. Dowd further criticizes disengagement theory for assuming that aging itself causes disengagement. He uses exchange theory to argue that disengagement occurs because the elderly have lost their power resources—in the sense that their skill or expertise has become outmoded—so that they have nothing to exchange with society for a higher status. Other sociologists contend that disengagement may be harmful to both society and the individual: it may mean losing the talent, energy, and expertise of the disengaged elderly, and it may contribute to poor health, poverty, and loneliness among some of them (Levin and Levin, 1980). Research has shown, however, that most older people do progressively disengage from most social activities, but there is no evidence to support the idea that disengagement leads to a healthier and happier life (Palmore, 1981).

Activity

In direct opposition to disengagement theorists, some sociologists argue that most of the elderly maintain their social involvement. Old people do lose certain roles when they retire or when their children leave home. But according to activity theorists, this loss does not necessarily produce disengagement. Instead, the elderly can invest more of their energies in the roles they retain, or they can find new activities. They might, for example, deepen relationships with grandchildren or spend more time on a hobby. They might make new friends, develop new hobbies, or join new voluntary organizations. By keeping active, say activity theorists, the elderly remain socially and psychologically fit—healthy, happy, and able to live a long life (Havighurst, 1963; Lemon, Bengston, and Peterson, 1972).

Critics have argued that the theory presents an often unattainable goal to the elderly, urging them to cling to an active role in life. Since it is hard for them to find activities that seem meaningful in comparison to their previous roles as workers or parents, they are likely to be left feeling like failures, useless, and worthless (Atchley, 1985). However, because of increased longevity, the elderly are becoming more and more active than their counterparts of the past. Not surprisingly, many elderly people today engage in activities, even as strenuous as marathon running, that the elderly of two decades ago would have considered beyond their reach. Research has also shown that social activity enhances life satisfaction, health, and longevity (Palmore, 1981; Longino and Kart, 1982).

Subculture

Many sociologists believe that the elderly in the United States have responded to their position in society by developing their own subculture. The bases for this development are the interests and experiences shared by the elderly as members of the same age group. Several factors increase interaction among the aged. First are social and demographic trends, including the increasing size of the elderly population, the growing concentration of old people in particular areas such as retirement communities and public housing for the elderly, and the proliferation of social services for the aged. Second, because of prejudice against the aged and

Claire Jacobs, age 80, graduating from college. In growing old, according to activity theorists, people have the time and opportunity to achieve goals that had to be set aside while raising a family or earning a living. Returning to college to take courses in a favorite subject or to earn a degree is an option for those who want to continue their education. By keeping busy, they are likely to remain mentally and socially fit—healthy, happy, and able to live a long life.

fear of aging, the old may find it difficult to interact with anyone but other old people. The result, according to subculture theory, is that the elderly interact with their peers more than with people of other ages, form a politically oriented consciousness of themselves as a group, and develop a stronger, more positive self-image (Rose, 1965).

It is not clear, however, whether the elderly prefer interaction with their peers. A recent study of retirement communities found evidence that the elderly did favor interaction with other old people (Longino, McClelland, and Peterson, 1980). But the people in this study may not have been typical of the elderly, most of whom do not live in retirement communities. Robert Atchley (1985) observes that "the *most valued* interactions for most older people are with members of their families, particularly their adult children." More important, it is not clear whether an elderly subculture actually exists. The theory's leading proponent, Arnold Rose (1965), did not show how the values, beliefs, and lifestyle of the elderly differ from those of the rest of the society.

Minority

Some sociologists believe that it is more accurate to talk of the aged as a minority. Like minority groups, they face prejudice and discrimination, which, by analogy to racism and sexism, is called **ageism.** Like race and gender, age is an ascribed status, over which the individual has no control. And like race and gender, age may be used as the basis for judging and reacting to people, whatever their individual characteristics.

Prejudice and discrimination against the aged can be seen in mandatory retirement laws, substandard nursing homes, and domestic neglect and abuse of elders (Levin and Levin, 1980; Douglass, 1983; Pillemer, 1985). Prejudice against the elderly is also evident in the popular beliefs that old people "are set in their ways, old fashioned, bossy, forgetful, and like to doze in a rocking chair." Some of these ageist beliefs are expressed in jokes such as "Old college presidents never die; they just lose their faculties." Prejudice can further be found in mass communication: in prime time television shows the aged tend to be depicted as evil, unsuccessful, and unhappy. Stereotypes about the aged being accident prone, rigid, dogmatic, and unproductive are often used to justify firing older workers, pressuring them to retire, or refusing to hire them. This is ironic, because, as has been suggested, many studies have shown job performance to increase with age (Levin and Levin, 1980; Meer, 1986). Even well-intentioned people may unconsciously patronize the elderly, treating them like children. This often comes across in the "baby talk" directed to the elderly. As the famous psychologist B. F. Skinner (1983) observes from his experience as a 79-year-old: "Beware of those who are trying to be helpful and too readily flatter you. Second childishness brings you back within range of those kindergarten teachers who exclaim, 'But *that* is very *good!*' Except that now, instead of saying, 'My, you are really growing up!' they will say, 'You are not really getting old!'" In fact, doctors often remark that "when they get old, we have to treat them like children." In a recent study, five physicians were audiotaped when interviewing eight patients each. Half the patients were 45 or younger and the other half 65 or older. In analyzing the tapes, the researchers found that the physicians were less egalitarian, patient, engaged, and respectful with their older patients. These elderly patients were much less successful than the younger ones in getting the doctors to answer their questions and address their own concerns (Schanback, 1987).

There are some problems with viewing the elderly as a minority, however. Contrary to what one would expect of a minority, the elderly have significant political power, because a high percentage of the elderly vote and because there are powerful groups with large memberships representing their interests, such as the National Council of Senior Citizens and the American Association of Retired Persons. Elderly people also hold some of the most powerful positions in the nation as governors, senators, Supreme Court justices, and even president. Even the average older American receives some social benefits from being old. There are many special programs and discounts for the elderly, and they are less likely to be victimized by crime than any other age group except very young children (Palmore, 1979).

QUESTIONS FOR DISCUSSION AND REVIEW

1. What is the focus of each of the theories of aging?
2. Why do many sociologists criticize disengagement theory?
3. Why does the subcultural theory complement the activity perspective on aging?
4. What beliefs make up the ideology of ageism, and why do they support the view that the elderly are members of a minority group?

THE LIFE OF THE ELDERLY

Many people would probably agree with the following statements about the elderly:

1. Old people are usually senile.
2. Older workers are not as productive as younger ones.
3. Most old people live in poverty.
4. Most old people are lonely.
5. Most old people end up in nursing homes and other institutions.
6. Most old people have no interest in or capacity for sexual relations.
7. Most old people are set in their ways and unable to change.
8. Most old people feel miserable (Palmore, 1977).

These statements both reflect and reinforce ageism, and, as we will see in the following sections, they are all false.

Health

Health takes on special importance for the elderly because they generally have more health problems than younger age groups. Americans as a whole average 5.1 visits a year to doctors, but among elderly Americans, the average is 6.6 visits per year. The elderly are also three times more likely than people under 17 to be hospitalized, even though most receive their medical care at home (Kart, 1981).

Compared with younger people, the elderly are less likely to suffer from acute (short-term) illnesses, but they are more likely to have chronic (long-term) ailments. The incidence of acute ailments, such as the common cold and infectious diseases, averages out to 3.6 occurrences a year for each youngster under age 7, but it drops with increasing age to only 1.1 for those aged 65 or older. These "youthful diseases" strike older women more often and harder than older men, disabling women, on average, for a longer time. In contrast, whereas only 20 percent of those under age 17 suffer from some chronic condition, about 85 percent of older people do. The most common chronic diseases are heart ailments, arthritis, rheumatism, and hypertension. Chronic conditions often do not restrict a person's daily activities, but as age increases, they are more likely to be disabling. Unlike acute ailments, chronic problems affect men more seriously than women. Men with chronic conditions are three times more likely than women to lose their capacity to carry on everyday activities (Atchley, 1985). For the chronically ill elderly, the increased longevity of recent years has been a scourge. After all, the longer they live, the longer they have to suffer—by living with chronic illnesses. This is why the suicide rate among the elderly, especially those older than 85, has risen significantly (Manton et al., 1987).

Patterns of mental illness also change with age. The aged are significantly more likely to suffer from a disabling type of mental illness. This is primarily because the prevalence of serious organic (physically caused) mental disorders increases with age. According to one study, chronic organic brain disorders occur in only about 2 percent of those under age 65 but in 20 percent of those 80 years old (Shanas and Maddox, 1976). The most familiar of these disorders is senility. As we noted earlier, senility is not a natural result of aging but instead an abnormal condition characterized by confusion, loss of memory, and loss of the ability to reason. Only about 10 percent of elderly Americans show even a mild loss of memory, much less senility. In fact, senility is not restricted to the elderly, although it is overdiagnosed in the aged. In 80 percent of the cases the symptoms—confusion and forgetfulness—result from *non*neurological problems that can be treated. Malnutrition, fever, and medication can make a person appear senile. If these underlying problems are not treated, the symptoms of senility may persist. In contrast to these cases of nonneurological problems, about 2.5 million Americans do suffer from neurological diseases. Most of these people are striken with **Alzheimer's disease,** an incurable disease of the brain. Scientists suspect that it is hereditary because half the immediate family members of the patient may develop the mental disorder if they live into their nineties. The disease can also strike the middle aged, although the symptoms usually do not appear before the age of 50. The victims progressively lose their memory, their ability "to think, to reason, to calculate, and, finally, to perform the simple chores of everyday life" (Henig, 1981; Fischman, 1984; Schmeck, 1987).

Despite the higher frequency of illness among the elderly, old age itself is not a disease. Thus old people cannot die of old age—just as young people cannot die of young age. In fact, the increasing life expectancy—due to improved sanitation, better health care, and healthier life-styles—will likely reduce the prevalence of chronic illness among the elderly (Palmore, 1986).

There are also large differences in the health of individuals among the elderly just as among younger people. This is why, as Matilda Riley (1982) points out, "even at the oldest ages there are some who can see as well, run as far, and perform as well on mental tests as younger people can." Also, most old people do not consider themselves in poor health. In fact, the majority (nearly 70 percent) of the elderly population consider their health good or excellent (Kart, 1981). Older people's perceptions of their own health are even more positive than those of younger people. This is, however, largely due to social comparison, whereby the elderly compare themselves with their age peers rather than with younger, healthier people. Thus we should be careful not to exaggerate the health of the elderly—they remain less healthy than younger individuals (Cockerham et al., 1983; Levkoff et al., 1987).

Work and Retirement

Thirty years ago, nearly 50 percent of all elderly men were employed. Today only 17 percent of them are in the labor force. However, elderly women's labor force participation has changed little, from 10 percent in 1950 to 8 percent today, largely because of ther traditionally low employment rates (Taeuber, 1983). The elderly as a whole have the lowest employment rate of any age group over 16 (Figure 12.2). In many other industrialized nations the elderly have similarly low rates of employment (see Table 12.1).

Factors in Declining Employment Several factors have contributed to this drop in employment among the elderly. First, industrialized economies increasingly demand more and more highly educated workers with the latest skills and knowledge, which places older workers at a competitive disadvantage with younger workers (Pampel and Weiss, 1983). Thus changing technology tends to make older people's skills obsolete, adding to their difficulties in retaining jobs or finding new ones. With the coming of nonmechanical watches, for example, the demand for skilled watchmakers who could repair the delicate mechanisms of conventional watches has dropped.

Figure 12.2 Employment Declines With Age

Rates of labor-force participation begin to decline slightly among those in their fifties but fall sharply among those in their sixties. This age-related downswing in employment has resulted from changing technology, age discrimination and pension programs.

Source: Census Bureau, *Statistical Abstract of the United States*, 1988, p. 366.

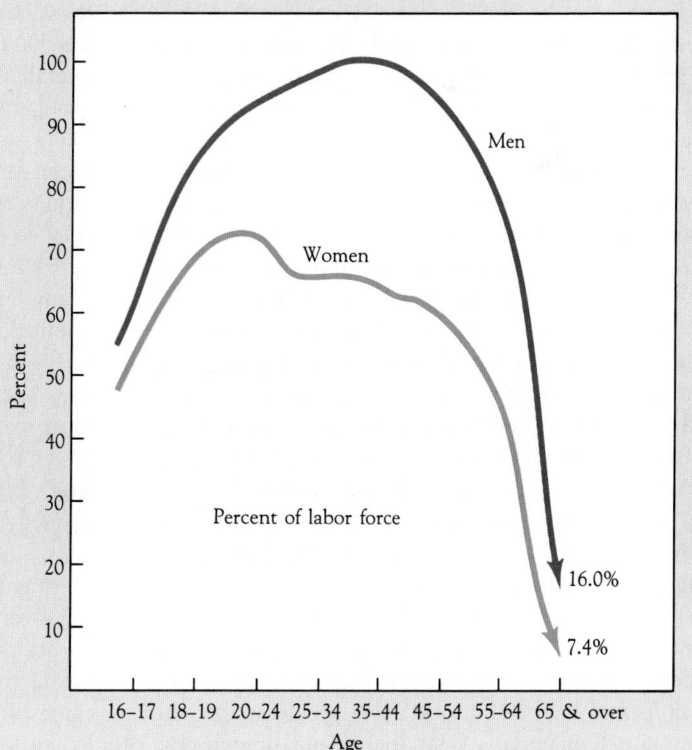

Table 12.1 Few Elderly Are Working

The majority of elderly people have always worked, especially in agricultural societies. Even in the United States 30 years ago, nearly half of all elderly men were employed. Today the proportion of elderly Americans working is much lower. A similar situation prevails in other industrial countries.

Country	Proportion of elderly working
Japan	25%
Norway	22
Israel	15
Portugal	14
United States	11
Canada	10
Switzerland	10
Australia	10
Sweden	9
Denmark	8
Italy	6
New Zealand	6
Spain	5
West Germany	4
France	3
Netherlands	2
Austria	2

Source: Year Book of Labour Statistics, 1983, Geneva: International Labour Office, 1983, pp. 13–37.

Second, because of ageism, older workers may be considered inefficient, whatever their actual skills are. The myth that older workers are not as productive as younger ones has been widespread. It has produced the conclusion that the economy benefited from a system of mandatory retirement, forcing workers to quit at a certain age and opening jobs to younger people. In fact, the aged do generally experience some decline in perception and reaction speed. But on most measures of productivity, they perform as well as younger workers. Sometimes, as in the garment manufacturing industry, older workers perform even better because of their greater experience. They show greater consistency of output, change jobs less, have fewer accidents, and are absent less often than younger workers (Giniger, Dispenzieri, and Eisenberg, 1983). Moreover, the elderly do not suffer an overall deterioration in intellectual performance. In fact, with age people show an improvement in acquired intellectual skills and in the ability to solve problems that involve visual materials (Hendricks and Hendricks, 1981). Still, age discrimination, though outlawed since 1967, makes it difficult for the elderly to get and keep jobs (Rones, 1983).

Finally, employment rates dropped because retirement became an established institution. The emergence of pension programs allowed workers to retire, and changing attitudes made it socially acceptable to do so. For the majority of American workers, retirement became economically feasible only after social security was established in 1935 as as way of opening up jobs for the vast number of younger unemployed workers during the Great Depression. Later, programs offering early retirement benefits further encouraged the exodus of older workers from the labor force (Atchley, 1982).

The Decision to Retire People may be forced to retire because of poor health, inability to find a job after being laid off, or mandatory retirement. When retirement is a matter of choice, both job satisfaction and retirement income play a part in the decision. Presumably, if we like our jobs now, we would not look forward to retirement. Evidence shows that this presumption is wrong. According to surveys, more than 80 percent of the American labor force are relatively satisfied with their jobs, but most have favorable attitudes toward retirement. Only a few dread it. On the other hand, professionals, managers, and others in high-status occupations overall like their jobs better than those in low-status occupations, and these higher-status workers are less likely to retire early. Physicians, for example, tend to prefer retiring in their late sixties, but male auto workers tend to retire in their mid-fifties (Atchley, 1982). When they do retire early, higher-status workers may continue to be involved in their professions. In one study, for example, the majority of retired scientists spent time on scientific research (Decker, 1980). The most important factor in deciding when to retire, however, is income. If they are eligible for adequate pay during retirement, most workers choose to retire early (Atchley, 1982).

The Effects of Retirement Retirement has been blamed for a variety of physical and psychological problems, including death. But research has shown that there is no causal relationship between retirement and illness or death. Of course, some people become ill and die after retirement, but usually they were in poor health before retirement. Indeed, they may have retired because of their health (Palmore, 1981; Minkler, 1981). In one survey about a third of the workers reported that retirement *improved* their health, and only about 3 per-

"Edgar, you've been retired for three years now. Why don't you loosen your tie?"

cent thought their health worsened (Rosenberg, 1970). A more recent study suggests that health improvement is especially likely to occur if retirement provides a release from the stress and strain of a job (Ekerdt, Bosse, and LoCastro, 1983).

Although a majority of retired people—70 percent in one study—are not completely satisfied with retirement, only a small minority—less than 12 percent—would want to return to a job or be able to do so (Motley, 1978). Most workers adapt to retirement in three months or less. According to a number of studies, for retired people *as a whole,* retirement does not cause low morale, low self-esteem, social isolation, or feelings of loneliness (Palmore, 1981). A major reason for the successful adjustment to retirement is the retiree's ability to keep busy. Under the influence of the "busy ethic," retirees keep busy by engaging in various activities, including part-time jobs, volunteer work, shopping, tasks around the home, and fishing or other leisure pursuits (Ekerdt, 1986).

But retirement does affect people's lives, and it tends to affect some groups more than others. For retirees as a whole, it tends to increase feelings of economic deprivation, because people's incomes usually drop when they retire—generally to about half of their preretirement income. In general, retirement seems to have more negative effects on women than men and on the lower classes than other groups. Retirement is more likely to produce, for example, poverty and social isolation among women and the lower classes. Blue-collar workers tend to be less satisfied with retirement than white-collar workers, even though white-collar workers tend to be more strongly committed to their jobs and less pleased with the prospect of retiring. Adjustment to retirement is especially difficult for those former blue-collar workers who have low income, poor health, and little education. The fact that men and white-collar workers are better adjusted to retirement than women and blue-collar workers has a lot to do with the former's superior financial situation (Atchley, 1985).

Financial Situation

The financial situations of old and young families are not strictly comparable. Usually the elderly's families are smaller, and they have fewer expenses than younger people. Most do not need to furnish a large new home, raise children, and pay their education expenses. Their expenses for work clothes and transportation are lower than those of younger people. They are also likely to have financial assets that younger people do not have. The majority of the aged own their homes, are free from mortgage payments, and have money in the bank. Many, though not a majority, own some U.S. savings bonds, stocks, and corporate bonds. Although the income from these assets is small, it does help offset slightly the gap between the incomes of middle-aged and older families. At the same time, however, the elderly are more likely than younger people to face huge medical bills, even beyond what government programs cover. And financial hardship is particularly difficult for the aged who have been accustomed to a better financial situation in their younger days (Decker, 1980).

The overwhelming majority (nearly 97 percent) of old people receive most of their income from social security benefits and private or public pensions. Of these programs social security is by far the most important source of income, because it is the *only* source of income for more than 80 percent of retirees. For many of the elderly, this income is supplemented by government benefits such as food stamps, Medicare, special property tax exemptions, public housing, and Supplemental Security Income for the elderly poor. Thus, the elderly are not so poor that they will pilfer food and medicine from a store (see box, p. 304).

Until recently the elderly were much more likely to be poor than most other Americans. In 1970 the propor-

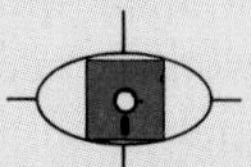

LOOKING AT CURRENT RESEARCH

Are Elderly Shoplifters Really Poor?

It is popularly believed that most elderly people are so poor that they resort to shoplifting. As the following report indicates, most of the elderly shoplifters have average or higher than average socioeconomic backgrounds. Their reasons for shoplifting are largely similar to those of younger offenders. What are these reasons?

Crime committed by the elderly has recently caught the attention of gerontologists, criminologists, and law enforcement officials. More than 200,000 elderly people are arrested each year in the United States for violations and crimes ranging from drunkenness and driving while intoxicated to homicide and aggravated assault. One crime particularly prevalent among the elderly is shoplifting.

While studies of shoplifting have covered its cost, causes, prevention and reporting, both the description and analysis of shoplifting by the elderly remains a relatively uncharted field. One exploratory study, undertaken in 1981, surveyed 191 cases of first-offender shoplifters aged 60 and over who were voluntarily participating in a rehabilitation program. The following characteristics of shoplifting by the elderly emerged from this survey:

Rates for elderly males slightly exceed those for elderly females.

Most offenders are of average or better than average socioeconomic status.

The majority of offenders are married or live with another individual.

Most offenders have lived two or more years in their communities, and many are 20-year residents.

Very few offenders suffer from a recent loss of a spouse, close friend or relative.

Very few offenders are plagued by serious health problems.

Offenders are as likely to feel optimistic as they are to feel alienated and pessimistic.

Offenders tend not to participate in religious, fraternal, or service associations, despite long-time residence in the community.

Food and drugs are less likely to be taken by elderly shoplifters than clothing or personal items.

The average value of goods stolen by elderly shoplifters is about $14—significantly less than that for all age groups.

While these findings are preliminary and further study is needed, they do begin to frame a portrait of shoplifting by the elderly.

Why people shoplift remains an open question. Some, in keeping with traditional psycho-social perspectives, content that shoplifters suffer from low frustration tolerance levels, lack of insight into realistic problem solving, poor self-images, feelings of inferiority, recent traumatic experiences, or a deeper psychopathology. Others assert that no pathological state underlies such acts. Instead, they are caused by the same economic forces which guide shopping behavior: getting the most goods for the least cost. Less analytical studies simply delineate the reasons typically given by shoplifters to account for their behavior, including, for example, desire for the item, lack of money, need for excitement, or an unexplained urge.

Source: Excerpted from Gary Feinberg, "Shoplifting by the Elderly," *Aging,* October/November 1983, pp. 20–24.

tion of the elderly living in poverty was nearly 25 percent, compared with 13 percent for the general population. A change came in the late 1970s: as inflation rose, the income of many Americans did not keep pace with the rising cost of living. Nor did many federal programs for the poor such as Aid for Families with Dependent Children. But social security did. Congress tied social security to increases in the consumer price index, so that benefits rose automatically as the cost of living rose. As a result, the poverty rate among the elderly declined, from 25 percent in 1970 to only 12 percent in 1987—compared with 14 percent for the general population (Herbers, 1982; Greer, 1987; Census Bureau, 1988).

The elderly are not exactly well off, though. Elderly households still had only 58 percent as much income as the average household in 1983 (Blotnick, 1984). It is true that the elderly do not need as much money as the average household to live comfortably—because they no longer have children to support, high mortgage payments, and other expenses that younger, larger households have. But a substantial proportion of the elderly—at least one-third—are living near the poverty line, though they are not officially considered poor (Binstock, 1983). Poverty is especially common among those older Americans who live alone, who are women, and who are members of minority groups, In 1982, for example, women accounted for nearly 71 percent of all elderly persons living in poverty, and about 38 percent of all elderly blacks were poor, compared with 12 percent of elderly whites (Census Bureau, 1985).

Personal Relationships

In several surveys, more than 70 percent of the elderly say they are never or hardly ever lonely. They often see close relatives, socialize with friends, go to church, and participate in voluntary organizations. At any one time, less than 5 percent of the elderly are living in a nursing home or other institution. During their whole lives, only about 20 percent of the elderly will ever spend time in an institution. Less than a tenth of older people have never married and, as lifelong loners, they are not likely to find old age a time of special isolation. About a quarter of the elderly—mostly women—live alone. Most of the aged live with their spouses, and their family relationships tend to be far more satisfying than stereotypes suggest (Gubrium, 1975; Palmore, 1977, 1981; Sanoff, 1983).

Marital Relationships More than half of the American elderly are married and living with their husbands or wives. But men are much more likely than women to be living with their spouses, because more than 70 percent of older men but less than 40 percent of older women still have a spouse alive to live with. One reason for this difference is that women tend to live longer than men. In addition, there is a greater tendency for men to marry younger women than for women to marry younger men.

The rate of divorce is extremely low among older people—about 3 percent. In one study 95 percent of the elderly rated their marriage as happy or very happy. Even more impressive is the finding that a majority (55 percent) reported that the happiest period of their marriage was the present (Decker, 1980).

Sexual Activity Contrary to popular stereotypes, most men and many women remain sexually active during their seventies and eighties. The availability of a partner and sexual experience in earlier life are the most important factors determining sexual activity among the aged. Those who are sexually active in old age generally were active when they were younger, and those who are less active sexually are likely to have shown this pattern, too, when they were younger. Other significant determinants of sexual frequency are health and socioeconomic status: better-educated, higher-income, and healthier elderly persons tend to be more sexually active. Although sexual activity does not guarantee longevity, it does tend to maintain or enhance both health and happiness among the elderly (Palmore, 1981). A continuing interest in sexuality does not occur only among the married elderly; it is also a significant part of their unmarried peers' dating experience. As a 77-year-old woman says, "Sex isn't as important when you're older, but in a way you need it more." The single elderly need the intimacy provided by sex because it helps raise their self-esteem, making them feel desired and needed (Bulcroft and O'Conner-Roden, 1986).

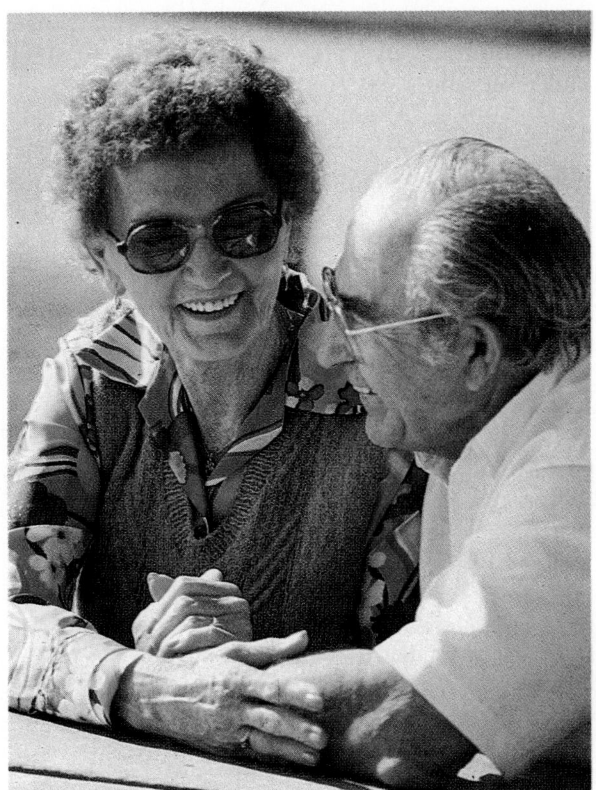

Most elderly people do not fit the stereotype of being sick and lonely. Most of the aged live with their spouses. They find their marriages quite satisfying. Most men and women also continue to be sexually active in their seventies and eighties.

Relationships with Children When the last child leaves home, most parents do not find the "empty nest" lonely or meaningless. They have anticipated their children's leaving, and they appreciate their own increased freedom. They also tend to maintain close ties with their children (Shanas, 1979).

About 85 to 90 percent of the aged who have children live less than an hour away from them, so they can visit each other easily. Indeed, they do see each other often, "maintaining intimacy at a distance." Several studies found that about 80 percent of older parents had seen one of their children within the last day or week (Kart, 1981). Elderly parents often give advice, gifts, even money. Some studies show that older parents in general are more likely to give money to their children than to receive it. The elderly parents' generosity often "takes the form of helping with college tuition, down payment on a house, furniture—not just a check every Christmas" (Gibbs, 1988). According to most estimates, about one out of ten older individuals receives cash from his or her adult children, but half of the elderly give cash to their children or grandchildren. More precisely, the flow of aid from parents to adult children occurs more often in the middle and upper classes, but the flow of aid from children to old parents happens more frequently in the working class (Atchley, 1985).

In short, the fact that few of the elderly live with their children apparently does not reflect an absence of feeling. Indeed, parents as well as children usually reject the idea of two or three generations living in the same household. According to one survey, most American adults believe it is a bad idea for parents to live with their children's families. But most say that a sick parent should live with a daughter rather than be placed in an institution (Wake and Sporakowski, 1972). In a more recent survey, most Americans also say that they would welcome their parents to live with them if they wanted to (Sussman and Romeis, 1982). There are several reasons for young adults' increasing support for multigenerational residence. First, the rising number of old people has sensitized Americans to the elderly's plight. Second, the decreasing dependence of older individuals due to improved health and financial status has made them more attractive as potential coresidents. And third, young people trying hard to succeed in their careers welcome the benefits of pooled economic resources and the help with child rearing and other domestic tasks (Okraku, 1987). But most of the elderly are reluctant to move in with their children, which may reflect the importance that American culture gives to independence and self-reliance. To many, it would be humiliating to accept help from their children.

Widowhood There are five times more widows than widowers. Men seem to adjust to widowhood more easily than women do. Among the possible reasons are the fact that, on the whole, men tend more to remarry, know more people, participate in more organizations, are more likely to own and drive a car, and most importantly, have higher incomes.

Even for men, losing a spouse can have serious consequences. Elderly widowers are seven times more likely than married men in the same age bracket to die. They are also three times more likely to die in a car accident, four times more likely to commit suicide, six times more likely to die from a heart attack, and ten times more likely to die from a stroke (Kucherov, 1981).

For women, widowhood brings different kinds of problems. The most serious is loneliness. This results mostly from having been accustomed to the traditional role of wife, having derived one's identity from being the wife of so-and-so. Widows who have been more independent are more able to cope with their loneliness. There are other factors that influence women's reactions to widowhood. Widows who live in large cities are more lonely than those who live in small towns. Compared with middle-class women, working-class women tend to be more lonely and isolated, because they have fewer

Widows outnumber widowers by 5 to 1. Widowhood weighs more heavily on elderly women than men. The women tend less to remarry, know fewer people, participate in fewer organizations, are less likely to own and drive a car, and have less income. The most serious problem besetting elderly widows is loneliness.

friends and associates and less money. Younger widows are more lonely than older ones. As Robert Atchley (1985) explains, "If [a woman] is one of the first in her group of friends to become widowed, she may find that her friends feel awkward talking about death and grief . . . if the widow is one of the last to become widowed in a group of friends, then she may find great comfort among friends who identify very well with the problems of grief and widowhood."

Myths and Realities

In summary, old age seems to look better to the elderly than it does to the young. Some studies have found no significant differences among age groups in happiness, morale, or satisfaction. In other studies the aged scored lower than younger people on various measures of happiness, but only 20 to 30 percent had low scores. In one recent national survey, less than a fourth of the elderly agreed with the statement that "This is the dreariest time of my life," and 87 percent agreed with the statement that "I am just as happy as when I was younger." In fact, a longitudinal study shows that psychological well-being does not decline with age, which suggests that old age by itself does not cause unhappiness (Novak, 1983; Baur and Okun, 1983; Costa et al., 1987). Since they feel that they have a good, full life, the elderly often accept death more readily than their young relatives. "Older people," said one gerontologist, "want to talk about death, but when they do, their 40-year-old children change the conversation" (Mayer, 1977).

The differences between popular myths and realities are summarized in Table 12.2. (See also box, p. 308.) But the fact that the position of the elderly as a whole is not as dreadful as stereotypes paint it should not obscure the difficulties that many of the elderly face. To a great extent, the position of elderly Americans mirrors their position earlier in life. Inequalities persist, or even worsen, during old age. The poor, minorities, and women living alone are likely to find old age a time of great economic difficulty. In fact, only a small portion of the tremendous increases in government expenditures for the aged goes to the poor, while most goes to the middle-class elderly (Cole, 1983; Haug and Folmar, 1986). Old people in nursing homes often find themselves being treated as mere objects. And most of the elderly must adjust to the loss of those they love, and the disappearance of the landmarks of their lives.

Table 12.2 The Aged: Myths and Realities

Myths	Realities
Old people are usually senile.	Most old people do not experience a loss of intelligence or rationality; only about 10 percent suffer even a mild loss of memory.
Older workers are not as productive as younger ones.	On most measures of productivity, older workers are as productive as younger ones, despite some decline in perception and reaction speed.
Most old people live in poverty.	Compared with the population as a whole, the aged are less likely to be poor, primarily because they have many sources of income.
Most old people are lonely.	In surveys the majority of the aged say they are never or hardly ever lonely.
Most old people end up in nursing homes and other institutions.	Although about a quarter of aged Americans will spend some time in a nursing home, less than 5 percent are institutionalized at any particular time.
Most old people have no interest in or capacity for sexual relations.	Most old people maintain their sexual interest and capacity.
Most old people are set in their ways and unable to change.	The majority of the aged manage to adjust to changes such as their children's leaving home, their own illness, and impending death.
Most old people feel miserable.	Some studies have found no significant difference among age groups in happiness, morale, or life satisfaction.

Source: Based largely on Erdman Palmore, "Facts on aging," *Gerontologist,* 17, August 1977, pp. 315–320.

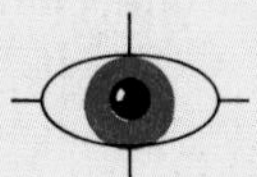

USING SOCIOLOGICAL INSIGHT

The Best Years of Their Lives

In the following article, Teresa Anderson presents some facts and figures to show that not all of the elderly require financial support from the government. Can the elderly continue to expect as much support in the future?

A while back, when I traveled with my husband and son to attend a family gathering, my parents, who were in an identical room in the same motel, were billed $5 less than I was. The reason? They are "senior citizens." Forget that they are both still very gainfully employed, have no dependents, own three pieces of property and had no intention of requesting a discount. In this country, anyone 62 or more is automatically entitled to a plethora of perks and subsidies, regardless of need.

The assumption now is that "old" equals "poor." But how needy are senior citizens? Families headed by a single woman, for example, have a per capita income less than half that of seniors. What's more, people 65 and older had a per capita after-tax income of $6299—$335 more than any age group except those over 50. Their poverty rate, 14 percent, only mirrors that of the general population.

Even that favorite phrase of politicians, "fixed income," has to be reconsidered. Retired persons often have stabilized, if not entirely rigid, expenses. Almost 70 percent own their own homes; others have a sizable nest egg from its sale. Their fixed incomes do not decrease because of a company layoff or because of increases in FICA [federal insurance contributions] withholding. Medicare covers major hospital expenses and private companies offer supplemental coverage. Public transportation is cheap, or nearly free. And virtually every amusement can be obtained for a discount.

Contrast this with the expenses of a 30-year-old "Yuppie" couple. The typical monthly mortgage payment in 1983 reached $741. Total income payments are higher. There is no rebate on your property tax, which many seniors in my city get. Or on a bus that costs 75 cents, but serves seniors for a dime.

This doesn't take into account the deductions for social security—my husband and I paid $3600 into the system in 1984. And that's just the amount deducted from our paychecks, not the equal employer contribution that we also had to earn. If we'd been allowed to invest this $3600 each year in an IRA earning 10 percent for 45 years, we could save more than $2.5 million dollars by retirement. Nausea prevents me from calculating the entire $7200.

Please don't confuse this questioning with a lack of respect for the aged. We should honor them for their wisdom and experience and attempt to meet their *real* needs. But senior citizens can't be lumped together into a homogenous blob of senile men and women eating cat food in lonely rented rooms. Some are bag ladies in need of a hearty meal and a safe house. But should Rose Kennedy and William Randolph Hearst, Jr., also be eligible for subsidized meals through congregate dining programs? Should a movie theater or restaurant be allowed to offer special rates to one population group? Would they get away with advertising "15 Percent Discount for Caucasians"? Why isn't it just as shocking to discriminate against the young as the old?

Young people have to lead the way in reform, hand in hand with those many older people who are tired of being treated like beggars. People like my grandmother, who just died at the age of 84. She served others by cooking, cleaning, baby-sitting, dog-walking and even by entertaining in nursing homes until the very day of her death. Her activities in many senior groups sometimes made her wonder, "Why should we expect things to be free? It's our grandchildren who will have to pay."

We need to untangle our social structure and separate the programs for the poor (both young and old) from the programs for the elderly (both poor and rich). We must not confuse perception with reality. After all, isn't there something strange about believing that a 73-year-old man can be president, but that he can't pay for his coffee at McDonald's?

Source: Reprinted from Teresa A. Anderson, "The Best Years of Their Lives," *Newsweek*, January 7, 1985, pp. 6–7. Reprinted by permission of Teresa Anderson.

QUESTIONS FOR DISCUSSION AND REVIEW

1. Why isn't old age a disease?
2. When do most elderly decide to retire, and how does this transition affect health and longevity?
3. Why do many elderly persons still live near the poverty line?
4. How do marital relationships, sexual activity, and relationships with children change when persons become elderly?
5. How do the myths about old age differ from the realities?

THE FUTURE OF AGING

What will aging be like 20 or 30 years from now? The educational level and occupational status of the elderly will probably be higher, perhaps destroying the stereotype of the aged as doddering, senile oldsters. The divorce rate of the elderly will probably increase, too, because as people expect to live longer, they may demand more from their marriages. Social pressure against early retirement will probably increase, because of the cost of providing income to the elderly (Decker, 1980; Williamson, Evans, and Munley, 1980; Kart, 1981).

The prediction that can be made with the most confidence, however, is that the size of the elderly population will grow. If present trends continue, by the year 2020 the elderly will make up 21 percent of the population, as opposed to about 11 percent today. There will also be far fewer elderly men than women. In 1983 there were already only about 67 American males aged 65 or older for every 100 females; in 2020 the sex ratio will even be smaller, with 65.5 men for every 100 women (Census Bureau, 1984). The political power of the elderly, already considerable, is likely to increase (Williamson et al., 1982). So, too, will the number of geriatric day-care centers, which offer part-time supervision and care including medical treatment, rehabilitation, and counseling. We now already have at least 1200 such centers, compared with only 12 in 1970 (Hey, 1986).

The proportion of elderly in the population is growing steadily. It is expected to reach 21 percent by the year 2020 from about 11 percent today. One major consequence will be a great increase in the elderly's political power, which is already considerable today. There will also be far more geriatric daycare centers providing medical treatment, rehabilitation, and counseling. It is difficult, though, to forecast whether ageism will wax or wane and whether the social security system will survive or collapse.

Other consequences of the growth in the elderly population are less certain. Some people argue that it will decrease prejudice against the aged. But prejudice against a minority often increases as the size of the group grows, because its members are then more likely to be seen by others as a threat. If unemployment goes up again in the future as it did in the early 1980s, then younger unemployed workers may resent older people who hold jobs. Even those who are employed may see older, high-status workers as obstacles to their own upward mobility. However, the economy may continue to be healthy. Besides, in the coming decades, labor is likely to be scarce because birth rates were low during the 1960s and 1970s. In that case, employment opportunities for the elderly may increase, and workers young and old should enjoy greater bargaining power with employers.

The shape of the economy and the size of the labor force are keys to another aspect of the elderly's well-being: social security. Social security benefits for those who are retired come from the social security taxes paid by *current* workers and their employers. If the workforce is small—because of slow population growth or high unemployment—or if wages are low, then social security funds will dry up. Any predictions about the state of social security in future decades therefore depend on how many people will be claiming benefits, how many people will be working, what their wages will be, and what the rate of inflation will be.

Today social security is in trouble. Created during the Depression of the 1930s as a small supplement to the elderly's own retirement savings, social security has now become the sole income for most retirees. It has also expanded its benefits to take care of disabled workers, sick employees, divorced spouses, full-time students, and dependent grandchildren. As a result, the number of beneficiaries on the rolls has shot up from fewer than 3 million 20 years ago to over 36 million today. Another problem has been the failure of workers' contributions to keep up with the soaring benefits. The tax rate has always been very low—no more than 7 percent of workers' income. Meanwhile, the elderly population has been growing larger while the number of workers has been shrinking. About 40 years ago there were 50 workers paying taxes to support each beneficiary, but today each beneficiary is supported by only three workers. Finally, the high rates of inflation and unemployment in the past ten years have reduced social security funds. One possible solution is to cut expenses by raising retirement age, decreasing benefits for early retirement, and encouraging IRA and other private pension plans. Another is to increase revenues by raising taxes and bringing more workers under social security. Whatever solutions are chosen will affect the economic well-being of many elderly Americans in the future (Anderson, 1983; Keyfitz, 1983; *Society*, 1983). Many observers, though, predict that when the baby-boom generation begins to retire in 2015, the far smaller baby-bust generation will refuse to pay the heavy taxes needed to support the hordes of elderly people. But such a pessimistic forecast fails to take into account several important factors. One, young adults realize that the government benefits from the taxes will go to their own parents and grandparents, whom they might have to support by themselves if the government did not. Two, the baby-bust generation will be in great demand as workers, so that they will be well-off enough to accept the tax increases necessary for supporting the elderly. Three, due to improved health, a growing number of older people will work past normal retirement, and these workers will pay taxes into the social security fund rather than draw benefits from it (Otten, 1987).

QUESTIONS FOR DISCUSSION AND REVIEW

1. How will the growing number of elderly persons change American society?
2. Why is the Social Security system in such trouble?

CHAPTER REVIEW

1. *What are the biological and psychological effects of aging?* With age, we become more vulnerable to disease and stress. There are many more specific changes that typically accompany old age—from wrinkled skin to declining visual acuity and slowing of psychomotor responses. These changes are usually inconveniences, not disabilities, and the rate of change varies from person to person.

2. *How does society influence aging?* It tends to magnify the biological and psychological effects of aging and underestimate individual differences in rates of aging. Society defines norms for people according to their chronological age groups. The elderly are usually accorded high status in preindustrial societies but lower status in industrial societies.

3. *How do the elderly respond to their social position?* According to disengagement theorists, society and the elderly withdraw from each other. In contrast, activity theorists argue that, instead of withdrawing from society, the elderly may turn to new activities to substitute for their lost roles as workers and parents. Subculture theorists claim that elderly Americans increase social interaction with each other and develop a distinctive subculture, which fosters political self-consciousness and a positive self-image. Other sociologists argue that interaction among the elderly results from their status as a minority group, facing prejudice and discrimination known as *ageism*.

4. *How do the elderly's health problems differ from those of younger people?* Overall, they tend to have more health problems. More specifically, they are less likely to suffer from acute problems but more likely to have chronic ailments. With increasing age, chronic conditions are more likely to be disabling. Although the overall rate of

mental illness is not higher among elderly people, the aged are more likely than younger people to suffer serious, physically caused mental disorders.

5. *Are older workers less productive than younger ones?* On most measures of productivity, no, although the elderly do generally experience a decline in perception and reaction speed. In a number of ways elderly workers tend to be more reliable than younger ones. *Does retirement harm people's health and self-image?* In general, retirement does not cause illness or low self-esteem, although it does tend to increase feelings of economic deprivation. But the effects of retirement vary. It is especially difficult for those with low income, poor health, and little education.

6. *How does old age affect Americans' financial situation?* Their incomes drop, but the needs of elderly families also tend to be less than those of younger ones. The overwhelming majority of the elderly receive most of their income from social security. In the last few years the poverty rate among the elderly has begun to dip below that of the population as a whole, but poverty is still common among the elderly who live alone, who are women, or who are black.

7. *Do elderly Americans live alone?* Most don't, but elderly women are far more likely than elderly men to live alone. In general, the divorce rate among the elderly is very low, and most of those with children see them frequently. *Are the elderly miserable?* Some researchers have found no significant difference among age groups in happiness, morale, or satisfaction.

8. *What is the status of aging likely to be a few decades from now?* The elderly are likely to make up a larger share of the U.S. population, and their educational level and occupational status are likely to be higher. Their divorce rate and pressures against early retirement might also increase. The economic status of the aged in the future may depend on the condition of the social security system at that time.

KEY TERMS

Ageism Prejudice and discrimination against people because of their age (p. 299).

Age norm A norm that defines what people at a given stage of life should or should not do (p. 295).

Alzheimer's disease An incurable disease of the brain, characterized by progressive loss of memory and other mental abilities (p. 300).

Crystalline intelligence Wisdom and insight into the human condition, as shown by one's skills in philosophy, language, music, or painting (p. 294).

Fluid intelligence Ability to comprehend abstract relationships, as in mathematics, physics, or some other science (p. 294).

Roleless role Being assigned no role in society's division of labor, a predicament of the elderly in industrial society (p. 297).

Senescence The natural physical process of aging (p. 292).

Senility An abnormal condition characterized by serious memory loss, confusion, and loss of the ability to reason; not a natural result of aging (p. 294).

SUGGESTED READINGS

Atchley, Robert C. 1985. *Social Forces and Aging,* 4th ed. Belmont, Calif.: Wadsworth. A comprehensive text on social gerontology—the sociological study of aging—one of the best in the field.

Davis-Friedmann, Deborah. 1983. *Long Lives: Chinese Elderly and the Communist Revolution.* Cambridge, Mass.: Harvard University Press. A highly readable account of how the status of the elderly in China has risen under communism.

Levin, Jack, and William C. Levin, 1980. *Ageism: Prejudice and Discrimination Against the Elderly.* Belmont, Calif.: Wadsworth. An important analysis of the elderly as a minority group, showing the characteristics and social implications of ageism as well as presenting a set of proposals for combating the problem.

Palmore, Erdman et al. (eds.) 1985. *Normal Aging III: Reports from the Duke Longitudinal Studies, 1975–1984.* Durham, N.C.: Duke University Press. A gold mine of data about the biological, psychological, and sociological aspects of aging.

Palmore, Erdman, and Daisaku Maeda. 1985. *The Honorable Elders Revisited: A Revised Cross-Cultural Analysis of Aging in Japan.* Durham, N.C.: Duke University Press. Shows how the elderly retain their traditionally high status in Japan despite the onslaught of modernization.

PART FOUR

Social Institutions

Virtually every society has evolved certain social institutions—sets of widely shared beliefs, norms, or procedures—for satisfying its members' basic needs. The most important institutions are the family, education, religion, politics, the economy, and medicine. Other institutions, especially science and sport, have recently become essential for living a comfortable and enjoyable life.

In Chapter 13 we discuss the family, which produces and socializes the society's new members. In Chapter 14 we focus on education, which transmits to the young the society's social and cultural values. In Chapter 15 we deal with religion, which fosters social integration through a sharing of sacred beliefs. In Chapter 16 we analyze politics, which regulates conflict and allocates resources to ensure social order. In Chapter 17 we examine the economy, which makes possible the production and distribution of goods and services. In Chapter 18 we look into the medical institution to see how social forces affect health and medical care. In Chapter 19 we turn to science, a relatively new institution of great importance to modern society. In Chapter 20 we zero in on sport, an institution whose influence on our lives has been growing increasingly bigger in recent years.

All these institutions are supposed to meet people's needs. But in what ways and how well do they carry out their functions? We will explore questions such as this in the following eight chapters.

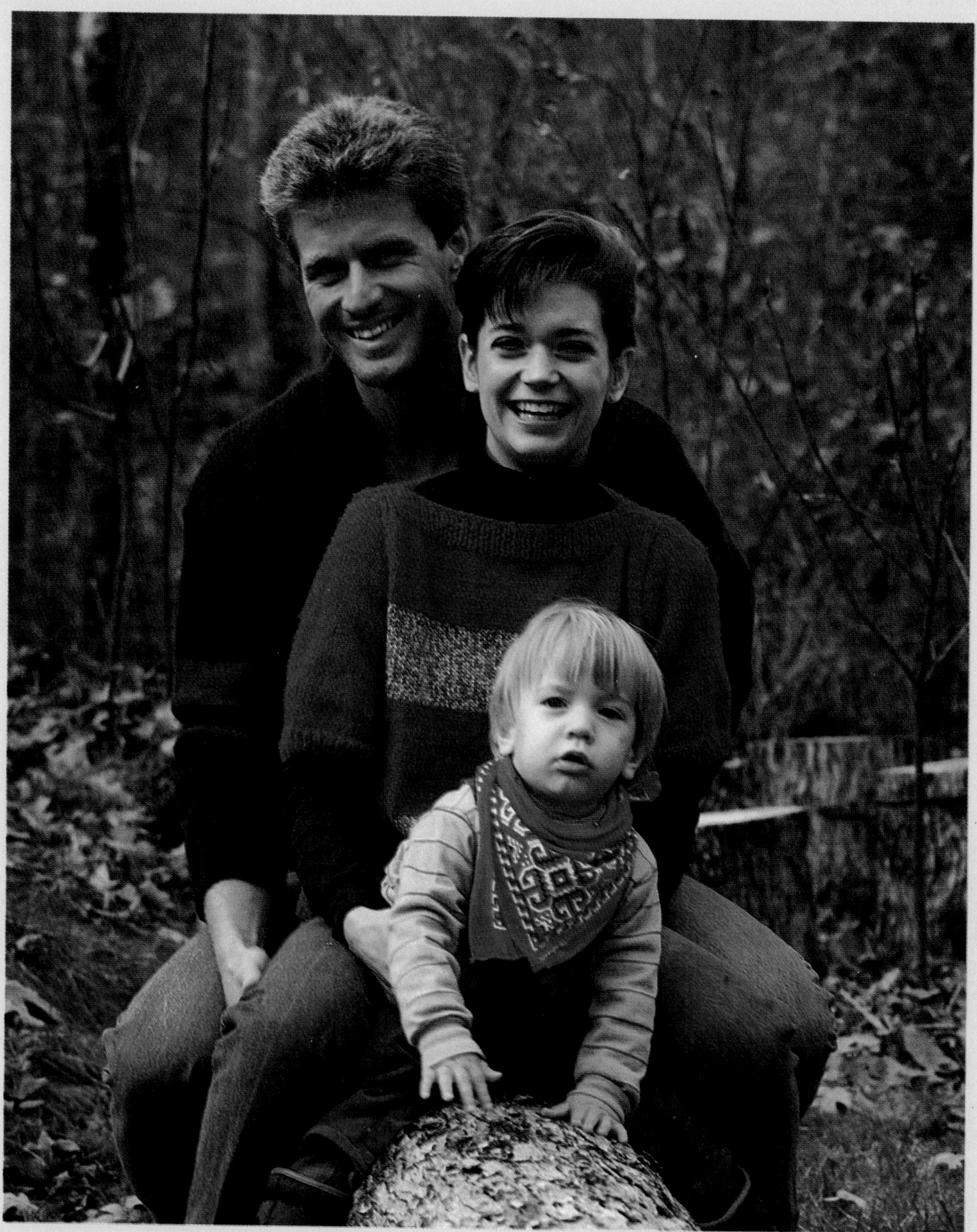

13 The Family

Although the United States has the highest divorce rate in the world, most American couples consider themselves happy with their marriages. Today, most American families no longer fit the traditional family model, in which only the wife keeps house and cares for the children while her husband goes out to work. Instead, the American family has taken on various forms, such as dual-career marriages, single-parent families, and living-together couples. Nevertheless, the basic family values, such as marrying and having children, are still very much alive today.

The family—a group of related individuals who live together and cooperate as a unit—has long been the basic building block of human societies. Its form and function have varied around the world over the centuries, but the family has been a universal, indispensable fact of life. It is probably the most important social institution.

Yet the American family seems to be falling apart. We have the world's highest divorce rate. A growing number of adults live alone, or live with members of the opposite sex without being married. Many more mothers are now working outside the home, turning their children into "latchkey kids." An increasing number of children grow up in single-parent families. There seems to be an epidemic of teenage pregnancies—and babies born out of wedlock. Many of these unwed mothers want to keep their children rather than give them up for adoption, which, along with the rising frequency of abortions, has reduced the number of adoptable children. Due to career pressure, more women are postponing childbirth, thus risking reduced fertility. The imbalance between many more infertile wives and fewer adoptable children has partly led to the popularity of surrogate motherhood. Given the surrogate mother's strong emotional attachment to her baby, she may refuse to give it up, as Mary Beth Whitehead recently demonstrated in the "Baby M" case. All these problems have alarmed people from all sides of the political spectrum. Many have urged the government to strengthen the family. Conservatives advocate that teenagers abstain from premarital sex, while also condemning sex education, birth control for minors, abortion, surrogate motherhood, and welfare for unwed mothers. Liberals take the opposite position on those issues while also supporting the idea of shoring up the family with more welfare and demanding income support, full employment, flexible work time, health care, and better child-care programs (Skolnick, 1983a; Cherlin and Furstenberg, 1983; Thornton and Freedman, 1983).

Is the family *really* breaking down? Is it *really* disappearing as an institution? To analyze questions like these, we need a clear idea of what the institution of family is and what American marriages and families are like today.

THE FAMILY AND SOCIETY

The family is an essential and universal institution, but this statement can be misleading. If, when you say "family," you see in your mind's eye Mom tending her two kids and a house in a suburb while Dad drives off to work, then you are thinking of a relatively rare phenomenon even in the United States. Throughout time and around the world, as societies have varied, so too have the forms of the family and the relative importance of its various functions. In this section we will look at these variations and how the American ideal of the family has emerged.

Varieties of the Family

Those who marry in effect have two families: the family in which they grew up, which is known as the **family of orientation,** and the family they establish through marriage, known as the **family of procreation.** As the abundance of jokes about mothers-in-law illustrates, the relationships between these two families can be complicated. Societies need norms that govern this relationship as well as norms that assign roles within the family of procreation. In effect, societies must answer questions such as: Who is part of my family? Who lives with whom? Who is an acceptable spouse? Who makes that decision?

All over the world, societies have given varied answers to these and other questions. If we go to Nyansongo, East Africa, we find that among the Gusii the husband rotates visits to his different wives. In Khalapur, India, we can find several generations of a family living together. We can also see that husbands and wives do not sleep together, men and women eat separately, and there is no family meal (Barnouw, 1973). In trying to understand such variations, sociologists have paid the most attention to family composition, norm of mate selection, rules of residence and descent, and rules of authority.

Family Composition Who makes up a family? Societies' definitions of a family can be classified into two basic types. In the United States we commonly define a "family" as being made up of a married couple and their young children—this group lives together apart from other relatives. Social scientists call this kind of family a **nuclear family.** In the nuclear family the relationship between husband and wife is the essential bond holding the family together. As a result, it is also called a *conjugal family,* quite common in Western industrialized societies.

In Western, industrialized societies such as ours, the ideal family consists of a married couple and their young children, living together as a group apart from other relatives. By contrast, the extended family, where a nuclear family lives with other relatives, is more common in the third world. Here is an extended family in Ivory Coast, West Africa.

The second type of family is more prevalent in the third world. It includes not only the nuclear family but also grandparents, uncles, aunts, and cousins. When a nuclear family lives in close proximity to other relatives, interacting with them frequently and acting together as a unit for some purposes, it is called an **extended family.** In this kind of family the blood tie among relatives is considered more important than the marital bond, so the extended family is also called the *consanguine family.* In traditional Chinese and Japanese extended families, for example, the tie between a married man and his mother is much stronger than his bond to his wife. In fact, if a mother does not like her son's wife, she can force him to divorce the wife.

Modernization, however, tends to break up the extended family. As a survey of workers in South America, Asia, and Africa suggests, people with more education and higher income are inclined to reject the extended family (Miller, 1984). But as a cultural heritage, coupled with its ability to reduce the high cost of living, the extended family is still going strong in the third world. Even in Japan, which is already extremely industrialized, nearly 30 percent of the households with preschool children are still extended. In such living arrangements, the

Although the extended family prevails in third-world countries, there are increasingly more nuclear families. A major force behind this change is modernization. Thus there are now many nuclear families in the newly industrialized nations of South Korea, Taiwan, Hong Kong, and Singapore. In other third-world countries, people with more education and higher income are also likely to have nuclear families.

elderly parents provide the young couple not only with free housing but also with child-care and housework aid so the young mother can work outside the home (Morgan and Hirosima, 1983). About the same cultural and economic factors lie behind the prevalence of extended households among poor blacks and Hispanics in the United States, especially those headed by young single women. These minorities have a long tradition of mutual aid among family members, and a relative in a female-headed extended household can release the young mother into the labor market by assisting with child care and other domestic tasks (Tienda and Angel, 1982; Angel and Tienda, 1982).

Mate Selection Societies differ, too, in their norms specifying who selects the marriage partner and who is an appropriate partner. In many traditional societies, **arranged marriages** are the rule. Parents choose mates for their children. The young couple may not even know each other until the wedding day, but they are expected to develop affection for each other during the marriage. They are considered too emotional to choose the "right," compatible mates. Usually the parents base their choice of a spouse on how financially secure the other family is, how agreeable the prospective daughter-in-law is to the young man's mother, and how compatible the couple's personalities are.

The selection of a partner depends, too, on the society's norms regarding what partners are appropriate. In most societies people are required to find their partners outside their clan, tribe, or village. This norm of mate selection is called **exogamy,** which literally means "marrying outward." Contrasted with exogamy is **endogamy,** which literally means "marrying within." In endogamous societies people must marry within their own clan, tribe, or village. Endogamy, however, stops short of violating the incest taboo, because endogamous societies do not encourage marriage between close relatives.

There are also norms governing the number of mates a person may have. **Monogamy**—the marriage of one man to one woman—is the most common form of marriage in the world. But many societies, especially small, premodern ones, allow people to have more than one spouse, a practice called **polygamy.** It is rare for a society to allow a woman to marry several men (a practice known as **polyandry**), but many societies allow a man to have more than one wife **(polygyny).** A new variant of polygamy has become increasingly common in the United States. Rather than having several spouses at the same time, many Americans go from one spouse to another—through a succession of marriage, divorce, and remarriage. American sociologists prefer to call this practice not polygamy but **serial monogamy.**

Societies differ in the norms that govern the number of spouses a person may have. Monogamy—the marriage of one man to one woman—is the most common practice in the world. Many small, premodern societies, however, allow people to have more than one spouse, a practice called *polygamy.* It is rare for such a society to permit a woman to practice *polyandry* by having more than one husband. It is far more common for polygamous societies to allow a man to practice *polygyny* by having more than one wife, as does this Bakhtiari chief in Iran, shown with his wives and children.

Rules of Residence, Descent, and Inheritance When most American couples marry, they establish a home of their own, away from both families of orientation. This pattern, called **neolocal residence,** is the least common rule of residence in the world. Most societies have a **patrilocal residence** pattern, which requires the bride to leave her family of orientation and live with her husband in the home of his family of orientation. Other societies have **matrilocal residence,** requiring the young couple to live with the bride's family of orientation.

Similar differences are found in rules of descent. Most societies trace a person's ancestry through the father's family. They follow the rule of **patrilineal descent.** They define the father's family as a child's close relatives. The children belong to their father's family of orientation, not that of their mother, and they adopt their father's family name. But daughters lose their family name when they marry, and their tie to their father's family is not permanent. Only sons, not daughters, may inherit property from the father in patrilineal societies. In such societies, there is a strong preference for sons in order to maintain the patrilineal line (Hirschman and Rindfuss, 1982).

Much less common is the rule of **matrilineal descent,** whereby descent is traced through the line of the mother's family. Only her relatives are considered kin. Even in matrilineal societies, however, daughters rarely have the right to inherit property. Usually, sons inherit property from their mother's brother.

American families seem to reflect the influence of patrilineal traditions. Wives and children still adopt the husband's family name. But generally Americans follow the rule of **bilateral descent,** tracing children's ancestry through both sides of the family. Children feel closely related to both their father's and their mother's kin, and both sons and daughters may inherit property from their mother's and their father's families.

Rules of Authority In most societies the eldest male dominates everyone else in the family. He allocates tasks, settles disputes, and makes other important decisions that affect family members. This kind of family is called **patriarchal.** In contrast, in a **matriarchal family** authority rests with the eldest female, and in an **egalitarian family,** authority is equally distributed between husband and wife.

Both matriarchal and egalitarian families are very rare. In the very few societies with matriarchal families, such as the Trobriand Islanders, the presumably dominant female does not actually exercise authority. Instead, she relegates it to her brother. To her children, the maternal uncle is the real authority figure. A variant of the matriarchal family, however, crops up in many industrialized countries. In the United States, for example, many poor families are matriarchal by default. Either the father is not present, or he has lost his dominant status because of chronic unemployment. Many other American families, though still dominated by husbands, are becoming increasingly egalitarian, as suggested in Chapter 11 (Gender Roles and Inequalities).

Functions of the Family

Behind all the variation in form, we do find a certain consistency in the institution of the family. In virtually all societies, the family serves the same basic functions. Although the importance of each function varies from one society to another, the family provides for sexual regulation, reproduction, socialization, economic cooperation, and emotional security.

Sexual Regulation No society advocates total sexual freedom. Although societies have very different sexual norms, all impose some control on who may have sex with whom. Even societies that encourage premarital and extramarital sex restrict and channel these activities so that they reinforce the social order. The Trobrianders of the South Pacific, for example, use premarital sex to determine whether a girl is fertile and to prepare adolescents for marriage. Traditional Eskimo society condones extramarital sex, but under conditions that do not disrupt family stability: as a gesture of hospitality, husbands offer their wives to overnight guests.

Traditionally, Western sexual norms have been relatively restrictive, demanding that people engage in sex only with their spouses. Tying sex to marriage seems to serve several functions. First, it helps minimize sexual competition, thereby contributing to social stability. Second, it gives young people an incentive to marry. Even today, most young adults eventually feel dissatisfied with unstable, temporary sexual liaisons and find a regular, secure sexual relationship in marriage an attractive prospect. Even most of the divorced, who usually find their postmarital sex lives very pleasurable, eventually remarry because they are more interested in sex with commitment, as available in marriage (see Chapter 8: Human Sexuality). Finally, encouraging people to marry and confining sexual intercourse to those who are married tends to ensure that children will be well cared for.

Reproduction In order to survive, a society must produce children to replace the adults and elderly who die, and practically all societies depend on the family to pro-

In virtually all societies, the family serves the same basic functions. It provides for sexual regulation, reproduction, socialization, economic support, and emotional security. In preindustrial societies, families usually operate as the center of diverse activities, where children receive their education and religious training from parents, and all family members work together to earn a living and entertain one another for relaxation. However, industrialized societies have undergone institutional differentiation, so that providing emotional security is now the family's main function, as shown by this family talking on their porch.

duce these new members. In some traditional societies, such as the Baganda of Uganda, children are considered so important that a marriage must be dissolved if the wife turns out to be barren. In many industrialized nations like the United States, families with children are rewarded with tax exemptions, and sexual acts that cannot produce pregnancy, such as homosexuality and anal intercourse, are condemned as perversions.

Socialization To replace its dead members, a society needs not just biological reproduction but also "sociological reproduction." It needs, in other words, to transmit its values to the new generation, to socialize them. As we saw in Chapter 6 (Socialization), the family is the most important agent of socialization. Because parents are likely to be deeply interested in their own children, they are generally more effective socializing agents than other adults.

Economic Cooperation Besides socialization, children also need physical care—food, clothing, and shelter. Fulfilling these needs is the core of the family's economic function, and it can facilitate effective socialization. Generally, however, the family's economic role goes beyond care for children and embraces the whole family. Family members cooperate as an economic unit. Each person's economic fate rises and falls with that of the family as a whole.

Emotional Security Finally, the family is the center of emotional life. As we saw in Chapter 6 (Socialization), the relationships we form in our families as children may shape our personalities and create hard-to-break patterns for all our relationships. Throughout life, the family is the most important source of primary relationships, the most likely place for us to turn to when we need comfort or reassurance.

Variations At various times and places some of these functions have been more important than others. In some societies in the past, the family was the center of educational, religious, political, economic, and recreational activities. Children received all their education from their parents. Religious practices were an integral part of family life. The head of the family assumed authority for allocating chores and settling disputes. The whole family pitched in to work on their farm or to make tools and other products in their home. Leisure activities were typically a family affair, with members entertaining one another. There was, however, little privacy and intimacy for husbands and wives (see box, p. 321).

Today, such all-embracing families still exist, especially in more traditional societies, but they are not typical of industrialized societies. Instead, specialized institutions have taken on a big share of the family's functions, a process called **institutional differentiation.** The schools educate children, and the media entertain

UNDERSTANDING OTHER SOCIETIES

Home

In the past, the household was largely a public place where business, entertainment, and work were conducted. The modern idea of home as a place of domestic privacy and intimacy began to emerge at the end of the seventeenth century. In this reading we see how the Bruns, a Norwegian family of that period, were going through the transition from the public household to the private home. How did the Bruns begin to find privacy and intimacy in their home?

Brun was a bookbinder, and he worked at home. A two-story half-timbered building contained the bindery, a stable, a barn, a hayloft, and many storerooms grouped around a courtyard. The dwelling itself faced the street. The house, which was the size of a small modern bungalow and would have been a tight squeeze for the Bruns and their eight children, actually housed fifteen persons; in addition to the Brun family, there were three employees and two servants.

The Brun home is an example of a "big house," which was the way that the prosperous bourgeois lived not just in the seventeenth but also in the sixteenth and fifteenth centuries. A chief characteristic of a big house was its public character. Like its medieval antecedent, it was the setting for all aspects of life—business, entertainment, and work. It was always full of relatives, guests, clients, friends, and acquaintances.

Following medieval tradition, most daytime activities took place in the large main room. A table with four chairs was in the center of the room; the rest of the furniture was placed around the walls. In addition to the large bed, there were eight chairs, the father's high-back armchair, a second armchair for visitors, a cupboard, and two chests. When guests came, chairs were placed in the bay window, which became an improvised conversation nook. The kitchen contained a large hearth and a small table with stools. There was no cupboard; the copper and pewter utensils hung on the walls.

The household awoke at dawn. Breakfast was an improvised affair and taken individually. Brun and his employees went next door to work in the shop. Food preparation occupied much time. Like most town-dwellers, the Bruns owned a small meadow outside the town where they grew hay (for their mare) and vegetables, which explains why a large amount of space in the house was devoted to food storage. Noon lunch at the Bruns was the main meal of the day and was shared by all fifteen persons. In the evening, only the immediate family ate together—the younger children and the apprentices ate in the kitchen. The day finished early, and people went to bed soon after dusk.

The Bruns lived and worked in the same premises, and most of their activities took place in one or two rooms, but this household was no longer medieval. There was more furniture (and) the use of stoves not only provided more convenience and comfort, it also allowed the house to be subdivided into many more rooms than would have been possible earlier. More important than the technical innovations were the changes in domestic arrangements. The parents still shared their bed with the infants, but the older children no longer slept in the same room. One can imagine the Bruns, after having sent the children upstairs to bed, sitting in the main room alone. The house is quiet, the day's work is done, and in the light of a candle they talk. A simple scene, and yet a revolution in human relations is taking place. The husband and wife have begun to think of themselves—perhaps for the first time—as a *couple.* Even their wedding night, twenty years before, would have been a public event, celebrated with boisterous, and medieval, informality. The opportunities to experience intimacy were rare and it was in such modest, bourgeois dwellings that family life began to acquire a private dimension. The importance of this event, which was taking place all over northern and central Europe, cannot be exaggerated. Before the idea of the home as the seat of family life could enter the human consciousness, it required the experience of both privacy and intimacy, neither of which had been possible in the medieval hall.

Comfort in the physical sense was still awaiting the eighteenth century and the improvement of such technologies as water supply and heating, as well as refinements to the internal subdivision of the home. But the transition from the public, feudal household to the private, family home was under way. The growing sense of domestic intimacy was a human invention as much as any technical device. Indeed, it may have been more important, for it affected not only our physical surroundings, but our consciousness as well.

Source: Adapted from Witold Rybczynski, *Home: A Short History of an Idea,* New York: Viking Press, 1986, pp. 44–49.

us all. Whereas once the whole family usually worked together to secure a livelihood, people now go outside the home to earn wages to support other family members. The family has ceased to be an economic unit that produces goods and services. At most it is a unit of consumption. Even its role in producing economic security has been reduced, as the government's role in aiding the poor and providing help in time of crisis has increased.

Although business, schools, churches, and government have taken over a large share of many of the family's functions, these impersonal organizations cannot provide intimate emotional support. This function still falls almost entirely on the family. A large extended family provides diffuse emotional security, in which the married couple expects companionship not only from each other but also from many other relatives. In the nuclear family, relations between husband and wife become more intense and exclusive. Their emotional importance is accentuated in societies such as the United States, which emphasizes individualism and privacy. Often, we view the world outside as a mass of strangers. We feel lonely, isolated, and alienated from that world, and see the family as a refuge. The emotional satisfactions of the family have become its main bond, its main reason for being.

The Conflict Perspective

We have just looked at the family from the functionalist perspective. Since it assumes that the family ensures the survival of society, it emphasizes only the positive functions of the family. But family life also has a dark side, which we can see through the conflict perspective.

First of all, the family, because of the strong feelings it generates, can be a powerful source of not just love and care but also pain and conflict. As a major study concludes, the family is "the most violent institution in American society except the military, and only then in time of war" (Straus, Gelles, and Steinmetz, 1980). The single most frequent type of murder involves family members—we are more likely to die at the hands of a relative than a stranger (see Chapter 7: Deviance and Control). In most families there can be found instances of conflict and violence such as anger, bitter feelings, hatred, physical punishment of children, or pokes and slaps of husbands and wives. In fact, the family is one of the few groups in society empowered by law and tradition to hit its members. It is, for example, legal for parents to spank their children as a form of punishment. Moreover, many husbands who strike their wives to keep them in line are not arrested, prosecuted, or imprisoned (Skolnick, 1983b). Domestic violence is indeed a serious problem. We should not, however, blow it out of proportion. It is not true that more police officers get killed dealing with family fights than die dealing with any other kind of crime. In fact, to the police, answering domestic disturbance calls is the least dangerous part of their job (Garner and Clemmer, 1986).

From the conflict perspective, we can also see family as a tool for men's exploitation of women. Housewives and mothers have greatly contributed to the rise and maintenance of capitalism with such forms of labor as reproduction and care of children, food preparation, daily health care, and emotional support. Without this "household production," men would not have been free to go out working. Yet, while men are paid for their jobs outside the home, women do not get any wages at all for their work in the home (Zaretsky, 1976; Himmelweit and Mohun, 1977; Hamilton, 1978). Ironically, women's household work is on the average worth more than men's paid employment. In 1981, for example, if a woman were paid for services as mother and housewife according to the wage scale for chauffeurs, baby sitters, cooks, and therapists, she would have earned over $40,000—more than most men made in that year (Strong et al., 1983). By demeaning women's housework, however, the family serves the interests of male domination. A century ago Karl Marx's collaborator, Friedrich Engels (1884), observed that the family is an arena of class conflict where "the well-being and development of one group are attained by the misery and repression of the other." That observation is apparently still relevant today. Although more than half of the married women are now gainfully employed, they still do most of the housework. It has been found that in an average dual-career household, the husband contributes only 11 hours a week to housework while the wife contributes 51 (Strong et al., 1983; see also Blumstein and Schwartz, 1983).

The American Experience

Both functionalist and conflict analyses have raised some questions about the American family: Is our nuclear family a new phenomenon, brought to us by industrialization? Has the American woman's domestic work always been downgraded? How has the provision of emotional support become the single most important function of the family? What other changes have occurred in the American family? The answers can be found in recent research on the history of the American family.

Industrialization seems a likely cause for the contraction of the extended family. In an industrial society workers go out of the home to work for a wage. They must be willing to go where the work is. That requires geographical mobility, which reduces interaction among relatives and makes it impossible to share routinely in the mutual obligations that mark the extended family. An industrial society also offers social mobility. Status comes to depend less on the family one is born into and more on what one achieves. Social mobility thus undermines the kinship ties that create the extended family. Other institutions have evolved to provide education, health care, and entertainment, so that they further reduce dependence on the kin network. Indeed, many developing countries in the third world have begun to see the substitution of the nuclear family for the extended family (Goode, 1982). But this has not been the case with the United States. The nuclear family had already existed before our country became industrialized. As historical demographers have found, most households in the preindustrial seventeenth and eighteenth centuries contained a nuclear family of husband, wife, and children, with no other relatives. One reason is that few people lived long enough to form an extended, three-generation family. Another reason is that impartible inheritance practices—which allow for only one heir to inherit all the property—forced sons who did not inherit the farm to leave and set up their own households (Cherlin, 1983).

On the farms of colonial America, men, women, and children helped produce the family's livelihood. The wife was typically an essential economic partner to the husband. If her husband was a farmer, she would run the household, make the clothes, raise cows, pigs, and poultry, tend a garden, and sell milk, vegetables, chickens, and eggs. If the husband was a skilled craftsman, she would work with him. Thus weavers' wives spun yarns, cutlers' wives polished metal, tailors' wives sewed buttonholes, and shoemakers' wives waxed shoes (Tilly and Scott, 1978). During the nineteenth century, the American "household ceased to be a center of production and devoted itself to child rearing instead" (Lasch, 1977). Industrialization took production out of the home. Initially husbands, wives, and children worked for wages in factories and workshops to contribute to the common family budget. But due to the difficulty of combining paid employment with domestic tasks, married women tended to work for wages irregularly. As wages rose, increasing numbers of families could earn enough without the wife's paid work. Then, increasingly, the home was seen as the emotional center of life and a private refuge from the competitive public world. The women's role became emotional and moral rather than economic. Women were expected to rear their children and comfort their husbands. This became the stereotype

In the colonial period, husbands, wives, and children all worked together as an economic unit to produce the family income. Most noteworthy was the role of the wife as her husband's equal partner. Later, during the nineteenth century, industrialization took production out of the home. Consequently, the American household stopped being the center of economic production and became devoted to providing emotional support. Women, then, assumed the task of rearing children and comforting husbands, serving solely as housewives.

of a typical and ideal American family. Thus it was after industrialization had been in full swing that women lost their status as their husbands' economic partners and acquired a subordinate status as housewives (Cherlin, 1983).

By the end of the last century, a decline in marriage and fertility rates and an increase in divorce, as well as the women's suffrage movement, fueled fears that the family was falling apart. Some social commentators worried that children, especially those of immigrants, were not being reared properly, and that social decline and moral decay would be the result. New groups and institutions stepped in where the family seemed to be failing. "The helping professions"—made up of teachers, social workers, doctors, psychologists—grew. Public education expanded, and the schools were forced to assume responsibilities formerly laid upon the home. As two educators wrote at that time, "Once the school had mainly to teach the elements of knowledge, now it is charged with the physical, mental, and social training of the child as well" (Lasch, 1979). Social workers and the juvenile courts took over in cases where even the schools failed. Eventually, "almost every other traditional function of the family passed out of the home and into the hands of institutions and professional providers, from the care of the sick to support of the poor, from the preparation of food to instruction in leisure activities" (Woodward, 1978).

From the functionalist point of view, these changes represent a natural, functional evolution in response to social and economic forces that exerted new pressures on the family. Schools, social workers, psychologists, and government moved to help individuals when family could no longer cope. Besides, women and children gained a measure of freedom from the father's authority.

Christopher Lasch (1977) presents a less benign conflict view of the transformation of the American family. Rather than being the result of inevitable social and economic forces, the changes reflect the outcome of capitalist exploitation:

> During the first stage of the industrial revolution, capitalists took production out of the household and [into] the factory. Then they proceeded to bring the workers' skills and technical knowledge [under managerial control]. Finally, they extended their control over the worker's private life as well, as doctors, psychiatrists, teachers, child guidance experts, officers of the juvenile courts, and other specialists began to supervise childrearing, formerly the business of the family. . . . They have made people more and more dependent on the managerial and professional classes—on the great business corporations and the state—and have thus eroded the capacity for self-help and social invention.

Throughout all the turmoil of this century, Americans by and large maintained the view that the typical and ideal family consisted of a breadwinning father and homemaking mother living with their children. Today, such a family is far from typical—only about 15 percent of American households fit this stereotype. About half of the mothers with young children are now working outside the home, while the proportions of such nontraditional households as single-parent families, unmarried couples living together, and individuals living alone have increased dramatically in the last 20 years (Busacca and Ryan, 1982; Census Bureau, 1988).

QUESTIONS FOR DISCUSSION AND REVIEW

1. How does a person's family of orientation differ from his or her family of procreation?
2. How do family composition and mate selection differ from one society to another?
3. What are the major social functions still performed by the institution of the family?
4. How does the conflict view of the family differ from the functionalist view, and what questions does each raise about the modern American family?
5. How have changes in the economy since colonial times led to several transformations of the family?

AMERICAN MARRIAGES

The American family is by and large nuclear, endogamous, monogamous, neolocal, and bilateral, and it has become increasingly egalitarian. Its cornerstone is the relationship between husband and wife. In this section we will discuss how Americans prepare for marriage, how most American couples achieve marital success, and how others fail.

Preparing for Marriage

Most Americans do not consciously prepare themselves for marriage or diligently seek a person to marry. Instead, they engage in activities that gradually build up a momentum that launches them into marriage. They date, they fall in love, they choose a mate, and in each of these steps they usually follow patterns set by society.

The Dating Ritual Developed largely after World War I, the American custom of dating has spread to many industrialized countries. It has also changed in the United States in the last decade. Before the 1970s, dating was more formal. Males had to ask for a date at least several days in advance. It was usually the male who decided where to go, paid for the date, opened doors, and acted chivalrous. The couple often went to an event, such as a movie, dance, concert, or ball game.

Today dating has become more casual. In fact, the word "date" now sounds a bit old-fashioned to many young people. "Getting together" or "hanging around" is more like it. Spontaneity is the name of the game. A young man may meet a young woman at a snack bar and strike up a brief conversation with her. If he bumps into her a day or two later, he may ask if she wants to go along to the beach, to the library, or to have some hamburgers. Males and females are also more likely than in the past to hang around—get involved in a group activity—rather than pair off for some seclusive intimacy. Neither has the responsibility to ask the other out, and both are spared much of the anxiety of formal dating. Getting together has also become less dominated by males. Females are more likely than before to ask a man out, to suggest activities, pay the expenses, or initiate sexual intimacies. Premarital sex has also increased, but it tends to reflect true feelings and desires rather than the need (for the male) to prove himself or (for the female) to show gratitude (Strong et al., 1983; Cox, 1984).

The functions of dating, however, have remained pretty constant. Obviously it is a form of entertainment. It is also a way of achieving status. By going out with a person of high prestige, an individual's own status may rise. Dating also provides people with opportunities for learning to get along with people of the opposite sex. Finally, it offers opportunities for courting, for falling in love with one's future spouse (Winch, 1974).

Romantic Love If someone is asked why he or she wants to get married, the answer is usually "Because I am in love." In American and other industrialized societies, love between husband and wife is the foundation of the nuclear family. In contrast, people in many traditional societies have believed that love is too irrational to form the basis for a marriage and that intense love between husband and wife may even threaten the stability of the extended family. To them, it is more rational to marry for such pragmatic considerations as economic security and good character.

But does romantic love really cause people to choose their mates irrationally? Many studies have suggested that the irrationality of love has been greatly exaggerated. An analysis of these studies has led William Kephart (1981) to reach this conclusion: "Movies and television to the contrary, American youth do not habitually fall in love with unworthy or undesirable characters. In fact, [they] normally make rather sound choices." In one study, when people in love were asked "Does your head rule your heart, or does your heart rule your head?" 60 percent answered "The head rules." Apparently, romantic love is not the same as infatuation, which involves physical attraction to a person and a tendency to idealize him or her. Romantic love is not as emotionalized as infatuation, but it is expected to provide intrinsic satisfactions such as happiness, closeness, personal growth, and sexual satisfaction. These are opposed to the extrinsic rewards offered by a pragmatic loveless marriage—rewards such as good earnings, a nice house, well-prepared meals, and overt respect. Due to improved economic and social conditions in the United States over the last twenty years, the belief in romantic love as the basis for marriage has grown more fervent than before. In several studies in the 1960s, 1970s, and 1980s, college men and women were asked "If a man (woman) had all the other qualities you desired, would you marry this person if you were not in love with him (her)?" Today, as opposed to earlier decades, a greater proportion of young people say no (Simpson et al., 1986).

The Influence of Homogamy Romantic love is not only far from blind, but it also does not develop in a social vacuum. Its development depends heavily on the partners' support from others, particularly family and friends (Parks, Stan, and Eggert, 1983). Such support is usually available if the couple goes along with the norm of **homogamy,** which requires people to marry those with social characteristics similar to their own.

Most marriages occur within the same social class. In a classic study, 55 percent of the couples came from the same class, 40 percent were one class apart, and only 5 percent were more than one class apart (Roth and Peck, 1951). Social class is still a significant factor in mate

Most people follow the norm of homogamy, which encourages individuals to marry those with social characteristics similar to their own. Thus most brides and their grooms are of the same race, the same class, the same faith, and about the same age—with most men only slightly older than their wives. Homogamy also reigns in regard to individual characteristics: people tend to marry those with similar personality traits and the same level of physical attractiveness.

selection today. "Most people marry within their own socioeconomic class," explain Bryan Strong and his associates (1983), "because of shared values, tastes, goals, occupations, and expectations."

Most marriages also involve members of the same race. Although there are now twice as many interracial marriages as in 1970, they constitute no more than 2 percent of all marriages (Census Bureau, 1988). Even these marriages may reflect the influence of homogamy. In most interracial marriages studied by Robert Merton (1941), the husband was an upper-class black and the wife a lower-status white. When severe racial prejudice entered into the calculation, the black husband's higher class position was balanced by the higher status of the wife's race. Thus the couple came out socially even. This may still be true today, but to a lesser degree because of a decreased prejudice against blacks. Since there is less prejudice against Asians and other nonblack minorities, the number of whites marrying them is more than three times the number of whites marrying blacks (Census Bureau, 1985).

Usually, people also choose mates of the same religious faith, although the frequency of intrafaith marriages varies from one group to another. The stronger the cohesion of the religious group and the higher the proportion of the group in a community, the more homogamous the group is. Jews are more likely to marry Jews than Catholics are to marry Catholics. Catholics, in turn, are more likely to marry Catholics than Protestants are to marry Protestants. Among Catholics, the lower the socioeconomic status, the higher the probability of homogamy. There are now more interfaith marriages than before, accounting for at least one-third of all marriages (Strong et al., 1983).

Americans also tend to marry people very close to their own ages. Most couples are only two years apart. If a man is 18 or younger when he marries, he is likely to marry a woman a few months older. But men older than 18 usually marry women slightly younger than they are. Most men who marry at 25 have wives three years younger; at 37, most men marry a woman six years younger. A major reason why older men tend to marry much younger women is that men generally place greater importance on their mates' physical attractiveness than women do. But the age difference between husbands and wives increases only until the men reach age 50. After this, most men marry women close to their own age (Schulz, 1982; Mensch, 1986).

People of similar race, religion, and class are also likely to live in close proximity to one another, so it is not surprising that people tend to marry someone who lives nearby. This tendency may be weakening as cars and airplanes continue to increase Americans' mobility, yet most couples still come from the same city, town, or even neighborhood. According to many studies, there is more than a fifty-fifty chance that one's future spouse lives within walking distance (Kephart, 1981). As James Bossard (1932) said, "Cupid may have wings, but apparently they are not adapted for long flights."

Homogamy applies to the *social* characteristics of couples. What about their individual characteristics, such as aggressive personalities and physical attractiveness? Do they also follow the same pattern? The answer is no, according to Robert Winch's (1971) famous theory of complementary needs. Winch argues that people with *different* personality traits are attracted to each other if these traits complement each other. This theory resembles the popular belief that "opposites attract." Thus aggressive men tend to marry passive women; weak men like strong women; talkative women go for quiet men; rational men find emotional women attractive; and so on. Winch's own research has supported the complementarity theory, but most of the studies by other investigators have backed the social psychological version of homogamy—the theory that people with similar traits are attracted to each other, much as "birds of a feather flock together." One study, for example, suggests that couples get along much better if both husbands and wives share the traditional feminine traits (such as being sensitive) than if one is aggressive and the other submissive (Antill, 1983). A more recent study shows that men and women who share a sense of humor are more likely to like, love, and want to marry each other than those who do not agree on what is funny (Bozzi, 1986). Homogamy also reigns in regard to physical attractiveness. Presumably, every man prefers a Snow White and every woman wants a Prince Charming. But most people end up marrying someone close to their own level of attractiveness. Interestingly, the similarity in attractiveness is greater among deeply committed couples than among casual ones. When people are playing the field, their looks may not match their dates'. But they are more likely to get serious with the dates who have about the same level of attractiveness (Kalick and Hamilton, 1986).

Marital Happiness

With time, both the physical attraction and the idealization of romantic love are likely to fade, so that marital love involves mostly commitment. Love may be less exciting after marriage, but as William Kephart (1981) observes, it "provides the individual with an emotional insight and a sense of self-sacrifice not otherwise attainable," qualities that may be keys to marital success.

How successful are American marriages? The answer obviously depends on how we define "successful." Gerald Leslie (1982) suggests that in a successful marriage the couple have few conflicts, basically agree on major issues, enjoy the same interests during their leisure time, and show confidence in and affection for each other. To others, this sounds like a static, spiritless relationship. Instead, some argue, a successful marriage is one that is zestful and provides opportunity for personal growth. Such disagreement among scholars suggests that a "successful marriage" is basically a value judgment, not an objective fact (Strong et al., 1983).

It is, therefore, best simply to look at whether people themselves consider their marriages successful, however experts might judge them. By this standard, most American marriages are successful. Several studies have shown that the overwhelming majority of Americans say they are either "very happy" or "pretty happy" with their marriages (Bradburn, 1969; Freedman, 1978). In fact, married couples are much more likely than single people to say that they are happy, whether it is about love, sense of recognition, personal growth, or even job satisfaction. Marriage, however, rather than parenthood, is the focal point of marital happiness. As research has suggested, the presence of children often detracts from marital happiness because the couple see their relationship less as a romance and more as a working partnership. According to one study, couples with children are less happy than childless couples. Another study indicates that while remarriages can be just as happy as first marriages, remarriages with stepchildren are twice as likely to end in divorce (Carlson and Stinson, 1982; Roberts, 1986; White and Booth, 1985).

What makes for marital happiness? By comparing happily married with unhappily married couples, researchers have come up with a long list of characteristics associated with happy marriages. Among these are having happily married parents; having known the prospective spouse for at least two years; having been engaged for at least two years; getting married at an age above the national average (about 23 for men and 20 for women); being religious or adhering to traditional values; having only little conflict with one's spouse before marriage; regarding one's spouse as a friend; being of the same religion and race; and having a college education, good health, a happy childhood, emotional stability, parental approval of the marriage, and an adaptable personality (Kephart, 1981; Hatch et al., 1986). Given the great complexity of marital happiness, however, conflicting findings always exist. While most social researchers have found richer and better educated people to be more happily married than poorer and less educated people, other investigators have not found this to be the case (Brandt, 1982). For many years researchers have also found that interaction between husband and wife causes marital happiness, but one study shows that spousal interaction is not the cause but instead the consequence of marital happiness (White, 1983). Thus we should regard the above list of characteristics as tentative rather than the final word on marital happiness.

Divorce

We often hear from the mass media that in the United States nearly one out of two marriages ends in divorce. Does this mean that half of all marriages end in divorce, or that you have a fifty-fifty chance of getting divorced when you marry? Not at all. It simply means that the number of divorces taking place in a given year is nearly half the number of marriages performed in the same year. In 1987, for example, there were 1,160,000 divorces and 2,414,000 marriages. If we compare these two figures, we will come up with an astounding divorce rate of 48 percent—by dividing the number of divorces by the number of marriages. But this is highly misleading because it fails to take into account the numerous existing marriages that had begun *before* 1987. If we include these marriages in computing the divorce rate for 1987, we will find that the rate was far lower than 48 percent. It was only 2 percent, namely, the number of divorces that occurred in 1987 divided by the number of all marriages that still existed in 1987:

$$\frac{1{,}160{,}000 \text{ divorces in } 1987}{54{,}600{,}000 \text{ existing marriages in } 1987} = 0.02 \text{ or } 2\%$$

Nevertheless, the current divorce rate is still high. Although it has begun to dip since 1982, it is still twice as high as it was in 1960—the year when the rate began to rise annually. It is also the highest in the world (United Nations, 1982; Thornton and Freedman, 1983; Census Bureau, 1988).

Although it provides an escape from a miserable marriage, divorce often brings new problems. Men from broken marriages are nine times as likely to be admitted to psychiatric hospitals as men from intact marriages. Hospital admission is three times more frequent for divorced women than for other women. Divorced people are also overrepresented in surveys on suicides, homicides, and deaths due to a variety of physical illnesses (Jacobs, 1982). Most experience an increase in such personal difficulties as depression, insomnia, loneliness, decreased efficiency, excessive smoking and drinking, or anger toward both themselves and their ex-spouses (Goode, 1982). Divorce hits women particularly hard in their purse strings. Their standard of living in the year after divorce falls by an average of 73 percent, while their former husbands' standard rises 42 percent. The 73 percent drop in living standard consigns many divorced women to a hand-to-mouth existence. As one of them describes it, "[My children and I] ate macaroni and cheese five nights a week. There was a Safeway special for 39 cents a box. We could eat seven dinners for $3.00 a week. I think that's all we ate for months" (Weitzman, 1985).

A marriage counselor. Many of the traditional functions of the family have passed out of the home into the hands of public or private institutions. Professional helpers—teachers, social workers, psychologists—have claimed a right to intervene in the relations between parents and children. Adults now turn to professionals for guidance not only on how to raise their families but also on how to get along with each other. To functionalists, the helping professions promote family unity. To conflict theorists, however, the professions undermine the family by eroding the capacity for self-help.

For children who think that they have a happy family, divorce may be especially traumatic. It now affects a large number of children (see box, p. 329). Boys from divorced families tend to become "undercontrolled"—taking out their frustration in school by bullying kids or disrupting classes. Girls are likely to become "overcontrolled"—anxious, withdrawn, or too well behaved. They apparently express their feelings in accordance with traditional gender roles (Emery, 1982). Even when

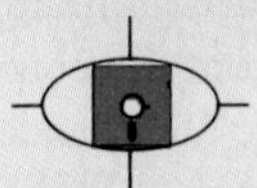

LOOKING AT CURRENT RESEARCH

Life Without Father

The high divorce rate in America has meant that numerous children grow up with little or no contact with their fathers. The following article presents data on the extent of this problem. It further suggests the reasons for the lack of contact between child and father. What impact can such a "life without father" have on the children?

Mom and Dad are divorced. Dad drops by on Saturdays to take the kids to the zoo. This stereotypical image softens the harsh realities of divorce. But most of the children of divorced parents must live with the realities: Over half see their absent parent (nine out of ten times their father) less than once a month. One-third never see their father.

Today, only 68 percent of children live with both biological parents. Twenty percent live in single-parent households, 9 percent live with one biological parent and a step-parent, and 4 percent live with neither parent. Even more dramatic than these cross-sectional statistics is the proportion of children who will live in a single-parent household sometime during their youth: 42 percent of white children and 86 percent of black children.

These statistics imply that almost one-quarter of white children and close to one-half of black children may lose regular, personal contact with their father at some point during their childhood. These children will see their fathers less than once a month or never see him. Does this mean that if parents and children do not live together, they are no longer part of the same family?

To address one aspect of this question, we used data from a special supplement to the National Health Interview Survey of 1981 which included information on the frequency of children's contact with absent parents and on the living arrangements, health, and well-being of children. The data, collected from a nationally representative sample of over 15,000 American children, show that the stereotypical image of how divorced parents relate to their children is far from the reality.

For children living with only one biological parent, their frequency of contact with the absent parent depends largely on whether the custodial parent has remarried. Among those living in a single-parent household headed by their biological mother, 24 percent see their father at least once a week. Only 31 percent never see their father. In comparison, among children living with a remarried biological mother, only 8 percent see their father at least once a week, while 46 percent—nearly half—never see their father.

We examined a variety of factors that might affect children's contact with an absent parent. We found only two factors that significantly affect the likelihood of weekly contact with an absent parent: the length of time that a child's parents have been separated, and the custodial parent's marital status. Children who have been living apart from a biological parent for one year or less are much more likely to see the parent weekly than children who have been separated from a parent for longer periods of time.

Children born outside of marriage are less likely to ever see an absent parent than children whose biological parents were married to each other. Children are more likely to have some contact with their absent biological mother than with their absent biological father. Children in households where there is a parent figure of the opposite sex (not a step-parent) are less likely to ever see their absent parent than children in households where there is no "substitute" parent figure. Also, our results show a positive link between the educational level of the householder in the child's household and the likelihood that the child will have some contact with an absent parent.

In sum, an increasing number of children are growing up in situations other than the "typical" two-parent nuclear family. Recent survey data suggest a surprisingly low level of contact between children and their absent parent once a divorce has occurred. *Kramer vs. Kramer* aside, most children still end up in their mother's custody when a marital break-up occurs and a sizable portion will have little or no contact with their father from that time on. In addition, family income in these mother-only households is low. And there is evidence of school problems and poorer health among children who are separated from one of their parents. Divorce may be the only realistic alternative for many unhappy marriages, but it is clear that monitoring what happens to children in its aftermath remains vitally important.

Source: Excerpted from Suzanne M. Bianchi and Judith A. Selzer, "Life without father," *American Demographics,* December 1986, pp. 43–46.

they become young adults, they still experience some of the negative effects of their parents' split. While they are more likely than those from intact families to engage in premarital intercourse and cohabitation, they are less satisfied with these activities (Booth, Brinkerhoff, and White, 1984). They are also likely to feel more distance and less affection from their mothers and fathers (Fine, Moreland, and Schwebel, 1983). However, getting stuck in a conflict-ridden home could have caused more unhappiness. Research has shown that children living in a two-parent home full of tension and conflict have greater emotional stress and lower self-esteem than children living in a supportive single-parent family (Lamanna and Riedmann, 1985). This may explain why, as one study indicates, most adolescents from divorced families prefer to live with a single parent than with two conflicting parents (McLoughlin and Whitfield, 1984).

Why do so many marriages end in divorce? Numerous studies have compared divorced couples with nondivorced couples and found a number of personal problems and social characteristics to be associated with divorce. Personal problems include infidelity, incompatibility, mental cruelty, personality problems, excessive drinking, and financial difficulties. Social characteristics are suggested by the higher divorce rates among certain groups, such as the very young (between ages 17 and 19), those with divorced parents, those who live in the city, those who do not go to church, those of lower socioeconomic status, blacks, and those having "mixed marriages"—whose husbands or wives come from different ethnic, religious, or economic backgrounds (Strong et al., 1983; Cox, 1984; South and Spitze, 1986; Breault and Kposowa, 1987). The personal and social characteristics are not necessarily related. Blacks, for example, have higher divorce rates than whites, not because of personality problems or excessive drinking but because of racial discrimination and economic deprivation.

But these data cannot explain why industrialized Western societies have higher divorce rates than traditional Eastern societies, or why the U.S. divorce rate today is far higher than it was a century ago. A cross-cultural analysis may suggest at least five larger social forces behind the current high divorce rate in the United States.

1. *Decreased social disapproval of divorce.* In many traditional societies, unhappily married couples stay married because of the stigma attached to divorce. In the United States, there is virtually no stigma. Divorce has gained wide acceptance as a solution to marital unhappiness, and it has become easier to obtain from the courts. As one sociologist says, "We, as a society, have made it too easy for people to divorce" (Kantrowitz, 1987).

2. *Greater availability of services and opportunities for the divorced.* In traditional societies men depend heavily on marriage for sexual gratification, cooking, and housecleaning, and women look to it for sex and financial security. Such services and opportunities are more easily available to American men and women *without* being married. American men can get sexual gratification outside marriage, and American women can become financially independent without husbands. In recent years fast-food restaurants have proliferated, with a growing number of businesses offering to clean homes, run errands, and provide other services for unmarried people. In addition, the higher divorce rate in the United States has expanded the pool of eligible new partners. All this makes divorce more attractive to unhappily married couples (Levitan and Belous, 1981; Udry, 1983).

3. *The increased specialization of the family in providing love and affection.* In societies with high divorce rates, such as the United States, the family has become specialized in offering love and affection, while the importance of its other functions has declined. When love and affection are gone, the modern couple are likely to break up their "empty shell" marriage. By contrast, in societies

"Hi, I'm Gilbert. I come with the territory."

with low divorce rates, the family's other functions—such as providing economic security and socializing many children—remain important. Thus even when little love remains between the parents, there are still many reasons for keeping the family together. Besides, since love is less reliable and less durable than the other, more mundane functions of marriage, the union based on love alone carries a higher risk of ending in divorce.

4. *Higher expectations about the quality of marital relationship.* Young people in traditional societies do not expect an exciting romantic experience with their spouses, especially if their marriages are arranged by their parents. But Americans expect a lot, such as an intense love relationship. These expectations are difficult to fulfill, and the chances of disillusionment with the partner are therefore great (Thornton and Freedman, 1983; Berger and Berger, 1983). Since young people have higher marital expectations than older ones, it is not surprising that most divorces occur within the first four years of marriage. It is also not surprising that the divorce rate has been falling in recent years. Today more brides and grooms are older when they first marry, and a growing number of couples want to improve their unhappy marriages rather than get out of them. The rising age at marriage and the increasing willingness to stay in unhappy marriages reflect a more realistic, less idealistic view (Glick and Lin, 1986; Kantrowitz, 1987).

5. *Increased individualism.* The rights of the individuals are considered far more important in high-divorce societies than in low-divorce societies. Individualism was so prominent in the United States during the late 1970s that it was called the "me decade." An individualistic society encourages people to put their own needs and privileges ahead of those of their spouses and to feel that if they want a divorce, they are entitled to get one. In more traditional societies with low divorce rates, people are more likely to subordinate their needs to those of the kinship group and thus to feel they have no right to seek a divorce. (For a closer look at how the last two social forces affect divorce, see box, p. 332.)

The current high divorce rate in the United States does not necessarily mean that our marriages are more unhappy than those in other societies. Often, low divorce rates reflect social disapproval of divorce—not a large number of happy marriages. High divorce rates also do not mean that marriage is on the way to extinction. In fact, Americans remain among the most marrying peoples in the world. The marriage rates are higher in the United States than in France, Hungary, Costa Rica, Panama, Japan, and Philippines (United Nations, 1982). While our divorce rates increased steadily over the last two decades, so did our marriage rates (Census Bureau, 1988). For Americans, divorce does not represent a rejection of marriage as an institution but only of a specific partner. That's why most divorced Americans eventually remarry. In fact, high divorce rates may mean that the American institution of marriage is strong rather than weak. Since unhappy marriages are weeded out through divorce, there are proportionately more happy ones in the society as a whole. For example, while the divorce rate rose from about 1 percent in 1957 to over 2 percent in 1976, the proportion of Americans saying that their marriage was very happy was 68 percent in 1957 and 80 percent in 1976, an increase of 12 percent (Veroff, Douvan, and Kulka, 1981). These happy marriages reflect a tremendous achievement on the part of the couples because, as we have suggested, they expect much more from each other than their counterparts do in other countries with lower divorce rates. But the fact that divorce has become commonplace does indicate significant changes in the American family, which we discuss in the next section.

QUESTIONS FOR DISCUSSION AND REVIEW

1. What roles do dating, romantic love, and homogamy play in preparing Americans for marriage?
2. What social factors are associated with marital happiness?
3. How many American couples divorce, and what are the principal causes of these marital breakups?

CHANGES IN THE AMERICAN FAMILY

When the Census Bureau counted American households in 1975, it found 81.2 percent living in "families," by which the Bureau means two or more persons living together who are related by birth or marriage. By 1983, only 73.2 percent of American households were families, and most of these were in many ways different from the traditional model of male breadwinner, full-time housewife, and two or more children (Rawlings, 1984). Increasingly, Americans are choosing either new patterns of family life, or life outside the family, while some are experiencing violence in the family.

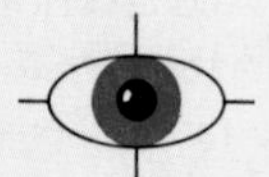

USING SOCIOLOGICAL INSIGHT

A Part-Time Marriage

Modern couples are finding it increasingly difficult to stay married. Some key social forces behind this problem seem to be the growing popular expectation for extended intense intimacy from marriage and heightened individualism. Here is a personal account of a divorce that reflects the impact of these social forces. The marriage breaks up because it fails to provide "seven-day-a-week high levels of intimacy" and because the woman leaves her husband "in order to find herself." How can expectations for marital intimacy and individualistic strivings be fulfilled at the same time?

When my wife told me she wanted a divorce, I responded like any normal college professor. I hurried to the college library. I wanted to get hold of some books on divorce and find out what was happening to me.

Over the next week . . . I read or skimmed about 20. Nineteen of them were no help at all. . . . The twentieth was a collection of essays by various sociologists, and one of the pieces took my breath away. It was like reading my own horoscope.

* * *

This is the story the essay told me. . . . Somewhere in some suburb or town or small city, a middle-class couple separate. They are probably between 30 and 40 years old. They own a house and have children. The conscious or official reason for their separation is quite different from what it would have been in their parents' generation. Then, it would have been a man leaving his wife for another, and usually younger, woman. Now it's a woman leaving her husband in order to find herself.

When they separate, the wife normally stays in the house they occupied as a married couple. Neither wants to uproot the children. The husband moves to an apartment . . .

Back when these two were married, they had an informal labor division. She did inside work, he did outside. Naturally, there were exceptions: She gardened, and he did his share of the dishes, maybe even baked bread. But mostly he mowed the lawn and fixed the lawn mower; she put up any new curtains, often enough ones she made herself.

One Saturday, six months or a year after they separated, he comes to see the kids. He plans also to mow the lawn. Before she leaves she says, "That damn overhead garage door you got is off the track again. Do you think you'd have time to fix it?" Apartment life makes him restless. He jumps at the chance.

She, just as honorable and straight-arrow as he, has no idea of asking for this as a favor. She invites him to stay for an early dinner. She may put it indirectly—"Michael and Sally want their daddy to have supper with them"—but it is clear that the invitation also proceeds from her.

* * *

One such evening, they both happen to be stirred not only by physical desire but by loneliness. "Oh, you might as well come upstairs," she says with a certain self-contempt. He needs no second invitation; they are upstairs in a flash. It is a delightful end to the evening. . . .

That, too, now becomes part of the pattern. He never stays the full night, because, good parents that they are, they don't want the children to get any false hopes up—as they would, seeing their father at breakfast.

* * *

What they have achieved post-divorce is what their marriage should have been like in the first place. Part-time. Seven days a week of marriage was too much. One afternoon and two evenings is just right.

* * *

. . . There are certainly people who thrive on seven-day-a-week marriages. They have a high level of intimacy and they may be better, warmer people than the rest of us. But there are millions and millions of us with medium, or low levels of intimacy. We find full-time family membership a strain. If we could enter marriage with more realistic expectations of what closeness means for us, I suspect the divorce rate might permanently turn downward. It's too bad there isn't a sort of glucose tolerance test for intimacy.

As for me personally, I still do want to get married again. About four days a week.

Source: Excerpted from Noel Perrin, "A part-time marriage," *The New York Times,* September 9, 1984, p. 122. Copyright © 1984 by The New York Times Company. Reprinted by permission.

Dual-Career Marriages

In the last 40 years there has been a tremendous surge of married women into the labor force. The proportion of gainfully employed wives shot up from only 14 percent in 1940 to 51 percent in 1982. While most work part time or occasionally take time out from the workforce for family-related reasons, their employment does make a handsome contribution to family income. In 1982 the median income of dual-career families ($30,300) was more than 40 percent higher than the median for one-career families ($21,300). At the low end of the income scale, the wife's contribution is so significant that relatively few dual-earner families fall below the poverty line (Thornton and Freedman, 1983).

Does this economic gain bring marital happiness? It apparently does for most dual-career couples. But when comparing them with one-career families, research has produced conflicting results. Some studies found that the wife's employment was good for her but not for her husband. In one such study, employed wives reported more marital happiness, more communication with husbands, fewer worries, and better health, while their husbands were less contented with their marriage and in poorer health (Burke and Weir, 1976). But other studies found more strain in dual-career marriages because the wife was still expected to be a housewife rather than a career seeker (Skinner, 1980). The strain is much heavier for the employed wife than for her husband because she does most of the housework, as we observed earlier. The effect of a wife's employment seems to depend on how much support she gets from her husband. Many husbands still find it difficult to render total support to their wives' careers, particularly if their wives earn more than they do. Understandably, in cases where the wife outperforms the husband, sex lives are more likely to suffer, feelings of love are more likely to diminish, and marriages are more likely to end in divorce. Moreover, premature death from heart disease is eleven times more frequent among husbands whose wives outshine them professionally (Rubenstein, 1982). On the other hand, in cases where the husbands fully support their wives' employment by doing their share of housecleaning and child care, the couples do head off marital stress and achieve marital happiness (Cooper et al., 1986). Presumably most dual-career couples are just like their single-career counterparts. This is why, as research has suggested, dual-worker marriages as a whole do not have much impact, either positive or negative, on the emotional, social, and educational development of children (Hayes and Kamerman, 1983).

Single-Parent Families

With increased divorce and out-of-wedlock birth, there has been a phenomenal rise in the number of children growing up in households with just one parent. As recently as 1970 the proportion of single-parent families was only 11 percent, but in 1983 it was 22 percent. The overwhelming majority (90 percent) of such families are headed by women. About a quarter of the children today live for some time in these female-headed families. It has been estimated that half of the children born in the 1970s will live with their mothers alone before they

With increased divorce and out-of-wedlock birth, single-parent families are now more than twice as common as they were two decades ago. The great majority are headed by women. A quarter of all children today live for some time in these female-headed families, and half of the children born in the 1970s are expected to live with their mothers alone before reaching age 18. Most of these families live below or near the poverty line. Women usually suffer a sharp drop in household income after divorce.

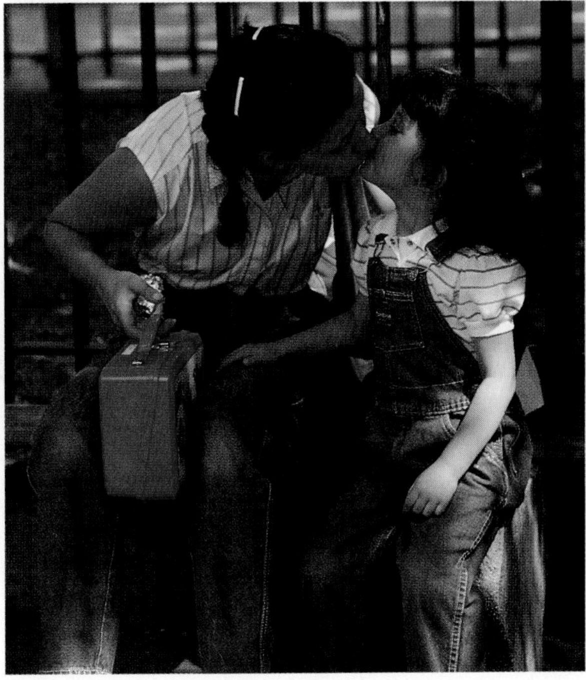

reach age 18 (Furstenberg and Nord, 1982; Thornton and Freedman, 1983; Rawlings, 1984). Black children are especially likely to live in female-headed families: in 1981 about 47 percent of all black families were headed by women, compared to 14 percent of white families. Most of these families, whether black or white, live below or near the poverty level. Even women of higher-income groups tend to suffer a sharp drop in household income as a result of marital breakup (Weiss, 1984). The higher black proportion of female-headed families, however, is a reflection of greater poverty among blacks—the effect of lingering racism and exclusion of blacks from economic opportunities (Comer, 1983).

Compared with two-parent families, female-headed families are more likely to experience social and psychological stress such as unemployment, job change, lack of social support (from friends and neighbors), negative self-image, and pessimism about the future (McLanahan, 1983). Children from single-parent families have also been found to have a larger share of such problems as juvenile delinquency, truancy, and poor class work. Whatever problems these children may have, however, they do not result directly from the absence of a father in a female-headed home, as popularly believed, but from factors that can also be found in a two-parent family, such as low income, poor living conditions, and lack of parental supervision (Eshleman, 1981). Since fewer than half of all divorced and separated women with children receive child-support payments, most of which are extremely inadequate, "the most detrimental effect for the children is not the lack of a male presence but the lack of a male income" (Cherlin and Furstenberg, 1983). A cross-cultural analysis indicates that in many tribal societies children from single-parent families generally do not have problems because of sufficient material resources, concerned and helpful relatives, and a culture of friendliness toward the youngsters (Bilge and Kaufman, 1983). Since our single mothers are often severely limited in financial resources, it is not surprising that they report greater stress and strains in their lives than other people (Thornton and Freedman, 1983).

Family Violence

As mentioned earlier, family violence is quite common in the United States. Its exact incidence is hard to pin down because various researchers do not define family violence in the same way. There is, of course, little disagreement about extreme cases where a family member is killed or seriously injured by another. But there is disagreement as to what kinds of behavior are acceptable for disciplining children or resolving spousal conflict. Some investigators consider spanking, for example, an act of violence, whereas others do not (Klaus and Rand, 1984). Thus there have been different estimates of the extent of family violence in the United States. According to one study, about 3 million Americans experience violence in the home each year, while another study puts the number at 8 million. The estimated proportions of families where violence occurs range from 10 to 20 percent a year, and anywhere between 25 and 50 percent of all couples have been estimated to undergo serious family violence during the course of their marriage (Straus et al., 1980; Levitan and Belous, 1981; Long, White, and Karr, 1983). More recent data suggest that the rates of family violence remain "extremely high," though they are lower than in the last decade (Straus and Gelles, 1986). All this should give us a sense of the enormity of the problem. After all, the family is supposed to be "home sweet home."

Why does violence occur in so many families? A major reason is stress. Research shows that the incidence of violence is highest among groups most likely to feel under stress, such as the urban poor, families with a jobless husband, and those with four to six children (Straus, Gelles, and Steinmetz, 1980). The stress that triggers violence can also be social-psychological. Husbands who have been socialized to play the dominant role are likely to feel uneasy if their wives have more education or higher-status occupations. Such husbands are more likely than others to assault their wives (Rubenstein, 1982). Stress by itself, however, does not necessarily cause violence. People would not resort to violence as a way of relieving stress if they were not culturally encouraged to do so. There seems to be a "culturally recognized script for behavior under stress" in American society. The violence on television, corporal punishment in schools, and the death penalty, for example, convey the idea that violence is an acceptable solution to problems (Straus et al., 1980). Research further suggests that a lot of marital violence is transmitted from one generation to another. It has been found that most of the violent couples have, as children, seen their parents hit each other (Kalmuss, 1984).

Living Together

In the past, very few couples lived together without a formal wedding ceremony or marriage license. These couples were said to be "living in sin." They were mostly the very rich, who could afford to ignore society's rules, and the very poor, who had little to lose by ignoring them. But today cohabitation has spread to other sectors of American society, including especially college students and young working adults. According to the Census Bureau (1988), the number of unmarried couples living together was slightly over half a million in 1970. Since then it has more than tripled to more than 2 million in 1986. Most of the increase has been among those under age 25 (from 11 percent of all cohabitants in 1970 to 19 percent in 1986) and those between ages 25 and 44 (from 20 percent in 1970 to 64 percent in 1986). They are now known as POSSLQ—Persons of Opposite Sexes Sharing Living Quarters—the acronym first introduced by the Census Bureau in 1980. Social disapproval has vastly diminished, and courts have stepped in to protect their rights as if they were legally married (Levitan and Belous, 1981).

Since the incidence of cohabitation continues to rise, there is some fear that it may undermine the institution of marriage. In Sweden, where cohabitation is already four times as prevalent as in the United States, living together does not pose a threat to marriage at all. Most cohabitants live like married couples, and intend to marry eventually (Lewin, 1982). About the same situation exists in the United States. Cohabitation as a permanent alternative to marriage, which is often called common-law marriage, is relatively rare today. It occurs mostly among the very poor. For most of the cohabitants, living together is a temporary arrangement which usually lasts for less than two years. Although it does not imply a commitment to marry later, cohabitation often leads to marriage. It is a modern extension of the courtship process, comparable to the traditional custom of "going steady" (Spanier, 1983; Gwartney-Gibbs, 1986; Tanfer, 1987).

Does living together lead to more marital happiness than the traditional courtship? Couples who live together often argue that cohabitation works like a trial marriage, preparing them for marital success. A study in Canada has indeed suggested that premarital cohabitation contributes to marital stability (White, 1987). But research in the United States generally suggests otherwise. In one study of couples who had been married for four years, those who had lived together before marriage had about the same rate of divorce as those who had not cohabited. Among those still married, both groups reported about the same amount of marital satisfaction (Newcomb and Bentler, 1980). This suggests that premarital cohabitation does not lead to more marital happiness. Other studies even show *less* marital satisfaction among couples who have lived together than among those who have not (Watson, 1983; DeMaris and Leslie, 1984). But this does not necessarily mean that marital dissatisfaction is the result of premarital cohabitation. It seems that the type of people who cohabit are likely to be poorly suited for marriage in the first place because they do not have as strong a commitment to marriage as other couples. As Alfred DeMaris and Gerald Leslie (1984) found, couples who have lived together before marriage are *less* likely to agree with the statement that "no matter how much trouble a husband and wife are having getting along, the best thing to do is to stay married and try to work out their problems." In short, premarital cohabitation by itself neither helps nor hurts married life (Watson and DeMeo, 1987).

Staying Single

Of the "alternatives" to marriage, staying single is by far the most common. In 1983 there were 48 million single adults in the United States. Many are young adults who live with their parents, and most will eventually get married. But in 1986 at least 21 million lived alone—about twice as many as in 1970—and many will stay single for a significant time. The live-aloners represented about 24 percent of all U.S. households in 1986 (Census Bureau, 1988).

Most singles are not actually opposed to marriage and expect to be married sooner or later. In a survey in Dayton, Ohio, the great majority of the respondents said that they would be married in five years (Cargan and Melko, 1982). According to one national survey, the majority of unmarried men and women said that they remain single because they have not met the right person (Simenauer and Carroll, 1982). However, the longer they wait, the harder it becomes to find that person. This is especially true for older, well-educated women. According to a famous Yale-Harvard study, single women reaching the age of 30 have only a 20 percent chance of marrying. Those who have reached age 35 have a 5 percent chance. The odds for 40-year-olds drop still further, to 2.6 percent. Given the increasing number of women who postpone marriage, the authors of the study conclude that "much of this marriage deferral is translating into marriage forgone" (Salholz, 1986; Greer, 1986). There are at least two reasons for the diffi-

Singles shopping at a grocery store. The number of singles who live alone has doubled over the last 20 years. Today they make up some 24 percent of American households. Most are not opposed to marriage; they expect to be married eventually. They remain single because they have not met the right person. However, the longer they wait, the harder it is to find that person. This is especially true for older, well-educated women because there are fewer marriageable men their age.

culty of finding Mr. Right. First, single women in their thirties and forties far outnumber marriageable men. This is partly because most women marry men several years their senior, and partly because the pool of these older men is smaller than that of the somewhat younger women. Second, since women tend to marry "up" not only in age but also in status and men tend to marry "down," the result is likely to be a surplus of well-educated, successful women. Many of these women will probably never marry. Seeing themselves as "the cream of the crop," they tend to see the remaining single men as being "at the bottom of the barrel" (Salholz, 1986).

Singleness, however, is not necessarily a scourge for women. A growing number of women—and men—choose to stay single. Some studies have found them to be happier than their married counterparts (Harayda, 1986). If asked why they are single, they are likely to say that "marriage entails too much commitment and responsibility" or "I prefer the life-style" (Simenauer and Carroll, 1982). There are several sociological reasons for the increase in committed singlehood. Basically, the social pressure to get married has fallen, and the opportunities for those who are single have grown. This is especially true for women. As educational and career opportunities open up for women, marriage stops being the only road to economic security, social respectability, and meaningful work. The influence of social pressure and opportunity on the popularity of the single life can also be seen in the fact that the single life tends to thrive in the big city and in the upper class. City dwellers face far less social pressure to marry than people in small towns, and the upper classes have money, an important weapon in combating loneliness, which is the chief drawback to being single. Many social scientists see another factor behind the rising number of people who prefer the single life-style. They perceive a "new narcissism," a total preoccupation with oneself. As sociologist Frank Furstenberg put it, "the institution of singledom is the symbolic recognition of the right of someone not to share his meal with someone else" (Francke, 1978).

Death of the Family?

Do the changes in the family signal its end? The death of the family has been predicted for decades. Nearly 40 years ago Carle Zimmerman (1949) concluded from his study on the family that "We must look upon the present confusion of family values as the beginning of violent breaking up of a system." By the "confusion of family values," Zimmerman referred to the threat that individualism presented to the tradition of paternalistic authority and filial duty. He assumed that individualism would eventually do the family in. Today many continue to predict the demise of the family, pointing out as evidence the increases in divorce, out-of-wedlock births, cohabitation, and singlehood.

But the family is alive and well, as we have suggested here and there. The problem with the gloomy forecast is that it confuses change with breakdown. Many of the traditional families—with husbands as breadwinners and wives as homemakers—have merely changed into two-worker families, which still hang together as nuclear families rather than disintegrate. Despite the increase in singlehood, an overwhelming majority of those who now live alone will eventually marry. Even in view of the "marriage squeeze" resulting from the shortage of marriageable men, 80 percent of female college graduates will also marry. In 1987 only 6 percent of men and 4 percent of women had remained single when they reached an age between 55 and 64 (Census Bureau, 1988). Although divorce rates have doubled over the last two decades, three out of four divorced people remarry, most doing so within three years of their marital breakup. Most of the young adults who live together before marriage will also marry eventually. However, as we have discussed, single-parent families, especially those resulting from out-of-wedlock births, do pose problems for many mothers and their children. But the problems have to do with economic deprivation rather than single parenthood as a new form of family.

Evidence from recent public opinion polls also points to the basic health of the American family. In one national survey, 78 percent of all adults said that they get "a great deal" of satisfaction from their family lives—only 3 percent said "a little" or "none." In the same survey, 66 percent of married adults said they are "very happy" with marriage—only 3 percent said "not too happy." In another survey, a large majority of children (71 percent) agreed that their family life is "close and intimate" (Cherlin and Furstenberg, 1983). According to a more recent poll, 85 percent of married Americans said that they would remarry their present spouses (Harris, 1987). Such a strong, enduring faith in marriage is indeed remarkable in view of the fact that we have the highest divorce rate in the world.

What will the American family be like in the next 20 years? It should be basically the same as it is today: continuing diversity without destroying the basic family values. As sociologists Andrew Cherlin and Frank Furstenberg (1983) sum it up, "'Diversity' is the word for the future of the American family. There will be more divorces, single-parent families, and mixed families from remarriages, but the ideal of marrying and having children is still very much a part of the American experience."

QUESTIONS FOR DISCUSSION AND REVIEW

1. How has the entry of large numbers of married women into the labor force changed the family?
2. What special problems do single parents face in raising children?
3. Why do American families experience so much violence?
4. How do sociologists interpret the dramatic increase in the numbers of Americans who cohabit?
5. What are the reasons so many Americans choose to stay single, and what are some consequences of this trend?
6. How will dual-career marriages and staying single affect the future of the family?

CHAPTER REVIEW

1. *In what ways does the family vary from one society to another?* Key variations occur in the definition of who makes up the family, in norms regarding who selects a marriage partner and who is an appropriate partner, and in rules of residence, descent, inheritance, and authority.

2. *What are the basic functions performed by the family?* Sexual regulation, reproduction, socialization, economic cooperation, and emotional security. The family's functions are not equally important in all societies, though. Preindustrial families tend to be all-purpose, operating as the center of educational, political, economic, and recreational activities. Industrial societies have undergone institutional differentiation, so that providing emotional support is now the family's main function.

3. *What does the family look like from the conflict perspective?* The family can be a source of pain and conflict and an opportunity for men to exploit women.

4. *How did industrialization change the American family in the nineteenth century?* In general, families were no longer centers of production. Family life and the world of work were increasingly separated. There emerged the stereotype of the ideal family that portrayed a wife as keeping house and caring for children while her husband went out to work.

5. *How do Americans prepare for marriage?* Usually, they do not prepare for marriage intentionally, but dating and falling in love are the traditional preparatory steps in the United States. *Is there any truth to the saying that opposites attract?* Winch believes so, but most studies support the

contrary saying that birds of a feather flock together. The theory that people of similar personality traits are attracted to each other gains further support from the norm of homogamy—that a person is likely to marry someone of the same class, race, religion, and other social characteristics.

6. *Are most American marriages successful?* Most married couples consider themselves happily married, although the United States has the highest divorce rate in the world. *Why do we have such a high divorce rate?* Among the likely social causes are (1) decreased social disapproval of divorce, (2) greater availability of services and opportunities for the divorced, (3) increased specialization of the family in providing love and affection, (4) higher expectations about the quality of marital relationships, and (5) increased individualism. Higher divorce rates, however, do not necessarily mean that marriages are more unhappy than those in other societies.

7. *What changes have taken place in the American family since 1970?* It has taken on diverse forms, such as dual-career marriages, single-parent families, living together, and staying single, while producing a great deal of marital and parental violence. But these changes do not reflect the end of the American family. The basic family values, such as marrying and having children, are still very much alive.

KEY TERMS

Arranged marriage A marriage in which the partners were selected by their parents (p. 318).

Bilateral descent Rule that recognizes both parents' families as a child's close relatives (p. 319).

Egalitarian family Family in which the husband and wife hold equal authority (p. 319).

Endogamy The norm of marrying someone from one's own group (p. 318).

Exogamy The norm of marrying someone outside one's group (p. 318).

Extended family Family that consists of two parents, their young children, and other relatives; also called *consanguine family* because its members are related by blood (p. 317).

Family of orientation Family in which one grows up, consisting of oneself and one's parents and siblings (p. 316).

Family of procreation Family that one establishes through marriage, consisting of oneself and one's spouse and children (p. 316).

Homogamy Marriage that involves two people having similar characteristics, or norm that requires such a marriage (p. 325).

Institutional differentiation The process by which the functions of one institution are gradually taken over by other institutions (p. 320).

Matriarchal family Family in which the dominant figure is the eldest female (p. 319).

Matrilineal descent Rule that recognizes only the mother's family as a child's close relatives (p. 319).

Matrilocal residence Rule that requires a married couple to live with the wife's family (p. 319).

Monogamy Marriage of one man to one woman (p. 318).

Neolocal residence Rule that requires a married couple to live by themselves, away from both husband's and wife's families (p. 318).

Nuclear family Family that consists of two parents and their unmarried children; also called *conjugal family* because its members are related by virtue of the marriage between the two adults (p. 316).

Patriarchal family Family in which the dominant figure is the eldest male (p. 319).

Patrilineal descent Rule that recognizes only the father's family as a child's close relatives (p. 319).

Patrilocal residence Rule that requires a married couple to live with the husband's family (p. 318).

Polyandry Marriage of one woman to two or more men (p. 318).

Polygamy Marriage of one person to two or more people of the opposite sex (p. 318).

Polygyny Marriage of one man to two or more women (p. 318).

Serial monogamy Marriage of one person to two or more people of the opposite sex but one at a time (p. 318).

SUGGESTED READINGS

Berger, Brigitte, and Peter L. Berger. 1983. *The War over the Family: Capturing the Middle Ground.* Garden City, N.Y. Anchor/Doubleday. A critique of both the radicals who favor individual liberation over family responsibilities and the conservatives who try to roll the family back to the traditional model of the past.

Blumstein, Philip, and Pepper Schwartz. 1983. *American Couples: Money, Work, and Sex.* New York: Morrow. A survey of mostly white, middle-class, and college-educated American couples, who report on how they put their lives together.

Levitan, Sar A., and Richard S. Belous. 1981. *What's Happening to the American Family?* Baltimore, Md.: Johns Hopkins University Press. An upbeat interpretation of the data on contemporary American families, presented with charm and humor.

Macklin, Eleanor D., and Roger H. Rubin (eds.). 1983. *Contemporary Families and Alternative Lifestyles.* Beverly Hills, Calif.: Sage. A highly useful collection of articles dealing with various forms of family and life-styles including singlehood, cohabitation, childless marriage, single-parent family, divorce, stepfamily, dual-career family, open marriage, gay relationship, commune, and traditional family.

Weitzman, Lenore J. 1985. *The Divorce Revolution: The Unexpected Social and Economic Consequences for Women and Children in America.* New York: Free Press. Initially intended to ensure equal treatment of men and women, the no-fault divorce law has ended up widening the income gap between the sexes, with the women and their children sinking into poverty.

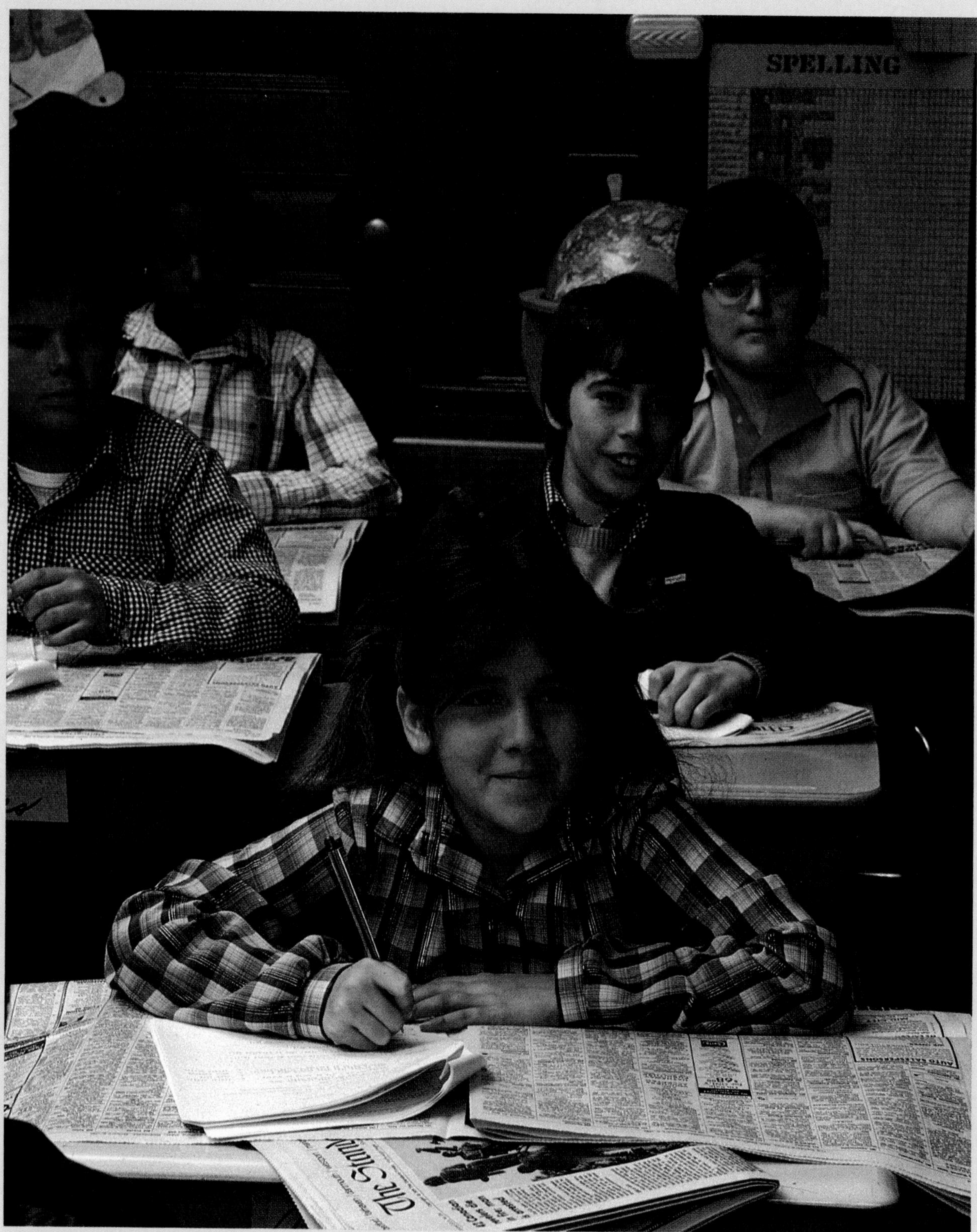
SPELLING

14 Education

From the functionalist perspective, we can see that education is important to society and individuals alike. It enables students to acquire knowledge and skills, promotes social mobility, fosters national unity, and provides custodial care for children. Moreover, by improving the life chances of poor and minority students, education can reduce social inequality. Conflict theorists disagree, arguing the American educational system reinforces inequality because it channels students of different socioeconomic backgrounds into different classes, colleges, and universities. The United States has nonetheless tried to achieve educational equality. It has bused schoolchildren to racially integrated schools, provided low-cost loans to poor and minority college students, and enforced affirmative action laws to open up various educational opportunities and programs for minorities and women.

When the young Frenchman Alexis de Tocqueville visited the United States in 1831, he was amazed at "the effort made . . . to spread instruction." Americans, he wrote to a friend, had a "universal and sincere faith" in education that was remarkable (Reeves, 1982). We seem to have maintained, or even strengthened, that faith. Name any problem, and we are likely to have heard a good many public commentators say that in order to fix it, we must have more education. According to a Gallup (1982) poll, we even consider education more important than having the best industrial system or the strongest military force. This is because, as the National Commission on Excellence in Education (1983) explains, both our industrial power and military might depend heavily on our schools. Education is indeed our biggest business. In 1986 we spent more than $300 billion on schools of all levels. Such expenditure is second only in size and growth to that of health care (Perelman, 1986). Other developed countries, as well as less developed ones, also give top priority to education (Ramirez and Meyer, 1980; Craig and Spear, 1982; Inkeles and Sirowy, 1983). But our expenditure on each student is the highest in the world: more than twice as high as in Europe or the Soviet Union and well over ten times as high as in Latin America, Asia, or Africa (Lerner, 1982).

Do we get our money's worth? In this chapter we examine what the functions of education are and how well they are being carried out. We also study the major components of the American educational system—teachers and students. We then analyze some aspects of the complex relationship between education and society and, finally, take a look at proposals for improving American education.

FUNCTIONS OF EDUCATION

According to the functionalist perspective, education performs many functions for us as individuals and for society as a whole. Here we will discuss only the most important functions: teaching knowledge and skills, enhancing social mobility, promoting national unity, and providing custodial care.

Knowledge and Skills

The most obvious function of education is to provide a new generation with the knowledge and skills necessary to maintain the society. Thanks to our schools, we have "a democratic system of government, a dynamic free enterprise economy, and an enduring social system, all of which are the envy of the world" (Warner, 1983).

But, oddly enough, over the last 20 years, there has been a lot of controversy over whether schools can help students develop cognitive skills. Since the late 1960s there have been many observers who believe that schools make little difference in how much we learn. This belief has largely stemmed from the works of James Coleman (1966), Christopher Jencks (1972), and their research associates. They found that raising the quality of high schools could improve academic performance by only 1 percent or less. They also found that school variables such as the quality of teachers and curricula accounted for a mere 2 to 3 percent of the variance in scholastic attainment, a figure way below the estimated 50 percent attributed to family background. All this was taken to mean that how much we learn depends far more on what kind of home we come from than on what kind of school we go to. If we are from middle-class families, we would do much better academically than our classmates from lower-class homes. The quality of the school has very little impact on our academic achievement. Such findings and interpretations have led to the conclusion that "additional school expenditures are unlikely to increase achievements, and redistributing resources will not reduce test score inequality" (Jencks et al., 1972).

Such a conclusion has recently been called into question. According to Michael Rutter (1983), the statistical method that Coleman and Jencks used in their studies was inappropriate for the subject under investigation. It produced misleading data, which suggest that schools have almost no influence on student achievement, while they in fact have a great deal of influence. Let's suppose (1) that German can be learned *only at school.* Let's also suppose (2) that all schools are equally good at teaching the language while students come from widely different family backgrounds. Because of the second condition, the statistical method that Coleman and Jencks used would have shown that schooling had a *zero* effect on the student's learning of German. This is obviously not true because we know from the first supposition that the language can be learned only at school.

More positively, many recent studies have shown real and substantial effects of schooling on student achievement. Of course, they do not discount completely the importance of family background. Given the greater learning resources—such as a daily newspaper, dictionary, and encyclopedia in their homes—upper- and middle-class students do have higher educational attainment than their lower-class peers (Teachman, 1987). But when researchers take family background into account, they still find that schools do make a difference in how much their students learn. Students from lower-income families attending "good" high schools, for example, have been found to learn more and have a better chance of going to college than other lower-income students attending "bad" schools (Brookover et al., 1979). Studies in developing countries, where schooling is not available to all children, have also shown that whether or not children attend school has a significant influence on their cognitive development (Stevenson et al., 1978; Sharp et al., 1979; Heyneman and Loxley, 1983). In fact, an extensive review of current studies concludes that schools can and do make a big difference in transmitting knowledge and skills to students (Rutter, 1983). Even James Coleman's recent study supports this conclusion (Coleman et al., 1982b).

Social Mobility

As individuals, Americans tend to value the knowledge and skills transmitted by the schools not for their own sake but because they hope to translate those skills into good jobs and money. As a recent study indicates, many students are attracted to college because of job and career considerations. Sixty percent of the college students and college-bound high school students in the study agreed that one must have a college education in order to make it in a career today (Widrick and Fram, 1984). Does education really enhance the individual's opportunity for social mobility?

The answer is no, according to a number of critics in the 1970s. Sociologist Randall Collins (1971; 1979) argued from the conflict perspective that formal education is often irrelevant to occupational achievement. Whatever training is needed comes more from work experience than from formal education. Even highly technical skills can be learned on the job. In 1970 about 40 percent of the practicing engineers did not have college degrees. Only 20 percent of the jobs available in the 1970s truly required a college education. For the most part, education seems to provide credentials rather than skills. In effect, a diploma or degree certifies to employers that the holder is employable. It gives them a place to start in screening potential employees, and those who have the right educational credentials are likely to make the "first cut" in competing for a job.

More blunt than Collins, social critic Caroline Bird (1975) blasted college education for being "the dumbest investment you can make." She estimated that if a Princeton freshman in 1972 had put the $34,181 needed

"First of all, I'd like to say I really feel I got my thirty-two thousand dollars' worth."

for four years of college into a savings account earning 7.5 percent interest compounded daily, then at age 64 he would have $1,129,200—which is $528,200 more than a college graduate could expect to earn between ages 22 and 64. According to Bird, college is not only a waste of money but also a waste of time because colleges do not prepare students for jobs. "The plain fact," she argues, "is that what doctors, nurses, lawyers, journalists, social workers, broadcasters, librarians, and executives do all day long isn't taught in classrooms."

But those criticisms are far off the mark. First, Bird underestimates the value of college education. The estimated lifetime earnings for college graduates as reported in government documents, from which Bird got her information, do *not* include various fringe benefits, periodic savings, and investments in stocks and bonds. These can be substantial when added up from age 22 to 64 (Burkhead, 1983). Second, she ignores the fact that a bird in the hand is worth two in the bush. After only four years of college education, a person can have an income every month for the next 42 years. But Bird's hypothetical Princeton freshman has to wait empty-handed for 46 years before he can get the money from his savings account. Third, both Bird and Collins gloss over the fact that most doctors, engineers, and other professionals can hardly do their jobs competently if they have not gone to college at all. While it is true that on-the-job training can enhance professional achievement, that training will be more beneficial if that individual has received the appropriate college education in the first place.

More positively, functionalist theory suggests that education serves a useful function by upgrading prospective workers' skills—human capital—which in turn boosts earnings for individuals and promotes economic growth for society. There is growing evidence to support this view. As Figure 14.1 shows, education and income are strongly related. In 1987 the average college graduate, for example, made $41,677, whereas the high school graduate earned $24,271. Economist Dan Burkhead (1983) estimates that a 25-year-old man with a college degree can expect to earn within 40 years $365,000 more than a man with a high school diploma can. A 25-year-old female college graduate also can expect to earn within 40 years $144,000 more than a female high school graduate. Another economist, Anne Young (1983), finds that higher education is not only a gateway to the most desirable jobs and career advancement but also provides considerable advantages in a sluggish economy, as demonstrated by the consistently lower-than-average jobless rates among college graduates. In analyzing the relationship between education and income from 1950 to 1970, sociologists Richard Wanner and Lionel Lewis (1982) conclude that "the overall trend is toward a stronger relationship." Most importantly, sociologists Pamela Walters and Richard

Figure 14.1 How Education Raises Our Income

A major function of education is to enhance the individual's opportunity for social mobility. Thus the more education people have, the bigger their earnings are.

Source: Census Bureau, *Statistical Abstract of the United States,* 1988, p. 423.

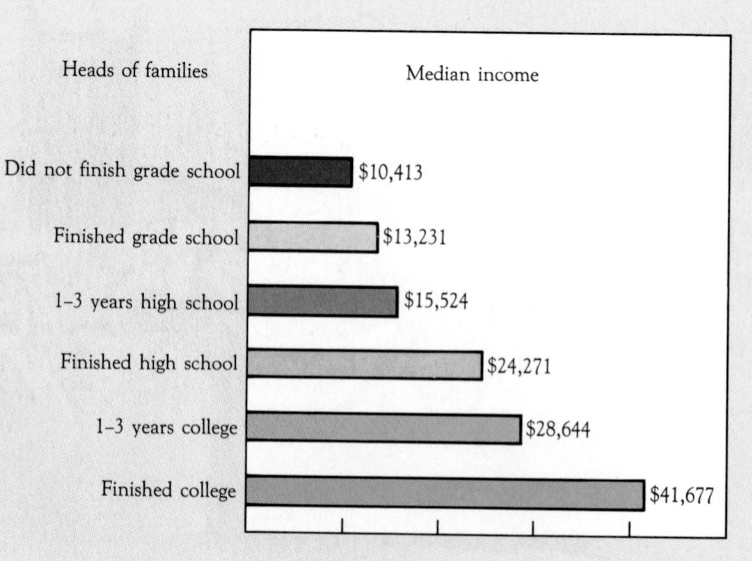

Rubinson (1983) find that the expansion of education in the United States since 1933 has contributed to the nation's economic growth. The reason is that educational expansion can increase worker productivity, develop more productive or labor-saving technology, and create a stable political climate.

We should note, however, that while schools may serve as a training ground for the world of work, they are not necessarily the product of industrial growth. Many social scientists erroneously assume that industrialization causes educational expansion because of its need for skilled workers. It is true that industry needs skilled workers, but research evidence suggests that industrialization does *not* cause educational expansion. Most empirical studies show, for example, that in the developing countries educational expansion often precedes rather than follows modernization. Historical evidence also indicates that mass schooling in Europe and Japan preceded industrialization (Ramirez and Meyer, 1980). What, then, has caused mass schooling to appear in the first place? It was probably the perceived need of a society to promote national unity, as suggested by the fact that mass education is more likely to originate in societies with states than in stateless societies (Ramirez and Meyer, 1980).

National Unity

To foster national unity, schools—mostly primary and secondary schools rather than colleges and universities—play an important role in transmitting the culture to a new generation. Students are taught to become good citizens, to love their country, to cherish their cultural values, and to be proud of their nationality—American, Mexican, Nigerian, Soviet, or whatever it may be. The teaching of good citizenship may involve the performance of rituals. In the United States, for example, schoolchildren are taught to recite the Pledge of Allegiance to the flag and to stand at attention to the playing of the "Star-Spangled Banner" before a ballgame. Schools also plant seeds of patriotism in their young charges by teaching civics, history, and other social studies. In these courses the glorious national achievements are played up. But the shameful acts, which can hardly inspire love and respect for one's own country, are watered down or left out. In Japan, for example, school textbooks do not contain information or pictures showing Japanese wartime atrocities in China, such as the slaughtering of 200,000 Chinese refugees, women, and children in the city of Nanjing, the bayoneting of Chinese civilians for practice, or Chinese civilians being buried alive. Recently, Japan's Ministry of Education even tried to soften the image of Japan as a World War II aggressor. It told textbook writers not to say "Japan invaded Korea, China, and Southeast Asia"—and instructed that the offensive word "invaded" be changed to "advanced into" or "sent troops to" (Sayle, 1982; Kim, 1983).

Like Japan and other countries, the United States has long recognized the importance of using education

An outdoor classroom in India. Research has shown that the expansion of education in the United States since 1933 has contributed to the nation's economic growth. Mass schooling has also been a driving force behind the industrialization in Europe and Japan. Similarly, educational expansion can be an impetus to modernization in third-world countries such as India.

to unify its people by teaching history from its own viewpoint. Our Founding Fathers believed that the schools should teach the American idea of democracy, ensuring individual freedom and good government. With the influx of immigrants getting larger and larger since 1860, more and more states found it necessary to enact compulsory education laws so that their children could become "Americanized." Americanization involves thinking of oneself as an American, supporting the American democratic idea, and becoming assimilated into the mainstream of American culture. Today the process of Americanization continues with the children of new immigrants, particularly those from Southeast Asia and Latin America. Americanization is also targeted to black, Hispanic, American Indian, and other minority children.

Seen from the functionalist perspective, Americanization is not only necessary for the nation as a whole but also useful to the immigrants and minorities. It enables the nation to enhance its unity and the minorities to improve their life chances. But conflict theorists argue that Americanization is cultural imperialism, forcibly imposing the WASP (White Anglo-Saxon Protestant) culture on non-WASP Americans. The typical American history textbook is written from the white's point of view so that it presents more white heroes than black heroes. Hispanic schoolchildren are expected to give up their Spanish and to be taught in English only. Thus the so-called Americanization not only threatens to destroy the minorities' cultural heritage but also encourages teachers to stereotype minority students as "culturally deprived."

Both functionalist and conflict views may be correct, but they are less relevant today than in the past. Since 1970, primarily due to the civil rights movement, such minority-oriented programs as black studies and bilingual education have been instituted in a number of schools. Respect for minorities' heritage is now a significant part of the American experience. At the same time, though, schools seem less effective in teaching the political culture of the nation. In the 1970s many polls showed that large numbers of Americans could not recognize the Bill of Rights when it was read to them. More important, they did not agree with major parts of it. Many teenagers also did not know how Congress or the president is selected (Yankelovich, 1974). The same situation may still exist in the 1980s.

Custodial Care

Another major but latent function of schooling is to offer custodial care of children, providing a place to put youngsters and someone to watch them. They keep children off the streets, presumably out of trouble (Rutter, 1983). The importance of this function has increased as more and more mothers have entered the labor market (see Chapter 13: The Family). Schools have traditionally done a good job performing their custodial role. As

A primary school classroom in Irvine, California. Primary and secondary schools play a key role in transmitting a nation's culture and values to young people. Schools usually pass on an idealistic version of the nation's history, so that students will love and respect their country. All this helps to foster and strengthen national unity.

A high school theater group in rehearsal. Schools serve a custodial role as well as an educational one. Because students must stay in school longer than the study of academic disciplines requires, there is time left over for extracurricular activities such as choral singing and theatrical performance. Students are also given the opportunities to take nonacademic electives such as cooking, driving, public speaking, leadership ("how to plan and conduct meetings") and "survival of singles."

research often showed, many schools were run almost like boot camps, where teachers diligently enforced rules and regulations and students obeyed them without question (Gracey, 1975). But since 1970 a fast-growing number of schools seem to have turned into "blackboard jungles," where violence and drugs are rampant. In 1976 there were about 150,000 cases of aggravated assaults in schools and the cost of vandalism on school property ran as high as $600 million—close to the amount spent on textbooks. In one month during 1978, nearly 16 percent of secondary-school students were victims of theft or physical attack. Although much of the violence was concentrated in inner-city schools, the same problem also plagued suburban and rural schools. There were, however, more problems in junior high school, because these schools contain more unwilling students who are forced by the compulsory attendance law to stay in school (Toby, 1983).

School violence continues to be a big problem in the 1980s. According to a Gallup poll, the public still ranks "lack of discipline" the number-one problem in schools, as it has done every year during the previous 14 years. The problem has become so serious that nearly a quarter of all teachers have been trained in how to deal with disruptive students. The Justice Department and Congress have also begun to tackle the problem (Solorzano, 1984a; Hartle, 1984). We should not, however, blow school violence out of proportion. While there is more of it today than before, an orderly routine still prevails in "most public schools—as well as in the overwhelming majority of private and parochial schools" (Toby, 1983). Teachers play a crucial part in maintaining this order. But some teachers find this custodial function degrading to their profession. They resent being "treated like babysitters." As Martha Fiske, a distinguished teacher who quit her high-paid position in one of the nation's best high schools, said, "If you want me to be a professional and publish articles on 'King Lear,' don't ask me to pick up litter in the girl's room, or catch potato puffs on lunch duty. Why not hire minimum-wage people? Isn't it counterproductive to pay someone $36,000 to supervise a bathroom?" (Marquand, 1986).

The custodial function of schools is important for yet another reason: it keeps the young out of the job market. Adults may find this reason embarrassing but it is quite real today. In the past, when unskilled labor was in great demand, children made up a large portion of the labor force. This is why for a long time farmers and manufacturers who needed child labor, as well as poor families who needed the money brought home by child labor, were opposed to mass compulsory education, which would take away the children from their jobs. Only when the need for unskilled labor began to diminish did they cooperate and send their children to school. Today there are so few unskilled jobs that if there were no compulsory school attendance to keep the youngsters from working, the nation's unemployment rate would shoot up dangerously. The need for keeping young people out of the job market, however, requires that they spend a lot of time in school—more than necessary for acquiring basic knowledge and skills. Thus most students take 12 years—from grades 1 through 12—to acquire basic reading and mathematical skills that can be achieved in about three years of intensive training between ages 15 and 18 (White, 1977). It is no wonder that students are given ample opportunities for recreational, extracurricular, or nonacademic activities. Their curriculum is often filled with such nonacademic electives as public speaking, putting out a yearbook, leadership ("how to plan and conduct meetings"), and "survival of singles" ("how to manage time and money while making wise choices in buying, preparing and selecting food, clothing, household furnishings, automobiles, and insurance"). In many schools, the time spent on learning to cook and drive even counts as much toward a high-school diploma as the time spent on studying English, mathematics, chemistry, American history, or biology (National Commission on Excellence in Education, 1983; Tharp, 1987). The schools apparently play their custodial role well, as most students consider games, sports, and friends—not books, classes, and teachers—the most important features of their school experience (Goodlad, 1984).

QUESTIONS FOR DISCUSSION AND REVIEW

1. What major functions does education perform for American society, and which of these are latent rather than manifest?
2. Why do critics charge that schools have failed to promote knowledge and skills?
3. What are some of the ways schools attempt to promote national unity, and why do some ethnic groups oppose this activity?
4. Why is the custodial care function of schools so important to American society?

EDUCATION AND INEQUALITY

If schools can serve all the functions that we have discussed, can they also reduce social inequality in the larger society? Most Americans seem to believe so, because they think that education can improve the life chances of the poor and minorities. But conflict theorists argue just the opposite—that schools reinforce the existing social structure of inequality.

The Conflict Perspective

Conflict theorists contend that American education supports the capitalist system by producing an array of skills and attitudes appropriate for maintaining social inequality. This is based on the assumption that the educational system gives children from different social classes different educational experiences, so that they develop skills and attitudes appropriate for their status. In elementary and secondary schools, lower-class children are trained to respect authority and obey orders—characteristics that employers like in menial laborers. In high school, higher-class youths are usually channeled into college preparatory courses, and thus eventually into higher-status jobs, while lower-class students are typically guided into vocational courses, which lead to lower-status jobs. After graduating from high school, higher-class students are more likely to attend college than lower-class students. Those in elite universities learn independent thinking and decision-making skills, which are useful for leadership positions. Meanwhile, in average universities and colleges, middle-class youth are taught responsibility, dependability, and the ability to work without close supervision—qualities needed for middle-level professions and occupations. In short, education teaches youth to know their place and fill it (Bowles and Gintis, 1976; Szymanski and Goertzel, 1979).

Conflict theorists do not, however, blame schools for producing inequality within themselves or in the larger society. As Samuel Bowles and Herbert Gintis (1976) wrote, "education is relatively powerless to correct economic inequality. The class, sex, and race biases in schooling do not produce, but rather reflect, the structure of privilege in society at large." In order for schools to reduce inequality, conflict theorists conclude, the capitalist society would have to change into a socialist one.

There is evidence to support the conflict argument about the relationship between social class and educational experience (Oakes, 1982; Goodlad, 1984; Colclough and Beck, 1986). In his study of nearly 900 high-school classes in various parts of the United States, John Goodlad (1984) consistently found that higher-track (higher-ability) and lower-track (lower-ability) classes were taught differently. There were disproportionately large numbers of higher-income students in higher-track classes and lower-class and minority students in lower-track classes. Higher-track, higher-income students were taught "a more independent type of thinking—self-direction, creativity, critical thinking, pursuing individual assignments, and active involvement in the process of learning." Lower-track, lower-class students were taught "a more conforming type of classroom behavior—working quietly, punctuality, cooperation, improving study habits, conforming to rules and expectations, and getting along with others."

But the conflict assumption that only capitalism is responsible for the inequality in schools is less convincing. To the extent that all societies are stratified, educational inequality exists everywhere, as evidence can be found in France and other societies. In fact, the division between elite schooling and mass education is sharper in Europe as a whole than it is in the United States (Garnier and Raffalovich, 1984; Rubinson, 1986). Even in the anticapitalist Soviet Union, an overwhelming majority of children from higher-status families (whose parents are government officials, scientists, and other members of the Soviet intelligentsia) attend elite schools that will lead them into a profession or government service. They avoid vocational schools that lead to farm or factory work, despite the government's urging that more Soviet youth switch to such schools and "give their strong young arms and hot hearts where they are most needed" (Williams, 1984a). More importantly, contrary to the conflict assumption, American schools can promote equality, as we will see in the following section.

Equalizing Education

Minorities have long faced discrimination when they sought formal education. Since Africans first arrived in America, for example, blacks have either been denied public education or allowed only an inferior variety. Although equal opportunities in education are not sufficient to produce social and economic equality, such equality is not likely to exist without them. Since the 1970s, minorities—especially blacks—have made considerable progress in attaining educational equality (see Chapter 10: Racial and Ethnic Minorities). Although large differences remain in the quality of the schools they attend and in their performance as a group, their test scores have improved, dropout rates have declined, and college attendance has increased. These improvements did not just happen. Behind them lies a broader social change: a decline in discrimination, accompanied by government actions to promote equality. Many of these actions have been very controversial, though.

Busing In 1954 the U.S. Supreme Court unanimously ruled segregated public schools unconstitutional and ordered them desegregated "with all deliberate speed." But progress has not been speedy. Although hundreds of school districts have been desegregated, a great deal of **de facto segregation** remains. Such school segregation results from existing social conditions, particularly residential segregation. Busing children to schools away from their own neighborhoods is therefore an important tool for desegregating schools. But it has encountered very strong opposition from parents, especially white parents. In 1982, 77 percent of whites opposed busing, compared with 43 percent for blacks (Gallup, 1982). Most of the white opposition appears to come from the working class in the cities. Having good intentions and high principles and seeking to do right, affluent suburban whites tend to characterize inner-city whites as bigots. Some social critics, however, suspect that many of the prosperous whites, ensconced in their privileged sanctuaries in the suburbs, might react in the same way if they were told to bus their children to a poor black neighborhood school (Lukas, 1985). Despite all this opposition to busing, the level of school integration has improved over the last two decades. Today both white and black pupils throughout the United States are more likely to attend integrated schools. Ironically, though, the South, formerly the most segregated region of our

Busing of black students and white students to achieve integrated schools has been controversial in both white and black communities. The benefits of busing have also been debated by sociologists. The debates center on whether busing causes white families to move to the suburbs to escape integrated schools and on whether black students in integrated schools do better academically than in nonintegrated schools. Today virtually all researchers agree that white flight has occurred, but there is still disagreement over whether school integration improves black students' grades.

country, is now the most integrated, while the Northeast, which used to be the most integrated region, is today the most segregated (Williams, 1987).

The controversy over busing has also embroiled sociologists. In the 1960s almost all sociologists supported busing because the research findings seemed to show desegregation as having beneficial effects on minority students. But in the 1970s several prominent sociologists opposed it, arguing from their research evidence that busing was not having the desired effects. The best example is James Coleman. In the mid-1960s he found that attending integrated schools would raise the achievement levels of black and other minority pupils. Ten years later he argued against mandatory integration and offered this reason for his about-face: "The achievement benefits of integrated schools appeared substantial when I studied them in the middle 1960s. But subsequent studies of achievement in actual systems that have desegregated, some with a more rigorous methodology than we were able to use in 1966, have found smaller effects, and in some cases, none at all" (Coleman, 1975). In addition, Coleman argued that busing is counterproductive, because it leads to massive "white flight" from the cities (where there are many blacks) to the suburbs (where there are fewer blacks). David Armor (1972) also found that busing was not raising black achievement but was depressing black aspirations and self-esteem and increasing black hostility toward whites. Coleman advocated that busing be made voluntary.

Other sociologists have vehemently disagreed with Coleman and Armor. Some argued that the data used by Coleman and Armor are not valid because of faulty research methods. Analyzing studies they considered methodologically superior, Thomas Pettigrew and his colleagues (1973, 1976) concluded that school desegregation does have some positive effects on black achievement. They also argued that shifts in black aspirations from unrealistically high levels to lower, more realistic levels during desegregation are beneficial. They can ward off disappointment and dropping out of school. Pettigrew and his associates further claimed that forced busing has little or no effect on white flight. Most of the movement of white residents out of central-city schools involved in busing, they contended, merely reflects the traditional migration to the suburbs of people who are entering the middle class.

Today the controversy is only partly resolved. There is no longer disagreement on the issue of white flight from desegregation. Even one of Coleman's harshest critics, Christine Rossell (1983), now agrees that the evidence shows white flight. The latest research report released by the U.S. Commission on Civil Rights also shows that all types of voluntary and mandatory desegregation were associated with a drop in the number of white students, with most of the decline being related to mandatory busing (Williams, 1987). But there is still disagreement on whether school desegregation benefits minority students. After reviewing numerous studies on the subject, Rita Mahard and Robert Crain (1983) conclude that desegregation indeed improves minority academic achievement. Analysis of about the same studies leads Nancy St. John (1981) to a different conclusion. She claims that there is no strong, clear evidence that desegregation closes the achievement gap between black and white students and explains that "moving children around like checkers will not in itself improve matters." Nevertheless, she still strongly believes that when schools become more thoroughly integrated than they are now, "all children will benefit, measurably and immeasurably." In her view, to be thoroughly integrated, the schools must have racially unbiased principals and teachers, multicultural curricula, and adequate amounts of equal-status racial contacts—interactions between students of different races with similar social backgrounds. Thus schools *can* equalize educational opportunities through proper desegregation.

Loans and Affirmative Action In higher education, the government policies most significant in promoting equality have been subsidized loans and affirmative action. The low-cost loans have aided not only minorities but all poor and even some middle-class students. Affirmative action has helped women at least as much as minorities with various educational opportunities and programs. Together, these policies have dramatically changed American colleges and universities since the early 1970s, making them more democratic institutions than before. In the early 1960s, only 30 to 35 percent of all black students attended predominantly white colleges, but by 1975–1976 the figure soared to 82 percent (Willie and Cunnigen, 1981; see also Muir and McGlamery, 1984).

Harvard can serve as an example. It has long been an institution that educates the sons of the elite and provides its graduates with an avenue to positions of power. Eight of 54 signers of the Declaration of Independence, 5 of the 40 U.S. presidents, and 6 of the 59 secretaries of state graduated from Harvard. As Richard Reeves (1982) puts it, "There are a lot of ways to make it economically, politically, intellectually, and socially in

America, but if there is a better place to start than Harvard—a better gateway than a Harvard education and Harvard connections—I have never noticed it." During the 1970s the percentage of applicants who were admitted to Harvard declined and the test scores of entering students rose. At the same time, "Harvard, which had admitted young men because of their privileged background, began accepting some because of their underprivileged background" (Reeves, 1982). The result has been encouraging. Less than 1 percent of the Harvard Class of 1961 was black; by the early 1980s, blacks made up almost 10 percent of the student body. The government's student loans and affirmative action helped spur this democratization, at Harvard and elsewhere (Reeves, 1982). But the pursuit of democracy has exacted a price from the American educational system, which we discuss in the following section.

QUESTIONS FOR DISCUSSION AND REVIEW

1. How does the conflict perspective on education differ from the functionalist approach?
2. What evidence supports the conflict view of the relationship between social class and educational experience?
3. What has resulted from efforts to promote equality in education such as busing and affirmative action?

AMERICAN EDUCATIONAL SYSTEM

In this decade there have been many critiques of education in the United States. They all document a decline in educational standards and achievement when compared with our past and other countries. As the National Commission on Excellence in Education (1983) points out, scores on Scholastic Aptitude Tests (SAT) taken by college-bound high school seniors fell continuously from 1963 to 1980, and in the early 1970s American students scored lower on 19 academic tests than their counterparts in Japan and other industrialized countries. In view of such facts, the National Commission warns that the United States is "a nation at risk" because "the educational foundations of our society are presently being eroded by a rising tide of mediocrity that threatens our very future as a nation and a people." Many other national task forces on education have raised about the same alarm (Davies and Slevin, 1984). The media have also fanned our fear with the warning that we are in danger of becoming a second-class economic power because of our students' poor showing on math and science tests (Lord and Horn, 1987). As if all this bad news were not enough, three publications in the summer of 1987 came out with new attacks on American education. One is the report from the National Endowment for the Humanities that most of the 8000 17-year-olds tested in 1986 flunked simple history and literature: 68 percent did not know when the Civil War happened and 84 percent had no idea who wrote *Crime and Punishment.* E. D. Hirsch (1987) documents the same ignorance of Western culture, calling the students "cultural illiterates." Allan Bloom (1987) blasts American universities for closing students' minds by focusing on trendy, "relevant," career-oriented studies rather than classical philosophy.

Problems in Perspective

Is American education really in a state of crisis? The answer is probably no if we put the discouraging data in proper perspective.

First, the decline of SAT scores may have partly resulted from the opening up of educational opportunities for larger numbers of the poor and minorities, who are

Scholastic Aptitude Test (SAT) scores fell steadily from 1963 to 1980 and were one of the components of a general perception that the quality of American education has been declining. But the decline may be more apparent than real. The democratization of education that began in the 1960s brought in large numbers of disadvantaged students whose lack of preparation partly caused an overall decline in measures of achievement such as test scores. As the educational system absorbs the disadvantaged, however, academic scores can be expected to rise. In fact, they have shown signs of doing so in recent years.

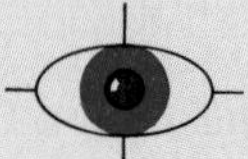

USING SOCIOLOGICAL INSIGHT

A Split Vision on American Schools

Our public schools, sometimes called common schools, are in a bind. They are expected to carry out their democratic mission by providing free education for everybody, including those without adequate intellectual preparation. Yet we are concerned that the emphasis on equality can hurt the quality of education. Here, David Cohen of Harvard University looks at the historical source of this split vision. How has this split vision affected today's public schools?

Americans celebrate common schools, but we also worry about them. Education in common means schools attended by all, open to all, supported by the state. We congratulate ourselves on the outstanding achievements of public education in this country and celebrate the egalitarian achievements of common schools. But when we worry about public schools, we think about that other meaning of the word, "common." We view our schools with a split vision—sometimes celebrating their commonness as an egalitarian achievement and sometimes worrying about their commonness as an unfortunate consequence of equality.

Our source of this split lies in two great patterns in American thought about schools. When public education was organized in this country in the 1830s and 1840s, there were two broadly different schools of thought about the virtues of common school education. One view was associated with the Workingmen's Associations. The Workingmen thought that America was on the verge of developing an aristocracy of wealth, and feared that inequalities of wealth would be reflected in the public domain. They foresaw class inequalities in political power, in part because wealthier citizens would have more political influence. Such citizens also could secure more political competence for their children by purchasing education for them. Families of what was then the artisan class would have only the political influence arising from their votes; they couldn't afford to purchase education. Lacking education, they would lack an essential resource—the skills of critical thought required for effective political participation.

The Workingmen argued that public education could remedy inequalities in political skills. If schools were public, open to all, supported by the state, then children from any family could attend and could gain those skills essential to democratic politics. They also argued that public, common schools could create bonds of mutual respect and perhaps even affection across social classes, because children of all classes would learn together before sentiment and prejudice hardened in their minds.

So one tradition of support for

encouraged to go to college. Perhaps due to inadequate academic preparation or the tests' cultural bias or both, the socially disadvantaged students did not do as well on the SAT as the socially advantaged, which helped bring down the average scores for the entire group. The democratization of education, because it tends initially to water down curriculum and teaching, has also caused many socially advantaged students to learn less than before. As educational psychologist Jerome Bruner (1982) said, "During the 1970s Americans responded to the perpetuation of class and caste by prescribing fair educational practices. We were in great part successful, but we almost killed ourselves with the prescription. In our effort to provide equal education, we so lowered standards that we're now facing a serious decline in educational quality." But the investment in equal education may have begun to pay off. Since 1980 the national SAT averages have begun to level off or pick up. Since 1976 the black-white gap in SAT scores has been closing. Mexican-American students have also made gains in recent years (I.B., 1982; Farrell, 1984).

Second, the lower academic achievement in the United States than in other industrialized nations may also reflect the impact of educational democratization in our society. Compared with the schools in other countries, our public schools are far less selective, containing a larger proportion of lower-class, minority, handicapped, foreign-language-speaking, immigrant, and other socially disadvantaged children (Wolf, 1983; Husen, 1983). (For the source of this dilemma, see box, above.) But the resulting lower achievement at the precollege level does not hurt the American educational common school education saw the schools as a critical resource for democratic politics. The very term "common school" referred to something noble, to the hope of equal political participation in what seemed a very unequal society.

But America's vision of the common school also has been shaped by another view—one that may have been important politically and in educational doctrine. This second school of thought was associated with more conservative men—New Englanders and others of substance—who worried about the influx of immigrants and commercial and manufacturing workers who were flooding cities like Boston, Philadelphia, New York, and Baltimore in the 1830s, 40s, and 50s. These reformers believed that the immigrants could corrupt the body politic, that their political expressions would be ill-informed and unrestrained, that they would give their votes to whomever appealed to their baser instincts or interests.

These conservatives also turned to the common schools, but they turned to them in a very particular spirit. They argued for compulsory education—not simply the provision of a free public education, but public education run by the state with mandated attendance. Their chief reason for such compulsion was the need to resocialize the strangers, literally to remake their minds, manners, and morals. In their view, the common school was an instrument the state created for its own protection against potentially dangerous citizens. According to this view, the common schools are necessary but not special, politically important but not noble.

If these visions seem to compete as a matter of principle, in the American educational past they often combined in practice. When educational reformers in the 1840s and 1860s argued for establishment of the schools, and when state legislators and chief state school officers took the steps toward public assumption of responsibility for education, they argued that the public schools would both remake the minds of strangers' children and help develop that critical intelligence required for democracy. If anything is characteristic of American educational dogma, it is the assumption that these are just two different aspects of the schools' complex mission.

Source: Excerpted from David K. Cohen, "The American common school—A divided vision," *Education and Urban Society*, vol. 16, no. 3, May 1984, pp. 253–261. Copyright © 1984 Sage Publications, Inc. Reprinted by permission of Sage Publications, Inc.

system as a whole, because the standard and quality of education become increasingly higher as we go from high school to college to graduate or professional school. This may explain why the United States produces the largest number of Nobel laureates and attracts a larger number of foreign students than any other country. As Professor Shibuya of Japan's Joetsu University says, "Consider the number of Nobel Prizes won so far by Japanese—fewer than ten. The number in the U.S.? More than 100" (Bowen, 1986).

Third, the United States is not alone in having some educational problems. Japan, which is often touted as taking over America's preeminence in science and technology, has serious problems with its higher education (see box, p. 354). While Japanese schoolchildren are under enormous pressures to study hard, university students are allowed to take it easy, as if in reward for having beaten their brains out before college. As Robert Christopher (1983) observes, "the great majority of Japanese universities are extraordinarily permissive: once you get into one, it takes real effort to get kicked out . . . Japanese university authorities do not regard a student's failure to attend classes or even to pass courses as a ground for dismissal." Moreover, many Japanese college students have little incentive to work hard because employers are more interested in the college from which potential recruits graduate than in their grades. Japanese political and business leaders are now concerned about the lax atmosphere in their colleges. They also worry that their schools' emphasis on conformity, such as finding the "single right answer" to a problem, is depriving their society of much-needed creativity, especially in the

UNDERSTANDING OTHER SOCIETIES

Japan: A Nation at Risk?

The United States is not alone in having educational problems. Japan also has its own problems, as the following article indicates. How does the American college life compare to that of the Japanese?

Since 1977, the Research Institute for Higher Education at Hiroshima University has been studying the Japanese university system. Its findings are being published in a series of reports which have already shocked the academic community. Foreign academics who teach at Japanese universities and a growing number of Japanese professors now believe the nation's colleges are failing to educate.

Students, once so zealous to enter, are indifferent to learning and professors are unenthusiastic about teaching. The drop-out rate is low. Classes are overcrowded with 100–200 students in a lecture. Students still learn by memory and notes are handed down from one generation of students to another. The curriculum is often adjusted to the interests of available professors. Many universities operate with a small staff of full-time professors and a large supply of poorly paid part-time lecturers. A university education will provide the credentials for entry into society, but the four years spent on campus are seen as a suspension between the grueling steps toward admission and entrance into professional life.

The national cliché is that Japanese universities are difficult to enter but easy to graduate from. A second-year student at a national university called it "leisure-land" and said: "Japanese children study, study, study; university students play, play, play."

Prerequisites for a university education are not simple. They make up a modern legend in Japan featuring the notorious *kyoiku mama* (education mother), a controlling woman who sacrifices her other interests to watch-dog her child's study for a year or two until he passes a set of entrance examinations, first to junior high school, later to senior high school.

Also included are the extra expenses of private tutors and *juku,* intensive preparatory schools which teach students how to pass examinations. There is the torment of *juku jigoku* (exam hell), a term reserved for university entrance examinations but also applicable to sitting for exams from elementary school to college.

Consider too, the high number of *ronin* (estimated at 200,000)—students who fail the exams and keep trying to pass two, three, four, even five years in a row; young suicides, depressed over failed or approaching examinations; and finally, the annual bribery scandals of private universities. . . .

The absence of an international character in universities bothers far-sighted men in government and private life. They have called for an "internationalization of higher education," saying Japan's commercial internationalism is not enough. Financed by grants from the Ministry of Education and the Ford Foundation, Hiroshima University undertook a special research project to discover why universities are parochial, how foreigners teaching in them evaluate them and in what ways the system can change. The results of the national opinion survey, among foreign teachers, were both shocking and gratifying.

"Foreign teachers are very critical of the teaching at Japan's universities and colleges. They say that professors are research-minded and indifferent to teaching, which seems a tiresome load. We were very much shocked at so much criticism," said Kazuyuki Kitamura, director of the project.

Out of 857 full-time foreign teachers in Japan, 371 responded to the five-page questionnaire which the institute prepared. The majority of the respondents were from North America or Europe.

Foreigners were as critical of Japanese students as they were of university teaching and claimed they lacked motivation. Passing seemed guaranteed because of the professor's sense of responsibility towards his students. Students did not show a similar responsibility towards their work. (Some Japanese students felt no shame in insisting on a passing C grade.) They were exam-oriented, cut classes freely, did not respond in class and expected to be lectured at instead of discussing or asking questions. Japanese professors enjoyed unquestioned authority and considered the situation with their students natural.

Source: Excerpted from Christine Chapman, "All play and no work," *Far Eastern Economic Review,* vol. 113, July 3, 1981, p. 32.

current age of rapid change. While Japanese colleges are generally inferior to ours, it is nevertheless true that their primary- and secondary-school students do outperform ours in academic achievement (Fiske, 1987).

Fourth, our schools are not to blame for the lower achievement of our students as compared with that of the Japanese. For one thing, our schools are expected to dilute their teaching resources by dealing with such social problems as alcohol and drug abuse and teenage pregnancy, which Japanese schools do not have. In fact, American teachers often have to spend 40 percent of their time on nonteaching tasks. Given the high rates of divorce, single parenthood, and two-worker couples, American parents are too stressed, tired, or self-absorbed to do what Japanese mothers do—helping with their children's homework and making sure they study three or four hours a night. Two-thirds of American teenagers hold part-time jobs, which significantly reduces their ability to hit the books after school. By contrast, working during the school year is virtually unheard of in Japan. American teenagers are also under great pressure from their peers not to be grinds but to look good, drink, socialize, date, and even have sex. This is the opposite of the Japanese adolescent peer culture, which pressures teenagers to study hard. Japanese students like to say, though a little facetiously, "Four you score; five you die," meaning "If you sleep five hours a night instead of four, you won't pass the exams" (Steinberg, 1987). In short, it is largely social problems and the lack of support from parents and the adolescent subculture that make it hard for American schools to compete with their Japanese counterparts. Our schools, then, are hardly to blame for our students' lower academic achievement.

Finally, while many problems can be found in America's schools, there is a lot of good in them, particularly in their mission of providing quality with equality (Goodlad, 1984). Although education researcher and reformist Theodore Sizer (1984) criticizes the nation's high schools for being rigid and impersonal, he still finds that "they are, on the whole, happy places, settings that most adolescents find inviting, staffed by adults who genuinely care for youngsters." In contrast, most Japanese students do not enjoy their school experience because they feel like robots or prisoners in a rigidly controlled environment. Moreover, some Japanese professors who have taught in the United States have observed that American students are more creative than their Japanese counterparts. As a math professor in Japan says, "Japanese kids at 18 know everything. But in terms of logical thinking, American kids can think better" (Tharp, 1987). It is ironic that, while Japanese school reformers are trying to emulate Americans by encouraging creativity and independent initiative in their students, Americans are trying to imitate Japanese by imposing stricter discipline and conformity on their students. The Japanese seem to be saying to their students "Sit back, relax, and discern," but the Americans' motto seems to be "Sit down, shut up, and learn" (Paleologos, 1986).

We may do well to keep all this in mind as we analyze critically the nature of our schools. In the next section we discuss the schools as formal, bureaucratic organizations with two major components, teachers and students. We also discuss higher education occasionally for comparison.

Bureaucracy

Today, school administrators, teachers, and students constitute more than a fifth of the entire U.S. population. If it is considered one unit, the school system has become the largest bureaucracy in the country. Within this giant bureaucracy, schools of various sizes and types are in a way remarkably similar. As Sizer (1984) concludes after studying 80 schools across the country, "Rural schools, city schools; rich schools, poor schools; public schools, private schools; big schools, little schools: the *framework* of grades, schedules, calendar, courses of study, even rituals, is astonishingly uniform and has been so for at least 40 years."

Like other bureaucracies, the schools have a clear-cut division of labor and hierarchy of authority. They are also largely impersonal, run in accordance with a set of formal rules. These rules dictate that administrators have authority over teachers who, in turn, have authority over students. Teachers must be assigned to teach certain subjects on the basis of skills rather than personal preferences. Students must be placed in classes according to age and ability. Forms must be filled out for just about any contingency. Of course, conditions vary from state to state and from school district to school district. But textbooks often are chosen by a state educational committee according to prescribed rules rather than by individual teachers. Even detailed curricula may be dictated to teachers by the educational bureaucracy. Budgets are likely to be drawn up by bureaucrats for an entire school district, and a school that saves money on, say, energy, might not be allowed to use the savings for some other purpose. In the educational bureaucracy as in other bureaucracies, little or no allowance is made for personalities, for the individual case, the unique event. That, after all, is the nature of bureaucracies.

All this is for the sake of efficiency, and the bureaucracy does have some advantages. The bureaucratic system ensures the provision of education for huge masses of children rather than only the few privileged ones. The larger school systems make it more likely that pupils can choose from a wide range of courses. The standardization that arises from bureaucracies allows children to adjust more easily to a new school, even when it is in a different part of the country. And bureaucratic rules offer administrators, teachers, and even students some protection from political pressures, racial and sexual prejudice, and the personal whims of those in authority.

It is the negative effects of bureaucracy, however, that are more apparent. Parents often complain that the bureaucracy leaves them out in the cold, frequently unable to influence their children's schooling. Students, too, may feel that they are treated like numbers—a situation that is not likely to inspire either respect for the school's authority or eagerness to learn. Some administrators may even find that they cannot fire incompetent teachers, and teachers, in turn, may occasionally throw up their hands from being mired in red tape. To the extent that the organization of a school system is bureaucratic, everyone is likely to lose the freedom to try innovations or to respond creatively to the unique aspects of a particular school or situation. Nevertheless, the educational bureaucracy continues to grow like a blob. Between 1960 and 1984, while the number of teachers rose by 57 percent, the number of principals and supervisors soared by 79 percent and the ranks of other staffers such as curriculum specialists and guidance counselors skyrocketed nearly 500 percent. Consequently, the proportion of funds devoted to teachers' salaries has dropped, from 55 percent of school budgets in 1955 to 41 percent in 1985. Moreover, since 1983, following the flurry of national reports on the decline in academic achievement, many states have enacted strict rules for schools. They have increased their programs for testing students in basic skills, raised their standards for licensing new teachers, and added new course requirements for getting a high school diploma. As a result, schools have added many administrators, ranging from "supervisors of instruction," who observe how teachers teach, to assistant principals who help with the yearly evaluations of teachers.

All this has caused an increasing number of teachers to complain that they have lost control over their jobs. As a teacher recently told a task force of the National Governors Association in Newark, "I no longer have autonomy over what is taught. I don't even have a lot of choice about how I teach . . . From 7:30 to 3 teachers can't even go to the bathroom without getting someone to take over their class." Agreeing that teachers are now largely governed by rules made by administrators who outrank them, the Carnegie Forum suggests that these conditions be radically altered to give teachers more leeway over how they teach (Solorzano, 1987). Other researchers have suggested that states, school boards, and superintendents give more power to each school so that it can take care of its own business, without having to do exactly what other schools are doing (Sizer, 1984). This is, in fact, a major characteristic of the better schools in Goodlad's (1984) massive study of schooling in the United States.

Teachers

Teachers play an important role in the educational system. As many recent studies indicate, teachers constitute the one single element of schooling that most influences students' learning (Goodlad, 1984). What kind of people are they?

Profile of Teachers Public-school teachers appear quite qualified for their jobs. Nearly all of the primary and secondary teachers have a bachelor's degree and slightly over half have a master's degree (Census Bureau, 1988). There is, of course, great variation in teacher qualifications among different schools. Compared with schools in lower-class communities, for example, schools in predominantly middle-class communities tend to have more teachers with an M.A. degree. While most of the college faculty have Ph.D. degrees, extremely few schoolteachers have the most advanced degrees. Ironically, these teachers—with the doctorates—tend not to teach but gravitate toward administration or out of the school system completely, for higher pay. As Goodlad (1984) writes, "Teaching is perhaps the only 'profession' where the preparation recognized as most advanced almost invariably removes the individual from the central role of teaching." In recent years, prospective teachers as a group have scored the lowest on SAT tests of all entrants to professional schools, fewer college students have planned to become teachers, and more women graduates have pursued careers with higher pay and status than teaching (Dollar, 1983).

What have the teachers learned while obtaining their college degrees? The curriculum for education majors includes practice teaching, which can be very valuable, but it also includes many courses on teaching methods. In fact, the method courses are often emphasized at the expense of courses in the specific subjects the prospective teachers will eventually teach. A survey of 1350 universities and colleges reveals that elementary education majors spend 41 percent of their time on method courses, which reduces the amount of time available for subject-matter courses. As a result, half of the recently employed English, science, and mathematics teachers are not qualified to teach these subjects, and in only one-third of high schools is physics taught by qualified teachers (National Commission, 1983). In 1986, however, more than 50 large universities already planned to phase out undergraduate education degrees and to require prospective teachers to major in subjects they plan to teach. This is, in effect, similar to the way prospective college professors are trained. While pursuing their doctorates, they focus on their chosen field, without taking any courses in teaching methods. Deans of 38 leading colleges of education have also recently proposed a three-tier hierarchy of schoolteachers. At the bottom would be "instructors." Any liberal arts graduate could become an instructor for up to five years, after which that person would either have to leave or begin graduate work in educational theory and methodology. Instructors would be supervised by teachers at the two higher levels, "professional" and "career professional," who have had extensive graduate training in pedagogy. This three-tier system is parallel to the ranking of college professors into instructors, assistant professors, associate professors, and professors. In the three-tier system, designed to attract and retain high-caliber teachers, the higher the level that is reached, the higher the salary, much the way college professors' salaries are determined. By 1987 this arrangement had been implemented in at least 11 states (Ricklefs, 1987).

Even if schoolteachers are qualified to teach a certain subject, they are not necessarily able to demonstrate their teaching effectiveness hour after hour in the classroom. In fact, many factors in the school environment—such as too many students in a confined space, too many hours each day with classes, administrative controls and restraints, interruptions, and students whose minds wander away from the subject matter before them—all these can throw a monkey wrench into the process of teaching (Goodlad, 1984). These obstructive forces, however, are less likely to operate in college teaching. Many college professors have used student evaluations to assess how well they have done in classrooms. So far many studies have failed to show any significant relationship between positive student evaluation and the amount of learning acquired. Some professors have also criticized student evaluations for measuring the teacher's skill as an actor with a box office appeal rather than as a teacher with an effective way of transmitting knowledge (Parelius and Parelius, 1978). It is possible, however, that the failure to find any value in student evaluations may reflect the researchers' bias against teaching. This bias is apparent from their definition of teaching effectiveness as ability to transmit knowledge, which ignores ability to inspire students. Moreover, many researchers have the attitude that teaching is not as important to their career as research.

It is tough to make a living as a schoolteacher. The salary for teaching is notoriously low, lower than for trucking and other occupations that require much less education. Many teachers are compelled to supplement their income with part-time and summer employment. Yet most are quite satisfied with their teaching career. According to a recent study, 74 percent of the teachers said that their career expectations had been fulfilled, and 69 percent reported that if they had it to do over again they would choose teaching as a career. Actually this need not be surprising because, for most teachers, money is not the primary reason for entering the teaching profession. Instead, the major reasons have to do with the nature of teaching itself: desire to teach in general or a particular subject, perception of teaching as a good and worthy profession, and desire to be of service to others (Goodlad, 1984).

Given the low pay, teachers do want higher salaries, along with more respect for their professionalism, more professional autonomy, and less administrative work, which they believe can help them do their jobs better. Thus powerful teachers' unions—to which over 90 percent of the nation's teachers belong—often negotiate for higher pay, smaller class size, fewer classes taught, and greater influence over hiring standards and textbook selection. They may resort to strikes as a way of enhancing their bargaining power. In fact, there are considerably more strikes today than there were in the recent past. Before 1970 there were no more than 10 strikes in any one year, but since then the number has soared to nearly 100 a year (Gollady, 1976; Hartle, 1984). Given a satisfying educational environment, teachers can teach more effectively. But they can also influence some of their students in a negative way, as we see in the following section.

The Pygmalion Effect In Greek mythology Pygmalion is a sculptor who created Galatea, an ivory statue of a beautiful woman. Pygmalion fell in love with his creation and prayed to the goddess of love, who brought the statue of Galatea to life. In educational psychology, the **Pygmalion effect** refers to the influence of teachers' expectations on students' academic performance. In a sense, teachers bring their expectations to life.

Basically, if a teacher expects certain students to fail, they are likely to do so. If a teacher expects them to succeed, then they are likely to succeed. Thus the Pygmalion effect is an example of a self-fulfilling prophecy. Robert Rosenthal and numerous other researchers have demonstrated the Pygmalion effect in a series of experiments, one of which was described briefly in Chapter 2 (Doing Sociology). The teachers' expectations do not affect the students' performance directly, but they do influence the teachers' behavior, which does affect students. Teachers tend to give attention, praise, and encouragement to students they consider bright. If the students fail to perform as well as expected, the teachers work extra hard to help them live up to expectations. But teachers tend to be uninterested, critical, and impatient with those they expect to do poorly in school. When these students have difficulty, teachers are likely to think it would be a waste of time trying to help them. And if they participate in class like a bright student, teachers are likely to put them down as smart alecks or troublemakers. As a result of this differential treatment, the differences in students' performances tend to match teachers' expectations: the "bright" students do better than the "poor" ones (Rosenthal, 1973; Harris and Rosenthal, 1985).

It is not surprising that in many schools the **tracking system,** which assigns students to different groups on the basis of their academic achievement, generally benefits higher-track students more than lower-track ones (Persell, 1984). The tracking system raises teacher expectations for higher track students and lowers teacher expectations for lower-track students. This may explain why Goodlad (1984) found that teachers in higher-track classes spent more time on instruction, expected students to study more at home, and were seen by students as more enthusiastic in teaching, more concerned about them, and less punitive toward them when compared with teachers in lower-track classes. Thus the good students tend to get better and the poor students poorer. As many studies have shown, higher-track students are more likely to go to college and lower-track students are more likely to have low self-esteem, drop out of school, or become delinquents (Alexander and Cook, 1982; Goodlad, 1984). In Israel, Yossi Shavit (1984) found similar effects of tracking: placement in the higher track enhances Ashkenazi students' eligibility for higher edu-

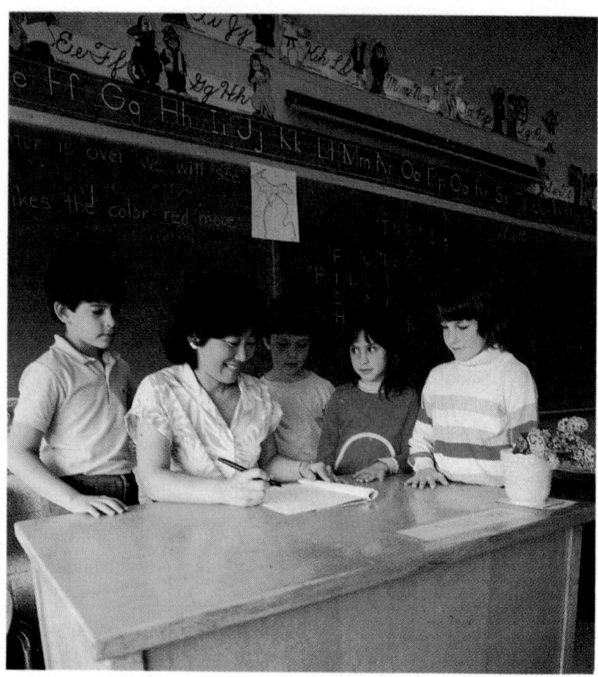

The classroom teacher is the most influential factor in the child's experience of school in the early grades. Teachers have a Pygmalion effect on their pupils. If a teacher expects a boy to do well in class, he is likely to do well. But if a teacher expects a girl to do poorly, she is likely to do poorly. The teacher's expectation does not by itself affect the pupil's performance. But the expectation can affect the teacher's behavior. It is this behavior, such as giving more attention and encouragement to a pupil expected to do well, that directly affects his or her academic performance.

cation while placement in the lower track decreases further Sephardi students' already low likelihood of going to college. A study in Great Britain also shows that students who have placed in high-ability groups score higher on reading and math tests than comparable ungrouped students, but students who have been segregated into low-ability groups perform more poorly on the tests than their ungrouped peers (Kerckhoff, 1986). All this demonstrates what symbolic interactionism suggests: in social interaction, people behave in accordance with how they think others see them (Chapter 1: Thinking Sociologically).

Students

Conflicting interests create a wide gulf between teachers and students. Unlike teachers, children are forced to be in school. Whereas teachers are duty-bound to press academic work on students, students are likely to resist. Long ago James Coleman (1961) found that high school boys aspired to be star athletes and girls wanted to be popular; neither wanted to be brilliant students. These attitudes were part and parcel of a youth culture. About the same culture still prevails today. Recently John Goodlad (1984) asked high school teenagers to choose from six categories of students they considered the most popular. A large majority (79 percent) selected "good-looking students" or "athletes," but very few (only 7 percent) picked "smart students." This and other similar data led to the conclusion that the youth "are excessively preoccupied with physical appearance, popularity in the peer group, and games and athletics." It is not surprising that most high school students are not fired up over their books, teachers, or the classes they are attending (Goodlad, 1984).

Among college students, who attend school by choice, there is more interest in intellectual pursuits. But they are not all cut from the same cloth. Burton Clark and Martin Trow (1966) found four distinct college subcultures. The *collegiate* subculture revolves around fraternities, sororities, parties, drinking, football, and similar activities. Its members tend to come from middle-class homes, and their parents are not particularly interested in intellectual matters. The *vocational* subculture is more serious, emphasizing hard work in order to get good jobs after graduation. Students in this subculture are stronger in mathematics than in verbal skills and are likely to major in science, engineering, law, and business. Today a growing number of students seem to be in this subculture (see box, p. 360). A recent study divides these students into "careerists" and "strivers." Careerists come largely from middle-class homes, while strivers are mostly members of minority groups, coming from homes with low socioeconomic status (Katchadourian and Boli, 1986). The *academic* subculture is less utilitarian, stressing the pursuit of scholarly achievement for its own sake. Its members tend to have upper-class, highly educated parents who are physicians, lawyers, or corporate executives. The *nonconformist* subculture repudiates the values of the other three subcultures, advocating rebellion from conventional society. These rebels come from all ethnic groups, from both high and low social status, but rarely from the middle class.

Given the lack of interest in academics among high-school students, how can teachers motivate them? By demanding more of them, research by Coleman and his associates (1982a, 1982b) suggests. These researchers surveyed tens of thousands of students in public and private schools and gave achievement tests to tenth and eleventh graders. They discovered that although the typical private school (a Catholic parochial school) had larger classes, lower-paid teachers, and substantially fewer resources than the average public school, the private-school students achieved more in vocabulary and mathematics. The investigators attribute this to private schools' "educational climate." Compared with public schools, private schools are more rigorous—their students are 50 percent more likely to have over an hour's worth of homework every night. Private schools impose stricter disciplinary rules and get more order in their classrooms. Most important, they put more emphasis on academic subjects, enrolling nearly 70 percent of their students in academic programs, compared with only 34 percent for public schools. A larger proportion of private-school students rated their teachers' interest in them as "excellent" than did public-school students (40 versus 10 percent). Another study also finds that private-school students rated the quality of their class instruction and strictness of discipline more highly than their peers in public schools (Morgan, 1983). Research by Barbara Falsey and Barbara Heyns (1984) demonstrates further the greater emphasis on academics in private schools: their students are much more likely to go to college than are public-school students with similar socioeconomic background, aspiration, and ability.

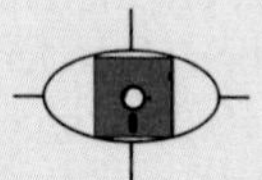

LOOKING AT CURRENT RESEARCH

The New Outsiders

Nowadays, an increasing number of college students are highly career-oriented. They study very hard to get good grades, hoping to land an excellent job after graduation. They are part of the vocational subculture that has been around on many campuses for a long time. According to the author of the following reading, such students used to be considered the outsiders, but the career-oriented students of today are quite different—hence the author calls them "the new outsiders." How does this subculture differ from the other three—collegiate, academic, and nonconformist—subcultures?

In the nineteenth and early twentieth centuries college men saw two alternatives: college life and the realm of the outsider. Intellectual achievement was valued largely by the outsiders—by poor country boys, who came to college to become ministers, and by Jews, who saw college as the stepping-stone to the professions. . . . The college men saw outsiders as grinds—rote learners and apple polishers. As it became clear to increasing numbers of students in the twentieth century that the collegiate way no longer offered the sure road to success, they looked to its flip side and sought to achieve through grinding the hoped-for future. The New Outsiders have simply accepted the terms of the past, only turning that which had once been despised into something dominant and positive.

College life had declared marks valueless. The New Outsiders reverse the judgment: grades are the ultimate value. Yet in making this shift, such students keep many of the elements of the old conception. Grades do not reflect innate differences in intelligence; rather, they result from figuring out what their professors want, spending long hours in study, and currying favor with their instructor. . . . Whereas the nineteenth-century college men scorned both the techniques and the goals of grade-grubbing, the New Outsider turns them into valued strategies and admirable ends.

The psychology of the New Outsider is more complicated than that of the college man. Nineteenth-century collegians owed individual professors respect, but could openly scorn them as a class. College men controlled the allocation of status because they chose those who led in sports and clubs. In the late twentieth century, professors hold the one judgment that matters to the New Outsiders—grades. The New Outsiders must therefore check any signs of open rebellion, even to the point of not allowing themselves to feel it. Hero worship has come to replace

Other sociologists, however, have criticized the Coleman study for being methodologically inadequate, which leads to misleading findings and interpretations (Heyns and Hilton, 1982; Alexander and Pallas, 1983, 1984; Cain and Goldberger, 1983). Karl Alexander and Aaron Pallas, for example, contend that private-school students score higher than public-school students on academic achievement tests because they are initially more capable and better motivated, not because private schools do a better job of educating them. But one of Coleman's associates, Sally Kilgore (1983, 1984) disagrees, sticking to the original position of the Coleman study. Nevertheless, while there is disagreement over the interpretation of the differences in achievement between private- and public-school students, everybody seems to agree that their school environments do differ. The key issue is not whether schools are private or public. Coleman found little difference between the achievement levels of students in high-performance public and private schools. What he found is that certain factors, such as a strict discipline, emphasis on academic subjects, and requiring considerable homework, are more likely to exist in private than in public schools. But the same conditions *can* be created in more public schools than we have today.

QUESTIONS FOR DISCUSSION AND REVIEW

1. Why do many of the recent criticisms of education misinterpret what happens in the schools?
2. How have schools become the largest bureaucracy in the country, and what are the educational consequences of this change?
3. What are some characteristics of modern public-school teachers?
4. How do the Pygmalion effect and the tracking system help explain the negative impact of teachers' expectations on some students' performance?
5. What are some characteristics of students in public and private schools and in colleges, and how do their experiences about education differ from those of teachers?

denigration. Professors assume an exalted status in such students' eyes. In the classroom they accept all the terms that the professor sets. . . . Such students do not seek to understand the nature of the universe or even to master a discipline or to deepen their knowledge in one of its areas. They are after grades.

Students entering college in the mid-1980s receive the New Outsiders' message to grind as surely as their nineteenth-century counterparts received the canons of the college man. This message has high personal costs.

As limiting as it was, traditional college life did create a time and place away from home where young men and women could try to define themselves. Distinctive dress marked the collegian: hedonism offered new experiences and, for some, struggle among peers opened new opportunities. . . . In different ways undergraduates worked for autonomy. But today's New Outsiders seem content to remain emotionally and economically dependent on their parents. College neither provides an alternative world of its own nor promises one in the future. Since they aspire to imitate their parents, the New Outsiders struggle in college to maintain the standards of home. . . . When undergraduates perceive college as mere preparation for professional school, they hold themselves in. They push themselves to make high grades and present an unblemished portrait before an admissions committee. This means they do not let themselves explore their inner selves or their world. . . .

Thus they fail to make a genuine choice. However messy for a grade point average, facing life during college gives a basis on which to make important decisions about the future. As today's New Outsiders calculate whether they want to be lawyers or bankers, they use language as abstract as high school seniors in a college interview committing themselves to a major. For the choice of vocation to be meaningful, it must grow out of deeply felt needs and intense interests. A true vocation comes out of a long and intricate process of maturation that the New Outsiders feel they cannot risk. Thus they prematurely commit themselves to an image, a career without content.

Source: From *Campus Life: Undergraduate Cultures from the 18th Century to the Present* by Helen Lefkowitz Horowitz. Copyright © 1987 by Helen Lefkowitz Horowitz. Reprinted by permission of Alfred A. Knopf, Inc.

REFORMS AND TRENDS

There are always ideas about how to improve America's schools. On the surface it sometimes seems as if ideas about educational reform change much like hemlines going up, then down, then up again. Discipline has been in fashion, then out of fashion, then "in" again. These shifts are often more than fads, though. They frequently reflect changing needs and changing problems. In the 1960s many people believed that the schools' main task was to promote individual development, but by the 1980s people seem most concerned that schools prepare students for jobs and strengthening the nation's economy. In the 1960s people awoke to the problem of educational inequalities, but by the 1980s a general decline in academic performance has become a pressing problem. Among the main reforms and trends that have emerged in the last two decades are compensatory education, alternative schools, "back to basics," voucher plans, and lifelong learning.

Compensatory Education

Coleman's (1966) research suggested that equalizing the quality of the nation's schools and educational opportunities would not bring educational equality, because children's family backgrounds could handicap them in school, even in kindergarten. Some youngsters never see a book at home and are never encouraged to do well at school. Others learn to read even before they enter school. What seemed needed were **compensatory education** programs—special teaching meant to compensate children who had a "culturally deprived" background. Some critics argued that compensatory education amounted to an attempt to impose white

Children in a Headstart program. Compensatory education programs are based on the belief that children who come from homes where learning is valued and reading is a frequent activity do better in school. Advocates of compensatory education believe that students from lower-class homes in poor neighborhoods will be helped academically by an early exposure to reading and verbal activities in school. Although the results of such programs have been disputed, current investigations support the idea that the programs do carry over into better academic performance in later years.

middle-class values on children from other backgrounds. Others believed that the federal government should not be involved in elementary and secondary education. But in the mid-1960s the federal government did begin funding compensatory education programs for the disadvantaged across the nation.

Some of these programs are remedial, designed to upgrade students' performance by giving them counselors and special teachers and special experiences such as field trips. Earlier studies of these programs were not encouraging. In one extraordinary experiment, a school system was given all the money it needed in order to offer disadvantaged students the best educational help that could be found, but the students' scholastic performance failed to improve (Martin and Harrison, 1972).

Another compensatory program, Headstart, is designed not to remedy but to prevent academic failure. It tries to ensure that disadvantaged children will be ready by the time they enter school. In general, Headstart provides children with rich verbal experiences such as by teaching them the alphabet and by telling stories. Again, earlier studies were not encouraging. They showed that although the training did raise children's IQ scores and scholastic achievement, these benefits were temporary. In the first grade, disadvantaged pupils who had had preschool training might perform better than those who did not, but by the third grade this difference tended to disappear, and both disadvantaged groups were equally likely to fall behind their grade level (Stearns, 1971).

Why did the advantages disappear, and why did students not respond better to remedial programs? In the 1970s researchers were not able to find a definitive answer. Most argued that the continuing influence of a poor family environment was the cause—it simply overwhelmed the influence of any educational program. Others contended that the preschool programs had been doomed to failure because of inadequate funding. A few argued that they had been unfairly evaluated before they had time to prove their effectiveness. The last argument turns out to be the one that hits the nail on the head. Recent studies show that the preschool programs do benefit low-income students in the long run. When poor youngsters who were in the preschool programs are 9 to 19 years old, they do better in school than their peers who did not participate in the programs (Bruner, 1982; Etzioni, 1982). Today the federal government has expanded compensatory education. Students whose school performance is below average are eligible for the added instruction regardless of their parents' income. Toward the end of 1986, the Reagan administration further proposed legislation providing parents with federally financed vouchers to pay for remedial education classes of their choice. If this bill becomes law, parents who find the remedial programs in their school district unsatisfactory will be able to send their children to those programs that work.

Alternative Schools

During the 1950s and much of the 1960s, rote learning and discipline were prominent features of many

American classrooms. Students generally had little if any choice about what they would be taught or how they should go about learning it. To some critics of the 1960s, the schools were repressive organizations that resembled boot camps: teachers were obsessed with rules and regulations, and students were forced to obey without question (Silberman, 1970; Gracey, 1975). The schools, said these critics, "destroy the hearts and minds of children" and in most, "children are treated, most of the time, like convicts in a jail" (Kozol, 1968; Holt, 1968). Their capacity for curiosity, creativity, self-direction, and learning itself was being stifled.

What was the alternative? Basically, the alternative-school movement emphasized personal choice for students. Its supporters believed that children would learn best if, rather than being processed from one structured program to another, they were free to choose to work on projects that interested them. In the **alternative school,** teachers do not lead, direct, or control the children. They are expected to "facilitate" activities that the child initiates and to help interpret materials that the child chooses. The classroom is supposed to be a "resource center," with a rich variety of educational materials such as tools, paints, musical instruments, writing materials, and books. It is supposed to be a place that pupils enjoy and that encourages them to be creative and to learn to direct their own lives. But once the students have decided to study a given subject, the teacher will give personal attention to each of them, creating a mentor system that emphasizes depth over breadth.

From small beginnings in the mid-1960s, the alternative-school movement grew to be a force with some influence by the mid-1970s. It was also called a movement for open education, open schools, open classrooms, or free schools. Today there are about 10,000 alternative schools, up from a few hundred in 1972. They have divided into three major types. Schools of the first type emphasize independent study, often carried out in an informal atmosphere. Such schools largely attract middle- and upper-class whites who plan to go to college. Schools of the second type primarily serve inner-city youths from low-income families, who have had problems in traditional public schools. These alternative schools focus on basic skills such as reading and writing. Schools of the third type emphasize certain sophisticated fields such as science and the arts in order to attract some of the ablest students. Also known as magnet schools, they have usually been set up as models by public school systems. They often have stiff entrance requirements.

Because of the focused, personal attention given to each student, made possible by the small size of the schools, alternative schools have generally produced gratifying results. The results can even be dramatic for students from educationally disadvantaged backgrounds. Consider the case of Edith Casimir. She dropped out of a traditional high school in the tenth grade. She explained, "School was such a strain on my system. I thought I was being degraded every day, treated like a sheep—hall monitors, passes. I was always being considered a troublemaker, talking back." Now, at 16, after switching to an alternative school, she bubbles with enthusiasm for school, saying, "It's brought new hope to me. I don't have such a sense of desperation. I'm free to make my own decision. I'm now planning to go to college" (Gruson, 1986).

Back to Basics

Educators and intellectuals have spearheaded most educational reforms, but during the late 1970s parents and politicians began to take the lead in pushing for major changes in American education. Angry about declining student achievement and discipline, functional illiteracy, and teacher incompetence, they blamed the educators, especially open-classroom advocates, and sought to gain some control over their children's education. What this movement proposed was a "return to the basics"—to basic subjects such as arithmetic and what they considered basic values such as obedience and respect for authority.

Around the country many schools have adopted at least some of the changes related to the back-to-basics movement. Many have placed greater emphasis on teaching basic skills in reading, writing, and arithmetic. They have reduced the students' freedom to choose elective courses, required students to take tests in basic skills, and stiffened the standards for grading. Discipline, too, has been intensified in some schools—partly just to bring order to the classroom and partly in hopes of thereby raising academic standards. Some schools have ended the policy of passing students from grade to grade whatever their achievement (the "social promotion" policy) and brought back the old practice of flunking students. In some states students must now pass standardized tests of minimum achievement before they can graduate from high school. Teachers, too, have come under similar pressures. Some states now require that applicants for teaching jobs pass standardized tests.

All these programs have received a tremendous boost from a flock of blue-ribbon study groups such as the National Commission on Excellence in Education and the Education Commission of the States' National Task Force on Education for Economic Growth. These commissions urged that schools stress more achievement, offer more demanding curricula, and stiffen graduation requirements. Teachers should be paid more, but they must pass competency tests and submit to periodic teaching evaluations. Students must have more homework, more discipline, better attendance, longer school days, and a longer school year (Dollar, 1983).

The back-to-basics movement has been sweeping the country since 1983. Many schools have begun to produce more orderly classrooms and higher test scores. According to former Secretary of Education Terrel Bell, the reform has benefited about 70 percent of the students but not the other 30 percent. The 30 percent come mostly from low-income or minority families. In some cases the new program of raising educational standards has exacerbated one of the most serious problems—the dropout rate (Reinhold, 1987). Moreover, if the back-to-basics movement is carried too far, we will, in a decade or so, hear that the schools are turning children into unthinking, conforming robots, and reforms will be called for. There is no final solution to educational problems, because there is a need to maintain a constantly shifting balance between the competing needs of the individual and society, the needs for creativity and conformity and for freedom and discipline.

Voucher Plans

In the late 1960s an idea began to receive considerable publicity. It was a very American idea: if there were more competition among schools, perhaps schools would be better. After all, Americans were entitled to more freedom in choosing where their children will be educated. This idea inspired proposals for voucher plans. Public schools have a virtual monopoly on public funds for education, and children attend schools depending, for the most part, on where they live. A voucher plan can change this situation. In a sense, parents, not schools, receive public money. They receive it in the form of a voucher which they use to pay for their children's attendance at the schools of their choice. The schools receive money from the government in return for the vouchers. The greater the number of parents who choose a particular school, the more money it receives. The idea is to force the public schools to compete with each other, and with private and parochial schools, for "customers." Presumably, good schools would attract plenty of students, and poor schools would be forced either to improve or to close.

But the majority of teachers and their unions, along with some civil rights groups, opposed vouchers for several reasons: Vouchers would encourage parents to choose schools on the basis of racial or ethnic prejudice. They would promote economic and racial segregation and, eventually, greater divisiveness in American society generally. If vouchers stimulated competition, they would probably also stimulate hucksterism. Since a voucher plan would mean giving government money to religious schools, it would violate the separation of church and state required by the Constitution (Hegedus, 1976). In any event, the voucher plan never caught on and finally the government let it die in the late 1970s.

Since the early 1980s, though, popular support for vouchers has been remarkable. In 1983, when asked in a Gallup poll whether they would favor a voucher system, more than 50 percent of the respondents said that they would. The Reagan administration and Congress also considered bringing vouchers back to life in the form of tuition tax credits for parents who enroll their children in private schools. Like the old voucher plan, tuition tax credits would allow parents to choose what they think is a good school for their children, except that it will not be a *public* school. Understandably, supporters of public education are afraid that tuition tax credits will cause an exodus from public to private schools. Indeed, a recent study by the National Commission on School Finance suggests that substantial movement to private schools would occur even with a small tax credit. The study also finds that the movement would be heaviest among low-income, minority students, whose parents are most critical of their public schools (Doyle, 1984). This finding is particularly ironic because supporters of public education are concerned that tuition tax credits would benefit the rich and white at the expense of the poor and minorities. More recently, the Reagan administration also proposed that vouchers be given to parents who may want to send their children to a public school outside their local district. The National Governors' Association endorses the concept of choice in that proposal. Even Albert Shanker, president of the American Federation of Teachers, supports it. As he said, "A professional must be seen to be acting in the interest of the client. But most clients choose the professionals they see—a doctor, a lawyer, an accountant. Children are the only clients who are perceived as the captives of the professionals who deal with them, captives of a given school and teacher." Nevertheless, most teachers reject this argument.

Lifelong Learning

Yet another trend in education has involved not children and adolescents but adults who have been out of school for some time. The appeal of "lifelong learning" has led many adults to return to the classroom, sometimes for formal college credits. Most of these lifelong learners are enrolled in two-year community colleges. In fact, they have been a major stimulus behind the tremendous growth of these schools. From a mere 600,000 in 1960, enrollment in community colleges increased sevenfold, to 4.1 million in 1976 (Van Dyne, 1978). By 1982 community colleges enrolled one-third of all students in higher education and more than 40 percent of the entering freshmen (Cohen and Brawer, 1982). This growth has influenced other colleges in at least two ways. First, community colleges have had a good deal of experience in providing remedial programs for students deficient in basic skills. As student achievement in high school declined during the 1970s, more and more community colleges faced the same problem of ill-prepared students. Many universities, even prestigious ones, turned to the community colleges, seeking to draw on their experience in setting up remedial programs. Second, seeing the popularity of adult education in community colleges and facing declining enrollments of traditional students, many four-year colleges and universities began offering their own continuing education programs (Van Dyne, 1978).

Among the students in continuing education programs are blue-collar workers seeking a promotion or raise or new career, housewives preparing to enter the job market at middle age, retired people seeking to pursue interests postponed or dormant during their working years, and people who want to enrich the quality of their personal, family, and social lives (Cohen and Brawer, 1982).

To accommodate their students' diverse responsibilities and interests, continuing education courses must be flexible. They offer courses at unusual times, even weekends, and sometimes outside conventional classrooms, in various community facilities such as libraries. Their requirements are flexible, too. Some programs allow students to earn college credits without taking a course, by

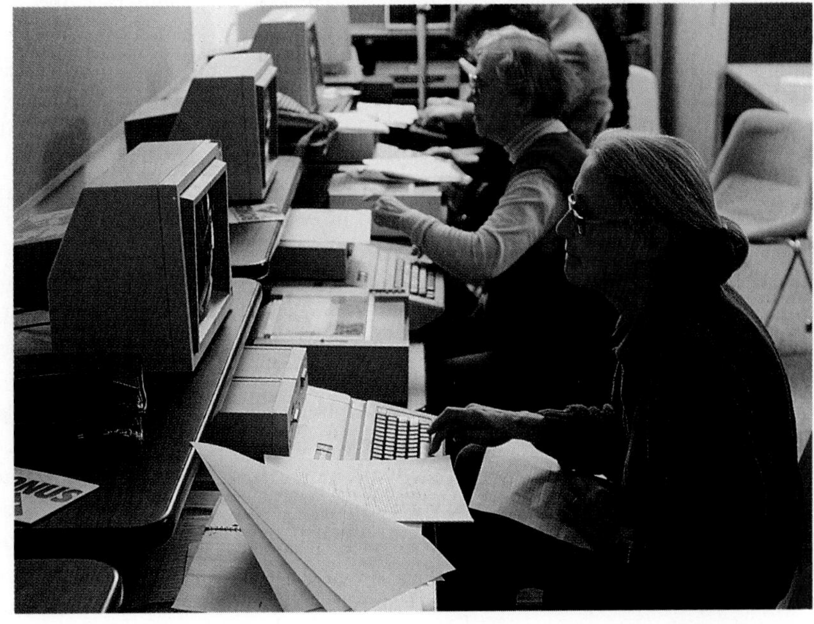

"Lifelong learning" is having a significant impact on the structure of the academic world. Most adults who return to school choose a two-year community college over a four-year school. Not only has this vastly increased enrollments in community colleges, it has also prompted them to offer innovations to accommodate their adult students' needs. Instruction is now offered during evening hours and on weekends for those who hold daytime jobs. Courses are frequently designed to focus on the adult student's specific career or life needs.

passing an examination or by proving their competency through their job, hobby, writing, and so on. In the future the students will also take courses by audiocassette, videocassette, and independent study. Many courses offered on the campus will be shorter and more focused than typical college courses. They will be "total immersion, high-impact courses that meet for about twelve hours per day for a period of two to five days" (Dunn, 1983). Since most of the students will be over age 25 and working full time, most of the courses currently designed for lifelong learners may well become the dominant feature of most colleges and universities (Dunn, 1983). These nontraditional students' high school grades are often lower than those of younger students, but their college grades tend to be higher. They also tend to feel isolated from the masses of traditional students. Some campuses, though, have taken big steps toward integrating them into the university mainstream (Rowe, 1986).

QUESTIONS FOR DISCUSSION AND REVIEW

1. How do the efforts to provide compensatory education within the traditional school compare with the alternative-school movement?
2. What factors have led many schools to "return to the basics"?
3. What is a voucher plan, and why do many teachers and some civil rights groups oppose this kind of educational reform?
4. How have community college and continuing education programs tried to meet the educational needs of adults?

CHAPTER REVIEW

1. *What are the functions of education?* The main functions today are teaching knowledge and skills, promoting social mobility, fostering national unity, and providing custodial care for children. *Do our public schools succeed in transmitting knowledge and skills?* Earlier studies showed that schools make little difference in how much the students learn, but recent analyses indicate otherwise. *Does our educational system promote social mobility?* In the 1970s critics argued that education by itself has little to do with occupational achievement. In the 1980s there is evidence to suggest that education not only raises the individual's income but stimulates the nation's economic growth. *How do our schools promote national unity?* By teaching the American idea of democracy and what it means to be an American. Conflict theorists, however, argue that the process of Americanization threatens minorities' cultural heritage. *What benefits does society gain from having the schools provide custodial care?* The schools keep children off the streets, presumably out of trouble. They also keep young people out of the labor market, which holds down the nation's jobless rates.

2. *Can education reduce social inequality?* No, according to some conflict theorists. They argued in the 1970s that the American educational system, as a reflection of the capitalist system, reinforces inequality by channeling students of different socioeconomic backgrounds into different classes, colleges, and universities. But the assumption that this can happen only in capitalist societies is not convincing because educational inequality can be found in communist countries as well. *How has the United States tried to achieve educational equality?* By busing schoolchildren to racially integrated schools and by providing low-cost loans to poor and minority college students and enforcing affirmative action laws to help minorities and women.

3. *Does the decline in educational standards and achievement mean that there is a crisis in American education?* Not necessarily. The drop in SAT scores may have reflected the opening up of educational opportunities for the poor and minorities. Lower achievement scores in the United States compared to other industrialized countries may have also reflected the impact of democratization. The United States is not the only country having some problems with its schools. All in all, American education is in good shape, though some people do not think so.

4. *What are the main features of American educational bureaucracy?* The bureaucracy is huge but the schools across the country are remarkably similar. It is operated with formal rules that dictate who has authority over whom. It is efficient in rendering education to masses of people, but its impersonality makes it difficult to deal with individuals' unique problems.

5. *What are American teachers like?* In view of their college degrees, they appear quite qualified for their jobs. Most teachers teach primarily because they like to do so rather than because they expect to earn much money. *How does the Pygmalion effect work?* Certain expectations

about students lead teachers to behave in a particular way that causes the students to live up to what the teachers have expected of them.

6. *What is the nature of the youth culture in high school?* It emphasizes the importance of looks, popularity, and athletics at the expense of intellectual pursuit. *What are the various college subcultures?* Collegiate, vocational, academic, and nonconformist. *Do private-school students have higher academic achievement than their peers in public schools?* Probably yes, because private schools demand more of their students.

7. *What are the major educational reforms and trends that have emerged in the last twenty years?* Compensatory education, designed to help disadvantaged children become better students; alternative schools, to foster student initiative and creativity; the back-to-basics movement, to teach discipline and basic skills; voucher plans, to improve schools by establishing competition among them for students; and lifelong learning programs, for adults who want to continue their education.

KEY TERMS

Alternative school A school representing an educational movement to enhance student creativity by allowing maximum freedom in choosing learning materials within the classroom (p. 363).

Compensatory education A school program intended to improve the academic performance of socially and educationally disadvantaged children (p. 361).

De facto segregation Segregation sanctioned by tradition and custom (p. 349).

Pygmalion effect The effect of a teacher's expectations on student performance (p. 358).

Tracking system A system in which students are assigned to different classes on the basis of ability (p. 358).

SUGGESTED READINGS

Burgess, Robert G. 1985. *Education, Schools, and Schooling.* London: Macmillan Education. A well-organized collection of excerpts from contemporary sociology of education, with such student-oriented devices as essay questions and further readings at the end of each chapter.

Clark, Reginald M. 1983. *Family Life and School Achievement: Why Poor Black Children Succeed or Fail.* Chicago: University of Chicago Press. An important study that shows how parents of poor black families, despite economic and other hardships, can produce children who do well in school.

Goodlad, John I. 1984. *A Place Called School: Prospects for the Future.* New York: McGraw-Hill. Presents a wealth of research findings about what goes on in our elementary and secondary schools.

Kohl, Herbert. 1984. *Growing Minds: On Becoming a Teacher.* New York: Harper & Row. An engrossing biographical account of what teaching is like.

Sizer, Theodore R. 1984. *Horace's Compromise: The Dilemma of the American High School.* Boston: Houghton Mifflin. A remarkable research report on 80 high schools throughout the United States, highly enjoyable to read because of its personal and lively style of writing.

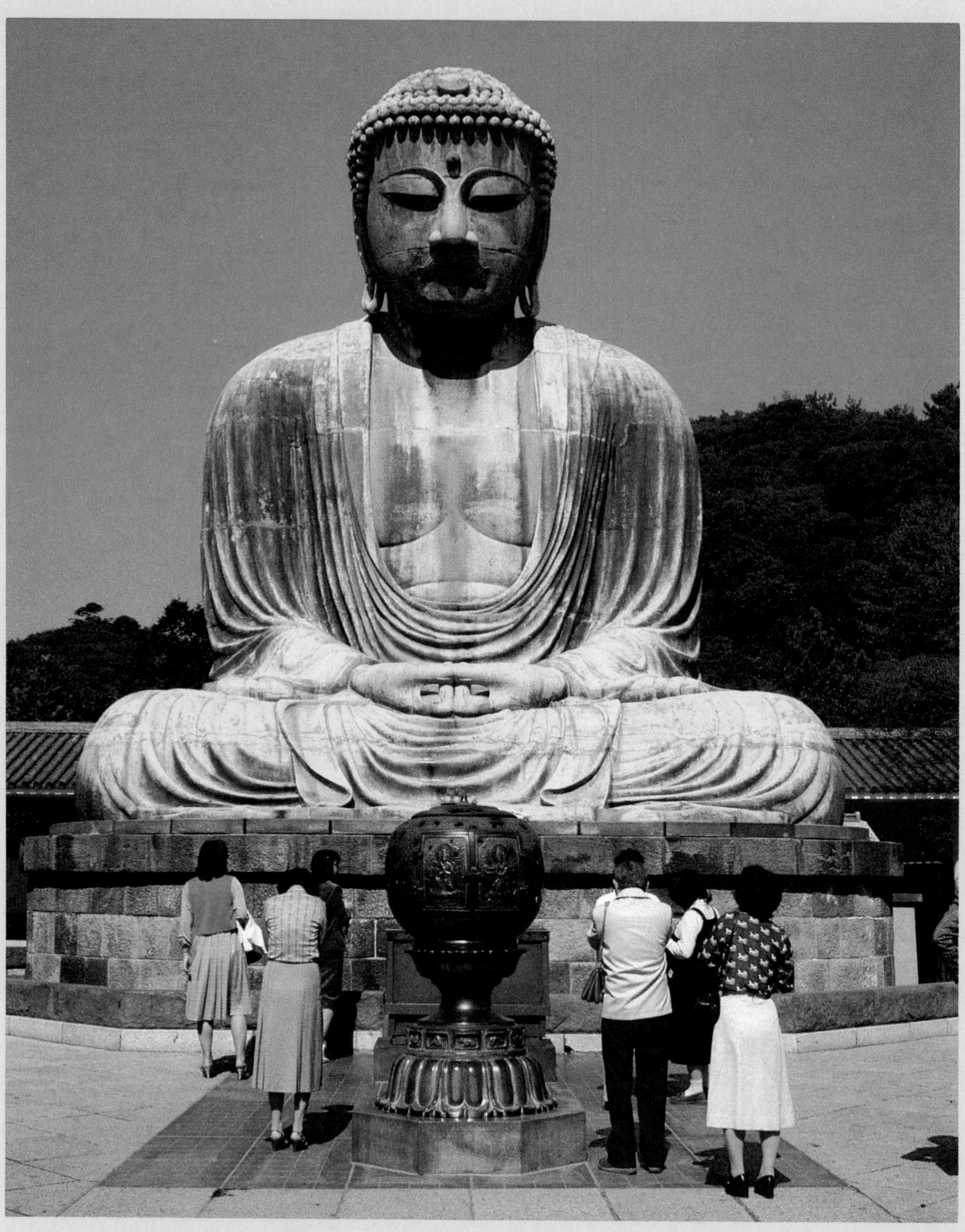

15 Religion

Religion is a universal phenomenon, but it appears in three major forms, with each centering on what it regards as sacred and distinguishing itself by its own beliefs, rituals, and community. Along with Confucianism, Taoism, and Shintoism, Buddhism, founded by the Buddha ("enlightened one"), is an ethical religion. It ascribes sacredness to moral principles rather than to a deity. On the other hand, Christianity, Judaism, Islam, and Hinduism are theistic religions. Believers worship a god or gods. A third type is animism, in which followers believe that spirits can help or harm people but can be manipulated to serve human needs. Regardless of its form, religion has a significant influence on believers' lives and their society.

Religion is everywhere. Some form of religious belief exists all over the world. It ranges from belief in an invisible deity to worship of an animal. Some people may think that religion is a carryover from the superstitious past, hence highly important for primitive, backward societies only. Actually, religion is also very much a part of our modern social life. While we are one of the world's most scientifically and technologically advanced societies, we are also one of the most religious. An overwhelming majority of Americans believe in God. Large numbers go to church on Sunday or attend other religious services regularly. The rise of religious fundamentalism helped make Ronald Reagan president, encouraged the Reverend Pat Robertson to run for the White House, and continues to influence the conservative trends in America today.

On the other hand, television evangelism has brought forth outrageous behavior. The Reverend Oral Roberts raised money by resorting to spiritual blackmail. He told his followers that God would "call him home" unless they sent in $8 million within two months. Another televangelist, Jim Bakker, scandalized the Christian community by fornicating with a church secretary; using $265,000 in church money to buy her silence; paying himself a $6.2 million salary over the course of four years; and splurging on two matching Rolls-Royces, $60,000 worth of gold plumbing fixtures, a large air-conditioned doghouse, and many other luxurious worldly possessions. After publicly calling Bakker "a cancer on the body of Christ," Jimmy Swaggart, another famous televangelist, was caught visiting prostitutes (Watson, 1987; King, 1988). In other countries, religion continues to fuel hostilities between Catholics and Protestants in Northern Ireland, Jews and Arabs in the Middle East, Christians and Moslems in Lebanon, Buddhists and Hindus in Sri Lanka, and Hindus and Sikhs in India.

Why do people lock horns over religion? Does religion necessarily lead to deviant behavior? What exactly do religious people believe? What can religion do to people? Why does religion continue to play a vital role in modern society? In trying to answer questions such as these, sociologists do not analyze religious beliefs for their truth or falsity. As a science, sociology can neither support nor undermine the validity of any religion. What sociologists do is study religion as a social institution—as an institution that, like the family or education, is created by human beings and fulfills human rather than divine needs. Thus, in this chapter, we deal with the human dimensions of religion. First we discuss the components and varieties of religion. Then we see what religion looks like through the eye of three sociological perspectives and how it is related to society in general. Finally we discuss religion in the United States.

VARIETIES OF RELIGION

According to some native religions of Africa, one god created the world, but he then withdrew. The spirits of ancestors and other gods now influence the world. These gods, as well as the creating god, are neither good nor evil, but they require animal sacrifices (Curtin et al., 1978). Christians hold that there is one all-powerful and all-good God and that one sacrifice—the death of Christ—was sufficient to redeem all people. Different as these religions are, they share several elements in common, elements characteristic of all religions.

Defining Religion

Although there is some disagreement about how to define religion, most sociologists accept Emile Durkheim's (1915) classic definition. According to Durkheim, **religion** is a unified system of beliefs and practices regarding sacred things that unites its adherents into a single moral community. Thus, by this definition, a religion consists of four basic elements.

1. *Something that is considered sacred.* This is the most distinctive characteristic of religion: it deals with the **sacred,** not the **profane.** The sacred is anything that inspires awe, mystery, and reverence. Sacredness, however, does not inhere in an object but in the minds and attitudes of believers. A god, a philosophy, an ideology, a stone, a tree, an animal—almost anything can be sacred as long as it is worshipped as such by a community of believers. The sacred is set apart from the profane—the mundane everyday world of eating, sleeping, or otherwise merely trying to survive like any other animals.

2. A *set of beliefs about the sacred thing.* Every religion has three types of beliefs. First are *justificatory* beliefs, which justify the existence of sacredness. Examples are the Christian beliefs in God, in the virgin birth, and in

A religious service in a Jewish synagogue. Most religions have ritual observances to mark the stages of life—birth, adulthood, marriage, parenthood, and death. By taking part in rituals, the individual affirms belief in the teachings of his or her religion and in this way feels part of an ancient tradition. Thus religious rituals can strengthen not only the faith of individual believers but also the solidarity of the moral community.

Christ and his miracles. Next are *purposive* beliefs, which suggest the rationale for embracing a religion. Beliefs in original sin, in eternal salvation or damnation, and in the possibility of redemption imply the purpose for adopting the Christian faith. Finally, there are *implementing* beliefs, which indicate the means for realizing the sacred purpose. They may include beliefs in submission to God, in self-sacrifice, in brotherhood, in chastity, and the like. In short, every religion has beliefs about the existence of some sacred object, the purpose of the religion, and the method for realizing that purpose (Glock, 1972).

3. *The affirmation of beliefs through rituals.* **Rituals** may involve communion with the sacred, such as through public prayer or church attendance. They may involve practicing prohibitions, such as those against eating pork or drinking alcoholic beverages. They may be acts of atonement for one's wrongful acts, such as baptism, confession, or penance. Some fundamentalist Christians in the American South handle venomous snakes as a ritual. The believer holds the poisonous snake, allowing its swaying head to come within a few inches of his or her face, and, when the snake stops moving, shouts, "Glory to God! The mighty power!" and passes the snake on to another person. This is an unusual ritual, but like other rituals it is an expression of belief, and it strengthens both the faith of individual believers and the solidarity of the religious group.

4. *An organization of believers who participate in the same rituals.* Religion is a social phenomenon, and an individual's private religious experience does not constitute a religion. The experience might not be repeated. At best, the individual's belief would vanish with his or her death. A religion must be sustained through a community of believers and through their rituals—what Durkheim called a "moral community." In Durkheim's (1915) words, "In all history, we do not find a single religion without a church"—that is, without some form of organization. But religion does not require any particular form of organization. A church may be large or small, its members may know each other intimately or hardly at all, and its administration may be centralized (as in the Roman Catholic Church) or decentralized (as among Southern Baptists).

We can easily spot these four elements in theistic, god-related religions such as Christianity, Judaism, and Islam. But the same elements can be found in beliefs that do not involve a deity. Democracy, communism, Confucianism, and humanism, for example, are just as sacred to their adherents as God is to his believers. The political ideologies and secular philosophies also have their own beliefs, rituals, and communities. Thus they can be considered religions in the same way as Christianity, Judaism, and Islam are. In fact, religion appears in many different forms, each with what it regards as sacred along with its own beliefs, rituals, and community. They can be classified into three major types: **theism, ethicalism,** and **animism.**

Theism

Theistic religions define the sacred as one or more supernatural beings. They center on the worship of a god or gods. There are two subtypes of theism: **monotheism,** or belief in one god, and **polytheism,** belief in more than one god.

Christianity, Judaism, Islam, and Zoroastrianism are all monotheistic. With over a billion followers, Christianity is the world's largest religion (see Table 15.1). It is split into three principal groups—Roman Catholic, Protestant, and Eastern Orthodox—but these groups share a belief in God as the Creator of the world and in Jesus as its savior. Judaism worships Yahweh, the God of the Old Testament, as the Creator of the universe and teaches that he chose the people of Israel as witness to his presence. Islam, the world's second-largest religion, was established by the prophet Muhammad in the seventh century A.D. It emphasizes that believers must surrender totally to the will of Allah (God), the Creator, Sustainer, and Restorer of the world. Zoroastrianism is an ancient, pre-Christian religion, which still has a quarter of a million followers known as Parsees in India. They believe in one supreme God whose omnipotence is, however, temporarily limited by an ongoing battle with evil—although God is assured of eventual victory. The faithful join forces with God by keeping themselves pure through ablution, penance, and prayers.

Table 15.1 Religions Around the World

The great variety of religions around the world can be divided into three major types: theism, ethicalism, and animism. Theists believe in the existence of a god or gods. Christians, Muslims, Hindus, Jews, and Zoroastrians are all theists. Ethicalists ascribe sacredness to moral principles, and ethicalists include Buddhists, Confucians, Shintoists, and Taoists. Animists believe that spirits capable of helping or harming people reside in animals, plants, or some other objects. Nobody knows how many animists there are in the world. Thus only the numbers of various theists and ethicalists are given below.

Total Christian		1,061,711,600
Roman Catholic	628,990,900	
Protestant	373,769,600	
Eastern Orthodox	58,951,100	
Muslim		554,700,200
Hindu		463,815,200
Buddhist		247,587,500
Confucian		150,984,000
Shinto		32,048,000
Taoist		20,056,000
Jewish		16,932,000
Zoroastrian		250,800

Source: Reprinted from the 1986 *Britannica Book of the Year,* copyright 1986, with the permission of Encyclopaedia Britannica, Inc., Chicago, Illinois.

The best-known polytheistic faith is Hinduism. The great majority of Hindus live in India. In small villages throughout India countless gods are worshipped. Each is believed to have a specific sphere of influence, such as childbirth, sickness, the harvest, or rain. These local deities are often looked on as manifestations of higher gods. Hinduism also teaches that we are *reincarnated*—born and reborn again and again—into new human or animal bodies. People may escape the cycle of reincarnation and achieve salvation by practicing mystical contemplation and steadfast endurance and by following traditional rules of conduct for their castes, families, and occupations.

Ethicalism

Some religions do not focus on supernatural beings. Instead, *ethical religions* ascribe sacredness to moral principles. The heart of these religions is the set of principles they offer as guides for living a righteous life. The best examples are Buddhism, Confucianism, Taoism, and Shintoism.

Buddhism was founded in India in the sixth century B.C. by Guatama, who is known as the Buddha ("enlightened one"). It is today the largest ethical religion. According to Buddhism, there is no independent, unchanging "self" and no physical world—both are illusions. Belief in their reality, attachment to them, and craving for human pleasures are, according to Buddhism, the source of human misery. To escape this misery is to attain Nirvana (salvation). It requires meditation—freeing one's mind from all worldly desires and ideas—and right thinking, right speech, right action, and the right mode of living.

Confucianism was founded by Confucius (551–479 B.C.) in China. For well over 2000 years it was practically the state religion of China. Confucianism stresses

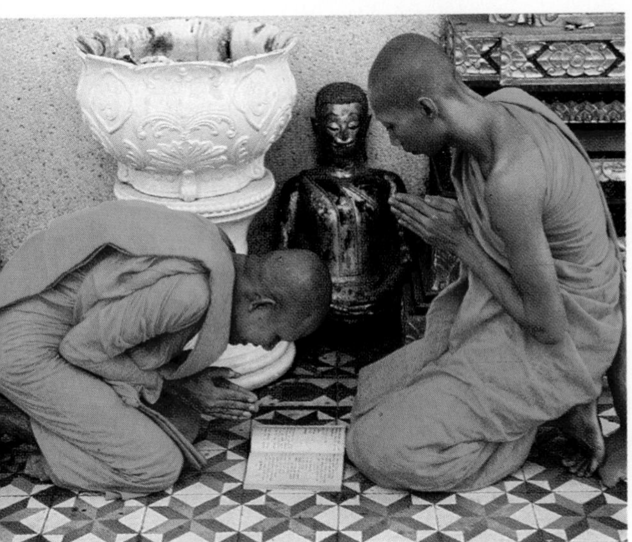

Young Buddhist monks in Thailand. In many countries where Buddhism is practiced, young men are encouraged to join a monastery, even if only for a short while. Life in the monastery is simple and ascetic. The young monks keep only a few personal possessions. They vow to abstain from drugs, liquor, and sex. They spend their time in meditation and in chanting religious rules and sacred texts. By doing so, they expect to free their minds from all worldly desires and ideas. The period they spend as monks affects all their subsequent behavior, making their Buddhist heritage an integral part of their lives.

personal cultivation through learning and self-examination, so that the individual becomes imbued with confidence and serenity. It also urges harmony between individuals. Confucius described proper social conduct as "reciprocity," which means, in his words, "Do not do to others what you would not want others to do to you."

Like Confucianism, Taoism has shaped the Chinese character for more than 2000 years, but today it has a much smaller following. Whereas Confucianism compels its adherents to be austere and duty-conscious, Taoism encourages joyful, carefree quietism, nonintervention, or "not overdoing." According to Taoism, every deliberate intervention in the natural course of events sooner or later turns into the opposite of what was intended. In essence, in a mystical manner, Taoism tells people to yield totally to the Tao ("the Way"), accepting what is natural and spontaneous in people. Actually, Taoism and Confucianism pursue the same goal—the subordination of individuals to groups such as families and society. They differ only in the means of achieving that goal. While Confucianism urges activism through performance of one's social duties, such as obeying one's own parents and being polite to others, Taoism teaches passivity through avoidance of self-indulgence, power-seeking, and self-aggrandizement.

Shintoism has always been a part of Japanese culture. It teaches that people should strive for *magokoro*—a "bright and pure mind" or "truthfulness, sincerity, or uprightness." This means that individuals must be sincerely interested in doing their best in whatever work they have chosen, and they must be truthful in their relationship with others. Purification, physical and spiritual, is the path to these goals. To remove the dust of humans' wickedness believed to cover their divine nature, purification rites are performed at Shinto shrines.

Animism

Belief in spirits capable of helping or harming people is the basis of *animism.* The spirits may reside in humans, animals, plants, rivers, or winds. They are not gods to be worshipped but supernatural forces that can be manipulated to serve human ends. Rituals such as feasting, dancing, fasting, and cleansing are often performed to appease the spirits, so that crops can be harvested, fish caught, illness cured, or danger averted.

Among tribal peoples in North and South America, a type of animism called **shamanism** is common. The shaman ("one who knows") is thought to communicate with the spirits, either by acting as their mouthpiece or by letting his soul leave his body and enter the spiritual world. The spirits, in effect, live in the shaman. By communicating with them, the shaman heals the sick, discovers lost animals, sees events in distant places, foresees those in the future, and forecasts prospects for farming, fishing, and hunting.

Another form of animism, **totemism,** is popular among native peoples of Australia and some Pacific islands. It is based on the belief that a kinship exists between humans and an animal (or less commonly, a plant). This animal, called a *totem,* represents a human family, a clan, or a group of ancestors. It is thought of as a person—but a person with superhuman power—and it must be treated with respect, awe, and fear. Killing, eating, touching, and even seeing the animal are prohib-

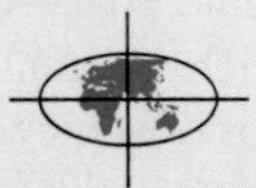

UNDERSTANDING OTHER SOCIETIES

Zombie Existence

We have seen the great variety of religions around the world. Many are quite different from the ones with which we are familiar in the United States. One such religion that may seem "far out" to us is voodoo, practiced mostly in Haiti. The following article describes the nature of its "zombification" ritual. How does voodoo differ from theistic, ethicalist, and animistic religions?

"This was only a dirt grave when I was buried here; they built this later," the heavy-set farmer said of the simple concrete tomb already cracked with age. Sitting on a neighboring tomb in the searing Haitian sun, he pointed to his epitaph written crudely in the wet cement 21 years ago: *"Ici Respose Clairvius Narcisse."* "When they buried me here I could hear everything that was happening but I couldn't move, speak or do anything." Pointing to a lumpy scar on his right cheek, Narcisse said in his slow deliberate manner: "One of the nails in my coffin did this; it went through my cheek."

Few Haitians in the Artibonite Valley or elsewhere question the fact that Clairvius Narcisse, 65, did "die" in 1962, spent two years as a zombie, and escaped to finally return home in 1980, after wandering for 16 years. Haitians don't have to see the hospital admission sheet noting that Clairvius Narcisse was admitted to the Albert Schweitzer hospital 30 April 1962 at 9:45 P.M. and died 2 May 1962 at 1:15 P.M. of "malignant hypertension and uremia." Nor do they need to see his death certificate which is on record at the National Archives; most Haitians believe in zombies.

In Haiti the supernatural is supreme, seldom challenged by the average Haitian. It is a land with an entire phantasmagoria of strange beliefs that can both baffle and handicap scientific investigators because so much of the imaginary is tightly woven with reality. Myth is as mighty as fact. The country's rich oral folkloric tradition is deeply embedded in the Haitian's mind and cannot easily be separated.

The idea of "zombie" comes from Africa and was probably transmitted to Haiti by Portuguese slave traders. One author writes, "zombie designates in general a revenant, a phantom, an otherwordly spirit. In popular belief, certain sorcerers have the power, by means of charms and spells, to cause apparent death to individuals and to bring them back to life again, even after they have been buried. These resuscitated persons, only half-conscious, are then isolated in distant parts of the country and utilized for field work. Nourished on food from which salt is rigorously excluded, they are thought to be able to regain their natural senses and all their mental faculties if they taste the least grain of this substance."

Dr. Lamarque Douyon, Haiti's leading psychiatrist and best known zombiologist, has studied the process of zombification. A local *bocor*

ited. The totem is relied on as a helper and protector, but it also punishes those who breach a taboo.

We have discussed the three major types of religion—theism, ethicalism, and animism. However, some religions cannot be considered to be any one of these types. A good example is voodoo (see box, above).

QUESTIONS FOR DISCUSSION AND REVIEW

1. What are the four basic elements of religion?
2. How do theistic religions differ from ethical and animistic beliefs?
3. To which varieties of religion do Buddhism, Shintoism, totemism, and Christianity belong?

RELIGION AND SOCIETY

Whatever the truth of any of those beliefs—and that is a matter of faith—a religion is of immense importance to the society as well as to its individual members. The nature of religion's relationship to society, as you probably suspect, has been much debated. Why do religions vary from one society to another? Does religion merely reflect the structure of a society, or can religion influence that structure? Durkheim, Marx, and Weber offered three very different sociological perspectives on religion.

(or witch doctor) agreed to allow him to witness the preparation process of zombie powder, which contains ground bone and dried animal parts.

The substance seems to be a skin-acting poison and is placed where it will come in contact with the victim's skin. The powder places the body in such a deep anaesthetic state that vital signs practically disappear and the metabolism and, therefore, oxygen requirements of the body are reduced to a minimum, making the "dead" able to survive up to eight hours on the air and oxygen trapped in the casket, Douyon hypothesizes. The bocors explain that the poison works for eight and a half hours and that if the person is not brought to the surface before the end of that period he dies of asphyxiation. After the poison wears off to a point, the "dead" can be revived.

The reanimation process Douyon observed was surrounded by rich voodoo ritual. "You must stay fully alert and able to discard what is ritual and what is really reanimation, as the bocors try to enmesh the two." After putting substances on the grave the bocor and his assistants take positions around the mound and begin to pound on the earth as if it were a drum in a voodoo service. They also begin calling the person's name. The earth is then by some magical means supposed to open up and the "dead" person spring up in a sitting position. Although the bocors give no explanation for this process, it is speculated that the beating on the earth and screams are amplified inside the wooden casket which becomes a kind of resonance box, thus stimulating the person's brain while the effects of the drug already have worn off. The person becomes excited and jumps out.

A Haitian ethnologist who has studied the voodoo structure explains that contrary to the folkloric explanation, zombies are not made to provide cheap labor. Because of his lethargic state the zombie is not a great worker and therefore is a burden, since he must be fed and sheltered.

The reason for zombifying a person is punishment, and perhaps the most terrible punishment for a Haitian—slavery. When someone transgresses a taboo within the community in which he lives, a religious or social transgression, or takes an action that is considered to endanger the harmony of the group, a secret society sits in judgment of him.

To Haitians, whose ancestors threw off their yoke in the only successful slave revolt in the New World, zombification is a fate worse than death.

Source: Excerpted from Bernard Diederich, "On the nature of zombie existence," *Caribbean Review*, Florida International University, Summer 1983. © Copyright 1983, Caribbean Review, Inc.

Society as God

Emile Durkheim presented his functionalist view of religion in *The Elementary Forms of Religious Life,* first published in 1912. It was Durkheim's aim to refute the popular view that God—or whatever is worshipped as sacred—is merely an illusion, a figment of human imagination. According to Durkheim, if religion were an illusion, it would have disappeared in rational modern societies. But it has not. "It is inadmissible," said Durkheim, "that systems of ideas like religion, which have held so considerable a place in history, and to which people have turned in all ages for the energy they need to live, should be mere tissues of illusion." If God were merely a product of the individual's imagination, Durkheim also argued, it would occupy the same status as any other idea—a part of the profane world incapable of inspiring reverence, awe, and worship. Instead, God must be sacred and far above humans, as demonstrated by the fact that the deity is widely worshipped.

If this revered entity is both real and superior to us, then what is God? Durkheim's answer: society. Society is more powerful than any of us and beyond our personal control. It is separate from us, yet we are part of it and it is part of our consciousness. It outlives each of us, and even our children. We are dependent on it, and it de-

An Episcopal service. There is evidence to support Durkheim's assumption that religion helps to preserve social order. Through their religious rituals, people can sanctify and renew their bonds to one another. But there is something wrong with Durkheim's theory that society is in effect our God. It is not empirically testable. The analogy that Durkheim drew between society and God—both exercising awesome power over us—merely shows that society is in some way similar to God, not that society is God.

mands our obedience to it. It is neither a person nor a thing, yet we feel and know its reality. These attributes of society are also characteristics of the sacred—in Western religions, of God. In short, the sacred, according to Durkheim, is the symbolic representation of society. By worshipping God we in effect are worshipping society.

Such a view of religion led Durkheim to emphasize that religion functions to preserve social order. Every religion, he argued, possesses both rituals and moral norms. Through their religion's rituals, people sanctify and renew their bonds to one another. Their belief in the sacred and acceptance of their common norms are strengthened. Thus religion binds the society and helps maintain it.

There is empirical support for the functionalist theory that religion helps maintain social order, as we will see later. But there is something wrong with Durkheim's argument that society is God. It is simply not empirically testable. The analogy that Durkheim drew between the characteristics of society and God may be interesting, but it cannot be used as scientific evidence to support his argument. The analogy only shows that society is in some ways *similar* to God, not that society *is* God.

People's Opium

Unlike Durkheim, Karl Marx considered religion an illusion. Writing before Durkheim, he presented the conflict theory that if a society is divided into classes, its dominant religion represents the interests of the ruling class. The religion disguises and justifies the power of that class, though. The deception is not deliberate. The ruling class is not conscious of the true state of things. Yet religion, argued Marx, is nonetheless a real and an oppressive illusion, one that helps the ruling class perpetuate its domination of the masses. In medieval Europe the Roman Catholic Church bolstered the feudal system by promoting the notion that kings ruled by divine right. In India the Hindu religion for thousands of years has provided religious justification for the caste system. Religion supports the ruling class by justifying existing inequalities.

If religion is merely an oppressive illusion, why would the masses support and even cling to it? The reason, according to Marx, is the prevailing social inequality and oppression, which drive the masses to seek solace somewhere. "Religion," Marx declared, "is the sigh of the oppressed creature, the heart of a heartless world, the soul of soulless circumstances. It is the opium of the people" (Acton, 1967). Opium offers relief and escape, and it drains one's will to find the source of problems. Similarly, religion brings relief to oppressed workers, dulls their sensitivity to suffering, and diverts them from attacking the root of their pain—their exploitation by the wealthy and powerful. Religion accomplishes all this by emphasizing the superiority of spiritual over earthly matters or promising eternal bliss in the afterlife with such doctrines as "Blessed are the poor." As a result, religion ends up "alienating" workers from themselves by acquiring a harmful power over them—causing them to develop a "false consciousness," to accept the dominance of their oppressors.

Many studies have supported Marx's assumption that poverty or oppression tends to make people embrace religion for consolation (Wimberley, 1984). But religion is not always the opiate of the people that makes them accept the status quo. Religion can and does inspire social movements that change society. The black civil rights movement in the 1960s and 1970s owed much of its success to Dr. Martin Luther King and other Christian ministers. In recent years the American Catholic bishops and the World Council of Churches have plunged themselves into the nuclear freeze movement by calling for a halt to the testing, production, and deployment of new nuclear weapons. Protestants, Catholics, and Jews have joined protests against South Africa's racist policies and U.S. ties with that country. Some church groups have picketed and lobbied against aid to Contra rebels in Nicaragua. Abroad, in the late 1970s, Moslem clergy spearheaded the revolution that has transformed Iran into a fanatically religious state. Many churches in Latin America today identify with guerrilla movements or revolutionary forces. Their "liberation theology" may sound ironically Marxist, but they claim that it draws its inspiration "from the Bible, where, they say, God always sides with the poor and the oppressed and topples the rich and powerful" (Marty, 1982). In 1986 the Vatican issued a document defending the right of the oppressed to revolt—even to use armed struggle, though only as a last resort. Earlier that year Catholics in the Philippines participated in the revolution that brought down the Marcos government. Churches in Poland, Chile, and South Korea have also been active against their repressive regimes, pressing for democratic reforms.

Origin of Capitalism

Marx assumed that there are two types of social forces: material (such as economic conditions) and ideal (such as religious beliefs). He contended that the material forces largely determine the character of the ideal forces, that the economic structure shapes religious belief. Max Weber took a different position, arguing that in some cases an ideal force can influence a material force. Religion, therefore, can influence economic structure, changing society.

Weber provided his best-known discussion of the influence of religion on economic behavior in *The Protestant Ethic and the Spirit of Capitalism.* This "spirit" elevates hard work to the status of a moral duty and produces the disciplined and rational, not speculative, pursuit of economic gain. In contrast, traditional economic activity was marked by easygoing work habits and speculative acquisition. Some way of life, certain ideas and habits, Weber argued, must have produced this change in economic activity. Protestantism was a likely place to look for one source of the change. In Germany, the largely Protestant regions around the turn of this century were more industrialized than the predominantly Catholic regions, and there was also a higher percentage of wealthy Protestants than Catholics. Although religion and the pursuit of wealth are usually considered contradictory, the Baptists and Quakers of the seventeenth century were known for both their piety and their wealth.

But how could Protestantism encourage the development of capitalism? The early Protestants—especially those of the Calvinist sect—believed that long before they were born, God had predestined them to either salvation in heaven or damnation in hell. But they could not know their eternal destiny. This generated a great deal of anxiety. But such doubt, Calvin taught, was a temptation. To relieve anxiety and resist temptation, the Calvinists could turn only to constant self-control and work. They further believed that, whether saved or damned, the faithful must work hard for the glory of God so as to establish his kingdom on earth. Work came to be seen as a "calling" from God, and the worldly success that work brought came to be interpreted as a sign of election to heaven. And the Calvinists did work hard.

The purpose of hard work, however, was to glorify God, not to indulge in one's own pleasures. Early Protestants believed that they should not spend their wealth on worldly pleasures. Instead, they reinvested their profits to make their businesses grow. The constant accumulation of wealth—the continual reinvestment of profit—is another foundation of capitalism. To paraphrase what Marx said in *Das Kapital,* "Accumulate, accumulate, this is the law of capitalism." This law, according to Weber, happened to be compatible with the Protestant ethic.

Weber further argued that capitalism did not emerge in predominantly Catholic countries or China or India because the religions in these countries had world views that differed from the Protestant ethic. Catholicism does not teach predestination. It encourages people to seek their rewards in heaven, and it does not view earthly success as a sign of God's favor. Confucianism values social harmony, not individualistic strivings. Taoism teaches acceptance of the world as it is and withdrawal from it. Buddhism views worldly things as illusory and encourages escape from them through meditation. Hinduism requires its believers to endure the hardships of life and fulfill the obligations of their respective castes. These religions, Weber argued, did not offer ideas and habits favorable to the development of capitalist industrialism, but Calvinist Protestantism did.

You may have noticed that Weber's theory is compatible with the symbolic interaction perspective discussed in Chapter 1 (Thinking Sociologically). As symbolic interactionism would suggest, religion as an interpretation of one's world influences one's behavior toward that world. This is the essence of Weber's theory. But since its appearance in 1904, it has provoked many criticisms and countercriticisms all the way down to this day (Gellner, 1982; Cohen, 1980, 1983; Holton, 1983). Jere Cohen (1980), for example, claims to have found evidence that rational capitalism had originated under Catholicism in Italy—before the emergence of Protestantism. But R. J. Holton (1983) disagrees, arguing in defense of Weber that the capitalist development in Catholic Italy was actually insignificant. At any rate, we can be sure about one thing: it is difficult to recognize either today's Protestantism or today's capitalism in Weber's description. Both have changed.

Most Protestant denominations today do not stress that most of us are predestined to hell. The "spirit" of modern American capitalism is based as much on consumption as on work and production and as much on spending as on investing. Capitalists need markets or buyers. Advertising that lures its audiences to indulge their desires and buy, to seek more leisure and buy, has become a major tool of American capitalism. These changes make it difficult to see how Weber's thesis can be valid today. In the late 1950s Gerhard Lenski (1961) did find that Protestants were more likely than Catholics to achieve upward mobility. But by the 1960s the difference had diminished, especially among the younger generation (Glenn and Hyland, 1967), and by the 1980s there is a higher percentage of well-off Catholics than Protestants (Gallup, 1984). Moreover, capitalism is booming in such non-Protestant countries as Japan, South Korea, Taiwan, Hong Kong, and Singapore.

Functions and Dysfunctions

Durkheim, Marx, and Weber pointed to some of the ways in which religion satisfies the needs of individuals and of society. Some of these functions are positive while others are negative (O'Dea and Aviad, 1983). Paradoxically, when a religion is too successful in carrying out its positive functions, it may become a negative force.

First, religion often performs a *supportive* function, by providing consolation, reconciliation, and relief from anxiety or fear. By praying, believers may become less fearful about losing their jobs or about old age and death. Faith may console those who have lost a loved one or are beset by loneliness, disappointment, frustration, or sorrow. Religion can reconcile people to the sinfulness of others, the hostility of enemies, the injustices of society, or other unpleasant aspects of this world. All this may explain why the more religious people are, the less likely they are to commit suicide (Stack, 1983a, 1983b; Stark, Doyle, and Rushing, 1983). As Rodney Stark and his fellow researchers conclude, religion helps "cushion the despair and desperation that can drive people to take their own lives."

However, if it offers *too much* support and consolation, it can impede useful social change. In Marx's terms, as we have discussed, religion can be an opiate for the pains created by society. Many religions urge their believers to see all worldly things as trivial compared with the life of the spirit. Others perceive this world as a mere way station, or a "vale of tears" that is meant to be a test of love and faith, or even as an illusion. All of these beliefs can encourage the faithful, not only to be consoled but also to endure their suffering docilely. Thus religions can discourage people from confronting the sources of their suffering, from joining a social or revolutionary movement that may help to alleviate their suffering.

Second, religion may perform a *social control* function, strengthening conformity to society's norms. Religion may sacralize (make sacred) the norms and values of society with such commandments as "Thou shalt not kill" and "Thou shalt not steal." Then the laws of the state may be taken to be the laws of God, fulfilling divine purposes. If believers are taught to accept the authority of their church, they may be more likely to obey the authority of the state and society's other norms. Indeed, over 50 research studies since 1970 have shown that religious participation inhibits crime, delinquency, and deviant behavior in general (Ellis, 1985; Peek et al., 1985). More positively, religion encourages good, friendly, or cooperative behavior with the story of the Good Samaritan, the proverb "do unto others as you would have others do unto you," and other such teachings. Research does show that more religious people seem more friendly and cooperative—more likely to stop and comfort a crying child, to be good listeners, and even to get along with loud-mouthed, obnoxious people (Morgan, 1983, 1984; but see King and Hunt, 1984). However, the *individual's* religiousness alone does not necessarily produce good behavior. One study by Rodney Stark and his colleagues (1982) suggests that religious individuals are more likely to refrain from deviant acts if they live in a community where the majority of the residents are also religious. Religious individuals are just as likely as others to engage in deviance if most of their friends are not religious. Thus religion inhibits deviance largely by influencing large numbers of people rather than just a few.

However, religion's power to reinforce social control may set up yet another roadblock to useful change. If religion completely sacralizes the norms and values of a society, it may help preserve unjust laws and harmful values, such as those supporting racial and sexual inequality. The extremely faithful may consider them too sacred to question or change, perhaps saying, for example, "it is God's will that women should stay home and be wives and mothers only."

Third, religion may be a source of social change. This is known as the *prophetic* function—recalling the role of the ancient Jewish prophets, who dared to challenge the society and political authorities of their day in order to call their people to fulfill their covenant with Yahweh. Similarly, Dr. Martin Luther King based his fight against racial discrimination on the ethical principles of Christianity. During the 1960s and 1970s, many religious leaders were in the forefront of the civil rights and anti-Vietnam War movements. More recently, in Poland, the late Stefan Cardinal Wyszynski, leader of the Roman Catholic Church, resisted the Communist government's restrictions on religious freedom; his successor, Archibishop Jozef Glemp, continues to fight. In the Philippines, Jaime Cardinal Sin, the church's leader, helped bring down Marcos's repressive government. In Latin America, the church's "liberation theology" is yet another example of the prophetic function of religion.

But prophetic calls for reform may produce violent fanaticism. During the seventeenth century, some 20,000 peasants in Russia were inspired to burn themselves as a way of protesting liturgical reforms in the

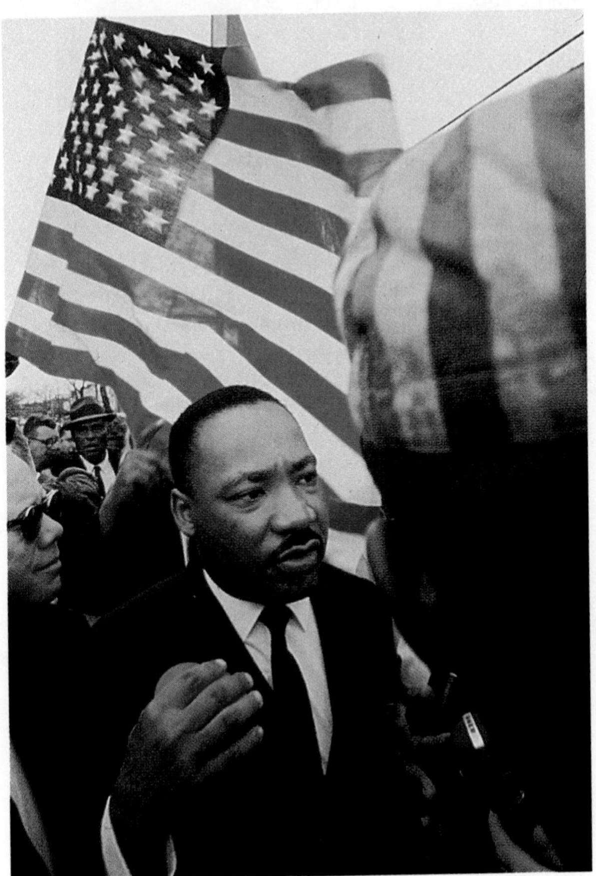

The Reverend Martin Luther King, Jr., speaking during the historic march for civil rights in Washington, D.C., in 1963. Religion has frequently been a powerful force for maintaining the status quo. When it is believed that God supports the established norms and values of society, then change is not welcomed. But when there is a perceived discrepancy between the way things are and the way God intends them to be, then religion can be a powerful force in favor of social change. Dr. King based his campaign to end legal segregation on ideas of equality embodied in the Judeo-Christian religion.

Religious differences lie behind many wars and social conflicts. The bitter war between Iraq and Iran has sources in differences over whose version of Islam should predominate in the Middle East. Iranians have been willing to recruit children of ten years of age, or younger, to take part in assaults on Iraqi positions. The guns carried by the children are not toys; they are real weapons loaded with live ammunition.

Russian Orthodox Church. In 1835 the Reverend Jan Bockelson incited his Anabaptist followers in Germany to "kill all monks and priests and all rulers that there are in the world, for our king alone is the rightful ruler." In 1420 the Adamites, a religious cult of Bohemians in Europe, set about making holy war to kill the unholy. They believed that they must continue killing until they could make the blood fill the world to "the height of a horse's head" (Morrow, 1978b). Today, in their holy war against semisecular Iraq, the Ayatollah Khomeini and other fundamentalist Shiite Muslim leaders tell their followers that they can find salvation in martyrdom. Thus, year after year, they have been sending teenage boys into the Iraqi minefields, which they give their lives to clear in the name of Allah. The Ayatollah's influence has also reached Lebanon, where the fanatic terrorists, including those who hold American and European hostages, welcome death as God's blessing for themselves while trying to kill their enemies. As a young Lebanese terrorist says, "I want to die before my friends. They want to die before me. We want to see God" (Galloway, 1987).

Fourth, religion may perform an *identity* function. By enabling individuals to consider themselves Baptist or Muslim, Catholic or Jewish, religion can tell believers who they are, what they are, and what the purpose of their lives is. In modern societies marked by impersonal relations and a confusing variety of values and norms, this function may be especially important to individuals. Without a religious identity, people may fall into an existential vacuum, finding life meaningless and merely muddling through.

However, if people identify too strongly with their own religion, social conflict may be intensified. In defining themselves by their religion, people tend to believe that there is only one true religion—their own—and become intolerant of all other, "false" religions. Loyalties to different religions may be yet one more factor dividing two groups and making compromise more difficult to achieve. In Africa's Sudan, since 1983, when the Moslem-led regime started a strict enforcement of Islamic law—which includes amputating the arms of robbers—animist and Christian rebels have reacted with shootings and terrorism (Maloney, 1984). Indeed, history is filled with persecutions and wars related to religious differences. Consider the medieval Christian Crusades against Muslim "heathens," the Thirty Years' War between Catholics and Protestants in seventeenth-century Europe, the persecution and slaughter of Mormons in the United States during the last century, the Hindu-Moslem conflicts that resulted in the creation of mostly Hindu India and a separate Islamic Republic of Pakistan in 1947, the strife between Protestants and Catholics in today's Northern Ireland, the violence between Christians and Moslems as well as between different Moslem sects that continues to tear Lebanon apart, and the clash between Buddhists and Hindus that plagues Sri Lanka today.

Confrontation and Compromise

A religion is concerned with the sacred, but it exists in this world, in an earthly rather than heavenly society. It must stand in some relation to that society—in harmony or confrontation, as an integral part of other institutions or withdrawn from them, or in some position in between these extremes. Even within Christianity, different groups have established different relations to society. Ernst Troeltsch, a friend of Max Weber, developed a classic analysis of these relationships. We will examine his classification, and then see the problems a religion faces as it becomes an accepted, established part of a society.

Church and Sect The two main categories in Troeltsch's (1931) classification of Christian religious bodies are the church and the sect. Speaking very generally, we can say that the church compromises with society; the sect confronts it. Many religious groups do not quite fit into either of these extreme categories, but we can think of main-line Protestant groups such as the Episcopal and Presbyterian churches as examples of what Troeltsch called a church, whereas Pentecostals and Jehovah's Witnesses are examples of sects.

A **church** tends to be a large, established religious group, with a formalized structure of belief, ritual, and authority. It is an inclusive organization, welcoming members from a wide spectrum of social backgrounds. Thus members often have little but their religion in common, and they may hardly know one another. Members tend to be born into the church, and the church sets up few if any requirements for membership. Its demands, on both its members and society, are not very exacting. Over the years the church has learned to take a relatively tolerant attitude toward its members' failings. It has learned to reconcile itself one way or another with the institutions of the society, coexisting in relative peace with society's values.

The church's compromises do not satisfy the **sect,** a relatively small religious movement that has broken away from an established church. Time and again, groups have split off from Christian churches because some members believed the church had become too worldly. The sect that results holds itself separate from society, and it demands from its members a deep religious experience, strong loyalty to the group, and rejection of the larger society and its values. The sect is a tightly knit community, offering close personal relations among its members.

The Dilemmas of Institutionalization Most pure sects do not last long. They either fail to maintain their membership and disappear, or they undergo change. Consider Methodism, which was founded in opposition to the Church of England. It was at first a sect that sought to correct social injustices and to aid the poor. Then Irish immigrants brought it to the United States, where it was initially associated with the lower classes. But it has become a highly institutionalized religion today—successful, respectable, middle-class, and less demanding of its members.

A paradoxical relation exists between religiousness and success. The more "successful" a religion is—in the sense of being more popular and more respectable in society as well as having more members—the less religious its members are. Established churches such as the Episcopalians, Methodists, and Catholics are more successful than sects such as the Amish and Jehovah's Witnesses. But members of sects tend to be more religious, devoting more of their time to such religious matters as reading the Bible, praying, and door-to-door evangelizing. They may even show greater willingness to suffer or even die for their beliefs, as their ancient counterparts such as Jesus, his disciples, and early Christians did. There are at least five dilemmas that accompany the success and institutionalization of a religion (O'Dea and Aviad, 1983).

1. *The dilemma of mixed motivation.* The success of a church offers its leaders new, self-centered motives for supporting the religion—motives such as power and prestige. A similar change may occur among the rank and file. Once a religion is institutionalized, its members may be born into the church rather than converted to it. The security, friendship, or prestige that the church offers may become a motive for membership greater in importance than religious conviction. These motives may be useful for ensuring the success of a church, but they are basically secular, opposed to the religious doctrines that stress single-minded devotion to God, that emphasize God-centered rather than human-centered needs.

2. *The dilemma of administrative order.* The organization that emerges with institutionalization brings another problem as well: bureaucracy. The Roman Catholic Church, for example, has a vast and complicated bureaucracy, with an elaborate hierarchy of authority including the pope, cardinals, archbishops, bishops, monsignors, priests—plus many other ranks and lines of authority. The development of a bureaucracy—which

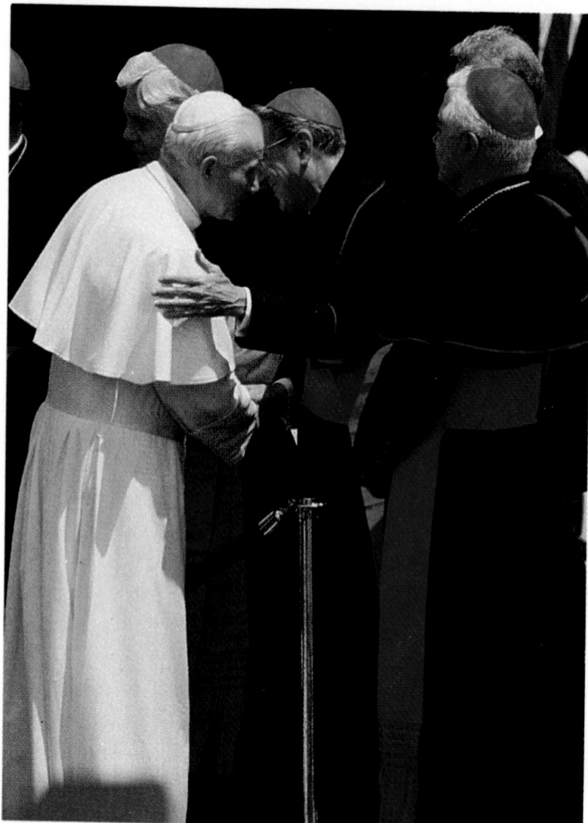

Pope John Paul II, the head of the Roman Catholic Church, being welcomed by American cardinals on a visit to the United States. The more successful and, therefore, the bigger a church becomes, the larger the bureaucratic structure needed to staff it. Such a bureaucracy, however, has an elaborate hierarchy of authority. It is, in effect, a form of social inequality, with some members occupying higher positions than others. This becomes a dilemma for the church because of its belief that all people are equal before God.

in essence practices social inequality—is contrary to the religious idea that all people are equal before God and should be treated as such.

3. *The symbolic dilemma.* At the heart of religions are symbolic expressions of the sacred. They are necessary for ensuring the success of a church, because they can make profound, complex religious concepts comprehensible and help people relate to God better. But people may end up misusing the symbols and missing the message behind them. The cross, for example, is a Christian symbol of God's love for humanity, which should cause us to accept and worship Christ with fervor. But illiterate Christians in traditional societies may be so awed by the cross that they worship it as an idol or use it as a talisman to ward off evil spirits. Better-educated Christians in traditional and industrial countries may find the cross so beautiful that they use it as a mere ornament. In short, the sacred symbols of a popular religion can lead to such irreligious behaviors as idolatry and vulgarization of God.

4. *The dilemma of oversimplification.* The oversimplification dilemma is similar to the symbolic dilemma. In order to ensure the success of its religion, the institutionalized church oversimplifies its teachings so that people can easily comprehend them. To make people understand how much God still loves us even though we are so wicked, worthless, or lost, Christian preachers may tell the story about the prodigal son or about the lost sheep. They would say that God is like the prodigal son's father, who still loves us despite our sins like those of the prodigal son, or that God is like the shepherd who is still looking everywhere for his one lost sheep, though he still has many sheep left. To show how much God supports the institution of marriage, the preachers may tell the story about Jesus turning water into wine at a wedding party. Just as symbols may be transformed into idols, however, the stories, parables, fables, and other preaching techniques of oversimplification may become mere objects of admiration and awe so that the faithful miss the message behind the stories. Thus some Christians may say "Oh, how moving the prodigal son story is!" but they continue to sin. Some married Christians may insist that Jesus actually turned water into wine, but instead of treating their marriages as sacred they opt for divorce.

5. *The dilemma of power.* To survive, the church makes accommodations with society. If it is successful, its values and society's may be increasingly similar. It may join forces with the secular authority, using the state to enforce religious conformity, and lending its authority to sanctify what the state does. Coercion may replace faith. In many places in the past, heresy was punished by torture and even death. All this may ensure the success of the church, but is basically irreligious because the church is supposed to show compassion, love, and forgiveness instead. A more subtle form of power—radio and television—is employed today to capture the souls of prospective followers. Those religious leaders who have easy access to this power of the mass media are more successful than those who do not. But the success is bought at the price of irreligiosity. The electronic

"A fantastic evangelist was on TV, and I sent him everything."

preachers must induce audiences to send in money. Thus their religious programs are, in effect, commercials. They may not look like commercials because they are much longer than most other advertisements. Nonetheless, these preachers expect people to buy their product (God) with money ("donation"), just as other advertisers do. In selling God like soap or pantyhose, though, they turn the holy into the profane. Here's how televangelist Richard Roberts does it: he urges his viewers to "sow a seed on your MasterCard, your Visa, or your American Express, and then when you do, expect God to open the windows of heaven and pour you out a blessing" (Woodward, 1987). As a group, TV evangelists use from 12 to 42.6 percent of their air time to explicitly appeal for funds. They do so by offering souvenirs and mementos, personal help or service, healing, and success (Marty, 1988).

Secularization

Successful or not, a religion today is likely to find itself at odds with society. Weber (1930) described the problem when he wrote, "The Puritans wanted to work in a calling; we are forced to do so." Their ethic "did its part in building the tremendous cosmos of the modern economic order," so that today, "material goods have gained an increasing and finally an inexorable power over the lives of men as at no previous period in history."

In short, our society has been secularized. In the past, religion suffused all aspects of many a society. But we have undergone **secularization.** It is the process by which nonreligious forces such as science, technology, and materialism exert their influence on a society's beliefs, norms, and values. Religious institutions and symbols no longer dominate the society. They become increasingly separated from other institutions, such as government and education, and the religious content of the culture's literature, art, and philosophy declines. Increasingly, people use other ideas and symbols, such as those of science, in order to interpret and guide their lives. Even "when Catholic or Anglican archbishops today wish to pronounce on social affairs," Bryan Wilson (1982) notes, "they rely neither on religious revelation nor on holy writ. They set up commissions, often with considerable reliance on the advice of sociologists." Periodically from 1952 to 1983 George Gallup (1984) asked Americans how important religion was in their lives. The percentage of the respondents saying "very important" fell from 75 percent in 1952 to 56 percent in

1983. All this, however, does not mean that religion is dying in the United States (Hadden, 1987; Sasaki and Suzuki, 1987). On the contrary, we are the most religious, while also being the most secular, among Western societies. A major reason for our comparatively high level of religiousness is the limited ability of secular forces to satisfy our needs. As political scientist Everett Ladd (1987) observes:

> If naturalism could explain everything, if science and technology could control everything, if the capacities of an industrial economy could solve all problems—there would be no place for religion, for belief in God, for what are sometimes referred to as the sacred and the transcendent. But none of the above apply.

Since those secular forces—science, technology, and industrialization—cannot provide everything we want, we tend to become religious while being secular at the same time. The upshot is the increasing worldliness of our religion—the emergence of secularized religion—which we will discuss later.

QUESTIONS FOR DISCUSSION AND REVIEW

1. Why did Emile Durkheim assert that the supreme objects of religious belief are really manifestations of society?
2. What arguments did Marx provide to support his view that religion is "the opium of the people"?
3. According to Weber, how did the Protestant ethic lead to the origin of capitalism?
4. What are the functions and dysfunctions of religion, and when does religion change from a positive to a negative force?
5. Why does the evolution of sects into churches create dilemmas of institutionalization for religions?
6. What is secularization, and what social forces help to create it?

RELIGION IN THE UNITED STATES

As early as 1835, Alexis de Tocqueville observed that "there is no country in the world in which the Christian religion retains a greater influence over the souls of men than in America." Still today, religion is pervasive in the United States. Recent surveys showed that 95 percent of Americans believed in God, compared with only 88 percent of Italians, 76 percent of Britons, and 65 percent of Scandinavians. The same surveys indicated that 56 percent of Americans considered religion "very important" in their lives, compared with only 36 percent of the people in Italy and Canada, 23 percent in Great Britain, and 17 percent in West Germany, the Scandinavian countries, and Japan (Benson, 1981; Gallup, 1984).

Just what is it all these Americans believe? There is an amazing diversity of religions in the United States. The tolerance for this diversity is one striking characteristic of American religion. Another is the paradoxical coexistence of a high level of religiousness and a very high degree of secularization. Let us, then, discuss these characteristics as well as the relationships between religion and other aspects of American society, particularly the state.

Religious Affiliation

There are more than 280 religious denominations in the country, but a few large churches have the allegiance of most Americans. Protestants constitute the largest group, although Catholics outnumber the largest Protestant denomination—the Baptists. According to the latest surveys, 91 percent of Americans have a specific religious preference, with 56 percent saying they are Protestants, 29 percent Catholics, and 2 percent Jews. The Baptists constitute 21 percent of all Americans (see Figure 15.1).

The correlation between affiliation with an organized religion and religious belief and practice is far from perfect. While 91 percent of Americans claim to have a religious preference, only 58 percent believe in life after death and 40 percent attend religious services regularly (Gallup, 1984). Among those who go to church, very few do so for strictly religious reasons. As a survey of Minnesota Christians shows, less than 10 percent cited worship as the primary reason they attend church (Bilheimer, 1983). Obviously, religious affiliation reflects something besides religious belief and practice. Belonging to a church can also afford a way of conforming to social norms or a way of obtaining fellowship. Various religions meet these and other needs in different ways. Some are more "respectable" than others, and some are more likely than others to offer friendship. Not surprisingly, the churches differ, too, in the typical social characteristics of their members.

Social Characteristics Catholics and Jews tend to be urban residents; Protestants tend to live in small towns

Figure 15.1 Most Americans Belong to a Few Major Churches

We are a "denominational society," having numerous religious denominations. Only a few, though, attract the majority of Americans into their fold. Protestants make up by far the largest group. But if Protestants are divided into different denominations, Catholics outnumber even the largest Protestant group—the Baptists.

Source: Census Bureau, *Statistical Abstract of the United States*, 1988, pp. 52–55.

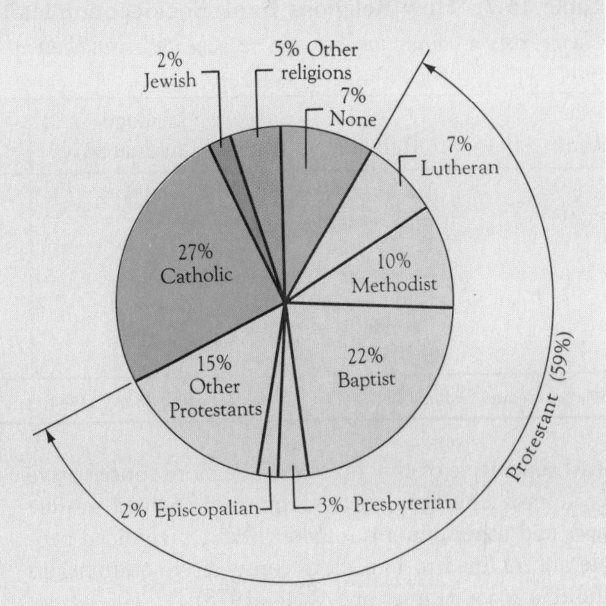

and rural areas. Catholics, Jews, Episcopalians, and Presbyterians can be found mostly in the Northeast. Baptists, Methodists, and Lutherans predominate in the South and West. The largest proportion of other religions such as the Mormons and Disciples of Christ are in the Midwest (Gallup, 1984). How religious Americans are varies also with the region where they live. Southerners seem to be the most religious, and Westerners the least, with Midwesterners ranking second and Easterners third.

Most religious groups favor the Democratic party over the Republican, just as the majority of Americans do. But Protestants are not as overwhelmingly Democratic as Catholics and Jews. In fact, Episcopalians and Presbyterians are more Republican than Democratic (Gallup, 1984). In general, Protestants are more socially conservative and less supportive of civil liberties than Catholics and Jews. Among Protestants, the most heavily Republican groups—Presbyterians and Episcopalians—are most likely to be socially liberal and pro-civil liberties, whereas the most staunchly Democratic—the Baptists—are most likely to be socially conservative and

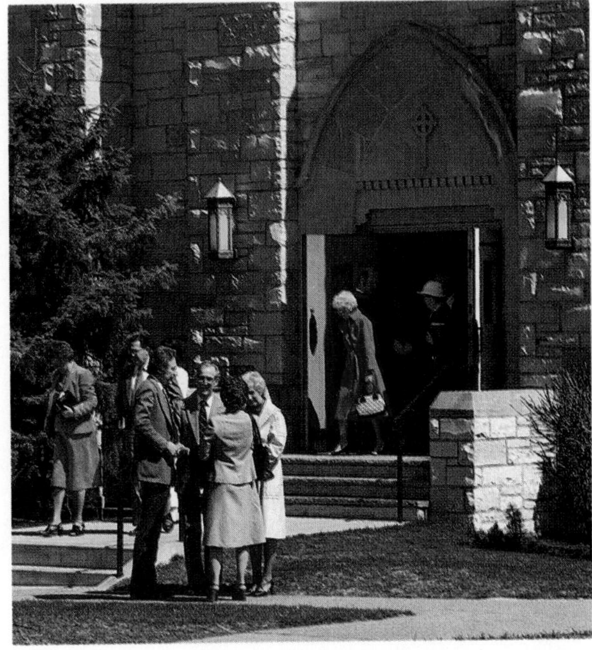

Religious participation varies with class. People of the higher social classes are more likely to attend church regularly. This does not necessarily mean that they are more religious. It seems to reflect merely their greater inclination to participate in all kinds of voluntary organizations. For many, going to church has a purpose beyond taking part in religious rites. It may enable them to appear respectable, or to obtain fellowship.

Table 15.2 How Religions Rank Socioeconomically

There exists a connection between religion and stratification. Despite their belief in equality before God, various religious groups are unequal socioeconomically.

Rank	Religion	College Graduates	Rank	Religion	Income of $15,000 or More
1	Jewish	43%	1	Jewish	80%
2	Episcopalian	38	2	Episcopalian	73
3	Presbyterian	27	3	Presbyterian	70
4	Methodist	17	4	Lutheran	67
5	Catholic	16	5	Catholic	65
6	Lutheran	15	6	Methodist	59
7	Baptist	8	7	Baptist	46

Source: George Gallup, *The Gallup Reports,* no. 222, March 1984, pp. 48, 49.

least supportive of civil liberties. The more conservative Protestant churches are also more prejudiced against Jews and other minorities. Most likely, prejudiced people are inclined to join more conservative churches in the first place (Lipset and Raab, 1978).

Social class may lie behind many of these associations. Although they may consider themselves equal before God, various religious groups are unequal socioeconomically. They have different statuses, and they tend to attract people from different educational and income levels. Usually, Jews, Episcopalians, and Presbyterians top the status hierarchy. They are followed by Methodists, Catholics, and Lutherans, trailed by Baptists (see Table 15.2).

Rates of religious participation also vary with social class. In general, the higher people's class, the more likely they are to attend church regularly. Moreover, upper-class people hold most of the leadership positions, such as membership on a church's board of trustees. But these facts do not mean that higher-status people are more religious. In fact, belief in God is more widespread among the poor than among the rich, and the lower classes are more likely to consider their religion a private affair and to be emotionally involved in it (Wilson, 1978). The high rate of participation by upper-status people seems to reflect the fact that they are more inclined than the lower classes to participate in *all* kinds of voluntary organizations. For many higher-status people, religious participation appears to be a public activity required for social respectability.

The Fundamentalist Revival Although religious membership among Americans remains high, the last decade has been a time of decline for many churches. Overall, the growth in church membership has not kept pace with the growth of the population. The American population has grown by 11.5 percent, but religious institutions have expanded by only 4.1 percent. Some churches have actually lost members. Others, however, have gained many members (Briggs, 1982; Hyer, 1982b).

Generally, the large main-line churches—Episcopalians, Lutherans, Presbyterians, Catholics—have either lost members or have grown only slightly. Those groups that have registered large gains tend to be smaller, less established religious groups. They are also the more conservative groups. Among them are fundamentalists, evangelicals, and charismatics or pentecostals (see Table 15.3). In contrast to main-line Protestants, fundamentalists emphasize a literal interpretation of everything in the Bible. Evangelical, "born again" Christians also stress emotional demonstrativeness rather than quiet devotion at church services. Through the experience of being "born again," they believe that their lives have been dramatically changed. Some of these groups, known as charismatics or pentecostals, also speak in tongues, utter prophecies, and heal the sick.

Southern Baptists, Jehovah's Witnesses, Mormons, the Church of God, and Catholic Pentecostals are among the groups participating in this revival. In the past, fundamentalist and evangelical Christianity was associated with the poor and uneducated. Today, however, its appeal has spread, and business executives and prominent politicians are among its advocates. The fundamentalist revival is a reflection of the conservative trend in society. It is also a culmination of a number of factors. One is the aggressive, skillful use of television, as illustrated by the popularity of such fundamentalist preachers as Jerry Falwell and Pat Robertson. Another is the social changes of the last two decades that have driven many conservative Americans into fundamentalist churches. These social changes have involved the women's movement, homosexuals, unmarried mothers, legalization of abortion, court decisions against school prayer, and affirmative action on behalf of blacks (Hammond, 1985). Moreover, the fundamentalist churches, because of their highly personal style of worship, tend to attract the casualties of this fast-changing, high-tech age—"people who are socially isolated, mentally depressed, alienated, and dehumanized by modern society" (Moberg, 1984). Finally, there is an organizational difference between main-line and fundamentalist churches. Main-line churches tend to be "religious audiences." Their members gather periodically to participate in worship services but often hardly know one another. But fundamentalist churches are closer to being "religious communities." Their members are more often likely to find their best friends within the congregation and to be deeply involved in the church's activities (Stark and Glock, 1968). Thus, for those who seek fellowship from a church, the fundamentalist groups are more attractive than main-line churches.

Many main-liners have begun to fight back, though. To increase its membership, one Episcopal church uses newspaper and direct-mail ads. One lampoons the fundamentalist competition by showing a man with his mouth taped. The accompanying caption says: "There's only one problem with religions that have all the answers. They don't allow questions." Another ad features six pallbearers carrying a coffin out of a church, for which the caption is "Will it take six strong men to bring you back to the church?" This campaign has worked for that particular church (Woodward, 1986). But it is too early to tell whether similar recruitment efforts can stop the "main-line" from drifting into the sideline all over the United States.

Cults Although some evangelical and charismatic groups represent a rebuke of main-line churches, they are not new religions. They remain Christian. In contrast, cults reject established religions. They usually claim to offer a new belief system. Like evangelical groups, American cults have been growing. Today there are about 2500 cults. They run the gamut from The Farm, which condemns all forms of violence, to the Bible of the Church of Satan, which teaches that "if a man smites you on the cheek, smash him on the other." Most are very small, and the total number of cultists is only about 3 million (Beck, 1978; Levine, 1984).

A **cult** is usually united by total rejection of society and extreme devotion to the cult's leader. The People's Temple is a dramatic example. In the 1970s their leader, Jim Jones, preached racial harmony, helped the poor, established drug-rehabilitation programs, staged protest demonstrations against social injustices, and helped

Table 15.3 Winners and Losers Among Churches

	1973	Latest	Change
Over the last decade, fundamentalist churches have gained members:			
Southern Baptist Convention	12,295,400	14,185,454	Up 15%
Church of Jesus Christ of Latter-Day Saints (Mormons)	2,569,000	3,593,000	Up 40%
Assemblies of God	1,099,606	1,879,182	Up 71%
Seventh-Day Adventists	464,276	623,563	Up 34%
Church of the Nazarene	417,732	507,574	Up 22%
In that same period, many main-line churches have declined:			
United Methodist Church	10,192,265	9,405,083	Down 8%
Presbyterian Church (U.S.A.)	3,715,301	3,157,372	Down 15%
Lutheran Church in America	3,017,778	2,925,655	Down 3%
Episcopal Church	2,917,165	2,794,139	Down 4%
Christian Church (Disciples of Christ)	1,330,747	1,156,458	Down 13%

Source: Copyright, 1984, *U.S. News & World Report.* Reprinted from issue of 4/30/84.

Followers of the Bhagwan Shree Rajneesh. Cults are new religions, usually made up of a small and dedicated group of believers. Members of the cult reject mainstream society and frequently choose an isolated spot in which to live. Their beliefs and practices are often at odds with those of conventional society. Contrary to popular belief, the young people who join a cult are mostly normal. They come from stable, religious families, have had good relationships with their parents, and have done particularly well in school. They have received a lot of material, social, and intellectual benefits from their parents.

elect sympathetic politicians. He moved his cult from San Francisco to Jonestown, Guyana, because, he said, evil people in the United States would try to destroy the Temple. He told his flock that to build a just society required a living God—namely, himself. To prove his divinity, he "healed" parishioners by appearing to draw forth "cancers" (which actually were bloody chicken gizzards). He claimed that he had extraordinary sexual gifts, required Temple members to turn over all their possessions to him, and insisted that they call him "Dad" or "Father." Then the People's Temple shocked the world. In November 1978 more than 900 members committed mass suicide at the order of their leader.

The Unification Church has been more successful. Its founder, Sun Myung Moon, a South Korean businessman, declares himself the New Messiah. He preaches a mixture of Christianity, Puritan morality, and Oriental philosophy—and the message that all the world's religions should be combined into one, headed by Moon himself. He teaches that sex is evil, demands that sexual feelings be totally repressed, and arranges all marriages within the cult. Members of the cult, most of whom are young, must break all ties with their families, work 18 hours a day soliciting donations, and give all their possessions to the church. The result is that Moon lives in splendor on a huge estate, owns several yachts, and controls an enormous business empire.

The cultists' lives are not easy at all. Why, then, would anyone want to join a cult? Primarily because it offers something that meets a specific need of the joiners, which cannot be found in traditional churches. The Synanon Church provides drug addicts with a home and rehabilitation program. The People's Temple emphasized egalitarianism and offered a communal home to the oppressed, especially poor blacks, prostitutes, and other outcasts. Most of the other cults, such as the Moonies, Hare Krishnas, and Children of God, are more popular with middle-class youth. Contrary to popular belief, the young people who join a cult are mostly normal and come from stable, religious families that uphold "traditional values of family life, morality, and decency." Most have maintained good relationships with their parents and have done particularly well in school. Indeed, their warm, concerned parents have given them every material, social, and intellectual benefit (Barker, 1984; Wright and Piper, 1986). What possible rewards can *they* find from joining a cult?

After studying at least 100 cults and interviewing more than 1000 individual members, Saul Levine (1984) concludes that the cults provide the youth with "desperate detours to growing up." Like most of their peers, the youthful joiners must grow up to be free and independent by leaving their parents. But they are more likely to lack the skill, confidence, or courage to strike out on their own in the harsh, cold world. They are more likely to find it too painful to leave their warm families for the cold world outside. For these youngsters, a cult provides separation without the accompanying pain, because the communal group typically operates as an exaggerated and idealized family that offers an enormous amount of love and care. It even gives careful attention to serving good, nutritious food, an emphasis that rivals a mother's care in assuring a wholesome diet for her children.

Serving as a halfway house between the parental home and the outside world, though not intentionally, the cult enables the young joiners to pick up skills for living an independent life. In observing the Moonies,

Rodney Stark discovered remarkable improvements in the way some of them managed interpersonal relations:

> They came to the group suffering from low self-esteem and lack of confidence that disrupted their interactions with others. For example, one man routinely whispered and looked only at his toes when he talked with others. Forging strong affective ties to other group members quite noticeably raised the self-esteem of new recruits. Indeed, the man just described "recovered" to the extent that he was able to preach in the streets after a period with the group (Stark and Bainbridge, 1980).

Once they have learned to take care of themselves, cult members usually leave the groups, resuming their previous lives and finding gratification in the middle-class world. In fact, more than 90 percent of the cult joiners return home within two years, and virtually all joiners eventually abandon their groups (Levine, 1984).

Secularized Religion

Common sense suggests that the more secular a society is, the less likely religion is to thrive. But the United States, as Will Herberg (1983) said, is "at once the most religious and the most secular of nations." The churches have retained large memberships despite the secularization of society. One reason may be the nature of most Americans' religion: it is, to a great extent, "secularized religion"—in effect, nonreligious religion. The religious elements are easy to see. But what are the nonreligious elements?

First, as we have seen, the high rate of religious affiliation does not reflect a strong commitment to religion. Close to half of Christian church members reject such traditional articles of faith as Christ's miracles, the resurrection, life after death, the virgin birth, and the second coming of Christ. An overwhelming majority do not believe that the devil exists. Neither do they consider divorce "always wrong or sinful." Many Catholics (at least 40 percent) ignore the church's ban on birth control and doubt that Jesus invested the church's leadership in the pope. Many Christians take little part in their church's rituals and do not seem to take seriously the Christian doctrine that the faithful should not be of this world. Most Catholics disagree with the pope on many issues. They reject the ban on birth control, and only a small minority (14 percent) accept the teaching that abortion should be totally illegal. More than half of all Catholics also favor permitting women to be priests, allowing priests to marry, and letting the divorced remarry, all of which the church does not allow. In other words, many religious people hold the same beliefs as secular, nonreligious people do. Yet they still consider themselves religious. As a recent poll shows, an overwhelming 93 percent of Catholics believe that "it is possible to disagree with the Pope and still be a good Catholic" (Bilheimer, 1983; Ostling, 1987).

Even the attitudes of the clergy reflect this retreat from religious belief. Hellfire-and-brimstone sermons are rare in most churches. The clergy refrain from emphasizing the uncompromising stands of Jesus, Isaiah, Amos, and other prophets in opposition to the "wicked" ways of this world. Some clerics, said Peter Berger (1967), even "proclaim the senselessness of prayer." In fact, the clergy are also more critical of the Bible than the laity (Bilheimer, 1983).

If traditional prayer and conviction are vanishing, what is left in the churches? In Herberg's (1983) words, there is "religiousness without religion . . . a way of sociability or belonging rather than a way of reorienting life to God." Without their traditional beliefs, some churches begin to look like social clubs, offering exercise classes, day-care programs, and singles' nights. In addition, some religions have turned to emphasizing ethics and social action, sometimes nonreligious in nature. They urge their congregations to strive not for personal holiness but for love of neighbors, social justice, international peace, the creation of a humane society, and the realization of the kingdom of God on earth. These could be the seeds of a shift from a theistic religion to an ethical one.

Secularism has not hit all religious bodies in the same way. In particular, most conservative groups have retained traditional beliefs. As we have noted, it is the conservative religious groups that have experienced growth during the last decade. However, their televangelists have secularized their religion to some degree. To have an authentic religious experience, we must have a special space for the performance of a religious service. A church, synagogue, temple, or mosque usually suffuses anything that happens there with a religious aura. But any other place will do if it is first decontaminated—divested of its secular, profane uses. Thus a gymnasium, dining hall, or hotel room can be sacralized with a cross on a wall, candles on a table, or a sacred document in public view. Moreover, our behavior must befit the otherworldliness of the space. This can be attained by sitting quietly, meditating, kneeling down at appropriate moments, wearing a skullcap, or some other religious conduct. But most people who watch a religious television program can hardly derive a real religious experience. They do not separate the sacred from the profane. They eat and drink and talk and occasionally walk to the refrigerator for more refreshments or to the bathroom for bodily relief—all these right in the middle of a religious service. Sometimes they even watch in the kitchen or bedroom, hardly a sacred place for worship. What they get from the TV religious program is, in effect, secularized religion, the experience being similar to watching a secular program such as *Dallas* or *The Cosby Show* (Postman, 1985).

Church and State

In the aftermath of the Jonestown bloodbath in late 1978, former President Carter commented, "I don't think we ought to have an overreaction because of the Jonestown tragedy by injecting government into trying to control people's religious beliefs." This is testimony to the unusually high degree of religious tolerance in America. Without this tolerance, the diversity of American religions would not be possible.

This diversity would have appalled some of the earliest settlers of America. They came to the New World in order to establish a "Holy Commonwealth," a community that would be ruled by church officials. In the Puritans' republic, "theology was wedded to politics and politics to the progress of the kingdom of God" (Bercovitch, 1978). Even after Independence was won, some of the states had official religions. But the Constitution guarantees religious freedom by forbidding government interference in religious activities. Eventually, the courts interpreted this guarantee to mean that church and state must be kept separate and that the government, including state governments, must refrain from promoting religion (see box, p. 391).

Thus the United States has no official religion. But, in practice, the separation of church and state is far from complete. In a sense, the U.S. government does support religion in general, by exempting religious organizations from taxation. It also sometimes intervenes in religious affairs. The government investigates church activities if it believes that a church is abusing its tax-exemption privileges or otherwise violating the law. The government has even, occasionally, forbidden activities that some groups consider religious. It has prohibited Mormons from practicing polygamy, forced Christian Scientists in some cases to accept blood transfusions, and prohibited a sect from letting children drink poison or handle venomous snakes.

Controversy continues to surround the question of where the line between church and state should be drawn. When church leaders of the 1960s and 1970s worked against racial discrimination and the Vietnam War, some people criticized them for interfering in politics. Today some religious groups take an even more active role in the nation's politics, by directly lobbying Congress and by promoting and opposing particular candidates.

Churches have been active on both sides of the political spectrum. Catholic and liberal Protestant groups have been visible for their opposition to nuclear-weapons production, U.S. involvement in El Salvador, and American aid to the Nicaraguan Contras. Conservative church groups have probably attracted more attention, thanks largely to their formation of political action groups such as the Moral Majority and Christian Voice. Interestingly, the political changes they seek often amount to increased government control of areas popularly considered the church's business—personal morality. They favor, for example, group prayer in public schools and laws against abortion, homosexuality, and pornography. To those opposed to these laws, they amount to government interference. But many conservative church groups interpret the government's failure to enforce such measures as a blow against religion, a promotion of antireligious forces. They wish to see the state allied with religion in promoting common values. Ironically, they also protest against what they consider to be government's intrusion into religion: the new federal law that requires churches to pay Social Security taxes for their employees, the withdrawal of federal tax breaks from fundamentalist Christian schools engaged in racial discrimination, and some states' attempts to close Christian schools for refusing to use state-approved teachers and courses.

There is, then, no strict separation between church and state in our society. Nevertheless, some Americans still insist that religion be completely removed from our public life. Thus they are opposed to government aid for religious schools, prayer in public schools, or any sign of endorsement or encouragement of religion in the public

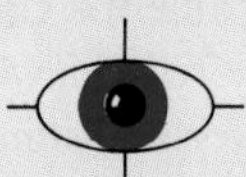

USING SOCIOLOGICAL INSIGHT

Disestablished Religion in America

By prohibiting the establishment of a state religion for all Americans, our Constitution has made it possible for many diverse religious beliefs to coexist in the United States. Yet in the midst of these potentially conflicting religions, there is a high level of political stability. How has this come about?

The United States continues to operate under the oldest written constitution still in force in the world today. At the same time, the United States remains the most religious country in the Western world—to judge, at least, by what people tell pollsters about their religious beliefs and practices. According to Gallup surveys, 95 percent of the American people profess belief in God, some 70 percent claim that they pray, and an equal proportion claim affiliation with a particular church or synagogue. Since the early nineteenth century, foreign visitors have been equally struck by America's unusual stability and its unusually pervasive public piety. The connection between them inevitably prompts reflection.

One connection has been stressed by public men in America from the outset. The constraints inculcated by religion may help people to develop the self-restraint required by a constitutional democracy. "Our Constitution was designed for a religious and moral people and for no other" was how John Adams put it. But such formulations, gratifying as they may be to the American self-image, tend to obscure an important fact about "religion": Not every kind of religion is compatible with a liberal constitutional order. The stability of our constitutional order owes much to the fact that the dominant religious tendencies through most of American history have, in fact, been quite compatible with liberal democracy and religious tolerance and have not, by and large, forced people to make wrenching choices between religious and civil obligations.

The connection no doubt has also worked in the opposite direction, however. The disestablishment of religion in our constitutional order has encouraged an extraordinary proliferation of religious sects and religious doctrines that has made sectarian repression seem impractical, even for those who did not regard it as improper. At the same time, religious diversity has encouraged a general blurring of the boundaries of "religion" and a weakening of church discipline, so that people of quite different character and outlook can all regard themselves as "religious in my own way." Perhaps most important, the condition of churches in our constitutional order—neither persecuted nor supported by government, and therefore neither goaded to a reactive rigor nor lulled into a complacent repose—has forced them to remain open to wider cultural trends in order to recruit or retain adherents and sympathizers. Disestablished religion has had to be more democratic religion, at least in the sense of being more attentive to the views and preferences of adherents. And while this has no doubt been a source of strength, it has often been a threat to religious integrity as well.

If this means that contemporary religion in America is in many ways not what it used to be, neither, of course, is the Constitution. The federal government has assumed a vast array of regulatory and social welfare responsibilities that would have seemed unthinkable under older understandings of the Constitution. And the federal courts have assumed an extraordinary role in monitoring the activities of state and local governments to ensure their conformity with current national ideals. The Constitution, like "religion," has endured in part because it has proved more elastic than anyone expected in earlier times. And although it may be impossible to disentangle historical cause and effect in these changes, there is surely more than mere parallelism in this.

Source: Reprinted with permission of the author from: *The Public Interest,* No. 86 (Winter 1987), pp. 124–139. © 1987 by National Affairs, Inc.

schools. But most Americans do not object to the inclusion of religion in the public realm as long as the religion involved represents all faiths rather than one particular faith. This is why polls continue to show majorities as large as 80 percent favoring some form of voluntary, nonsectarian prayer in public schools. After all, public schools practice a nonsectarian religion every day by saluting the flag with the affirmation of America as "one nation, *under God.*" Even at the opening of legislative sessions, presidential inaugurations, and other public ceremonial occasions, ministers, priests, and rabbis offer their religious invocations or benedictions (Rabkin, 1987). In fact, the joining of church and state can best be seen in what sociologist Robert Bellah has called "the American civil religion."

Civil Religion

Groups such as the Moral Majority are calling for the moral reform of the nation, but they do not condemn the country itself. Indeed, according to the Reverend Jerry Falwell (1981), the United States is "the only logical launching pad for the world evangelization" because it is a "great nation . . . founded by godly men upon godly principles to be a Christian nation"—but it has been corrupted. What the Moral Majority and similar groups appear to be seeking is a renewal of America's old civil religion.

Every nation has its own **civil religion,** a collection of beliefs, symbols, and rituals that sanctify the dominant values of the society. The civil religion is a hybrid of religion and politics. The state takes up certain religious ideas and symbols, and religion sacralizes certain political principles, backing up the government's claim to a right to rule with its own moral authority. Falwell, for example, has argued that the free-enterprise system is outlined in the Bible's Book of Proverbs. Thus aspects of political institutions take on religious overtones. The civil religion links religion and politics, harmonizing them (Bellah and Hammond, 1980). Whatever its content, a civil religion can unify the citizens of a country by heightening their sense of patriotism.

What is the content of this civil religion in the United States? It includes, first of all, faith in the American way of life, with freedom, democracy, equality, individualism, efficiency, and other typically American values as its creeds. The "American way of life," said Herberg (1983), is the common religion of American society by which Americans define themselves and establish their unity. Protestantism, Catholicism, and Judaism are its "subfaiths."

God plays an important role in this civil religion. He is cited on our coins ("In God We Trust") and in national hymns ("God Bless America"). References to God are made in all oaths of office, in courtroom procedures, at political conventions, in the inaugural address of every president, and on practically all formal public occasions.

But the God of American civil religion is not the god of any particular church. Adherence to American civil

Anthony Kennedy being sworn in as a Justice of the Supreme Court. The United States has no official religion. In practice, though, the separation of church and state is far from complete. The government supports religion in general by exempting religious organizations from taxation. The government sometimes intervenes in religious affairs by, for example, investigating church activities for possible violations of law. One of the most obvious illustrations of the unity between church and state is the swearing-in ceremony, where God and the Bible are called upon to help administer the oath.

religion requires only our belief in God, however we choose to define him—as a personal God, an impersonal force, a supreme power, an ideal, or whatever. We do not have to believe in Moses, Jesus, the Bible, heaven and hell, or any other doctrine of a particular religion. We are instead exhorted to "go to the church of your choice." "Our government makes no sense," President Eisenhower is reported to have said, "unless it is founded on a deeply felt religious faith—*and I don't care what it is.*" The civil religion does not favor one particular church but religion in general. Everyone is expected at least to pay lip service to religious principles, if not to join a church or synagogue. It is considered un-American to be godless, or, worse, to attack religion.

Like a genuine religion, American civil religion contains symbols, rituals, and scriptures. Its sacred writings are the Declaration of Independence and the Constitution. George Washington is seen as the Moses who led his people out of the hands of tyranny. Abraham Lincoln, our martyred president, is seen as the crucified Jesus; his Gettysburg Address is a New Testament. The civil religion's holy days are the Fourth of July, Thanksgiving, Memorial Day, and Veterans Day, when we sing sacred hymns such as "The Star-Spangled Banner" and "America the Beautiful," invoke the name of God, listen to sermonlike speeches, and watch ritualistic parades. The American flag, like the Christian cross, is supposed to inspire devotion.

It is popularly believed that religion is less relevant to our lives as we become more scientifically and technologically sophisticated. This turns out to be a myth. As we have seen, the United States, despite its being the world's leader in science and technology, is more religious than many other nations. Americans are also more religious today than they were some 60 years ago. There are now proportionately more churches, more people attending religious services, and more money donated to churches (Caplow, Bahr, and Chadwick, 1983). Since 1975 there has also been no decline in church attendance among Catholics, despite their growing opposition to the pope's teachings. "In their hearts," conclude Michael Hout and Andrew Greeley (1987), "they are as Catholic as the Pope, whether he thinks so or not." Why is religion so popular in the United States? The answer could be found in the unique nature of American religion. As has been discussed, we have a tremendous diversity of religious beliefs, a high level of religious tolerance, a secularized religion, the Constitutional protection of religious freedom, and a civil religion. All this makes it easy for all kinds of individuals to be religious *in their own way.* That's probably why, as we have noted, most Americans can claim to believe in God or have a religion, but without much commitment.

QUESTIONS FOR DISCUSSION AND REVIEW

1. What are the traditional religious affiliations of Americans?
2. What does the current fundamentalist religious revival have in common with the upsurge in cults, and how do these two types of religious movements differ?
3. What contributes to the development of secularized religion in American society?
4. How has the political activity of many religions challenged America's traditional commitment to the separation of church and state?
5. What is civil religion, and what beliefs are included in the American version of this religion?

CHAPTER REVIEW

1. *What is religion?* A religion is a unified system of beliefs and practices regarding sacred things that unites its adherents into a single community. *Are there religions without churches?* No, religion is a social institution. For a religion to be sustained, there must be an organization of believers who participate in the same rituals. *Must a religion focus on the worship of a god?* No, only theistic religions do so. Ethical and animistic religions define the sacred in a different way.

2. *According to Durkheim, what is God?* He argued that God is a symbolic representation of society. By their worship, members of society strengthen their bonds to each other and their acceptance of the society's norms. Thus religion helps preserve social order. *How did Marx view religion?* To him, religion is an oppressive illusion, which helps the rich and powerful to perpetuate their domination of the masses. He argued that religion justifies society's inequalities and gives solace to the masses, diverting their attention from the source of their oppression. *Can religion influence economic structure, or do material forces always determine ideal forces?* Unlike Marx, Weber argued that in some cases religion can influence economic structure, changing society, and he contended that Protestantism was one force that encouraged the development of capitalism.

3. *What functions does religion serve, for individuals and for society as a whole?* It can support and console people, provide social control, stimulate social change, and provide individuals with a sense of identity. If these functions are carried too far, however, religion can become dysfunctional. By offering too much solace and maximizing social control, religion can impede social change. Crusades for social reform can develop into violent fanaticism. Too strong an identification with a religion can lead to conflict with other groups.

4. *How can "success" sap a religion of its vitality?* As a religious group grows and becomes institutionalized, it faces dilemmas involving mixed motivation, administrative order, symbols, oversimplification, and power. *What challenge confronts all religions in industrialized societies?* These societies have been secularized. Religion occupies just one part of their social life, and its influence is frequently overshadowed by that of nonreligious ideas and symbols.

5. *What are some distinguishing characteristics of religion in the United States?* A high percentage of Americans belong to some church, even though we are a very secular society. Many religions have themselves been secularized. And there is great diversity of religions and religious tolerance. *Are American religious groups growing?* Overall, their membership is not increasing as fast as the population. But less established, more conservative religious groups have recently experienced considerable growth, while more liberal, main-line churches have suffered a decline. *In what ways are many of our Christian churches secularized religions?* Many Christians reject the traditional doctrines of their faith and seem to turn to their churches for the sake of fellowship, not commitment to God. Many churches now stress social reform rather than worship—an emphasis that might indicate evolution from a theistic to an ethical religion.

6. *How are church and state related in the United States?* There is no official church, and freedom of religion is guaranteed by the Constitution, but the separation between church and state is not absolute. *What is the American civil religion?* It includes belief in God, support for religion in general—but not for any particular religion—and celebration of the "American way of life."

KEY TERMS

Animism The belief in spirits capable of helping or harming people (p. 373).

Church A well-established religious organization that is integrated into the society and does not make strict demands on its members (p. 381).

Civil religion A collection of beliefs, symbols, and rituals that sanctify the dominant values of society (p. 392).

Cult A religious group that professes new religious beliefs, rejects society, and demands extreme loyalty from its members (p. 387).

Ethicalism The type of religion that emphasizes moral principles as guides for living a righteous life (p. 372).

Monotheism The belief in one god (p. 372).

Polytheism The belief in more than one god (p. 372).

Profane The everyday life experience, which is mundane, ordinary, and utilitarian (p. 370).

Religion A unified system of beliefs and practices regarding sacred things that unites its adherents into a single moral community (p. 370).

Ritual Behavioral expression of a religious belief (p. 371).

Sacred Whatever transcends the everyday world and inspires awe and reverence (p. 370).

Sect A religious group that sets itself apart from society and makes heavy demands on its members (p. 381).

Secularization The process by which nonreligious forces exert their influence on society (p. 383).

Shamanism The belief that a spiritual leader can communicate with the spirits, by acting as their mouthpiece or letting his soul leave his body and enter the spiritual world (p. 373).

Theism The type of religion that centers on the worship of a god or gods (p. 372).

Totemism The belief that a kinship exists between humans and an animal or a plant (p. 373).

SUGGESTED READINGS

Douglas, Mary, and Steven M. Tipton (eds.). 1983. *Religion and America: Spirituality in a Secular Age.* Boston: Beacon. A useful collection of essays by leading social scientists on the current trends in American religion.

Ladd, Everett Carll. 1987. "Secular and Religious America." *Society,* March/April, pp. 63–68. A useful analysis of how our society can be both highly secular and highly religious.

Levine, Saul V. 1984. *Radical Departures: Desperate Detours to Growing Up.* New York: Harcourt Brace Jovanovich. A remarkably interesting research report on why some middle-class youngsters join cults.

Marshall, Gordon. 1982. *In Search of the Spirit of Capitalism.* New York: Columbia University Press. Well-reasoned analysis of Weber's thesis about the Protestantism-capitalism connection, showing where its strengths and weaknesses lie.

McBrien, Richard P. 1987. *Caesar's Coin: Religion and Politics in America.* New York: Macmillan. An excellent presentation of the messy relationship between church and state in our society.

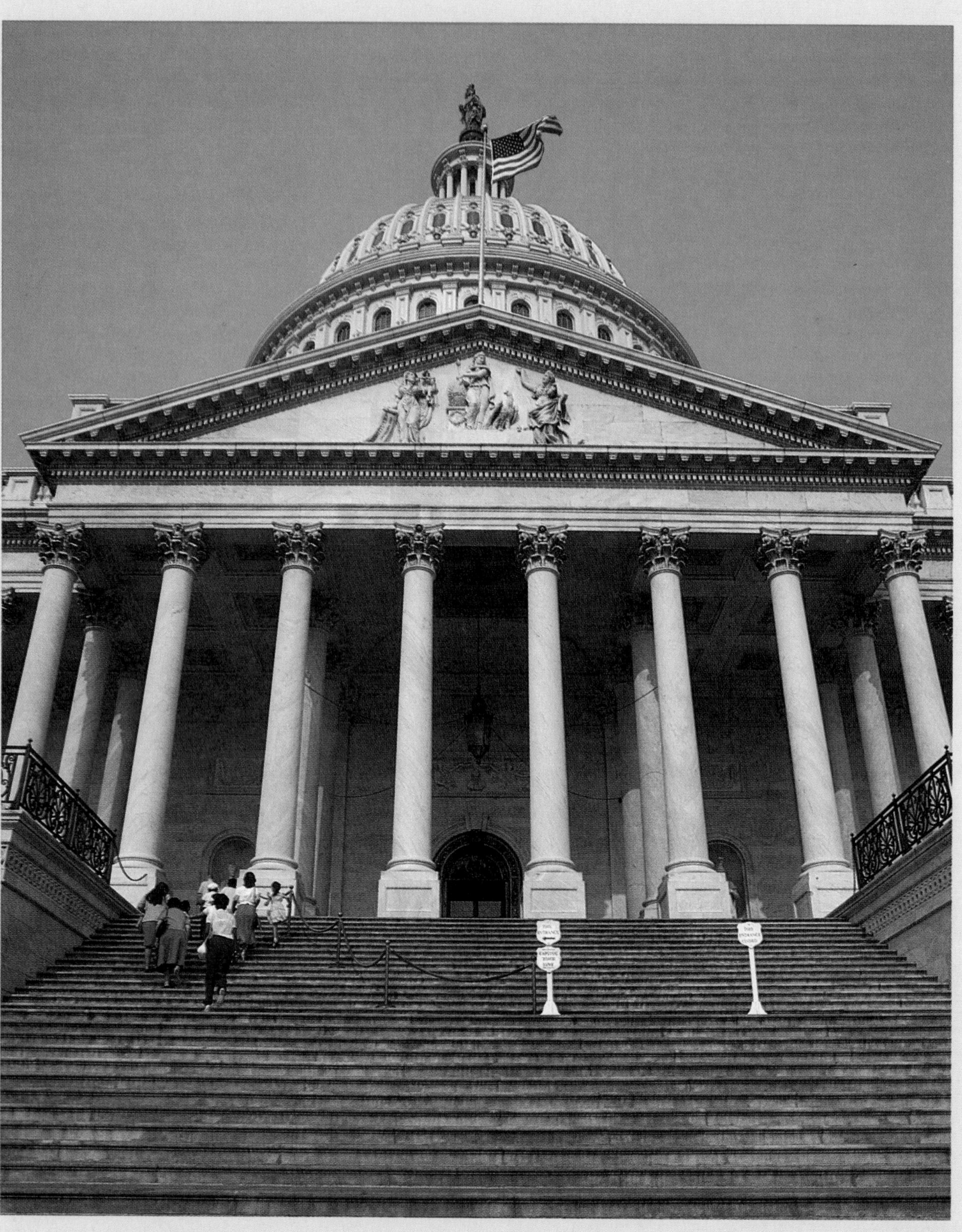

16 Politics and the State

Most nations are not democracies. Democracy is apparently a fragile, unruly kind of political system. Yet the American democracy seems remarkably strong. It is, after all, the oldest democracy on earth despite our relatively short history as a nation. Two kinds of political organizations—political parties and interest groups—help keep American democracy alive by providing links between the people and their government. They are especially important because most Americans do not actively participate in the political process. They may vote, but at a lower rate than the citizens in many other democracies.

Human beings are "political animals," said Aristotle more than 2000 years ago. In every society the scarcity of valued resources compels people to play politics, to determine who gets what, when, and how (Lasswell, 1936). **Politics** is the type of human interaction that involves one party acquiring and exercising power over the other. If left to the individuals themselves, politics can become a nasty game, with the players trying to get at each other's throats in order to protect their interests. It would be, in the words of Thomas Hobbes (1651), a "war of all against all." If violence is not resorted to, politics among unrestrained individuals can at least be, as John Locke (1690) observed, too inconvenient, too chaotic, and too time-consuming. It is little wonder that in most societies the state steps in to dictate how politics should be played.

The state is a political institution that regulates conflict and allocates resources among the citizens of a country. We often equate the state with the government, but the two words have somewhat different meanings. The state is an *abstract entity,* such as the U.S. presidency, Congress, and Supreme Court combined. The government consists of *specific individuals* who run the affairs of the state, such as the president, Supreme Court justices, and so on. Government officials come and go, but the state remains.

In this chapter we see how the state has the power to carry out its task and how it varies from one society to another. Then we take a closer look at the American political system and ask who controls it. Finally, we study how people respond to their government.

POWER AND THE STATE

The state can do its job of regulating conflict and allocating resources only because it has a tremendous amount of power. In some societies the government has the power to tell citizens what work they will do and what god, if any, they can worship. Governments take their citizens' money and spend it to educate their children or to overthrow a foreign government or to do many other things. Max Weber argued that the modern state is distinguished from other institutions by its power to monopolize the use of physical force. To understand the state, we therefore begin by taking a closer look at what power is and, more specifically, what kinds of power governments may wield.

The Nature of Power

Weber (1954) defined **power** as "the possibility of imposing one's will upon the behavior of other persons." If a robber forces you to hand over your wallet, that is an example of power. If your friends convince you to cancel a dinner and help them move, that is power. Power is at work when you pay taxes and when you write a term paper. It is an aspect of all kinds of social interaction, but obviously there are important differences in the types of power people can exercise.

The most basic difference is between illegitimate and legitimate power. *Illegitimate power* is control that is exercised over people who do not recognize the right of those exercising the power to do so. Thus illegitimate power requires the use or the threat of physical force in order to compel obedience. Weber called it **coercion.** In contrast, *legitimate power* is control that is exercised over people with their consent; they believe that those exercising power have the right to do so.

Exercising power through coercion requires constant vigilance. If it is the only source of power leaders possess, they are not likely to be able to sustain their power for long. In contrast, legitimate power can often be exercised with little effort, and it can be very stable. Employers, for example, often need do little more than circulate a memo in order to control their employees' behavior. A memo goes out telling workers to stop making personal telephone calls or to request vacations in writing a month in advance and, at least for a while, workers are likely to obey.

There are at least two kinds of legitimate power. One is **influence,** which is based on persuasion. Frequently, those who wield other types of power also exercise influence. They may acquire influence because of wealth, fame, charm, knowledge, persuasiveness, or any admired quality. Business executives may use their wealth to achieve influence over politicians through campaign contributions. Television reporters may acquire the ability to influence public opinion because of their personal attractiveness and journalistic skill. In general, influence is less formal and direct, and more subtle, than other forms of power. Moreover, there is **authority,** the type of legitimate power institutionalized in organizations. When authority exists, people grant others the right to power because they believe that those in power have the right to command and that they themselves have a duty to obey. Authority is essential to the state.

Types of Authority

What is the source of the state's authority? For an answer, we turn again to Weber (1957). He described three possible sources of the right to command, which produce what he called traditional authority, charismatic authority, and legal authority.

Traditional Authority In many societies people have obeyed those in power because, in essence, "that is the way it has always been." Thus kings, queens, feudal lords, and tribal chiefs did not need written rules in order to govern. Their authority was based on tradition, on long-standing customs, and it was handed down from parent to child, maintaining traditional authority from one generation to the next. Often, traditional authority has been justified by religious tradition. For example, medieval European kings were said to rule by divine right and Japanese emperors were considered the embodiment of heaven.

Charismatic Authority People may also submit to authority not because of tradition but because of the extraordinary attraction of an individual. Napoleon, Gandhi, Mao Zedong, and Ayatollah Khomeini all illustrate authority that derives its legitimacy from **charisma**—an exceptional personal quality popularly attributed to certain individuals. Their followers perceive charismatic leaders as persons of destiny endowed with remarkable vision, the power of a savior, or God's grace. Charismatic authority is inherently unstable. It cannot be transferred to another person. If a political system is

There are three types of authority. (a) Catherine the Great, Empress of Russia (reigned 1762–1796), represents *traditional authority*. Her power over all her subjects was absolute, subject only to traditional but not binding restraints. (b) Napoleon Bonaparte (1769–1821) represents *charismatic authority*. He began his career as a junior officer in the French army and seized on opportunities to make himself ruler of France and, ultimately, head of an empire that he himself founded. His authority depended on his talents and his ability to inspire people to follow him personally. (c) Franklin D. Roosevelt (1882–1945), thirty-second president of the United States, serving from 1933 to 1945, represents *legal authority*. Although he was highly popular, the only president elected four times, his authority remained the same as that of any other American president. It is prescribed by law and belongs to the office rather than to the officeholder personally. If Roosevelt had not died during his fourth term, his authority, though not his influence, would have ended when he left office.

a

b

c

based on charismatic authority, it will collapse when the leader dies. Otherwise, it will go through a process of "routinization," in which the followers switch from "personal attachment" to "organizational commitment," their personal devotion to a leader being replaced by formal commitment to a political system (Madsen and Snow, 1983). In essence, charismatic authority is transformed into legal authority.

Legal Authority The political systems of industrial states are based largely on a third type of authority: legal authority, which Weber also called rational authority. These systems derive legitimacy from a set of explicit rules and procedures that spell out the ruler's rights and duties. Typically, the rules and procedures are put in writing. The people grant their obedience to "the law." It specifies procedures by which certain individuals hold offices of power, such as governor or president or prime minister. But the authority is vested in those offices, not in the individuals who temporarily hold the offices. Thus a political system based on legal authority is often called a "government of laws, not of men." Individuals come and go, as American presidents have come and gone, but the office, "the presidency," remains. If individual officeholders overstep their authority, they may be forced out of office and replaced.

In practice, these three types of authority occur in combinations. The American presidency, for example, is based on legal authority, but the office also has considerable traditional authority. Executive privilege, whereby a president can keep certain documents secret, even from Congress, acquired force from tradition, not through the Constitution or laws. Some presidents, like Abraham Lincoln and Franklin Roosevelt, have also possessed charismatic authority. Still, the primary basis of the power of the president is legal authority. In general, when societies industrialize, traditional and charismatic authority tends to give way and legal authority becomes dominant.

Politics and Economics

While societies differ from one another in what form of authority is dominant, they also differ in the scope of the authority claimed by the state. In totalitarian nations such as the Soviet Union, the state claims the right to exercise considerable control over its citizens. In democratic nations such as the United States, the state claims less control over its people. Seymour Martin Lipset (1981) and other sociologists have found that democratic countries generally have achieved a higher level of economic development (see Figure 16.1). According to Lipset, a nation's economic development tends to bring forth in its citizens such characteristics as personal satisfaction, self-confidence, antiauthoritarianism, and being trustful and tolerant of others, which, in turn, stimulate and reinforce popular demands for democracy. The correlation between economic development and democracy is not perfect, though. The Soviet Union is more advanced economically than India, but India is a more democratic society. Another exceptional case involves the oil-rich Arab states, which remain authoritarian despite their wealth.

Democratic states also have a different kind of economic system than totalitarian states. The totalitarian state tries to control the economy, along with every-

Figure 16.1 Most Wealthy Countries Are Democratic

There is a strong relationship between economic development and democracy. The richer the countries, the more likely that they are democratic.

Source: Larry J. Diamond, "The social foundations of democracy: The case of Nigeria," (Ph.D. dissertation, Department of Sociology, Stanford University, 1980), p. 91, reported in Seymour Martin Lipset, *Political Man: The Social Bases of Politics* (Baltimore/London: Johns Hopkins University Press, 1981), p. 471.

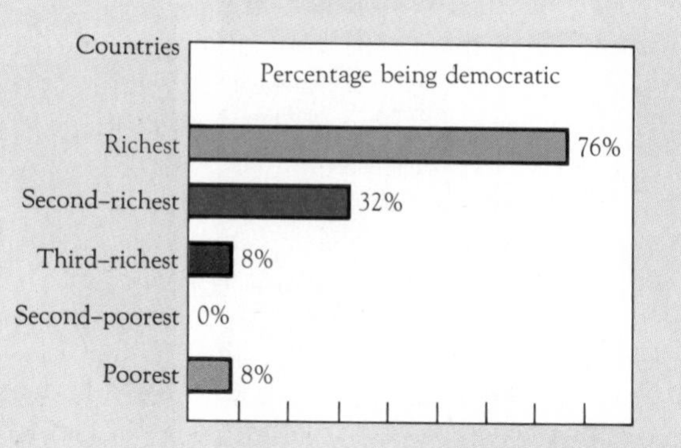

Too much governmental control of the economy has stunted the economic growth of many communist countries such as China, the Soviet Union, and Cuba. But these countries have been able to deliver extensive, state-supported social services to their citizens. One of these services is the provision of state-run day-care centers for the very young children of working parents. Above is such a center in China.

thing else. The government owns industry and other means of production. It plans economic goals, determines how much is to be produced of what, sets wages and prices, and so on. In contrast, all democratic nations have allowed at least a significant part of their economies to be determined by the market—by the decisions of countless individuals who buy and sell without government control. All this may explain why democratic states are generally more prosperous than totalitarian states (Weede, 1982).

While too much government control of the economy has retarded many communist countries' economic growth, it has helped reduce economic inequalities. In China, for example, the highest-paid people earn only ten times more than the average Chinese. By contrast, the wealthiest people in the United States earn over a hundred thousand times more than the average American (Kondracke, 1979; Page, 1983). In addition, states with centrally controlled economies generally deliver more social services to their citizens. Cuba, for example, has cut the illiteracy rate to 4 percent, decreased infant mortality to 29 per 1000 live births, and extended average life expectancy to 70 years. This compares favorably against the nearby Dominican Republic, a noncommunist country with a market economy, which has much higher rates of illiteracy and infant mortality and a much shorter life expectancy (Elson, 1978).

In short, the economic system of socialism in communist countries tends to bring a lot of social equality but also a low standard of living for the society as a whole. By contrast, the economic system of capitalism in democratic societies produces much wealth but also substantial inequality. This is part of what Winston Churchill, the British prime minister during World War II, had in mind when he said: "The vice of capitalism is the unequal distribution of blessings, but the virtue of socialism is the equal distribution of miseries."

War and Peace

Tied to the "misery" of relatively low living standards in communist countries is the political "misery" of not being able to enjoy as much individual freedom as in democratic societies. The wide-ranging control over the economy merely reflects the state's nearly total control over the political and other aspects of its citizens' lives.

The bombing of Cologne, Germany, during World War II. For 95 percent of the last 5600 years, war has occurred somewhere in the world. To functionalists, war occurs because it serves useful functions such as strengthening national unity and stimulating technological progress. But to conflict theorists, the loss of lives and property outweighs the benefits of war. Conflict theorists argue that war primarily serves the interests of the ruling class. It enables the government to divert citizens' attention from domestic problems, military leaders to become heroes, and business tycoons to profit from sales of military hardware.

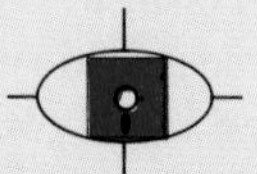

LOOKING AT CURRENT RESEARCH

Sociobiological Theory of War

There are various theories about the causes of war. The most controversial is probably the sociobiological argument that war arises from people's struggle to enhance their chances of transmitting more of their genes to the next generation. The following is a report on how a recent study of an extremely violent society will reignite the debate among anthropologists over the sociobiological theory of war. Do you see anything wrong with this theory?

They are probably not the kind of people you would invite over for afternoon tea. They are quick to anger, will bear a grudge for years and often launch violent attacks on members of their own tribe.

Anthropologist Napoleon Chagnon is talking about the Yanomamo, fierce Indians who live in the forests near the Venezuela-Brazil border. But his description might also apply to the anthropologists who study the natives. The Yanomamo are one of the most violent societies on earth, and they have long been the subject of intense scrutiny—and heated debate—by anthropologists searching for the roots of human conflict.

A recent study by Chagnon is sure to inflame the debate further. He suggests that the Yanomamo warriors fight not over scarce resources or political and cultural differences, as many anthropologists have long believed, but because their violence results, however indirectly, in their having more children.

Chagnon says that despite the toll the violence takes on the Yanomamo—nearly 70 percent of them have lost a close relative, and more than 50 percent have lost two or more—war is perpetuated in the society because a reputation for violence gives a Yanomamo warrior a high social status, which makes him an attractive candidate for arranged marriages.

"We have the same thing in our society," Chagnon points out. "Of course, here it's much more complex. We don't reward our war heroes with additional wives—we give them Cadillacs or a seat in the Senate." The military experiences of George Bush, Bob Dole, and Albert Gore, for example, are often brought up in considering their qualifications as candidates for public office.

Chagnon's explanation of human violence has its roots in sociobiology: the theory that some aspects of human behavior result from the competition between individuals for reproductive success. People sometimes will fight even though their resources are plentiful, sociobiologists explain, if fighting increases the chances of putting more of their genes—in their offspring or the offspring of close relatives—into the next generation.

Among the Yanomamo, a fight will typically begin over infidelity or the abduction of a woman from a neighboring village. The two men take turns pounding each other in the chest with their fists or hitting each other on the head with long wooden poles. Often, relatives of the protagonists are drawn in and the fight erupts into a brawl. If

Does this totalitarian policy encourage domination over other countries? If it does, the totalitarian state is likely to resort to war, because no country is willing to hand itself over to a foreign power. Moreover, totalitarian states have a history of killing large numbers of their own citizens. From 1918 to 1953, for example, "the Soviet government executed, slaughtered, starved, beat or tortured to death, or otherwise killed some 39.5 million of its own people. Other estimates vary from 20 to 83 million" (Rummel, 1986). If the Soviet government could kill that many of its own people—far more than the 20 million Soviet lives lost in World War II—in order to ensure complete control over its citizens, would it use similar violence—war—to apply its totalitarian policy to other countries? The answer is probably yes, because, as the nineteenth-century military strategist Karl von Clausewitz said, "War is simply the continuation of state policy by other means." Moreover, having far more power than their democratic counterparts, totalitarian rulers find it easier to wage war. The Soviet leader, for example, does not have to grapple with antiwar groups, as the American president and other Western leaders do. There is indeed some evidence that totalitarian states are more likely than democratic nations to start a war (Rummel, 1985). Of course, war is a complex phenomenon. It cannot be attributed to totalitarianism someone is killed, it can trigger a Hatfield-and-McCoy feud between villages as relatives of the victims seek revenge. Because most Yanomamo have many kin—more than 80 percent of the people are related in one way or another to 75 percent of the others—the feud can continue for years.

Chagnon found that Yanomamo men who have killed at least one other person have more than twice the number of wives and children as those who have not killed. An especially successful warrior may have as many as six wives. "I went down there looking for shortages of resources," says Chagnon, who has spent 23 years studying the tribe. "But it turns out they are fighting like hell over women."

While sociobiology has been generally accepted among scientists investigating animal populations, the theory's relevance in explaining human behavior has been hotly contested—particularly among anthropologists. One opposing camp, for example, believes that beneath all human conflict lies a fundamental struggle not for reproduction but for resources such as food, land or oil. Cast in Marxist economics, the so-called cultural materialist theory proposes that war is a byproduct of the ever changing relationship between groups of people and the limited resources in their environment.

When resources become scarce, the shortages lead to tensions that sometimes erupt in war. Such conflicts reduce the population and create no man's lands where game can become abundant again and the population restores its balance with the environment. "Cultural materialists believe that war is like a thermostat," says anthropologist Brian Ferguson. "It keeps the environment and the population in check."

Another group of anthropologists believes that while a conflict may contribute to an individual's reproductive success or maintain a balance between the environment and a population, those are merely the results of war, not its causes. These anthropologists argue that conflicts are primarily the result of historical and cultural forces in a society—rather than being an unconscious struggle over resources or reproduction. "People don't fight over things they don't know about," says researcher Clayton Robarchek. "If someone gets up in the morning and decides to launch an attack, he usually has a reason for doing it." As evidence for his theory, Robarchek cites two other primitive societies that he has recently studied, one in Asia and one in South America. Both of these tribes have similar amounts of resources, he says; yet one tribe is extremely violent, while the other hardly ever fights.

Source: William F. Allman, "A Laboratory of Human Conflict," *U.S. News & World Report,* April 11, 1988, pp. 57–58. Copyright, April 11, 1988, *U.S. News & World Report.*

alone. After all, democratic societies such as the United States have engaged in many wars. What, then, are other reasons for nations going to war?

The general public assumes that war is part of "human nature," that humans are naturally warlike (Zur, 1987). Similarly, sociobiologists believe that warfare arises from people struggling for reproductive success (see box, above). Ethologists, who specialize in the study of animal behavior, observe that the human species is the most warlike in the animal kingdom. Tigers, lions, and other beasts rarely kill members of their own species. By contrast, humans often kill one another because they have failed to evolve the instinct to neutralize the killer instinct they share with the lower animals (Lorenz, 1966). To support these biological theories, advocates emphasize the prevalence of war or the rarity of peace in world history. One points out that in the last 5600 years there have been only 292 years when peace reigned in the world (Farley, 1987). In other words, for an astounding 95 percent of that long history, war has occurred somewhere in the world. Sociologists, however, discount the biological theories because all societies are not equally warlike. As we observed in Chapter 3 (Culture), the Yanomamo are warlike but the Eskimos are peaceful. Even if all societies were warlike, the universality of human aggression does not necessarily suggest that the behavior derives from human nature, just as the universal incest taboo is not biologically determined (see Chapter 8: Human Sexuality).

Sociologists maintain that the prevalence of war can be explained sociologically. Using the functionalist perspective, we can argue that war occurs because it serves some useful functions for society. Most notably, it enhances social solidarity by focusing people's attention on fighting a common enemy. Another function of war that is often mentioned is the stimulation of scientific and technological development. War has made possible, for example, "the improvement of airplanes, the invention of new surgical techniques, and the harnessing of nuclear energy" (Coleman and Cressey, 1987). But the loss of lives and property may outweigh the benefits of war for the society as a whole. If this is the case, another sociological perspective may be a better guide to understanding war. The conflict perspective suggests that war reflects an exploitation of the masses by the ruling elite. Political leaders have been known to whip up a war frenzy against some foreign enemy as a way of regaining popular support or diverting people's attention from domestic problems. Other members of the power elite also benefit, with military brass becoming heroes and business tycoons reaping profits from sales of military hardware.

While these sociological perspectives suggest the general forces that may lead to war, they cannot predict precisely when a nation will start a war. This is because many other factors may be involved. If two countries are traditional, long-standing enemies, as in the case of Israel and its Arab neighbors, they are likely to attack each other every now and then. If nations have become polarized into two hostile camps, a single incident may trigger a world war. Given the polarization between Germany, Austria, and Hungary on one side and Great Britain, France, and Russia on the other, World War I broke out when an Austrian duke was assassinated. A combination of an inflammatory ideology and a charismatic leader can also be a powerful recipe for war. Nazi Germany started World War II by invading its neighbors because the Germans, under Hitler's strong, mesmeric leadership, came to believe that they were the "master race," destined to rule the world. In the early 1980s, Iran started its holy war against neighboring Iraq because the Iranians had been galvanized by their leader, the Ayatollah Khomeini, with the belief that their brand of Moslem religion must dominate semisecular Iraq. Finally, if nations are militarily prepared to defend themselves or their allies, they are likely to engage in war. Fortified with huge armies and enormous stockpiles of weapons, the United States and the Soviet Union stand ready to "defend" themselves against each other. The United States has done so by sending troops to Vietnam in the 1960s and, more recently, by supporting Israel in its conflicts with Syria and aiding the Contra rebels in their attempt to overthrow the pro-Soviet Sandinista government of Nicaragua. Similarly, the Soviet Union has dispatched troops to Afghanistan, supported Syria, and aided the rebels in El Salvador in their effort to topple pro-American governments.

In such warfare, the two superpowers have scrupulously avoided a direct confrontation. When the Soviet Union invaded Afghanistan, the United States protested loudly but did not send troops there to confront the Soviets. When the United States invaded South Vietnam, the Soviet Union protested loudly but did not send troops there to fight the Americans. Apparently, the two superpowers are afraid that, if they fight each other directly, they might start a nuclear war that would destroy them both and much of the rest of the world as well. The fear of nuclear war has also led them to negotiate a series of arms-control treaties, the latest one calling for the elimination of both American and Soviet medium-range missiles in Europe. Although both governments favor this treaty, it can reduce their enormous nuclear arsenals by only 4 percent (Watson, 1987). Thus the possibility of a nuclear holocaust continues to hang like the sword of Damocles over both countries.

QUESTIONS FOR DISCUSSION AND REVIEW

1. How do sociologists define politics and powers?
2. How does legitimate power differ from illegitimate power, and what is the difference between influence and authority?
3. Why do democratic states claim authority over fewer activities than states like the Soviet Union?
4. What factors help explain why war is more prevalent in some societies than others?

AMERICAN POLITICAL STRUCTURE

Most of the world's nations are not democracies. Many that established democratic institutions after they achieved independence soon turned to authoritarian rule. Apparently, democracy is a fragile as well as an unruly kind of system. Yet the American democracy seems remarkably strong. It is the oldest democracy in the world. What is the nature of this political structure? Its government consists of three branches of power: the executive (including the president), the legislative (Congress), and the judiciary (the Supreme Court). They check and balance each other so that none can become too powerful. Thus gross abuse of power can be avoided and democracy can be preserved. But we can also learn much about the American political structure by analyzing its political parties and interest groups. These are very important political organizations that provide links between the government and the people.

"Ladies and gentlemen, I've put aside my prepared speech. All I want to say is I'm proud to be an American. I love my mother, I love apple pie—and I love you all!"

Political Parties

Political parties are not mentioned in the U.S. Constitution, but it is difficult to imagine the government running today without them. A **political party** is a group organized for the purpose of gaining government offices. In seeking this goal for themselves, political parties also perform several functions vital to the operation of a democracy. First, parties recruit adherents, nominate candidates, and raise campaign money to support their choices for public office. Without the parties, the process of electing officials would be chaotic, as hundreds of people might offer themselves as candidates for each office. Second, parties formulate and promote policies. The desire to seek voters' support ensures that these policies reflect public opinion. This is one way in which the parties serve as a link between the people and their government. Finally, the parties help organize the main institutions of government. Leadership positions in the legislature and its committees are parceled out on the basis of which party holds the allegiance of most members of Congress.

The Two-Party System The American political party system is quite different from its counterpart in European democracies, each of which often has ten or more political parties. In contrast, we have a two-party system. For more than a century, the Democratic and Republican parties have held unquestioned dominance over the political system. Of course, there are many other parties, which we collectively call "third parties." Occasionally, a third-party candidate wins a local or even a state election, as some socialist party candidates have done. Sometimes a third party, such as John Anderson's in 1980, threatens to influence the outcome of a national election—not by winning but by taking votes that would otherwise go to one of the majority party candidates. But not since Abraham Lincoln won for the Republicans has a new party emerged that had a chance of winning the presidency. No third party has any influence in Congress, either. In contrast, "third parties" in other countries hold seats in the national parliaments, and they may have a strong influence on policy.

Generally, the Republicans are more conservative than the Democrats. The Republicans tend to advocate tax breaks for the wealthy, reduction in government spending, more local control, and less government interference with the economy. Consequently, the Republican party usually gets more support from the economically advantaged, Anglo-Saxon whites, members of major Protestant churches, and suburban and small town residents. The Democrats, on the other hand, are inclined to emphasize the need for government to combat unemployment, relieve poverty, and institute various social welfare programs. Therefore, the Democratic party tends to gain more support from the economically disadvantaged, minority groups, and residents of the central-city areas in large metropolitan regions (Lipset, 1981; Ladd, 1983a). But party differences, when all is said and done, are actually not very great. Consider tax policies, for example. In 1954 the Republican administration offered large tax breaks to big business, but in 1969, 1974, 1975, and 1976 Republican presidents also signed rather than vetoed tax bills that gave tax credits to low-income people and increased payroll taxes for high incomes. In a similar zigzag, compromising manner, Democratic administrations enacted tax cuts for low incomes in 1964 but also tax cuts for the rich in 1962 and 1978. In the early 1980s, the Democrats even tried to out-Reagan Reagan by offering more lucrative tax breaks to business (Page, 1983).

In fact, the two-party system requires that each party represent as many Americans as possible if it is to win election or reelection. Thus both parties usually aim for the center of political opinion, trying to appeal to everyone and offend no one. They take in a broad coalition of politicians with many viewpoints. We can find such strange bedfellows as conservatives and liberals in each party. When they look for presidential candidates, both parties usually look to the centers of their own parties. This has led to the charge that there is "not a dime's worth of difference" between them. Yet if the Republican party overemphasizes its conservatism and the Democratic party its liberalism, both parties are certain to turn off many voters and get a severe beating at the polls. This is what happened when the conservative wing seized control of the Republican party and nominated Barry Goldwater for president in 1964; Democratic liberals did the same with George McGovern in 1972. Both choices led to landslide defeats in the general election.

Since it seeks as broad a consensus as possible, the two-party system in the United States is more likely to produce a stable government than the multiparty systems in European democracies. In a multiparty system, extremist parties such as communists and monarchists, though very small in membership, can easily get elected into the government. If they receive only 5 percent of the votes, they will get 5 percent of the seats in the legislature. Their uncompromising opposition to other parties threatens the stability of the government. Thus, it is not unusual for a multiparty government to change hands two or three times a year. To the Europeans, though, the frequent change in government is no cause for concern. It has not created any crisis or revolution. It is no wonder that Italians consider their last 40 years of changing governments like musical chairs as a period of "extremely stable instability" (Levi, 1987).

Are the Parties Over? For more than two decades, commentators have been talking about the decline of the U.S. political parties. More and more voters identify themselves as "independents" rather than as Democrats or Republicans. In 1980 about 77 percent of American voters identified themselves with one of the two major parties, but in 1986 only 58 percent did so. Between those two years the proportion of independents had grown from 23 to 42 percent (Lamar, 1986). Even those who say they are Democrats or Republicans often split their vote, choosing some candidates from one party and some from another. In a recent survey, a representative sample of Americans were asked which of the two parties can do a better job of handling the nation's problems. Those who answered "Republicans" or "Democrats" were outnumbered by those who said they could not tell which party did a better job (White and Morris, 1984). Most politicians still call themselves Democrats or Republicans, but they often act like independents, refusing to follow the direction of party leaders in Congress, or even the president from their party. As former House Speaker Tip O'Neill complained, "If this were France, the Democratic party would be five parties" (Morrow, 1978a).

There are several possible forces behind this decline. One is television, which enables candidates, if they have the money, to reach voters directly rather than through an organized army of volunteers and party activists knocking on doors. Another is the spread of party primaries, which increasingly put the choice of candidates in the hands of voters rather than party leaders and activists. Thus the party organization has less control over who its candidates are. A third factor is the increasing cost of elections and the rise of political action committees (PACs) as a big source of that campaign money. **PACs** are political organizations that funnel money from business, labor, and other special-interest groups into election campaigns to help elect or defeat candidates. PACs act independently of the parties. Finally, pollsters and political consultants have emerged as the wise men of politics, telling the politician what the public is thinking and feeling. Politicians turn to them, not the local party precinct captain or state party chairperson, for news of how the political winds are blowing. In short, whatever the parties can offer, politicians can find elsewhere. The parties have fewer carrots and sticks to control politicians. But if politicians do not follow a party's position, then the party labels mean less and less and voters have little reason to pay attention to them (Wattenberg, 1981).

In recent years there have been some signs that the parties are coming back to life. In both the Republican and Democratic parties the organizational activity at the grass-roots level is higher than before. State parties are better staffed, better funded, and more efficient. At the national level, the parties have their own large headquarters in Washington, with huge budgets (as much as $40 million a year) and lengthy direct mail lists. They are active all the time rather than only every four years. They have also improved their ability to recruit, train, and then assist candidates for office—with polling, advertising, advice, and money (Pomper, 1984; Herrnson, 1986).

No Wild,
No Wildlife.

Life in the wild can be pretty tough these days. Without the necessary habitat to live in, some species like the Grizzly Bears that inhabit Yellowstone National Park are severely threatened.
Over 80% of the national forest lands that border Yellowstone and are not specifically put out-of-reach for oil development, have been leased: habitat that the Grizzlies rely on, as do elk, moose and deer.
If their refuges are replaced with roads, oil rigs and gas pipelines, they too will become victims of senseless and thoughtless development. The Sierra Club's work to protect public lands from development also helps preserve the habitat of these Grizzlies, saving the wilderness they need in order to survive.
To learn more about our work protecting endangered species such as the Grizzly Bear in Yellowstone or to take part in it through membership, please write us at: Sierra Club, 730 Polk Street, San Francisco, CA 94109, (415) 776-2211.

SIERRA
CLUB

The Sierra Club, which seeks to protect the environment, is an example of an interest group that works on many levels to have its views heard and to influence government action. Through its nationwide grass-roots network of members, it generates public support, helps elect sympathetic candidates, files lawsuits against those who destroy the environment, and hires lobbyists to influence lawmakers directly.

Interest Groups

For those Americans who find neither party to be an effective representative of their concerns, there is another alternative: interest groups. An **interest group** is an organized collection of people who attempt to influence the government's policies. If you are a hog farmer interested in keeping the price of hogs high, there is a group for you. If you are a hunter interested in preventing the regulation of firearms or a baseball bat manufacturer interested in breaking into the Japanese market, there are groups for you, too. There are business groups like the U.S. Chamber of Commerce and the National Association of Manufacturers; labor groups like the AFL-CIO; professional groups like the American Medical Association; as well as civil rights groups, civil liberties groups, environmental groups, consumers' groups, and religious groups.

All these groups use the same basic methods in trying to influence the government's policies. First, they try to influence public opinion. They advertise in the media, collect petitions, and send out letters urging people to write or call their legislators. Second, they help elect sympathetic candidates by endorsing them, urging their members to support those candidates, and donating money to their campaigns. Third, interest groups frequently file lawsuits to further their goals. Finally, interest groups hire lobbyists, people who deal directly with government officials, attempting to influence them on behalf of the groups.

There are at least 15,000 lobbyists in Washington today, which average out to nearly 30 lobbyists working on each member of Congress. Former House Speaker Tip O'Neill once grumbled, "Everyone in America has a lobby" (*Time,* 1978a). Even the Gift Fashion Shop Association from the Virgin Islands has a lobbyist. Together, lobbyists spend about a billion dollars a year to influence officials in Washington and another billion to pressure legislators indirectly by drumming up public opinion in their home districts.

Is all this activity good or bad? Interest groups undoubtedly serve some useful functions. They provide a way for millions of citizens to make their voices heard. Civil rights, environmental issues, and a nuclear "freeze" are but a few examples of issues that were first put on the political agenda by interest groups. To the political parties and those in office, these issues were either unimportant or too controversial to warrant action until interest groups forced the politicians to address them. Thus interest groups prevent the political parties, the media, or officials from monopolizing control over just what policies and viewpoints the government should consider. By organizing into an interest group, an otherwise voiceless association gains a voice in government, and just about any collection of citizens can increase their clout.

Interest groups also inform and advise lawmakers. Being masters of their subject, lobbyists, in effect, become technical advisers to legislators and their staffs, supplying them with information vital to wise decision making and to the writing of workable laws. Of course, lobbyists are likely to slant the information they present to favor their interest group, but lawmakers know that as well as we do. Thus they rely on a multitude of lobbyists with different views that counterbalance one another.

If interest groups are so good, why do so many people fear and criticize them? Why do Democrats and Republicans both rail against the "special interests"? One concern is that they are corrupting the process of government through back-room dealings of one sort or another—through secret meetings between lobbyists and regulatory officials, or through outright bribery of members of Congress. Such explicit deals seem to be an infrequent exception in the political process, however. More serious is the concern that through relentless pursuit of their narrow goals, some interest groups are thwarting the will of the majority and harming the public good. Although polls have consistently shown broad support for gun control, for example, the National Rifle Association (NRA) persuaded Congress to reject gun-control bills fourteen times in ten years. The NRA managed to organize an avalanche of angry mail from citizens to persuade Congress. Money is another powerful tool. Interest groups have increasingly used PACs to give money to sympathetic candidates. The total amount of PAC money given to members of Congress shot up from $34.1 million in 1978 to $132.2 million in 1986 (Gopoian, 1984; Plattner, 1987).

As the saying goes, we seem to be getting the best Congress money can buy. Elected officials often have good reason to believe that a vote will influence how much money they can obtain from PACs for their next campaign. There have been cases in which PAC money clearly influenced votes, as the following instances illustrate (Green, 1982):

> —A New York Democrat admitted that he voted for the Alaska Gas Pipeline, even though he opposed it on the merits, because "I didn't want the construction unions contributing to my opponent."
> —Representative Mike Synar, Democrat of Oklahoma, says, "I go out on the floor and say to a member, 'I need your help on this bill,' and often he will say, 'I can't do that, I got $5,000 from a special interest.' So I no longer lobby Congressmen. I lobby the lobbyists to lobby the Congressmen."

In short, as the power of interest groups grows, the government may end up being for sale to whatever group has the most money or the best organization. Federal tax policy, for example, favors business more often than labor because business has about 22 times as large a budget as labor to spend on tax lobbying (Page, 1983). Of course, no one interest group can always have its way on every issue. Still, the growth of interest groups raises the question: Who really rules the country?

QUESTIONS FOR DISCUSSION AND REVIEW

1. What are some functions of political parties?
2. How do interest groups influence legislation and executive policies?

WHO REALLY GOVERNS?

The emergence of political parties and interest groups has brought us a long way from the government envisioned by James Madison. It was his hope to exclude "interests" and "factions" from the government. Legislators were to represent and vote for the public good, not one interest or the other. Where has this evolution brought us? Are the interest groups and parties mechanisms through which the people gain more effective control of government, or have the people lost control? Who in fact has **political power,** the capacity to use the government to make decisions that affect the whole society? Let us look again at the three views introduced in Chapter 9 (Social Stratification).

The Pluralist View

A pluralist looking at American government sees many centers of power and many competing interest groups. Government reflects the outcome of their conflict. In this view the interest groups are central to American democracy. Together they create a mutually restraining influence. No one group can always prevail. Thus through their competition the interests of the public are reflected in government policy.

We have seen in Chapter 9 (Social Stratification), however, that there are large inequalities of wealth, power, and prestige in the United States. How, in the face of such inequality, can pluralism be maintained? Cannot one group marshal its resources to dominate others? Why doesn't one group or one coalition of groups gradually achieve a concentration of power?

The reason, according to Robert Dahl (1981), is that inequalities are *dispersed,* not cumulative. Inequalities would be cumulative if a group rich in one resource (wealth, for example) were also better off than other groups in almost every other resource—political power, social standing, prestige, legitimacy, knowledge, and control over religious, educational, and other institutions. In the United States, however, one group may hold most of one of these resources, but other groups may have the lion's share of others. What the upper middle class lacks in wealth, for example, it makes up for in knowledge and legitimacy. Power over economic institutions may be concentrated in the hands of corporations, but U.S. religious institutions elude their grasp.

This dispersal of power in society is reflected in a dispersal of political clout. The country's many competing groups vie for control over government policy, and end up dominating different spheres. Corporations may dominate the government's decisions on taxes but not on crime. Even tax policy is not dictated solely by corporations, because labor unions and other groups fight with the corporations for influence on politicians and voters. The structure of the government, with its separation of powers, promotes this pluralism. What civil rights groups could not win in Congress in the 1950s, they sometimes won in the courts. Corporations that have lost a battle in Congress may win the war by influencing regulations issued by the executive branch. In the end, in Dahl's view, competing groups usually compromise and share power. Thus there is no ruling group in the United States. It is instead a pluralist democracy dominated by many different sets of leaders.

David Riesman (1950) and Arnold Rose (1967) have developed a somewhat different analysis. In their view, America has become so pluralistic that various interest groups constitute *veto groups.* They are powerful enough to block each other's actions. To get anything done, the veto groups must seek support from the unorganized public. The masses, then, have the ultimate power to ensure that their interests and concerns are protected. The bottom line is that the overall leadership is weak, stalemate is frequent, and no one elite can emerge to dominate the others.

The Elitist View

It is obvious that there are many competing groups in the United States. But does their competition actually determine policy? Is the government merely the neutral arbitrator among these conflicting interests? According to elitist theorists, the answer is no.

Many years ago Italian sociologists Vilfredo Pareto (1848–1923) and Gaetano Mosca (1858–1941) argued that a small elite has governed the masses in all societies. Why should this be so? If a nation is set up along truly democratic lines, isn't control by an elite avoidable? According to German sociologist Robert Michels (1915), there is an "iron law of oligarchy" by which even a democracy inevitably degenerates into an oligarchy, which is rule by a few. A democracy is an organization, and according to Michels, "who says organization says oligarchy."

In Michels's view, three characteristics of organizations eventually produce rule by the elite. First, to work efficiently, even a democratic organization must allow a few leaders to make the decisions. Second, through their positions of leadership, the leaders accumulate skills and knowledge that make them indispensable to the rank and file. Third, the rank and file lack the time, inclination, or knowledge to master the complex tasks of government, and they become politically apathetic. Thus, in time, even a democracy yields to rule by an elite.

How does this view apply to the United States? According to C. Wright Mills (1916–1962), there are three levels of power in this country. At the bottom are ordinary people—powerless, unorganized, fragmented, and manipulated by the mass media into believing in democracy. In the middle are Congress, the political parties, interest groups, and most political leaders. At this level, pluralism reigns. The middle groups form "a drifting set of stalemated, balancing forces" (Mills, 1959a). Above them, however, ignored by pluralist theorists, is an elite—what Mills called the *power elite*—that makes the most important decisions.

The base of the elite's power lies in three institutions: the federal government, the military, and the

George Shultz's career illustrates how a member of the elite moves easily from one important position of power to another. Among the posts he has held are secretary of state (1982–1988), president of Bechtel Corporation (1975–1980), secretary of the treasury (1974–1975), director of the Office of Management and Budget (1970–1972), secretary of labor (1969–1970), and dean of the University of Chicago's Graduate School of Business (1962–1968).

large corporations. According to Mills, power in the United States is increasingly concentrated in these three institutions, and those who lead them control the nation. Further, those leaders now form a cohesive, unified group. They are unified first because they share many social and psychological characteristics. They are mostly WASPs (white Anglo-Saxon Protestants) who attended Ivy League universities, belong to the same exclusive clubs, have similar values and attitudes, and know each other personally. They are unified, too, in that they form an "interlocking directorate" over the three key institutions. The three key institutions are increasingly interdependent: the government, the economy, and the military are tightly linked. Decisions by one affect the others, and the leaders of these institutions increasingly coordinate their decisions. Moreover, the *same* people move back and forth between leadership positions in the military, corporations, and the federal government. Corporate executives head the Department of Defense; high government officials routinely become corporate lawyers or executives; and generals easily exchange their uniforms for civilian clothes to head federal commissions or join the boards of directors of huge corporations. Thus the country is ruled by "a handful of men" who head the federal government, military, and large corporations and form a cohesive, united group—the power elite.

If Mills is correct, all the hoopla of campaigns and debates, all the fund-raising by interest groups and earnest debate in the media, are but so much sound and fury. The power elite is free to do as it chooses. The government can allocate billions to defense to strengthen the military and to enrich the corporations from which the weapons are purchased. Big business can support political leaders with campaign money. The politicians can aid business with favorable legislation. Where is the evidence to support Mills's view?

There is indeed evidence that the three institutions Mills singled out have accumulated increasing power. There is also evidence for Mills's view that a cohesive elite exists. Time and again researchers have found that top officials in both Democratic and Republican administrations previously held high positions in corporations, that they return to corporations after leaving the government, and that leaders come disproportionately from upper-class backgrounds (Mintz, 1975; Dye, 1976; Useem, 1979, 1980). Ronald Brownstein and Nina Easton (1982), for example, profiled 100 officials in the Reagan administration and found 28 millionaires, 22 multimillionaires, and several "likely millionaires." After collecting data to show that a power elite exists within the upper class, William Domhoff (1978, 1983) argued that no more than 0.5 percent of the population owns about 25 percent of all privately held wealth, controls major banks and corporations, runs the executive and judiciary branches of federal government, heavily influences the federal legislature and most state governments, and dominates the formulation of national economic and political policies.

The Marxist View

Power-elite theory has been criticized by pluralists and Marxists. Pluralists argue that an elite does not enact policies only in its own interests. It may hold liberal values, trying to eliminate racism, abolish poverty, educate the masses, and generally do good (Dye, 1976). Even if an elite is quite conservative, it may also keep the public interest in mind when formulating policies. The framers of the U.S. Constitution, for example, were quite "pro-rich." Nevertheless, they believed that "a strong national government, protection of private property, and opening of national markets would benefit everyone," not just themselves as wealthy landowners and capitalists (Page, 1983). According to the Marxists, Mills's analysis confuses the issue. They argue that his political and military elites are not free to act in their own interests—they are merely agents of the corporate elite. What we have are not three elites that come together but one ruling class.

American sociologist Albert Szymanski (1978) provides an example of this approach. According to Szymanski, there are four classes in the United States. The first is the capitalist class, which owns and controls the major means of production and is commonly known as big business. The second is the petty bourgeoisie, which includes professionals, small-business people, and independent farmers. Some of these people own the "means of production," but they must work with it themselves. The third class is the working class, including industrial, white-collar, and rural workers; they must sell their physical or mental labor to live. The fourth is the lumpen proletariat, which consists of the unemployed, welfare recipients, criminals, and down-and-outs. Szymanski argues that the capitalist class uses the state as an instrument for exploiting the other three economically subordinate classes. Unlike Mills, Szymanski does not argue that the masses are hopelessly passive and manipulated. Instead, in his view, there is a constant "class struggle" in which the capitalists try to dominate the masses who, in turn, continually resist the domination. But the capitalist class more often wins than loses because it has the state do its bidding.

To control the state, capitalists may use the same methods employed by interest groups, such as lobbying and supporting sympathetic candidates. In using these tools, however, the capitalist class has a big advantage over the run-of-the-mill interest group: they have more money. The capitalist class also has indirect methods that give it a position far superior to that of any interest group. First, its values—such as free enterprise, economic growth, and competition—permeate society. They are propagated by the media, schools, churches, and other institutions. Violations of the values that further the interests of the capitalist class are often taken to be un-American, giving capitalist interests a potent weapon against unsympathetic politicians. Few American politicians want to be branded as antigrowth and antibusiness—or as socialists. Second, if the government acts against the interests of capitalists, they can, in effect, go on strike: they can refuse to put their capital to work. They might close plants or stop investing or send their money abroad. As a result, "business can extort favors, virtually without limit, from the political authorities. For . . . governments have a deep interest in continued and increasing productivity, but they have very little power over the owners of capital. In order to get businessmen to do their job, they must provide extensive protection, not only against violence but also against economic risk" (Walzer, 1978).

Thus in the 1980s politicians of all stripes have talked about molding an economic policy that would "send a message" to "reassure Wall Street." In state after state in recent years, gubernatorial and mayoral campaigns have been fought over the issue of whether a particular candidate would create a good or bad "business climate," over which candidate had the best plan of subsidies and tax breaks to lure business into the city or state. The public interest is identified with business interests, and political choices thus become hostages to the decisions of capitalists. Marxist theorists do not claim that capitalists dictate government policy or have their way on every issue, but they do argue that the capitalist class sets the limits to change and controls the "big" issues.

The issue of who really governs in American society boils down to three questions: Which group holds the most power? Where does it get the power? And what role do the masses play in the government? The three views that we have discussed are different in some respects and similar in others. Both elitists and Marxists see power concentrated in the hands of a small group and hardly any influence by the masses on the government. These theorists differ, however, in regard to the key source of power. To elitists, the ruling elite's power comes from its leadership in business, government, and the military, while to Marxists, the ruling class gets its power from controlling the economy. On the other hand, pluralists disagree with both. They argue that political leaders ultimately derive their power from the citizenry and they must compete among themselves to stay at the top (see Table 16.1).

Which view, then, most accurately represents the

Table 16.1 Who Really Governs?

View	Key Ruling Group	Chief Source of Power	Role of Masses
Pluralist	Elected officials; interest groups and their leaders	Various political resources, including wealth, authority, and votes	Indirectly control leaders through competitive elections and interest group pressures
Elitist	Cohesive power elite, made of top corporate, government, and military leaders	Control of key institutions, primarily the corporation and the executive branch of government	Manipulated and exploited by the power elite
Marxist	Capitalists, owners and controllers of the corporate world	Wealth and control of society's productive resources	Manipulated and exploited by the capitalist class

Source: Adapted from Martin N. Marger, *Elites and Masses*. Copyright © 1981 by Litton Educational Publishing Company, Inc. Used by permission of Wadsworth Publishing Company, Inc.

reality of American government? It is difficult, if not impossible, to answer the question because relevant data are unavailable. But it seems obvious that each of the three views captures only a small portion, rather than the complex whole, of the political reality. Pluralists are most likely to hit the bull's eye in regard to most domestic issues, such as jobs and inflation, about which the public feels strongly. In these cases the government tends to do what the people want (Burstein, 1981). Elitists and Marxists are more likely to be correct on most foreign and military policy matters, about which the masses are less concerned and knowledgeable. This explains why defense contractors are able to sell the U.S. government far more arms than are needed (Page, 1983). The three views may be oversimplistic and one-sided, but they are basically complementary, helping to enlarge our understanding of the complex, shifting nature of political power.

QUESTIONS FOR DISCUSSION AND REVIEW

1. What is political power, and what are the different theories about who exercises power in the United States?
2. How does the elitist view of who exercises political power differ from the pluralist view?
3. According to the Marxist view, which elites make the most important decisions, and how do they exercise power?

THE PEOPLE'S RESPONSE

Each of the three theories we have discussed focuses on the decision makers. Here we turn to those who are governed. What influences their attitudes toward government, and what are those attitudes? Are most Americans as powerless and passive as elitists and Marxists suggest, or are they potentially powerful and capable of taking an active part in government?

Political Socialization

In politics as in other spheres of life, socialization is one key to behavior. **Political socialization** is the process by which individuals acquire political knowledge, beliefs, and attitudes. It begins at a very young age, when the family is the major socializing agent. As children grow up, schools, peer groups, and the media also become important agents of political socialization.

What is it that children learn? Before they are 9 years old, most American children know who the U.S. president is, and they are aware of the Democratic and Republican parties. Childhood socialization also appears to shape several important political attitudes. Schools and parents begin to influence children's sense of political efficacy—their belief that they can participate in politics and that their participation can make a difference. In addition, parents often transmit their party identification (their support of a political party) to their children. If both their parents support the same party, children are likely to support that party. With age, however, their identification with their parent's party tends to decline. Parental influence is generally stronger among conservative Republicans than liberal Democrats. As sociologist Frederic Koenig (1982a) explains,

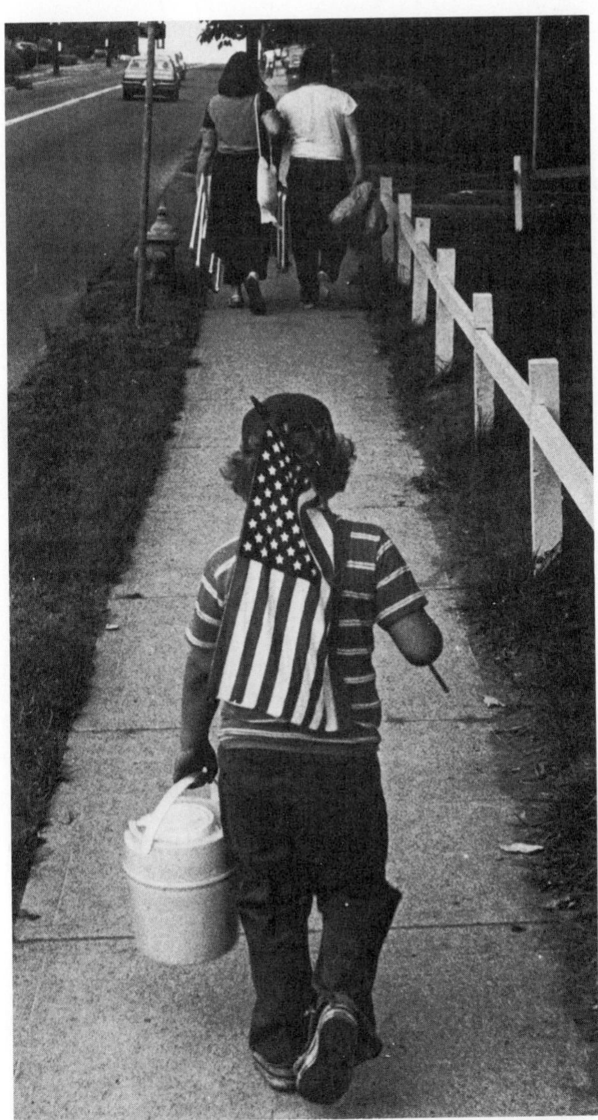

Parents are the first important agent in the political socialization of children. As children grow up, schools, peer groups, and the media also influence their political knowledge, beliefs, and attitudes. As a result, most American children know the name of the U.S. president and the two major political parties. Children also believe in political participation and support their parents' party.

conservative children feel more strongly about preserving traditions across generations and have greater respect for authority figures like parents.

Children also develop attitudes toward the government in general and politicians in particular. With age, support for the political system tends to grow, but faith in government officials seems to decline. In one survey students were asked whether they agreed with the statement "Democracy is the best form of government." Only 46 percent of third-grade students said yes, but 74 percent of seventh-graders did. In contrast, 90 percent of third-graders felt that government officials generally did a good job, but only 76 percent of eighth-graders thought so (Segal, 1974). This age difference seems to reflect older children's increased ability to understand abstract concepts such as democracy as well as their increased exposure to information about specific politicians (Meadow, 1982).

Socialization continues in adulthood, when our political beliefs may be influenced by friends, families, and co-workers. Thus where we live may affect our political attitudes. One study has found that people who live in predominantly Democratic neighborhoods are mostly Democrats themselves but the likelihood of their becoming Republicans increases significantly if they move into Republican neighborhoods. This suggests that people tend to accept their neighbors' choices of a political party (Segal, 1974; Weatherford, 1982; Himmelweit, 1983).

Political Attitudes

Social class seems to play a leading role in shaping attitudes toward government and its policies. Members of the working class tend to be economic liberals and social conservatives. They are, for example, likely to support social programs and intervention in the economy by the government but to oppose efforts to guarantee equal treatment for homosexuals. In contrast, higher-income groups tend to be economic conservatives, opposing social programs and government intervention, and social liberals, supporting equal treatment (Lipset, 1981).

There is more consensus and less consistency in public opinion, however, than those statements may suggest. Polls find wide support among all classes for government spending to clean up the environment, improve the nation's health, combat crime, strengthen the educational and social security system, improve the situation of minorities, and provide medical care and legal assistance for the poor. But while they support all these government services, Americans are highly critical of the government itself. A majority tell pollsters that the government has become too powerful, too intrusive, and too wasteful, and that it creates more problems than it solves. Most respondents to the polls agree that "the government is run by people who don't know what they are doing," that "the government cannot be trusted to do what is right," and "the government wants a lot of tax dollars." Americans often say they want lower taxes—but also more and better government services (Lipset and Schneider, 1983; Ladd, 1978, 1983b).

In short, most Americans are angry over "big government" and high taxes, yet they support big government by demanding more services. This inconsistency reflects a uniquely American political character. A political analyst has described it as "a classic case of people wanting their cake and eating it too" (Lamar, 1986). But it is more complicated than that. Americans are **ideological conservatives,** believing in free enterprise, rugged individualism, and capitalism (Chong, McClosky, and Zaller, 1983). They are, in theory, opposed to big government. At the same time, Americans are **operational liberals,** who, in effect, support big government by backing government programs that render service to the public. Such mixed, ambivalent attitudes do not only have to do with those economic issues. They are just as real in regard to social issues. Many Americans today want to "get government off our backs," but at the same time they support school prayer and antiabortion laws, which, in effect, advocates government intervention in our private lives (Ladd, 1978, 1983b).

Still, despite criticisms of their government, Americans are more likely than the people of other nations to take pride in their country and to say they would be willing to fight for it if there were a war. One survey found that 80 percent of Americans are proud of their country, compared with 66 percent of the Irish, 55 percent of the British, 30 percent of the Japanese, and 21 percent of the West Germans (Hyer, 1982a).

Political Participation

Americans can participate in government and politics in numerous ways. They can attend a rally or run for office, form an interest group or send money to a candidate, write to their representatives or work for their opponents. But it seems that few Americans choose to take an active role in their government. Compared with people elsewhere, though, we are more interested in public affairs, more politically active, prouder of our governmental institutions, more satisfied with the way our political system works, and less suspicious of our politicians (Wolfinger, 1986).

The most popular form of political participation is probably the easiest: voting. According to many election specialists, the percentage of people who bother to vote is lower in the United States than in nearly all other Western nations (see left column in Table 16.2). Actually our voting performance is not that bad, because the percent of our *voting-age population* who vote is unjustifiably compared with the turnout rate of *registered voters* in each of the other countries. Registered voters include only those people who are legally qualified to vote in an election. But the voting-age population includes many people who could not possibly vote, such as millions of aliens, citizens who are ex-convicts and inmates of prisons and mental hospitals, and citizens who fail to register. The apples-and-oranges comparison is bound to make our voter participation appear extremely

Voter participation is relatively low in the United States. A large number of citizens who are eligible to vote do not do so. As a result, many elected officials in the United States at every level of government are chosen by a small minority of citizens. The low voter turnout is due to residency requirements, the inconvenience of voter registration, voting as voluntary rather than compulsory, and too many elections. But compared with citizens of other nations, Americans are more interested in public affairs, prouder of their governmental institutions, and less suspicious of their politicians.

dismal (Glass, Squire, and Wolfinger, 1984). However, if the same criterion of analysis is applied to all countries, by counting only *registered voters,* then the United States looks considerably better. It now ranks eleventh among the 24 nations, a definite move up from its earlier twenty-third place (see Table 16.2).

Nevertheless, we may still consider our voter participation quite low, especially when we are not electing a president. In 1980, for example, only 38 percent of voting-age Americans voted for members of Congress, compared with 53 percent for president. As a consequence, our officials are usually put into office by a minority of Americans eligible to vote. In 1980 Reagan's victory was often called a landslide because he beat Carter by a wide margin. But most Americans either voted for someone else or did not bother to vote at all. Only about 20 percent of eligible voters chose to vote for him (Ranney, 1983). Even when we use the same criterion to compare our voting rate with that in other Western nations, we still fall behind nearly half of the other democracies. Why the lower turnout of American voters?

One reason is that, although it is easy to vote, it is not as easy in the United States as in most other Western countries. Voting laws vary from one state to another, but Americans must meet residency requirements and must register to vote some time before an election. The biggest obstacle to voting is the requirement that every time you change residence you must sign up all over again. The nuisance of reregistration reduces voting turnout because a great many Americans move. In

Table 16.2 Is Our Voter Turnout Really Small?

If the rate of voter participation in the United States is calculated as the percentage of the voting-age population who vote, while the turnout in other countries is computed as the percentage of registered voters who vote, as is popularly done, then we rank near the bottom (see left column below). If the same yardstick is used for all countries, as it should be, the United States looks much better, as the right column shows. Nevertheless, we still rank below nearly half of the nations.

Popular Measure of Turnout		Turnout of Those Who Are Registered	
1. Belgium	94.6%	1. Belgium	94.6%
2. Australia	94.5	2. Australia	94.5
3. Austria	91.6	3. Austria	91.6
4. Sweden	90.7	4. Sweden	90.7
5. Italy	90.4	5. Italy	90.4
6. Iceland	89.3	6. Iceland	89.3
7. New Zealand	89.0	7. New Zealand	89.0
8. Luxembourg	88.9	8. Luxembourg	88.9
9. W. Germany	88.6	9. W. Germany	88.6
10. Netherlands	87.0	10. Netherlands	87.0
11. France	85.9	11. United States	86.8
12. Portugal	84.2	12. France	85.9
13. Denmark	83.2	13. Portugal	84.2
14. Norway	82.0	14. Denmark	83.2
15. Greece	78.6	15. Norway	82.0
16. Israel	78.5	16. Greece	78.6
17. United Kingdom	76.3	17. Israel	78.5
18. Japan	74.5	18. United Kingdom	76.3
19. Canada	69.3	19. Japan	74.5
20. Spain	68.1	20. Canada	69.3
21. Finland	64.3	21. Spain	68.1
22. Ireland	62.2	22. Finland	64.3
23. United States	52.6	23. Ireland	62.2
24. Switzerland	48.3	24. Switzerland	48.3

Source: David Glass, Peverill Squire, and Raymond Wolfinger, "Voter turnout: An international comparison," *Public Opinion,* December/January 1984, pp. 50, 52.

UNDERSTANDING OTHER SOCIETIES

Political Funerals

Sociologists have discovered that political protests in countries with repressive governments can take unusual forms. Here the political funeral is analyzed as a vehicle of political protest. What other kinds of ceremonies might political protestors use to oppose repressive governments?

The Philippine mass outpouring during ceremonies honoring the martyred opposition leader Benigno Aquino is only the latest of what might be called "political funerals" in repressive regimes. A political funeral, simply put, is the transformation of burial services and associated ceremonies into opposition political demonstrations. Political funerals occur almost exclusively in authoritarian regimes, where they are one of the few means by which dissent can be expressed without much fear of reprisals.

The mysterious assassination of Aquino upon his return to Manila on August 21, 1983, after years of imprisonment and exile, touched off months of antigovernment demonstrations. Fully realizing the opportunity presented by the murder, Aquino's family and supporters delayed his formal funeral for ten days and in the meantime placed the body on display in three different sites, transporting the coffin in elaborate processions which attracted huge crowds chanting such slogans as Free Our Country! and Marcos Resign! Since the funeral, massive demonstrations centering around Aquino and expressing opposition to Marcos have been almost daily occurrences, indicating, as one prominent Filipino stated, that the public mood had "changed drastically" since the assassination. Previously, people were "afraid to express their feelings," but the "shock of Aquino's murder set people free to say what they felt."

Careful readers of the press will note that political funerals have also been very common of late in other authoritarian regimes. On April 17, 1983, for example, the *New York Times* reported the politicized funeral of Saul Mkhize, a leader in the black resistance to South African government attempts to remove blacks from officially proclaimed "white" lands they had been occupying. Mkhize had been shot by police two weeks earlier, when a disturbance broke out as the authorities tried to claim the land from its black occupants. Even though the family homestead where Mkhize was buried was more than ten miles from the nearest surfaced highway, more than 1500 mourners, many of whom, reported the *Times,* "had never heard of him or his struggle" before the shooting, came to the funeral.

A month after the Mkhize funeral in South Africa, the news media reported that the Warsaw funeral of Grzegorz Przemyk (a high school student allegedly beaten to death by the Polish police) had been transformed into a major antigovernment demonstration by pro-Solidarity activists, with an estimated 20,000 Poles in

contrast, voter registration in other democracies is automatic—otherwise, public officials go out to register citizens at their homes. In some of these countries, such as Belgium and Australia, voting is compulsory, which may further explain their higher voter-participation rates than ours. Finally, American voters may simply get tired of voting because there are many more elections in the United States than in other countries (Wolfinger, 1986; Powell, 1986).

Those reasons, however, cannot explain the significant differences in the voting turnout of various groups of Americans. In general, those who are poorer, younger, or less educated are less likely to vote. Blacks also have lower voting rates than whites, but class, not race, seems to be the primary factor. When blacks and whites of similar education and income are compared, there is hardly any gap between the turnout of blacks and whites (Kourvetaris and Dobratz, 1982; Glass et al., 1984). Traditionally, lower-status Americans' lack of political participation is blamed on their feelings of apathy, alienation, and distrust. Recent research suggests that the fault lies more with political parties and candidates, who are less likely to write or speak personally to the poor than the rich. Voter contact by a political party or candidate does encourage voter participation (Zipp, Landerman, and Luebke, 1982).

Political Violence

There is yet another form of political participation: political violence. In 1786 armed mobs of American attendance. The huge turnout resulted in one of the largest antigovernment demonstrations in Poland since the proclamation of martial law seventeen months earlier. This was especially remarkable since news of the funeral was spread entirely by word of mouth and clandestine notice. Although the demonstration was manifestly illegal under martial law regulations, Polish police and troops were nowhere to be seen during the funeral. Many of the mourners who crowded into St. Stanislaw Kostka Church for the ceremony wept openly when Warsaw's suffragan bishop said that Przemyk would "have to finish his final exam in heaven."

The political funeral is in many ways a tribute to the indomitable desire of human beings around the world to obtain political freedom. It is a means of outfoxing the political authorities by creating an outlet for the expression of opposition that is extraordinarily hard to suppress, akin to other forms of dissent manifested even in such repressive states as Poland, where crosses of flowers are formed outside of churches and where many Poles take ostentatious walks when the official news is broadcast on television.

I have been struck by the similarities between the use of political funerals in contemporary authoritarian regimes and their widespread use in Europe between 1815 and 1914, when many countries on that continent found themselves under the heel of repressive regimes which, for example, allowed only the very wealthy to vote, censored the press, and banned trade unions and unauthorized political demonstrations. While definite statements about the nature, numbers, and role of political funerals must await a full-blown scholarly treatment, it seems safe to say that in Europe such manifestations probably reached their height during the nineteenth century, for the same reasons that they are now so common in the Third World. As a result of modernizing advances in such areas as education, transportation, communication, and urbanization, the potential for mass political dissatisfaction and mobilization reached levels previously unknown; at the same time, most European governments were not willing to allow opposition organizations to meet, demonstrate, or otherwise protest in more "normal" ways. Thus, the political funeral is a means by which opposition can be thinly disguised, yet still expressed, and usually in a manner too truly spontaneous and under circumstances too sacred for the authorities to intervene effectively.

Source: Excerpted from Robert Justin Goldstein, "Political Funerals." Published by permission of Transaction Publishers, from *Society*, Vol. 21, No. 3, pp. 13–17. Copyright © 1984 by Transaction Publishers.

farmers, angry about foreclosures on their farms, forcibly prevented county courts from convening. In 1877 railroad workers, incensed over wage cuts and increased working hours, seized railroad facilities in several cities and confronted armed militias of local governments. In the 1960s, after years of nonviolent protest, some civil rights and antiwar protestors turned to violence. Throughout American history, various groups have resorted to one form of violence or another, generally because they believed the government would not respond to their needs. After analyzing 50 U.S. protest movements, William Gamson (1975) concluded that 75 percent of those groups which used violence got what they wanted, compared with only 53 percent of those which were nonviolent. Violence, it seems, can pay off. In other, repressive regimes, however, it seems safer and more effective to stage nonviolent protests, as in the form of political funerals (see box, above).

Much of the violence in American history has taken the form of riots or brief, violent seizures of property for limited aims, inspired by specific grievances. Violent as our history is, we have seen rather little of two forms of political violence—revolution and terrorism—that have the broader aim of overthrowing the government.

Revolution If a protest movement turns to violence, it may produce a **revolution**—the violent overthrow of the existing government and drastic change in social and political order. There have been numerous studies on revolutions in many different societies. They differ in explaining the causes of revolution, but they all suggest in one way or another that a revolution is likely to occur if the following conditions are met (Goldstone, 1982).

1. *A group of rather well-off and well-educated individuals feel extremely dissatisfied with the society.* They may be intellectuals or opinion leaders such as journalists, poets, playwrights, teachers, clergy, and lawyers. These people would withdraw support from the government, criticize it, and demand reforms. Discontent may also exist within such elites as wealthy landowners, industrialists, leading bureaucrats, and military officials. It is from among all these people that revolutionary leaders emerge.

2. *Revolutionary leaders rely on the masses' rising expectation to convince them that they can end their oppression by bringing down the existing government.* By itself, poverty does not produce revolution. Most of the world, after all, is poor. When people have long lived with misery, they may become fatalists, resigned to their suffering. They may starve without raising a fist or even a whisper against the government. But if their living conditions improve, then fatalism may give way to hope. They may expect a better life. It is in times of such a *rising expectation* that revolutionary leaders may succeed in attracting mass support.

3. *A sudden economic crisis triggers peasant revolts and urban uprisings.* In a social climate of rising expectation, large masses of peasants and workers tend to respond explosively to serious economic problems. When the state raises taxes too high and landlords, in turn, jack up the dues of tenant farmers or take over their lands, the peasants are likely to revolt. When the cost of food and the rate of unemployment soar, food riots and large-scale antigovernment protests would erupt in the cities.

4. *The existing government is weak.* Usually, before a government is overthrown, it has failed to resolve one problem after another and gradually lost legitimacy. As the crisis mounts, the government often tries to initiate reforms. But the effort tends to be too little or too late. It only reinforces people's conviction that the regime is flawed, and encourages demands for even bigger reforms. All this can quicken the government's downfall. As Machiavelli (1469–1527) said in his warning to rulers, "If the necessity for [reforms] comes in troubled times, you are too late for harsh measures. Mild ones will not help you, for they will be considered as forced from you, and no one will be under obligation to you" (Goldstone, 1982).

Terrorism What if the masses do not support the opposition to the government and the government is not weak? In that case, a violent protest is likely to produce not revolution but terrorism. The would-be leaders of a revolution become terrorists, trying on their own to destabilize, if not to topple, the government through violence. Their methods include bombing, kidnapping, airline hijacking, and armed assault. There are more than 100 terrorist groups today. But only a few are well known, such as the anti-Israeli Palestinians, anti-British

On September 17, 1986 a terrorist tossed a bomb from a car into a crowded clothing store in Paris. Four people were killed and at least 50 wounded. The blast was the fifth and last in a ten-day wave of bombings in the city that had left 10 dead and more than 160 injured. Terrorists resemble revolutionaries in being young and well-educated. There is, however, a basic difference between them: while revolutionaries usually have the support of the masses in their attempt to topple a weak government, terrorists do not have mass support in their futile battle against a strong government.

Irish, anti-Turkish Armenians, and anti-Yugoslavian Croatians. Most terrorists are in their early twenties and have attended college. They almost always come from the middle or upper classes (Lodge, 1981). In short, their background resembles that of leaders of revolutions—but the terrorists are self-styled leaders without followers.

In recent years another kind of terrorist has emerged. These terrorists are not powerless individuals futilely fighting a government. Instead, they are individuals carrying out their governments' policies. There are, in effect, terrorist governments. They represent a wide spectrum of international politics, from the radical right to the far left. Militant regimes in Libya, Syria, and Iran—known as the "League of Terror" to the U.S. State Department—have sent terrorists to assassinate their opponents in foreign countries. Syria and Iran may have encouraged the 1983 bombing of the U.S. Marine barracks in Beirut that took 241 lives. Iran is also known to support the terrorists holding American and European hostages in Lebanon. In Argentina, El Salvador, and other rightist-regime countries in Latin America, death squads, with varying degrees of implicit or explicit government support, have kidnapped, tortured, and even killed people. The Soviet Union has long been suspected of funding and arming terrorists, and its most loyal satellite, Bulgaria, has been suspected of masterminding the attempted assassination of John Paul II. In 1983 North Korea dispatched its terrorists to the Burmese capital of Rangoon when South Korea's president and his top officials paid a state visit there. The terrorists succeeded in killing 21 people, including two top presidential advisers and four cabinet officers of the South Korean government (Kelly, 1984).

The rise of terrorism has generated much attention, sparked national and international crises, and boosted the security industry. In 1978 alone, American businesses paid more than $7 billion for security against terrorism abroad (Jenkins, 1979). In 1986 the U.S. Congress appropriated a record $10 million for efforts against terrorism. Our government has also spent huge sums of money training some 3000 people for counterterrorist activities (Thatcher, 1987). In 1986, in response to Libya's terrorist attacks on the Vienna and Rome airports, the United States bombed terrorist-related installations in the Libyan cities of Tripoli and Benghazi. Not surprisingly, the Soviet Union, Syria, and Iran vociferously denounced the air strikes, but our European allies also voiced their criticisms. With heavy media coverage, terrorist activities have created an atmosphere of fear among Americans traveling abroad. After seeing on TV the dead and wounded strewn on bloodstained airport floors, hijacked planes blowing up, frightened hostages and their anguished family members, American tourists find it hard not to fear that they are all at risk. This is what the terrorists have hoped to achieve.

Our government and European governments, however, have generally adopted hard-line, "no ransom, no concessions" policies on terrorism. Since 1986, they have also stepped up their cooperative efforts against terrorism. They have imposed arms embargoes, improved extradition procedures, reduced the size of diplomatic missions of terrorism-supporting countries, and refused to admit any person expelled from another country due to suspected involvement in terrorist activities. These efforts have so far caused a decline in terrorism worldwide—the drop being as much as 40 percent between 1986 and 1987 in Europe (Thatcher, 1987). Nevertheless, "get tough" policies do not always translate into practice in a democratic society like ours. Under the pressure of public opinion, the Reagan administration for several years took a posture of strength, proclaiming a no-concessions all-out war against terrorists. But in 1986 the plight of the hostages and the appeals of their families finally compelled Reagan to secretly swap arms with Iran for the hostages. The Iranians got the weapons but the hostages were not released. The failed ransom attempt brought the president tremendous political embarrassment here and abroad. Humanitarian concerns have also compromised the Israeli government's tough, no-concession stance against terrorists. In 1984, pressured by appeals from hostage families, Israeli officials secretly negotiated with the Palestinian organizations. This resulted in the freeing of nearly 1200 Palestinian prisoners—including terrorists convicted of killing Israeli citizens—in exchange for three Israeli soldiers held by the Palestinians. In early 1986 the prime minister of France also compromised his strong public position against concessions to terrorists. He got the release of French hostages by agreeing to return to Iran the late Shah's billion-dollar investment in France (Oakley, 1987).

QUESTIONS FOR DISCUSSION AND REVIEW

1. What is the process through which individuals acquire political knowledge, beliefs, and attitudes?
2. What forces seem to shape attitudes toward government and its policies?

3. Why do so many Americans fail to participate in politics and government?
4. What social conditions must usually exist before a revolution can occur?
5. When does terrorism emerge as a form of political participation, and why has it become such a problem today?

CHAPTER REVIEW

1. *What are states?* They are political institutions that regulate conflict and allocate resources among citizens. They dictate how the game of politics—the process of determining who gets what, when, how—is to be played. *How is legitimate power different from illegitimate power?* When power is exercised over people with their consent, the power is called legitimate. The legitimate power institutionalized in the state is called authority. It may be derived from tradition, from the charisma of a leader, or from a set of legal rules. *Is economics related to politics?* Yes. In general, the more economically developed a country is, the more likely it is to be a democracy. *Is war "the continuation of state policy by other means"?* Probably yes, because a state's use of mass killings as a way to impose its will on its own citizens is akin to a country's use of war to impose its will on a foreign nation. This may explain the research finding that totalitarian states are more likely than their democratic counterparts to wage war. In addition to totalitarianism, the causes of war include the society's attempt to seek solidarity and other benefits from war, the power elite's exploitation of the masses, a long-standing hostility between two nations, a combination of a fiery ideology and a strong leader, and a high level of military preparedness.

2. *How do American political parties differ from those in Europe?* European democracies typically have several important political parties, and those parties have a rather well-defined political ideology. In contrast, in the United States only two parties have influence in national politics, and each usually avoids adhering to a well-defined ideology because each tries to appeal to people with a wide range of interests and opinions. Consequently, the American government is more stable. *How do interest groups influence government?* They try to sway public opinion, support sympathetic candidates, file lawsuits, and hire lobbyists to deal personally with government officials.

3. *According to pluralist theory, who governs America?* Diverse interest groups share power. *Who controls the government according to Mills?* A power elite made up of those who hold top positions in the federal government, the military, and corporations. Mills believed that pluralism reigns in the middle levels of power, but that, above the competing interest groups, there is an elite that makes the important decisions. *According to Marxists, what is wrong with Mills's power-elite theory?* It does not recognize that the power elite serves as the agent for the capitalist class. In Marxists' view, capitalists use the state to maintain their dominance over the other classes.

4. *What are some results of political socialization during childhood?* Children acquire both political information and political attitudes from their families, schools, peers, and the media. *Are political attitudes in the United States divided along class lines?* The upper class tends to be more conservative on economic issues and more liberal on social issues than other classes. But there is wide support among all social classes for a great variety of government programs—and widespread opposition to big government. Thus there is a tendency, across class lines, for Americans to be ideological conservatives but operational liberals. *Are Americans active participants in their government?* No, most limit their participation to voting, and the percentage of those who bother to vote has been low compared with the voting rates in other democracies. In general, those who are poor, young, or have little education vote less than other Americans.

5. *What conditions make revolution likely?* There are four: (1) some disgruntled, well-off, and well-educated individuals; (2) the masses' rising expectation; (3) a sudden economic crisis; and (4) weak government. *What about terrorism?* It is likely to occur if the would-be leader of a revolution does not have the support of the masses and if the government is strong.

KEY TERMS

Authority Legitimate power that derives from traditions, leader's charisma, or laws (p. 398).

Charisma An exceptional personal quality popularly attributed to certain individuals (p. 399).

Coercion Illegitimate use of force or threat of force to compel obedience (p. 398).

Ideological conservative A person who opposes the idea of government intervention in citizens' affairs (p. 414).

Influence The ability to control others' behavior through persuasion rather than coercion or authority (p. 398).

Interest group An organized collection of people who attempt to influence government policy (p. 407).

Operational liberal One who is in favor of governmental programs serving the public (p. 414).

PACs Acronym of political action committees, which are political organizations that funnel money from business, labor, and other special interest groups into election campaigns to help elect or defeat candidates (p. 406).

Political party A group organized for the purpose of gaining government offices (p. 405).

Political power The capacity to use the government to make decisions that affect the whole society (p. 408).

Political socialization A learning process by which a person acquires political knowledge, beliefs, and attitudes (p. 413).

Politics Process in which people acquire and exercise power, determining who gets what, when, and how (p. 398).

Power The ability to control the behavior of others, even against their will (p. 398).

Revolution The violent overthrow of an existing government and drastic change in the social and political order (p. 417).

SUGGESTED READINGS

Domhoff, G. William. 1983. *Who Rules America Now? A View for the Eighties.* Englewood Cliffs, N.J.: Prentice-Hall. An excellent update on Domhoff's classic theory that the upper class rules America.

Hollander, Paul. 1983. *The Many Faces of Socialism.* New Brunswick, N.J.: Transaction Books. A foremost specialist's critical essays on the totalitarian nature of the Soviet Union and Eastern European societies.

Kelley, Stanley, Jr. 1983. *Interpreting Elections.* Princeton, N.J.: Princeton University Press. A data-packed, well-written analysis of U.S. presidential elections and their significance for American democracy.

Lipset, Seymour Martin. 1981. *Political Man: The Social Bases of Politics.* Baltimore, Md.: Johns Hopkins University Press. Originally published in 1960, this important sociological analysis of politics has been expanded to deal with recent political developments here and abroad.

Page, Benjamin I. 1983. *Who Gets What from Government.* Berkeley: University of California Press. Full of interesting data on how American government policies affect people's income and how political factors such as political parties, interest groups, and public opinion influence the policies.

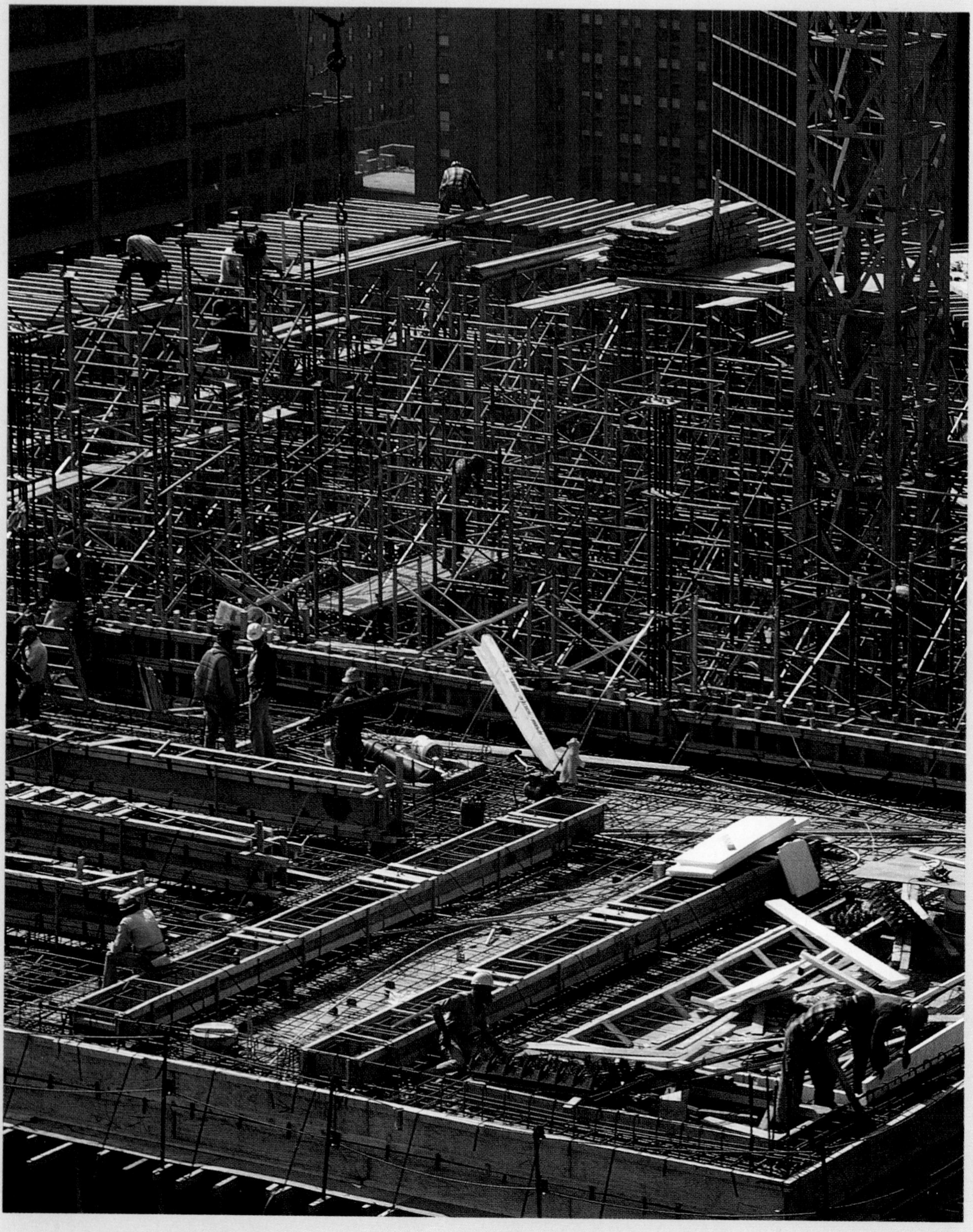

17 The Economy and Work

Thanks to technological innovations, today one farmer can produce enough food for more than 60 people. Such a high agricultural productivity has pushed numerous workers off the farm. In earlier decades many of them went to work in construction and in manufacturing industries, making cars, clothes, and the like. Since 1945, however, the share of jobs held by these blue-collar workers has begun to shrink, while the number of jobs held by white-collar workers—such as managers, salespersons, and clerical workers—has steadily increased. Today white-collar workers outnumber blue collars by 3 to 1.

We must eat in order to survive. Beyond basic needs of this kind, we have developed countless others—needs for clothing, housing, schooling, medical care, entertainment, and innumerable other goods and services. To meet these needs, societies evolve systems for producing goods and services and distributing them. These systems are called **economic institutions.** In studying them, economists tend to focus on impersonal economic factors like productivity, wages, prices, and profits. Sociologists are more interested in the social aspects of the economy—in how people work, how their occupations affect their lives, and how the economy is related to other aspects of society (Granovetter, 1985). Thus we begin this chapter by discussing how the industrial revolution changed human societies. Then we examine contemporary economic systems. Finally, we look at the economic situation in the United States through its big corporations and labor force.

CONTEMPORARY ECONOMIC SYSTEM

To understand the economic world today, we need to look back at least to the eighteenth century, when the **Industrial Revolution** took hold in England. That revolution transformed not only the world's economies but also its societies.

The Industrial Revolution

For 98 percent of the last 10,000 years, the pattern of economic life changed rather little: practically all our ancestors eked out a mere subsistence living from relatively primitive economies such as hunting and gathering or agriculture (see Chapter 4: Social Structure). During all those years, as sociologists Raymond Mack and Calvin Bradford (1979) pointed out, "the whole economic process was wrapped up in the individual." This was especially true for craftworkers: they owned their own tools, secured their own raw materials, worked in their homes, set their own working hours, and found their own markets for finished products.

But gradually, as the population grew and the demand for goods increased, individual craftworkers became more and more dependent on middlemen to find raw materials and to sell their finished products. Some of these intermediaries took over the economic process, telling craftworkers what to produce and how much. In essence, these intermediaries became capitalists, and the formerly independent craftworkers became employees. Craftworkers, however, still worked separately in their own homes, forming what is called a cottage industry.

As the Industrial Revolution was about to dawn in England, cottage industry began to give way to a factory system. Capitalists found it more economical to hire people to work together in one building than to collect goods from many scattered cottages. They began to own every part of the manufacturing process: the factory, the tools, the raw materials, and the finished products. In effect, they even owned the landless workers, who had only their labor to sell in order to survive. (For the working conditions of these laborers, see box, p. 425.) To make the process more efficient, capitalists increased the division of labor. Some individuals were hired to spin thread, others to weave cloth, and one person to oversee all the workers as their supervisor.

Then, with the invention of steam engines, spinning jennies, and other machines, mass production became possible, and the Industrial Revolution was under way. It began in England around 1760, and during the following century it profoundly changed the economic structure of Western Europe and North America. The Industrial Revolution brought the substitution of machines for human labor to perform many tasks, the great improvement in the getting and working of raw materials, the widespread development of railroad and steamship to transport huge quantities of raw materials and manufactured goods, and the movement of labor and resources from agriculture to industry. All this created tremendous wealth in the West. At the same time, the small machines were replaced by big ones, the little mills became giant factories, and the modest partnerships changed into large corporations.

Consequences The results of industrialization are far-reaching. First, it changes the nature of work. The mechanization of agriculture calls for few operators, causing most people to leave farming for industrial work. Bigger and better machines in the factory, in the mines, and at construction sites further require fewer workers, which reduces the number of blue-collar jobs. But since technology is highly productive, it brings prosperity, which increases the demand for all kinds of services from

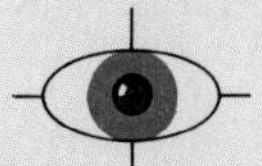

USING SOCIOLOGICAL INSIGHT

Work in the Eighteenth Century

The early days of industrialism were marked by great social changes and harsh working conditions. In England, where the Industrial Revolution began, these changes touched every aspect of life. The following account provides a glimpse of the conditions of work in the mid-eighteenth century. How are today's conditions of the workplace different?

Duty hours—especially for servants-of-all-works—were gruellingly long. Dawn to dusk was a common span, though in certain trades journeymen's combinations [unions] had secured a ten-hour day. Household servants were hardly allowed lives of their own. Working conditions were often hellish—the flames and sulphurous fumes of vats and furnaces, the lethal damps and gases of the coal-field, the perils of the sea, doubled by undermanned, water-logged but well-insured vessels. Workmen in physical trades such as sawyers became prematurely wizened, succumbing to ghastly industrial diseases; fumes and dust brought on lung and bronchial conditions, many lead-miners for example contracting plumbism, and no new legislation protecting against occupational diseases and hazards was introduced. Around ports, common seamen were never safe from the shanghai'ing press-gangs. Women's earnings in particular were derisory; they got only about two-thirds the wages of men. Workers had no compensation against slumps or seasonal under-employment, when snow, floods, or drought halted trade (the well-off working man was the one in employment twelve months in the year). Men were subjected to brutality from their masters (soldiers and sailors were flogged as matters of routine), women, especially servants, were prey to sexual exploitation. Further hardships were piled on, for instance payment by truck [in goods] rather than in coin, or long in arrears (though this did enforce a form of savings). Even Dean Tucker, a friend of capitalism, admitted that in some industries the relationship between master and worker "approached much nearer to that of a planter and slaves in our American colonies than might be expected of such a country as England."

Source: Reprinted from Roy Porter, *English Society in the Eighteenth Century*, Baltimore, Md.: Penguin Books, 1984, p. 101.

education and health to entertainment and money management. Thus white-collar occupations proliferate. Even in manufacturing companies, white-collar workers outnumber blue collars. The General Electric Company, for example, produces numerous different items from turbines to light bulbs, but the majority of its employees are engaged in services from accounting to marketing—less than 40 percent work in production. Of the factory workers in the United States today, no more than 7 percent are subjected to the physical and psychological strain of working on the assembly line. Better-educated white-collar workers tend to be self-directed, demanding the freedom to decide what work to do, how to do it, and even when to do it. Increasingly, their bosses let them have considerable autonomy in their work—and address requests rather than give orders to them (Ginzberg, 1982).

Industrialization also brings about demographic changes—changes in the characteristics of a population. In general, as a society industrializes, cities grow, and fewer people live on farms. The population as a whole further increases when a society industrializes. But once a society has developed an industrialized economy, population growth tends to slow, and the percentage of elderly people in the population rises.

Industrialization also changes human relations. In industrial societies people usually spend much of their time in huge, bureaucratic organizations. They interact with a broad range of people, but their relationships with these people tend to be formal, fragmentary, and superficial. Ties to primary groups loosen (see Chapter 4: Social Structure). Industrialization alters other institutions as well. Formal schooling tends to become more important, and functions once served by the family are taken over by other institutions, such as business and government (see Chapter 13: The Family). According to a study of 50 countries, industrialization also creates international inequality, with highly industrialized nations enjoying higher status and more power than the less industrialized (Rau and Roncek, 1987).

Finally, industrialization changes the values of a society. Traditional values and ways of living are discredited. People learn to view change as natural and to hope for a better future. Thus industrialization brings a dynamism into society. It produces greater energy and openmindedness but also restlessness and discontent. Social and political conflict often follows. So, too, does the "social notion of gain." In Robert Heilbroner's (1972) words, "The idea of gain, the idea that each man not only may, but should, constantly strive to better his material lot, . . . [as] an ubiquitous characteristic of society, is as modern an invention as printing."

A *Postindustrial World* Many countries have been trying to achieve in a few years the industrialization that developed over two centuries in the West. Social instability has been one result. In Iran, for example, the clash between the new values encouraged by industrialization and the values of traditional Islam helped bring on a revolution. Many developing countries are plagued by widespread poverty, high rates of unemployment, military coups, and wars. A basic cause is "the partial character of their modernization." They have imported Western technology to lower death rates but not birth rates, so that population growth has eaten up or outstripped their gains in income. They have instituted Western-style education, enough to let people dream of a better life but not enough to create and operate a modern economy. They have seen the rewards of an industrial technology—and developed a craving for what they believe to be a material paradise—but they do not have the means to satisfy their appetite (Landes, 1969).

Meanwhile, the advanced countries continue to industrialize and have taken the process a step further. During industrialization, machines take over tasks that humans have performed, and people control the machines. Now the task of controlling the machines is increasingly given over to computers. A growing number of factory workers will sit at computer terminals in clean, quiet offices. They will monitor tireless, precise robots doing the kind of work that assembly-line workers do with dirty, noisy machines. It seems that the advanced nations such as the United States are moving into a new era, a "postindustrial" age. Postindustrial societies are marked by a high degree of affluence and leisure, the rise of technical and professional people to a dominant social position, and extensive reliance on automation (Bell, 1973).

One major characteristic of the "postindustrial" age will be widespread reliance on automation. We will interact frequently with computers or machines controlled by computers, where previously we would have expected to deal with a person. Of course, many transactions will become more impersonal. The automatic bank teller (above) won't smile and talk about the weather when you step up to it. Nevertheless, it is more convenient for customers, since it provides service 24 hours a day, even when the bank is closed. Automation will free many employees from monotonous work and contribute to a higher degree of affluence and leisure for society as a whole.

Capitalism and Socialism

No factory exists on its own. It must buy raw materials and sell its products. It is enmeshed in a complicated network of exchanges. This network must be organized in some way, but how? There are two basic alternatives. The economy may be organized through markets. A market economy is driven by the countless decisions made by individuals to buy and sell. This is **capitalism.** Alternatively, the economy may be controlled by the authority of the government. This is **socialism.** In fact, all economies in the world represent some mixture of these basic alternatives. But to understand them better, we look first at how two great theorists interpreted the essence of capitalism.

Adam Smith and Capitalism At the core of capitalism lies a belief about the psychology of human beings: we are inherently selfish and act to serve our own interests. Capitalism works by allowing this pursuit of self-interest to flourish. It does so through two key characteristics: (1) private ownership of property and (2) free competition in buying and selling goods and services. Without these, capitalism does not exist.

Private ownership is considered important for the health of the economy because it motivates people to be efficient and productive. This is often taken to explain why Federal Express and other private companies in the United States are generally more successful than the U.S. Postal Service and other government-owned enterprises. Private ownership is also used to explain why the small, privately owned lands in the Soviet Union and China are far more productive than the large state-owned farms. Although private plots make up less than 3 percent of Russia's arable land, they produce about 50 percent of the country's meat, milk, and green vegetables and about 80 percent of its eggs and potatoes. In China the private plots constitute only 5 percent of all cultivated land but produce some 25 percent of noncereal products (Hollander, 1982).

Free competition is also believed beneficial to the economy because it compels businesses to make the most efficient use of resources, to produce the best possible goods and services, and to sell them at the lowest price possible. Only by doing so can they expect to beat their competitors. Competition, then, acts like an "invisible hand," bringing profits to the efficient producers and putting the inefficient ones out of business.

Doesn't the pursuit of self-interest reduce society to a jungle and harm the public good? Adam Smith argued that the answer is a resounding no. In 1776, in *The Wealth of Nations,* he argued that when there is free competition, the self-serving decisions of individuals to buy and sell end up promoting the public good. How does this work? Because there is competition, people must take account of others' interests in order to serve their own. If Apple Computer does not meet your needs, you can buy a product from Texas Instruments or IBM—and Apple knows it. It is in their interest to serve your interests. Since many businesses strive to serve their own interests by serving those of the public, the whole society will benefit. There will be an abundance of high-quality, low-priced goods and services, which will entice many people to buy. Businesses will then produce more to meet consumers' increased demand, which will create more jobs and raise wages. The result is a prosperous economy for the society as a whole. As the editors of the *Wall Street Journal* (1986) say, "By doing well for themselves, capitalists as risk-taking entrepreneurs create jobs and new opportunities for others. A rising tide does lift all boats."

The government, in Smith's view, should therefore adopt a *laissez-faire,* or hands-off, policy toward markets. Left to themselves, the markets will provide a self-regulating mechanism that serves society's interests. If government interferes by, say, imposing price control, businesses will lose their incentive to produce. The energy shortage in the 1970s, for example, has been blamed on government control of oil and gas prices.

Karl Marx and Socialism When Smith looked at specialized division of labor in industrial capitalism, he saw a key unlocking economic well-being to masses of ordinary people. To Smith, specialization enhances *efficiency* in the generation of wealth. When Karl Marx looked at specialization, he saw a source of **alienation of labor.** Because workers own neither their tools nor the products they make and because they cannot exercise all their capacities as they choose but are forced to perform an isolated, specific task, their work is no longer their own. Instead, it becomes a separate, alien thing.

Other aspects of industrial capitalism also looked starkly different to Marx than they did to Smith. Where Smith saw a self-regulating system internally propelled on an upward spiral of prosperity, Marx saw a system that had within it severe contradictions and would create "its own gravediggers." One contradiction grows from capitalism's devotion to individualism. As Heilbroner (1972) said, "factories necessitated social planning, and private property abhorred it; *capitalism* had become so complex that it needed direction, but *capitalists* insisted on a ruinous freedom." Marx saw another contradiction as well. Capitalists depend on profit, but according to Marx, their profit comes from the fact that workers put more value into products than they are given in the form of wages. To increase their profits, capitalists often hold down wages, and, whenever possible, substitute machines for human labor as well. As a result, the poor get poorer from lower wages or job loss. This, in turn, reduces the demand for the capitalists' products, thereby decreasing their profits. The economy can work itself out of this crisis, but such crises will recur, with each one getting worse until the workers revolt.

Ultimately, Marx believed, the contradictions of capitalism would lead to communism, to a classless society that would operate on the principle of "from each according to his ability, to each according to his needs." In this society the state would wither away. First, however, the destruction of capitalism would be followed by a temporary era of socialism.

No state, including the so-called communist countries such as the Soviet Union and China, has reached communism yet, but many have tried socialism. In a socialist economy, the state owns and operates the means of production and distribution, such as land, factories, railroads, airlines, banks, and stores. It determines what the nation's economic needs are and develops plans to meet those goals. It sets wages and prices. Individual interests are subordinate to those of society.

Economies in the Real World

In fact, no state has a purely socialist or purely capitalist economy. In all socialist economies, there is still some buying and selling outside of government control and individual ownership of property. In Poland, for example, independent-minded farmers produce much of the country's food supplies on private plots. In the cities of Hungary, taxi drivers, artisans, shopkeepers, and restaurants operate almost as freely as their counterparts in the capitalist West. In China a growing number of peasants own farms and sell their produce in a free market, and an increasing number of privately owned retail stores, restaurants, and service shops have opened up in the cities. Even in the Soviet Union, perhaps the most anticapitalist, some service industries keep the profits they earn, rather than turning them over to the government. Nevertheless, in all the communist countries, the state still owns and controls key industries such as steel and oil, and bans large, privately owned companies (Knight, 1985).

On the other hand, no government in capitalist societies has followed a strictly laissez-faire policy. In the United States, for example, government policies provided the canals, roads, railroads, cheap land, and education that laid the foundation for America's economic growth. When the American public became disgusted with outrageous railroad freight fares, contaminated meat, and similar problems around the turn of the century, the government stepped in with new laws to regulate business. When capitalism failed in the Great Depression of the 1930s, the government established an array of programs to regulate business practices and to provide people with a cushion against the impact of hard times. When people realized that Smith's "invisible hand" did not prevent business from producing dangerous levels of pollution and wasted resources, environmental regulations were passed.

Classifying Economies Although all economic systems are **mixed economies,** containing elements of both capitalism and socialism, the "mix" between these elements varies considerably. Thus we can arrange economies along a continuum from most capitalist to most socialist.

All economies are mixed. The United States is committed to a capitalist philosophy, but the government continually intervenes in the economy on every level. Usually it establishes rules by which business may be conducted. However, in the 1930s, when the government was faced with widespread unemployment, it created various agencies that hired the jobless to work for the government directly. The Civilian Conservation Corps (below) hired young men to help build the national parks system and to reclaim land ruined by destructive farming methods.

The United States and Japan are among the most capitalist. Yet, as we have seen, the United States does not follow a laissez-faire policy, and competition is limited in many ways. In Japan the government takes a leading role in planning investment for the future, in turning corporations toward industries that are likely to grow.

Ranging along the middle of the continuum are the European democracies. From time to time, several of these democracies have had socialist governments. In general, these nations have combined capitalist enterprise with wide-ranging government control—and high taxes. They tend to establish stricter controls on business and more extensive social services than the United States. All these states, for example, provide a national system of health insurance. Over the years their governments have owned and managed many industries. Great Britain, for example, has had the coal, steel, automobile, and television industries under government control at various times. Even before France elected a socialist government in 1981, its government had created subway and aerospace industries. Nevertheless, these European democracies are so much more capitalist than socialist that they are usually considered capitalist.

At the socialist end of the continuum we find the Soviet Union, China, Cuba, and Eastern European nations. Their government clearly controls the economy. But some—particularly Hungary, Yugoslavia, and China—have experimented with a new economic arrangement in which centralized direction of the economy by the government is reduced. The most dramatic is China's recent adoption of some free-enterprise practices. It has abolished most rural communes, restored family farms, established a free market in agricultural and consumer goods, granted state-owned enterprises wide autonomy in running their business, and opened up its coastal regions to foreign investors. A major reason for this experiment with capitalism has been the poor performance of China's socialist economy (Knight, 1985).

Economic Performance The socialist economies have a decidedly mixed record. Their total wealth is generally far below that of capitalist countries (see Figure 17.1). True, under socialism, nations such as Cuba and China have improved the standard of living for vast numbers of people who had been destitute. In general, socialist nations have reduced the extremes of poverty, inflation, or

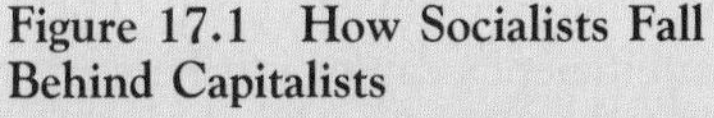

Figure 17.1 How Socialists Fall Behind Capitalists

The total wealth of socialist economies is far below that of capitalist nations. Using the value of a country's gross national product for each person (GNP per capita) as an indicator of its wealth, we can see that socialist economies fall considerably behind capitalist ones.

Source: The World Factbook: 1987 (Washington, D.C.: U.S. Government Printing Office, 1987).

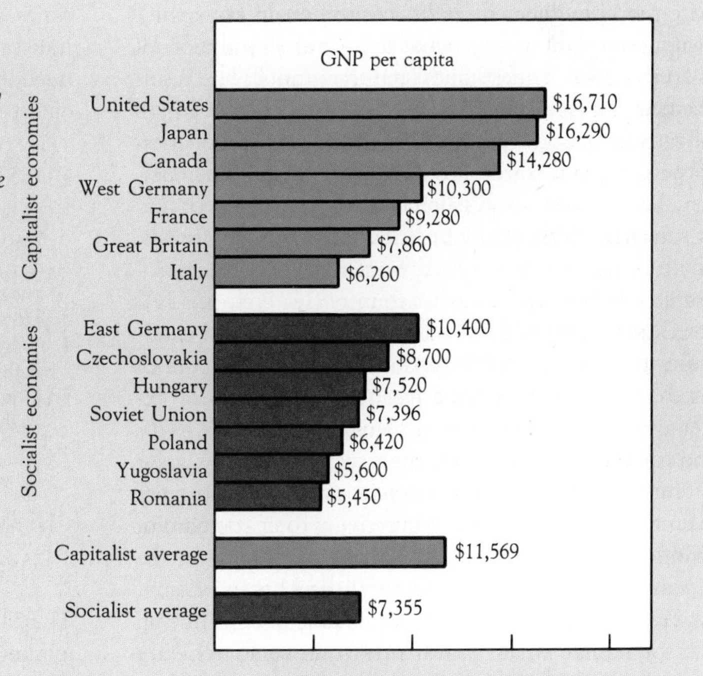

In general, socialist countries have reduced the extremes of poverty, inflation, or unemployment that occasionally hit capitalist nations. But their state-run, centralized economies are far from efficient and productive. Thus severe shortages of consumer goods and foodstuffs are common. Ordinary citizens must spend hours in line, waiting to buy goods that are easily available in capitalist countries. The people above are waiting to get into a butcher shop in Warsaw, Poland.

unemployment that occasionally hit capitalist states. But significant economic inequalities still remain. Managers make much more money than ordinary workers. They also have special privileges and access to luxury goods that ordinary citizens cannot get. Furthermore, the central planning of socialist states often creates inefficiencies and bottlenecks. Perhaps their greatest problem is production. Severe shortages plague many socialist states, especially Poland and the Soviet Union. The absence of adequate incentives comparable to private-property ownership, as we have observed, is the major cause of the low productivity of the Soviet Union's state-run farms. In China, after it began to dismantle its state-run communes in 1979, farmers could have their own farms, plant more of what they wanted, sell more of it on the open market, and keep the profits. The result has been encouraging. Between 1981 and 1985 China's wheat production went up 43 percent, meat production 39 percent, and cotton production 40 percent (Samuelson, 1987). After seeing such benefits from the adoption of some capitalist practices, the new Soviet leader Mikhail Gorbachev has started to agitate for similar economic reforms in his socialist country (see box, p. 431).

Gorbachev could also have seen that capitalist economies have little trouble producing ample quantities of goods, although they have faced periodic bouts of extreme inflation and unemployment, as in the late 1970s and early 1980s. Moreover, their social peace to a great extent has depended on economic growth, which gives even the poor some hope of improving their standard of living. Their ability to sustain this growth may not be certain all the time. Around 1980 the U.S. economy, for example, seemed to get stuck, unable to continue up the spiral that Adam Smith predicted would generate more productivity and more wealth. In fact, its productivity went down, increasing unemployment as well as inflation. But in 1983 the U.S. economy began to make a dramatic comeback, showing a substantial growth in productivity and a decline in unemployment and inflation. The economies in Canada, Western Europe, and Japan also rebounded (Alvarez and Cooper, 1984; Knight, 1984). Despite the ups and downs of their economic conditions, these capitalist countries always remain considerably more productive than their socialist counterparts. According to a recent study by the Worldwatch Institute, Western European countries' labor productivity rates are often twice as high as those of Eastern Europe, and the United States is nearly 20 times more productive than the Soviet Union. The capitalist system's higher efficiency can be attributed to the freedom for pursuing personal gain or the absence of socialist-style government control (Rheem, 1986).

QUESTIONS FOR DISCUSSION AND REVIEW

1. How did the Industrial Revolution change the economic institutions of societies?
2. Why do some sociologists feel that advanced societies have now developed postindustrial economies?
3. How does capitalism differ from socialism?
4. Why do economies in the real world incorporate both socialist and capitalist principles?
5. How do sociologists classify economies, and how well has each type performed in recent history?

THE DOMINANCE OF BIG CORPORATIONS

There is an inherent contradiction in the competitive market system: the more efficient it is, the more it threatens to destroy itself. Through free competition,

UNDERSTANDING OTHER SOCIETIES

Can the Russians Reform?

The Soviet Union has the world's largest centrally planned economy, and it has long encountered severe problems such as low worker productivity and poor management. The current leadership is attempting to reform the economy, and in this reading, the famous economist John Kenneth Galbraith discusses the nature of the problems that the Soviets face. What impact might these economic reforms have on Soviet society?

There is no doubt that economic and political changes in the Soviet Union, or, in any case, the effort to bring them about, are very great. I am not sure that our press and television have even yet given them wholly adequate emphasis. Certainly in Russia these changes are the topic of unprecedented comment and conversation. A young Soviet economist told me that for the first time in his life he was turning each day to the political news rather than to sports or cultural affairs. Nothing else at the moment seemed so exciting.

The Soviet bureaucratic problem is our own, writ large. The Gorbachev reforms, nearly all of them, will run up against the tendencies and compulsions of bureaucracy. Gorbachev seeks to reduce the personnel and power of the great ministerial bureaucracies by giving industrial enterprises the right to determine what they will produce and how much, and by giving them the encouragement of having and sharing the resulting return. With this would go the right to pay workers in accordance with their productivity.

All of this is, or *sounds*, eminently sensible; but here enters the dynamics of bureaucracy, or, more literally, the absence thereof. In the vast Soviet organization are many people, many in positions of comfort and security as well as power, who find things eminently satisfactory as they are, and who rejoice in the power they now exercise, the privileges they now enjoy. On such persons and their initiative rests in no small part the responsibility for change. Thus a formidable contradiction: change must come in some measure from those who least want change.

Matters are made worse, as Russians are not hesitant to say, by memories of past reforms. There have been movements for change before—more freedom to make production decisions at the plant level, more relief from upstream control. And then there have been pullbacks, with rebuke, possibly even punishment, for those who exploited self-interest, reaped the resulting economic rewards, and were thus visibly unfaithful to socialist principle. Now it behooves one to be cautious; perhaps, the Gorbachev eloquence notwithstanding, there will be another reversal. To bureaucratic inertia is added the force of personal caution.

There is a powerful force working for reform that receives little mention. This is the tendency for American and Western European living standards to become, relentlessly and inescapably, the test of Soviet performance. Western living standards embrace a vast diversity of goods and services, with an even greater diversity of styles and designs and with a huge and intricate structure of support and maintenance services. For a rigid planning system as has existed in Russia, these are difficult, perhaps even impossible, to replicate. The answer, the only answer, is to release production to independent response to demand—in some measure, to the market.

As to the prospect for reform, no one can be sure despite the many who are available to say. I would not be entirely pessimistic. At the top and also at the bottom there clearly are many who want change. This pressure will surely continue. I see no reason why Americans should not wish the effort well. I cannot think that a contented and prosperous Russia would be a menace to us. The menace will be those Americans whose intellectual capital, as it is often called, is locked into an assumption of failure, into the belief that whatever happens in the Soviet Union must somehow be bad for the rest of the world.

Source: Adapted from John Kenneth Galbraith, "Can the Russians reform?" *Harper's Magazine,* June 1987, pp. 52–55. Copyright © 1987 by *Harper's Magazine.* All rights reserved. Reprinted from the June issue by special permission.

the best producers gain more resources, which gives them an edge on their competitors. They may use this edge to drive their competitors out of business or to buy them out and prevent other potential producers from entering the market. Eventually, just one firm might dominate production of a product, achieving a **monopoly.** It is far more likely that a handful of firms control a certain market, forming an **oligopoly.** The number of car companies, for example, plummeted from hundreds in the early 1900s to only three today. As sociologists Al-

GRIFFITH COLLEGE DUBLIN South Circular Road, Dublin 8. Tel.4545640 Fax.4549265 bert Szymanski and Ted Goertzel (1979) have observed, "A similar concentration goes on in almost every industry, although it is often concealed from the consumers by a proliferation of brand names used by the same company. Independent grocers are driven out of business by supermarkets, family restaurants by franchised fast food outlets, small shops by shopping centers. Small business survives only by filling odd niches in the economy, or by picking up the less profitable fringes of the business."

Indeed, big corporations dominate the economy in the United States and other capitalist countries today. In the United States, for example, 2000 corporations, which represent only 0.1 percent of all companies in the country, own 40 percent of all company assets and 88 percent of all business income (Useem, 1980). The largest 100—considerably less than 1 percent—of the manufacturing companies hold more than 47 percent of the nation's manufacturing assets (Census Bureau, 1988). (For the top 50 corporations, see Table 17.1.)

The Nature of Big Corporations

A big corporation does not have a single owner. Instead, it has thousands or even hundreds of thousands of stockholders. They do not communicate with one another, much less organize to control the corporation. But they can exercise their right to vote—usually for electing a board of directors to run the corporation. The directors make overall plans for the company. They may decide how to raise money, how to expand the company, or what dividends are to be paid to shareowners. The directors also appoint the president, vice president, and other officers to conduct the company's day-to-day operations. In corporations, then, ownership and control are separated.

Perhaps more important, neither owners nor managers are personally responsible for what the corporation does. The law treats the corporation as a "fictitious legal person," existing independently of its owners and managers. The latter are granted a right to profit from the

Table 17.1 The Top 50 American Corporations

Rank	Company	Sales ($million)	Rank	Company	Sales ($million)
1	General Motors	101,782	26	Atlantic Richfield	16,282
2	Exxon	76,416	27	Wal-Mart Stores	16,065
3	Ford Motor	73,145	28	RJR Nabisco	15,766
4	IBM	54,217	29	GTE	15,421
5	Mobil	51,223	30	Boeing	15,355
6	Sears, Roebuck	48,440	31	JC Penney	15,332
7	General Electric	39,315	32	Xerox	15,125
8	Texaco	34,372	33	Tenneco	14,790
9	American Tel & Tel	33,598	34	American Stores	14,272
10	EI du Pont	30,224	35	USX	13,898
11	Citicorp	27,519	36	Dow Chemical	13,377
12	Chrysler	26,277	37	Eastman Kodak	13,305
13	Chevron	26,015	38	McDonnell Douglas	13,146
14	K mart	25,864	39	BellSouth	12,269
15	Philip Morris Cos	22,279	40	Nynex	12,084
16	Aetna Life & Cas	22,114	41	Rockwell Intl	11,936
17	Amoco	20,174	42	PepsiCo	11,485
18	ITT	19,525	43	Lockheed	11,321
19	Procter & Gamble	17,892	44	American Intl Group	11,278
20	American Express	17,768	45	Federated Dept Stores	11,118
21	Kroger	17,660	46	Allied-Signal	11,116
22	Travelers	17,459	47	Chase Manhattan	10,745
23	United Technologies	17,170	48	Phillips Petroleum	10,721
24	Occidental Petroleum	17,096	49	Westinghouse	10,679
25	Cigna	16,909	50	Dayton Hudson	10,677

Source: Excerpted by permission of *Forbes* magazine, April 25, 1988, pp. 136–137. © Forbes, Inc., 1988.

corporation's assets, but their responsibility for its liabilities is limited. If a company goes bankrupt as a result of mismanagement, the creditors may get what they can from the assets of the corporation—but they may not touch the personal property of the managers and shareholders. Only the managers are personally liable for breaking the law, such as fixing prices or defrauding investors (Aram, 1983).

The corporation has proved to be an ingenious creation for the accumulation of wealth. It may, of course, simply increase its profits through more sales and more efficient operations. But many corporations have chosen to grow primarily through other means. They merge with other companies, or they buy up smaller ones. Since the early 1970s mergers and acquisitions have been redrawing the map of corporate America. In 1975 there were only 14 mergers involving a purchase price of more than $100 million; in 1977 there were 41 mergers of that size; in 1978 the number soared to 80, and in 1980 to 94 (Wingo, 1981). In 1983 there were a total of 2533 mergers of all sizes. To the corporations involved in these activities, it is cheaper to buy an existing company than to start a new one or expand the one they have, because interest rates are high and investment in new ventures or in research and development is risky (Greenwald, 1984b). Most mergers and acquisitions make the corporations more efficient, more competitive with their Japanese and European rivals. But a new breed of corporate raider has emerged in recent years. Such raiders are more interested in making a quick profit than cleansing the economy of inefficient managers. This can have crippling consequences. Many corporate executives are preoccupied with these raiders, wasting huge resources to ward off takeover attempts rather than concentrating on competing more successfully abroad (Etzioni, 1987).

"The merger has been approved in principle. The hang-up is over who is swallowing who."

The big corporation is a far cry from what Adam Smith expected. To him, a typical company would be small, started by one or a few individuals with their personal savings. These entrepreneurs would personally manage it and reap profits or suffer losses, depending on how well they would do in a competitive market. Thus the rise of giant corporations today can have serious consequences that Smith did not anticipate. First, the few dominant companies, relatively free from competitive challenges, can force consumers to pay high prices for their products. They may slow down production and then increase the prices for their "scarce" goods. This is what the oil, steel, and other mining and manufacturing companies did in the 1970s. More recently, according to Paul McGrath (1984), head of the Justice Department's Antitrust Division, protection from foreign competition has enabled the three giant American automobile companies to charge for each car about $1000 more than they would have if there were no restraints on imports of Japanese cars. Price hikes can generate inflation, and production slowdowns can cause unemployment, both of which can throw society into an economic crisis as they did in the 1970s.

Moreover, given their control over large shares of the market, giant corporations may not have the incentives to build new plants, increase research and development of new products, make themselves more efficient, and offer consumers better goods and services. This may partly explain why some giant U.S. industries—cars and steel in particular—have had a hard time competing with Japanese and other foreign firms. Huge corporations also pour too much money into sales efforts. Through massive advertising, they persuade people that one never has enough or one can always consume more. Consequently, Americans spend far more than they earn and fall deeply into debt. In 1986, for example, their disposable personal income was $2,645 billion, but their total consumer debt amounted to $2,741 billion (Census Bureau, 1988). The government is also a superconsumer, spending enormous sums on defense, health, and welfare. The whole country has been spending so much that by the end of 1986 its net foreign debts soared to more than $200 billion. This is astounding because, four years earlier, our country had net foreign *assets* of almost $150 billion. All those huge debts will eventually come home to roost—depressing our economy and lowering our living standard—unless we spend less, save more, and produce more (Clark, 1987).

However, big corporations also contribute to the well-being of the U.S. economy and society. As historian Robert Hessen (1979) has observed, "combining the capital of millions of investors and the talents of millions of workers, giant corporations are a testament to the ability of free people, motivated by self-interest, to engage in sustained, large-scale, peaceful cooperation for their mutual benefit and enrichment." Of course, not all the U.S. corporations are equally successful. In some corporations, management and workers are indeed not cooperative enough. On the whole, however, American corporations have made it possible for us to "enjoy a standard of living—of luxury, leisure, and longevity—that is unprecedented in world history and unparalleled in contemporary socialist societies" (Hessen, 1979).

While cooperation *within* the corporations helps ensure our prosperity, perhaps more beneficial to our economy is the fierce competition that still exists *between* corporations. Despite their giant status, most American corporations do compete with each other and with foreign companies. Zenith and RCA cannot ignore Sony's and Panasonic's sales inroads; Kodak must respond to Polaroid's challenge; Wilkinson blades must slug it out with Gillette and Schick; and Xerox, the pioneer of photocopying, now faces stiff competition from Ricoh, Canon, and other corporations. In their battle for customers, big corporations do not restrict themselves to producing the best products and selling them at the lowest price possible. They also contribute over a billion dollars a year to universities and colleges, charitable organizations, and public-service projects. Corporate philanthropy may be intended to stimulate sales by generating good will, but it does help improve the nation's health, education, and welfare (Burt, 1983). Since corporations are considered vitally important, they receive a great deal of help from the government as we will see next.

Welfare for the Rich

Corporations are a product of law and thus of government. By establishing property rights and enforcing contracts, governments provided the economic security that allowed corporations and other aspects of the market system to arise in the first place. They also set the laws under which corporations operate today. The U.S. government uses antitrust laws to prevent monopolies and preserve competition. It enacts environmental, health, and labor laws to control the effect of corporate activities on resources, workers, and the population at large.

Being the corporate police, however, is only a small part of the government's role in the economy. It is itself a large buyer, seller, and producer of goods and services, and it is a huge employer. Through these economic activities, it has an effect on the economy much as a large corporation does. In addition, through its taxing and spending policies and its control of the nation's monetary system, the government influences the economic environment for the nation as a whole. The government can use its policies to encourage or discourage economic growth, to favor the rich or the poor, to encourage investment in homes or in industries, among other things.

How does it use this power? The answer varies somewhat from administration to administration. Occasionally, mostly in wartime, the government has imposed wage and price controls in order to prevent shortages and control inflation. Several times since the Great Depression it has stimulated the economy to increase the number of jobs. It has enacted many programs that help the disadvantaged and an income tax system that, theoretically, takes the most from those who are most able to pay.

Does this mean that the government uses its economic power primarily to the benefit of the poor, equalizing the unequal distribution of economic power created by the market system? No. The distribution of income and wealth in the United States has remained essentially the same for decades. Many Americans still live in poverty, and the number of homeless people is growing. The Reagan administration's economic program has further shifted the tax burden. When a Wall

Street firm tallied and analyzed the net effects of the 1981 and 1982 tax and budget cuts, it found that well-off families (with annual incomes of more than $47,900) would gain $9.2 billion, while middle-income and poor families would lose $8 billion (Rowan, 1982).

The net effect of the government's many policies is extremely difficult to measure, but consider the nation's two welfare systems. One is the well-known welfare system for the poor and the other is that for the rich. When government help goes to rich individuals, it is usually through a tax credit or deduction or other "loopholes"; when it goes to corporations, it is usually called not welfare but a subsidy. Welfare for the rich is far more generous than welfare for the poor. In 1981, for example, when Uncle Sam doled out about $36 billion in food stamps, Medicaid, and welfare payments to the poor, it gave more than $112 billion in tax breaks to people making more than $50,000 a year. The government is even more generous to big corporations. Corporate income taxes have always been proportionately smaller than personal income taxes. In the last 20 years the corporate income tax as a fraction of the federal revenue has steadily declined, from 23.0 percent in 1966 to 10.2 percent in 1986 (Auerbach, 1983; Census Bureau, 1988). The government also supplies big business with more dollars in direct loans and loan guarantees than all the commercial and industrial loans provided by private banks. Every year the government also pays an enormous sum ($48.5 billion in 1987) for research and development projects in areas such as the military, space, and atomic energy. After developing the technology at taxpayer's expense, corporations are allowed to use it to earn a profit.

The government can even bail out a corporation on the verge of bankruptcy. Generally, the larger a corporation, the larger the number of people who would be hurt by its failure, and the more likely the government is to rescue the corporation from its own mistakes. In 1979, for example, Chrysler had a $4.1 billion payroll, with about 130,000 workers in the United States. In addition, the economic fate of automobile suppliers and dealers scattered across the country was tied to Chrysler. Hundreds of companies fail every year, but when Chrysler seemed about to go under, the government offered a helping hand with $1.5 billion in loan guarantees (Gregg, 1980). Thus our free enterprise system might be called "corporate socialism." To some extent risk has been "socialized"—borne by all of us—but profit remains "privatized," claimed by corporate stockholders. Giant corporations are even more likely to get substantial government support if they operate all over the world.

Multinational Corporations

In many big corporate mergers, corporations buy others that operate in unrelated industries, producing a **conglomerate.** A striking example is the International Telephone and Telegraph Corporation (IT&T). In the last two decades IT&T has bought a long string of companies that had nothing to do with telephones and telegraphs. Its acquisitions included Sheraton Hotels, Avis car rentals, Bobbs-Merrill publishers, Hartford Insurance, Levitt and Sons builders, Continental bakeries, and Smithfield hams, as well as firms that manufacture cellulose, vending machines, and other products. Another conglomerate, the cigarette manufacturer R. J. Reynolds Industries, now owns subsidiaries in various businesses such as Del Monte dealing in primary commodities, Heublein and its cigarette operations, Kentucky Fried Chicken, and some shipping and petroleum companies (Clairmonte and Cavanagh, 1983).

Most of these conglomerates have further expanded by establishing subsidiaries abroad, becoming **multinational corporations.** IT&T, for example, employs over 425,000 workers in at least 70 countries. Many multinationals have more economic power than a medium-sized nation. One way to measure their power is to compare the annual sales of a corporation with the gross national product of a nation. By this standard, in 1985, General Motors was more powerful than Ireland, Greece, Pakistan, and Nicaragua combined, and Exxon was more powerful than Israel, Jordan, the Philippines, and Guatemala (*Forbes,* 1986; *World Factbook,* 1987).

In search of lower labor costs, lower taxes, and larger markets, many multinational corporations have shifted their assets out of their industrialized birthplaces into the developing world. In the early 1970s the pharmaceutical industry already had located 33 percent of its total assets outside the United States; for the consumer goods industry, the figure was 40 percent; and for the electrical industry, 70 percent (Barnet and Müller, 1974). Overall, while American firms increased their investment in foreign operations sixteenfold between 1950 and 1980, their investments in this country increased only half that much (Boyle, 1982). From these foreign invest-

A Colonel Sanders outlet in Japan. The majority of huge American companies have become multinational corporations by establishing subsidiaries abroad. Many are wealthier than a medium-sized nation such as Greece or Pakistan. They also earn substantial profits from their foreign investments. In 1981, these profits accounted for nearly 40 percent of the multinationals' total net profits.

ments the American corporation as a whole earned nearly 40 percent of their net profits in 1981. Some companies earned much more than that. For example, Exxon received 70.1 percent of its total earnings from foreign investments, Texaco 67 percent, and Chase Manhattan Bank 65 percent (Clairmonte and Cavanaugh, 1983).

These profits, however, are not easy to come by. The competition for global markets is so fierce that managers of multinational corporations increasingly turn to military science for tips on how to develop competitor-centered strategies to win market shares. They often use military talk to describe their activities. Computer manufacturers engage in "price wars," "border clashes," and "skirmishes." Cigarette manufacturers "escalate arms race." There are "market invasion" and "guerilla warfare" in the coffee market. A corporation's advertising is its "propaganda arm," its salespersons are its "shock troops," and its market research is its "intelligence." The managers must face or use "confrontation," "brinkmanship," "superweapons," "reprisals," and "psychological warfare" (Clairmonte and Cavanaugh, 1983). To win market shares or simply to survive in this economic war, corporations get significant help from their governments. The help usually comes in the form of export subsidies, loans at preferential rates, cash grants, subsidization of research and development, and dismantling or reshaping of antitrust, banking, and tax laws.

Multinational corporations can have far-reaching effects on developing nations. They can promote social conflict by bringing in elements of a foreign culture. They can promote dangerous practices such as smoking and the use of powdered milk formulas to feed infants. (The milk formula is dangerous for the poor in developing countries because the water is often contaminated, sterilization procedures are seldom carried out, and poor people often stretch the expensive milk supply by over-diluting the baby formula. As a result, millions of infants have suffered severe malnutrition and diarrhea.) The corporations may end up reducing a nation's economic, social, and political independence. In the 1960s, for example, U.S. firms controlled 80 percent of Chile's most important industry: copper production. In both the 1964 and 1970 Chilean elections, American corporations funneled millions of dollars to their favored presidential candidate (Hersh, 1982). As Richard Barnet and Ronald Müller (1974) have written, "the managers of firms like GM, IBM, Pepsico, GE, Pfizer, Shell, Volkswagen, Exxon, and a few hundred others are making daily business decisions which have more impact than those of most sovereign governments on where people live; what work, if any, they will do; what they will eat, drink and wear; what sorts of knowledge schools and universities will encourage; and what kind of society their children will inherit."

We should not, however, exaggerate the power of multinational corporations. Developing nations can reduce it or take it away. In 1980, for example, Saudi Arabia took over the powerful Aramco, a consortium of three American giant corporations. Some developing countries prohibit Western corporations from sending their profits home. Others require the corporations to share ownership with local interests (Katrak, 1983). But most welcome multinationals. They often try to attract more foreign investment with a wide array of incentives, ranging from extensive tax benefits to subsidized labor, including the elimination of militant trade unions (Clairmonte and Cavanagh, 1983). Apparently they appreciate the fact that multinationals usually create many badly needed jobs, transfer modern technology to them, and stimulate their economic growth (Rowley, 1983).

QUESTIONS FOR DISCUSSION AND REVIEW

1. When does the competitive market system lead to oligopoly or monopoly?
2. What are the characteristics of big corporations, and how do they contribute to the American economy?
3. Why does American society have two welfare systems, one for the rich and one for the poor?
4. Why do large corporations today form conglomerates and multinational corporations, and how do these organizations subsequently change the economies of America and developing nations?

WORK IN AMERICA

When Americans meet strangers, one of their first questions is likely to be, "What do you do?" We answer, "I am a salesperson" or "I am a cabdriver" or a doctor or lawyer, whatever. Work is not just a way to make enough money to pay the bills. For many of us, work helps define our identity and our sense of self-worth. Just what it is we are able to do, however, depends to a great extent on the economic institutions we have described. As we will see in the following sections, the kinds of workers needed by our complex economy further affect labor unions, unemployment, job satisfaction, and the workplace.

The Labor Force

The labor force includes all those over 16 years of age who are gainfully employed as well as those who are jobless but are actively seeking paid employment. It excludes full-time housewives, students, and retired people—anyone who is not paid for his or her work and is not seeking a paying job. In 1986 about 65.3 percent of Americans over the age of 16 were in the work force—compared with about 55 percent in 1940 (Labor Dept., 1984a; Census Bureau, 1988). This increase has been accompanied by dramatic shifts in what American workers do and who makes up the work force.

Occupations The stage was set for the appearance of today's labor force by the industrialization of the farm, a process that accelerated greatly after World War II. Thanks to technological innovations ranging from new machinery to new fertilizers to new breeding techniques, agricultural productivity has soared during this century. In 1900 one American farmer on average produced enough food to support seven other people. Today, one farmer produces enough for more than 60 people.

This increasing agricultural productivity pushed many workers off the farm. In just five years, from 1950 to 1955, a million workers migrated out of agriculture. As a result, less than 3 percent of the American labor force works on the farm today, compared with nearly 60 percent in 1870 and 30.2 percent in 1920. The percentage will probably fall to 1 percent by 1990 (Rosenthal and Pilot, 1983; Labor Dept., 1984b). The continuing farm exodus also reflects the increasing failure of small family farms to survive. Government subsidies and other "save the family farm" programs such as crop insurance, production control, food stamps, school lunches, and distribution of surplus butter and cheese to low-income families have largely come to naught. What remains is the increasingly smaller number of highly efficient farms that need only few workers to produce enough food for the whole nation (Peterson, 1986).

Many of those who left the farm in earlier decades went to work in manufacturing industries, producing clothes, furniture, cars. But major changes were under way in manufacturing as well. As in agriculture, new machines decreased the number of people needed to produce one item or another. Since World War II, the share of jobs in manufacturing held by white-collar workers—managers, professionals, clerical workers, salespersons—rather than blue-collar workers has increased greatly. Before 1945, blue-collar workers had long outnumbered white-collar workers, but then white collars began to grow so fast in numbers that today they are three times as numerous as blue collars (Killingsworth, 1981; Census Bureau, 1988).

Meanwhile, the growth in jobs in manufacturing and other goods-producing industries has slowed, but jobs in service industries—education, health care, banking, real estate, insurance—have increased. In 1900 about 75 percent of the labor force was employed in production and fewer than 25 percent in service. But by 1982 the situation was reversed—74 percent in service and 26 percent in production. In the last ten years the largest job growth in service industries has been among secretaries, followed by cashiers and then registered nurses. Contrary to popular belief, though, not too many new jobs have come from high technology, which is often regarded as "the soul of the new U.S. economy." While high-tech positions have been growing fast, they still make up a small portion (13 percent) of the labor force. Their growth in the last decade was less than one-third the job gains experienced by cooks (Greenwald, 1984a). The major factors that have contributed to the rapid growth in the service sector as a whole are rising income and living standards that increase demand for health care, entertainment, and business and financial services (Labor Dept., 1984b).

The Workers The composition of the American labor force has changed, too. The most publicized change has occurred in its sexual makeup. In 1984 the U.S. Department of Labor announced that since 1960 the number of women in the labor force had nearly doubled. Today about 53 percent of women are in the labor force, compared with just 33 percent in 1960. The number of women workers will continue to rise, which is projected to account for about two-thirds of the entire labor force growth between 1982 and 1995 (see box, p. 439). The feminist movement—through its publicizing and legitimizing of the rights and needs of women to earn enough money to support themselves and contribute to total family income—has largely contributed to the increase (see Chapter 11: Gender Roles and Inequalities).

Important though less visible changes have occurred in the age and racial composition of the work force. From 1960 to 1984, the employment rate for men more than 54 years old declined significantly. Age discrimination and retirement programs such as social security and private pension plans have probably played a part in these declines, as we saw in Chapter 12 (The Elderly). During the last two decades there has also been a slight increase in white participation in the work force and a decrease in that by blacks. The overall decline among blacks is due to a decrease in employment among black males. Black females, like their white peers, have increased their participation in the labor force (Labor Dept., 1984a, 1984b).

These breakdowns by gender, race, and age do not tell us much about what is actually going on in the American economy. We have a "dual" economy, with a "core" of giant corporations dominating the market and a "periphery" of small firms competing for the remaining smaller shares of business. In addition, there is a third sector, consisting of various government agencies. About 30 percent of the American labor force work in the third, state sector, and the rest are employed in the private core and peripheral sector. Contrary to popular belief, most of the privately employed Americans do not work in the core's huge companies (with more than 1000 employees each). Only 30 to 40 percent do so. Most work in the peripheral sector, especially in small firms with fewer than 100 employees (Granovetter, 1984). Whatever sector they work in, American workers are now better educated than before. In 1940 most workers had just slightly more than a grade-school education. Today more than half have some college and three out of four are high-school graduates (Levitan, 1984). As we will see in the next section, the growing number of better-educated workers affects labor unions in some way.

Labor Unions

As an individual, the worker usually has little if any power. Of course, workers at least theoretically can leave their jobs if they don't like them, but many workers cannot afford to take that risk, especially when unemployment is high. A few workers may have some bargaining power with their employers if their skills are rare and in great demand. If workers are very scarce, employers may compete to offer the best conditions and salaries. More often, workers compete for jobs and employers have the upper hand.

To balance the scales of power in the workplace, millions of workers have joined labor unions. Both business and government long fought their establishment in the United States, sometimes violently. Between 1933 and 1936, for example, more than 100 workers were killed while striking for union recognition. Only toward the late 1930s did the federal government change sides and back the right of workers to join unions and bargain collectively with their employers. Since then the unions organized more and more workers, so that the percentage of the work force that was unionized climbed from only 12 percent in the 1930s to a peak of 35 percent in the 1950s. The unions won for their workers higher wages, shorter working hours, safer working conditions, and fringe benefits such as health insurance, pensions, and vacations. All these did cost individual companies by eating into their profits, but that cost was more than

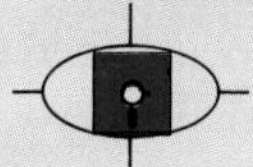

LOOKING AT CURRENT RESEARCH

The Unique U.S. Labor Force

The number of Americans seeking work has dramatically grown in the past several years, but this growth has created new problems. The following reading documents this increase and its causes and consequences. What new groups are seeking employment, and how might governmental action deal with the pressures they have created?

Since the mid-1970s, the civilian labor force of the United States has been growing at a sustained pace of about 2.2 million net additional job seekers a year (from 93 million in 1975 to 117.8 million in 1986). In terms of those actually able to find employment, their numbers also have increased significantly from 85.8 million to 109.5 million over this same time span. This growth in absolute numbers is not found in comparisons with any of the other major industrial powers of the free world. Only Canada and Japan have shown any appreciable absolute increases in the size of their respective labor forces over this period.

Three major forces have contributed to the rapid growth of the U.S. labor force over the past decade. Each of these pressures has also exerted significant influences on the gender, age, and ethnic composition of the labor force. The forces are the unprecedented number of women who have sought entry into the labor market, the maturing of the post-World War II "baby boom" population cohort, and the acceleration in the number of immigrants coming to the United States. All of these factors are likely in varying degrees to continue to exert considerable influence into the 1990s.

More women in both absolute and relative terms have been entering and staying longer in the labor force than at any previous time in the nation's history. The movement has been so abrupt and so large that it can be fairly described as being a "social revolution" in its own right. Two out of every three new labor market entrants since 1975 have been women, and the same pattern is forecast to continue through 1995.

The contributing factors for this growth rest with the rapidly increasing participation rate of married women in general and married women with children in particular. It is the labor market behavior of the latter female workers that presents the dramatic departure from the past.

The rapid growth of the labor force has also been significantly affected by the age distribution of the U.S. population. It currently contains a large "bulge" in the age range between 25 and 44 years of age. Not only is it the largest cohort of the population, but it is also the most rapidly growing. If ever a person is going to seek work, it is most probable he or she will do so between these ages.

The last factor contributing to the rapid growth of the U.S. labor force is a phenomenon unique to the experience of the U.S. economy. It is immigration. Since the mid-1960s, immigration has slowly reemerged as a key characteristic of the U.S. population and labor force. In contrast to all other advanced nations, the United States stands virtually alone in its willingness to admit each year hundreds of thousands of legal immigrants and refugees for permanent settlement as well as to tolerate mass abuse of its laws by an even larger annual number of illegal immigrants.

The continuing growth of the civilian labor force has placed the U.S. economy under severe strain to provide a sufficient number of jobs for those who seek them. Moreover, matching job seekers with jobs is not automatic. The rapidly changing composition of the civilian labor force has complicated the matching process. It is anticipated that 80% of the labor force entrants for the remainder of this century will be composed of women, minorities, and immigrants. For historical and institutional reasons, members of these groups have usually had difficulty securing the necessary job preparation and receiving fair opportunities to compete for available jobs. Hence, these changes in the size and composition of the labor force dictate that qualitative human resource policies—such as education, training, retraining, labor information, and labor mobility programs—become integral components of national economic policy. If such policy endeavors are undertaken on an enlarged scale from what currently exists and if they are combined with rigid enforcement of the nation's equal employment opportunity and immigration laws, the prospects for full employment, general prosperity, and domestic tranquility are good.

Source: Excerpted from Vernon M. Briggs, Jr., "The growth and composition of the U.S. labor force," *Science*, October 9, 1987, pp. 176–180.

offset by the beneficial results of collective bargaining—better morale and increased productivity (Freeman and Medoff, 1984).

Once the undisputed underdogs, unions have become "Big Labor." If all the unions in the nation united into one organization, it would be a wealthy organization indeed. In 1975 unions collected $4.5 billion through dues, fees, and investments—which is more than that year's net income for Exxon, the largest American corporation at the time (*Nation's Business,* 1979a). But, of course, unions are not one organization. Sometimes they fight over which union will represent certain workers, as the United Farm Workers and Teamsters fought to represent California farmworkers in the 1970s. Members of the same union may even fight among themselves, as demonstrated in 1986 by the Hormel meatpackers' strike in Austin, Minnesota, which infuriated its parent union. Often unions, like corporations, disagree about government policies and even support different candidates. In 1984, for example, the Teamsters and several construction unions supported Reagan while AFL-CIO endorsed Mondale. Most significantly, the power of unions has declined steadily since the 1950s.

By 1985 union members made up only about 14 percent of the work force, compared with 25 percent in 1970 and 35 percent in 1954. Union membership is expected to continue shrinking, reaching about 5 percent by the year 2010—only two decades away. While losing members, the unions have also been losing their traditional power of gaining concessions from employers. From the 1950s through the 1970s, employers could rarely operate during labor strikes. This is no longer the case today. In 1986, for example, when 6000 flight attendants struck Trans World Airlines, the employer hired new workers, and 4400 of the strikers lost their jobs. Also in 1986, when 150,000 communication workers struck the American Telephone and Telegraph Company, service continued with little disruption because, along with supervisors filling in, new workers were hired to replace the strikers. It is no wonder that, according to the Department of Labor, the frequency of major strikes has fallen sharply—from 424 in 1974 to only 67 in 1986. Why have unions been losing members and power?

A major reason is that unions were born among blue-collar workers, and these workers have long been the bulwark of the unions. But, as we have seen, it is white-collar employment that has been growing while blue-collar jobs have been increasingly scarce. Further, many blue-collar workers have lost their jobs to their counterparts in foreign countries. In 1980 the U.S. trade *surplus*

Union membership has declined substantially over the last thirty years. Unions have also largely lost their traditional power of gaining concessions from employers, who before 1980 rarely could operate during a labor strike. Consequently, when workers go on strikes today, they tend more to lose than win. In 1986, 4400 of the striking TWA flight attendants, some shown here, lost their jobs because their employers could hire new workers to replace them.

in goods was $40 billion, but only five years later our trade *deficit* hit $140 billion. This deficit represents nearly 4 million jobs that have left the United States. It also means that American employers have been facing tougher competition in the international market. To be more competitive, they are compelled to reduce costs by hiring permanent replacements at lower wages to fill the jobs of union members who strike. All this has caused a sharp decline in the number and power of blue-collar union workers, so that today only about 60 percent of the union members work in blue-collar jobs (Kirkland, 1986; Drucker, 1987). While about 40 percent of union members now work in white-collar jobs, the unions still have a hard time recruiting white-collar workers as well as blue-collar workers. The reason can be found in their past successes and failures.

The unions' earlier victories in raising wages for members and convincing the government to increase the minimum wage had rippling effects throughout the economy. They created a new middle class of union members and put upward pressure on the wages of nonunion workers as well. But as middle-class prosperity and status spreads, union solidarity tends to weaken. Many middle-class union members, like their nonunion neighbors, resent strikes by garbage collectors and teachers and firefighters and the higher taxes needed to meet their wage demands. A significant number of union members have moved away from the unions' traditional political orientation and became more conservative, seeking to preserve their own comfort by defending the status quo. Meanwhile, many lower-paid, nonunion workers resent the comparatively high pay earned by unionized steel workers and auto workers. As the nation's economic troubles piled up in the 1970s, some people looked for a simple answer and a villain, and blamed the unions.

The unions' own failures also played a big role in their decline. Some were slow to open their rolls to blacks and women and were late in responding to the growing importance of white-collar and service workers. There have been well-publicized cases of union corruption. Although most unions are not corrupt at all, repeated disclosures of a few union officers' gangland-style killings, ripoffs of union pension funds, payroll padding, bribes, and shakedowns have made many workers wary of union membership. Richly paid union leaders also appear to have more in common with their supposed foes, corporate executives, than with the rank and file. Individualistic workers resist the notion of working under the countless rules that may come with union contracts. On the whole, polls indicate the public's low opinion of unions—only 55 percent approved of labor organizations in 1981 compared with 76 percent in 1957—a fact that complicates the unions' task of organizing new workers and regaining their power (Craver, 1983).

The unions are far from giving up the fight, however. They have begun to use new tactics to recruit members. In their attempt to sign up service workers, white-collar workers, and even professionals such as engineers, scientists, and college professors, they focus on more than the traditional bread-and-butter concerns. They now also emphasize quality-of-work concerns such as career development, professional autonomy, and dealing with technological change. Thus they seek pay equity, career ladders, child care, job training, and ways of combating stress in the workplace. They further try to overcome skepticism about unions by presenting themselves as salespersons offering a service to prospective members rather than as militant crusaders fighting for economic justice. They will offer new members such benefits as low-interest credit cards, low-cost legal services, and home and auto insurance (Trost, 1986). Unions have also advised their members to stage work slowdowns as a new tactic to gain concessions without the risk of getting fired that the traditional strikes often incur. By working to the minimum of their job requirements, employees have succeeded in squeezing benefits from their employers. Several years ago at Boston's City Hospital, 700 nurses engaged in a work slowdown by adhering strictly to contract rules. They refused to work overtime, answer phones, move beds, or do other work outside their job classification. Within two weeks, the administration was forced to give a 23 percent pay raise over two years (Kotlowitz, 1987).

These efforts have brought unions some signs of a revival. The American Federation of State, County, and Municipal Employees (AFSCME) has more than doubled in size in the last decade. The National Education Association (NEA) has increased its membership by 48 percent. In 1973 clerk-typist Karen Nussbaum founded an organization known as "9 to 5" with just ten female clerical workers, but ten years later its membership zoomed to 12,000. Since its recent affiliation with the Service Employees International Union it has further gained 5000 members. (For the rise of these white-collar, service-sector unions, see Table 17.2.) When the 1979–1981 recession found one union after another

Table 17.2 How Occupations Change Unions

Shrinking blue-collar employment, among other factors, has caused blue-collar unions to lose many members. By contrast, the growth in white-collar jobs, coupled with increased recruitment, has resulted in larger white-collar unions.

	Membership (in thousands)		
	1970	1982	Percent change
Winners: white-collar unions			
American Federation of State, County, and Municipal Employees	444	956	+115.3
National Education Association	1100	1625	+47.7
Communication Workers of America	422	583	+38.0
Service Employees International Union	435	576	+32.4
Losers: blue-collar unions			
Amalgamated Clothing and Textile Workers Union	564	224	−60.2
United Steelworkers of America	1410	693	−50.8
International Ladies' Garment Workers' Union	442	253	−42.7
United Auto Workers	1486	1010	−32.0
International Brotherhood of Electrical Workers	992	824	−10.6

Source: U.S. Bureau of National Affairs, U.S. Bureau of Labor Statistics, and AFL-CIO, reprinted in *Newsweek*, September 5, 1983, p. 52. Copyright © 1983, by Newsweek, Inc. All rights reserved. Reprinted by permission.

making concessions to industry in order to preserve jobs, some unions showed a capacity for moving in new directions. The United Auto Workers (UAW), in particular, negotiated contracts that helped the industry hold down labor costs while exacting in return other changes that improved working conditions. Today Ford and General Motors avoid closing plants, minimize outsourcing (subcontracting of work to foreign countries), experiment with profit sharing, and make available training and retraining for jobs *outside* the auto industry (Shostak, 1983). Nevertheless, unions still have a hard time reversing the basic trend toward shrinking membership and influence. Many workers simply feel that unions are not right for them. According to a recent Harris survey, most nonunion workers believe that "unions force members to go along with decisions they don't like" and that "unions stifle individual initiative" and "fight change" (Trost, 1986).

Unemployment

Many unions fear that widespread joblessness discourages people from joining them. As Vicki Saporta, the Teamsters' director of organizing, explains, "In periods of real high unemployment, people oftentimes are just happy to have a job, and they don't want to rock the boat" (English, 1984). Indeed, the unemployment rate has been higher in the United States than in other industrialized countries. From 1970 to 1982, for example, the jobless rate in the United States averaged 6.7 percent, compared with 3.5 percent in Italy, 2.6 in West Germany, and 1.8 in Japan. In 1982 our jobless rate soared about 10 percent. But by mid-1987 it had come down to 6.2 percent, lower than the rate in other industrialized countries except Japan. Nevertheless, many—over 8 million—Americans are still out of work (Labor Dept., 1983; Norwood, 1983; Devens, 1984; Klott, 1987).

Unemployment is especially likely to hit blue-collar workers. In 1986 blue collars' jobless rate was three times as high as that of white collars (Census Bureau, 1988). As we have observed, industrial reorganization has diminished production industries and hence blue-collar jobs. The loss of such jobs will continue. The already small blue-collar work force is expected to shrink from its present 25 percent of the labor market to only 10 percent in the next two decades. Joblessness is also higher among teenagers (16 to 19 years old), minorities, and Americans with less than three years of high school (Young, 1983; Devens, 1984). A chief contributing factor is again the shrinkage of blue-collar employment, combined with lack of skill, lack of education, and racial discrimination.

Joblessness obviously brings economic deprivation, but it can also produce emotional, physical, and social problems. Many studies have shown that the unemployed typically suffer a loss of self-esteem. They feel ashamed and humiliated, avoid seeing friends, and sink into depression. They seem to blame themselves for losing their jobs. Some are ready to blame "the system" instead. Expressing this loss of faith in the social order, one unemployed man said: "I thought my conscientiousness and diligence would pay off. Hard work, you know, the old go go go. Nothing could be more erroneous" (Braginsky and Braginsky, 1975).

In any event, the cumulative effect of unemployment on society is great. It is associated with an increase in a broad range of social difficulties, from burglary to suicide. Unemployment may not be a direct cause of all these problems. Instead, it may often be a trigger, setting off problem-prone people. The damage is nonetheless significant. After analyzing various studies, Harvey Brenner (1976) concluded that a 1 percent rise in the U.S. unemployment rate is associated with increases of

4.3 percent in admissions to mental hospitals
8.6 percent in narcotics violations
4.1 percent in homicides
2.2 percent in reported burglaries
2.8 percent in larceny cases
6.0 percent in embezzlement cases

In 1970 alone, according to Brenner, joblessness contributed to 1740 homicides, 1540 suicides, 870 deaths from alcoholism, and 26,440 deaths from heart attacks. During the 1981–1982 recession, Brenner found that the sharp rise in unemployment contributed to as many as 75,000 additional deaths (*Scientific American,* 1984). Studies by other social scientists have largely confirmed Brenner's conclusion that unemployment has serious health and social costs not only for individual workers but for their families and communities as well (Catalano and Dooley, 1983; Baum et al., 1986; Atkinson et al., 1986; Warner, 1986).

To soften the impact of unemployment, the government provides unemployment compensation, food stamps, and other transfer payments. In fact, spending on entitlement programs has grown from 26.7 percent of the national budget in 1967 to 46.7 percent in 1977 and to 49.1 percent in 1982 (Yankelovich and Immerwahr, 1984). Even the Supreme Court ruled in 1987 that employers be required to pay severance benefits to some workers laid off in plant closings. Moreover, increasing numbers of people and organizations are working to help the jobless and their families. The United Community Services of Metropolitan Detroit has distributed some 4.5 million pamphlets advising people on how to survive unemployment and personal crises, how to cope with the emotional trauma of unemployment, how to search for jobs, and where to find opportunities for retraining. There are also organizations that distribute food to needy families. Some laid-off workers respond to the crisis by spending more time with their families (Riegle, 1982). GM, UAW, and the State of California have also jointly started a $10 million program to train 8400 ex-auto workers for high-tech reemployment as machinists, data processors, aerospace equipment builders, and the like (Shostak, 1983). Training for high-skilled jobs is increasingly important these days. Since the early 1980s there has been a substantial growth in jobs that require higher skills. But our society has not been training people fast enough to fill those jobs. There is currently a shortage of skilled labor, as indicated by numerous help-wanted ads offering high-skilled jobs. Much of this problem, though, is demographic. Given the earlier "baby bust"—the sharp decline in the birth rate since the late 1950s—our labor force today is increasing at a snail's pace. It grows at an annual rate of about 1.3 percent only, which is about half the rate of the last decade when the labor market bulged with the postwar "baby boom" workers. The labor shortage is expected to continue into the 1990s, which should alleviate the unemployment problems (Bacon, 1986).

Job Satisfaction

While it is miserable to be laid off, does being employed bring happiness? Are Americans really happy with their jobs? In many studies during the last two decades, representative samples of workers have been asked whether they would continue to work if they inherited enough money to live comfortably without working. More than 70 percent replied that they would. When asked how satisfied they were with their jobs, even more—from 80 to 90 percent—replied that they were very or moderately satisfied (O'Toole, 1973; Chelte, Wright, Tausky, 1982; Bridgwater, 1984). But when asked whether they would choose the same line of work if they could begin all over again, most said no. Only 43 percent of white-collar workers and 24 percent of blue collars said yes (O'Toole, 1973). More recently, when asked "Do you enjoy your work so much that you have a hard time putting it aside?" only 34 percent of men and 32 percent of women answered affirmatively (Glenn and Weaver, 1982). In short, most Americans seem to like their jobs but are not too excited about them.

Studies have also shown that job satisfaction varies from one group to another. Generally, older workers are more satisfied than younger ones. One reason is that older workers, being more advanced in their careers, have better jobs. Another reason is that younger workers are more likely to expect their jobs to be highly interesting and stimulating, hence are more likely to be disillusioned because of the difficulty in realizing high aspirations (Kalleberg and Loscocco, 1983; but see Janson and Martin, 1982). White-collar workers, especially professionals and businesspeople, are also more likely than blue collars to feel genuinely satisfied with their jobs (O'Toole, 1983; Glenn and Weaver, 1982). Among blue-collar workers, union members report significantly *less* job satisfaction than nonmembers, which reflects job dissatisfaction as the primary reason for joining unions (Schwochau, 1987). Women, however, are about as satisfied with their jobs as men are with theirs. Isn't this puzzling? After all, women are generally paid less and have less prestigious jobs than men, as we have seen in Chapter 11 (Gender Roles and Inequalities). Why, then, are women not less happy with their jobs? A major reason is that they expect less than men from the job market and so can more easily fulfill their lower expectation. If they get jobs that are as good as men have, which goes beyond their expectation, they are likely to express more satisfaction than men (Murray and Atkinson, 1981; D'Arcy, Syrotuik, and Siddique, 1984). Indeed, as more recent studies have shown, women are more involved than men with their jobs when provided similar autonomy in task performance (Lorence, 1987). In general, workers who enjoy greater autonomy or self-management are more satisfied with their jobs (Taylor et al., 1987).

People with satisfying jobs have better mental health than those with less satisfying work. Thus white-collar workers are less likely than blue collars to suffer from psychosomatic illnesses, low self-esteem, worry, anxiety, and impaired interpersonal relationships. People who are happy with their jobs also tend to have better physical health and to live longer. Although diet, exercise, medical care, and genetics are all related to the incidence of heart disease, job dissatisfaction is more closely linked to the cause of death (O'Toole, 1973).

A fundamental cause of dissatisfaction could be the increasing specialization of work. For doctors and lawyers and other professionals, specialization may stimulate the mind while it fattens the checkbook. But for less-educated manual workers, specialization can be numbing. It can produce monotonous, repetitive tasks. A person working in the slaughter and meatpacking industry, for example, can be a large stock scalper, belly shaver, crotch buster, gut snatcher, gut sorter, snout puller, ear cutter, eyelid remover, stomach washer, hindleg-toenail puller, frontleg-toenail puller, or oxtail washer. Sorting the guts of hogs eight hours a day is far from an interesting job. Neither is identification of oneself as a gut sorter likely to boost one's ego.

Specialization of work, if carried too far, leaves little room for responsibility or initiative by the worker. It can mean that some people are assigned the job of controlling those who actually produce goods or deliver services. When Studs Terkel (1974) interviewed workers, he found "the most profound complaint is 'being spied on.' There's the foreman at the plant, the supervisor listening in at Ma Bell's, the checker who gives the bus driver a hard time. . . ." Moreover, by tying the worker to an isolated task, to a small part of some large task, specialization can empty jobs of their meaning. The result can be dehumanizing for some workers, as Terkel (1974) found when he interviewed people across the country: "'I'm a machine,' says the spotwelder. 'I'm caged,' says the bank teller. 'I'm a mule,' says the steelworker. 'A monkey can do what I do,' says the receptionist. . . ."

What, then, can generate job satisfaction? In a recent study researchers asked 64 workers to define what constitutes a good working life (Levine et al., 1984; see also Mottaz and Potts, 1986). They came up with 34 items. Then the investigators presented these items to 450 other employees, asking them to choose the ones that they thought reflect a high quality of work life. Only seven conditions were found to be significant. They are, in the order of importance:

1. My superiors treat me with respect and have confidence in my abilities (similar to work autonomy).

The nature of the rewards associated with a job has much to do with a worker's job satisfaction. (a) Workers such as the men on the oil rig (right), who have to do strenuous physical labor or boring repetitive tasks, may find the job worthwhile if they feel they are receiving an adequate wage. (b) But people such as this artist (below) may be willing to forgo a high salary in order to continue with work that they love. In fact, the artist and other white-collar workers are more likely than blue collars to feel genuinely satisfied with their jobs. Generally, white collars like their jobs because they can enjoy a great deal of autonomy or self-management.

a

b

2. Variety in my daily work routine (the opposite of specialization).
3. Challenge in my work.
4. Work at present leads to good future work opportunities.
5. Self-esteem.
6. My work can be enhanced by my nonwork life.
7. The work I do contributes to society.

Note that the list does not include a big paycheck. In the past, most jobholders regarded work as a business transaction for pay only. They would be satisfied even if their work was disagreeable, unpleasant, or degrading, as long as they were adequately paid. Today most Americans expect more. They want their work to be pleasant and interesting. Indeed, in the last 20 years there have been significant changes in worker attitudes, aspirations, and values.

The Changing Workplace

In a recent survey only 26 percent of American workers still hold the traditional view of work. Some of these workers said that "the more I get paid, the more I do." Others agreed that "work is one of life's unpleasant necessities. I wouldn't work if I didn't have to." A bumper sticker on a car says it all: "Work sucks, but I need the bucks." In contrast, a large majority (73 percent) of the respondents expressed more positive attitudes toward work. Many agreed with the statement: "I have an inner need to do the very best I can, regardless of pay." They most frequently rated as "very important" certain nonmonetary, inherent qualities of work, such as interesting jobs, developing their own skills, and seeing how good the results of their work are (Yankelovich and Immerwahr, 1984). The American work ethic has taken on a new quality.

As we noted in Chapter 15 (Religion), the Protestant ethic elevated hard work to the status of a moral duty. Working hard was seen as a way of serving God. This work ethic motivated the early Protestants. But as the power of religion declined, so did the influence of ideas about moral duty. As a result, as Max Weber (1930) wrote, "the idea of duty in one's calling prowls about in our lives like the ghost of dead religious beliefs." Although work lost its religious idea of serving God, the Protestant ethic of self-denial—the notion of sacrificing for others—continued to hold sway. Thus more Americans have until recently worked hard to support their families, disregarding how unpleasant and boring their work might be. They believed that "a man with a family has a responsibility to choose the job that pays the most, rather than one that is more satisfying but pays less." Today, however, a majority of Americans reject that view. Instead, they seek interesting jobs that allow for personal growth and self-fulfillment (Yankelovich and Immerwahr, 1984). There is, then, a shift in the work ethic, from an emphasis on self-sacrifice to a stress on self-development as the primary motive for hard work.

How has this new ethic come about? As we have observed, the number of white-collar workers and the amount of average workers' education have increased substantially over the last several decades. It is these white-collar and better-educated workers who value autonomy and personal growth in the workplace. Hasn't this new focus on the self led to the death of the American work ethic? No. According to a Gallup study, an overwhelming 88 percent of all working Americans feel that it is important for them to "work hard and to do their best on the job." The work ethic is particularly strong among college graduates. In one survey, 63 percent of college-educated jobholders feel a sense of dedication to their work, compared with only 47 percent for those who never went to college. The better-educated are more likely to have a strong commitment to work because they have more satisfying, challenging, or interesting jobs (Yankelovich and Immerwahr, 1984).

There is, however, a problem in the workplace. Many people are not working as hard as they should in accordance with their belief in the work ethic. In one survey, only 23 percent of workers say that they are performing to their full capacity, and nearly half (44 percent) say that they do not put much effort into their jobs. Another study finds that a considerable portion (49 percent) of work time is spent on nonproductive activities—coffee breaks, late starts, early quits, personal activities, waiting around, and otherwise idling (Yankelovich and Immerwahr, 1984; but see Hedges, 1983). If Americans believe in the work ethic, why are they not giving their best to the jobs?

A key source of the problem could be management's failure to motivate employees to perform effectively. Many workers feel that they do not get enough recognition for good work. In one survey, 58 percent of working

Americans say that they would work harder if they did receive more recognition. Employees often get the implicit message from management that "we don't care about extra effort, so why should you?" This comes through clearly when management gives the same raise to all employees although some have worked harder than others. This is, in fact, a serious problem. As Daniel Yankelovich and John Immerwahr (1984) note, "One of the most startling findings of the national survey of working Americans is the degree to which the American workplace has undercut the link between a jobholder's pay and his or her performance." According to the survey, nearly half of the work force (45 percent) believe that there is no connection between their effort and their pay, another 28 percent say there is some connection, and only 22 percent see a close relationship. Under such conditions, trying to live up to one's belief in the work ethic can make one feel like a fool.

Efforts have been made, however, to tie pay closer to performance. Other reward systems are also used to motivate employees, such as earned time off, profit sharing, bonuses, and recognition as employee of the month, best service team, or the like (Horn, 1987). Further attempts have been made to reorganize the workplace. They usually include offering workers more interesting jobs, more autonomy, and increased participation in decision making. To make their jobs more interesting, for example, employers allow employees to work on a whole product rather than a minute portion of it. At Motorola, each worker produces an entire stereo speaker, putting together 80 components rather than working on just one or two. Furthermore, the workers' names are engraved on their products, indicating their personal responsibility for the quality. A growing number of companies give workers some freedom to set their own working hours within specified limits. Some have introduced mechanisms that allow workers to take part in decisions about production methods, promotions, hiring, and firing. These efforts have boosted productivity by 5 to 40 percent (Yankelovich and Immerwahr, 1984). This can be exemplified by the GM–Toyota Motor Company joint venture. In 1984 it reopened a GM factory in Fremont, California, that had been closed two years earlier. It was managed with flexible work rules and significant worker control over operations. By 1987 the factory was about 50 percent more efficient than before and 40 percent more efficient than the average, traditionally managed GM plant (Schlesinger, 1987).

QUESTIONS FOR DISCUSSION AND REVIEW

1. What occupations make up the American labor force, and what kinds of Americans fill these positions?
2. Why do so few workers join labor unions today, and how have these organizations tried to attract new members?
3. What is the overall impact of unemployment on individuals and society, and what groups have suffered the most from this economic problem?
4. Why does specialization lessen the satisfaction of workers with their jobs?
5. What factors have contributed to the changes in the American work ethic?

CHAPTER REVIEW

1. *How did the Industrial Revolution change the economic process?* Machines replaced much human labor, mass production in factories displaced cottage industry, and agriculture lost ground to industry. *What are some effects of industrialization?* Industrialization speeds up production, shrinking blue-collar employment and enlarging white-collar work. It further changes demographic features, human relations, and the values of society.

2. *What are two basic types of economic organization?* Capitalism and socialism. Capitalism is based on private ownership of property and on competition in the buying and selling of goods and services. Its driving force is the self-interest of individuals. In contrast, socialism subordinates the individual's interests to those of society and puts the ownership and control of the economy in the hands of the state. *How do real economies differ from the models offered by capitalist and socialist theories?* No economy is purely capitalist or purely socialist. All economies have capitalist and socialist elements. They only differ in degree, ranging on a continuum from the most capitalist to the most socialist. Generally, capitalist economies are more productive than socialist ones.

3. *What is a big corporation like?* The numerous shareholders who own the corporation do not run it. A small group of directors and managers do. Owners and managers may profit from corporate assets but may not be held responsible for its liabilities. Corporations tend to grow into giants through mergers and acquisitions. The rise of giant corporations has both positive and negative consequences for the economy and society.

4. *What is the government's role in the economy?* The government sets the terms that allow corporations to exist and thrive. It regulates them and other economic factors. It is itself a buyer, seller, and employer. It shapes the economic environment as a whole. Since the U.S. government depends on corporations to keep the economic machine going, it gives billions each year to help corporations stay healthy and profitable.

5. *What are some characteristics of multinational corporations?* They reap huge profits from abroad, but they must battle among themselves for those profits. Since multinationals are more powerful than some nations, they can reduce the ability of nations to control their own economic fate. To many developing countries, however, multinationals bring needed jobs, technology, and economic growth.

6. *How has the American labor force changed in recent years?* The number of jobs in agriculture has dropped sharply, the number in service industries has risen, and the population of white-collar workers has expanded. Meanwhile, the employment rate for women has soared, the rate for older men has declined significantly, and the rate for blacks has fallen off slightly.

7. *Why has union membership dwindled?* Much of the recent industrial growth has occurred in the Sunbelt, which is historically hostile to labor unions. The traditional source of unionization—blue-collar employment—has shrunk. The spread of middle-class prosperity has diminished union appeal. Unions have been slow to recruit minority and white-collar workers and have created a poor public image.

8. *How does unemployment affect society?* The effects are more than economic. With even a 1 percent rise in unemployment, there is a significant rise in numerous problems such as crime, alcoholism, and suicide.

9. *Who are more likely to be satisfied with their work?* Older and white-collar workers. Given the same kinds of jobs, women are happier than men. *What is the basic cause of job dissatisfaction?* Extreme specialization of work.

10. *How has the American workplace changed?* Workers are less willing to accept unpleasant jobs and more likely to expect meaningful ones. They continue to want to work hard, but management has failed to give them enough recognition for hard work. However, efforts have been made to give employees more interesting jobs, more freedom, and more power in the workplace.

KEY TERMS

Alienation of labor Marx's term for laborers' loss of control over their work process (p. 427).

Capitalism An economic system based on private ownership of property and competition in producing and selling goods and services (p. 426).

Conglomerate A corporation that owns companies in various unrelated industries (p. 435).

Economic institution A system for producing and distributing goods and services (p. 424).

Industrial Revolution The dramatic economic change brought about by the introduction of machines into the work process about 200 years ago (p. 424).

Mixed economy An economic system that includes both capitalist and socialist elements (p. 428).

Monopoly Situation in which one firm controls the output of an industry (p. 431).

Multinational corporation A corporation that has subsidiaries in several nations (p. 435).

Oligopoly Situation in which a very few companies control the output of an industry (p. 431).

Socialism An economic system based on public ownership and control of the economy (p. 427).

SUGGESTED READINGS

Freeman, Richard B., and James L. Medoff. 1984. *What Do Unions Do?* New York: Basic Books. An interesting, data-packed book that shows what big labor has done for society as a whole and what it has done to individual companies.

Fuchs, Victor R. 1983. *How We Live: An Economic Perspective on Americans from Birth to Death.* Cambridge, Mass.: Harvard University Press. An easy-to-read analysis of how the economy affects individual choices regarding work, family, schooling, and health.

Ginsburg, Helen. 1983. *Full Employment and Public Policy: The United States and Sweden.* Lexington, Mass.: Lexington Books. Analyzes why unemployment is so much higher in the United States than in Sweden and discusses the economic and social effects of unemployment in our society.

Halal, William E. 1986. *The New Capitalism.* New York: Wiley. Discusses the emergence of a new American capitalism that combines the conservative spirit of laissez-faire "corporate America" and the liberal spirit of big-government "regulated America."

Rose, Michael. 1985. *Reworking the Work Ethic.* New York: Schocken. A critical examination of popular beliefs about the current work ethic in the United States.

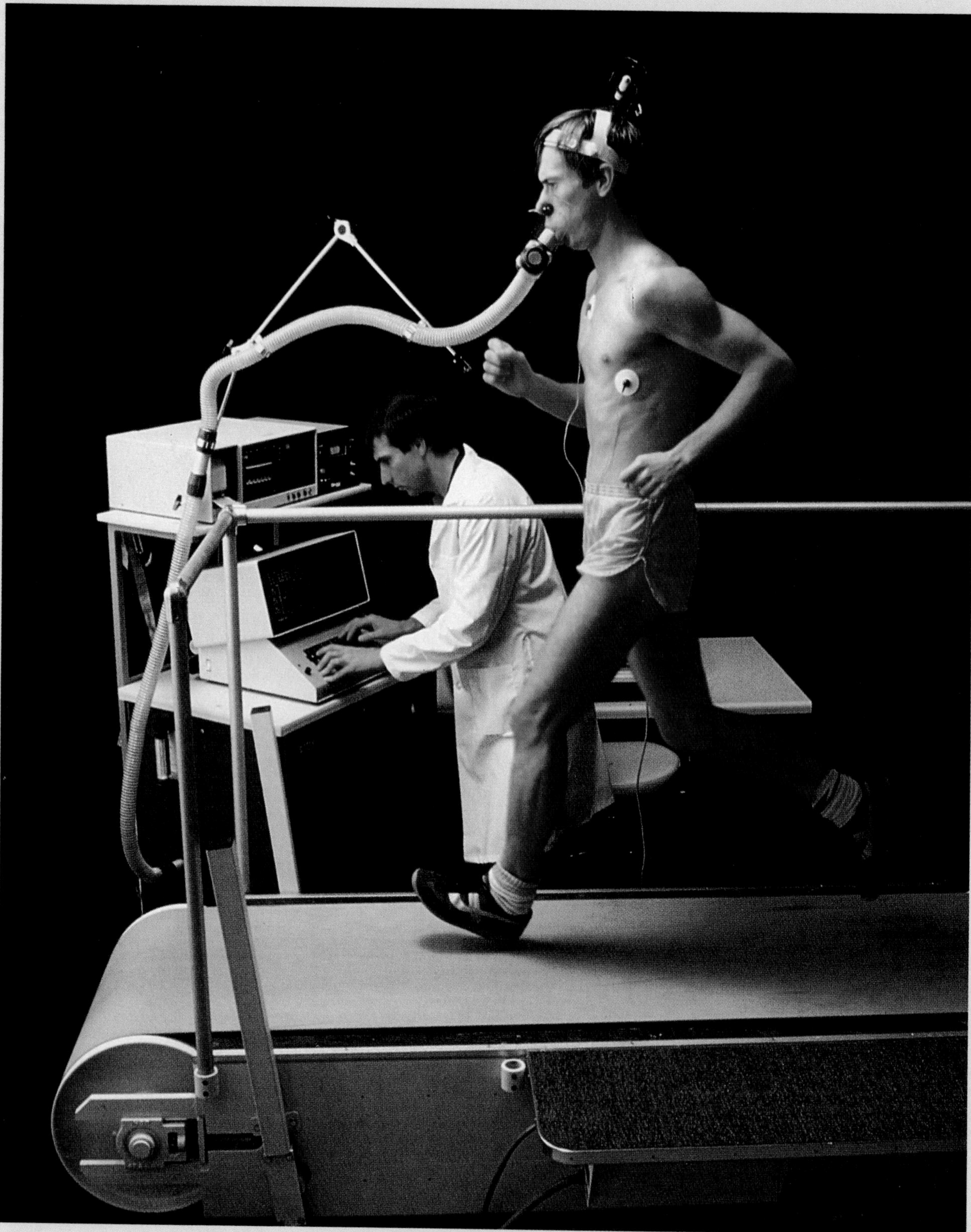

18 Health and Medical Care

Americans are much healthier than before. Our life expectancy has increased substantially. Acute illnesses such as pneumonia and smallpox no longer seriously threaten us today as they did our ancestors around 1900. But chronic illnesses such as heart disease, cancer, and stroke have become the major killers of today. This can be traced to the impact of our longer life span and higher living standard. As people live beyond age 55, they tend more to have high cholesterol levels. High cholesterol increases the risk of developing chronic illnesses. So do the affluence-related habits of excessive eating, smoking, and drinking.

In recent years there have been many tragedies like the following:

> An American soldier stationed in Africa in the late 1970s had sex with prostitutes there. On returning to the U.S., he married and fathered three children. At age 37, almost a decade after his African tour of duty, he developed AIDS and died. His widow and their youngest child—a 15-month-old toddler—are fatally ill with AIDS (McAuliffe, 1987).

Casual, promiscuous sex is a major social contributor to the spread of AIDS (acquired immune deficiency syndrome). Through sex with multiple partners, individuals increase their chances of being infected with the virus that directly causes the deadly disease. An increasing number of other diseases these days can also be traced to specific social behavior. Consider the popular habit of smoking. It contributes to 350,000 deaths every year in the United States. The 51 million adult Americans who continue to puff—some 32 percent of our population—enormously multiply their chances of dying prematurely from lung cancer. For men, the risk is ten times greater; for women, it is four. Smoking is also a heavy contributor to heart disease, accidents, stroke, influenza, and pneumonia (Carey and Silberner, 1987). It is obvious that our health is more than an individual matter and depends on more than the biological functioning of our body machinery. Dealing with many of our current health problems, then, requires that we look beyond the body to society—to our ways of life, our social structure, and our medical institutions, all of which powerfully influence our health.

It should be obvious that recovery from illness also depends on the availability and quality of medical care. Our society spends more on medical care than on our national defense. Individual Americans spend more on medical care than on automobiles and gasoline combined. Ironically, while military affairs, gas prices, and the latest car-styling gimmicks are often analyzed fully in public discourse, medical care is shunted aside as a vast, unapproachable mystery. As a cancer patient says, "You can get elaborate star ratings on restaurants, movies, any kind of product. But on one of the central issues affecting your life—which doctor is good, what treatment is right—you're totally in the dark" (Easterbrook, 1987). Sociology can demystify the nature of health and medical care. In this chapter we examine the relationship between health and society, the medical profession, and the consumption and delivery of medical care.

HEALTH AND SOCIETY

As a social phenomenon, health varies from one society to another and from one group to another within the same society. From these variations we can see how social factors affect health and what consequences an outbreak of illness has for society. We can also track down the origin of a disease by examining all its victims for something that they have in common as a social group.

American Health

As the Population Reference Bureau has shown, Americans are much healthier than ever before. Since 1900 our life expectancy has increased by more than 50 percent, from about 49 years in 1900 to 75 today. At birth we can expect to live 26 more years than did our counterparts in 1900—more than 1½ times as long as they did then. Another indicator of our health, the infant mortality rate, has shown even more dramatic improvement. While about 15 percent of all American babies died during the first year of life at the turn of this century, only 1 percent die today. All this can be chalked up to healthier living conditions, better diet, immunization, and penicillin and other antibiotics.

These breakthroughs have further vanquished most

"Everything that was bad for you is now good for you."

of the major killer diseases around 1900—particularly pneumonia, influenza, and tuberculosis—along with such infectious childhood diseases as smallpox and measles. Most of these diseases are acute. **Acute diseases,** usually caused by invading viruses or bacteria, last for a short time, during which the victims either recover or die. Such diseases have been replaced by the major killers of today—heart disease, cancer, and stroke. These **chronic diseases** last for a long time before the victims die. They usually cannot be cured, but the pain and suffering that they bring can be reduced. To a certain extent, the emergence of the chronic diseases as today's big killers is, ironically, due to our increased longevity and rising living standard. Because of our high living standard, we tend to eat, smoke, and drink too much. When these self-indulgent behaviors are carried on for a long time, made possible by the rising life expectancy, chronic illnesses such as heart disease and cancer are likely to occur. It is no wonder that older Americans—above age 55—are far more likely than younger Americans to have high blood cholesterol levels and to suffer from those chronic diseases (Thompson, 1987).

Even our increased life expectancy by itself loses its impressiveness in comparison with that of other industrialized countries. Among 12 such nations, the United States ranks close to the bottom rather than near the top. People in at least 7 industrialized countries live longer than do Americans. Our standing in regard to infant mortality is the same. Proportionately more babies die in the United States than in 8 out of 12 industrialized nations, which puts our health condition near the bottom of the ranking system (see Table 18.1). This is ironic, because we spend more money on health care than any of these nations. As Joseph Califano recently pointed out, "Although the U.S. spent $1,600 for the health care of each person in 1984 and Singapore [a newly industrialized country] spent only $200, residents of both nations have the same life expectancy" (*Medical World News,* 1987). However, compared with the developing countries in the third world, the United States has a much higher life expectancy and considerably lower infant mortality rate (Census Bureau, 1988).

Social Factors

Americans are not all equally likely to get sick. Instead, the incidence of sickness varies from one group to another. Old people are less likely than younger people to suffer from acute and infectious illnesses such as measles and pneumonia. But they are more susceptible to chronic illnesses such as arthritis, heart disease, and cancer (Census Bureau, 1988).

Health also varies with gender. Women have higher rates of both chronic and acute illnesses than men of the

Table 18.1 Life Expectancies and Infant Mortality Rates

Our health record is far from impressive. Among industrialized nations in 1986, the United States ranked near the bottom in life expectancy and infant mortality.

Country	Life expectancy	Country	Infant mortality rate
Japan	78	Japan	6
Netherlands	77	Netherlands	8
Canada	77	Canada	8
Spain	77	Australia	8
Australia	76	West Germany	8
West Germany	76	Italy	9
Italy	76	France	10
France	75	Great Britain	10
United States	75	United States	11
Great Britain	75	East Germany	11
East Germany	73	Spain	12
Soviet Union	68	Soviet Union	27

Source: Statistical Abstract of the United States, 1988, p. 800.

In addition to men's biological inferiority to women, certain social factors can explain why men die sooner than women do. Men have weaker emotional ties with others; smoke, drink, or drive more often; and tend more to work in stressful and hazardous occupations, as shown here.

same age, yet women live longer than men. Why? One reason is biological superiority. Women are more able to endure sickness and survive. They also are less likely to develop hemophilia and other diseases linked to the X chromosome. Their sex hormones further protect them from cardiovascular morbidity up to the time of menopause. A second reason is that women maintain stronger emotional ties with more people than men do. By offering social support and deterring loneliness, intimate human relationships can reduce the severity and duration of illness. A third reason is the greater tendency of men to smoke, drink, and drive. Such behaviors increase the risk of serious chronic diseases and physical injuries (Verbrugge, 1985). It is also possible that women are more attuned to their bodies and thus more likely to sense problems and seek medical help before an illness becomes serious. Stress and health hazards in the workplace—from noise, vibration, fumes, and the like—may further shorten men's lives.

Race and ethnicity are also correlated with health. Blacks, Hispanics, and American Indians all have shorter life expectancies than do Anglo Americans. While white women have a life expectancy four years longer than that of black women, white men have a life expectancy five years longer than that of black men. Blacks are far more likely than whites to suffer from cirrhosis, influenza, pneumonia, and hypertension (high blood pressure). Blacks are twice as likely as whites in the same age bracket to die from disease. Hispanics are much more likely than Anglo Americans to die from influenza, pneumonia, and tuberculosis. Both blacks and Hispanics are twice as likely as whites to get AIDS—about 40 percent of the nation's 38,000 diagnosed AIDS cases are black or Hispanic, although these minorities make up only 20 percent of the U.S. population. The racial disparity is even more striking among babies: black infants are 25 times more likely to fall victim to AIDS than are white infants. American Indians suffer the most from acute diseases. They are ten times more likely than other Americans to get tuberculosis, 30 times more likely to get strep throat, and 66 times more likely to get dysentery. Both Hispanics and American Indians, however, are less likely than Anglos to die from heart disease and cancer (Cockerham, 1986; Koskenvuo et al., 1986; Levine, 1987).

These racial and ethnic differences may largely reflect another social factor that influences health: social class. The diseases that hit minority groups the hardest are those associated with poverty. In particular, acute and infectious diseases such as tuberculosis and influenza are more prevalent among the lower social classes. Chronic illnesses such as heart disease and cancer also strike the lower classes more often, but the class differentials in these diseases are smaller than those in acute and infectious illnesses. Researchers have attributed the higher rates of disease among the lower classes to several related factors: toxic, hazardous, and unhygienic environments; stress resulting from such life changes as job loss and divorce; and inadequate medical care (Syme and Berkman, 1987).

There are many other instances in which social factors strongly influence health condition. Of course, we should not deny the crucial role of natural, biological factors in the development of disease. The point to be emphasized here is that social factors can aggravate, soften, or even neutralize the biological impact on health. A medical researcher recently identified four Mormon families who carry a gene for a dangerously high cholesterol level. Since 1900 the men in these families have died from heart disease, on average, by age 45. But the researcher discovered that, before 1880, the men lived up to age 62 or even 81. They lived longer because their life-style included a more healthful diet and physically active occupations (Carey and Silberner, 1987). This illustrates how social factors can sidetrack a gene from producing a disease. Social factors can also make the body susceptible to disease. However, to track them down requires a kind of detective work called **epidemiology,** the study of the origin or spread of disease in a given population.

Epidemiology

In searching for clues to the origin and spread of a disease within a given population, sociologists join forces with physicians, public health workers, biochemists, and other medical scientists. These epidemiologists first hunt down all the people who already have the disease. Then they ask the victims where they were and what they did before they got sick. The epidemiologists also collect data on the victims' age, gender, marital status, occupation, and other characteristics. The aim is to find out what all the victims have in common besides the disease so that its cause can be identified and eliminated. Usually the common factor that ties all the victims together provides the essential clue (Cockerham, 1986).

Epidemiology emerged as an applied science in 1854, when the English physician John Snow discovered the source of one of London's periodic cholera epidemics. He had gone to the neighborhoods where the victims lived and asked them what they did every day, where they worked, what they ate and drank, and many other questions about their lives and activities. Finally, after sifting through this huge pile of information, Snow hit upon the clue to the origin of the disease. He found that all the victims had one thing in common: they had drunk water from a particular pump on Broad Street. Snow simply shut off the pump and, with that single act, stopped the epidemic in its tracks. Not till many years later, with the discovery of germs, could anyone explain why shutting down the pump was effective: he had removed the source of the cholera bacteria (Cockerham, 1986).

Since then, there have been numerous social and medical scientists who have used epidemiology to trace the origins of many different diseases such as cancer and heart disease. In investigating heart disease, for example, epidemiologists have discovered that the majority of victims have eaten high-cholesterol foods, smoked and drunk heavily, and failed to get enough exercise. But heart disease and other present-day illnesses are far more complex than cholera. Unlike Snow, today's epidemiologists rarely find that all the victims of a disease have had exactly the same experiences. Unlike cholera, heart disease can occur from many different causes rather than a single cause. But every now and then, even today, an epidemic like cholera does erupt and spread through a population.

In July 1976 over 200 people became seriously ill and more than 30 of them died. The victims suffered from such symptoms as headaches, muscle and chest pains, abnormally high fever, and pneumonia, but doctors felt helpless because they did not know their cause. However, epidemiologists discovered that all the victims had one thing in common: they had attended a convention of the American Legion in a Philadelphia hotel. The medical detectives contacted all the people who had attended the convention—both those who had fallen ill and those who had not. These legionnaires were asked "again and again what they ate, what they drank, where they went, what they did when they got to the hotel, and what time they did it, and so forth" (Cockerham, 1986). The investigators finally nailed the culprit—a bacterium lurking in the hotel's air-conditioning system. Since then, an antibiotic has been used effectively to treat the illness, now known as legionnaires' disease. No such cure, however, has so far been available for another, more recent epidemic, AIDS.

AIDS: An Epidemiological Analysis

This is a deadly disease that destroys the body's immune system, leaving the victim defenseless against such conditions as pneumonia, meningitis, and a cancer called Kaposi's sarcoma. Common symptoms include a persistent cough, prolonged fever, chronic diarrhea, difficulty in breathing, and multiple purplish blotches and bumps on the skin. AIDS is also known, in Africa, as a "slim disease," for its victims' emaciated appearance, the result of a painful wasting away of body tissues and uncontrolled weight loss. The disease was originally

Figure 18.1 AIDS Numbers: A Rapid Rise

Source: U.S. Centers for Disease Control, 1988.

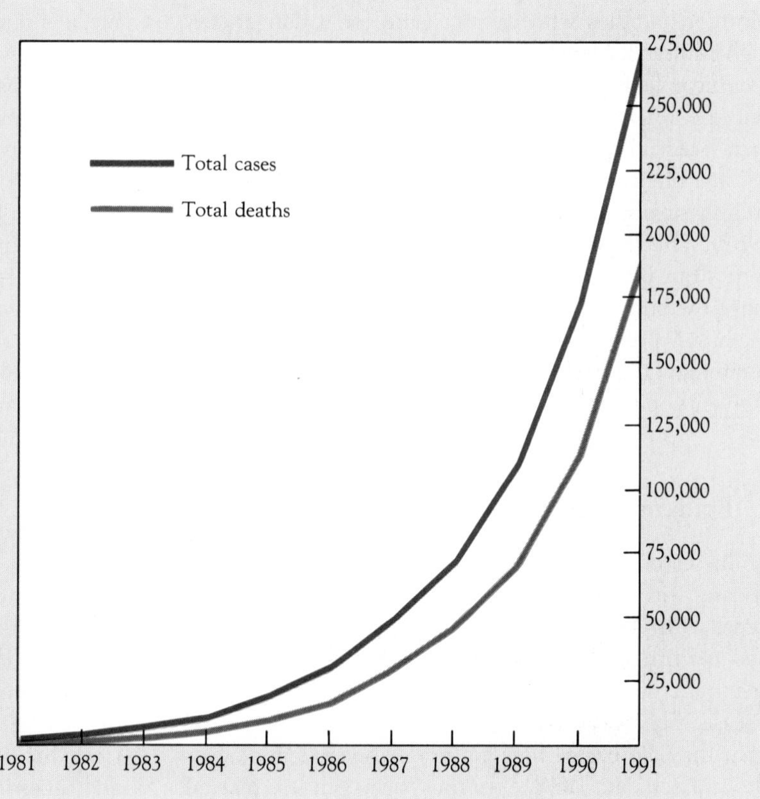

brought to the United States by American tourists returning from Haiti, where it had come from Central Africa. It first came to the attention of American physicians in early 1981. Since then, the disease has spread rapidly. In 1981 only about 50 people were identified as having the disease. At the end of 1987 the number had shot up to more than 49,743, and 27,909 had died. By 1991, according to the most conservative estimates, 270,000 Americans will have been stricken with AIDS and 179,000 will have died (see Figure 18.1). Moreover, considerably more Americans carry the AIDS virus without yet displaying any symptoms. Their number is estimated to range from 1 to 4 million. Conceivably, all of these people could eventually get the full-blown, lethal disease. At least 25 to 50 percent will certainly get it within 4 to 10 years (McAuliffe, 1987; Pear, 1988).

The AIDS virus, referred to by medical investigators as the human immunodeficiency virus (HIV), has been shown to be the direct cause of the disease and this discovery has made it possible to determine infection before the disease symptoms appear. The virus is so elusive, though, that there are as yet no tests that can detect the virus directly in the infected person. The currently available tests are designed to identify antibodies specific to the virus; their presence can be safely taken to suggest that the individual has been infected with the virus. This is because when a foreign germ invades the blood, the body's immune system produces antibodies specific to that type of germ. The immune system of a child with measles, for example, produces antibodies that specifically fight measles.

To test for antibodies to the AIDS virus, the **ELISA** test is most widely used. (ELISA is the acronym for "enzyme-linked immunosorbent assay.") The ELISA is extremely sensitive; it almost always reacts positively to blood that has been infected. The problem is that it sometimes also reacts positively to virus-free blood—if, that is, the blood carries proteins similar to those of the AIDS virus antibodies. Thus the ELISA, while mostly accurate, may sometimes produce a **false-positive** outcome, indicating that the antibodies are present when in fact they are not. Because of the possibility of false posi-

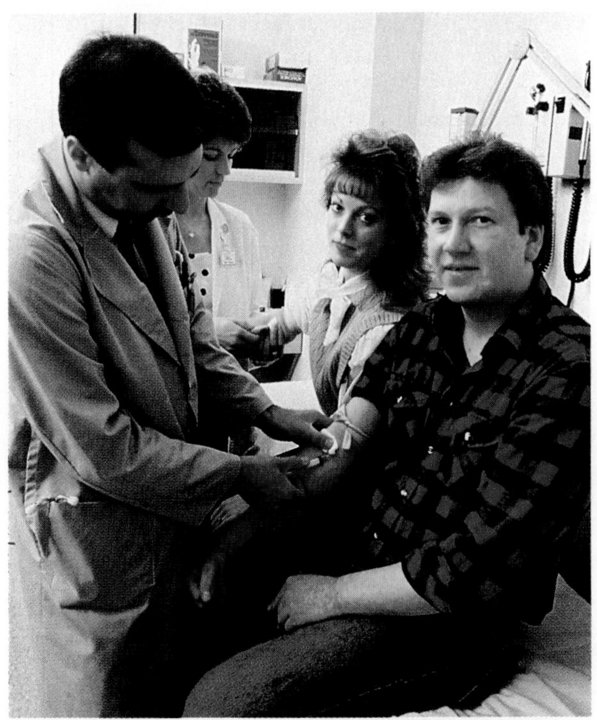

Man and woman being tested for AIDS. The most widely used test for determining whether a person is infected with the AIDS virus is the ELISA. Actually, it is the antibodies to the virus, rather than the virus itself, that show up on the test. But the presence of those antibodies in the blood means that the person is infected with the AIDS virus, which is the direct cause of the deadly disease. The ELISA is in most cases highly accurate, but it may occasionally produce false results.

tives, anyone who gets a positive result must be tested two more times. If a person tests positive two out of three times, he or she must be subjected to a different analysis called the Western blot test, which is more accurate but more difficult to run and therefore more expensive than the ELISA. When a person has tested positive at least twice on the ELISA with a positive confirmation by the Western blot, that person can be said with confidence though not complete certainty to be infected with the virus. Even such careful testing can sometimes produce a **false negative,** showing no antibodies while in fact the person has been infected. This is because the virus can live in the blood for as long as six months without setting off the production of antibodies (Slaff and Brubaker, 1985). In sum, testing for AIDS is highly complicated, time-consuming, and expensive. It is in most cases very accurate, but it may sometimes produce false results.

In searching for the cause of AIDS, epidemiologists have found the clues in the social characteristics and behaviors of the victims. So far most of the victims (65 percent in 1987) have been homosexual or bisexual men. The second largest group (25 percent) have been intravenous drug users. The rest are non–drug-using heterosexuals (3 percent); people who have received blood or blood products (3 percent), one third of whom have suffered from hemophilia or other blood disorders; and children born to mothers with AIDS and other unidentified individuals (4 percent).

In recent years, however, the number of *new* victims among homosexual men has fallen sharply. This is largely because gay men have drastically changed their sexual behavior. As surveys of the large homosexual community in San Francisco indicate, from 1978 to 1985 the median number of sexual partners during a four-month period dropped from 16 to 1, and the incidence of anal intercourse was down 96 percent (Holzman, 1988). In contrast, new infection among intravenous drug users has skyrocketed, so that most of the new cases of AIDS now appear among drug users. Toward the end of 1987, more than half of New York City's estimated 200,000 drug addicts were already infected with the virus (Joseph, 1987). Most of these are poor blacks and Hispanics in the inner city; they often share contaminated needles when shooting drugs and pass the virus on to one another. New infection has also risen significantly among poor black and Hispanic children whose mothers acquired the virus from shooting drugs themselves or having sex with infected male addicts (Thomas, 1988). But the AIDS infection has stabilized among drug-free heterosexuals and recipients of blood transfusions. Apparently scared by earlier warnings that AIDS would "break out" into the heterosexual population, many sexually active men and women have practiced monogamy or safer sex. Due to new, stringent blood-screening procedures, hemophiliacs and others who need blood transfusions have their risk of infection significantly reduced (Gorman, 1987; Levine, 1988).

All those epidemiogical facts clearly suggest that AIDS spreads mostly through sexual intercourse with an infected person and through the sharing of a hypodermic needle that has been contaminated with the virus. By examining the blood, semen, or vaginal secretions of AIDS victims, medical scientists were able to discover

Anti-AIDS parade by San Francisco's gays. In recent years, the number of new AIDS victims among homosexual men has declined significantly. A major reason has been a drastic change in sexual behavior. According to surveys of male homosexuals in San Francisco, from 1978 to 1985 the median number of sexual partners during a four-month period plummeted from 16 to 1, and the incidence of anal intercourse fell by 96 percent. Multiple partners and anal sex had been a major contributor to the spread of AIDS in the homosexual community.

HIV, the virus that causes AIDS. Studies in other societies can also be useful. For example, epidemiologists have discovered some similarities and differences between African AIDS victims and their American counterparts. Unlike the American victims, the African patients do not have histories of intravenous drug use, homosexuality, or blood transfusion. But like American homosexuals with AIDS, African heterosexuals with the disease are mostly upper-middle-class, live in large cities, and have been promiscuous. Thus AIDS has spread among Africans in the same way as it has among homosexuals in the United States: through sex with multiple partners. By itself, though, promiscuity is not the source of the virus. It is largely due to the law of probability that the more sexual partners one has, the more likely one is to pick up the infection. In other words, becoming infected through promiscuity "is not due to the cumulative effect of sex with 'too many partners.' It is due to the increased possibility of having sex with the 'wrong partner'" (Slaff and Brubaker, 1985). The risk of infection from a single act of sexual intercourse with an infected partner is 1 in 500, which is a million times as high as the risk from one sexual encounter with a partner who has been tested negative (Hearst and Hulley, 1988).

Unfortunately, it is not as easy to stop the spread of AIDS as it was for Dr. Snow to stop the spread of cholera in 1854. As we have observed, he simply shut down the Broad Street water pump. This simple action worked because the water pump was the only source of the cholera that struck the Broad Street residents. But today, according to the Centers for Disease Control in Atlanta, there are at least a million carriers of the AIDS virus in the United States (Ricklefs, 1988). There are, in effect, a million sources of the disease. It is difficult to stop all of them from spreading the virus, especially since most of them have not shown any symptoms and even they themselves generally do not know they have the virus.

The epidemiology of AIDS, however, suggests that behavioral changes can slow the spread of the disease. As has been noted, the rate of new infection has plummeted among homosexual men because they have largely given up sexual promiscuity and practiced safer sex. Similar changes in sexual behavior among heterosexuals may explain why "there are no signs of the much feared 'breakout' of AIDS into the heterosexual population" (Gorman, 1987). But the soaring rate of new infection among intravenous drug addicts suggests that this high-risk group continues to use contaminated needles. If clean needles are used, infection can be reduced not only for drug addicts themselves but for their sex partners and unborn babies as well. There is as yet no certainty that addicts will stop sharing needles.

Social Consequences of AIDS

Unlike such familiar killers as cancer and heart disease, AIDS is mysterious and has had an unusual impact on our society. As we have seen, the disease is not only lethal but can be transmitted through life's most basic human interaction—sex and procreation. Understandably, the general public is gripped with the fear of contagion. The initial appearance of AIDS among two groups of which society disapproves—homosexuals and drug addicts—has added to the fear, as prejudice discourages any understanding of "their" disease.

According to a series of surveys by the U.S. Public Health Service, a growing number of Americans have quickly learned the risk factors for AIDS, but misinformation about the disease's transmission remains a major problem. In late 1987, 91 to 97 percent of the respondents knew that AIDS could be transmitted by way of sex, through the use of shared needles, or from an infected woman to her unborn child. Seventy-seven percent also correctly said that someone could carry the AIDS virus without having the disease. But a substantial minority (21 to 47 percent) said that (1) a person could get AIDS by donating blood, (2) transmission could occur through the sharing of utensils or the use of public toilets, and (3) they could get AIDS from a co-worker (*Medical World News,* 1987). Many journalists have also reported that some people are even afraid that AIDS can be spread by casual contact—through shaking hands, hugging, kissing, or sitting next to an infected person. There is also fear that crying, coughing, sneezing, spitting, or eating food prepared by an AIDS carrier can spread the disease. Such fears, according to health authorities, are groundless.

Nevertheless, the fears have spawned strange and sad actions against AIDS victims. In 1987 the school board in Arcadia, Florida, barred three hemophiliac brothers—Richard, Robert, and Randy Ray—who had been infected with the virus through blood transfusions. When the boys were ordered admitted to class by a court, many parents boycotted the school. The Ray family received telephone threats and lost their home to arson, which forced them to leave the town. Parents in many other places have also demanded mandatory testing of all schoolchildren and segregation of those with AIDS. Even some high-ranking government officials have supported mandatory testing as a way of stopping the spread of AIDS. In 1987 Secretary of Education William Bennett called for mandatory tests of hospital patients, couples seeking marriage licenses, prison inmates, and foreigners who want to immigrate into the United States. Although Bennett did not go so far as to advocate quarantining AIDS victims, his proposal on compulsory testing shocked public health experts and some lawyers, politicians, and ethicists.

Some people are afraid that AIDS can be spread by casual contact such as shaking hands, hugging, or sitting next to an infected person. Although such fears are groundless, they have generated strange and sad actions against AIDS victims. Some parents have pressured school boards to bar AIDS-infected children, and other parents have demanded mandatory testing of all schoolchildren and segregation of those with AIDS.

As has been suggested, while present tests for AIDS are highly accurate, they are not foolproof. The tests are particularly reliable when applied to such high-risk groups as gay men and drug abusers. They produce only a minute number of false positives among these people, which is dwarfed by the large number of true positives (obtained among those who test positive and actually have the virus). By contrast, the same tests applied to the general population, which is at low risk for AIDS, would produce more false positives than true positives. According to the congressional Office of Technology Assessment, if a low-risk group were screened for AIDS by the ELISA test, with its positive results confirmed by the Western blot test, 89 out of 100,000 people would be labeled as carrying the virus. Of these 89 positives, 80 would be false and only 9 true. This means that "in screening a low-risk population, up to 90 percent of people confirmed by the two tests as infected will not be" (*New York Times,* 1987).

Mandatory testing can further wreak havoc in the lives of those who test positive. Individuals who have tested positive from voluntary testing have been known to say: "Hardly an hour goes by when I don't think about it," "I feel like a leper," or "I am frightened of being rejected." Some have even killed themselves or tried to do so. A person who tested positive said, "At first, I thought I had AIDS and was going to die. Later I tried to kill myself, but a friend and a fireman rescued me." Many carry their burden secretly for fear of losing friends, lovers, jobs, homes, and health insurance (Ricklefs, 1988). Such fear is far from groundless, because these people really are vulnerable to rejection and discrimination. Life is already wrenching enough to those who have tested truly positive and must carry the stigma of their disease. It would be tragically ironic to cause the same suffering in those who happened to test falsely positive in a mandatory mass screening.

Mandatory testing could also drive high-risk and infected people underground. They would be frightened away from counseling, treatment, and other disease-control programs. Even if they were assured that their diagnoses would be kept confidential, they would not have much confidence in such assurances. They are typically the people most suspicious of authority because, as homosexuals or drug users, they have not been viewed kindly by society. The cost of screening low-risk populations is also too high. Given the enormous number of low-risk people to be tested, the cost could be over $50,000 for each true positive detected. The money could better be spent on research to find a cure for the disease. And there is a cheaper alternative for finding infected individuals: tracing the sexual and needle contacts of those already diagnosed. Finally, mandatory testing may violate the constitutional right to privacy. It is better to set up *voluntary* testing programs with a guarantee of confidentiality, which virtually nobody would oppose. In sum, opponents of mandatory testing have "condemned the idea as prohibitively expensive, morally and legally wrong and, as a practical matter, unworkable" (Seligman, 1987).

Despite the legal issues, medical questions, and economic costs brought up by opponents, most Americans still support mandatory testing. In a 1987 *Newsweek* poll, more than 75 percent of those surveyed favored testing for people who apply for marriage licenses or who enter hospitals for treatment, and slightly more than 50 percent agreed that the entire U.S. population should be tested. The largest percentage (87 percent) of the respondents supported the idea that high-risk groups should be tested (see Table 18.2).

In addition to the controversy over testing, there is the conflict of opinion over what else can be done to stop the spread of AIDS. Liberals advocate "safer sex," such as condom use and careful selection of sex partners. But conservatives insist that abstinence ("no sex") is better than safer sex because it is the only certain method to prevent the sexual transmission of AIDS. Moreover, there is a controversy over the distribution of free clean needles to drug addicts. This conflict has erupted between public-health officials and law-enforcement agents. Public-health officials believe that distribution of clean needles will slow the spread of AIDS, but law enforcers argue that drug addicts would sell rather than use the free needles because they are hooked on needle sharing.

The AIDS fear has also generated a host of legal conflicts. The largest number of cases involve jobs. When AIDS struck schoolteacher Vincent Chalk, he was transferred to office duties working on grant proposals. The school board feared that he might endanger his students' lives. But Chalk was infuriated. Armed with doctors' statements that he posed no health threat, he sued the school board and got his job back. Another common lawsuit arises when employers require employees and job applicants to take blood tests for the AIDS virus. The American Federation of Government Em-

Table 18.2 The Public Says Yes to Mandatory Testing

Despite complicated civil liberties issues and medical questions, there is widespread support for broader AIDS testing. Below are the responses of people who were asked which of the following groups should have their blood tested for AIDS:

Percent saying yes	Groups the public says should be tested
87%	High-risk groups such as homosexuals, intravenous drug users, and their sex partners
71%	People in certain occupations such as food handlers, teachers, and health-care workers
80%	People applying for marriage licenses
77%	People entering hospitals for treatment
52%	Everyone

Source: From *Newsweek*, February 16, 1987, p. 22. Copyright © 1987 by NEWSWEEK, Inc. All rights reserved. Reprinted by permission.

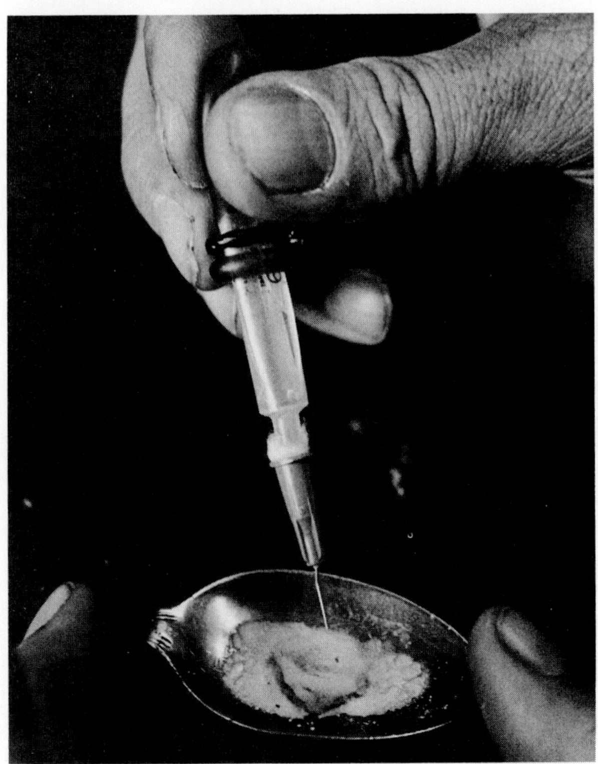

The sharing of contaminated needles among drug users has contributed to the large increase in new cases of AIDS. But controversy has erupted over the distribution of free, clean needles to drug addicts. Public-health officials contend that distributing needles will slow the spread of AIDS. But law enforcers argue that drug addicts would sell rather than use the free needles because they are addicted to needle sharing as much as to drugs.

ployees, for example, recently sued the U.S. State Department to stop mandatory testing. In some states, AIDS patients charge that they are denied services by businesses. In West Hollywood, California, a man sued Jessica's Nail Clinic for refusing to give him a pedicure after the clinic heard that he had AIDS. Homosexuals have also sued insurance companies for discriminating against them in issuing health insurance—by requiring them, for example, to fill out a special supplementary health questionnaire. Some cases hinge on the question of whether transmitting the disease is itself a criminal offense. A Chicago woman has sued American Airlines for reckless hiring because one of its ticket agents, who carries the AIDS virus, bit her in a scuffle over a boarding pass. A woman in St. Paul, Minnesota, has sued the estate of her former fiancé—now dead—for allegedly giving her the AIDS virus through sexual intercourse (Ricklefs, 1987).

AIDS has further reinforced the homophobia—fear of homosexuals—that haunts the general public. Before AIDS made headlines, most Americans would not have denied gays their civil rights, although they considered homosexuality wrong. In the mid-1980s, however, the fear of AIDS as a major health crisis changed public attitudes. People blamed homosexuals for causing the disease, called it the "gay plague." Violence against homosexuals has been rising significantly. In New York City, reported attacks on gays nearly tripled from 176 in 1984 to 517 in 1987. Not surprisingly, a majority of Americans agreed that governmental restrictions should be placed on the sexual and workplace activities of known carriers of AIDS (Schneider and Lewis, 1984; Zuckerman, 1988). Nevertheless, as the disease has been spreading among an ever-widening pool of victims, American society has begun to come to terms with the AIDS epidemic as an unprecedented health and social crisis. The federal government has begun to fund anti-AIDS programs. It increased its AIDS budget from only $5.5 million to $950 million over five years. AIDS has become the number-one priority of the Department of Health and Human Services (HHS). In 1988 Dr. Otis Bowen, the Secretary of HHS, requested a further increase in funds to fight AIDS in 1989. The requested $1.145 billion would be used for AIDS-related research, treatment, and education (Pear, 1988). Under pressure from gays, 21 states have passed laws protecting AIDS victims against job dismissal and other forms of discrimination, and other states seem to be moving in the same direction (Morganthau, 1986).

Compared with the epidemics of the past, however, AIDS pales in significance. In only three years, between 1347 and 1350, the Black Death, or bubonic plague, killed 25 to 50 million people in Europe. At its height in the eighteenth century, smallpox killed some 400,000 Europeans a year. In two years, from early 1917 to late 1918, an influenza outbreak took 22 million lives. Some ancient epidemics even wiped out entire populations or civilizations. The whole Aztec civilization in what is now Mexico collapsed in the wake of a smallpox epidemic started by a Spanish soldier. When the Dutch colonists brought smallpox to South Africa in the eighteenth century, Africa's entire Hottentot population soon died out. By contrast, between 1981 and 1986, the death toll from AIDS in this country stood at about 20,000 (Wells, 1987). If the comparatively small epidemic of AIDS could cause the social turmoil that we have observed, we can imagine how much more disastrous the social impact of past epidemics must have been. With cases doubling every 13 weeks, AIDS may well have the same cataclysmic consequences for our society at the turn of the century, when, if no vaccine has yet appeared, tens of millions of Americans might die.

QUESTIONS FOR DISCUSSION AND REVIEW

1. Why have chronic diseases replaced acute diseases as the chief threat to Americans' health?
2. How do social factors like gender, race and ethnicity, and social class influence a person's health?
3. What is epidemiology, and how does it help doctors locate the causes of disease?
4. What have epidemiologists discovered about the social characteristics and behaviors of the victims of the AIDS virus?
5. Why do most Americans support mandatory testing for the AIDS virus, and what problems could such a policy create?

THE MEDICAL PROFESSION

Until fairly recently, doctoring was a lowly profession. Many of the doctors were more like quacks than true medical scientists. They had little knowledge of how the various body systems worked or of how diseases developed. In the face of such ignorance, doctors could easily be a menace. For numerous ailments, they bled patients profusely; evacuated their bowels, often until they passed out; stuffed them with poisons; and tormented them with various ghastly appliances. One treatment for syphilis was to roast the patient in an oven. Sometimes the patients survived despite all this assistance, but more often they died. Either way, the doctors learned a great deal from them. In time, they developed a store of knowledge that eventually enabled them to practice a highly respectable profession (Blundell, 1987).

The Emergence of Modern Medicine

Modern medicine has a short history, since medical schools only began to turn out competent doctors less than 80 years ago. Before then, the vast majority of such schools did not even teach the basic sciences. Most operated like the barbers' colleges and other trade schools of today; they were not affiliated with universities or hospitals. Some were simply diploma mills, selling medical degrees. At the turn of the century, there was a widespread perception among physicians themselves that medical education needed to be reformed, and the Carnegie Foundation commissioned Abraham Flexner to investigate. Flexner's report, which came out in 1910, was a stinging condemnation of medical training. In its wake, bogus medical schools—some two-thirds of all the medical schools in the United States and Canada—were closed, standards for admitting students became stringent, and basic sciences as well as real medical courses were offered. Soon the schools were graduating competent doctors, and by the 1920s the medical societies, through physician licensing, had driven the quacks from the profession. "For the first time in human history," observed a medical historian, "a random patient with a random disease consulting a doctor chosen at random stood better than a 50-50 chance of benefiting from the encounter" (Twaddle and Hessler, 1987).

All this did not result solely from the reorganization of medical training and the profession. The birth of modern medicine would not have taken place without the development of the germ theory of disease in the 1850s. For centuries before then, physicians never suspected that germs could cause disease. Without microscopes, which only became available during the last century, they could not see the tiny disease-causing organisms. More importantly, physicians were not empirically inclined—they were reluctant to cut up human bodies to observe what was inside. Instead, they accepted the medical theories of the ancient Greek philosophers. They were most impressed by the theories that the Greek physician Hippocrates formulated some 2500 years ago.

According to Hippocrates, a person's health depended on a delicate balance among four "humors": blood, phlegm, yellow bile, and black bile. If these bodily fluids were in equilibrium, the individual was healthy. But any imbalance, with one fluid being more abundant than the others, led to illness. Thus fever, a common symptom of many diseases, was attributed to an excess of "hot blood." Logically, the patient should be bled. Bloodletting, then, became a popular method of treatment, although it did more harm than good. Other aspects of Hippocrates' philosophy, however, have benefited humanity even to this day. The most famous is the

Hippocratic oath, which requires physicians always to help the sick, avoid harming people, and keep confidential what goes on between doctor and patient. Another useful legacy from Hippocrates is his observation that human health depends on a totality of personal and environmental factors: mental state, life-style, climate, and the quality of air and water. This knowledge has been employed to improve health and prevent disease. Even in the old days, when physicians did not know anything about germs as the cause of disease, they did know that a contaminated, polluted environment could make people sick. In the Middle Ages, for example, physicians knew why cities were not as healthy as farmlands. They could see sewage running in the streets, water supplies that were dirty and smelly, and houses that were cramped, with too little light and ventilation. When they occasionally succeeded in cleaning up such an environment, they could see an improvement in the residents' health.

But up until about 1850, physicians were generally unconcerned about the sanitary condition of their practice. Knowing nothing about germs, they did not bother to scrub before they operated on a patient. After patching up wounds or dissecting corpses, they would proceed to deliver babies—without first washing their hands. Hospitals were filthy places where patients were left unwashed on vermin-infested beds. Indeed, hospitals were notorious for spreading diseases more than curing them. Not surprisingly, most people turned to family members for care at times of sickness, and hospitals operated mostly as charity wards for those urban poor who had no families to care for them (Rosenberg, 1987). In 1867, however, French chemist Louis Pasteur revolutionized medicine with his discovery of germs as the cause of cholera, anthrax, chickenpox, and other common infectious diseases. Surgeons then began to scrub and hospitals became sanitary. To further stop the infection and spread of diseases, people were immunized against them. Toward the end of the last century, physicians were able to treat many more ailments, thanks to the introduction of medical technology like X-ray examinations and of synthetic drugs like barbital and quinine.

It was, however, in this century that the medical profession took a quantum leap in fighting diseases. By the 1920s the hospital had supplanted the home as the preferred place in which to receive medical care. Most Americans no longer regarded the hospital as a refuge for the poor but as a place where genuine medical treatment was offered (see box, p. 464). In the 1930s the development of penicillin and sulfa drugs began to give physicians their first true power to cure. They would soon be able to eliminate nearly every infectious disease. Tending the wounds of combat during World War II, they received ample opportunity to hone their skills and develop new techniques. In the 1950s and 1960s, vaccines became available for preventing polio and measles, and high medical technology—respirators, dialyzers, and CAT scans—began to appear everywhere. By now these vaccines and medical machines, along with antibiotics, have transformed our image of doctors. They are ex-

French chemist Louis Pasteur (1822–1895). In 1867 Pasteur revolutionized medicine with his discovery that microorganisms, or germs, cause such infectious diseases as cholera, anthrax, and chicken pox. Since then, surgeons scrub before operations, and hospitals have taken steps to become sanitary. Vaccination has also been used to stop infection and the spread of diseases.

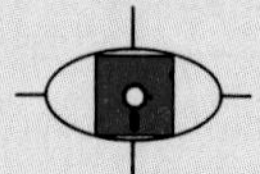

LOOKING AT CURRENT RESEARCH

The Care of Strangers

Before 1920, most Americans, when they became ill, depended on their families for care at home. Hospitals served primarily to care for strangers—that is, for people who could not be cared for at home and who were not known personally by the hospital staff. Usually only the urban poor fell into this category. But today, the situation is reversed; nearly everyone, of every class, expects to be treated for serious ailments in a hospital. This change came about gradually, as outlined in the following reading. What are the most significant differences between care of the sick before the 1920s and today?

In 1800, the hospital was still an insignificant aspect of American medical care. No gentlemen of property or standing would have found himself in a hospital unless striken with insanity or felled by epidemic or accident in a strange city. When respectable persons or members of their family fell ill, they would be treated at home. In those days, every educated gentleman was presumed to know something about medicine, and every woman was something of a general practitioner.

If too sick to be cared for at home, urban workers were most likely to find themselves in an almshouse, not a hospital. Although envisioned as a "receptacle" for the dependent and indigent, the almshouse had by the late eighteenth century become in part a municipal hospital in function if not in name. Growing numbers of sick in the almshouses of America's seaport cities required the development of separate wards for their care—separate from the simply destitute, the orphaned, the marginally criminal, and the permanently incapacitated who also populated their warehouse for the dependent.

All of this had changed drastically by 1920. The hospital had become a national institution, no longer a refuge for the urban poor alone. It had become a potential recourse for a much larger proportion of Americans. The prosperous and respectable as well as the indigent were now treated in hospitals, frequently by their regular physicians.

Many social functions had been moving from the home and neighborhood to institutional sites in early-twentieth-century America—but none more categorically than medical care. And in no other case was the technical rationale more compelling. From today's perspective, the resources of hospital medicine in 1920 may seem primitive, but they were impressive to contemporaries. Antiseptic surgery, the x-ray, and the clinical laboratory seemed to represent a newly scientific and efficacious medicine—a

pected to heal their patients. As a consequence, medicine has become the most respected profession (Starr, 1983; Easterbrook, 1987).

Training for a Medical Career

So far in this decade about half of the applicants to medical schools have been admitted. Most of these students are white males, although they are increasingly joined by women and minorities. In the United States, medicine is still widely considered a masculine profession, since the majority of doctors are men. This contrasts with the popular image of medicine as a feminine occupation in the Soviet Union and Eastern Europe, where the majority of doctors are women. Nonwhites are still underrepresented among medical students partly because of inadequate financial resources. There are other social determinants of who is likely to go to medical school. One is age. Compared with their peers in other fields, medical students decide on their career choice very early. Slightly more than half made that decision before they were 14 years old, and about one-fifth did so before age 16. Family influence is also a major factor. The fathers or other relatives of many medical students are physicians. For other students, the decision to enter medical school is likely to have been influenced by family doctors or family friends who are doctors. Altogether, according to one study, 71 percent of medical students have had some contact with members of the medical profession. Influenced by these doctors and fueled by their youthful commitment to medicine, medical students are generally ready to put in an medicine necessarily based in the hospital. Few practitioners could duplicate these resources in their offices or make them easily available in the homes of even their wealthiest patients. Successful physicians had come to assume, and had convinced their patients, that the hospital was the best place to undergo surgery and in fact to treat any acute ailment.

However, costs began to rise steadily. Although simple and technologically unadorned by contemporary standards, the hospital of the 1920s was a capital-intensive institution, certainly by comparison with its mid-nineteenth-century predecessors. An increasingly sophisticated technology, both medical and nonmedical, implied higher capital and operating costs and thus a ceaseless quest for reliable sources of income and endowment. Moreover, most hospitals continued the traditional mission of caring for the needy. Treating the poor and lower middle class inevitably threatened unending deficits. Administrators of nonprofit hospitals thus energetically sought to maximize private patient income.

The increasing prominence of technology and the physicians who employed these impressive new tools expressed itself in another and particularly tenacious way. This was the prominent role of acute care in the nonprofit hospital, and a parallel lack of interest in the chronically ill. Such patients were expensive and fit uncomfortably into the priorities of an increasingly self-confident medical profession. Most chronic facilities, for example, found it difficult to attract housestaff; the duties were depressing and the cases "uninteresting."

From 1920 to the present, the emergence of third-party payment, government involvement, technological change, and general economic growth has stimulated a rapid development of the hospital. At the same time, scientific medicine has raised expectations and costs. We are still wedded to acute care and episodic, specialized contacts with physicians. There is a great deal of evidence that indicates widespread dissatisfaction with the quality of care as it is experienced by Americans. Chronic and geriatric care still constitute a problem—as they always did. We cannot seem to live without high-technology medicine; we cannot seem to live amicably with it, either. Yet, for the great majority of Americans, divorce is unthinkable.

Source: Adapted from *The Care of Strangers: The Rise of America's Hospital System,* by Charles E. Rosenberg. Copyright © 1987 by Basic Books, Inc. Reprinted by permission of Basic Books, Inc., Publishers.

eight-hour day of classes and laboratories plus four to five hours of study every night. Not surprisingly, an overwhelming majority (about 95 percent) of all entering medical students will eventually graduate with the M.D. degree (Cockerham, 1986).

The first two years of medical school are taken up with basic sciences: anatomy, physiology, biochemistry, pharmacology, microbiology, and pathology. The next two years are devoted to clinical training. Under the supervision of interns, residents, and faculty, students serve as junior physicians, learning to collect samples for laboratory analysis, examine patients, diagnose diseases, and suggest treatments. In these four years students acquire the scientific knowledge and clinical skills they will need as doctors. But their attitudes and values also change significantly. During the first year, they bubble with idealism, determined to learn it all so that they can later serve humanity. Soon they realize that there is too much information for them to absorb. After feverishly—but to no avail—trying to memorize everything, they throw in the towel. They begin to study only that fraction of the material which they think will appear on the exams (Becker et al., 1961).

They also learn to be egalitarian with patients, allowing them to have a voice in their own care, especially in these days, when some patients are quite knowledgeable and critical—unwilling to rely on the physician's authority alone (Lavin et al., 1987). At the same time, however, students learn to avoid emotional involvement with patients. They learn to maintain professional objectivity, seeing disease and death as medical problems rather than emotional issues. Since this involves suppressing empathy and compassion, it is bound to throw cold water on their earlier fiery enthusiasm

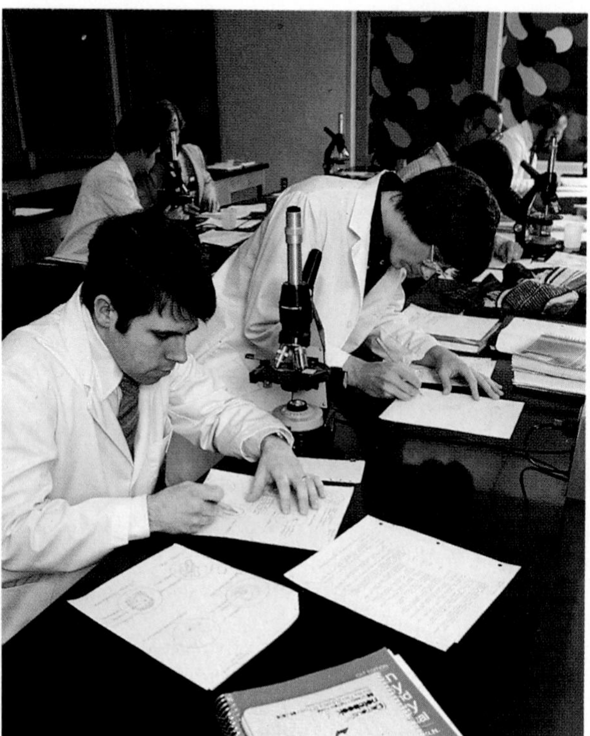

During the four years of medical school, students learn the scientific knowledge and clinical skills they will need as doctors. But their attitudes and values tend to change. During the first year, they are determined to learn everything so that they can later serve humanity. Soon their idealism wanes and practicality prevails: they study only what they think will appear on the exams. After they graduate and serve as interns and, often, residents, they expect to have a profitable practice.

about serving humanity. Having lost much of their idealism, they begin to think more about making money. Thus many would not choose to help the poor by providing basic medical care or to practice medicine in the small towns and rural areas where doctors are needed desperately (Broadhead, 1983). After graduation, they learn doctoring by serving as interns for a year, after which they take an exam leading to a license to practice medicine.

An increasing number of these new physicians continue their training by taking a residency at a hospital for one to five years. Typically they work 12 hours straight each day, not by sitting behind desks but by doing the hard labor of tending people in pain. In addition, every third night or so they must interrupt their sleep to answer the dreaded emergency calls. Despite their overwork, young doctors are paid only about $22,000 yearly, much less than the average physician's salary of $113,000. Then, after spending a small fortune on medical school, residents are further burdened with an average debt of $33,000. Even more significantly, they must forgo their young adulthood, since the brutalizing learning process does not stop until age 30. Understandably, many are determined to make up for lost youth by earning high fees when they set up their own medical practices (Easterbrook, 1987).

A Symbolic Interactionist View

An important aspect of medical practice is the relationship between doctor and patient. Research has suggested that patients tend to evaluate warm, friendly doctors favorably even when these doctors have not provided successful treatment. By contrast, patients are most likely to sue for malpractice those physicians who are the most highly trained and who practice in the most sophisticated hospitals. Although these physicians are not intentionally negligent, they are most likely to be viewed by their patients—not just the ones that sue them—as cold and bureaucratic (Twaddle and Hessler, 1987). It is the friendly doctor's "affiliative style" of communication that enhances patient satisfaction and it is the highly competent but bureaucratic doctor's "dominant style" that alienates patients. "Affiliative style" involves behaviors that communicate honesty, compassion, humor, and a nonjudgmental attitude. "Dominant style" involves the manifestation of power, authority, professional detachment, and status in the physician's interaction with the patient (Buller and Buller, 1987).

Why does the doctor's communication style affect patient satisfaction? Why are patients likely to be satisfied with the friendly doctor's treatment even if it has failed to cure the disease? Why do patients tend to sue highly competent but dominant doctors? From the perspective of symbolic interactionism (see Chapter 1: Thinking Sociologically), we can assume that, in interacting with patients, friendly doctors are more likely than dominant doctors to take into account the views, feelings, and expectations held by the patients about themselves, their illnesses, and their doctors. To the patients, the illness is unusual, as it does not happen to them every day. Moreover, their suffering is a highly intimate, emotional reality. Thus they expect their doctors to show a great deal of concern. They obviously want a cure, but they also crave emotional support. If doctors attune themselves to these expectations, they can develop warm relationships with their patients (see box, p. 468). But this is no easy task because physicians have been trained to take an objective, dispassionate approach to disease. They have learned to view patients unemotionally, especially in cases where they must perform surgeries that cause considerable pain. After all, they have learned "to perform acts unpleasant to them personally—sticking your hands inside diseased strangers is not many people's idea of a good time—without flinching or losing their nerves" (Easterbrook, 1987).

Such emotional detachment often intrudes into the medical interview. According to the National Task Force on Medical Interviews, "In the typical doctor-patient encounter, all too often the doctor dominates with questions based on his technical understanding of the cause and treatment of the illness, while the patient, often in vain, tries to get the doctor to pay attention to his very personal sense of the illness" (Goleman, 1988). In one study, average patients were found to have three different problems on their minds when they went to see their doctors, but their efforts to tell their stories were cut off by the doctors within the first 18 seconds of the interview. In fact, most patients never got beyond the first question. Moreover, when the patients were allowed to talk, the physician often responded only with an "um hum." Such a response is noncommittal and indicates only minimal interest (Goleman, 1988). Detached professionalism may be effective for diagnosing and treating disease, but it tends to exact a price by alienating patients. They often feel that they are being treated as mere diseases rather than as people. Thus such patients are likely to be dissatisfied with the medical care they receive.

QUESTIONS FOR DISCUSSION AND REVIEW

1. What events that occurred during the nineteenth and early twentieth centuries helped shape the emergence of modern medicine?
2. Who decides to pursue a medical career, and what experiences during and after medical school shape the practice of medicine?
3. How do symbolic interactionists describe and explain the doctor-patient relationship?

In order to be objective, doctors tend to be emotionally detached in dealing with patients. In typical doctor-patient encounters, doctors usually dominate with questions based on their knowledge of the disease, while patients futilely try to get the doctors to appreciate their personal sense of the illness. Detached professionalism tends to alienate patients because they feel that they are being treated as mere diseases rather than as people.

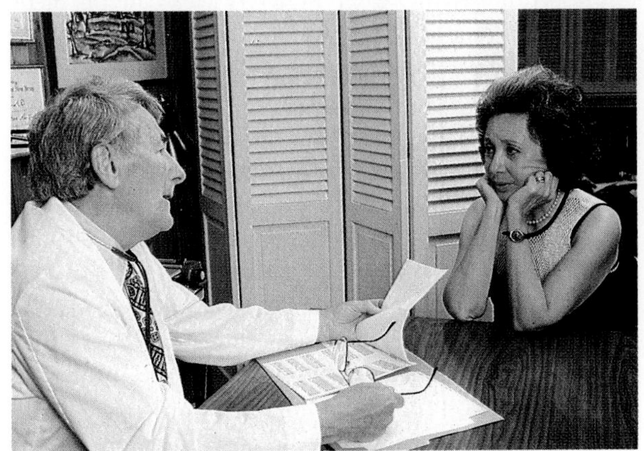

MEDICAL CARE

When people feel sick, they obviously want to get well again. But they do not automatically go to see a doctor. Some may simply shrug off their illness, feeling that it is not serious enough. But it is more than the severity of illness that motivates people to seek medical care. Social factors are also involved. They help determine who is likely to see a doctor and who is not.

Seeking Medical Care

It is common knowledge that the elderly are more often ill than are younger people (see Chapter 12: The Elderly). It is, therefore, not surprising that the elderly are the most likely of all age groups to seek medical care. There is also a gender factor: women are more likely than men to use health services. Like the elderly, women suffer from a higher rate of illness.

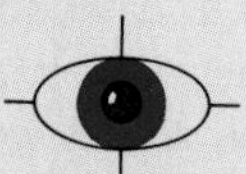

USING SOCIOLOGICAL INSIGHT

The Doctor as Dramatist

As symbolic interactionism suggests, doctors can interact smoothly with their patients if they correctly interpret the way their patients think and feel about their illness, themselves, and their doctors. We can see such a symbolic interaction in the following account by a doctor. How do this doctor and his patient interpret each other's behavior?

"Your next patient is a lady with a weak foot," the charge nurse informs me. I'm the doctor on duty in a hospital emergency ward and, as I walk to the room she's pointed to, I take a moment to prepare myself. First, I've got to have the right diagnostic mind-set as I enter: the weakness means I must think about stroke, multiple sclerosis and heart disease, among other things. I must also lead off with the right persona. Each type of patient—the adolescent with a drug overdose, the middle-aged man with chest pain or the depressed elderly woman—calls for a certain demeanor. A doctor tries to assume it from the outset, adjusting it as he goes on, as he would the fit of his white coat.

My patient turns out to be 27; she started on the Pill five days before and has had trouble with her right foot off and on ever since. She's worried about a stroke.

Hoping to put her at ease, I adopt a calming manner. After I'm far enough into my examination to see that her strength and sensation are normal, I tell her I understand why she came in; that many women who start the Pill are concerned about developing a stroke, a heart attack or a blood clot. Then, pausing for effect, I smile and give the good news, thinking it will allay her fears: "Fortunately, it takes much longer for the risk of a stroke to increase."

"It's not in my head, if that's what you mean," she snaps.

When I try to persuade her that nothing seems amiss, she balks. "Well, something is definitely wrong!"

I stall for a second, realizing that I've failed. I haven't responded to the need that brought her to the hospital late on a Sunday night. Even though I've done what was medically called for, I never like it when a patient leaves feeling angry or dissatisfied; I tend to take such reactions personally. What's more, the threat of malpractice is seldom far from my mind. While I believe I've exercised proper judgment, I know that in the charged atmosphere of the courtroom, good judgment alone doesn't always suffice. It's time, then, to improvise. Like Prospero in "The Tempest," only through "some vanity of mine art" can I make "my project gather to a head."

And so, I resort to theater. I stage a dazzlingly detailed neurolog-

Women's greater tendency to seek medical attention does not always lead them to obtain the proper care. Under the influence of sexual prejudice, doctors tend to dismiss women's complaints with such terms as "overstress," "back strain," "could be just the heat," or "nothing to worry about." Even when a patient presents complaints such as chest pains and other symptoms of heart disease, the doctor is less likely to take them seriously coming from a woman than from a man. As Jonathan Tobin and his colleagues (1987) found, doctors are twice as likely to label women's chest pains as a psychiatric complaint or something other than a sign of heart disease. Nevertheless, when they feel ill, women are still more likely than men to consult doctors.

Certain racial and ethnic minorities, however, are less inclined to consult physicians. Compared with other groups, Mexican-Americans have lower rates of physician utilization. They tend more to see the doctor as a last resort, preferring, when ill, to try Mexican folk medicine first. Their relatives, friends, neighbors, or *curanderos* (folk healers) are generally ready to provide certain patent medicines, herbs, and teas along with massages or manipulation of the body and the performance of religious rituals. American Indians also have a similar system of folk medicine which involves the use of herbal drugs, religious rituals, and physical manipulations. This sort of medicine is believed to be capable of restoring health by bringing back a harmonious balance of various biological and spiritual forces in the sick person's life. About the same principles of harmonious balance can be found in traditional Chinese medicine, which is popular with residents in America's Chinatowns. According to ic exam. There are props: a reflex hammer and an ophthalmoscope, each of which I move about in carefully choreographed patterns. There are dramatic asides—thoughtful "hmmm's"—and flourishes, too, like the motions I put my patient through to test for rare, abnormal reflexes. I even bring in special effects, such as a black and white striped tape which I move back and forth hypnotically before the woman's eyes, testing for subtle changes in her vision. Throughout it all, I'm careful to concentrate on my delivery, timing my words, smiles and gestures for best effect. My last act is to order an X-ray of the neck to make absolutely sure that impingement on a nerve root isn't the cause of her problems.

It's often said that doctors "play God," but the comment misses the point. Whether or not we're trying to be God's understudies, we always play to our audience. The truth is that people expect it of us. Despite the pressure to demystify what we do (we're increasingly asked to let our patients in on what's going on), we're still called on to perform. All cultures, at all times, have asked their healers to do so, and though we may not dance or play the drums or chant over a magic fire, we are still medicine men.

In offices, clinics and hospitals, we give performances calculated to make people feel better. We take full advantage of spectacle in the testing lab. When we perform physical exams, we resort to the ritual laying on of hands. Dialogue is another useful device. A doctor often moves his patient through an artful soliloquy or by conferring a fancy attribution on ailment either because it's common and we don't want the patient to feel unimportant, or because we don't have a name for it, and we don't want to deprive it of legitimacy.

My patient has arrived back from the X-ray suite and, as expected, the film shows no abnormality. Returning to her side, I sit down, maintain eye contact and explain as gently as I can that a thorough workup has shown that nothing is awry. Yet I carefully try to deal with her concern and to leave the door open to further care. "These symptoms are clearly bothering you a lot and they will hopefully resolve on their own," I say, "but we should consider doing more studies if they persist." I encourage her to call, shake her hand and wish her well. She's clearly pleased and thanks me profusely.

Source: Stephen A. Hoffman, "The doctor as dramatist," *Newsweek,* February 1, 1988, p. 10.

the Chinese, illness results from an imbalance between *yin* (the female, "cold" force) and *yang* (the male, "hot" force). If illness is due to an excess of (cold) yin over (hot) yang, certain herbs and foods that are classified as hot should be taken to bring back the balance between yin and yang—and hence health. If illness results from too much (hot) yang, "cold" herbs and foods should be taken.

To a large extent, however, the reluctance of racial and ethnic minorities to use a doctor also stems from their lack of financial resources or health insurance coverage. Nearly 30 percent of Mexican-Americans, for example, do not have health insurance. Many blacks—about 20 percent of all blacks under age 65—do not have insurance either. But blacks, without the folk medicine available to other minorities, are nearly as likely as whites to visit physicians. There is, though, a difference in the type of physician services used by the two racial groups. Blacks are two or three times more likely than whites to receive treatment in hospital outpatient clinics or emergency rooms, which are more often public than private. Whites are more likely to go to a private doctor's office. This is largely because a greater proportion of blacks than whites are poor.

The poor are more likely than the rich to get medical treatment in public clinics and emergency rooms. They are also more likely to visit the doctor, though in public hospitals. This may appear remarkable in view of their underutilization of physician services for many years in the past. After Medicaid was put into effect in the 1960s, and since 1970, the poor have been having higher rates of physician use than all of the higher-income groups. This does not mean, however, that the poor have enough medical care to meet their health needs. Although they see doctors more often than higher-income people do, the poor are also much more often sick. If the need for medical care is taken into account, the poor are actually less likely than the rich to receive adequate care. It is no wonder that the poor are more inclined to brush off illness or to treat themselves and delay seeking professional help. Moreover, since they typically receive treatment in public hospitals, the poor tend to get inferior care and to spend more time in waiting rooms. They are also less likely to have a personal physician and must wrestle with more bureaucratic agencies (Dutton, 1978; Cockerham, 1986). Apparently, the problem does not lie with unconcern among the poor about their health; instead, it lies in the health-care system. Let us take a closer look at it.

People waiting for treatment in a public clinic. One major problem with the health-care system is the unequal distribution of medical resources. There are proportionately far more doctors in affluent areas than in poor segments of the inner cities and countryside. Although the poor see doctors more often because of their higher incidence of illness, they tend more to receive treatment in public clinics and emergency rooms. The care is generally not as good as that available to affluent Americans in their doctors' offices.

Health-Care Delivery

One major problem with the health-care system in the United States is unequal access to care. There is no scarcity of medical resources. In fact, we have more doctors per person than many other industrial countries, as well as an abundance of medical technology and hospitals. But the distribution of these resources is very unequal. Doctors are plentiful in affluent areas but often scarce in poverty-stricken parts of the inner cities and countryside. Overall, there is one physician for every 4000 relatively poor Americans compared with one for every 500 affluent Americans.

During the late 1960s and the 1970s, government programs, with some success, sought to bring greater equality in medical care. Nutritional programs to supplement the diets of pregnant and nursing women and infants have been credited with lowering the infant mortality rate. The billions spent on Medicare and Medicaid allowed millions of elderly and poor Americans to receive more of the medical care they needed. Today, as we have observed, poor people have higher rates of physician use than other Americans. Now, even rates of surgery are about equal among the classes (Macrae, 1984). Typically, however, the poor receive treatment in public clinics and emergency rooms, where medical care is often inferior to that received by better-off Americans in their doctors' offices. Most of this care of the poor in inner cities and rural areas is delivered by city and county hospitals. A majority of these treatment centers are "Medicaid mills," run by dropouts from the respectable parts of the health-care system—doctors with questionable credentials and businessmen with little concern for their clientele.

Even this mediocre health care is not available to some 35 percent of the 33.1 million Americans below the poverty line. Many of the working poor and members of the lower middle class, being technically above the poverty line, do not qualify for Medicaid. But they are for all practical purposes "medically indigent": they can pay for their basic needs, but a medical expense can wipe them out. Also, ironically, our government spends about twice as much on medical care for the affluent middle class as for the poor. In 1985, for example, the federal government spent $70.5 billion on Medicare—for the elderly, many of whom are middle-class—and granted $30 million in tax breaks to corporations for private group health insurance. The total health-care assistance for people of means, then, amounted to roughly $100 billion. This contrasts with about $47 billion spent on Medicaid—for the poor—with the federal government doling out $21.9 billion and state and local governments contributing the rest (Easterbrook, 1987).

Another problem with our health-care system is soaring costs. In the last 27 years, medical costs have gone up faster than the rate of inflation for other goods and services. By 1987 medical care was already consuming over 10 percent of our national income, about $1200 for each American, compared with only $126 in 1960. Medical costs are expected to keep on rising.

Why have health-care costs escalated so rapidly? The aging of the American population may be one contributing factor, and the proliferation of medical technology may be another. New drugs and treatments and expensive new technologies appear every year. During the last decade, for example, hospitals began buying $700,000 CAT scanners to improve on what X-ray machines could do. Now there are $1.5-million NMRs (nuclear magnetic resonators) improving on the CAT scanners. There have also been significant advances in keeping coma and stroke victims alive—but they may then require extremely expensive medical care for years. According to officials at the Mayo Clinic in Rochester, Minnesota, "it costs as much as $9 million to add a year of life to the seriously ill patient through such ultramodern technologies as kidney dialysis and organ transplants" (Greenwald, 1982).

Thus there are some good reasons for rising costs, but these do not account for all of the increase. An additional, highly important reason is that the medical establishment has emphasized curing illness rather than preventing it and maintaining health. Most significantly, medical care in the United States is organized as a business, but it is quite different from other businesses. Medical "customers" have little say about what they buy because they usually cannot judge what they need. They rely on doctors to tell them what they need and how much they must pay. Meanwhile, doctors, hospitals, and consumers have few incentives to keep prices down. Consumers pay only a small share (about a third) of the cost directly. Most of it is passed on to third parties—insurance companies, employers, and the government. Understandably, consumers are not too concerned about medical costs. As for doctors and hospitals, they rarely feel the pressure felt by other businesses to keep their prices reasonable. Rarely is there competition to deliver medical services at a lower price.

Since 1983, however, efforts have been made to crack down on rampaging medical costs and with some success. Instead of paying hospitals whatever they want to charge Medicare patients, the federal government now pays them according to its own predetermined prices. In the private sector, the big corporations, labor unions, and insurance companies have joined forces to fight runaway health costs, forcing many employees to pay a larger share of their medical bills. This has reduced the use of expensive medical services and caused people to shop for cheaper health care. The coalition of business, labor, and insurance companies has also amassed and publicized data as to which doctors overcharge and which hospitals are the most expensive, so as to pressure them to compete and cut costs. An increasing number of companies require or encourage employees to join health-maintenance organizations (HMOs), whose medical services generally cost less than those provided by doctors in private practice. All this has begun to slow down the rise of health-care expenses. But the rise continues to be high. In 1986 the cost of medical care rose 7.7 percent, seven times more than the general inflation rate (Dentzer, 1984; Pear, 1987).

QUESTIONS FOR DISCUSSION AND REVIEW

1. How do social factors determine who might seek medical care?
2. What medical and social factors contribute to the difficulties some Americans have in seeking medical care?
3. Why has the cost of health care risen so dramatically during recent years?

PERSPECTIVES ON HEALTH AND MEDICAL CARE

From the functionalist perspective, we can see the positive aspects of medical care and even the positive functions of sickness for society. By contrast, the conflict perspective directs our attention to the negative side of health and medical care.

The Functionalist Perspective

According to functionalists, both physicians and patients play roles that contribute to social order. Patients must play the **sick role,** a pattern of expectation regarding how an ill person should behave. As discussed in Chapter 4 (Social Structure), role is associated with status, which in turn presents the person with a set of rights and obligations. In his classic definition of the sick role, Talcott Parsons (1975) essentially laid out what rights a sick person can claim and what obligations he or she should discharge. First, the sick should not be blamed for their illness, because they do not choose to be sick. They are not responsible for their illness. Therefore, they have the right to be taken care of by others. Second, the sick have the right to be exempted from certain social duties. They should not be forced to go to work. In the case of students, they should be allowed to miss an exam and take it later. Third, the sick are obligated to want to get well. They should not expect to remain ill and use the illness to take advantage of others' love, concern, and care for them and to shirk their work and other social responsibilities. And fourth, the sick are obligated to seek technically competent help. In seeing a doctor, they must cooperate to help ensure their recovery.

On the other hand, doctors have their own rights and obligations in playing the **healing role,** which is necessary to the orderly functioning of society. Basically, doctors are obligated to help the sick get well, as required by the Hippocratic oath, which they take when embarking on their medical career. At the same time, however, they have the right to receive appropriate compensation for their work. Since their work is widely regarded as highly important, they may expect to make a great deal of money and enjoy considerable prestige.

Seen from the functionalist perspective, both the sick and healing roles serve a social control function. They help to prevent illnesses from disrupting economic production, family relations, and social activities. Many sociologists, though, have criticized Parsons's theory of the sick role for a number of reasons. First, the theory may be relevant to Western societies but not necessarily to non-Western societies, where the sick are more likely to turn to folk medicine rather than seeking technically competent treatment. Second, even within a Western society, the sick role does not affect all social groups in the same way. As we have noted, racial and ethnic minorities, for example, are less likely than whites to seek treatment from physicians. Third, the sick role may apply to serious illnesses but not to mild ailments, because the latter do not lead to exemption from normal activities or contact with a physician (Twaddle and Hessler, 1987). Nevertheless, the critics do not question the basic point of Parsons's functionalist theory—namely, that the sick role serves a social control function for society, as previously indicated.

Moreover, the functionalist perspective suggests that the system of medical care helps maintain the health of society. Thus functionalists tend to attribute an improvement in the nation's health or a decline in mortality, when it occurs, to medicine, the physician, the medical profession, or some new technology of treatment. Such medical discoveries as the germ theory and such medical interventions as vaccines and drugs are credited for our great victory over infectious diseases. All this, however, is a myth to conflict theorists.

The Conflict Perspective

According to conflict theorists, improvements in the social environment contribute far more than do medical interventions to the reduction of illness and mortality. As one study shows, only about 3.5 percent of the total decline in mortality from five infectious diseases (influenza, pneumonia, diphtheria, whooping cough, and poliomyelitis) since 1900 can be attributed to medical measures. In many instances, the new chemotherapeutic and prophylactic measures to combat those diseases were introduced several decades *after* a substantial decline in mortality from the diseases had set in (McKinlay and McKinlay, 1987). According to the conflict perspective, this decline in mortality has been brought about mostly by several social and environmental factors: (1) a rising standard of living, (2) better sanitation and hygiene, and (3) improved housing and nutrition (Conrad and Kern, 1986). Moreover, since 1950, the year when the nearly unrestrained, precipitous rise in medical expenditure began, the health of Americans has *not* improved significantly. Most of the marked increase in longevity or decline in mortality in this century occurred before 1950. Since that year, the death rates of middle-aged men have actually risen (Hollingsworth, 1986).

Conflict theorists, however, do not mean to suggest that modern clinical medicine does not alleviate pain or cure disease in some individuals. Their point is that the medical institution fails to bring about significant improvements in the health of the population as a whole. Why, then, does our society continue to spend such vast

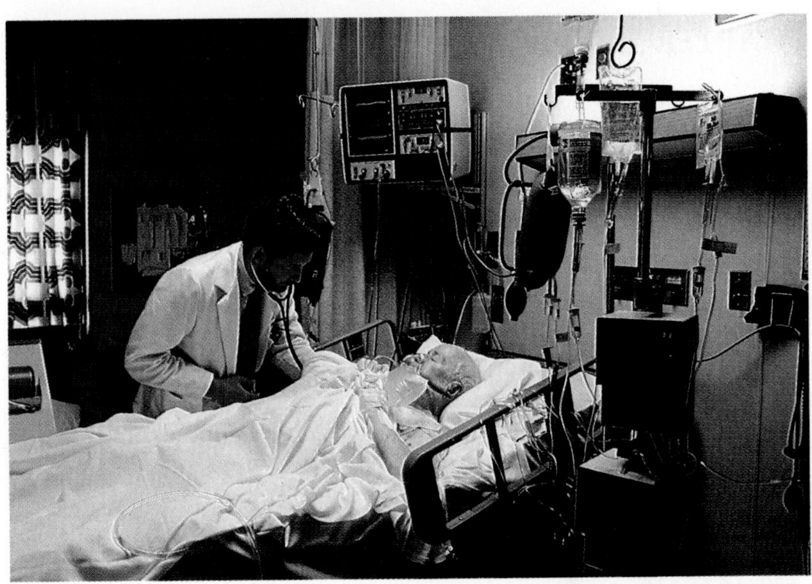

Since their introduction in the 1960s, highly expensive coronary-care units have become so popular that today they can be found in half of all the acute-care hospitals in the United States. But, according to a Marxist analysis, they have not been proven more effective than simple rest at home. Nonetheless, the profit motive has driven corporations to oversell them.

sums of money on medical care? This, according to conflict theorists, has much to do with the pursuit of private profit in our capitalist society.

In his Marxist analysis of coronary-care technology, for example, Howard Waitzkin (1987) finds that since its introduction in the 1960s, the highly expensive coronary-care units have become so popular that today they can be found in half of all the acute-care hospitals in the United States. But the intensive care provided by that medical technology has not been proven more effective than simple rest at home. Waitzkin argues that the proliferation of this highly expensive but relatively ineffective form of treatment can be traced to the profit motive. He finds that corporations such as Warner-Lambert Pharmaceutical Company and the Hewlett-Packard Company have participated in every phase of the research, development, promotion, and dissemination of today's coronary-care technology, which produces huge profits for them. Waitzkin also points out that the same profit motive has driven corporations to oversell many other highly expensive technological advances such as computerized axial tomography and fetal monitoring, even though these devices have not significantly improved the nation's health; they have benefited only a limited number of patients.

It is also the profit motive that has led many doctors—and more recently big corporations—to turn medical care into a lucrative business more than a social service. This is why, for example, some physicians tend to increase their already high incomes by performing more surgeries than necessary, as indicated by the fact that about half of all the highly expensive cardiac pacemaker and coronary bypass operations have been estimated to be unnecessary. By itself, though, the profit motive does not necessarily result in the exploitation of patients as consumers. A more important factor is the great power that the medical establishment and huge corporations have over patients as consumers.

The conflict perspective further suggests that the unequal distribution of health and medical care reflects the larger social inequality. We have discussed in some detail how health and medical care are unequally distributed. First, wealthy, industrialized countries have considerably lower infant mortality rates and higher life expectancies than do poor, developing countries. Second, in the United States, the lower classes suffer from higher rates of most diseases than do the middle and upper classes. Third, the poor are more likely to receive inadequate medical care.

QUESTIONS FOR DISCUSSION AND REVIEW

1. How do the roles played by patients and physicians contribute to the social order?
2. What facts about American health care do followers of conflict theory emphasize?

CHAPTER REVIEW

1. *How healthy are Americans?* Americans are much healthier than before. Our life expectancy has increased substantially. But while acute diseases were more common in the past, chronic illnesses are more prevalent today. Compared with most other industrialized countries, the United States has a higher infant mortality rate.

2. *What social factors influence our health?* One is gender: women are more likely than men to experience chronic and acute illnesses, though they do live longer. Blacks, Hispanics, and American Indians also have lower life expectancies and higher illness rates than whites. Poor people, too, are more likely than higher-income groups to become ill. *Can epidemiology track down the social causes of diseases?* Yes. It can do so by finding out who has the disease and what all the victims have in common.

3. *What causes AIDS and how has the disease spread?* The cause of AIDS is the human immunodeficiency virus (HIV), popularly known as the AIDS virus, which can be found in the blood, semen, or vaginal secretions of those who are infected. The disease was brought into the United States by American tourists returning from Haiti, where the virus had come from Central Africa. In the early 1980s the disease spread rapidly in homosexual communities. It then arose among intravenous drug addicts, their sex partners, and their unborn children as well as among heterosexuals who had received blood transfusions. Today, new infection has dropped sharply among homosexuals and blood recipients but has increased dramatically among drug addicts and their sex partners and unborn children. The AIDS virus is transmitted largely through sexual intercourse and needle sharing. *What social consequences have ensued from the AIDS epidemic?* The spread of AIDS has created a lot of fear about the disease, stirred up some hostility toward homosexuals, and contributed to other social conflicts. But the AIDS epidemic has also led to less promiscuity and "safer sex."

4. *What triggered the emergence of modern medicine?* The discovery of the germ theory in the middle of the last century and the reorganization of medical training and the medical profession in the early part of this century led to the emergence of modern medicine. *What have doctors learned from their medical training?* The first two years of medical school are devoted to courses in the basic sciences and the next two years focus on clinical training. As freshmen, medical students are eager to learn everything about medicine so as to be able, eventually, to serve humanity. But many soon lose their idealism and study only enough to pass exams. During their residency, after graduating from medical school, these physicians continue to develop an emotionless professionalism, becoming less idealistic and more concerned with their earnings. *How can symbolic interactionism shed light on the doctor-patient relationship?* If doctors take into account the views held by patients about themselves, their illnesses, and their doctors, patients are likely to be happy with the medical treatment they receive.

5. *Who is likely to seek medical care when ill?* Those who have higher rates of physician utilization are the elderly, women, and the poor. But if actual needs for medical care are taken into account, the poor are less likely than the rich to see a doctor. Mexican-Americans, American Indians, and the residents of Chinatowns are less likely than other Americans to visit physicians because they can rely on folk medicine. Blacks are more likely than whites to seek medical care, but blacks tend to go to public clinics and emergency rooms rather than a physician's private office. *What is wrong with the health-care system?* One problem is the unequal access to medical care, with the poor receiving inadequate and poor-quality care and the affluent getting better care. Another problem is the soaring cost of health care.

6. *How do functionalists and conflict theorists view health and medical care?* To functionalists, the sick role and the healing role contribute to social order, and the system of medical care significantly maintains health or reduces illness. But to conflict theorists, change in the social environment reduces mortality from diseases much more than medicine does. In this view, medical care and technology serve mostly the interests of doctors and corporations, and there is considerable social inequality in health and medical care.

KEY TERMS

Acute disease A disease that lasts for a short time, during which the victim either recovers or dies (p. 452).

Chronic disease A disease that lasts for a long time before the victim dies (p. 452).

Epidemiology The study of the origin and spread of disease within a population (p. 455).

ELISA Acronym for "enzyme-linked immunosorbent assay," a widely used test for antibodies to the AIDS virus (p. 456).

False negative The result of a blood test indicating an incorrect negative result—for example, that the body does not have AIDS-virus antibodies when in fact it does (p. 457).

False positive The result of a blood test indicating an incorrect positive result—for example, that the body has AIDS-virus antibodies when in fact it does not (p. 456).

Healing role A set of social expectations that defines the doctor's rights and obligations (p. 472).

Sick role A pattern of expectations regarding how a sick person should behave (p. 472).

SUGGESTED READINGS

Cockerham, William C. 1986. *Medical Sociology*, 3rd ed. Englewood Cliffs, N.J.: Prentice-Hall. A good, compact text from which the reader can get a quick and yet fully adequate overview of various social aspects of medicine.

Conrad, Peter, and Rochelle Kern (eds.). 1986. *The Sociology of Health and Illness*, 2nd ed. New York: St. Martin's. A collection of articles that present medical sociology largely from the conflict perspective.

Greenberg, Michael R. 1983. *Urbanization and Cancer Mobility*. New York: Oxford University Press. A careful analysis of the relationship between urbanization and cancer not only in the United States but in other countries as well.

Shilts, Randy. 1987. *And the Band Played On: People, Politics and the AIDS Epidemic.* New York: St. Martin's. A revealing look into the social and political aspects of the AIDS crisis during its earlier phases.

Starr, Paul. 1983. *The Social Transformation of American Medicine.* New York: Basic Books. A scholarly but highly readable account of how the medical profession has emerged from a widely distrusted, unprofitable line of work in the last century to a widely respected, profitable business today.

19 Science and Technology

Since World War II, billions of dollars have been poured into scientific research, and the number and prestige of scientists have soared. Today, the United States continues to lead the world on nearly all scientific frontiers. For the general public, the benefits of this scientific leadership are everywhere. They include various physical comforts and conveniences from such innovations as television, computers, and the cure and treatment of diseases. The costs, however, may not be known until years later. It is quite possible, for example, that computers will enable government and business to take away our privacy and that some new chemicals will endanger our health in unexpected ways.

The family, religion, economy, and other institutions have been around for thousands of years. But science began to emerge as a social institution only 300 years ago. Only then did it begin to become widely accepted as a necessary means of satisfying societal needs. This came about when scientific knowledge was used to improve technology, which led to improvements in daily life. Today science and technology are so intertwined that we often use the words interchangeably, but they do refer to different things. **Science** is a body of knowledge developed through systematic methods. **Technology** can mean any kind of tool or practical know-how, but it has come to mean the practical application of scientific principles.

Everywhere we look today, we see technology based on science, for good or ill. Thanks to scientific and technological advances, we now live longer and more comfortably than our ancestors did. We benefit from computers, telephones, airplanes, cars, electricity. In fact, industrial society would break down without these and other devices made possible by science. We also fear many of the effects of scientists' achievements, from thermonuclear bombs to toxic synthetic chemicals. All the other social institutions we have examined have been altered by the rise of science.

In this chapter we first see how science is related to technology, how science advances, and how it has developed into a powerful institution. Then we examine the ideals and realities of the scientific profession today. Finally, we analyze the impact science has on society.

THE EMERGENCE OF SCIENCE

If science did not have practical uses, it would probably have little influence or prestige. It has become an important social institution primarily through its marriage to technology. How did this come about?

Science and Technology

Through trial and error, ancient peoples discovered how to light a fire, build huts, make bows and arrows, and so on. Some 3000 years ago they even learned to mix tin with copper in order to produce a stronger metal, bronze. All this and more they did without benefit of science. They created and used technologies without knowing the principles behind their inventions. Even the Industrial Revolution owed little if anything to science. The steam engine was invented and used before people understood how it worked. The rapid technological progress of modern societies, however, has depended on the rise of science.

The First Scientists Like technology, science has ancient roots. We can trace it back to Greeks such as Plato, who advocated mathematics as a means of disciplining the mind, and Aristotle, who classified animals and plants. But as we saw in Chapter 1 (Thinking Sociologically), their science was not based on what is now called the scientific method. It was not until the seventeenth century that the seed of modern science began to grow in Western Europe, especially in England. Then "a growing habit of testing theories against careful measurement, observation, and upon occasion, experiment" spurred rapid progress in the natural sciences (McNeill, 1963).

A radical change in philosophical ideas about nature was a key factor stimulating scientific growth. Earlier students of nature had seen it as a living cosmos, filled with spiritual or human qualities. The new scientists treated the universe as a dead thing. Natural phenomena were no longer believed to act randomly, on their own whim, or by the will of a supernatural power. Instead, scientists now regarded nature as an object that behaves predictably, like a machine. It could be studied through direct observation, measured, and controlled. Respect for nature gave way to the quest to dominate, control, and use it.

A second factor in the development of modern science was the emergence of cooperative scholarship among those who regarded themselves as scientists. Through cooperative communication, scientists can expand their knowledge more easily and quickly and avoid repeating the work and the mistakes of others. The world's first example of cooperative scholarship among scientists came into being in 1662 when the Royal Society of London was organized. Its members, being gentlemen of wealth and leisure, could afford to spend long hours studying nature and discussing their findings with each other. But unlike their scholarly predecessors, they were not prejudiced against "dirtying their hands with anything but ink" (McNeill, 1963). They not only shared the new, mechanistic philosophy of nature but also believed that experiments provided the path to knowledge.

These early scientists were also for the most part deeply religious Protestants. We might expect that their dedication to science would clash with their religion. But two characteristics allowed them to maintain fidelity to both religion and science. First, the potential for conflict was eased by the fact that the early scientists "were content with striving to understand only a small segment of reality at a time, leaving the great questions of religion and philosophy to one side" (McNeill, 1963). A second characteristic reconciling their religion and their science, according to Robert Merton (1973, 1984), was the Protestant ethic. They believed that their scientific activity fulfilled the demands of this ethic, which, as we have seen, required them to work hard for the glory of God. They reasoned that "the scientific study of nature enables a fuller appreciation of His works and thus leads us to admire and praise the Power, Wisdom, and Goodness of God as manifested in His creation." Furthermore, the scientists believed that their experiments would eventually lead to improvements in the human condition. Thus through their scientific endeavors they were also heeding the Christian tenet to serve their neighbors. In Merton's view, the Protestant ethic helped make science a legitimate activity in the eyes of both the public and scientists themselves (see also Webster, 1975; Becker, 1984).

The Institutionalization of Science The members of the Royal Society had a committee devoted to improving "mechanical inventions," but for many years science did little to aid technology. In fact, it was technology that aided science. Galileo, for example, was able to make his astronomical observations because a Dutchman playing with lenses had invented the telescope.

Lewis Mumford (1963) has dated the beginning of the modern technological age to around 1832, when a huge water turbine was perfected as a result of scientific studies. This marked, in Mumford's view, the emergence of a new pattern, in which science drives technology onward. In the modern age, there is "deliberate and systematic invention" based on "the direct application of scientific knowledge to technics and the conduct of life." The Germans pioneered in giving this new approach institutional form. Their chemical and electrical companies created research laboratories, staffed them with chemists and physicists, and made invention a "deliberate, expected, normal affair." Science and technology, then, were not only wedded to each other but also embedded into the routines of economic life.

Today, science and technology depend on each other, as we depend on both of them. Modern technological developments such as computers and nuclear reactors could not have been invented through trial and error. Their invention required an understanding of scientific principles. To carry on their work, however,

Science and technology help each other advance. Scientists develop new principles that enable technicians to build more sophisticated equipment. The new equipment, in turn, permits scientists to conduct experiments that yield data for testing existing theories or developing new ones. Most advanced research requires extraordinarily large, expensive, and sophisticated equipment like the vacuum chamber shown here. The chamber can create a condition of extremely low pressure and reduce hydrocarbons and oxygen in residual gases to an absolute minimum. This ensures that the results of scientific experiments conducted in the chamber are reliable.

most scientists require extremely complicated technology. Biologists use electron microscopes, physicists use particle accelerators, and astronomers use NASA's satellites—all extremely sophisticated technology. While it enables these various scientists to do their research, technology can also by itself suggest new scientific ideas. For example, the search to eliminate a technological problem—static in radiotelephony—led to the birth of the science of radio astronomy and hence to the discovery of quasars and other astronomical phenomena. Thus the flow of knowledge goes not only from science to technology but also from technology to science.

There would not have been much progress in both science and technology if they had been differentiated—with one being highly developed to the neglect of the other. Scientific ideas, especially mathematics and logical proof, reached great heights in ancient Greece, but science never flourished there for want of interest in technical problem solving. The technology in ancient China was highly sophisticated, which brought forth papermaking, gunpowder, iron casting, and many other inventions long before they appeared in the West. But these technical innovations later fell far behind Western technology because the Chinese failed to pursue conceptual abstraction and theoretical generalization—the essence of science (Münch, 1983). In contrast, as we have seen, Westerners have shown much interest in both science and technology since the seventeenth century, which may explain why both are so highly advanced in the West today.

Scientific Progress

Science is so much a part of modern society that it is easy to take it for granted. Defining just what it is scientists do, and explaining how science advances, however, is not easy. We frequently say, for example, that science depends on not accepting facts or ideas on the basis of faith. Instead, scientists must subject everything to the test of observation and experiment. Taken literally, however, this would mean that scientists would be repeating each other's experiments endlessly. In fact, scientists often find replication an impractical undertaking. One reason is the incompleteness of many published descriptions of experiments. Just as cookbook recipes cannot include all the tiny details that every good cook knows, neither can scientists be exhaustive in describing their experiments. But these little technical points are often necessary for a successful replication. Many scientists would rather do original research. In science, the prizes go for originality, not for repeating someone else's experiment. Besides, replication may require just as much time, effort, and money as original research. Contrary to popular belief, then, most scientists seldom repeat each other's experiments (Broad and Wade, 1983).

If they do not constantly replicate experiments, scientists must make certain assumptions, taking certain things on faith, just like everyone else. Most biologists today accept as a basic assumption Darwin's theory of natural selection. Physicists use the theory of quantum mechanics as a working assumption. Each of these constitutes what Thomas Kuhn (1970) calls a **paradigm,** a model for defining, studying, and solving problems. For

An artist's view of Galileo's trial for heresy. Galileo Galilei (1564–1642), an Italian astronomer, was one of the most original thinkers of all time. For hundreds of years, astronomers had shared the Ptolemaic system of the heavens as their *paradigm,* assuming, as did the Church, that the earth was the center of the universe and that the sun revolved around the earth. Galileo, however, started a *scientific revolution* by demolishing this assumption with proof that the earth and other planets circle the sun. Since this was contrary to the Church's belief, Galileo was accused of heresy and was forced to deny what he had discovered to be true.

hundreds of years, for example, astronomers shared the Ptolemaic system of the heavens as their paradigm. They believed that the earth was the center of the universe and the sun revolved around it. Most scientists work within the paradigm of their discipline. They are not inclined to doubt its basic assumptions. How, then, does science advance? How do innovations—new facts and ideas—appear?

Kuhn divides innovation into two types: ordinary innovation and scientific revolution. Ordinary innovation is the product of everyday research, such as Foucault's discovery in 1850 that light travels faster in air than in water, or the invention of the transistor in 1949 by a team of scientists at Bell Labs. Journeymen scientists produce these innovations all the time, and Kuhn calls them **normal science.** As normal science keeps producing new ideas and data, however, some of these create problems for the existing paradigm. They are **anomalies,** incompatible with or unexplainable by the paradigm. If these anomalies keep piling up, they generate a "crisis" that compels some very innovative scientists to develop a new paradigm, which initiates a **scientific revolution,** such as Newton's law of gravity or Einstein's theory of relativity (Kuhn, 1970).

All this suggests the importance of cultural accumulation. Normal science does not operate in an intellectual vacuum but through the guidance of a paradigm. The paradigm itself is a product of an earlier scientific revolution, which, in turn, resulted from the accumulation of anomalous theories and data, the fallout of routine research. At each stage of cultural accumulation, there is a storehouse of scientific ideas and facts that can be used to fashion an innovation. Even Isaac Newton acknowledged a debt to this cultural storehouse, claiming in great modesty, "If I have seen farther, it is by standing on the shoulders of giants." This cultural accumulation explains why science is full of multiple discoveries—the same discoveries being made independently by different scientists. Calculus, for example, was discovered independently by Isaac Newton and Gottfried Leibniz. The theory of evolution was developed independently by Charles Darwin and Alfred Russel Wallace. The basic laws of genetics were discovered independently by Gregor Mendel and, later, by three other scientists. Of course, not all scientific discoveries are multiples. There are singletons—discoveries made by individual scientists alone (Patinkin, 1983). But multiples are numerous enough to suggest the importance of cultural accumulation for scientific progress.

Modern Science

As science advanced over the years, its methods were applied to more and more areas of life, and it achieved great prestige in Western society. As recently as 40 years ago, however, scientists were poorly paid, worked alone on shoestring budgets, and were popularly viewed as eccentric characters. This era of "little science" ended in the United States with World War II and the development of the atomic bomb. In a sense, scientists had enabled the United States to end the war. The Cold War and the arms race with the Soviet Union that followed ensured that the government, like industry, would continue to have a large interest in fostering scientific development. When, in 1957, the Soviet Union surprised Americans by launching the first satellite into space, the government intensified its role in science. It poured new money into research and scientific education.

Explosion of an atomic bomb in 1950 near the Western Pacific island of Bikini. The development of the atomic bomb during World War II ended the era of "little science," which had been marked by inadequate government support for scientific research. Then the Cold War and the arms race with the Soviet Union in the 1950s, especially the surprising launch of the first satellite into space by Russia in 1957, caused the U.S. government to pour more money into scientific research and education.

The billions of dollars that the government, industry, and private foundations spent on research after the war gave birth to the era of "big science." The number of scientists as well as the prestige and influence of science have soared. Increasingly, scientists work as narrow specialists within huge bureaucracies. In Jacques Ellul's (1964) words, "the research worker is no longer a solitary genius." For the most part, scientists work as members of teams. Only by joining the "team" of a bureaucracy can they gain access to the expensive, sophisticated equipment most scientists require. Since the 1920s the percentage of papers written by one person has declined substantially. Now it is very common for two or more scientists to collaborate on a paper. It is also very common for several scientists to make the same discovery independently (Merton, 1976).

Big science has brought about some unintended consequences. One is an increase in trivial research by the expanding ranks of narrow specialists. Because of this, the scientific community risks losing financial support from the government. "The triumphs of discovery," biophysicist W. B. Gratzer (1984) complains, "are obscured by an unwholesome miasma of triviality and duplication. The suspicions of intelligent outsiders are aroused. Senator Proxmire bares his teeth and science trembles." (A member of the Senate Appropriation Committee, Proxmire periodically criticizes scientists who use large government grants to do trivial research by "giving" them his Golden Fleece Award. Once a scientist received such an award for his research designed to determine how much alcohol a goldfish can drink without getting drunk.) Another spin-off of big science is the emergence of many scientists "busily running conferences, setting up nomenclature committees, and starting unwanted journals. The most voracious and fecund of the new breed of pseudoprofessionals are the administrators" (Gratzer, 1984). But big science is big enough to accommodate scientists of various stripes. Thus it manages to keep the United States in the forefront of scientific research, as most of the Nobel prizes go to American scientists every year (see Figure 19.1).

QUESTIONS FOR DISCUSSION AND REVIEW

1. How does technology differ from science?
2. Who were the first scientists, and what happened when the activities of scientists became institutionalized?
3. How do scientific anomalies sometimes lead to scientific revolutions?
4. What are the characteristics of "big science," and what are some of its unintended consequences?

THE SCIENTIFIC PROFESSION

More than half of all American scientists work in business and industry. Fewer than one-fifth work in universities and colleges and even fewer in the federal government and other organizations (see Figure 19.2). Those working in educational institutions are much more likely

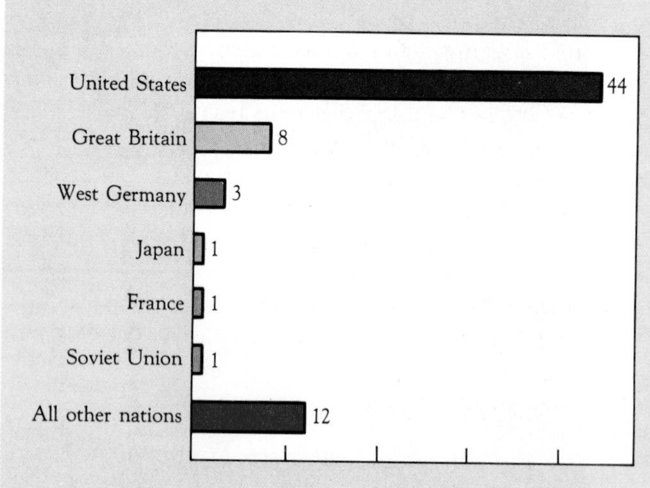

Figure 19.1 U.S. Leads World in Science

The United States continues to be in the forefront of scientific research. The latest data show that between 1976 and 1985 American scientists won far more Nobel prizes than their peers in any other country.

Source: Census Bureau, *Statistical Abstract of the United States,* 1988, p. 561.

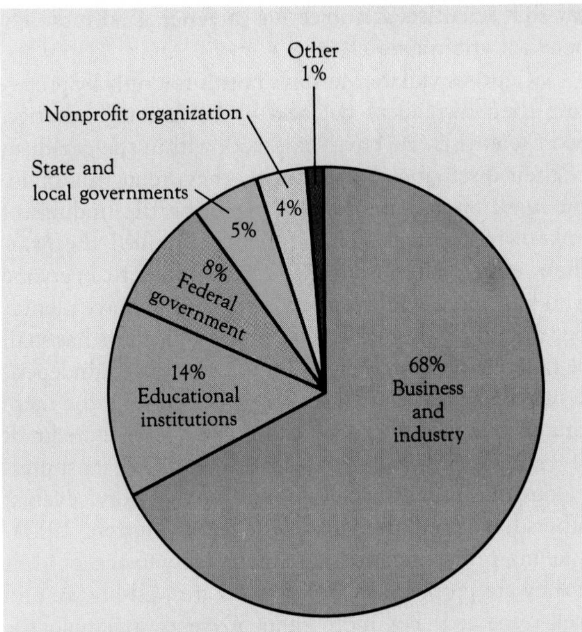

Figure 19.2 Where Scientists Work

There are far more scientists working in business and industry than in universities and colleges. The scientists in educational institutions are much more likely to do basic research, while those in industry and government tend more to do applied research.

Source: Statistical Abstract of the United States, 1988, p. 562.

to do basic research ("pure science") than scientists in government or business, many of whom work on technology, often called "applied research." Wherever they work, many scientists spend little time on research, though. Some manage or administer research programs; others spend much of their time teaching. Still, scientists tend to share certain norms, patterns of interaction, and paths to success.

Scientific Ideals

Unlike their seventeenth-century predecessors, modern scientists do not need to justify their work to themselves or others by saying that it glorifies God. From the outset of their training, scientists are socialized to consider science worthy of their dedication for its own sake and to keep it "pure": "Science must not suffer itself to become the handmaiden of theology or economy or state" (Merton, 1973). The self-confident insistence on autonomy attests to the power and influence of science today. Robert Merton argues that the autonomy and purity of science is maintained through four norms which are "binding on the man of science" and "in varying degrees internalized by the scientist."

The first norm is **universalism,** which holds that scientific ideas should be evaluated by impersonal criteria. When they evaluate ideas or findings, scientists should not consider the author's personality, race, age, sex, or other personal characteristics. Instead, they should evaluate ideas by considering only their consistency with logic and observations. Scientists, as Alfred Maurice Taylor (1967) says, "must hold scientific theories in judicial detachment. Scientists must be passionless observers, unbiased by emotion, intellectually cold"—toward their own work as well as that of others.

A second norm, **organized skepticism,** sets science apart from other institutions. Whereas the church and the state often ask people to bow to their authority, and may see skepticism as a sign of disloyalty, science elevates skepticism to the status of a virtue. According to this norm, scientists should take nothing in science at face value and should carefully scrutinize all findings, even those by the most respected scientists, for faulty logic or factual error. They must be prepared "to drop a theory the moment an observation turns up to conflict with it" (Taylor, 1967).

A third norm, **communality,** requires scientists to share their knowledge and to regard discoveries as public property, not as private property which they might keep secret or sell to the highest bidder. As a result, their discoveries can provide springboards for further knowledge, just as past discoveries made today's advances possible. The only "property right" scientists may claim is professional recognition and esteem.

A final norm, **disinterestedness,** governs motives for engaging in scientific work. Scientists should not expect to gain great wealth, fame, or power. Seeking these rewards may be appropriate for businesspeople, politicians, lawyers, and others—but not for scientists. They must seek the truth and only the truth, and they should consider the thrill of making a discovery sufficient reward for their work. So long as scientists follow this norm, it is unlikely that they will be tempted to falsify data.

Scientific Realities

Contemplating his colleagues' denial of any interest in fame, one modern scientist wondered, "Why do even the greatest minds stoop to such falsehood? For, without being conscious lies, these denials are undoubtedly false" (Merton, 1973). The denials suggest that the norm of disinterestedness does influence scientists, but they are ambivalent toward it. Scientists do not totally reject this and the other norms Merton identified, but they do not enthusiastically support them either. In fact, they find these norms irrelevant to their everyday scientific activities and tend to break all of them.

Consider the norm of universality, for example. Ian Mitroff (1974) found clear violations of this norm by the scientists who analyzed lunar rocks brought back by Apollo astronauts. Instead of being impersonal, objective, or emotionally neutral, the Apollo scientists, especially the best ones, "were emotionally involved with their ideas, were reluctant to part with them, and did everything in their power to confirm them." Every one of the scientists considered it naive and nonsensical to say that scientists are objective. Science is an intensely personal enterprise.

Ideally, scientists should follow the norm of universalism, which requires that they be passionless observers, unbiased by emotion or intellectually cold. But, in reality, they often violate the norm. A good example is the scientists who analyzed the rocks brought back from the moon by Apollo astronauts (below). The scientists were far from impersonal, objective, or emotionally neutral. Instead, they were emotionally involved with their ideas and did everything to prove them correct.

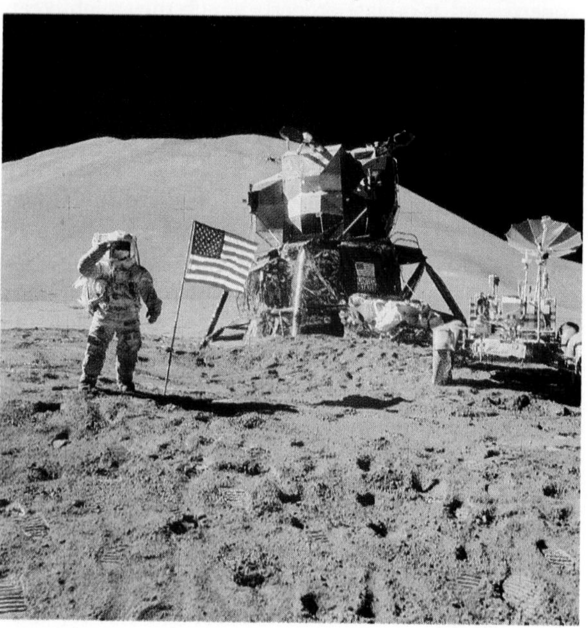

Scientists violate Merton's norms not only by preferring their own ideas but also by bowing to authority. Most scientists, we have said, work within the paradigm of their discipline. Furthermore, they frequently praise the work of the famous while ignoring the findings of unknown scientists. The tendency is called the **Matthew effect,** after Matthew 25:29—"For to everyone who has, more shall be given, and he shall have plenty. But from him who has not, even that which he has shall be taken away from him." When two scientists independently make the same discovery, for example, the more famous one is likely to get most if not all the credit. If several scientists collaborate on a subject, the most prestigious one usually receives more of the glory, even if others have done the bulk of the work (Merton, 1973). Like most of us, scientists are more likely to accept ideas if they are proposed by people who are well-known and well-respected. For more than 30 years, psychologists accepted the renowned Cyril Burt's data on the heritability of IQ, until the data were revealed as fraudulent in 1972 (Weinstein, 1979). All this clearly violates the norms of skepticism and of universalism, which require scientists to evaluate ideas and research without considering the personal characteristics of the author.

Personal characteristics and emotions may also play a part in the resistance with which scientists commonly greet revolutionary ideas and discoveries. Of course, they may resist a new idea because of justified skepticism, especially when that idea contradicts a paradigm that has long seemed accurate. But the emotional reaction that frequently greets new scientific ideas suggests that less objective factors are at work. Darwin's theory of evolution, for example, aroused considerable hostility. In a debate on the theory between Bishop Wilberforce, who had been carefully coached by a leading biologist, and T. H. Huxley, who supported Darwin's theory, the bishop attacked both Huxley and the theory contemptuously. The bishop asked Huxley, "Are you related to an ape on your father's or your mother's side?" Huxley replied that if he had to choose for a grandfather either an ape or a man who resorted to ridicule rather than reason in a scientific discussion, then "I unhesitatingly affirm my preference for the ape."

Such emotional behavior suggests that scientists are just as human as the rest of us. They may reject scientific ideas not because of objective and scientific considerations but because of their nonscientific beliefs. The fact that Darwin's evolutionary theory contradicted a literal reading of the Bible fueled opposition to his ideas. Professional specialization and jealousies may be another cause of resistance. Physicians used to reject Pasteur's germ theory because they regarded him as "a mere chemist poaching on their scientific preserves, not worthy of their attention" (Barber, 1961).

Violations of the norms Merton described do not bring science to a halt. In fact, they sometimes promote scientific progress. Being emotionally involved with one's work, for example, may pay off. In Mitroff's study the three scientists perceived by their colleagues to be the most emotionally committed to their own hypotheses were also judged the most outstanding and creative of those in the program. "Without emotional commitment," one of the scientists said, "one couldn't have the energy, the drive to press forward, sometimes against extremely difficult odds."

If we compare Merton's other norms with scientists' actual behavior, we find similar violations, and, sometimes, beneficial results. Perhaps most striking are violations of the norm of disinterestedness. Far from being motivated only by an idealistic quest for knowledge, most scientists take part in a very competitive game.

Since the birth of science in the seventeenth century, scientists have not sought the advance of science alone. They have also sought to advance their own interests. They have battled each other to claim the glory of being recognized as the first to make a scientific discovery. Since 1983, after the French scientist Dr. Luc Montagnier (left) and his American rival Dr. Robert Gallo (right) independently discovered the AIDS virus, each has been claiming to have made the discovery first. In 1985, Montagnier even sued Gallo for using the French virus samples to develop the blood test kits for identifying antibodies to the AIDS virus.

Competition

Since the birth of science in the seventeenth century, scientists have sought to advance their own interests as well as those of science. Three hundred years ago the English mathematician Newton and the German Leibniz battled each other to claim the glory of being recognized as the first to discover calculus. They attacked "each other with injurious epithets" and encouraged "their partisans to publish scurrilous innuendos in learned journals" (Merton, 1973). They eventually accused each other of plagiarism—stealing the idea of calculus from each other and then publishing it as their own (Collins and Restivo, 1983). A similar incident erupted only several years ago between American and French medical scientists. In 1983 Dr. Luc Montagnier and his French colleagues reported that they had discovered the AIDS virus, which they called LAV. Then, in 1984, Dr. Robert Gallo and his American colleagues discovered an apparently different virus called HTLV-3. They quickly used this finding to develop blood test kits for identifying antibodies to the AIDS virus. A year later, when it turned out that the American and French viruses were practically identical, the French filed a lawsuit, claiming that the Americans had used the French virus samples to develop the test. The court later dismissed the suit, which the French appealed to a higher court. But finally, in 1987, President Reagan and French Prime Minister Jacques Chirac announced that both countries agreed to share profits from the blood test—while leaving it to historians to decide who discovered the AIDS virus first.

For a scientist wishing to gain recognition from the scientific community, making a breakthrough is not enough. The work must be published first. If two or more scientists make the same discovery independently, the one who publishes first gets the credit. Scientists, then, often compete fiercely to be the one who "got there first." Such competition brings some benefits, as it can motivate scientists to work harder. Researchers have found that stiff competition in American universities, and in German universities during the nineteenth century, helped make them more productive than French and British universities (Hagstrom, 1974). Competition may also discourage scientists from delaying the publication of their findings. After considering his theory for 20 years, Charles Darwin finally published his ideas about evolution when he learned that Alfred Russel Wallace had independently reached the same conclusions. By spurring scientists to publish their work quickly, competition may promote the diffusion of ideas and thus hasten the advance of science.

On the other hand, competition can deter this diffusion by inhibiting cooperation and communication. Scientists eager for recognition and afraid of being beaten into print often keep their work secret until it is published. Before winning a Nobel prize, biophysicist Maurice Wilkins was so possessive of an x-ray study of DNA that James Watson, his Nobel cowinner, used his sister's charms and other devious means to gain entrance to Wilkins's lab (Watson, 1968). Scientists' employers are also engaged in their own competition, and it too leads to secrecy. The U.S. government fears that scientific reports may include material useful to its rival, the Soviet Union. Businesses want to protect industrial secrets from their competitors.

Such secretive behavior has both personal and social costs. By depriving people of valuable ideas, it both reduces individual productivity and slows down scientific progress as a whole. Another social cost is wasteful duplication of effort by scientists working on the same problem. Finally, competition may strain social relations, discouraging scientists from giving the encouragement and advice that some of their colleagues sorely need. Sometimes, professional jealousies and ego clashes directly hamper research. In 1986 it was reported that the scientists working on AIDS research at the Centers for Disease Control often sabotaged each other's experiments. A senior scientist, when his colleagues were away, ordered a technician to throw into the garbage the AIDS viruses they were nurturing because he wanted them to do research with a strain he himself had isolated. Another senior scientist found that his viral cultures were rearranged at night and contaminated—possibly by someone spitting into them (Kwitny, 1986). Similar problems have plagued the industrial research institutes in the Soviet Union. There have been bitter infighting, sabotage of lab equipment and records, alteration of rival experiments, and faking of entire theses. The Soviet press has blamed these problems for the backwardness of the Soviet economy (Sullivan, 1986).

The pressures of competition may also produce deviant behavior. Some scientific deviance is serious, such as plagiarism and falsification of data. As we have suggested, about 40 years ago the renowned psychologist Cyril Burt published phony data to prove the heritability of intelligence. More recently, in the early 1980s, Mark Spector, a Cornell University graduate student, forged data to support a remarkable new theory of cancer causation. A dozen other cases of fraud took place in institutions like Harvard and Yale, where there is tremendous pressure to get ahead (Broad and Wade, 1983). Over the last few years many episodes of fraud have come to light. Consider the following cases, which surfaced in 1986 alone:

1. After a painstaking 2½ year investigation, the National Institute of Mental Health concluded that a leading psychiatrist, Stephen Breuning, had published numerous research studies that he never carried out. Before being discovered to be fake, this research had led to widespread use of stimulant drugs for severely retarded children in institutions.
2. A research physician, Dr. Robert Slutsky, committed extensive fraud in heart research. Over a six-year period, he had produced 161 scientific papers—sometimes turning out a paper every 10 days. But many of these papers reported studies that were never done.
3. A cancer research team at Harvard published reports of what was widely regarded as a major scientific breakthrough in highly prestigious journals—the discovery of a molecule vital to the immune system. But they later retracted those reports after discovering that a member of the team had faked the research (Greenberg, 1987).

These cases of scientific fraud are rare. Far more common are less serious actions. To avoid being "scooped," scientists may publish partial findings as quickly as possible, even if their data are shaky. They may simply announce that they are working on a project, hoping to discourage other scientists from proceeding with similar research. Reporting successful experiments but not unsuccessful ones is a common practice. Scientists trade favors by having each other's names listed as coauthors, though only one of them has done the work. Even more prevalent is the practice of publishing one study in many places. A scientist may publish a piece of research first in a report to the agency that funded the study, then in papers presented at professional meetings, then in scientific journals, then in a book edited by a good friend. Finally, all these slightly different versions of the same study are collected into a book. Thus the scientist creates the illusion that he or she is prolific—and wastes a lot of paper as well as the readers' time. This kind of behavior occurs because scientific competence is often judged by the quantity of a scientist's publications, which is easy to measure, rather than by their quality, which is difficult to measure.

Success in Science

In the scientific profession as elsewhere, competition produces a stratification system. For science, that system is shaped like a pyramid: there are a very few scientists at the top and a great many at the bottom. Most scientists never make a great discovery and go unnoticed by the rest of the scientific community. No more than 5 percent publish more than half of the scientific literature.

Who are the successful scientists? Most scientists consistently did well in school. Because they outshone other students in mathematics, they were encouraged to work toward a career in science, engineering, or a related field. But even the most productive scientists are

"A penny for your thoughts."

not necessarily much smarter than the common run of scientists and other people. Nobel prize winner James Watson (1968) has noted that it is not unusual for him to find an article or book too difficult to understand. "One could not be a successful scientist," he has written, "without realizing that . . . a good number of scientists are not only narrow-minded and dull, but also just stupid."

In fact, several studies have shown that measures of intellectual ability have very low correlations with scientific productivity (Bayer and Folger, 1966). Although personal factors such as talent, motivation, and training contribute to scientific success, social factors also play a significant role. One study of all Nobel prize winners up to 1977 shows that most are Jewish, followed by Protestants and then Catholics. The majority of American-born Nobel scientists hail from New York City, which has a large Jewish population, and from the Midwest, which is predominantly Protestant. The Nobel scientists all over the world have come overwhelmingly from families of higher social classes, most of their fathers having been professionals or businessmen. Nobel scientists, however, have had different childhood experiences than Nobel writers. Many of the writers (over 30 percent) have lost at least one parent through death or desertion or experienced their father's bankruptcy or impoverishment, but extremely few of the scientists have suffered the same ordeal. The physicists, in particular, have led "remarkably uneventful lives" (Berry, 1981; see also Silver, 1983). Other social factors that have been found to influence scientific success are social interaction, marital fertility, and the reward system of science.

Social Interaction Interaction in which scientists exchange information and ideas presumably stimulates creativity and productivity. Most scientists have only limited opportunities for this kind of interaction. Their employers—whether a university, or industry, or government—restrict the use of long-distance calls and limit travel to meetings. Research facilities are often organized to encourage an isolated, solitary existence (Kasperson, 1978). Their limited interaction with other scientists may provide a partial explanation for the fact that most scientists are uncreative and unproductive. In contrast, creative and productive scientists tend to be those who have considerable interaction with other scientists. They are more likely than unproductive scientists to form a kind of "invisible college," an informal group of scientists scattered across the country who communicate with each other regularly by writing letters, attending meetings, visiting each other's laboratories, and making telephone calls. Such social interaction enables the scientists to learn from one another. It may also enhance their chances of getting research grants, because their trusted friends are likely to be members of the committees that review research proposals. Members of the committees are typically drawn from the same groups of scientists that win most grants.

Marital Fertility Another social factor related to scientific success is children. The more children a scientist has, the less likely he or she is to be productive. According to one study, within a two-year period, childless scientists published about 1.5 more research papers than those with children. The publications by childless scientists were also more frequently cited in scientific journals, which suggests that their quality was superior. Most likely, childless scientists are more successful than those with children because the absence of children allows them to devote more time and energy to their work (Hargens, McCann, and Reskin, 1978).

The Reward System Age appears related to scientific productivity. Newton developed his laws of gravity and his calculus when he was 24; Einstein was 26 when he formulated his theory of relativity. A huge majority of modern scientists published their first significant work when they were between 25 and 35 years old (Cole, 1979). Many people have therefore concluded that science is a "young person's game." T. H. Huxley declared that scientists should be strangled on their sixtieth birthday before "age hardens them against the reception of new truths, making them clogs upon progress" (Merton, 1973). In fact, recent research has shown that older Nobel laureates are just as receptive to innovation as younger scientists (Hull, Tessner, and Diamond, 1978). Less productive scientists do become even less productive as they grow older. But more productive scientists become more productive with advancing age (Allison and Stewart, 1974).

The scientific reward system, not age, actually accounts for changes in productivity as a scientist grows older. The gap between more productive scientists and less productive ones increases with age because the productive ones have been rewarded with recognition, which motivates them to be more productive. Meanwhile less productive scientists go unrecognized, and so their productivity continues to decline (Cole, 1979). Because of the Matthew effect, the productive scientists are likely to receive even more recognition than they deserve, further widening the gulf between the elite and the masses in the scientific community. But the quality of scientific work is more powerful than the Matthew effect in shaping the stratification in science. Thus scientists who have made a significant discovery are usually rewarded with recognition, even if they have not been famous (Stewart, 1983). Another powerful influence on stratification is the growth rate of a scientific field. Generally, reward differentials among scientists are greater in rapidly growing, more developed fields such as physics and chemistry than in more slowly growing, less developed fields such as the social sciences (Hargens and Felmlee, 1984). Apparently, in a fast-growing field, creative scientists have the opportunity to show their "right stuff" and stand out.

QUESTIONS FOR DISCUSSION AND REVIEW

1. What four key norms make up the ideals of science, and why do scientists often fail to follow them?
2. Why does competition among scientists often inhibit communication and distort research results?
3. How do successful scientists differ from less productive ones?

SCIENCE AND SOCIETY

A former Soviet journalist reports:

> A huge crowd of women is huddled outside a grocery store in Kirov, a city in northern Russia. They have heard that fresh supplies are en route to this store. Half an hour later, only the first 15 people get butter and meat. The rest leave empty-handed and bitter. Six hundred miles to the west, another crowd files silently into a huge electronics store in Leningrad. Everyone here is looking for quality goods, but that means either shelling out a month's salary for a Sanyo radio, a Philips dictation machine or a Texas Instruments calculator, or dealing with the black marketeers who hover nearby . . . (Reichlin, 1984).

Why is it so hard for Soviet people to buy bread, meat, and butter? Why do they have to pay a fortune for gadgets readily available in the United States? An important reason is that the Soviet government had until the late 1950s backed biologist Trofim Lysenko's dubious genetic theory and also discouraged the development of cybernetics—the foundation of computer science. Lysenko believed that acquired characteristics could be genetically inherited, which was compatible with communist ideology. The Soviet Union applied Lysenko's theory on the farm, with disastrous consequences that are still felt in Soviet grocery stores today (see box, p. 490). Russian officials condemned cybernetics as the worst aberration of the corrupt West's scientific thought because they found its mechanistic view of people contrary to communist thinking. As a result, the Soviets today are desperately trying to catch up with the United States, even by stealing our latest computers (Reichlin, 1984).

There is, indeed, a close relationship between science and society. A country can retard or advance its science, which in turn can affect the lives of its citizens. How well does our science serve us?

Benefits and Costs

Our scientific advances produce both beneficial and harmful effects. The benefits are often immediately attainable or at least apparent. In contrast, the costs may not be understood until years later.

Thanks to science, we can pamper ourselves with cultural delights provided by radio, stereo, and television. We can get in touch instantly with someone far away through a telephone. We can have ourselves speedily and comfortably transported over vast distances by jet. Economists observe that growth in economic productivity has depended on earlier investments in research and development. We not only live better than before but also longer. Thanks to advances in biomedical science, the percentage of deaths caused by major diseases has declined substantially over the past 20 years. Heart disease has dropped 11 percent, deaths due to stroke have gone down 37 percent, influenza mortality has decreased 50 percent, deaths from hardening of the arteries have declined 31 percent, and even deaths due to diabetes have dropped 18 percent (Census Bureau, 1988).

Many dramatic advances have burst on the scientific scene in the last decade. Electronics has given us pocket calculators, electronic games, and sophisticated home computers; it may soon radically change everything from the way we study, work, and think to how we travel, shop, vote, and play. Another scientific revolution is under way in genetics. Scientists are learning to manipulate genes and create new organisms, such as genetically reprogrammed bacteria that are able to produce insulin for use by diabetics, to manufacture antibiotics, to devour oil slicks, or to turn chemical wastes into usable plastics. Scientists may soon be able to cure some genetic diseases such as sickle cell anemia and thalassemia. (For other biological discoveries and their potential uses, see box, p. 492.) To ward off death, human organs are already increasingly transplanted from one person to another. The era of the test-tube baby is also fast developing. Science has offered growing numbers of childless couples various options, including in-vitro fertilization,

The benefits of science can be seen in the many dramatic advances that have recently burst on the scientific scene. One example is test-tube babies like the one shown here with its joyful parents. Increasing numbers of childless couples now have various options such as in-vitro fertilization, artificial insemination, and the use of surrogate mothers. Within a few years, the recently discovered superconductors will probably be used to produce cheaper electricity, tiny computers, "floating" trains, and more efficient ways to launch satellites. But science can also create risks such as the computer's invasion of our privacy.

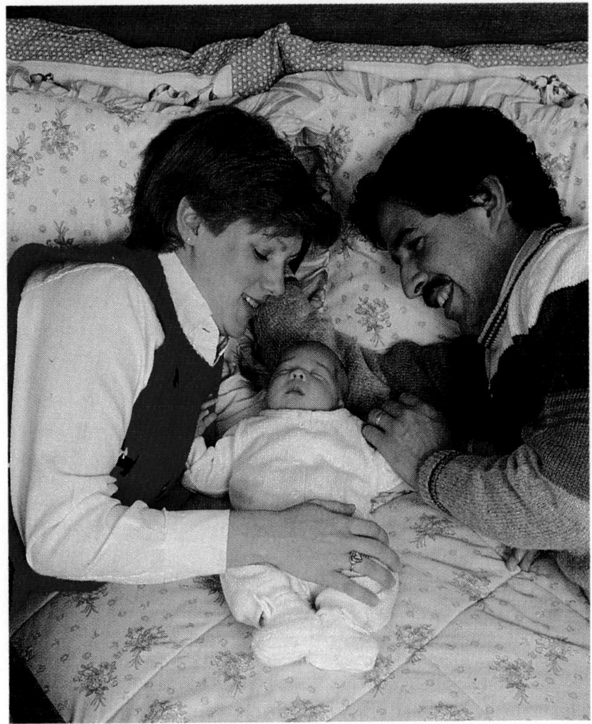

UNDERSTANDING OTHER SOCIETIES

How Dogma Cripples Soviet Science

Science and society are closely interrelated. A society can retard or advance its science, which in turn can affect the lives of its citizens. We can see this in the following account of Soviet science. What norms of American science have helped avoid most of the problems created by Soviet politics and dogma?

Few Soviet people know why it is so hard for them to buy bread, meat and butter for their families or why they pay a fortune for gadgets readily available in the West. Fewer still would blame this hardship on Soviet genetics or cybernetics, and hardly anyone at all blames Soviet ideology.

Yet top Russian officials know, as do most foreign observers, that Marxism has cast a blight on Soviet science. It has caused Sigmund Freud's monumental theories of the human psyche to be either ignored or vilified. In genetics, Soviet research was long crippled by official backing of Trofim Lysenko's eccentric theories, so that today Russian genetics lags painfully behind the West. And ideological bias so undercut early Soviet studies of cybernetics—the theory underlying computer research—that today the USSR is trying desperately to catch up with the United States by copying or stealing our latest computers.

Perhaps surprisingly, some Russian officials grudgingly agree that the current ills of the Soviet economy may be the result of past attacks on Soviet science by Kremlin zealots. Soviet science was dealt a number of crippling blows in the late 1940s and early 1950s. Although aimed at science across the board, the blows fell most heavily on genetics, biology and cybernetics, which in the Russian usage of the word includes most applications of computer technology.

The irony of all this is that Karl Marx and Friedrich Engels, the founding fathers of Communism, had proclaimed that science would enable the working class to beat capitalism and achieve peace and productivity. In the USSR, all other sciences *are subordinate to philosophy's findings.* If the results of research in the natural or social sciences do not conform to Communist philosophy, ideologues believe that these sciences are at fault, not the philosophy. This in turn has created a uniquely Soviet concept of "Party spirit" or "Partyness"—a fairly complex idea. "The principle of Partyness demands devotion to the ideals of Communism and an actively effective participation in their realization," write Soviet political scientists P. V. Alekseev and A. I. Ilyin. According to them, Partyness does not in any way hinder the creativity of scientists, since the interests of Communist ideology

artificial insemination, and the use of surrogate mothers. We may even enter a new technological age within a few years when the recently discovered superconductors come into use. The superconductors are basically made up of ceramics that do not resist the flow of electric current as do ordinary conductors, such as copper wire (Spotts, 1987). They will make possible cheaper electricity, tiny computers, "floating" trains, and new ways to launch satellites.

The same scientific innovations that improve our lives, however, also threaten us with their unintended harmful effects. The spread of electronic computers throughout society is eroding our long-cherished right to privacy because our personal records are easily accessible to the curious. If we sue a doctor for medical malpractice, we are likely to go into a computer blacklist and suffer more than the loss of privacy rights. One woman in Joliet, Illinois, filed a malpractice suit and later found that 30 other doctors refused to treat her when she became ill again (Elmer-DeWitt, 1986). Another example of the harmful consequences of our scientific breakthroughs is the constant possibility of dying in a nuclear holocaust. Furthermore, we are threatened with nuclear wastes buried in our soil, with asbestos-dust particles in our schools and workplaces, and with other cancer-causing pollutants in our air, water, and food. "We live in a sea of chemicals," Frank Press (1978), former President Carter's adviser on science and technology, wrote. "The latest computer registry of the Chemical Abstract Service contains some 4,039,907 distinct entities, and the number of entries is now growing at the rate of 6000 per week." Many of these chemicals have some immediate benefits, but in the long run some may generate unforeseen damage. Millions of tons of the powerful com-

and science coincide when one is searching for the objective truth.

It was this outlook that made it possible for Trofim Lysenko, a biologist from a Ukrainian village, and a host of quasi scientists who followed him to climb to power. In the opinion of MIT science historian Loren Graham, the Lysenko affair is a prime example of how an opportunist armed with Partyness can succeed in Soviet society.

The strategy used by Lysenko was simple: He promised to deliver the results the Party, i.e., Stalin, asked for. In the 1930s, for example, Nikolai Vavilov, then president for the Academy of Agricultural Sciences, promised bumper crops in 10 to 15 years from some potentially highly productive breeds of corn and wheat. Lysenko, already popular with the Party bosses for this eagerness to please, brazenly vowed to produce the same kind of crop in 2 or 3 years. At the same time, Lysenko actively promoted his "theory" that acquired characteristics could be genetically inherited—a view consistent with Marxist outlook. Lysenko eventually won in his battle with Vavilov. In 1940, Vavilov lost his job and was later arrested and died in prison. In 1948, again bolstered by Stalin's support of his position, Lysenko finally denounced Soviet genetics. Stalin closed the Medical-Genetic Institute and declared its director an enemy of the people. Most of Russia's top geneticists were jailed.

Meanwhile, Lysenko was dabbling in animal husbandry. Pushing the same idea of genetic inheritance of acquired characteristics, he crossbred imported Jersey bulls, whose cows have a high-butterfat milk, with high-yield milk cows. He claimed that if such cows were copiously fed during gestation, and the bull is of large stature, the calves will take after the larger parent, combining the best qualities of both. The idea appealed to Khrushchev, Stalin's successor, who encouraged farms to adopt the procedure. Unfortunately, it destroyed decades of breeding work; its consequences are still felt in Soviet grocery stores.

After Khrushchev was forced out in 1964, Soviet scientists finally managed to retire Lysenko. Another 10 to 15 years were needed, however, to raise a new generation of geneticists.

Source: Excerpted from Igor Reichlin, "How dogma cripples Soviet science," *Science Digest,* March 1984, pp. 66–69, 101–103.

pound DBCP were spread on croplands to control pests before it was discovered that workers at Occidental Chemical Company became sterile after handling the compound. Given the positive and negative consequences of science, how do we react to it?

Societal Reaction

According to several surveys, the American public has more trust in science and technology than in any other institution. Trust is highest among those Americans who are comparatively young, well educated and affluent and who live in large cities (Etzioni and Nunn, 1974; Pion and Lipsey, 1981). The level of public confidence, however, is lower than in the 1950s and 1960s, when American scientists enjoyed almost total autonomy and unquestioning respect. There was widespread support for nuclear energy in those two decades, for example, but today most Americans are opposed to it even though most scientists consider it relatively safe (Rothman, 1983). The decline in part reflects a general loss of confidence in our social institutions: while confidence in science sagged during the 1970s, trust in other institutions plunged. But the loss of confidence may also reflect a new appreciation for the cost that comes with scientific advances (Pion and Lipsey, 1981).

Actually, we are ambivalent toward science. Just as science can have good and bad consequences, Americans respond to it with mixed emotions—trust and distrust. Consider, for example, our attitude toward computers. Many Americans have so much faith in computers that they would take the machines' words

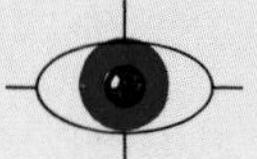

USING SOCIOLOGICAL INSIGHT

The Challenge of Biotechnology

Society is created by the interplay between humanity's biological and social natures. Today, through advances in biotechnology, scientists are beginning to change the biological structure of humans, and such developments could change the nature of human society. This reading, written by one of the century's most famous scientists, describes the potential and impact of genetic engineering. Should biotechnology be more fully regulated? How do changes in biological makeup potentially alter people's relationships to each other?

In the broadest sense, the manipulation of biological organisms is almost as old as humanity itself. Humankind's early efforts—the making of wine, cheese, and bread; the domestication and breeding of plants and animals—were almost entirely empirical. What has transformed the subject has been the discoveries of modern science and, in particular, the rapid development of molecular biology, based upon our deep understanding of modern physics and chemistry. In the past few years, this understanding has led to a series of new and powerful techniques which are likely to transform the whole of biological research.

Recent developments are often referred to as *recombinant DNA* discoveries. With these techniques, a particular piece of DNA can, with a little luck, be recognized, cut out, joined to other bits of DNA, added to other cells, and often incorporated in the cell so that it can function there. Other techniques allow us to sequence rapidly any particular stretch of DNA. These DNA sequences are now recorded in central computers. So far, the total length stored there, from all over the world, amounts to about six million base pairs.

Where are these new techniques likely to lead? In the immediate future, we may expect to see better methods of diagnosing diseases and, hopefully, of curing some of them. The cure or prevention of at least the most widespread tropical diseases, for example, would be possible, given sufficient effort, and is very likely to have a very large social impact. We can already recognize certain genetic abnormalities in the early fetus, and we may expect to be able to recognize many more. We should be able to improve plants, for example, by making them resistant to certain insect pests, and to improve our domestic animals, for example, by improving milk yields. Eventually we may be able to make proteins cheaply enough that they can be used in industrial processes.

Before long we may expect to be able to recognize the biological basis and, with luck, to cure or prevent types of senility such as Alzheimer's disease. We may expect much better methods of coping with cancer and cardiovascular disease. Eventually the process of

over their own. If their bank statements do not seem right to them, they are likely to scratch their heads and assume that the bank's computer is right. According to one study, almost one-quarter of men and two-thirds of women did not question the accuracy of a calculator that the researcher had secretly programmed to make errors. Instead, they blamed themselves, as one said, "I must have entered it wrong on the calculator; either that or I'm thinking wrong." At the same time, though, disenchantment with computers may be on the rise, after an initial burst of enthusiasm or an increase in machine errors and breakdowns (Timnick, 1982).

Our ambivalence toward technology can show itself in another way. We have the largest automobile ownership in the world, yet it does not keep us from walking, running, and bicycling, and even from rebuilding the centers of our cities on a scale convenient to pedestrians. In fact, we have learned to use technology to enhance our enjoyment of nontechnological things. As Canadian architect Witold Rybczynski (1983) observes,

> It is no coincidence that the hang glider, the dune buggy, the surfboard and the sailboat were all invented in the United States, because they characteristically combine enjoyment of nature with enjoyment of technique. . . . The American is never happy as when he can bring the machine into the garden and marry both

aging, which is unlikely to be simple, should be understandable. Hopefully some of its processes can be slowed down or avoided. In fact, in the next century, we shall have to tackle the question of the preferred form of death. Moreover, the increasing age of the population will transform the nature of society.

It is possible that we can add genes to an adult human being to correct some genetic defect, but altering a gene in the gene line to produce improved offspring is likely to be very difficult because of the danger of unwanted side effects. It would also raise obvious ethical problems; however, such problems are already with us since we can eliminate certain defective genes using fetal diagnosis and early abortion. But, would it be ethical for parents to choose the sex of their unborn child in this way—for example, by aborting the fetus if it were the unwanted sex?

In the long run, these new methods will lead to an extraordinary explosion of detailed knowledge in many branches of biology. We can expect very rapid advances in developmental biology and neurobiology, although a detailed understanding of the brain will probably have to wait until well into the next century.

It seems probable that brains are nothing more than neuronal machines. Eventually, our new knowledge of the precise workings of the brain may make any other hypotheses quite superfluous. This is likely to produce an even greater cultural shock than Darwin's suggestion that we have evolved from apelike ancestors.

In short, these new developments will allow us to acquire almost unlimited information about the biological nature of humanity. Knowledge brings power, and power brings both benefits and risks. There is little doubt that by these discoveries society will be transformed before the end of the next century.

It should be realized that, for much of our evolution as human beings, our ancestors were hunter-gatherers. Many of our ways of thinking, including the obvious human desire for a religion of some sort, were evolved to help us survive during this period. Humankind did not evolve in order to cope with a scientific view of the world, since that is far too recent. . . . We must face the fact that scientific knowledge has led us into ways of thinking which are only partly in harmony with our genetic heritage. Are we prepared to face up to this very difficult problem?

Source: Adapted from Francis Crick, "The challenge of biotechnology," *Humanist*, July/August 1986, pp. 8–11.

parts of the American myth: American know-how and America-the-beautiful.

Thus we have the power to control technology, to make it work for us. But some social scientists fear that our life can be "ordered in all its important aspects by mechanical regulation" (Bittner, 1983). As sociologist Sherry Turkle (1984) argues, computers have begun to make people compare their own intellectual workings with those of the machine, with many preferring mechanistic models of thought to more traditional humanistic ones. Heavy users of computers, according to psychologist Craig Brod (1984), tend to be impatient and contemptuous when other humans fail to show the speed, efficiency, and unambiguity of the machine. Ultimately, however, it is humans who determine how technology is to be used because it is by itself neither good nor bad—only neutral.

QUESTIONS FOR DISCUSSION AND REVIEW

1. What are the beneficial and harmful effects of scientific advances?
2. Why do so many Americans have more trust in science and technology than in other social institutions?
3. Why do some sociologists fear technology's impact on society?

CHAPTER REVIEW

1. *When did modern science begin to develop?* In seventeenth-century Europe. Its development was nurtured by the emergence of a mechanistic philosophy of nature, cooperation among the new scientists, and the achievement of social legitimacy by scientists. Science became established as a social institution, however, only as scientists began to achieve success in applying their knowledge to improve technology. *How are science and technology related today?* They are virtually inseparable, and technology has come to mean the application of scientific knowledge to practical purposes. Science is routinely applied to technological problems today, and most current technological advances could not occur without science. But to carry on their work, most scientists today require complicated technology, and the flow of knowledge goes from technology to science as well as from science to technology.

2. *How is scientific knowledge advanced?* Cultural accumulation is fundamental. Most scientists work within the reigning paradigm of their discipline. The paradigm is a cultural product, a heritage scientists share as a result of the work of earlier scientists. Normal research produces an accumulation of scientific ideas and findings. Some of these will be anomalies, from which a new paradigm is eventually fashioned, and thus a scientific revolution occurs.

3. *When did the era of "big science" begin?* After World War II. Billions of dollars were poured into scientific research, and the number and prestige of scientists soared. Increasingly, they worked as narrow specialists with huge bureaucracies. Collaboration and multiple, independent discoveries have become common. Big science has also brought about triviality in research and substantial administrative work, but it continues to make the United States the leader on all scientific frontiers.

4. *What norms help preserve the integrity of science?* Robert Merton identified four: universalism, organized skepticism, communality, and disinterestedness. *Do scientists follow the norms Merton identified?* They frequently violate them. Scientists are often emotional about their work, more enthusiastic about their own discoveries than those of others, strongly motivated to seek recognition, and ready to accept or reject new ideas for nonscientific reasons. *Did scientists of the past observe the norm of disinterestedness?* In the past as now, scientists have been very competitive. Getting published is a key to gaining the recognition that determines who wins this competitive game. Although competition can benefit science by motivating scientists to work hard and by discouraging them from delaying publication, it can also slow scientific progress by encouraging secrecy, discouraging cooperation, and increasing the frequency of deviant behavior such as falsification of data.

5. *What sort of stratification system does scientific competition produce?* There is a very, very small elite. Most scientists never make a great discovery, are unnoticed by the scientific community, and publish little. *Does success in science depend on intelligence?* Measures of intellectual ability have very low correlations with scientific productivity. Several social factors—including family background, interaction among scientists, marital fertility, and the scientific reward system—have an important influence on scientific achievement.

6. *What are the benefits and costs of science?* The benefits are often attainable right away. They include physical comforts and conveniences from such innovations as television and computers as well as the curing of diseases. The costs may not be known until years later, such as the computer's invasion of our privacy and some chemicals' threat to our health. *How does the American public react to science and technology?* It is ambivalent toward them, trusting and yet not trusting them, enjoying them but also enjoying nature.

KEY TERMS

Anomaly Kuhn's term for a research finding that cannot be fitted into the existing paradigm and thus cannot be explained by it (p. 481).

Communality The norm that requires scientists to share their knowledge freely with each other (p. 483).

Disinterestedness The norm that requires scientists to pursue truth rather than self-interest (p. 483).

Matthew effect The tendency to praise famous scientists and to ignore the contributions of those who are not well known (p. 484).

Normal science Kuhn's term for routine research (p. 481).

Organized skepticism The norm that requires scientists to be critical of any scientific idea or finding (p. 483).

Paradigm A model for defining, studying, and solving problems in accordance with certain basic assumptions (p. 480).

Science A body of knowledge about natural phenomena that is acquired through the systematic use of objective methods (p. 478).

Scientific revolution Kuhn's term for the replacement of an old paradigm by a new one (p. 481).

Technology The application of scientific knowledge for practical purposes (p. 478).

Universalism The norm that requires scientists to evaluate ideas in accordance with impersonal criteria (p. 483).

SUGGESTED READINGS

Brannigan, Augustine, 1981. *The Social Basis of Scientific Discoveries.* New York: Cambridge University Press. Shows how scientific achievements are socially defined as discoveries, with insightful analyses of such subjects as multiple discoveries, priority disputes, and deception in science.

Knorr-Cetina, Karin D., and Michael Mulkay (eds.). 1983. *Science Observed: Perspectives on the Social Study of Science.* Beverly Hills, Calif.: Sage. A collection of articles presenting various approaches to the sociology of science.

Rybczynski, Witold. 1983. *Taming the Tiger: The Struggle to Control Technology.* New York: Viking. An interesting study of technology and its users, full of case histories showing that humans are in charge.

Taubes, Gary. 1987. *Nobel Dreams: Power, Deceit, and the Ultimate Experiment.* New York: Random House. A fascinating, revealing case study of a 1984 Nobel-prize winner's brilliant and distinguished career tainted by such scientifically unseemly behavior as manipulation, bullying, corner cutting, and data fabrication.

Turkle, Sherry. 1984. *The Second Self: Computers and the Human Spirit.* New York: Simon & Schuster. A highly stimulating analysis of how computers can make people think and behave like them.

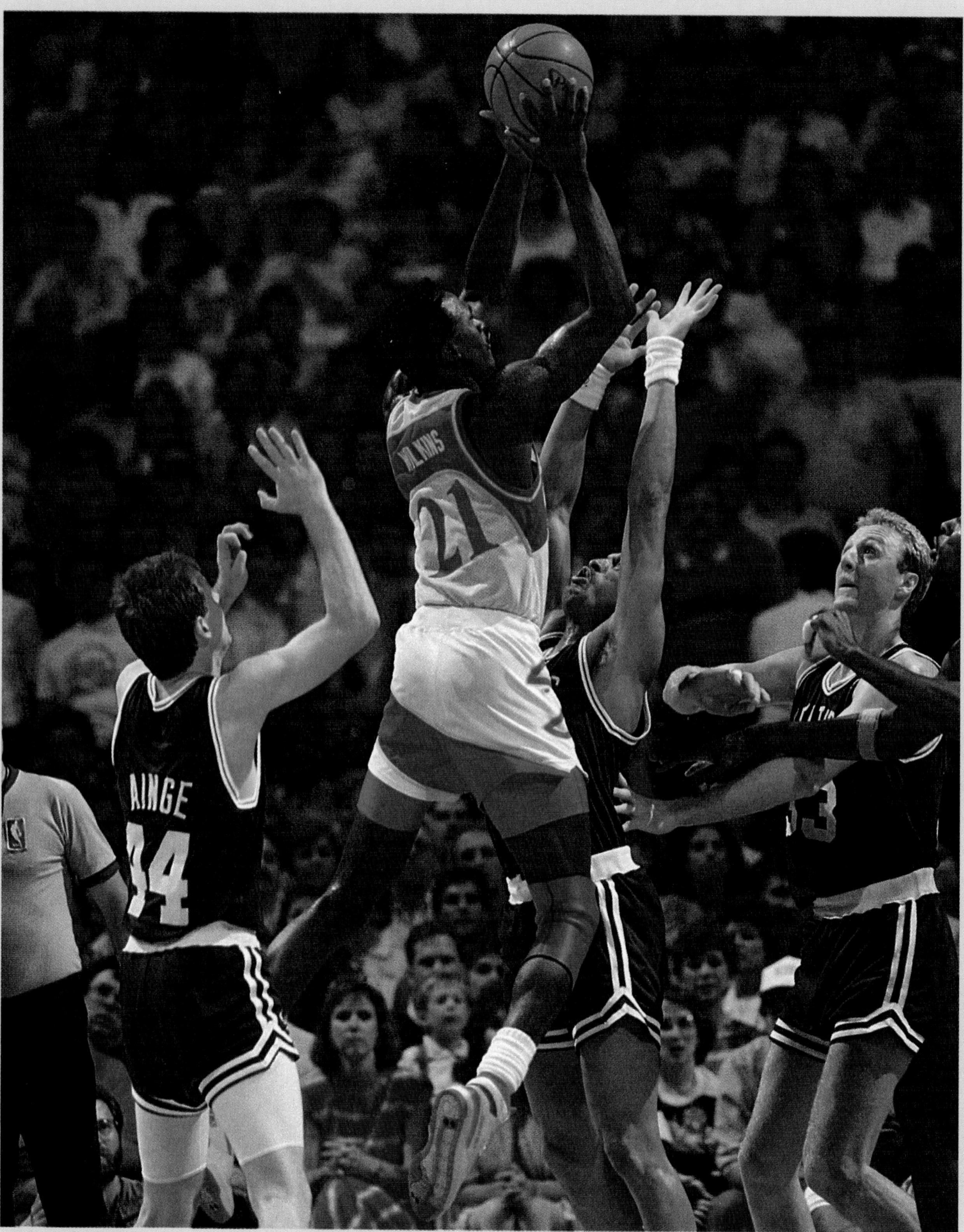
21
AINGE

20 Sport

Sport and society are interrelated. On the one hand, we can see the influence of society on sport. Basketball, for example, is a game of physical skill, strategy, and chance combined. This popular sport reflects the larger game of life in our complex society. Just as we need a good deal of skill and strategy and some luck to make it in our society, basketball players need the same things to win on the court. On the other hand, we can see the impact of sport on people. Moderate physical activities can keep us in shape, but fiercely competitive sports can wreck our bodies. Playing football or basketball tends to hurt academic performance in college, though not in high school. Sports violence tends to produce fan violence. Finally, sport and various other social institutions such as the family and politics affect each other.

Sport is a social institution whose influence reaches far and wide. This is especially true in an increasingly leisure-oriented society like our own. Most of us have had some experience with sport, either as participants or spectators. Schools, from kindergarten to college, provide many opportunities for sport activities. Newspapers carry more news about sports than about politics, the economy, crime, or practically any other event. Radio and television newscasts rarely go on the air without any sports reporting. Football, baseball, and other games are often broadcast in their entirety, which sometimes preempts regular programming. Sport exerts so much influence on our lives that our everyday speech often carries such sport imageries as "struck out," "touch base," "ballpark figure," "game plan," "teamwork," and "cheap shot."

In the last decade, the pervasive influence of sport has attracted serious attention from sociologists. As a result, there has emerged a rapidly growing literature on sport. In this chapter we analyze the relationship between sport and the larger society; the impact of sport on academic achievement, social mobility, and violent behavior; the connection between sport and other institutions; and black and women athletes.

SPORT AND SOCIETY

There is an immediate relationship between the sports world and the larger society. Our favorite sports and beliefs about them reflect as well as influence the culture of our society.

Sports in Various Countries

The strong connection between sport and society can be seen from the popularity of different kinds of sport in various countries. While football and baseball are extremely popular in the United States, soccer is equally so throughout Latin America and other parts of the world. Baseball is also "big" in Cuba, Nicaragua, and other Latin American countries, and boxing is especially so in Panama, but these sports have not caught on in Asia. There, other sports are more popular. Sumo wrestling, in which two incredibly bulky opponents try to push each other out of a very small ring, is unique to Japan. Cockfighting is so popular in the Philippines that it is televised in some parts of the country. Fish fighting

World Cup soccer game in Mexico between France and Italy. The popularity of particular sports varies from country to country. Although soccer is only a minor activity in the United States, it is the national game of many countries in Europe and Latin America. Individuals identify so strongly with their country's team that riots often break out when teams take part in international competitions.

is a fascinating spectator sport to the people of Thailand. Kite fighting, in which contestants try to cut down each other's kites with glass fragments glued to their strings, is also popular in Thailand as well as in Indonesia and Malaysia (MacLachlan, 1982).

A classic anthropological study has systematically demonstrated the close link between sport and society (Sutton-Smith and Roberts, 1970; Roberts and Cosper, 1987): The games of *physical skill* (such as swimming and canoeing) tend to be popular in tropical countries, where the weather is easily predictable, the economy is relatively simple, social stratification and political institutions are practically absent, social conflict and war are rare, and child-rearing practices are relaxed. Games of *chance* (such as cockfighting and dice) are more popular in places with a harsh, unpredictable environment, where drastic seasonal changes are common, food shortages are frequent, child-rearing practices are punitive, and belief in the benevolence of gods is widespread. Games of *strategy* (chess, checkers) are more popular in societies with more complex cultures—with larger populations, more occupational specialization, more highly developed social stratification, and greater emphasis on achievement and self-reliance in child-rearing practices. Games of physical skills, chance, and strategy *combined* (football, basketball) tend to characterize the most highly industrialized societies, such as the United States. In football, for example, physical skill and strategy are heavily emphasized, while a residue of chance is expected to make the game interesting due to its unpredictable outcome. This game reflects the larger game of life in our complex society. We need a good deal of skill and strategy to make it in our society, but we also need some luck to enhance our chances of success despite the advanced forms of our science and technology.

While skill and strategy can be developed through hard work, what about the element of chance? In cultures where chance plays a part in the outcome of a game, a ritual is typically performed to increase the probability of victory. The sports ritual, however, differs from one society to another. In Thai boxing, before a bout begins, each boxer prays to his deity, pays his respects to his mentor, and whips himself into a frenzy by performing a war dance. The Japanese sumo wrestlers also perform a ritual before each fight, which culminates in the sprinkling of salt to enhance the chance of winning. In the United States, where individualism reigns, each player tends to carry out a different ritual, often referred to by sportswriters as a "personality quirk." Thus Dave Murphy, a marathon runner from England, always listens to a tape of The Who one hour before every race. Elaine Zayak, a former national figure skating champion, often brought the same stuffed monkey to every competition (Zimmer, 1984). Pat Haden, a former Rams quarterback, always slept in the bed next to the door and drove the same way to the stadium before every game. Mark Fidrych, a former Detroit pitcher, had the habit of talking to the ball. Al Hrabosky, when pitching for the Kansas City Royals, never failed to stare menacingly at the hitter while jerking his head back and forth. Hockey goalie Giles Gratton, when he was with the New York Rangers, wore a mask that made him look like a snarling lion with bared fangs (Womack, 1978).

With a diverse population and culture, American society has also encouraged the development of various

With a diverse population and culture, American society has developed various sports that appeal to different audiences. Football is in effect a war game full of violent action. It is, therefore, highly popular among macho men, who like to play generals by planning one strategy after another for their warriors on the field. This sport contrasts with golf and tennis, which hold more attraction for country club members and other genteel people.

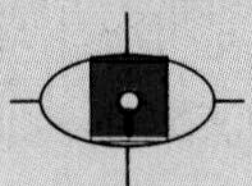

LOOKING AT CURRENT RESEARCH

The Pigskin Cult

The popularity of a sport usually reflects the culture in which the athletes and their fans live. This reading shows how southerners have developed a strong devotion to football. What is it in the culture of the South that contributes to the "pigskin cult"?

In the Deep South, football is number one. Baseball and basketball are second-string pastimes. Football is more important to Dixie than it is to any other region of the country, and its dominance there has increased during the last three decades.

The rise of the pigskin cult in the South represents a major geographic shift. Football is a northern game, but southerners adopted it, absorbing it into their macho culture. The process began when the famous coaches Heisman and Warner brought Ivy League innovation to Georgia early in the century, and it accelerated as established coaches moved to southern colleges. When the southwestern oil boom pulled workers from northeastern football hearths like Ohio and Pennsylvania to Texas, Louisiana, and Oklahoma, high-quality football spread into those southern states.

Yet it was not until 1951, when Ivy League schools decided to deemphasize the college game, that the balance of power began to shift southward. Since then, southern high school football and college football have grown in quality and social importance.

The fever now crosses class and racial lines. Well-to-do southern white children with football potential are routinely held back—"redshirted in the eighth grade"—so they will be more mature when the time comes to play ball. Blacks now have full access to the university of their choice, and they are choosing big-name football schools with increasing regularity. The evidence suggests that the number of southern black football players has increased by at least 50 percent in the past decade.

Regional sports cultures are easy to see but hard to measure because they depend on the accumulation of individual attitudes and feelings. The ideal measuring system would track the behavior of a geographically varied sample of Americans, including data on their sports participation, sports spectating, media choices, attitudes and values. Such a survey does not exist, but there is another way to go.

If regional differences in the ability to develop high-quality athletes mirror regional attitudes toward different sports, then a study of the hometown origins of top college and professional athletes should reveal the sports attitudes of each region. In fact, pronounced regional variations in origin do exist, with the Deep South clearly at the top of the football heap.

Using college football rosters from top football schools in the

sports to appeal to different audiences. For those living in small towns and rural areas, baseball offers a great attraction because it represents a slow, relaxed experience. In contrast, basketball is comparable to the hustle and bustle of big city life, thus greatly appealing to urbanites. Football, in effect a war game full of violent action, excites those who like to play generals, planning one strategy after another for their warriors on the field. It is likely to be highly popular in a macho culture (see box, above). Golf and tennis appeal to country club members and other genteel people, horse racing to those folks hooked on gambling, and auto racing to those who admire the drivers' roaring machines and death-defying antics (Axthelm, 1970). Sociologists have also found a class factor in Americans' preference for particular sports: the upper classes prefer golf and tennis; the middle classes football, baseball, bowling, and hunting; and the lower classes boxing, wrestling, and horse racing (Stone, 1969; Eitzen and Sage, 1982).

Mass Participation in Sports

We are probably the most sports-crazy people in the world. Although a number of countries, such as the Soviet Union and Brazil, have impressed some observers as more enthusiastic about sports, their enthusiasm is largely confined to being spectators rather than participants (Michener, 1976). We participate in sports nearly as often as we watch them. As the Miller Lite Report (1983) shows, 71 percent of Americans engage in physical exercises at least once a week, compared with 73

National Collegiate Athletic Association, I assembled data on the hometown high school, home county, metropolitan area, and race of 50,300 college football players during several time periods. The origins of professional football players are based solely on 1981 rosters.

Southern dominance was firmly in place by 1976. The entire southern tier, from Virginia to California, was above the national average. On balance, the South was producing twice as many college football players per capita as the North. The South also dominated pro football rosters.

The South's single-minded emphasis on football has produced a new cultural hearth for America's top football players—Texas, Mississippi, and Louisiana. One researcher has estimated that 13 of the top 20 college football squads between 1953 and 1983 were in the Sunbelt. Between 1973 and 1983, 17 of the top 25 were Sunbelt schools.

How an area becomes infatuated with football, or any other sport, cannot be easily explained. Something intangible accounts for the great interest and prolific output of talent from certain area. Such factors as economic and occupational structure, ethnic and racial composition, and climate surely play a role. But perhaps most important is the degree to which a community provides social and financial support for its schoolboy warriors.

Texas and Oklahoma towns are the epitome of the high school football culture. Over 1,000 Texas high schools, 2,000 junior high schools, and multitudes of elementary schools field football teams. In many towns the game is life's biggest diversion, and in the autumn the game schedule controls the tempo of activity from Friday evening to Sunday afternoon.

High school sports programs are a mirror of community attitudes and values. Some are designed to breed major college and pro athletes who will bring prestige to the homeland and win at all costs. Others promote mass participation and encourage a lifetime of physical activity. An analysis of state school statistics reveals the regions where each philosophy dominates.

In the Deep South, the breeding program reigns supreme. A typical high school will offer only basic sports like football, basketball, baseball, and track. Attempts to expand the sports program by diluting the football effort usually meet with strong opposition. Women's programs generally have meager resources and low participation, and cheerleading brings girls higher status than playing on a team.

Source: Excerpted from John F. Rooney, Jr., "The pigskin cult and other Sunbelt sports," *American Demographics,* September 1986, pp. 38–43.

percent watching sports on television that often. The great mass participation may reflect the general affluence of American society. In fact, there is evidence to suggest a significant link between economic success and sports participation. Generally, higher-income Americans are more likely to participate in sports than lower-income Americans (Anderson and Stone, 1979; Miller Lite Report, 1983).

Today the passion for sports is running high throughout the United States. The latest Gallup poll shows that 59 percent of American adults exercise daily, up 12 percent from two years ago and more than twice the figure for 1961 (Huntley, 1984). They participate in many kinds of sports, ranging from swimming to jogging to calisthenics (see Table 20.1). Some are so obsessed with sports that they often overdo it and incur injury. The number of Americans getting hurt in recreational athletics has risen significantly. Some of these injuries result from "overuse syndrome"—pushing the aging out-of-condition body too far. Nearing middle age, most of these athletes seem reluctant to accept the inevitable changes of growing older (Hathaway, 1984). Here is a typical example:

> He could hear them yelling "Slide! Slide!" Home plate was only a few feet away. So what if he hadn't played softball since college 20 years ago? So what if he now weighed 275 lbs.? He could do it. He knew he could. He slid. . . . They carried him off the field (*Time,* 1978b).

Other injuries, such as shinsplints, tendinitis, and stress fractures, which can persist for a lifetime, often afflict

Table 20.1 How We Keep Fit

Percentages of Americans 7 years of age or older participating in:

	Percent
Swimming	33.8%
Exercise walking	24.9
Bicycle riding	23.1
Fishing	19.0
Bowling	15.9
Exercising with equipment	14.9
Running/jogging	10.8
Aerobic exercising	10.2
Basketball	9.9
Softball	9.7
Golf	9.3
Tennis	8.4
Hiking	6.7
Calisthenics	6.5

Source: Census Bureau, *Statistical Abstract of the United States*, 1988, p. 220.

Spectator sports are popular throughout the world, but Americans are distinguished by also being great participants in sports. Activities such as cycling, bowling, jogging, or just stretching and exercising are popular in the United States. According to a Miller Lite report, for example, 71 percent of Americans engage in physical exercise at least once a week. Such a massive participation in sports may reflect the general affluence of American society.

younger people who are addicted to exercise. They are unable to stop jogging or doing aerobics even when it hurts. Consider the experience of an exercise addict: "Every time she lifted her legs to step over a curb, Lois Deville grimaced with the pain of her shinsplints. The Miamian, in New York City on business, was frantic over missing her daily aerobics classes. To compensate, she paced the streets for hours, even though the pain was so excruciating she couldn't put a sheet on her legs at night" (Charlier, 1987).

Behind the mass participation in sports lies something more than the pursuit of physical fitness. Under the influence of our competitive society, most Americans seek the thrill of competition. According to a poll, 86 percent of men and 71 percent of women said that they almost always or often try their best to win in a game (*Public Opinion*, 1983). A large majority also look upon sports participation as a type of beauty, an artistic expression, or a way of having a good time with friends (Spreitzer and Snyder, 1983). Most Americans enjoy physical activity probably because they get the same feeling of mental well-being as joggers often do. Runners find that their sport releases tension and anger as well as relieves anxiety and depression (Hathaway, 1984). Research has suggested other reasons for adult participation in sports: parental encouragement and youth participation in athletics; reading and talking about sports; and feelings of pride, competence, relaxation, and satisfaction from physical activities (Spreitzer and Snyder, 1983; see also box, p. 504). It is quite possible that mass participation in sports gets a boost from the increased popularity of spectator sports. Although research in Israel has failed to show a clear connection between sports participation and spectatorship (Shamir and Ruskin, 1984), attendance at most sports events in the United States has gone up significantly (see Table 20.2). All this can ultimately be traced to the American **ideology of sport,** the popular belief that athletic competition can do wonders for our health and character.

American Ideology of Sport

American athletes and their coaches and fans hold certain beliefs about sports that reflect the dominant values of the larger society. Just as success is most heavily emphasized in our culture, so it is in the American ideology of sport. Success in sports means winning, the

Table 20.2 Rising Attendance at Sport Events

	1983 Attendance	Change From 1973
Baseball*	78.1 mil.	Up 85.2%
Horseracing	75.8 mil.	Down 1.3%
Auto racing	55.1 mil.	Up 19.8%
Football*	54.4 mil.	Up 24.8%
Basketball*	41.7 mil.	Up 19.1%
Greyhound racing	22.1 mil.	Up 46.6%
Hockey*	20.3 mil.	Down 3.9%
Wrestling	9.5 mil.	Up 85.1%
Soccer	8.4 mil.	Up 67.1%
Boxing	7.1 mil.	Up 229.5%
Tennis	4.2 mil.	Not available

* Both professional and collegiate events.

Source: Daily Racing Form. Reprinted from *U.S. News & World Report* issue of 8/13/84. Copyright, 1984, U.S. News & World Report, Inc.

importance of which is well expressed by the late football coach Vince Lombardi's immortal words: "Winning isn't everything, it is the only thing." In order to win, athletes must have great discipline and work extremely hard. Such personal traits and acts are popularly believed to be the results of sports participation. Sociologist Harry Edwards (1973) has analyzed these and other widely held beliefs.

First, sport is believed capable of building character. This, in effect, means that athletes are supposed to be clean-cut, wholesome, red-blooded, loyal to their team, and altruistic toward their teammates. They are, in other words, expected to be conventional, conforming to popular American values. Thus, in the 1960s, when short haircuts were the norm, athletes with long hair were often censured or barred from sports participation. Muhammad Ali was stripped of his boxing title for refusing to be drafted into the army, which was then fighting a war that he opposed. Ballplayers and their coaches often used slogans to express their beliefs in loyalty and altruism, such as "An ounce of loyalty is worth a pound of cleverness," "There is no U in team—there is no I in team," and "Cooperate—remember the banana, every time it leaves the bunch, it gets skinned."

Second, sport is believed capable of developing self-discipline. This, in practice, pressures athletes to accept strict discipline. Coaches are fond of repeating such slogans as "Live by the code or get out" and "He who flies with the owls at night cannot keep up with the eagles during the day." Players are even ordered not to have sex the night before a game, which has led to the popular myth that sex the night before competition will hurt athletic performance.

Third, through its emphasis on competition, sport is believed capable of developing fortitude and preparing one for life, thus enabling the young athletes to overcome the challenges in the competitive society at large. Such a faith in sport is expressed by coaches assuring the public: "Send us a boy; we'll return him a man." Trying to realize this goal, the coaches often exhort their players to develop courage, perseverance, and aggressiveness with such slogans as "When the going gets tough, the tough get going" and "It's easy to be ordinary, but it takes guts to excel."

Fourth, sport is believed capable of producing physical fitness and mental alertness. Thus athletes, particularly in competitive sports, are expected to push themselves to the limit of fatigue, as expressed by the slogans: "Fatigue makes cowards of us all" and "No one ever drowns in sweat." Although the games may strain their muscles or crush their bones, the athletes apparently are impressed with their toughness into believing that their sports activities make them physically strong and mentally alert.

There is evidence to suggest that the general public by and large supports the ideology of sport. Sociologists Eldon Snyder and Elmer Spreitzer (1983) found that most people consider sports beneficial not only for individual athletes but for society as a whole. In their study, nearly 90 percent of the people interviewed said that sport was useful for teaching self-discipline, 80 percent stated that sport was valuable for promoting the sense of fair play, and 70 percent indicated that sport was helpful

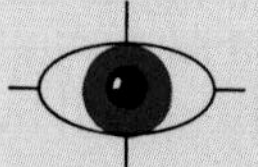

USING SOCIOLOGICAL INSIGHT

How to Keep on Exercising

Sociologists have discovered that most people exercise not because it is good for them but because it feels good. According to the study reported here, the good feelings often come from the ability to demonstrate one's athletic competence, enjoy being physically active, and find relaxation from sports. Such findings can be used to help people keep on exercising. How do these benefits of exercise contribute to America's sports ideology?

A serious concern of our society involves the maintenance of physical and mental health. Legislators develop proposals for public health programs, insurance companies charge higher rates to cover rising health costs, and physical therapists, educators, and medical specialists emphasize the need for increased attention to the prevention of physical and mental disabilities. These specialists emphasize the importance of exercise on a regular basis in order to enhance one's physical and mental health. In 1982 the National Academy of Sciences' Institute of Medicine estimated that 50 percent of the mortality from the ten leading causes of death in the United States could be traced to life-style. Curiously, there is little research concerning the more important issue of (a) why some individuals prefer sedentary life-styles, (b) why others choose to become physically active, and (c) why some individuals adhere to vigorous exercise programs once they are adopted whereas others discontinue.

The scientific literature shows a clear relationship between regular physical activity and holistic health. The implications for preventive health are very evident. The literature shows that vigorous physical activity can reduce anxiety, depression, tension, and coronary risk factors such as obesity and hypertension. Unfortunately, adherence to a program of physical activity is relatively low. Organized exercise programs typically do not succeed in producing adherence to physical activity on an ongoing basis. The literature shows that about half the participants who begin an exercise program discontinue exercising within the first six months.

The present study, then, attempts to identify factors that affect both initial and continued participation by adults in physical fitness activities. An increased understanding of the factors associated with involvement and adherence in physical fitness activities is an important step in achieving those health care goals.

Data for this study were collected through questionnaires, which were sent to persons who had voluntarily taken a physical fitness stress test at the Bowling Green State University Fitness and Sports Physiology Laboratory.

in teaching youngsters to respect authority and to be good citizens (see also Dodder, Fromme, and Holland, 1982).

It is a well-known fact that moderate physical activities can keep us in shape. But the ideology of sport is largely what it is—an ideology. There has been no conclusive evidence to substantiate it. What are believed to be the consequences of highly competitive sports often do not result from participation but from selectivity. Coaches, for example, are inclined to recruit individuals with good character and screen out those with bad character. Moreover, sports do not always enhance physical fitness. In fact, football often causes head and spinal injuries, largely because the players routinely resort to "spearing"—blocking or tackling head first. Baseball, too, tends to damage the bones in the players' shoulders, elbows, fingers, and toes. The greatest threat to health is probably boxing, as tragically demonstrated by Muhammad Ali's recent symptoms of Parkinson's disease—slurred speech, trembling hands, and masklike face—brought on by years of fighting in the ring. Nevertheless, the ideology of sport is important for understanding why sport is so popular in the United States.

QUESTIONS FOR DISCUSSION AND REVIEW

1. How do sports in various countries demonstrate the link between sport and society?
2. Why are Americans probably the most sports-crazy people in the world?
3. What components make up the American ideology of sport, and how do they promote mass participation in athletic activities?

These persons had taken the test over a period of approximately five years, and with the completion of the physical work-up each individual was advised about the appropriate physical activity for his or her level of fitness. An important aspect of this study is that the subjects in the present sample expressed their initial concern for physical fitness by making an appointment, paying a fee, and undergoing the physical test. In short, the respondents in this survey had been tested and prescribed an individualized physical regimen. The goal of this follow-up study was to analyze the variables associated with adherence to the prescribed program.

Our findings showed that 31 percent of the individuals in our sample who had undergone a physical fitness assessment and stress test were subsequently inactive in terms of regular exercise. On the more optimistic side, 40 percent reported that they engage in at least five hours of exercise per week. The demographic variables of age, education, occupation, and income showed little correlation with adherence to an exercise program. The three strongest predictors of physical activity were perceived athletic ability, an intrinsic orientation toward physical activity as an end in itself, and an orientation toward sports as a means of relaxation.

Our research concurs with previous studies showing that most people do not exercise because it is good for them; rather, they exercise because it feels good. In fact, some research suggests that participants can become emotionally dependent on, even addicted to, regular exercise. William Glasser suggests that physical activity can alter an individual's consciousness under the following conditions.

1. The activity must be uncompetitive and voluntarily selected.
2. It should be something that can be done easily and without much mental effort for at least an hour a day.
3. The activity should be one that can be done alone and does not depend upon the participation of others.
4. The activity must have some physical, emotional, or spiritual value for the participant.
5. The participant must believe that persistence will result in improvement.
6. The activity must be one that can be done without self-criticism.

If we can meet these conditions, we will keep on exercising.

Source: Excerpted and adapted from Eldon E. Snyder and Elmer Spreitzer, "Patterns of adherence to a physical conditioning program," *Sociology of Sport Journal*, vol. 1, 1984, pp. 103–116.

THE IMPACT OF SPORT

There have been many studies about the impact of sport on academic achievement, social mobility, and violent behavior. Before we deal with these issues, let us examine two sociological perspectives that have been used to view the effect of sport on the society at large.

Perspectives on Sport

In the sociology of sport, there are two ways of looking at the impact of sport on society. One is the functionalist perspective, which sees sport as functional for society. The other is the conflict perspective, which views sports as dysfunctional (Theberge, 1981; Young, 1986; Wilkerson and Doddler, 1987). Functionalists assume that sport serves at least two major positive functions:

1. Sport is an integrating force for society, thereby contributing to social order and stability. Sport is seen as a social mechanism for uniting otherwise disunited Americans. Through their common interest in a famous athlete or team, Americans of diverse racial, social, and cultural backgrounds can feel a sense of homogeneity that they can acquire in no other way.

2. Due to its competitive nature, sport inspires individuals to do their utmost to win. In so doing, they will develop skill and ability, mental alertness, and physical prowess. These qualities are believed to ensure success in

the larger society, as has been expressed by Douglas MacArthur's famous statement: "Upon the fields of friendly strife are sown the seeds that, upon other fields, on other days, will bear the fruits of victory." Personal success, perhaps needless to say, is assumed to contribute to the overall success of the society as a prosperous and happy one.

Conflict theorists are sharply critical of the functionalist view. They argue that sport in American society is a harmful force for the masses.

1. By serving as an integrating force, sport, in effect, acts as an opiate, numbing the masses' sense of dissatisfaction with capitalist society. Through their involvement in sport as spectators, workers tend to distract their minds from their tedious and dehumanizing jobs. At the same time they tend not to criticize the status quo. The consequence is the perpetuation of an unjust, racist, male-dominated, capitalist society.

2. Due to its heavy emphasis on competition and winning, sport has lost its original elements of play and fun, which all the participants can enjoy equally. Sport has now become big business, enabling the powerful owners of professional teams to exploit the public. Being professionalized and bureaucratized, sport has generated an elitist system, whereby a very tiny number of players become superstars and the huge number of potential players are turned into mere spectators. In such a system, according to two critics of sport, the superstar tends to become a superjerk. They describe him as "the superstar who won't simply kick, hit, throw, or maim someone, and call it a day. The superjerk is not content with earning large sums of money while getting wholesome exercise. He must constantly display his superego, indulge in superwinning, superbragging, superspending, and superpointing" (Tutko and Bruns, 1976).

Academic Achievement

The student athlete is widely stereotyped as the "dumb jock" because it is assumed that sport participation interferes with schoolwork. There is, however, no truth in this stereotype and assumption when applied to *high-school* athletes. In fact, many studies have consistently demonstrated a positive relationship between athletic participation and academic performance. Most impressive is the classic study by Walter Schafer and Michael Armer (1968). They discovered that high-school athletes had higher grade point averages than nonathletes. They further found that the athletes' greater academic achievement was not due to such factors as being from higher-income families or taking easy courses. Similar findings have emerged in more recent studies (Wells and Picou, 1980; Braddock, 1981; Sage, 1982).

What, then, could explain the athletes' better scholastic records? According to those researchers, higher educational aspirations motivated the athletes to study harder, as they were found to be more likely than nonathletes to plan to finish four years of college. High educational aspiration is apparently not the only intervening variable between sport participation and academic achievement. Other factors, particularly lower socioeconomic status and rural background, have been found to have a positive impact on the athletes' schoolwork. As research has shown, athletes from poor families are more motivated to do well academically than athletes from affluent homes. The latter tend to take their academic work for granted, nonchalantly assuming that they will attend college later. But the poorer athletes are more inclined to take their studies seriously because athletic involvement is often the most important means for them "to gain social recognition and acceptance, and through it, greater academic aspirations and higher scholarship" (Buhrmann, 1972). Student athletes with rural backgrounds are encouraged in the same way to study harder (Picou and Curry, 1974).

Studies about the impact of athletic participation at the *college* level, however, present a mixed, conflicting picture. Some show that college athletes have higher grade-point averages and better chances of graduating than nonathletes. Other studies indicate just the opposite: athletes are poor students. Thus a review of some studies has led to the conclusion "that college athletes as a group tend on the average to beat their academic predictions and to have a higher persistence [to graduation] rate than students not engaged in intercollegiate sports" (Hanford, 1974). A more recent study, however, casts doubt on this conclusion. After analyzing more than 2000 athletes over ten years at a major university, sociologists Dean Purdy, Stanley Eitzen, and Rick Hufnagel (1982) found that athletes entered the university with poor academic backgrounds, received lower grades, and were less likely to graduate than the general student population. Scholarship athletes and participants in the revenue-producing sports of football and basketball had the poorest academic potential and performance, primarily

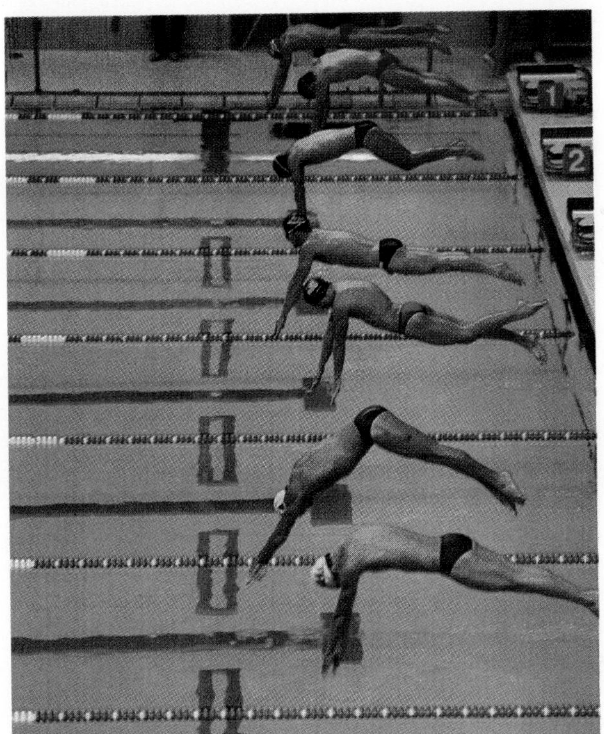

Student athletes are often stereotyped as "dumb jocks." It is assumed that participation in sports hurts academic achievement. This is not true in regard to high-school athletes, who generally show better academic performance than other students. In college, though, scholarship athletes and participants in revenue-producing sports—football and basketball—tend to do poorly in class. But college athletes in nonrevenue sports such as swimming have better scholastic records.

because they were under tremendous pressures to win at the expense of their schoolwork. But athletes in nonrevenue sports as well as female athletes had the same scholastic achievement as their nonathlete peers. In short, college athletes' academic performance depends to a significant degree on how much time and energy they are required to put into their sports.

Social Mobility

The mass media regularly publicize famous ballplayers' enormous salaries and glamorous life-styles. Many biographies and autobiographies show how sport heroes rise from rags to riches. As a result, many people believe that sport provides an easy access to fabulous success. One writer, for example, states enthusiastically that "football would enable a whole generation of young men in the coal fields of Pennsylvania to turn their backs on the mines that had employed their fathers" (Rudolph, 1962).

Black youngsters, in particular, are often so impressed with black star athletes' spectacular flight from ghetto denizen to millionaire superstar that they channel their energies toward becoming great athletes. It is little wonder that there are proportionately far more blacks in professional sports than in nonathletic occupations. As the black tennis champion Arthur Ashe (1977) points out, "While we are 60 percent of the National Basketball Association, we are less than 4 percent of the doctors and lawyers. While we are about 35 percent of major league baseball, we are less than 2 percent of the engineers. While we are about 40 percent of the National Football League, we are less than 11 percent of construction workers such as carpenters and bricklayers." But Ashe is so worried about the use of sport to escape the ghetto that he urges black youth to spend two hours in the library for every hour spent on the athletic field. He is acutely aware of the tremendous odds against making it to professional sports. "Even if you make it as a pro athlete," Ashe says, "your career will be over by the time you are 35. So you will need that diploma."

It is indeed a myth that sport offers talented athletes an excellent opportunity for social mobility. Of the high-school football players, for example, less than 2 percent will eventually receive scholarships to play college football. Of these college players, even fewer—only about 1 percent—will finally be lucky enough to turn professional. "For every 'Broadway' Joe Namath," observes Jack Scott (1971), "there are hundreds of sad, disillusioned men standing on the street corners and sitting in the beer halls of Pennsylvania towns such as Scranton, Beaver Falls, and Altoona." Ashe is correct in suggesting that the average sport career is not only short-lived but also promises to impoverish the athlete soon after retirement—if there is no college diploma to fall back on. Studies on professional boxers, soccer players, and hockey players have documented retired athletes' sharp downward mobility (Loy, McPherson, and Kenyon, 1978).

Although most college athletes do not end up with riches and fame as professional players, high-school athletes do tend to get better jobs and higher incomes outside sports than nonathletes. Several studies have shown that former high-school athletes earn more than nonathletes 11 or 15 years after they graduated, though not 5 years after graduation (Otto and Alwin, 1977; Howell and Picou, 1983; Howell, Miracle, and Rees, 1984). According to Luther Otto and Duane Alwin (1977), high-school sports can sharpen interpersonal skills, reinforce success drives, and provide beneficial interpersonal networks, all of which can give student athletes an edge over nonathletes in their future careers. Such a benefit from high-school sports, however, will not accrue equally to all students. White males will likely benefit the most and black females the least. This is possibly because black female athletes tend to suffer the stigma of being labeled unfeminine (Picou et al., 1987).

Violent Behavior

Violence is an integral part of many contact sports such as football, basketball, and hockey. Under great pressure to win, players are inclined to assault their opponents. They are further encouraged to do so by their coaches, who believe that violence is necessary for winning a game. As Vince Lombardi said, "To play football you must have that fire in you and there is nothing that stokes fire like hate." Leo Durocher, a baseball coach, expressed the same kind of attitude when he said, "If I were playing third base and my mother was rounding third with the run that was going to beat us . . . I would trip her. Oh, I'd pick her up, and I'd brush her off, and then I'd say, 'Sorry, Mom,' But nobody beats me!" (Coakley, 1982). Fans also tend to prod the players to play nasty. In the eyes of spectators, as a college basketball coach says, "the more blood, the better the show" (Snyder and Spreitzer, 1983).

It has long been a popular theory that violent sports are good for society. They are assumed to serve as a catharsis, enabling spectators to release pent-up aggression in a socially acceptable way. Fans may jump up and down, screaming and yelling, but without hurting anybody. Or they may simply watch the game quietly. Either way, viewing violent action in sports is assumed to drain away feelings of violence. When fans go home, they are believed to become less violent.

But evidence shows just the opposite: sport violence breeds fan violence. In investigating newspaper accounts of 68 episodes of violence among spectators during or after sporting events, Canadian sociologist Michael Smith (1983) found that in three-quarters of them the precipitating event was violence in the game. Other sociologists have discovered that after a sporting event hostility tends to rise among fans of football—a violent sport—but not among spectators of gymnastics—a nonviolent sport (Goldstein and Arms, 1971). Soccer games are especially likely to trigger fan violence in other countries. In Great Britain soccer fans tend to engage in "fighting on the field, street killings, assaults on public transportation to and from games, or attacks on police." When there is a major soccer game, people who live near the field would "evacuate their children, barricade doors and windows, swallow Valium tablets, or pray that the soccer hooligans pass peacefully by." In 1985 during a soccer game in Bradford, England, some fans set fire to the stadium, burning 57 people to death. Later in the same year, when a British soccer team played an Italian team in Brussels, Belgium, hundreds of English fans charged toward the Italian fans. The retreating Italian crowd was pushed against a retaining wall of the stand, causing it to collapse and crush 38 people to death. In Lima, Peru, too, a soccer match once precipitated a riot, killing 318 people and injuring another 500 (Hughes, 1983; Taylor, 1987). Finally, as we observed in Chapter 7 (Deviance and Control), watching a prizefight on television can lead some members of the audience to commit murder. However, today's sports violence pales in comparison with that in ancient societies. Chariot racing in the Byzantine Empire, for example, often provoked massive bloodshed among its fans. One rioting at a chariot race in Constantinople in A.D. 532 resulted in the loss of some 30,000 lives (Guttmann, 1986). While most of the violent sports tend to incite violence among the *audience,* some violent sports may have an opposite, positive impact on the *participants.* Karate, for example, teaches self-control and thus reduces aggressiveness in the participants (Trulson et al., 1985).

QUESTIONS FOR DISCUSSION AND REVIEW

1. In what ways does the functional perspective on sport differ from the conflict perspective?
2. Why do athletics promote scholastic achievement in high school but not in college?
3. What belies the belief that sport offers athletes an excellent chance for social mobility?
4. What impact does sports violence have on players and fans?

SPORT AND OTHER INSTITUTIONS

Sport is not a trivial artifact of our culture. It is not, as Howard Cosell once said, "the toy department of life." Instead it is of great significance to our lives because it is deeply involved with various highly important social institutions of our society.

Family Influence

Most American parents (76 percent) encourage their children to participate in sports (Miller Lite Report, 1983). The family is one of the most important influences on sport participation. Children tend to take up sports if their parents strongly encourage them or set an example. In a study on elite male athletes at the University of Wisconsin, the investigators sought to find out which socializing agents—parents, siblings, friends, teachers, school coaches, and counselors—encourage sport participation the most. Not surprisingly, coaches were found to exert the greatest influence. But the next most influential agents were parents, whose impact on their sons' sports involvement even increased as they rose from grade school to college. Similar results have appeared in another study, which compared high-school female athletes with nonathletes in Ohio. The female athletes were shown to have received greater parental encouragement than nonathletes (Snyder and Spreitzer, 1983).

There is, however, a pattern of gender-role socialization in regard to what types of sports are encouraged. Parents tend to emphasize gymnastics as more appropriate for their daughters than basketball. As for boys, parents are likely to prefer swimming, tennis, and hockey over baseball and football (Snyder and Spreitzer, 1983). In a national survey, Louis Harris found that parents object most strongly to certain sports for their children: football for both sons and daughters, wrestling for girls, and boxing for boys (*Time,* 1979).

Parents' tendency to socialize sons and daughters into different sports may reflect the residual influence of the traditional gender-role perceptions. Basketball or wrestling, for example, has traditionally been considered all right for boys but too "unfeminine" for girls. At the same time, though, parents do not always stick to this stereotyped view about masculinity or femininity. After all, they oppose football for boys and girls alike. They seem to have rejected the traditional view of football as a masculine sport—as suitable for boys only—probably because football has become too violent.

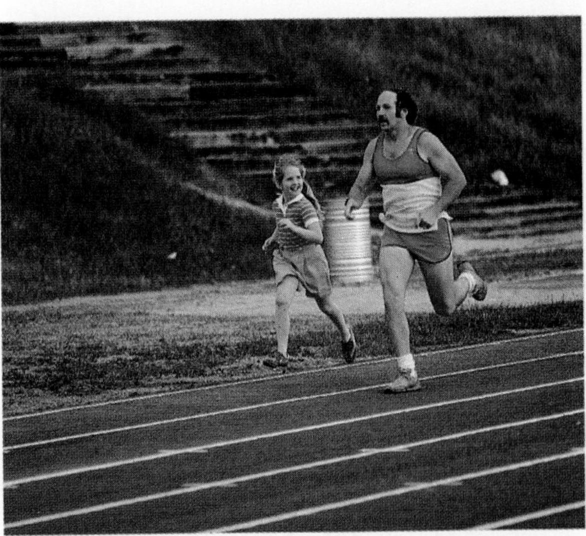

Most American parents encourage their children to participate in sports, often by being the child's first instructor. Parents direct their children toward or away from certain sports, depending on whether they consider the sport suitable for a girl or a boy, or too dangerous. Parents are also likely to teach their children different sport values, such as aggressiveness and fair play, on the basis of their gender.

Parents also influence their children's sport orientations on the basis of their gender. Boys are more likely to be taught traditional male sport orientations, such as aggressiveness, competitiveness, and toughness. Girls are more apt to learn the traditional female sport values of "fair play" and "everyone should participate." Fathers, however, are more influential than mothers in transmitting these sex-appropriate values to both boys and girls (McElroy, 1983).

Sports in Schools

In the United States, athletic contests between schools were first organized by college students about 100 years ago. The students felt that sport was a good way for relieving the pressure or boredom of their schoolwork. But in the early part of this century, school officials began to take over the organization of student sports. It was felt that the youth needed sports to improve their physical condition, as many of them had failed physical examinations. It was further believed that sports could help students become good citizens. Today sports have become extremely popular in schools from the lowest grade level to college. Especially in the last decade, students' participation in sports has experienced an explosive growth (Snyder and Spreitzer, 1983).

To high-school students, sport is considerably more important than scholarship as a source of prestige. The students admire the brilliant athletes far more than the studious nonathletes in their midst. There are also many more male students who wish to be remembered as athletic stars than there are those who would prefer to be remembered as brilliant students (Coleman, 1961; Thirer and Wright, 1985). How does scholarship, supposedly the central objective of education, come to take a back seat to athletics in high school? The answer, according to James Coleman (1961), lies in the fact that academic achievements can only make the student look smart and others dumb—while the athlete's efforts can bring glory to the entire school.

It is not only students who attribute so much importance to sport. School administrators feel the same way. But the nature of sport varies from one level of school to another. In elementary school, sport participation is meant to provide fun and to teach fair play. As students progress to higher levels, they as well as school officials increasingly emphasize the development of skill and the achievement of victory as the goal of sport. Once they reach the highest level, as students of a major university, the athletes stop playing sport for fun and turn it into serious hard work. The major reason is that college sports have become a big business. They are highly profitable in attracting alumni support, receipts at the gate, and television payments. Coaches are paid far more than distinguished professors, often more than $150,000 and sometimes as much as $500,000 a year. In 1986 the 105 most competitive football colleges alone raised and spent about a billion dollars. As in professional sports, reaching "the pot of gold" depends on winning. As Florida State University's athletic director said, "You show me a program that doesn't emphasize winning, and I'll show you a program that doesn't have any money" (Goodwin, 1986).

With so much at stake, the pressure to win is bound to be heavy. The result is the tendency to engage in unethical practices. Thus coaches are inclined to use shady methods to enlist and keep outstanding student athletes. They may recruit with such illegal offers as money, cars, and clothing, and have substitutes take admission tests for the athletes. They may alter their athletes' transcripts, help them get credits for courses they have not taken, pay them for nonexistent jobs, or offer jobs to their parents. Illegal drugs are sometimes used to improve the chances of winning. Some offensive linemen in football are instructed to use such illegal tactics as holding and tripping. Basketball players are coached to fake being fouled (Eitzen and Sage, 1982). The pressure to win weighs most heavily on the average scholarship football player at a major university. He is expected to put in 49 hours a week preparing for, participating in, and recovering from the games. Yet he is required to carry a full academic load while also being among the least scholastically prepared students on campus (Edwards, 1982).

The National Collegiate Athletic Association (NCAA) has recently tried to deal with those problems. It required a C average in high school and a combined score of at least 700 on the Scholastic Aptitude Test or 15 on the American College Test for a freshman to be eligible for varsity competition. The NCAA has also punished or sanctioned universities for violating its rules. In 1987 Virginia Tech's basketball team was barred from postseason play for a recruiting violation, and Southern Methodist University was suspended from fielding its football team for the 1987 season because 13 of its players had received cash payments from university alumni. A year earlier, Memphis State University was punished for illegal payments to players; Texas Christian University was sanctioned for more than 60 offenses; the University of Georgia was compelled by court order to pay a million dollars in damages to a teacher dismissed for protesting favoritism to athletes. However, a growing number of critics argue that similar scandals will continue unless far more drastic measures are taken. The chancellor of the University of California at Berkeley, Ira Michael Heyman (1987), observes that the root of the problem is "the extreme commercialization of college sports." He proposes that financial aid should be awarded on the basis of need rather than athletic ability, that freshmen should be ineligible for varsity competition so that they can first establish themselves as students, and that bowl games and postseason basketball tournaments should be abolished. He further suggests that minor leagues be set up for football and basketball so that aspiring athletes do not have to attend college if they plan to turn professional. In essence, Heyman wants colleges to engage in education, not the entertainment business. But such ideas, though reasonable, are too radical to be acceptable to many Division I schools.

Courting the Gods of Sport

Athletic contests were an integral part of the religious festivals in ancient Greece. The Olympic games, in particular, were periodically held to honor Zeus, the king of all the Greek gods. But the games, which had been started in 776 B.C., were abolished in A.D. 393, when Greece was conquered by a Roman emperor. Being a Christian, the emperor associated the games with paganism. Since then, for over 1500 years the Christians in Western societies condemned sporting activities as sinful for pleasing the flesh at the expense of the soul. It was not until 1896, the year when the Olympic games were revived, that many Christians changed their attitude toward sports. This turnaround was largely due to the impact of industrialization. The long hours of toiling under extremely harsh working conditions caused poor health to become a great urban problem. Social reformers, including many religious leaders, came to believe that sport activities could alleviate the health problem.

Nowadays sport has become so intertwined with religion that it is difficult to separate them. In fact, sport has become, in the eyes of many observers, an American religion. First of all, sports heroes are widely idolized. Second, the sports slogans that come down from the saintly or priestly coaches are in effect the religious commandments of the sports world. Athletes must learn by heart and put into practice such slogans as "Lose is a four-letter word" and "Good, better, best; never rest until your good is better and your better best." Third, many shrines are put up throughout the country to commemorate and glorify highly successful sports figures. These shrines are popularly known as the "sports halls of fame." Fourth, athletes are expected to practice their faith in sport as a religion. They are supposed to live a clean life, abstaining from smoking, alcohol, and, in the case of the fanatic ones, sex. On the other hand, sports fans are expected to show their devotion to their favorite teams. Thus they do a lot of loud chanting to support their teams and sometimes go on pilgrimages to faraway places to see their teams play (Eitzen and Sage, 1982).

Given those religious elements of sports, churches are inclined to use athletic activities to promote their religious cause. They may sponsor sport and recreation programs in order to attract and maintain membership. Church-supported universities and colleges may beef up their athletic teams in hopes of becoming famous and prestigious. Such fame and prestige often turn an academically mediocre school into a top-notch university.

Sport has become so intertwined with religion that it is hard to separate them. On the one hand, sport has become an American religion, as suggested by the well-documented devotion of athletes, fans, and churches to sports. On the other hand, athletes often rely on religion to enhance their chances of winning. Many major league baseball or football teams attend a Sunday church service before the game. Many college coaches and athletes also pray for a winning performance.

A good example is Notre Dame. As the chaplain of its athletic department says, "Of course, Catholic schools used athletes for prestige. Notre Dame would not be the great school it is today, the great academic institution, were it not for football" (Deford, 1976a). Some religious groups, such as Athletes In Action and the Fellowship of Christian Athletes, try to use sport to establish a Christian denomination, which the sportswriter Frank Deford (1976b) calls "Sportianity." This new brand of Christianity is engaged in converting famous athletes and then getting them to do missionary work among the fans—by endorsing Jesus in about the same way as they would a new sneaker. In their public team prayers, the Sportians loudly address Jesus as the Divine Goalie or the Head Coach in the Sky.

The Christian athletes also use God to enhance their chances of winning. Although they normally would not pray flat out for victory, they ask God to help them practice the "try ethic" to the fullest. They will try their hardest to win, because they believe in maximum performance as part of the Christian tenets. Many major-league baseball and football teams hold a Sunday chapel service before the game. Many college coaches and athletes also pray for winning performance or personal excellence. Some athletes, as we have suggested, resort to magic to increase their chances of winning. In fact, the more unpredictable the outcome of an athletic contest, the more likely the players will court the gods of sport. In professional baseball, for example, hitters and pitchers are more likely than fielders to engage in magic because the chances of success in hitting and pitching are far smaller than in fielding (Gmelch, 1972).

The Politics of Sport

Sport is fair game for political intrusion and manipulation. Politicians regularly use sport to enhance their political fortunes. The recent U.S. presidents as well as presidential candidates have always identified themselves as great sports fans. They watch football and other games; talk with athletic superstars and their coaches; play golf, ski, or jog; and recruit sports heroes to drum up public support for their political office or candidacy. Not only politicians exploit sport, though. Famous athletes themselves use their fame as sports heroes to get elected to political office. The former basketball star Bill Bradley is now a U.S. senator and the former football star Jack Kemp is a prominent U.S. congressman.

Sport also plays an important role in international politics. First of all, sport competition among nations is used as a vehicle of propaganda. Individual participants in an international athletic contest are always made to feel that they represent their own countries rather than themselves only. At the Olympic games, contestants are separated into national groups so that athletes from the same country stay in the same dorm, march together with their flag waving, have the name of their country emblazoned on their clothing, and stand at attention to the playing of their national anthem when receiving medals. All this is bound to stir up nationalistic fervor among not only the athletes but also their fellow citizens. The rulers of many countries also regard their athletes' outstanding performances as demonstrable proof of the adequacy, if not superiority, of their political systems.

This may explain why the governments of the Soviet Union and East Germany have gone all out to train their athletes, making their sport activities a paid full-time occupation, providing them with the best coaches that can be found, and supporting them with excellent medical sports programs. After being turned into professional athletes so that they can compete successfully with amateurs at the Olympic games, the Soviets and East Germans are sometimes even given drugs to maximize their athletic prowess. East German women swimmers, for example, often take anabolic steroids (male hormones) to toughen their bodies. One major side effect is that the women not only tend to become as muscular and powerful as men but also tend to develop a deep voice pitch. But this does not seem to bother the East German sports authorities. As their coach once told reporters at the 1976 Montreal Olympics, "We have come here to swim, not to sing." Apparently the Soviet and East German governments intend to have their athletes show the whole world the triumph of their socialist workers' paradise over the decadent, capitalist nations of the West. The U.S. government, too, wants to use the Olympic games to enhance its prestige as a prosperous capitalistic society. As General MacArthur (1965) said, "Nothing is more synonymous with our national success than is our national success in athletics."

International sport is further used as a tool of diplomatic recognition or nonrecognition. When a country chooses to have its athletes compete with those of another state, that contact is usually seen as tacit recognition of the state and its government. Conversely, refusal to compete with a given country is seen as diplomatic nonrecognition. Communist East Germany has been most successful in using sport to gain recognition. In 1969 only 13 states—mostly in the communist world—had diplomatic relations with East Germany. But five years later, through its "diplomats in track suits," East Germany ended up establishing relations with the rest of the international community. A similar case was the "ping-pong diplomacy," where a series of table tennis matches between American and Chinese players in the early 1970s broke the decades-long silence between the governments of the United States and China. It was this contact that eventually led to the establishment of full diplomatic relations between the two countries. On the other hand, Israeli athletes were barred from the 1974 Asian games, because many of the participating countries refused to recognize Israel. The Asian Games Federation expelled Taiwan in 1974 and Canada refused to admit the Taiwanese athletes to the Montreal Olympics in 1976, because Taiwan's claim to represent China was rejected (Strenk, 1978).

International sport is also used as a means of political struggle. In the 1960s and 1970s black African states successfully used international sports to protest against the racist policies in white-dominated South Africa. They did so by threatening to boycott the Olympic and non-Olympic games if South Africa were not ousted. At the 1968 Mexico City Olympics, the victorious American runners Tommie Smith and John Carlos protested against racism in the United States by raising their gloved fists during the playing of the American national anthem. In 1969 a soccer game between Honduras and El Salvador ended with fans of the home team assaulting and killing the players of the visiting team, which soon culminated in a real war between the two countries. In 1972 Palestinian guerillas called "Black September" carried their war against Israel to the Munich Olympics, where they killed 11 Israeli athletes. In 1976 28 African nations boycotted the Montreal Olympics when New Zealand, which had sent a rugby team to South Africa, was allowed to participate in the Games. In 1980 the United States led a 55-nation boycott of the Moscow Olympics in response to the Soviet Union's invasion of Afghanistan, and four years later the Soviets retaliated by heading up a 15-nation boycott of the Los Angeles Olympics. Throughout 1986 and 1987 it was feared that North Korea, if not allowed to cohost the 1988 Olympics with South Korea, might lead a boycott or even try to disrupt the games with terrorist acts similar to its 1983 bombing in Rangoon, Burma, which killed six high South Korean officials (Strenk, 1978; Edwards, 1984b; Christie, 1984; Holmes, 1987). Indeed, toward the end of 1987, after North Korea's demand to cohost the Olympics was denied, it sent two agents to blow up a South Korean jetliner, killing all 115 people on board. North Korea also pulled out of the Games, followed by another communist country, Cuba.

In spite of the political influence on athletic contests, many sports authorities such as the International Olympic Committee still insist that athletics has nothing to do with politics. Sport is seen as promoting friendship, peace, and understanding only. The insistence on sport as nonpolitical in effect reflects the conservative mood of the sports world. After all, being apolitical—refusing to acknowledge the political nature of sport, much less take a political stand in sport—is actually being political, subscribing to the conservative idea that the status quo should not be disturbed, least of all by sport. In the United States, coaches are generally more conservative than most people in other occupations. A survey by the Carnegie Commission on Higher Education shows that physical education teachers—many of them coaches or ex-coaches—rank second in conservatism among the faculties in 30 academic fields (Snyder and Spreitzer, 1983).

Sport as Big Business

Sports is big business. In the United States alone, over $100 billion is invested in sport and related enterprises. The big business of sport significantly affects not only professional athletes but amateur ones as well. To most Americans—including a majority of coaches—sports have become more entertainment than athletics, so that they have lost the spirit of the game (Miller Lite Report, 1983).

Owners of professional teams like to tell the public that they often lose a lot of money from their investment in sports. They argue, however, that they do not mind the losses because they are not in the sports business for profit anyway—only for the joy of the games. As Ted Turner, an owner, once said, "Professional sport is not my primary source of income, thank God. Most owners have made lots of money in other businesses. For me, owning two professional teams is nothing more than a hobby. Otherwise, I couldn't justify the losses or the agony and grief that go along with owning them" (*Nation's Business,* 1979b).

Nevertheless, evidence suggests that the sports business is highly profitable. First of all, much money can be

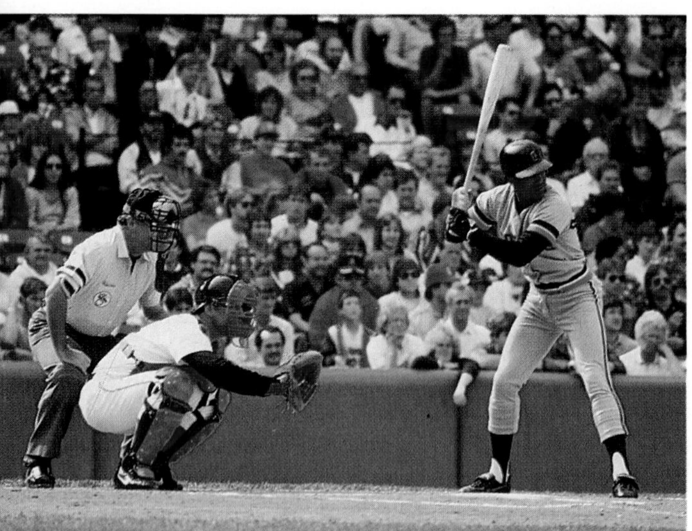

Sport is big business, primarily because it has become more entertainment than athletics. Much money can be made from ticket sales and such related enterprises as sales of food and beverages at the games, operations of parking lots, and sales of programs and souvenirs. The largest profits come from sales of radio and television rights for broadcasting the games. Huge chunks of all that money go to the team owners and their athletes.

made from ticket sales and such ancillary enterprises as sales of food and beverages at the games, operation of parking lots, and sales of programs and souvenirs. The biggest profits come from the sale of radio and television rights for broadcasting the games. These rights are extremely expensive, but broadcasting networks are glad to purchase them because TV ads can be sold to sponsors at even higher prices. The air time for a mere one-minute TV commercial may cost hundreds of thousands of dollars (Loy, McPherson, and Kenyon, 1978). In addition, team owners receive many tax benefits from Uncle Sam and do not pay much for renting stadiums from city halls—which consider sports franchises good for the morale and economy of their communities. The sports industry also enjoys the enviable position of being the only self-regulated monopoly in the United States. Team owners are allowed to decide among themselves whether to admit or deny new teams and how to divide media markets and negotiate media rights (Flint and Eitzen, 1987). Big earnings are, therefore, common in the world of professional sports. In the late 1970s the annual profit was already sky-high—about $200,000 for the average owner of a basketball team, $500,000 for the owner of a baseball team, and $2 million for a football-team owner (Loy, McPherson, and Kenyon, 1978). It is little wonder that, while owners keep on complaining that professional sport is a losing business, new stadiums continue to be built and more entrepreneurs are trying to purchase sports franchises (Alm, 1984).

Professional athletes earn a lot of money, too. Before 1976, when the **reserve system** gave a team monopoly rights to a player for life, athletes received relatively low salaries. Since 1976, the **free-agent system** has enabled many athletes to seek the best deal from among competing teams. The upshot is that their salaries have been skyrocketing (see Figure 20.1), although team owners have in recent years tried to keep their costs down by refusing to bid for players. Moreover, some earn large incomes off the playing field by endorsing products for various sports-related companies. The superstars make even more money from outside sources than from playing the sport. Yet they still demand bigger salaries, sometimes resorting to strikes to get them.

Since most of the profits in professional sports come from television contracts, sports executives and players have virtually sold their souls to the demands of television. They have let TV producers determine the schedules, time-outs, and the like. Such a surrender to television has prompted Bill Russell, former player and coach for the Boston Celtics, to say: "If you don't watch those TV people, they will devour you. First they ask you to call time-outs so that they can get in their commercials. Then they tell you when to call them. Then they want to get into the locker room at half-time. Then more and more and more" (Shecter, 1969). But most sports executives, including those in intercollegiate athletics, do not mind doing television's bidding. As the late Alabama coach Bear Bryant once growled, "We think TV exposure is so important to our program and so important to this university that we will schedule ourselves to fit the medium. I'll play at midnight if that's what TV wants" (Michener, 1976).

The commercialization of sport has also spilled into intercollegiate and international athletic contests. Various colleges and universities spend millions on athletic programs and earn millions from gate receipts and television contracts. Cash payments are often made to college scholarship athletes. The result is the blurring of the

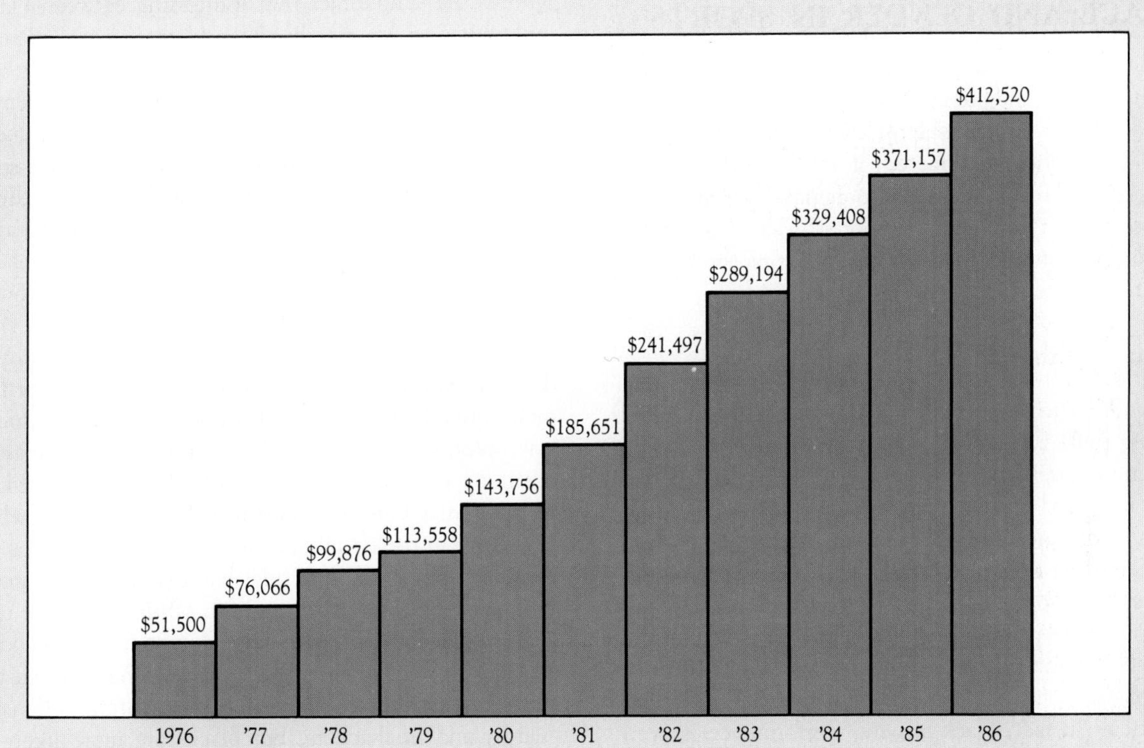

Figure 20.1 Skyrocketing Salaries in Baseball

The free-agent system has enabled professional athletes to seek the best deal possible. As a result, their salaries have been rising sharply every year. Here is how the average salary of major-league baseball players has been going up.

Source: Major League Baseball Players Association, 1987.

traditional distinction between **amateur sport,** which is supposed to be played for fun, and **professional sport,** which is played for money. But there still remain significant differences between collegiate and professional sports. The college athletic budgets are smaller than those of professional sports. Student athletes' pay is far lower than that of professionals. College players are not as free as professionals to devote full time to perfecting their athletic performance. However, the supposedly amateur participants in international sports, such as the Olympic games, are more like professionals. The American athletes are often given scholarship or expense money while in training for the Olympics. They usually train several hours a day. Their counterparts in Russia and other communist countries have gone even further: they have practically become professionals by receiving full financial support from their governments and training full time for the Olympics.

QUESTIONS FOR DISCUSSION AND REVIEW

1. What do parents teach their male and female children about sports?
2. Why is sport often more important than scholarship for many school administrators and students, and what problems does this imbalance create?
3. In what ways have sports become intertwined with religion?
4. How do the Olympics serve as an example of how politicians and political movements use sport to further their causes?
5. What impact has the commercialization of sports had on amateur sports and sports careers?

RACE AND GENDER IN SPORTS

A growing number of women are participating in sports long held as a male preserve. It is, therefore, important to find out how female athletes are viewed by their society and how they are affected, if at all, by their sports involvement. Black athletes also demand our attention because of their dominance in sports. What accounts for this black dominance? Does it mean that racism has disappeared in the sport arenas?

Black Athletes

In 1960 the proportion of blacks in the sports world was less than 10 percent—the proportion of blacks in the general population. Since then, the black involvement in sports has increased dramatically. In 1983, blacks constituted only 12 percent of the population, but they made up 74 percent of professional basketball players, more than 55 percent of professional football players, and 19 percent of major-league baseball players. High-school and college athletes are also disproportionately black. The black dominance in sports is more than numerical. In fact, black athletes' performance is even more impressive. Of the collegiate football players who won the last 11 Heisman trophy awards, 10 are black. Similarly, in 1982, all the athletes named to the first team of a major Division I all-American basketball roster were black. Blacks also constituted 88 percent of the athletes selected for the 1982 National Basketball Association (NBA) All-Star game. Since 1958, blacks have won the NBA's Most Valuable Player title 20 times as opposed to only three times for whites (Edwards, 1984a).

Two explanations have been given for the dominance of blacks in sports. One is the idea, popular with the general public, that blacks are born to be greater athletes than whites. There have been attempts to support this theory by arguing that if not for their innate physical superiority, the blacks in our society would not have survived to this day. "I have a theory about why so many sports stars are black," contended a professional football player. "I think it boils down to the survival of the fittest. Think of what African slaves were forced to endure in this country merely to survive. Well, black athletes are their descendants. They are the offspring of those who were physically tough enough to survive" (Kane, 1971). Black sociologist Harry Edwards (1973) has criticized the biological argument as naive because it ignores the simple fact that inbreeding between blacks and whites in America has been so extensive that many black Americans today are not 100 percent black.

Another explanation for the black athletic dominance is the sociological theory that most blacks, due to their experience of job discrimination, believe in sport as one of the few ladders of social mobility open to them. This has led black society to emphasize the importance of physical skills, thereby motivating many young blacks to spend long hours developing their athletic prowess (Edwards, 1973; 1984a; Rudman, 1986).

The remarkable success of black athletes, however, does not mean that the sports world has rid itself of racial prejudice. Racism still exists, though in a subtle way. We can detect it in the racial patterns of playing positions in major ballgames—whites being more likely to be in the central, more important positions while blacks are in the peripheral, less important positions. In baseball, whites typically play such central positions as infielders, catchers, and pitchers, while blacks are usually relegated to the peripheral positions of outfielders (see Figure 20.2). In football, whites tend to be in the central positions of quarterbacks, centers, offensive guards, and linebackers, but blacks are more likely to play the peripheral positions as offensive tackles, running backs, and defensive backs. The central positions are considered more important because they represent a higher degree of leadership or ability for affecting the outcome of the game (Loy and McElvogue, 1970; Phillips, 1983).

Another sign of racism is the fact that black athletes must outperform their white peers in order to play in the major leagues. As a former Chicago Cubs star Billy Williams, who is black, says, "We had to be twice as good as the white guys just to sit on the bench." After examining the rosters of all major-league baseball teams, sociologists John Phillips and Lenny Mendonca conclude that most of the black players today are standouts and outshine their white teammates. In 1986, for example, twice as many black baseball players as whites had career averages greater than .281; by contrast, three times as many whites as blacks had averages below .241 (Meer, 1984b; Rosellini, 1987). Moreover, blacks rarely assume such important roles as owners, managers, and coaches of professional teams. But sports have also removed racial barriers: blacks and whites now have more opportunities to interact on the playing fields, in the grandstands, and through a common interest in the games (Miller Lite Report, 1983).

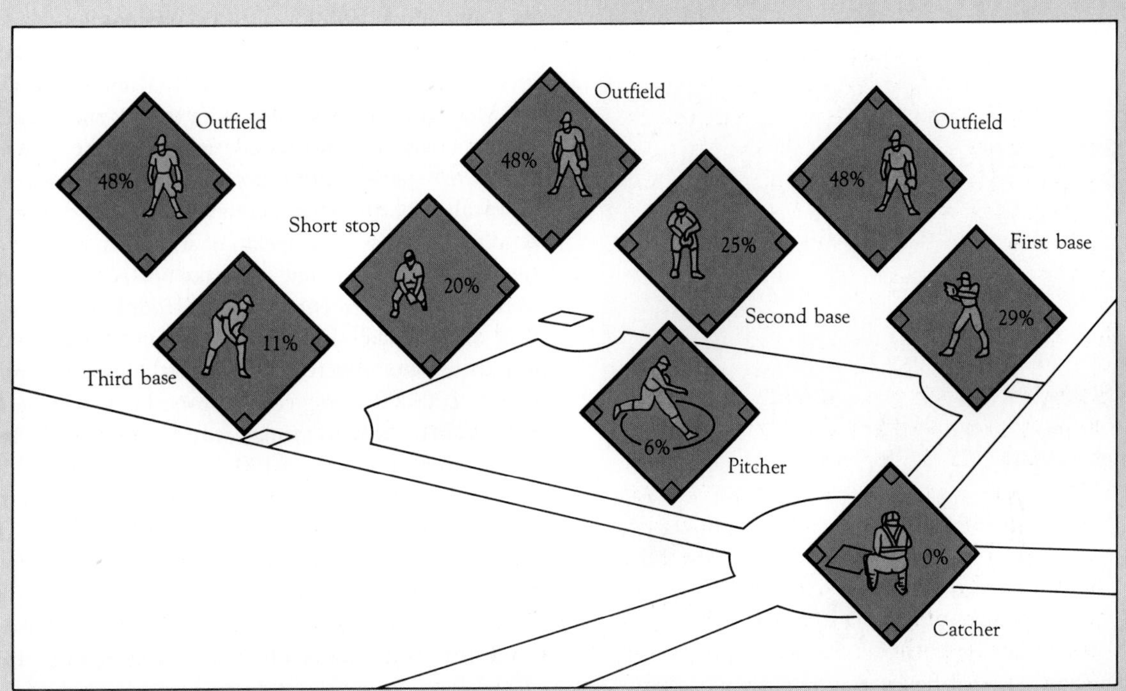

Figure 20.2 Blacks in Baseball

Racism shows through the racial pattern of playing positions in major-league ballgames. While whites are more likely to be in the central, more important positions, blacks tend to be in the peripheral, less important positions. In baseball, whites usually play such key positions as pitcher, catcher, and infielder, but blacks are often relegated to the outfield. Here are the percentages of major-league baseball players who are black.

Source: Center for the Study of Sport in Society, Northeastern University, reprinted in *U.S. News & World Report,* July 27, 1987, p. 53. Copyright, July 27, 1987, *U.S. News & World Report.*

Female Athletes

The recent increase in female sports participation is extraordinary. Since the early 1970s female involvement in collegiate sports has jumped by over 100 percent, and female participation in high-school athletic programs has zoomed more than 600 percent. Although similar statistics for professional sports are not available, it is clear from reading the sports pages and watching sports on television that there are now many more women in sports than before. The trend is apparently a spin-off from the women's liberation movement and the 1972 law (Title IX of the Educational Amendment Act) that prohibits sex discrimination in school sports (Flygare, 1979; Snyder and Spreitzer, 1983). Nevertheless, Title IX has not been fully enforced because unequal expenditures for male and female athletics are still legally acceptable. This means, among other things, that more funds may continue to be spent on men's sports, such as football and basketball, than on women's athletic programs.

In fact, society still differentiates between male and female sports. Generally, the so-called male sports involve bodily contact during competition, the handling of a heavy object, the propelling of the body through space over long distances, and the employment of physical force to overpower an opponent. Examples are football, basketball, baseball, wrestling, boxing, weightlifting, and long-distance running. Women are expected to stay away from these supposedly men's sports. If they do

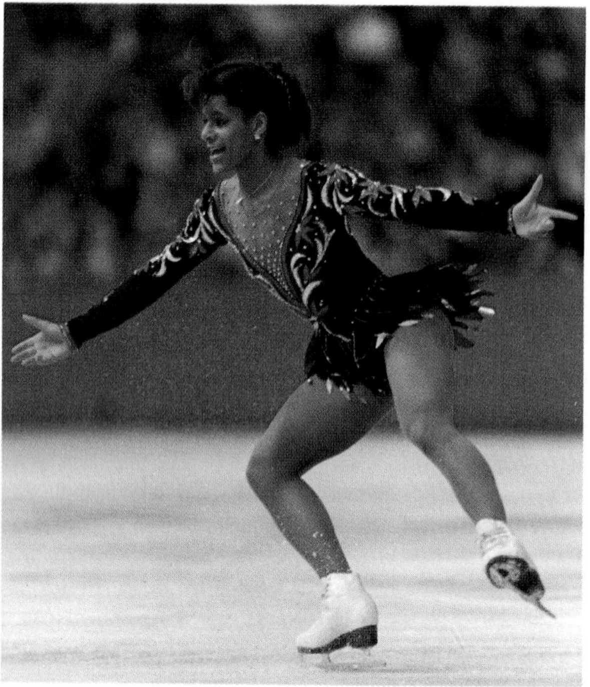

Debi Thomas, national figure-skating champion. Society differentiates between male and female sports. Women are usually encouraged to avoid violent sports. Instead, they are directed to sports that are believed to enhance their femininity by emphasizing grace and beauty in the body's movement, such as figure skating, swimming, gymnastics, and tennis.

not, they are popularly believed to be losing their feminine qualities. To maintain or enhance their femininity, women are expected to stick to the so-called women's sports, such as aerobic dancing, swimming, diving, gymnastics, racquetball, and tennis, all of which emphasize grace and beauty in the body's movement (Snyder and Spreitzer, 1983).

These sexist attitudes seem to have affected women who participate in "masculine" sports. They tend to feel that they are less feminine than other women. According to one study, 70 percent of female gymnasts perceived themselves as being "very feminine," but only 44 percent of women basketball players saw themselves in the same way (Snyder and Spreitzer, 1983). Many female athletes seem so afraid of losing their femininity in "male" sports that they try to protect it by "wearing hair ribbons, pastel-colored outfits, or 'feminine' hairstyles." As Vicki Foltz, a long-distance runner, says, "I suppose it's because so many people have said women athletes look masculine. So a lot of us try, subconsciously maybe, to look as feminine as possible in a race. There's always lots of hair ribbons in the races" (Rohrbaugh, 1979).

Most girls under 15 also seem to lack the confidence to participate in traditionally male contact sports. Research has suggested that if young girls are asked to take physical tests that they perceive to be masculine, they tend to have less expectation of success than their abilities merit. Thus very few girls take up "boy" sports. Girls join less than 1 percent of the Amateur Hockey Association of America's 11,104 teams. Pop Warner Football found that there were only 24 girls among its approximately 200,000 young competitors. Little League Baseball has been able to attract only 1 girl for every two or three hardball leagues of 100 or more boys. Instead, the girls overwhelmingly choose to play on all-female Little League softball teams (Monagan, 1983).

Sports in general, however, do benefit women athletes. According to one study, they are far more likely than nonathletes to experience a heightened sense of confidence and well-being. They are more likely to find themselves "generally feeling in good spirits," "being very satisfied with life," and "finding much happiness in life" (Snyder and Spreitzer, 1983). Sexual liberation may have brought these women into the sports world, but as athletes they are more conservative than nonathletes. They are more likely to agree that "the responsibility of a wife is to keep her husband and children happy" and "a woman's personal ambition should be subordinated to her family" (Snyder and Spreitzer, 1983). Apparently, the conservative nature of sports has affected them as much as it has male athletes. As we have suggested, coaches are mostly conservative, and they compel their athletes to obey authority. Athletes themselves have long been socialized to accept the decisions of umpires. They rarely behave like the tennis star John McEnroe, who is notorious for arguing with referees. Those in team sports are further indoctrinated to subordinate themselves to teams. They are taught, for example, that "a player doesn't make the team, the team makes the player" (Eitzen and Sage, 1982).

QUESTIONS FOR DISCUSSION AND REVIEW

1. What factors help explain the wide participation of blacks in sports since the 1960s?
2. How has sport enhanced the confidence and well-being of women?
3. To what extent do sexism and racism still influence sports careers and the world of sport?

CHAPTER REVIEW

1. *How are sports related to society?* Some sports are more popular in some societies than in others. Games of physical skill are popular in tropical countries. Games of chance are often played in harsh environments. Games of strategy are a great favorite in more complex cultures. Games with a combination of physical skill, chance, and strategy have a large following in highly industrialized countries.

2. *What do Americans think of sports?* They enjoy watching and participating in sports. They also believe that sports can build character, develop self-discipline, prepare one for life's challenges, and produce physical fitness and mental alertness.

3. *What are the sociological perspectives on sport?* Functionalists view sport as performing positive functions for society, but conflict theorists stress the harmful effects of sport. *Does sport hurt academic performance?* Not necessarily. In fact, high-school athletes are better students than nonathletes. But college athletes tend to be poor students, compared with the general student population. *Do most talented athletes strike it rich after they graduate?* No. Only about 1 percent of college student athletes will turn professional. *Does sports violence release our tension safely and make us less violent?* No. It tends to produce fan violence.

4. *How is sport related to various social institutions?* Parents have a hand in their children's sport participation, by encouraging it or by setting an example. Schools place a high premium on sport but tend to turn it into serious work rather than pure fun. Religion often uses sport to help spread the gospel, and athletes rely on religion to improve their chances of winning. Politics plays an important role in athletic contests, which, however, is denied by many sports authorities. Sport is big business, easily succumbing to the dictates of commercial sponsors of television sports.

5. *Do blacks dominate the sport scene in the United States?* Yes. There are more blacks than whites in sports. Their athletic performance also surpasses that of whites. The general public often attributes blacks' dominance in sports to their natural inheritance of athletic skills. But sociologists explain it as a consequence of oppressed black society's emphasis on athletic skills as a key avenue to fame and riches. The remarkable success of black athletes, however, has not totally banished racism from the playing field.

6. *Are women becoming increasingly involved in sports?* Yes, but society still expects men to engage in "male" sports and women in "female" sports. Consequently, women tend to feel unfeminine if they participate in so-called men's sports. Young girls also avoid "boy" sports. Generally, women athletes do feel better and happier than nonathletes, but they are also more conservative.

KEY TERMS

Amateur sports Sport that is played for fun (p. 515).

Free-agent system The practice of permitting professional athletes to leave one team and choose a better deal from another (p. 514).

Ideology of sport A set of popular beliefs that emphasizes the positive functions of sport (p. 502).

Professional sport Sport that is played for money (p. 515).

Reserve system The practice of forcing professional athletes to play for their team for as long as the owner wants them to (p. 514).

SUGGESTED READINGS

Guttmann, Allen. 1986. *Sports Spectators.* New York: Columbia University Press. An interesting sociological and historical analysis of sports spectators' behavior, especially violence.

Hoberman, John M. 1984. *Sport and Political Ideology.* Austin: University of Texas Press. Analyzing the political interpretations of sport by Western scholars and, more interestingly, the official attitudes toward sport in Nazi Germany, the Soviet Union, East Germany, and China.

Lever, Janet. 1983. *Soccer Madness.* Chicago: University of Chicago Press. A well-written analysis of the popularity of soccer in Brazil, showing how it helps integrate people, groups, towns, cities, and regions into a single nation.

Nixon, Howard L, II. 1984. *Sport and the American Dream.* New York: Leisure Press. Showing clearly how the American Dream of rising from rags to riches influences our athletic activities in schools and colleges as well as professional and Olympic sports—and how rarely the Dream turns into reality.

Smith, Michael D. 1983. *Violence and Sport.* Toronto: Butterworths. Highly informative, this first English text on sports violence discusses, among other things, the impact of violence in professional sports on young athletes, the role of media coverage in sports violence, and violence among the fans.

PART FIVE

Moving into the Future

Our world has always been in a state of change. But the pace of change is much faster today, especially in industrial societies such as ours. We are so caught up in the many changes in our society that we rarely stand back to reflect on the forces that are moving us into the future. This is what we do in this last part of the book.

As our population increases, we are more likely to diminish our natural resources and pollute our environment. Environmental pollution further threatens our health, making us susceptible to various diseases including cancer. We therefore examine population growth and ecological problems in Chapter 21. Population growth often occurs in the form of urbanization, the movement of people from the countryside to the city. The city, in turn, affects how people live. Thus we discuss urbanization and city life in Chapter 22. Then, in Chapter 23, we switch to collective behavior and social change. Collective behavior occurs outside the bounds of social norms and often directly changes society. We will examine various forms of collective behavior, such as panics and social movements. Then we will analyze the major theories about how and why social change occurs.

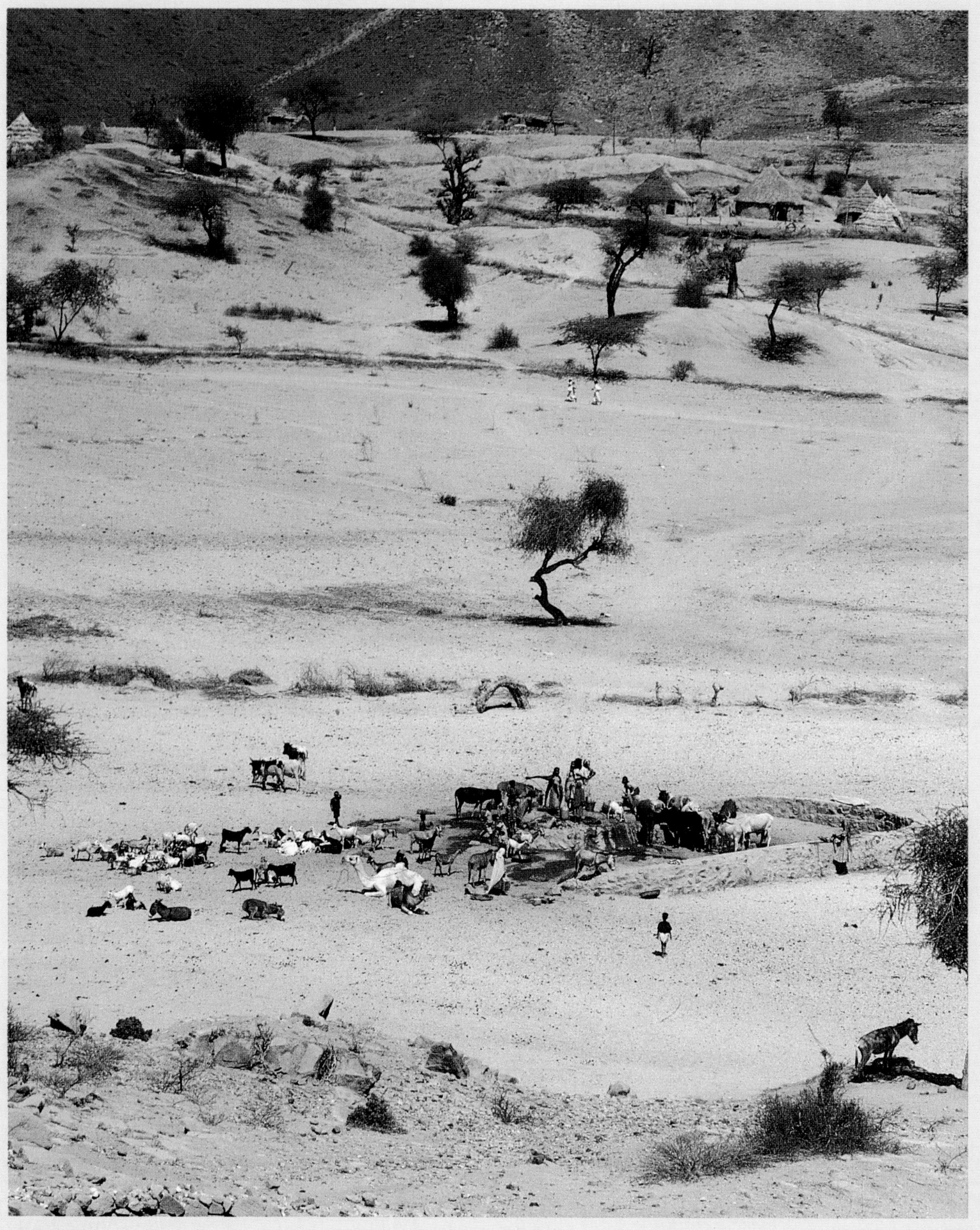

21 Population and Ecology

Population and ecology are closely related to each other. The growth of population puts pressures on the environment, depleting its resources and threatening human life. This problem is particularly serious for many poor, developing countries. For example, their great population growth has substantially increased the use of firewood for fuel. This in turn has caused deforestation and soil erosion. Unrestrained population growth has also led to overcultivation of farmland, which causes the soil to lose its fertility and to dry up and blow away in the wind. Moreover, overgrazing has already caused the deserts of Africa to expand. The effects on population are devastating, as the continuing famine in Africa illustrates.

By the time you finish reading this sentence, there will be about 20 more people in this world than when you began. Twenty more people will have been born than will have died. Every day, at least 200,000 babies are born around the world. Meanwhile, an increasing number of people live longer than their parents. The result is a population explosion. If present trends continue, the world's population will double, to about 8.3 billion, in just 40 years. Nearly all of the population increase is occurring in the poor, developing nations of Asia, Africa, and Latin America (McNamara, 1984).

How will all these people live? Even with today's population, there are more people than there are jobs, and there is too little food for so many. Almost two-thirds of the world's people go to bed hungry every night. Moreover, both poor and rich nations, capitalist and communist nations, are disrupting the natural systems essential for life. In the United States alone about 800 species of plants and animals have become extinct during the last two centuries. In such countries as Tanzania and India, dependence on firewood for fuel has caused substantial deforestation. This has damaged flood control, sped up erosion, and increased the hardship of simply staying alive (Russell, 1984). Unless there are massive changes in societies around the world, population growth will help not only to diminish natural resources but also to pollute the environment, with serious consequences for our health. Thus, in this chapter, we examine how and why populations change, what difficulties result, and how governments have responded to these problems. We also look at the nature of ecology, environmental pollution, causes of environmental problems, and how governments deal with these problems.

POPULATION CHANGE

The scientific study of population is called **demography.** More than any other area of sociology, demography is based on a large body of reasonably accurate data. Most of these data come from censuses and vital statistics.

A **census** is a periodic head count of the entire population of a country. It includes a wealth of information, such as age, sex, education, occupation, and residence. Most early censuses were incomplete and unreliable, but the quality of modern census data is far better. The latest U.S. census, for example, missed only about 2 percent of the population. Among the people not counted are mostly the homeless, hoboes, criminals, illegal immigrants, and minorities in tough ghetto neighborhoods, who are difficult for census takers to track down.

The other source of population data, **vital statistics,** consists of information about births, marriages, deaths, and migrations into and out of a country. The U.S. government did not require the states to record these data until 1933.

From all this information, demographers can tell us a great deal about what the characteristics of a population are and how the population changes. These variables are greatly influenced by social factors, and they vary from one society to another.

Demographic Processes

The world's population is increasing about 1.73 percent a year. This means that there are about 17 new members a year for every 1000 people in the world. This growth rate may appear small, but it represents an enormous addition of people—some 87 million, nearly a third of the U.S. population, being added in 1987 alone. Moreover, given the same growth rate every year, population does not increase linearly, with the *same* number of people added annually. Instead, it grows exponentially, with an *increasingly larger* number of new people appearing in each succeeding year. (It works like your savings account, which earns an increasingly larger rather than the same interest in each succeeding year.) Thus the world's current growth rate of 1.73 percent a year means that there will be about 86 million more next year, 88 million more the following year, 90 million more the year after that, and so on. This is why, given the same annual growth rate of 1.73 percent, global population will double in only about 40 years—instead of 60 years if it grew linearly.

Increases in population are therefore far more dramatic in modern times of big populations than in ancient times of small populations. Before the year 1600 it took more than 500,000 years for the human population to reach about 500 million. Thereafter, the population skyrocketed to 5.06 *billion* in less than 400 years. Today it takes only 5 or 6 years, as opposed to the 500,000 years before 1600, for the world to produce 500 million people. (See Figure 21.1 for the remarkable population growth in the modern era.)

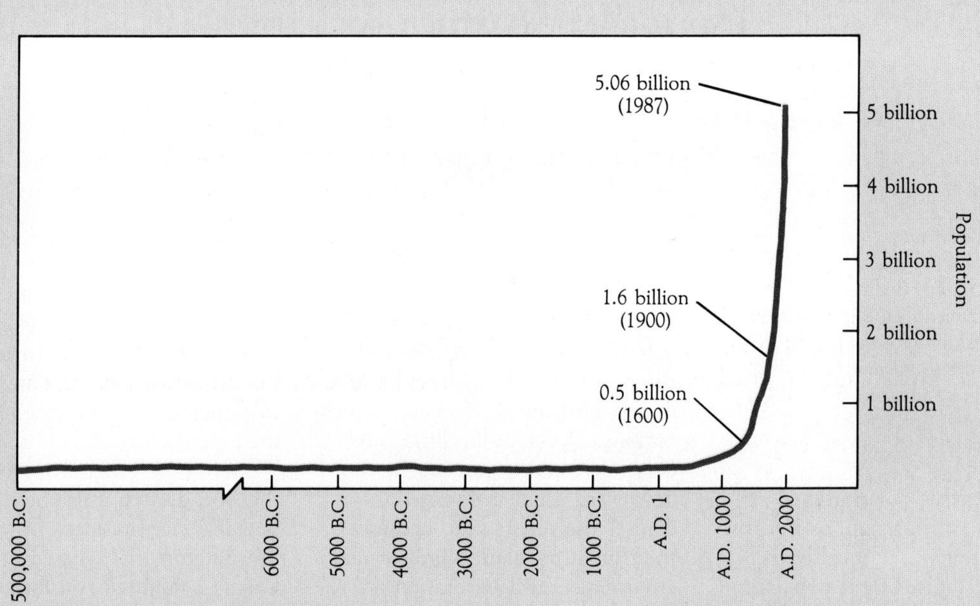

Figure 21.1 How World's Population Grows

In recent history the world's population has experienced a tremendous, exponential growth. Before the modern era began in 1600, it had taken more than 500,000 years for global population to reach only about half a billion. But since then it has taken less than 400 years for the population to skyrocket to more than 5.06 billion today.

Source: Population Reference Bureau, "How Many People Have Ever Lived on Earth?" *Population Bulletin,* Feb. 1962, p. 5; Census Bureau, *Statistical Abstract of the United States,* 1988, p. 794.

In general, populations are growing much faster in poor, developing countries than in rich, developed ones. Between 1982 and 1987, for example, the United States and Canada each had a growth rate of only 1.0 percent, compared to Venezuela's 2.8 percent, Nicaragua's 3.4 percent, and Kenya's 4.0 percent. The rich nations generally have an annual growth rate of 1 percent or less. In contrast, the poor nations typically grow at a rate far above 2 percent (see box, p. 526).

The growth of a nation's population is determined by the number of births minus the number of deaths plus the net immigration rate—the excess of people moving into a country (immigrants) over those leaving it (emigrants). Thus the growth rate of a nation's population equals the birth rate plus the net immigration rate minus the death rate (see Figure 21.2). Because births, deaths, and migrations are population changes that take place continually, demographers call them **demographic processes.**

Birth rates The **birth rate** is the number of babies born every year for every thousand members of a given population:

$$\frac{\text{Births}}{\text{Total population}} \times 1000$$

For many years the birth rates of most industrialized nations have been far lower than 20 per 1000 population, while those of most agricultural countries have far exceeded 30 per 1000.

Indeed, people in poor countries do tend to have larger families—an average of four or more children—than people in rich countries, who have an average of about two children per family. Because of high birth rates in past years, the poor countries also have a very large number of women entering their childbearing years. As a result, even if these women average fewer children than their mothers did, their nations' birth

UNDERSTANDING OTHER SOCIETIES

Population Growth Sharply Divides the World

Birth and death rates shape the demography of a country, which, in turn, influences its economy and ecology. This reading documents an important trend in world population growth, that of the division of the world into high- and low-growth-rate nations. What might result from this great division?

A demographic polarization is dividing the world's nations into two distinct groups: the roughly half who have limited their population growth rates to about 0.8 percent annually, and the other half whose average population growth is triple that, according to a new report by the Washington, D.C.-based Worldwatch Institute. Nations in the second group tend to be experiencing grave economic and ecological trouble. And they will likely continue to do so, the report says, until they put a brake on their population growth.

The problem, explains Worldwatch President Lester R. Brown, one of the study's authors, is that the high-growth group—now doubling its population every 20 to 28 years—is beginning to outstrip its environment's capacity to provide food, energy and jobs. Ironically, this is partly a result of modernized health care, which has dramatically cut the death rate from disease. Unlike the low-population-growth group (especially industrial nations), high-growth nations have not compensated for their declining death rates by reducing birth rates. Now many such nations, especially in Africa and Central America, are caught "in a downward spiral in living standards," the report says, because their rapid population growth and environmental deterioration are feeding on one another.

In recent years, several developing countries—most notably China but also Cuba and Thailand—have moved from the high-growth group to the low-growth group. Though each solution was different, all relied on making birth control technologies widely available. They also tended to include social and political incentives, like tax advantages for one- or two-child families, the report notes. While such strategies can be economically costly, Brown says, these nations recognized that the alternative would be even more costly—declining living standards for the entire society as a fixed or dwindling resource base was shared by an ever larger number of people.

Each of these recent population growth declines was achieved while local economic conditions were improving—a situation in sharp contrast to that facing most high-growth countries today. What the high-growth nations must learn, the report says, is how to slow population increases in the face of declining conditions.

While he generally agrees with the Worldwatch assessment, Joseph Speidel, vice-president of the Washington, D.C.-based Population Crisis Committee and former deputy director of the U.S. Agency for International Development's population program, believes there is also reason for optimism. Dramatically declining economic and environmental conditions in many of the high-growth societies provide a potent motivator both for changing attitudes and policies about birth control, he says. However, he adds, without increased international aid for family planning, even a highly motivated country will have a hard time reducing its population growth.

Source: Excerpted from "Birth rates sharply divide the world," *Science News*, January 10, 1987, p. 25. Reprinted with permission from *Science News*, the weekly newsmagazine of science, copyright 1987 by Science Service, Inc.

rates will remain high. Meanwhile, developed countries are close to zero population growth, a situation in which the population stops growing. Consequently, well over 90 percent of the world's population increase in coming decades will occur in the poorest nations. By the year 2000 the United States will probably account for only about 4 percent of the total population (Census Bureau, 1988).

Death Rates The **death rate** is the number of deaths in a year for every 1000 members of a population. The rich nations have an average of 10 deaths per 1000 population and the poor nations have 13. The difference is surprisingly small. In fact, death rates obscure the large gap between rich and poor nations in health and living conditions. Because the percentage of young people is much higher in developing countries than in developed

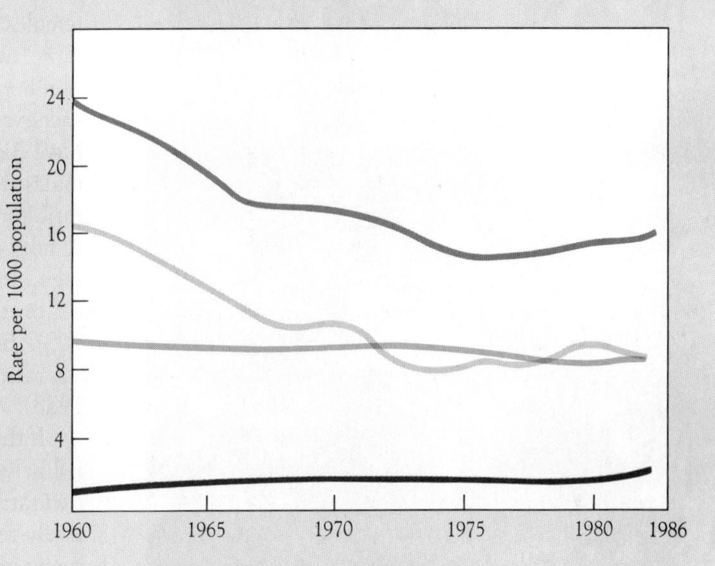

Figure 21.2 How to Calculate Population Growth

The growth rate of a population is determined by the birth rate minus the death rate plus the net immigration rate. In 1986, for example, the U.S. growth rate was 15.3 (birth rate) − 8.7 (death rate) + 2.6 (net immigration rate) = 9.2 (growth rate).

Source: Statistical Abstract of the United States, 1988, p. 9.

ones and the percentage of old people much lower, the death rates in these nations are more similar than we might expect.

To compare the health and living conditions of nations, demographers therefore use refined rates, especially the **infant mortality rate,** which shows the number of deaths among infants less than one year old for every thousand live births. In many developed countries the infant mortality rate is far lower than 20. In many developing countries it is far higher than 30 (Census Bureau, 1988).

Another indicator of health conditions is **life expectancy,** which is the average number of years that a group of people can expect to live. If the group being considered is a nation's newborn infants, then life expectancy rates reflect infant mortality rates. In developing nations, the average life expectancy is 56 years. In the United States, the life expectancy has soared from 40 years at the turn of the century to 75.5 years for those born in 1987. The National Center for Health Statistics has reported that Americans 65 to 70 years old can expect to live to be almost 82. All over the world, however, females tend to live longer than males. As we have seen in Chapter 18 (Health and Medical Care), various categories of Americans have significantly different life expectancies.

Migration International migration—movement of people from one country to another—obviously does not increase or decrease the world's population, but it may greatly alter the population of a specific country. Israel is a case in point. For several years after it was established in 1948, Israel experienced a tremendous annual population growth of 24 percent. Ninety percent of this growth was due to immigration by European Jews. Another notable example is the United States. Between 1880 and 1910 more than 28 million European immigrants settled in the United States. More recently, during the 1970s, many European countries attracted millions of immigrants from the Middle East, North Africa, Turkey, Greece, and Yugoslavia (Wrong, 1977).

The effect of immigration goes beyond the immediate addition to the population. Most immigrants are young adults from lower-class families—categories with relatively high fertility rates. As a result, through their children and grandchildren the immigrants multiply population growth, producing an effect that echoes through the years.

Unlike international migration, internal migration—movement within a country—does not affect the size of a country's population. But it obviously changes the populations of regions and communities. Through internal migrations cities have been created and frontiers conquered. The United States is probably the most mobile country in the world. Since the nation was founded, people have migrated westward. For many years after the Civil War, there was also significant migration out of the rural South to the industrial North

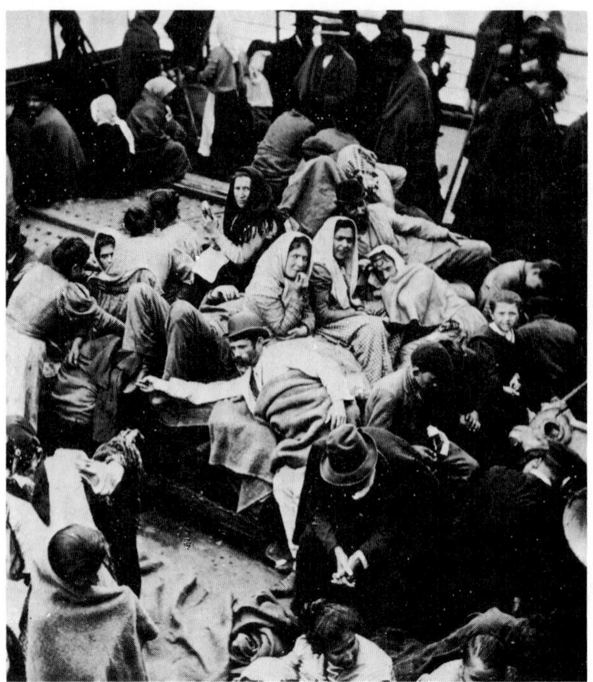

Population growth in the United States has traditionally depended on massive immigration. Between 1880 and 1910 more than 28 million immigrants came here from Europe. The result was a rapidly expanding population. The influx of new people immediately swells the host country's population. But another, less obvious factor is also at work: the immigrants are usually in their peak child-bearing years, and their children in turn contribute to population growth.

and from rural areas to the cities and then to the suburbs. Recently, while westward migration continues, other migration patterns have changed. During the 1970s many people moved into the South as well as the West, the so-called Sunbelt. Meanwhile, migration to large industrial centers of the North and West essentially stopped, and rural areas and small towns grew at a faster rate than cities and suburbs (Census Bureau, 1985).

Population Characteristics

Many characteristics of a population influence its growth and related aspects of society. Among the most important are the sex ratio, marriage rate, and age structure.

The **sex ratio** indicates the number of males per 100 females. A sex ratio of more than 100 means there are more males than females. If the sex ratio is 100, the number of males equals the number of females. In most societies slightly more boys are born than girls, but males have higher death rates. As a result, there are more females than males in the population as a whole. The sex ratio for young adults is about even in normal times, but it falls in wartime because wars are waged mainly by men. In the United States, about 105 males are born for every 100 females each year (giving a sex ratio of 105), but because males die sooner than females, the sex ratio for the entire population is 94 (Census Bureau, 1988).

If the sex ratio is close to 100, then the **marriage rate** is likely to be high. Since most babies are born to married rather than unmarried women, the birth rate is positively related to the marriage rate. When soldiers came home from World War II, for example, our marriage rate went up, and the "baby boom" followed. Since 1960 the numbers of unmarried adults, late marriages, and divorces in the United States have all increased, partly causing our low birth rates.

The **age structure** of a population also shapes birth rates. If there are many women of childbearing age, the birth rate is likely to be high. As we noted earlier, this is one reason for the high birth rates in developing countries. Typically, these countries have a very low percentage of old people and a high percentage of young people compared with developed countries (see Figure 21.3). Since the current large numbers of children will grow up to produce children themselves, future birth rates in these nations are likely to be high as well. The age structure also affects death rates. If two nations have equally healthy populations and living conditions, the country with the higher percentage of older people will have a higher death rate.

Social Characteristics

The population characteristics of a society explain only a small part of the variation in demographic processes among societies. In the United States, for example, there is now a very large number of women of childbearing age (due to the baby boom that followed World War II), yet birth rates have increased only slightly. To understand birth rates, and other demographic proc-

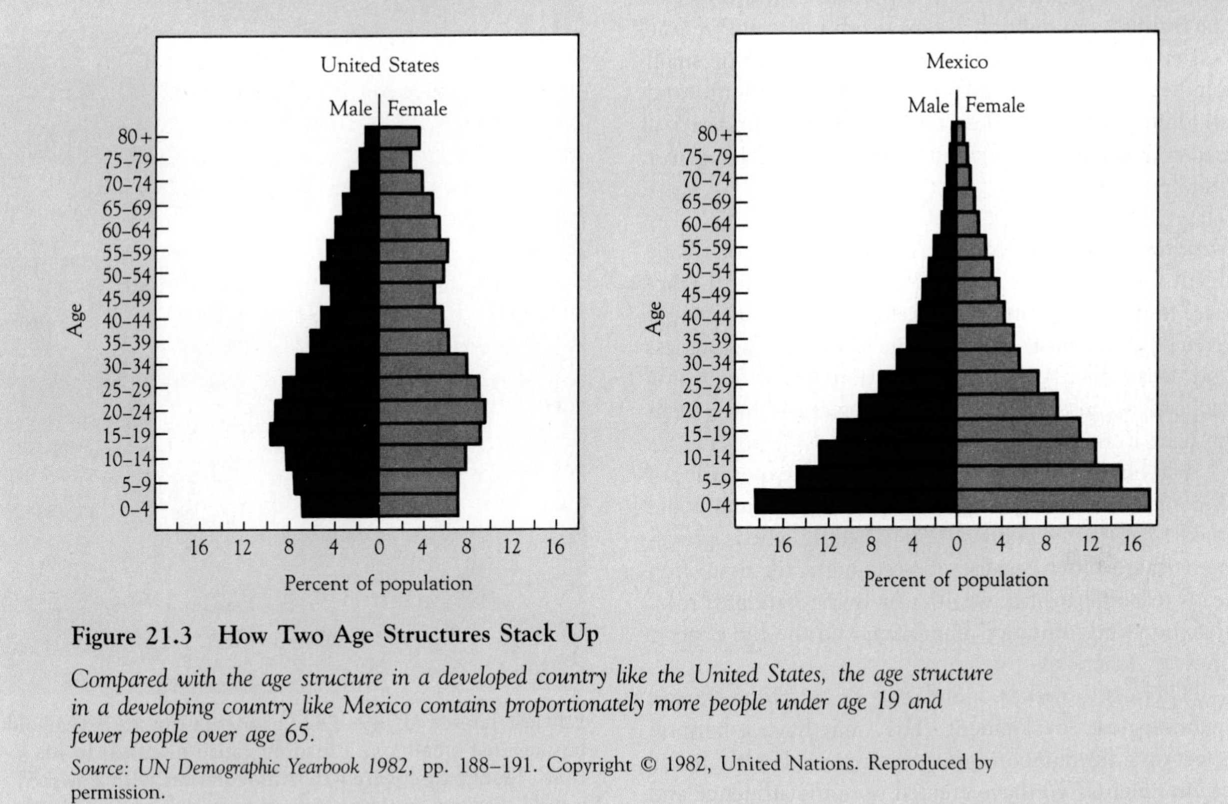

Figure 21.3 How Two Age Structures Stack Up

Compared with the age structure in a developed country like the United States, the age structure in a developing country like Mexico contains proportionately more people under age 19 and fewer people over age 65.

Source: UN Demographic Yearbook 1982, pp. 188–191. Copyright © 1982, United Nations. Reproduced by permission.

esses, we need to look beyond age structure and other population characteristics to more general social characteristics.

Variations in Birth Rates Why do people in rich nations have fewer babies than those in poor countries? Biology cannot explain the difference. The average woman has the biological capacity to produce about twenty children, but in every society **fertility,** the actual number of babies born to the average woman of childbearing age, is lower than **fecundity,** the potential number of babies the average woman can bear. Several social factors ensure that women have fewer children than biology permits. These factors appear to exert a greater influence on societies with relatively low birth rates than on those with higher birth rates.

Access to effective and convenient methods of birth control is one social factor that lowers fertility rates. The nuclear family system is another factor. Unlike the married couple in the extended family with many relatives to help raise their children, couples in nuclear families must assume all the responsibility for their children's care. More fundamental than these two factors is a third—industrialization. In agricultural societies children are economic assets; they can help with the farmwork. In industrialized societies, however, children have become economic liabilities. They depend on their families for financial support, but they cannot contribute significantly to the family's income.

Industrialization is also associated with two other factors that hold down fertility: the entrance of women into the work force, and a preference for small families. If women join the labor force outside the home, they may find the prospect of raising children too difficult, or they may find childbearing uninteresting compared with their careers. A preference for small families is then more likely to take hold. Other cultural values and norms also affect this preference. Some societies, for example, encourage high fertility by judging a man's virility by the number of children he has, and many religions urge their members, in the words of the Bible, to "be fruitful, and multiply." Low death rates remove one barrier to the development of a preference for small families. So long as death rates among infants and children are high, as they tend to be in nonindustrialized countries, high birth rates serve as a hedge against childlessness.

Variations in Death Rates At least three factors shape death rates and life expectancies. One is medical practice. Immunization of children, for example, has greatly reduced the number of deaths due to infectious diseases, and death rates in many poor nations today are being reduced because modern medical practices have been brought into these countries.

Early in this century, however, the life expectancy of Americans improved *before* modern medicine could make a substantial contribution to health. The improvement came about because of a second factor that often leads to better health: wealth. As living standards rose, nutrition and sanitation improved, and the life expectancy of Americans rose.

There is, however, a dark side to our affluence and technological development. They may have a harmful effect on a third important determinant of health: living environments. We have created not only affluence and technological wonders but also a polluted environment and a culture in which stress and unhealthy eating habits have become common. These characteristics have been tied to cancer, heart disease, and stroke—diseases which account for about 70 percent of all deaths in the United States. Automobile accidents have also become the major cause of death among children, adolescents, and young adults (Census Bureau, 1988).

Causes of Migration Both "pushes" and "pulls" stimulate international and internal migrations. The "push" typically comes from economic hardship which compels people to leave their community or even their country; the "pull" comes from economic opportunity elsewhere. A hundred years ago, nearly half of Ireland's population was "pushed" out of the country by its great potato famine and "pulled" into the United States by its reputation for providing economic opportunity. During the Great Depression of the 1930s, farmers left the American dustbowl and headed West in search of jobs. The recession of 1981 brought another migration, this time mostly of blue-collar workers from the Midwest hoping for better times in oil-rich states like Texas, Oklahoma, and Alaska.

Edward Jenner (1749–1823) inoculating an 8-year-old boy against smallpox, a leading cause of death in his time. Jenner discovered that inoculation with cowpox, a mild disease, could prevent a person from contracting smallpox, a deadly disease. In 1803 Jenner inoculated some 12,000 people, causing the number of deaths from smallpox to plunge from 2018 in the previous year to 622. Due to his hard work, the practice of vaccinating against smallpox became widespread, and the death rate from the disease fell sharply. Improved medical practices such as Jenner's is one of at least three factors that greatly reduce death rates. The other two factors are relatively high standards of living and healthful living environments.

Economics, however, does not motivate all migrations. Political and religious oppression has pushed many people to brave the uncertainties of a new land. Examples include the Jews fleeing persecution in Nazi Germany and, more recently, Vietnamese and Cuban refugees escaping communist oppression.

Patterns of Population Change

Demographers can tell us a great deal about the populations of the past, and about how populations are changing. But what about the future? Will there be another baby boom like that of the late 1940s and 1950s? Will the population explosion in the developing world continue? If a pattern can be deciphered in the varying strands of population change, then we might have a theory that could allow demographers to predict more accurately what lies in store for us. The most influential descriptions of population patterns are Malthusian theory and the theory of demographic transition.

Malthusian Theory In 1798 the English clergyman and economist Thomas Malthus (1766–1834) published a truly dismal portrait of population dynamics in *An Essay on the Principles of Population*. He argued that population grows much faster than the production of food supplies, because a population *multiplies* itself but it can increase food production only by *addition*—by cultivating more land. Thus population typically increases geometrically (2, 4, 8, 16), but food supplies increase only arithmetically (2, 3, 4, 5). As a population outstrips food supplies, it is afflicted by war, disease, and poverty. Eventually, population growth must stop.

People might halt this growth through what Malthus called "preventive checks," by which he meant late marriage and sexual restraint, which would reduce birth rates. But Malthus doubted that people, especially the lower classes, had the will to exercise this restraint. Instead, he argue, population growth would eventually be stopped by nature. Its tools would be what Malthus called "positive checks"—disease and famine:

> Premature death must in some shape or other visit the human race. The vices of mankind [such as war] are active and able ministers of depopulation. . . . But should they fail in this war of extermination, sickly seasons, epidemics, pestilence, and plague advance in terrific array. . . . Should success still be incomplete, gigantic inevitable famine stalks in the rear, and with one mighty blow, levels the population (Malthus, 1798).

Malthus failed to foresee three revolutions that undermined his theory: the revolutions in contraception, agricultural technology, and medicine. He did not anticipate the development of very effective and convenient contraceptives such as the pill and the IUD (intrauterine contraceptive device). He did not expect that birth control, which he condemned as a vice, would become widespread. Especially in the West, the use of contraceptives has helped bring birth rates down to a point lower than Malthus thought possible. Meanwhile, the technological revolution has allowed farmers to increase production by raising the yield of their land, not just by adding farmland. Finally, medical advances have given us an arsenal of effective weapons against the contagious diseases that Malthus expected would devastate overpopulated nations. As a result, instead of being reduced by disease, overpopulated nations continue to grow more crowded. Thus the awful fate Malthus predicted has not come to pass—or at least, not yet. His theory, however, has served as a warning to nations that populations cannot expand indefinitely, because natural resources are finite.

The Demographic Transition Most demographers subscribe to the theory that human populations tend to go through specific, demographic stages and that these stages are tied to a society's economic development. This theory of **demographic transition** is based on the population changes that occurred in Western Europe during the past 300 years. According to the theory, there are four demographic stages (see Figure 21.4).

In the first stage both birth rates and death rates are high. Because the two rates more or less balance each other, the population is fairly stable, neither growing nor declining rapidly. This was the stage of the populations in western Europe in 1650, before industrialization began. Today the least industrialized societies, such as those of Central Africa, are still in this stage.

During the second stage the birth rate remains high but the death rate declines sharply. This stage occurred in western Europe after it had become industrialized, and it is occurring today in many developing nations. The introduction of modern medicine, along with better hygiene and sanitation, has decreased their death rates. Their economies and values, however, are still essentially traditional, so their birth rates remain high. As a result, their populations grow rapidly.

During the third stage, both birth rates and death rates decline. Western countries found themselves in this stage after they reached a rather high level of industrialization. Today Taiwan, South Korea, and Argentina are among the developing nations that have reached this stage. Their birth rates have declined significantly. The population still grows because the birth rate continues to exceed the death rate, but growth is slower than during the second stage.

The fourth stage is marked by a low birth rate and a low death rate. Only the most modernized nations of western Europe, North America, and Japan have reached this stage. They have fairly stable populations

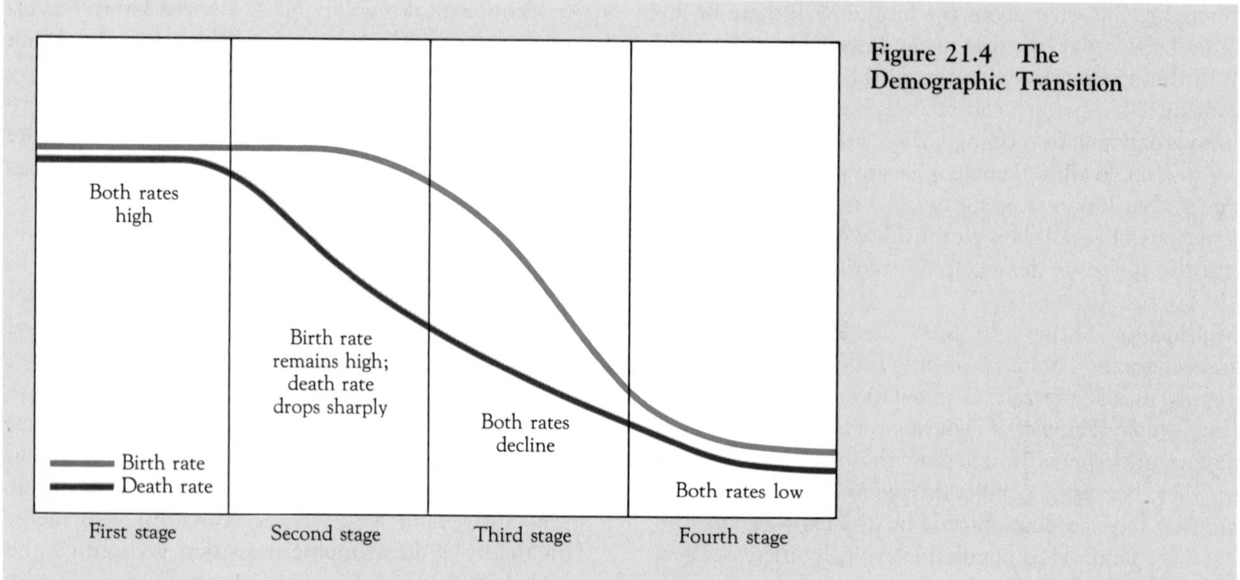

Figure 21.4 The Demographic Transition

and are moving close to zero population growth. Some countries, such as Hungary, Sweden, Denmark, and West Germany, have fallen below zero growth, with birth rates being lower than death rates (Lunde, 1984). The other industrialized countries may eventually follow suit (see box, p. 534).

To proponents of the demographic transition theory, the future of human populations looks bright. They believe that when developing countries match the level of modernization found in the West and Japan, they too will have stable populations. To critics of the theory, the future is far less certain. There is at least one major difference between contemporary third-world countries and the condition of European nations when they began to industrialize: thanks to modern medicine, death rates in developing countries have declined far more rapidly than they did in nineteenth-century Europe. While it took Europe 200 years to lower its mortality, it takes developing countries today only a year or so to lower theirs. In these countries, demographer William Petersen (1982) notes, "the latest life-saving advances become available immediately so that in extreme cases populations went in one step from witch doctor to antibiotics." As a result, there is a population explosion in the third world today, a condition that did not occur in nineteenth-century Europe.

Demographic "Fallout"

The composition of a society's population shapes the demands placed on that society. If the youthful population in a society is large, it needs many maternity wards, schools, family housing, and job opportunities. If the percentage of elderly people is high, the society needs many heart and cancer surgeons, extended-care nursing facilities, and pensions. If the percentage of children and young people in a society increases, it is likely to face lower economic productivity (because the children consume resources without producing any) and higher crime rates (because youths commit more crimes than people in other age groups).

Any relatively swift change in the characteristics of a population can create many difficulties. A sudden exodus of people from a region may leave those who stay behind with a devastated economy and little money to maintain public services. Internal migration can also produce sudden "booms" in a city or region. Demands for schools, for water supplies, for roads and other government services then soar. Often "booms" are also accompanied by increases in crime, divorce rates, and other social difficulties.

Even without a marked change in population trends, growth in a population today is likely to have important consequences. The effects are greatest in the developing nations, but they are also significant in the developed nations.

The Fallout on Developing Countries The most dramatic population change today is the population explosion in many developing countries. Its consequences are most visible in the oppressive poverty of many of these

Starvation in Ethiopia. The major consequence of population explosion in many developing countries is oppressive poverty. Given their fast-growing populations, these nations' efforts to fight poverty often come to naught. Instead of climbing up the economic ladder, they find themselves remaining on a treadmill, constantly in danger of slipping backward to the Malthusian famine. Occasionally, they do suffer massive starvation.

nations. Their cities are filled with people who live in overcrowded shacks, and others who must live on the streets, sidewalks, vacant lots, rooftops, and cemeteries. About two-thirds of the people in the world are undernourished, and malnutrition is devastating millions of children, weakening their bodies and their minds. Some 15 million children die of starvation every year (Ehrlich, 1984).

The rapidly growing populations of developing nations greatly complicate their efforts to fight poverty. Instead of climbing up the economic ladder, they find themselves standing on a treadmill, constantly in danger of slipping backward to the Malthusian famine. According to economists, a country whose population grows 3 percent a year must invest up to 20 percent of its national income in economic development in order to raise its per capita income by just 1 percent a year. This increase would mean that an average person who earned $100 one year would earn $101 the next year. That is not much of a gain, yet most developing nations find even this goal too optimistic. They find it difficult to invest even 10 percent a year in economic development. But at this rate of investment, if the population grows at 3 percent, the average person can expect to receive only an additional 50 cents for every $100 earned. Economic investment can barely keep up with the rapid population growth. More than half of Africa's economic expansion has been used just to maintain the expanding population at a subsistence level. Some have already experienced massive starvation. In fact, most of the poor third-world nations cannot survive without economic assistance from the West (Davis, 1976b; Ward, 1984).

Without economic growth, rapid population growth is eventually reflected in rising unemployment. The result is more poverty, plus the threat of social unrest and political instability. In the years ahead the gap between rich and poor nations is expected to widen. According to the World Bank's calculations, while per-capita income in the United States should rise to $9000 by the year 2000, in India it should climb to just $200. All over the world the number of people living in absolute poverty—"without sufficient food to keep body and soul together"—will rise from about 800 million today to between 1.3 and 1.7 billion (Barraclough, 1978; Bessis, 1984).

The Fallout on Developed Countries For the United States, the plight of the poor nations threatens to bring increased immigration, problems in dealing with economic turmoil around the world, and increased competition for minerals and fuels. Furthermore, even the small population growth within developed nations such as ours has unhappy repercussions. While developed countries contain only 25 percent of the world's population, they account for 75 to 90 percent of the world's annual use of mineral and commercial energy resources. Small increases in these nations' populations, then, have resulted in "drawing resources from every region on Earth while dispersing air and water pollutants and toxic

I'VE NEVER THOUGHT THAT MUCH ABOUT EATING...

YOU DO WHEN YOUR DISH IS EMPTY!
11-28 ©1985 United Feature Syndicate,Inc.

Reprinted by permission of NEA, Inc.

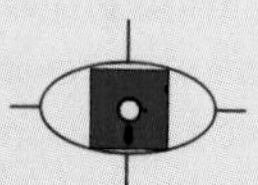

LOOKING AT CURRENT RESEARCH

Population in the Year 2034

What will the world be like in 50 years? One aspect of the future that can be estimated is world population. Using statistical techniques, demographers can project present population trends into the future to suggest the size, density, and distribution of future populations. Here a demographer attempts a glimpse at the year 2034 and considers how different countries will change as a result of their current population trends. What demographic forces will most likely play the greatest role in creating these future population patterns?

According to the 2034 *World Population Data Sheet,* only about 7 percent of the people on this planet live in what were once called the "more developed" nations, compared to the 25 percent included in this category 50 years ago in 1984. We have long since changed our categorization of world population by "more developed" and "less developed" regions, however, and now classify nations into four types: the service/information societies, with a mere 4 percent of the world's population; the new industrialized nations, with 38 percent of the total; the developing regions, with 43 percent; and the least developed nations, with about 15 percent. Let us examine each of the four types of societies to understand both the situation in 2034 and how it evolved over the past 50 years.

Service/Information Societies

This group includes all of Europe except the Soviet Union and a few other Eastern European countries; the United States and Canada; Australia and New Zealand; and Japan. The Soviet Union has changed dramatically over the past 50 years but is still struggling to become truly service oriented.

The service/information countries have witnessed below-replacement fertility for at least 60 years. This has been appropriate, given the exceedingly low demand for manual labor and, indeed, for human labor in general. The robotic revolution, together with the information revolution, has resulted in increasing numbers of jobs being performed first by mechanical robots and more recently by robots capable of decisionmaking.

Such societies have little incentive for population growth. Many people have opted not to have children (or even to marry). Most couples who do have children are satisfied with one. Productivity has increased considerably as a result of more and more reliance on "steel-collar" robots (replacing the blue-collar workers of 50 years ago) and "thinking" robots (displacing many of the service and professional workers of days gone by). By the year 2000, almost all Northern and Western European countries had joined the few European countries where births already fell short of deaths in the early 1980s. Despite the reduced need for workers, concern about diminishing numbers

wastes around the globe" (Ehrlich, 1984). Despite their efforts to help feed the world, rich nations also consume 40 to 85 percent of the world's agricultural supplies. This, too, increases desertification—the spread of desert—in the western United States through overgrazing, unwise cultivation, and poor irrigation practices. Our groundwater is further being sacrificed to the agricultural push. This has intensified competition for water in the western states (Ehrlich, 1984). Our population growth has also increased our dependence on other countries for raw materials. Forty-five years ago the United States was a net exporter of raw materials but today we have to import half of them in order to maintain our current standard of living (McFalls, Jones, and Gallagher, 1984).

QUESTIONS FOR DISCUSSION AND REVIEW

1. What is demography, and why are its data more accurate than those in other areas of sociology?
2. How do birth rates, death rates, and migration influence the demographic characteristics of a society?
3. How do social characteristics such as wealth and industrialization influence birth rates, death rates, and migration?
4. How would a Malthusian theorist's view of current world population patterns differ from that of a demographic transitionist?
5. What is demographic "fallout," and how do these sudden shifts in population affect developing and developed countries?

grew. Further, with so few children being born, such societies inevitably are top-heavy with older people and have a median population age approaching 45 or even 50. These nations began to ask themselves: How can we survive with falling numbers and without youth to develop new ideas to carry on the service/information revolution? One option was to rely increasingly on robots to replace the young population. The other option was to allow more immigration from countries with surplus populations.

Industrialized Nations

Over the last 50 years, population growth, combined with the aspirations of less developed nations, has fueled tremendous growth of the demand for and thus manufacture of industrialized products of all kinds—machinery, clothing, high-tech products. With the hitherto industrialized nations of Europe and North America abandoning that manufacturing role, other nations might have been expected to rush to fill the breach. In the vanguard were the "less developed" nations already approaching industrialization 50 years ago: the Philippines, for example, as well as what were then South Korea, Taiwan, and Hong Kong.

Developing Countries

This category includes the largest proportion of world population (43 percent) and the most countries. These countries remain to this day somewhat more rural than urban. But the cities are growing, close to three-quarters of the adult population is now literate, and fertility has fallen rapidly, particularly in the last one or two decades. With any good fortune, some such nations could advance to industrialized status within the next 50 years. The category includes India, Pakistan, Kenya, Egypt, and Latin American countries.

Least Developed Nations

The last category, with about 15 percent of Earth's population, includes most of sub-Saharan Africa other than the five developing nations listed above, Bangladesh, and some Middle Eastern countries. These nations present planet Earth with its most critical demographic problems in 2034. In most, fertility has only recently fallen below four births per woman and mortality is still falling; thus, population growth is rapid. Mass deaths from starvation and epidemics bred by overcrowding are a constant threat and sometimes a reality, as in Bangladesh in 2015.

Source: Excerpted from Leon F. Bouvier, "Planet Earth 1984–2034: A demographic vision," *Population Bulletin* (Population Reference Bureau, Inc., Washington, D.C., February 1984), pp. 24–31.

COMBATING POPULATION GROWTH

For thousands of years there have been individuals who practiced birth control, but many nations at various times in their histories have sought to *increase* their population because they associated big population with great military power and national security. Religious, medical, and political authorities often argued against birth control. For more than a century, the United States even had laws that prohibited the mailing of birth control information and devices. During the 1950s and 1960s, however, many governments began to see population growth as a social problem. By 1984 most countries, representing about 95 percent of the world's population, had formulated official policies to combat population growth (Davis, 1976b; Russell, 1984). These policies can be classified into two types: encouragement of voluntary family planning and compulsory population control.

Family Planning

A number of governments make contraceptives available to anyone who wants them. They encourage birth control, but they do not try to impose a limit on how many children a couple may have. In order for this voluntary family planning to work, however, people must prefer small families to large ones—otherwise they will not use birth control.

This is the heart of the problem with family planning. Industrialized societies typically value small families, and family planning programs therefore have reduced birth rates significantly in advanced developing countries such as Taiwan and South Korea. Family planning is even more successful in the more industrialized nations in the West, where the preference for small families is strong. Many less advanced developing countries, however, retain the preference for large families that is typical of agricultural societies. As a result, voluntary planning programs in these nations have failed to reduce birth rates as significantly as they have in developed countries (Ainsworth, 1984).

During the last decade, for example, there has been no fertility decline in Africa. There have been substantial fertility declines, though, in the developing countries in Asia, the Pacific, Latin America, the Caribbean, and the Middle East. Still, among these countries none has reached a birth rate of under 20 births per 1000 population—the level of all developed countries—and a third of them still have birth rates above 40. Obviously, their family planning programs have not worked well enough. Their preferred family size is simply too high, ranging from an average of 4.0 children per family in Asia to 7.1 in Africa—far above the average of 2 in developed countries (Lightbourne and Singh, 1982). Especially in Africa, having many children is a status enhancer, particularly for the less educated. Moreover, the extended family that is common in third-world countries reverses some of the direct economic penalty of a large family. In fact, children are considered a form of old-age pension because there are no social welfare systems like the one we have in the United States. Since many children die early, parents are even more anxious to have a large family to increase their chances of being looked after in their senior years (Francis, 1986). As a result of the relative ineffectiveness of family planning in the developing countries, several have tried compulsory programs.

Population Control

In the early 1970s India forced government employees who had more than two children to undergo sterilization. With the encouragement of the central government, some states in India also forced men to be sterilized after their second child was born. If the men refused, they could be fined $250 and imprisoned for up to a year. In some villages overzealous government officials rounded up and sterilized all the men, without checking how many children they had. The program stirred up widespread opposition. Demographer Frank Notestein had predicted in 1971 that if a developing country tried to force its people to practice birth control, it "would be more likely to bring down the government than the birth rate." Indeed, the sterilization program apparently contributed to the fall of Prime Minister Indira Gandhi's government in 1977. Since then India has returned to a voluntary program (Landman, 1977; Petersen, 1982). India now has a fertility rate of 4.7 children per woman (compared with 1.8 in the United States) and it will become the world's most populous nation by about 2045 (Russell, 1984).

In 1983, as part of an ongoing battle against its population explosion, Bangladesh also launched a campaign of compulsory sterilization. Soldiers rounded up villagers—mostly poor women—having more than three children, and took them in trucks to a clinic where they were sterilized against their will. The U.S. Agency for International Development, which backed the population control program there with $24.8 million in 1983, eventually pressured the Bangladesh government to stop that brutal campaign. Today Bangladesh uses financial incentives to encourage sterilization. Each person who agrees to be sterilized receives a payment of $7 (less than one-tenth the annual per capita income in Bangladesh) and new clothing worth about $4 (Hartmann and Hughes, 1984). But the fertility remains very high, with 6.3 children per woman. This means that the Bangladesh population will nearly triple to 266 million (more than the current U.S. population) within 40 years, and they will be squeezed into an area the size of Wisconsin (Russell, 1984).

Singapore has had more success with its compulsory program. Its goal in the 1970s was to establish the two-child family as the social norm, and its methods included both rewards and punishments. The first two children born to a family were given top priority in admission to school, with increasingly lower priority given to additional children. Higher government fees for hospital deliveries were charged for each additional child. Paid maternity leave was given to women with three or fewer children, but it was abolished after three births. Large families were denied government-subsidized housing. In government and in some businesses, employees with many children had a hard time getting promotions. As a result of these measures, Singapore's birth rate de-

A one-child family poster in China. With a population of over one billion, mainland China faces a staggering problem of population control. In 1980 the Chinese government announced an official program to stabilize the population by the year 2000. The program aims at establishing the one-child family as the social norm. The government rewards parents of one-child families with free schooling, priority access to medical care, and preferences in employment. Conversely, parents who have more than one child are penalized economically. They must, for example, pay income taxes, which is not required of most citizens. The Chinese also rely on social pressure—the approval or disapproval of neighbors and fellow workers—to make parents conform. The program has been quite successful in reducing the birth rate. But since 1986 the birth rate has begun to inch up because the government has relaxed its one-child policy.

clined significantly. It fell by 8.1 percent in 1973 and another 8.4 percent in 1974 (Saw, 1975). In the early 1980s its population grew by only 1.2 percent a year, less than the world's growth rate of 1.8 percent (Census Bureau, 1985). In fact, by 1986 Singapore had produced fewer babies than needed to prevent a long-term decline in the population. Thus, ironically, in 1987 the Singapore government reversed its earlier population control policy by encouraging parents to have more babies. Its slogan now is "Have three, and more if you can afford it," backed up with generous tax rebates and other incentives similar to those used in the past to restrict birth (Holloway, 1987).

China has also tried to reduce its birth rate by using a similar strategy, combining rewards and punishments. For a couple with only one child, rewards are substantial. The parents get a salary bonus, and the child receives free schooling, priority in medical care, admission to the best schools and universities, and preference in employment. In contrast, multichild parents are severely penalized. They must pay all costs for each additional child, are taxed about 10 percent of their income, and are often denied promotion for two years. Since it started this "one-child family" campaign in 1979, China has halved its birth rate, a record unmatched by any other developing nation (Lader, 1983). Beginning in 1986, though, the birth rate began to rise again because the government relaxed its one-child policy. One reason for the relaxation is the increasing prosperity among the Chinese, who are often willing to pay the fines for having more than one child. Another reason is the international criticism that China has received for pressuring women to abort fetuses even late in pregnancy. A third reason is that the one-child policy has encouraged, albeit unintentionally, the killing of female infants by parents who hope to have sons. Nevertheless, China continues to exhort couples to have only one child, though it now focuses on persuasion, education, and publicity campaigns rather than coercion and penalties (Kristof, 1987).

U.S. Population Policy

During the 1960s the U.S. government began to recognize global population growth as a potential problem, and by 1968 it had spent several hundred million dollars to help developing nations control their population growth. However, in the early 1970s, a number of leftist governments in the third world dismissed population control as an imperialist ploy by rich countries to keep poor nations' populations down in order to perpetuate Western dominance over the globe. They argued that poor nations should be more concerned with economic development because "development is the best contraceptive," that is, elimination of poverty will lead to lower birth rates. Later those leftist governments reversed themselves and pursued population control—with a vengeance in China's communist regime.

Ironically, the conservative Reagan administration also saw economic growth as the answer to world overpopulation. But it held that only a free-market economy can guarantee economic growth as well as low birth rates. It cited as supporting evidence the experiences of Western European nations, Canada, the United States, Japan, Singapore, Hong Kong, South Korea, Taiwan, and New Zealand. All these countries have free-market economies, are highly prosperous, and have very low birth rates (Abraham, 1984). The Reagan administration also favored the cutting of family-planning aid to organizations or countries if they continued to include abortion in their population-control programs. This is because the administration found abortion morally offensive, seeing it as a form of infanticide (Russell, 1984). Thus, the administration ended its $15-million-a-year support for the London-based International Parenthood Federation in 1985 and suspended $25 million in aid to the United Nations Family Planning Agency in 1986 because these two international organizations advocated abortion as an option. A similar attempt to withdraw funds from family planning agencies within the United States, however, was defeated by Congress (Lewis, 1987).

In the United States the government has been spending over $100 million a year to assist family planning centers. But our population growth has slowed primarily because of social and economic factors, not government action. In fact, family planning has become the norm rather than the exception. Even the majority of American Catholics practice forms of birth control forbidden by their church. Today sterilization is the most popular type of birth control in the United States, closely followed by the pill and the condom. The use of sterilization and the condom has increased faster than that of any other method because of concern and controversy over the side-effects of the pill and the IUD. The use of abortion as a birth control method has also increased, despite restrictions by the federal government and many state governments on the use of Medicaid funds for abortions (NCHS, 1984; Lederer, 1983).

Still, in 1980 the fertility rate increased to its highest rate in 17 years because of a rise in the fertility rate of unmarried white women and because of the increased number of women from the baby-boom generation. Nevertheless, the Census Bureau believes that in the coming decades American women in their childbearing years will average just 1.8 births—less than the replacement rate of 2.1. Such a "birth dearth," according to the controversial scenario painted by Ben Wattenberg (1987), will spell trouble for the future of the United States. With a shrinking population, the U.S. economy will decline for lack of consumers. With the declining birth rate, there will be too few young workers to pay enough Social Security taxes to support the bulging elderly population. If we are not a populous nation, we will lose our position as a superpower in the world, because only a large society can tax its people enough to finance expensive research and development for the military and to maintain large armed forces. For numerous people, growing old without offspring will be quite sad, because when you get old the people who will care about you most dearly will be your children or grandchildren. The loss of population will even cause the United States to lose its cultural, ideological dominance in the world, making it difficult for Americans to promote and defend liberty. Therefore, Wattenberg proposes that Americans produce more babies. But some demographers point out the difficulty of predicting long-term population trends. In the 1920s and 1940s, for example, many population experts anxiously predicted decline, but they were later totally surprised by the postwar baby boom. Many scholars also argue that it is racist for Wattenberg to assume that white, Western values should prevail in the United States. He has observed that the rising tide of third-world immigrants in this country, combined with higher birth rates of Hispanic and black Americans, will reduce the proportion of European-descended Americans from the present 80 percent to 60 percent by 2080. He considers the growing proportion of nonwhites a threat to Western culture, such a view being regarded by his critics as inappropriate to America's pluralism (Bowen, 1987).

It seems inevitable that if the birth dearth continues, our society will rely increasingly on immigration to stop the population from declining. Today immigration—both legal and illegal—accounts for about 26 percent of the nation's population growth. But that proportion will rise to 50 percent early in the next century, and then immigration will provide the bulk of the nation's population growth in the second half of the twenty-first century. History has shown the great contribution of immigrants to the prosperity of this country. As President Reagan's Council of Economic Advisers wrote in its 1986 annual report, "the economic benefits of immigration are spread throughout the economy. These include increased job opportunities and higher wages for some workers as well as the widely diffused benefits of lower product prices and higher profits" (Bacon, 1986). But since most of the immigrants come from the third world rather than Europe, there is resentment among some Americans against them, especially the illegal aliens.

Every year more people enter this country illegally than legally, and the growth in the number of illegal aliens has accelerated in recent years. Partly to avoid appearing racist or jingoist, however, the U.S. Congress in late 1986 passed a law that offers amnesty—in effect, legal residency status—to aliens who have been living in this country since January 1, 1982. But at the same time the United States will beef up its efforts to stop foreigners from entering the country illegally. Since the small number of agents of the U.S. Immigration and Naturalization Service (INS) cannot by themselves stop the vast number of aliens flooding illegally into this country, Congress has also passed a law that prohibits employers from hiring illegal aliens. This law has, in effect, forced the nation's 7 million employers to work for free as agents of the INS. They must ask for a job applicant's proof of citizenship or legal residency. They must further keep detailed new records documenting their efforts to maintain their workplace free of illegal aliens. Can this law successfully cut off the economic lure for illegal immigrants? According to a study by the General Accounting Office, sanctions against employers for hiring illegals have failed to be an effective deterrent in 20 other nations. Canada convicted only 40 employers under its law in the past three years (Solis et al., 1987). The problem is that it is difficult to enforce the law against the numerous employers who have greatly profited from a ready supply of inexpensive and hard-working laborers, which illegal immigrants are likely to be.

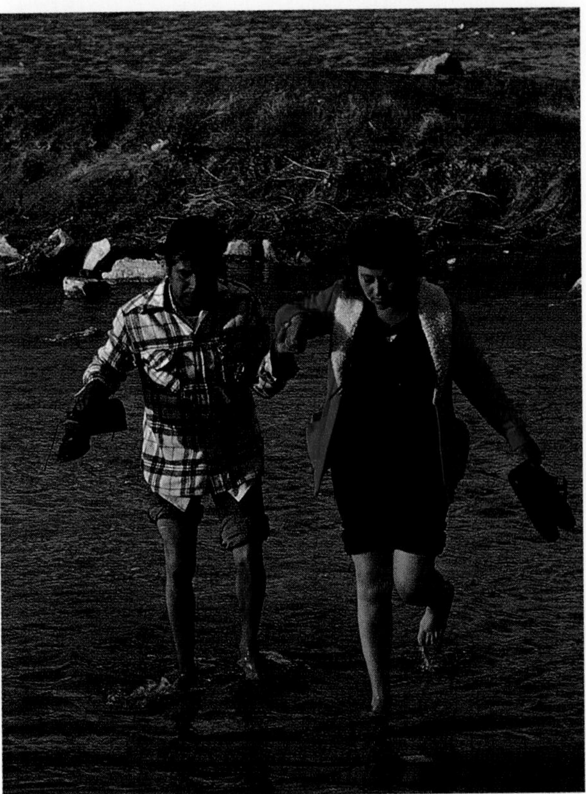

Lured by better job opportunities, more people enter the United States illegally than legally. The growth in the number of illegal aliens has accelerated in recent years. In late 1986 an amnesty law was passed, granting legal residency status to illegal aliens who have been living here since 1982. But the government has also vowed to increase efforts to stop illegal immigration by patrolling the borders and prohibiting the hiring of illegal aliens. Since most of the illegal aliens come from third-world rather than European countries, there is resentment against them among some Americans.

QUESTIONS FOR DISCUSSION AND REVIEW

1. What are the two basic strategies that governments can use to control population, and what are the pros and cons of each?
2. What has been the result of compulsory birth control programs in over-populated countries like China?
3. How does U.S. population policy differ from that of other societies?
4. What roles might the birth dearth and immigration play in determining the composition of the American population in the future?

ECOLOGY

To understand how the growth of population and consumption can damage the environment and thus endanger us, we look to **ecology.** It is a subfield of biology that examines the interactions among organisms and between organisms and their physical environment.

Despite all the amazing things humans have managed to do, we are still limited by these ecological principles. We are still living organisms, dependent like other organisms on ecosystems. However, we have tried to ignore that dependence and act in defiance of nature's limits. Two basic kinds of environmental problems result: a depletion of natural resources, and pollution.

Elements of Ecology

Like all organisms, humans exist within a thin layer of air, soil, and water known as the **biosphere.** Within the biosphere we can isolate countless **ecosystems,** communities of living things interacting with the physical environment. An ecosystem may be as small as a puddle in a forest or as large as the biosphere itself. But whatever ecosystem we choose to look at, we find that the organisms within it depend on each other and on the physical environment for their survival. They are bound together by mutual interdependence. Energy and matter are constantly being transformed and transferred by the components of an ecosystem, providing the organisms with the essentials of life. Plants, for example, take in carbon dioxide and give off oxygen, which humans and other animals require for survival, and animals exhale carbon dioxide. Plants, in turn, use carbon dioxide in photosynthesis, the process by which they convert solar energy into carbohydrates and become food for animals. When animals die, their decomposed bodies provide nutrients to the soil, which plants then use.

From an examination of ecosystems we can isolate two simple principles. First, natural resources are finite. Every ecosystem therefore has a limited "carrying capacity," a limited number of living things that it can support. Second, we can never do just one thing, because everything is related to everything else. If we try to alter one aspect of an ecosystem, we end up changing others as well. When farmers used DDT, for example, they meant merely to kill pests. But DDT also got into the soil and water, from there into plankton, into fish that ate plankton, and into birds that ate the fish. The DDT eventually damaged the ability of some birds to reproduce. The chemical also found its way into our food. Some American women had so much DDT in their systems that their milk would be legally prohibited from sale in interstate commerce (Ehrlich, Ehrlich, and Holdren, 1977).

Diminishing Resources

Although Americans make up less than 6 percent of the world's population, each year the United States consumes about 30 percent of the world's energy and raw materials. We use more than 40 percent of the earth's aluminum and coal and about 30 percent of the platinum and copper (Ehrlich et al., 1977). Economist Wassily Leontief calculated that at present rates of consumption, by the year 2000 the world will "use up three to four times the volume of mineral resources that humans consumed during the whole previous history of civilization" (Barraclough, 1978). According to some estimates, the world's reserves of lead, silver, tungsten, mercury, and other precious resources will be depleted within 40 years. Even if new discoveries increase oil reserves fivefold, the global supply of oil will last only 50 years (Meadows et al., 1974). Poor nations fear that by the time they become fully industrialized, the resources they hope to enjoy will be gone.

Closer to home, we are endangering our own supplies of arable land and water. We are losing topsoil to erosion at an alarming rate—about 4 to 5 billion tons a year. In the worst cases, an inch of topsoil, which nature takes 100 to 1500 years to form, is being destroyed in 10 to 20 years. At the same time, homes and stores and businesses are taking over millions of acres of farmland each year. The National Agricultural Lands Study has estimated that by the year 2000 there will be a "shortfall of 10 million to 46 million acres" of farmland. Meanwhile, in the western United States underground water reservoirs are being depleted. In the East thousands of gallons of water are wasted because of leaking city pipes (Kneeland, 1981).

In short, we are fast running out of natural resources. "Barring revolutionary advances in technology," concludes the *Global 2000 Report,* "life for most people on earth will be more precarious in 2000 than it is now." Economist Julian Simon (1982), however, disagrees. He argues that the future is likely to be better "because our powers to manage our environment have been increasing throughout human history." This may be correct, but only because of analyses like *Global 2000* that open our eyes to serious resource problems and stimulate the necessary technological progress to solve them (Aage, 1984).

Most ecologists, however, believe that technology cannot solve all the problems. Once nonrenewable resources such as minerals, metals, coal, and oil are used up, they are gone forever. Simon (1983) disagrees again, arguing that these resources can always be replaced through technology. We can capture solar energy to replace coal and oil. We can also find substitutes for metals, such as plastics for tin cans or satellites for copper telephone wire. Simon even contends that copper can be made from cheaper metals. The problem, according to ecologists, is that the cost of producing these substitutes is prohibitive. As ecologist Garrett Hardin (1982) points out, it is possible to make copper from nickel-62 but the process will require $2 billion worth of electricity to produce one pound of copper—which sold for 80 cents in 1982. Moreover, turning solar energy into electricity or producing substitutes for natural resources requires the use of materials that already exist in finite supply (Mann, 1983).

Environmental Pollution

To consume more, we must produce more and create more wastes. These by-products of our consumption must go somewhere. Nature has many cycles for transforming wastes to be used in some other form, but we are overtaxing nature's recycling capacity. We put too much waste, such as automobile emissions, in one place at the same time, and we have created new substances, such as dioxin and PCBs, that cannot be recycled safely. The result is pollution.

Pollution of the air has many sources. Power-generating plants, oil refineries, chemical plants, steel mills, and the like spew about 140 million tons of pollutants into the air every year. The heaviest polluter is the automobile, which accounts for at least 80 percent of air pollution. The pollutants irritate our eyes, noses, and throats; damage buildings; lower the productivity of the soil; and may cause serious illnesses such as bronchitis, emphysema, and lung cancer. In 1948 a low-hanging mass of hot air trapped pollutants over Donora, Pennsylvania, producing severe air pollution that killed 20 people and made nearly half of Donora's residents sick. In 1952 about 4000 people were killed in London by what the British called the "Black Fog" (Ehrlich et al., 1977). Most recently, in 1984, the escape of poisonous gas from a chemical plant in Bhopal, India left 2500 people dead and 100,000 disabled with blindness, sterility, kidney and liver infections, tuberculosis, and brain damage (Whitaker, 1984). In 1986 the nuclear power plant in Chernobyl in the Soviet Union exploded, spreading a cloud of dangerous radioactivity over large parts of the country and much of Eastern and Western Europe. Although the Soviet government reported that only two died and fewer than 200 were injured, Western experts believe that "the disaster was catastrophic, possibly causing thousands of casualties and contaminating an area the size of Rhode Island" (Gabor, 1986).

Another kind of air pollution, called *acid rain,* has also aroused concern. When sulfur and nitrogen compounds are emitted by factories and automobiles, chemical reactions in the atmosphere may convert them to acidic compounds that can be carried hundreds of miles which then fall to the earth in rain and snow. Rain as acidic as vinegar has been recorded. This acid rain can kill fish and aquatic vegetation. It damages forests, crops, and soils. It corrodes buildings and water pipes and tanks because it can erode limestone, marble, and even metal surfaces. Due to acid rain, thousands of lakes and rivers in North America and Europe are now "dead," unable to support fish and plant life. In Sweden, for example, damage to fisheries attributed to acidification has been found in 2500 lakes and signs of the process have been observed in another 6500. In southern Norway, out of 5000 lakes, 1750 have lost all their fish and 900 others are seriously affected. In Canada, nearly 20 percent of all the lakes in Ontario have been turned acid (*UN Chronicle,* 1983). In the United States the acidity of rain has increased during the last 10 to 15 years over a broad area extending from the Southeast to the Northwest (*Earth Science,* 1983).

Lakes, rivers, underground wells, and even the oceans are further polluted every day by tons of garbage. The greatest dumpers are industry and agriculture. An average paper mill, for example, produces as much organic waste as the human sewage of a large city. Modern farmers apply huge quantities of nitrate and phosphate fertilizers to their land—chemicals that are often washed by rain and irrigation into lakes and rivers.

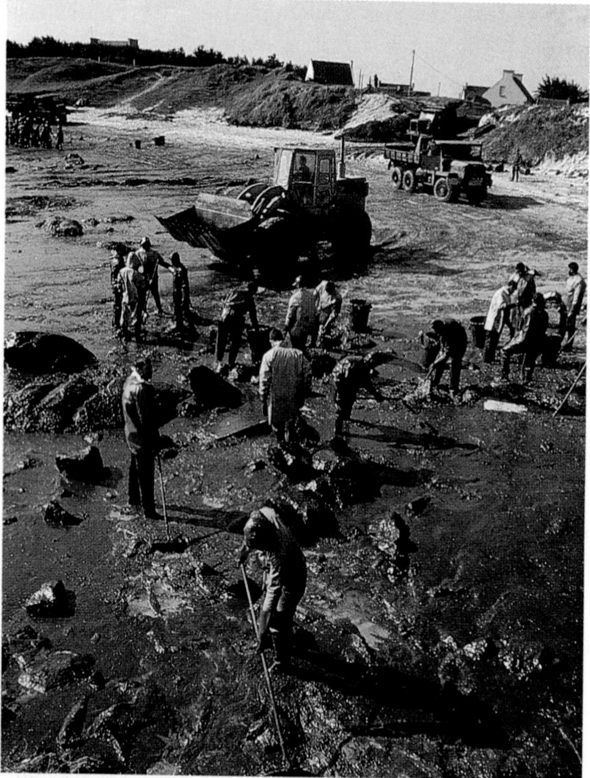

Cleaning up after Amoco Cadiz oil spill, off the coast of Brittany in France. In addition to this kind of occasional water pollution, every day tons of garbage are thrown into lakes, rivers, and oceans. The greatest dumpers are industry and agriculture. Water pollution not only fouls the air, it also kills the fish. Even human lives are threatened. Nearly half the population regularly swallows some pollutants because the groundwater from which we get our drinking water has slowly been contaminated over the years by chemicals, gasoline, and industrial wastes.

Nearly 16 million gallons of such pollutants were dumped into the Great Lakes in 1976, and the layer of fish-killing muck at the bottom of Lake Erie once reached 125 feet. Billions of tons of industrial waste and human sewage are also thrown into the sea. When adventurer Thor Heyerdahl crossed the Atlantic by raft in 1970, he found garbage floating all around him (Ehrlich et al., 1977; Smith, 1984).

Water pollution does not merely foul the air and kill the fish. It may also threaten human lives. When a Japanese chemical plant dumped organic wastes containing mercury into a nearby bay, more than a hundred people died or suffered severe damage to their nervous systems from eating the polluted seafood. In fact, nearly half of the U.S. population (some 108 million) ingest some pollutants every day because the groundwater from which they get their supplies of drinking water has slowly been contaminated over the years by an array of chemicals, gasoline, and industrial wastes (Abelson, 1984; Dorfman, 1984).

Nuclear pollution has also become a source of special concern. The accident at the Chernobyl nuclear power plant in 1986 made it clear that, contrary to all the assurances experts had given, serious nuclear disasters can happen. Even without a major accident, nuclear power poses environmental hazards. People living near a nuclear plant may be subject to routine releases of low-level radiation, and workers in the plants may receive dangerous doses of radioactivity. Transporting uranium to nuclear plants and disposing of radioactive wastes pose other problems. The mining and refining of uranium has produced millions of tons of radioactive tailings which can be spread by the wind and contaminate drinking water. The nuclear power plants themselves are running out of storage space for their wastes. Some of this material will remain radioactive and very dangerous for thousands of years.

Chemical industries also produce hazardous wastes. About 60 million tons a year are generated in the United States, compared with 20 to 30 million tons in Europe. Hazardous wastes represent 10 to 20 percent of the world's manufacturing wastes. Careless disposal of hazardous wastes has caused fires; explosions; air, water and land pollution; contamination of food and drinking water; and harm to humans, animals, and plants. People exposed to poisonous vapors from hazardous wastes have suffered headaches, nausea, dizziness, skin rash, and numbness of the limbs. Exposure to dioxin, in particular, has been found to cause cancer, organ damage, weakening of the immune system, and reproductive failure in women. In 1983, after a flood, the community of Times Beach, Missouri, was found to be contaminated with dioxin, which had come from the waste oil sprayed earlier on unpaved roads to hold down dust. Within two years all the 2242 residents except one old couple had left the town. There are so far 37 confirmed dioxin sites in Missouri, and dozens more are suspected. In fact, since the Love Canal tragedy was widely publicized in 1978, communities across the country have been discovering the toxic contamination of their land (*UN Chronicle*, 1983; Barnes, 1983; Shipp, 1986).

In 1986 the nuclear power plant in the Soviet town of Chernobyl exploded, spewing dangerous radioactivity into the air over large parts of the country and much of Eastern and Western Europe. According to Western experts, the disaster probably caused thousands of casualties and contaminated an area as big as Rhode Island. Even without such an accident, nuclear power may already pose environmental hazards. People living near a nuclear plant may be routinely exposed to radiation, and workers in the plant may receive higher, more dangerous doses of radioactivity.

Causes of Environmental Problems

Polluting our environment and depleting its resources may amount to a slow form of suicide. Sometimes the cause is ignorance; sometimes it is poverty. In many developing nations, rivers and streams are polluted by human wastes. Poor people desperate for fuel in developing countries have stripped mountainsides of trees, clearing the way for massive erosion. Overgrazing is expanding the deserts of Africa.

Neither ignorance nor poverty, however, can explain much of the environmental damage now being done around the world. One source of the problem is the fact that clean air, clean rivers, and other environmental resources are public, not private, goods. In Aristotle's words, "What is common to the greatest number gets the least amount of care." Garrett Hardin (1980) has used a parable called the "Tragedy of the Commons" to illustrate why this is so, and how damage to the environment results. Suppose you are raising sheep, and you and your neighbors share a commons, a common piece of land for grazing. To increase your income, you want to raise more sheep and graze them on the commons. If you do, you may damage the commons by overgrazing, but you will gain the entire benefit of raising additional sheep, and share only part of the cost of the damage done to the commons. So you add another sheep to your herd, and then perhaps another. Everyone else using the commons makes the same calculation, however, and in their own self-interests, add to their herds. Eventually, overgrazing is severe enough to destroy the commons.

Without government intervention, the physical environment is much like this grazing commons. Individuals gain by using, even polluting, it, but society as a whole bears the cost of the damage. When people act on the basis of their individual self-interests, they end up degrading the environment. Hardin has put the case far more dramatically: "Ruin is the destination toward which all men rush, each pursuing his own best interests in a society that believes in the freedom of the commons. Freedom in a commons brings ruin to all."

The environmental destruction wrought by industrialized nations, however, also has more specific causes. One is the Western attitude toward nature. It is different from traditional non-Western attitudes. Non-Western religions, for example, consider nature the equal or even the superior of humanity. Animals, trees, mountains, streams, and other parts of nature are respected or even worshipped. To tamper with them is to risk terrible consequences. Eastern philosophies typically portray humans as an integral part of nature and urge people to live in harmony with the natural world. In contrast, Western culture justifies the exploitation of nature and views humans as nature's masters. In Western religions, humans are believed to have been created in God's own image, hence a special creation set apart from and above nature. People are therefore encouraged to subdue and use nature for their own benefit.

The exploitative attitude toward nature freed America's settlers to cut across and "conquer" the continent. Considering the white settler, Chief Luther Standing Bear mused, "One portion of the land is the same to him as the next, for he is a stranger who comes in the night and takes whatever he needs. The earth is not his brother but his enemy, and when he conquers it he moves on" (Hayden, 1980). This attitude toward nature also provided the soil in which science and modern technology grew (see Chapter 19: Science and Technology), and they in turn have vastly increased our impact on the environment. The impact derives partly from the power of today's technology, and partly from the types of technology we have chosen to develop. We have forged ahead to unleash the awesome power of the atom, and thereby created hazards of radiation, but we have not yet been able to harness the energy of the sun for efficient large-scale use. With today's strip-mining machinery, more than 200 cubic yards of earth can be hauled away in one scoop, but we have not developed methods to ensure protection against soil erosion.

Modern technology has also increased our impact on the environment indirectly, by spurring increased wealth and increased consumption. An American living in a private home with electricity generated by nuclear power and a furnace heated with natural gas, with an automobile guzzling gasoline and a lawn fertilized with chemicals, eating food packaged in plastic and transported hundreds of miles, has far more impact on the environment than a poor Indian farmer in the Andes. By one estimate, each American uses more resources than 14 people in a developing country (Ehrlich, 1984).

These effects of our exploitative attitude toward nature are compounded by the definition of progress as growth in material wealth. We tend to measure one another's worth in terms of how much we are capable of acquiring: the more wealth we have, the higher our social status. Modern societies, whether they are capitalist or communist, relentlessly pursue economic growth (Jones, 1987).

Wealth and technology, however, are not always the environment's destroyers. As a nation develops economically, it gains more leeway to divert money from sustenance to improvement and protection of the environment. As it advances technologically, it can devise new ways to correct environmental problems, such as improved methods of treating sewage. In fact, some people argue that economic growth and technological progress can eventually solve our environmental problems. As Malthus was wrong, they argue, so today's doomsayers are wrong. The problems technology has created, technology can solve. To stimulate technology, economic growth should be encouraged (Simon, 1982). There may be some truth in this argument. But nature *is* limited. To date, the most obvious effects of economic growth and modern technology have been increased pressure on the environment.

Environmental Policies

During the 1970s the federal and state governments in this country took many steps to bring environmental problems under control. The main approaches to these problems include antipollution laws, conservation, alternative technologies, and limitations on economic and population growth. Some of these approaches have worked because the governments have been able to anticipate how disastrous the consequences would be if the environmental problems were ignored (see box, p. 546).

Antipollution laws have attracted the most attention. Industry resisted them because of their expense. Unions sometimes opposed them because they feared jobs would be lost as a result of the cost to industry. Some consumers objected to these laws because they feared prices would rise too high once industry was forced to reduce pollution. State governments were often reluctant to make or enforce their own pollution-control laws for fear that companies would move their business elsewhere.

Despite all these concerns, laws regulating air and water pollution, pesticide use, and the disposal of hazardous wastes were passed during the late 1960s and 1970s, and they now enjoy wide public support (Ladd, 1982). The laws are often flouted and poorly enforced, but they have had some success. The carbon monoxide levels in eight major cities declined 46 percent from 1972 to 1976 (Kelman, 1978). Emissions of lead into the atmosphere were cut by more than 60 percent from 1971 to 1981 (Barringer, 1981). In the early 1980s the Reagan administration relaxed antipollution standards, which it considered too costly for industry to meet. But in 1983, when William Ruckelshaus took over leadership of the Environmental Protection Agency (EPA), the quality of the environment began to improve significantly. Nevertheless, the administration still held EPA's budget and staff at insufficient levels. Therefore, environmental monitoring and research have been inadequate (Sun, 1984). Interestingly, since the Reagan administration has been widely perceived as antienvironment, many environmental groups such as the Sierra Club and the Environmental Defense Fund have attracted a lot of new members, which has added significantly to their political clout. Consequently, they have been able to lobby Congress into passing proenvironment legislation even in the face of veto threats by the president. Quite often the president was forced to drop his veto threats, as he did in 1986 when he signed the $9 billion superfund bill passed by well over the vetoproof two-thirds majority. The bill was designed to clean up the nation's worst hazardous waste sites (Rheem, 1986).

Conservation provides a second method of reducing our impact on the environment. During the late 1970s the federal and state governments took many steps to encourage the conservation of energy. People were urged to insulate their homes, turn down the thermostat in cold months, drive smaller cars at lower speeds, and ride buses and trains. The government began to offer tax credits and direct subsidies to encourage energy conservation. Americans were reminded that most European countries use far less energy than the United States while maintaining a high standard of living. Conservation efforts combined with rising energy prices and economic recession to produce a drop in Americans' energy use from 1979 to 1982 that was greater than experts had thought possible. Recycling provided another means of conserving energy and raw materials, and of combating pollution.

A third approach to environmental problems focuses on the development of new technology that is efficient, safe, and clean. Changes in automobiles illustrate this approach. Since the early 1970s, their fuel efficiency has been increased, while their polluting emissions have been reduced. These improvements represent only a small part of what might be done to improve the efficiency of transportation and reduce its damage to the environment. Less reliance on automobiles and increased use of railroads, subways, buses, and even bikes would conserve resources and reduce pollution. If we developed the technology to allow the large-scale substitution of solar, water, wind, and other renewable sources of energy for coal, gas, and nuclear power, then we could be much more optimistic about our future.

A fourth way of solving environmental problems is to limit both population growth and economic growth. If growth continues at the present rate, in a hundred years or less we will deplete natural resources and pollute the environment so much that massive numbers of people will die (Barney et al., 1982). Some people have proposed drastic methods to limit population growth—such as adding a birth control chemical to the water supply. But in the real world, as we noted, many nations are eagerly pursuing economic growth, and efforts to control population barely make a dent in the problem. In the United States, we have kept down our population growth, but our economic growth has remained high, posing a threat to our environment. Research has shown that the more highly industrialized areas have higher levels of environmental pollution, which, in turn, are associated with higher rates of cancer and other diseases (Greenberg, 1983, 1984).

QUESTIONS FOR DISCUSSION AND REVIEW

1. What major environmental problems now challenge the ecosystems of modern industrial societies?
2. Why can't technology solve all the problems of diminishing resources and environmental pollution?
3. How does the "Tragedy of the Commons" help explain environmental destruction and an exploitive attitude toward nature?
4. Which environmental policies might work best to bring environmental destruction under control?

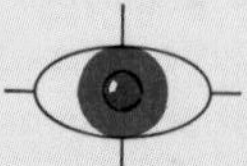

USING SOCIOLOGICAL INSIGHT

Social Adaptations to the Future

Many people feel pessimistic about humankind's ability to save the world's environment. Others, though, conclude that humans can change their behavior and reverse the deterioration of the air and water. Among the latter is the famous biologist Rene Dubos, who argues that humans have the unique capacity to anticipate the future and change their behavior accordingly. Is this human capacity enough to solve the problems discussed in this chapter?

We adapt to heat, cold, crowding, poverty and other environmental and social conditions when we experience these conditions and minimize their effects by appropriate changes in our physiological mechanisms and our ways of life. The phrase "social adaptations *to the future*" therefore sounds nonsensical since societies have not experienced the conditions, largely unpredictable, to which they will have to adapt in years to come. However, human societies can adapt to the future, even a distant one, by *anticipating* the probable effects of situations they are likely to encounter in times to come, and by taking in advance adequate measures in the light of these anticipations.

Until our times, most important changes took the world by surprise. Consequently there was no possibility of affecting their occurrence and it was difficult to control their manifestations. Now, in contrast, the possible effects of technological and social innovations are discussed long before they become manifest, especially if they are likely to be dangerous. We try to imagine the "future shocks" that humankind will experience when its ways of life and its environments are altered, at some undetermined time in the future. Anticipation has of course always influenced human activities, but it is only during recent decades that a significant number of important anticipations can be based on a wide range of reliable information and at times on precise scientific knowledge.

Anticipating the likely consequences of natural processes and of human activities is quite different from predicting the future. The future cannot be predicted for two different reasons. One is that prediction would require complete knowledge of the past as well as of the present, which is impossible. The other is that human beings practically always impose a pattern of their own choice on the natural course of events. There is a "willed" future that is first imagined and decided in human minds and that comes into being only through systematic planning and efforts. The optimists, among whom I try to be, are those who believe that the willed future based on humanistic values can be successfully integrated with the effects of natural forces and with the social structures emerging from scientific technology. The following examples illustrate that the willed future is bringing about, in many situations, desirable changes which are based on effects and events that have not

CHAPTER REVIEW

1. *How fast are populations around the world growing?* Overall, global population is growing by about 1.7 percent a year, which means it should double in about 40 years. Most of this growth, however, is occurring in poor, nonindustrialized countries. *What elements determine a nation's growth rate?* It is the birth rate plus the net immigration rate minus the death rate.

2. *Are there population characteristics that contribute to the variations in demographic processes?* Yes. The sex ratio, marriage rate, and age structure are among the most significant. If there are many young people in the population, for example, future birth rates are likely to be high.

3. *What social factors hold down birth rates?* Access to effective birth control methods, substitution of nuclear for extended families, industrialization, movement of women into the labor force, and a preference for small families are all significant factors. *What social factors lower death rates?* The availability of modern medicine, high living standards, and healthful ways of living have an important influence. *What motivates migrations?* The

yet occurred. In other words, social adaptations to the future are taking place now.

The North American continent has never had a high population density but it might have become overpopulated if the high birth rates of the past continued for a few more decades. The writing of demographers created a widespread awareness of the threats to the quality of life posed by uncontrolled population growth. Thus, while there is still much empty space and unused resources in the United States and Canada, the anticipation that North America could become overpopulated in the *next century* has significantly contributed to the decrease in average family size. Birth rates are now so low in many social groups that the North American continent may achieve Zero Population Growth some time next century.

Ever since the beginning of the Industrial Revolution and until the late 1950s, London was the most polluted large city of the Western world. As a result of the control measures taken by the London City Council under the Clean Air and Clean Water Act of 1957, the annual amount of sunshine over London has now increased by some fifty percent, there has not been a single case of "pea soup" smog during the past ten years, the songbirds mentioned in Shakespeare can once more be heard in the city parks, and salmon—that most fastidious of fish—has returned to the Thames. In New York City, Jamaica Bay used to be grossly polluted with garbage and sewage, but thanks to a variety of antipollution measures it is now in such good condition that fin fish and shellfish, including oysters, are sufficiently abundant to support a fishing industry. Furthermore, the bay has become a rich bird sanctuary and a most attractive part of the Gateway National Recreation Area.

The ability to anticipate long-range consequences does not mean that modern societies will necessarily be able or willing to act early and vigorously enough to prevent deleterious effects. Pessimists have good reason to believe that someday, somewhere, a social or technological innovation will be carried so far so fast that it will cause irreversible damage to the human species or to global ecology. However, while a catastrophe following overshoot cannot be ruled out, there is reason for hope in the wonderful resiliency of human beings. Advances in knowledge will facilitate anticipating the long-range consequences of technological and social innovations and may thus enable us to overcome the myth of inevitability.

Source: Adapted from René Dubos, *Celebrations of Life,* New York: McGraw-Hill, Inc., 1981, pp. 145–151. Reprinted by permission of The René Dubos Center for Human Environments, Inc.

"push" of deprivation and oppression and the "pull" of opportunity and freedom elsewhere are often the key motive.

4. *What are two prominent theories regarding population patterns?* Malthusian and demographic transition theories. According to Malthus, human populations tend to grow faster than food supplies. As a population outstrips its supply of food, it is afflicted by war, disease, poverty, and even famine, which eventually stop population growth. Malthus's predictions have been derailed by contraceptive, technological, and medical revolutions. According to the theory of demographic transition, human populations go through specific stages, which are tied to economic development.

5. *How does population growth affect poor countries?* It tends to perpetuate poverty or retard economic progress. *Is population growth a problem for industrialized countries?* Yes, even moderate population growth can cause environmental problems.

6. *How can governments control population growth?* By encouraging voluntary family planning and setting up

compulsory population programs. But family planning programs work only if people prefer to have small families, and compulsory programs may meet stiff opposition. Both Singapore and China, however, have reduced birth rates through basically compulsory programs that combine rewards for small families and punishments for large families. *Does the U.S. government control population growth?* No, but it does give some aid to family planning centers. Social and economic factors, not government action, keep birth rates low.

7. *Why are sociologists interested in ecology?* Humans, like other organisms, live within ecosystems, dependent on other organisms and on the physical environment. Thus we are limited by two ecological principles. One, natural resources are finite. Two, if we alter one aspect of our environment, we end up changing others as well. *What are our basic environmental problems?* The depletion of natural resources and pollution. *How is pollution related to consumption?* To consume we must produce, and both production and consumption create waste materials that must go somewhere. When our creation of wastes exceeds nature's capacity to recycle the material, pollution results. *What are the main causes of environmental problems?* Poverty, ignorance, and overconsumption and pollution are among the causes. In industrialized societies the tendency to despoil the environment has been increased by an exploitative attitude toward nature and by an emphasis on material wealth as the chief indicator of human progress. *What are the main methods of dealing with environmental problems?* Antipollution laws, conservation, development of more efficient, less polluting technology, and a slowing of economic and population growth.

KEY TERMS

Age structure The pattern of the proportions of different age groups within a population (p. 528).

Biosphere A thin film of air, water, and soil surrounding the earth (p. 540).

Birth rate The number of births for every 1000 people in a given year (p. 525).

Census A periodic head count of the entire population of a country (p. 524).

Death rate The number of deaths for every 1000 people in a given year (p. 526).

Demographic process An aspect of a population that is always changing, such as the birth rate, death rate, or net migration rate (p. 525).

Demographic transition The process of going through various stages of population change, with each stage being determined by a certain level of economic development (p. 531).

Demography The scientific study of population (p. 524).

Ecology The study of the interrelationships among organisms and between organisms and their environment (p. 540).

Ecosystem A self-sufficient community of organisms depending for survival on one another and on the environment (p. 540).

Fecundity The number of babies that the average woman has the biological capacity to bear (p. 529).

Fertility The actual number of babies born to the average woman of childbearing age (p. 529).

Infant mortality rate The number of deaths among infants less than one year old for every 1000 live births (p. 527).

Life expectancy The average number of years that a group of people can expect to live (p. 527).

Marriage rate The number of marriages for every 1000 people in a given year (p. 528).

Sex ratio The number of males per 100 females (p. 528).

Vital statistics Data about births, marriages, deaths, and migrations into and out of a country (p. 524).

SUGGESTED READINGS

Gray, David B., Richard J. Borden, and Russell H. Weigel. 1985. *Ecological Beliefs and Behaviors: Assessments and Change.* Westport, Conn.: Greenwood. An analysis of social research on ecological beliefs and behaviors, with advice on how to use such research to promote proenvironment attitudes and actions.

Guttentag, Marcia, and Paul F. Secord. 1983. *Too Many Women? The Sex Ratio Question.* Beverly Hills, Calif.: Sage. An interesting, provocative analysis of how the sex ratio affects such social phenomena as marriage, divorce, work, childbearing practices, and family stability.

Keyfitz, Nathan. 1982. *Population Change and Social Policy*. Cambridge, Mass.: Abt Books. A highly useful collection of articles by a renowned demographer, dealing with population theory, methods and data of demography, and such policy issues as social security and birth control.

Simon, Julian L. 1981. *The Ultimate Resource*. Princeton, N.J.: Princeton University Press. Presents the controversial argument that resources are limitless because of human beings' technological ingenuity.

Wattenberg, Ben J. 1987. *The Birth Dearth*. New York: Pharos Books. A highly provocative, controversial speculation on the disastrous social, cultural, economic, and military consequences of population decline.

22 Urbanization and City Life

Many people believe that a city is an unpleasant place to live in because it is too crowded, too noisy, too impersonal, and too stressful. Therefore, they conclude, the urban environment harms the people who live there, by producing both social and psychological disorders such as high rates of crime and mental illness. Such a view was expressed in the 1930s in sociologist Louis Wirth's urban anomie theory. Today, many sociologists reject this theory. Some—the compositional theorists—argue that the city does not make much difference to people's lives. They maintain that city dwellers' social lives, as they are centered in small groups of neighbors, relatives, and friends, are much like those of people living in small towns. Other sociologists—the subcultural theorists—contend that the city enriches people's lives by creating various subcultures and diverse opportunities. In fact, these three theories are equally convincing, but each captures only a slice of city life. Crime rates are indeed higher in cities than in small towns, as urban anomie theory suggests. Most people, however, do lead a normal, pleasant life in the city, as the other two theories imply.

One of the powerful social forces that can change the face of a society is **urbanization.** It involves the migration of people from the countryside to cities, increasing the proportion of a population that lives in cities. Throughout history most human beings lived in small isolated groups, but only about a hundred years ago urbanization began to transform many societies. Today, most people in the industrialized world, and an increasing number in the developing nations, live in urban areas.

The influence of urbanization goes beyond the cities to touch all of society. In this chapter we discuss how urbanization occurred and how it has affected society, as well as what lies ahead for American cities.

STAGES OF URBANIZATION

In 1693 William Penn wrote that "the country life is to be preferred for there we see the works of God, but in cities little else than the work of man." Most people at the time probably agreed with him. Less than 2 percent of the world's population were urban dwellers. By 1900, however, Great Britain had become the first predominantly urban society. By 1920 the United States had followed suit. Since then, urbanization around the world has been occurring at an increasingly rapid pace. Today about 39 percent of the world's population lives in urban areas, and more than 50 percent will do so by the end of the century (Fischer, 1984).

While urban populations have grown, the cities themselves have changed. We can identify three periods in their history: the preindustrial, industrial, and metropolitan-megalopolitan stages.

The Preindustrial City

For more than 99 percent of the time since human beings appeared on earth, our ancestors roamed about in search of food. They were able to hunt, fish, and gather edible plants, but they could never find enough food in one place to sustain them for very long. They had to move on, traveling in small bands from one place to another.

Then, about 10,000 years ago, technological advances allowed people to stop their wandering. This was the dawn of what is called the Neolithic period. People now had the simple tools and the know-how to cultivate plants and domesticate animals. They could produce their food supplies in one locale, and they settled down and built villages. The villages were very small—only about 200 to 400 residents each. For the next 5000 years villagers produced just enough food to feed themselves.

By about 5000 years ago humans had developed more powerful technologies. Thanks to innovations like the ox-drawn plow, irrigation, and metallurgy, farmers could produce more food than they needed to sustain themselves and their families. Because of this food surplus, some people abandoned agriculture and made their living by weaving, pottery, and other specialized crafts. Methods of transporting and storing food were also improved. The result was the emergence of cities (Childe, 1952).

Cities first arose on the fertile banks of such rivers as the Nile of Egypt, the Euphrates and Tigris in the Middle East, the Indus in Pakistan, and the Yellow River in China. Similar urban settlements later appeared in other parts of the world. These preindustrial cities were very small compared with the cities of today. Most had populations of 5000 to 10,000 people. Only a very few cities had more than 100,000 people, and even Rome never had more than several hundred thousand.

Several factors prevented expansion of the preindustrial city. By modern standards, agricultural techniques were still very primitive. It took at least 75 farmers to produce enough of a surplus to support just one city dweller. For transportation, people had to depend on their own muscle power or that of animals. It was difficult to carry food supplies from farms to cities, and even more difficult to transport heavy materials for construction in the cities. Poor sanitation, lack of sewer facilities, and ineffective medicine kept death rates high. Epidemics regularly killed as much as half of a city's population. Moreover, families still had a strong attachment to the land, which discouraged immigration to the cities. All these characteristics of preindustrial society kept the cities small (Davis, 1955).

Preindustrial cities differed in other ways from their larger counterparts today. First, their role in society was different. The countryside, not the city, was the dominant social and cultural force. City people still lived like farmers, in the shadow of extended family and large kinship networks. Second, living patterns in the preindustrial city were strikingly different from those typical of modern cities. The commercial district and residential areas were not segregated as they tend to be today. Artisans and traders worked at home. But other types of segregation were very marked. People with different crafts or trades lived in different sections of the city. Blacksmiths made their living and their homes in one quarter; tailors in another. Each occupational group had its own quarter. In most cases these areas were walled off from one another, with their gates locked at night. People were further segregated into classes or castes, with little or no opportunity for social mobility. Residents were geographically separated into ethnic or religious groups, with little or no interaction with one another (Sjoberg, 1966).

The Industrial City

For almost 5000 years the nature of the cities changed little. Then their growth, in size and number, was so rapid it has been called an urban revolution or urban explosion. In 1700 less than 2 percent of the population in Great Britain lived in cities, but by 1900 the majority of the British did so. Other European countries and the United States soon achieved the same level of urbanization even in a shorter period.

The major stimulus to this urban explosion was the Industrial Revolution. It triggered a series of related events which sociologist Philip Hauser (1981) has termed a population explosion, population implosion, population displosion, and technoplosion. Industrialization is at first accompanied by a rise in production growth, and the mechanization of agriculture brings about a farm surplus. Fewer farmers can support more people—and thus larger urban populations. Workers no longer needed on the farms move to the city. There is, then, displacement of people from rural to urban areas *(population displosion)* and a greater concentration of people in a limited area *(population implosion)*. The development of other new technologies (a *technoplosion*) spurs urbanization on. Improved transportation, for example, speeds the movement of food and other materials to urban centers.

The outcome of these events was the industrial city. Compared with the preindustrial city, the industrial city was larger, more densely settled, and more diverse. It was a place where large numbers of people—with different skills, interests, and cultural backgrounds—could live and work together in a limited space. Also unlike the preindustrial city, which had served primarily as a religious or governmental center, the industrial city was a commercial hub. In fact, its abundant job opportunities attracted so many rural migrants that migration accounted for the largest share of its population growth. Without these migrants, the city would not have grown at all, because of its high mortality rate brought about by extremely poor sanitary conditions.

The quick pace of urbanization can be seen in U.S. history. In 1790 only 5 percent of Americans lived in urban areas. In 1860, when industrialization was confined largely to the northeast coast, only about 20 percent did so. But by 1920 more than half of the population was urban. Today, urban areas take up only about 1.5 percent of the nation's land area, but about 75 percent of the population lives in them. By specializing in finance, the oil industry, or some other sector of the world economy, New York, Houston, and other American cities exert a powerful influence on the world. As global cities, they attract foreign migrant labor, engage in international commerce, and search out raw materials and markets in all parts of the world (Rodriguez and Feagin, 1986).

Urbanization of the developing nations of Africa, Asia, and Latin America has been even more dramatic. Between 1950 and 1960 the proportion of their population living in cities rose twice as fast as in the industrialized countries. From 1960 to 1984 the population of Calcutta increased from 6 to 10 million, and Mexico City's population rose from 5 million to 17 million. Efforts to industrialize rapidly have helped produce what might be called premature urbanization or overurbanization in the third world. This is made possible by state policies on investment, pricing, and taxation that encourage economic development in urban areas. The resulting higher standard of living in the city draws migrants from poorer, rural areas. In addition, American and other foreign corporations, seeking cheap labor, invest heavily in urban manufacturing, which creates jobs that lure rural workers to the city (Bradshaw, 1987). Much of the urban growth, however, comes not entirely from migration to the city, but also to a large extent from high birth rates coupled with declining death rates. As a result, their cities are growing faster than the supply of jobs and housing. Makeshift squatters' settlements have proliferated in the cities. In India's largest city, Calcutta, most of the residents live in slums, and it is common to see other people—600,000 of

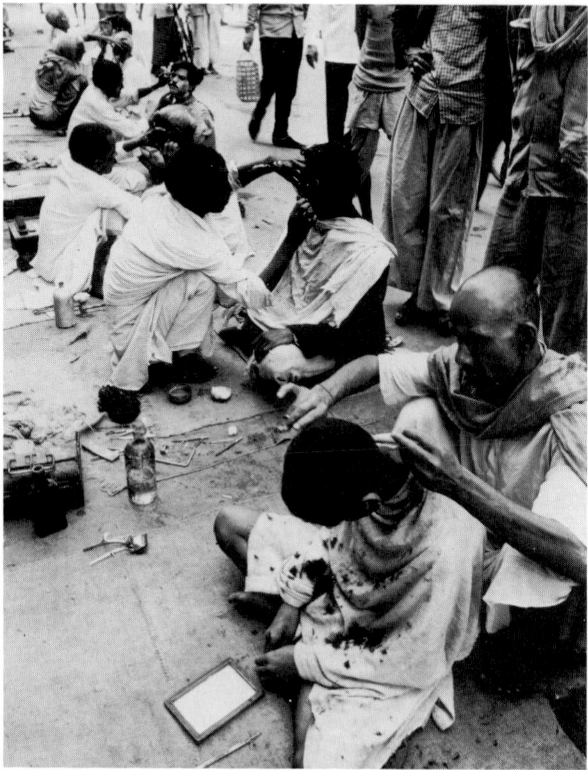

Barbers at work on a street in Benares, India. The population in third-world cities often grows at a phenomenal rate. Much of the urban growth comes from the migration of villagers to the city, coupled with high birth rates and declining death rates. As a result, the city cannot physically accommodate the people who live there. The shortage of space has forced many people to work, and even to live, on the streets.

them—living on the streets. Yet Calcutta continues to grow at an explosive rate (Davis, 1974; Barney et al., 1982; Friedrich, 1984).

Metropolis and Megalopolis

Early in this century the large cities of the industrialized nations began to spread outward. They formed **metropolises,** large urban areas that include a city and its surrounding suburbs. Some of these suburbs are politically separate from their central cities, but socially, economically, and geographically, the suburbs and city are tied together. The U.S. Census Bureau recognizes this unity by defining what is called a *Standard Metropolitan Statistical Area,* which cuts across political boundaries.

In the United States the upper and middle classes usually sparked this expansion of cities outward. As migrants from rural areas moved into the central city, the better-off classes moved to the surrounding suburbs. The automobile greatly facilitated this development. It encouraged people to leave the crowded inner city for the more comfortable life of the suburbs, if they could afford it. As the number of cars increased, so did the size of suburbs and metropolises. (See box, p. 555, for a similar situation in fast-growing Mexico City, where cars are now so many that they cause 70 percent of the metropolis's air pollution.) In 1900 there were only 8000 cars in the United States, but by 1930 the number had soared to more than 26 million. Meanwhile the percentage of Americans living in the suburbs grew from only 15.7 percent in 1910 to 48.6 percent in 1950 (Glaab and Brown, 1983).

Since 1950 virtually all the growth in metropolitan areas has occurred in the suburbs. During the 1960s American suburbs grew four times faster than inner cities, and stores and entertainment facilities followed the people there. Suburban jobs increased 44 percent, while inner city employment dropped 7 percent. Suburbanites now outnumber city residents three to two. Traditional sociologists have attributed this suburban growth to transport technology. But Marxists explain it as the result of capitalists moving their factories to suburban areas—in order to avoid labor unrest in central cities, high city taxes, or other financial costs (Jaret, 1983; Gottdiener, 1983).

As the suburbs expanded, they merged with the suburbs of adjacent metropolitan areas, creating a vast urban complex called a **megalopolis.** For hundreds of miles from one major city to the next, suburbs and cities have merged with one another to form a continuous region in which distinctions between suburban, urban, and rural areas are blurred. The hundreds of miles from Boston to Washington, D.C. form one such megalopolis, another stretches from Detroit through Chicago to Milwaukee in the Midwest, and another goes from San Francisco to San Diego.

Demographics of American Cities What kinds of people live in these urban areas? In general, the poor and minority groups concentrate in the inner cities while more affluent people live in the suburbs. A closer look, however, led sociologist Herbert Gans (1968) to find five types of people in many central cities:

UNDERSTANDING OTHER SOCIETIES

Mexico City: An Alarming Giant

The rapid growth of metropolises in developing countries continues, creating a host of social problems. As population explodes and massive movements of people from rural areas to cities continue, feeding, housing, and employing millions of new people become increasingly difficult. We can get a sense of the seriousness of these problems from the following account of life in Mexico City, Mexico. What steps should countries like Mexico take to control these patterns of large-scale, destructive growth?

Whatever you have heard about Mexico City—good or bad—may well be true. It is, or soon will become, the world's largest city, growing tumorously from some 16 million now toward 30 million inhabitants by the end of the century.

One demographer jokes, "Our optimists count on an earthquake or the atom bomb."

I am not that kind of an optimist. As an old and worried friend of Mexico City, I have lately examined the worst deformities of its slums—lost cities, as they're called—and sampled its enduring pleasures in streetside restaurants, markets, and museums. Most of all, I have talked to all kinds of *chilangos,* as residents of the capital are often called. From them I perceive the one fact that confirms both optimism and pessimism: This city is still very Mexican. And if Mexicans seem short on self-restraint, they are brilliant at improvising.

Mexicans are gregarious and warm-blooded. Thus they have a scary national birthrate—34 per thousand population in 1980 (more than twice that of the U.S.). It is estimated that in the capital 30 percent of the families sleep in a single room—and those families average five people. Aside from Roman Catholic tradition, numerous children prove a man's machismo and a woman's fertility. "But children are also an investment for old age," a student told me.

Recent trends suggest significant change. "Mexico's family-planning program is a model for the Third World," an international expert asserts. Nationwide, population growth is slowing, from 3.5 percent in 1970 to 2.4 in 1982.

If large families bring large problems, they also furnish some solutions. Relatives take care of each other, and in a land lacking unemployment insurance, this is a fact of survival.

But the very population density—along with a Mexican sense of neighborhood and a year-round outdoor climate—provides another service, creating the condition that urbanist Jane Jacobs calls "eyes on the street."

Sidewalks are alive and noisy with vendors selling tacos and lottery tickets, children at play, gossipy nursemaids and loiterers, and shops with open doors. Day or night, little escapes notice on Mexico City's informally self-patrolled streets. Sometimes a *ratero,* or pickpocket, does his light-fingered work. But violent crime is rare. I feel safer in the capital of Mexico than in any large U.S. city.

Even so, along with unemployment, some sorts of crime have risen—especially auto thefts, an appropriate felony since greater Mexico City is both shaped and afflicted by the motorcar. (Motor vehicles, for example, cause 70 percent of the air pollution, widely regarded as the world's worst.)

City planners conservatively estimate that half of the city's population lives in irregular housing. "Either the title is faulty or construction does not comply with the code—*something* is wrong," notes one planner. Although city records are being computerized, land tenure is the major problem of urban development here. "No one puts his best effort into a house if his ownership is insecure." Scientific city planning in Mexico City dates only from 1980.

I recall a dismal community of shacks at the bottom of a 500-foot ravine. Living there were 87 families, some with as many as 14 children. By stairsteps carved into the clay, I descended their hill in the dry season, marveling that anyone could manage that slope carrying bundles and babies in the rain.

Once there, I talked with the residents. "We used to live up there," Señora Rebeca González gestured toward some mountaintop sand quarries, "in those caves. Our only hope was one day to have a place to live. And now we do!" She smiled with pride at the jerry-built shacks. They stood in neat rows, I had to admit, and each one had a collection of flowers planted in tin cups. "One day, we hope to extend the water pipes and drainage—perhaps even pave . . ."

And what was the name of her community? Señora González beamed: "Esperanza!" The name means hope.

Source: Excerpted from Bart McDowell, "Mexico City: An alarming giant," *National Geographic,* August 1984, pp. 139–172.

1. Cosmopolites—artists, intellectuals, professionals
2. Unmarried individuals and childless couples
3. "Ethnic villagers"—immigrants from other countries
4. The deprived—the poor, blacks, other minorities
5. The trapped—poor elderly people

These groups are not likely to feel strong ties to each other or to the city as a whole. The deprived and the trapped are too poor to move—they live in the city by necessity, not choice. The ethnic villagers are likely to be strongly tied only to fellow immigrants in their neighborhoods. The unmarried and childless have ties mostly to those who share their life-style. Cosmopolites associate primarily with those who share their interests.

The movement of blacks into the central city has been especially striking. Just 45 years ago less than half of the black population was urban. By 1982, 76 percent of black Americans lived in urban areas, and most of these in the inner cities. For years blacks entering the city had come from the rural South, but today most black migrants come form other urban areas. Compared with the inner-city natives, they rank higher in education and employment, and have lower rates of crime. Some middle-class blacks have joined the exodus to the suburbs, but they move mostly to black suburbs. Thus the different black and white migration patterns reinforce segregation. In 1982 blacks made up only 6 percent of suburban dwellers but 24 percent of central-city residents. Several large cities are now predominantly black, and one out of three black Americans lives in just 15 central cities (Pettigrew, 1981; Logan and Schneider, 1984).

Workers renovating an old building in Boston. Cities resemble living organisms that grow and change. Just as a person can get sick and recover, some neighborhoods decline and then experience a revival. The process of restoring a rundown area is called *gentrification* if poor people move out and affluent people (the "gentry") move in.

A Postindustrial City? Since 1970 the exodus to suburbia has slowed. Before 1970 the suburban population grew by an average of 2.4 percent a year, but since then it has increased by only 1.3 percent (Census Bureau, 1987). Meanwhile, the number of cosmopolites, young professionals, adult singles, and childless couples in the inner city has grown significantly. Increasing numbers of these affluent people now choose to remain in the inner city. They buy run-down buildings and renovate them into elegant townhouses and expensive condominiums. This urban revival, called **gentrification,** has transformed slums into such stylish enclaves as Capitol Hill in Washington, Philadelphia's Queen Village, Boston's South End, Cincinnati's Mount Adams, and Chicago's New Town. To a large extent, urban rehabilitation programs have stimulated gentrification. They have turned over abandoned homes and stores for the price of a few dollars and offered low-interest mortgage loans. Ironically, though, gentrification tends to drive up rents and property taxes; forcing poor and elderly residents to give up their homes to the well-off gentrifiers. Every year as many as 2 million people are displaced (Smith, 1982). However, gentrification has not been extensive enough to transform most of the city. In the last decade nearly twice as many people have been moving from central cities to suburbs as those moving in the opposite direction. Central cities continue to lose residents, a trend that began in the early 1970s (Tobin and Judd, 1982; Census Bureau, 1988).

Most suburbs still offer better schools, more living space, less pollution, and less crime than the central city, so that people continue to "vote with their feet," heading for suburbia. Especially in recent years, there has emerged a "second suburban migration" from the cities—involving not only people and homes but offices and jobs. The proportion of all new office construction that took place in the suburbs jumped from 46 percent in 1980 to 66 percent in 1985. Even more new office build-

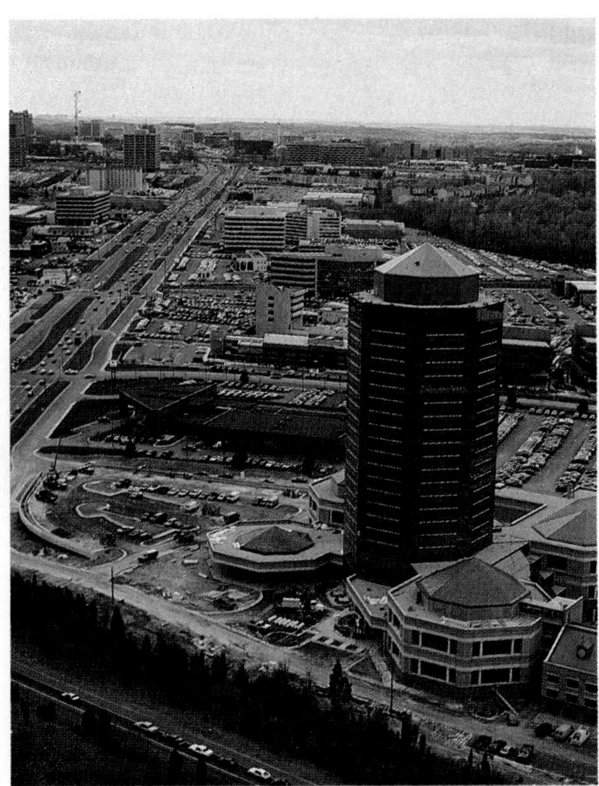

Sprawling office development at Tyson Corner, Virginia, near Arlington. For decades many people have moved from the city to a suburb to live while continuing to work in the city. In recent years, however, there has emerged a "second suburban migration"—huge numbers of urbanites moving to the suburbs for jobs as well as places to live. As a result, many suburbs have developed problems once considered "urban," such as traffic jams and noise, air and water pollution, and crime.

ings are expected to be built in the suburbs in the next few years. Developers have already created vast clusters of big buildings, people, and cars (Dentzer, 1986). But many suburbs have developed problems once considered "urban," such as congestion, pollution, and crime. Rapid, unregulated growth has created some of these problems. When industry and stores moved to the suburbs to be near people's homes, they often brought with them traffic jams and noise, air pollution and water pollution, not to mention landscape "pollution." Suffering through traffic snarls now afflicts many suburban workers, as it does inner-city commuters. "For Pat Widmer," for example, "driving to work in north Dallas can take the determination of General Patton and the patience of a saint. She leaves at about 7:30 a.m. for the drive to her office—a gleaming 16-story high-rise in what once was a sleepy suburb. Cruising at 7 miles per hour on the congested expressway, she passes the wrecks from early morning accidents. The trip takes about 40 minutes" (Dentzer, 1986). Although most of the suburbs are prosperous, an increasing number are not. The Los Angeles suburbs have more poor families than the city, and there is more substandard housing in the suburbs of Pittsburgh than in the city itself. Poor suburbs tend to be predominantly black or Hispanic. Among the ten poorest suburbs, half are mostly black, such as Ford Heights, Illinois (outside Chicago), Kinlock, Missouri (outside St. Louis), and Florida City, Florida (outside Miami). The other five poorest suburbs are predominantly Hispanic, all near Los Angeles, including Cudahy, Bell Gardens, and Coachella (Johnson, 1987).

As suburbs and cities have become more similar, many Americans have looked elsewhere for their homes. During the last decade rural areas and small towns have grown at a much faster rate than before. This is highly significant in view of the steady decline among cities. In fact, some observers have called it "the latest geographic revolution" and "a craze or mass movement" (Bryan, 1982; Campbell and Garkovich, 1984). Since most of this metropolitan depopulation involves workers and consumers seeking good climate, more space, clean air, fewer crimes, and the other pleasant attributes of rural

"It has been moved and seconded that we transfer our headquarters back to the city. All in favor?"

areas and small towns, industries tend to relocate into those places. By providing employment opportunities and a wide range of consumer goods, these industries further attract city folks out of the urban areas (Frey, 1987).

QUESTIONS FOR DISCUSSION AND REVIEW

1. What stages give rise to urbanization, and why has it spread so rapidly in the twentieth century?
2. How does the industrial city differ from the preindustrial city?
3. What forces have led to the development of suburbs, metropolises and, finally, megalopolises?
4. How have the shifts of persons and jobs into and out of the city changed the nature of modern metropolitan areas?

URBAN ECOLOGY

As we observed in the previous chapter, ecologists study the natural world and tell us that everything in it is related to everything else. Organisms affect other organisms and they all affect the environment, which in turn affects them. During the 1920s and 1930s some sociologists at the University of Chicago began to look at the urban world in a similar way. They initiated a new approach to the study of cities called **urban ecology,** the study of the relationship between people and the urban environment. More specifically, the Chicago school of urban ecologists believed that human behavior determines the overall spatial pattern of the urban environment, which in turn has a powerful effect on people.

Spatial Patterns

Like a natural environment, the urban environment is not a random arrangement of elements. If you walk around a city, you will rarely see a mansion next to a slum, or an apartment next to a factory. Different areas tend to be used for different purposes. As a result, the people, activities, and buildings within a city are distributed in a certain pattern. The urban ecologists tried to describe what this pattern is and how it arose. Three prominent theories came out of their efforts: the **concentric zone theory,** the **sector theory,** and the **multiple nuclei theory** (see Figure 22.1).

Concentric Zone Theory In the 1920s Ernest Burgess suggested that a typical industrial city spreads outward from the center, forming a series of concentric zones. Each zone is used for a different purpose. The heart of the city, for example, is the central business district. The innermost zone is occupied by shops, banks, offices, hotels, and government buildings. The next zone is the transition zone, characterized by shabby rooming houses, deteriorating apartments, and high crime rates. The third zone is in better shape. It is made up of working people's homes. Beyond it is a zone that houses mostly middle-class people, and beyond that is the commuters' zone, with large homes and plenty of open space. The rich live here, and commute to the city to work (Burgess, 1967).

Obviously, according to this theory, social class has a lot to do with spatial distribution: the farther a piece of land is from the center of the city, the higher the status of those using it. But land values tend to *drop* with distance from the center of the city. Thus the pattern of land use has a rather perverse result: the poor live on expensive land and the rich on relatively cheap land (Alonso, 1964).

The concentric zone theory describes some American cities fairly well, especially those such as Chicago and St. Louis that grew rapidly early in this century under the stimulus of intense industrialization and the automobile. But many cities do not have concentric zones.

Sector Theory San Francisco and Minneapolis illustrate a pattern described by Henry Hoyt in the late 1930s. He agreed with concentric zone theorists that a city grows outward from the center, and that the center is occupied by the central business district. But, Hoyt said, growth occurs, not in concentric circles, but in wedge-shaped sectors that extend outward from the city. As a result, low-class housing occurs not just close to the business district but in a band extending from the center outward, perhaps to the rim of the city. The key to the extension of a sector is transportation. If, say, warehouses are built along a railroad, they tend to expand along the length of the railroad toward the periphery of the city. Similarly, a retail district might expand along a highway. The poor tend to live along transportation lines near factories, while the rich tend to choose areas that are on the fastest lines of transportation and occupy high ground, safe from floods and offering a beautiful view (Hoyt, 1943).

Figure 22.1 Theories of Cities' Spatial Patterns

On the right is a diagrammatic representation of the three theories about the shapes and locations of various districts within a typical American city.

Source: Reprinted from "The Nature of Cities," by Chauncy D. Harris and Edward L. Ullman, in *Annals of the American Academy of Political and Social Sciences,* Nov. 1945, p. 13.

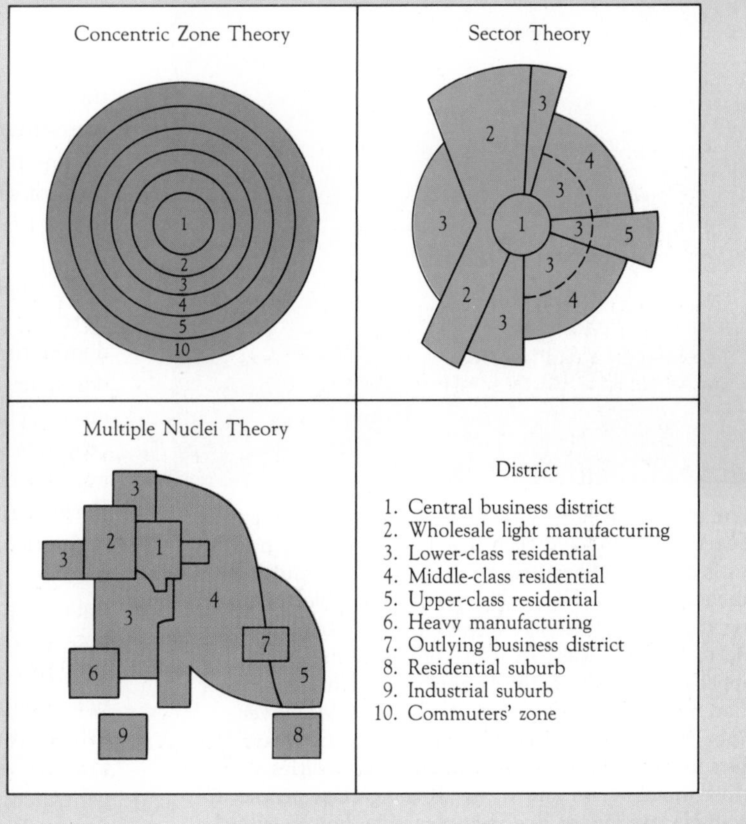

Multiple Nuclei Theory Boston is one of many cities that do not show either wedge-shaped sectors or concentric zones. It seems to be described better by yet a third theory, which was proposed by Chauncy Harris and Edward Ullman in the 1940s. Unlike the concentric and sector theorists, who hold that each city is built around one center, they believe that many cities are built around discrete centers, or nuclei. Each nucleus is the center of specialized activities. There are centers of finance and commerce, which are separate from the political center, which in turn is separate from the center of heavy industries, and so on.

These separate nuclei, according to Harris and Ullman, arise as a result of four factors. First, some activities require specialized facilities. Manufacturing districts must be located on large blocks of land with easy connections to railroads or water transportation, or a port district must be attached to a suitable waterfront. Second, similar activities often profit from being grouped together. If retail stores are concentrated in one district, they all profit from an increased number of potential customers, who are usually attracted by the chance to compare the offerings of various stores. Third, putting dissimilar activities together in one location often harms them. Factories and homes do not mix well. Wholesale districts, which require street loading and rail facilities, stay away from retail districts, which need many pedestrians, cars, and buses. Fourth, people locate certain activities at undesirable sites because they cannot afford the high rents of more desirable places. Bulk wholesaling, for example, requires a lot of space. Renting or buying the necessary space in the central business district would be too expensive (Harris and Ullman, 1945).

These theories are largely valuable for depicting the major patterns of some of our cities such as Chicago, San Francisco, and Boston. But since the theories were based on studies of American cities, they are less applicable to land-use patterns in other countries. Upper-class resi-

The growth of large cities is not entirely random. Three theories have been developed to depict how cities grow: the concentric zone, sector, and multiple-nuclei theories. These theories are valuable for describing the major patterns of our cities but are less applicable to foreign cities. In many other countries, upper-class families, for example, live close to, rather than away from, the center of the city. Moreover, since the theories were developed 40 to 60 years ago, they are less relevant to many American cities today. Most middle-class and white working-class people, for example, no longer live in inner cities but in suburbs.

dences, for example, are close to the center in many cities around the world. Moreover, since the theories were developed some 40 to 60 years ago, they are less accurate in describing many American cities today. Most of the middle and white working classes no longer live in inner cities but in the suburbs. Many factories, office complexes, wholesale and retail trade, and jobs involving people (retail sales, medical services, food service) have also moved out of the urban center (Edmonston and Guterbock, 1984). Contemporary Marxist urbanists further point out that a city's spatial pattern depends significantly on "capitalists' need for a large, cheap, easily controlled labor force and ever increased production" (Jaret, 1983). Thus inner cities were filled with factories and working-class homes in the past because industrialists had found it profitable to operate there. In recent years, however, they have moved many plants out of the urban center because it was more profitable to do so.

The Ecological Processes

How do these spatial patterns come about? Nowadays, city governments often use zoning laws and building codes to determine the patterns of land use and to segregate activities. But many patterns arose without anyone planning them, forming what are called *natural areas* of segregated activities. The urban ecologists believed that two forms of human behavior are most important in shaping the urban environment: dominance and competition. A group of people typically concentrate in a particular area of the city for a specific purpose, dominating that area. Businesses, for example, usually dominate the center of American cities. Sometimes, a group achieves dominance only after competing with others to determine how the land will be used. Businesses and residents often clash over land use in a city. Businesses can usually win by buying out the land at a high price, forcing residents to move. Universities often engage in a similar competition with residents. Thus the use of land in a city is determined directly by *dominance* and indirectly by *competition.*

The city, however, is not static. Instead, over time a new group or type of land use will move into an established area, a process called *invasion.* If the new group forces others out, *succession* has occurred. The process of gentrification discussed earlier is an example: young professionals invade an urban neighborhood, raising land values and rents, and eventually they push out its lower-income residents, who can no longer afford the neighborhood. This reverses the pattern of succession that shaped many American cities. Traditionally, as industries and immigrants moved into American cities, those who were better-off moved out to the suburbs, and their neighborhoods "filtered down" to the lower class. In recent years, however, most of this ecological process has involved blacks moving into inner cities with whites moving out of them (Massey, 1983).

Dominance, competition, invasion, and succession constitute what are called the **ecological processes.** The Chicago school used these, and particularly competition, to explain the spatial patterns they perceived in American cities. As we have seen, however, their theories cannot account fully for the distribution of activities in American cities. Today urban ecologists recognize that they must look beyond the four ecological processes to explain a city's evolution. Dominance and competition, for example, cannot explain why Los Angeles has grown into a huge, smog-filled metropolis. Today's urban ecologists emphasize interdependence more than competition. They argue that the pattern of a modern city depends on a complex of relationships among population, organization, environment, and technology ("POET"). As John Palen (1981) describes it,

> In Los Angeles a favorable natural environment led to large-scale increase in population, which resulted in organizational problems (civic and governmental) and technological changes (freeways and factories). These in turn led to environmental changes (smog), which resulted in organizational changes (new pollution laws), which in turn resulted in technological changes (antipollution devices on automobiles).

The Nature of City Life

In 1964 Americans were horrified by a story that many took as typical of life in New York City—or any large city. A young woman named Catherine Genovese was walking home from work in the early morning hours when she was attacked. Her murderer stabbed her repeatedly for more than half an hour. Thirty-eight neighbors heard her screams or witnessed the attack. But no one helped or even called the police. Most of the neighbors later explained that they did not want to "get involved."

What could cause such cold-bloodedness? Many commentators of the time blamed the city. Living in a city, they believed, changes people for the worse. This charge echoed what some sociologists had long been saying. Louis Wirth, for example, contended in the 1930s that the conditions of the city produce a distinctive way of life, *urbanism,* and that the urban environment harms the people who live there. His analysis represented the ecological approach of the Chicago School. Since Wirth's time, however, many sociologists have rejected this view. Some have argued that the city does not make much difference to people's lives, and others contend that the urban environment enriches people's lives by creating and strengthening subcultures. These three theories about the nature of urban life are called urban anomie theory, compositional theory, and subcultural theory.

Urban Anomie Theory Louis Wirth presented **urban anomie theory** in 1938 in his essay "Urbanism as a Way of Life." According to Wirth, the urban environment has three distinctive features: huge population size, high population density, and great social diversity. These characteristics, Wirth argued, have both a sociological and a psychological impact, producing both social and personality disorders.

Wirth drew on the work of Ferdinand Tönnies (1855–1936) to analyze the sociological impact of the urban environment. As we discussed in Chapter 4 (Social Structure), Tönnies contrasted large industrial societies, which he called *Gesellschaft,* with small rural communities, which he called *Gemeinschaft.* In rural communities, according to Tönnies, people feel bound to each other and relate to each other in a personal way. In industrial societies, people are alienated from one another and their relationships are impersonal. In the country people help their neighbors build a barn. In the city they stand by passively while a neighbor is mugged, or even murdered.

Wirth essentially agreed with Tönnies's analysis and argued that the size, density, and diversity of the city create the alienation that marks industrial societies. In the city people are physically close but socially distant. Every day they encounter strangers. They become accustomed to dealing with people only in terms of their roles. Their relationships tend to be impersonal. In other words, much of their lives are filled not with primary relations with neighbors, who are also relatives and friends, but with secondary relations. Moreover, these people are separated by their diverse religious, ethnic, and racial backgrounds. It is difficult for people in the city to form friendships across these lines or to develop a moral consensus. Under these circumstances people can no longer ensure social order by relying on informal controls such as tradition and gossip. Instead they turn to formal controls, such as the police. Rather than talking to a young troublemaker's parents, they call the police. But formal controls, Wirth argued, are less effective than informal controls, so crimes and other forms of deviance are more frequent in the city than in the countryside.

The size, density, and diversity of the city, according to Wirth, also affect the psychological health of its residents. Drawing on the ideas of Georg Simmel (1858–1918), Wirth argued that because of these characteristics people in the city are bombarded with stimuli. Sights, sounds, and smells assault them virtually every minute of their waking hours. Wherever they turn, they must contend with the actions of others. They are jostled on the street and in the elevator. They wake to the sound of their neighbor's radio and fall asleep despite screaming sirens. Beggars and drunks and crazy people are a common sight. To protect themselves from what Stanley Milgram (1970) called "psychic overload," city people learn to shut out as many sensations as possible—sometimes even the call of a neighbor for help. They deal with the unremitting assault of stimuli by becoming emotionally aloof from one another, concerned only with calculating their own interests. Despite this adaptation, the constant bombardment is still stressful. People become irritable, nervous, anxious. The result, Wirth claimed, is that mental disorders are more common in the city than in rural areas.

Compositional Theory Wirth's description of the urban environment and its effects sounds reasonable. But is it accurate? Many empirical studies of cities have shown that his portrait amounts to an overdrawn stereotype. Some sociologists have therefore proposed a **compositional theory.** They argue that the urban environment does not fundamentally alter how people live their lives, because most urbanites are enmeshed in a network of primary relations with people like themselves.

Perhaps the crucial difference between the urban anomie and compositional theorists concerns the influence of the urban environment on primary relations. Wirth argued that a city life is an impersonal one, that the city erodes primary relations. But compositional theorists contend that no matter how big, how dense, how diverse the city is, people continue to be deeply involved with a small circle of friends and relatives and others who have similar life-styles, backgrounds, or personalities. In this small social world they find protection from the harsher, impersonal world of strangers. The streets of the city may seem cold and impersonal, but urban people's lives are not. As one exponent of compositional theory wrote:

> Social life is not a mass phenomenon. It occurs for the most part in small groups, within the family, within neighborhoods, within the church, formal and informal groups, and so on. The variables of number, density, and heterogeneity are, therefore, not crucial determinants of social life and personality (Lewis, 1965).

Many studies show that there is indeed a significant amount of social cohesion within cities, as compositional theorists contend. Herbert Gans (1982a) found that people in ethnic neighborhoods of large cities have a strong sense of community loyalty. He found the solidarity in these neighborhoods impressive enough to call them "ethnic villages." When Scott Greer (1956) studied two Los Angeles neighborhoods, he discovered that the residents carried on their personal lives much as people in rural areas do, such as visiting relatives at least once a week. In their cross-cultural analysis of London, Los Angeles, and Sydney, Bartolomeo Palisi and Claire Canning (1983) also found that "people who live in more-urban settings visit friends as much or more frequently and share as much or more marriage companionship as people in less-urban environments." Even in slum neighborhoods Gerald Suttles (1968) found strong feelings of community solidarity.

It is true that rates of crime and mental illness are usually higher in urban than in rural areas. But compositional theorists argue that these disorders are not created by the urban environment itself. Instead they result from the demographic makeup of the city—from the fact that the urban population includes a high percentage of those categories of people who are likely to suffer from social and mental disorders. Examples are young unmarried individuals, the lower classes, and minority groups.

Subcultural Theory Claude Fischer (1982, 1984) has presented in his **subcultural theory** yet another view of city life. Like urban anomie theorists, he has argued that the urban ecology significantly affects city life, but unlike them he believes that the effect is positive. Instead of destroying social groups, the urban environment creates and strengthens them. These social groups are, in effect, subcultures—culturally distinctive groups, such as college students, black Americans, artists, corporate executives, and so forth. These subcultures are able to emerge because of the great population size, density, and diversity of the city, and the clash of subcultures within a city may strengthen each of them. When people come in contact with individuals from other subcultures, Fischer (1984) wrote, they "sometimes rub against one another only to recoil, with sparks flying . . . People from one subculture often find people in another subculture threatening, offensive, or both. A common reaction is to embrace one's own social world all the more firmly, thus contributing to its further intensification." (For a closer look at such a subculture, see box, p. 563).

Fischer has also argued that the urban experience brings some personal benefits to city dwellers. Urban housing, when compared to rural housing, generally has better plumbing facilities and is less crowded. Compared with people in the country, city people have access to far more facilities, services, and opportunities. As Harvey Cox (1966) noted, "Residents of a city of 10,000 may be

LOOKING AT CURRENT RESEARCH

Subculture Flourishes in Times Square

Fischer's subcultural theory suggests that the city helps create various subcultures by offering all kinds of opportunities. One of these can be a deviant subculture, which people from other subcultures find "threatening, offensive, or both." The following are some findings about the nature of this subculture in New York City. What ecological forces in the urban environment help to create and sustain this deviant subculture?

If the outsider sees Forty-second Street as a place where violent and exotic creatures tear at one another and at a victimized public in a fierce struggle to survive, those who make their homes there experience a way of life that is ordered, predictable, and controlled. There is a human ecology in Times Square that is at least as elaborate and as fascinating as the ecology of the tropical jungle to which the area has often been compared. What appears to be chaos and confusion is actually a complex interaction of social groups, each with its codes and rituals.

To members of New York's urban middle class, a city street—and Forty-second Street in particular—is fraught with danger, a place to be passed through alertly and left quickly for the comfort and security of home. But for others, the street is a home.

Street people are all around Manhattan, but the Times Square area is among the few places where they have staked out territories. Prostitutes, drug dealers, and bottle gangs all have their "strolls," or regularly traveled routes, each with its "stations," or oases of rest. Liquor stores, dark corners, and doorways serve as stations for the alcoholic derelicts who haunt the narrower, less populous side streets. Corners where a waiting woman can pick up a trick are the stations along the prostitutes' stroll on the west side of Eighth Avenue, north of Forty-second Street. For the drug peddlers, whose stroll is the Deuce itself, the stations are recesses and courtyards where their transactions can be made out of sight.

Different territories in Times Square mark not only different occupations but different levels of status as well. Through the city, street people rank themselves according to a hierarchy. Alcoholics and the mentally ill occupy the bottom rungs. The young men who hustle for their living are further up. And the pimps who set up shop in bars, safe from arrest and other dangers outside, are at the top—in the street world, an admired elite.

By far the largest and most complex of these status groups is the hustlers. Hustling in Times Square involves running con games, selling phony jewelry, shoplifting, and a host of other activities requiring good street sense and an aptitude for calculating the risks of arrest, injury, or being taken in by somebody else's "game." Large numbers of passersby offer a ready market for a wide variety of goods and services that the hustler can provide.

Hustling zones often overlap, and the various players sometimes try to hustle one another. But not all the relationships of hustlers are exploitative. Regulars on the street know and depend on one another. Some drug dealers are related by family ties, others are acquaintances from prison; a number live in the same buildings nearby. Though at a glance it may seem that every hustler on the stroll is fiercely competing with every other, hustlers actually belong to identifiable cliques, whose members can be seen sharing drugs, loaning one another money, and calling out one another's names. They often arrive at a station on their stroll the same time every morning, as if they were going to an entirely routine job.

Though prostitutes, drug dealers, and con men are well dispersed throughout Manhattan, their concentration in Times Square creates a permanent marketplace, the likes of which exists nowhere else in the city.

Source: Excerpted from Vernon Boggs and William Kornblum, "Symbiosis in the city: The human ecology of Times Square," *The Sciences,* January/February 1985, pp. 25–30. Copyright © by the New York Academy of Science.

limited to one or two theaters, while people who live in a city of a million can choose among perhaps 50 films on a given night. The same principle holds for restaurants, schools, and even in some measure for job opportunities or prospective marriage partners."

The three theories present partial truths about city life, and their conflicting judgments reflect the ambivalence most Americans feel toward the city. Migration has almost always been from country to city. But, as urban anomie theory suggests, residents of large cities are usually much less satisfied with their neighborhoods than are their counterparts in small towns (Lee and Guest, 1983). Why do people condemn the city but continue to live in it? Opportunity is the most important reason. The city provides a better chance than the farm or small town for jobs and economic advancement. As Fischer (1984) writes, "Most people see residence in cities as a necessary evil—necessary to achieve a desired standard of living, but not desirable in its own right."

All in all, however, city life is not as bad as popularly believed. People do lead a normal, pleasant life in the city as compositional and subcultural theories suggest. Many urban people even enjoy what are often considered the city's negative features—large, busy, noisy, and impersonal downtown areas—which they find exciting (Reitzes, 1983). As urban sociologist William Whyte has found, city dwellers may complain about crowds, but they will mingle happily with others to watch a performer or buy food from a street vendor. They will even "chat in the middle of a teeming department store or stop to talk by a busy intersection, while avoiding quieter, emptier spaces nearby" (*Science Digest,* 1984). According to a recent poll, most New Yorkers consider their city an urban hellhole, with all its crime, filth, and official corruption. Nevertheless, they like living in the Big Apple very much. To them, "the pulse and pace and convenient, go-all-night action of the city, its rich ethnic and cultural stew, still outweigh its horrors" (Blundell, 1986).

The Suburban Experience

About 2000 years ago the poet Horace expressed feelings familiar to many Americans: "In Rome you long for the country; in the country—oh inconstant!—you praise the city to the stars." Many Americans have tried to solve this ancient dilemma by moving to the suburbs. They hope to leave noise, pollution, crowds, and crimes behind—but to keep their jobs in the city and their access to its stores and museums and nightlife. They hope in the suburbs to find the best of both worlds—the open space, quiet, comfort, and wholesomeness of the country and the economic and recreational opportunities of the city.

Americans have expressed their preference for suburban life in many opinion polls and, more dramatically, by moving to the suburbs in droves. Unlike the public at large, however, many intellectuals have seen little good in the suburbs. Particularly in the 1950s, it was common to criticize the suburbs as wastelands of bland, shallow conformity. Suburbanites, in this view, are a homogeneous lot, and their lives are ruled by the need to conform. They spend backbreaking hours trying to impress one another with their spic-and-span homes and perfect lawns, and their houses are all the same, inside and out. They seem very friendly, but they form no deep friendships. They are bored, lonely, and depressed. The wives are domineering, the husbands absent, and the children spoiled. Behind the green lawns, barbecue pits, and two-car garages one finds marital friction, adultery, divorce, drunkenness, and mental breakdown (Gans, 1982b).

In the 1960s these notions about suburbia were discredited as either gross exaggerations or totally unfounded. Suburbs are not all alike. There are predominantly white-collar suburbs, blue-collar suburbs, and various ethnic suburbs, much like the different neighborhoods within a central city. Even within a suburb, total homogeneity is very rare—there are almost always a few families of different ethnic, religious, or occupational backgrounds. Contrary to the old stereotypes, suburbanites are more likely than city residents to find their friends among their neighbors. Unwanted conformity to neighborhood pressures is rare. Suburbanites keep their houses and lawns clean and neat because of their social backgrounds and personal habits, not out of a slavish desire to conform (Berger, 1971).

Most Americans feel happier after they move out of the inner city into the suburbs. They are proud of their suburban homes, and they enjoy the open space that enables them to garden and their children to play safely. The move to the suburb tends to increase the time that parents spend with children and husbands spend with wives. Most suburbanites are less lonely and bored after their move. As we noted, however, many suburbs have becomes less "suburban" and more "urban." As they have grown, many suburbs have found themselves with problems once considered the special burden of cities. Especially in the larger, sprawling suburbs, the way of life has become much less centered on community, and much more on work, entrepreneurship, and the private life, with neighborhood groceries and gathering spots giving way to superstores and fast-food franchises. The potential for being lonely and friendless is therefore considerably greater (Morris, 1987). Still, suburban homes remain the overwhelming choice of most Americans (Clay and Frieden, 1984). Moreover, there are ways to solve or alleviate those problems (see box, p. 566).

a

b

The suburban experience has changed over the last three decades. (a) In the 1950s most suburbanites enjoyed the open space that enabled them to garden and their children to play safely. They were less lonely after moving from the city, though they were often criticized as mindless conformists. This experience still prevails in most suburbs today. But (b) many suburbs have recently become huge and sprawling. As a consequence, the way of life has become less centered on community and more on work and private life. The potential for being lonely and friendless is greater.

QUESTIONS FOR DISCUSSION AND REVIEW

1. How do the concentric zone, sector, and multiple-nuclei theories each explain the spatial patterns of cities?
2. What are the different urban ecological processes, and how do they shape the development of cities?
3. Why do the different theories about the nature of city life make such conflicting judgments?
4. How have the features that have attracted many Americans to the suburbs changed in recent years?

TRENDS AND PROBLEMS

In 1975 New York City was broke and deeply in debt. A year later it laid off 44,275 people—15 percent of the municipal work force—and imposed a three-year freeze on the city budget. As a result, the police department was understaffed. Garbage piled up, uncollected and rotting in the streets. Too few firefighters were available to protect homes, particularly the firetraps in poor neighborhoods. Private businesses began to leave the city, causing hundreds of thousands of workers to lose their jobs. Only a $2.3 billion loan from the federal government and help from New York State saved New York City from bankruptcy. By 1980 New York appeared to have weathered its financial crisis. But then the nationwide recession and cutbacks in federal aid struck. By 1982 New York was again struggling to reduce its budget, and planning new reductions in its work force. All across the country, other cities have faced similar cutbacks in their budgets and services (Bradbury, Downs, and Small, 1982; Clark and Ferguson, 1983).

New York's near bankruptcy was just the most dramatic of its many difficulties. Almost every problem in American society—drug abuse and crime, racism and poverty, poor education and environmental pollution—seems more severe in the cities, particularly in the older and more congested ones. As Sunbelt cities age and grow, their problems are likely to become more like those of New York. The difficulties the cities face and their ability to deal with them are shaped to a great extent by the intertwining effects of demographics, economics, and politics.

Demographics, Economics, and Politics

In the last 20 years Buffalo, Cleveland, Pittsburgh, St. Louis, and other big cities have lost more than 20

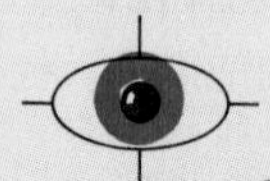

USING SOCIOLOGICAL INSIGHT

Suburban Renewal: The Task Ahead

Much of the growth in American metropolitan areas has taken place in the suburbs, but poor planning and development have created many problems. This reading suggests how the suburb can be turned into a nice place to live again. How does this proposed suburban renewal differ from the failed urban renewal of the 1950s and 1960s?

For a long time, the suburban pattern seemed to be the perfect expression of the American ideal: a healthy, secure, convenient, and pleasing place for young families to fulfill their aspirations for the good life. The frequent moves demanded by the job meant that one could move from one familiar environment to another three thousand miles away. The goal was few surprises, a ready-made community of people with similar backgrounds and jobs, and steady progress toward material well-being: a mass participation in the American dream. But the present form of the suburban city is grossly wasteful in its use of energy, materials, and land. Changing demography and living patterns further render the present form increasingly unstable and dysfunctional. How, then, can existing suburban form begin to adapt to another set of values—conservation, cooperation, place-centeredness, more social activities—values which we believe will become more important in the coming years?

A first strategy is to deemphasize the importance of the street. In the typical suburban block, much of the total land area is wasted. Streets that serve only local traffic are usually oversized. Typically, there are two lanes for traffic, each 12 feet wide, and two parking lanes each eight feet wide, for a total width of forty feet, not including sidewalks. One design solution is to remove many of these through streets, limiting parking to clusters at the end of the now dead-ended streets. The results would be fewer accidents, a better use of outdoor space, and a greater neighborliness, in addition to making land available for other uses such as food production and common outdoor activities.

A second strategy is to encourage densification and diversification of the suburban neighborhood. The original idea of the suburb was to provide separate homes for nuclear families, but social structure has been changing rapidly. While the family consisting of man and woman and one or more children is with us to stay, the number of households composed of unattached individuals of one or both sexes has increased dramatically, as has the number of single-parent households. Housing costs have also risen far more rapidly than real income. Yet, most single-family housing is underused, when it is still occupied by parents whose children have left. Single parents have to band together to share child-rearing, and singles find that they must share housing and use facilities cooperatively. All of these trends point to opportunities to redesign the suburban block pattern toward greater density of use and more adaptable housing forms. Thus owners eager for some added income, or to accommodate the housing needs of a child or relative, should be allowed to turn basements, attics, and garages into "in-law" units. And people should be permitted to run small businesses out of their home.

In the renewed suburb, cars will no longer be the exclusive means of transportation for all trips, and the space devoted to the car will be reduced and turned over to more productive uses, such as gardens or playing areas. People will spend more time at home and spend more of their "leisure" time on activities such as maintenance, gardening, and improvements. People will band together in cooperative projects involving the use of common space, such as a sauna, or a home cannery, or a basketball court, on what was once a street. More people, representing more diverse age grouping and income mix, will be living there in a greater variety of living accommodations.

Source: Adapted from *Sustainable Communities*, by Sim Van Der Ryn and Peter Calthorpe. Copyright © 1986 by Sim Van Der Ryn and Peter Calthorpe. Reprinted with permission of Sierra Club Books.

percent of their population. In fact, of the 60 cities that have more than 200,000 people, 73 percent have suffered population declines (Baldassare, 1983). On the face of it, this may look like good news for the cities' finances. It seems as if fewer people should mean less demand for, and less spending on, police protection, fire protection, education, and other public services. But, in reality, the population decreases have created a financial squeeze.

As a city ages, it must spend more to maintain its

road, sewer, and water networks, even if it has fewer people to pay for these services. Similarly, when families abandon the central city, the need for police and fire protection increases because abandoned homes usually become targets for vandalism and crime. They become fire hazards, and finally must be torn down at the city's expense. Furthermore, behind the statistics of declining populations lies the fact that those who move out of the cities are largely middle-class whites, and with them go many businesses. Thus the cities have fewer private-sector jobs and declining revenues. Those left behind in the city are typically less educated, poorer, and disproportionately nonwhite and elderly. They are the people most in need of government spending for education, housing, health services, and welfare. High crime rates also impose costs on the city—for more police services and more employees to deal with the increased incidence of false alarms, housing code violations, and the wear and tear on parks and other public facilities.

These needs and the loss of private-sector jobs create pressures to retain and even increase public employment. Moreover, the urban decline has coincided with the rising power of public employees' unions. Using strikes as a weapon, such unions have boosted their members' salaries above those for comparable jobs in private industry. As a result, spending by big cities jumped dramatically in recent decades. From 1951 to 1985 expenditures by all city governments rose by about 7.5 percent a year, twice the growth rate of the entire economy. The increase looks more dramatic when viewed in another way: between 1960 and 1970 city expenditures zoomed up by nearly 500 percent. Big cities experienced the most rapid rise (Census Bureau, 1988).

If the cities are in deep financial trouble, where do they get this money? According to the U.S. Census Bureau, cities raised about 22 percent of their general revenues from property taxes in 1981; another 19 percent came from income taxes, sales taxes, and corporate taxes. The cities also raised some money by charging fees for services. Since the 1960s, however, cities have come to depend increasingly on the state and federal governments to help pay their bills. In fact, during the last 20 years the big cities that were losing population received two-thirds of their revenues from these outside sources. In the early 1980s about 36 percent of all the cities' general revenues came from the federal and state governments (UPI, 1983).

All this money triggered rises in spending not only by troubled cities but also by the cities as a whole and by the states. It is, after all, far more tempting to spend other people's money than one's own, and far easier for politicians to spend money when they are not required to impose the taxes that raise the funds. By the 1980s some people saw the cities as a bottomless pit that could consume billions of taxpayers' dollars to no good end, and the federal government began cutting back on its aid to the states and cities. In 1986 the federal government was forced by its huge budget deficit to end its revenue-sharing program, which had delivered $85 billion to all the cities since 1972. Poor cities, which had to rely on revenue sharing much more than richer ones, may have to choose between two equally unpleasant options—raising taxes and reducing government services.

In fairness, however, we should admit that there were some valid reasons for the rise in spending by cities during the 1970s. Governments around the nation took on new responsibilities during the 1970s—to protect the environment, improve health care, enforce civil rights laws, and so on. More importantly, cities' weak political position makes economic independence an extremely difficult goal. Many states refuse to allow cities much power to raise taxes themselves, often giving the cities little choice but to beg for money elsewhere. Their lack of control over their own fate can leave the cities, in effect, paying other people's bills. Federal and state governments use city property but receive tax exemptions worth billions of dollars. Suburbanites come into town, adding to traffic congestion and garbage and the wear and tear on roads and parks. They also benefit from police protection and other urban services. But few cities are allowed to tax the suburbanites who use these services. Meanwhile, the suburbs have drained off much of the cities' tax base—by attracting industries and stores and middle-class and upper-class people. This gives the suburbs increased clout with politicians, since these are the people most likely to vote. That clout is reflected in the fact that the suburbs often receive more federal and state aid, per capita, than the hard-pressed central cities (Loewenstein, 1977).

The cities' financial problems further get worse due to city politicians' unwillingness to raise taxes even if they have the power to do so and their citizens have the ability to pay. Politicians are often no braver than the rest of us, and may not be willing to risk taxpayers' anger even when taxes are low and necessary. Despite all their begging for aid from the state, Los Angeles officials decided in 1982 to continue to exempt newspapers, radio, and television stations from a business license tax. Furthermore, the cities find themselves in competition with other cities to keep or attract businesses and industries. They use low taxes and tax exemptions to win this competition. By thus undermining their tax base, they hope to build a larger tax base, through an increased number of jobs, for the future. Unfortunately, research has shown a tendency for rapid urban growth to be associated with higher rates of unemployment. As jobs develop in a fast-growing city, it will attract the unemployed from other cities, adding to the local unemployed work force (Molotch, 1983). In the mid-1980s President Reagan proposed setting up **enterprise zones** in a number of cities to revitalize their economically depressed areas. Businesses that create jobs in those areas would be rewarded with generous tax credits. But critics argued that the major beneficiaries would be big corporations, not workers, whose jobs would be mostly "low-skilled, low-wage, even degraded" (Walton, 1982; Malone, 1982). Eventually Congress voted against a bill designed to create 75 enterprise zones around the country. Some 20 states, however, have proceeded on their own. Most seem to have been successful, creating thousands of jobs for the poor residents of the special zones. But some have failed, largely due to the states' half-hearted, inadequate support. It is hard to predict whether most states will even try to establish enterprise zones in the near future.

Housing Problems

Every year Americans spend billions of dollars on housing. The government helps out by granting billions of dollars in tax deductions to landlords and homeowners. As a result, we are among the best-housed people in the world, with over 64 percent of the nation's families owning their own homes. But since the early 1970s it has become increasingly difficult to own or rent a home. At the same time, large numbers of houses—more than 8 million or 10.6 percent of them—are dilapidated or lacking plumbing (Nenno, 1984). Much of this inferior housing is concentrated in the cities, forming slums in which jobs and public services are few and crime is common.

Racial Segregation Housing problems are most severe for the nation's minorities. For one thing, minorities, especially blacks, make up a very high percentage of the population of the inner cities, where good housing at reasonable prices is increasingly scarce. While most of the blacks living in metropolitan areas are concentrated in the inner cities, most of the metropolitan whites are spread out in the surrounding suburbs. Washington, D.C., Baltimore, Newark, New Orleans, Detroit, and St. Louis are among the nine major cities that have become predominantly black. In both the inner cities and in the suburbs, blacks are frequently segregated from whites (Farley et al., 1983).

Economics is one cause of the segregation. Because blacks and other minorities as a whole are economically deprived, they often cannot afford to move into white neighborhoods. In addition, there is voluntary segregation by blacks themselves. Most middle-income families in Roxbury, a black ghetto in Boston, for example, choose to remain there rather than move to a predominantly white neighborhood. Sometimes blacks prefer to stay in an inner-city ghetto because the price of housing there is low and the area is close to cultural, shopping, and transportation facilities. They may also prefer segregated areas because they wish to avoid confronting hostility from whites, especially if the neighborhoods are completely or predominantly white (Farley et al., 1983).

Discrimination, however, continues to force segregation on blacks and other minorities. There are laws against racial discrimination in housing, and there are signs that prejudice against blacks has declined. In a series of national surveys conducted between 1942 and 1968, for example, white Americans were asked whether it would make any difference to them if a black family moved into their neighborhood. The percentage of people answering yes fell sharply from 62 percent in 1942 to 21 percent in 1968 (de Leeuw, Schnare, and Struyk, 1976). A more recent study, however, shows that most whites would move out of their neighborhood if it becomes more than one-third black (Farley et al., 1983). Moreover, real estate agents tend to steer potential black buyers and renters away from white neighborhoods, perpetuating segregation. Conscious or unconscious discrimination by banks in granting loans also contributes to segregation and to the housing problems of minorities. Banks have long been more cautious, at the least, in granting loans to blacks than to whites, making it difficult for blacks to own or rehabilitate homes and thus encouraging the deterioration of black neighborhoods.

Government Programs The nation's housing problems have not gone unnoticed by the government. In fact,

Housing problems are most severe for minorities. While discrimination is illegal, de facto segregation prevents many minority people from moving into white neighborhoods. Economics is also a factor in segregation. Poverty compels many minority people to remain in substandard housing.

over the decades the government has tried many approaches in an effort to eliminate slums and to provide better housing for the poor. One of the oldest programs is public housing, which essentially began during the Depression of the 1930s. The federal government gives subsidies to local housing authorities, which develop, own, and manage apartment buildings. The apartments are offered at low, subsidized rents to designated categories of people such as the elderly and the poor.

Unfortunately, public housing projects have dramatized the tendency of government programs to backfire, making social problems worse. Eventually, many projects themselves become no better than slums. The most notorious example is the Pruitt-Igo project in St. Louis. Completed in 1955 at a cost of $52 million, the Pruitt-Igo project consisted of 33 eleven-story apartment buildings. The project won an architectural award, but it soon became a slum. Elevators and laundry rooms were filthy. Light fixtures were ripped out. Walls were smeared and cracked. Hallways were filled with garbage and reeked of urine. Children risked burning themselves on exposed pipes and falling out of windows. According to a 1969 survey, 20 percent of the adults in the project had been physically assaulted, 39 percent had been insulted or harassed by teenagers, and 41 percent had been robbed (Rainwater, 1970). By 1972 most residents had found the project unsafe and uninhabitable. They abandoned it, and the government finally demolished the buildings.

The deterioration of public housing is sometimes due to shoddy construction and inadequate funds for maintenance, but two other factors also play an important role. First, the physical design of housing projects often promotes social conflict. They usually fail to provide what urban ecologists call "defensible space"—some open space in which neighbors may develop informal networks of social interaction. Thus there are "frequent and escalating conflicts between neighbors, fears of vulnerability to the human danger in the environment, and withdrawal to the last line of defense—into the single-family dwelling unit" (Yancey, 1971). Second, over the years the population living in housing projects changed. At first they were occupied mainly by basically middle-class people made temporarily poor by the Great Depression, then by working families who were poor, and then by the "problem" poor—those who were unemployed, those who had given up looking for work, and single mothers on welfare. As Herbert Gans (1974) noted, "Ultimately a house is only a physical shell for people's lives; it cannot affect the deprivation forced by unemployment or underemployment; or lessen the anxiety of an unstable or underpaid job; or reduce the stigma and dependency of being on welfare; or keep out pathology." Public housing became so unpopular that in the 1970s

Scudder Homes housing project in Newark, New Jersey, where living conditions became so bad that the buildings had to be destroyed. The federal government has often subsidized housing for the poor. But such public housing tends to deteriorate because of shoddy construction and inadequate funds for maintenance. There are also two other important reasons: (1) the physical design of housing projects often promotes social conflict, and (2) the building tends to become merely a physical shell for the poor.

many communities halted construction except for housing set aside for the elderly.

Housing problems in the cities were increased by urban renewal, which was promoted during the 1950s and 1960s as a solution to the problem of slums. Old buildings were simply torn down. The government bought up the land, cleared it, improved it, and sold it to private developers who then built offices, stores, and apartments for the middle class. The idea was to rejuvenate the city, make it more attractive, and thus halt the exodus of businesses and middle-class whites. In the process the developers received subsidies, poor people lost their homes, and rarely was new housing built that they could afford. Often these displaced slum dwellers had first claim on public housing, and often the result was deterioration of these projects, less housing for working poor families, and long waiting lists for public housing.

Toward the end of the 1960s a new program was initiated. Low-income families were given subsidies to buy their own homes. But the program, which relied on private corporations to construct and manage the housing, soon fell apart. Real estate speculators, in collusion with housing officials, had defrauded the government of millions of dollars. They had bought up dilapidated houses at rock-bottom prices, and sold them for a huge profit after making only a few cosmetic repairs, such as sprucing them up with a fresh coat of paint. In 1974 Congress came up with another program, called Section 8, which provides rental assistance to low-income families. Under this program, tenants pay only 25 percent of their income for housing, the rest being paid by the government to the landlord. The purpose is for the government to get out of public housing and let private developers provide subsidized tenants with housing.

In the early 1980s, the Reagan administration further reduced the government's role in public housing. At first, low-income tenants were required to pay 30 rather than 25 percent of their income for rents. This rent subsidy was later replaced with smaller housing vouchers—direct cash payments to poor households who can use the money to find housing on the private market. The voucher program was intended to save the government millions of dollars. It was estimated that for every family put in a newly constructed public-housing unit, three families could be helped with rent vouchers at the same cost. The voucher recipients were also expected to get the same quality of housing on the private market as subsidized housing. In addition, private housing generally costs 20 percent less than subsidized housing, because landlords must compete for private housing consumers but not for subsidized tenants (Muth, 1984; Clay and Frieden, 1984). Thus the Reagan administration practically stopped financing large-scale public housing projects. The resulting shortage of public housing has forced a growing number of poor families onto the streets. These homeless are not the stereotyped winos and bag ladies but men who are jobless, women on welfare unable to pay soaring rents, and mothers with children whose husbands have deserted them. The housing-voucher system has so far worked only in the few places where housing is plentiful and rents are low. For many poor families, the vouchers are useless because private rental units are scarce and too expensive (Hull, 1987).

The Future of American Cities

Where are American cities headed? We can extrapolate from the previously discussed facts and observations and offer some predictions for the urban future.

Most cities, particularly those in the Northeast and Midwest, will continue to lose population to the suburbs and the country. Most of these migrants are whites and middle class, leaving behind in inner cities a large concentration of black, poor, and elderly people. The trend toward racially separate communities will produce more "chocolate cities" and "vanilla suburbs" (Farley et al., 1983). Gentrification will continue, but it will not be enough to revive the decaying inner cities. The gentrifiers will only create small enclaves of residential wealth—with luxury apartments, townhouses, and condominiums—segregated from the urban poor. Their expensive homes will increasingly be "fortified by electric door locks, security guards, closed-circuit television, and what otherwise has come to be known as the 'architecture of defense'" (Kasarda, 1983).

Central cities will suffer more than population loss. As the nation's economy shifts from manufacturing to service, informational, and high-technology industries, businesses will build their plants in suburban areas, where most white-collar workers live. If enterprise zones fail, the continuing loss of blue-collar manufacturing jobs will increase unemployment and poverty in inner cities. Moreover, the new, high-tech industries, lower living costs, and higher incomes in the Sunbelt states will continue to attract immigration from the Frostbelt states. But the fast-growing Sunbelt cities will have more unemployment, crime, and other social problems, due to the huge influx of jobless workers.

Finally, with the end of the Reagan era, the federal government might stop cutting its financial support for the cities. But if its budget deficit and the nation's economy worsen, it can hardly be expected to pump more money into urban programs. As suggested earlier, Congress already refused to restore the revenue-sharing program when its authorization ran out in late 1986. Besides, the reductions in city services and increases in local taxes that had resulted from the Reagan policies, though substantial, had not been as drastic as many city officials had feared (Caputo, 1985; Wolman, 1986). On the other hand, the federal government cannot leave the cities out in the cold. Thus there will always be a tension between the conservative impulse toward local control and the liberal tendency toward federal intervention. We can sense this tension in the recent proposal that Senator Daniel Evans of Washington gave for solving urban problems. He argued that "the federal government ought to take on those responsibilities that are essentially nationwide in scope," such as welfare, Medicaid, and long-term health care. He also proposed returning to state and local governments those programs that are local in nature, such as community-development block grants, mass transit, rural waste-water grants, and vocational education (Hey, 1986). Even with federal aid, however, the city governments themselves still have to tackle the problem of how to provide adequate services without raising taxes too much.

QUESTIONS FOR DISCUSSION AND REVIEW

1. What changes have occurred in the demographics, economics, and politics of cities?
2. How have racial segregation and poverty contributed to housing problems in cities, and what has the government done to help provide more housing for all?
3. How might future changes in governmental policy and population composition transform the nature of American cities?

CHAPTER REVIEW

1. *What are the main stages in the history of cities?* Preindustrial, industrial, and metropolitan-megalopolitan. Preindustrial cities began developing about 5000 years ago. They were very small, with people living where they worked. The industrial city developed when the Industrial Revolution triggered urbanization. During the twentieth century the industrial city spread outward, and the city and its suburbs became interdependent, forming a metropolis. *Who usually lives in the city and who lives in the suburbs?* Generally, more affluent people live in the suburbs. The poor and minority groups tend to concentrate in central cities. But typical urban residents

also include immigrants, professionals, unmarried individuals, and childless couples. *Do the suburbs provide a refuge from urban problems?* To some extent, but some suburbs have become more like the cities, suffering from congestion, pollution, poverty, and crime.

2. *Is there a pattern behind land use in a city?* Yes, but no one pattern characterizes all cities. Three prominent theories explain the patterns found in many American cities. According to concentric zone theory, cities spread outward from a central business district, forming a series of concentric zones. Each zone is used for a distinct purpose, and the farther the land is from the center, the higher the status of those using it. According to sector theory, cities expand from a central business district not in concentric circles but in wedge-shaped sectors. Transportation lines are the main determinants of this expansion. In contrast, multiple nuclei theory holds that a city is not built around one center but around discrete nuclei, each of which is the center of specialized activities. *What determines the spatial pattern of a city?* Dominance, competition, invasion, and succession.

3. *Does the urban environment make city people different from other people?* Three prominent theories offer different answers. According to urban anomie theory, the large population size, high population density, and great social diversity create a unique way of life. It is filled with alienation, impersonal relations, and reliance on formal social control as well as psychic overload, emotional aloofness, and stress. In contrast, compositional theorists argue that city dwellers' social lives, centered in small groups of friends, relatives, and neighbors, are much like those of people outside the city. Subcultural theorists contend that the city enriches people's lives by offering them diverse opportunities and by promoting the development of subcultures.

4. *What is the nature of suburban life?* A stereotype of suburbia holds that the suburbs are homogeneous places in which people are dominated by the need to conform and social relations are shallow and short-lived. Research, however, does not support this stereotype, and most Americans who move from inner cities to suburbs are happier and less lonely after the move.

5. *If large American cities have been losing populations, why has their spending risen?* The costs of maintaining streets, sewers, public buildings, and so on have risen as these age. Many who remain in the city depend on its services to survive. Federal and state aid to cities may also encourage spending. *Why is it very difficult for cities to be financially independent?* The state and federal governments decide what financial power the cities may exercise, and many cities have been granted little power. When they lose middle-class and upper-class residents, their political clout and their revenues generally decline further. Moreover, low taxes are one of the few means they have for attracting and keeping businesses and upper-class residents. *Why does public housing often deteriorate into a slum?* Shoddy construction and poor maintenance sometimes contribute to the decay, but social processes are also a factor. Public housing is often designed without areas of "defensible space" in which networks of informal social interaction might develop. As a result, there are frequent conflicts. In addition, public housing has increasingly become the home of the "problem" poor. *What is the future of American cities?* Separation between whites and minorities and between rich and poor will continue within cities. Population and job loss will also continue. Both the federal and local governments will continue to find ways to solve the urban problems.

KEY TERMS

Compositional theory The theory that city dwellers are as involved with small groups of friends, relatives, and neighbors as are noncity people (p. 562).

Concentric zone theory Model of land use in which the city spreads out from the center in a series of concentric zones, each of which is used for a particular kind of activity (p. 558).

Ecological processes Processes in which people compete for certain land use, one group dominates another, and a particular group moves into an area and takes it over from others (p. 560).

Enterprise zone President Reagan's term for the depressed urban area that businesses, with the help of generous tax credits, will revive by creating jobs (p. 568).

Gentrification The movement of affluent people into urban neighborhoods, displacing poor and working-class residents (p. 556).

Megalopolis A vast area in which many metropolises merge (p. 554).

Metropolis A large urban area including a city and its surrounding suburbs (p. 554).

Multiple nuclei theory Model in which the land-use pattern of a city is built around many discrete nuclei, each being the center of some specialized activity (p. 559).

Sector theory Model in which a city grows outward in wedge-shaped sectors from the center (p. 558).

Subcultural theory Fischer's theory that the city enriches people's lives by offering diverse opportunities and developing various subcultures (p. 562).

Urban ecology The study of the relationship between people and their urban environment (p. 558).

Urban anomie theory Wirth's theory that city people have a unique way of life, characterized by alienation, impersonal relations, and stress (p. 561).

Urbanization Migration of people from the countryside to cities, increasing the percentage of the population that lives in cities (p. 552).

SUGGESTED READINGS

Baldassare, Mark (ed.) 1983. *Cities and Urban Living.* New York: Columbia University Press. A useful collection of articles on such topics as inner-city revitalization, rural population growth, urban overcrowding, and the city's vulnerable populations—the elderly, Mexican women, and blacks.

Fischer, Claude. 1982. *To Dwell among Friends: Personal Networks in Town and City.* Chicago: University of Chicago Press. Marshaling data to drive home the subcultural theory that city life is highly rewarding.

Goetze, Rolf. 1983. *Rescuing the American Dream: Public Policy and the Crisis in Housing.* New York: Holmes and Meier. Shows how past housing policies have been ineffective and counterproductive.

Krupat, Edward. 1985. *People in Cities: The Urban Environment and Its Effects.* New York: Cambridge University Press. A social-psychological approach to the experience of living in the cities.

Mollenkopf, John H. 1983. *The Contested City.* Princeton, N.J.: Princeton University Press. An urban-policy analysis showing how politics helps determine whether a city grows or declines.

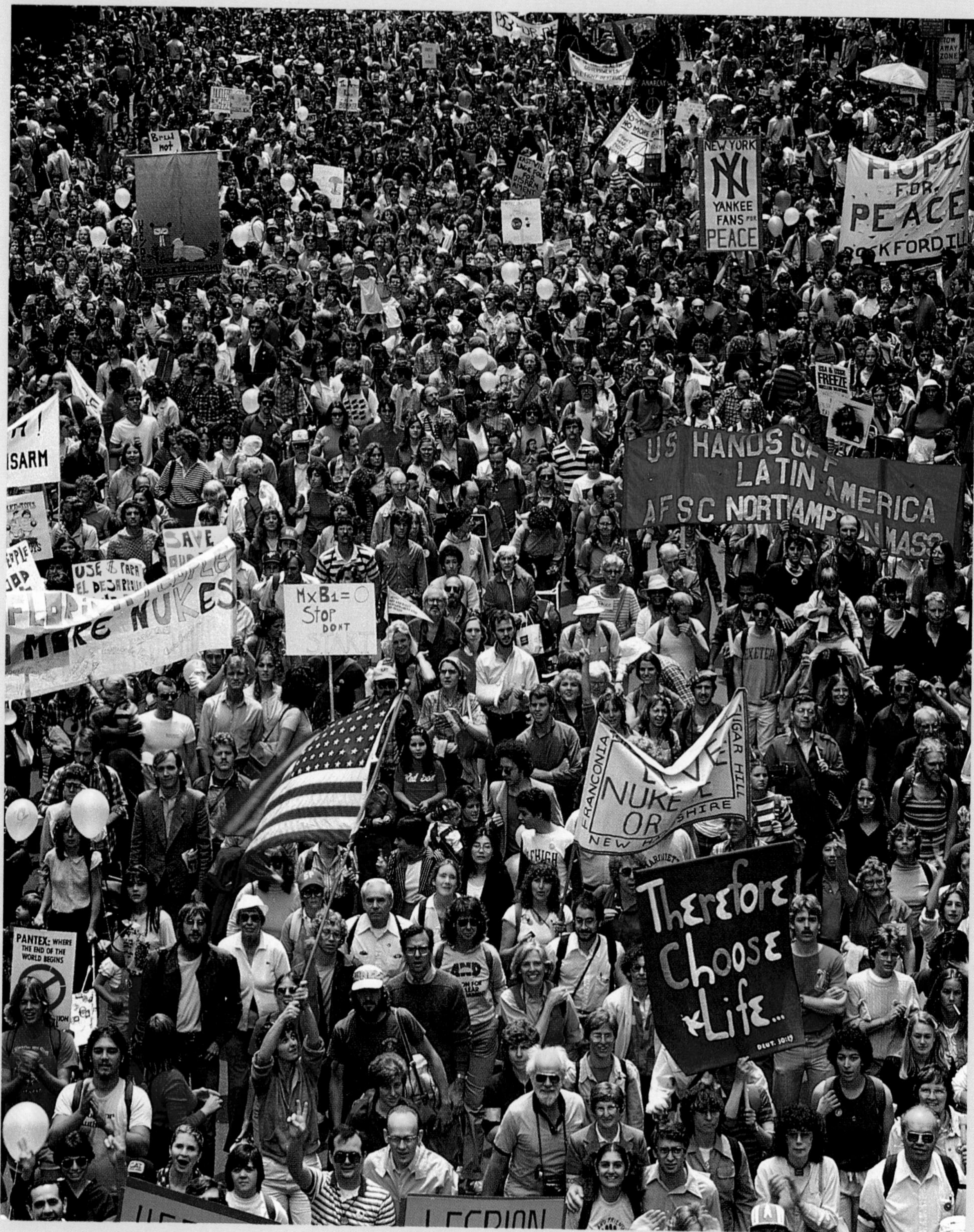

NEW YORK
NY
YANKEE FANS FOR PEACE
HOPE FOR PEACE
US HANDS OFF
LATIN AMERICA
AFSC NORTHAMPTON MASS
FREEZE
SAVE
NUKES
MxB1=0
Stop DONT START
PANTEX: WHERE THE END OF THE WORLD BEGINS
Therefore Choose Life..
EXETER
LEGION

23 Collective Behavior and Social Change

When people jostle and scream in a stampede to get out of a burning theater, that is an example of collective behavior. When people rush to attend a Michael Jackson concert, that is another example of collective behavior. Collective behavior is taking place, too, when people take to the streets to protest abortion, nuclear arms, or apartheid in South Africa. Despite its diversity, all forms of collective behavior have one thing in common. They represent an attempt to deal with a situation of strain, such as danger to life, fear of missing out on an exciting concert, or some kind of social injustice. Collective behavior often leads to social change. According to various theories, societies may change gradually from simple to complex forms, change in a rise-and-fall cycle, change peacefully, or change violently. Each theory of social change can also explain modernization—the transformation of agricultural societies into industrial ones. But specific conditions, such as technological revolution and capital accumulation, have been found to be the more immediate causes of modernization.

When a rather large number of people do something together, they may act either in a well-organized, rather predictable way or in a spontaneous, unorganized, unpredictable manner. Organized social behavior occurs frequently and routinely. Every Sunday groups of people gather in church. Every weekday masses of people hurry to work. On every campus groups of students attend classes during the week. These predictable patterns of group actions are basically governed by social norms. They illustrate what we call institutionalized behavior. This kind of behavior is the bedrock of social order. In contrast, spontaneous,unstructured social behavior that operates largely outside the confines of social norms is called **collective behavior.** When spectators at a ball game angrily hurl insults and objects at an incompetent player, that is an example of collective behavior. When people develop a passion for funny-looking dolls called Cabbage Patch Kids, that is another example of collective behavior. Collective behavior is occurring, too, when investors sell their shares in panic and cause the stock market to crash. This kind of social behavior may stimulate social change.

However, **social change**—the alteration of society over time—is nothing new. During just the last three decades, the first black American was allowed into a white Alabama university, and the first black was appointed to the Supreme Court. Space travel passed from the pages of science fiction novels to those of newspapers. In the last few years we have seen the emergence of various opportunities for having babies: through the use of a test tube, by renting the womb of a surrogate mother, or by buying the sperm of a Nobel prize winner. Where is all this social change taking us? Is there some general pattern behind the way societies change? Where can we expect future changes to come from, and can they be controlled? To understand these issues better, we look at several theories of social change. We also examine modernization—a particular social change that shaped many features of our society and is now reshaping many societies around the world. But let us first take a look at six major forms of collective behavior: panics, crowds, fashions, rumor, public opinion, and social movements.

COLLECTIVE BEHAVIOR

Sociologists who study collective behavior face two special difficulties. First, collective behavior is relatively unstructured, spontaneous, and unpredictable, whereas scientific analysis seeks out predictable, regular patterns. Second, collective behavior includes a wide, varied range of social behavior. What, for example, do break dancing and a riot have in common? Is a social movement such as the prolife, antiabortion movement an example of collective behavior? Some sociologists say yes. Others say that social movements are a different, though related, category of human action.

Despite these difficulties, the sociological analysis of collective behavior has been fruitful. Although collective behavior is relatively unstructured compared with institutionalized behavior, it does have a structure, which sociologists have been able to illuminate. Even rumor, for example, involves some division of labor, as some people are its messengers while others are interpreters, skeptics, or merely an audience. The difference between institutionalized and collective behavior is not absolute. Instead, these are classifications based on the relative degree of control exercised by traditional norms. Thus we can arrange social behaviors on a continuum like that shown in Figure 23.1. As we move from left to right on the figure, the behavior noted is increasingly subject to traditional norms. Thus institutionalized behavior is at the far right of the continuum and collective behavior lies to the left.

Only the main forms of collective behavior are shown on the continuum. At the far left, for example, is panic, the least structured, most transitory, and rarest form of mass action. When people in a burning theater rush to the same exit, losing their capacity to cooperate and reducing their chance of escape, that is a panic. Next on the continuum are crowds, which are somewhat more structured than panics, more subject to the influence of social norms. As a result, members of a crowd can be persuaded to work toward a common goal. Social movements are even more structured than crowds. Their members consciously work together to achieve a common objective.

Preconditions

Despite its diversity, all forms of collective behavior are basically an attempt to deal with a situation of strain, such as danger to life, threat of loss of money, or social injustice. The specific form such behavior takes depends largely on how the people involved define the problem. If they see it as a simple matter, they are likely to engage

Degrees of normative regulation →

Collective behavior						Institutionalized behavior	
Panics	Crowds	Fashions	Rumors	Public opinion	Social movements	Small groups	Large organizations
Behavior less regulated by traditional norms						Behavior more regulated by traditional norms	

Figure 23.1 A Continuum of Normative Regulation

There are two kinds of social behavior, collective and institutionalized. The difference is not absolute but relative to normative regulation. Collective behavior is less strongly controlled by traditional norms. Collective behavior may further be divided into different forms, which vary from one another in the degree to which they are regulated by traditional norms.

in such "clumsy" or "primitive" behavior as a panic or riot. If they believe the problem is complex enough to require an elaborate analysis, they are more prone to respond through a social movement. Thus, the more complex the situation of strain is believed to be, the more structured the collective behavior. Whatever the form of the collective behavior, six factors, according to Neil Smelser (1971), are necessary to produce the behavior. By itself no one of these factors can generate collective behavior. Only the combination of all six factors, occurring in sequence, creates the conditions necessary for any kind of collective behavior to happen. The six factors are presented below, fleshed out with some facts about the recent anti-Sikh riots in India.

1. *Structural conduciveness.* The social organization must permit collective action to occur. Individuals by themselves cannot start a collective action. Some condition, such as living in the same neighborhood, must exist for them to assemble and communicate with each other before they can take part in collective behavior. In India, the Hindus that joined the riots against Sikhs were brought together by the media reporting that their prime minister had been assassinated by her Sikh bodyguards.

2. *Social strain.* The strain may arise from a conflict between different groups, from the failure of a government to meet its citizens' needs, or from the society's inability to solve a social problem. Some strain has long existed between the Hindu majority and the Sikh minority. Militant Sikhs have often agitated for an independent Sikh nation, but without success. In June 1984 the Indian Army attacked the Sikhs' holiest Golden Temple, in which the Sikh militants had been holed up. But this incident helped unite moderate and militant Sikhs in anger.

3. *The growth and spread of a generalized belief.* Participants in a collective action come to share some belief about the social strain. The Sikhs are a prosperous minority, who account for only 2 percent of India's population but make up a much higher proportion of its business, professional, and military leaders. Their efficient farming in their home state of Punjab has provided much of India's food supply but they have felt that they have received too little in return from India. On the other hand, the Hindus have resented the Sikhs' affluence, power, and influence.

4. *A precipitating factor.* Some event brings the social strain to a high pitch and confirms the generalized belief about it. In November 1984, Prime Minister Gandhi's assassination provoked the Hindus' indignation at the Sikhs.

5. *The mobilization of participants for action.* Ringleaders or some rudimentary form of organization move people to take a specific action. Small groups of hoodlums have been reported to be the leaders of many anti-Sikh riots. They whipped up feelings of revenge against Sikhs by shouting: "Long Live Mrs. Gandhi!" and "Let's kill Sikhs!"

6. *Inadequate social control.* Agents of control such as the police fail to prevent the collective action, or even take action that ends up encouraging it. The Indian police looked the other way during the riots. Some officers even encouraged anti-Sikh mobs. As a result, numerous Sikh homes and stores were burned down; some 2000 people, mostly Sikhs, were killed, many burned alive; and an additional 1000 or so were listed as missing (Watson, 1984).

We can also see all six of these conditions in the 1943 race riot in Detroit (Brown, 1965):

1. *Structural conduciveness.* The concentration of a large black population in a ghetto was the structural feature conducive to collective behavior, although by itself it did not cause the riot.

2. *Social strain.* The strain arose from the conflict between the American belief in equality and the reality of racism and discrimination. Again, this factor by itself did not cause the riot because, usually, blacks reacted to the strain in other ways.

3. *A generalized belief.* It took the form of hostile and fearful beliefs among both blacks and whites in Detroit in 1943. The whites believed that the blacks "are pushing us off the sidewalks, running down the value of our property, and trying to rape our women. We must get rid of them." The blacks believed that the whites "hate us and will never give us our rights. We must do something about it."

4. *A precipitating factor.* Then, on June 20, 1943, a humid Sunday afternoon, fistfights broke out between whites and blacks on a bridge connecting the city to Belle Isle, an island park. Rumors spread among whites that a white baby had been thrown off the bridge and among blacks that a black baby had been thrown off.

5. *Mobilization for action.* Before the riot exploded, a black man is said to have grabbed a microphone in a black nightclub and urged some 500 people there "to take care of a bunch of whites who killed a colored woman and her baby at Belle Isle Park."

6. *Inadequate social control.* The police were poorly trained, often acting like a mob themselves. They beat blacks savagely for minor violations of the law. The local authorities hesitated before requesting riot-control help from more disciplined federal troops. Thirty-four people were killed in the riot.

If we look at many other riots such as those in the Liberty City section of Miami in 1980 and in the Overtown section in 1982, we can find a similar sequence of events (Porter and Dunn, 1984). We should note, however, that in most riots the violence is not "mutually inclusive"—not all participants engage in violence. Many simply watch (McPhail and Wohlstein, 1983).

The 1982 riot in the Overtown section of Miami. Riots may be the least structured form of collective behavior, the least subject to control by traditional norms. Yet, as Neil Smelser has observed, riots, like other forms of collective behavior, can take place if six factors occur in sequence. These six factors are structural conduciveness, social strain, a generalized or widespread belief, a precipitating event, mobilization of participants for action, and weak social control.

Panics

On a December afternoon in 1903 a fire broke out in Chicago's Iroquois Theater. According to an eyewitness,

> Somebody had of course yelled "Fire!" . . . The horror in the auditorium was beyond all description. . . . The fire-escape ladders could not accommodate the crowd, and many fell or jumped to death on the pavement below. Some were not killed only because they landed on the cushion of bodies of those who had gone before. But it was inside the house that the greatest loss of life occurred, especially on the stairways. Here most of the dead were trampled or smothered, though many jumped or fell to the floor. In places on the stairways, particularly where a turn caused a jam, bodies were piled seven or eight feet deep. . . . An occasional liv-

> ing person was found in the heap, but most of these were terribly injured. The heel prints on the dead faces mutely testified to the cruel fact that human animals stricken by terror are as mad and ruthless as stampeding cattle. Many bodies had the clothes torn from them, and some had the flesh trodden from their bones (Schultz, 1964).

The theater did not burn down. Firefighters arrived quickly after the alarm and extinguished the flames so promptly that no more than the seats' upholstery was burned. But 602 people died and many more were injured. Panic, not the fire itself, largely accounted for the tragedy.

The people in the Iroquois Theater behaved as people often do when faced with unexpected threats such as fires, earthquakes, floods, and other disasters: they exhibited panic behavior. A **panic** is the type of collective behavior characterized by a maladaptive, fruitless response to a serious threat. That response generally involves flight, but it is a special kind of flight. In many situations flight is a rational, adaptive response: it is perfectly sensible to flee a burning house or an oncoming car. In these cases flight is the only appropriate way of achieving a goal—successful escape from danger. In panic behavior, however, the flight is irrational and uncooperative. It follows a loss of self-control and it increases, rather than reduces, danger to oneself and others. If people in a burning theater panic, they stampede each other, rather than filing out in an orderly way, and produce the kind of unnecessary loss of life that occurred in the Iroquois Theater.

Preconditions When five knife-wielding hijackers took over a Chinese airplane bound for Shanghai in 1982, the passengers did not panic. Instead, they cooperated and, with mop handles, soda bottles, and other objects, overpowered the hijackers. About 20 years ago during a performance of *Long Day's Journey into Night* in Boston, word spread through the audience that there was a fire. But the audience did not stampede to the exits. One of the actors "stepped to the footlights and calmly said, 'Please be seated, ladies and gentlemen, nothing serious has happened. Just a little accident with a cigarette. . . . The fire is out now and if you will sit down again we can resume.' The audience laughed and sat down." In this case, as in the Iroquois fire, the audience had an impulse to flee for their lives. But a contradictory impulse, to follow the norms of polite society and remain calm and quiet, won out (Brown, 1965).

In short, the existence of a crowd and a threat does not ensure that people will panic. There are several preconditions for the development of a panic. First, there must be a perception that a crisis exists. Second, there must be intense fear of the perceived danger. This fear is typically compounded by a feeling of *possible* entrapment. If people believed they were *certainly* trapped, as in the case of prisoners who are about to be executed by a firing squad, they would give in to calm resignation rather than wild panic. Third, there must be some panic-prone individuals. Typically they are very self-centered persons whose frantic desire to save themselves makes them oblivious to the fate of others and to the self-destructive consequences of their panic. Fourth, there must be mutual emotional facilitation. The people in the crowd must spread and enhance each other's terror. Finally, there must be a lack of cooperation among people. Cooperation typically breaks down in a panic because no norms exist to tell people how to behave appropriately in an unusual, unanticipated situation (Schultz, 1964). But most crowds are made up of many small, primary groups of relatives or friends rather than strangers. Constrained by the bonds of these primary groups, members of crowds usually do not panic and stampede each other to death (Johnson, 1987).

Mass Hysteria Panic sometimes takes the form of **mass hysteria,** in which numerous people engage in a frenzied activity without bothering to check the source of their anxiety. A classic case occurred in 1938 when the play *War of the Worlds* was broadcast on the radio. Many people thought that they were hearing a news report. While listening to music on the radio, they suddenly heard an announcement that Martians had invaded the earth:

> Ladies and gentlemen, I have a grave announcement to make. Incredible as it may seem, both the observations of science and the evidence of our eyes lead to the inescapable assumption that those strange beings who landed in the New Jersey farmlands tonight are the vanguard of an invading army from the planet Mars. The battle which took place tonight . . . has ended in one of the most startling defeats ever suffered by an army in modern times; seven thousand men armed with rifles and machine guns pitted against a single fighting machine of the invaders from Mars. One hundred and twenty known survivors. The rest strewn over the battle area . . . and trampled to death under the metal feet of the monster, or burned to cinders by its heat ray (Cantril, 1982).

Long before the broadcast ended, at least a million of the 6 million listeners were swept away by panic. Many prayed, cried, or fled, frantic to escape death from the Martians. Some hid in cellars. Young men tried to rescue girlfriends. Parents woke their sleeping children. People telephoned friends to share the bad news or to say good-bye. Many called hospitals for ambulances, and others tried to summon police cars.

Why did the mass hysteria occur? As much as 42 percent of the audience tuned in to the program late and thus never heard the opening explanation that the broadcast was only a play. Moreover, the play was presented as a series of special news bulletins, and they were very believable. The actors were very convincing as news announcers, scientific and military experts, and witnesses to the Martian invasion. In addition, economic crisis and political turmoil abroad had created a great deal of insecurity and had accustomed Americans to bad news. Many were therefore ready to believe horrifying reports.

But not everyone who tuned in late to the broadcast panicked. Hadley Cantril directed a study to find out who panicked, who didn't, and why. Those who did not were found to have what Cantril called *critical ability.* Some of these people found the broadcast simply too fantastic to believe. As one of them reported, "I heard the announcer say that he saw a Martian standing in the middle of Times Square and he was as tall as a skyscraper. *That's all I had to hear*—just the word Martian was enough even without the fantastic and incredible description." Others with critical ability had sufficient specific knowledge to recognize the broadcast as a play. They were familiar with Orson Welles's story or recognized that he was acting the role of Professor Pierson. Still others tried to check the accuracy of the broadcast by looking up newspaper listings of radio schedules and programs. These people, on the whole, had more years of education than those who did panic. The less educated, aside from lacking critical ability, were found to have a feeling of personal inadequacy and emotional insecurity (Cantril, 1982).

Crowds

A **crowd** is a collection of people temporarily doing something while in close proximity to one another. They may be gathered on a streetcorner, watching a fire. They may be in a theater, watching an opera. They may be on a street, throwing rocks at police. Nearly all crowds share a few characteristics. One is *uncertainty:* the participants do not share clear expectations about how to behave or about the outcome of their collective behavior. Another element common to most crowds is a *sense of urgency.* The people in the crowd feel that something must be done right away to solve a common problem. The third characteristic of crowds is the *communication* of mood, attitude, and idea among the members, which pressures them to conform. Crowds are also marked by *heightened suggestibility.* Those in the crowd tend to respond uncritically to the suggestions of others and to go along impulsively with their actions. Finally, crowds are characterized by *permissiveness,* by freedom from the constraint of conventional norms. Thus people tend to express feelings and take actions that under ordinary circumstances they would suppress (Turner and Killian, 1972).

Beyond these similarities among crowds, there are significant differences. Sociologist Herbert Blumer (1978) has classified crowds into four types: casual, conventional, acting, and expressive. The *casual crowd* is the type with the shortest existence and loosest organization. It emerges spontaneously. "Its members," wrote Blumer, "come and go, giving but temporary attention to the object which has awakened the interest of the crowd, and entering into only feeble association with one another." People collecting at a streetcorner to watch a burning building, a traffic accident, or a street musician constitute a casual crowd. The *conventional crowd,* unlike the casual crowd, occurs in a planned, regularized manner. Examples include the audience in a theater and the spectators at a football game. Whereas the conventional crowd assembles to observe some activity, the *acting crowd* is involved in a basically hostile or destructive activity, and its members focus their energy on one particular goal. Rioters, a lynching mob, and a revolutionary crowd are all examples. The *expressive crowd* has no goal. Its members plunge themselves into some unrestrained activity, releasing emotions and tensions. Examples include people at a rock concert or at a religious revival.

Both acting and expressive crowds tend to be irrational or destructive. Consider American lynching mobs. Before 1900 many thousands of whites and blacks were lynched. The number of lynchings dropped during this century, but still, between 1900 and 1950 there were more than 3000 victims, nearly all of them black.

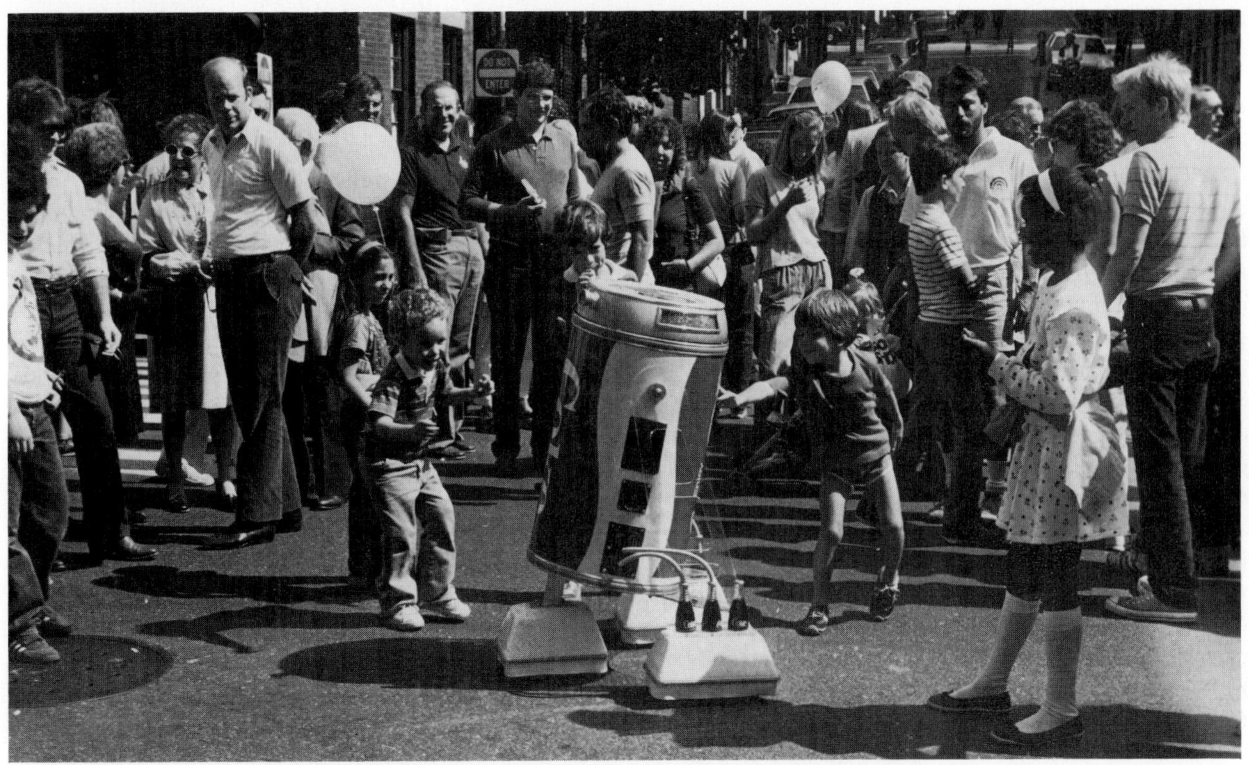

A crowd is a temporary gathering of people. Sociologist Herbert Blumer has identified four types of crowd. The *casual crowd,* such as the group of people watching the toy robot, has the shortest existence and the loosest organization. The members have little purpose in common except the brief distraction offered by the transitory event. The other three types of crowd are *conventional crowd, acting crowd,* and *expressive crowd.*

The alleged crimes of the black victims were often trivial, such as trying to act like a white man, making boastful remarks, winking at a white man's wife, or being too ambitious. For these "crimes" the blacks were hanged, shot, burned to death, or mutilated (Raper, 1970).

Why did the members of the lynch mob behave so irrationally and destructively? In particular, why did otherwise civilized whites act like beasts as members of the lynch mob? There are two prominent theories that try to explain this kind of crowd behavior. One, based on the classic work of Gustave Le Bon, describes a psychology unique to crowds. A second theory focuses on the social interactions within crowds.

Social Contagion and the Collective Mind The French social psychologist Gustave Le Bon proposed his theory of crowds in 1896. According to Le Bon, a crowd is homogeneous in thought and action. All the people in a crowd think, feel, and act alike. Regardless of who the individuals are, "however like or unlike be their mode of life, their occupations, their character, or their intelligence, the fact that they have been transformed into a crowd puts them in possession of a sort of collective mind" (Le Bon, 1976). If we assume that, as Le Bon claimed, a crowd does share a "collective mind," then we are left with two questions: what is this collective mind like, and how does it come about?

According to Le Bon, the collective mind of crowds is emotional and irrational. It represents the human personality stripped bare of all civilizing restraints. Beneath those restraints, Le Bon believed, hides a barbarian. All the members of a crowd bring to the situation this hiding barbarian with its primitive instincts. Normally, they suppress these instincts, wearing the mask of civilized behavior. But a crowd provides them with a different sort of mask: the large numbers of people give individuals a cloak of anonymity that weakens their restraining sense of responsibility and releases primitive emotions.

Individuals give up their individuality and are transformed into part of this collective mind, in Le Bon's view, as a result of **social contagion**—the spreading of a certain emotion and action from one member of the crowd to another. Many other sociologists have identified processes that can produce this contagion. One is *imitation,* the tendency of an individual to imitate another person in a crowd, especially a leader. Another is *suggestibility,* the psychological readiness to be influenced by the images, feelings, and actions of others. Still another process that produces contagion is called a *circular reaction:* the members of a crowd intensify their emotional excitement further and further by stimulating one another's feelings. An interested crowd is likely to applaud heated rhetoric, for example, which is likely to encourage the speaker to yet more inflamed talk, which stimulates the crowd's emotions further (Turner and Killian, 1972). Research has further uncovered factors that can facilitate these processes of contagion. Among these factors are crowd size and noise. When people are viewing a humorous movie in a theater, the larger the audience, the more frequent the laughter. If a person coughs in a room full of people, others are more likely to cough as well than they would if there were only a few people around. In watching a videotaped arm-wrestling match, subjects' tendency to imitate the wrestlers increases with higher levels of audience noise (Levy and Fenley, 1979; Pennebaker, 1980; Markovsky and Berger, 1983).

The Emergent-Norm Theory To most sociologists today, Le Bon's notion of a collective mind is valid only as a loose metaphor for what happens in crowds. Members of a crowd may appear homogeneous. They may seem to have given up their individuality and become absorbed into a "collective mind." But beneath these appearances the members of a crowd are basically just individuals engaged in a particular kind of interaction. Whereas Le Bon set the behavior of crowds apart from normal social interaction as a sort of bizarre regression to almost subhuman behavior, other sociologists have found that routine and orderly behavior prevails in most crowds (McPhail and Wohlstein, 1983).

American sociologists Ralph Turner and Lewis Killian (1972), for example, accept Le Bon's fundamental idea that a crowd appears to act as a homogeneous group, but they have argued that Le Bon exaggerated its homogeneity. In a lynch mob, for example, not all the members think or act in the same way. Some individuals storm the jail, others drag out the prisoner, others bring ropes, others hang the victim, and some just stand by and watch. Even those engaged in the same act may have different feelings, attitudes, or beliefs, and they participate because of diverse motives. How, then, does the apparent unanimity among the participants develop?

Turner and Killian proposed the **emergent-norm theory** to answer this question. The crowd finds itself in an unconventional situation, in which existing norms provide inadequate guidelines. Eventually, through social interaction, members develop a new norm appropriate for the situation. This norm encourages the participants to behave in a certain way, such as praying loudly at a religious revival meeting. Because of the norm, people feel pressed to conform with the crowd's outward behavior, even if they disagree with the action. The result, according to Turner and Killian, is the appearance of unanimity, which may be more illusion than reality. Indeed, many studies have found the "illusion of unanimity" in most crowds (McPhail and Wohlstein, 1983).

Fashions

Practically all aspects of human life—clothes, hairstyle, architecture, philosophy, and the arts—are influenced by fashions. A **fashion** is a great though brief enthusiasm among a relatively large number of people for a particular innovation. Because their novelty wears off quickly, fashions are very short-lived. Most are related to clothes, but as long as there is something new about any artifact that strikes many people's fancy, it can become a fashion.

Why do fashions occur in the first place? One reason is that some cultures, like ours, value change: what is new is good. Thus in many modern societies clothing styles change yearly, while people in traditional societies may wear the same style of clothing for many generations. Many industries promote quick changes in fashions to increase their sales. Fashions are stimulated, too, by the quest for prestige and social mobility. Although a new style occasionally originates from lower-status groups, as blue jeans did, most fashions trickle down from the top. Upper-class people adopt some style or artifact as a badge of their status, but they cannot monopolize most status symbols for long. The style or object is adopted by the middle class, maybe copied and modified for use by lower-status groups, providing people with the prestige of possessing a high-status symbol. By trickling down, however, the symbol eventually loses its prestige. The upper class adopts a new style, until it too "trickles down" and must be replaced by another (Turner and Killian, 1972).

Fads and **crazes** are similar to fashions, but they occur less predictably, have an even shorter life, and are less socially respectable. Examples of fads include hula hoops, goldfish-swallowing, telephone booth stuffing, streaking, and pet rocks. (If these things mean nothing to you, that is testimony to how fast the magic of fads can fade.) Fads are basically trivial, but they can be a source of status to some people. Certain individuals get a sense of being part of an in-group by playing the game of Trivial Pursuit or growing a stubbly beard to look like Don Johnson of "Miami Vice." They also like being part of something new, creative, or avant-garde (Santiano, 1985). Fads are basically less bizarre and less harmful than crazes, which are a kind of contagious folly with serious consequences. Usually crazes are economic in nature, including a *boom* in which many people frantically try to buy something of madly exaggerated value, and a *bust* in which many frantically try to sell a worthless thing.

The most famous craze is probably the tulip mania that swept Holland in 1634. For some unknown reason the Dutch developed a passion for tulips. Eventually one bulb would cost as much as a large house. Soon the Dutch were more interested in making a fortune out of tulips than in growing them. People bought bulbs only to sell them for a huge profit. The Dutch even expected to grow wealthy by exporting bulbs to other countries, but to their great surprise they discovered that other people found tulip bulbs less precious. They were astonished when people who returned from long trips abroad did not appreciate the tulip bulbs at all. It was widely known that a sailor mistook a valuable tulip for an onion and ate it with his herring. Eventually, people began to realize that the price of tulips could not keep rising forever. Thus the boom was broken and the price of tulips fell sharply, bankrupting thousands.

Like an epidemic disease, a fashion, fad, or craze usually goes through five phases. First, during the latent phase, the new idea exists in the minds of a few but shows little sign of spreading. Then the idea spreads rapidly. In the third phase the idea reaches a peak and begins to go downhill. Then, its newness wearing thin, resistance to it develops, rather like immunity to an infectious disease. The final phase, quiescence, is much like the first phase. Most people no longer share the enthusiasm, but it is embedded in the lives of a few. The tulip craze, for example, is long gone, but the Dutch are still known for their fine tulips. Similarly, such American toy fads and crazes as Slinky, Silly Putty, Barbie dolls, and Pac-Man have died down, but some people still buy or play with them (Penrose, 1981; Simon, 1981).

A tulip field in Holland. A craze is a kind of contagious folly with relatively serious consequences. Most crazes are economic in nature, including a *boom* in which people rush to buy something of madly exaggerated value, and a *bust* in which hordes of people futilely try to sell a worthless thing. A classic example is the tulip mania that swept Holland in 1634. It started out as a boom, with many people willing to buy a bulb even at the price of a large house. It finally turned into a bust, with the price of tulips tumbling to rock bottom, which bankrupted thousands of tulip owners.

Rumor

A **rumor** is an unverified story that is spread from one person to another. Social psychologists have often examined false rumors. According to one theory, they occur because, as a story is relayed from one person to another, each person distorts the account by dropping some items and adding his or her own interpretations

(Allport and Postman, 1975). But a rumor is not necessarily false. It may turn out to be true. It is unverified *not* because it is necessarily a distortion but because people do not bother to check it against facts.

In fact, we all act every day on the basis of unverified reports. Sociologists therefore view rumors as a normal form of communication. Tamotsu Shibutani (1966), for example, wrote that rumor is "a communication pattern that develops when people who are involved together in a situation in which something out of the ordinary has happened pool their intellectual resources in an effort to orient themselves." Rumor, then, is a process in which many individuals try together to construct a definition of an ambiguous situation.

Why do rumors emerge? According to Shibutani, a rumor is likely to develop and circulate if people's demand for news about an ambiguous situation is not met by institutionalized channels of communication such as newspapers, government announcements, television and radio newscasts. The more ambiguous a situation is and the greater a public's anxiety about it, the greater the chance for a rumor to develop. Thus rumor is much more a part of interpersonal communications in police states and totalitarian societies. In such countries people do not trust the media because the government controls them. Not long ago widespread anxiety over economic problems also made the United States ripe for the rumor mill. Americans who had lost or were afraid of losing their jobs, according to social psychologist Fredrick Koenig (1982b), were especially likely to believe or pass on damaging rumors about big companies. Seeing a corporate giant in trouble seemed to make them feel better. All this provided fertile ground for the growth of the rumor in 1978 that McDonald's added earthworms to its hamburgers. In 1982 another rumor had it that Procter & Gamble's logo, showing 13 stars and a man in the moon, was a sign of devil worship. Although both rumors were false, they spread like a prairie fire throughout the country.

Public Opinion

When we talk about "the public," we usually mean the population at large. In sociology, however, **public** also has a different, more limited meaning. It is a dispersed collection of people who share some interest or concern, such as an interest in environmental issues, or in civil rights, or in outlawing pornography. Thus there are a great many publics within the population at large.

Whenever a public comes into being, it forms an opinion. **Public opinion** is the collection of ideas and attitudes shared by the members of a particular public. As measured by polls and surveys, public opinion often seems fickle, changing easily even while values appear constant. This fickleness may reflect the difference between private and public opinion. "What a person says only to his wife, himself, or in his sleep," wrote Turner and Killian (1972), "constitutes his private opinion. What he will say to a stranger is public opinion." In private many people will express doubts about an opinion. In public they might state an opinion shared by others.

Most pollsters and researchers assume that the public consists of individuals only. To them, the public does not include groups, organizations, societies, or any other collectivity because they do not really have opinions—only individual members in a group do. Thus in public opinion polling only individuals are interviewed. The summation of individual opinions is then taken to represent the opinion of the group. But sociologists Zvi Namenwirth, Randi Miller, and Robert Weber (1981) argued that it is unrealistic for pollsters to exclude organizations such as chambers of commerce, labor unions, corporations, and churches. Through their spokespersons, organizations may express opinions that differ from those of their individual members. Even if the opinions of organizations and individuals are the same, the social consequences are not, because the opinion of organizations generally counts more. Being more influential or having more resources, "organizations are better able to translate opinions into effective action." However, organizations and individuals are equally subject to change or manipulation by the mass media. Newspapers, magazines, movies, television, and radio can reach millions of Americans very rapidly, and there is no doubt that they have some influence on public opinion. Let us take a close look at the nature and extent of that influence.

Propaganda The American media generally have no special interest in building support for one opinion or another. For the most part, they share one overriding goal: to make a profit. But the mass media are the main instruments by which others do try to manipulate public opinion. Politicians want to win our hearts and minds and businesses want to win our dollars. Both use the media to try to gain mass support by manipulating public opinion. In other words, they generate **propaganda**—communication tailored to influence opinion. Propaganda may be true or false. What sets it apart from other communications is the intent to change opinion.

There are scores of devices for manipulating opinion, some subtle, some crude. When the Reagan administration renamed the MX missile the "Peacekeeper" or when tax increases were called "revenue enhancers" or "user fees," everyone knew what was going on. Alfred and Elizabeth Lee (1979) identified seven methods that are frequently used to sway public opinion:

1. *Name calling,* or giving something a very negative label. This method is designed to make the audience reject an idea or person or product without analysis. If a candidate is "ultraconservative," "ultraliberal," "flaky," or a "big spender," why bother to consider his or her qualifications seriously? If abortion is "murder," who can support its legalization?

2. *Glittering generality,* which is the opposite of name calling. An idea or product is associated with a very general, ambiguous, but extremely popular concept or belief. If a war represents the defense of democracy and freedom, who can oppose it?

3. *Transfer,* or associating an idea or product with something else that is widely respected or admired. Beautiful, scantily clad actresses sell cars and mattresses on television commercials. Ed McMahon became a celebrity just by being associated with Johnny Carson on the "Tonight" show. Presidents give television speeches with the American flag prominently displayed behind them.

4. *Testimonial,* or presenting a respected or at least famous person to endorse or oppose some idea or product. Top athletes tell us to use a certain shampoo or shaving cream. Famous politicians travel to towns they never heard of to urge people to vote for obscure candidates.

5. *Plain folks,* or identifying the propagandist with the average person. Former President Carter made sure people saw him playing softball and going fishing—doing what ordinary Americans do. He frequently presented himself as a mere peanut farmer, not much different from average-income Americans, even though he was a wealthy man.

6. *Card stacking,* in which one fact or falsehood supporting a point of view is piled on top of another. Commercials do not tell us both the strengths and weaknesses of a product or a candidate. Instead we read that a brand-new car, for example, is "Quiet. Smooth riding. Full size. With comfort and luxury for six passengers. . . . Rich velour fabrics, thick carpeting and warm woodtones. . . . A truly fine automobile."

7. *Bandwagon,* creating the impression that everyone is using a product or supporting an idea or person. Soft-drink companies have often used commercials in which a horde of young, happy people are drinking their product and singing its praises. Political candidates are usually quick to announce favorable poll results. Thus the propagandist creates pressure to conform to a real or illusory norm.

Influence of the Media Despite such manipulations, the effect of propaganda, like the effect of any communication, is limited. Because we are not computers to be programmed or clay to be molded, neither propagandists nor the media can simply insert opinions into our heads or erase previously held beliefs.

In general, at least three factors limit the influence of the American media on public opinion (Turner and Killian, 1972). First, a multitude of independent organizations make up what we call the American media, and they present a variety of viewpoints. People select the media they will pay attention to, and thus the media that have the chance to influence them. Second, because most of the media are interested in making a profit, not in convincing the public, they often present what listeners or readers want to see or hear. They try to gauge and match public opinion, not mold it. Third, the effects of the media are often indirect because communication frequently occurs, not in only one step from the media to an individual, but through what is called the *two-step flow* of influence. A neighbor hears an analysis of an issue on television, and we hear about it from that neighbor. Often people are most influenced by communication received, not directly from the media, but from **opinion leaders,** individuals whose opinions they respect.

The media do influence public opinion. Their power comes largely from their role as gatekeepers—determining what information will be passed on to large numbers of Americans. We can identify at least five ways in which the media affect opinion (Turner and Killian, 1972). First, they *authenticate* information, making it more credible to the audience. A news item reported in the mass media often seems more believable than one passed by word of mouth. Second, the media *validate* private opinions, preferences, and values. If a famous commentator offers a view similar to our own, we are likely to feel more confident of our own opinion. Third, the media *legitimize* unconventional viewpoints. The wildest idea may eventually sound reasonable, or at least worth considering, if we read it repeatedly on the editorial pages of newspapers or hear it from the mouths of 50-year-old men in pin-striped suits on the evening news. Fourth, the mass media *concretize* free-floating anxieties and ill-defined preferences. By supplying such labels as "the crime wave," "the nuclear freeze," and "the Moral Majority," the media in effect create a world of objects against which feelings can be specifically expressed. Fifth, the mass media help *establish a hierarchy* of importance and prestige among persons, objects, and opinions. If the national media never interview the senators from your state, the public is not likely to consider them important, even if they are very influential among their colleagues in the Senate. While the media can influence public opinion in these five ways, all people who appear on television do not have the same impact on the audience. According to a recent study, news commentators, experts, and popular presidents influence public opinion much more than do unpopular presidents as well as such interest groups as business corporations and organizations that represent organized labor and the poor. Those who have a greater influence on public opinion share a higher level of credibility (Page et al., 1987).

QUESTIONS FOR DISCUSSION AND REVIEW

1. What makes collective behavior different from institutionalized behavior, and why is it difficult to study its forms?
2. According to Smelser, what are the six factors that together can generate collective behavior?
3. How do panics differ from other types of crowd behavior, and what preconditions must exist before they occur?
4. What are the different types of crowds, and how do the social contagion and emergent-norm theories explain crowd behavior?
5. Why do sociologists regard fashions and rumors as collective behavior?
6. How do people use propaganda and the media to mold public opinion?

SOCIAL MOVEMENTS

A hundred years ago American women could not vote. Fifty years ago paid vacations for workers were almost unheard of. A little more than two decades ago, George Wallace took office as governor of Alabama, declaring "segregation now, segregation tomorrow, segregation forever." These features of American society were transformed through **social movements,** conscious efforts to bring about or prevent change.

Social movements may be considered a form of collective behavior because they operate at least in part outside society's recognized institutions and outside at least some of its norms. Members of a social movement may send letters to members of Congress, but they may also block the entrance to a government building. They may organize a strike, but if it fails, they may also resort to more violent action.

Compared with the forms of collective behavior we have so far discussed, however, social movements are, first of all, far more purposive. A bank run or stock market crash, for example, unfolds without plan. A social movement develops as a result of purposive effort. Social movements are also far more structured than other forms of collective behavior, even if they are not centrally coordinated. A lynch mob may develop a division of labor, but it is an informal division with a very short life. In contrast, although the civil rights movement does not have one headquarters or one set of officers, it does have within it numerous organizations that have recognized leaders and sets of roles and statuses. Finally, a social movement is also more enduring than other forms of collective behavior. A crowd may stay together for a few hours, but a movement may endure for years. These characteristics give social movements the potential to build a membership in the thousands or even millions.

Types

Most social movements aim to change society, but they seek varying degrees of change. If we classify them by their aims, we find four types of social movements.

1. *Revolutionary movements* seek total, radical change in society. Their goal is to overthrow the existing form of government and replace it with a new one. Revolutionary movements typically resort to violence or some other illegal action. Examples include the American revolution, the Bolshevik Revolution in Russia, the Chinese Communist Revolution, and the Castro-led revolution in Cuba.

2. *Reform movements* seek only a partial change in society. They support the existing social system as a

whole and want to preserve it, but they aim to improve it by removing its blemishes, typically through legal methods. Each reform movement usually focuses on just one issue. The civil rights movement seeks to rid society of racial discrimination. The women's movement seeks to eliminate gender inequality. The ecology movement seeks to put a stop to environmental pollution.

3. *Resistance movements* cherish an existing system and try to reverse trends that threaten to change that system. The Ku Klux Klan and the American Nazi party, for example, try to stop racial integration. The Moral Majority aims to stop changes in the nature of family life and gender roles.

4. *Expressive movements* seek to change the individual, not society. Many are religious, aimed at converting individuals to a particular faith. These movements enable their members to express their sense of guilt, their joy of redemption, and their devotion to their religion. Examples include the Moonies, Hare Krishnas, and other sects (for further discussion, see Chapter 15: Religion). Sometimes, an expressive movement can turn into a revolutionary movement, as shown by the Islamic revolution in Iran (see box, p. 588). Expressive movements may also be secular, like the human potential movement of the 1970s. The movement included numerous groups advocating various therapies, from the outrageous to the commonplace, that promised to clear the path to self-fulfillment.

Causes

There are many things to do in this world. You can spend your time making money, or fishing, or whatever. Why would people instead spend their time pushing a social movement? Eric Hoffer (1966) argued that those who participate in social movements are frustrated and troubled. They use social movements as a diversion, enabling them to hide from themselves their personal problems, such as a sense of inadequacy and inferiority. Furthermore, through such a social movement they can gain a sense of being noble and magnanimous, as they fight a good cause beyond their own self-interest. A social movement can also provide a sense of belonging and a way of identifying oneself. According to Hoffer, members are therefore strongly dedicated to their movement's objective, following their leaders blindly as "true believers."

There are, however, some holes in Hoffer's psychological theory. For one thing, he in effect blames movement participants rather than society for their frustration. The fact is that it is often the unpleasant social conditions, such as social injustice or racial discrimination, that have brought about the discontent in the first place, as is obvious in the case of the civil rights movement. Another problem with Hoffer's view is that, although frustration may motivate people to join a social movement, it cannot explain why some participate in the *pro*abortion movement while others take part in the *anti*abortion movement.

Whatever the role of psychological variables in determining movement participation, we cannot explain this social phenomenon unless we look as well at the role of social variables. As we have observed in the discussion of revolutions (Chapter 16: Politics and the State), deprivation alone cannot explain people's participation in these movements. If it could, most of the world would be constantly at the barricades, seeking change. Instead, we can say that social movements are unlikely to arise unless social conditions produce frustration among masses of people. This appears to be the first condition necessary for the emergence of a movement. According to the traditional sociological perspective, social movements develop when discontented individuals identify a common frustration, work out a plan to change the offending conditions, and band together to carry out that plan (Turner and Killian, 1972).

Consider the antinuclear movement, for example. Since the late 1970s a fast-growing number of people have been increasingly worried about the prospect of a nuclear holocaust resulting from the continuing buildup of Soviet and U.S. nuclear arsenals. Initially, various groups, including Physicians for Social Responsibility, lawyers, performing artists, computer operators, labor leaders, churches, and even grandparents, called for an immediate halt to the nuclear arms race. Then many individuals came together in church basements and city meeting halls across the country to discuss ways to make the freeze an issue in their area. In June 1982 they converged in New York's Central Park to mount the largest protest rally in the U.S. history to demonstrate their support for the freeze. By late 1982 they successfully urged nine state legislatures along with city councils in such places as Philadelphia, Chicago, and Denver to endorse the freeze. A national poll also revealed that 76 percent of Americans supported the freeze idea. Finally, the various antinuclear groups—26 of them with some 20 million members—were united into a national organization called Citizens Against Nuclear War in order to

UNDERSTANDING OTHER SOCIETIES

Islamic Revolution

Revolutions are social movements that seek radical changes in society. The attempts by Iran and some other Islamic countries to create massive social changes form the most important revolution under way today. The following reading explores these recent events and compares them to the French and Russian revolutions. How closely does the recent history of Iran fit into the classic model of a revolutionary social movement?

In revolutions, even more than in other forms of political activity, there is an element of theater. This is evidenced by the almost universal use of such words as *drama, stage, scene, role,* even *actor,* in speaking of revolutionary events. Revolutionaries are, of course, conscious of this dramatic element.

Playwrights and actors alike are especially aware of their audiences, both present and future. This awareness affects revolutionaries as they write, direct, interpret, and perform their roles in the revolutionary drama. The theater of revolution is essentially participatory, requiring more than the usual rapport between actors and audience. It depends on knowledge and empathy on the part of the public, who are not just spectators. The audience must know, preferably know intimately, the essentials of the plot, the characters and roles of good and evil figures, and the desired, indeed the inevitable, outcome. The dramatist, the director, and the actors can appeal to a shared frame of reference and of allusion, of memories; symbols that they can invoke to gain the interest, sympathy, and finally the enthusiastic participation of the audience.

During the last two hundred years, the dominant models of successful revolution in most of the world have been those of France and Russia. In the nineteenth and early twentieth centuries, many revolutionary leaders attempted, in differing conditions of their own countries, to reenact the magnificent climax of the storming of the Bastille and the proclamation of the Republic. These models were most influential in societies that shared with France and Russia a common heritage of usable allusions and symbols, drawn from their European or Europe-derived culture.

The Islamic revolution which won power in Iran in 1979 and continues to offer a major challenge to existing regimes in other Islamic lands uses none of these symbols. This of course does not mean that they have none. Islam has its own scriptures and classics. Islamic history provides its own models of revolution; its own prescriptions on the theory and practice of dissent, disobedience, resistance, and revolt; its own memories of past revolutions, some ending in success, others ending in failure and martyrdom. It is against this background of Islamic action and ideas that the Islamic revolution must be studied and may be understood.

The Islamic revolution in Iran is as authentic a revolution as the French or the Russian. For better or for worse, what happened in Iran was a revolution in the classical sense, a mass movement with wide popular participation that resulted in a major shift in economic as well as political power, and that inaugurated a process of vast social

enhance the chance of achieving their objective (Price, 1982; van Voorst, 1982; Magnuson, 1982).

For a more specific set of conditions, we can apply Smelser's theory about the preconditions of collective behavior to social movements. Again, we can see each of these conditions in the nuclear freeze movement.

1. *Structural conduciveness.* Before the freeze movement began in 1980, there had been some activity stirring in at least four areas. In academia, quite a few colleges had started peace-studies programs. Among retired defense officials, in the medical profession, and in the churches, there had been a growing concern with the nuclear arms race between the United States and Soviet Union.

2. *Social strain.* In the wake of the Carter administration's failure to get SALT II ratified in 1979 and the increasing hostility between the two superpowers, many Americans were under some strain. They were fearful that a nuclear holocaust might materialize.

3. *Generalized belief.* Since 1980 an increasing proportion of the American public has begun to believe that President Reagan would lead the country into war and that nuclear war with the Russians is imminent. This is largely the result of the president's repeated refer-

transformation. As with other revolutions, it was preceded by a long period of preparation in which the transfer of power was merely a stage, introduced by what went before and facilitating what came after. It arose from deep discontents; it was inspired by passionate beliefs and driven by ardent hopes. And it still has a long way to go before it works itself out, and before one can determine its nature and consequences.

The Islamic revolution in Iran was the first truly modern revolution of the electronic age. Khomeini was the first charismatic orator who sent his oratory to millions of his compatriots at home on cassettes; he was the first revolutionary leader in exile who directed his followers at home by telephone, thanks to the direct dialing that the Shah had introduced in Iran and that was available to him in France. Needless to say, in the long war in which they have been engaged with Iraq, the Iranian revolutionary leaders have made the fullest use of such weapons as the West and its imitators are willing to supply—guns, rockets, tanks, and planes on the one hand, radio, television, and the printing press on the other.

Like the French and the Russian in their time, the Iranian revolutionaries play to international as well as domestic audiences, and their revolution exercises a powerful fascination over other peoples outside Iran, in other countries within the same culture, within the same universe of discourse. It was and remains very strong in the greater part of the Muslim world. In these, the sectarian difference is unimportant: Khomeini can be seen as an Islamic revolutionary leader. The Western radicals, in their day, responded with almost messianic enthusiasm to the events in Paris and Petrograd, events "that shook the world." Similarly, millions of young and not so young men and women all over the world of Islam from West Africa to Indonesia and, more recently, millions of Muslim immigrants and guest workers in Western Europe responded enthusiastically to the Iranian revolution.

The parallel is again very close between what happened in the Islamic world in our day and what happened in Europe and beyond following the Russian and French revolutions—the same upsurge of emotion, the same uplifting of hearts, the same boundless hopes, the same willingness to excuse and condone all kinds of horrors, and the same questions. Where next? Who could have predicted in 1795 or in 1925 the further development of the French or the Russian revolutions? I shall not attempt it for Iran. Only this much can be said: that what is in progress is producing vast, deep, and irreversible changes, that the forces that are causing these changes are not yet spent and that their destination is still unknown.

Source: Adapted from Bernard Lewis, "Islamic revolution," *The New York Review of Books,* January 21, 1988, pp. 46–49.

ences to a "window of vulnerability," his impassioned campaign to strengthen defense and increase nuclear weaponry, his vice president's belief that nuclear war is winnable, and his former secretary of state's remark that a nuclear warning blast may be necessary in the event of a conventional war in Europe.

4. *Precipitating factors.* One such factor was the peace movement in Western Europe. Another was the easily comprehensible freeze proposal, which calls upon both the United States and the Soviet Union to stop the testing, production, and deployment of nuclear weapons. This simple "freeze manifesto," as opposed to the complicated SALT treaties, was effective in stimulating nuclear awareness, generating grass-roots interest, and attracting hard-working volunteers.

5. *Mobilization for action.* Various groups and individuals, as has been discussed, joined the movement, with the result that in late 1982 a large majority of Americans supported the movement.

6. *Inadequate social control.* Given the increased popularity of the movement, the Reagan administration's opposition to the freeze has not been effective. In fact, Reagan might have unwittingly given a boost to the movement in late 1982 when he charged that it was

"inspired not by the sincere, honest people who want peace, but by some who want the weakening of America and who are manipulating many honest people and sincere people." Such an outburst might have strengthened the movement because many supporters, especially lawyers, doctors, professors, and other well-educated people, resented the insinuation that they were dupes.

This classical analysis, however, does not sit well with proponents of contemporary **resource mobilization theory.** They particularly find fault with the notion of "structural strain," which they equate with the psychological concept of frustration, deprivation, or discontent. They argue that what sparks a movement is not discontent but the availability of resources for mobilization such as strong organization, effective leadership, money, and media access (Gurney and Tierney, 1982; Jenkins, 1983; Wood and Hughes, 1984; Barkan, 1984). But these theorists have in turn been criticized for virtually ignoring the place of discontent in social movements (Law and Walsh, 1983; Klandermans, 1984). In fact, both resource mobilization and discontent can be found in practically all movements. But the importance of each varies from one movement to another. As Harold Kerbo (1982) notes, discontent plays a larger role in "crisis movements" involving blacks, the unemployed, or poor people, while resource mobilization figures more in "affluence movements" such as environmental and antinuclear movements, which involve mostly affluent Americans. More recent studies have produced other explanations as to why social movements occur or why some individuals participate in them. Nancy Langton (1987) suggests that social movements arise from three conditions:

1. A group objectively receiving fewer resources than others.
2. Members of that group experiencing relative deprivation, which results from their perception of the unequal distribution of resources.
3. A good communication network that enables the oppressed individuals to identify with one another.

On the other hand, Bert Klandermans and Dirk Oegema (1987) have found that individuals would participate in a social movement under four conditions:

1. "Becoming part of the mobilization potential": they are thinking of joining a movement because of their relative deprivation or disenchantment with authorities.
2. "Becoming target of mobilization attempts": they are encouraged by friends, organizations, direct-mail campaigns, and mass media to participate.
3. "Becoming motivated to participate": they are led to perceive that the benefits of participation outweigh the costs.
4. "Overcoming barriers to participation": they are able to take some time off from work or solve whatever problems that prevent them from participating.

Recent studies such as these suggest both social and psychological factors as causes of social movements or individual participation in them.

QUESTIONS FOR DISCUSSION AND REVIEW

1. How do sociologists define and categorize social movements and distinguish them from other types of collective behavior?
2. What roles do social discontent, leadership, and effective communication play in successful social movements?

THEORIES OF SOCIAL CHANGE

Modern sociology was born in a time of great social tumult, and its founding fathers developed many of their ideas as a result of trying to understand the vast social changes of their time. Anthropologists and historians, too, were intrigued by the question of how societies change. To some, human society seemed like a one-way train, headed toward eventual Utopia. To others, it was like a human being, passing inevitably from innocent childhood to decrepit old age. To yet others, it was rather like an ocean tide, rising and falling and then rising again. No one theory has emerged that can adequately account for all social change. We look here at four views that have had great influence on sociology: the evolutionary, cyclical, equilibrium, and conflict theories.

Evolutionary Theory

Human horizons expanded greatly during the nineteenth century, as Europeans discovered and studied "exotic" peoples of other lands and of the distant past. The early anthropologists believed that these peoples offered a portrait of their own ancestors. Most agreed that all societies progressed, or evolved, through three stages of development: savagery, barbarism, and civilization. Western societies, of course, were deemed civilized. All other peoples were considered savages or barbarians.

This was the origin of **evolutionary theory.** One of its early exponents was Herbert Spencer (1820–1903). He believed that all societies followed uniform, natural laws of evolution. These laws decreed "survival of the fittest": those aspects of society that worked well would survive; those that did not would die out. Thus over time societies would naturally and inevitably improve.

This early version of evolutionary theory received a boost from its similarities to Darwin's theory of biological evolution (see Chapter 3: Culture). It was also buttressed by the fact that it justified the Europeans' exploitation of people in other lands. These people, after all, had supposedly not yet "evolved" to a "civilized" stage. It seemed therefore natural for them to be ruled by the civilized white man and for their lands to be held as colonies.

Behind this simplistic form of evolutionary theory there were three unsupported assumptions. First, it assumed that Western culture represents the height of human civilization—an extremely ethnocentric position. Second, it assumed that widely different non-Western societies could be lumped together. For example, peoples of Mexico who had developed empires, cities, astronomy, and mathematics were put in the same stage of barbarism as simple Pueblo peasants. Third, the early evolutionists insisted that all societies independently went through an identical, unilinear process of evolution. But societies do not evolve independently. Most borrow many elements of their neighbors' culture. Moreover, evolution is multilinear, not unilinear. Societies evolve along different paths. Hunting societies, for example, make adaptations to their environments different from those made by agricultural societies (Steward, 1973).

Modern evolutionary theorists have discarded these assumptions. In general, they argue that societies tend to change gradually from simple to complex forms. Pastoral societies may be considered simple; modern industrial societies, complex. But evolutionary theorists no longer imply that the change represents an improvement. Neither do they assume that all societies change in the same way or at the same rate (Lenski and Lenski, 1987). Evolving complexity can be seen in the change Durkheim described from mechanical solidarity to organic solidarity (see Chapter 4: Social Structure). But organic solidarity is not necessarily "better" than mechanical solidarity. A modern life-style is not always an improvement over a traditional one. Moreover, among developing countries today some are industrializing at a snail's pace, while others are catching up with the West. In a recent study, Gerhard Lenski and Patrick Nolan (1984) found that industrializing agricultural societies such as Mexico, Brazil, and South Korea show a higher level of technological and economic development than industrializing horticultural societies such as Ghana, Chad, and Uganda (for a discussion of agricultural and horticultural societies, see Chapter 4: Social Structure).

Cyclical Theory

Evolutionists assume that social change has only one direction. They believe that when societies change they, in effect, burn their bridges behind them—they cannot return to their previous states. In contrast, proponents of **cyclical theory** believe that societies move forward and backward, up and down, in an endless series of cycles.

Spengler's "Majestic Cycles" German historian Oswald Spengler (1880–1936) was the first to make this assumption explicit. Like many of his contemporaries in the early twentieth century, Spengler was led by the savagery of World War I to question the belief in progress and the supremacy of Western civilization. As suggested by the title of his 1918 book, *The Decline of the West,* Spengler believed that Western civilization was headed downhill and would soon die out, just as the Greek and Egyptian civilizations had. "The great cultures," he wrote, "accomplish their majestic wave cycles. They appear suddenly, swell in splendid lines, flatten again, and vanish, and the face of the waters is once more a sleeping waste." More often, Spengler likened a culture to an organism. Like any living thing, a culture, he believed, went through a life cycle of birth, youth, maturity, old age, and death. Western civilization as he saw it had reached old age and was tottering toward death.

Spengler's theory was very popular for a time. But to

An artist's reconstruction of an ancient Incan Temple in Peru, South America. According to Spengler's cyclical theory, great cultures go through "majestic wave cycles." As Spengler wrote, "they appear suddenly, swell in splendid lines, flatten again, and vanish, and the face of the waters is once more a sleeping waste." He believed that Western civilization was headed downhill and would soon die out, just as the Incan culture had. Modern sociologists find too much poetry and too little science in Spengler's argument, but his basic concept of social change as cyclical has left its mark on more recent studies in the social sciences.

modern sociologists there is too much poetry and too little science in his argument, and the analogy between societies and biological organisms is more misleading than useful. Nevertheless, Spengler's basic idea that social change is cyclical has influenced social science. Recently, for example, Paul Kennedy (1987) argued that the United States is losing its superpower status in the world just as other powerful nations like Spain, the Netherlands, France, and Britain did in the last 300 years (see box, p. 594). Other social scientists, particularly Arnold Toynbee and Pitirim Sorokin, had earlier offered their famous versions of the cyclical theory.

Toynbee's "Challenge" and "Response" From 1934 to 1961 the British historian Arnold Toynbee (1889–1975) formulated a cyclical theory in his multivolume work *A Study of History*. Like Spengler, Toynbee believed that all civilizations rise and fall. But in his view the rise and fall do not result from some inevitable, biologically determined life cycle. Instead, they depend both on human beings and on their environments. Environments present "challenges," and humans choose "responses" to those challenges. The fate of a civilization, according to Toynbee, depends on both the challenges presented to a civilization and the responses it devises.

The challenge may come from the natural environment or from human sources. Barren land, a frigid climate, and war, for example, all represent "challenges." A civilization arises out of a society's successful response to a challenge. A civilization declines, though, if the challenge it faces is either too weak or too severe. Suppose food is extremely abundant; people may become lazy, and their civilization will decline. But if food is very scarce, starvation may kill the people, and their civilization as well. A moderate challenge is likely to stimulate a civilization to grow and flourish. The relatively large population and relatively scarce natural resources of Japan might represent a "moderate" challenge.

The fate of a civilization, however, depends not just on the challenge from the environment but also on the people's response. Whether a successful response comes about usually hinges on the actions of a creative minority. They develop new ideas and lead the masses to meet the challenge. The founders of the Chinese civilization, for example, emerged from among those who lived along the Yellow River rather than the far more numerous peoples occupying the vast region to the south and southwest of China. Toynbee called them the creative minority because they responded successfully to the challenge presented by the river. It was unnavigable most of the time. In the winter it was either frozen or choked with floating ice. In the spring the melting ice produced devastating floods. The people were compelled to devise means to navigate the river and control the flood. Thus the rise and fall of a civilization depend both on the severity of the challenge offered by the environment and on the creativity of people's response to it.

Toynbee's theory provides an interesting way of looking at the history of civilizations, but it does not give us a means of predicting how societies will change. What, after all, is a "severe" challenge? Will the depletion of oil and minerals represent a "moderate" or an overly "severe" challenge for Western civilization? We know the answer only after the fact. If a civilization falls, we may assume that the challenge was not moderate and the response was not adequate. Before a civilization rises or falls, we have no way of testing Toynbee's theory. But it still can be considered a useful theory. According to French sociologist Raymond Boudon (1983a, 1983b), social change is so complex that the best we can expect from a theory is whether it can help us understand what has happened rather than predict what will happen. That's what Toynbee's theory does.

Sorokin's Principle of Immanent Change Another cyclical theory was offered by Pitirim Sorokin (1889–1968), a Russian-American sociologist. In essence, Sorokin argued that societies fluctuate between two extreme forms of culture, which he called ideational and sensate. **Ideational culture** emphasizes faith or religion as the key to knowledge and encourages people to value spiritual life. **Sensate culture** stresses empirical evidence or science as the path to knowledge and urges people to favor a practical, materialistic, and hedonistic way of life.

External forces such as international conflict or contact with another culture may force change on a society, but Sorokin believed that internal forces—forces within the society itself—are more powerful in bringing about social change. As he wrote, "One of the most important 'determinators' of the course of any system lies within the system itself, is inherent in it. . . . Its life course is set down in its essentials when the system is born" (Sorokin, 1967). Hence Sorokin called his theory the **principle of immanent change.** When the time has come for a society's "inwardly ordained change," all the main aspects of the culture change. Thus society eventually reacts against one extreme form of culture, and swings to the other extreme. Sorokin regarded the Western culture of his time, for example, as sensate, and like Spengler he thought it was declining. In the widespread pursuit of pleasure, proliferation of fraud and crime, and deterioration of the family, Sorokin saw signs that Western culture was "overripe" and ready to swing to the other extreme—ideational culture.

To most sociologists today, Sorokin's theory is too speculative, impossible to test scientifically. Although Sorokin supported his theory with a mountain of historical data, he seems to have selected those facts which supported his view and ignored those which did not. Nevertheless, Sorokin's theory, like Toynbee's, can help us understand some of the changes in our history, such as the rise of fundamentalist religion in the last decade (see Chapter 15: Religion). It can be interpreted as a reflection of the shift from a sensate to an ideational culture.

Equilibrium Theory

American sociologist Talcott Parsons developed yet another theory of social change, one that remains influential today. According to **equilibrium theory,** which is a version of functionalist theory, all the parts of society serve some function and are interdependent (Chapter 1: Thinking Sociologically). As a result, a change in one part produces compensatory changes throughout society. Both the family and the school, for example, play an important part in socializing children, instilling in them the norms of society. If the family's role changes, then the school's role is also likely to change, ensuring that

According to Talcott Parsons' equilibrium theory, a change in one part of society produces compensatory changes elsewhere. It has recently become necessary, for example, for both parents to work in order to earn enough income to support a family. But if both parents must leave the home, who will care for their children? Society has responded with the increased availability of day-care services. Many day-care centers are now open in the workplace. Here parents are joining children for lunch in their company's day-care center.

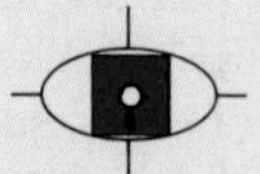

LOOKING AT CURRENT RESEARCH

Is America in Decline?

The United States today faces many problems like those that have beset other powerful nations in the past. These other nations, one after another, eventually lost their power and influence in the world. Is the United States about to stop being a superpower too? Historian Paul Kennedy says yes in Imperial Cycles, *his recent analysis of the rise and fall of powerful nations. The following reading by Michael Howard summarizes Kennedy's argument. How does Kennedy's version of the cyclical theory of social change compare with those of Spengler, Toynbee, and Sorokin?*

Paul Kennedy of Yale University . . . in a work of almost Toynbeean sweep, describes a pattern of past development that is not only directly relevant to our times but is clearly intended to be read by policy makers, particularly American policy makers. . . . His thesis can be easily summarized: The more states increase their power, the larger the proportion of their resources they devote to maintaining it. If too large a proportion of national resources is diverted to military purposes, this in the long run leads to a weakening of power. The capacity to sustain a conflict with a comparable state or coalition of states ultimately depends on economic strength; but states apparently at the zenith of their political power are usually already in a condition of comparative economic decline, and the United States is no exception to this rule. Power can be maintained only by a prudent balance between the creation of wealth and military expenditure, and great powers in decline almost always hasten their demise by shifting expenditure from the former to the latter. Spain, the Netherlands, France and Britain did exactly that. Now it is the turn of the Soviet Union and the United States. . . .

Mr. Kennedy clearly sets out his pattern of over-extension and decline. At the beginning of the 16th century, Spain, the first European great power, inherited vast commitments in Europe and overseas. In spite of the excellence of Spain's armed forces, defending those commitments involved expenditure on a scale that could not be met from Spain's own mismanaged resources . . . and had to be met by an ultimately lethal mixture of deficit budgeting and inflation. Spain's preponderance lasted as long as it did only because her principal adversary, France, mismanaged her resources even more badly. By the end of the 17th century, however, France had developed a system of bureaucratic and military management that enabled her to exploit her economic resources to such military effect that it required a coalition of all other European powers to prevent her from establishing a permanent hegemony over the continent.

Then France in her turn became overextended, her economy unable to support increasingly expensive regular armed forces, until her participation in the American

functions essential to society are performed. Such changes keep the various parts of the social system in balance, ensuring social order and stability.

In this view of society, social change seems rather like an infection invading the body. Just as an infection triggers the body's immune system to fight it, so too a change in one part of the social system triggers other parts of the system to make adjustments.

Many sociologists have argued that the equilibrium theory may explain social stability but that it cannot explain social change. Parsons (1964), however, insisted that his theory is "*equally* applicable to the problems of change and to those of process within a stabilized system." To Parsons social change is not the overthrow of the old and creation of something wholly new. Instead, new elements are integrated with aspects of the old society through a "moving equilibrium," or movement to a new equilibrium.

Like evolutionary theorists, Parsons (1966) believed that societies evolve from simpler to more complex forms. He argued that the most important type of change represented an "enhancement of adaptive capacity," and that evolutionary changes follow a common pattern. First, there is **differentiation,** in which one unit of society divides into two or more. In a simple society, for example, the family serves as the unit of residence *and* of production, of kinship and occupation (Chapter 13: The Family). But as a society evolves, production moves out of the household. An additional, separate social unit—an economic institution such as the factory—is then formed, and the family itself is altered. Thus the family has become differentiated from its origi-

Revolutionary War created the bankruptcy that led to the French Revolution. . . .

The United States emerged as supreme from the two world wars as Britain had from the Napoleonic wars, her economy stimulated rather than debilitated by the conflict. That supremacy, like Britain's before, was temporary and relative, created by the eclipse of old competitors and the only gradual emergence of new ones. But while the supremacy lasted, the United States assumed a range of global commitments about which, in Mr. Kennedy's words, "Louis XIV or Palmerston would have felt a little nervous."

By now, European, Soviet and Japanese recovery, together with the slower emergence of the People's Republic of China, has gradually reduced American ascendancy . . . and, like other great powers in the past, in order to preserve her hegemonial status the United States has felt it necessary to allocate an increasing share of her resources to defense expenditure. Now she finds herself in the position of Spain and France before her. Unwilling to defray the costs of empire by an equitable system of domestic taxation, she has tried to pay for it by a combination of deficit financing and external indebtedness which in her case threatens the stability of the whole free-market system. And as was the case with Hapsburg Spain, she preserves her ascendancy only because the condition of her major adversary is even worse.

Unlike Toynbee or Spengler, Mr. Kennedy does not conclude that the West is doomed to cyclical decay. . . . What the United States needs, he concludes, is the wisdom to recognize its problem, the will to come to terms with it, and the kind of political skills that in the past have enabled lesser powers to maximize their advantages and minimize their defects.

He is not, it must be said, optimistic about the capacity of the American political system over the long term to engender such virtues in its leaders. The thought indeed obtrudes itself . . . that if the Soviet leadership were to prove better able to develop such qualities and operate more skillfully in an increasingly multipolar world, the outlook for the United States would be bleak. No amount of defense expenditure could then save it from the consequences of that unhappy isolation into which so many great powers have found themselves driven in the past and from which they have emerged, chastened and defeated, as second- or third-rank powers. There are lessons to be learned from the past . . . and the American leadership would do well to heed them.

Source: Excerpted from Michael Howard, "Imperial Cycles: Bucks, Bullets and Bust," January 10, 1988 Book Review. Copyright © 1988 by The New York Times Company. Reprinted by permission.

nal function as a production unit, which is now taken over by the economic institution. Differentiation, however, poses problems of **integration.** The new social units—such as the modern family and the economic institution—must be coordinated. As a result, other changes will occur within the society. Social status becomes more dependent on work than on family background. Young people are now more likely to choose the jobs they prefer than those their parents prefer. Families become smaller. Individuals tend more to identify with their country as opposed to their village. In short, traditionalism has given way to modernism, a new social equilibrium in which various parts, such as the family, the economic institution, and nationhood, are integrated with each other (Inkeles, 1983).

Parsons' theory is useful for describing gradual change. According to its critics, however, it fails to explain why social change occurs, does not deal with *revolutionary* change, and portrays societies as far more stable and harmonious than they are.

Conflict Theory

Whereas equilibrium theory portrays stability as the pervasive characteristic of societies, conflict theorists believe that societies are always marked by conflict and that conflict is the key to change. Karl Marx (1818–1883) is the father of **conflict theory.** We have discussed some aspects of his work several times in previous chapters, especially his prediction of the downfall of capitalism.

A mechanized automobile plant. Conflict theorists believe that societies are marked by conflict and that conflict is the key to change. Workers in heavy industry organized unions in order to get better working conditions, higher pay, and job security. Owners and managers responded by introducing new machinery to take over the most unpleasant physical jobs and to lower labor costs. Now workers feel threatened by the machines, which may take away their jobs.

According to Marx, a capitalist society includes two classes: the owners of the means of production (the bourgeoisie or capitalists) and those who must sell their labor (the proletariat or workers). These classes are in constant conflict with each other. The capitalists are determined to keep wages low in order to maximize their profits while the workers resist this exploitation. The capitalists have the upper hand, but they unwittingly sow the seeds of their own destruction. By completely controlling the labor of workers, capitalists further their alienation. By exploiting workers mercilessly, capitalists fuel rage and resentment among workers, and lead them to feel that they have nothing to gain from the present system. And through factories and improved transportation and communication, the capitalist society brings workers together and helps them share their sufferings with one another. As a result, the workers develop a consciousness of themselves as a class. According to Marx, the alienation, resentment, and class consciousness eventually lead workers to revolt against capitalist society.

History has not fulfilled these predictions. Marx failed to anticipate the emergence of a large middle class, made up largely of white-collar workers. He also failed to see that governments might respond to social conflict by improving the condition of workers. In fact, Marx's dire predictions about the future of capitalism helped spur governments to ease the suffering of workers. In a sense, by predicting that capitalism carried the seeds of its destruction, Marx sowed seeds that would help destroy his own prediction. Through the emergence of the welfare state as well as the growth of the middle class, workers in capitalist societies have grown richer, not poorer as Marx predicted. They have thus gained a stake in the system and are not likely to overthrow it by supporting revolution.

Other aspects of Marx's work have stood up better against the test of time. Marx did accurately predict the rise of large-scale industry, the emergence of multinational corporations, the continuous squeeze of technology on employees. His analysis further implied the concentration of capital in a few giant corporations, which is evident in the United States today. Moreover, many social scientists agree with Marx that material conditions—economic production in particular—shape intellectual, political, and social life. They also accept his view that "the innermost nature of things" is dynamic and filled with conflict (Heilbroner, 1980).

QUESTIONS FOR DISCUSSION AND REVIEW

1. What are the four major theories of social change, and what factor does each consider to be the basic agency of change?
2. Why do only a few people still believe in the evolutionary theory of social change?
3. How do the separate versions of cyclical theory differ from each other, and how does each contribute to sociology's understanding of social change?
4. Why are differentiation and integration important processes in the equilibrium theory of social change?
5. What are the strengths and weaknesses of Marx's approach to social change?

MODERNIZATION

A typical American farmer and, say, a Guatemalan peasant seem to be separated not just by hundreds of miles but by hundreds of years. Behind this gap lies a set of social changes that goes by the name of **modernization.** Its key element is the change from an agricultural society to an industrial one. Whenever this transformation has occurred, many other changes have swept through various spheres of social life.

Societies that have undergone modernization are those which we have at various times called "developed," "industrialized," and "rich," as well as "modern." Examples are the United States, Japan, and Western European countries. Those societies that have not modernized or are still undergoing modernization we have previously described as "developing," "poor," "third world," or "traditional" societies. They are mostly in Africa, Asia, and Latin America. Here we look at the characteristics, causes, and consequences of modernization. We see just what separates modern from traditional societies. But keep in mind that our descriptions represent ideal types. They are not descriptions of actual societies but an attempt to capture the essence of each type of society. In reality, every society includes both modern and traditional elements. Keep in mind, too, that modern does not necessarily mean something better than traditional. What is traditional may be confining but it may also offer stability and meaning. What is modern may be powerful but it may also be destructive. We are not using these terms as a form of value judgment.

Characteristics

Modernity is simply the condition of advanced industrial societies such as the United States around the middle of the twentieth century. In general, compared with a traditional society, a modern society is more economically rational, more progressive, more "developed," and more innovative. But what about the average modern individual? Through extensive research in six developing countries, sociologist Alex Inkeles (1983) has provided a portrait of what the "modern" person looks like. According to Inkeles, a modern individual shows

1. Openness to new experiences and ideas. A modern person, for example, is willing to try birth control and to meet new people.
2. Independence from traditional authority figures such as priests and elders, and allegiance instead to leaders in government, trade unions, and the like.
3. Rejection of fatalism and passivity in the face of life's difficulties and confidence in one's own efficacy and that of science.
4. Ambition to achieve high occupational and educational goals, and to see one's children achieve these goals.

The conventional wisdom long held that modernization had another effect on individuals: psychological stress. But Inkeles's research casts doubt on this assumption. He studied people from six developing countries and divided them into two categories. One category was considered modernized and the other not. Specifically, people in the modernized group had moved to a city, whereas those considered nonmodernized remained in their villages. Furthermore, compared with the nonmodernized group, modernized individuals had worked more years in factories and had much more exposure to the mass media. Inkeles then gave both groups the same psychological test. He found that they showed about the same number of symptoms of stress. Inkeles therefore concluded that modernization does not produce stress.

But modernization does not necessarily bring greater happiness, either. As one study in Libya has shown, there has not been a significant increase in the Libyans' satisfaction with their lives despite dramatic improvement in education, health care, housing, and other social services during the last decade (Attir and Peterson, 1981). Research in developed countries has also shown that the level of satisfaction and happiness has not grown with respect to earlier times. One reason can be illustrated by the fable of Buridan's donkey: faced with many piles of hay, it suffers the burden of decision. Another reason is that affluence usually increases expectations for a happy life. When expectations rise faster than actual life improvements, satisfactions may decline. Modernization also produces role conflicts. Career ambitions, for example, undermine efforts to spend time with children, making it difficult to be good parents (Kutsch, 1981). Worse yet, in third-world countries, modernization has meant higher crime rates, weakening of family and kinship ties, and increasing rates of environmental pollution. Modernization has further caused massive migrations from rural to urban areas so that many cities are overpopulated and full of overcrowded slums and shantytowns (Stone, 1983).

Causes

How do such far-reaching changes come about? First, several economic developments must occur if a society is to modernize. According to a classical economic theory, modernization requires the following:

1. A technological revolution in agriculture, which permits, and even forces, workers to move off the farms and into industry.
2. An accumulation of capital and of money that

can be loaned to exploit natural resources and manufacture consumer goods.

3. An expansion of foreign trade, which provides an export market for the country's manufactured goods as well as foreign funds and technology.
4. The emergence of entrepreneurs—of people who are willing to take risks to invest in new business ventures (Rostow, 1960).

For modernization to occur, these economic factors must be accompanied by sociological and psychological changes. The people of a society must themselves become modern and committed to modernization. In fact, recently, most development experts in the third world have found that economic development projects have benefited the elites but not the masses. They have therefore shifted attention away from economic to social emphasis by providing more and better education and health care to the people (Stone, 1983). More important, Inkeles (1983) has found four social factors—education, the factory, urbanism, and mass communication—to be the strongest stimulants to modernization. He discovered, for example, that the more years of formal schooling a person had, the higher he or she scored on the "modernity test." Industrial workers also scored higher on the test than peasants. Working in a factory apparently can increase "a man's sense of efficacy, make him less fearful of innovation, and impress on him the value of education as a general qualification for competence and advancement"—qualities typical of a modern person. Thus Inkeles called the factory "a school of modernization."

Other researchers have found that nationalism has become the most powerful of the "ideologies of development" in the third world, replacing the Protestant ethic and individualistic values that have contributed to the economic success in the West (Germani, 1981). Nationalism can stimulate modernization because both are compatible. Nationalism involves a transfer of allegiance from tribes to a nation-state, and modernization requires participation of diverse groups in the national mainstream. This is why developing nations often try to promote modernization by appealing to nationalism. The leaders of Kenya, for example, have long adopted the policy of *harambee* ("let us pull together") in order to unify various tribes, blacks and whites, and villagers and urbanites (Segal, 1982).

Marxist analysts, however, argue that it is difficult for third-world countries to modernize because of their "inherited dependency" on or exploitation by rich nations. They cannot acquire enough loans or aid from industrial nations to finance their development projects. The level of development assistance that they need should be at least 2 percent of the rich nations' GNP, but they get less than 1 percent. They also find it difficult to export their manufactured goods to rich countries because of the latter's protectionist restrictions. This is why in the last 25 years the developing countries as a whole have not increased their share in gross world product. In fact, for the 33 poorest countries containing 47 percent of the world's population, the share dropped from 8.1 percent in 1955 to 4.8 percent in 1980 (Stone, 1983; Chilcote and Johnson, 1983; Wood, 1984).

Toward One World Society?

Discussions about modernization often make three assumptions. One, all societies will, sooner or later, modernize and follow the path forged by Western industrial nations. Two, modernization destroys traditions. And three, as a result, eventually there will be just one worldwide society. All these assumptions are worth examining.

Barriers to Industrialization There is no certainty that developing countries will mimic the social history of nineteenth-century Western nations, or that if they do industrialize, they will also modernize in the same way Western nations did. In fact, they face several barriers to industrialization, and there are significant differences between their situation today and the world in which Western societies industrialized.

In the West the transformation of an agricultural society into an industrialized one using high technology took more than 300 years. The governments of most developing countries today believe that the needs of their people require that they achieve similar technological development within just a few decades. Their efforts are hindered, however, by a population explosion that Western nations did not face at a similar point in their development. As the population grows, economic gains must be used to sustain the increased numbers of people, rather than to fund investments for continued economic development. The economic pie may grow, but it must be divided into ever more slices. Little is left for the improved transportation or machinery or other capital that would aid future growth.

A second barrier to industrialization of the third world is **neocolonialism**—economic dominance by the West, which once held most of the developing world as colonies. While the Western nations were industrializing, they used their colonies as a source of cheap raw materials. Today, developing nations lack a comparable outside source of cheap raw materials. They also must compete with the modernized West in selling their manufactured goods. Many are still finding it difficult to break out of the pattern of a colonial economy, in which the colony exports raw materials and imports manufactured goods. Often developing nations must sell their raw materials cheaply, and pay high prices for the manufactured goods they import. This makes it impossible for them to earn enough to build up their own countries.

Finally, the developing world faces dilemmas in choosing a path to modernization. The economic success of Western nations makes them an alluring model. But efforts to imitate the West can be counterproductive. Developing nations seeking to copy the mass education system of the United States, for example, may divert money badly needed for industrial investments into expensive education that has little practical value to their people and little relation to the job opportunities within their nations. They may also find, as the Shah of Iran did, that their people perceive modernization on the Western model as a betrayal of their own values and way of life, a new colonization by the West.

If, on the other hand, developing nations resist the temptation to mimic the West, they face another set of problems. One is that the United States in particular and Western investors in general may view their policies with suspicion, as a move toward socialism and perhaps anti-Americanism. They may then find it difficult to attract foreign investment and to secure favorable trade policies. Even if Western nations remain friendly, however, developing nations that spurn imitation of existing economic systems face the difficulty of being in largely uncharted waters, of having no good guide to tell them how else they might achieve economic development. During the 1960s, for example, China rejected both Soviet-style socialism and Western-style capitalism, seeking an ideologically pure socialism. One slogan declared, "We would prefer a poor society under socialism to a rich one under capitalism." The effort destroyed the economy and was abandoned in the 1970s.

It has long been assumed that modernization inevitably demolishes tradition. But some studies suggest that the traditions of many developing countries are surviving the onslaught of modernization. The Saudi Arabian technicians shown here, for example, still wear traditional clothing adapted for life in the desert, although they are working on a modern device for utilizing solar energy.

Traditions and Modernization Many sociologists have assumed that modernization inevitably destroys tradition. But some studies suggest that the traditions of developing societies are surviving the onslaught of modernization. Anthropologist Stephen Lansing (1978), for example, has found that economic development has not dismantled Balinese culture. Instead, economic development through tourism has stimulated the traditional Balinese art of woodcarving.

This survival of traditions is really not surprising. Even in the very modernized United States, after all, we find cultural elements, such as religion, that predated modernization. As Inkeles (1983) notes, we are by any measure one of the most modern nations in the world and yet we have one of the highest rates of church membership and attendance (see Chapter 15: Religion). When sociologist Theodore Caplow and his colleagues (1983) studied a midwestern community, they found that the cultural values of high-school students were not significantly different from those of earlier generations. In any society some people are likely to be more "modern" than others, but some aspects of society are more likely than others to endure.

Furthermore, traditions and industrialization do not always clash. As Joseph Gusfield (1967b) has pointed out, they may reinforce each other. In studying the impact of modernization on India, Gusfield found a reinforcement of traditions. When Indians of middle and lower levels seek upward mobility, they do so by "becoming more devoutly Hinduistic," by being as genuinely Indian as possible. Even among very Westernized elites, the native culture still exerts a powerful influence. Nearly all Indian intellectuals speak a regional language as their mother tongue, are steeped in classical

Workers at a Matsushita TV factory in Japan gather every morning to recite the company creed and to sing the company song. The tradition of cooperation, obedience to authority, and the sacrifice of individual wishes for the public good have all contributed to Japan's phenomenal industrial growth. Tradition, then, can advance rather than retard modernization.

Sanskrit literature, are strongly tied to an extended family, and are likely to find a spouse through parental arrangements. The men marry very traditional wives.

We can also see the impact of tradition on modernization in Japan. Without its traditional culture, Japan would not have become an industrial giant. The Japanese culture emphasizes the importance of social relations and collective welfare. It encourages consensus rather than conflict, deference to rather than disrespect for authority, and paternalism rather than indifference by those in authority. These cultural values saturate Japan's economic system. A business enterprise, no matter how large, is run like a household, with the accompanying interdependence and loyalty characteristic of the family. Since the company takes care of its workers by giving them lifetime employment, employees tend to identify strongly with employers and work as hard as they can. Moreover, the traditional emphasis on collective welfare serves more than just enhancing productivity through cooperation between managers and workers. It causes society to favor business and industry at the expense of individuals, transferring funds and wealth from individuals to industries. This can be seen in the fact that factories and company apartments are mostly grand and imposing while private homes are cramped yet highly expensive (Clark, 1979).

Convergence Theory Political scientist Zbigniew Brzezinski once predicted that exposure to supersonic aircraft, satellite communication, and multinational companies would eventually Westernize Asia. This reflects the view known as **convergence theory.** It assumes that modernization will break down the cultural barriers between the third world and the West and that the third world will adopt Western ways of living and virtually all the values of the West. Under the influence of modernization, technocrats and leaders in Asia, Africa, and South America will become a "cosmopolitan elite." They will abandon their own cultures and will be capable of dissolving the cultural differences between their countries and the West.

It is true that third-world countries have acquired many social and cultural characteristics of the West. But as we have noted, there is also evidence that non-Western traditions are surviving and that at least some elites remain closely tied to their native cultures. Convergence theory seems to assume that modernization is a uniform, all-embracing, all-powerful process. But when historian Selig Harrison (1979) evaluated the application of convergence theory to Asia, he found, instead of a convergence toward Western culture,

> an altogether different prospect. Cultural divisions are hardening rather than dissolving. Economic and social change is generating unprecedented pressures for the democratization of cultural life and the reinforcement of cultural identities. While cosmopolitan elites are growing in absolute numbers, their ability to serve as effective mediators is steadily declining. Increasingly, these Westernized elites find themselves isolated and engulfed by rising tides of cultural nationalism.

Sociologist Wilbert Moore (1979) also failed to see the trend toward a common destination. Aside from the failures of most developing countries to catch up economically with the developed nations, Moore offered some instances where convergence is unlikely to happen. Saudi Arabia and other mideastern countries preserve their traditional Islamic way of life despite their efforts at modernization. Nationalism, the antithesis of a world-society concept, has become the "secular religion" of new nations while it continues to be alive in older nations. Finally, the Soviet Union and the United States, though equally far ahead of the third world in modernization, are hardly converging on a common ideological position. They are still at loggerheads, making many people nervous about the prospect of a nuclear war.

If Harrison and Moore are correct, we can expect conflict and misunderstanding between cultures to continue and probably even increase. But we can also look forward to a far more diverse, more interesting, and richer world than the look-alike world predicted by convergence theory.

QUESTIONS FOR DISCUSSION AND REVIEW

1. What key changes occur as a society undergoes modernization?
2. Why must individuals change their outlook on life before they can participate in efforts to modernize?
3. What roles do entrepreneurs, technology, and nationalism play in helping a society become more modern?
4. How do population explosions and neocolonialism create barriers to industrialization in the third world?
5. Why do beliefs in traditions and nationalism challenge the assumptions of the convergence theory of modernization?

MAJOR CHANGES IN OUR FUTURE

What is in store for us in the remainder of this century? Demographic changes should have a marked impact on American society (*Society,* 1984). Working adults and the elderly will each make up a larger share of the population, while the young will constitute a smaller share. With fewer youth, we can expect crime and competition for entry-level jobs to decrease. With more working and elderly adults, productivity and political conservatism would increase. The conservatism may find expression in an emphasis on the basics in education, in toughness toward criminals, in heartlessness toward the poor, and in resistance to efforts by women and minorities to achieve social and economic equality. Brought up in such an environment, young people would also become more conservative. Political conflict between elderly and younger Americans may increase, as the interests of those receiving social security and those paying the taxes clash. People would continue to migrate from the Frostbelt to the Sunbelt, so that the South and West would grow richer at the expense of the Northeast and Midwest. But Sunbelt cities would eventually have higher unemployment, more crime, greater traffic congestion, and more pollution, while Frostbelt states would gradually strengthen their economy by offering tax benefits and other incentives to attract industry, especially electronics and other high-tech firms.

Technology will also stimulate change. Many social scientists and commentators have described how technology is moving us into a new era through a "revolution" as momentous as the Industrial Revolution. This new era has been called the *postindustrial age* by sociologist Daniel Bell (1973) and the *Third Wave era* by journalist Alvin Toffler (1980). According to Toffler, the First Wave era was launched by the agricultural revolution around 8000 B.C. and ended around A.D. 1750. Then the Second Wave, set off by the Industrial Revolution, shaped the world until about 1955. A new civilization then began to emerge out of the old, sparked by computers, jets, space exploration, genetic engineering, the electronic mass media, and other manifestations of high technology. While the industrial era revolved around the machine and the production of goods, this new era, which Toffler called the Third Wave, will revolve around computers and the production of information. Industrial societies, Bell noted, "are goods-producing societies. Life is a game against fabricated nature. . . . A postindustrial society is based on services. Life becomes a game between persons. What counts is not raw muscle power, or energy; what counts is information." Today, about 40 to 45 percent of the American labor force works on information-related ac-

The brokerage office at Merrill Lynch in New York. Information-related activities, as in the financial industry, are becoming the major source of jobs for the American labor force. What will the effects on society be when most people will have to earn a living by doing mental work of some kind? What will happen to those people who are not equipped for such tasks? This profound shift in the nature of work may well generate many social problems in the future. Society will probably become more fragmented or less cohesive. The gap between rich and poor will also widen.

"Roger, it won't kill you to help your own father with his computer."

tivities, such as management, design, high technology, and the mass media. By the year 2000, 85 percent of the American labor force will work in jobs related to information (Spieler, 1980).

What difference will these changes make? More specifically, how will the computer revolution affect us? Computers will probably make our lives more comfortable. After all, they can perform many routine tasks such as managing payrolls, checking inventories, planning family budgets, banking and shopping without leaving the home, and cooking and doing other domestic chores. Physicians can rely on computers to diagnose diseases, monitor pulse and blood pressure, and even make electronic house calls. Computerized robots can be used to handle tedious, dirty, or dangerous jobs such as assembling cars and working with radiation-rich plutonium. We can also use the greatly increased leisure time made possible by the computer to play video games and enjoy ourselves with a myriad of other entertainment options. All this may exact a price, though. Since people can make their living at home and bring all kinds of information and entertainment into their homes, our society will become more individualistic, more fragmented, less cohesive. The gulf between rich and poor will widen, as the schoolchildren now learning to use computers are generally from upper- and middle-class families. Also, blue-collar workers will feel threatened by computerized robots. Such a splintering of society, coupled with the increasing conservatism that we have observed, may well produce more social conflict.

QUESTIONS FOR DISCUSSION AND REVIEW

1. How might demographic changes and technological development influence the future of American society?
2. Why might the new era of computers lead to more personal isolation and social conflict?

CHAPTER REVIEW

1. *According to Smelser, what are the preconditions for the appearance of collective behavior?* Six conditions must appear, in the following sequence: (1) structural conduciveness, (2) social strain, (3) the spread of a generalized belief, (4) a precipitating factor, (5) mobilization of participants, and (6) inadequate social control.

2. *How does a panic come about?* There must be a perception of a crisis, intense fear of possible entrapment, some panic-prone individuals, mutual emotional facilitation, and a lack of cooperation among people. *Which type of people are most likely to succumb to mass hysteria?* Those with little critical ability and little education.

3. *Why do crowds sometimes act irrationally, even violently?* Le Bon argued that as a result of the anonymity of a crowd, people give up their individuality and release their primitive instincts. Then as a result of social contagion, they become part of a collective mind that is irrational. Many sociologists today believe that Le Bon's "collective mind" is a fiction and that crowds are not as homogeneous as they appear. Instead, as Turner and Killian have argued, they appear homogeneous because they conform to a new norm that emerges to deal with the unconventional situation in which the crowd finds itself.

4. *Do fashions affect many aspects of life?* Yes, in fact, almost all aspects of life are influenced by fashion. *How do fashions, fads, and crazes differ?* Fashions occur more predictably, last longer, and are more socially respectable than fads and crazes. Fads are less outrageous and less harmful than crazes.

5. *Are rumors always distortions?* No, they are merely unverified. They may turn out to be true. *When are rumors likely to develop?* If a situation is ambiguous and

institutionalized channels of communication do not satisfy the demand for news about it, then a rumor is likely to emerge.

6. *How does propaganda differ from other types of communication?* It is designed to influence opinion. *Why is the influence of the American media limited?* There are several reasons: the multitude of viewpoints presented by the media; its tendency to try to match rather than mold opinion, telling people what they want to hear; and the frequency with which communication occurs by a two-step flow—from the media to opinion leaders and only then to the public. *What influence do the media have?* They frequently authenticate information; validate private opinions, preferences, and values; legitimize unconventional viewpoints and behavior; concretize ill-defined anxieties and preferences; and establish a hierarchy of importance and prestige among people, objects, or ideas.

7. *What are the aims of social movements?* Generally, they seek some sort of change. Revolutionary movements seek total, radical change of society. Reform movements seek a partial change in society. Resistance movements try to turn back some ongoing social change. Expressive movements seek to change individuals, not society. *What are the social causes of social movements?* According to the traditional perspective, social conditions must first frustrate masses of people, then people must identify a common frustration and work out a plan and band together to change the offending conditions. Smelser's theory regarding six preconditions of collective behavior can be applied to social movements. But resource mobilization theory emphasizes the importance of resources at the expense of discontent as the cause of social movements.

8. *How do modern evolutionary theorists describe social change?* They argue that societies tend to change gradually from simple to complex forms. *What is a primary difference between evolutionary and cyclical theorists?* Evolutionary theorists see social change as having one principal direction: toward increased complexity. Cyclical theorists portray social change as reversible: societies may move "forward" and "backward," they may rise and fall, in cycles. *What is equilibrium theory?* It holds that the various parts of society are all interdependent and that a change in any one part stimulates compensatory changes in other parts of the system. *What, in Parson's view, are two basic processes in the evolution of societies?* Differentiation and integration. *How does conflict theory differ from equilibrium theory?* Whereas equilibrium theory portrays stability as the pervasive characteristic of societies, conflict theorists believe that societies are always marked by conflict and that conflict is the key to change.

9. *What is modernization?* It is the set of social changes that has accompanied the transformation of agricultural societies into industrial ones. *What characteristics are typical of a modern individual?* Openness to new experience and ideas, independence from traditional authority figures, rejection of fatalism and passivity, and ambition. *What conditions are necessary for modernization to occur?* Several economic developments are necessary: (1) a technological revolution in agriculture, (2) an accumulation of capital, (3) an expansion of foreign trade, and (4) the emergence of entrepreneurs. The people of a society must also become modern, be committed to modernization, and harbor feelings of nationalism. *Will modernization produce one worldwide society?* Not necessarily. Modernization of the third world along Western lines is not inevitable, and modernization does not always destroy traditions. In some nations undergoing industrialization today, cultural differences with the West are increasing rather than decreasing.

10. *What effects are demographic changes in the United States likely to produce in the near future?* The aging of the population seems likely to lead to lower crime rates and increased productivity and conservatism. Political conflict between racial and ethnic groups, sexes, and generations may increase. Migration from the Frostbelt to the Sunbelt will continue. *How is technology changing the society?* It is carrying us into a "postindustrial age" or a "third wave" era in which information, not goods, will be the most important product. The computer technology will substantially improve our living conditions but not social life.

KEY TERMS

Collective behavior Relatively spontaneous, unorganized, and unpredictable social behavior (p. 576).

Conflict theory The theory that societies are always marked by conflict and that conflict is the key to change (p. 595).

Convergence theory The theory that modernization

will bring the third world and the West together by breaking down their cultural barriers (p. 600).

Craze A fad with serious consequences (p. 583).

Crowd A collection of people who for a brief time do something in close proximity to one another (p. 580).

Cyclical theory The theory that societies change in an endless series of cycles, by growing, maturing, and declining and then starting over with a new form (p. 591).

Differentiation The process by which one unit of society divides into two or more (p. 594).

Emergent-norm theory Turner and Killian's theory that members of a crowd develop, through interaction, a new norm to deal with the unconventional situation facing them (p. 582).

Equilibrium theory The theory that various parts of a society are so interdependent that changes in one part produce compensatory changes in others, thereby ensuring social order and stability (p. 593).

Evolutionary theory The theory that societies change gradually from simple to complex forms (p. 591).

Fad A temporary enthusiasm for an innovation less respectable than a fashion (p. 583).

Fashion A great though brief enthusiasm among a relatively large number of people for some innovation (p. 582).

Ideational culture Sorokin's term for the culture that emphasizes faith as the key to knowledge (p. 593).

Integration The process by which various units of society are coordinated (p. 595).

Mass hysteria A form of collective behavior in which numerous people engage in a frenzied activity without checking the source of their fear (p. 579).

Modernization The set of social changes that has accompanied the transformation of agricultural societies into industrial societies (p. 596).

Neocolonialism The economic dependence of third-world countries on their former colonial rulers, the current Western industrial powers (p. 598).

Opinion leader A person whose opinion is respected by others and influences them (p. 585).

Panic A form of collective behavior characterized by a maladaptive, fruitless response to a serious threat (p. 579).

Principle of immanent change Sorokin's term for social change being the product of the social forces that exist within a society (p. 593).

Propaganda Communication tailored to influence opinion (p. 585).

Public A dispersed collection of people who share some interest or concern (p. 584).

Public opinion The collection of ideas and attitudes shared by members of a particular public (p. 584).

Resource mobilization theory The theory that social movement results from the availability of resources for mobilization such as strong organization, effective leadership, money, and media access (p. 590).

Rumor An unverified story passed from one person to another (p. 583).

Sensate culture Sorokin's term for the culture that emphasizes empiricism or science as the key to knowledge (p. 593).

Social change The alteration of society over time (p. 576).

Social contagion The spreading of a certain emotion and action from one member of a crowd to another (p. 582).

Social movement An activity in which many people jointly struggle to bring about or resist social change (p. 586).

SUGGESTED READINGS

Chirot, Daniel. 1986. *Social Change in the Modern Era.* New York: Harcourt Brace Jovanovich. A sociohistorical analysis of social change, focusing on the past and present conditions of Western societies.

Glynn, Prudence. 1982. *Skin to Skin: Eroticism in Dress.* New York: Oxford University Press. An insightful, entertaining panorama of how fashions vary across time and space.

Hewlett, Sylvia Ann. 1980. *The Cruel Dilemmas of Development.* New York: Basic Books. A provocative study of modernization, showing how massive poverty, increasing inequality, and political repression can result from economic development.

Inkeles, Alex. 1983. *Exploring Individual Modernity.* New York: Columbia University Press. A well-integrated collection of articles that reports and analyzes findings from the author's famous studies on becoming modern in six third-world countries.

Porter, Bruce, and Marvin Dunn. 1984. *The Miami Riot of 1980.* Lexington, Mass.: Lexington Books. A useful, data-packed analysis of the "McDuffie" riot that resulted in 18 dead, $80 million in property damage, and 1000 arrests.

Glossary

Achieved status A status that is attained through an individual's own action.

Acute disease A disease that lasts for a short time, during which the victim either recovers or dies.

Ad-hocracy Toffler's term for an organization that assembles temporary groups of experts for solving specific problems.

Ageism Prejudice and discrimination against people because of their age.

Age norm A norm that defines what people at a given stage of life should or should not do.

Age structure The pattern of the proportions of different age groups within a population.

Agricultural society A society that produces food by relying on plows and draft animals.

Alienation of labor Marx's term for laborers' loss of control over their work process.

Alternative school A school representing an educational movement designed to enhance student creativity by allowing maximum freedom in choosing learning materials within the classroom.

Alzheimer's disease An incurable disease of the brain, characterized by progressive loss of memory and other mental abilities.

Amalgamation The process by which the subcultures of various groups are blended together, forming a new culture.

Amateur sport Sport that is played for fun.

Androgynous role A pattern of attitudes and behaviors combining elements of what are usually considered masculine and feminine patterns.

Animism The belief in spirits capable of helping or harming people.

Anomaly Kuhn's term for a research finding that cannot be fitted into the existing paradigm and thus cannot be explained by it.

Anomie A condition in which social norms are absent, weak, or in conflict.

Anticipatory socialization Socialization that prepares a person to assume a role in the future.

Anti-Semitism Prejudice or discrimination against Jews.

Applied science The type of science that puts knowledge to use.

Aptitude The capacity for developing physical or social skills.

Arranged marriage A marriage in which the partners were selected by their parents.

Ascribed status A status that one has no control over, such as status based on race, sex, or age.

Assimilation The process by which a minority adopts the dominant group's culture, fading into the larger society.

Authority Legitimate power that derives from traditions, a leader's charisma, or laws.

Basic science The type of science that seeks knowledge for its own sake.

Behavioral assimilation The minorities' adoption of the dominant group's language, values, and behavioral patterns.

Behaviorism The school of psychology that regards behavior as the product of conditioning.

Belief An idea that is relatively subjective, unreliable, or unverifiable.

Bilateral descent Rule that recognizes both parents' families as a child's close relatives.

Biosphere A thin film of air, water, and soil surrounding the earth.

Birth rate The number of births for every 1000 people in a given year.

Bureaucracy An organization characterized by a division of labor, hierarchy of authority, the hiring of employees on the basis of impersonal procedures and technical qualifications, and reliance on formal rules.

Capitalism An economic system based on private ownership of property and competition in producing and selling goods and services.

Caste system A relatively rigid stratification system in which one's position is ascribed and there is almost no mobility.

Castration anxiety A psychiatric term for the male homosexual's fear of getting castrated while having sex with a woman.

Catch-22 Novelist Joseph Heller's term for the situation in which the very compliance with one rule results in violating another.

Census A periodic head count of the entire population of a country.

Charisma An exceptional personal quality popularly attributed to certain individuals.

Chromosomes The materials in a cell that transmit hereditary traits to the carrier from his or her parents.

Chronic disease A disease that lasts for a long time before the victim dies.

Church A well-established religious organization that is integrated into the society and does not make strict demands on its members.

Civil religion A collection of beliefs, symbols, and rituals that sanctify the dominant values of society.

Class A category of people who own or do not own the means of production, or have about the same amount of income, power, and prestige.

Class conflict Marx's term for the struggle between capitalists, who own the means of production, and the proletariat, who do not.

Classical conditioning The type of conditioning that involves training the subject to associate two inherently unrelated stimuli.

Class system A stratification system in which achieved characteristics play a large role in determining one's position and in which there is considerable social mobility.

Coercion Illegitimate use of force or threat of force to compel obedience.

Coercive organization An organization in which force or threat of force is applied to the lower participants, who in turn are alienated from the organization.

Collective behavior Relatively spontaneous, unorganized, and unpredictable social behavior.

Coming out The process of publicly identifying oneself as a homosexual.

Communality The norm that requires scientists to share their knowledge freely with each other.

Compensatory education A school program intended to improve the academic performance of socially and educationally disadvantaged children.

Competition A relationship in which two individuals or groups strive to achieve the same goal before the other does.

Compositional theory The theory that city dwellers are as involved with small groups of friends, relatives, and neighbors as are noncity people.

Concentric-zone theory Model of land use in which the city spreads out from the center in a series of concentric zones, each of which is used for a particular kind of activity.

Conditioning The process by which associations are formed between stimuli and responses.

Conflict A relationship in which two individuals or groups struggle to achieve a goal by defeating each other without regard to rules.

Conflict perspective A theoretical perspective that focuses on conflict and change in society, particularly conflict between a dominant and a subordinate group, and emphasizes that conflict is a constant fact of social life.

Conflict theory The theory that societies are always marked by conflict and that conflict is the key to change.

Conglomerate A corporation that owns companies in various unrelated industries.

Constant A phenomenon or characteristic whose value does not change from one individual or group to another within the population being studied.

Content analysis The analysis of a communication by searching for its specific words or ideas and then turning them into numbers.

Control group The subjects in an experiment who are not exposed to the independent variable.

Convergence theory The theory that modernization will bring the third world and the West together by breaking down their cultural barriers.

Cooperation A relationship in which two or more persons work together to achieve a common goal.

Correlation A consistent association between two or more variables, which may or may not be causal.

Counterculture A subculture whose norms and values sharply contradict those of the larger society but are basically not criminal or illegal.

Craze A fad with serious consequences.

Crowd A collection of people who for a brief time do something in close proximity to one another.

Crystalline intelligence Wisdom and insight into the human condition, as shown by one's skills in philosophy, language, music, or painting.

Cult A religious group that professes new religious beliefs, rejects society, and demands extreme loyalty from its members.

Cultural determinism The view that cultural and subcultural factors are the most important determinants of human personality.

Cultural diffusion The spread of cultural traits from one society to another, largely through contact between them.

Cultural lag Ogburn's term for the tendency of values and beliefs and other nonmaterial aspects of our culture to lag behind technological change.

Cultural pluralism The peaceful coexistence of various racial and ethnic groups, with each retaining its own subculture.

Cultural relativism Evaluating other cultures on their own terms, with the result of not passing judgment on them.

Cultural transmission The process by which the values of crime and delinquency are transmitted from one group to another.

Cultural universal A practice that is found in all cultures as a means for meeting the same human need.

Culture A complex whole consisting of objects, values, and other characteristics that people have acquired as members of society.

Cyclical theory The theory that societies change in an endless series of cycles by growing, maturing, and declining, and then starting over with a new form.

Date rape Rape committed by a man against a woman he is out with.

Death rate The number of deaths for every 1000 people in a given year.

De facto segregation Segregation sanctioned by tradition and custom.

De jure segregation Segregation sanctioned by law.

Demographic process An aspect of a population that is always changing, such as the birth rate, death rate, or net migration rate.

Demographic transition The process of going through various stages of population change, with each stage being determined by a certain level of economic development.

Demography The scientific study of population.

Dependent variable A variable that is considered the effect of another variable.

Descriptive research Research aimed at gathering information in order to describe a phenomenon.

Detached observation A method of observation in which the researcher stands apart from the subjects.

Developmental socialization The kind of socialization that teaches a person to be more adequate in playing his or her currently assumed role.

Deviant behavior An act that is considered deviant by public consensus or the powerful at a given place and time.

Deviant subculture A subculture whose values are in conflict with those of the dominant culture and that tends to be illegal or criminal.

Differential association The process by which potential deviants associate more with criminal elements than with noncriminal elements.

Differentiation The process by which one unit of society divides into two or more.

Discrimination An unfavorable action against individuals that is taken because they are members of some category.

Disinterestedness The norm that requires scientists to pursue truth rather than self-interest.

Double standard The social norm that allows males but not females to engage in nonmarital sex.

Ecological processes Processes in which people compete for certain land use, one group dominates another, and a particular group moves into an area and takes it over from others.

Ecology The study of the interrelationships among organisms and between organisms and their environments.

Economic institution A system for producing and distributing goods and services.

Ecosystem A self-sufficient community of organisms depending for survival on one another and on the environment.

Egalitarian family Family in which the husband and wife hold equal authority.

Ego According to Freud, the rational part of the personality which mediates between the id and superego.

Electra complex According to Freud, the girl's sexual love for her father and hostility for her mother.

ELISA Acronym for "enzyme-linked immunosorbent assay," a widely used test for antibodies to the AIDS virus.

Emergent-norm theory Turner and Killian's theory that members of a crowd develop, through interaction, a new norm to deal with the unconventional situation facing them.

Empirical indicator An observable and measurable thing that represents a basically unobservable phenomenon.

Endogamy The norm of marrying someone from one's own group.

Enterprise zone President Reagan's term for the depressed urban area that businesses, with the help of generous tax credits, will revive by creating jobs.

Epidemiology The study of the origin and spread of disease within a population.

Equilibrium theory The theory that various parts of a society are so interdependent that changes in one part produce compensatory changes in others, thereby ensuring social order and stability.

ERA Equal Rights Amendment to the U.S. Constitution, intended to prohibit denial of legal rights by the United States or any state on account of gender.

Ethicalism The type of religion that emphasizes moral principles as guides for living a righteous life.

Ethnic group People who share a distinctive cultural heritage.

Ethnocentrism The attitude that one's own culture is superior to that of others.

Evolutionary theory The theory that societies change gradually from simple to complex forms.

Exchange A reciprocal transaction between individuals, groups, or societies.

Exogamy The norm of marrying someone outside one's group.

Experiment A research method in which the researcher manipulates variables so that their influence can be determined.

Experimental group The subjects in an experiment who are exposed to the independent variables.

Explanatory research Research designed to test a hypothesis in order to explain a phenomenon.

Expressive role Role that requires taking care of personal relationships.

Extended family Family that consists of two parents, their young children, and other relatives; also called *consanguine family* because its members are related by blood.

Extramarital sex Having sex with a person who is not one's spouse, popularly called adultery or marital infidelity.

Fad A temporary enthusiasm for an innovation less respectable than a fashion.

False negative The result of a blood test indicating an incorrect negative result—for example, that the body does not have AIDS-virus antibodies when in fact it does.

False positive The result of a blood test indicating an incorrect positive result—for example, that the body has AIDS-virus antibodies when in fact it does not.

Family of orientation Family in which one grows up, consisting of oneself and one's parents and siblings.

Family of procreation Family that one establishes through marriage, consisting of oneself and one's spouse and children.

Fashion A great though brief enthusiasm among a relatively large number of people for some innovation.

Fecundity The number of babies that the average woman has the biological capacity to bear.

Fertility The actual number of babies born to the average woman of childbearing age.

Fluid intelligence Ability to comprehend abstract relationships as in mathematics, physics, or some other science.

Folk society Redfield's term for a society that is small, nonliterate, and homogeneous, with a strong group solidarity; used to distinguish preindustrial from industrial societies.

Folkways "Weak" norms that specify expectations about proper behavior.

Formal organization A group whose activities are rationally designed to achieve specific goals.

Free-agent system The practice of permitting professional athletes to leave one team and choose a better deal from another.

Gemeinschaft Tönnies's term for a type of society marked by a strong sense of community and by personal interactions among its members.

Gender role The pattern of attitudes and behaviors that a society expects of its members because of their gender.

Generalized others Mead's term for people whose names are unknown to the child but who influence the child's internalization of the values of society.

Genocide Wholesale killing of a racial or ethnic group.

Gentrification The movement of affluent people into urban neighborhoods, displacing poor and working-class residents.

Gesellschaft Tönnies's term for a type of society characterized by individualism and by impersonal interactions.

Groupthink The tendency for members of a group to maintain consensus to the extent of ignoring the truth.

Hawthorne effect The unintended effect of the researcher's presence on the subjects' behavior.

Healing role A set of social expectations that defines the doctor's rights and obligations.

Homogamy Marriage that involves two people having similar characteristics, or norm that requires such a marriage.

Horizontal mobility The movement of a person from one job to another within the same status category.

Hormones Chemical substances that stimulate or inhibit vital biological processes.

Horticultural society A society that depends on growing plants in small gardens for its survival.

Hunting-gathering society A society that hunts animals and gathers plants to survive.

Hypothesis A tentative statement about how various events are related to one another.

Id According to Freud, the irrational, pleasure-seeking component of personality.

Ideal type Weber's term for a description of what are theorized to be the essential characteristics of a phenomenon, with which actual phenomena can be compared.

Ideational culture Sorokin's term for the culture that emphasizes faith as the key to knowledge.

Ideological conservative A person who opposes the idea of governmental intervention in citizens' affairs.

Ideology of sport A set of popular beliefs that emphasizes the positive functions of sport.

Impression management The act of presenting one's "self" in such a way as to make others form the desired impression.

Incest taboo The social norm that strongly prohibits sexual relations between close relatives.

Independent variable A variable that is the cause of another variable.

Index offense The FBI's term for a major, serious crime such as murder, rape, or robbery.

Individual mobility Social mobility related to an individual's personal achievement and characteristics.

Industrial Revolution The dramatic economic change brought about by the introduction of machines into the work process about 200 years ago.

Infant mortality rate The number of deaths among infants less than one year old for every 1000 live births.

Influence The ability to control others' behavior through persuasion rather than coercion or authority.

Informal organization A group formed by the informal relations among members of an organization; based on personal interactions, not on any plan by the organization.

Ingroup The group to which an individual is strongly tied as a member.

Instincts Fixed traits that are inherited and enable the carrier to perform complex tasks.

Institutional differentiation The process by which the functions of one institution are gradually taken over by other institutions.

Institutionalized discrimination The persistence of discrimination in social institutions, not necessarily known to everybody as discrimination.

Instrumental role Role that requires performing a task.

Integration The process by which various units of society are coordinated.

Intelligence The capacity for mental or intellectual achievement.

Interest group An organized collection of people who attempt to influence government policy.

Intergenerational mobility A change in social standing from one generation to the next.

Internalization The process by which individuals incorporate the values of society into their personalities, accepting the norms of society as their own.

Intragenerational mobility A change in an individual's social standing, also called career mobility.

Jim Crow The system of laws made in the late nineteenth century in the South for segregating blacks from whites in all kinds of public and private facilities.

Kinesics Use of body movements as a means of communication.

Knowledge A collection of relatively objective ideas and facts about the physical and social world.

Latent function A function that is unintended and thus often unrecognized.

Laws Norms that are specified formally in writing and backed by the power of the state.

Life chances Opportunities for living a good, long, or successful life in a society.

Life expectancy The average number of years that a group of people can expect to live.

Life-styles Tastes, preferences, and ways of living.

Looking-glass self Cooley's term for the self-image that we develop from the way others treat us.

Manifest function A function that is intended and thus seems obvious.

Marginal surplus population Marxist term for unemployed workers who are useless to the capitalist economy.

Marriage rate The number of marriages for every 1000 people in a given year.

Mass hysteria A form of collective behavior in which numerous people engage in a frenzied activity without checking the source of their fear.

Master status A status that dominates a relationship.

Material culture All the physical objects produced by humans as members of society.

Matriarchal family Family in which the dominant figure is the eldest female.

Matrilineal descent Rule that recognizes only the mother's family as a child's close relatives.

Matrilocal residence Rule that requires a married couple to live with the wife's family.

Matthew effect The tendency to praise famous scientists and to ignore the contributions of those who are not well-known.

Mechanical solidarity A form of social cohesion that develops when people do similar work and have similar beliefs and values, characteristic of simple, traditional societies.

Megalopolis A vast area in which many metropolises merge.

Men's liberation A quiet movement among some men not to play the traditional dominant male role.

Metropolis A large urban area including a city and its surrounding suburbs.

Minority A group of people who share distinctive physical or cultural characteristics and who are subjected to prejudice and discrimination.

Mixed economy An economic system that includes both capitalist and socialist elements.

Modernization The set of social changes that has accompanied the transformation of agricultural societies into industrial societies.

Monogamy Marriage of one man to one woman.

Monopoly Situation in which one firm controls the output of an industry.

Monotheism The belief in one god.

Mores "Strong" norms that specify normal behavior and constitute demands, not just expectations.

Multinational corporation A corporation that has subsidiaries in several nations.

Multiple-nuclei theory Model in which the land-use pattern of a city is built around many discrete nuclei, each being the center of some specialized activity.

Natural selection Process in which organisms that are well adapted to their environment have more offspring than the less well adapted, thereby producing evolution.

Negative imprinting A biological mechanism that suppresses erotic feelings for individuals with whom one has become familiar since early childhood.

Neocolonialism The economic dependence of third-world countries on their former colonial rulers, the current Western industrial powers.

Neolocal residence Rule that requires a married couple to live by themselves, away from both husband's and wife's families.

Neurosis Mental problem characterized by a persistent fear, anxiety, or worry about trivial matters.

Nonmaterial culture Norms, values, and all the other intangible components of culture.

Norm A social rule that directs people to behave in a certain way.

Normal science Kuhn's term for routine research.

Normative organization An organization in which normative power is exercised over the lower participants, who are deeply committed to the organization.

Nuclear family Family that consists of two parents and their unmarried children; also called *conjugal family* because its members are related by virtue of the marriage between the two adults.

Objective method The method of identifying social classes by using occupation, income, and education to rank people.

Oedipus complex According to Freud, the young boy's sexual love for his mother and jealousy of his father.

Oligopoly Situation in which a very few companies control the output of an industry.

Operant conditioning The type of conditioning that involves administering rewards for desired behavior and punishment for undesired behavior.

Operational definition A specification of the action needed to translate what is basically unobservable into what can be observed and measured.

Operational liberal One who is in favor of governmental programs serving the public.

Opinion leader A person whose opinion is respected by others and influences them.

Organic solidarity A form of social cohesion that develops when the differences among occupations make people depend on each other; characteristic of complex, industrialized societies.

Organized skepticism The norm that requires scientists to be critical of any scientific idea or finding.

Outgroup The group of which an individual is not a member.

PACs Acronym of political action committees, which are political organizations that funnel money from business, labor, and other special interest groups into election campaigns in order to elect or defeat candidates.

Panic A form of collective behavior characterized by a maladaptive, fruitless response to a serious threat.

Paradigm A model for defining, studying, and solving problems in accordance with certain basic assumptions.

Parkinson's Law Parkinson's observation—that "work expands to fill the time available for its completion"—for explaining why bureaucracy tends to keep growing.

Participant observation A method of observation in which the researcher takes part in the activities of the group being studied.

Pastoral society A society that domesticates and herds animals for food.

Patriarchal family Family in which the dominant figure is the eldest male.

Patrilineal descent Rule that recognizes only the father's family as a child's close relatives.

Patrilocal residence Rule that requires a married couple to live with the husband's family.

Personality A fairly stable configuration of feelings, attitudes, ideas, and behaviors that characterizes an individual.

Peter Principle Peter's observation—that "in a hierarchy every employee tends to rise to his level of incompetence"—for explaining the prevalence of incompetence among bureaucrats.

Plea bargaining A pretrial negotiation in which the defendant agrees to plead guilty to a lesser charge in exchange for a less severe penalty.

Political party A group organized for the purpose of gaining government offices.

Political power The capacity to use the government to make decisions that affect the whole society.

Political socialization A learning process by which a person acquires political knowledge, beliefs, and attitudes.

Politics Process in which people acquire and exercise power, determining who gets what, when, and how.

Polyandry Marriage of one woman to two or more men.

Polygamy Marriage of one person to two or more people of the opposite sex.

Polygyny Marriage of one man to two or more women.

Polytheism The belief in more than one god.

Population The entire group of people to be studied.

Postmarital sex The sexual experience of the divorced or widowed.

Power The ability to control the behavior of others, even against their wills.

Power elite A small group of individuals who hold top positions in the federal government, military, and corporations, having similar backgrounds, values, and interests.

Prejudice A negative attitude toward some category of people.

Premarital sex Sex before marriage.

Prescribed role A set of expectations held by society regarding how an individual with a particular status should behave.

Primary deviance An isolated violation of a norm that is not considered deviant by the person committing the act.

Primary group A group whose members interact informally, relate to each other as whole persons, and enjoy their relationship for its own sake.

Principle of immanent change Sorokin's term for the idea that social change is the product of the social forces existing within a society.

Profane The everyday life experience, which is mundane, ordinary, and utilitarian.

Professional sport Sport that is played for money.

Propaganda Communication tailored to influence opinion.

Proxemics Perception and use of space as a means of communication.

Psychosis Mental disorder typified by loss of touch with reality.

Public A dispersed collection of people who share some interest or concern.

Public opinion The collection of ideas and attitudes shared by members of a particular public.

Pygmalion effect The effect of a teacher's expectations on student performance.

Race People who share inherited physical characteristics and who are looked upon as forming a distinct biological group.

Random sample A sample drawn in such a way that all members of the population had an equal chance of being selected.

Rationalization Weber's term for the tendency to replace traditional, spontaneous, informal, and diverse ways of doing things with a planned, formally unified method based on abstract rules.

Recidivism Repeated commission of crimes.

Reference group A group that is used as the frame of reference for evaluating one's own behavior.

Reliability The extent to which a study produces the same findings when repeated by the original or other researchers; popularly known as "consistency."

Religion A unified system of beliefs and practices regarding sacred things that unites its adherents into a single moral community.

Reputational method The method of identifying social classes by selecting a group of people and then asking them to rank others.

Reserve system The practice of forcing professional athletes to play for their team for as long as the owner wants them to.

Resocialization The kind of socialization that is aimed at replacing one's old self with a new self.

Resource-mobilization theory The theory that social movement results from the availability of resources for mobilization, such as strong organization, effective leadership, money, and media access.

Revolution The violent overthrow of an existing government and drastic change in the social and political order.

Ritual Behavioral expression of a religious belief.

Role A set of behaviors associated with a particular status.

Role conflict Conflict between two roles being played simultaneously.

Roleless role Being assigned no role in society's division of labor, a predicament of the elderly in industrial society.

Role performance Actual performance of a role.

Role strain Stress caused by incompatible demands built into a role.

Rumor An unverified story passed from one person to another.

Sacred Whatever transcends the everyday world and inspires awe and reverence.

Sample A relatively small number of people selected from a larger population.

Sanction Formal or informal rewards for conformity to norms, or punishments for violation of norms.

Scapegoat The minority that the dominant group's frustrated members blame for their own failures.

Science A body of knowledge about natural phenomena that is acquired through the systematic use of objective methods.

Scientific revolution Kuhn's term for the replacement of an old paradigm by a new one.

Secondary analysis The analysis of existing data collected by somebody else.

Secondary deviance Habitual norm violations that the person recognizes as deviant and commits in conformity with his or her self-image as a deviant.

Secondary group A group in which the individuals interact formally, relate to each other as players of particular roles and expect to profit from each other.

Sect A religious group that sets itself apart from society and makes heavy demands on its members.

Sector theory Model in which a city grows outward in wedge-shaped sectors from the center.

Secularization The process by which nonreligious forces exert their influence on society.

Segregation The spatial and social separation of a minority group from the dominant group, forcing the minority to live in inferior conditions.

Senescence The natural physical process of aging.

Senility An abnormal condition characterized by serious memory loss, confusion, and loss of the ability to reason; not a natural result of aging.

Sensate culture Sorokin's term for the culture that emphasizes empiricism or science as the key to knowledge.

Sequential orgasms One partner reaching sexual climax after the other does.

Serial monogamy Marriage of one person to two or more people of the opposite sex but one at a time.

Sex drive A biological potential for, rather than determinant of, sexual desire or behavior.

Sex instinct An innate biological mechanism that causes its carrier to have sexual relations in a certain way and at a definite time.

Sexism Prejudice and discrimination against women.

Sex ratio The number of males per hundred females.

Shamanism The belief that a spiritual leader can communicate with the spirits by acting as their mouthpiece or letting his soul leave his body and enter the spiritual world.

Sick role A pattern of expectation regarding how a sick person should behave.

Significant others Mead's term for specific persons, such as parents, who have a significant influence on the child because the child interacts mainly with them in his or her early years and plays at being these adults.

Simultaneous orgasms Both partners reaching sexual climax at the same time.

Social aggregate A collection of people who happen to be in one place but do not interact with one another.

Social category A number of people who happen to share some characteristics but do not interact with one another or gather in one place.

Social change The alteration of society over time.

Social consensus Condition in which most members of society agree on what is good for everybody to have and cooperate to achieve it.

Social contagion The spreading of a certain emotion and action from one member of a crowd to another.

Social control Process by which individuals are pressured by others such as teachers, peers, and police to conform to social norms.

Social forces Forces that arise from the society we are part of.

Social group A collection of people who share some characteristics, interact with one another, and have some feeling of unity.

Social institution A set of widely shared beliefs, norms, or procedures necessary for meeting the needs of a society.

Social integration The degree to which people are related to a social group.

Social interaction The process by which individuals act toward and react to one another.

Socialism An economic system based on public ownership and control of the economy.

Socialization The process by which a society transmits its cultural values to its members.

Social mobility The movement from one social standing to another.

Social movement An activity in which many people jointly struggle to bring about or resist social change.

Social network A web of social relationships that connects specific individuals or groups to one another.

Social stratification A system in which people are ranked into categories with some getting more social rewards than others.

Social structure A recurrent pattern in the ways people relate to each other.

Society A collection of interacting individuals sharing the same culture and territory.

Sociological imagination C. Wright Mills's term for the ability to see the impact of social forces on individuals, especially on their private lives.

Sociology The scientific study of human social behavior.

Spurious correlation The appearance of a correlation between two variables that are not causally related.

Status A position in a group or society.

Status inconsistency The condition in which the individual is given a different ranking in various social categories, such as being high in occupation but low in income.

Status system System in which people are stratified according to their social prestige.

Stratified sampling The process of drawing a random sample in which various categories of people are represented in proportions equal to their presence in the population.

Structural assimilation Social condition in which minority groups cease to be minorities and are accepted on equal terms with the rest of society.

Structural functionalism A theoretical perspective that focuses on social order, which is assumed to be based on the positive functions performed by the interdependent parts of society.

Structural mobility A change in social standing that affects many people at the same time and results from changes in the structure of society.

Structured interview The interview in which the researcher asks standardized questions that require respondents to choose from among several standardized answers.

Subcultural theory Fischer's theory that the city enriches people's lives by offering diverse opportunities and developing various subcultures.

Subculture A culture within a larger culture.

Subjective method The method of identifying social classes by asking people to rank themselves.

Subordinate status A status that does not influence a particular relationship.

Superego In Freud's theory, that component of the personality which approximates what is traditionally called conscience. It represents an internalization of the parents' ideals and prohibitions and restrains the id.

Survey A research method that involves asking questions about opinions, beliefs, or behavior.

Symbol A thing that stands for some other thing.

Symbolic interactionism A theoretical perspective that focuses on the interaction between individuals and is based on the assumption that their subjective interpretations of each other's actions influence their interaction.

Systematic sampling The process of drawing a random sample systematically rather than haphazardly.

Technology The application of scientific knowledge for practical purposes.

Theism The type of religion that centers on the worship of a god or gods.

Theoretical perspective A set of broad assumptions, which cannot be proven true or false, about the nature of a subject.

Theory A set of logically related hypotheses that explains the relationship among various phenomena.

Third variable A hidden variable that is responsible for the occurrence of a relation between two other variables that are not causally related.

Totemism The belief that a kinship exists between humans and an animal or a plant.

Tracking system A system in which students are assigned to different classes on the basis of ability.

Universalism The norm that requires scientists to evaluate ideas in accordance with impersonal criteria.

Unstructured interview The interview in which open-ended questions are asked and the respondent is allowed to answer freely.

Urban anomie theory Wirth's theory that city people have a unique way of life, characterized by alienation, impersonal relations, and stress.

Urban ecology The study of the relationship between people and their urban environment.

Urbanization Migration of people from the countryside to cities, increasing the percentage of the population that lives in cities.

Urban society Redfield's term for societies that are large, literate, and heterogeneous, with little group solidarity.

Utilitarian organization An organization in which remuneration is used to control the lower participants, who show calculative involvement in the organization.

Validity The extent to which a study measures what it is supposed to measure; popularly known as "accuracy."

Value A socially shared idea that something is good, desirable, or important.

Variable A characteristic that varies from one individual or group to another within the population being studied.

Variant subculture A subculture that is different from but acceptable to the dominant culture.

Verstehen Weber's term for the subjective method, which requires sociologists to adopt an attitude of understanding or empathy toward their subjects.

Vertical mobility The movement of people up or down the status ladder.

Victimless crimes Crimes that are without any victim because the offender does not harm another person.

Vital statistics Data about births, marriages, deaths, and migrations into and out of a country.

White ethnics Americans of eastern and southern European origins.

Women's ghettos Traditionally female low-paying occupations that are subordinate to positions held by men.

References

Aage, Hans. 1984. "Economic arguments on the sufficiency of natural resources." *Cambridge Journal of Economics,* 8, pp. 105–113.

Abelson, Philip H. 1984. "Groundwater contamination." *Science,* 224, p. 673.

Abraham, A. S. 1984. "The north-south gap." *World Press Review,* 31, October, p. 39.

Acton, H. B. 1967. *What Marx Really Said.* New York: Schocken.

Adorno, Theodore W., et al. 1950. *The Authoritarian Personality.* New York: Harper & Row.

Ainsworth, Martha. 1984. "Population policy: Country experience." *Finance & Development,* 21, pp. 18–20.

Akiyama, Yoshio. 1981. "Murder victimization: A statistical analysis." *FBI Law Enforcement Bulletin,* 50, pp. 8–11.

Alba, Richard D. 1981. "The twilight of ethnicity among American Catholics of European ancestry." *The Annals,* 454, March, pp. 86–97.

———. 1985. "The twilight of ethnicity among Americans of European ancestry: The case of Italians." *Ethnic and Racial Studies,* 8, pp. 134–58.

Albert, Ethel M. 1963. "Women of Burundi: A study of social values," in Denise Pauline (ed.), *Women of Tropical Africa.* Berkeley: University of California.

Albrecht, Terrance L., et al. 1982. "Integration in a communication network as a mediator of stress." *Social Work,* 27, pp. 229–234.

Alder, Christine. 1985. "An exploration of self-reported sexually aggressive behavior." *Crime & Delinquency,* 31, pp. 306–331.

Aldrich, Howard E. 1979. *Organizations and Environments.* Englewood Cliffs, N.J.: Prentice-Hall.

———, and Jane Weiss. 1981. "Differentiation within the United States capitalist class: Workforce size and income differences." *American Sociological Review,* 46, pp. 279–290.

Alexander, Karl L., and Martha A. Cook. 1982. "Curricula and coursework: A surprise ending to a familiar story." *American Sociological Review,* 47, pp. 626–640.

———, and Aaron M. Pallas. 1983. "Private schools and public policy: New evidence on cognitive achievement in public and private schools." *Sociology of Education,* 56, pp. 170–182.

———. 1984. "In defense of 'private schools and public policy': Reply to Kilgore." *Sociology of Education,* 57, pp. 56–58.

Allison, Paul D., and John A. Stewart. 1974. "Productivity differences among scientists." *American Sociological Review,* 39, pp. 596–606.

Allport, Gordon W., and Leo Postman. 1975/1947. *The Psychology of Rumor.* New York: Russell & Russell.

Alm, Richard. 1984. "Sports stadiums: Is the U.S. overdoing it?" *U.S. News & World Report,* May 21, pp. 51–52.

Alonso, William. 1964. "The historic and the structural theories of urban form: Their implications for urban renewal." *Journal of Land Economics,* 40, pp. 227–231.

Alter, Jonathan. 1983. "Hispanic power at the polls." *Newsweek,* July 4, pp. 23–24.

Altman, Lawrence K. 1988. "AIDS researchers frustrated in hunt for genetic factors." *New York Times,* January 12, p. 16.

Alvarez, Donato, and Brian Cooper. 1984. "Productivity trends in manufacturing in the U.S. and 11 other countries." *Monthly Labor Review,* 107, January, pp. 52–57.

Alvesson, Mats. 1982. "The limits and shortcomings of humanistic organization theory." *Acta Sociologica,* 25, pp. 117–131.

Alwin, Duane F. 1984. "Trends in parental socialization values: Detroit, 1958–1983." *American Journal of Sociology,* 90, pp. 359–382.

Amir, Menachem. 1971. *Patterns in Forcible Rape.* Chicago: University of Chicago Press.

Anderson, Dean, and Gregory P. Stone. 1979. "A fifteen year analysis of socioeconomic strata differences in the meaning given to sport by metropolitans," in M. Krotee (ed.), *The Dimensions of Sport Sociology.* West Point, N.Y.: Leisure Press.

Anderson, George M. 1981. "White-collar crime." *America,* May 30, pp. 446–447.

Anderson, Harry. 1983. "The Social-Security crisis." *Newsweek,* January 24, pp. 18–28.

Anderson, Linda S., Theodore G. Chiricos, and Gordon P. Waldo. 1977. "Formal and informal sanctions: A comparison of deterrent effects." *Social Problems,* 25, pp. 103–114.

Andreski, Stanislav. 1968. "Method and substantive theory in Max Weber," in S. N. Eisenstadt (ed.), *The Protestant Ethic and Modernization.* New York: Basic Books.

Angel, Ronald, and Marta Tienda. 1982. "Determinants of extended household structure: Cultural pattern or economic need?" *American Journal of Sociology,* 87, pp. 1360–1383.

Antill, John K. 1983. "Sex role complementarity versus similarity in married couples." *Journal of Personality and Social Psychology,* 45, pp. 145–155.

Apte, Mahadev L. 1987. "Ethnic humor versus sense of humor." *American Behavioral Scientist,* 30, pp. 27–41.

Aram, John D. 1983. *Managing Business and Public Policy.* Boston: Pitman.

Archer, Margaret S. 1985. "The myth of cultural integration." *British Journal of Sociology,* 36, pp. 333–353.

Armor, David J. 1972. "The evidence on busing." *Public Interest,* Summer, pp. 90–126.

Aronoff, Joel, and William D. Crano. 1975. A re-examination of the cross-cultural principles of task segregation and sex role differentiation in the family." *American Sociological Review,* 40, pp. 12–20.

Asch, Solomon E. 1955. "Opinions and social pressure." *Scientific American,* 193, pp. 31–35.

Ashe, Arthur. 1977. "An open letter to black parents: Send your children to the libraries." *New York Times,* February 6, section 5, p. 2.

Atchley, Robert C. 1982. "Retirement: Leaving the world of work." *Annals,* 464, November, pp. 120–131.

———. 1985. *Social Forces and Aging,* 4th ed. Belmont, Calif.: Wadsworth.

Athanasiou, Robert, Phillip Shaver, and Carol Tavris. 1970. "Sex." *Psychology Today,* July, pp. 37–52.

Atkinson, Thomas, Ramsay Liem, and Joan H. Liem. 1986. "The social costs of unemployment: Implications for social support." *Journal of Health and Social Behavior,* 27, pp. 217–331.

Attir, Mustafa O., and Robert A. Peterson. 1981. "Socioeconomic development plans and individual satisfaction in Libya," in Mustafa O. Attir, Burkart Holzner, and Zdenek Suda (eds.), *Directions of Change.* Boulder, Colo.: Westview.

Auerbach, Alan J. 1983. "Welfare aspects of current U.S. corporate taxation." *American Economic Review Papers and Proceedings,* 73, pp. 76–81.

Axthelm, Pete. 1970. *The City Game.* New York: Harper & Row.

Babbie, Earl R. 1986. *The Practice of Social Research,* 4th ed. Belmont, Calif.: Wadsworth.

Bacon, Kenneth H. 1986. "The 1990s economy: Impact of 'baby bust.'" *Wall Street Journal,* April 14, p. 1.

Bailey, Kenneth D. 1987. *Methods for Social Research,* 3rd ed. New York: Free Press.

Baldassare, Mark. 1983. "Introduction: Urban change and continuity," in Mark Baldassare (ed.), *Cities and Urban Living.* New York: Columbia University Press.

Balkan, Sheila, Ronald J. Berger, and Janet Schmidt. 1980. *Crime and Deviance in America: A Critical Approach.* Belmont, Calif.: Wadsworth.

Ball, Richard A. 1968. "A poverty case: The analgesic subculture of the Southern Appalachians." *American Sociological Review,* 33, pp. 885–895.

Bandura, Albert. 1977. *Social Learning Theory.* Englewood Cliffs, N.J.: Prentice-Hall.

Barber, Bernard. 1961. "Resistance by scientists to scientific discovery." *Science,* 134, pp. 596–602.

Barden, J. C. 1987. "Marital rape: Drive for tougher laws is pressed." *New York Times,* May 13, p. 10.

Barkan, Steven E. 1984. "Legal control of the Southern Civil Rights movement." *American Sociological Review*, 49, pp. 552–565.

Barker, Eileen. 1984. *The Making of a Moonie*. New York: Basil Blackwell.

Barnes, Donald. 1983. "An overview on dioxin." *EPA Journal*, 9, November, pp. 16–19.

Barnet, Richard J., and Ronald E. Müller. 1974. *Global Reach: The Power of the Multinational Corporations*. New York: Simon & Schuster.

Barney, G. O., et al. 1982. *The Global 2000 Report to the President of the United States: Entering the 21st Century*, vol. 1. London: Penguin Books.

Barnouw, Victor. 1973. *Culture and Personality*, rev. ed. Homewood, Ill.: Dorsey.

Barraclough, Geoffrey. 1978. "The struggle for the third world." *New York Review of Books*, November 9, pp. 47–58.

Barringer, Felicity. 1981. "Debate over lead in gasoline revs up again." *Washington Post*, October 5, p. A11.

Bart, Pauline B. 1975. "Rape doesn't end with a kiss." *Viva*, June, pp. 39–42, 100–101.

Bartell, Gilbert D. 1971. *Group Sex*. New York: Signet.

Baruch, Grace K., and Rosalind C. Barnett. 1986. "Consequences of fathers' participation in family work: Parents' role strain and well-being." *Journal of Personality and Social Psychology*, 51, pp. 983–992.

Basow, Susan A. 1980. *Sex-Role Stereotypes*. Monterey, Calif.: Brooks/Cole.

Baum, Andrew, Raymond Fleming, and Diane M. Reddy. 1986. "Unemployment stress: Loss of control, reactance and learned helplessness." *Social Science and Medicine*, 22, pp. 509–516.

Baumrind, Diana. 1985. "Research using intentional deception: Ethical issues revisited." *American Psychologist*, 40, pp. 165–174.

Baur, Patricia A., and Morris A. Okun. 1983. "Stability of life satisfaction in late life." *Gerontologist*, 23, pp. 261–265.

Baven, Ezra. 1987. "Battling over birth policy." *Time*, August 24, p. 58.

Bayer, Alan E., and John Folger. 1966. "Some correlates of a citation measure of productivity in science." *Sociology of Education*, 39, pp. 381–389.

Beck, Lois. 1982. "Nomads and urbanites, involuntary hosts and uninvited guests." *Middle Eastern Studies*, 18, pp. 426–444.

Beck, Melinda. 1978. "The world of cults." *Newsweek*, December 4, pp. 78–81.

———. 1982. "Reservations on Reaganomics." *Newsweek*, November 29, pp. 49–50.

Becker, George. 1984. "Pietism and science: A critique of Robert K. Merton's hypothesis." *American Journal of Sociology*, 89, p. 1065–1090.

Becker, Howard S. 1963. *Outsiders*. New York: Free Press.

———. 1967. "Whose side are we on?" *Social Problems*, 14, pp. 239–247.

———, et al. 1961. *Boys in White: Student Culture in Medical School*. Chicago: University of Chicago Press.

Beeghley, Leonard. 1984. "Illusion and reality in the measurement of poverty." *Social Problems*, 31, pp. 322–333.

Beer, William R. 1987. "The wages of discrimination." *Public Opinion*, July/August, pp. 17–19, 58.

Beilin, Robert. 1982. "Social functions of denial of death." *Omega*, 12(1), pp. 25–35.

Belcastro, Philip A. 1985. "Sexual behavior differences between black and white students." *Journal of Sex Research*, 21, pp. 56–67.

Bell, Alan P., and Martin S. Weinberg. 1978. *Homosexualities: A Study of Diversity Among Men and Women*. New York: Simon & Schuster.

———, and Sue Kiefer Hammersmith. 1981. *Sexual Preference: Its Development in Men and Women*. Bloomington: Indiana University Press.

Bell, Daniel, 1973. *The Coming of Post-Industrial Society*. New York: Basic Books.

Bellah, Robert N., and Phillip E. Hammond. 1980. *Varieties of Civil Religion*. New York: Harper & Row.

———, et al. 1986. *Habits of the Heart: Individualism and Commitment in American Life*. New York: Harper & Row, 1986.

Bem, Sandra Lipsitz. 1975. "Androgyny vs. the tight little lives of fluffy women and chesty men." *Psychology Today*, September 1975, pp. 58–62.

Bendix, Reinhard. 1962. *Max Weber: An Intellectual Portrait*. New York: Anchor Books.

Bengston, Vern L., Jose B. Cuellar, and Pauline K. Ragan. 1977. "Stratum contrasts and similarities in attitudes toward death." *Journal of Gerontology*, 32, pp. 76–88.

Bennis, Warren G., and Philip E. Slater. 1968. *The Temporary Society*. New York: Harper Colophon.

Benson, John M. 1981. "The polls: A rebirth of religion?" *Public Opinion Quarterly*, 45, pp. 576–585.

Bercovitch, Sarcan. 1978. *The American Jeremiad*. Madison: University of Wisconsin Press.

Berger, Bennett M. 1971. *Working-Class Suburb: A Study of Auto Workers in Suburbia*. Berkeley: University of California Press.

Berger, Brigitte, and Peter L. Berger. 1983. *The War over the Family: Capturing the Middle Ground*. Garden City, N.Y.: Anchor/Doubleday.

Berger, Joseph. 1986. "Split widens on a basic issue: What is a Jew?" *New York Times*, February 2, pp. 1, 18.

Berger, Peter L. 1963. *Invitation to Sociology*. Garden City, N.Y.: Anchor/Doubleday.

———. 1967. "A sociological view of the secularization of theology." *Journal for the Scientific Study of Religion*, 6, pp. 3–16.

Berkowitz, Leonard. 1969. "The frustration-aggression hypothesis revisited," in Leonard Berkowitz (ed.), *Roots of Aggression*. New York: Atherton.

Bernard, Jessie. 1981. *The Female World*. New York: Free Press.

Bernard, L. L. 1924. *Instinct*. New York: Holt, Rinehart and Winston.

Berry, Colin. 1981. "The Nobel scientists and the origins of scientific achievement." *British Journal of Sociology*, 32, pp. 381–391.

Bessis, Sophie. 1984. "Tomorrow's world." *World Press Review*, 31, October, p. 40.

Bianchi, Suzanne M., Reynolds Farley, and Daphne Spain. 1982. "Racial inequalities in housing: An examination of recent trends." *Demography*, 19, pp. 37–51.

Biddle, B. J. 1986. "Recent developments in role theory." *Annual Review of Sociology*, 12, pp. 67–92.

Bieber, Irving, et al. 1962. *Homosexuality*. New York: Basic Books.

Bienen, Leigh, Alicia Ostriker, and J. P. Ostriker. 1977. "Sex discrimination in the universities," in Nona Glazer and Helen Youngelson Waehrer (eds.), *Women in a Man-Made World*, 2nd ed. Chicago: Rand McNally.

Bilge, Barbara, and Gladis Kaufman. 1983. "Children of divorce and one-parent families: Cross-cultural perspectives." *Family Relations*, 32, pp. 59–71.

Bilheimer, Robert S. (ed.) 1983. *Faith and Ferment: An Interdisciplinary Study of Christian Beliefs and Practices*. Minneapolis, Minn.: Augsburg.

Billy, John O. G., and J. Richard Udry. 1985. "Patterns of adolescent friendship and effects on sexual behavior." *Social Psychology Quarterly*, 48, pp. 27–41.

Binstock, Robert H. 1983. "The aged as scapegoat." *Gerontologist*, 23, pp. 136–143.

Bird, Caroline. 1975. *The Case Against College*. New York: McKay.

Bittner, Egon. 1983. "Technique and the conduct of life." *Social Problems*, 30, pp. 249–261.

Black, Donald. 1970. "Production of crime rates." *American Sociological Review*, 35, pp. 733–748.

———. 1983. "Crime as social control." *American Sociological Review*, 48, pp. 34–45.

Blackwell, James E. 1982. "Persistence and change in intergroup relations: The crisis upon us." *Social Problems*, 29, pp. 325–346.

Blake, Judith. 1981. "Family size and the quality of children." *Demography*, 18, pp. 421–442.

Blalock, Hubert M., Jr. 1982. *Race and Ethnic Relations*. Englewood Cliffs, N.J.: Prentice-Hall.

———. 1984. *Basic Dilemmas in the Social Sciences*. Beverly Hills, Calif.: Sage.

Blau, Peter M. 1977. *Inequality and Heterogeneity: A Primitive Theory of Social Structure*. New York: Free Press.

———, and Otis Dudley Duncan. 1967. *The American Occupational Structure*. New York: Wiley.

———, and W. Richard Scott. 1962. *Formal Organizations*. San Francisco: Chandler.

Bloom, Allan. 1987. *The Closing of the American Mind*. New York: Simon & Schuster.

Blotnick, Srully. 1984. "Older and wiser." *Forbes*, February 27, pp. 204–205.

Blumberg, Paul. 1980. *Inequality in an Age of Decline*. New York: Oxford University Press.

Blumer, Herbert. 1978. "Elementary collective groupings," in Louis E. Genevie (ed.), *Collective Behavior and Social Movements*. Itasca, Ill.: Peacock.

Blumstein, Philip, and Pepper Schwartz. 1983. *American Couples: Money, Work, and Sex*. New York: Morrow.

Blundell, William E. 1986. "Gripe session." *Wall Street Journal*, May 9, pp. 1, 9.

———. 1987. "When the patient takes charge." *Wall Street Journal,* April 24, pp. 5D–6D.

Bodard, Lucien. 1972. *Green Hell.* New York: Dutton.

Booth, Alan, David B. Brinkerhoff, and Lynn K. White. 1984. "The impact of parental divorce on courtship." *Journal of Marriage and the Family,* 46, pp. 85–94.

Borman, Kathryn M., Margaret D. LeCompte, and Judith Preissle Goetz. 1986. "Ethnographic and qualitative research design and why it doesn't work." *American Behavioral Scientist,* 30, pp. 42–57.

Bossard, James. 1932. "Residential propinquity as a factor in marriage selection." *American Journal of Sociology,* 38, pp. 219–244.

Boudon, Raymond. 1983a. "Individual action and social change: A no-theory of social change." *British Journal of Sociology,* 34, pp. 1–18.

———. 1983b. "Why theories of social change fail: Some methodological thoughts." *Public Opinion Quarterly,* 47, pp. 143–160.

Boulding, Kenneth E. 1981. "On the virtues of muddling through." *Technology Review,* 83, pp. 6–7.

Bowen, Ezra. 1986. "Nakasone's world-class blunder." *Time,* October 6, pp. 66–67.

Bowen, Ezra. 1987. "Battling over birth policy." *Time,* August 24, p. 58.

Bowles, Samuel, and Herbert Gintis. 1976. *Schooling in Capitalist America.* New York: Basic Books.

Box, Steven. 1983. *Power, Crime, and Mystification.* London: Tavistock.

Boyle, Patrick. 1982. "Cutbacks in factory jobs taking toll in California." *Los Angeles Times,* November 29, p. A24.

Bozzi, Vincent. 1986. "Laughing all the way down the aisle." *Psychology Today,* August, p. 8.

———. 1987. "The macho man behind the beard." *Psychology Today,* May, p. 20.

Brabant, Sarah, and Linda Mooney. 1986. "Sex role stereotyping in the Sunday comics: Ten years later." *Sex Roles,* 14, pp. 141–148.

Bradburd, Daniel. 1982. "Volatility of animal wealth among Southwest Asian pastoralists." *Human Ecology,* 10, pp. 85–106.

Bradburn, Norman M. 1969. *The Structure of Psychological Well-Being.* Chicago: Aldine.

Bradbury, Katharine L., Anthony Downs, and Kenneth A. Small. 1982. *Urban Decline and the Future of American Cities.* Washington, D.C.: Brookings Institution.

Braddock, Jomills H. 1981. "Race, athletics, and educational attainment—dispelling the myths." *Youth and Society,* 12, pp. 335–350.

Bradshaw, York W. 1987. "Urbanization and underdevelopment: A global study of modernization, urban bias, and economic dependency." *American Sociological Review,* 52, pp. 224–239.

Braginsky, D. D., and B. M. Braginsky. 1975. "Surplus people: Their lost faith in self and system." *Psychology Today,* August, pp. 68–72.

Braithwaite, John. 1981. "The myth of social class and criminality reconsidered." *American Sociological Review,* 46, pp. 36–58.

———, and Gilbert Geis. 1982. "On theory and action for corporate crime control." *Crime and Delinquency,* 28, pp. 292–314.

Brandt, Anthony. 1982. "Avoiding couple karate." *Psychology Today,* October, pp. 38–43.

Breault, K. D., and Augustine J. Kposowa. 1987. "Explaining divorce in the United States: A study of 3,111 counties, 1980." *Journal of Marriage and the Family,* 49, pp. 549–558.

Brenner, Harvey. 1976. *Hearings of the Joint Congressional Economic Committee.* Washington, D.C.: U.S. Government Printing Office.

Bridges, William P., and Wayne J. Villemez. 1986. "Informal hiring and income in the labor market." *American Sociological Review,* 51, pp. 574–582.

Bridgwater, Carol Austin. 1980. "When a man talks, you listen." *Psychology Today,* December, p. 25.

———. 1984. "The work ethic lives." *Psychology Today,* February, p. 17.

Briggs, Kenneth A. 1982. "Church growth lags behind that of U.S." *New York Times,* September 24, p. D19.

Brim, John, et al. 1982. "Social network characteristics of hospitalized depressed patients." *Psychological Reports,* 50, pp. 423–433.

Broad, William J., and Nicholas Wade. 1983. *Betrayers of the Truth.* New York: Simon & Schuster.

Broadhead, Robert S. 1983. *The Private Lives and Professional Identity of Medical Students.* New Brunswick, N.J.: Transaction.

Brod, Craig. 1984. *Technostress: The Human Cost of the Computer Revolution.* Reading, Mass.: Addison-Wesley.

Broderick, Carlfred. 1972. "How young people are creating a new morality." *Sexual Behavior,* 2, April, pp. 24–30.

Brooke, James. 1987. "In Burundi, minority persists in control of nation." *New York Times,* June 5, p. 8.

Brookover, W., et al. 1979. *School Social Systems Student Achievement: Schools Can Make a Difference.* New York: Praeger.

Brown, B. Bradford, Sue Ann Eicher, and Sandra Petrie. 1986. "The importance of peer group ('crowd') affiliation in adolescence." *Journal of Adolescence,* 9, pp. 73–96.

Brown, Roger. 1958. *Words and Things.* New York: Free Press.

———. 1965. *Social Psychology.* New York: Free Press.

Brownmiller, Susan. 1976. *Against Our Will: Men, Women and Rape.* New York: Simon & Schuster.

———. 1984. *Feminity.* New York: Simon & Schuster.

Brownstein, Ronald, and Nina Easton. 1982. "The culture of Reaganism." *New Republic,* October 25, pp. 15–24.

Bruner, Jerome. 1982. "Schooling children in a nasty climate." *Psychology Today,* January, pp. 57–63.

Bryan, Frank. 1982. "Rural renaissance: Is America on the move again?" *Public Opinion,* June/July, pp. 16–20.

Bryan, James H. 1965. "Apprenticeships in prostitution." *Social Problems,* 12, pp. 287–297.

Buhrmann, H. 1972. "Scholarship and athletics in junior high school." *International Review of Sport Sociology,* 7, pp. 119–131.

Bulcroft, Kris, and Margaret O'Conner-Roden. 1986. "Never too late." *Psychology Today,* June, pp. 66–69.

Buller, Mary Klein, and David B. Buller. 1987. "Physicians' communication style and patient satisfaction." *Journal of Health and Social Behavior,* 28, pp. 275–388.

Burgess, Ernest W. 1967/1925. "The growth of the city: An introduction to a research project," in R. E. Park, E. W. Burgess, and R. D. McKenzie (eds.), *The City.* Chicago: University of Chicago Press.

Burke, Ronald J., and Tamara Weir. 1976. "Relationship of wives' employment status to husband, wife, and pair satisfaction and performance." *Journal of Marriage and the Family,* 38, pp. 279–287.

Burkhardt, William R. 1983. "Institutional barriers, marginality, and adaptation among the American-Japanese mixed bloods in Japan." *Journal of Asian Studies,* 42, pp. 519–544.

Burkhead, Dan L. 1983. *Lifetime Earnings Estimates for Men and Women in the United States:* 1979. Current Population Reports, Series P-60, No. 139. Washington, D.C.: U.S. Government Printing Office.

Burns, John F. 1982. "An apron awaits Soviet cosmonaut." *New York Times,* August 29, p. 3.

Burrough, Bryan. 1987. "Broken Barrier: More women join ranks of white-collar criminals." *Wall Street Journal,* May 29, p. 19.

Burstein, Paul. 1981. "The sociology of democratic politics and government" *Annual Review of Sociology,* 7, pp. 291–319.

Burt, Martha R. 1980. "Cultural myths and supports for rape." *Journal of Personality and Social Psychology,* 38, pp. 217–230.

Burt, Ronald S. 1983. "Corporate philanthropy as a cooptive relation." *Social Forces,* 62, pp. 419–449.

Busacca, Richard, and Mary P. Ryan. 1982. "Beyond the family crisis." *Democracy,* Fall, pp. 79–92.

Bush, Diane Mitsch, and Roberta G. Simmons. 1981. "Socialization processes over the life course," in Morris Rosenberg and Ralph H. Turner (eds.), *Social Psychology: Sociological Perspectives.* New York: Basic Books.

Butler, Robert. 1984. Interviewed in *U.S. News & World Report,* July 2, pp. 51–52.

Cain, G. G., and A. S. Goldberger. 1983. "Public and private schools revisited." *Sociology of Education,* 56, pp. 208–218.

Camer, Richard. 1983. "Class notes." *Psychology Today,* October, p. 21.

Campbell, Colin. 1982. "A dubious distinction? An inquiry into the value and use of Merton's concepts of manifest and latent function." *American Sociological Review,* 47, pp. 29–44.

Campbell, Rex R., and Lorraine Garkovich. 1984. "Turnaround migration as an episode of collective behavior." *Rural Sociology,* 49, pp. 89–105.

Cantril, Hadley, with Hazel Gaudet and Herta Herzog. 1982/1940. *The Invasion from Mars.* Princeton, N.J.: Princeton University Press.

Caplow, Theodore, et al. 1983. *Middletown Families: Fifty Years of Change and Continuity.* Minneapolis: University of Minnesota Press.

———, Howard M. Bahr, and Bruce A. Chadwick. 1983. *All Faithful People: Change and Continuity in Middletown's Religion.* Minneapolis: University of Minnesota Press.

Caputo, David A. 1985. "American cities and the future." *Society,* January/February, pp. 59–64.

Carey, Joseph, and Joanne Silberner. 1987. "Fending off the leading killers." *U.S. News & World Reports,* August 17, pp. 56–64.

Cargan, Leonard, and Matthew Melko. 1982. *Singles: Myths and Realities.* Beverly Hills, Calif.: Sage.

Carlson, Elwood, and Kandi Stinson. 1982. "Motherhood, marriage timing, and marital stability: A research note." *Social Forces,* 61, pp. 258–267.

Catalano, Ralph, and David Dooley. 1983. "Health effects of economic instability: A test of economic stress hypothesis." *Journal of Health and Social Behavior,* 24, pp. 46–60.

Census Bureau. 1982. *Population Profile of the United States.* Series P-23, No. 130. December 1982. Washington, D.C.: U.S. Government Printing Office.

———. 1984. *Statistical Abstract of the United States.* Washington, D.C.: U.S. Government Printing Office.

———. 1985. *Statistical Abstract of the United States.* Washington, D.C.: U.S. Government Printing Office.

———. 1986. "Households, Families, Marital Status, and Living Arrangements: March 1986." *Current Population Reports: Population Characteristics,* Series P-60, No. 382. Washington, D.C.: U.S. Government Printing Office.

———. 1987. *Population Profile of the United States 1984/85.* Series P-23, No. 150. Washington, D.C.: Government Printing Office.

———. 1988. *Statistical Abstract of the United States.* Washington, D.C.: U.S. Government Printing Office.

Centers, Richard. 1949. *The Psychology of Social Classes.* Princeton, N.J.: Princeton University Press.

Chafetz, Janet Saltzman. 1978. *Masculine, Feminine or Human?* Itasca, Ill.: Peacock.

———. 1984. *Sex and Advantage: A Comparative, Macro-Structural Theory of Sex Stratification.* Totowa, N.J.: Rowman & Allanheld.

Chagnon, Napoleon A. 1968. *Yanomamo: The Fierce People.* New York: Holt, Rinehart and Winston.

Chambliss, William J. 1969. *Crime and the Legal Process.* New York: McGraw-Hill.

———. 1973. "The saints and the roughnecks." *Society,* November/December, pp. 24–31.

Champion, Dean J. 1975. *The Sociology of Organizations.* New York: McGraw-Hill

Chance, Paul, and Joshua Fischman. 1987. "The magic of childhood." *Psychology Today,* May, pp. 48–58.

Charlier, Marj. 1987. "Overdoing it." *Wall Street Journal,* October 1, pp. 1, 24.

Chelte, Anthony F., James Wright, and Curt Tausky. 1982. "Did job satisfaction really drop duing the 1970s?" *Monthly Labor Review,* 105, November, pp. 33–36.

Cheney, Lynne V. 1986. "Students of success." *Newsweek,* September 1, p. 7.

Cherlin, Andrew J. 1981. *Marriage, Divorce, Remarriage.* Cambridge, Mass.: Harvard University Press.

———, 1983. "Changing family and household: Contemporary lessons from historical research." *Annual Review of Sociology,* 9, pp. 51–66.

———, and Frank F. Furstenberg, Jr. 1983. "The American family in the year 2000." *Futurist,* 18, June, pp. 7–14.

Chilcote, Ronald H., and Dale L. Johnson, (eds.) 1983. *Theories of Development: Mode of Production or Dependency?* Beverly Hills, Calif.: Sage.

Childe, Gordon. 1952. *Man Makes Himself.* New York: New American Library.

Chong, Dennis, Herbert McClosky, and John Zaller. 1983. "Patterns of support for democratic and capitalist values in the United States." *British Journal of Political Science,* 13, pp. 401–440.

Christie, James. 1984. "The politics of sport." *World Press Review,* 31, July, pp. 39–40.

Christopher, Robert C. 1983. *The Japanese Mind: The Goliath Explained.* New York: Linden/Simon & Schuster.

Church, George. 1979. "How gay is gay?" *Time,* April 23, pp. 72–76.

Clairmonte, Frederick F., and John H. Cavanagh. 1983. "Transnational corporations and the struggle for the global market." *Journal of Contemporary Asia,* 13, pp. 446–480.

Clark, Burton R., and Martin Trow. 1966. "The organizational context," in Theodore M. Newcomb and Everett K. Wilson (eds.), *College Peer Groups.* Chicago: Aldine.

Clark, Kenneth B., and Mamie P. Clark. 1947. "Racial identification and preferences in Negro children," in Theodore M. Newcomb and Eugene L. Harley (eds.), *Readings in Social Psychology.* New York: Holt, Rinehart and Winston.

Clark, Lindley H., Jr. 1987. "Our problem is that we consume too much." *Wall Street Journal,* April 24, p. 10.

Clark, Margaret S. 1981. "Noncomparability of benefits given and received: A cue to the existence of friendship." *Social Psychology Quarterly,* 44, pp. 375–381.

Clark, Matt. 1986. "Running for your life." *Newsweek,* March 17, p. 70.

Clark, Ramsey. 1971. *Crime in America.* New York: Pocket Books.

Clark, Rodney. 1979. *The Japanese Company.* New Haven, Conn.: Yale University Press.

Clark, Terry Nichols, and Lorna Crowley Ferguson. 1983. *City Money: Political Processes, Fiscal Strain, and Retrenchment.* New York: Columbia University Press.

Clay, Phillip L., and Bernard J. Frieden. 1984. "A plea for less regulation." *Society,* March/April, pp. 48–53.

Clifford, Margaret M., and Elaine Walster. 1973. "The effect of physical attractiveness on teacher expectation." *Sociology of Education,* 46, pp. 248–258.

Clinard, Marshall B. 1979. *Illegal Corporate Behavior.* Washington, D.C.: U.S. Government Printing Office.

———, and Peter C. Yeager. 1978. "Corporate crime: Issues in research." *Criminology,* 16, pp. 255–272.

Coakley, Jay J. 1982. *Sport in Society: Issues and Controversies,* 2nd ed. St. Louis: Mosby.

Cobb, Stephen. 1983. "So you want a job: Sociology, liberating skills, and experiential learning." *ASA Teaching Newsletter,* February, p. 11.

Cockerham, William C. 1986. *Medical Sociology,* 3rd ed. Englewood Cliffs, N.J.: Prentice-Hall.

———, Kimberly Sharp, and Julie A. Wilcox. 1983. "Aging and perceived health status." *Journal of Gerontology,* 38, pp. 349–355.

Cohen, Albert K. 1956. *Delinquent Boys.* Glencoe, Ill.: Free Press.

———. 1966. *Deviance and Control.* Englewood Cliffs, N.J.: Prentice-Hall.

———, and Harold M. Hodges. 1963. "Characteristics of the lower-blue-collar class." *Social Problems,* 10, pp. 303–334.

Cohen, Arthur M., and Florence B. Brawer. 1982. "The community college as college." *Change,* March, pp. 39–42.

Cohen, Debra Rae. 1978. "To avoid rape, be ready to struggle at home." *Psychology Today,* November, pp. 124–125.

Cohen, Jere. 1980. "Rational capitalism in renaissance Italy." *American Journal of Sociology,* 85, pp. 1340–1355.

———. 1983. "Reply to Holton." *American Journal of Sociology,* 89, pp. 181–187.

Cohen, Lawrence E., James R. Kluegel, and Kenneth C. Land. 1981. "Social inequality and predatory criminal victimization: An exposition and test of a formal theory." *American Sociological Review,* 46, pp. 505–524.

Colclough, Glenna, and E. M. Beck. 1986. "The American educational structure and the reproduction of social class." *Sociological Inquiry,* 56, pp. 456–476.

Cole, Stephen. 1976. *The Sociological Method.* Chicago: Rand McNally.

———. 1979. "Age and scientific performance." *American Journal of Sociology,* 84, pp. 958–977.

Cole, Thomas R. 1983. "The 'enlightened' view of aging: Victorian morality in a new key." *Hastings Center Report,* 13, pp. 34–40.

Coleman, Eli. 1982. "Developmental stages of the coming out process." *American Behavioral Scientist,* 25, pp. 269–482.

Coleman, James S. 1961. *The Adolescent Society.* Glencoe, Ill.: Free Press.

———. 1975. "Racial segregation in the schools: New research with new policy implications." *Phi Delta Kappan,* 57, pp. 75–78.

———. 1982. *The Asymmetric Society.* Syracuse, N.Y.: Syracuse University Press.

———, et al. 1966. *Equality of Educational Opportunity.* Washington, D.C.: U.S. Government Printing Office.

———, Thomas Hoffer, and Sally Kilgore. 1982a. "Cognitive outcomes in public and private schools." *Sociology of Education*, 55, pp. 65–76.

———. 1982b. *High School Achievement: Public, Catholic, and Private Schools Compared.* New York: Basic Books.

Coleman, James William, and Donald R. Cressey. 1987. *Social Problems*, 3rd ed. New York: Harper & Row.

Coleman, Richard P., and Lee Rainwater. 1978. *Social Standing in America: New Dimensions of Class.* New York: Basic Books.

Collins, Randall. 1971. "Functional and conflict theories of educational stratification." *American Sociological Review*, 36, pp. 1002–1019.

———. 1975. *Conflict Sociology.* New York: Academic Press.

———. 1979. *The Credential Society: An Historical Sociology of Education and Stratification.* New York: Academic Press.

———. 1986. "Is 1980s sociology in the doldrums?" *American Journal of Sociology*, 91, pp. 1336–1355.

———, and Sal Restivo. 1983. "Robber barons and politicians in mathematics: A conflict model of science." *Canadian Journal of Sociology*, 8, pp. 199–227.

Comer, James P. 1983. "Single-parent black families." *Crisis*, 90, pp. 510–515.

Commission on Civil Rights. 1981. *Affirmative Action in the 1980s: Dismantling the Process of Discrimination.* Washington, D.C.: U.S. Government Printing Office.

Conant, Jennet. 1987. "What women want to read." *Newsweek*, February 23, p. 61.

Conklin, John E. 1977. *"Illegal But Not Criminal": Business Crime in America.* Englewood Cliffs, N.J.: Prentice-Hall.

Connor, Jane, et al. 1986. "Use of the titles Ms., Miss, or Mrs.: Does it make a difference?" *Sex Roles*, 14, pp. 545–549.

Conrad, Peter, and Rochelle Kern (eds.). 1986. *Sociology of Health and Illness: Critical Perspectives*, 2nd ed. New York: St. Martin's Press.

Cook, Karen S., et al. 1983. "The distribution of power in exchange networks: Theory and experimental results." *American Journal of Sociology*, 89, pp. 275–304.

Cooley, Charles H. 1909. *Social Organization.* New York: Scribner's.

Cory, Christopher T. 1979. "Women smile less for success." *Psychology Today*, March, p. 16.

Cooper, Kristina, et al. 1986. "Correlates of mood and marital satisfaction among dual-worker and single-worker couples." *Social Psychology Quarterly*, 49, pp. 322–329.

Cornell, Stephen. 1986. "The new Indian politics." *The Wilson Quarterly*, New Year's 1986, pp. 113–131.

Corzine, Jay, James Creech, and Lin Corzine. 1983. "Black concentration and lynchings in the South: Testing Blalock's power-threat hypothesis." *Social Forces*, 61, pp. 774–796.

Costa, Paul T., Jr., et al. 1987. "Longitudinal analyses of psychological well-being in a national sample: Stability of mean levels." *Journal of Gerontology*, 42, p. 50–55.

Cowgill, Donald O. 1974. "Aging and modernization: A revision of the theory," in J. F. Gubrium (ed.). *Late Life: Communities and Environmental Policy.* Springfield, Ill.: Thomas.

———, and Llewelyn Holmes. 1972. *Aging and Modernization.* New York: Appleton-Century-Crofts.

Cox, Frank D. 1984. *Human Intimacy: Marriage, the Family, and Its Meaning.* St. Paul, Minn.: West.

Cox, Harvey. 1966. *The Secular City.* New York: Macmillan.

Craig, J., and N. Spear. 1982. "Explaining educational expansion: An agenda for historical and comparative research," in M. S. Archer (ed.), *The Sociology of Educational Expansion.* Beverly Hills, Calif.: Sage.

Crane, L. Ben, Edward Yeager, and Randal L. Whitman. 1981. *An Introduction to Linguistics.* Boston: Little, Brown.

Craver, Charles B. 1983. "The future of the American labor movement." *The Futurist*, 17, October, pp. 70–76.

Cullen, Francis T., Bruce G. Link, and Craig W. Polanzi. 1982. "The seriousness of cime revisited: Have attitudes toward white-collar crime changed?" *Criminology*, 20, pp. 83–102.

Cumming, Elaine. 1963. "Further thoughts on the theory of disengagement." *International Social Science*, 15, pp. 377–393.

———, and William E. Henry. 1961. *Growing Old: The Process of Disengagement.* New York: Basic Books.

Cummings, Scott. 1980. "White ethnics, racial prejudice, and labor market segmentation." *American Journal of Sociology*, 85, pp. 938–950.

Curtin, Philip D., et al. 1978. *African History.* Boston: Little, Brown.

Dabbs, James M., Jr., and Neil A. Stokes. 1975. "Beauty is power: The use of space on the sidewalk." *Sociometry*, 38, pp. 551–557.

Dahl, Robert A. 1981. *Democracy in the United States: Promise and Performance*, 4th ed. Boston, Mass.: Houghton Mifflin.

Dahrendorf, Ralf. 1984. "The new underclass." *World Press Review*, 31, April, pp. 21–23.

Dank, Barry M. 1971. "Coming out in the gay world." *Psychiatry*, 34, pp. 180–197.

Dannefer, Dale. 1984. "Adult development and social theory: A paradigmatic reappraisal." *American Sociological Review*, 49, pp. 100–116.

D'Arcy, Carl, John Syrotuik, and C. M. Siddique. 1984. "Perceived job attributes, job satisfaction, and psychological distress: A comparison of working men and women." *Human Relations*, 37, pp. 603–611.

Dardis, Rachel, et al. 1981. "Cross-section studies of recreation expenditures in the United States." *Journal of Leisure Research* 13, pp. 181–194.

Davies, Gordon K., and Kathleen F. Slevin. 1984. "Babel or opportunity?" *College Board Review*, No. 130, Winter, pp. 18–21, 37.

Davies, Leland J. 1977. "Attitudes toward old age and aging as shown by humor." *Gerontologist*, 17, pp. 220–226.

Davies, Mark and Denise B. Kandel. 1981. "Parental and peer influences on adolescents, educational plans: some further evidence." *American Journal of Sociology*, 87, pp. 363–387.

Davis, Cary, Carl Haub, and JoAnne Willette. 1983. "U.S. Hispanics: Changing the face of America." *Population Bulletin*, 39, June, pp. 1–45.

Davis, James. 1982. "Up and down opportunity's ladder." *Public Opinion*, June/July, pp. 11–15, 48–51.

Davis, Kingsley. 1947. "Final note on a case of extreme isolation." *American Journal of Sociology*, 52, pp. 432–437.

———. 1949, *Human Society.* New York: Macmillan.

———. 1955. "The origin and growth of urbanization in the world." *American Journal of Sociology*, 60, pp. 429–437.

———. 1974. "The urbanization of the human population," in Charles Tilly (ed.), *An Urban World.* Boston: Little, Brown.

———. 1976a. "Sexual behavior," in Robert K. Merton and Robert Nisbet (eds.), *Contemporary Social Problems.* 4th ed. New York: Harcourt Brace Jovanovich.

———. 1976b. "The world's population crises," in Robert K. Merton and Robert Nisbet (eds.), *Contemporary Social Problems*, 4th ed. New York: Harcourt Brace Jovanovich.

———, and Wilbert E. Moore. 1945. "Some principles of stratification." *American Sociological Review*, 10, pp. 242–249.

Decker, David L. 1980. *Social Gerontology.* Boston: Little, Brown.

Deford, Frank. 1976a. "Religion in sport." *Sports Illustrated*, April 19, pp. 92–96.

———. 1976b. "The world according to Tom." *Sports Illustrated*, April 26, pp. 54–69.

DeLamater, John. 1981. "The social control of sexuality." *Annual Review of Sociology*, 7, pp. 263–290.

de Leeuw, Frank, Anne B. Schnare, and Raymond J. Struyk. 1976. "Housing," in William Gorham and Nathan Glazer (eds.), *The Urban Predicament.* Washington, D.C.: The Urban Institute.

DeLeon, George. 1982. "The decriminalization issue revisited." *Social Policy*, Fall, pp. 46–48.

Deloria, Vine, J. 1981. "Native Americans: The American Indian today." *The Annals of the American Academy of Political and Social Science*, 454, March, pp. 139–149.

DeMaris, Alfred, and Gerald R. Leslie. 1984. "Cohabitation with the future spouse: Its influence upon martial satisfaction and communication." *Journal of Marriage and the Family*, 46, pp. 77–84.

DeMause, Lloyd. 1975. "Our forebears made childhood a nightmare." *Psychology Today*, April, pp. 85–86.

DeMott, Benjamin. 1980. "The pro-incest lobby." *Psychology Today*, March, pp. 11–16.

Denfeld, Duane. 1974. "Dropouts from swinging." *The Family Coordinator*, January, pp. 45–49.

Dentzer, Susan. 1984. "Hospitals take the cure." *Newsweek*, July 2, pp. 56–57.

———. 1986. "Back to the suburbs." *Newsweek,* April 21, pp. 60–62.
Derber, Charles, and William Schwartz. 1983. "Toward a theory of worker participation." *Sociological Inquiry,* 53, pp. 61–77.
Devens, Richard M., Jr. 1984. "Employment in the first half: Robust recovery continues." *Monthly Labor Review,* 107, August, pp. 3–7.
Dion, Kenneth L. 1987. "What's in a title: The Ms. stereotype and images of women's titles of address." *Psychology of Women Quarterly,* 11, pp. 21–36.
Dodder, Richard A., Marie Lim Fromme, and Lorell Holland. 1982. "Psychosocial functions of sport." *Journal of Social Psychology,* 116, pp. 143–144.
Doleschal, Eugene. 1979. "Crime—some popular beliefs." *Crime and Delinquency,* 25, pp. 1–8.
Dollar, Bruce. 1983. "What is really going on in schools." *Social Policy,* 14, Fall, pp. 7–19.
Dollard, John, et al. 1939. *Frustration and Aggression.* New Haven: Yale University Press.
Domhoff, G. William. 1978. *The Powers That Be: Processes of Ruling-Class Domination in America.* New York: Radom House.
———. 1983. *Who Rules America Now? A View for the Eighties.* Englewood Cliffs, N.J.: Prentice-Hall.
Dorfman, Andrea. 1984. "Danger: Don't drink this water." *Science Digest,* 92, March, p. 28.
Douglass, Richard L. 1983. "Domestic neglect and abuse of the elderly: Implications for research and service." *Family Relations,* 32, pp. 395–402.
Dowd, James J. 1975. "Aging as exchange: A preface to theory." *Journal of Gerontology,* 30, pp. 584–594.
———. 1980. "Exchange rates and old people." *Journal of Gerontology,* 35, pp. 596–602.
Dowd, Maureen. 1983. "Rape: The sexual weapon." *Time,* September 5, pp. 27–29.
Doyle, Denis P. 1984. "Tuition tax credits and education vouchers: Private interests and the public good." *College Board Review,* No. 130, Winter, pp. 6–11.
Drucker, Peter. 1986. "Goodbye to the old personnel department." *Wall Street Journal,* May 22, p. 24.
Duchon, Dennis, et al. 1986. "Vertical dyad linkage: A longitudinal assessment of antecedents, measures, and consequences." *Journal of Applied Psychology,* 71, pp. 56–60.
Dunn, Samuel L. 1983. "The changing university: survival in the information society." *Futurist,* 17, pp. 55–60.
Durkheim, Emile. 1915/1965. *The Elementary Forms of the Religious Life.* New York: Free Press.
———. 1966. *The Rules of Sociological Method.* New York: Macmillan.
———. 1951/1897. *Suicide.* New York: Free Press.
Dutton, Diana B. 1978. "Explaining the low use of health services by the poor: Costs, attitudes, or delivery system?" *American Sociological Review,* 43, pp. 348–368.
Dye, Thomas R. 1976. *Who's Running America? Institutional Leadership in the United States.* Englewood Cliffs, N.J.: Prentice-Hall.

Earth Science. 1983. "Trends in acid-rain patterns have shifted across U.S." 36, Winter, pp. 9–10.
Easterbrook, Gregg. 1987. "The revolution in medicine." *Newsweek,* January 26, pp. 40–74.
Edmonston, Barry, and Thomas M. Guterbock. 1984. "Is suburbanization slowing down? Recent trends in population deconcentration in U.S. metropolitan areas." *Social Forces,* 62, pp. 905–925.
Edwards, Harry. 1973. *Sociology of Sport.* Homewood, Ill.: Dorsey.
———. 1982. "Common myths hide flaws in the athletic system." *Center Magazine,* January/February, pp. 17–21.
———. 1984a. "The black 'dumb jock': An American sports tragedy." *College Board Review,* 131, pp. 8–13.
———. 1984b. "Sportpolitics: Los Angeles, 1984—'The olympic tradition continues'." *Sociology of Sport Journal,* 1, pp. 172–183.
Ehrenreich, Barbara, and Karin Stallard. 1982. "The nouveau poor." *Ms.,* July/August, pp. 217–224.
Ehrlich, Anne. 1984. "Critical masses: World population 1984." *Sierra,* July/August, pp. 36–40.
Ehrlich, Paul R., Anne H. Ehrlich, and John P. Holdren. 1977. *Ecoscience: Population, Resources, Environment.* San Francisco: Freeman.
Eitzen, D. Stanley, and George H. Sage. 1982. *Sociology of American Sport,* 2nd ed. Dubuque, Iowa: Brown.
Ekerdt, David J. 1986. "The busy ethic: Moral continuity between work and retirement." *The Gerontologist,* 26, pp. 239–247.
Ekerdt, David J., Raymond Bosse, and Joseph S. LoCastro. 1983. "Claims that retirement improves health." *Journal of Gerontology,* 38, pp. 231–236.
Elkin, Frederick, and Gerald Handel. 1984. *The Child and Society,* 4th ed. New York: Random House.
Elliott, Delbert S., and Suzanne S. Ageton. 1980. "Reconciling race and class differences in self-reported and official estimates of delinquency." *American Sociological Review,* 45, pp. 95–110.
Ellis, Godfrey J., Gary R. Lee, and Larry R. Petersen. 1978. "Supervision and conformity: A cross-cultural analysis of parental socialization values." *American Journal of Sociology,* 84, pp. 386–403.
Ellis, Lee. 1985. "Religiosity and criminality." *Sociological Perspectives,* 28, pp. 501–520.
Ellul, Jacques. 1964. *The Technological Society.* Translated by John Wilkinson. New York: Vintage Books.
Elmer-DeWitt, Philip. 1986. "An electronic assault on privacy?" *Time,* May 19, p. 104.
Elson, John, (ed.) 1978. "Socialism: Trials and errors." *Time,* March 13, pp. 24–36.
Ember, Carol R., and Melvin Ember. 1977. *Anthropology.* Englewood Cliffs, N.J.: Prentice-Hall.
Emery, Robert E. 1982. "Interparental conflict and the children of discord and divorce." *Psychological Bulletin,* 92, pp. 310–330.
Engels, Friedrich. 1884, 1942. *The Origin of the Family, Private Property, and the State.* New York: International Publishing.
English, Carey W. 1984. "Why unions are running scared." *U.S. News & World Report,* September 10, pp. 62–65.
Epstein, Cynthia Fuchs. 1976. "Sex roles," in Robert K. Merton and Robert Nisbet (eds.), *Contemporary Social Problems.* New York: Harcourt Brace Jovanovich.
Erikson, Erik H. 1963. *Childhood and Society.* New York: Norton.
———. 1975. *Life History and Historical Moment.* New York: Norton.
Erikson, Kai T. 1966. *Wayward Puritans.* New York: Wiley.
Eron, Leonard D., and Rolf A. Peterson. 1982. "Abnormal behavior: Social approaches." *Annual Review of Psychology,* 33, pp. 231–264.
Eshleman, J. Ross. 1981. *The Family.* Boston: Allyn and Bacon.
Etzioni, Amitai. 1975. *A Comparative Analysis of Complex Organizations,* rev. ed. New York: Free Press.
———. 1982. "Education for mutuality and civility." *Futurist,* 16, October, pp. 4–7.
———. 1987. "In praise of public humiliation." *Wall Street Journal,* April 2, p. 26.
———. 1987. "The party, like Reagan's era, is over." *New York Times,* February 16, p. 17.
———, and Clyde Nunn. 1974. "The public appreciation of science in contemporary America." *Daedalus,* Summer, pp. 191–205.

Fader, Shirley Sloan. 1987. "Men lose freedom if women lose ground." *Wall Street Journal,* February 2, p. 14.
Falsey, Barbara, and Barbara Heyns. 1984. "The college channel: Private and public schools reconsidered." *Sociology of Education,* 57, pp. 111–122.
Falwell, Jerry. 1981. *Listen America!* New York: Bantam Books.
Faris, Robert E. L., and H. Warren Dunham. 1939. *Mental Disorders in Urban Areas.* Chicago: University of Chicago Press.
Farley, John E. 1987. *American Social Problems: An Institutional Analysis.* Englewood Cliffs, N.J.: Prentice-Hall.
Farley, Reynolds. 1980. "Homicide trends in the United States." *Demography,* 17, pp. 177–188.
———, et al. 1983. "Chocolate city, vanilla suburbs: Will the trend toward racially separate communities continue?" In Mark Baldassare (ed.), *Cities and Urban Living.* New York: Columbia University Press.
Farley, Reynolds. 1985. "Three steps forward and two back? Recent changes in the social and economic status of blacks." *Ethnic and Racial Studies,* 8, pp. 4–28.
Farran, D. C., and R. Haskins. 1980. "Reciprocal influence in the social interactions of mothers and three-year-old children from different socioeconomic backgrounds." *Child Development,* 51, pp. 780–791.
Farrell, Charles S. 1984. "Black students im-

prove scores on mathematics section of SAT." *Chronicle of Higher Education,* March 28, p. 11.

Fasteau, Marc Feigen. 1975. "The high price of macho." *Psychology Today,* September, p. 60.

Feagin, Joe R., and Douglas Lee Eckberg. 1980. "Discrimination: Motivation, action, effects, and context." *Annual Review of Sociology,* 6, pp. 1–20.

Featherman, David L., and Robert M. Hauser. 1976. "Sexual inequalities and socioeconomic achievement in the United States, 1962–1973." *American Sociological Review,* 41, pp. 462–483.

———. 1978. *Opportunity and Change.* New York: Academic Press.

———, and Richard M. Lerner. 1985. "Otogenesis and sociogenesis: Problematics for theory and research about development and socialization across the lifespan." *American Sociological Review,* 50, pp. 659–676.

FBI (Federal Bureau of Investigation). 1988. *Uniform Crime Reports.* Washington, D.C.: U.S. Government Printing Office.

Feeney, Floyd, and Adrianne Weir. 1975. "The prevention and control of robbery." *Criminology,* 13, pp. 87–92.

Feld, Scott L. 1982. "Social structural determinants of similarity among associates." *American Sociological Review,* 47, pp. 797–801.

Felson, Richard B., and Mark D. Reed. 1986. "Reference groups and self-appraisals of academic ability and performance." *Social Psychology Quarterly,* 49, pp. 103–109.

Fernichel, Otto. 1945. *The Psychoanalytic Theory of Neurosis.* New York: Norton.

Ferro-Luzzi, Gabriella Eichinger. 1986. "Language, thought, and Tamil verbal humor." *Current Anthropology,* 27, pp. 265–272.

Festinger, Leon. 1957. *A Theory of Cognitive Dissonance.* Stanford, Calif.: Stanford University Press.

Fidell, Linda. 1970. "Empirical verification of sex discrimination in hiring practices in psychology." *American Psychologist,* 25, pp. 1094–1098.

Fine, Mark A., John R. Moreland, and Andrew I. Schwebel. 1983. "Long-term effects of divorce on parent-child relationships." *Developmental Psychology,* 19, pp. 703–713.

Finkelhor, David, and Kersti Yllo. 1982. "Forced sex in marriage: A preliminary research report." *Crime and Delinquency,* 28, pp. 459–478.

Fiorina, Morris P. 1983. "Flagellating the federal bureaucracy." *Society,* March/April, pp. 66–73.

Fischer, Claude. 1982. *To Dwell Among Friends: Personal Networks in Town and City.* Chicago: University of Chicago Press.

———. 1984. *The Urban Experience,* 2nd ed. San Diego: Harcourt Brace Jovanovich.

Fischer, David Hackett. 1977. *Growing Old in America.* New York: Oxford University Press.

Fischman, Joshua. 1984. "The mystery of Alzheimer's." *Psychology Today,* January, p. 27.

———. 1986. "What are friends for?" *Psychology Today,* September, pp. 70–71.

Fiske, Edward B. 1987. "Global focus on quality in education." *New York Times,* June 1, pp. 19, 23.

Fitzpatrick, Joseph P., and Lourdes Travieso Parker. 1981. "Hispanic-Americans in the Eastern United States." *Annals,* 454, March, pp. 98–110.

Fligstein, Neil. 1987. "The intraorganizational power struggle: Rise of finance personnel to top leadership in large corporations, 1919–1979." *American Sociological Review,* 52, pp. 44–58.

Flint, William C., and D. Stanley Eitzen. 1987. "Professional sports team ownership and entrepreneurial capitalism." *Sociology of Sport Journal,* 4, pp. 17–27.

Flygare, Thomas J. 1979. "Schools and the law." *Phi Delta Kappan,* 60, pp. 529–530.

Foner, Anne. 1979. "Ascribed and achieved bases of stratification." *Annual Review of Sociology,* 5, pp. 219–242.

Forbes. 1986. "Forbes sales 500." April 30, pp. 172–173.

Ford, Clellan S., and Frank A. Beach. 1951. *Patterns of Sexual Behavior.* New York: Harper & Row.

Ford, Maureen Rose, and Carol Rotter Lowery. 1986. "Gender differences in moral reasoning: A comparison of the use of justice and care orientations." *Journal of Personality and Social Psychology,* 50, pp. 777–783.

Form, William. 1982. "Self-employed manual workers: Petty bourgeois or working class?" *Social Forces,* 60, pp. 1050–1069.

Fox, Richard G. 1971. "The XYZ offender: A modern myth?" *Journal of Criminal Law, Criminology, and Police Science,* 62, pp. 59–73.

Francis, David R. 1987. "Despite concern, black Africa's population picture grows worse." *Christian Science Monitor,* November 7, p. 22.

Francke, Linda Bird. 1978. "Going it alone." *Newsweek,* September 4, pp. 76–78.

Franklin, John Hope. 1981. "The land of room enough." *Daedalus,* 110, pp. 1–12.

Freedman, Jonathan L. 1978. *Happy People: What Happiness Is, Who Has It, and Why.* New York: Harcourt Brace Jovanovich.

———. 1986. "Television violence and aggression: A rejoinder." *Psychological Bulletin,* 100, pp. 372–378.

Freeman, John, and Michael T. Hannan. 1983. "Niche width and the dynamics of organizational population." *American Journal of Sociology,* 88, p. 1116–1145.

Freeman, Richard B., and James L. Medoff. 1984. *What Do Unions Do?* New York: Basic Books.

Freud, Sigmund. 1961. *Civilization and Its Discontent.* Translated and edited by James Strachey. New York: Norton.

Frey, David L., and Samuel L. Gaertner. 1986. "Helping and the avoidance of inappropriate interracial behavior: A strategy that perpetuates a nonprejudiced self-image." *Journal of Personality and Social Psychology,* 50, pp. 1083–1090.

Frey, William H. 1987. "Migration and depopulation of the metropolis: Regional restructuring or rural renaissance?" *American Sociological Review,* 52, pp. 240–257.

Friedman, Richard C., et al. 1977. "Hormones and sexual orientation in man." *American Journal of Psychiatry,* 134, pp. 571–572.

Friedrich, Otto. 1984. "A proud capital's distress." *Time,* August 6, pp. 26–39.

Friedrich-Cofer, Lynette, and Aletha C. Huston. 1986. "Television violence and aggression: The debate continues." *Psychological Bulletin,* 100, pp. 364–371.

Furstenberg, Frank F., Jr., and C. W. Nord. 1982. "The life course of children of divorce: Marital disruption and parental contact." Paper presented at the annual meeting of the Population Association of America, San Diego, April 29–May 1, 1982.

Fussell, Paul. 1983. *Class: A Guide Through the American Status System.* New York: Summit.

Gabor, Andrea. 1986. "Stark fallout from Chernobyl." *U.S. News & World Report,* May 12, pp. 18–23.

Gaertner, Samuel L., and John P. McLaughlin. 1983. "Racial stereotypes: Associations and ascriptions of positive and negative characteristics." *Social Psychology Quarterly,* 46, pp. 23–30.

Gagliani, Giorgio. 1981. "How many working classes?" *American Journal of Sociology,* 87, pp. 259–285.

Gagnon, John H., and William Simon. 1967. "Homosexuality: The formulation of a sociological perspective." *Journal of Health and Social Behavior,* 8, pp. 177–185.

Galloway, Joseph L. 1987. "Islam: Seeking the future in the past." *U.S. News & World Report,* July 6, pp. 33–35.

Gambino, Richard. 1974. *Blood of My Blood.* New York: Doubleday.

Gamson, William A. 1975. *The Strategy of Social Protest.* Homewood, Ill.: Dorsey.

Gans, Herbert J. 1968. *People and Plans.* New York: Basic Books.

———. 1974. "A poor man's home is his poorhouse." *New York Times Magazine,* March 31, p. 58.

———. 1982a. *The Urban Villagers.* New York: Free Press.

———. 1982b. *The Levittowners: Ways of Life and Politics in a New Suburban Community.* New York: Columbia University Press.

Garbarino, James, and Gwen Gilliam. 1980. *Understanding Abusive Families.* Lexington, Mass.: Lexington Press.

Gardner, Howard. 1972. *The Quest for Mind: Piaget, Levi-Strauss, and the Structuralist Movement.* New York: Vintage Books.

———. 1978. *Developmental Psychology.* Boston: Little, Brown.

Garner, Joel, and Elizabeth Clemmer. 1986. *Danger to Police in Domestic Disturbances—A New Look.* Washington, D.C.: U.S. Department of Justice.

Garnier, Maurice A., and Lawrence E. Raffalovich. 1984. "The evolution of equality of educational opportunities in France." *Sociology of Education,* 57, pp. 1–11.

Gartrell, Nanette K., Lynn Loreaux, and Thomas N. Chase. 1977. "Plasma testosterone in homosexual and heterosexual women." *American Journal of Psychiatry,* 134, pp. 1117–1119.

Gaulin, Steven J. C., and Alice Schlegel. 1980. "Paternal confidence and paternal investment: A cross cultural test of a sociobiological hypothesis." *Ethology and Sociobiology*, 1, pp. 301–309.

Gebhard, Paul. 1970. "Postmarital coitus among widows and divorcees," in Paul Bohannan (ed.), *Divorce and After.* New York: Doubleday.

Gecas, Viktor. 1981. "Contexts of Socialization," in Morris Rosenberg and Ralph H. Turner (eds.), *Social Psychology: Sociological Perspectives.* New York: Basic Books.

———. 1982. "The self-concept." *Annual Review of Sociology*, 8, pp. 1–33.

Gellner, David. 1982. "Max Weber: Capitalism and the religion of India." *Sociology*, 16, pp. 526–543.

Gelman, David. 1980. "The games teen-agers play." *Newsweek*, September 1, pp. 48–53.

———. 1986. "Why we age differently." *Newsweek*, October 20, pp. 60–61.

———. 1988. "Black and White in America." *Newsweek*, March 7, pp. 18–23.

Germani, Gino. 1981. *The Sociology of Modernization.* New Brunswick, N.J.: Transaction.

Gest, Ted. 1984. "Battle of the sexes over comparable worth." *U.S. News & World Report*, February 20, pp. 73–74.

Gibbs, Nancy R. 1988. "Grays on the go." *Time*, Feruary 22, pp. 66–75.

Gilbert, Dennis, and Joseph A. Kahl. 1987. *The American Class Structure: A New Synthesis*, 3rd ed. Homewood, Ill.: Dorsey.

Giles, Michael W., and Arthur Evans. 1986. "The power approach to intergroup hostility." *Journal of Conflict Resolution*, 30, pp. 469–486.

Gilleard, Christopher John, and Ali Aslan Gurkan. 1987. "Socioeconomic development and the status of elderly men in Turkey: A test of modernization theory." *Journal of Gerontology*, 42, pp. 353–357.

Gillespie, Dair L., and Ann Leffler. 1983. "Theories of nonverbal behavior: A critical review of proxemics research," in Randall Collins (ed.), *Sociological Theory* 1983. San Francisco, Calif.: Jossey-Bass.

Gilligan, Carol. 1982. *In a Different Voice: Psychological Theory and Women's Development.* Cambridge: Harvard University Press.

Gilman, Hank. 1986. "Marketers court older consumers as balance of buying power shifts." *Wall Street Journal*, April 23, p. 37.

Gilmartin, Brian G. 1975. "That swinging couple down the block." *Psychology Today*, February, pp. 54–58.

Giniger, Seymour, Angelo Dispenzieri, and Joseph Eisenberg. 1983. "Age, experience, and performance on speed and skill jobs in an applied setting." *Journal of Applied Psychology*, 68, pp. 469–475.

Ginzberg, Eli. 1982. "The mechanization of work." *Scientific American* 247, September, pp. 66–75.

Giordano, Joseph. 1987. "The Mafia mystique." *U.S. News & World Report*, February 16, p. 6.

Glaab, Charles N., and A. Theodore Brown. 1983. *A History of Urban America*, 3rd ed. New York: Macmillan.

Glass, David, Peverill Squire, and Raymond Wolfinger. 1984. "Voter turnout: An international comparison." *Public Opinion*, December/January, pp. 49–55.

Glazer, Nona. 1980. "Overworking the working woman: The double day in a Mass Magazine." *Women's Studies International Quarterly*, 3, pp. 79–83.

Glenn, Norval D., and Ruth Hyland. 1967. "Religious preference and worldly success: Some evidence from national surveys." *American Sociological Review*, 32, pp. 73–75.

Glick, Paul C., and Sung-Ling Lin. 1986. "Recent changes in divorce and remarriage." *Journal of Marriage and the Family*, 48, pp. 737–747.

———, and Charles N. Weaver. 1982. "Enjoyment of work by full-time workers in the U.S., 1955 and 1980." *Public Opinion Quarterly*, 46, pp. 459–470.

Glock, Charles Y. 1972. "On the study of religious commitment," in Joseph E. Faulkner (ed.), *Religion's Influence in Contemporary Society.* Columbus, Ohio: Merrill.

Glueck, Sheldon, and Eleanor Glueck. 1956. *Physique and Delinquency.* New York: Harper & Row.

Gmelch, George. 1972. "Magic in professional baseball," in Gregory Stone (ed.), *Games, Sport, and Power.* New Brunswick, N.J.: Dutton.

Goethals, George W. 1971. "Factors affecting permissive and nonpermissive rules regarding premarital sex," in James M. Henslin (ed.), *Studies in the Sociology of Sex.* New York: Appleton-Century-Crofts.

Goffman, Erving. 1959. *The Presentation of Self in Everyday Life.* Garden City, N.Y.: Doubleday/Anchor.

Goldberg, Gertrude S., and Eleanor Kremen. 1987. "The feminization of poverty: Only in America." *Social Policy*, Spring, pp. 3–14.

Goldberg, Herb. 1976. *The Hazards of Being Male.* New York: Signet.

Goldberg, Phillip. 1968. "Are women prejudiced against women?" *Transaction*, 6, April, pp. 28–30.

Goldman, Ari L. 1987. "Tailoring Catholic theology in a time of modern plague." *New York Times*, December 20, p. 20.

Goldman, Morton, et al. 1981. "Factors affecting courteous behavior." *Journal of Social Psychology*, 115, pp. 169–174.

Goldstein, Jeffrey H., and Robert L. Arms. 1971. "Effects of observing athletic contests on hostility." *Sociometry*, 34, pp. 83–90.

Goldstein, Melvyn C., and Cynthia M. Beall. 1982. "Indirect modernization and the status of the elderly in a rural third-world setting." *Journal of Gerontology*, 37, pp. 743–748.

Goldstone, Jack A. 1982. "The comparative and historical study of revolutions." *Annual Review of Sociology*, 8, pp. 187–207.

Goleman, Daniel. 1988. "Physicians may bungle part of treatment: Medical interview." *New York Times*, January 21, p. 12.

Gollady, Mary A. 1976. *The Condition of Education.* Washington, D.C.: U.S. Government Printing Office.

Goode, Erich. 1984a. *Drugs in American Society*, 2nd ed. New York: Knopf.

———. 1984b. *Deviant Behavior*, 2nd ed. Englewood Cliffs, N.J.: Prentice-Hall.

Goode, William J. 1982. *The Family*, 2nd ed. Englewood Cliffs, N.J.: Prentice-Hall.

Goodlad, John I. 1984. *A Place Called School: Prospects for the Future.* New York: McGraw-Hill.

Goodman, Norman, and Gary T. Marx. 1982. *Sociology Today*, 4th ed. New York: Random House.

Goodwin, Michael. 1986. "When the cash register is the scoreboard." *New York Times*, June 8, pp. 27–28.

Gootlieb, Annie. 1971. "Female human beings." *New York Times Book Review*, February 21, sec. 2, p. 1.

Gopoian, J. David. 1984. "What makes PACs tick? An analysis of the allocation patterns of economic interest groups." *American Journal of Political Science*, 28, pp. 259–281.

Gordon, David M. 1973. "Capitalism, class and crime in America." *Crime and Delinquency*, 19, pp. 163–186.

Gordon, Michael. 1978. *The American Family in Social-Historical Perspective*, 2nd ed. New York: St. Martin's.

Gorman, Christine. 1987. "Step in the right direction," *Time*, December 14, p. 75.

Gortmaker, Steven L. 1979. "Poverty and infant mortality in the U.S." *American Sociological Review*, 44, pp. 280–297.

Gottdiener, Mark. 1983. "Understanding metropolitan deconcentration: A clash of paradigms." *Social Science Quarterly*, 64, pp. 227–246.

Gottfredson, Michael R., and Michael J. Hinderlang. 1981. "Sociological aspects of criminal victimization." *Annual Review of Sociology*, 7, pp. 107–128.

Gould, Robert E. 1974. "What we don't know about homosexuality." *New York Times Magazine*, February 24, p. 12.

Gouldner, Alvin W. 1979. *The Future of Intellectuals and the Rise of the New Class.* New York: Seabury.

Goy, R. W., and B. S. McEwen. 1980. *Sexual Differentiation of the Brain.* Cambridge, Mass.: MIT Press.

Gracey, Harry L. 1975. "Learning the student role: Kindergarten as academic boot camp," in Holger R. Stub (ed.), *The Sociology of Education.* Homewood, Ill.: Dorsey.

Granovetter, Mark. 1983. "The strength of weak ties: A network theory revisited," in Randall Collins (ed.), *Sociological Theory 1983.* San Francisco: Jossey-Bass.

———. 1984. "Small is bountiful: Labor markets and establishment size." *American Sociological Review*, 49, 323–334.

———. 1985. "Economic action and social structure: The problem of embeddedness." *American Journal of Sociology*, 91, pp. 481–510.

Grant, W. Vance, and Thomas D. Snyder. 1984. *Digest of Education Statistics 1983–84.* Washington, D.C.: U.S. Government Printing Office.

Gratzer, W. B. 1984. "Science has lost its virtue, not its value." *Science 1984*, January/February, p. 17.

Greeley, Andrew M., and William C. McCready. 1974. *Ethnicity in the United States: A Preliminary Reconnaissance.* New York: Wiley.

Green, Edward, and Russell P. Wakefield. 1979. "Patterns of middle and upper class homicide." *Journal of Criminal Law and Criminology*, 70, pp. 172–181.

Green, Mark. 1982. "Political PAC-man." *New Republic;* December 13, pp. 18–25.

Greenberg, Daniel. 1987. "Publish or perish—or fake it." *U.S. News & World Report,* June 8, pp. 72–73.

Greenberg, David. 1981. *Crime and Capitalism: Readings in Marxist Criminology.* Palo Alto, Calif.: Mayfield.

Greenberg, Michael R. 1983. *Urbanization and Cancer Mobility.* New York: Oxford University Press.

———. 1984. "Sunbelt, Frostbelt and public health." *Society,* July/August, pp. 68–75.

Greene, Michele G. 1987. "No patience for elder patients." *Psychology Today,* February, p. 22.

Greenwald, John. 1982. "Those sky-high health costs." *Time,* July 12, pp. 54–55.

———. 1984a. "A remarkable job machine." *Time,* June 25, pp. 52–54.

———. 1984b. "Swallowing up one another." *Time,* February 6, pp. 46–48.

Greer, Scott. 1956. "Urbanism reconsidered: A comparative study of local areas in a metropolis." *American Sociological Review,* 21, pp. 19–25.

Greer, William R. 1986. "The changing women's marriage market." *New York Times,* February 22, p. 16.

———. 1987. "Big gains in income are seen by elderly." *New York Times,* April 23, pp. 17–18.

Gregg, Gail. 1980. "Chrysler aid cleared in final day's session." *Congressional Quarterly Alamanac 1979,* pp. 285–292.

Grimshaw, Allen D. 1982. "Whose privacy? What harm?" *Sociological Methods and Research,* 11, pp. 233–247.

Groth, A. Nicholas, and H. Jean Birnbaum. 1980. "The rapist: Motivations for sexual violence," in S. L. McCombie (ed.), *The Rape Crisis Intervention Handbook.* New York: Plenum.

Grusky, David B., and Robert M. Hauser. 1984. "Comparative social mobility revisited: Models of convergence and divergence in 16 countries." *American Sociological Review,* 49, pp. 19–38.

Gruson, Lindsey. 1986. "Alternative schools' revisited." *New York Times,* April 8, p. 17.

Gubrium, Jaber F. 1975. "Being single in old age." *International Journal of Aging and Human Development,* 6, pp. 29–41.

Gurney, Joan Neff, and Kathleen J. Tierney. 1982. "Relative deprivation and social movements: A critical look at twenty years of theory and research." *Sociological Quarterly,* 23, pp. 33–47.

Gusfield, Joseph R. 1967a. "Moral passage: The symbolic process in public designations of deviance." *Social Problems,* 15, pp. 175–188.

———. 1967b. "Tradition and modernity: Misplaced polarities in the study of social change." *American Journal of Sociology,* 72, pp. 351–362.

Guttman, Allen. 1986. *Sports Spectators.* New York: Columbia University Press.

Gwartney-Gibbs, Patricia A. 1986. "The institutionalization of premarital cohabitation: Estimates from marriage license applications, 1970 and 1980." *Journal of Marriage and the Family,* 48, pp. 423–434.

Hacker, Andrew. 1983. "What the very rich really think." *Forbes,* Fall, pp. 66–70.

Hadden, Jeffrey K. 1987. "Toward desacralizing secularization theory." *Social Forces,* 65, pp. 587–611.

Hage, Jerald. 1980. *Theories of Organizations: Form, Process, and Transformation.* New York: Wiley.

Hagstrom, Warren O. 1974. "Competition in science." *American Sociological Review,* 39, pp. 1–18.

Hall, Edward T. 1966. *The Hidden Dimension.* New York: Anchor/Doubleday.

———. 1976. "How cultures collide." *Psychology Today,* July, p. 66.

Hall, Wayne. 1986. "Social class and survival on the *S.S. Titanic.*" *Social Science and Medicine,* 22, pp. 687–690.

Haller, Archibald O., and David B. Bills. 1979. "Occupational prestige hierarchies: Theory and evidence." *Contemporary Sociology,* 8, pp. 721–734.

Haller, Max, et al. 1985. "Patterns of career mobility and structural positions in advanced capitalist societies: A comparison of men in Austria, France, and the United States." *American Sociological Review,* 50, p. 579–603.

Hamilton, Roberta H. 1978. *The Liberation of Women: A Study of Psychiatry and Capitalism.* London: George Allen and Unwin.

Hammond, Phillip E. 1985. "The curious path of conservative Protestantism." *Annals of American Academy of Political and Social Science,* 480, July, pp. 53–62.

Hancock, R. Kelly. 1980. "The social life of the modern corporation: Changing resources and forms." *Journal of Applied Behavioral Science,* 16, pp. 279–298.

Handwerker, W. Penn, and Paul V. Crosbie. 1982. "Sex and dominance." *American Anthropologist,* 84, pp. 97–104.

Hanford, George H. 1974. *The Need for and Feasibility of a National Study of Intercollegiate Athletics.* Washington, D.C.: American Council of Education.

Hanlon, Martin D. 1982. "Primary group assistance during unemployment." *Human Organization,* 41, pp. 156–161.

Harayda, Janice. 1986. *The Joy of Being Single.* Garden City, N.Y.: Doubleday.

Hardin, Garrett. 1980. "Tragedy of the commons" (Sound recording). Glendale, Calif.: Mobiltape.

———. 1982. "Is the era of limits running out?" *Public Opinion,* February/March, pp. 48–54.

Hare, A. Paul. 1962. *Handbook of Small Group Research.* Glencoe, Ill.: Free Press.

Hargens, Lowell L., and Diane H. Felmlee. 1984. "Structural determinants of stratification in science." *American Sociological Review,* 49, pp. 685–697.

———, James C. McCann, and Barbara F. Reskin. 1978. "Productivity and reproductivity." *Social Forces,* 57, pp. 154–163.

Harkins, Stephen G., et al. 1979. "Social loafing: Allocating effort or taking it easy." *Journal of Experimental Social Psychology,* 16, pp. 457–465.

Harmatz, Morton G., and Melinda A. Novak. 1983. *Human Sexuality.* New York: Harper & Row.

Harrington, Michael. 1962. *The Other America: Poverty in the United States.* New York: Macmillan.

Harris, Anthony R., and Gary D. Hill. 1982. "The social psychology of deviance: Toward a reconciliation with social structure." *Annual Review of Sociology,* 8, pp. 161–186.

Harris, Chauncy D., and Edward L. Ullman. 1945. "The nature of cities." *Annals of the American Academy of Political and Social Science,* 242, pp. 7–17.

Harris, Louis. 1987. *Inside America.* New York: Vintage.

Harris, Marvin. 1974. *Cows, Pigs, Wars and Witches.* New York: Random House.

———. 1980. *Cultural Materialism.* New York: Vintage.

———. 1981. *America Now: The Anthropology of a Changing Culture.* New York: Simon & Schuster.

———. 1985. *Good to Eat: Riddles of Foods and Culture.* New York: Simon & Schuster.

Harris, Monica J., and Robert Rosenthal. 1985. "Mediation of interpersonal expectancy effects: 31 meta-analyses." *Psychological Bulletin,* 97, pp. 363–386.

Harrison, Selig S. 1979. "Why they won't speak our language in Asia." *Asia,* March/April, pp. 3–7.

Hasenfeld, Yeheskel. 1987. "Is bureaucratic growth inevitable?" *Contemporary Sociology,* 16, pp. 316–318.

Hartle, Terry. 1984. "The public and the teacher unions: Out of step on the basics?" *Public Opinion,* April/May, pp. 55–58.

Hartmann, Betsy, and Jane Hughes. 1984. "And the poor get sterilized." *The Nation,* 238, pp. 798–800.

Hatch, Ruth C., Dorothy E. James, and Walter R. Schumm. 1986. "Spiritual intimacy and marital satisfaction." *Family Relations,* 35, pp. 539–545.

Hathaway, Bruce. 1984. "Running to ruin." *Psychology Today,* July, pp. 14–15.

Haug, Marie R., and Steven J. Folmar. 1986. "Longevity, gender, and life quality." *Journal of Health and Social Behavior,* 27, pp. 332–345.

Hauser, Philip M. 1981. "Chicago—urban crisis exemplar," in J. John Palen (ed.), *City Scenes,* 2nd ed. Boston: Little, Brown.

Havighurst, Robert J. 1963. "Successful aging," in Richard H. Williams, Clark Tibbitts, and William Donahue (eds.), *Processes of Aging,* vol. 1. New York: Atherton.

Haviland, William A. 1985. *Anthropology,* 4th ed. New York: Holt, Rinehart & Winston.

Hawkes, Kristen, and James F. O'Connell. 1981. "Affluent hunters? Some comments in light of the Alyawara case." *American Anthropologist,* 83, pp. 622–626.

Hayden, Tom. 1980. *The American Future: New Visions Beyond Old Frontiers.* Boston: South End Press.

Hayes, Cheryl D., and Sheila B. Kamerman. 1983. *Children of Working Parents: Experiences and Outcomes.* Washington, D.C.: National Academy Press.

Hays, Laurie. 1987. "Pay problems: How couples react when wives out-earn husbands." *Wall Street Journal,* June 19, p. 19.

Hays, Robert B., and Diana Oxley. 1986.

"Social network development and functioning during a life transition." *Journal of Personality and Social Psychology,* 50, pp. 305–313.

Hearn, John. 1978. "Rationality and bureaucracy: Maoist contributions to a Marxist theory of bureaucracy." *Sociological Quarterly,* 19, pp. 37–54.

Hearst, Norman, and Stephen B. Hulley. 1988. "Preventing the heterosexual spread of AIDS." *Journal of American Medical Association,* 259, pp. 2428–2432.

Hedges, Janice Neipert. 1983. "Job commitment in America: Is it waxing or waning?" *Monthly Labor Review,* 106, July, pp. 17–24.

Hegedus, Rita. 1976. "Voucher plans," in Steven E. Goodman (ed.), *Handbook on Contemporary Education.* New York: Bowker.

Heilbroner, Robert L. 1972. *The Worldly Philosophers: The Lives, Times, and Ideas of the Great Economic Thinkers,* 4th ed. New York: Simon & Schuster.

———. 1980. *Marxism: For and Against.* New York: Norton.

Heilman, Samuel C. 1982. "The sociology of American Jewry: The last ten years." *Annual Review of Sociology,* 8, pp. 135–160.

Helprin, Mark. 1986. "Harvard's point of order." *Wall Street Journal,* March 12, p. 34.

Hemming, Jan. 1980. "A clue to homosexuality? Stress during pregnancy." *Science,* August, pp. 69–70.

Hendricks, Jon, and C. Davis Hendricks. 1981. *Aging in Mass Society: Myths and Realities,* 2nd ed. Cambridge, Mass.: Winthrop.

Henig, Jeffrey R. 1982. "Neighborhood response to gentrification: Conditions of mobilization." *Urban Affairs Quarterly,* 17, pp. 343–358.

Henig, Robin Marantz. 1981. *The Myth of Senility: Misconceptions about the Brain and Aging.* Garden City, N.Y.: Anchor/Doubleday.

Hensley, Thomas R., and Glen W. Griffin. 1986. "Victims of groupthink: The Kent State University board of trustees and the 1977 gymnasium controversy." *Journal of Conflict Resolution,* 30, pp. 497–531.

Henslin, James, and Mae A. Briggs. 1971. "Dramaturgical desexualization: The sociology of the vaginal examination." In James M. Henslin (ed.), *Studies in the Sociology of Sex.* New York: Appleton-Century-Crofts.

Herberg, Will. 1983. *Protestant-Catholic-Jew: An Essay in American Religions.* Chicago: University of Chicago.

Herbers, John. 1982. "Experts say 4 million more Americans may join poverty ranks this year." *New York Times,* July 27, p. D22.

Herbert, Wray. 1983. "Curing femininity." *Science News,* 124, pp. 170–171.

———, and Joel Greenberg. 1983. "Fatherhood in transition." *Science News,* 124, p. 172.

Herrnson, Paul S. 1986. "Do parties make a difference? The role of party organizations in congressional elections." *Journal of Politics,* 48, pp. 589–615.

Hersh, Seymour M. 1982. "The price of power: Kissinger, Nixon, and Chile." *Atlantic Monthly,* December, pp. 31–58.

Hertzberg, Rabbi. 1984. "The plight of the Jewish voter." *Newsweek,* June 18, pp. 12–13.

Hess, Robert D. 1970. "The transmission of cognitive strategies in poor families: The socialization of apathy and underachievement," in Vernon L. Allen (ed.), *Psychological Factors in Poverty.* Chicago: Markham.

Hess, Robert D., et al. 1968. *The Cognitive Environments of Urban Preschool Children.* Chicago: University of Chicago Press.

Hessen, Robert. 1979. *In Defense of the Corporation.* Stanford, Calif.: Hoover Institution Press.

Hewlett, Sylvia Ann. 1986. *A Lesser Life: The Myth of Women's Liberation in America.* New York: William Morrow.

Hey, Robert P. 1986. "New federalism ideas in wake of revenue sharing." *Christian Science Monitor,* October 9, pp. 3–4.

Heyl, Barbara. 1979. *The Madam as Entrepreneur: Career Management in House Prostitution.* New Brunswick, N.J.: Transaction.

Heyman, Ira Michael. 1987. "Trapped in an 'athletics arms race.'" *U.S. News & World Report,* July 20, p. 7.

Heyneman, Stephen P., and William A. Loxley. 1983. "The effect of primary-school quality on academic achievement across twenty-nine high- and low-income countries." *American Journal of Sociology,* 88, pp. 1162–1194.

Heyns, Barbara, and T. L. Hilton. 1982. "The cognitive tests for high school and beyond: An assessment." *Sociology of Education,* 55, pp. 89–102.

Hill, Martha S. 1985. "The changing nature of poverty." *The Annals of the American Academy of Political and Social Sciences,* 479, pp. 31–47.

Himmelfarb, Milton. 1986. "Porn, AIDS and the public health." *Wall Street Journal,* January 8, p. 22.

Himmelweit, Hilde T. 1983. "Political socialization." *International Social Science Journal,* 35, pp. 237–256.

Himmelweit, Susan, and Simon Mohun. 1977. "Domestic labor and capital." *Cambridge Journal of Economics,* 1, pp. 15–31.

Hippler, Arthur E. 1978. "Culture and personality perspective of the Yolngu of Northeastern Arnhem Land. Part I—Early socialization." *Journal of Psychological Anthropology,* 1, pp. 221–244.

Hirsch, E. D., Jr. 1987. *Cultural Literacy.* Boston: Houghton Mifflin.

Hirschman, Charles. 1983. "America's melting pot reconsidered." *Annual Review of Sociology,* 9, pp. 397–423.

———, and Ronald Rindfuss. 1982. "The sequence and timing of family formation events in Asia." *American Sociological Review,* 47, pp. 660–680.

Hitching, Francis. 1982. *The Neck of the Giraffe.* New Haven, Conn.: Ticknor & Fields.

Hite, Shere. 1976. *The Hite Report.* New York: Macmillan.

Hobbes, Thomas. 1651. *Leviathan.* London: Crooke.

Hodge, Robert W., Paul M. Siegel, and Peter H. Rossi. 1964. "Occupational prestige in the United States: 1925–1963." *American Journal of Sociology,* 70, pp. 286–302.

Hodge, Robert W., and Donald J. Treiman. 1968. "Class identification in the United States." *American Journal of Sociology,* 73, pp. 535–547.

Hodges, Donald C. 1981. *The Bureaucratization of Socialism.* Amherst: University of Massachusetts Press.

Hoetler, John W. 1982. "Race differences in selective credulity and self-esteem." *Sociological Quarterly,* 23, pp. 527–537.

Hoffer, Eric. 1966. *The True Believer: Thoughts on the Nature of Mass Movements.* New York: Harper & Row.

Hoffman, Martin. 1968. *The Gay World.* New York: Basic Books.

Hollander, Edwin P. 1964. *Leaders, Groups, and Influence.* New York: Oxford University Press.

Hollander, Paul. 1982. "Research on Marxist societies: The relationship between theory and practice." *Annual Review of Sociology,* 8, pp. 319–351.

Hollinger, Richard C., and John P. Clark. 1982. "Formal and informal social controls of employee deviance." *Sociological Quarterly,* 23, pp. 333–343.

Hollingshead, August B., and Frederick C. Redlich. 1958. *Social Class and Mental Illness.* New York: Wiley.

Hollingsworth, J. Rogers. 1986. *A Political Economy of Medicine: Great Britain and the United States.* Baltimore, Md: Johns Hopkins University Press.

Holloway, Nigel. 1987. "All you can afford." *Far Eastern Economic Review,* March 19, p. 45.

Holmes, John. 1987. "International matches made nasty." *Insight,* October 26, pp. 49–51.

Holt, John. 1968. "Education for the future," in Robert Theobald (ed.), *Social Policies for America in the Seventies.* Garden City, N.Y.: Doubleday.

Holton, R. J. 1983. "Max Weber, 'rational capitalism,' and renaissance Italy: A critique of Cohen." *American Journal of Sociology,* 89, pp. 166–180.

Holzman, David. 1988. "Signs of a break in AIDS epidemic." *Insight,* January 15, pp. 52–53.

Hooker, Evelyn. 1969. "Parental relations and male homosexuality in patient and nonpatient samples." *Journal of Consulting and Clinical Psychology,* 138, pp. 140–142.

Hoover, Kenneth R. 1984. *The Elements of Social Scientific Thinking,* 3rd ed. New York: St. Martin's.

Hopper, Earl. 1981. *Social Mobility: A Study of Social Control and Insatiability.* Oxford: Blackwell.

Horai, Joanne, Nicholas Naccari, and Elliot Fatoullan. 1974. "The effects of expertise and physical attractiveness upon opinion agreement and liking." *Sociometry,* 37, pp. 601–606.

Horn, Jack C. 1987. "Bigger pay for better work." *Psychology Today,* July, pp. 54–57.

Horner, Matina S. 1969. "Fail: Bright women." *Psychology Today,* November, pp. 36–38.

Horowitz, Helen Lefkowitz. 1987. *Campus Life.* New York: Knopf.
Hotz, Louis. 1984. "South Africa." *1984 Britannica Book of the Year,* pp. 621–624.
Hougland, James G., Jr., and James R. Wood. 1980. "Control in organizations and the commitment of members." *Social Forces,* 59, p. 85–105.
Hoult, Thomas Ford. 1974, 1979. *Sociology for a New Day,* 1st and 2nd eds. New York: Random House.
House, James S. 1981. "Social structure and personality," in Morris Rosenberg, and Ralph H. Turner (eds.), *Social Psychology.* New York: Basic Books.
Houseknecht, Sharon K., Suzanne Vaughan, and Anne S. Macke. 1984. "Marital disruption among professional women: The timing of career and family events." *Social Problems,* 31, pp. 273–284.
Hout, Michael, and Andrew M. Greeley. 1987. "The center doesn't hold: Church attendance in the United States, 1940–1984." *American Sociological Review,* 52, pp. 325–345.
Howell, Frank M., and J. Steven Picou. 1983. "Athletics and income achievements." Paper presented at annual meeting of Southwestern Sociological Association, Houston.
———, Andrew W. Miracle, and C. Roger Rees. 1984. "Do high school athletics pay?: The effects of varsity participation on socioeconomic attainment." *Sociology of Sport Journal,* 1, pp. 15–25.
Hoyt, Homer. 1943. "The structure of American cities in the post-war era." *American Journal of Sociology,* 48, pp. 475–492.
Hraba, Joseph. 1979. *American Ethnicity.* Itasca, Ill.: Peacock.
Hsu, Cheng-Kuang, Robert M. Marsh, and Hiroshi Mannari. 1983. "An examination of the determinants of organization structure." *American Journal of Sociology,* 88, pp. 975–996.
Hsu, Francis L. K. 1979. "The cultural problem of the cultural anthropologist." *American Anthropologist,* 81, pp. 517–532.
Huber, Bettina J. 1983a. "Helping undergraduate students with careers." *ASA Teaching Newsletter,* February, p. 14.
———, 1983b. "Sociological practitioners: Their characteristics and role in the profession." *ASA Footnotes,* May, pp. 1, 6–8.
———. 1984. "Career possibilities for sociology graduates." *ASA Footnotes,* December, pp. 6–7.
Huber, Joan and Glenna Spitze. 1983. *Sex Stratification: Children, Housework, and Jobs.* New York: Academic Press.
Hughes, Rob. 1983. "Britain's soccer violence." *World Press Review,* December, p. 61.
Hull, David L., Peter D. Tessner, and Arthur M. Diamond. 1978. "Planck's principle." *Science,* 151, pp. 717–723.
Hull, Jennifer. 1987. "Freedom of choice." *Time,* February 9, p. 23.
Humphreys, Laud. 1970. *Tearoom Trade: Impersonal Sex in Public Places.* Chicago: Aldine.
Hunt, Morton M. 1975. *Sexual Behavior in the 1970s.* New York: Dell.
Huntley, Steve. 1983. "America's Indians: 'Beggars in our own land'." *U.S. News & World Report,* May 23, pp. 70–72.
———. 1984. "Keeping in shape—everybody's doing it." *U.S. News & World Report,* August 13, pp. 24–25.
Husen, Torsten. 1983. "Are standards in U.S. schools really lagging behind those in other countries?" *Phi Delta Kappan,* 64, pp. 455–461.
Hyer, Marjorie. 1982a. "Americans willing to fight, proud of U.S." *Washington Post,* October 9, p. 2.
———. 1982b. "U.S. churchgoing habits changing." *Boston Globe,* October 24, p. 10.

I.B. 1982. "SAT verbal, math scores up for first time in 19 years." *Chronicle of Higher Education,* 25, September 29, pp. 1, 6.
Inkeles, Alex. 1983. *Exploring Individual Modernity.* New York: Columbia University Press.
———, and Larry Sirowy. 1983. "Convergent and divergent trends in national educational systems." *Social Forces,* 62, pp. 303–333.
Inwald, Robin Hurwitz, and N. Dale Bryant. 1981. "The effect of sex of participants on decision making in small teacher groups." *Psychology of Women Quarterly,* 5, pp. 532–542.
Irwin, Victoria. 1987. "Taint of racism persists." *Christian Science Monitor,* February 2, p. 1.

Jackson, Elton F., and Richard F. Curtis. 1972. "Effects of vertical mobility and status inconsistency: A body of negative evidence." *American Sociological Review,* 37, pp. 701–713.
Jacobs, Jerry. 1983. "Industrial sector and career mobility reconsidered." *American Sociological Review,* 48, pp. 415–421.
Jacobs, John W. 1982. "The effect of divorce on fathers: An overview of the literature." *American Journal of Psychiatry,* 139, pp. 1235–1241.
Jacoby, Neil H., et al. 1977. *Bribery and Extortion in World Business: A Study of Corporate Political Payments Abroad.* New York: Macmillan.
Jacquard, Albert. 1983. "Myths under the microscope." *UNESCO Courier,* 36, November, pp. 25–27.
Jaggar, Alison M., and Paula Rothenberg Struhl. 1978. *Feminist Frameworks.* New York: McGraw-Hill.
Janis, Irving L. 1982. *Groupthink: Psychological Studies of Policy Decisions and Fiascos.* Boston: Houghton Mifflin.
Janson, Philip, and Jack K. Martin. 1982. "Job satisfaction and age: A test of two views." *Social Forces,* 60, pp. 1089–1102.
Jaret, Charles. 1983. "Recent neo-Marxist urban analysis." *Annual Review of Sociology,* 9, pp. 499–525.
Jarvenpa, Robert. 1985. "The political economy and political ethnicity of American Indian adaptations and identities." *Ethnic and Racial Studies,* 8, pp. 29–48.
Jasso, Guillermina. 1985. "Marital coital frequency and the passage of time: Estimating the separate effects of spouses' ages and marital duration, birth and marriage cohorts, and period influences." *American Sociological Review,* 50, pp. 224–241.
Jencks, Christopher, et al. 1972. *Inequality: A Reassessment of the Effect of Family and Schooling in America.* New York: Basic Books.
———. 1979. *Who Gets Ahead?* New York: Basic Books.
Jenkins, Brian M. 1979. "International terrorism." *The Americana,* p. 49.
Jenkins, J. Craig. 1983. "Resource mobilization theory and the study of social movements." *Annual Review of Sociology,* 9, pp. 527–553.
Jessor, Richard, et al. 1983. "Time of first intercourse: A prospective study." *Journal of Personality and Social Psychology,* 44, pp. 608–626.
Johnson, Allan Griswold. 1980. "On the prevalence of rape in the United States." *Signs,* 6, pp. 136–145.
Johnson, David W., and Roger T. Johnson. 1984. "The effects of intergroup cooperation and intergroup competition on ingroup and outgroup cross-handicap relationships." *Journal of Social Psychology,* 124, pp. 85–94.
Johnson, Dirk. 1987. "The view from poorest U.S. suburb." *New York Times,* April 30, p. 10.
Johnson, Marguerite. 1984. "This is all so painful." *Time,* June 4, p. 36.
Johnson, Miriam M. 1982. "Fathers and 'femininity' in daughters: A review of the research." *Sociology and Social Research,* 67, pp. 1–17.
Johnson, Norris R. 1987. "Panic at 'The Who concert stampede': An empirical assessment." *Social Problems,* 34, pp. 362–373.
Johnson, Richard E. 1980. "Social class and delinquent behavior: A new test." *Criminology,* 18, pp. 86–93.
Johnson, Sterling, Jr. 1987. "This is the wrong message to give." *New York Times,* December 20, p. 20E.
Johnston, Lloyd D. 1980. "Marijuana use and the effects of decriminalization." Testimony before the Subcommittee on Criminal Justice, Judiciary Committee, U.S. Senate, January 16, Washington, D.C.
Jones, Alwyn. 1987. "The violence of materialism in advanced industrial society: An eco-sociological approach." *The Sociological Review,* 35, pp. 19–47.
Joseph, Stephen C. 1987. "50 to 60 percent are infected." *New York Times,* December 20, p. 20.

Kaagan, Lawrence. 1983. "Are the parties over?" *Psychology Today,* April, p. 8.
Kalick, S. Michael, and Thomas E. Hamilton III. 1986. "The matching hypothesis reexamined." *Journal of Personality and Social Psychology,* 51, pp. 673–682.
Kalisch, Philip A., and Beatrice J. Kalisch. 1984. "Sex-role stereotyping of nurses and physicians on prime-time television: A dichotomy of occupational portrayals." *Sex Roles,* 10, pp. 533–553.
Kalleberg, Arne L., and Karyn A. Loscocco.

1983. "Aging, values, and rewards: Explaining age differences in job satisfaction." *American Sociological Review,* 48, pp. 78–90.

Kallman, Franz J. 1952. "Comparative twin study on the genetic aspects of male homosexuality. *Journal of Nervous and Mental Disease,* 115, pp. 283–298.

Kalmuss, Debra. 1984. "The intergenerational transmission of marital aggression." *Journal of Marriage and the Family,* 46, pp. 11–19.

Kane, Martin. 1971. "An assessment of black is best." *Sports Illustrated,* January 18, p. 76.

Kanin, Eugene J. 1983. "Rape as a function of relative sexual frustration." *Psychological Reports,* 52, pp. 133–134.

Kanin, Eugene J. 1985. "Date rapists: differential sexual socialization and relative deprivation." *Archives of Sexual Behavior,* 14, pp. 219–231.

———, and Stanley R. Parcell. 1981. "Sexual aggression: A second look at the offended female," in Lee H. Bowker (ed.), *Women and Crime in America.* New York: Macmillan.

Kanter, Rosabeth Moss. 1977. *Men and Women of the Corporation.* New York: Basic Books.

Kantrowitz, Barbara. 1987. "How to stay married." *Time,* August, pp. 52–57.

———. 1987. "Kids and contraceptives." *Newsweek,* February 16, pp. 54–65.

Kaplan, Howard B., et al. 1987. "The sociological study of AIDS: A critical review of the literature and suggested research agenda." *Journal of Health and Social Behavior,* 28, pp. 140–157.

Kardiner, Abram, and Lionel Ovesey. 1962. *The Mark of Oppression.* New York: Meridian.

Kart, Gary S. 1981. *The Realities of Aging.* Boston: Allyn and Bacon.

Kasarda, John D. 1983. "Urbanization, community, and the metropolitan problem," in Mark Baldassare (ed.), *Cities and Urban Living.* New York: Columbia University Press.

———, and John O. G. Billy. 1985. "Social mobility and fertility." *Annual Review of Sociology,* 11, pp. 305–328.

Kasindorf, Martin. 1982. "Asian-Americans: A 'model minority'." *Newsweek,* December 6, pp. 47–51.

Kasperson, Conrad J. 1978. "Scientific creativity: A relationship with information channels." *Psychological Reports,* 42, pp. 691–694.

Katchadourian, Herant A. 1985. *Fundamentals of Human Sexuality,* 4th ed. New York: Holt, Rinehart and Winston.

———, and John Boli. 1986. *Careerism and Intellectualism Among College Students.* San Francisco: Jossey-Bass.

Katrak, Homi. 1983. "Multinational firms' global strategies, host country indigenisation of ownership and welfare." *Journal of Development Economics,* 13, pp. 331–348.

Kaufman, Herbert. 1977. *Red Tape.* Washington, D.C.: Brookings Institution.

Keller, Helen. 1954. *The Story of My Life.* Garden City, N.Y.: Doubleday.

Keller, James F., Stephen S. Elliott, and Edwin Gunberg. 1982. "Premarital sexual intercourse among single college students: A discriminant analysis." *Sex Roles,* 8, pp. 21–32.

Kelman, Herbert C. 1986. "When scholars work with the C.I.A." *New York Times,* March 5, p. 27.

Kelly, Orr. 1984. "Rash of terrorism ahead? Is U.S. ready?" *U.S. News & World Report,* July 16, pp. 28–30.

Kelman, Steven. 1978. "Regulation that works." *New Republic,* November 25, p. 18.

Kelvin, Alice J. 1983. "Anti-Climax." *Psychology Today,* April, p. 66.

Kemper, Susan. 1984. "When to speak like a lady." *Sex Roles,* 10, pp. 435–443.

Kenna, John T. 1983. "The Latinization of the U.S." *1983 Britannica Book of the Year,* pp. 586–587.

Kennedy, Paul M. 1988. *The Rise and Fall of the Great Powers.* New York: Random House.

Kephart, William M. 1981. *The Family, Society, and the Individual,* 5th ed. Boston: Houghton Mifflin.

Kerbo, Harold R. 1982. "Movements of 'crisis' and movements of 'affluence': A critique of deprivation and resource mobilization theories." *Journal of Conflict Resolution,* 26, pp. 645–663.

———. 1983. *Social Stratification and Inequality: Class Conflict in the United States.* New York: McGraw-Hill.

Kerckhoff, Alan C. 1986. "Effects of ability grouping in British secondary schools." *American Sociological Review,* 51, pp. 842–858.

———, Richard T. Campbell, and Idee Winfield-Laird. 1985. "Social mobility in Great Britain and the United States." *American Journal of Sociology,* 91, pp. 281–308.

Kessin, Kenneth. 1971. "Social and psychological consequences of intergenerational occupational mobility." *American Journal of Sociology,* 77, pp. 1–18.

Kessler, Ronald C. 1979. "Stress, social status, and psychological distress." *Journal of Health and Social Behavior,* 20, pp. 259–272.

———, Richard H. Price, and Camille B. Wortman. 1985. "Social factors in psychopathology: Stress, social support, and coping processes." *Annual Review of Psychology,* 36, pp. 560–561.

Keyfitz, Nathan. 1983. "Age, work, and social security." *Society,* 20, July/August, pp. 45–51.

Kidder, Rushworth. 1987. "Amitai Etzioni." *Christian Science Monitor,* April 3, pp. 16–17.

Kilgore, Sally B. 1983. "Statistical evidence, selectivity effects, and program placement: Response to Alexander and Pallas." *Sociology of Education,* 56, pp. 182–186.

———. 1984. "Schooling effects: Reply to Alexander and Pallas." *Sociology of Education,* 57, pp. 59–61.

Killingsworth, Charles C. 1981. "The development of employment policy," in Michael Carter and William Leahy (eds.), *New Directions in Labor Economics and Industrial Relations.* Notre Dame: University of Notre Dame Press.

Kim, Paul S. 1983. "Japan's bureaucratic decision-making on the textbook." *Public Administration,* 61, pp. 283–294.

Kimmel, Michael S. 1986. "A prejudice against prejudice." *Psychology Today,* December, pp. 47–52.

King, Anthony. 1985. "Transatlantic transgressions: A comparison of British and American scandals." *Public Opinion,* January, pp. 20–22, 64.

King, Morton B., and Richard A. Hunt. 1984. "Measuring religion: A comment on Morgan." *Social Forces,* 62, pp. 1087–1088.

King, Wayne. 1988. "Swaggart says he has sinned; will step down." *New York Times,* February 2, 1988, pp. 1, 11.

Kinsey, Alfred C., Wardell B. Pomeroy, and Clyde E. Martin. 1948. *Sexual Behavior in the Human Male.* Philadelphia: Saunders.

———, Wardell B. Pomeroy, Clyde E. Martin, and Paul H. Gebhard. 1953. *Sexual Behavior in the Human Female.* Philadelphia: Saunders.

Kirkland, Lane. 1986. "Labor unions look ahead." *The Futurist,* May/June, pp. 48–49.

Kirkpatrick, Clifford, and Eugene Kanin. 1957. "Male sex aggression on a university campus." *American Sociological Review,* 22, pp. 52–58.

Kirkpatrick, Jeane J. 1982. *Dictatorships and Double Standards: Rationalism and Reason in Politics.* New York: Simon & Schuster.

Kitagawa, Evelyn M., and Philip M. Hauser. 1968. "Education differentials in mortality by cause of death, United States 1960." *Demography,* 5, pp. 318–353.

Kitahara, Michio. 1982. "Menstrual taboos and the importance of hunting." *American Anthropologist,* 84, pp. 901–903.

Kitano, Harry H. L. 1981. "Asian-Americans: The Chinese, Japanese, Koreans, Philipinos [*sic*], and Southeast Asians." *Annals,* 454, March, pp. 125–149.

Kitcher, Philip. 1985. *Vaulting Ambition: Sociology and the Quest for Human Nature.* Cambridge, Mass.: MIT Press.

Klandermans, Bert. 1984. "Mobilization and participation: Social-psychological expansions of resource mobilization theory." *American Sociological Review,* 49, pp. 583–600.

Klandermans, Bert, and Dirk Oegema. 1987. "Potentials, networks, motivations, and barriers: Steps towards participation in social movements." *American Sociological Review,* 52, pp. 519–531.

Klaus, Patsy A., and Michael R. Rand. 1984. "Family violence." *Bureau of Justice Statistics Special Report.* U.S. Department of Justice.

Klott, Gary. 1987. "Unemployment declines to 6.2%, reaching lowest level in 7 years." *New York Times,* May 9, pp. 1, 10.

Kluckhohn, Clyde. 1948. "As an anthropologist views it," in Albert Deutsch (ed.), *Sex Habits of American Men.* Englewood Cliffs, N.J.: Prentice-Hall.

———, 1949. *Mirror for Man.* New York: McGraw-Hill.

Kluegel, James R., and Eliot R. Smith. 1981. "Beliefs about stratification." *Annual Review of Sociology,* 7, pp. 29–56.

———. 1982. "Whites' beliefs about blacks' opportunities." *American Sociological Review,* 47, pp. 518–532.

———. 1983. "Affirmative action attitudes: Effects of self-interest, racial affect, and stratification beliefs on whites' views." *Social Forces,* 61, pp. 797–823.

Kneale, Dennis. 1986. "Working at IBM: Intense loyalty in a rigid culture." *Wall Street Journal,* April 7, p. 17.

Kneeland, Douglas E. 1981. "Urbanization of rural U.S. called peril to farmland." *New York Times,* June 16, p. B8.

Knight, Robin. 1984. "Up from recession—U.S. leads the way." *U.S. News & World Report,* June 11, pp. 26–27.

———. 1985. "The Marxist world: Lure of capitalism." *U.S. News & World Report,* February 4, pp. 36–42.

Knoke, David, and James H. Kuklinski. 1982. *Network Analysis.* Beverly Hills, Calif.: Sage.

Koenig, Fredrick. 1982a. "Preferences for candidates of college students and their parents in two presidential elections." *Psychological Reports,* 50, pp. 335–336.

———. 1982b. "Today's conditions make U.S. 'ripe for the rumor mill'." *U.S. News & World Report,* December 6, p. 42.

Koepp, Stephen. 1986. "Is the middle class shrinking?" *Time,* November 3, pp. 54–56.

Kohlberg, Lawrence. 1963. "The development of children's orientations toward a moral order: 1. Sequence in the development of moral thought." *Human Development,* 6, pp. 11–33.

———. 1966. "A cognitive-developmental analysis of children's sex-role concepts and attitudes," in Eleanor E. Maccoby (ed.), *The Development of Sex Differences.* Stanford, Calif.: Stanford University Press.

———. 1969. "Stage and sequence: The cognitive-developmental approach to socialization," in David A. Goslin (ed.), *Handbook of Socialization Theory and Research.* Chicago: Rand McNally.

———. 1981. *The Philosophy of Moral Development: Moral Stages and the Idea of Justice.* New York: Harper & Row.

Kohn, Melvin L. 1963. "Social class and parent-child relations: An interpretation." *American Journal of Sociology,* 68, pp. 471–480.

———. 1982. "The benefits of bureaucracy." In Melvin L. Kohn and Schooler (eds.), *Occupational Structure and Personality.* Norwood, N.J.: Ablex.

———. 1977. *Class and Conformity,* 2nd ed. Homewood, Ill. Dorsey.

———. 1980. "Job complexity and adult personality," in Neal Smelser and Erik Erikson (eds.), *Themes of Love and Work in Adulthood.* Cambridge, Mass.: Harvard University Press.

Kohn, Alfie. 1986. *No Contest: The Case Against Competition.* Boston: Houghton Mifflin.

Kolata, Gina. 1988. "AIDS research on our drugs bypasses addicts and women." *New York Times,* January 5, pp. 15, 19.

Kolata, Gina Bari. 1979. "Sex hormones and brain development." *Science,* September 7, pp. 985–987.

Kolb, L. Coleman. 1963. *Modern Clinical Psychiatry.* Philadelphia: Saunders.

Koller, Marvin R., and Oscar W. Ritchie. 1978. *Sociology of Childhood,* 2nd ed. Englewood Cliffs, N.J.: Prentice-Hall.

Kondracke, Morton. 1979. "China diarist: Rich and poor." *New Republic,* April, p. 42.

Koskenvuo, Markku, et al. 1986. "Social factors and the gender differences in mortality." *Social Science and Medicine,* 23, pp. 605–609.

Kotlowitz, Alex. 1987. "Labor's Shift." *Wall Street Journal,* May 22, pp. 1, 6.

Kourvetaris, George A., and Betty A. Dobratz. 1982. "Political power and conventional political participation." *Annual Review of Sociology,* 8, pp. 289–317.

Kozol, Jonathan. 1968. *Death at an Early Age.* Boston: Houghton Mifflin.

Kraut, Robert E. 1976. "Deterrent and definitional influences on shoplifting." *Social Problems,* 23, pp. 358–368.

Krenz, Claudia, and Gilbert Sax. 1986. "What quantitative research is and why it doesn't work." *American Behavioral Scientist,* 30, pp. 58–69.

Kristof, Nicholas D. 1987. "China's birth rate on rise again as official sanctions are ignored." *New York Times,* April 21, pp. 1, 6.

Krivo, Lauren. 1986. "Home ownership differences between Hispanics and Anglos in the United States." *Social Problems,* 33, pp. 319–334.

Krohn, Marvin D., et al. 1980. "Social status and deviance." *Criminology,* 18, pp. 303–318.

Kübler-Ross, Elisabeth. 1969. *On Death and Dying.* New York: Macmillan.

Kucherov, Alex. 1981. "Now help is on the way for neglected widowers." *U.S. News & World Report,* June 22, pp. 47, 48.

Kuhn, Thomas S. 1970. *The Structure of Scientific Revolutions,* 2nd ed. Chicago: University of Chicago Press.

Kutsch, Thomas. 1981. "Modernization, everyday life, and social roles: Benefits and costs of life in 'developed' societies." In Mustafa O. Attir, Burkart Holzner, and Zdenek Suda (eds.), *Directions of Change.* Boulder, Colo.: Westview.

Kwitny, Jonathan. 1986. "Science follies." *Wall Street Journal,* December 12, pp. 1, 14.

LaBarre, Weston. 1954. *The Human Animal.* Chicago: University of Chicago.

Labor Department. 1983. *Handbook of Labor Statistics.* Washington, D.C.: U.S. Government Printing Office.

———. 1984a. *Employment and Earnings: August 1984.* Washington, D.C.: U.S. Government Printing Office.

———. 1984b. *Occupational Outlook Handbook.* Washington, D.C.: U.S. Government Printing Office.

Lacayo, Richard. 1987. "Considering the alternatives." *Time,* February 2, pp. 60–61.

———. 1987. "Whose trial is it anyway?" *Time,* May 25, p. 62.

Ladd, Everett Carll. 1978. "What the voters really want." *Fortune,* December 18, pp. 40–48.

———. 1982. "Clearing the air: Public opinion and public policy on the environment." *Public Opinion,* February/March, pp. 16–20.

———. 1983a. "A party primer." *Public Opinion,* October/November, p. 20.

———. 1983b. "Politics in the 80's: An electorate at odds with itself." *Public Opinion,* December/January, pp. 2–5.

———. 1987. "The prejudices of a tolerant society." *Public Opinion,* July/August, pp. 2–3, 56.

———. 1987. "Secular and religious America." *Society,* March/April, pp. 63–68.

Lader, Lawrence. 1983. "The China solution." *Science Digest,* April, p. 78.

Lamanna, Mary Ann, and Agnes Riedman. 1985. *Marriages and Families: Making Choices Throughout the Life Cycle.* Belmont, Calif.: Wadsworth.

Lamar, Jacob V. 1986. "Suspending their judgment." *Time,* September 29, pp. 31–32.

Lamberti, Joseph W., Nathan Blackman, and James M. A. Weiss. 1967. "The sudden murderer," in Marvin E. Wolfgang (ed.), *Studies in Homicide.* New York: Harper & Row.

Landecker, Werner S. 1981. *Class Crystallization.* New Brunswick, N.J.: Rutgers University Press.

Landes, David S. 1969. *The Unbound Prometheus: Technological Change and Industrial Development in Western Europe from 1750 to the Present.* London: Cambridge University Press.

Landman, Lynn C. 1977. "Birth control in India: The carrot and the rod?" *Family Planning Perspective,* 9, pp. 101–110.

Landy, David, and Harold Sigall. 1974. "Beauty is talent—Task evaluation as a function of the performer's physical attractiveness." *Journal of Personality and Social Psychology,* 29, pp. 299–304.

Lane, Harlan. 1976. *The Wild Boy of Aveyron.* Cambridge, Mass.: Harvard University Press.

Langton, Nancy. 1987. "Niche theory and social movement: A population ecology approach." *The Sociological Quarterly,* 28, pp. 51–70.

Lansing, J. Stephen. 1978. "Economic growth and traditional society: A cautionary tale from Bali." *Human Organization,* 37, pp. 391–394.

Larsen, Otto. 1981. "Need for continuing support for social sciences." *ASA Footnotes,* 9, March, p. 8.

Lasch, Christopher. 1977. *Haven in a Heartless World: The Family Besieged.* New York. Basic Books.

———. 1979. *The Culture of Narcissism: American Life in an Age of Diminishing Expectations.* New York: Norton.

Lasswell, Harold D. 1936. *Politics: Who Gets What, When, How?* New York: McGraw-Hill.

Latané, Bibb, et al. 1979. "Many hands make light work: The causes and consequences of social loafing." *Journal of Personality and Social Psychology,* 37, pp. 822–832.

———, and Steve Nida. 1981. "Ten years of research on group size and helping." *Psychological Bulletin,* 89, pp. 308–324.

Lauer, Robert H. 1982. *Perspectives on Social Change,* 3rd ed. Boston: Allyn and Bacon.

Lavin, Bebe, et al. 1987. "Change in student physicians' views on authority relationships with patients." *Journal of Health and Social Behavior*, 28, pp. 258–272.

Law, Kim S., and Edward J. Walsh. 1983. "The interaction of grievances and structures in social movement analysis: The case of JUST." *Sociological Quarterly*, 24, pp. 123–136.

Layton, Robert. 1986. "Political and territorial structures among hunter-gatherers." *Man*, 21, pp. 18–33.

Leach, Edmund. 1981. "Biology and social science: Wedding or rape?" *Nature*, 291, p. 268.

Leakey, Richard E., and Roger Lewin. 1977. *Origins*. New York: Dutton.

Le Bon, Gustave. 1976/1960. *The Crowd: A Study of the Popular-Mind*. New York: Viking.

Lederer, Joseph. 1983. "Birth-control decisions: Hidden factors in contraceptive choices." *Psychology Today*, June, pp. 32–38.

Lee, Alfred McClung, and Elizabeth Briant Lee. 1979. *The Fine Art of Propaganda*. San Francisco: International Society for General Semantics.

Lee, Barrett A., and Avery M. Guest. 1983. "Determinants of neighborhood satisfaction: A metropolitan-level analysis." *Sociological Quarterly*, 24, pp. 287–303.

Lee, Elliott D. 1987. "Female tenants battle increased sex harassment." *Wall Street Journal*, January 30, p. 19.

Lee, John Alan. 1982. "Three paradigms of childhood." *Canadian Review of Sociology and Anthropology*, 19, pp. 591–608.

Lee, Richard B. 1979. *The !Kung San: Men, Women and Work in a Foraging Society*. New York: Cambridge University Press.

Lefkowitz, Monroe, Robert R. Blacke, and Jane S. Moutin. 1955. "Status factors in pedestrian violation of traffic signals." *Journal of Abnormal and Social Psychology*, 51, pp. 704–706.

Lemert, Edwin M. 1951. *Social Pathology*. New York: McGraw-Hill.

Lemon, B. W., K. L. Bengston, and J. A. Peterson. 1972. "An exploration of the activity theory of aging: Activity types and life satisfaction among in-movers to a retirement community." *Journal of Gerontology*, 27, pp. 511–523.

Lenski, Gerhard. 1961. *The Religious Factor*. Garden City, N.Y.: Anchor/Doubleday.

———. 1966. *Power and Privilege*. New York: McGraw-Hill.

———, and Jean Lenski. 1987. *Human Societies*, 5th ed. New York: McGraw-Hill.

———, and Patrick D. Nolan. 1984. "Trajectories of development: A test of ecological-evolutionary theory." *Social Forces*, 63, pp. 1–23.

Leo, John. 1979. "Homosexuality: Tolerance vs. approval." *Time*, January 8, pp. 48–51.

———. 1986. "Are women 'male clones'?" *Time*, August 18, pp. 63–64.

———. 1987. "Exploring the traits of twins." *Time*, January 12, p. 63.

Leonard, George. 1983. *The End of Sex*. Boston: Houghton Mifflin.

Leslie, Gerald R. 1982. *The Family in Social Context*. New York: Oxford University Press.

Levi, Arrigo. 1987. "Italy's stable instability." *World Press Review*, June, pp. 22–24.

Levi, Ken. 1981. "Becoming a hit man: Neutralization in a very deviant career." *Urban Life*, 10, pp. 47–63.

Levin, Jack, and James Alan Fox. 1985. *Mass Murder: America's Growing Menace*. New York: Plenum.

Levin, Jack, and William C. Levin. 1980. *Ageism: Prejudice and Discrimination Against the Elderly*. Belmont, Calif.: Wadsworth.

Levine, Art. 1987. "The uneven odds." *U.S. News & World Report*, August 17, pp. 31–33.

———. 1988. "AIDS and the innocents." *U.S. News & World Report*, February 1, pp. 49–51.

Levine, Mark F., James C. Taylor, and Louis E. Davis. 1984. "Defining quality of working life." *Human Relations*, 37, pp. 81–104.

Levine, Saul V. 1984. *Radical Departures: Desperate Detours to Growing Up*. New York: Harcourt Brace Jovanovich.

Levinson, Daniel J. 1978. *The Seasons of a Man's Life*. New York: Knopf.

Levitan, Sar A. 1984. "The changing workplace." *Society*, September/October, pp. 41–48.

———, and Richard S. Belous. 1981. *What's Happening to the American Family?* Baltimore, Md.: Johns Hopkins University Press.

Levkoff, Sue E. 1987. "Differences in the appraisal of health between aged and middle-aged adults." *Journal of Gerontology*, 42, pp. 114–120.

Levy, S. G., and W. F. Fenley, Jr. 1979. "Audience size and likelihood and intensity of response during a humorous movie." *Bulletin of Psychonomic Society*, 13, pp. 409–412.

Lewin, Bo. 1982. "Unmarried cohabitation: A marriage form in a changing society." *Journal of Marriage and the Family*, 44, pp. 763–773.

Lewis, Lionel S. 1982. "Working at leisure." *Society*, July/August, pp. 27–32.

Lewis, Neil A. 1987. "White House and pro-choice groups wage battle over abortions abroad." *New York Times*, June 1, p. 8.

Lewis, Oscar. 1965. "Further observations on the folk-urban continuum and urbanization," in Philip M. Hauser and Leo F. Schnore (eds.), *The Study of Urbanization*. New York: Wiley.

Lewontin, R. C., Steven Rose, and Leon J. Kamin. 1984. *Not in Our Genes*. New York: Pantheon.

Liem, Ramsay, and Joan Liem. 1978. "Social class and mental illness reconsidered: The role of economic stress and social support." *Journal of Health and Social Behavior*, 19, pp. 139–156.

Lightbourne, Robert Jr., and Susheela Singh, with Cynthia P. Green. 1982. "The world fertility survey: Charting global childbearing." *Population Bulletin*, 37, March, pp. 1–54.

Lin, Nan. 1982. "Social resources and instrumental action." In Peter V. Marsden and Nan Lin (eds.), *Social Structure and Network Analysis*. Beverly Hills, Calif.: Sage, pp. 131–145.

Lincoln, James R., and Arne L. Kalleberg. 1985. "Work organization and workforce commitment: A study of plants and employees in the U.S. and Japan." *American Sociological Review*, 50, pp. 738–760.

Link, Bruce. 1982. "Mental patient status, work, and income: An examination of the effects of a psychiatric label." *American Sociological Review*, 47, pp. 202–215.

Lipset, Seymour Martin. 1976. "Equality and inequality," in Robert K. Merton and Robert Nisbet (eds.), *Contemporary Social Problems*. New York: Harcourt Brace Jovanovich.

———. 1981. *Political Man: the Social Bases of Politics*. Baltimore, Md.: John Hopkins University Press.

———. 1982. "Social mobility in industrial societies." *Public Opinion*, June/July, pp. 41–44.

———. 1987. "Blacks and Jews: How much bias?" *Public Opinion*, July/August, pp. 4–5; 57–58.

———, and Earl Raab, 1978. *The Politics of Unreason*, 2nd ed. New York: Harper & Row.

———, and William Schneider. 1983. *The Confidence Gap: Business, Labor, and Government in the Public Mind*. New York: Free Press.

Littler, Craig R. 1978. "Understanding Taylorism." *British Journal of Sociology*, 29, pp. 185–202.

Locke, John. 1690. *Two Treatises of Government*. London: Churchill.

Lodge, Juliet. 1981. *Terrorism: A Challenge to the State*. New York: St. Martin's.

Loevinger, Jane, and Elizabeth Knoll. 1983. "Personality: Stages, traits, and the self." *Annual Review of Psychology*, 34, pp. 195–222.

Loewenstein, Louis K. 1977. *Urban Studies*, 2nd ed. New York: Free Press.

Logan, John R., and Mark Schneider. 1984. "Racial segregation and racial change in American suburbs, 1970–1980." *American Journal of Sociology*, 89, pp. 874–888.

Lombroso, Cesare. 1918. *Crime: Its Causes and Remedies*. Boston: Little, Brown.

Long, Sharon K., Ann D. White, and Patrice Karr. 1983. "Family violence: A microeconomic approach." *Social Science Research*, 12, pp. 363–392.

Longino, Charles F., and Gary S. Kart. 1982. "Explicating activity theory: A formal replication." *Journal of Gerontology*, 37, pp. 713–722.

———, Kent A. McClelland, and Warren A. Peterson. 1980. "The age subculture hypothesis." *Journal of Gerontology*, 35, pp. 758–767.

Lord, Lewis. 1986. "Sex, with care." *U.S. News & World Report*, June 2, pp. 53–57.

Lord, Lewis J., and Miriam Horn. 1987. "The brain battle." *U.S. News & World Report*, January 19, pp. 58–64.

Lord, Walter. 1981. *A Night to Remember*. New York: Penguin.

Lorence, Jon. 1987. "A test of 'gender' and 'job' models of sex differences in job involvement." *Social Forces*, 66, pp. 121–142.

Lorenz, Konrad. 1966. *On Aggression*. New

York: Harcourt, Brace and World.
Loy, John W., and Joseph F. McElvogue. 1970. "Racial segregation in American sport." *International Review of Sport Sociology*, 5, pp. 5–24.
———, Barry D. McPherson, and Gerald Kenyon. 1978. *Sport and Social Systems: A Guide to the Analysis, Problems, and Literature.* Reading, Mass.: Addison-Wesley.
Lukas, Anthony. 1985. *Common Ground: A Turbulent Decade in the Lives of Three American Families.* New York: Knopf.
Lunde, Anders S. 1984. "Demography." *1984 Britannica Book of the Year*, pp. 284–289.
Lunde, Donald T. 1975. "Our murder boom." *Psychology Today*, pp. 40–42.
Luria, Zella, Susan Friedman, and Mitchel D. Rose. 1987. *Human Sexuality.* New York: Wiley.
Lüschen, Günther. 1980. "Sociology of sport: Development, present state, and prospects." *Annual Review of Sociology*, 6, pp. 315–347.

Mabry, Edward A., and Richard E. Barnes. 1980. *The Dynamics of Small Group Communication.* Englewood Cliffs, N.J.: Prentice-Hall.
MacArthur, Douglas. 1965. *A Soldier Speaks.* New York: Praeger.
Maccoby, Eleanor E., and Carol N. Jacklin. 1975. *The Psychology of Sex Differences.* Stanford, Calif.: Stanford University Press.
Mack, Raymond W., and Calvin P. Bradford. 1979. *Transforming America.* New York: Random House.
MacLachlan, Mike. 1982. "The game's the thing." *Far Eastern Economic Review*, January 22, pp. 28–30.
Macrae, Norman. 1984. "Reducing medical costs." *World Press Review*, 31, July, pp. 27–29.
Madsen, Douglas, and Peter G. Snow. 1983. "The dispersion of charisma." *Comparative Political Studies*, 16, pp. 337–362.
Madsen, Jane M. 1982. "Racist images." *USA Today*, 111, p. 14.
Magnuson, Ed. 1982. "Unease among the freezers." *Time*, October 25, p. 33.
Mahard, Rita E., and Robert L. Crain. 1983. "Research on minority achievement in desegregated schools," in Christine H. Rossell and Willis D. Hawley (eds.), *The Consequences of School Desegregation.* Philadelphia: Temple University Press.
Malamuth, Neil M. 1981. "Rape proclivity among males." *Journal of Social Issues*, 37, pp. 138–157.
Malone, Janet H. 1982. "The questionable promise of enterprise zones: Lessons from England and Italy." *Urban Affairs Quarterly*, 18, pp. 19–30.
Maloney, Lawrence D. 1984. "Plague of religious wars around the globe." *U.S. News & World Report*, June 25, pp. 24–26.
Malson, Lucien. 1972. *Wolf Children and the Problem of Human Nature.* New York: Monthly Review.
Malthus, Thomas. 1798. *An Essay on the Principles of Population.* London: Reeves and Turner.
Mann, Donald. 1983. "Growth means doom." *Science Digest*, 91, April, pp. 79–81.
Manton, Kenneth G., Dan G. Blazer, and Max A. Woodbury. 1987. "Suicide in middle age and later life: Sex and race specific life table and cohort analyses." *Journal of Gerontology*, 24, pp. 219–227.
Marden, Charles F., and Gladys Meyer. 1978. *Minorities in American Society.* New York: Van Nostrand.
Mare, Robert D., and Christopher Winship. 1984. "The paradox of lessening racial inequality and joblessness among black youth: Enrollment, enlistment, and employment, 1964–1981." *American Sociological Review*, 49, pp. 39–55.
Markides, Kyriacos C., and Steven F. Cohn. 1982. "External conflict/internal cohesion: A reevaluation of an old theory." *American Sociological Review*, 47, pp. 88–98.
Markovsky, Barry, and Seymour M. Berger. 1983. "Crowd noise and mimicry." *Personality and Social Psychology Bulletin*, 9, pp. 90–96.
Marple, David. 1982. "Technological innovation and organizational survival: A population ecology study of nineteenth-century American railroads." *Sociological Quarterly*, 23, pp. 107–116.
Marquand, Robert. 1986. "Speaking for teacher 'professionalism'." *Christian Science Monitor*, October 6, pp. 27, 30.
Marsden, Peter V., John Shelton Reed, Michael D. Kennedy, et al. 1982. "American regional cultures and differences in leisure time activities." *Social Forces*, 60, pp. 1023–1049.
Martin, John H., and Charles H. Harrison. 1972. *Free to Learn.* Englewood Cliffs, N.J.: Prentice-Hall.
Martin, M. Kay, and Barbara Voorhies. 1975. *Female of the Species.* New York: Columbia University Press.
Marty, Martin E. 1982. "Religious growth in a new area." *Encyclopedia Britannica, 1984*, pp. 606–607.
———. 1988. "Religion, television, and money." *Encyclopedia Britannica*, pp. 294–295.
Marwick, Arthur. 1986. *Class in the Twentieth Century.* New York: St. Martin's.
Marx, Gary T. 1967. *Protest and Prejudice.* New York: Harper & Row.
Marx, Karl. 1866 (1967). *Capital*, vol. 1. New York: International Publishers.
———. 1964. *Theories of Surplus Value*, vol. 1. London: Lawrence & Wishart.
Massey, Douglas S. 1983. "A research note on residential succession: The Hispanic case." *Social Forces*, 61, pp. 825–833.
———, and Brendan P. Mullan. 1984. "Processes of Hispanic and Black spatial assimilation." *American Journal of Sociology*, 89, pp. 836–873.
Masters, William H., and Virginia E. Johnson. 1979. *Homosexuality in Perspective.* Boston: Little, Brown.
———, and Robert Kolodny. 1988. *Crisis: Heterosexual Behavior in the Age of AIDS.* New York: Grove Press.
Mathison, David L. 1986. "Sex differences in the perception of assertiveness among female managers." *Journal of Social Psychology*, 126, pp. 599–606.
Mayer, Allan J. 1977. "The graying of America." *Newsweek*, February 28, pp. 50–64.
Mazur, Allan. 1986. "U.S. trends in feminine beauty and overadaptation." *Journal of Sex Research*, 22, pp. 281–303.
McAuliffe, Kathleen. 1987. "AIDS: At the dawn of fear." *U.S. News & World Report*, January 12, pp. 60–69.
McBee, Susanna. 1984. "Asian-Americans: Are they making the grade?" *U.S. News & World Report*, April 2, pp. 41–47.
McCabe, Justine. 1983. "FBD marriage: Further support for the Westermarck hypothesis of the incest taboo?" *American Anthropologist*, 85, pp. 50–69.
McClearn, Gerald E. 1969. "Biological bases of social behavior with specific reference to violent behavior," in Donald J. Mulvihill et al., *Crimes of Violence*, vol. 13. Washington, D.C.: U.S. Government Printing Office.
McConahay, John B., Betty B. Hardee, and Valerie Batts. 1981. "Has racism declined in America?" *Journal of Conflict Resolution*, 25, pp. 563–579.
McDonald, John M. 1971. *Rape.* Springfield, Ill.: Thomas.
McDonald, Laughlin. 1979. "The legal barriers crumble." *Southern Exposure*, 7, Summer, pp. 18–31.
McElroy, Mary A. 1983. "Parent-child relations and orientations toward sport." *Sex Roles*, 9, pp. 997–1004.
McFalls, Joseph A., Jr., Brian Jones, and Bernard J. Gallagher III. 1984. "U.S. population growth: Prospects and policy." *USA Today*, 112, January pp. 30–34.
McGrath, Ellie. 1983. "Confucian work ethic." *Time*, March 28, p. 52.
McGrath, J. Paul. 1984. "We harm the economy if we artifically restrict mergers." *U.S. News & World Report*, August 6, pp. 77–78.
McKinlay, John B., and Sonja M. McKinlay. 1987. "Medical measures and the decline of mortality," in Howard D. Schwartz (ed.), *Dominant Issues in Medical Sociology*, 2nd ed. New York: Random House.
McLanahan, Sara S. 1983. "Family structure and stress: A longitudinal comparison of two-parent and female-headed families." *Journal of Marriage and the Family*, 45, pp. 347–357.
McLoughlin, David, and Richard Whitfield. 1984. "Adolescents and their experience of parental divorce." *Journal of Adolescence*, 7, pp. 155–170.
McNamara, Robert S. 1984. "Time bomb or myth: The population problem." *Foreign Affairs*, 62, pp. 1107–1131.
McNeill, William H. 1963. *The Rise of The West: A History of the Human Community.* Chicago: University of Chicago Press.
McPhail, Clark, and Ronald T. Wohlstein. 1983. "Individual and collective behaviors within gatherings, demonstrations, and riots." *Annual Review of Sociology*, 9, pp. 579–600.
McWilliams, Carey. 1948. *A Mask for Privilege.* Boston: Little, Brown.
Mead, Margaret. 1935. *Sex and Temperament in Three Primitive Societies.* New York: Mentor.
Meadow, Robert G. 1982. "Information and maturation in children's evaluation of gov-

ernment leadership during Watergate." *Western Political Quarterly*, 35, pp. 539–553.

Meadows, Donella H., et al. 1974. *The Limits to Growth*, 2nd ed. New York: Universe Books.

Medea, Andra, and Kathleen Thompson. 1974. *Against Rape*. New York: Farrar, Straus and Giroux.

Medical World News. 1987. "U.S. gets good health report." February 9, pp. 85–86.

Mednick, Sarnoff A., and J. Volavaka. 1980. "Biology and crime," in N. Morris and M. Tonry (eds.), *Crime and Justice: An Annual Review of Research*, volume 2. Chicago: University of Chicago Press.

Meer, Jeff. 1984a. "Civil rights indicators." *Psychology Today*, June, pp. 49, 50.

———. 1984b. "Hard line up the middle." *Psychology Today*, July, p. 69.

———. 1986. "The reason of age." *Psychology Today*, June, pp. 60–64.

———. 1987. "Date rape: Familiar strangers." *Psychology Today*, July, p. 10.

Mensch, Barbara. 1986. "Age differences between spouses in first marriages." *Social Biology*, 33, pp. 229–240.

Meredith, Nikki. 1984. "The gay dilemma." *Psychology Today*, January, pp. 56–62.

Merton, Robert K. 1938. "Social structure and anomie." *American Sociological Review*, 3, pp. 672–682.

———. 1941. "Intermarriage and the social structure: Fact and theory." *Psychology*, 4, pp. 361–374.

———. 1957. *Social Theory and Social Structure*. New York: Free Press.

———. 1973. *The Sociology of Science: Theoretical and Empirical Investigations*. Edited by Norman Storer. Chicago: University of Chicago Press.

———. 1976. *Sociological Ambivalence and Other Essays*. New York: Free Press.

———. 1984. "The fallacy of the latest word: The case of 'pietism and science'." *American Journal of Sociology*, 89, pp. 1091–1121.

Messner, Steven F. 1986. "Television violence and violent crime: An aggregate analysis." *Social Problems*, 33, pp. 218–235.

———, and Judith R. Blau. 1987. "Routine leisure activities and rates of crime: A macro-level analysis." *Social Forces*, 65, pp. 1035–1052.

Meyer, Marshall W. 1985. *The Limits to Bureaucratic Growth*. New York: de Gruyter.

Michels, Robert. 1915/1949. *Political Parties*. Glencoe, Ill.: Free Press.

Michener, James A. 1976. *Sports in America*. New York: Random House.

Mikulski, Barbara. 1970. "Who speaks for ethnic America?" *New York Times*, September 28, p. 72.

Milgram, Stanley. 1970. "The experience of living in cities." *Science*, March, pp. 1461–1468.

———. 1974. *Obedience to Authority*. New York: Harper & Row.

———. 1967. "The small-world problem." *Psychology Today*, 1, pp. 61–67.

Miller, Arthur G. 1970. "Role of physical attractiveness in impression formation." *Psychonomic Science*, 19, pp. 241–243.

Miller, Joanne, and Howard H. Garrison. 1982. "Sex roles: The division of labor at home and in the workplace." *Annual Review of Sociology*, 8, pp. 237–262.

Miller, Karen A. 1984. "The effects of industrialization on men's attitudes toward the extended family and women's rights: A cross-national study." *Journal of Marriage and the Family*, 46, pp. 153–160.

———, Melvin L. Kohn, and Carmi Schooler. 1986. "Educational self-direction and personality." *American Sociological Review*, 51, pp. 372–390.

Miller Lite Report. 1983. *American Attitudes Toward Sports*. Milwaukee, Wis.: Miller Brewing Co.

Mills, C. Wright. 1959a. *The Power Elite*. New York: Oxford University Press.

———. 1959b. *The Sociological Imagination*. New York: Grove.

Mills, Theodore M. 1967. *The Sociology of Small Groups*. Englewood Cliffs, N.J.: Prentice-Hall.

Miner, Horace. 1956. "Body ritual among the Nacirema." *American Anthropologist*, 58, pp. 503–507.

Minkler, Meredith. 1981. "Research on the health effects of retirement: An uncertain legacy." *Journal of Health and Social Behavior*, 22, pp. 117–130.

Mintz, Beth. 1975. "The president's cabinet, 1897–1972: A contribution to the power structure debate." *Insurgent Sociologist*, 5, pp. 131–148.

Mintzberg, Henry. 1983. *Power In and Around Organizations*. Englewood Cliffs, N.J.: Prentice-Hall.

Mirowsky, John, and Catherine E. Ross. 1983. "Paranoia and the structure of powerlessness." *American Sociological Review*, 48, pp. 228–239.

Mitroff, Ian I. 1974. "Norms and counternorms in a select group of the Apollo moon scientists." *American Sociological Review*, 39, pp. 579–595.

Moberg, David O. 1984. "Review of James Hunter's *American Evangelicalism*." *Contemporary Sociology*, 13, pp. 371, 372.

Molotch, Harvey. 1983. "The city as a growth machine: Toward a political economy of place," in Mark Baldassare (ed.), *Cities and Urban Living*. New York: Columbia University Press.

Molotsky, Irvin, "Senate votes to compensate Japanese-American internees," *New York Times*, April 21, 1988, pp. 1, 9.

Monagan, David. 1983. "The failure of coed sports." *Psychology Today*, March, pp. 58–63.

Money, John, and Anke A. Ehrhardt. 1972. *Man and Woman/Boy and Girl*. Baltimore, Md.: Johns Hopkins University Press.

Monmaney, Terence. 1987. "AIDS: Who should be tested?" *Newsweek*, May 11, pp. 64–65.

Montana, Constanza. 1986. "Latino schism." *Wall Street Journal*, October 21, pp. 1, 25.

Montgomery, Robert L. 1980. "Reference groups as anchors in judgments of other groups: A biasing factor in 'rating tasks'?" *Psychological Reports*, 47, pp. 967–975.

Moore, Wilbert E. 1979. *World Modernization: The Limits of Convergence*. New York: Elsevier.

Morgan, Carolyn Stout, and Alexis J. Walker. 1983. "Predicting sex role attitudes." *Social Psychology Quarterly*, 46, pp. 148–151.

Morgan, S. Philip. 1983. "A research note on religion and morality: Are religious people nice people?" *Social Forces*, 61, pp. 683–692.

———. 1984. "Reply to King and Hunt." *Social Forces*, 62, pp. 1089–1090.

———, and Kiyoshi Hirosima. 1983. "The persistence of extended family residence in Japan: Anachronism or alternative strategy?" *American Sociological Review*, 48, pp. 269–281.

Morgan, William R. 1983. "Learning and student life quality of public and private school youth." *Sociology of Education*, 56, pp. 187–202.

Morganthau, Tom. 1986. "Future shock." *Newsweek*, November 24, p. 39.

Morris, Betsy. 1987. "Shallow roots." *Wall Street Journal*, March 27, pp. 1, 7.

Morrow, Lance. 1978a. "The decline of the parties." *Time*, November 20, p. 42.

———. 1978b. "The lure of doomsday." *Time*, December 4, p. 30.

———, 1984a. "The Powers of racial example." *Time*, April 16, p. 84.

———. 1984b. "Why not a woman?" *Time*, June 4, pp. 18–22.

Mortimer, Jeylan T., and Roberta G. Simmons. 1978. "Adult socialization." *Annual Review of Sociology*, 4, pp. 421–454.

Moskin, J. Robert. 1980. "Chinese politesse." *World Press Review*, December, p. 8.

Motley, Dena K. 1978. "Availability of retired persons for work: Findings from the retirement history study." *Social Security Bulletin*, 41, pp. 18–28.

Mottaz, Clifford, and Glenn Potts. 1986. "An empirical evaluation of models of work satisfaction." *Social Science Research*, 15, pp. 153–173.

Moyer, Kathryn Johnston, and Gordon L. McAndrew. 1978. "Is this what schools are for?" *Saturday Review*, December, p. 58.

Muir, Donald E., and C. Donald McGlamery. 1984. "Trends in integration attitudes on a deep-South campus during the first two decades of desegregation." *Social Forces*, 62, pp. 963–972.

Mulvihill, Donald J., and Melvin M. Tumin, with Lynn A. Curtis. 1969. *Crimes of Violence*, vol. 11. Washington, D.C.: U.S. Government Printing Office.

Mumford, Lewis. 1963. *Technics and Civilization*. New York: Harcourt, Brace and World.

Münch, Richard. 1983. "Modern science and technology: Differentiation or interpenetration?" *International Journal of Comparative Sociology*, 24, pp. 157–175.

Murdock, George Peter. 1937. "Comparative data on the division of labor by sex." *Social Forces*, 15, pp. 551–553.

———. 1945. "The common denominator of cultures," in Ralph Linton (ed.), *The Science of Man in World Crisis*. New York: Columbia University Press.

———. 1967. *Ethnographic Atlas*. Pittsburgh: University of Pittsburgh Press.

Murray, M. A., and T. Atkinson. 1981. "Gender differences in correlates of job satisfaction." *Canadian Journal of Behavioral Science,* 13, pp. 44–52.

Mussen, Paul H. 1963. *The Psychological Development of the Child.* Englewood Cliffs, N.J.: Prentice-Hall.

Muth, Richard F. 1984. "Is more really better?" *Society,* 21, March/April, pp. 35–39.

Myers, J. K., et al. 1984. "Six-month prevalence of psychiatric disorders in three communities." *Archives of General Psychiatry,* 41, pp. 959–967.

Myrdal, Gunnar. 1973. "How scientific are the social sciences?" *Bulletin of the Atomic Scientists,* January, p. 34.

Namenwirth, J. Zvi, Randi Lynn Miller, and Robert Philip Weber. 1981. "Organizations have opinions: A redefinition of publics." *Public Opinion Quarterly,* 45, pp. 463–476.

National Center for Health Statistics. 1984. *Monthly Vital Statistics Report,* vol. 33, no. 9, December 26. Washington, D.C.: Government Printing Office.

National Commission on Excellence in Education. 1983. *A Nation at Risk: The Imperative for Educational Reform.* Washington, D.C.: U.S. Government Printing Office.

National Opinion Research Center. 1986. *General Social Surveys, 1983–1986: Cumulative Codebook.* Chicago: University of Chicago Press.

Nation's Business. 1979a. "Labor's changing profile." April, pp. 30–35.

———. 1979b. "Sportsmen for all seasons." March, p. 30.

NCHS (National Center for Health Statistics). 1984. *Use of Contraception in the United States, 1982.* NCHS Advancedata, 102, December 4. Washington, D.C.: U.S. Government Printing Office.

Nelson, Candace, and Marta Tienda. 1985. "The structuring of Hispanic ethnicity: Historical and contemporary perspectives." *Ethnic and Racial Studies,* 8, pp. 49–74.

Nenno, Mary K. 1984. "Housing allowances are not enough." *Society,* 21, March/April, pp. 54–57.

Newcomb, Michael D., and Peter M. Bentler. 1980. "Cohabitation before marriage: A comparison of married couples who did and did not cohabit." *Alternative Lifestyles,* 3, pp. 65–85.

Newcomb, Theodore. 1958. "Attitude development as a function of reference group: The Bennington study," in Guy E. Swanson et al. (eds.), *Readings in Social Psychology.* New York: Holt, Rinehart and Winston.

Newman, William M. 1973. *American Pluralism: A Study of Minority Groups and Social Theory.* New York: Harper & Row.

Newsweek. 1975. "The pride of Olean." January 13, p. 27.

Newton, George D., Jr., and Franklin E. Zimring. 1969. *Firearms and Violence in American Life.* Washington, D.C.: U.S. Government Printing Office.

New York Times. 1966. "Dr. King addresses an integrated junior chamber in Atlanta." October 21, p. 28.

———. 1987. "A treacherous paradox: AIDS tests." November 30, p. 18.

Nielson, John. 1984. "Rising racism on the continent." *Time,* February 6, pp. 40–45.

Nisbet, Robert A. 1970. *The Social Bond.* New York: Knopf.

———. 1982. "Genius." *Wilson Quarterly,* special issue, pp. 98–107.

Norwood, Janet L. 1983. "Labor market contrasts: United States and Europe." *Monthly Labor Review,* 106, August, pp. 3–7.

Novak, Mark. 1983. "Discovering a good age." *International Journal of Aging and Human Development,* 16, pp. 231–239.

Novak, Michael. 1973. *The Rise of the Unmeltable Ethnics: Politics and Culture in the Seventies.* New York: Collier.

NOW (National Organization for Women). 1977. *Dick and Jane as Victims.* Princeton, N.J.: NOW.

Oakes, Jeannie. 1982. "Classroom social relationships: Exploring the Bowles and Gintis hypothesis." *Sociology of Education,* 55, pp. 197–212.

Oakes, Russell C. 1985. "Individual Piagetian epistemological development of children from ages 6 to 11." *Journal of Genetic Psychology,* 146, pp. 367–377.

Oakley, Robert. 1987. "International terrorism." *Foreign Affairs,* 65, pp. 611–629.

Ochse, Rhona, and Cornelis Plug. 1986. "Cross-cultural investigation of the validity of Erikson's theory of personality development." *Journal of Personality and Social Psychology,* 50, pp. 1240–1252.

O'Dea, Thomas F., and Janet O'Dea Aviad. 1983. *The Sociology of Religion,* 2nd ed. Englewood Cliffs, N.J.: Prentice-Hall.

Okraku, Ishmael O. 1987. "Age and attitudes toward multigenerational residence, 1973 to 1983." *Journal of Gerontology,* 42, pp. 280–287.

Orwell, George. 1949. *1984.* New York: Signet.

Ostling, Richard N. 1987. "John Paul's fiesty flock." *Time,* September 7, pp. 46–51.

O'Toole, James. 1973. *Work in America.* Cambridge, Mass.: MIT Press.

Otten, Alan L. 1987. "Warning of generational fighting draws critics—led by the elderly." *Wall Street Journal,* January 13, p. 35.

Otto, Luther B., and Duane F. Alwin. 1977. "Athletics, aspirations, and attainments." *Sociology of Education,* 42, pp. 102–113.

Ouchi, William G., and Alan L. Wilkins. 1985. "Organizational culture." *Annual Review of Sociology,* 11, pp. 457–483.

Page, Benjamin I. 1983. *Who Gets What from Government.* Berkeley: University of California Press.

———, Robert Y. Shapiro, and Glenn R. Dempsey. 1987. "What moves public opinion?" *American Political Science Review,* 81, pp. 23–43.

Palelogos, Nicholas. 1986. "American school reform: Those Pacific overtures." *Christian Science Monitor,* August 28, p. 15.

Palen, I. John. 1981. *The Urban World,* 2nd ed. New York: McGraw-Hill.

Palisi, Bartolomeo J., and Claire Canning. 1983. "Urbanism and social psychological well-being: A cross-cultural test of three theories." *Sociological Quarterly,* 24, pp. 527–543.

Palmore, Erdman. 1975. *The Honorable Elders.* Durham, N.C.: Duke University Press.

———. 1977. "Facts on aging." *Gerontologist,* 17, pp. 315–320.

———. 1979. "Advantages of aging." *Gerontologist,* 19, pp. 220–221.

———. 1981. *Social Patterns in Normal Aging: Findings from the Duke Longitudinal Study.* Durham, N.C.: Duke University Press.

———, and Daisaku Maeda. 1985. *The Honorable Elders Revisited: A Revised Cross-Cultural Analysis of Aging in Japan.* Durham, N.C.: Duke University Press.

———. 1986. "Trends in the health of the aged." *The Gerontologist,* 26, p. 298–302.

Pampel, Fred C., and Jane A. Weiss. 1983. "Economic development, pension policies, and the labor force participation of aged males: A cross-national, longitudinal approach." *American Journal of Sociology,* 89, pp. 350–372.

Parelius, Anna Parker, and Robert J. Parelius. 1978. *The Sociology of Education.* Englewood Cliffs, N.J.: Prentice-Hall.

Parenti, Michael. 1977. *Democracy for the Few.* New York: St. Martin's.

Parker, Seymour, and Hilda Parker. 1979. "The myth of male superiority: Rise and demise." *American Anthropologist,* 81, pp. 289–309.

Parkinson, C. Northcote. 1957. *Parkinson's Law.* Boston: Houghton Mifflin.

Parks, Malcolm, Charlotte M. Stan, and Leona L. Eggert. 1983. "Romantic involvement and social network involvement." *Social Psychology Quarterly,* 46, pp. 116–131.

Parsons, Talcott. 1964/1951. *The Social System.* Glencoe, Ill.: Free Press.

———. 1966. *Societies: Evolutionary and Comparative Perspectives.* Englewood Cliffs, N.J.: Prentice-Hall.

———. 1975. "The sick role and the role of the physician reconsidered." *Millbank Memorial Fund Quarterly,* 53, pp. 257–278.

———, and Robert F. Bales. 1953. *Family, Socialization, and Interaction Process.* Glencoe, Ill. Free Press.

Patinkin, Don. 1983. "Multiple discoveries and the central message." *American Journal of Sociology,* 89, pp. 306–323.

Pauly, David, 1979. "Crime in the suites: On the rise." *Newsweek,* December 3, pp. 114–121.

Pear, Robert. 1987. "Medical-care cost rose 7.7% in '86." *New York Times,* January 9, pp. 1, 9.

———. 1988. "Substantial rise sought next year in outlay on AIDS." *New York Times,* January 5, pp. 1, 19.

Pedersen, Darhl M., and Barbara L. Bond. 1985. "Shifts in sex-role after a decade of cultural change." *Psychological Reports,* 57, pp. 43–48.

Peek, Charles W., and Sharon Brown. 1980. "Sex prejudice among white Protestants: Like or unlike ethnic prejudice?" *Social Forces,* 59, pp. 169–185.

———, Evans W. Curry, and H. Paul Chalfant. 1985. "Religiosity and delinquency over time: Deviance deterrence and deviance amplification." *Social Science Quarterly,* 66, pp. 120–131.

Pennebaker, J. W. 1980. "Perceptual and environmental determinants of coughing."

Basic Applied Social Psychology, 1, pp. 83–91.
Penrose, L. S. 1981/1952. *On the Objective Study of Crowd Behavior.* London: H. K. Lewis.
Peplau, Letitia Anne. 1981. "What homosexuals want." *Psychology Today*, March, pp. 28–38.
Perelman, Lewis J. 1986. "Learning our lesson: Why school is out." *The Futurist,* March-April, pp. 13–16.
Perrow, Charles. 1979. *Complex Organizations,* 2nd ed. Glenview, Ill: Scott, Foresman.
Perrucci, Robert, et al. 1980. "Whistle-blowing: Professionals' resistance to organizational authority." *Social Problems,* 28, pp. 149–164.
Persell, Caroline Hodges. 1984. *Understanding Society.* New York: Harper & Row.
Peter, Laurence J. 1978. "Bureaucratic bungling." *Human Behavior,* April, p. 70.
———, and Raymond Hull. 1969. *The Peter Principle.* New York: Morrow.
Peters, Thomas J., and Robert H. Waterman, Jr. 1982. *In Search of Excellence: Lessons from America's Best-Run Companies.* New York: Harper & Row.
Petersen, Larry R., Gary R. Lee, and Godfrey J. Ellis. 1982. "Social structure, socialization values, and disciplinary techniques: A cross-culture analysis." *Journal of Marriage and the Family,* 44, pp. 131–142.
Petersen, William. 1982. "The social roots of hunger and overpopulation." *Public Interest,* 68, Summer, pp. 37–52.
Peterson, Candida C., James L. Peterson, and John Carroll. 1986. "Television viewing and imaginative problem solving during preadolescence." *Journal of Genetic Psychology,* 147, pp. 61–67.
Peterson, Iver. 1987. "Feminists discern a bias in Baby M. custody case." *New York Times,* March 20, p. 16.
Peterson, Janice. 1987. "The feminization of poverty." *Journal of Economic Issues,* March, pp. 329–337.
Peterson, Richard A. 1979. "Revitalizing the culture concept." *Annual Review of Sociology,* 5, pp. 137–166.
Peterson, William H. 1986. "Why not save the 31,000 top farmers?" *Wall Street Journal,* October 8, p. 28.
Pettigrew, Thomas F. 1981. "Race and class in the 1980s: An interactive view." *Daedalus,* 110, pp. 233–255.
———, et al. 1973. "Busing: A review of 'the evidence'." *Public Interest,* Winter, pp. 88–118.
———, and Robert L. Green. 1976. "Urban desegregation and white flight: A response to Coleman." *Phi Delta Kappan,* February, pp. 399–402.
Phillips, David P. 1982. "The behavioral impact of violence in the mass media: A review of the evidence from laboratory and nonlaboratory investigations." *Sociology and Social Research,* 66, pp. 387–398.
Phillips, John C. 1983. "Race and career opportunities in major league baseball 1960–1980." *Journal of Sport and Social Issues,* 7, Summer/Fall, pp. 1–12.
Picou, J. Steven, and E. W. Curry. 1974. "Residence and the athletic participation-aspiration hypothesis." *Social Science Quarterly,* 55, pp. 768–776.
———, Virginia McCarter, and Frank M. Howell. 1987. "Do high school athletics pay? Some further evidence." *Sociology of Sport Journal,* 2, pp. 72–76.
Pierson, Elaine C., and William V. D'Antonio. 1974. *Female and Male.* Philadelphia: Lippincott.
Pietropinto, Anthony, and Jacqueline Simenauer. 1977. *Beyond the Male Myth.* New York: Times Books.
Pillemer, Karl. 1985. "The dangers of dependency: New findings on domestic violence against the elderly." *Social Problems,* 33, pp. 146–158.
Pines, Maya. 1981. "The civilizing of Genie." *Psychology Today,* September, pp. 28–34.
———. 1983. "Can a rock walk?" *Psychology Today,* November, pp. 46–54.
Pion, Georgian M., and Mark W. Lipsey. 1981. "Public attitudes toward science and technology: What have the surveys told us?" *Public Opinion Quarterly,* 45, pp. 303–316.
Plattner, Andy. 1987. "The high cost of holding—and keeping—public office." *U.S. News & World Report,* June 22, p. 30.
Plisko, Valena White (ed.) 1984. *The Condition of Education.* Washington, D.C.: U.S. Government Printing Office.
Plog, Fred, and Daniel G. Bates. 1980. *Cultural Anthropology,* 2nd ed. New York: Knopf.
Pogrebin, Letty Cottin. 1982. "A conversation with pollster Dan Yankelovich." *Ms.,* July/August, p. 140.
Polk, Kenneth. 1983. "Curriculum tracking and delinquency: Some observations." *American Sociological Review,* 48, pp. 282–284.
Pomeroy, Wardell B. 1969. "Homosexuality," in Ralph W. Weltge (ed.), *The Same Sex.* Philadelphia: Pilgrim Press.
———. 1977. "The new sexual myths." *McCall's,* October, pp. 102–106.
Pomper, Gerald M. 1984. "Party politics." *Society,* September/October, pp. 61–67.
Porter, Bruce, and Marvin Dunn. 1984. *The Miami Riot of 1980.* Lexington, Mass.: Lexington Books.
Porter, Judith R., and Robert E. Washington. 1979. "Black identity and self-esteem: A review of studies of black self-concept." *Annual Review of Sociology,* 5, pp. 53–74.
Post, Shelley. 1982. "Adolescent parricide in abusive families." *Child Welfare,* 61, pp. 445–455.
Postman, Neil. 1985. *Amusing Ourselves to Death: Public Discourse in the Age of Show Business.* New York: Viking.
Powell, Brian, and Lala Carr Steelman. 1982. "Fundamentalism and sexism: A reanalysis of Peek and Brown." *Social Forces,* 60, pp. 1154–1158.
Powell, G. Bingham, Jr. 1986. "American voter turnout in comparative perspective." *American Political Science Review,* March, pp. 17–43.
Prerost, Frank J., and Robert E. Brewer. 1980. "The appreciation of humor by males and females during conditions of crowding experimentally induced." *Psychology,* 17, pp. 15–17.
Press, Aric. 1985. "The war against pornography." *Newsweek,* March 18, pp. 58–66.
Press, Frank. 1978. "Science and technology: the road ahead." *Science 200,* May 19, pp. 737–741.
Price, Jerome. 1982. *The Antinuclear Movement.* Boston: Twayne.
Provence, Sally, and Rose C. Lipton. 1962. *Infants in Institutions.* New York: International Universities Press.
Public Opinion. 1978. "Opinion roundup." July/August, p. 38.
———. 1981. "Opinion roundup." October/November, pp. 21–40.
———, 1982. "Opinion roundup." June/July, p. 30.
———. 1983. "The sports pages." August/September, pp. 32–33.
Purdy, Dean A., D. Stanley Eitzen, and Rick Hufnagel. 1982. "Are athletes also students? The educational attainment of college athletes." *Social Problems,* 29, pp. 439–448.

Quinney, Richard. 1974. *Critique of Legal Order.* Boston: Little, Brown.
———. 1975. *Criminology.* Boston: Little, Brown.

Rabkin, Jeremy. 1987. "Disestablished religion in America." *Public Interest,* Winter, pp. 124–139.
Rainwater, Lee. 1964. "Marital sexuality in four cultures of poverty." *Journal of Marriage and the Family,* 26, pp. 457–466.
———. 1970. *Behind Ghetto Walls.* Chicago: Aldine.
———. 1974. *What Money Buys.* New York: Basic Books.
Ramirez, Francisco O., and John W. Meyer. 1980. "Comparative education: The social construction of the modern world system." *Annual Review of Sociology,* 6, pp. 369–399.
Ranney, Austin. 1983. "Nonvoting is not a social disease." *Public Opinion,* October/November, pp. 16–19.
Ransford, H. Edward, and Jon Miller. 1983. "Race, sex, and feminist outlooks." *American Sociological Review,* 48, pp. 46–59.
Raper, Arthur F. 1970. *The Tragedy of Lynching.* New York: Dover.
Rau, William, and Dennis W. Roncek. 1987. "Industrialization and world inequality: The transformation of the division of labor in 59 nations, 1960–1981." *American Sociological Review,* 52, pp. 359–369.
Rawlings, Steve W. 1984. "Household and family characteristics: March 1983." Census Bureau's *Current Population Survey.* Washington, D.C.: U.S. Government Printing Office.
Reeves, Richard. 1982. "An American journey, II." *New Yorker,* April 12, pp. 53–124.
Reich, Michael. 1981. *Racial Inequality: A Political-Economic Analysis.* Princeton N.J.: Princeton University Press.
Reich, Robert B. 1987. "The new 'competitiveness' fad." *New York Times,* January 14, p. 19.
Reichlin, Igor. 1984. "How dogma cripples Soviet science." *Science Digest,* March, p. 66.
Reid, John. 1982. "Black America in the

1980s." *Population Bulletin,* 37, December, pp. 1–38.
Reiman, Jeffrey H., and Sue Headlee. 1981. "Marxism and criminal justice policy." *Crime and Delinquency,* 27, pp. 24–47.
Reinhold, Robert. 1987. "School reform: 4 years of tumult, mixed results." *New York Times,* August 10, pp. 1, 11.
Reiss, Ira L. 1986. *Journey into Sexuality: An Exploratory Voyage.* Englewood Cliffs, N.J.: Prentice-Hall.
———, Ronald E. Anderson, and G. C. Sponaugle. 1980. "A multivariate model of the determinants of extramarital sexual permissiveness." *Journal of Marriage and the Family,* 42, pp. 395–411.
Reissman, Leonard 1959. *Class in American Society.* New York: Free Press.
Reitzes, Donald C. 1981. "Role-identity correspondence in the college student role." *Sociological Quarterly,* 22, pp. 607–620.
———. 1983. "Urban images: A social psychological approach." *Sociological Inquiry,* 53, pp. 314–332.
Rensberger, Boyce. 1984. "What made humans human." *New York Times Magazine,* April 8, pp. 80–92.
Reser, Joseph. 1981. "Australian aboriginal man's inhumanity to man: A case of cultural distortion." *American Anthropologist,* 83, pp. 387–393.
Restak, Richard M. 1979. *The Brain: The Last Frontier.* New York: Doubleday.
Revlin, Leanne G. 1986. "A new look at the homeless." *Social Policy,* 16, pp. 3–10.
Reynolds, Paul Davidson. 1982. *Ethics and Social Science Research.* Englewood Cliffs, N.J.: Prentice-Hall.
Rheem, Donald L. 1986. "Free market system said to be more efficient than state planning." *Christian Science Monitor,* September 22, p. 7.
———. 1986. "Superfund clears way for cleanup of most hazardous waste sites." *Christian Science Monitor,* October 20, p. 7.
Rich, Spencer. 1982. "Single parent families rise dramatically." *Washington Post,* May 2, p. A5.
Richardson, Laurel Walum. 1981. *The Dynamics of Sex and Gender.* Boston: Houghton Mifflin.
———. 1986. *The New Other Woman.* New York: Free Press.
Richman, Joseph. 1977. "The foolishness and wisdom of age: Attitudes toward the elderly as reflected in jokes." *The Gerontologist,* 17, pp. 210–219.
Ricklefs, Roger. 1987. "AIDS cases prompt a host of lawsuits." *Wall Street Journal,* October 7, p. 31.
———. 1987. "Career ladder plans for teacher offer incentives other than cash." *Wall Street Journal,* May 8, p. 17.
———. 1988. "The specter of AIDS is haunting the lives of the 'HIV positive.'" *Wall Street Journal,* February 11, pp. 1, 14.
Ridgeway, Cecilia L. 1981. "Nonconformity, competence, and influence in groups: A test of two theories." *American Sociological Review,* 46, pp. 333–347.
———. 1982. "Status in groups: The importance of motivation." *American Sociological Review,* 47, pp. 76–88.
Riegle, Donald W. 1982. "The psychological and social effects of unemployment." *American Psychologist,* 10, pp. 1113–1115.
Riesman, David. 1950. *The Lonely Crowd.* New Haven, Conn.: Yale University Press.
Riley, John W., Jr. 1983. "Dying and the meanings of death: Sociological inquiries." *Annual Review of Sociology,* 9, pp. 191–216.
Riley, Matilda White. 1982. "Aging and health in modern communities." *Ekistics,* 296, pp. 381–383.
Rindos, David. 1986. "The evolution of the capacity for culture: Sociobiology, structuralism, and cultural selectionism." *Current Anthropology,* 27, pp. 315–332.
Ritzer, George. 1983. "The 'McDonaldization' of society." *Journal of American Culture,* 6, pp. 100–107.
Roach, Jack L., Llewellyn Gross, and Orville R. Gursslin, eds. 1969. *Social Stratification in the United States.* Englewood Cliffs, N.J.: Prentice-Hall.
Roberts, John M., and Ronald L. Cosper. 1987. "Variation in strategic involvement in games for three blue collar occupations." *Journal of Leisure Research,* 19, pp. 131–148.
Roberts, Marjory. 1986. "A parent is born." *Psychology Today,* December, pp. 18–20.
Robinson, Ira E., and Davor Jedlicka. 1982. "Change in sexual attitudes and behavior of college students from 1965 to 1980: A research note." *Journal of Marriage and the Family,* 44, pp. 237–240.
Robinson, Robert V., and Jonathan Kelley. 1979. "Class as conceived by Marx and Dahrendorf: Effects on income inequality and politics in the United States and Great Britain." *American Sociological Review,* 44, pp. 38–58.
———. 1980. "Synthesis and comparison of stratification theories: A reply." *American Sociological Review,* 45, pp. 325–333.
Rodgers, Harrell R., Jr. 1982. *The Cost of Human Neglect.* Armonk, N.Y.: M. E. Sharpe, Inc.
Rodino, Peter W. 1986. "Will handgun foes be over a barrel?" *New York Times,* March 28, p. 27.
Rodriguez, Nestor P., and Joe R. Feagin. 1986. "Urban specialization in the world-system: An investigation of historical cases." *Urban Affairs Quarterly,* 22, pp. 187–220.
Roethlisberger, Fritz J., and William J. Dickson. 1939. *Management and the Worker.* Cambridge, Mass.: Harvard University Press.
Rohrbaugh, Joanna Bunker. 1979. "Femininity on the line." *Psychology Today,* August, pp. 30–42.
Rones, Philip L. 1983. "The labor market problems of older workers." *Monthly Labor Review,* 106, pp. 3–12.
Rose, Arnold M. 1965. "The subculture of aging," in Arnold M. Rose and Warren A. Peterson (eds.), *Older People and Their Social World.* Philadelphia: F. A. Davis.
———. Arnold 1967. *The Power Structure.* New York: Oxford University Press.
Rose, Peter I. 1981. *They and We: Racial and Ethnic Relations in the United States.* New York: Random House.
———. 1983. *Mainstream and Margins: Jews, Blacks, and Other Americans.* New Brunswick, N.J.: Transaction.
Rosellini, Lynn. 1987. "Strike one and you're out." *U.S. News & World Report,* July 27, pp. 52–57.
Rosenberg, Charles E. 1987. *The Care of Strangers.* New York: Basic Books.
Rosenberg, George S. 1970. *The Worker Grows Old.* San Francisco: Jossey-Bass.
Rosenfeld, Anne, and Elizabeth Stark. 1987. "The prime of our lives." *Psychology Today,* May, pp. 62–72.
Rosenthal, Neal H. 1985. "The shrinking middle class: Myth or reality?" *Monthly Labor Review,* March, pp. 3–10.
———, and Michael Pilot. 1983. *National Occupational Projections for Vocational Education Planning.* Columbus, Ohio: National Center for Research in Vocational Education, O.S.U.
Rosenthal, Robert. 1973. "The pgymalion effect lives." *Psychology Today,* pp. 56–63.
Rossell, Christine H. 1983. "Desegregation plans, racial isolation, white flight, and community response," in Christine H. Rossell and Willis D. Hawley (eds.), *The Consequences of School Desegregation.* Philadelphia: Temple University Press.
Rossi, Alice S. 1964. "Equality between the sexes: An immodest proposal." *Daedalus,* 93, pp. 607–652.
———. 1984. "Gender and parenthood." *American Sociological Review,* 49, pp. 1–19.
Rossi, Peter H., and William Foote Whyte. 1983. "The applied side of sociology," in Howard E. Freeman et al. (eds.), *Applied Sociology.* San Francisco: Jossey-Bass.
Rossides, Daniel W. 1976. *The American Class System.* Boston: Houghton Mifflin.
Rostow, Walt W. 1960. *The Process of Economic Growth.* New York: Norton.
Roth, Julius, and Robert Peck. 1951. "Social class and social mobility factors related to marital adjustment." *American Sociological Review,* 16, pp. 478–487.
Rothman, Stanley. 1983. "Contorting scientific controversies." *Society,* 20, July/August, pp. 25–32.
Rothschild, Joyce, and Raymond Russell. 1986. "Alternatives to bureaucracy: Democratic participation in the economy." *Annual Review of Sociology,* 12, pp. 307–328.
Rothschild-Whitt, Joyce. 1982. "The collectivist organization: An alternative to bureaucratic models," in Frank Lindenfeld and Joyce Rothschild-Whitt (eds.), *Workplace Democracy and Social Change.* Boston: Porter Sargent.
———, and Frank Lindenfeld. 1982. "Reshaping work: Prospects and problems of workplace democracy," in Frank Lindenfeld and Joyce Rothschild-Whitt (eds.), *Workplace Democracy and Social Change.* Boston: Porter Sargent.
Rowan, Hobart. 1982. "A widening gap between rich and poor." *Washington Post,* March 11, p. A29.
Rowe, Jonathan. 1986. "Older college students add to campus diversity." *Christian Science Monitor,* November 7, pp. 23–24.
Rowley, Anthony. 1983. "The multinational

myth." *Far Eastern Economic Review*, September 15, p. 84.
Rubenstein, Carin. 1980. "An evolutionary basis for stepparents' neglect?" *Psychology Today*, December, pp. 31, 32.
———. 1982. "Real men don't earn less than their wives." *Psychology Today*, November, pp. 36–41.
Rubin, Lillian Breslow. 1976. *Worlds of Pain: Life in the Working-Class Family*. New York: Basic Books.
Rubinson, Richard. 1986. "Class formation, politics, and institutions: Schooling in the United States." *American Journal of Sociology*, 92, pp. 519–548.
Rudman, William J. 1986. "The sport mystique in black culture." *Sociology of Sport Journal*, 3, pp. 305–319.
Rudolph, Frederick. 1962. *The American College and University*. New York: Random House.
Rummel, R. J. 1985. "Libertarian propositions on violence within and between nations: A test against published research results." *Journal of Conflict Resolution*, 29, pp. 419–455.
———. 1986. "War isn't this century's biggest killer." *Wall Street Journal*, July 7, p. 10.
Rushing, William A., and Suzanne T. Ortega. 1979. "Socioeconomic status and mental disorder: New evidence and a sociomedical formula." *American Journal of Sociology*, 84, pp. 1175–1200.
Russell, Diana E. H., and Nancy Howell. 1983. "The prevalence of rape in the United States revisted." *Signs*, 8, pp. 688–695.
Russell, George. 1984. "People, people, people." *Time*, August 6, pp. 24–25.
Rutter, Michael. 1983. "School effects on pupil progress: Research findings and policy implications." *Child Development*, 54, pp. 1–29.
Rybczynski, Witold. 1983. "Our love affair with technology." *Science Digest*, December, pp. 14–15.

Sacks, Karen, and Mary Rubin. 1982. "The then, now, and future of women." *Ms.*, August, p. 130–131.
Sage, George H. 1982. "Sociocultural aspects of physical activity: Significant research traditions, 1972–1983." *American Academy of Physical Education Academy Papers*, 16, pp. 59–66.
Sahlins, Marshall. 1972. *Stone Age Economics*. Chicago: Aldine.
Salholz, Eloise. 1986. "Too late for prince charming?" *Newsweek*, June 2, pp. 54–61.
Samuelson, Robert J. 1987. "The ghost of Adam Smith." *Newsweek*, February 9, p. 54.
Sanday, Peggy Reeves. 1981. "The sociocultural context of rape: A cross-cultural study." *Journal of Social Issues*, 37, pp. 5–27.
Sanoff, Alvin P. 1983. "Millions who are old and alone." *U.S. News & World Report*, February 21, p. 56.
Santino, Jack. 1985. "A conversation with Jack Santino: From jogging to trivial games, fads create status." *U.S., News & World Report*, February 11, p. 44.
Sapir, Edward. 1929. "The status of linguistics as a science." *Language*, 5, pp. 207–214.
Sasaki, Masamichi, and Tatsuzo Suzuki. 1987. "Changes in religious commitment in the United States, Holland, and Japan." *American Journal of Sociology*, 92, pp. 1055–1076.
Saw, Swee-Hock. 1975. "Singapore: Resumption of rapid fertility decline in 1973." *Studies in Family Planning*, 6, pp. 166–169.
Sayle, Murray. 1982. "A textbook case of aggression." *Far Eastern Economic Review*, 117, August 20, pp. 36–38.
Schaefer, Richard T. 1984. *Racial and Ethnic Groups*, 2nd ed. Boston: Little, Brown.
Schafer, Walter E., and Michael Armer. 1968. "Athletes are not inferior students." *Transaction*, 5, November, pp. 21–26.
Schanback, Mindy. 1987. "No patience for elder patients." *Psychology Today*, February, p. 22.
Schlesinger, Jacob M. 1987. "Going local." *Wall Street Journal*, March 16, pp. 1, 13.
Schmeck, Harold M., Jr. 1987. "Strong new evidence found of inherited Alzheimer risk." *New York Times*, May 22, p. 8.
Schneider, William, and I. A. Lewis. 1984. "The straight story on homosexuality and gay rights." *Public Opinion*, February/March, pp. 16–20, 59–60.
Schultz, Duane P. 1964. *Panic Behavior*. New York: Random House.
Schulz, David A. 1982. *The Changing Family*, 3rd ed. Englewood Cliffs, N.J.: Prentice-Hall.
Schuman, Howard, Charlotte Steeh, and Lawrence Bobo. 1985. *Racial Attitudes in America: Trends and Interpretations*. Cambridge, Mass.: Harvard University Press.
Schur, Edwin M. 1979. *Interpreting Deviance*. New York: Harper & Row.
———. 1984. *Labeling Women Deviant: Gender, Stigma, and Social Control*. New York: Random House.
Schwartz, John. 1987. "A 'superminority' tops out." *Newsweek*, May 11, pp. 48–49.
Schwochau, Susan. 1987. "Union effects on job attitudes." *Industrial and Labor Relations Review*, 40, pp. 209–224.
Science Digest. 1984. "Newscience/update: William H. Whyte observes the teeming tribes of urban jungles." March, p. 17.
Scientific American. 1984. "And the poor get sicker." September, p. 82.
Scott, David Clark. 1986. "How 'quality circles' move from the assembly line to the office." *Christian Science Monitor*, August 4, p. 18.
Scott, Jack. 1971. *The Athletic Revolution*. New York: Free Press.
Scully, Diana, and Joseph Marolla. 1984. "Convicted rapists' vocabulary of motive: Excuses and justifications." *Social Problems*, 31, pp. 530–544.
Sebald, Hans. 1986. "Adolescents' shifting orientation toward parents and peers: A curvilinear trend over recent decades." *Journal of Marriage and Family*, 48, pp. 5–13.
Segal, Aaron. 1982. "Kenya," in Carol L. Thompson, Mary M. Anderberg, and Joan B. Antell (eds.), *The Current History of Developing Countries*. New York: McGraw-Hill.
Segal, David R. 1974. *Society and Politics: Uniformity and Diversity in Modern Democracy*. Glencoe, Ill.: Scott, Foresman.
Seligmann, Jean. 1987. "Mandatory testing for AIDS?" *Newsweek*, February 16, p. 22.
Selkin, James. 1975. "Rape." *Psychology Today*, January, pp. 70–74.
Sellin, Thorsten. 1938. *Culture Conflict and Crime*. New York: Social Science Research Council.
Serrill, Michael S. 1987. "In the grip of the scourge." *Time*, February 16, pp. 58–59.
Shah, Farida, and Melvin Zelnik. 1981. "Parent and peer influence on sexual behavior, contraceptive use, and pregnancy experience of young women." *Journal of Marriage and the Family*, 43, pp. 339–348.
Shah, Saleem A., and Loren H. Roth. 1974. "Biological and psychophysiological factors in criminality," in Daniel Glaser (ed.), *Handbook of Criminology*. Chicago: Rand McNally.
Shamir, Boas, and Hillel Ruskin. 1984. "Sport participation vs. sport spectatorship: Two modes of leisure behavior." *Journal of Leisure Research*, 16, pp. 9–21.
Shanas, Ethel. 1979. "The family as a social support system in old age." *Gerontologist*, 19, pp. 169–174.
———, and George L. Maddox. 1976. "Aging, health, and the organization of health resources," in Robert H. Binstock and Ethel Shanas (eds.), *Handbook of Aging and the Social Sciences*. New York: Van Nostrand Reinhold.
Shariff, Zahid. 1979. "The persistence of bureaucracy." *Social Science Quarterly*, 60, pp. 3–19.
Sharp, D., et al. 1979. "Education and cognitive development: The evidence from experimental research." *Monographs of the Society for Research in Child Development*, 44 (178), pp. 1–2.
Shavit, Yossi. 1984. "Tracking and ethnicity in Israeli secondary education." *American Sociological Review*, 49, pp. 210–220.
Shaw, Clifford R., and Henry D. McKay. 1929. *Delinquency Areas*. Chicago: University of Chicago Press.
Shecter, Leonard. 1969. *The Jocks*. Indianapolis: Bobbs-Merrill.
Sheldon, William H. 1949. *Varieties of Delinquent Youth*. New York: Harper.
Shepher, Joseph. 1971. "Mate selection among second generation kibbutz adolescents and adults: Incest avoidance and negative imprinting." *Archives of Sexual Behavior*, 1, pp. 293–307.
———. 1983. *Incest: A Biosocial View*. New York: Academic Press.
Sherif, Muzafer. 1956. "Experiments in group conflict." *Scientific American*, 195, pp. 54–58.
Sherman, Mark A., and Adelaide Haas. 1984. "Man to man, woman to woman." *Psychology Today*, June, pp. 72, 73.
Shibutani, Tamotsu. 1966. *Improvised News*. Indianapolis: Bobbs-Merrill.
Shipp, E. R. 1986. "Only 2 remain in dioxin ghost town." *New York Times*, April 8, p. 9.
Shornack, Lawrence L., and Ellen McRoberts

Shornack. 1982. "The new sex education and the sexual revolution: A critical view." *Family Relations,* 31, pp. 531–544.
Shostak, Arthur B. 1983. "High tech, high touch, and labor." *Social Policy,* 13, pp. 20–23.
Shrauger, J. Sidney, and Thomas J. Schoeneman. 1979. "Symbolic interactionist view of self-concept: Through the looking glass darkly." *Psychological Bulletin,* 86, pp. 549–573.
Shrum, Wesley, and Neil H. Cheek, Jr. 1987. "Social structure during the school years: Onset of the degrouping process." *American Sociological Review,* 52, pp. 218–223.
Silberman, Charles E. 1970. *Crisis in the Classroom.* New York: Vintage Books.
Silver, Harry R. 1983. "Scientific achievement and the concept of risk." *British Journal of Sociology,* 34, pp. 39–43.
Simenauer, Jacqueline, and David Carroll. 1982. *Singles: The New Americans.* New York: Simon & Schuster.
Simkus, Albert A. 1981. "Comparative stratification and mobility." *International Journal of Comparative Sociology,* 22, pp. 213–236.
Simmons, Jerry L. 1969. *Deviants.* Berkeley, Calif. Glendessary Press.
Simon, Armando. 1981. "A quantitative, nonreactive study of mass behavior with emphasis on the cinema as behavioral catalyst." *Psychological Reports,* 48, pp. 775–785.
Simon, David R., and D. Stanley Eitzen. 1986, *Elite Deviance,* 2nd ed. Boston: Allyn and Bacon.
Simon, Julian. 1982. "Is the era of limits running out?" *Public Opinion,* February/March, pp. 48–54.
———. 1983. "Growth means progress." *Science Digest,* 91, April, pp. 76–79.
Simpson, Janice C. 1987. "Campus barrier?" *Wall Street Journal,* April 3, pp. 1, 23.
Simpson, Jeffry A., Bruce Campbell, and Ellen Berscheid. 1986. "The association between romantic love and marriage: Kephart (1967) twice revisited." *Personality and Social Psychology Bulletin,* 12, pp. 363–372.
Simpson, Miles. 1980. "The sociology of cognitive development." *Annual Review of Sociology,* 6, pp. 287–313.
Singh, J. A. L., and Robert M. Zingg. 1942. *Wolf Children and Feral Man.* New York: Harper.
Single, Eric W. 1981. "The impact of marijuana decriminalization," in Yedy Israel et al. (eds.), *Research Advances in Alcohol and Drug Problems.* New York: Plenum Press.
Sizer, Theodore R. 1984. *Horace's Compromise: The Dilemma of the American High School.* Boston: Houghton Mifflin.
Sjoberg, Gideon. 1966. *The Preindustrial City: Past and Present.* New York: Free Press.
Skinner, B. F. 1983. "Creativity in old age." *Psychology Today,* September, pp. 28, 29.
Skinner, Denise. 1980. "Dual-career family stress and coping: A literature review." *Family Relations,* 29, pp. 473–480.
Skolnick, Arlene. 1983a. "Review on 'What's happening to the American family'?" *Society,* 20, May/June, pp. 102–103.
———. 1983b. *The Intimate Environment: Exploring Marriage and the Family,* 3rd ed. Boston: Little, Brown.
Slaff, James, and John K. Brubaker. 1985. *The AIDS Epidemic.* New York: Warner Books.
Slater, Philip E. 1955. "Role differentiation in small groups," in Paul Hare et al. (eds.), *Small Group: Studies in Social Interaction.* New York: Knopf.
Smelser, Neil J. 1971/1962. *Theory of Collective Behavior.* New York: Free Press.
Smilgis, Martha. 1987. "The big chill: fear of AIDS." *Time,* February 16, pp. 50–53.
Smith, A. Wade. 1981. "Tolerance of school desegregation, 1954–77." *Social Forces,* 59, pp. 1256–1274.
Smith, D. Randall. 1983. "Mobility in professional occupational-internal labor markets: Stratification, segmentation, and vacancy chains." *American Sociological Review,* 48, pp. 289–305.
Smith, Douglas A. 1987. "Police response to interpersonal violence: Defining the parameters of legal control." *Social Forces,* 65, pp. 767–782.
Smith, Eleanor. 1984. "Midnight dumping." *Omni,* 6, March, p. 18.
Smith, Kevin B. 1981. "Class structure and intergenerational mobility from a Marxian perspective." *The Sociological Quarterly,* 22, pp. 384–401.
Smith, Michael D. 1983. *Violence and Sport.* Toronto: Butterworths.
Smith, Neil. 1982. "Gentrification and uneven development." *Economic Geography,* 58, pp. 139–155.
Smolowe, Jill. 1987. "Those 24 words are back." *Time,* July 6, p. 91.
Snarey, John. 1987. "A question of morality." *Psychology Today,* June, pp. 6–8.
Snyder, Eldon E., and Elmer A. Spreitzer. 1983. *Social Aspects of Sport.* 2nd ed. Englewood Cliffs. N.J.: Prentice-Hall.
Socarides, Charles W. 1978. *Homosexuality.* New York: Jason Aronson.
Society. 1983. "Parenting and discipline," 21, November/December, p. 2.
———. 1984. "Optimistic forecast." 22, November/December, pp. 2–3.
Solis, Dianna, et al. 1987. "Changing the rules." *Wall Street Journal,* June 5, pp. 1, 12.
Solorzano, Lucia. 1984a. "Schools draw the line on troublemakers." *U.S. News & World Report,* January 23, p. 65.
———. 1984b. "A second look at bilingual education." *U.S. News & World Report,* June 11, p. 78.
———. 1987. "Beating back the education 'blob.'" *U.S. News & World Report,* April 27, p. 74.
Sorokin, Pitirim. 1967. "Causal-functional and logico-meaningful integration," in N.J. Demerath and Richard A. Peterson (eds.), *System, Change, and Conflict.* New York: Free Press.
South, Scott J., and Glenna Spitze. 1986. "Determinants of divorce over the marital life course." *American Sociological Review,* 51, pp. 583–590.
Sowell, Thomas. 1981. *Ethnic America: A History.* New York: Basic Books.
———. 1983. *The Economics and Politics of Race: An International Perspective.* New York: Morrow.
Spada, James. 1979. *The Spada Report.* New York: New American Library.
Spanier, Graham B. 1983. "Married and unmarried cohabitation in the United States: 1980." *Journal of Marriage and the Family,* 45, pp. 277–288.
Spates, James L. 1983. "The sociology of values." *Annual Review of Sociology,* 9, pp. 27–49.
Spieler, Joseph. 1980. "After the recession." *Quest/80,* September, pp. 26–33.
Spindler, George D., and Louise Spindler. 1983. "Anthropologists view American culture." *Annual Review of Anthropology,* 12, pp. 49–78.
Spitz, René A. 1945. "Hospitalism." *Psychoanalytic Study of the Child,* 1, pp. 53–72.
Spitzer, Robert L. 1981. "The diagnostic status of homosexuality in DSM-III: A reformulation of the issues." *American Journal of Psychiatry,* 138, pp. 210–215.
Spotts, Peter N. 1987. "The disk that's turning science on its ear." *Christian Science Monitor,* July 13, pp. 1, 5.
Spreitzer, Elmer, and Eldon E. Snyder. 1983. "Correlates of participation in adult recreational sports." *Journal of Leisure Research,* 15, pp. 27–38.
Srole, Leo, et al. 1962. *Mental Health in the Metropolis.* New York: McGraw-Hill.
Stack, Steven. 1983a. "The effect of the decline in institutionalized religion on suicide, 1954–1978." *Journal for the Scientific Study of Religion,* 22, pp. 239–252.
———. 1983b. "The effect of religious commitment on suicide. A cross-national analysis." *Journal of Health and Social Behavior,* 24, pp. 362–374.
St. John, Nancy H. 1981. "The effects of school desegregation on children: A new look at the research evidence," in Adam Yarmolinsky, Lance Liebman, and Corinne S. Schelling (eds.), *Race and Schooling in the City.* Cambridge, Mass.: Harvard University Press.
Starbuck, William H. 1983. "Organizations as action generators." *American Sociological Review,* 48, pp. 91–102.
Stark, Elizabeth. 1986. "Stand up to your man." *Psychology Today,* April, p. 68.
Stark, Rodney. 1972. "The economics of piety: Religious commitment and social class," in Gerald Thielbar and Saul Feldman (eds.), *Issues in Social Inequality.* Boston: Little, Brown.
———, Lori Kent, and Daniel P. Doyle. 1982. "Religion and delinquency: The ecology of a 'lost' relationship." *Journal of Research in Crime and Delinquency,* 19, pp. 4–24.
———, and William Sims Bainbridge. 1980. "Networks of faith: Interpersonal bonds and recruitment to cults and sects." *American Journal of Sociology,* 85, pp. 1376–1395.
———, and Charles Y. Glock. 1968. *American Piety.* Berkeley: University of California Press.
———, Daniel P. Doyle, and Jesse Lynn Rushing. 1983. "Beyond Durkheim: Religion and suicide." *Journal for the Scientific Study of Religion,* 22, pp. 120–131.
Starr, Paul. 1983. *The Social Transformation of American Medicine.* New York: Basic Books.

Stearns, Marion S. 1971. *Report on Preschool Programs.* Washington, D.C.: U.S. Government Printing Office.

Steinberg, Laurence. 1987. "Why Japan's students outdo ours." *New York Times,* April 25, p. 15.

Steinberg, Stephen. 1981. *The Ethnic Myth: Race, Ethnicity, and Class in America.* New York: Atheneum.

Steiner, Stan. 1979. *Fusang: The Chinese who Built America.* New York: Harper & Row.

Stevens, Gillian. 1981. "Social mobility and fertility: Two effects in one." *American Sociological Review,* 46, pp. 573–585.

Stevens, William K. 1982. "Rise in 'dowry deaths' alarms Indian women." *The New York Times,* September 12, p. 20.

Stevenson, H. W., et al. 1978. "Schooling, environment, and cognitive development: A cross-cultural study." *Monographs of the Society for Research in Child Development,* 43 (175), p. 3.

Steward, Julian H. 1973. "A Neo-evolutionist approach," in Amitai Etzioni and Eva Etzioni-Halevy (eds.), *Social Change,* 2nd ed. New York: Basic Books.

Stewart, John A. 1983. "Achievement and ascriptive processes in the recognition of scientific articles." *Social Forces,* 62, pp. 166–189.

Stoll, Clarice Stasz. 1978. *Female & Male.* Dubuque, Iowa: Brown.

Stone, Gregory P. 1969. "Some meanings of American sport: An extended view," in Gerald S. Kenyon (ed.), *Aspects of Contemporary Sport Sociology.* Chicago: Athletic Institute.

Stone, P. B. 1983. "Development at a crossroads." *World Press Review,* March, pp. 33–35.

Storms, Michael D. 1980. "Theories of sexual orientation," *Journal of Personality and Social Psychology,* 38, pp. 783–792.

Straus, Murray A., Richard J. Gelles, and Suzanne K. Steinmetz. 1980. *Behind Closed Doors: Violence in the American Family.* New York: Anchor/Doubleday.

———. 1986. "Societal change and change in family violence from 1975 to 1985 as revealed by two national surveys." *Journal of Marriage and the Family,* 48, pp. 465–479.

Strenk, Andrew. 1978. "The thrill of victory and the agony of defeat." *Orbis,* Summer, pp. 453–457.

Strong, Bryan, Christine DeVault, Murray Suid, et al. 1983. *The Marriage and Family Experience.* St. Paul, Minn.: West.

Suh, Sung-Hee. 1986. "The cost of being an Asian-American superachiever." *New York Times,* August 15, p. 22.

Sullerot, Evelyn. 1971. *Women, Society, and Change.* New York: McGraw-Hill.

Sullivan, Walter. 1986. "Soviet scientists often thwarted, study says." *New York Times,* October 7, pp. 19, 22.

Sun, Marjorie. 1984. "Environment 1984 gets mixed marks by report." *Science,* 224, p. 1324.

Suransky, Valerie Polakow. 1982. *The Erosion of Childhood.* Chicago: University of Chicago Press.

Sussman, Marvin B., and James C. Romeis. 1982. "Willingness to assist one's elderly parents: Responses from United States and Japanese families." *Human Organization,* 41, pp. 256–259.

Sussman, Nan M., and Howard M. Rosenfeld. 1982. "Influence of culture, language, and sex on conversational distance." *Journal of Personality and Social Psychology,* 42, pp. 66–74.

Sutherland, Edwin E., and Donald R. Cressey. 1978. *Criminology,* 9th ed. Philadelphia: Lippincott.

Suttles, Gerald D. 1968. *The Social Order of the Slum.* Chicago: University of Chicago Press.

Sutton-Smith, Brian, and John M. Roberts. 1970. "The cross-cultural and psychological study of games," in Günther Lüschen (ed.), *The Cross-Cultural Analysis of Sport and Games.* Champaign, Ill.: Stipes.

Swigert, Victoria Lynn, and Ronald A. Farrell. 1976. *Murder, Inequality, and the Law.* Lexington, Mass: Heath.

Sykes, Gresham M. 1978. *Criminology.* New York: Harcourt Brace Jovanovich.

Syme, S. Leonard, and Lisa F. Berkman. 1987. "Social class, susceptibility, and sickness," in Howard D. Schwartz (ed.), *Dominant Issues in Medical Sociology,* 2nd ed. New York: Random House.

Szymanski, Albert. 1978. *The Capitalist State and the Politics of Class.* Cambridge, Mass.: Winthrop.

———, and Ted George Goertzel. 1979. *Sociology: Class, Consciousness, and Contradictions.* New York: Van Nostrand.

Taeuber, Cynthia M. 1983. "America in transition: An aging society." *Current Population Reports Series,* No. 128, p. 23. Washington, D.C.: U.S. Government Printing Office.

Talmon, Yonina. 1964. "Mate selection in collective settlements." *American Sociological Review,* 29, pp. 491–508.

Tanfer, Koray. 1987. "Patterns of premarital cohabitation among never-married women in the United States." *Journal of Marriage and the Family,* 49, pp. 483–497.

Tannenbaum, Frank. 1938. *Crime and the Community.* New York: Columbia University Press.

Tanner, Nancy Makepeace. 1983. "Hunters, gatherers, and sex roles in space and time." *American Anthropologist,* 85, pp. 335–341.

Tavris, Carol, and Carole Wade. 1984. *The Longest War: Sex Differences in Perspective,* 2nd ed. New York: Harcourt Brace Jovanovich.

———, and Susan Sadd. 1978. *The Redbook Report on Female Sexuality.* New York: Dell.

Taylor, Alfred Maurice. 1967. *Imagination and the Growth of Science.* New York: Schocken.

Taylor, Frederick W. 1911. *Scientific Management.* New York: Harper.

Taylor, Ian. 1987. "Putting the boot into a working-class sport: British soccer after Bradford and Brussels." *Sociology of Sport Journal,* 4, pp. 171–191.

Taylor, Patricia A., Burke D. Grandjean, and Niko Tos. 1987. "Work satisfaction under Yugoslav self-management: On participation, authority, and ownership." *Social Forces,* 65, pp. 1020–1034.

Taylor, Ralph B., et al. 1979. "Sharing secrets: Disclosure and discretion in dyads and triads." *Journal of Personality and Social Psychology,* 37, pp. 1196–1203.

———, and Joseph C. Lanni. 1981. "Territorial dominance: The influence of the resident advantage in triadic decision making." *Journal of Personality and Social Psychology,* 41, pp. 909–915.

Taylor, Ronald A. 1980. "End a federal rule and a new one replaces it." *U.S. News & World Report,* March 3, pp. 61, 62.

———. 1987. "Why fewer blacks are graduating." *U.S. News & World Report,* June 8, 1987.

Taylor, Stuart, Jr. 1987. "High court deals setback to suit on Japanese-American detention." *New York Times,* June 2, p. 15.

Teachman, Jay D. 1987. "Family background, educational resources, and educational attainment." *American Sociological Review,* 52, pp. 548–557.

Terkel, Studs. 1974. *Working.* New York: Pantheon.

Terrace, Herbert S., et al. 1979. "Can an ape create a sentence?" *Science,* 206, pp. 891–902.

Testa, Ronald J., Bill N. Kinder, and Gail Ironson. 1987. "Heterosexual bias in the perception of loving relationships of gay males and lesbians." *Journal of Sex Research,* 23, pp. 163–172.

Testart, Alain. 1982. "Significance of food storage among hunter-gatherers." *Current Anthropology,* 23, pp. 523–530.

Tharp, Mike. 1987. "Academic debate." *Wall Street Journal,* March 10, p. 1.

Thatcher, Gary. 1987. "New U.S. data show terrorism ebbed in 1987." *Christian Science Monitor,* February 3, pp. 3, 4.

Theberge, Nancy. 1981. "A critique of critiques: Radical and feminist writings on sport." *Social Forces,* 60, pp. 341–353.

Thio, Alex. 1972. "Toward a fuller view of American success ideology." *Pacific Sociological Review,* 15, pp. 381–393.

———. 1973. "Class bias in the sociology of deviance." *The American Sociologist,* 8, pp. 1–12.

———. 1975. "A critical look at Merton's anomie theory." *Pacific Sociological Review,* 18, pp. 139–158.

———. 1988. *Deviant Behavior,* 3rd ed. New York: Harper & Row.

Thirer, Joel, and Stephen D. Wright. 1985. "Sport and social status for adolescent males and females." *Sociology of Sport Journal,* 2, pp. 164–171.

Thomas, Charles W., and John R. Hepburn. 1983. *Crime, Criminal Law, and Criminology.* Dubuque, Iowa: Brown.

Thomas, Melvin E., and Michael Hughes. 1986. "The continuing significance of race: A study of race, class, and quality of life in America, 1972–1985." *American Sociological Review,* 51, pp. 830–841.

Thomas, Patricia. 1988. "The second wave of AIDS: IV drug users and their kin." *Medical World News,* January 11, pp. 76–77.

Thompson, Dick. 1987. "A how-to guide on cholesterol." *Time,* October 19, p. 45.

Thornberry, Terence P., and Margaret Farnworth. 1982. "Social correlates of criminal involvement: Further evidence on the relationship between social status and criminal behavior." *American Sociological Review,* 47, pp. 505–518.

Thornton, Arland, Duane F. Alwin, and Donald Camburn. 1983. "Causes and consequences of sex-role attitudes and attitude change." *American Sociological Review,* 48, pp. 211–227.

———, and Deborah Freedman. 1983. "The changing American family." *Population Bulletin,* 38, October, pp. 1–43.

Thurow, Roger, 1987. "Keeping control." *Wall Street Journal,* March 11, pp. 1, 26.

Tienda, Marta, and Ronald Angel. 1982. "Headship and household composition among blacks, Hispanics, and other whites." *Social Forces,* 61, pp. 508–531.

Tift, Susan. 1984. "Filling the Democratic pipeline." *Time,* June 4, pp. 28, 29.

Tilly, Charles. 1979. "Race and migration to the American city," in Joe R. Feagin (ed.), *The Urban Scene,* 2nd ed. New York: Random House.

Tilly, Louise A., and Joan W. Scott. 1978. *Women, Work, and the Family.* New York: Holt, Rinehart and Winston.

Time. 1978a. "The swarming lobbyists." August 7, pp. 14–22.

———. 1978b. "Woes of the weekend jock." August 21, pp. 40–50.

———. 1979. "Running battle: Fitness and its discontents." February 5, p. 140.

Timnick, Lois. 1982. "Electronic bullies." *Psychology Today,* February, pp. 10–15.

Tittle, Charles R. 1983. "Social class and criminal behavior: A critique of the theoretical foundation." *Social Forces,* 62, pp. 334–358.

Tobin, Gary A., and Dennis R. Judd. 1982. "Moving the suburbs to the city: Neighborhood revitalization and the 'amenities bundle'." *Social Science Quarterly,* 63, pp. 771–779.

Tobin, Jonathan N., et al. 1987. "Sex bias in considering coronary bypass surgery." *Annals of Internal Medicine,* 107, pp. 19–25.

Toby, Jackson. 1983. *Violence in School.* U.S. Department of Justice, National Institute of Justice. Washington, D.C.: Government Printing Office.

Tocqueville, Alexis de. 1835/1899. *Democracy in America.* New York: Colonial.

Toffler, Alvin. 1970. *Future Shock.* New York: Bantam Books.

———. 1980. *The Third Wave.* New York: Morrow.

Tolbert, Charles M., II. 1982. "Industrial segmentation and men's career mobility." *American Sociological Review,* 47, pp. 457–477.

Train, John. 1986. "Parkinson's laws aren't by popular vote." *Wall Street Journal,* May 15, p. 28.

Travers, Jeffrey, and Stanley Milgram. 1969. "An experimental study of the small world problem." Sociometry, 32, pp. 425–443.

Treiman, Donald J. 1977. *Occupational Prestige in Comparative Perspective.* New York: Academic Press.

———, and Patricia A. Roos. 1983. "Sex and earnings in industrial society: A nine-nation comparison." *American Journal of Sociology,* 89, pp. 612–650.

Tresemer, David. 1974. "Fear of success: Popular but unproven." *Psychology Today,* March, pp. 82–85.

Troeltsch, Ernst. 1931. *The Social Teaching of the Christian Churches.* New York: Macmillan.

Troiden, Richard R. 1979. "Becoming homosexual: A model of gay identity acquisition." *Psychiatry,* 42, pp. 362–373.

Trost, Cathy. 1986. "New-collar jobs." *Wall Street Journal,* September 19, pp. 1, 12.

Trost, Jan. 1985. "Swedish solutions." *Society,* November, pp. 44–48.

Trott, Stephen S. 1985. "Implementing criminal justice reform." *Public Administration Review,* 45, pp. 795–800.

Trotter, Robert J. 1987. "Mathematics: A male advantage?" *Psychology Today,* January, pp. 66–67.

Trulson, Michael E., et al. 1985. "That mild-mannered Bruce Lee." *Psychology Today,* January, p. 79.

Tumin, Melvin M. 1953. "Some principles of stratification: A critical analysis." *American Sociological Review,* 18, pp. 387–393.

———, 1967. *Social Stratification: The Forms and Functions of Inequality.* Englewood Cliffs, N.J.: Prentice-Hall.

Turkle, Sherry. 1984. *The Second Self: Computers and the Human Spirit.* New York: Simon & Schuster.

Turner, Paul R. 1982. "Anthropological value positions." *Human Organization,* 41, pp. 76–79.

Turner, R. Jay, and John W. Gartrell. 1978. "Social factors in psychiatric outcome: Toward the resolution of interpretive controversies." *American Sociological Review,* 43, pp. 368–382.

Turner, Ralph H., and Lewis M. Killian. 1972. *Collective Behavior,* 2nd ed. Englewood Cliffs, N.J.: Prentice-Hall.

Tutko, Thomas, and William Bruns. 1976. *Winning Is Everything and Other American Myths.* New York: Macmillan.

Twaddle, Andrew, and Richard Hessler. 1987. *A Sociology of Health,* 2nd ed. New York: Macmillan.

Tylor, Edward B. 1871. *Primitive Culture.* London: Murray.

Tyree, Andrea, Moshe Semyonov, and Robert W. Hodge. 1979. "Gaps and glissandos: Inequality, economic development, and social mobility in 24 countries." *American Sociological Review,* 44, pp. 410–424.

———, and Moshe Semyonov. 1983. "Social mobility and immigrants or immigrants and social mobility." *American Sociological Review,* 48, pp. 583–584.

Udry, J. Richard. 1983. "The marital happiness/disruption relationship by level of marital alternatives." *Journal of Marriage and the Family,* 45, pp. 221–222.

UN Chronicle. 1983. "State of the world environment." Vol. 20, May, pp. 33–46.

Unger, Irwin. 1982. *These United States: The Questions of Our Past,* vol. 1, 2nd ed. Boston: Little, Brown.

United Nations. 1982. *United Nations Demographic Yearbook 1982.*

UPI. 1983. "Property tax role drops in cities." *Washington Post,* January 12, p. A8.

U'Ren, Marjorie B. 1971. "The image of women in textbooks," in Vivian Gornick and Barbara K. Moran (eds.), *Women in Sexist Society.* New York: Basic Books.

U.S. Commission on Civil Rights. 1981. *Affirmative Action in the 1980s: Dismantling the Process of Discrimination.* Washington, D.C.: U.S. Government Printing Office.

U.S. Department of Justice, Bureau of Justice Statistics. 1983. *Report to the Nation on Crime and Justice: The Data.* Washington, D.C.: Government Printing Office.

U.S. Department of Labor. 1983. *Handbook of Labor Statistics.* Washington, D.C.: U.S. Government Printing Office.

———. 1984a. *Employment and Earnings: August 1984.* Washington, D.C.: U.S. Government Printing Office.

———. 1984b. *Occupational Outlook Handbook.* Washington, D.C.: U.S. Government Printing Office.

U.S. Office of Management and Budget. 1984. *Budget of the United States Government, 1985.* Washington, D.C.: U.S. Government Printing Office.

Useem, Michael. 1979. "Which business leaders help govern?" *Insurgent Sociologist,* 9, Fall, pp. 107–120.

———. 1980. "Corporations and the corporate elite." *Annual Review of Sociology,* 6, pp. 41–77.

Van den Berghe, Pierre L. 1978. *Race and Racism: A Comparative Perspective.* Huntington, N.Y.: Krieger.

Van Dyne, Larry. 1978. "The latest wave: Community colleges." *The Wilson Quarterly,* 2, Autumn, pp. 81–87.

van Voorst, L. Bruce. 1982. "The critical masses." *Foreign Policy,* No. 48, Fall, pp. 82–93.

Vander Zanden, James W. 1987. *Social Psychology,* 4th ed. New York: Random House.

Vandewiele, Michel. 1981. "Influence on family, peers, and school on Senegalese adolescents." *Psychological Reports,* 48, pp. 807–810.

Vanek, Joann. 1978. "Housewives as workers," in Ann H. Stromberg and Shirley Harkess (eds.), *Women Working: Theories and Facts in Perspective.* Palo Alto, Calif.: Mayfield.

Varghese, Raju. 1981. "An empirical analysis of the Eriksonian bipolar theory of personality." *Psychological Reports,* 49, pp. 819–822.

Velo, Joseph. 1983. "On 'material' and 'nonmaterial' aspects of culture." *Cultural Anthropology,* 24, p. 126.

Ventimiglia, J. C. 1982. "Sex roles and chivalry: Some conditions of gratitude to altruism." *Sex Roles,* 8, p. 1107–1122.

Verbrugge, Lois M. 1985. "Gender and health: An update on hypotheses and evidence." *Journal of Health and Social Behavior,* 26, pp. 156–182.

Veroff, Joseph, Elizabeth Douvan, and Richard A. Kulka. 1981. *The Inner American: A*

Self-Portrait from 1957 to 1976. New York: Basic Books.

Vidich, Arthur J., and Stanford M. Lyman. 1985. *American Sociology: Worldly Rejections of Religion and Their Directions*. New Haven, Conn.: Yale University Press.

Vora, Erika. 1981. "Evolution of race: A synthesis of social and biological concepts." *Journal of Black Studies*, 12, pp. 182–192.

Wagner, David G., and Joseph Berger. 1985. "Do sociological theories grow?" *American Journal of Sociology*, 90, pp. 697–728.

———, Rebecca S. Ford, and Thomas W. Ford. 1986. "Can gender inequality be reduced?" *American Sociological Review*, 51, pp. 47–61.

Waitzkin, Howard. 1987. "A Marxian interpretation of the growth and development of coronary care technology," in Howard D. Schwartz (ed.), *Dominant Issues in Medical Sociology*, 2nd ed. New York. Random House.

Wake, Sandra Byford, and Michael J. Sporakowski. 1972. "An intergenerational comparison of attitudes toward supporting aged parents." *Journal of Marriage and the Family*, 34, pp. 42–48.

Walker, Lawrence J. 1984. "Sex differences in the development of moral reasoning: A critical review." *Child Development*, 55, pp. 677–691.

———. 1986. "Sex differences in the development of moral reasoning: A rejoinder to Baumrind." *Child Development*, 57, pp. 522–526.

Wall Street Journal. 1986. "Das Kapital (revised ed.)," p. 32.

Wallerstein, James S., and Clement J. Wyle. 1947. "Our law-abiding law-breakers." *Probation*, 25, pp. 107–112.

Walters, Pamela Barnhouse, and Richard Rubinson. 1983. "Educational expansion and economic output in the United States, 1890–1969: A production function analysis." *American Sociological Review*, 48, pp. 480–493.

Walton, John. 1982. "Cities and jobs and politics." *Urban Affairs Quarterly*, 18, pp. 5–17.

Walzer, Michael. 1978. "Must democracy be capitalist?" *New York Review of Books*, July 20, p. 41.

Wanner, Richard A., and Lionel S. Lewis. 1982. "Trends in education and earnings, 1950–70: A structural analysis." *Social Forces*, 61, pp. 436–455.

Ward, Olivia. 1984. "Life without work?" *World Press Review*, 31, October, p. 41.

Warner, Carolyn. 1983. "Tuition tax credits: The death of private schooling." *College Board Review*, No. 129, Fall, pp. 26–30.

Warner, Richard. 1986. "Hard times and schizophrenia." *Psychology Today*, June, pp. 50–52.

Waters, Harry F. 1977. "What TV does to kids." *Newsweek*, February 21, pp. 63–70.

———. 1982. "Life according to TV." *Newsweek*, December 6, pp. 136–140.

Watkins, Linda M. 1986. "Liberal-arts graduates' prospects in the job market grow brighter." *Wall Street Journal*, May 6, p. 33.

Watson, James D. 1968. *The Double Helix*. New York: New American Library.

Watson, John B. 1924. *Behaviorism*. Chicago: University of Chicago Press.

Watson, Robert I. 1965. *Psychology of the Child*. New York: Wiley.

Watson, Roy E. L. 1983. "Premarital cohabitation vs. traditional courtship: Their effects on subsequent marital adjustment." *Family Relations*, 32, pp. 139–147.

———, and Peter W. DeMeo. 1987. "Premarital cohabitation vs. traditional courtship and subsequent marital adjustment: A replication and follow-up." *Family Relations*, 36, pp. 193–197.

Watson, Russell, 1984. "India: Putting back the lid." *Newsweek*, November 19, pp. 64–66.

———. 1987. "At long last, an arms deal." *Newsweek*, September 28, pp. 18–21.

———. 1987. "Heaven can wait." *Newsweek*, pp. 58–65.

Wattenberg, Ben J. 1987. *The Birth Dearth*. New York: Pharos Books.

Wattenberg, Martin P. 1981. "The decline of political partisanship in the United States: Negativity or neutrality?" *American Political Science Review*, 75, pp. 941–950.

Waxman, Chaim I. 1981. "The fourth generation grows up: The contemporary American Jewish community." *The Annals*, 454, March, pp. 70–85.

Weatherford, M. Stephen. 1982. "Interpersonal networks and political behavior." *American Journal of Political Science*, 26, pp. 116–143.

Weber, Max. 1930. *The Protestant Ethic and the Spirit of Capitalism*. New York: Scribner's.

———. 1954. *Max Weber on Law and Sociology*. Cambridge, Mass.: Harvard University Press.

———. 1957. *The Theory of Social and Economic Organization*. New York: Free Press.

Webster, Charles, 1975. *The Great Instauration: Science, Medicine and Reform, 1626–70*. London: Duckworth.

Webster, Murray, Jr., and James E. Driskell. 1983. "Beauty as status." *American Journal of Sociology*, 89, pp. 140–165.

Weede, Erich. 1982. "The effects of democracy and socialist strength on the size distribution of income: Some more evidence." *International Journal of Comparative Sociology*, 23, pp. 151–165.

Weinberg, Martin S., and Colin J. Williams. 1975. *Male Homosexuals*. New York: Penguin Books.

Weinstein, Deena. 1979. "Fraud in science." *Social Science Quarterly*, 59, pp. 644–645.

Weiss, Robert S. 1984. "The impact of marital dissolution on income and consumption in single-parent households." *Journal of Marriage and the Family*, 46, pp. 115–127.

Weissman, M. M., et al. 1978. "Psychiatric disorders in a U.S. urban community: 1975–1976." *American Journal of Psychiatry*, 135, pp. 459–462.

Weitzman, Lenore. 1981. *The Marriage Contract: Spouses, Lovers, and the Law*. New York: Free Press.

———. 1985. *The Divorce Revolution: The Unexpected Social and Economic Consequences for Women and Children in America*. New York: Free Press.

Wellborn, Stanley. 1987. "How genes shape personality." *U.S. News & World Report*, April 13, pp. 58–62.

Wells, Richard H., and J. Steven Picou. 1980. "Interscholastic athletes and socialization for educational achievement." *Journal of Sport Behavior*, 3, pp. 119–128.

Wells, Stacy. 1987. "Killer illnesses of history." *U.S. News & World Report*, January 12, p. 69.

Welniak, Edward J., and Mary F. Henson. 1984. *Money Income of Households, Families, and Persons in the United States: 1982*. Washington, D.C.: U.S. Government Printing Office.

Werner, Leslie Maitland. 1986. "Philosopher warns West of 'idolatry of politics.'" *New York Times*, May 13, p. 9.

Wessel, David. 1986. "Growing gap." *Wall Street Journal*, September 22, pp. 1, 16.

Westermarck, Edward A. 1922. *The History of Human Marriage*, vol. 2. 5th ed. New York: Allerton.

Wheaton, Blair. 1978. "The sociogenesis of psychological disorder: Reexamining the causal issues with longitudinal data." *American Sociological Review*, 43, pp. 383–403.

———. 1980. "The sociogenesis of psychological disorder: An attributional theory." *Journal of Health and Social Behavior*, 21, pp. 100–124.

Whitaker, Mark. 1984. "It was like breathing fire . . ." *Newsweek*, December 17, pp. 26–32.

White, James M. 1987. "Premarital cohabitation and marital stability in Canada." *Journal of Marriage and the Family*, 49, pp. 641–647.

White, John Kenneth, and Dwight Morris. 1984. "Shattered images: Political parties in the 1984 election." *Public Opinion*, December/January, pp. 44–48.

White, Leslie A. 1969. *The Science of Culture*. New York: Farrar, Straus and Giroux.

White, Lynn K. 1983. "Determinants of spousal interaction: Marital structure or marital happiness." *Journal of Marriage and the Family*, 45, pp. 511–519.

———, and Alan Booth. 1985. "The quality and stability of remarriages: The role of stepchildren." *American Sociological Review*, 50, pp. 689–698.

White, Sheldon H. 1977. "The paradox of American education." *National Elementary Principal*, 56, May/June, pp. 9, 10.

Whorf, Benjamin. 1956. *Language, Thought, and Reality*. New York: Wiley.

Whyte, Martin King. 1973. "Bureaucracy and modernization in China: The Maoist critique." *American Sociological Review*, 38, pp. 149–163.

Whyte, William Foote. 1986. "On the uses of social science research." *American Sociological Review*, 51, pp. 555–563.

Wiatrowski, Michael D., et al. 1982. "Curriculum tracking and delinquency." *American Sociological Review*, 47, pp. 151–160.

Widrick, Stanley, and Eugene Fram. 1984. "Is higher education a negative product?" *Col-*

lege Board Review, 130, Winter, pp. 27–29.

Wiener, Leonard. 1984. "Standing up to the IRS." *U.S. News & World Report,* March 26, pp. 38–41.

Wiener, Robert. 1953. *Ex-Prodigy: My Childhood and Youth.* New York: Simon & Schuster.

Wierzbicka, Anna. 1986. "Human emotions: Universal or culture-specific?" *American Anthropology,* 88, pp. 584–594.

Wiley, Norbert. 1979. "Notes on self genesis: From me to we to I." *Studies in Symbolic Interaction,* 2, pp. 87–105.

Wilkerson, Martha, and Richard A. Doddler. 1987. "Collective conscience and sport in modern society: An empirical test of a model." *Journal of Leisure Reserch,* 19, pp. 35–40.

Willey, Fay. 1980. "A plea from Soviet women." *Newsweek,* April 7, p. 50.

Willhelm, Sidney M. 1980. "Can Marxism explain America's racism?" *Social Problems,* 29, pp. 98–112.

Williams, Dennis A. 1984a. "Class conscious in Moscow." *Newsweek,* June 11, p. 73.

———. 1984b. "A formula for success." *Newsweek,* April 23, pp. 77–78.

Williams, J. Allen, Jr., et al. 1987. "Sex role socialization in picture books: An update." *Social Science Quarterly,* 68, pp. 148–156.

Williams, Kirk R. 1984. "Economic sources of homicide: Reestimating the effects of poverty and inequality." *American Sociological Review,* 49, pp. 283–289.

Williams, Lena. 1987. "Study cites gains on race in schools." *New York Times,* May 20, p. 16.

Williams, Robin M., Jr. 1970. *American Society: A Sociological Interpretation,* 3rd ed. New York: Knopf.

Williams, Roger M. 1983. "White help still wanted." *Psychology Today,* November, p. 16.

Williamson, John B., Linda Evans, and Ann Munley. 1980. *Aging and Society.* New York: Holt, Rinehart and Winston.

Williamson, John B., et al. 1982. *The Politics of Aging: Power and Policy.* Springfield, Ill.: Charles C. Thomas.

Willie, Charles V., and Donald Cunnigen. 1981. "Black students in higher education: A review of studies, 1965–1980." *Annual Review of Sociology,* 7, pp. 177–198.

Willner, Dorothy. 1983. "Definition and violation: Incest and the incest taboos." *Man,* 18, pp. 134–159.

Wilson, Bryan. 1982. *Religion in Sociological Perspective.* New York: Oxford University Press.

Wilson, Edward O. 1980. *Sociobiology: The Abridged Edition.* Cambridge, Mass.: Harvard University Press.

———. 1984. *Biophilia: The Human Bond to Other Species.* Cambridge: Mass.: Harvard University Press.

Wilson, John. 1978. *Religion in American Society.* Englewood Cliffs, N.J.: Prentice-Hall.

Wilson, William Julius. 1980. *The Declining Significance of Race: Blacks and Changing American Institutions,* 2nd ed. Chicago: University of Chicago Press.

———. 1987. *The Truly Disadvantaged: The Inner City, the Underclass, and Public Policy.* Chicago: University of Chicago Press.

Wimberley, Dale W. 1984. "Socioeconomic deprivation and religious salience: A cognitive behavioral approach." *Sociological Quarterly,* 25, pp. 223–238.

Winch, Robert F. 1971. *The Modern Family.* New York: Holt, Rinehart and Winston.

———. 1974. "The functions of dating," in Robert Winch and Graham Spanier (eds.), *Selected Studies in Marriage and the Family.* New York: Holt, Rinehart and Winston.

Wingo, Walter S. 1981. "Behind the boom in big-company mergers." *U.S. News & World Report,* April 6, pp. 79–80.

Wirth, Louis. 1945. "The problems of minority groups," in Ralph Linton (ed.), *The Science of Man in the World Crisis.* New York: Columbia University Press.

Wolf, Arthur P. 1966. "Childhood association, sexual attraction, and the incest taboo: A Chinese case." *American Anthropologist,* 68, pp. 883–898.

———. 1970. "Childhood association and sexual attraction: A further test of the Westermarck hypothesis." *American Anthropologist,* 72, pp. 503–515.

Wolf, Richard M. 1983. "American education: The record is mixed." *Public Interest,* No. 72, pp. 124–128.

Wolfe, Tom. 1979. *The Right Stuff.* New York: Farrar, Straus, and Giroux.

Wolfinger, Raymond E. 1986. "Registration creates an obstacle." *New York Times,* November 4, p. 31.

Wolff, Kurt H., ed. 1950. *The Sociology of Georg Simmel.* New York: Free Press.

Wolfgang, Marvin E. 1958. *Patterns of Criminal Homicide.* Philadelphia: University of Pennsylvania Press.

Wolman, Harold. 1986. "The Reagan urban policy and its impacts." *Urban Affairs Quarterly,* 21, pp. 311–335.

Womack, Mari. 1978. "Sports magic." *Human Behavior,* September, pp. 43–44.

Wood, Michael, and Michael Hughes. 1984. "The moral basis of moral reform: Status discontent vs. culture and socialization as explanations of anti-pornography social movement adherence." *American Sociological Review,* 49, pp. 86–99.

Wood, Robert E. 1984. "Development ledger." *Comtemporary Sociology,* 13, pp. 700–702.

Woodburn, James. 1982. "Egalitarian societies." *Man,* 17, pp. 431–451.

Woodward, Kenneth L. 1978. "Saving the family." *Newsweek,* May 15, pp. 63–73.

———. 1986. "From 'mainline' to sideline." *Newsweek,* December 22, pp. 54–56.

———. 1987. "Saving souls—or a ministry?" *Newsweek,* July 13, pp. 52–53.

World Factbook. 1987. Washington, D.C.: U.S. Government Printing Office.

Wright, Erik Olin. 1985. *Classes.* London: Verso.

———, and Bill Martin. 1987. "The transformation of the American class structure, 1960–1980." *American Journal of Sociology,* 93, pp. 1–29.

Wright, James D., Peter H. Rossi, and Kathleen Daly. 1983. *Under the Gun: Weapons, Crime, and Violence in America.* New York: Aldine.

Wright, Stuart A., and Elizabeth S. Piper. 1986. 1986. "Families and cults: Familial factors related to youth leaving or remaining in deviant religious groups." *Journal of Marriage and the Family,* 48, pp. 15–25.

Wriston, Michael J. 1980. "In defense of bureaucracy." *Public Administration Review,* 40, pp. 179–183.

Wrong, Dennis H. 1961. "The oversocialized conception of man in modern sociology." *American Sociological Review,* 26, pp. 183–193.

———. 1977. *Population and Society,* 4th ed. New York: Random House.

Yancey, William L. 1971. *Environment and Behavior.* Beverly Hills, Calif.: Sage.

Yankelovich, Daniel. 1974. *The New Morality.* New York: McGraw-Hill.

———. 1981. *New Rules: Searching for Self-Fulfillment in a World Turned Upside Down.* New York: Random House.

———, and John Immerwahr. 1984. "Putting the work ethic to work." *Society,* 21, January/February, pp. 58–76.

Yeracaris, Constantine A., and Jay H. Kim. 1978. "Socioeconomic differentials in selected causes of death." *American Journal of Public Health,* 68, pp. 342–351.

Yesner, David R. 1983. "On food storage among hunter-gatherers." *Current Anthropology,* 24, p. 119.

Yin, Peter, and Kwok Hung Lai. 1983. "A reconceptualization of age stratification in China." *Journal of Gerontology,* 38, pp. 608–613.

Yinger, J. Milton. 1982. *Countercultures: The Promise and the Peril of a World Turned Upside Down.* New York: Free Press.

Young, Anne McDougall. 1983. "Recent trends in higher education and labor force activity." *Monthly Labor Review,* 106, February, pp. 39–41.

Young, T. R. 1984. "Crime and capitalism." Livermore, Colo.: Red Feather Institute.

———. 1986. "The sociology of sport: Structural Marxist and cultural Marxist approaches." *Sociological Perspectives,* 29, pp. 3–28.

Zangwill, Israel. 1909. *The Melting Pot.* New York: Macmillan.

Zaretsky, Eli. 1976. *Capitalism, the Family, and Personal Life.* New York: Harper & Row.

Zeitz, Gerald. 1983. "Structural and individual determinants of organization morale and satisfaction." *Social Forces,* 61, pp. 1088–1108.

Zelnick, Melvin, and John F. Kantner. 1980. "Sexual activity, contraceptive use, and pregnancy among metropolitan-area teenagers: 1971–1979." *Family Planning Perspectives,* 12, pp. 230–237.

Zenner, Walter P. 1985. "Jewishness in America: Ascription and choice." *Ethnic and Racial Studies,* 8, pp. 117–133.

Zerubavel, Eviatar. 1982. "Easter and passover: On calendars and group identity." *American Sociological Review,* 47, pp. 284–289.

Zimbardo, Philip G. 1972. "Pathology of im-

prisonment." *Society,* April, pp. 4–8.
Zimmer, Judith. 1984. "Courting the gods of sport." *Psychology Today,* July, pp. 36–39.
Zimmerman, Carle C. 1949. *The Family of Tomorrow.* New York: Harper & Brothers.
Zinsmeister, Karl. 1987. "Asians: Prejudice from top and bottom." *Public Opinion,* July/August, pp. 8–10, 59.
Zipp, John F., Richard Landerman, and Paul Luebke. 1982. "Political parties and political participation: A reexamination of the standard socioeconomic model." *Social Forces,* 60, pp. 1140–1153.
Zucker, Lynn. 1983. "Organizations as institutions." in Samuel B. Bacharach (ed.), *Research in the Sociology of Organizations,* vol. 2. Greenwich, Conn.: JAI Press.
Zuckerman, Laurence. 1988. "Open season on gays." *Time,* March 7, p. 24.
Zuern, Ted. 1983. "Indian nations, American citizens." *America,* 148, pp. 412–416.
Zur, Offer. 1987. "The psychohistory of warfare: The co-evolution of culture, psyche and enemy." *Journal of Peace Research,* 24, pp. 125–134.
Zurcher, Louis A. 1983. *Social Roles: Conformity, Conflict, and Creativity.* Beverly Hills, Calif.: Sage.

Photo and Cartoon Credits

CONTENTS

Page iv, © William Strode/Woodfin Camp & Assoc.; p. v, Joan Liftin/Archives; p. vi, © Carol Lee/The Picture Cube; p. vii, © Gabe Palmer 1985/The Stock Market; p. viii, © Meryl Joseph 1984/The Stock Market; p. ix, © Suzanne A. Vlamis/International Stock Photo; p. x, © Tom Tracy/Black Star; p. xi, © Jay Nadelson 1982/The Stock Market.

CHAPTER 1

Page 2, © William Strode/Woodfin Camp & Assoc.; p. 4, © Bob Daemmrich; p. 7, © Kevin Horan/Picture Group; p. 9, Bettmann Archive/BBC Hulton; p. 10, (bottom left) Culver Pictures, (top right) Bettmann Archive; p. 11, German Information Center; p. 12, (top) Bettmann Archive, (bottom) Culver Pictures; p. 13, drawing by Handelsman, © 1987 Harvard Business Review; p. 15, (top left) © Michael Grecco/Stock, Boston, (bottom right) © 1986 Anthony Suau/ Black Star; p. 17, Robert Eckert/The Picture Cube.

CHAPTER 2

Page 24, Elliot Varner-Smith/International Stock Photo; p. 27, © 1987 David Stoecklein/The Stock Market; p. 33, drawing by Stevenson, © 1980 The New Yorker Magazine, Inc.; p. 34, Paul Conklin/ Monkmeyer; p. 36, Mimi Forsyth/Monkmeyer; p. 38, Rick Browne/ Stock, Boston; p. 39, © 1965 by Stanley Milgram, from the film *Obedience,* distributed by the Pennsylvania State University, PCR; p. 46, Owen Franken/Stock, Boston.

CHAPTER 3

Page 52, © Marc & Evelyne Bernheim/Woodfin Camp & Assoc.; p. 55, © Roy Morsch/The Stock Market; p. 58 © Lynn Johnson/ Stock, Boston; p. 62, © Robert Azzi/Woodfin Camp & Assoc.; p. 64, © Burt Glinn/Magnum; p. 65, © Mark Boulton/Photo Researchers; p. 67, (top left) © Marc & Evelyne Bernheim/Woodfin Camp & Assoc., (top right) © Arthur d'Arazien/The Image Bank, (bottom left) © Greg Davis/Black Star, (bottom right) © Catherine Ursillo/ Photo Researchers; p. 69, © Marc & Evelyne Bernheim/Woodfin Camp & Assoc.; p. 70, Napoleon Chagnon/Anthro-Photo; p. 71, drawing by Gahan Wilson, © 1987 The New Yorker Magazine, Inc.; p. 73, Michael Putnam/Peter Arnold, Inc.; p. 74, Tony Korody/ Sygma.

CHAPTER 4

Page 78, Brett Palmer/The Stock Market; p. 81, Rolf Hamilton-Pressensbild/Photoreporters; p. 83, (top) © Eugene Richards/Magnum, (bottom) © Steven McCurry/Magnum; p. 86, Irven DeVore/Anthro-Photo; p. 87, © Marc & Evelyne Bernheim/Woodfin Camp & Assoc.; p. 89, © 1986 David Pollack/The Stock Market; p. 90, © Jim Brown 1986/The Stock Market; p. 94, (top left) David Strickler/The Picture Cube, (bottom right) © Eve Arnold/Magnum; p. 95, Christopher Brown/Stock, Boston.

CHAPTER 5

Page 102, © Joan Liftin/Archive; p. 106, © Miro Vintoniv/Stock, Boston; p. 111, © 1984 Chuck Kneyse/Black Star; p. 113, (top) Markel/Gamma-Liaison, (bottom) Abraham & Dunn/The Stock Market; p. 116, © Rick Browne/Stock, Boston; p. 117, drawing by Handelsman, © 1987 The New Yorker Magazine, Inc.; p. 120, © Richard Kalvar/Magnum; p. 122, Nik Wheeler/Black Star; p. 126, © Tom Tracy/The Stock Market.

CHAPTER 6

Page 130, © M. W. Peterson/The Image Bank; p. 134, © Erika Stone 1982; p. 138, © David Lissy 1987/The Picture Cube; p. 139, © Michal Heron 1983/Woodfin Camp & Assoc.; p. 142, Mimi Forsyth/Monkmeyer; p. 146, (top) Terry Eiler/Stock, Boston, (bottom) drawing by Weber, © 1984 The New Yorker Magazine, Inc.; p. 147, © Michal Heron 1983/Woodfin Camp & Assoc.; p. 150, Mark Antman/The Image Works; p. 154, © Erika Stone 1985.

CHAPTER 7

Page 158, A. Tannenbaum/Sygma; p. 161, Markel/Gamma-Liaison; p. 162, (top) Wide World, (bottom) Bob Fitch/Black Star; p. 166, © Raghu Rai/Magnum; p. 167, Sidney Harris; p. 169, Michelle Borgre/ Black Star; p. 174, Mimi Forsyth/Monkmeyer; p. 175, Bettmann Archive; p. 179, Stephen Ferry/Gamma-Liaison; p. 181, © Ellis Herwig/ Stock, Boston.

CHAPTER 8

Page 184, © Carol Lee/The Picture Cube; p. 187, Alain Keler/Black Star; p. 189, © Catherine Ursillo/Photo Researchers; p. 192, Sidney Harris; p. 194, © Joel Gordon; p. 196, © Serraillier/Photo Researchers; p. 198, © Matthew McVay/Picture Group.

CHAPTER 9

Page 208, © 1988 Andrew Holbrooke/Black Star; p. 210, Lewis Hine/ Bettmann Archive; p. 212, (top left) A. Tannenbaum/Sygma, (top right) © 1987 Xenophon A. Beake/The Stock Market, (bottom left) © 1988 Andrew Holbrooke/Black Star, (bottom right) © Rick Browne 1987/Stock, Boston; p. 218, © 1986 Charles Gupton/Stock, Boston; p. 221, © Mark Godfrey/Archive; p. 222, (top) © Michal Heron/ Woodfin Camp & Assoc.; (bottom) © Michael O'Brien/Archive; p. 225, © William Campbell/Sygma; p. 228, © Fredrik D. Bodin/ Stock, Boston; p. 229, (left) © Peter Menzel/Stock, Boston, (right) © Michal Heron/Woodfin Camp & Assoc.; p. 232, drawing by Handelsman, © 1984 The New Yorker Magazine, Inc.

CHAPTER 10

Page 236, © Gabe Palmer 1985/The Stock Market; p. 239, © Henley & Savage/Click/Chicago; p. 241, Paul Dagys; p. 245, © Dan Ford Connolly 1987/Picture Group; p. 247, drawing by Modell, © 1984 The New Yorker Magazine, Inc.; p. 249, Catherine Ursillo/Photo Researchers; p. 250, © Michal Heron/Woodfin Camp & Assoc.; p. 252, Wide World; p. 256, © Mario Ruiz/Picture Group; p. 259, J.-L.Atlan/ Sygma; p. 260, UPI/Bettmann Newsphotos.

CHAPTER 11

Page 266, © Susan Van Etten/The Picture Cube; p. 271, Owen Franken/Stock, Boston; p. 273, © Stephanie Maze 1985/Woodfin Camp & Assoc.; p. 275, Cynthia Johnson/TIME Magazine; p. 277, Tass/Sovfoto; p. 278, © Bob Daemmrich/Stock, Boston; p. 279, drawing by Ross, © 1987 The New Yorker Magazine, Inc.; p. 283, Cynthia Johnson/Time Magazine; p. 286, © Lester Sloan 1985/Woodfin Camp & Assoc.

CHAPTER 12

Page 290, © Dahlgren/The Stock Market; p. 292, Nancy Coplon/Newsweek; p. 294, Guido Alberto Rossi/The Image Bank; p. 298, Tannenbaum/Sygma; p. 303, drawing by Mankoff, © 1979 The New Yorker Magazine, Inc.; p. 305, © Ellis Herwig/The Picture Cube; p. 306, © Jim Goodwin 1982/Photo Researchers; p. 309, © Bettye Lane/Photo Researchers.

CHAPTER 13

Page 314, © Meryl Joseph 1984/The Stock Market; p. 317, (top) © Marc & Evelyne Bernheim/Woodfin Camp & Assoc., (bottom) © Michal Heron 1983/Woodfin Camp & Assoc.; p. 318, © Tony Howarth/Woodfin Camp & Assoc.; p. 320, © Leif Skoogfors/Woodfin Camp & Assoc.; p. 323, The Metropolitan Museum of Art, Gift of Miss A. S. Colgate, 1951; p. 326, © Chuck Fishman 1986/Woodfin Camp & Assoc.; p. 328, © David M. Grossman/Photo Researchers; p. 330, drawing by Bernard Schooenbaum, © 1987 The New Yorker Magazine, Inc.; p. 333, © Lenore Weber/Taurus; p. 336, © Brad C. Bower/Picture Group.

CHAPTER 14

Page 340, © Charles Harbutt/Archive; p. 343, drawing by Lorenz, © 1978 The New Yorker Magazine, Inc.; p. 345, © Marc & Evelyne Bernheim/Woodfin Camp & Assoc.; p. 346, © Spencer Grant/The Picture Cube; p. 347, © Ann Hagen Griffiths/Omni Photo-Communications; p. 349, © Susan Van Etten/The Picture Cube; p. 351, © Alan Carey/The Image Works; p. 358, © Macdonald/The Picture Cube; p. 362, © Ann Hagen Griffiths/Omni Photo-Communications; p. 365, © 1986 Alan Goldsmith/The Stock Market.

CHAPTER 15

Page 368, © Suzanne A. Vlamis/International Stock Photo; p. 371, © 1985 John Bryson/The Image Bank; p. 373, © J-L Dugast/Sygma; p. 376, © 1981 Larry Mulvehill/Photo Researchers; p. 379, © Flip Schulke/Black Star; p. 380, Sygma; p. 382, © 1987 Christopher Morris/Black Star; p. 383, drawing by W. Miller, © 1987 The New Yorker Magazine, Inc.; p. 385, © Betsy Lee 1984/Taurus Photos; p. 388, J. P. Laffont/Sygma; p. 392, UPI/Bettmann Newsphotos.

CHAPTER 16

Page 396, © 1981 Fred Ward/Black Star; p. 399, (left) Bettmann Archive, (center) Culver Pictures, (right) UPI/Bettman Newsphotos; p. 401, (top left) © M. Durrance/Black Star, (bottom) Wide World; p. 405, drawing by Tobey, © 1984 The New Yorker Magazine, Inc.; p. 407, courtesy, The Sierra Club; p. 410, © Susan Steinkamp/Picture Group; p. 413, © George E. Jones III/Photo Researchers; p. 414, © Christina Thomson 1984/Woodfin Camp & Assoc.; p. 418, Mouchet/Gamma-Liaison.

CHAPTER 17

Page 422, © Guy Gillette 1981/Photo Researchers; p. 426, © Sandra Johnson/The Picture Cube; p. 428, Wide World Photos; p. 430, © 1981 Chris Niedenthal/Black Star; p. 433, from *The Wall Street Journal*—permission, Cartoon Features Syndicate; p. 436, © Don Smetzer/Click/Chicago; p. 440, UPI/Bettmann Newsphotos; p. 445, (top) © Jim Olive/Peter Arnold, Inc., (bottom) Judy Gurovitz/International Stock Photo.

CHAPTER 18

Page 450, © Tom Tracy/Black Star; p. 452, drawing by Sauers, © 1984 The New Yorker Magazine, Inc.; p. 454, © 1986 Ted Clutter/Photo Researchers; p. 457, Arthur Schay/Time Magazine; p. 458, de Sheulles/SIPA; p. 459, UPI/Bettmann Newsphotos; p. 461, © Richard Frear/Photo Researchers; p. 463, Bettmann Archive; p. 466, © Bill Stanton 1983/International Stock Photo; p. 467, © Rhoda Sidney/Monkmeyer; p. 470, © Catherine Ursillo/Photo Researchers; p. 473, © Susan Leavines/Photo Researchers.

CHAPTER 19

Page 476, © Chuck O'Rear/Click/Chicago; p. 479, © Tom Tracy/Black Star; p. 480, Culver; p. 481, UPI/Bettmann Newsphotos; p. 484, NASA; p. 485, Wide World; p. 487, drawing by Chas. Addams, © 1987 The New Yorker Magazine, Inc.; p. 489, © Hank Morgan/Science Source/Photo Researchers.

CHAPTER 20

Page 496, Focus on Sports; p. 498, P. Perrin/Sygma; p. 499, Al Brodsky/Taurus; p. 502, © Bernard Gotfryd/Woodfin Camp & Assoc.; p. 503, drawing by W. Miller, © 1987 The New Yorker Magazine, Inc.; p. 507, © Bob Daemmrich/Stock, Boston; p. 509, © Jeff Persons/Stock, Boston; p. 511, © Gilles Peress/Magnum; p. 514, John Coletti/Stock, Boston; p. 518, UPI/Bettmann Newsphotos.

CHAPTER 21

Page 522, Anthony Suau/Black Star; p. 528, Library of Congress; p. 530, Bettmann Archive; p. 533, (top left) © 1984 David Burnett/Contact/Woodfin Camp & Assoc. (bottom right) © 1985 United Feature Syndicate, Inc.; p. 537, © 1985 Alon Reininger Woodfin Camp & Assoc.; p. 539, Zigy Kaluzny/Gamma-Liaison; p. 542, © Martin Rogers/Woodfin Camp & Assoc.; p. 543, Tass/Sovfoto.

CHAPTER 22

Page 550, © Wes Thompson 1986/The Stock Market; p. 554 United Nations Photo by Jongen; p. 556, Jonathan L. Barkan/The Picture Cube; p. 557, (top) © John Troha/Black Star, (bottom) drawing by P. Steiner, © 1983 The New Yorker Magazine, Inc.; p. 560, © 1984 Saloutos/The Stock Market; p. 565, (top) Ralph Crane for LIFE Magazine, © 1958 Time Inc., (bottom) © Renate Hiller/Monkmeyer; p. 569, © John Lei/Stock, Boston; p. 570, UPI/Bettmann Newsphotos.

CHAPTER 23

Page 574, © Jay Nadelson 1982/The Stock Market; p. 578, © 1981 Miami Herald/Black Star; p. 581, © J. R. Holland/Stock, Boston; p. 583, Netherlands Board of Tourism; p. 592, Culver; p. 593, © Richard Howard 1984/Black Star; p. 596, © Peter Yates 1987/Picture Group; p. 599, Minosa-Scorpio/Sygma; p. 600, © Chie Nishio/Omni Photo Communications; p. 601, © Nubar Alexanian/Woodfin Camp & Assoc.; p. 602, drawing by Modell, © 1984 The New Yorker Magazine, Inc.

Name Index

Subject Index